Writers of the Restoration and Eighteenth Century, 1660-1789

Concise Dictionary of British Literary Biography
Volume Two

Writers of the Restoration and Eighteenth Century, 1660-1789

A Bruccoli Clark Layman Book
Gale Research Inc.
Detroit, London

Advisory Board for
CONCISE DICTIONARY
OF BRITISH LITERARY BIOGRAPHY

Printed in the United States of America

Published simultaneously in the United Kingdom
by Gale Research International Limited
(An affiliated company of Gale Research Inc.)

The paper used in this publication meets the minimum requirements
of American National Standard for Information Sciences—Permanence
Paper for Printed Library Materials, ANSI Z39.48-1984. ∞™

Copyright © 1992
Gale Research Inc.
835 Penobscot Bldg.
Detroit, MI 48226-4094

ISBN 0-8103-7980-5
ISBN 0-8103-7982-1

10 9 8 7 6 5 4

Contents of Volume 2

Authors Included in This Series

Volume 1
Writers of the Middle Ages and Renaissance
Before 1660

Francis Bacon
Francis Beaumont & John Fletcher
Beowulf
Thomas Campion
Geoffrey Chaucer
Thomas Dekker
John Donne
John Ford
George Herbert
Ben Jonson

Sir Thomas Malory
Christopher Marlowe
Sir Walter Ralegh
William Shakespeare
Sir Philip Sidney
Edmund Spenser
Izaak Walton
John Webster

Volume 3
Writers of the Romantic Period, 1789-1832

Jane Austen
William Blake
Robert Burns
George Gordon, Lord Byron
Thomas Carlyle
Samuel Taylor Coleridge
Thomas De Quincey
William Godwin

John Keats
Charles Lamb
Sir Walter Scott
Mary Shelley
Percy Bysshe Shelley
Mary Wollstonecraft
William Wordsworth

Volume 4
Victorian Writers, 1832-1890

Volume 5
Late Victorian and Edwardian Writers, 1890-1914

Volume 6
Modern Writers, 1914-1945

Volume 7
Writers After World War II, 1945-1960

Volume 8
Contemporary Writers, 1960-Present

Plan of the Work

The eight-volume *Concise Dictionary of British Literary Biography* was developed in response to requests from school and college teachers and librarians, and from small- to medium-sized public libraries, for a compilation of entries from the standard *Dictionary of Literary Biography* chosen to meet their needs and their budgets. The *DLB*, which comprises more than one hundred volumes as of the end of 1991, is moving steadily toward its goal of providing a history of literature in all languages developed through the biographies of writers. Basic as the *DLB* is, many librarians have expressed the need for a less comprehensive reference work which in other respects retains the merits of the *DLB*. The *Concise DBLB* provides this resource.

The *Concise* series was planned by an eight-member advisory board, consisting primarily of secondary-school educators, who developed a method of organization and presentation for selected *DLB* entries suitable for high-school and beginning college students. Their preliminary plan was circulated to some five thousand school librarians and English teachers, who were asked to respond to the organization of the series. Those responses were incorporated into the plan described here.

Uses for the Concise DBLB

Students are the primary audience for the *Concise DBLB*. The stated purpose of the standard *DLB* is to make our literary heritage more accessible. *Concise DBLB* has the same goal and seeks a wider audience. What the author wrote; what the facts of his or her life are; a description of his or her literary works; a discussion of the critical response to his or her works; and a bibliography of critical works to be consulted for further information: these are the elements of a *Concise DBLB* entry.

The first step in the planning process for this series, after identifying the audience, was to contemplate its uses. The advisory board acknowledged that the integrity of *Concise DBLB* as a reference book is crucial to its utility. The *Concise DBLB* adheres to the scholarly standards established by the parent series; the *Concise DBLB* is a ready-reference source of established value, providing reliable biographical and bibliographical information.

It is anticipated that this series will not be confined to uses within the library. Just as the *DLB* has been a tool for stimulating students' literary interests in the college classroom—for comparative studies of authors, for example, and, through its ample illustrations, as a means of invigorating literary study—the *Concise DBLB* is a primary resource for high-school and junior-college educators.

Organization

The advisory board further determined that entries from the standard *DLB* should be presented complete—without abridgment. The board's feeling was that the utility of the *DLB* format has been proven, and that only minimal changes should be made.

The advisory board further decided that the organization of the *Concise DBLB* should be chronological to emphasize the historical development of British literature. Each volume is devoted to a single historical period and includes the most significant literary figures from all genres who were active during that time.

The eight period volumes of the *Concise DBLB* are: *Writers of the Middle Ages and Renaissance Before 1660; Writers of the Restoration and Eighteenth Century, 1660-1789; Writers of the Romantic Period, 1789-1832; Victorian Writers, 1832-1890; Late Victorian and Edwardian Writers, 1890-1914; Modern Writers, 1914-1945; Writers After World War II, 1945-1960; Contemporary Writers, 1960-Present.*

Form of Entry

The form of entry in the *Concise DBLB* is substantially the same as in the standard series. Entries have been updated and, where necessary, corrected.

It is anticipated that users of this series will find it useful to consult the standard *DLB* for information about those writers omitted from the *Concise DBLB* whose significance to contemporary readers may have faded but whose contribution to our cultural heritage remains meaningful.

Comments about the series and suggestions for its improvement are earnestly invited.

A Note to Students

The purpose of the *Concise DBLB* is to enrich the study of British literature. Besides being inherently interesting, biographies of writers provide a basic understanding of the various ways writers react in their works to the circumstances of their lives, the events of their times, and the cultures that envelop them.

Concise DBLB entries start with the most important facts about writers: what they wrote. We strongly recommend that you also start there. The chronological listing of an author's works is an outline for the examination of his or her career achievements. The biography that follows sets the stage for the presentation of the works. Each of the author's important works and the most respected critical evaluations of them are discussed in *Concise DBLB*. If you require more information about the author or fuller critical studies of the author's works, the references section at the end of the entry will guide you.

Illustrations are an integral element of *Concise DBLB* entries. Photographs of the author are reminders that literature is the product of a writer's imagination; facsimiles of the author's working drafts are the best evidence available for understanding the act of composition—the author in the process of refining his or her work and acting as self-editor; dust jackets and advertisements demonstrate how literature comes to us through the marketplace, which sometimes serves to alter our perceptions of the works.

Literary study is a complex and immensely rewarding endeavor. Our goal is to provide you with the information you need to make that experience as rich as possible.

Acknowledgments

This book was produced by Bruccoli Clark Layman, Inc. Karen L. Rood is senior editor for the *Dictionary of Literary Biography* series. David Marshall James was the in-house editor.

Production coordinator is James W. Hipp. Projects manager is Charles D. Brower. Photography editors are Edward Scott and Timothy C. Lundy. Layout and graphics supervisor is Penney L. Haughton. Copyediting supervisor is Bill Adams. Typesetting supervisor is Kathleen M. Flanagan. Systems manager is George F. Dodge. The production staff includes Rowena Betts, Patricia Coate, Gail Crouch, Margaret McGinty Cureton, Bonita Dingle, Mary Scott Dye, Sarah A. Estes, Robert Fowler, Cynthia Hallman, Ellen McCracken, Kathy Lawler Merlette, John Myrick, Pamela D. Norton, Jean W. Ross, Laurrè Sinckler-Reeder, Thomasina Singleton, Maxine K. Smalls, and Betsy L. Weinberg.

Walter W. Ross and Henry Cunningham did library research. They were assisted by the following librarians at the Thomas Cooper Library of the University of South Carolina: Jens Holley and the interlibrary-loan staff; reference librarians Gwen Baxter, Daniel Boice, Faye Chadwell, Jo Cottingham, Cathy Eckman, Rhonda Felder, Gary Geer, Jackie Kinder, Laurie Preston, Jean Rhyne, Carol Tobin, Virginia Weathers, and Connie Widney; circulation-department head Thomas Marcil; and acquisitions-searching supervisor David Haggard.

Concise Dictionary of British Literary Biography
Volume Two

Writers of the Restoration and Eighteenth Century, 1660-1789

Concise Dictionary of British Literary Biography

Joseph Addison
(1 May 1672 - 17 June 1719)

This entry was written by Lillian D. Bloom (Research Scholar, Henry E. Huntington Library and Art Gallery) for DLB 101: British Prose Writers, 1660-1800: First Series.

BOOKS: *Nova philosophia veteri praeferenda. In Theatri oxoniensis encaenia: sive comitia philologica 1693 celebrata* (Oxford: e Theatro Sheldoniano, 1693);

A Poem to His Majesty, Presented to the Lord Keeper (London: Printed for J. Tonson, 1695);

The Campaign, A Poem, To His Grace the Duke of Marlborough (London: Printed for Jacob Tonson, 1705);

Remarks on Several Parts of Italy, &c. in the years, 1701, 1702, 1703 (London: Printed for Jacob Tonson, 1705; revised, 1718);

Rosamond: An Opera, humbly inscribed to her Grace the Duchess of Marlborough (London: Printed for J. Tonson, 1707);

The Present State of the War and the Necessity of an Augmentation Consider'd (London: Printed & sold by J. Morphew, 1708);

The Tatler. By Isaac Bickerstaff, Esq., nos. 1-271, by Addison and Richard Steele (London: Printed by John Nutt for John Morphew, 12 April 1709 - 2 January 1711);

The Whig Examiner, nos. 1-5 (London: Sold by A. Baldwin, 14 September - 12 October 1710);

The Spectator, nos. 1-555, by Addison and Steele (London: Printed for Samuel Buckley & Jacob Tonson & sold by A. Baldwin, 1 March 1711 - 6 December 1712); second series, nos. 556-635, by Addison (London: Printed for Samuel Buckley & Jacob Tonson & sold by A. Baldwin, 18 June - 20 December 1714);

The Guardian, nos. 1-175, by Addison, Steele, and others (London: Printed for J. Tonson, 12 March - 1 October 1713);

Cato: A tragedy, as it is acted at the Theatre-Royal in Drury Lane (London: Printed for J. Tonson, 1713);

The Late Tryal and Conviction of Count Tariff (London: Printed for A. Baldwin, 1713);

The Lover. By Marmaduke Myrtle, Gent., 40 nos., nos. 10 and 39 by Addison, others by Steele (London: Printed & sold by Ferd, Burleigh, 25 February - 27 March 1714);

The Free-holder, nos. 1-55 (London: Printed & sold by S. Gray, 23 December 1715 - 29 June 1716);

The Drummer; or, The Haunted House. A Comedy. As it is acted at the Theatre-Royal in Drury-Lane (London: Printed for Jacob Tonson, 1716);

To Her Royal Highness the Princess of Wales, with the tragedy of Cato. Nov. 1714. To Sir Godfrey Kneller on his Picture of the King (London: Printed for J. Tonson, 1716);

A Dissertation upon the Most Celebrated Roman Poets. Written originally in Latin by Joseph Addison, Esq.; Made English by Christopher Hayes, Esq. [Latin and English texts] (London: Printed for E. Curll, 1718);

Two Poems, viz. I. On the Deluge, Paradise, the Burning of the World, and of the New Heavens and New Earth. An Ode to Dr. Burnett. II. In Praise of Physic and Poetry. An Ode to Dr. Hannes [Latin texts followed by English translations

Joseph Addison (portrait by Sir Godfrey Kneller; National Portrait Gallery, London)

by Thomas Newcomb] (London: Printed for E. Curll, 1718);

The Resurrection. A Poem. Written by Mr. Addison [Latin text followed by an English translation by Nicholas Amhurst] (London: Printed for E. Curll, 1718);

Poems on Several Occasions, With A Dissertation Upon the Roman Poets (London: Printed for E. Curll, 1719);

The Old Whig, nos. 1 and 2 (London: Sold by J. Roberts & A. Dodd, 19 March and 2 April 1719);

Notes upon the twelve books of Paradise Lost (London: Printed for Jacob Tonson, 1719);

Miscellanies, in Verse and Prose (London: Printed for E. Curll, 1725);

The Christian Poet. A Miscellany of Divine Poems (London: Printed for E. Curll, 1728);

The Evidences of the Christian Religion (London: Printed for J. Tonson, 1730);

A Discourse on Antient and Modern Learning (London: Printed for T. Osborne, 1734);

The Poems of Addison, volume 23 of *The Works of the English Poets,* edited by Samuel Johnson (London: H. Baldwin, 1781).

Editions: *The Works of the Right Honourable Joseph Addison,* 4 volumes, edited by Thomas Tickell (London: Printed for Jacob Tonson, 1721)—includes the first printings of "Dialogues upon the Usefulness of Ancient Medals, Especially in Relation to Latin and Greek Poets" and "Of the Christian Religion";

Miscellaneous Works in Verse and Prose, 3 volumes (London: Printed for Jacob Tonson, 1726);

The Works of the Right Honourable Joseph Addison, A New Edition, 6 volumes, notes by Richard Hurd (London: Printed for T. Cadell & W. Davies, 1811);

The Miscellaneous Works of Joseph Addison, 2 volumes, edited by A. C. Guthkelch (London: Bell, 1914);

The Spectator, 5 volumes, edited by Donald F. Bond (Oxford: Clarendon Press, 1965);

The Freeholder, edited by James Leheny (Oxford: Clarendon Press, 1979);

The Guardian, edited by John Calhoun Stephens (Lexington: University Press of Kentucky, 1982);

The Tatler, 3 volumes, edited by Bond (Oxford: Clarendon Press, 1987).

PLAY PRODUCTIONS: *Rosamond*, libretto by Addison and music by Thomas Clayton, London, Theatre Royal, Drury Lane, 4 March 1707;

Cato, London, Theatre Royal, Drury Lane, 14 April 1713;

The Drummer, London, Theatre Royal, Drury Lane, 10 March 1716.

OTHER: "Tityrus et Mopsus" ("Hic inter corylos"), in *Vota Oxoniensia pro serenissimis Guilhelmo rege et Maria regina M. Britanniæ . . . Nuncupata* (Oxford: e Theatro Sheldoniano, 1689);

"Gratulatio" ("Cum Domini"), in *Academiæ Oxoniensis Gratulatio pro exoptato serenissimi regis Guilielmo ex Hibernia reditu* (Oxford: e Theatro Sheldoniano, 1690);

"To Mr. Dryden," in *Examen Poeticum: Being the third Part of Miscellany Poems*, dedication signed by John Dryden (London: Printed by R. E. for Jacob Tonson, 1693);

"Virgil's Fourth Georgic" (translation), "A Song for St. Cecilia's Day at Oxford," "The Story of Salmacis and Hermaphroditus" (translation, from Ovid's *Metamorphoses*, book 4), and "An Account of the Greatest English Poets," in *The Annual Miscellany: for the Year 1694. Being the Fourth Part of Miscellany Poems* (London: Printed by R. E. for Jacob Tonson, 1694);

"An Essay on Virgil's Georgics," in *The Works of Virgil: Containing His Pastorals, Georgics, Æneis. Translated into English Verse; By Mr. Dryden* (London: Printed for Jacob Tonson, 1697);

"Sphæristerium," "Resurrectio Delineata ad altare Col. Magd.," "Machinæ gesticulantes, Anglicè A Puppet-Show," "Insignissimo Viro Thomæ Burnet D.D. Theoriæ Sacræ Telluris Autori," "Barometri descriptio," "Prælium inter pygmæ & grues commissum," and "Ad medicum et poetam ingeniosum" [anonymous], unauthorized versions, in *Examen Poeticum Duplex: sive musarum anglicanarum delectus alter* (London: Impensis Ric. Wellington, 1698); authorized versions published in

Musarum Anglicanarum Analecta, volume 2 (1699);

"Ad D. D. Hannes, Insignissimum Medicum et Poetam," "Pax Gulielmi Auspiciis Europæ redditta, 1697," and "Honoratissimo Viro Carolo Montagu, Armigero, Scaccharii Cancellario, Ærarii præfecto, Regi à Secretioribus Consiliis, &c." [dedication], in *Musarum Anglicanarum Analecta: sive poemata quædam melioris notæ, seu hactenus inedita, seu sparsim edita*, volume 2 (Oxford: e Theatro Sheldoniano, impensis John Crosley, 1699);

"A Letter from Italy, to the Right Honourable Charles Lord Hallifax," "Milton's Stile Imitated," and translations, with notes, from Ovid's *Metamorphoses*, books 2 and 3, in *Poetical Miscellanies: the fifth Part*, edited by John Dryden [and Nicholas Rowe] (London: Printed for Jacob Tonson, 1704);

Prologue to *The Tender Husband, or, The Accomplish'd Fools*, by Richard Steele (London: Printed for Jacob Tonson, 1705);

George Granville, Baron Lansdowne, *The British Enchanters: or, No Magick like Love. A Tragedy*, epilogue by Addison (London: Printed for Jacob Tonson, 1706);

Prologue to *Phædra and Hippolitus. A Tragedy*, by Edmund Smith (London: Printed for Bernard Lintott, 1709);

"Epilogue Spoken at Censorium on the King's Birthday," in *Town-Talk*, by Steele, no. 4 (London: Printed by R. Burleigh & sold by Burleigh, Anne Dodd, James Roberts & J. Graves, 6 January 1716);

"Verses written for the Toasting Glasses of the Kit-Kat Club in the Year 1703" and "Lady Manchester," in *The First [-Sixth] Part of Miscellany Poems. Containing Variety of New Translations of the Ancient Poets: Together with Several Original Poems* (London: Printed for Jacob Tonson, 1716);

Sir Samuel Garth, ed., *Ovid's Metamorphoses in Fifteen Books. Translated by the most Eminent Hands*, includes translations by Addison, Dryden, and others (London: Printed for Jacob Tonson, 1717).

Nathan Drake keened in 1805 that Joseph Addison for all his literary achievement and "moral dominion" frustrated biographers, who stood helpless before his reticence and distrust of self-revelation. Time and scholarship have not made the private individual more accessible. *The Letters of Joseph Addison*, for example, scrupulously gathered and edited by Walter Graham for publication in 1941, exposed a cinematic "Thin Man," a largely nonexistent personality clothed and bewigged. Almost as if his personal papers had been censored, not a single piece of correspondence between him and his family has been preserved. Peter Smithers's second edition of a full-scale biography (1968) unearthed few significant clues to Addisonian uniqueness. Only surface details about the public figure, who apparently forfeited depth for appearance and impact, have been perpetuated.

A mélange of paradoxes, he made his artistic life fuel his political career so that a rapid symbiotic association developed between artistry and politics. He began by composing poetry, not because his mind teemed with images but because his was a poetic age, and he had no quarrel with its conventions. From start to finish—from 1689 ("Tityrus et Mopsus") to 1716 ("To Sir Godfrey Kneller")—his poetry lacked an imaginative passion, a reflection perhaps of the peace he made with the uninterrupted containment of his own mind. He experimented with several genres of drama: opera, tragedy, and comedy. Unable to write a fifth act for *Cato* when he had presumably plotted it in 1699 at Magdalen, he nonetheless finished it in little more than a week's time to satisfy the importunate pleadings of the Whigs about a decade later. *Cato* (1713) became the most controversial theatrical success of the first half of the eighteenth century.

A dull, hesitant speaker among strangers, Addison was purportedly mute among superiors. Yet in the course of a relatively few years, from 1710 to 1719, he devised a prose style that suggested uncluttered, good-humored talk. The fact that he presented little of his buried self gave a pleasurable dimension to his periodical writing, particularly to the essays of *The Spectator* (1711-1712, 1714). Such an abeyance of ego forced no new complications or intimacy onto his audience. Indeed, no barriers of angst stood between author and reader; each responded to the other in a near-perfect rapport of measured empathy. Addison's genius finally found itself in the undefined art of popular journalism.

He was born on May Day 1672 in the rectory at Milston, Wiltshire. He nurtured through time and inner necessity a dignified restraint which Alexander Pope later denigrated as a "stiff sort of silence," presumably an even tenor of disciplined emotion that gave little away and so protected the armored individual. Throughout his

life, he cultivated prudence, recoiled from financial pressure, and usually agreed to any offer of "employment" with an annual stipend. He accepted his ambition and a corollary quest for acclaim. He depended on "great men" because they were great; he could be useful to them and they to him. The point remains that he wore many masks as he tempered personality to the moment, and who the man really was has evaded definition.

Much of this expedient latency he absorbed from his father, Lancelot, who had been granted a B.A. at Queen's College, Oxford. Once ordained, the elder Addison responded to money problems with political sensitivity; he accepted his first clerical appointment among Royalist families in Sussex. Shortly after the Restoration, he secured, perhaps as a royal reward, the chaplaincy of the British garrison at Dunkirk. Serving there and then in Tangier from 1661 to 1670, he returned to England, married Jane Gulston, and settled down in the village rectory. No simple country priest ready for a remote parish in southwestern England, Lancelot Addison—a scholar, writer, and traveler—identified himself as "a Chaplain in Ordinary to his Majesty" on the title page of his first book, *West Barbary, or a Short Narrative of the Revolutions of the Kingdoms of Fez and Morocco* (1671).

The Addisons' first child died in infancy. Their second, Joseph, wailed so piteously that he was baptized on the day of his birth. But he survived, and several more siblings followed him. Lancelot Addison in the meanwhile maneuvered for a place within the ecclesiastical hierarchy; in 1683 he became dean of Lichfield Cathedral. Because of his father's elevation, the eleven-year-old Joseph without demur enrolled at the Lichfield Grammar School, an institution in the Midlands that grounded its pupils in the classics. The school helped the bashful but precocious boy to stock his mind with knowledge, to think in terms of a career, and to plan on political preferment by advertising his talents among powerful men in government.

In 1686 Lancelot Addison, now the holder of four offices in the Church, took his son out of what he dismissed as a provincial grammar school and sent the withdrawn adolescent to Charterhouse in London. Here the "gentleman scholar" stayed for a year, just time enough to meet Richard Steele, a "poor scholar" from Ireland. According to the speculative, if exaggerated, reconstruction of Thomas Babington Ma-

Portrait of Addison by W. Sonmans, probably painted at Oxford before 1700 (Collection of Viscount Devonport)

caulay, Joseph Addison, aged fifteen, had the classical expertise of "a Master of Arts." Apparently Lancelot recognized his son's scholarly nimbleness, felt that it had been little encouraged or challenged, even at Charterhouse. Again the boy was moved, this time to Oxford, where without choice he matriculated at his father's college (Queen's) on 18 May 1687.

He found quick collegiate distinction with a Latin verse dialogue, "Tityrus et Mopsus," published in *Vota Oxoniensia pro serenissimis Guilhelmo rege et Maria regina M. Britanniæ* (1689), a compendium of encomia on the royal couple's Protestant triumph over James, the Old Pretender. The dialogue, Addison's first extant composition, offers insight into the deftness of his political timing: it voices his allegiance to a dominant party and especially to its establishment, a loyalty that marked his authorship until the last publication in his life-

time, *The Old Whig*, in March and April 1719. The dialogue probably nailed down his election as a demy (a foundation scholar) at Magdalen College on 30 July 1689 with its small stipend and promise of a fellowship to come.

At Oxford, where he took his B.A. on 6 May 1691, he enjoyed the reputation of being a fluent Latin poet. Yet he doffed his hat to the new scientific spirit. At the encaenia on 7 July 1693, with the relaxed stance of an avant-garde intellectual, he delivered an oration using a gerundive imperative, "Nova Philosophia Veteri præferenda est" (that is, the new philosophy or science must be chosen over an outdated scholastic methodology). At Magdalen, particularly, he "fashioned" an adult personality. He was tactful, financially alert, obedient to the political order both in the university and in the wider reaches of the state. He realized that his search for identity

Charles Montagu, Baron Halifax (later first Earl of Halifax), circa 1703-1710 (portrait by Sir Godfrey Kneller; National Portrait Gallery, London). Halifax and another powerful Whig, John Somers, arranged a treasury grant to subsidize Addison's travels on the Continent in 1699-1703.

and reward had to continue despite a want of brashness, a hesitance to talk and push himself forward. He accepted such a conflict of psyche, came to terms with it, and inched his way upward.

On 14 February 1693, when he took his M.A., he calculated the limits of his current life. Comfortable as he was at Magdalen, he felt driven to prove himself with more than imitative Latin verse and to pledge fealty to patrons beyond college walls. He consequently tried his hand at English couplets addressed "To Mr. Dryden." Casting aside subtlety as counter to his purpose, he lauded the elder poet's "sacred Lays," "poetick Heat," and holy "Rage." The sledgehammer praise did not embarrass the recipi-

ent; rather, John Dryden printed it in his *Examen Poeticum: Being the third Part of Miscellany Poems* (1693).

Goaded by a desire for attention, if only to the extent that his name be echoed in literary conversation, Addison found space for four other poetic orts in *The Annual Miscellany: for the Year 1694.* Of these only "An Account of the Greatest English Poets" adds to the biography, providing a clue to his reading and taste. Like his contemporaries, he admired Abraham Cowley, William Congreve, and Edmund Waller. Atypically, however, he asserted the epic greatness of John Milton but immediately thereafter used his own literary affirmation for a political statement. While Miltonic verse scanned "serene and bright," the poet's republicanism—unlike Addisonian adherence to the Revolution Settlement—"Betray[ed] a bottom odious to the Sight." Textually the last of the "Greatest English Poets" was the Whig minister Charles Montagu, Baron Halifax, who presumptively suppressed his art of "negligent grace" for service in "*Nassau*'s secret councils." From this time onward Addison recognized that he could not make his way alone: that for himself no separation existed between art and a commitment to faction, that talent and propaganda were indivisible, and that even as an artist he required party sanctuary.

In 1695 he searched for a new patron in the Whig hierarchy, one even more powerful than Halifax. He dedicated *A Poem to His Majesty* to John Somers, Lord Keeper of the Great Seal, whom he entreated to "receive the present of a Muse Unknown." Addison piled flattery on flattery to etch the portrait of Somers, "the great man" who dispenses favor and office. "On You, my Lord, with anxious Fear I wait, / And from your Judgment must expect my Fate." With the entreaty versified, a subtheme in the poem proper cautiously emerged. The accomplishments of William's ministry, led by Somers, called for a publicist's muse to sing "in daring numbers" the subtle, understated glories of king and party.

The flattery and proposal worked well together. Somers sent for Addison who, when only twenty-four, had access to the two most stalwart Whigs in England. His deference paid off: it secured the fellowship at Magdalen he had long anticipated; it made possible the publication of the second volume of *Musarum Anglicanarum Analecta* (1699), for which he wrote the dedication and edited sixteen pieces, eight of them his own. The edition advertised the Whig poet whose subdued glibness rarely jarred or antagonized. As a literary experience it merited, according to Samuel Johnson, "particular praise," possibly because it borrowed words and styles from no one classical source but from many, all judiciously interwoven and attuned to matters meaningful in 1699.

If Addison's patrons gave him a leg up at Oxford, they also pushed him away from Magdalen's cloisters and shady walks. Aware of his literary potential and political adroitness, Halifax and Somers arranged for him to receive a treasury grant for travel abroad. By the late summer of 1699 he had crossed the Channel. The push that forced his vagrancy, antithetical to the stability of the "middle condition" he admired, was a pragmatic foresight which insisted on an end to

penny-pinching. He saw his travels as an assignment that ideally would serve the king and his ministers but, more immediately, would insure a paid "employment." The assignment, he knew, specified tasks from the menial (perhaps even reprehensible) to the elegant. Since he traveled under the patronage of the crown's chief ministers, he had entry into diplomatic missions. His tasks multiplied, imposing on the young man the technique of sophisticated watchfulness. For his sponsors he had to ferret out the names of friends and enemies abroad; for himself he had to eradicate hints of parochial behavior with a diplomat's polished caution.

Addison journeyed on the Continent for almost four years, from 1699 through 1703. However far from home, he never lost sight of political friendships or the opportunity to celebrate those friendships. Allegedly while crossing snow-covered Mount Cenis in the early winter of 1701, he reworked the formula of *A Poem to His Majesty*. He roughed out his new effort and entitled it—while yet in manuscript—"A Letter from Italy," addressing it to Charles, Lord Halifax.

In both poems the persona continues unchanged since the poet and his circumstances have not substantively altered: both are humble, diffident men, chosen celebrants of English "Liberty," the catchword of Whig polemic. Both are "ravish'd" pleaders. "A Letter" apostrophizes Halifax as one hallowed by sacrifice. The second paragraph of the poem in manuscript at the Bodleian Library (MS. Rawl. Poet. 17) in a rhetoric of omission limns a statesman idled during a Parliamentary investigation. The charges leveled against him in the spring of 1701 are poetically unvoiced. Instead the poet relies on a series of polarities to emphasize the wasted greatness of a great man. The persona therefore stands dwarfed alongside the fallen leader whose contributions to government deserve what he had never received: the grandeur of "Advent'rous song" and "Majestic Lays."

The bibliographical history of "A Letter from Italy" and the poem's place in the biography require reconstruction. Dating the manuscript poem "From Italy / 19 February 1702," Addison, temporarily housed in Geneva, sent it to Edward Wortley, who passed it to their mutual friends at court and to Wortley's relative baron Halifax, still a shadowy manipulator of the king's diplomatic appointments. The poet had set his political hopes not on a printed text but on a handwritten copy. (Indeed, "A Letter from Italy" was

To you, my Lord, my Gratefull Muse conveys
Soft gentle sounds and Unambitious Lays,
That big with Lansskips, paint the happy place
Where all the best of the Melodious Race,
By more than mortal Inspirations warm'd,
From Age to Age the Listning world have charm'd.
    On evry side I turn my ravisht Eyes
Gay Gilded Scenes and shining Prospects rise,
Poetick fields encompass me around,
And still I seem to tread on Classic ground:
For here the Muse so oft her Harp has strung,
That not a Mountain rears his head Unsung,
Renown'd in Verse each shady Thicket grows,
And evry stream in Heavnly numbers flows.
How am I pleas'd to search the Hills and woods
For Rising springs and celebrated floods!
To view the Nar, Impetuous in his course,
And trace the smooth Clitumnus to his source,
To see the Mincio draw his watry store
Through the long windings of a fruitfull shore,
And hoary Albula's Infected Tide
O'er the warm Bed of smoaking Sulphur glide:
Sometimes, misguided by the Tunefull throng,
I look for streams Immortalis'd in Song,
That lost in silence and Oblivion lye,
(Dumb are their fountains and their Currents Dry)
Yet run for ever by the Muses skill,
And in the smooth Description murmure still.
Sometimes to Gentle Tiber I retire,
And the fam'd Rivers empty shores admire,
That, destitute of strength, derives its course
From thrifty Urns, and an Unfruitfull source,
Yet, sung so often in Poetick Lays,
With scorn the Danube and the Nile surveys:

So high

Page from the manuscript for "A Letter from Italy," written in winter 1701 and addressed to Charles Montagu, Baron Halifax (MS. Rawl. Poet. 17; Bodleian Library, Oxford) first published in December 1703 in the elder Jacob Tonson's *Poetical Miscellanies: the fifth Part*, with the year 1704 on its title page.) Revealed to William by a courtier—more likely by Halifax himself—the manuscript reminded the monarch of the young versifier and his eagerness for assignment. But before Addison could be named officially field secretary to Prince Eugene, the imperial commander readying for an Italian campaign, William died unexpectedly on 8 March 1702, and the Whigs, confronted by a suspicious Queen Anne, seemed disarrayed.

Addison must have been distressed at losing a diplomatic post of value, one that could have led to a safe and permanent secretaryship in an English embassy. More dependent than ever on his dwindling grant from the royal treasury, he played out his role as a reluctant Ulysses. At the same time he translated his travel notes into a book padded with familiar quotations drawn from Virgil, Ovid, Silius Italicus, or whoever else rated a place in schoolboy texts. Concerned with places—a kind of classical tourism—rather than with people, he did not seek originality in his descriptions but a conventional resonance that reminded readers subliminally and comfortably of what they already knew. Published by Tonson, the book, a prose parallel to "A Letter from Italy," appeared circa 22 November 1705 as *Remarks on Several Parts of Italy, &c. in the years, 1701, 1702, 1703*. Ambiguously dated in the title and never clarified, even in the revised edition of 1718, this volume—perhaps the first of the two projected—spun an impersonal travelogue that began 12 December 1699 in medias res ("Monaco and Genoa"); it ended precipitously some vague years later with the narrator "coasting" through the "Tirol, Inspruck, Hall, &c.," never, at least in the text, to find his way homeward.

Addison came home in either February or March 1704. If his travels did nothing else, they strengthened the confidence that sometimes accompanies self-awareness. He had established several things about himself: he could write poems of flattery that lulled an audience of hardened politicians, and he could move with inconspicuous ease in diplomatic circles. No longer tempted by a collegiate refuge, he gambled on a Haymarket garret near government offices in Whitehall and waited for an appointment with official status. In the meanwhile he took his seat among the Whigs in the Kit-Cat Club and in congenial coffeehouses, such as St. James's. The London milieu, however, did not alleviate his financial anxiety.

Thrift was an ever-present familiar. In his mind he at first equated political employment with survival, only later with the quiet wealth and status he craved.

Unexpectedly, foreign affairs rescued Addison. In August 1704—some eight days after the battle on the thirteenth—all London learned of the triumph at Blenheim in Bavaria. Halifax, mindful of a patron's duty toward a disciple, thought a poetic celebration in order even when sponsored by a Tory ministry. He suggested as much to Sidney, Lord Godolphin, the lord treasurer, who was unfettered by precise party designation and who was probably one of the closest friends of John Churchill, the great Duke of Marlborough. The idea of an ode moved through ministerial channels until Henry Boyle, the chancellor of the exchequer, asked Addison to poetize the victory over France. The request was honored, a rough draft rather quickly turned over to Godolphin who, satisfied with it, appointed the no-longer "ravish'd" pleader a commissioner of appeal in excise with a yearly stipend of two hundred pounds.

The Campaign was published by Jacob Tonson on 14 December 1705, soon enough for the event to animate conversation and yet retrospective enough for the talkers to perceive its significance. The poem further captured a serendipitous moment with its appearance on the day that Marlborough landed at Greenwich with his prisoners, almost forty high-ranking French officers. *The Campaign* is both an overt paean and a muted dirge, cast loosely as a moral exercise with Marlborough the hero and Tallard the villain in a struggle for the souls and bodies of British troops. Refining a method that he had tried in his earlier political poems, Addison does not appropriate detailed fact or historical perspective: rather he generalizes an incontrovertible truth that young men, victims of the patriotic moment, died for military gain; he glorifies and so renders null a possible source of shame, Marlborough's scorched-earth policy in Bavaria.

Cleansed of potential improprieties, the English general, "Calm and serene" amid the carnage of "the furious blast," functions poetically like a brilliant integer within a scheme, "th' Almighty's orders to perform." Addison projects the metaphor of a "god-like leader" who rode *alone* across the front and gave the order to sound the charge. Within this metaphor of apotheosis there is no room for others such as John Cutts, Richard Ingoldsby, and William, Earl of

John Churchill, first Duke of Marlborough, whose military triumph at Blenheim is the subject of Addison's poem The Campaign, *and his wife, Sarah (portraits attributed to J. Closterman [left] and after Sir Godfrey Kneller [right]; National Portrait Gallery, London)*

Cadogan, all of whom had leadership roles in the struggle; even Prince Eugene carries off "Only the second honours of the day."

In *The Campaign* history undergoes no substantive distortion to the extent that the victory at Blenheim happened. But certain telling details are either minimized or set aside because they undercut what Addison intends as the theme of his Virgilian song: the military brilliance of Marlborough, who tightly controlled the battle in all its stages, who turned a tattered army into a unique weapon of high morale and single-minded pursuit. Unmentioned, for example, is Marshal Camille Tallard's accidental capture by some Hessian troops, who led him to the nearest allied camp, Marlborough's. The surrender, purposely not dramatized in the text, becomes the unvoiced climax of the poem, the abbreviated instant of Tallard's ruin and Marlborough's exaltation.

Similarly, to enhance the ethical dimension of British troops at Blenheim, Addison likens them to "martyrs that in exile groan'd," marching through "various realms" of inspirational nomenclature, an implicit *via dolorosa*. While he sounds the muffled beat of "Confed'rate drums" vaguely "terrible from far," he obscures the real-

ity of a polyglot fighting force (some fifty thousand) of whom not more than nine thousand were British. Since the allied armies have no place within the context of the poem, he can celebrate the campaign as a British venture in heroism and pious commitment.

He does not romanticize the "gore" of victory. He does not use the term as a poetic euphemism for dung and slime smeared with blood. The connotations of filth in clotted blood are present in his frequent repetition of the word. He does not gloss over images that catch the indiscriminate butchery of war, even at Blenheim, where "Nations with nations mix'd confus'dly die, / And lost in one promiscuous carnage lye." But he concentrates mainly on "the Gallic squadrons" in rout, pushed into the Danube. Here whole cavalry regiments perished, men and horses alike, the mangled bodies of beast and master, intermingled, swept away in "floods of gore" that mock the presumed dignity of death. Still, since he writes as a publicist, he cunningly subsumes the moment of mourning for fallen Britons—like "the noble Dormer"—by narrating the poem as a series of "wond'rous ... exploits ... divinely bright," much like a fairy "tale" with an unusual happy ending.

Jealous of Addison as "The Towring Youth" who had never known either "Envy or Party Spleen," Daniel Defoe, a ministerial hireling, in *The Double Welcome* (1705) excoriated *The Campaign* and denounced Addison as a servile hack before whom "Maecenas" (Halifax) dangled not a paltry carrot but a "Pension":

> Let *Addison* our Modern *Virgil* sing,
> For he's a Poet fitted for a King;
> No Hero will his mighty Flight disdain,
> The first, as thou *the Last* of the Inspir'd Train;
> Maecenas has his Modern Fancy strung,
> And fix'd his Pension first, or he had never sung.
> . . . .
> The Towring Youth with high Success aspires,
> And sings as one whose Song the World admires.

Such naysayers were few in 1705. Known for its larger-than-life portrait of Marlborough, *The Campaign* won applause for more than two centuries with at least two authorized editions in Addison's lifetime. Joseph Warton in his *Essay on the Writings and Genius of Pope* (1756) might have tried to question its success as a mere "Gazette in Rhyme," but for the most part its drumbeat of selective history and crisp heroic couplets depicted a romantic notion of battle. Yet the idealized images of poetry shrank before the stark realities of modern warfare early on in the twentieth century. No longer wholly credible is the portrayal of fearless military composure within sound of the "dreadful burst of cannon" and of a near-mythic leader marked, in the words of Samuel Johnson, by "deliberate intrepidity, a calm command of his passions . . . in the midst of danger."

Addison's life as a Whig publicist became busier than ever with the continuation of the War of the Spanish Succession. In November 1707 he wrote *The Present State of the War* and saw it published early in the next year. The pamphlet was his first journalistic commitment to the Anglo-French struggle, a logical successor to *The Campaign*, which focused on a single battle and its preliminary skirmishes. The format itself served him well: it let him work in a genre which he had not tried before but which gave a happy boldness to political editorializing. Designed for a large, mixed audience, the pamphlet commanded rapid composition at the expense of nuance. It therefore encouraged the anonymous Addison to speak paradoxically in propria persona and to argue for a party platform more openly than he

could in simulated verse epic or in any government publication, such as the *London Gazette*. Finally it gave him the chance to treat a single subject with persuasive intimacy, as he would do later in *The Spectator*.

The Present State of the War deals with material no longer pertinent to twentieth-century readers. What does give it interest today is Addison's out-and-out emergence as a propagandist. Like the fictive undeviating patriot of *The Campaign*, the pamphlet's persona or Addison himself, the two having merged intellectual identities, assumes a ramrod militarism that stifles controversy: the war against France has not only to be prosecuted but "augmented." The organization of the pamphlet, its emotional logic of cause and effect, is Addison's contrivance, but its policy had been hammered out by the Whig junto. Nowhere in the pamphlet, however, does he speak of party because he wants the theme philosophically enlarged, freed from the bickering and self-interest of faction. The pamphleteer promises to set before British patriots, and therefore people of his own mind, data which offer a rationale for the war and, more to the point, for its escalation. "Let it not . . . enter into the heart of any one, that hath the least zeal for his religion, or love of liberty . . . to think of peace with *France*, till the *Spanish* monarchy be entirely torn from it, and the house of *Bourbon* disabled from ever giving the law to Europe." His presentation—direct, repetitive, and flag-waving in a rousing wind—tacitly phrases a question: who but a traitor would look to peace? The answer is self-evident.

Early in his tract Addison asserts certain a priori premises, that the War of the Spanish Succession, specifically the conflict with "the Gallic Tyranny," is a live-or-die contest for England and so beyond negotiation. Still, some Britons in 1707 muttered about the desirability of peace. They believed that the military objectives of the 1701 Treaty of Grand Alliance had been fulfilled: that France's fleet had been virtually destroyed, her troops ousted from Italy and the Spanish Netherlands. Apparently dismissive of the peace-mongers and their arguments, Addison heard not the voice of the turtledove but only that of Whig councils that dreaded "the evil empire" of an insatiable France and her Jacobite allies in Scotland. What the pamphlet holds out to its readers is the prophecy of Whig merchants and their dream visions of Britain's untold wealth accumulated from and during conflict.

13

The war placed a halo on greed and beatified it with respectability. The Addison who mourned the dead in 1704 now accepted war itself as so many investments, whether of men or of bullion, as so many cautious risks when weighed against the financial gains that victory brought. "It may be necessary," he confessed, insensitive to his bloodletting analogy, "for a person languishing under an ill habit of body to lose several ounces of blood, notwithstanding it will weaken him for a time, in order to put a new ferment into the remaining mass, and draw into it fresh supplies."

Several years later—perhaps in 1718—Addison considered his pamphlet a successful foray in a paper war since he authorized Thomas Tickell to include it in his edition. Never republished before then, it has not withstood time's obliteration, in part because it wants the moral substance and goodwill of issue that perpetuate political writing; it wants the vibrancy that he projected in certain *Freeholder* essays. If the pamphlet occupies little space in the Addisonian canon today, it did in its time satisfy the martial determination of Whiggish Britons, prepared to gamble on the prospect of a mercantile empire.

The Present State of the War was, in November 1707, written to order by a polemicist impervious to war as a threat to social and moral order. For some forty-four pages he suggests the energy and rhetoric of a zealot calling for violence in the name of principle. "The only means therefore for bringing *France* to our conditions, and what appears to me, in all human probability, a sure and infallible expedient, is to throw in multitudes upon them, and overpower them with numbers . . . and in one summer overset the whole power of *France*." What his optimistic timetable deliberately obscures is a new scheme for replacing costly foreign mercenaries with native conscripts, for dehumanizing British lives as an "expedient," as so many "multitudes" and "numbers."

The year 1708 was a good one for Joseph Addison. He proved his loyalty to the Whigs as a poet, a pamphleteer, and an able civil servant. His political rise depended upon himself and his push but also upon circumstances. In February of that same year the Whigs and moderate Tories called for the dismissal of Robert Harley, secretary of state for the northern department, who had leaked secrets to France. Queen Anne, despite misgivings, acceded to their politely couched imperative. When Parliament was dissolved on 4 April, Whig candidates—Addison among them—faced the polls with jauntiness. He probably wanted elected office as another forward movement in his career: one that made his name as familiar as his literary output and enhanced his reputation as an administrator and a "man of business." In the spring of 1708 he sought the Parliamentary seat of Lostwithiel, which lay in a strong Tory landscape in Cornwall. When the contest ended and the declaration was announced on 17 May, Addison came in one of the winners with thirteen votes. Too Whiggish for minuscule Tory Lostwithiel, he willy-nilly became the target of several recall petitions. Not ready to surrender what he considered rightly his, he was nevertheless unseated more than a year later, on 20 December 1709.

Visibly unperturbed by this defeat, he had in late 1708 won a grander prize as secretary to Thomas, Lord Wharton, Lord Lieutenant of Ireland. Other employments followed inevitably from this association: he represented Cavan in the Irish House of Commons from 1709 to 1713; he became a privy councillor in Ireland and the keeper of records in Dublin Castle. On 11 March 1710 he was returned to the English Parliament on Lord Wharton's interest at a by-election for Malmesbury, a seat which he held until his death.

But to move back to 1709. Planning a London holiday, Addison arrived there in September and found that Richard Steele had already launched *The Tatler* on 12 April. Printed on both sides of a folio half-sheet, it offered a journalistic grab bag of political news, social gossip, wit, and unobtrusive tutoring. The first issue of *The Tatler* or *The Lucubrations of Isaac Bickerstaff* (as some later editions were titled) explained the diversity of each number and hence its fragmented format. "*All Accounts of* " genteel amusement "*shall be under the Article of* White's Chocolate-house"; poetry from Will's Coffee-house; learning from the Græcian; "Foreign *and* Domestick News, *you will have from St.* James's Coffee-house; *and what else I have to offer on any other subject, shall be dated from my own Apartment.*" In its beginnings *The Tatler* was considered another miscellany in the style of the *Mercure Gallant* and the *Gentleman's Journal*.

Even before Addison's arrival in London, *The Tatler* had become politically suspect, guilty by association with the former editor of the *London Gazette* and with Sidney, Lord Godolphin, who had from time to time allied himself with the Whigs, offended Queen Anne, and the Church of England. Tory Grubeans stood ready to attack the new periodical, but they could not

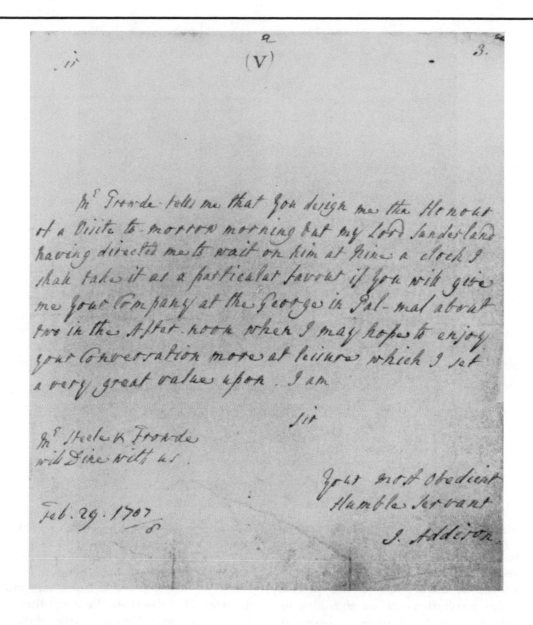

Letter from Addison to Jonathan Swift (Add. MS. 4804; British Library)

anticipate the variable and transparent fictions through which Bickerstaff or the author's surrogate sounded political principle without party label. For example, in number 4, dated 19 April 1709, Steele presents the parable of "*Felicia*, an Island in *America*" recovering from the "Death of [its] late glorious King." Felicia is of course Great Britain, whose "Chief Minister has enter'd into a Firm League with the ablest and best Men of the Nation [obviously members of the Whig junto], to carry on the Cause of Liberty, to the Encouragement of Religion, Virtue, and Honour." Before

the end of its second week, then, *The Tatler* made the late King William its mythic protector and the Revolution Settlement its talismanic rule of law.

Steele relished the challenge of outwitting Tory propagandists. But the thrice-weekly publication of the journal exacted a heavy price of concentration and ingenuity. As soon as he could, he bamboozled or begged contributions from friends and especially from Addison, who appreciated the maneuverability of *The Tatler* as a party vehicle with the further flair of authorial anonymity.

Robert Harley, first Earl of Oxford, who supported Tory journalists in their campaign against The Tatler
(portrait after Sir Godfrey Kneller; National Portrait Gallery, London)

Just when he first contributed to *The Tatler* remains unsure; debatable, too, is the precise number of his contributions (about sixty-nine in whole or part). Even what he wrote or suggested for it cannot be absolutely determined. An exegesis of the papers during his English visits (September or October 1709 to April 1710 and 19 August to the close of the journal) suggests that in these months the full-length essay became the favored form, that the characters of Tom Folio, Ned Softly, Sir Timothy Tittle, and "the Political Upholsterer" are in all likelihood his creations. Whatever Addison's effort in *The Tatler*, Steele admitted in the preface to volume 4 of the collected essays that his part-time collaborator "performed with such Force of Genius, Humour, Wit, and Learning, that I fared like a distressed Prince who calls in a powerful Neighbour to his aid; I was undone by my Auxiliary; when I had once called him in, I could not sub-

sist without Dependance on him."

The Tatler ran for 271 numbers, ending on 2 January 1711, perhaps because Tory journalists had by now zeroed in on its political slant and perhaps because the collaborators had already contemplated the start of *The Spectator*. However clouded the "Auxiliary" contribution is to *The Tatler*, John Gay in *The Present State of Wit* (dated 3 May 1711) wondered at the nature of a personality "who refuse[d] to have his Name set before those Pieces which the greatest Pens in England would be Proud to own." Trying to second-guess the reasons for Addison's self-effacement, Gay instead identified his essays with vague accuracy: "I am assur'd, from good hands, That all the Visions, and other Tracts in that way of Writing, with a very great number of the most exquisite Pieces of Wit and Raillery throughout the Lucubrations are entirely of this Gentleman's Composing, which may, in some Measure, account for that different Genius, which appears in the Winter Papers, from those of the Summer; at which time the Examiner often hinted, this Friend of Mr. Steele's was in Ireland."

Despite Gay's appreciation of Addison's performance in *The Tatler*, the periodical itself served as an adjunct of Whiggery. Almost from its introduction, the editors used their skill on and off, directly or indirectly, to frustrate the propaganda machine of Robert Harley (later Earl of Oxford) and Henry St. John (later Viscount Bolingbroke), who supported—according to *Tatler* 92—a "low Race" of scribblers (by implication, Tories) in their war against "great and heroic Spirits" (by reversal, Whigs).

Unlike Steele, who accepted the inevitable scars of editorial jousting, Addison resented journalistic assault or, indeed, any kind of censure. He particularly despised the opponent of *The Tatler*, the weekly *Examiner*, which St. John founded on 3 August to disseminate the Tory advocacy of peace while it hacked away at Whig warmongering. Then—between 2 November 1710 and 14 June 1711 (nos. 13-45)—Jonathan Swift edited the papers, which depicted the City Whigs as cannibalistic republicans whose fingers dripped with "the gore" of British lives spent in futile battle.

Not by accident, Addison in 1710 met Arthur Mainwaring, the Whig junto's chief propagandist, who presumably "could not suffer [*The Examiner's*] insolence to pass, without animadversion." As a consequence of this meeting, Addison published *The Whig Examiner*, whose title defined its purpose: from its very first number "to give all persons a rehearing, who have suffered under any unjust sentence of *The Examiner*. As that author has hitherto proceeded his paper would have been more properly entitled the *Executioner*. At least, his examination is like that which is made by the rack and wheel."

In terms of the image which he manufactured, Addison saw himself as a victim, destined to unmask the primitive brutality of *The Examiner*. His strategy, to laugh the Tories into oblivion, derived from confidence in his sense of comedy and timing, but in this case he fulfilled neither the strategy nor the assignment. For a short time *The Whig Examiner* stumbled on without vigor or direction. Perhaps Addison was too fastidious for sustained name-calling or for the dirty game of political invective. Perhaps his genius needed a cloak of invisibility, not the well-bruited secret of his authorship. Whatever the reasons

for Addisonian inadequacy, the periodical failed, historically askew with the moment of publication.

Between *The Present State of the War* and the ditto-like *Whig Examiner* Addison foundered as a Whig journalist. He could not humanize the slogan of "No Peace without Spain" which thematically framed both works. He could not make less predatory his Exchange-minded intimation that Britain's new plenty rose proportionately to the depletion of allied wealth. The truth is that *The Whig Examiner* did not excite a people tired of rations, high taxes, casualty lists, and, as he later wrote in *Spectator* 26, of "uninhabited Monuments." Addison's periodical in 1710 satisfied a handful of "new" men, of Whig merchants engaged in international commerce. But they required no more satisfaction than their bank accounts, their "fleets," and inventories.

Without the rage and manic sarcasm of *The Examiner*, *The Whig Examiner* became its own worst enemy. Too finicky for effectiveness, it left only a faint smudge in the paper war. For five numbers—from start to close—from 14 September to 12 October, Addison intuited the journal's end, since the cause it espoused had already tottered. Whether indifferent to or bored by *The Whig Examiner's* repetition of stale material and its deadly awful sameness, Addison committed a journalistic sin. He left unmentioned one of the reasons for the periodical's being: to promote the Whig cause at the Parliamentary election ordered by the queen for October. Such neglect stunned Maynwaring, especially in view of the Parliamentary campaign begun by the third *Examiner* in late summer.

He quickly realized Addison's lack of editorial belligerence, the rapid-fire attack that was called for in a crisis year. He understood that it would not do to match the "rack and wheel" techniques of *The Examiner* with the gentle and genteel defense of Samuel Garth's poetry or Tory calumny with an analysis of the clichés, passive obedience and nonresistance. Involved himself in writing some portions of *The Whig Examiner*, Maynwaring had to question himself: why would a reading public, eager for plowshares and pruning hooks, rise in anger when *The Whig Examiner* mocked its opponent's misuse of classical allusions, mixed metaphors, and improprieties of speech? The propagandist, who suffered no sentimentality, permitted Addison's periodical to die without an obituary; he simply supplanted it with another, *The Medley* (5 October 1710 - 6 August

1711). But like its predecessor this effort contradicted historical inevitability, and it too died, or as Swift wrote in the *Journal to Stella*, "Grub Street is dead." A Tory peace, in spirit, if not in actuality, broke out in 1711.

The Tatler, as we have seen, closed down on 2 January 1711. For the next two months Addison and Steele undoubtedly planned the character and makeup of another periodical to be printed and sold by Samuel Buckley and Jacob Tonson the younger, as well as distributed by Anne Baldwin in Warwick Lane and (somewhat later) by Charles Lillie, "Perfumer," in the Strand. *The Spectator* immediately distanced itself from the earlier journal by an avowal of political objectivity, an "exact Neutrality between Whigs and Tories" (number 1). Indeed, in several other numbers (16, 262, 556) Addison repeated his persona's disclaimer of partisanship. Forbearance became a lighthearted mode of deception operative on need. Almost as if to test the quick of his audience, he drafted the third number to intimate a party affiliation; that is, he mocked what he judged a bizarre Tory whim to capture the directorship of the Bank of England, which had been established in 1694 through the economic foresight of Charles Montagu. To emphasize the incongruity of the aspiration, he created a dream allegory that centered on the further incongruity of the romance figure, Public Credit.

Unlike the squat, leaden "Old Lady of Threadneedle Street," the allegory's young heroine sat on a gold throne in the Great Hall of the Bank. As mysterious as she was "infinitely timorous [that is, conservative] in all her Behaviour," she nonetheless decorated her salon with the Magna Carta and the Act of Settlement, with the Acts of Toleration and Uniformity. Suddenly Public Credit faced three pairs of mismatched dancing phantoms: Tyranny and Anarchy; Bigotry and Atheism; and the last couple, the Genius of the Commonwealth hand in hand with a young man, probably the Stuart Pretender. Brandishing a sponge and sword, he began to erase the documents that protected Britain's heritage of liberty. At this moment of crisis Public Credit did what any genteel maiden would do—at least in the masculine vision of international banking. She fainted, and her moneybags, demurely inconspicuous behind the throne, flattened.

In the nick of melodramatic time, predictably, "a second Dance of Apparitions very agreeably matched together" tiptoed into the Great Hall. "The first Pair was Liberty, with Monarchy at her right Hand: The second was Moderation leading in Religion"; and the third was the Hanoverian heir with the Genius of Great Britain. What had once seemed desolate, now revived: "the Bags swell'd to their former Bulk, the Piles of Faggots and Heaps of Paper changed into Pyramids of Guineas." Public Credit assumed once more her role of chaste mistress to Great Britain's wealth. Within a few days after the introduction of *The Spectator*, then, Addison chanced and won a Whig controversy without strident ado. The journal immediately thereafter resumed its posture of neutrality, and the readership grew.

The Spectator also differed from *The Tatler* in that it rejected a medley format for its papers. Probably at Addison's insistence, the new periodical offered a single unified essay in each number. The format itself projected a oneness of thematic purpose whereby the essayist would enlighten both men and women while he painlessly entertained them. He realized that his intention needed a lightness of touch. To achieve such delicacy in "distinct Sheets" published "as it were by Piece-meal," he would eschew mere descriptive prose and laboring digression, would instead "immediately fall into our Subject and treat every part of it in a lively Manner." He would reduce the material of his papers—no matter what its scope or profundity—"to their Quintessence" (124). All this he would "endeavour" to do within a folio half sheet, printed on both sides, two columns to the page, with advertisements filling the whole or part of the last column.

The Spectator built upon the reputation of *The Tatler*, and so it began with a ready-made audience of possibly "Three Thousand" disciples, "with Twenty Readers to every Paper" sold. During the first year of publication Addison repeated that the "Demand for my Papers has encreased every Month since their first Appearance in the World" (10, 124, 262). He emphasized the circulation figures to puff *The Spectator*, to sweeten his bitter recollection of *The Whig Examiner*, and to reassure an ego momentarily rattled but not muddled in the early years of the St. John-Harley ministry (later the Lords Bolingbroke-Oxford ministry until the summer of 1714).

The first series of *The Spectator*, the collaboration of Addison and Steele, consisted of 555 numbers, printed in sheets and distributed daily (Sundays excepted) from March 1711 to December 1712 and later collected in seven volumes. Of the 555, Addison wrote 202 independent essays with no help from others; Steele only 89. Hence Macaulay's mathematically just panegyric: "Addison is the Spectator." The continuation of *The Spectator*, or the second series (556-635), was Addison's with assistance from Eustace Budgell, Thomas Tickell, and others. It appeared three times a week from June to December 1714 and later as volume 8. Of the 79 essays, 25 were written by Addison, who in August had been named secretary to the Lords Justices (the Regents), about 10 by Budgell in whole or in part, and about 26 by Tickell.

To suggest the coherence of the journal's 635 papers the writers in the first series emphasize a few themes. So Steele and Addison in 1711 and 1712—Steele more than his former "Auxiliary"—delineated the world of London, "this great City," as they reacted to it. Still another theme—this time an Addisonian offering—concerns literary criticism, an unexpectedly popular feature of the periodical. The essays number about sixty, divisible into four groups: English tragedy (39, 40, 42, 44, and 548); true and false wit (58-63); "The Pleasures of the Imagination or Fancy" (411-421); the eighteen Saturday papers on *Paradise Lost* that begin with number 267; scattered essays on ballads (70, 74, 85), Sappho (223 and 229), humor (35, 47, 249), modern poetry (523). What these critical papers give to a spectatorial audience is a tidy package of fashionable criticism without either condescension or pedantry.

Fortifying the semblance of thematic wholeness are the Saturday issues on philosophy and devotion, formulated as lay sermons prefatory to weekend or Sunday meditation. Very much the contribution of Addison, they serve both a pragmatic and religious intention. They document the time-tested rational arguments for divine existence (459, 465); they give preference to natural religion over faith and therefore espouse a rational Anglicanism attuned to moderate government. The Saturday papers also deal with specific subjects such as immorality (111), zeal (185), atheism (186), enthusiasm and superstition (201, 458), with their implications of republicanism, on the one hand, and arbitrary government on the other; the nature of prayer (207); good intentions (213); God in nature, or cheerfulness as a "kind of worship to the great Author of Nature" (393); the scale of being (519); the divine attributes (531). To give these and other lessons in piety a charisma of their own, Addison composed five hymns (441, 453, 465, 489, 519), most of

them a reworking of favorite psalms in *The Book of Common Prayer.*

Dependent in part on the repetition of certain themes, the journal's unity is further manipulated by the presence of seven type figures who meet twice a week as members of the Spectator Club: the silent, featureless Mr. Spectator, whose voice blends with both Steele's and Addison's; Will Honeycomb; the Templar; the Clergyman; Sir Andrew Freeport; and Sir Roger de Coverley. The club provides a congenial narrative in support of the putative political and consequent social neutrality of the periodical.

Despite the persona's flim-flam promise to give each "Rank or Degree" of society a hearing, the journal deliberately cultivates a myopic perspective of classes, but deepens it into a narrative symbolism by the friendly conflict between the squire Sir Roger de Coverley and the international merchant Sir Andrew Freeport. By knighting the two men and making them clubbable—hence equal, or almost so, in a social hierarchy—Addison and Steele predicate an accommodation between "the landed" and "the money" interests in which each shares or exchanges benefits, "their just Rights and Privileges" (34).

Addison preferred Sir Andrew to all the other club members since he had already proved himself a person of accomplishment, a doer, who saw that his ships blown home from every "Point in the Compass" profited the public as well as himself. The preference is muted so that, like the others, Sir Andrew plays a comic role. What elevates him above jest is the fact that he "made his Fortunes himself" and his "Notions of Trade" (perhaps his only "Notions") are "noble and generous."

Contrasted with him is Sir Roger, who, "the descendant of worthy ancestors," has pride of place in the club's roster of membership. When Steele introduces him, he is a hearty bachelor, but out of step with the world of London in his rustic Toryism and even with himself in his showy parade of old-fashioned manners and clothing. Given more space and detail than Sir Andrew, the figure of "the good old Knight" is constructed upon a series of interconnecting polarities.

The squire's virtues both nourish and feed upon his eccentricities. When, for example, he and Mr. Spectator traveled from London to the country, they did "not so much as bait at a Whig Inn. . . . for we were not so inquisitive about the

Addison in 1716 (portrait by Sir Godfrey Kneller; Yale University Library)

Inn as the Inn-keeper, and provided our Land-lord's Principles were sound, did not take any No-tice of the Staleness of his Provisions" (126). Yet in the essay just previous to this mockery of the squire's blinkered Toryism, Mr. Spectator stresses Sir Roger's "Reflections on the Mischief that Par-ties do in the Country; how they spoil good Neigh-bourhood, and make honest Gentlemen hate one another." Ultimately the squire's capacity for friendship transcends bigotry and the "Malice of Parties." He loves Sir Andrew, although he sus-pects that the merchant holds "Republican Doc-trines" and even has "a Hand in the Pope's Procession," which the Tory ministry in 1711 cited as an example of "Presbyterian" subversion (269).

Even Sir Roger's death reveals the split within the personality. At once selfless and vain,

he "caught his Death at the last County Sessions, when he would go to see Justice done to a poor Widow Woman, and her Fatherless Children that had been wronged by a Neighbouring Gentle-man" (517). Addison perforce killed him off be-cause Sir Roger had no place to go; figuratively he clung to his ancestry much like a limpet to a rock. In a society that gauged everyone on per-formance, he did not perform. In a time of enter-prise, he bustled about to have antlers hung on the walls of his estate and a patchwork of fox noses on the stable doors (112). Addison enjoyed the knight's garrulous, if naïf, goodness; he re-spected his sense of a vital past. He knew, as he later stated in *Guardian* 137, that "a Man of Merit [and certainly the squire is such], who is derived from an Illustrious Line, is very justly to be re-garded more than a Man of equal Merit who has no Claim to Hereditary Honours."

Addison in 1719 (portrait by Michael Dahl; National Portrait Gallery, London)

Unlike Sir Roger, Sir Andrew Freeport, whose very name risibly allies him to mercantilist theory, did not die. When the latter makes his final appearance in *Spectator* 549, he feels comfortable with himself; he contemplates a life well spent in an "abundance of those lucky Hits, which at another time he would have called pieces of Good Fortune," and a retirement well earned. In withdrawing from the City to a rural estate, he insinuates that the time has come to cap his career and convert energy into a canny investment "in Substantial Acres and Tenements." In fact, he has the last realistic word in the survey and judgment of his life. There is really no more to be said on the subject. "I remember," he comments, "an excellent Saying . . . *Finis coronat opus.* You know best whether it be in *Virgil* or in *Horace*, it is my business to apply it." That the "Saying" comes from Ovid's *Heroides* in no way diminishes the old

man's strength or subtracts from his "Acres and Tenements."

The year 1713 was a time of shuttling literary activity for Addison. In that spring he composed, as we have seen, a fifth act for *Cato* and from a side box or backstage watched its first performance. That night and the drama's extraordinary reception brought him all the handclapping he ever desired and possibly a bit he preferred to shun. Whatever its reputation today, his one tragic verse drama made history in the first half of the eighteenth century. The reasons for such acclaim are atextual, lying not in spectacular or innovative dramaturgy but in its partisan theme.

But what is its "message"? When he hastily drafted the first four acts of *Cato*, he could not plot a conclusion and therefore could not conceive a thematic intent. While he had already turned out successful political verse, he probably had not affiliated a large and costly enterprise like the drama with faction's support. Wasting nothing, he continued to struggle with it intermittently and dully, unable to finish what had begun as an academic exercise contrary to his slowly emerging comic talent. He contrived a last act only in 1713, written—said Steele in a "Dedication" to *The Drummer*—"in less than a Week's time."

In preparation for the election of 1713, Addison was prodded to see in *Cato* the latent political texture which, with honing, could be made apparent to an audience set up for it. Lady Mary Wortley Montagu thought it deserved a place on the stage. So did the actress Anne Oldfield, wise in the ways of the theater and, as the former mistress of Arthur Mainwaring, experienced in the techniques of thought control. Other Whigs urged that the playwright complete the tragedy quickly, that he flesh out the declamatory figure of Marcus Porcius Cato of Utica, the stoic peculiarly unrestrained in his denunciation of Julius Caesar's tyranny.

Several individuals convinced Addison that the drama called for production as both a literary and party investment. Once committed by wishful thinking to assurances of alleged theatricality in *Cato*, he enhanced its twofold function. When he added the lines on the necessity of civil freedom, he hoped that an audience would recall buried memories of 1688, how the Whigs upheld the Revolution Settlement against Tory attacks. When he "flung" in "the love part," he capitulated to popular taste.

Whatever changes Addison made to *Cato* before 14 April 1713, he seemed compulsively eager to escape the charge of political bias for himself and his tragedy. He therefore approached Alexander Pope, an ambivalent Tory or a Whig, for an opinion of the play. Pope reported that certain lines had poetical merit but that the piece as a whole suffered from dramatic stasis. Addison seemingly agreed with this verdict but admitted "that some particular friends of his whom he could not disoblige insisted on its being acted."

Fostering his own "insistence" was a tangle of motives and pressures: his hope for literary adulation accompanied by financial advantage, his slow recognition of *Cato* as pointed dramatic propaganda, and, above all, his determination that no infighting among parties detract from a box-office success in whose proceeds he would share. Nonetheless, when with Pope—and with Swift as

well—he assumed the part of an anxiety-ridden dramatist who wished that the Lords Bolingbroke and Oxford would reject any invidious rumor that *Cato* was a "party play." In truth, he wanted the play understood precisely as such but as a "party play" that offended no party, especially the "opposite faction." At first he had it his way. Steele's crew, adroitly spaced throughout the pit, cheered every mention of the word "Liberty," while several of the queen's advisers were ostentatiously seated at the Drury Lane on Tuesday, 14 April, during Easter week.

Before that Tuesday, interest in the play—at least to Swift—was one of amused tolerance. He saw no party involvement in it. The debut of *Cato*, however, silenced Swift's forbearance and disciplined the response of faction. In a letter to John Caryll, dated 30 April, Pope described the event: "The numerous and violent claps of the Whig party on one side of the Theatre, were echoed back by the Tories on the other, while the author sweated behind the scenes with concern to find their applause proceeded more [from] the hand than the head."

In the first year of its run, *Cato* was unstoppable. It played in London some twenty times. After 1713 it became a standard repertory piece presented every season until 1750 and staged about 234 times by 1797. (It was printed with and without the love scenes some 111 times between 1713 and 1799.) Long before the end of the century, Voltaire in his *Letters concerning the English Nation* (1733) dismissed the love scenes as distasteful artifice but credited Addison with being "the first *English* writer who compos'd a Regular Tragedy thro' every part of it." By the time of the Regency, nearly a hundred years after the first night, it became the closet drama that Pope had initially said it was. Maynard Mack, in the spirit of a Popean biographer, recently described it as a "vast echoing museum filled with plaster casts."

After the triumph of *Cato*, Addison faced new literary demands but experienced few winning moments except perhaps as a "man of business." While he busied himself with the play at Drury Lane, Steele had begun *The Guardian*, which lasted for 175 numbers from 12 March to 1 October 1713 under the fictive editorship of Nestor Ironside, whose relatives in the Lizard family occasionally helped him with journalistic chores. Addison made his first contribution to *The Guardian* on 28 May with number 67. Presumably during July he oversaw the periodical when Steele

Addison late in life (portrait by Sir Godfrey Kneller; from Peter Smithers, The Life of Joseph Addison, *second edition, 1968)*

readied himself for the hustings and the seat at Stockbridge which he won on 25 August 1713.

As overseer, Addison sought to moderate Whig pugnacity in *The Guardian* with a series of playful essays on a lady's tucker, the "ruffle around the uppermost Verge of the Woman's Stays" (100, 109), on the parodic antics of lions and jackals (71), on a lion's head for a postbox at Button's (98). Even with these essays he could not give the fledgling journal an aura of neutrality. Clearly by August, Steele again set its tone by publishing on the seventh his combative number 128 on Dunkirk, an attack on the Tory ministry for not forcing the French "demolition" of the harbor there, as the Peace of Utrecht specified.

The spring and summer of 1713 involved Addison in a fever of politico-literary composition. He could not escape the ubiquitous *Cato* with its coupling of Whiggism and "Liberty" or Toryism and "Tyranny." Yet just before he substituted for Steele on *The Guardian*, he made a

blatant offering to the Whig platform. This time it was *The Late Tryal and Conviction of Count Tariff*, a pamphlet allegory which broadcast England's maritime trading victory over the French and, more significantly, the Parliamentary defeat of the eighth and ninth articles of the Tory-sponsored Treaty of Navigation between Great Britain and France. He wrote the allegory speedily between 18 and 28 June, saw to its publication on the last day of the month. He did not disguise its intention: its economic patriotism was designed as rhetoric for the Whigs. If it survived only as long as the issue which produced it, that was the necessary exorbitancy of to-the-moment journalism. Addison did not fantasize its place in literary history. Nor did he overstate the artistry of *The Guardian*, which, unlike *The Spectator* and even *The Tatler*, thought of itself as a partisan periodical. He watched *The Guardian* blaze into faction and consume itself. Unlike the phoenix, however, it died, a sacrifice to party. He could do nothing more for Nestor Ironside and the Lizards. He had contributed some fifty-two or fifty-three essays to the periodical, about thirty percent of the total number.

After Queen Anne died on 1 August 1714, England looked to George's arrival from Hanover on 18 September and his coronation on 20 October. In that interval authority lodged in a Regency. On Halifax's recommendation, Addison drew on 3 August an appointment as secretary to this governing committee. He accepted the stop-gap employment as he did most others during his political lifetime. But in a period of burgeoning hope, he anticipated one of the several high offices of government. He had, he confessed, serious "pretensions to the Board of Trade." But passed over, he suffered a bitter autumn—he wrote in carefully measured petulance to Lord Halifax on 30 October 1714—and felt weighted down like "an old sergeant or corporal." With the coming of the new year and for months thereafter, he swallowed "resentment," stood hat in hand, watching for a royal nod and a place that fulfilled "pretensions."

George in the first year of his reign presented an unpopular Germanic figure, reclusive and almost speechless if only because he knew so little English. His ministry set about gathering middle-of-the-road opinion on his behalf while shredding the Jacobite image of James as the legitimate monarch of Great Britain. They therefore turned to a publicist whose modulated voice carried conviction without intemperance. They asked Addison to create a Whig journal with a large circulation, one that could assuage extremes and bring them nearer to the center, purportedly to George. Almost as if in advance payment, he was named on 20 December 1715 a member of a significant trade commission with an annual salary of one thousand pounds. Three days later, the first number of the thrice-weekly *Free-holder* had been printed and readied for sale by Samuel Gray, publisher of the *Daily Courant*.

The fifty-five numbers of *The Free-holder* ran a sustained advertisement of the Whigs—their great men, their quasiphilosophical policies, and their Parliamentary programs. It circulated from 23 December 1715 (the day after James Stuart landed in Scotland) to 29 June 1716 (three days after Parliament rose). The reasons for its birth were several, both personal and political. Throughout most of 1715 Addison had searched for advantage. Before he agreed to undertake the journal as a solo enterprise, he demanded

and received—as we have already noted—a position on the commission for trade and plantations, which brought him early information on profitable exports and imports. He also stayed with the periodical out of an indebtedness to party, those "particular friends of his whom he could not disoblige." Finally, *The Free-holder* arose from his own creative urgency. For many years he had submitted to the fact that his fate, tied to the vagaries of Whig fortune, left him little time for serious composition, free of a propagandist's concern with the state of the parties. He had to grab at whatever opportunity came along, and the journal in 1715 promised such an opportunity. Hence, he considered it an artistic effort in which each essay, polished and complete, made a statement "upon Government, but with a View to the present Situation of affairs in *Great Britain*," endangered by "unnatural Rebellion" (55).

For a little more than six months, Addison touched upon or gave over entire numbers to Parliamentary problems: for example, to the suspension of habeas corpus (16), the passage of the Septennial Act (25, 28), and the increase in the Land Tax (20). With greater success, however—at least for today's readers—he wrote about the structure of the state: the principle of natural law and the doctrine of consent, their assimilation into the unwritten British constitution and the near-subversion of that framework by the Jacobites or the Tory High Fliers who screened their revolutionary motives behind the pietistic slogan, "the Church is in danger" (32, 37). Addison probed these matters Whiggishly but usually without "that Mixture of Violence and Passion, which so often creeps into the Works of Political Writers" (55).

He was undeniably one of those "Political Writers" who regarded *The Free-holder* as a supplement to his office in the commission of trade and plantations. As meaningful as the journal was to him, he remained conscious of his audience for whom he would lighten sobriety and enliven the dry materials of theory, polemic, and legalistic proceedings with witty equivalents of short fiction and characterization. He "sacrificed to the Graces" with what he called "proper Scenes and Decorations" (45), with the transmutation of political clichés into a narrative of stock figures—the Tory Fox Hunter and his Inn-keeper, Second Sighted Sawney, "Stateswomen" whose tuckers did them no good since their "Stays [were] ready to burst with Sedition" (26). The satire which energizes these types forfeited fine-tuning but never compromised criticism with belittlement or with invective.

Addison accepted the reality of party journalism even as he had become, on the death of Arthur Mainwaring in November 1712, a covert manager or an untitled director of Whig propaganda. For several years he recruited, advised, wined, and housed his hirelings. He himself enjoyed anonymity as a participant in paper wars, but even without anonymity he seldom retreated from a position or sought shelter behind the walls of the Cockpit. Rather he stayed in the field as long as he could. Almost three years after the last *Free-holder*, when he was dying, he took part in a journalistic contretemps over the peerage bill, an internecine crisis that camouflaged a struggle for leadership within the Whig party. From his couch in the spring of 1719 he actively organized an impressive group of pamphleteers and dictated *The Old Whig* (19 March and 2 April) in defense of the Whig establishment led by Charles Spencer, Earl of Sunderland, and James, Earl Stanhope. In the course of the verbal feints that followed, Addison's journal confronted *The Plebeian* (14 March - 6 April), written in four numbers by Steele in support of Robert Walpole and progressive Whiggism. The bill, never important except to a handful of aggressive politicians, failed of final passage. Indeed, the whole war of words has relevance only as a biographical moment, as a squabble between onetime collaborators whose friendship began some three decades earlier at Charterhouse. And that too was the price of political journalism.

In the last five years of his life little happened to Addison except that he married and died—but not necessarily effect from cause. On 9 August 1716 he celebrated his wedding to Charlotte, the widow of Edward Rich, the tempestuous sixth Earl of Warwick. While the match probably did not do much for his emotional life, it gave him access to the splendors of Holland House in Kensington, particularly to the library and galleries there. It probably brought him one of the great offices of government. On 6 April 1717 Lord Sunderland named him secretary of state for the southern department. Even some who were Whig-shy cheered the appointment. In a letter dated 9 July 1717, Swift congratulated the new secretary with an ironical caveat: "I am only a little concerned to see you stand single, for it is a prodigious singularity in any Court to owe ones Rise entirely to Merit."

Having deferred to party superiors for so long, Addison had little time to be "a great man." He suffered from a degenerative heart condition and dropsy, wrongly diagnosed from the symptoms of a cough and shortness of breath as asthma. By March 1718 he reluctantly retired with an annual pension of £1,500. Perhaps brooding on his physical decline—despite the birth of his only child, Charlotte, on 30 January 1719—he had few doubts about his literary immortality. In his will, signed 14 May 1719, he bequeathed his literary remains to James Craggs the younger (his successor as one of the principal secretaries of state) but assigned the task of editing them to Thomas Tickell, a professional Whig protégé. In the last month of his life he kept tight control of his emotions by contemplating and deciding on the order of his collected works to be published posthumously. The ultimate choice was his. He worked with whatever energy a self-employment demanded or the gasping for breath permitted. On 17 June 1719 he died at Holland House. The funeral, if he could have stage-managed it from a side box or the wings, was all he desired for himself, the fifth act in a life dedicated to the pursuit of fame and reward. He lay in state in the Jerusalem Chamber of Westminster Abbey during the day of 26 June. That night he was interred in King Henry VII's Chapel in the Albemarle vault "next [his] lov'd Montagu," according to Tickell's "Dirge."

The Addisonian personality has remained aloof, perhaps as secretive as the man who has always seemed a prepared surface with invisible, well-manned defenses. But the artist deliberatively left behind a record of performance—how he wished to be known and remembered. The best of his art is *The Spectator*, a collaboration which by comparative test pinpoints the nature of his achievement. Steele buttonholed his audience with an ingratiating openness and a hint—real or invented—of troubled immediacy: he "stumbled and got up again and got into jail and out again, and sinned and repented." In such a manner William Makepeace Thackeray synthesized his appreciation of "this amiable creature" in *The English Humourists of the Eighteenth Century* (1853). Indeed, he urged all "to think gently of one who was so gentle . . . [to] speak kindly of one whose own breast exuberated with human kindness."

What Thackeray missed in the interest of descriptive parallelism is the fact that Addison had greater perspective and comic instinct, greater

Charlotte Myddelton of Chirk (later Countess of Warwick), who married Addison on 9 August 1716
(Collection of Col. R. Myddelton at Chirk Castle)

agility of mind than did Steele. The "Auxiliary" brought the range of topics to *The Spectator* in language that approximates the easy drift of rational conversation. He perfected a "middle style," the verbal equivalent of his journalistic ethos. He wrote much like a literate reporter who never lost sight of his general audience. He was for the most part comfortable with the spectatorial world and its values. He did not ignore the truth that folly existed there, that time and effort, paradoxically, nurtured the trivial, the silly, and the downright nasty. Far from being the best of all possible worlds, it nonetheless allowed him sufficient space and privacy for a hidden spirit that had to be embattled. Because he lived in intimacy with this fictional world—possibly the only intimacy he required—he managed to catch the defining qualities of the age of Anne as few others could do.

Addison created a new journalism, one which painlessly ensnared and projected the ideas and sentiments of his readers. In a rhetoric that muffles the assertions of opinion and commitment—although both are there—he identified with his readers even as they identified with the pied-piper persuasiveness of his delicately crafted *Spectator* essays. Finally, author and audience possessed a mutuality of taste, which he articulated as a first step in a melioristic process of refinement—but he made no guarantee.

Letters:

The Letters of Joseph Addison, edited by Walter Graham (Oxford: Clarendon Press, 1941);

The Correspondence of Richard Steele, edited by Rae Blanchard (Oxford: Oxford University Press, 1941; reprinted, with a new appendix, Oxford: Clarendon Press, 1968).

Bibliographies:

Samuel J. Rogal, "Joseph Addison (1672-1719): A Check List of Works and Major Scholarship," *Bulletin of the New York Public Library*, 77 (Winter 1974): 236-250;

Robin Carfrae Alston, *A Check List of the Works of Joseph Addison* (Leeds: Printed by the compiler for private circulation, 1976).

Biographies:

G. J. [Giles Jacob], *Memoirs of the Life and Writings of the Right Honourable Joseph Addison esq., with his Character by Sir Richard Steele, and a true Copy of his Last Will and Testament* (London: Printed for E. Curll, 1719);

[T. Birch and J. Lockman], *The Life of J. Addison, Esq. extracted from No. III. and IV. of the General Dictionary, Historical and Critical To which is prefixed the Life of Dr. Lancelot Addison, Dean of Litchfield, his Father* (London: Printed for N. Prevost, 1733);

John Campbell, "Addison," in *Biographia Britannica* (London: Printed for W. Innys, W. Meadows, J. Walthoe, T. Cox, A. Ward & others, 1747);

Samuel Johnson, "Addison," in his *Lives of the English Poets* (1781), edited by George Birkbeck Hill, 3 volumes (Oxford: Clarendon Press, 1905), II: 79-158;

[Thomas Tyers], *An Historical Essay on Mr. Addison* (London: Printed by J. Nichols for the author, 1783);

Richard Phillips, *Addisoniana*, 2 volumes (London: Printed for Richard Phillips by T. Davison, 1803);

Nathan Drake, *Essays, Biographical, Critical, and Historical, illustrative of the "Tatler," "Spectator" and "Guardian,"* 3 volumes (London: Printed by C. Whittingham for J. Sharpe, 1805);

Joseph Spence, *Observations, Anecdotes, and Characters of Books and Men* (1820), edited by James M. Osborn, 2 volumes (Oxford: Clarendon Press, 1966);

Nathaniel Ogle, *The Life of Addison* (London: Printed by Thomas Davison, 1826);

Lucy Aikin, *The Life of Joseph Addison*, 2 volumes (London: Longman, Brown, Green & Longmans, 1843);

Thomas Babington Macaulay, "Life and Writings of Addison," review of *The Life of Joseph Addison*, by Lucy Aikin, *Edinburgh Review*, 78 (July 1843): 193-260;

Arthur L. Cooke, "Addison's Aristocratic Wife," *PMLA*, 72, part 1 (June 1957): 373-389;

Peter Smithers, *The Life of Joseph Addison*, second edition, revised (Oxford: Clarendon Press, 1968);

James L. Battersby, "Johnson and Shiels: Biographers of Addison," *Studies in English Literature*, 9 (1969): 521-537.

References:

George A. Aitkin, *The Life of Richard Steele*, 2 volumes (London: William Isbister, 1889);

J. D. Alsop, "New Light on Joseph Addison," *Modern Philology*, 80 (August 1982): 13-34;

P. B. Anderson, "Addison's Letter from Italy," *Modern Language Notes*, 47 (May 1932): 318;

Norman Ault, "Pope and Addison," in his *New Light on Pope* (London: Methuen, 1949), pp. 101-127;

Edward A. and Lillian D. Bloom, *Joseph Addison's Sociable Animal* (Providence: Brown University Press, 1971);

Edward A. and Lillian D. Bloom, eds., *Addison and Steele: The Critical Heritage* (London, Boston & Henley: Routledge & Kegan Paul, 1980);

Edward A. and Lillian D. Bloom, and Edmund Leites, *Educating an Audience: Addison, Steele, and Eighteenth-Century Culture* (Los Angeles: William Andrews Clark Memorial Library, 1984);

Lillian D. Bloom, "Addison's Popular Aesthetic: the Rhetoric of the 'Paradise Lost' Papers," in *The Author in his Work*, edited by Louis L. Martz and Aubrey Williams (New Haven & London: Yale University Press, 1978), pp. 263-281;

Donald F. Bond, "Addison in Perspective," *Modern Philology*, 54 (November 1956): 124-128;

Richmond P. Bond, *The Tatler. The Making of a Literary Journal* (Cambridge, Mass.: Harvard University Press, 1971);

Leicester Bradner, "The Composition and Publication of Addison's *Latin* Poems," *Modern Philology*, 35 (May 1938): 353-367;

Bradner, *Musae Anglicanae / A History of Anglo-Latin Poetry / 1925-1950* (New York: Modern Language Society of America / London: Oxford University Press, 1940);

Daniel Defoe, *The Double Welcome. A Poem to the Duke of Marlbro* (London: Printed & sold by B. Bragg, 1705);

John Dennis, *Remarks upon Cato, A Tragedy* (London: Printed for B. Lintot, 1713);

Bonamy Dobrée, *English Literature in the Early Eighteenth Century 1700-1740* (Oxford: Clarendon Press, 1959), pp. 102-120;

Dobrée, "The First Victorian," in his *Essays in Biography* (Oxford: Clarendon Press, 1925), pp. 201-345;

Irvin Ehrenpreis, *Swift the Man, His Works, and The Age*, 3 volumes (Cambridge, Mass.: Harvard University Press / London: Methuen, 1967-1983);

Lee Andrew Elioseff, *The Cultural Milieu of Addison's Literary Criticism* (Austin: University of Texas Press, 1963);

Albert Furtwangler, "Mr. Spectator, Sir Roger and Good Humour," *University of Toronto Quarterly*, 46 (Fall 1976): 31-50;

John Gay, *The Present State of Wit* (London, 1711); edited by Donald F. Bond in *Publications of the Augustan Reprint Society*, series 1, no. 3 (May 1947);

Bertrand A. Goldgar, *The Curse of Party. Swift's Relations with Addison and Steele* (Lincoln: University of Nebraska Press, 1961);

Robert Halsband, "Addison's *Cato* and Lady Mary Wortley Montagu," *PMLA*, 65 (December 1950): 1122-1129;

Donald Kay, *Short Fiction in "The Spectator"* (Tuscaloosa: University of Alabama Press, 1975);

Michael G. Ketcham, *Transparent Designs: Reading, Performance, and Form in the "Spectator" Papers* (Athens: University of Georgia Press, 1985);

C. S. Lewis, "Addison," in *Essays on the Eighteenth Century Presented to David Nichol Smith in Honour of His Seventieth Birthday* (Oxford: Clarendon Press, 1945), pp. 1-14;

Maynard Mack, *Alexander Pope / A Life* (New Haven & London: Yale University Press /

New York & London: W. W. Norton, 1985);

Brian McCrea, *Addison and Steele Are Dead* (Newark: University of Delaware Press / London & Toronto: Associated University Presses, 1990);

Allan Ramsay, *Richy and Sandy, A Pastoral on the Death of Mr. Joseph Addison* (Edinburgh, 1719);

Robert W. Rogers, *The Major Satires of Alexander Pope* (Urbana: University of Illinois Press, 1955);

George Sherburn, *The Early Career of Alexander Pope* (Oxford: Clarendon Press, 1934);

Sherburn, ed., *The Correspondence of Alexander Pope*, 5 volumes (Oxford: Clarendon Press, 1956);

Sir Richard Steele, "Epistle Dedicatory to Mr. Congreve—occasioned by Mr. Tickell's Preface to the four volumes of Mr. Addison's Works," in *The Drummer*, second edition (London: Printed for John Darby & sold by J. Roberts, 1722);

James Sutherland, "The Last Years of Joseph Addison," in his *Background for Queen Anne* (London: Methuen, 1939), pp. 127-144;

Jonathan Swift, *Journal to Stella* (1784), edited by Harold Williams, 2 volumes (Oxford: Clarendon Press, 1948);

William Makepeace Thackeray, *The English Humourists of the Eighteenth Century* (London: Smith, Elder, 1853);

Calhoun Winton, *Captain Steele: The Early Career of Richard Steele* (Baltimore: Johns Hopkins University Press, 1964);

Winton, *Sir Richard Steele, M.P.: The Later Career* (Baltimore & London: Johns Hopkins University Press, 1970).

James Boswell

(29 October 1740 - 19 May 1795)

This entry was updated by John J. Burke, Jr. (University of Alabama) from his entry in
DLB 104: British Prose Writers: 1660-1800: Second Series.

BOOKS: *Observations, Good or Bad, Stupid or Clever, Serious or Jocular, on Squire Foote's Dramatic Entertainment, Intituled, The Minor. By a Genius* (Edinburgh, 1760; London: Printed for J. Wilkie, 1761);

An Elegy on the Death of an Amiable Young Lady. With an Epistle from Menalcas to Lycidas [i.e., Lycidas to Menalcas] (Edinburgh: Printed by A. Donaldson & J. Reid for Alex Donaldson, 1761);

An Ode to Tragedy. By a Gentleman of Scotland (Edinburgh: Printed by A. Donaldson & J. Reid for Alex Donaldson, 1661 [i.e., 1761]);

The Cub, at Newmarket: A Tale (London: Printed for R. & J. Dodsley, 1762);

Critical Strictures on the New Tragedy of Elvira, Written by Mr. David Malloch, by Boswell, Andrew Erskine, and George Dempster (London: Printed for W. Flexney, 1763);

Letters between the Honourable Andrew Erskine, and James Boswell, Esq. (London: Printed by Samuel Chandler for W. Flexney, 1763);

Disputatio juridica, ad Tit. X. Lib. XXIII. Pand. de supellectile Jegata quam . . . publicae disquisitioni subjicit Jacobus Boswell (Edinburgh: Apud Alexandrum Kincaid, 1766);

Dorando, A Spanish Tale (London: Printed for J. Wilkie, sold also by J. Dodsley, T. Davies, and by the booksellers of Scotland, 1767);

The Essence of the Douglas Cause (London: Printed for J. Wilkie, 1767);

An Account of Corsica, the Journal of a Tour to that Island; and Memoirs of Pascal Paoli (Glasgow: Printed by Robert & Andrew Foulis for Edward & Charles Dilly, London, 1768);

A Letter to Robert Macqueen, Lord Braxfield, on His Promotion to Be One of the Judges of the High Court of Justiciary (Edinburgh: Sold by all the booksellers, 1780);

A Letter to the People of Scotland, on the Present State of the Nation (Edinburgh: Printed & sold by all the booksellers, 1783; London: Printed for C. Dilly, 1784);

James Boswell (portrait by Sir Joshua Reynolds; National Portrait Gallery, London)

A Letter to the People of Scotland on the Alarming Attempt to Infringe the Articles of the Union, and Introduce a Most Pernicious Innovation, by Diminishing the Number of the Lords of Sessions (London: Printed for Charles Dilly, 1785);

The Journal of a Tour to the Hebrides with Samuel Johnson, LL.D. (London: Printed by Henry Baldwin for Charles Dilly, 1785);

Ode by Dr. Samuel Johnson to Mrs. Thrale, upon Their Supposed Approaching Nuptials (London: Printed for R. Faulder, 1784 [i.e., 1788]);

A Conversation between His Most Sacred Majesty George III. and Samuel Johnson, LL.D. Illustrated with observations by James Boswell, Esq. (London: Printed by Henry Baldwin for Charles Dilly, 1790);

No Abolition of Slavery; or, The Universal Empire of Love (London: Printed for R. Faulder, 1791);

The Life of Samuel Johnson, LL.D. (2 volumes, London: Printed by Henry Baldwin for Charles Dilly, 1791; revised and augmented, 3 volumes, 1793);

The Principal Corrections and Additions to the First Edition of Mr. Boswell's Life of Johnson (London: Printed for C. Dilly, 1793);

Boswelliana: The Commonplace Book of Boswell, edited by Charles Rogers (London: Grampian Club, 1874);

Private Papers of James Boswell from Malahide Castle; in the Collection of Lt.-Colonel Ralph Heyward Isham, 18 volumes: volumes 1-6 edited by Geoffrey Scott, volumes 7-18 edited by Scott and Frederick A. Pottle (Mount Vernon, N.Y.: Privately printed by W. E. Rudge, 1928-1934).

The Yale Edition of the Private Papers of James Boswell:

Boswell's London Journal, 1762-1763, edited by Pottle (New York: McGraw-Hill, 1950; London: Heinemann, 1950);

Boswell in Holland, 1763-1764, Including His Correspondence with Belle de Zuylen (Zélide), edited by Pottle (New York: McGraw-Hill, 1952; London: Heinemann, 1952);

Boswell on the Grand Tour: Germany and Switzerland, 1764, edited by Pottle (New York: McGraw-Hill, 1953; London: Heinemann, 1953);

Boswell on the Grand Tour: Italy, Corsica, and France, 1765-1766, edited by Frank Brady and Pottle (New York: McGraw-Hill, 1955; London: Heinemann, 1956);

Boswell in Search of a Wife, 1766-1769, edited by Brady and Pottle (New York: McGraw-Hill, 1956; London: Heinemann, 1957);

Boswell for the Defense, 1769-1774, edited by W. K. Wimsatt and Pottle (New York: McGraw-Hill, 1959; London: Heinemann, 1960);

Boswell's Journal of a Tour to the Hebrides with Samuel Johnson, LL.D., edited by Pottle and Charles H. Bennett (1936), revised by Pottle (New York: McGraw-Hill, 1961; London: Heinemann, 1963);

Boswell: The Ominous Years, 1774-1776, edited by Charles Ryskamp and Pottle (New York: McGraw-Hill, 1963; London: Heinemann, 1963);

Boswell in Extremes, 1776-1778, edited by Charles McC. Weis and Pottle (New York & London: McGraw-Hill, 1970; London: Heinemann, 1971);

Boswell: Laird of Auchinleck, 1778-1782, edited by Joseph W. Reed and Pottle (New York & London: McGraw-Hill, 1977);

Boswell: The Applause of the Jury, 1782-1785, edited by Irma S. Lustig and Pottle (New York & London: McGraw-Hill, 1981);

Boswell: The English Experiment, 1785-1789, edited by Lustig and Pottle (New York & London: McGraw-Hill, 1986);

Boswell: The Great Biographer, 1789-1795, edited by Marlies K. Danziger and Brady (New York & London: McGraw-Hill, 1989).

Editions: *Boswell's Life of Samuel Johnson, Together with Boswell's Journal of a Tour to the Hebrides and Johnson's Diary of a Journey into North Wales*, 6 volumes, edited by George Birkbeck Hill, revised by L. F. Powell (Oxford: Clarendon Press, 1934-1964);

The Journal of a Tour to Corsica; and Memoirs of Pascal Paoli, edited by Morchard Bishop (London: Williams & Norgate, 1951).

James Boswell is important for several reasons. His biography of Samuel Johnson is undoubtedly his most celebrated work, and for it he has traditionally been assigned pride of place among biographers. *The Life of Samuel Johnson, LL.D.* (1791) is often said to mark the boundary between old and new biography just as surely as the contemporary revolution in France marked the boundary between old and new political arrangements. But Boswell the writer did much more than just create the most significant biography in modern times. He electrified Great Britain in 1768 with an account of the revolutionary events then taking place on the Mediterranean island of Corsica and later played a significant role in helping Gen. Pasquale di Paoli set up a government in exile in London. In 1785 he enlarged the dimensions of travel literature significantly when he published his *Journal of a Tour to the Hebrides*, a work that recounts a trip he had taken with Johnson through Scotland and some of her western islands in 1773. But Boswell's most striking achievement may be the private journals that he kept during most of his adult life. They were discovered only in the twentieth century, and are only now fully published. Taken together they constitute the greatest diary ever written in English.

Apart from his stunning literary achievements, Boswell's life was often characterized by frustration and disappointment. He was born to

Boswell's parents: Alexander Boswell, Lord Auchinleck (painting by Allan Ramsay); and Euphemia Erskine Boswell, Lady Auchinleck (painting by an unknown artist). Both portraits are in the collection of Sir Arthur Eliott of Stobs, Bart.

Alexander and Euphemia Erskine Boswell in Edinburgh on 29 October 1740. He was raised in a Whiggish household that adhered to the strict Presbyterian tenets of the Church of Scotland. When he was eight the family moved to Auchinleck, the ancestral estate in the western part of the Scottish lowlands, not far from Glasgow and Ayr. When he was thirteen he entered the University of Edinburgh, where he studied for the next five years, before going on to the University of Glasgow (1759-1760). Apart from his early love of literature, there were no signs that he was an exceptional student. While at the University of Edinburgh, though, he was to meet other young men who would later play a significant part in his life, most notably William Johnston Temple and John Johnstone of Grange. The young Boswell, if anything, was far more interested in becoming a swashbuckling soldier, and his desire for a military career was only one of many youthful conflicts with his stern and proper father. Alexander Boswell, Lord Auchinleck, wanted his son to follow his own path, to become a lawyer and settle down on their ancestral estate in Ayrshire as the next laird of Auchinleck.

Young James Boswell's response to his father's demands was to flee to London, some four hundred miles to the south, first in 1760 and again in 1762. Boswell's early journals have an intoxicating sense of freedom about them. In London he became acquainted with the people who would make such a difference in his life, John Wilkes, David Garrick, Edmund Burke, Joshua Reynolds, Topham Beauclerk, Bennet Langton, and above all, Samuel Johnson. Late in the summer of 1763 Boswell moved to Holland ostensibly to study law at the University of Utrecht but actually to be in an appropriate place for beginning a Grand Tour of the Continent that would bring him to Germany, Switzerland, Italy, Corsica, and France, and would include interviews with Jean-Jacques Rousseau, Voltaire, and Pasquale di Paoli.

Boswell returned home in 1766, shortly after his mother died, to the insistent demands from his father that he settle down. Before he could do that, though, he had to decide about a wife. He spent some time on this endeavor, finally settling his affections upon his first cousin Margaret Montgomerie. This decision may have been the best one he ever made, but from his father's point of view it was the worst. Margaret Montgomerie had barely a penny to her name. To underscore his paternal displeasure Alexander Boswell did not attend the ceremony and arranged to marry a second time, on 25 November 1769, the very day his son took Margaret for his bride. However, Margaret Boswell was to prove a loving and devoted wife, a true companion and friend to someone who would have exasperated even a saint. Together they had five children: Veronica (born in 1773), Euphemia (born in 1774), Alexander (born in 1775), James, Jr. (born in 1778), and Elizabeth (born in 1780).

Boswell's father died in 1782, and James succeeded him as laird of Auchinleck with an income that has been estimated as £1,600 a year, though most of that amount was tied up in paying for the expenses that came with the position he now had in society. The story of the rest of James Boswell's life is the story of ceaseless efforts to augment his income so that he could support his life-style and the ever-expanding needs of his five children. He enjoyed some success as a lawyer with the Scottish bar (to which he had been admitted in 1766), but the sums he earned were so modest that he determined to move himself and his family to London so that he could try his hand at the English bar (to which he was admitted in 1786). That proved to be a disastrous decision. Margaret died in 1789 from tuberculosis, and from that time on Boswell had to face life as a widower. He had enjoyed some success with the publication of his *Account of Corsica* in 1768 and *The Journal of a Tour to the Hebrides* in 1785, but neither publication brought in the kind of money that would leave him financially secure. To remedy this situation, he sought preferment. Yet, except for a brief stint as recorder for Carlisle, he failed to get a position that would bring in the additional income he so desperately needed. To be sure, there was a moment of glory in 1791 when he published his *Life of Samuel Johnson*, which had been seven years in the making. Nevertheless, Boswell's last years were by and large a gloomy affair, marked by various bouts of illness, constant financial difficulties, and psychological depression. He died in London on 19 May 1795. Three weeks later he was laid to rest in the family vault on his ancestral estate in Scotland.

Boswell did publish three major works during his lifetime, and they were sufficient to give him a measure of literary immortality. The publication of his *Account of Corsica* in 1768 first brought him to the attention of the public at large. The spirit of revolution that would become so palpable as the century came to a close was most apparent then in a backward island off the coasts of Italy and France. At that time Corsica was claimed by Genoa. However, a hardy group of native Corsicans, led by the virtuous and courageous Pasquale di Paoli, was struggling to throw off the Genoese yoke. Boswell, then only twenty-four years old, had visited with Jean-Jacques Rousseau. He was well acquainted with the conclusion to chapter 10 in part 2 of *The Social Contract* (1762), which pointed to Corsica as a shining example of what other European countries could become if they threw off the chains of tyranny. Boswell, then on his Grand Tour, was scheduled to spend almost all of 1765 in Italy, but he could not resist the chance to go to Corsica. He wanted to see for himself what this movement of national liberation was all about. He got aboard a boat in Leghorn that brought him to the Corsican coast, then made the rugged journey into the interior. He eventually made his way to the small village of Sollacarò, where he was able to spend almost a week in Paoli's company. After returning to Britain in 1766 he began to write an account from the notes he had taken at the time; then he added some two hundred pages of Corsican history digested from the work of others; at the end he attached a sketch of his meetings and conversations with Paoli. The book was published on 18 February 1768.

Boswell's *Account of Corsica* forces us to revise some commonly mistaken notions. It is easy enough when reading or hearing about Boswell's journals to come away with the impression that he was a frivolous character who was always chasing women or getting drunk. But whatever Boswell's follies, there was clearly an underlying seriousness in his character that makes him stand out from his contemporaries in a completely admirable light. It was not unusual in the eighteenth century for a young man of Boswell's class to go on a Grand Tour of the Continent, but it certainly was unusual for a young man to take the time and trouble to visit a backwater place such as Corsica on the chance that he might find something interesting there. On such a journey Boswell had to endure primitive living conditions, extreme physical pain, and serious danger to his life. It would be hard to think of a Horace Walpole or a Thomas Gray making such a trip. However, the young James Boswell did, and the burning curiosity that drove him on remains one of his most attractive qualities.

It also becomes clear from studying this work that Boswell would have achieved some measure of renown if he had never met Samuel Johnson. We can recognize in his portrait of Paoli many of the features that were to be used to much better effect in the later *Life of Johnson*, but which still win our admiration in their early form. There are, for instance, the deft verbal portraits, with an emphasis on dramatizing his material, often with sly humor. He vividly conveys the first moments of his meeting with Paoli, which are at once naive and uneasy; only later does he reveal that Paoli at first thought the preposterous figure who had come among them was a Genoese spy. There is also his record of conversation. It is clear enough from this work that Boswell was already interested in learning how to record conversation and that he could do so creditably. There is also the matter of autobiography. In *An Account of Corsica* there is a Paoli's Boswell, just as there is a Johnson's Boswell in *The Journal of a Tour to the Hebrides* and in *The Life of Samuel Johnson*. The important thing to notice about Boswell's autobiographical portraits is that they are rhetorical. Boswell did not use his published works as a way of shamelessly flaunting himself before an uneager and uninterested world. The autobiography grounds the reality of the events in Boswell's personal experience, as is right and proper. Moreover, it provides the artistic contrast that allows us to get a better gauge of who Pasquale di Paoli is.

Boswell's *Account of Corsica* is a remarkable achievement by almost any count. It is certainly one of the few occasions when a literary figure actually shaped events in the world outside the world of letters. Boswell certainly was not able to prevent the Genoese from crushing Paoli's rebellion. They achieved that by turning the island over to the French. Nevertheless, Boswell's book aroused considerable support for Paoli in England. He would later be given a pension of £1,200 a year by the government, and he would run a government in exile in London until his unfortunate decision to return to Corsica in 1790. If Paoli had been successful, if he had become the liberator of his people and the father of one of the first true republics in Europe, he would loom much larger today on the historical scene, and what Boswell had written about him would necessarily be of more interest. However, posterity is rarely interested in those on the losing sides

of conflicts in the distant past. To a very real extent the fortunes of Boswell's first major work were tied to the declining fortunes of the man he wrote about. As Paoli has continued to shrink in significance, so too has Boswell's *Account of Corsica*.

That was not, however, to be the fate of the subject of Boswell's next major book, *The Journal of a Tour to the Hebrides with Samuel Johnson, LL.D.*, first published near the end of September 1785, some ten months after Johnson's death on 13 December 1784. *The Journal of a Tour to the Hebrides* may well be the most important single work in Boswell's canon; yet it does not have a fixed identity. It is often printed separately as a piece of travel literature, which it is. But it is also a portion of the *Life* which would be published in 1791, more than six years later, and is in fact printed as a part of the *Life* (volume 5) in the Hill and Powell edition, the single most important edition of Boswell's works. As remarkable as *The Journal of a Tour to the Hebrides* might seem to be at first, it is actually a culmination of what Boswell had been doing for years. Thanks to the documents recovered from Malahide Castle, we now know that Boswell had been keeping a journal well before he met Samuel Johnson. If we did not have his private journals, we would still know from *An Account of Corsica* that he kept a journal at times, just as we would know that he was adept at recording conversation and that he had an eye for significant details and a gift for dramatizing his materials. What is new in *The Journal of a Tour to the Hebrides* is the figure of Samuel Johnson, and that seems to have been difference enough.

But why Johnson and not someone else? To understand Boswell's attraction to Johnson, we must attend to the serious side of his character. Boswell's initial acquaintance with Johnson was apparently through Johnson's *Rambler* papers (1750-1752), and they are not usually thought of as fare for the light-headed or light-hearted. From the beginning Johnson represented to Boswell something that he wanted and needed in his own life, a firm sense of direction, a rational control over the riotous urges of fancy and emotion. Of course, Johnson was also famous, and Boswell was always curious about the people he read and heard about. Following the publication of Johnson's *Dictionary* in 1755 Boswell heard more and more of Johnson. That is undoubtedly why he wanted to meet him as early as his first jaunt to London in 1762, and why he had asked first

*James Boswell (engraving by E. Finden after a portrait
by G. Langton)*

Thomas Sheridan and then Andrew Erskine to arrange a meeting for him. Boswell was not, of
course, to meet Johnson by those means, but instead almost incidentally on 16 May 1763, while
he was sipping tea in the room behind Tom
Davies's bookshop. Their first meeting was not
auspicious. Boswell was a callow youth of twenty-
two and much too bent on making a good impression, while Johnson at fifty-three was not the
kind to be easily impressed under the best of circumstances. He certainly was not ready to be told
by a youngster, and a Scots youngster at that,
how he should handle his relations with David
Garrick.

The real story of their relationship probably
begins with the follow-up meeting at Johnson's
quarters in the Inner Temple. There the two
discovered that they enjoyed one another's
company, undoubtedly with Boswell seeing in

Johnson the kind of father figure he had always
wanted, while Johnson saw in Boswell the son he
had never had. Those, of course, are overtones
in their relationship, but they were never prisoners of narrow psychological roles. First and foremost, they became friends, in the deepest and
truest sense of that word. For a while that friendship could only be continued by letter, because
Boswell was to set off on a Grand Tour that
would take him through Germany, Italy, France,
and, of course, to Corsica, and therefore away
from Great Britain for more than two years.
When Boswell returned there was a noticeable improvement in his ability to record Johnson's conversations, something he could not do so easily at
first. Recording conversation is no easy matter. It
is an art that has to be learned, and one that can
be improved through practice. Boswell practiced
his art in his journals, and gradually got better.

His growing skill at recording conversation
made the idea of a trip to Scotland by Johnson
all the more pivotal. The eighteenth century, as
is so often noted, was an age of travel; travel was
a tool for exploration and investigation and thus
an important part of the intellectual debates of
the time. The thirst for knowledge could well be
Johnson's most conspicuous trait, but limited by
circumstances and also by poverty, he had not
been able to travel to any significant extent. A
trip to Scotland, and particularly to the Hebrides,
offered him the opportunity to do something he
had always wanted to do, to travel about and test
for himself the current social theories, particularly those that argued for the superiority of primitive societies. With Boswell for a traveling
companion he knew he would have somebody
with him who would make the journey as enjoyable as possible. For Boswell it was an opportunity to be in Johnson's company on an uninterrupted basis. It was also to be a kind of
experiment. He would get to see what this literary lion would be like away from the familiar circumstances of London.

We do not know exactly when Boswell decided that his way to literary fame would be
as Johnson's biographer. According to Marshall
Waingrow, the first written evidence occurs in
1769 when Boswell asked Johnson if it would be
all right to publish his letters after his death. Boswell first indicated that he had something far
grander in mind on 31 March 1772, when he
wrote in his journal: "I have a constant plan to
write the life of Mr. Johnson. I have not told him
of it yet, nor do I know if I should tell him." By

31 March 1772 Boswell had also obtained Johnson's agreement to come to Scotland. The journey was to be delayed, but Johnson came on 19 August 1773, after first accompanying his friend Robert Chambers to Newcastle.

Johnson's visit to Scotland was successful beyond Boswell's wildest dreams. It gave him time to know Johnson better than ever because he had 101 days in his company without any significant interruptions. It allowed him to see Johnson in a variety of circumstances: from poking about inside a smoky hut on the edge of Loch Ness to elegant dining with the duke and duchess of Argyll; from the salty company of illiterate boatmen as they sailed from isle to isle to that of cerebral university dons in Glasgow; from spirited conversations with such intellectually sophisticated figures as William Robertson and James Burnett, Lord Monboddo, to heated political arguments with Lord Auchinleck, Boswell's stubbornly Whiggish father. On land and on sea, through valleys and over mountains they traveled, but above all they talked: talked about trees, talked about turnips, talked about Ossian, talked about social theories, talked about government. It was out of the record of these days that Boswell, with help from Edmond Malone, would carve out *The Journal of a Tour to the Hebrides* that he published in 1785. More important, it was at this moment that he decided he had whatever it would take to write the "life" of Samuel Johnson. Nevertheless, writing a "life" necessarily involved a much larger scale than the limited dimensions of a "tour" or "journey," so Boswell faced an immensely more difficult and daunting task.

Boswell worked on shaping and refining his *Life of Johnson* for the better part of the six and a half years that passed between the death of Johnson on 13 December 1784 and its publication on 16 May 1791. By almost all measures it is an admirable achievement, one of the greatest books to be published in eighteenth-century England, and undoubtedly the most famous biography in the English-speaking world. It is a remarkable achievement even by what could be described as the scientific standards of biography. The basic arrangement of the *Life* is chronological, and that is because Boswell more than any other single person established the chronology of the events in Johnson's life. There have been some notable modern successes at filling in the gaps in that chronology—for example, Johnson's secret collaboration with Robert Chambers on the Vinerian Law Lectures in the late 1760s—but the basic chronology that Boswell established has not been seriously challenged. Boswell also added to the dimensions of the Johnson canon, giving emphasis to the many unsigned pieces Johnson published during his first years in London. There have been other additions to the canon. We have learned, for instance, that Johnson was responsible for the sections on foreign books and foreign history in the *Gentleman's Magazine*, that he wrote electoral addresses for Henry Thrale, and that he helped Bishop Thomas Percy with the *Reliques of Ancient English Poetry* (1765). None of these, however, have substantially altered our picture of his interests and achievements, though they have enlarged it.

Boswell's *Life* also contains a substantial collection of Johnson's letters, 344 in all. This is particularly important to Boswell's method because he had claimed that he adopted the example of William Mason in his *Memoirs of the Life and Writings of Thomas Gray* (1775)—that is, he intended to let Johnson speak in his own voice so that where and when possible he would be telling his own story. This is a clear advantage, for instance, over Sir John Hawkins, who, though he quoted generously from Johnson's writings in his biography, quoted only sparingly from letters because he had so few to quote from. In 1788, the year after Hawkins's biography appeared, Hester Thrale Piozzi published an edition of Johnson's letters, mostly to herself. Boswell's contribution would of course include a generous number of letters to and from himself, but it also includes many letters to and from other correspondents, including the well-known letter to Philip Dormer Stanhope, Lord Chesterfield, as well as letters to and from Bennet Langton, Charles Burney, Sir Joshua Reynolds, and Thomas Warton, among others. The fact that he could publish these letters is powerful testimony to his industry and his diligence.

Boswell's *Life of Johnson*, like any biography, is basically a record of facts. The excellence of a biography is measured first by the accuracy with which it records the facts of its subject's life. It must, however, be more than accurate; it must also be full; that is, it must record all the facts that we would want to know. To assess Boswell's *Life of Johnson* as a record of facts properly requires an understanding of the nature of the task Boswell faced as he set out to account for the whole of Johnson's life. Boswell was certainly acquainted with him during the later part of his life, but he had no personal knowledge of John-

(56.)

this morning with the illustrious
Donaldson. In the evening I went
to Temple's: he brought me ac:
quainted with a Mr Claxton a
very good sort of a young man tho
reserved at first. Mr Nicholls was
there too. Our conversation was
sensible & lively. I wish I could
spend my time allways in such company.

     Monday 16 May.

Temple & his Brother breakfas:
ted with me. I went to Love's
to try to recover some of the mo:
ney which he owes me. But alas
a single guinea was all I could
get. He was just going to dinner,
so I stayed & eat a bit, tho I was
angry at myself afterwards.
I drank tea at Davies's in Russ:
el Street and about seven came
in the great Mr Samuel John:
son, whom I have so long wished
to see. Mr Davies introduced
me to him. As I knew his mortal
antipathy at the Scotch, I said
to

Description of Boswell's first meeting with Samuel Johnson, from Boswell's journal entry for 16 May 1763
(Yale University Library)

36

(563)

to Davies; don't tell where I come
from. However he said From Scotland.
Mr Johnson said I indeed I come
from Scotland, but I cannot help
it. : Sir replied he. : That I find
is what a very great many of
your countrymen cannot help.
Mr Johnson is a man of a most
dreadfull appearance. He is a
very big man is troubled with sore
eyes, the Palsy & the King's
evil. He is very slovenly in
his dress & speaks with a
most uncouth voice. Yet his
great knowledge, and strength
of expression command vast
respect and render him very
excellent company. He has
great humour and is a worthy
man. But his dogmatical rough:
:ness of manners is disagreable.
I

son during his early years or even when he first became a celebrated public figure.

The first problem then was lack of information on the period of Johnson's life before Boswell met him in 1763. Johnson's early years were particularly obscure. Since only about one-fifth of the *Life* is devoted to the first fifty-three years of Johnson's life, which included his schooling up through his thirteen months at Pembroke College, Oxford, his several failed attempts at finding a way to earn a living, his marriage to the widowed Elizabeth Porter, his early literary successes, his triumph as a public figure with the *Dictionary*, and the granting of his pension, it is clear enough that Boswell did not fully succeed with the task he had set for himself. Modern scholars have understandably focused on the early and middle years as the areas where the Boswellian record might be improved, and they have drawn attention to some obvious gaps and occasional mistakes.

It has been argued, and argued rightly, that we do not learn all we might need to know or all we would like to know about Johnson from the pages of Boswell's biography. Certainly we have only an imperfect notion of how Johnson was formed by family life, what his relationships must or could have been with his father, Michael; his mother, Sarah; and his brother, Nathaniel. It is also true that we have little sense of Johnson as a married man, though he was married for more than seventeen years. We can develop a somewhat better sense of his intellectual development, but even here there is much more that we would like to know. Boswell reported correctly that Johnson had left Oxford before taking a degree, but he did make a mistake in relying on information he had received from the Reverend William Adams, who was the master of Pembroke College when Boswell knew him. As a result Boswell left the young Samuel Johnson at Pembroke for "little more than three years," when, according to the information supplied by Pembroke's buttery books, Johnson actually resided at Oxford for only thirteen months before returning to Lichfield. There are mistakes in Boswell's *Life*, but they are not numerous. More important, what mistakes there are not of the kind that would dramatically alter our understanding of Johnson.

What is all too easily forgotten when enumerating Boswell's relatively few lapses is how much he got right. Just how much he did get right becomes readily apparent when Boswell's work is compared with that of other of his contemporaries. Between Johnson's death on 13 December 1784 and the publication of Boswell's *Life* on 16 May 1791, roughly sixteen biographical accounts of Johnson were published. At least two of them—Hester Thrale Piozzi's *Anecdotes of the Late Samuel Johnson*, published in 1786, and Sir John Hawkins's *Life of Samuel Johnson*, published in 1787—can be considered major works. If we compare what we learn from them about Johnson's early years, including how long he attended Pembroke College, we quickly see that Boswell stands out as the most reliable of the early biographers. We learn about his family—father, mother, and brother—from all the major biographers. We learn from each of them, for instance, that young Samuel contracted scrofula from his wet nurse and that his mother brought him to London so that he could be touched by the queen. But both Hawkins and Piozzi repeat the story of a three-year-old child prodigy composing verses on a duck, while we learn from Boswell that the verses were really composed by Johnson's father. Hester Thrale Piozzi retells some anecdotes about Johnson's days at Oxford but is vague about the details of his residence there, while Sir John Hawkins leaves Johnson at Oxford just as long as Boswell did. Hawkins noted that Johnson had left Oxford for Lichfield in December of 1729, but he was sure that he had returned to Oxford and "made up the whole of his residence in the university, about three years." If Boswell is occasionally unreliable, so are his chief rivals. It is in the early years that modern scholars have been most successful in adding to and completing the Boswellian record, but that is largely because the Boswellian record has always been so reliable to begin with.

Johnson's middle years represent a different problem. The middle years refer to the time when Johnson became a public figure and acquired the reputation of being the greatest literary figure in England, in other words, the time of *The Rambler* (1750-1752) and the *Dictionary* (1755), of *Rasselas* (1759) and *The Idler* (1758-1760). The middle years are usually dated from 1749, the year when Johnson published *The Vanity of Human Wishes*, the first publication to have his name on the title page, to the year 1763, when he first met Boswell. Boswell was not, of course, personally acquainted with Johnson during those years either, but many of the people he knew best were, and he relied upon them for accurate information. This is part of the importance, for instance, of Sir Joshua Reynolds, Frank

Boswell in Rome, 1765 (painting by George Willison; Scottish National Portrait Gallery)

Barber, Oliver Goldsmith, David Garrick, Dr. Charles Burney, Arthur Murphy, William Maxwell, Topham Beauclerk, and Bennet Langton. Boswell collected information from each of these, and fleshed out his record with their testimony.

Boswell's method can be illustrated in his reconstruction of the events that led up to Johnson's quarrel with Lord Chesterfield just before the publication of his *Dictionary* on 15 April 1755. The origins of that quarrel were in Johnson's dedication of his original *Plan of a Dictionary* to Lord Chesterfield in August 1747. Johnson, young and still relatively unknown, hungry and poor, undoubtedly expected further interest and favors for his work from the earl. Chesterfield meanwhile believed that he had shown all the interest and encouragement that was appropriate with a gift of ten pounds to the starving author. Somehow, contrary to expectations, Johnson pushed on and eventually completed his work on the *Dictionary*, and according to all the reports had completed it brilliantly. The earl of

Chesterfield, hearing those reports, and with a clear and distinct memory of the dedication of the *Plan* still in his head, near the end of 1754 composed two highly flattering essays on the approaching publication of Johnson's *Dictionary* for a periodical called the *World*. Johnson responded to the essays in the *World* with his now-famous letter rejecting Lord Chesterfield's flatteries as belated attempts to have the *Dictionary* dedicated to him: "Is not a Patron, my Lord, one who looks with unconcern on a man struggling for life in the water, and, when he has reached ground, encumbers him with help?"

To appreciate Boswell's achievement in this account we need only compare his version with the mangled versions we find in all other contemporary biographies. All of Johnson's first biographers were aware that there had been a serious quarrel between Johnson and Lord Chesterfield, and most of them knew that there had been some kind of letter, though they were not sure when the letter was sent, nor what it said. Almost everybody believed that the quarrel had been started when Lord Chesterfield had snubbed Johnson for Colley Cibber, a man with a reputation as the prince of dunces. Some of the early biographers, though not all, mention the publication of the two essays in the *World*, but for the most part they thought the essays were published after the quarrel rather than before it. This led them to see the essays in the *World* as Lord Chesterfield's failed attempt to patch up the quarrel, whereas actually they were what triggered it. The principal source for Boswell's account in the *Life* is unimpeachable because it was Johnson himself. He denied that Lord Chesterfield had ever preferred Colley Cibber before him, and in fact denied that there had ever been a single incident that had brought about the rupture between them. It was Boswell who persuaded Johnson to dictate from memory a copy of the letter he had written to Lord Chesterfield in the first week of February 1755 repudiating his patronage. It was Boswell who first published that letter along with suitable excerpts from Lord Chesterfield's essays in the *World*. Boswell fleshed out some of the details from Johnson's friend the Reverend William Adams, who was residing in London at the time. He may also have relied on, directly or indirectly, Robert Dodsley, who played a part, too, in these events. It is much in the same vein that he reconstructed other key events during Johnson's middle years, such as the death of his wife and the awarding of his pension.

If Boswell as Johnson's biographer had done no more than what he did for Johnson's early and middle years, he would undoubtedly have won some form of immortality. But it is his account of the later years, the last twenty-one years of Johnson's life, that earned him literary greatness and forever changed the meaning of what constitutes a biography. He did this because of his record of conversations, the most celebrated part of his *Life of Johnson* and Boswell's most distinctive contribution to the art of biography. Any just estimate of his artistic stature must make this a center of concern because here Boswell was doing what nobody else had ever done. It is not even an exaggeration to add that this part of his achievement has never yet been matched, and that it may not ever be done so well again.

The key to Boswell's ability to record conversation was his habit of keeping a journal. Often but not always he would write up daily accounts of what had happened to him. He had begun re-

Pasquale di Paoli, leader of the Corsican independence movement (engraving by John Raphael Smith, from a painting commissioned by Boswell from Henry Benbridge). His conversations with Paoli in Corsica in October and November 1765 inspired Boswell to write An Account of Corsica.

cording conversation before he ever met Johnson. One of the most memorable moments in the *London Journal* occurs in January of 1763. Boswell, after gaining all that he had wished from an actress he calls "Louisa," discovers that he has a bad case of gonorrhea. He is at once angry, frustrated, and deflated by the realization that he had been deceived. He decides that he must confront Louisa and make her face her guilt. He records the moment of that confrontation in his journal as a dialogue or conversation between the two of them.

Of course, he also recorded his first meeting with Johnson on 16 May 1763 in his journal. What we see in the journal are the elements of what will later appear in the *Life* in more polished form. According to the *London Journal*:

> I drank tea at Davies's in Russell Street, and about seven came in the great Mr. Samuel Johnson, whom I have so long wished to see. Mr. Davies introduced me to him. As I knew his mortal

antipathy at the Scotch, I cried to Davies, "Don't tell where I come from." However, he said, "From Scotland." "Mr. Johnson," said I, "indeed I come from Scotland, but I cannot help it." "Sir," replied he, "that, I find, is what a very great many of your countrymen cannot help."

Boswell goes on to describe Johnson's "dreadful appearance" and to register his distaste for his "dogmatical roughness of manners," but then goes on to record what he remembers of Johnson's conversation on that day. What he has recorded consists of Johnson talking about how much authors are like other men and how little real distinction they enjoy in modern times; a favorable but qualified comment on *The Elements of Criticism* (1762) by Henry Home, Lord Kames; his dislike of some of the recent behavior of John Wilkes; his distaste for the cant of liberty; and brief critical comments on both Thomas Sheridan and Samuel Derrick.

Changes were made when this entry was transferred into the *Life of Johnson*. Most noticeably, the remarks about Johnson's unpleasant, even frightening, appearance have been eliminated and replaced by a statement about how much Sir Joshua Reynolds's portrait of Johnson had prepared him for his first glimpse of the living man. What may be more significant is that there is no explicit statement expressing Boswell's resentment against his dogmatic roughness. The preparation for their first exchange is more elaborate, with a greater effort at painting the scene, establishing, for instance, a dramatic parallel with *Hamlet* to fix such nonverbal elements as tone, gesture, and expression.

> At last, on Monday the 16th of May, when I was sitting in Mr. Davies's back-parlour, after having drunk tea with him and Mrs. Davies, Johnson unexpectedly came into the shop; and Mr. Davies having perceived him through the glass-door in the room in which we were sitting, advancing towards us,—he announced his aweful approach to me, somewhat in the manner of an actor in the part of Horatio, when he addresses Hamlet on the appearance of his father's ghost, "Look, my Lord, it comes."
>
> . . . .
>
> Mr. Davies mentioned my name, and respectfully introduced me to him. I was much agitated; and recollecting his prejudice against the Scotch, of which I had heard much, I said to Davies, "Don't tell where I come from."—"From Scotland," cried Davies, roguishly. "Mr. Johnson, (said I) I do indeed come from Scotland, but I can-

not help it." I am willing to flatter myself that I meant this as a light pleasantry to sooth and conciliate him, and not as a humiliating abasement at the expence of my country. But however that might be, this speech was somewhat unlucky; for with that quickness of wit for which he was so remarkable he seized the expression "come from Scotland," which I used in the sense of being of that country; and, as if I had said that I had come away from it, or left it, retorted, "That, Sir, I find, is what a very great many of your countrymen cannot help."

This more polished version illustrates something important about Boswell's record of conversation. It can be naively thought that for the Boswellian record to pass muster, Boswell had to have functioned as a kind of eighteenth-century tape recorder, and that only the words, the very words that Johnson and his interlocutors spoke can be accepted as an accurate and authentic account of what actually happened. But that would be a naive view of conversation in general and of Boswell's record of Johnson's conversation in particular. A transcript of any ordinary, everyday conversation in the eighteenth century would not look like the polished dialogue in an eighteenth-century play. Sentences in conversation are not always perfectly formed, and diction is often far from exact. There are pauses, stumblings, coughs, throat clearings, smiles. Much of the meaning in most spoken exchanges is in fact conveyed by nonverbal means, through the eyes, movements of the head, and gestures with the hands. None of these can appear as such on the printed page.

Moreover, even if it were possible to have a completely faithful transcript of a conversation, the bare printed words could easily be subject to misinterpretation. Part of what we notice when we compare the version in the *Journal* with the version in the *Life* are the efforts Boswell makes to see that neither he nor Johnson is misinterpreted. He wants to assure his fellow Scots that he was not slighting his native land when he begged Tom Davies not to tell Johnson that he was from Scotland. He also provides commentary on Johnson's reply to show it as an example of wit rather than of dogmatic roughness. The adverb "roguishly" is added to Davies's reply, and helps us better catch the tone of teasing that evidently was part of the interaction between Boswell and Tom Davies.

The rest of the entry is more interesting. It reveals that from the very start, even one as inaus-

James and Margaret Boswell with their three eldest children, Alexander, Veronica, and Euphemia
(painting by Henry Singleton; Scottish National Portrait Gallery)

picious as this, Boswell is captivated by Johnson's talk and feels compelled to record what he said, but not all of what he said. Johnson walked in at seven, and Boswell was forced to leave at ten because of a prior appointment. What appears in Boswell's journal clearly does not represent three hours of conversation. The art of recording conversation necessarily begins with selection and requires judgment from the recorder. The six topics Boswell recorded at their first meeting reflect what he found most interesting in those three hours of talk. Lord Kames, a Scotsman who sat with Boswell's father on the Court of Sessions, was clearly one of them. It is worth noting the slight modifications in this entry as it passed from his journal into the text of the *Life*. In the journal what reads as "Lord Kames's *Elements* is a pretty essay and deserves to be held in some estimation, though it is chimerical" becomes " 'Sir, this book ("The Elements of Criticism," which he had taken up,) is a pretty essay, and deserves to be held in some estimation, though much of it is chimerical.' " In the later version Boswell tells us

that Johnson "had taken up" a copy of Lord Kames's *Elements of Criticism* before making his remark. This added touch provides us with a context that tells us how Kames's book became a topic of conversation. He also has the words "much of " before "it is chimerical," undoubtedly having noticed that there would be no good reason to hold it "in some estimation" if the book were totally chimerical. There might be some who would argue that such changes are distortions of the original record, but it seems more reasonable to see them as part of an honest effort to provide a faithful record of what was actually said.

It is also worth noting that John Wilkes was one of the topics of conversation at this first meeting between Johnson and Boswell. Earlier in his journal, Boswell had mentioned having seen Wilkes, but he had not yet actually met and talked with him. He would do that for the first time eight days later, on 24 May 1763, and he would find himself completely charmed by Wilkes. On 16 May 1763, however, Wilkes was a topic of conversation because of the attacks he had been making upon the royal family in the *North Briton*. Boswell had been following these events and had even gone out on one occasion to observe the commotion Wilkes was causing, so he was bound to be interested in what Johnson had to say on these matters. It seems prescient that Wilkes should figure so immediately in the relationship between the two men, given the fairly large part he would later play in both their lives and given the very large one he would play in the greatest single scene in the *Life of Johnson*.

What the record in the *London Journal* indicates is that Boswell had already acquired considerable skill in recording conversation but that he was not yet at the peak of his ability in this difficult art. After presenting us with his record of Johnson's conversation during June and early July of 1763, he says: "Let me here apologize for the imperfect manner in which I am obliged to exhibit Johnson's conversation. In the early part of my acquaintance with him, I was so wrapt in admiration of his extraordinary colloquial talents, and so little accustomed to his peculiar mode of expression, that I found it extremely difficult to recollect and record his conversation with its genuine vigour and vivacity. In progress of time, when my mind was, as it were, *strongly impregnated with the Johnsonian aether*, I could with much more facility and exactness carry in my memory and commit to paper the exuberant variety of his wisdom and wit."

Boswell did gain more facility and exactness as time went on, in part because of his habit of writing down the important events of each day in his journal and in part because he grew accustomed to Johnson's characteristic manner of speaking. The transition from journeyman to master would occur during the 101 days they spent together when touring Scotland and her western islands in 1773. During that time Boswell let Johnson read what he was writing in his journal. He tells us that Johnson made a few small corrections but for the most part seemed genuinely impressed with Boswell's record of his talk and satisfied with its accuracy. Boswell's full mastery of the art of recording conversation is probably seen most easily in the unusually full record he kept during 1778. Here he is not just recording Johnson talking, or even two speakers talking with one another, but actually recording the conversation of several speakers. On 9 April 1778, for instance, he and Johnson dined at Sir Joshua Reynolds's, where the guests included Dr. Shipley, the

Bishop of St. Asaph, and Allan Ramsay, who had just returned from a trip to Italy where he had visited Horace's villa. Here is Boswell's rendition of how the conversation evolved:

> The Bishop said, it appeared from Horace's writings that he was a cheerful contented man. JOHNSON. "We have no reason to believe that, my Lord. Are we to think Pope was happy, because he says so in his writings? We see in his writings what he wishes the state of his mind to appear. Dr. Young, who pined for preferment, talks with contempt of it in his writings, and affects to despise every thing that he did not despise." BISHOP OF ST. ASAPH. "He was like other chaplains, looking for vacancies: but that is not peculiar to the clergy. I remember when I was with the army, after the battle of Lafeldt, the officers seriously grumbled that no general was killed." BOSWELL. "How hard is it that man can never be at rest." RAMSAY. "It is not in his nature to be at rest. When he is at rest, he is in the worst state that he can be in; for he has nothing to agitate him."

This picture of civilized talk is a large part of the reason Boswell's *Life of Johnson* has entranced generation after generation of readers. It is in fact so graceful and so entrancing that it is easy to forget just how much skill was necessary to record it and then render it in a way that would be comprehensible to people who were not there.

There are other features which set Boswell's *Life of Johnson* apart and which belong more to its art than to its science. One of these is Boswell's Boswell. This refers to the Boswell who appears as a character in the *Life*, a Boswell that is quite different from Boswell the narrator or Boswell the author of the *Life*. To those who feel that it is the biographer's duty to efface him- or herself from the biography in the interests of objectivity, Boswell's method of including himself in the story will seem to be little more than an exercise in vanity, the biographer using the biography as a means for drawing attention to himself. But a careful look at when and how Boswell appears in the *Life* reveals that Boswell's Boswell is intended to serve the interests of objectivity. Boswell, after all, was part of Johnson's *Life*, and his presence is a reminder of his credentials for writing this biography, for he is someone who, in Johnson's words, "had eaten," "drunk," and "lived in social intercourse" with the subject about whom he was writing, as Johnson had required he should. If conversations were to be presented as taking place between people, the interlocutors were often enough Johnson and Boswell. The conversations are more meaningful because we hear them as exchanges between two very different men whom we have come to know in the process of reading the book. Boswell often disagrees with Johnson, in his opinion on Henry Fielding, or on slavery, or on the justice of the American cause, but those disagreements are important too. They help us to mark the boundary between Boswell and Johnson, and reassure us that Boswell has made an effort to be objective, that the Johnson he presents to us is not a Johnson who simply thinks and acts like himself.

Another creative aspect of Boswell's *Life* is revealed in those moments when Boswell's very presence produces something that might not otherwise have taken place. This can be as small and as trivial as Boswell asking Johnson why a fox's tail is bushy, or as large and revealing as coaxing Johnson into stating his serious thoughts on marriage or government. For lack of a better word, these could be called Boswell's "experiments" referring to events arranged by Boswell, events that would not have occurred if he had not been there, but because he was there and did arrange them they became part of Johnson's biography. Boswell's tactics were not without their risk, but when they do work they represent the grandest moments of the *Life*. The tour of Scotland and the Hebrides could, in fact, be described as one grand experiment. Johnson would never have made that trip if Boswell had not made the arrangements and graciously served as his host and traveling companion. And who would want to argue that the life and the *Life* of Johnson are not the richer for the 101 days he spent in Scotland?

All of these features, those that belong to the art of the *Life*, are clearly evident in one of the supreme moments in Boswell's biography, the meeting between Johnson and Wilkes at Dilly's on 15 May 1776. This moment in the *Life* proceeded from a kind of scientific curiosity on Boswell's part, a desire to see what would happen if he put one element of a possibly explosive compound into contact with another. It was necessarily a high-risk strategy. It was always possible that an experiment might blow up in his face. He experienced a taste of what might happen when on 22 September 1777 he had unwisely expressed a desire to see Johnson and the Whiggish Catharine Macaulay together. Johnson had turned on him with a stinging rebuke, "No, Sir, you would not see us quarrel, to make you sport.

Don't you know that it is very uncivil to *pit* two people against one another?"

The possibility of an explosive quarrel in a meeting between Johnson and Wilkes was even more palpable. As Boswell himself says of them without much exaggeration, "two men more different could perhaps not be selected out of all mankind": Johnson the sturdy Tory, Wilkes the arch-Whig; Johnson the stoic, Wilkes the epicurean; Johnson the moralist and devout believer, Wilkes the rake, thoroughly secular and almost certainly an agnostic. Moreover, the differences between the two had taken a sharply personal turn in the past. Wilkes had had little difficulty turning Johnson's eccentricities into ridicule, while Johnson had leveled an attack of breathtaking ferocity on Wilkes and his supporters in *The False Alarm*, a political pamphlet he had published in 1770. Incredible as it may seem, Boswell had been on very friendly terms with both men for more than a decade, and somehow had managed to keep these two different parts of his life totally separate. Now, however, he conceived, as he says, "an irresistible wish" to bring the two of them together.

Boswell set about his task as though he were writing a script, though it was a script where the denouement could not be foreseen. A chance had come his way when he learned that his friend Edward Dilly would be hosting a dinner to which Wilkes had been invited. Boswell then persuaded Dilly to invite Johnson to the dinner too. Once he had the invitation in hand, he then had to persuade Johnson to attend, and that was no easy task. His strategy was to play upon the pride Johnson took in his good manners, slyly suggesting that Johnson might not want to attend a dinner where there might be people in attendance he did not like. Johnson caught the innuendo exactly as Boswell had hoped he would, and quickly responded that he would never be so ill-mannered as to dictate who the other guests might be.

At this point all was going according to script. But when Boswell appeared at Johnson's door on the evening of the dinner party he found that Johnson had forgotten about the invitation from Dilly and had agreed instead to have dinner with his housemate, the blind Anna Williams. All seemed lost. Boswell, though, ever resourceful, begged permission from the peevish Mrs. Williams for Johnson to attend the dinner at Dilly's. When she gave it, Johnson called out

Engravings from Thomas Rowlandson's Picturesque Beauties of Boswell *(1786), caricatures illustrating passages from Boswell's* Journal of a Tour to the Hebrides: *Boswell at Auchinleck; Samuel Johnson and Boswell beginning their tour, accompanied by Boswell's manservant, Joseph Ritter; Boswell doing a Highland dance; Johnson discovering Boswell with a headache after a night of drinking, and commenting, "What, drunk yet?"; Boswell holding a rope to keep him out of the sailors' way during a storm; Boswell's father and Johnson exchanging Whig and Tory views on Oliver Cromwell and Charles I (Boswell reports the argument as heated but nonviolent)*

for a clean shirt, and Boswell had regained the victory he had just been about to lose.

Total triumph, however, was not yet in hand. The most dangerous moment lay ahead at Dilly's. When Johnson entered the room he realized immediately he did not fit in with the company. As soon as he caught sight of Wilkes, he picked up a book and withdrew. A breakthrough only became possible when dinner was announced. At this point Boswell lets himself disappear from the picture and keeps our eyes on the two major actors. Wilkes sat down next to Johnson and started to win him over by helping him to some fine veal, a process Boswell dramatizes vividly in the following conversation: " 'Pray give me leave, Sir:—It is better here—A little of the brown—Some fat, Sir—A little of the stuffing—Some gravy—Let me have the pleasure of giving you some butter—Allow me to recommend a squeeze of this orange;—or the lemon, perhaps, may have more zest'—'Sir, Sir, I am obliged to you, Sir,' cried Johnson, bowing, and turning his head to him with a look for some time of 'surly virtue,' but, in a short while, of complacency."

Boswell has just brought off the most brilliant truce, as Edmund Burke would say, in the history of world diplomacy. The scene continues for several more pages, and Boswell records the various topics of their conversation, the buffoonery of Samuel Foote, Garrick's reputation for avarice, the interpretation of a difficult line in Horace, jokes about Scotland, and a considerable amount of kidding at Boswell's expense. Finally, the tables are completely turned when Johnson gets in some sly pokes at the libertine life-styles of both Boswell and Wilkes: " 'You must know, Sir, I lately took my friend Boswell and shewed him genuine civilised life in an English provincial town. I turned him loose at Lichfield, my native city, that he might see for once real civility: for you know he lives among savages in Scotland, and among rakes in London.' WILKES. 'Except when he is with grave, sober, decent people like you and me.' JOHNSON (smiling). 'And we ashamed of him.' "

Not only is this arguably Boswell at his best, it is also an instance of when the phrase "Boswell's Johnson" has its most accurate meaning. The meeting between Johnson and Wilkes would never have taken place if Boswell had not been there to arrange it. Thus in a very real sense he was not only recording Johnson's life: he was actually creating it. It seems fair enough to say that Johnson surprises us with his good-

natured response and by the resourcefulness with which he turns the tables on his creator. It is clear enough that Boswell's purpose in this scene is not to draw attention to himself, but to help us see something that is very much to Johnson's credit.

The achievement of the *Life* is realized in moments such as the dinner with Wilkes, but it can also be experienced in its cumulative effect. The chief virtue of the *Life* is its variety, a sense of roundedness, a sense that if we can ever come to know a fellow human being through a book, we have come to know Samuel Johnson through Boswell's great biography. It has been said that Boswell's *Life* leads us to hero worship, but that of course is nonsense. There are too many moments—Johnson quarreling, Johnson whining, Johnson being grumpy, Johnson acting strangely—when Boswell's Johnson is in short merely acting like the rest of us. The obverse argument is that Boswell's *Life* subtly debunks Johnson, making him look narrow-minded and foolish when he was no such thing. These critics lay particular stress on the seeming emphasis in the *Life* on Johnson's explosive High Church zeal or his hot-headed Toryism.

But it ought to be crystal clear that Boswell's purpose was no more to discredit Johnson than it was to exalt him beyond the dimensions of the human. Being human can mean being thoughtful, kind, warm, and generous, but it can also mean being testy, grouchy, inconsiderate, lazy, and selfish. Boswell's Johnson is by turn all of these because Boswell wanted to present him to us as fully human. The nature of Boswell's intentions in the *Life* can perhaps be clarified by the testimony of Fanny Burney, someone who is not likely to be numbered among his admirers. She recorded in her diaries a moment when, much to her embarrassment, Boswell approached her, hoping to secure her help for the biography he was then writing: "Yes, madam; you must give me some of your choice little notes of the Doctor's; we have seen him long enough upon stilts; I want to show him a new light. Grave Sam, and great Sam, and solemn Sam, and learned Sam,—all these he has appeared over and over. Now I want to entwine a wreath of the graces across his brow; I want to show him as gay Sam, agreeable Sam, pleasant Sam; so you must help me with some of his beautiful billets to yourself." These are not the words of a debunking biographer nor are they the words of a hero worshiper. They serve rather as unambiguous evidence about Bos-

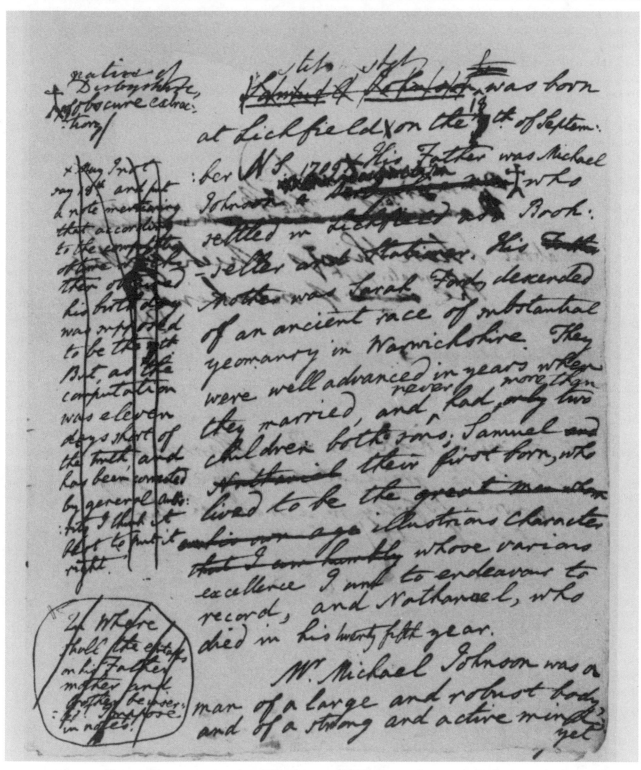

Page from the manuscript for Boswell's Life of Johnson *(Yale University Library)*

well's intentions in the *Life*. Fanny Burney's testimony on this matter is all the more persuasive both because she is recording an exchange that had taken place spontaneously and because it was recorded by someone who was not at all friendly to Boswell's interests.

The Life of Johnson was the last work to be published by Boswell during his lifetime, and the one most responsible for his enduring literary reputation. Yet Boswell's reputation in the twentieth century is no longer tied to a single work, and that is the result of one of the most astounding stories in the annals of literary scholarship. As Richard Altick retells the story in *The Scholar Adventurers* (1950), one day in 1850 in the French town of Boulogne-sur-Mer an English gentleman otherwise unknown to history came away from a small shop with some purchases wrapped in old paper. When unwrapping one of the parcels he happened to notice the name of James Boswell was signed to the end of a letter. This chance occurrence was to lead to the publication in 1856 of Boswell's letters to the Reverend William Temple, and the revelation of a James Boswell who existed quite apart from his role as the biographer of Samuel Johnson.

Just how much of that James Boswell existed would become even more visible with further discoveries. When Boswell died in 1795 he had left behind an enormous store of papers. He had appointed the Reverend William Temple, Edmond Malone, and Sir William Forbes as his literary executors and had left them the charge of determining what if anything from this huge store of papers could be published for the benefit of his children. Some of those papers were stored at the Boswell home in Auchinleck, and a part of them in an ebony cabinet mentioned in Boswell's will. Others were stored at the home of Sir William Forbes, who after he had examined them under the terms of the will had kept them by him, and never had an opportunity to return them to Auchinleck. Wherever the papers were, though, they were inaccessible to outsiders.

Eventually the papers stored at Auchinleck, including those in the ebony cabinet, were moved to Ireland, to Malahide Castle just outside of Dublin, where the last direct descendant of James Boswell had taken up residence. In 1927 James Boswell Talbot, sixth Lord Talbot de Malahide, agreed to sell the Boswell papers in his possession to Lt. Col. Ralph Heyward Isham, an American collector, with the understanding that the papers would be kept together and would be published in a dignified scholarly edition. This original purchase included some of Boswell's letters and a few leaves from the manuscript version of the *Life*, but most important were the journals that Boswell had kept for almost thirty-three years. These would form the basis of the elegant eighteen-volume edition of *Private Papers of James Boswell* that was privately printed for Colonel Isham between 1928 and 1934.

But even as Isham's edition was going forward under the editorship first of Geoffrey Scott and then of Frederick A. Pottle, new discoveries were being made. In April 1930 the Talbot family discovered more papers in a croquet box, papers that included the manuscript version of Boswell's *Journal of a Tour to the Hebrides*. Later in the same year Claude Colleer Abbott, working independently of all the others, came across a new cache of Boswell papers at Fettercairn House in Kincardineshire, nowhere near the ancestral Boswell home at Auchinleck. A substantial portion of Boswell's papers had come to be stored at Fettercairn because this house had become the residence of the direct descendants of Sir William Forbes, one of the three men Boswell had named as his literary executors, and who had physical possession of some of the papers. Abbott came upon hundreds of letters, originals and copies, that testify to Boswell's vast correspondence. Among them were the letters of Temple to Boswell, the other side of the correspondence that had been found in Boulogne in 1850. There were also letters from Johnson to various correspondents. And, perhaps most important, the manuscript of what would become known as *Boswell's London Journal, 1762-1763*, thus bridging what had been an awkward gap in the documentary record.

There is a gap in the chronology here that had awkward implications for modern scholarship. Though Abbott made these discoveries in the late fall and early winter of 1930, he did not make them public until 1936. This delay was going to prove embarrassing to two monuments of modern scholarship, Colonel Isham's edition of the *Private Papers* and the Hill and Powell edition of Boswell's *Life*. Both had in good faith represented themselves as the latest in Boswell scholarship, but the latest in Boswell scholarship was without their knowledge already something different from what they were presenting to the public because of the new discoveries at Fettercairn.

Incredibly enough, the story of these discoveries does not even end here. In March 1937 Colonel Isham, with permission from the Talbots, made another search of the residence at Malahide and came upon more papers in a tin dispatch box. This find included Johnson's diary and the register of the letters Boswell had sent and received between 1782 and 1790. In the fall of 1940 the Talbots were to find yet more Boswell papers, this time stored in the hayloft of an old barn that had not been used for more than twenty years. This find recovered a large number of letters, including more letters from Temple to Boswell, and the sketch Boswell had written of his own life for Rousseau in Switzerland in 1764.

Colonel Isham somehow managed to keep the collection of the Boswell papers intact, in spite of the financial hardships brought on by the constant stream of new discoveries and the burden of the complex legal wranglings that were to follow. In 1949 Colonel Isham turned his collection over to his alma mater, Yale University. As a result, Yale now houses what is beyond doubt the world's finest single collection of Boswell's papers. Yale's collection has formed the basis of what is referred to as the trade edition of Boswell's journals, an edition that began with the publication of the *London Journal* in 1950 and is now complete with the publication in 1989 of the last volume of the journals, entitled *Boswell: The Great Biographer*.

The publication of the journals has affected Boswell's literary reputation in the twentieth century more than anything else. The journals are, of course, invaluable for source studies. We now have the means, for instance, to compare the public versions of events in *The Journal of a Tour to the Hebrides* and in the *Life* with what was originally entered into the journals. What we have found has for the most part increased our esteem for Boswell's intelligence and deepened our respect for his integrity. Some scholars are more in awe than ever of the industry he employed in writing, collecting, and preserving so much.

Above all, Boswell can no longer be seen as the author of one great book. He is now the author of absorbing and vivid journals, someone who set a new standard in the genre of autobiography, or, as some would have it, someone who is responsible for the greatest diary ever written. In other words, Boswell's Boswell is now as important as Boswell's Johnson, and with good reason. In the journals we see better than ever what battles must be fought in the effort to be human in the modern world. Moreover, Boswell is a ready-made example for postmodernism with its empha-

sis on the role of writing in our lives. He seems to embody as well as anyone our struggle to overcome emptiness and meaninglessness through a heroic will to write.

Curiously enough, we do not know where Boswell got his original notion to keep a journal, nor what precedent if any he had in mind. What we do know is that at first he kept some diaries, but to quote Frederick Pottle, whose familiarity with the Boswell papers was nonpareil, "to judge from the surviving specimens [from the diaries], they had all been concise and unambitious." However, not long before his twenty-second birthday, on 14 September 1762, more than two months before he would set out for London, Boswell began something which he titled "Journal of My Jaunt, Harvest 1762." It was, says Pottle, "consciously begun as prologue to and training for the swelling act which he planned to record in London. It was the inception of an elaborate literary journal which he was to keep without the gap of a single day at least to the end of January 1765—nearly two thousand quarto pages of careful manuscript. It is the first of his writings in which he demonstrates his power to write so that others must read what he has written."

Perhaps the first and most striking impression we have when we begin to read in the journals is how different this Boswell is from the Boswell we thought we knew from the *Life* or from the *Tour*. Those of us who have formed our picture of Boswell on those books cannot help but think of him as someone who followed a great man around, trying to record whatever wit or wisdom he was willing to utter. It comes as a surprise to learn that Boswell led a full existence quite apart from Samuel Johnson. Perhaps this comes through most forcefully in the *London Journal*, which records that time in his life—Boswell was only twenty-two—before he even met Samuel Johnson. His relish for London is obvious. His rebellion against his father is smoldering. More than anything he wants a career as a soldier in the guards, but he is never successful in winning the appointment that he seeks.

Most of all, though, Boswell is interested in women, or at least in recording his interest in women. Whether or not Boswell was more highly sexed than other men may be open for question. What is clear is that he found sanction, or thought he found sanction, from the company of men, for believing that a man was entitled to, or even required to, seek relief with a woman several times a week. What may be most significant

Auchinleck House, the ancestral home Boswell inherited after his father's death in 1782

is a note of boasting in his description of his sexual intrigues. That note makes it hard to escape the inference that he wrote these down fully believing that his record of his encounters with prostitutes would win the approval of his fellow males, and perhaps even their grudging admiration. This may tell us a good deal about how men talked to one another "off the record" in the eighteenth century, but it does not seem to be all that different from how they talk among themselves in the twentieth.

The most memorable moments in the *London Journal* come during Boswell's intrigue with an actress he calls "Louisa." It is formed like a miniature play. In the first two acts, we find Boswell scheming and plotting to win the lady's favor. After some complications he finally wins what he has been seeking. He performs in bed as a prodigy of nature, pleasing Louisa by coming to a climax five times in a single night. It would seem as though life could not be better. Then comes the downturn. Shortly after his night of lovemaking he begins to experience familiar symptoms. The realization slowly grows that, prodigy of nature though he may be, he has just contracted a very ordinary case of gonorrhea. Venereal disease means being bedridden for at least a month, and considerable expense for the attentions of a physi-

cian. In the final act he chooses to confront Louisa with the facts of her duplicity and corruption. She protests her innocence, but this time he does not fall for the bait. There is a somewhat unexpected twist at the end when the two guineas he had earlier "lent" Louisa are returned to him wrapped in plain paper, without a note of explanation or apology. It is vivid writing, and we might even note that the confrontation scene is rendered in dialogue. Yet despite its theatrical elements or perhaps because of them, it is hard to shake off the sense that we come extraordinarily close to the experience of day-to-day life in the eighteenth century in this journal, and the taste proves to be rather tart.

There are other moments in the journals that have become part of our legend and lore, but none perhaps more celebrated than Boswell's interviews with Rousseau and Voltaire. He reveals in these many of the same qualities that he would later employ in the *Life of Johnson*, and to much the same effect. The theatrical element is undoubtedly the most important. We know from Boswell's own testimony early in the journal that he had every intention of stopping to see both Rousseau and Voltaire, two of Europe's most famous men, when he began his Grand Tour. Both men lived near the border between France and

Boswell's ebony cabinet, in which some of his papers were stored at Auchinleck House. During the first decade of the twentieth century the papers and cabinet were taken to Malahide Castle, near Dublin, Ireland, where they remained inaccessible to scholars until Lt. Col. Ralph Heyward Isham bought them from Boswell's descendants in 1927 and published them as Private Papers of James Boswell *(1928-1934).*

Switzerland, and thus on his route south from Germany into Italy. He had even secured a letter of introduction to Rousseau from George Keith, Earl Marischal, but in December 1764, when Boswell got close to Rousseau's home near Neuchâtel, he learned that the great man was suffering badly from several physical ailments and that he was constantly plagued by visitors. This meant that he might not get to see Rousseau, letter or no letter. Boswell decided that he had to do something that would win Rousseau's interest, so he sat down and composed a letter that contained a portrait of his life and explained why at twenty-four he needed the guidance of an older, wiser man. It turned out that Rousseau, then fifty-two, was captivated by such unusual tactics. Boswell won permission to visit, and ended up winning the affection of both his host and his host's mistress, Thérèse le Vasseur.

Boswell would follow a similar strategy to gain entrance to Voltaire's mansion at Ferney, just outside of Geneva. Boswell spent his first day at Voltaire's residence on 24 December 1764. He started up a conversation with the great man in the afternoon, talking with him about Johnson and Lord Kames, especially about Kames's *Elements of Criticism*, in part because Boswell suspected Voltaire did not like it. He had to break off his visit in order to get back to Geneva before five o'clock when the gates of the city were shut for the night. As a result he decided to write a letter to Voltaire's niece Madame Denis, asking for permission to stay overnight at Ferney. Permission was quickly granted because Boswell had made such a positive impression upon the seventy-two-year-old Voltaire.

The success of both interviews depends upon the sense of drama. That drama in turn depends upon Boswell himself. He becomes a kind of stand-in for all of us, slowly laying the groundwork for his meetings with both men. In both cases Boswell's youthful exuberance proves irresistible to the older men, and they find themselves charmed by an unlikely source. There are exchanges of views which are interesting in themselves, but the most interesting are those that come in the confrontations over religion. With Rousseau, the question is the character of his religious beliefs, when Boswell, looking steadily into his eye, asks him: "But tell me sincerely, are you a Christian?" With Voltaire, he approaches the same subject a bit more indirectly, but once the subject does come up he reports with some satisfaction how Voltaire did "rage," eventually falling back exhausted upon his chair and holding his head. Under further prodding from Boswell, Voltaire finally acknowledges the deistic beliefs for which he was famous: the existence of a supreme being, but without any necessity for churches and a clergy, nor for any of the doctrines of supernatural revelation. Boswell is particularly horrified when Voltaire expresses his indifference to the notion of personal immortality. This was the religious doctrine that mattered most to Boswell. But his wavering confidence in the doctrine of immortality provides no more of an explanation for his bizarre religious behavior than any other.

Anyone who reads in Boswell's journals is bound to feel jolted by the experience of reading in one paragraph how nothing seems to matter more than the exalted devotion he feels at a liturgy or a sermon, only to find him roaring about in search of a whore in the next. Boswell's religious practices, like so much else in his life, were part of his rebellion against his father. He was of course raised according to the strict Presbyterian practices of his parents. Almost as soon as he was on his own, he converted to Roman Catholicism, only to recant shortly after, due to pressure from his family. Despite his recantation he retained an attraction to Catholicism, and perhaps even a sympathy with it. That would explain why he was so much at ease and so well accepted as a traveler in Italy, France, and Corsica. Ultimately, in line with his Anglophilia, Boswell found his richest satisfactions in the religious practices of High Church Anglicanism, and this was to provide yet another bond between him and Samuel Johnson.

There are other moments in the journals that have acquired a fame of their own. Many find themselves fascinated with Boswell's complex relationship with Belle de Zuylen, a captivating woman known as Zélide, whom he came to know while in Holland. His relationship with Margaret Montgomerie, the woman who would become his wife and mother of his five children, has its own attraction. His efforts in behalf of the sheep stealer John Reid are deeply moving and a convincing evidence that there was more to Boswell than a foolish pride in his aristocratic rank. His interview in 1778 with Margaret Caroline Rudd, the woman who charmed her way out of a capital conviction for forgery, is a revelation of yet another side of that nature.

The later journals, though always interesting, are less engaging and somewhat less full. By and large they recount Boswell's disastrous decision to pursue a career at the English bar and later to seek political advancement by means of favor from the powerful. Eventually they recount the painful story of the wasting away of his wife, Margaret, who had contracted tuberculosis. Her premature death adds another sorrowful burden to the growing gloom of his final years. Near the end we see Boswell shamed and humiliated when younger men steal his wig, forcing him to travel a dozen miles in order to appear properly attired before the imperious Sir James Lowther, Lord Lonsdale. Later still we hear about a drunken Boswell being mugged and rolled while on his way home late at night. His last days are the story of the disintegration of what had once been a superbly healthy body, one that had withstood incredible amounts of abuse. Eventually, though, even Boswell's body proved to be mortal. He died on 19 May 1795, his death the result of a kidney infection that could be traced easily enough to multiple incidents of venereal disease.

A recounting of the sad events at the close of Boswell's life should serve as a reminder about the nature of Boswell's journals. Autobiography ought not to be confused with biography. While Boswell is recording instance after instance of his personal decline and degradation, he is at work producing one of the glories of English literature. The discrepancy between this idea of himself and the reality we know to be true, between his sense of himself as a failure and the success he was then creating in *The Life of Samuel Johnson* is something that surely ought to interest scholars and critics alike. We cannot and should not equate the flesh-and-blood Boswell with the Boswell of the journals. As much as Boswell recorded about himself, he clearly did not record all, nor even much, of what we might find most interesting about him. It will be the business of his future biographers to take more careful note of these discrepancies, to investigate them, and to debate how we might account for them. When we do, we may have a better understanding of the curious combinations of weakness and strength that can constitute genius.

Letters:
Letters of James Boswell, Addressed to the Rev. W. J. Temple, edited by Sir Philip Francis (London: Bentley, 1857 [i.e., 1856]);

The Letters of James Boswell, 2 volumes, edited by Chauncey Brewster Tinker (Oxford: Clarendon Press, 1924);

The Correspondence of James Boswell and John Johnston of Grange, edited by Ralph S. Walker (New York: McGraw-Hill, 1966; London: Heinemann, 1966);

The Correspondence and Other Papers of James Boswell Relating to the Making of the "Life of Johnson," edited by Marshall Waingrow (New York: McGraw-Hill, 1969; London: Heinemann, 1969);

Boswell's Correspondence with Certain Members of the Club, edited by Charles N. Fifer (New York: McGraw-Hill, 1976; London: Heinemann, 1976);

The Correspondence of James Boswell with David Garrick, Edmund Burke, and Edmond Malone, edited by George M. Kahrl, Rachel McClellan, Thomas W. Copeland, Peter S. Baker, and James M. Osborn (London: Heinemann, 1987; New York: McGraw-Hill, 1988).

Bibliographies:

Frederick A. Pottle, *The Literary Career of James Boswell, Esq., Being the Bibliographical Materials for a Life of Boswell* (Oxford: Clarendon Press, 1929);

Anthony E. Brown, *Boswellian Studies*, second edition, revised (Hamden, Conn.: Archon, 1972);

Marion S. Pottle, *Catalogue of the Papers of James Boswell at Yale University* (New York: McGraw-Hill, 1992).

Biographies:

Frederick A. Pottle, *James Boswell: The Earlier Years, 1740-1769* (New York: McGraw-Hill, 1966);

Frank Brady, *James Boswell: The Later Years, 1769-1795* (New York: McGraw-Hill, 1984);

Iain Finlayson, *The Moth and the Candle: A Life of James Boswell* (London: Constable, 1984).

References:

Harold Bloom, ed., *Dr. Samuel Johnson and James Boswell*, Modern Critical Views (New York: Chelsea House, 1986);

Bloom, ed., *James Boswell's "Life of Samuel Johnson,"* Modern Critical Interpretations (New York: Chelsea House, 1985);

Bertrand Bronson, "Boswell's Boswell," in his *Johnson and Boswell*, University of California Publications in English, volume 4, no. 9

(Berkeley: University of California Press, 1944); republished as *Johnson Agonistes & Other Essays* (Berkeley & Los Angeles: University of California Press, 1965), pp. 53-99;

David Buchanan, *The Treasure of Auchinleck: The Story of the Boswell Papers* (New York: McGraw-Hill, 1974);

John J. Burke, Jr., "The Documentary Value of Boswell's *Journal of a Tour to the Hebrides*," in *Fresh Reflections on Samuel Johnson*, edited by Prem Nath (New York: Whitston, 1987), pp. 349-372;

James L. Clifford, ed., *Twentieth Century Interpretations of Boswell's "Life of Johnson"* (Englewood Cliffs, N.J.: Prentice-Hall, 1970);

Greg Clingham, *Boswell: The Life of Johnson* (Cambridge: Cambridge University Press, 1991);

Clingham, ed., *New Light on Boswell: Critical and Historical Essays on the Occasion of the Bicentenary of the "Life of Johnson"* (Cambridge: Cambridge University Press, 1991);

William C. Dowling, *The Boswellian Hero* (Athens: University of Georgia, 1979);

Joseph Foladare, *Boswell's Paoli* (Hamden, Conn.: Archon, 1979);

Mary Hyde, *The Impossible Friendship: Boswell and Mrs. Thrale* (Cambridge, Mass.: Harvard University Press, 1972);

Allan Ingram, *Boswell's Creative Gloom: A Study of Imagery and Melancholy in the Writings of James Boswell* (New York: Barnes & Noble, 1982);

Donald Kay, "Boswell in the Green Room," *Philological Quarterly*, 57 (Spring 1978): 195-212;

Irma S. Lustig, "Fact into Art: James Boswell's Notes, Journals, and the *Life of Johnson*," in *Biography in the Eighteenth Century*, edited by John D. Browning (New York: Garland, 1980), pp. 128-146;

Maximillian Novak, "James Boswell's *Life of Johnson*," in *The Biographer's Art: New Essays*, edited by Jeffrey Meyers (London: Macmillan / New York: New Amsterdam, 1989), pp. 31-52;

Frederick A. Pottle, "James Boswell, Journalist," in *The Age of Johnson: Essays Presented to Chauncey Brewster Tinker* (New Haven: Yale University Press, 1949), pp. 15-25;

Pottle, "The Power of Memory in Boswell and Scott," in *Essays on the Eighteenth Century Presented to David Nichol Smith* (Oxford: Clarendon Press, 1945), pp. 168-189;

Pottle, *Pride and Negligence: The History of the Boswell Papers* (New York: McGraw-Hill, 1982);

William S. Siebenschuh, *Form and Purpose in Boswell's Biographical Works* (Berkeley & Los Angeles: University of California Press, 1972);

John A. Vance, ed., *Boswell's "Life of Johnson": New Questions, New Answers* (Athens: University of Georgia Press, 1985).

Papers:

Most of the Boswell papers are at Yale University. That they are for the most part in one place is due largely to the heroic efforts of Lt. Col. Ralph Isham to keep the collection together, and to the noble way Yale has continued to carry out its responsibilities as custodian. After Yale, to quote the words of David Buchanan in *The Treasure of Auchinleck*, "the largest and finest Boswellian collection in the world is to be found in the Hyde Library at Four Oaks Farm in New Jersey." There are also important Boswell papers at the National Library of Scotland.

John Bunyan

(November 1628 - 31 August 1688)

This entry was written by Leopold Damrosch, Jr. (University of Maryland) for DLB 39: British Novelists: 1660-1800: Part One.

BOOKS: *Some Gospel-Truths Opened According to the Scriptures* (London & Newport Pagnell: Printed for J. Wright the Younger, 1656);

A Vindication of the Book Called Some Gospel-Truths Opened (London & Newport Pagnell: Printed for Giles Calvert, 1657);

A Few Sighs from Hell; or, The Groans of a Damned Soul (London: Printed by Ralph Wood for M. Wright, 1658; Boston: J. Allen, 1708);

The Doctrine of the Law and Grace Unfolded (London & Newport Pagnell: Printed for M. Wright, 1659; Boston: Sold by D. Henchman, 1742);

Profitable Meditations Fitted to Mans Different Condition (London: Printed for Francis Smith, 1661);

I Will Pray with the Spirit, and I Will Pray with the Understanding Also (London: Printed for the author, 1663);

Christian Behaviour; or, The Fruits of True Christianity (London: Printed for Francis Smith, 1663);

A Mapp Shewing the Order and Causes of Salvation and Damnation (London, 1664?);

One Thing Is Needful; or, Serious Meditations upon the Four Last Things (London: Printed for Francis Smith, 1665?);

John Bunyan (Cracherode Collection, British Museum)

The Holy City; or, The New Jerusalem (London: J. Dover, 1665),

Prison Meditations (London, 1665);

The Resurrection of the Dead and Eternall Judgement (London: Printed for Francis Smith, 1665?);

Grace Abounding to the Chief of Sinners; or, A Brief and Faithful Relation of the Exceeding Mercy of God in Christ to His Poor Servant John Bunyan (London: George Larkin, 1666; Boston: J. Allen, 1717);

A Confession of My Faith and a Reason of My Practice (London: Printed for Francis Smith, 1672);

A Christian Dialogue (London, 1672?);

A New and Useful Concordance to the Holy Bible (London, 1672?);

A Defence of the Doctrine of Justification by Faith in Jesus Christ (London: Printed for Francis Smith, 1672);

Differences in Judgment about Water-Baptism (London: Printed for John Wilkins, 1673);

The Barren Fig-Tree; or, The Doom and Downfall of the Fruitless Professor (London: Printed for J. Robinson, 1673; New York: Printed for J. Tiebout, 1806);

Peaceable Principles and True; or, A Brief Answer to Mr. D'Anvers and Mr. Paul's Books (London, 1674);

Light for Them That Sit in Darkness (London: Printed for Francis Smith, 1675);

Instruction for the Ignorant (London, 1675);

Saved by Grace; or, A Discourse of the Grace of God (London, 1676?);

The Strait Gate; or, Great Difficulty of Going to Heaven (London, 1676);

The Pilgrim's Progress from This World to That Which Is to Come, Delivered under the Similitude of a Dream Wherein Is Discovered, the Manner of His Setting Out, His Dangerous Journey, and Safe Arrival at the Desired Countrey (London: Printed for Nathaniel Ponder, 1678; Boston: Printed by S. Green, 1681);

Come and Welcome, to Jesus Christ (London: Printed for B. Harris, 1678; Boston: N. Boone, 1728);

A Treatise of the Fear of God (London: Printed for N. Ponder, 1679);

The Life and Death of Mr. Badman Presented to the World in a Familiar Dialogue between Mr. Wiseman, and Mr. Attentive (London: Printed by J. A. for Nathaniel Ponder, 1680; New York: R. H. Russell, 1900);

The Holy War Made by Shaddai upon Diabolus for the Regaining of the Metropolis of the World; or, the Losing and Taking Again of the Town of Mansoul (London: Printed for Dorman New-man and Benjamin Alsop, 1682; Boston: T. Fleet, 1736);

The Greatness of the Soul and the Unspeakableness of the Loss Thereof (London: Printed for Ben Alsop, 1683);

A Case of Conscience Resolved (London, 1683);

A Holy Life, the Beauty of Christianity (London: Printed by B. W. for Benj. Alsop, 1684);

Seasonable Counsel; or, Advice to Sufferers (London: Printed for B. Alsop, 1684);

The Pilgrim's Progress from This World to That Which Is to Come: The Second Part, Delivered under the Similitude of a Dream Wherein Is Set Forth the Manner of the Setting out of Christian's Wife and Children, Their Dangerous Journey and Safe Arrival at the Desired Countrey (London: Printed for Nathaniel Ponder, 1684);

A Caution to Stir up to Watch against Sin (London: N. Ponder, 1684);

A Discourse upon the Pharisee and the Publicane (London: Printed for John Harris, 1685);

Questions about the Nature and Perpetuity of the Seventh-Day Sabbath (London: Printed for N. Ponder, 1685);

A Book for Boys and Girls; or, Country Rhimes for Children, as J. B. (London: N. Ponder, 1686);

Good News for the Vilest of Men (London: George Larkin, 1688; Boston: Printed for J. Edwards & H. Foster, 1733);

The Advocateship of Jesus Christ Clearly Explained and Largely Improved (London: Printed for Dorman Newman, 1688);

A Discourse of the Building, Nature, Excellency and Government of the House of God (London: George Larkin, 1688);

The Water of Life (London: Printed for N. Ponder, 1688; Boston: Manning & Loring, 1807);

Solomon's Temple Spiritualiz'd; or, Gospel Light Fetcht out of the Temple at Jerusalem (London: Printed for George Larkin, 1688; Hartford, Conn.: J. Babcock, 1802);

The Acceptable Sacrifice (London: Printed for G. Larkin, 1689);

Mr. John Bunyan's Last Sermon (London, 1689);

The Heavenly Footman (London: Printed for Charles Doe, 1698);

A Relation of the Imprisonment of Mr. John Bunyan (London: James Buckland, 1765).

Editions and Collections: *The Works of That Eminent Servant of Christ, Mr. John Bunyan,* edited by Charles Doe (London: William Marshall, 1692; 3 volumes, New Haven, Conn.: N. Whiting, 1830);

The Works of John Bunyan, 3 volumes, edited by
George Offor (Glasgow: Blackie, 1853);

The Life and Death of Mr. Badman, edited by G. B.
Harrison (Oxford: Oxford University Press,
1929);

The Pilgrim's Progress, edited by James B. Wharey,
revised by Roger Sharrock (Oxford: Clarendon Press, 1960);

Grace Abounding to the Chief of Sinners, edited by
Sharrock (Oxford: Clarendon Press, 1962);

The Miscellaneous Works of John Bunyan, 11 volumes, edited by Sharrock (London: Oxford
University Press, 1976-1989);

The Holy War, edited by James F. Forrest and
Sharrock (Oxford: Clarendon Press, 1980).

John Bunyan, author of the immortal allegory *The Pilgrim's Progress* (1678, 1684), was born
in November 1628 in Elstow, near Bedford, to
Thomas Bunyan and his second wife, Margaret
Bentley Bunyan. Not much is known about the details of Bunyan's life; his autobiographical memoir, *Grace Abounding to the Chief of Sinners* (1666),
is concerned with external events only as they im-
pinge upon spiritual experience. His family was
humble though not wholly impoverished, and
after learning to read at a grammar school he became a brazier or tinker like his father, following
an itinerant trade that seems to have been much
despised at the time.

The year 1644, when Bunyan turned sixteen, proved shockingly eventful. Within a few
months his mother and sister died; his father married for the third time; and Bunyan was drafted
into the Parliamentary army, in which he did garrison duty for the next three years. He never saw
combat, from which he seems to have thought himself providentially spared, since he reports that a
soldier was killed who was sent in his place to a
siege. Nothing more is known about Bunyan's
military service, but he was unquestionably impressed by a church that was military as well as militant, and his exposure to Puritan ideas and
preaching presumably dates from this time.

The central event in Bunyan's life, as he describes it in *Grace Abounding to the Chief of Sinners,*
was his religious conversion. This was both preceded and followed by extreme psychic torment.
Under the influence of his first wife (whose
name is not known) Bunyan began to read works
of popular piety and to attend services regularly
in Elstow Church. At this point he was still a member of the Church of England, in which he had
been baptized. One Sunday, however, while play-

ing a game called "cat" on the village green, he
was suddenly arrested by an interior voice that demanded, "Wilt thou leave thy sins and go to
heaven, or have thy sins and go to hell?" Since Puritans were bitterly opposed to indulgence in Sunday sports, the occasion of this intervention was
no accident, and Bunyan's conduct thereafter
was "Puritan" in two essential respects. First, he
wrestled inwardly with the guilt and self-doubt
that William James, writing of Bunyan in *The Varieties of Religious Experience* (1929), characterized as
symptomatic of "the divided self." Second, he
based his religion upon the Bible rather than
upon traditions or ceremonies. For years afterward, specific scriptural texts would speak themselves unbidden in his head, some threatening
damnation and others promising salvation. Suspended between the two, Bunyan came close to despair, and his anxiety was reflected in physical as
well as mental suffering. At last he happened to
overhear some old women, sitting in the sun,
speak eloquently of their own abject unworthi-
ness, and this liberated him into an intuition that
those who feel their guilt most deeply have been
chosen by God for special attention. Like St. Paul
and like many other Puritans, he could proclaim
himself the "chief of sinners" and thereby declare himself one of the elect.

While he was never wholly free from inner
disquiet, Bunyan's gaze thenceforward was directed outward rather than inward, and he
soon gained a considerable local reputation as a
preacher and spiritual counselor. In 1653 he
joined the Baptist congregation of John Gifford
in Bedford; Gifford was a remarkable pastor
who greatly assisted Bunyan's progress toward
spiritual stability and encouraged him to speak to
the congregation. After Gifford's death in 1655
Bunyan began to preach in public, and his ministrations were so energetic that he gained the nickname "Bishop Bunyan." Among Puritan sects,
the Bedford Baptists were moderate and pacific
in their attitude. Doctrinally they stood to the
left of the Presbyterians, who differed from the
Anglicans mainly on points of church government, but to the right of the many "antinomian"
sects that rejected dogma or revised it in a myriad of imaginative ways. Bunyan's first published
work, *Some Gospel-Truths Opened* (1656), was an attack on the Quakers for their reliance on inner
light rather than on the strict interpretation of
Scripture. Above all Bunyan's theology asserted
the impotence of man unless assisted by the unmerited gift of divine grace. Both his inner experi-

The village green at Elstow, where Bunyan heard the voice that led to his conversion to Puritanism

ence and his theological position encouraged a view of the self as the passive battleground of mighty forces, a fact which is of primary importance in considering the fictional narratives he went on to write.

Bunyan's wife died in 1658, leaving four children, including a daughter who had been born blind and whose welfare remained a constant worry. He remarried the following year; it is known that his second wife was named Elizabeth, that she bore two children, and that she spoke eloquently on his behalf when he was in prison. The imprisonment is the central event of his later career: it was at once a martyrdom that he seems to have sought and a liberation from outward concerns that inspired him to write literary works. Once the Stuart monarchy had been reestablished in 1660, it was illegal for anyone to preach who was not an ordained clergyman in the Church of England, and Bunyan spent most of the next twelve years in Bedford Gaol because he would not undertake to give up preaching, although the confinement was not onerous and he was out on parole on several occasions. After 1672 the political situation changed, and except for a six-month return to prison in 1677, Bunyan was relatively free to travel and preach, which he did with immense energy and goodwill. Bunyan's principal fictional works were published during the postimprisonment period: the two parts of *The Pilgrim's Progress, The Life and Death of Mr. Badman* in 1680, and *The Holy War* in 1682. Most of the rest of Bunyan's sixty publications were doctrinal and homiletic in nature.

Bunyan died on 31 August 1688, after catching cold while riding through a rainstorm on a journey to reconcile a quarreling family, and was buried at the Nonconformist cemetery of Bunhill Fields in London. By 1692 a folio edition of his works had been published, together with a biographical sketch that includes this portrait: "As for his person he was tall of stature, strong boned though not corpulent, somewhat of a ruddy face, with sparkling eyes, wearing his hair on his upper lip after the old British fashion; his hair reddish, but in his latter days time had sprinkled it with grey; his nose well set, but not declining or bending; and his mouth moderate large, his forehead something high, and his habit always plain and modest."

Grace Abounding to the Chief of Sinners, a relatively short narrative of about a hundred pages, stands unchallenged as the finest achievement in the Puritan genre of spiritual autobiography. Its origins lie in the personal testimony that each new member was required to present before being admitted to the Bedford congregation, and Bunyan's allusions to St. Paul in the preface sug-

Bunyan's cottage in Elstow

gest that he intended the published work as a kind of modern-day Epistle for the encouragement of believers. Determined to tell his story exactly and without rhetorical artfulness, Bunyan promises to "be plain and simple, and lay down the thing as it was." What follows is a deeply moving account of inner torment, in which God and Satan vie for possession of the anguished sinner by causing particular Biblical texts to come into his head; Bunyan exclaims grimly, "Woe be to him against whom the Scriptures bend themselves."

Bunyan conveys a strong impression of a life filled with outward troubles. He speaks of "my poor blind child, who lay nearer my heart than all I had besides; O the thoughts of the hardship I thought my blind one might go under, would break my heart to pieces." But biographical details are mentioned only when they are necessary to explain spiritual experience, which is described with harrowing clarity and honesty. Many Puritans suffered as Bunyan suffered, but only Bunyan had the gift of expressing his story in unforgettable metaphors. "O how gingerly did I then go, in all I did or said! I found myself as on a miry bog, that shook if I did but stir." Again, "I did liken myself in this condition unto the case of some child that was fallen into a mill-pit, who though it could make some shift to scrabble and sprawl in the water, yet because it could

find neither hold for hand nor foot, therefore at last it must die in that condition."

For Bunyan, salvation is attainable only through the most strenuous effort, effort made possible only by the unmerited grace of God. Bunyan recounts "a kind of vision" in which the Bedford believers were separated from him by a high mountain with a narrow door in it. Repeated assaults on the door were in vain, until at last "me-thought I at first did get in my head, and after that, by a sideling striving, my shoulders, and my whole body; then I was exceeding glad, and went and sat down in the midst of them, and so was comforted with the light and heat of their sun." But this experience occurs relatively early in the narrative, and one's final impression is of an unceasing oscillation between hope and fear, from which Bunyan is liberated only by energetic labor on behalf of other people and by unflinching commitment to an existential leap of faith. "If God doth not come in, thought I, I will leap off the ladder [gallows] even blindfold into eternity, sink or swim, come heaven, come hell; Lord Jesus, if thou wilt catch me, do; if not, I will venture for thy name."

Experience in *Grace Abounding* is represented as a succession of discrete moments, each of which is pregnant with spiritual significance. Other kinds of experience are largely ignored, and no attempt is made to organize the narrative as a causal sequence. *The Pilgrim's Progress,* Bunyan's fictional masterpiece, is committed to the same way of representing life: individual moments are elaborated in themselves rather than connected after the fashion of a conventional plot. Although Bunyan's allegory is an important ancestor of the eighteenth-century novel, it uses the realistic world of everyday experience only as a metaphor for the world of the spirit. The title page clearly announces Bunyan's subject: *The Pilgrim's Progress from This World to That Which Is to Come, Delivered under the Similitude of a Dream.* A set of verses that concludes the book emphasizes the didactic message, and also the reader's obligation to detect that message: "Put by the curtains, look within my veil; / Turn up my metaphors, and do not fail. . . ." Bunyan's metaphors, and the language in which they are expressed, are drawn directly from the Bible, and specific texts are frequently invoked (often in marginal annotation) to ensure that the reader gets the interpretation right.

Bunyan's allegory derives its power from the imaginative force with which he brings didactic themes to life and the wonderfully living prose in which he dramatizes the conflicts of the spirit. The unforgettable opening paragraph, with its strong monosyllables and active verbs, surrounds the reader at once with the atmosphere of urgency: "As I walked through the wilderness of this world, I lighted on a certain place, where was a den; and I laid me down in that place to sleep: and as I slept I dreamed a dream. I dreamed, and behold I saw a man clothed with rags, standing in a certain place, with his face from his own house, a book in his hand, and a great burden upon his back. I looked, and saw him open the book, and read therein; and as he read, he wept and trembled: and not being able longer to contain, he brake out with a lamentable cry; saying, 'What shall I do?' " The den is Bedford Gaol, in which Bunyan found himself inspired to develop this artistic "dream"; the book is the Bible; the burden is the sinfulness of Christian, the hero of the story. Whereas *Grace Abounding* was explicitly about Bunyan himself, *The Pilgrim's Progress* is about Everyman.

From Bunyan's point of view the normal world of most novels would belong to the City of Destruction from which Christian flees, putting his fingers in his ears to block out the pleas of his family. He leaves them behind and enters a world of mental space, in which interior experience is given external embodiment. His trials and

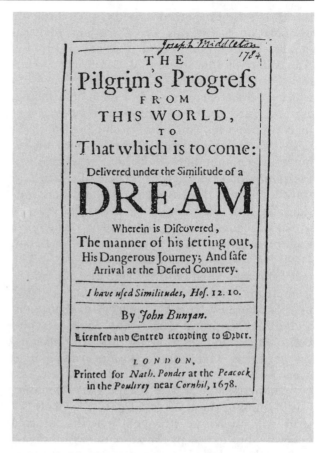

Title page for Bunyan's religious allegory, which remained a best-seller for more than two centuries

adventures follow no particular sequence, for life itself is full of repetitive challenges. Sometimes he fights against armed men or ogres or beasts; at other times he engages in debate with plausible tempters such as Talkative and Mr. Worldlywiseman, or enters into companionship with a fellow pilgrim such as Faithful. Certain moments, however, are crucial: after his conversion Christian goes through the Wicket Gate (the "strait and narrow" entrance of the Gospel) and sets out along the Way; when he reaches a cross, he sees a vision (as he later explains) of the crucified Christ, and the burden falls from his back; and after long journeying he reaches the tranquillity of Beulah Land, where he can wait at his ease until it is time to cross the river of death and enter the heavenly city.

Three of the most famous episodes can serve as instances of Bunyan's allegorical method: Christian is benighted in the Valley of the Shadow of Death, mocked in Vanity Fair, and imprisoned by the Giant Despair in Doubting Castle. Vanity Fair represents everything in this world that the Puritans despised, and accordingly it holds no attractions for Christian, who patiently endures humiliation until he is set free. The Valley of the Shadow of Death and Doubting Castle represent spiritual conditions into which Puritans were in serious danger of falling, and they are therefore represented as frighteningly oppressive. Christian, stumbling in darkness, cannot hope to prevail by his own efforts, but must commit himself without reservation to the power of God's grace. "When Christian had travelled in this disconsolate condition some considerable time, he thought he heard the voice of a man, as going before him, saying, 'Though I walk through the Valley of the Shadow of Death, I will fear none ill, for thou art with me.'" The text from the Twenty-third Psalm liberates the pilgrim from a scene that had been, in the first place, elaborated from the imagery of that psalm and other scriptural texts. The Bible provides both context and solution for Bunyan's allegorical narrative, surrounding and pervading it at every point.

Similarly, the way to escape from Doubting Castle is not to stand up and fight—the Giant Despair will always be stronger than the afflicted believer—but to accept the absoluteness of divine grace. "Now a little before it was day, good Christian, as one half amazed, brake out in this passionate speech, 'What a fool,' quoth he, 'am I, thus to lie in a stinking dungeon, when I may as well walk at liberty. I have a key in my bosom, called promise, that will (I am persuaded) open any lock in Doubting-Castle.'"

Episodes such as these treat despair and similar states of mind as entirely external: despair is a giant who attacks one, not an intimate part of oneself. They accurately reflect Bunyan's psychological experience, in which he did indeed feel helpless in the face of external threats, so that the very words that occurred to his imagination seemed to enter his mind from outside. The allegory of *The Pilgrim's Progress* offers a means of clarifying and understanding that experience. The self is seen as unified and determined—Christian manfully fighting the good fight—while those aspects of the self that seem unacceptable are projected outside and thereby made manageable. If despair is within one, then it is hard to know how to fight it; if despair is an alien persecutor, then it is possible to unlock the prison door and leave it behind. This was also the message of *Grace Abounding*, but that book was filled with the relapses and anxieties of an author who could

never be sure that he was free. *The Pilgrim's Progress* translates spiritual suffering into terms that are more universal and also more aggressively positive, intended for the encouragement of its readers.

The Puritans were assiduous autobiographers: life, as they saw it, cried out for interpretation, containing hidden clues to God's will and to their own election or reprobation. Just as the reader is expected to interpret the incidents in *The Pilgrim's Progress*, Christian himself receives an extended tutorial in interpretation when he visits Interpreter's House. A series of emblematic scenes is presented to him, and each scene is expounded by Interpreter, who quotes a crucial text from 2 Corinthians: "For the things that are seen, are temporal; but the things that are not seen, are eternal." *The Pilgrim's Progress* derives its energy and interest from the vividness of its narrative, but that narrative is only a screen, as it were, behind which the true story waits to be revealed. In the concluding verses Bunyan explicitly counsels the reader to do what Christian has done:

> Now reader, I have told my dream to thee,
> See if thou canst interpret it to me,
> Or to thyself or neighbour: but take heed
> Of misinterpreting; for that instead
> Of doing good, will but thyself abuse:
> By misinterpreting evil ensues.

Later novels, even those with didactic intent, offered tales of "real" life and allowed the reader to enjoy them for themselves, meanwhile imbibing moral lessons along with the story. Bunyan, who loved romances of knights and dragons but like other Puritans rejected them as immoral fictions, adapted their techniques to an allegorical mode in which the visible is only a mask for the invisible, and in which everything depends on interpreting rightly. One of the most persuasive speakers in the book is the "very brisk lad" Ignorance, who remains ignorant because he has not opened his heart to the sole truth of the Word, and who disappears at the end into a trapdoor that leads to damnation. "Then I saw that there was a way to Hell, even from the Gates of Heaven, as well as from the City of Destruction. So I awoke, and behold it was a dream."

The second part of *The Pilgrim's Progress* (1684) can be dealt with more briefly. Whereas the first part represents the private experience of the solitary soul, the second part dramatizes collective experience. Christiana and her children

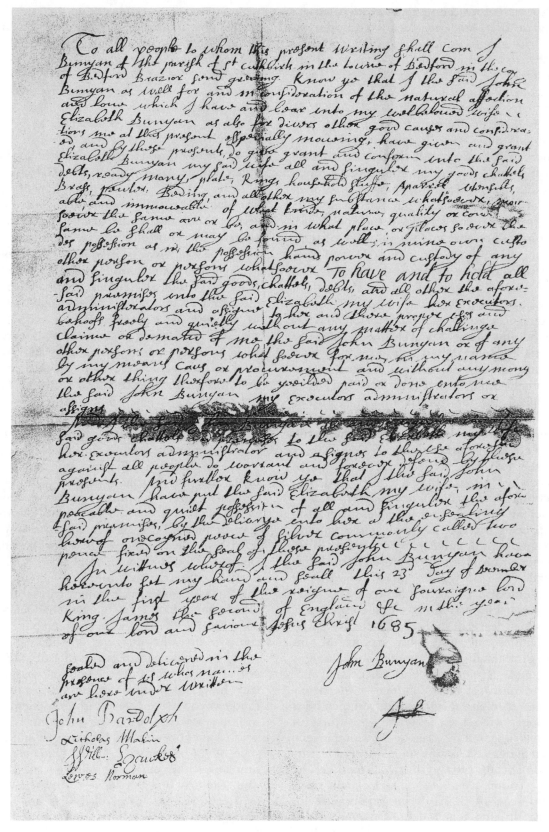

Bunyan's will

entrust themselves to the wise guidance of an experienced leader, Mr. Great-heart, and with his help they are able to avoid many of the trials into which Christian had impetuously stumbled. Bunyan felt greatly tempted by the sin of pride, and it may be surmised that he is here recommending the submissive course that he himself, like Christian, often failed to follow. Mr. Great-heart says that religious experience is not unvarying, and that a person will meet with those trials that he or she deserves. "For the common people when they hear that some frightful thing has befallen such an one in such a place, are of an opinion that that place is haunted with some foul fiend, or evil spirit; when alas it is for the fruit of their doing, that such things do befall them there." The cast of characters grows in the second part, and most of the newcomers sustain the pattern of patient obedience: Christiana's humble companion Mercy is hesitant even to attempt the journey lest she be unworthy; Mr. Fearing trembles at every hint of danger but is assured of safe passage to heaven. The second part is more like a novel than the first, in that it displays its characters in collective action. But the first part, with its profound dramatization of psychic disturbance and recovery, has much more to offer the novelists who were later to draw upon it.

In the six years between the two parts of *The Pilgrim's Progress,* Bunyan published two other fictional works. *The Life and Death of Mr. Badman* is not an allegory, and its novelistic realism has often been noted. The scene is the familiar world of shops and family life, and questions of social and mercantile ethics are explored at considerable length. The story is distanced, however, by being presented in a dialogue between Mr. Wiseman, who provides a running moral commentary on the events he relates, and Mr. Attentive, who interjects questions and observations of his own, and occasionally shows understandable signs of impatience. If Christian and Christiana were among the Calvinist elect, Badman is decisively one of the reprobate. From earliest infancy he is unremittingly wicked, in spite of the efforts of pious and loving family, friends, and employers. Badman marries (to the subsequent grief of his virtuous wife) from purely financial motives; he cheats his customers ruthlessly; he is sexually profligate; and worst of all, he dies unrepentantly but peacefully, proving that the Lord's vengeance is not always visibly enacted in this world. Much of the book is filled out, however, with alarming anecdotes from published collections in which notori-

ous sinners are swallowed up by the earth or snatched through barred windows in a flurry of blood. Whereas *The Pilgrim's Progress* is preeminently the story of the aspiring soul as seen from within, *The Life and Death of Mr. Badman* is a meditation, entirely from the outside, upon the behavior of the damned.

Less known than it deserves to be is Bunyan's other great allegory, *The Holy War.* If *The Pilgrim's Progress* dramatizes the popular Puritan metaphor of life as wayfaring, *The Holy War* develops the equally popular metaphor of spiritual warfaring. The tale is at once an allegory of the individual soul and of the history of the Christian church. The town of Mansoul is infiltrated by the agents of Diabolus, who win over the governor, Mr. Willbewill, and various other characters representative of mental faculties. Shaddai (God), who dwells far away, sends his son Prince Emmanuel to win back the town, but after a temporary period of rejoicing it relapses, he departs, and Diabolus reappears in force, entering the town after a successful assault on the Eargate. This time it is far more difficult to recover from slavery to sin, and when Emmanuel at last consents to return, he can only conquer Mansoul after an extended battle, and after abject protestations of repentance on the part of the citizens.

The allegory of *The Holy War* derives from a medieval tradition that symbolized the self as an embattled fortress, while its narrative details are drawn directly from the civil wars Bunyan had seen firsthand. "Oh, the fearful state of Mansoul now! Now every corner swarmed with outlandish Doubters; red-coats and black-coats walked the town by clusters, and filled up all the houses with hideous noises, vain songs, lying stories, and blasphemous language against Shaddai and his Son." During the civil wars the metaphor had become reality; the imagery of spiritual combat, which is as old as the Epistles of Paul, enacted itself in a war that Puritan militants regarded as truly holy. But Bunyan, writing during the Restoration when Puritans were enduring relentless persecution, was drawn to the metaphor above all because it expressed the fragmented and helpless state of the embattled self. *The Pilgrim's Progress* dramatizes the outward militancy of the elect soul, *The Holy War* its passive endurance in a state of siege that its own disloyalty to God has brought about. Here, more than ever, Bunyan's tendency to externalize unwanted impulses finds expression: just as in *The Pilgrim's Progress* despair was projected outward as a brutal giant, so

Effigy of Bunyan on his tomb in Bunhill Fields, London. The face was damaged by shrapnel from British antiaircraft guns during World War II.

in *The Holy War* the doubts that afflict Mansoul are "outlandish," alien invaders from without.

In *The Pilgrim's Progress* grace is a mysterious power, usually mediated by agents such as Evangelist or Mr. Great-heart, who help Christian and the other pilgrims successfully confront their trials. In *The Holy War* it is visibly embodied in the direct agency of God, operating in the form of Christ (Emmanuel), that must overwhelm the sinful resistance that prevents even the elect soul from freely opening its gates to Him. In *The Pilgrim's Progress* man does the fighting; in *The Holy War* God does. "Yea, let him conquer us with his love and overcome us with his grace, and then surely shall he be but with us and help us, as he was and did that morning that our pardon was read unto us." In *The Pilgrim's Progress* man keeps constantly on the move in a pilgrimage whose goal is the heavenly city, even if at times the "progress" is repetitive and obstructed. In *The Holy War* man can do nothing but wait, trusting to the savior who will one day return and put the besieging forces to rout. As Emmanuel says at the very end, in language drawn from the Book of Revelation, "O my Mansoul, how have I set my heart, my love upon thee, watch! Behold, I lay none other burden

upon thee than what thou hast already. Hold fast till I come."

Bunyan's fictions arise from a particular religious faith in a particular historical setting. *The Life and Death of Mr. Badman* is the most conventional, and the least energetic dramatically. *The Pilgrim's Progress* and *The Holy War* serve as complementary expressions of Puritan experience, and if *The Pilgrim's Progress* has turned out to have the most lasting appeal, that is not necessarily because it is more accomplished as a work of literature. *The Holy War*, despite its imaginative power, is imprisoned within a deterministic Calvinism that few readers, from the eighteenth century onward, have found appealing. The embattled yet passive self continues to exist as a psychological type but in fiction is best suited to the kind of narrative that explores personality (or character) in a quasi-biographical manner. In *The Holy War*, where the self is dispersed into a host of warring factions, modern readers tend to find the treatment disappointing or disturbing or both.

The Pilgrim's Progress, on the other hand, though no longer the best-seller that it was for more than two centuries, presents a permanently attractive image of fighting the good fight, confronting the never-ending threats and confusions that attack the self both from within and without, and winning through to a condition of permanent peace. It too is founded firmly upon Calvinist theology, but its positive emphasis, together with its superb use of traditional romance and adventure motifs, has made it attractive to readers who share few of Bunyan's beliefs. And its allegorical presentation of inner life proved seminal in the conception, sixty years later, of the first English novel. *Robinson Crusoe,* Daniel Defoe makes his hero say in a later work, is "an allusive allegoric history" of a traditional kind: "Such are the historical parables in the Holy Scriptures, such *The Pilgrim's Progress,* and such, in a word, the adventures of your fugitive friend, Robinson Crusoe."

Bibliographies:

Frank Mott Harrison, *A Bibliography of the Works of John Bunyan* (Oxford: Oxford University Press, 1932);

James F. Forrest, *John Bunyan: A Reference Guide* (Boston: G. K. Hall, 1982);

E. Beatrice Batson, *John Bunyan's Grace Abounding and The Pilgrim's Progress: An Overview of Literary Studies, 1960-1987* (New York: Garland, 1988).

References:

Margaret Bottrall, *Every Man a Phoenix: Studies in Seventeenth-Century Autobiography* (London: Murray, 1958), pp. 82-110;

John Brown, *John Bunyan: His Life, Times, and Work,* revised by Frank Mott Harrison (London: Marshall, Morgan & Scott, 1928);

Leopold Damrosch, Jr., *God's Plot and Man's Stories: Studies in the Fictional Imagination from Milton to Fielding* (Chicago: University of Chicago Press, 1985), pp. 121-186;

Richard A. Dutton, " 'Interesting, but Tough': Reading *The Pilgrim's Progress,*" *Studies in English Literature,* 18 (Summer 1978): 439-456;

Stanley Fish, *Self-Consuming Artifacts: The Experience of Seventeenth-Century Literature* (Berkeley: University of California Press, 1972), pp. 224-264;

Monica Furlong, *Puritan's Progress: A Study of John Bunyan* (London: Hodder & Stoughton, 1975);

Harold Golder, "Bunyan and Spenser," *PMLA,* 45 (March 1930): 216-237;

Golder, "Bunyan's Valley of the Shadow," *Modern Philology,* 27 (August 1929): 55-72;

Richard L. Greaves, *John Bunyan* (Grand Rapids, Mich.: Eerdmans, 1969);

G. B. Harrison, *John Bunyan: A Study in Personality* (London: Dent, 1928);

Anne Hawkins, *Archetypes of Conversion: The Autobiographies of Augustine, Bunyan, and Merton* (Lewisburg, Pa.: Bucknell University Press, 1985);

Wolfgang Iser, *The Implied Reader: Patterns of Communication in Prose Fiction from Bunyan to Beckett* (Baltimore: Johns Hopkins University Press, 1974), pp. 1-28;

William James, *The Varieties of Religious Experience* (New York: Random House, 1929), pp. 125-185;

U. Milo Kaufmann, *The Pilgrim's Progress and Traditions in Puritan Meditation* (New Haven: Yale University Press, 1966);

John R. Knott, *The Sword of the Spirit: Puritan Responses to the Bible* (Chicago: University of Chicago Press, 1980), pp. 131-163;

Edmund A. Knox, *John Bunyan in Relation to His Times* (London: Longmans, 1928);

Thomas Babington Macaulay, "John Bunyan" (1831), in *The Works of Lord Macaulay,* volume 5 (New York: Longmans, Green, 1897), pp. 445-457;

Macaulay, "John Bunyan" (1854), in *The Works of Lord Macaulay,* volume 7, pp. 297-309;

John N. Morris, *Versions of the Self: Studies in English Autobiography from John Bunyan to John Stuart Mill* (New York: Basic Books, 1966), pp. 89-104;

Vincent Newey, ed., *The Pilgrim's Progress: Critical and Historical Views* (Liverpool: University of Liverpool Press, 1980);

Lynn Veach Sadler, *John Bunyan* (Boston: Twayne, 1979);

Roger Sharrock, *John Bunyan* (London: Macmillan, 1954);

Sharrock, "Spiritual Autobiography in *The Pilgrim's Progress,*" *Review of English Studies,* 24 (April 1948): 102-120;

Stuart Sim, *Negotiations with Paradox: Narrative Practice and Narrative Form in Bunyan and Defoe* (London: Harvester Wheatsheaf, 1990);

James Sutherland, *Restoration Literature, 1660-1700: Dryden, Bunyan, and Pepys* (London: Oxford University Press, 1990);

Henri Talon, *John Bunyan: The Man and His Works,* translated by Barbara Wall (Cambridge, Mass.: Harvard University Press, 1951);

William York Tindall, *John Bunyan: Mechanick Preacher* (New York: Russell & Russell, 1934);

Dorothy Van Ghent, *The English Novel: Form and Function* (New York: Rinehart, 1953), pp. 21-32;

Owen C. Watkins, *The Puritan Experience: Studies in Spiritual Autobiography* (New York: Schocken, 1972);

Joan Webber, *The Eloquent "I": Style and Self in Seventeenth-Century Prose* (Madison: University of Wisconsin Press, 1968), pp. 15-52;

Ola Elizabeth Winslow, *John Bunyan* (New York: Macmillan, 1961).

William Congreve

(24 January 1670 - 19 January 1729)

This entry was written by Peter Holland (Cambridge University) for
DLB 84: Restoration and Eighteenth-Century Dramatists: Second Series.

See also the Congreve entry in DLB 39: British Novelists, 1660-1800: Part One.

BOOKS: *Incognita: or, Love and Duty Reconcil'd. A Novel* (London: Printed for Peter Buck, 1692);

The Old Batchelour, A Comedy. As it is Acted at the Theatre Royal, by Their Majesties Servants (London: Printed for Peter Buck, 1693);

The Double-Dealer, A Comedy. Acted at the Theatre Royal, by their Majesties Servants (London: Printed for Jacob Tonson, 1694);

The Mourning Muse of Alexis. A Pastoral. Lamenting the Death of our late Gracious Queen Mary of ever Blessed Memory (London: Printed for Jacob Tonson, 1695);

Love for Love: A Comedy. Acted at the Theatre in Little Lincoln's-Inn Fields, By His Majesty's Servants (London: Printed for Jacob Tonson, 1695);

A Pindarique Ode, Humbly Offer'd to the King on his Taking Namure (London: Printed for Jacob Tonson, 1695);

The Mourning Bride, A Tragedy. As it is Acted at the Theatre in Lincoln's-Inn-Fields, By His Majesty's Servants (London: Printed for Jacob Tonson, 1697);

The Birth of the Muse. A Poem. To the Right Honourable Charles Montague, Chancellour of the Exchequer, &c. (London: Printed for Jacob Tonson, 1698);

Amendments of Mr. Collier's False and Imperfect Citations &c., from the Old Batchelour, Double Dealer, Love for Love, Mourning Bride (London: Printed for Jacob Tonson, 1698);

The Way of the World, A Comedy. As it is Acted at the Theatre in Lincoln's-Inn-Fields, By His Majesty's Servants (London: Printed for Jacob Tonson, 1700);

The Judgment of Paris: A Masque (London: Printed for Jacob Tonson, 1701);

A Hymn to Harmony, Written in Honour of St. Cecilia's Day (London: Printed for Jacob Tonson, 1703);

The Tears of Amaryllis for Amyntas. A Pastoral. Lamenting the Death of the late Lord Marquis of Blandford (London: Printed for Jacob Tonson, 1703);

A Pindarique Ode, Humbly Offer'd to the Queen, on the Victorious Progress of her Majesty's Arms, Under the Conduct of the Duke of Marlborough. To which is Prefixed a Discourse on the Pindarique Ode (London: Printed for Jacob Tonson, 1706);

An Impossible Thing. A Tale (London: Printed for J. Roberts, 1720);

A Letter from Mr Congreve to the Right Honourable the Lord Viscount Cobham (London: Printed for A. Dodd & E. Nutt, 1729);

Mr Congreve's Last Will and Testament, with Characters of his Writings (London: Printed for E. Curll, 1729).

Collections: *The Works of Mr William Congreve*, 3 volumes (London: Printed for Jacob Tonson, 1710);

The Complete Works of William Congreve, 4 volumes, edited by Montague Summers (London: Nonesuch Press, 1923);

The Comedies; The Mourning Bride, Poems and Miscellanies, 2 volumes, edited by Bonamy Dobrée (London: Oxford University Press, 1925, 1928);

The Complete Plays of William Congreve, edited by Herbert Davies (Chicago & London: University of Chicago Press, 1967);

The Complete Works, 3 volumes, edited by D. F. McKenzie (Oxford: Clarendon Press, 1990).

PLAY PRODUCTIONS: *The Old Bachelor*, London, Theatre Royal in Drury Lane, 9 March 1693;

The Double Dealer, London, Theatre Royal in Drury Lane, October 1693;

Love for Love, London, Lincoln's Inn Fields, 30 April 1695;

The Mourning Bride, London, Lincoln's Inn Fields, February 1697;

The Way of the World, London, Lincoln's Inn Fields, March 1700;

The Judgment of Paris, London, Dorset Garden Theatre, 21 March 1701 (with music by John Eccles); 28 March 1701 (with music by Godfrey Finger); April 1701 (with music by Daniel Purcell); 6 May 1701 (with music by John Weldon);

Squire Trelooby, adapted from Molière's *Monsieur de Pourceaugnac*, by Congreve, John Vanbrugh, and William Walsh, London, Lincoln's Inn Fields, 30 March 1704.

OTHER: Satire XI and "To Mr Dryden," in *The Satires of Decimus Junius Juvenalis. Translated into English Verse. By Mr Dryden, and Several other Eminent Hands. Together with the Satires of Aulus Persius Flaccus. Made English by Mr. Dryden* (London: Printed for Jacob Tonson, 1693);

"An Essay Concerning Humour in Comedy," in *Letters upon Several Occasions*, edited by John Dennis (London: Printed for Sam. Briscoe, 1696);

Book III, in *Ovid's Art of Love*, translated by Congreve and others (London: Printed for Jacob Tonson, 1709),

"Dedication," in *The Dramatick Works of John Dryden, Esq.*, 6 volumes (London: Printed for Jacob Tonson, 1717);

"The Story of Orpheus and Eurydice" and "The Fable of Cyparissus," in Book III of *Ovid's Metamorphoses in Fifteen Books. Translated by the most Eminent Hands* (London: Printed for Jacob Tonson, 1717).

William Congreve is, by common consent, the greatest writer of comedies in the late seventeenth century. *The Way of the World* (1700), above all, has come to represent the standard against which all other comedies of the period have to be measured, the crowning glory of Restoration comedy and of "the comedy of manners," whatever that title may be supposed to represent. His dialogue, usually praised in ecstatic terms for its dazzling or even coruscating wit, and the comedy of his fools who pretend to wit, have been the prime qualities that have secured his preeminence. Yet every revival, especially of *The Way of the World*, is greeted by theater reviewers with an automatic response of incomprehension at the daunting complexities of Congreve's plots, the price the audience supposedly has to pay to be allowed to listen to the subtlety and sophistication of his lovers' speeches. Recent academic criticism has taken the brilliance of the dramatic language for granted and has set itself to puzzle out the extraordinarily individualistic way Congreve turns the materials of his plays into complete and coherent actions. On rare occasions when directors have been prepared to take the plots seriously, as, for example, in John Barton's excellent production of *The Way of the World* for the Royal Shakespeare Company in London in 1978, the seriousness of Congreve's concerns, of which the wit is only a small part, has been revealed with startling clarity. For Congreve is a serious writer who uses comedy to examine the potentialities of human behavior in ways that the audience comes to respect. As Horace commented, in a phrase from his *Ars Poetica* that Congreve put as a motto on the title page of *The Double-Dealer* (1694), "sometimes however even comedy raises its voice."

Congreve was born at Bardsey in Yorkshire on 24 January 1670. His father, William, came from a staunchly Royalist family, while his mother, Mary Browning Congreve, was connected to the Lewis family whose wealth derived from trade with India and Persia. His parents lived in a house on the Lewis estate, but his fa-

from John C. Hodges, William Congreve
The Man, *1941*

ther, as a younger brother, had little expectation from his family. By 1672 the Congreves were in London, where his elder sister, Elizabeth, was buried. In 1674 his father joined the army in Ireland as a lieutenant and moved the family to Youghal, an Irish seaport. Congreve lived in Ireland until 1691, leading many contemporaries to assume him to be Irish, in spite of his protestations, and allowing Samuel Johnson to assume that Congreve's claim to an English birth was a "falsehood of convenience or vanity." In Youghal

the family established a friendship with the Boyle family, including Charles, the dedicatee of Congreve's first play. In 1678 the family moved to Carrickfergus and then, in 1681, to Kilkenny. Congreve may have gone to school in Youghal, but he was certainly at Kilkenny College, one of the greatest schools in Ireland, from 1682 to 1686. Jonathan Swift, a few years his senior, was at the same school, and there Congreve also began his enduring friendship with Joseph Keally, the recipient of many of his best letters. His time at Kil-

William Congreve during his attendance at Kilkenny College (portrait by W. D. Clarea; from John C. Hodges, William Congreve The Man, *1941)*

kenny College was the beginning of many other significant recurrent events in his life: his near-sightedness, which led to operations in later life; his interest in Greek; his writing poetry (his earliest known composition is on the death of a master's magpie); and, above all, his contact with drama. The school had a long tradition of performing plays, but Congreve may also have seen the Smock Alley Players, the professional theater company from Dublin, on one of their visits to perform at the Castle in Kilkenny.

In 1686 Congreve entered Trinity College, Dublin, where he pursued his study in Greek and his interest in eating well and drinking substantially, practices he never gave up. His regular absences from college on Saturday afternoons were probably spent at the Smock Alley Theatre, run by Joseph Ashbury, who had been, like Congreve's father, a lieutenant in the regiment of James Butler, first Duke of Ormonde. The Smock Alley company included players such as

Thomas Doggett, Joseph Trefusis, and William Bowen, who later moved to London and for whom Congreve wrote parts. At Smock Alley, Congreve could have seen plays that had recently been successful on the London stage. But alongside this introduction to contemporary drama by Thomas Shadwell, Thomas Southerne, Thomas Otway, or John Dryden, Congreve began to read in literary and dramatic theory. The catalogue of his library indicates that he had probably already purchased copies of Dryden's *Essay of Dramatic Poesie* (1668), Wentworth Dillon, fourth Earl of Roscommon's 1680 translation of Horace's *Ars Poetica*, and such French theorists as René Rapin and François Hédelin, author of *The Whole Art of the Stage* (1684).

Congreve left Trinity College in 1689 and was soon in London. In March 1691 he entered the Middle Temple, one of the Inns of Court, using the opportunity, as did so many other young men, less to study law than to join fashionable London society, particularly, in Congreve's case, the literary circles centered on Will's Coffee-house.

Though he had probably already completed *The Old Bachelor*, Congreve's first published work was a short novel, *Incognita* (1692). Its action is an intricate maze of disguises and mistakes, set against the background of carnival in Florence, Italy, and following the adventures of two young men, Aurelian and Hippolito, as they fall in love with Incognita and Leonora. Entangled by Aurelian's father's intention to marry his son to Juliana in order to resolve a long-standing family feud, the two men take each other's names with inevitable confusions. Equally inevitable is the final discovery, long anticipated by the reader, that Incognita's real name is Juliana, the intended bride of Aurelian, and hence that his attempts to avoid being found by his father prove to have been totally unnecessary, since his love for Incognita and his duty to his father are not in opposition (as the novel's subtitle forewarns: *"Love and Duty Reconcil'd"*). The twists and turns of the narrative, complete with masked balls, wedding tournaments, duels, attempted rape, letters, and dozens of chance meetings, sound irredeemably trivial, and *Incognita* has usually been written off as a youthful foray enlivened only by an energetic exuberance, wit, and amused observation of the contortions forced on its characters.

Congreve also gives *Incognita* an extraordinary and unprecedented self-consciousness. No sooner has he indulged in an elaborate set-piece description of dusk, couched in flowery language of painful pretentiousness, than the narrator intervenes to apologize for such "impertinent digressions" and to differentiate sharply between the author's pleasure and the reader's:

> I think it fit to acquaint him, that when I degress, I am at that time writing to please my self, when I continue the Thread of the Story, I write to please him; supposing him a reasonable Man, I conclude him satisfied to allow me this liberty, and so I proceed.

This wry control over the reader's irritations extends into the narrative itself in its consideration of the characters' psychology. If on the one hand the maneuverings of the plot treat the characters as puppets at the behest of the author's will, on the other their reactions are offered from a sophisticated perception of individual motive. Don Fabio's concern for Aurelian's education is complexly self-directed, a consequence of seeing his son as "the Type of himself," so that his sus-

tained gazing on his son at dinner is offered by the narrator as the result either of "regret, at the Recollection of his former self, or for the Joy he conceiv'd in being, as it were, reviv'd in the Person of his Son."

There is nothing heavy-handed about this concern with the novel's own progress. Throughout there is a deft lightness that anticipates the brilliance of Congreve's dramatic dialogue. Congreve's serious consideration of the methods of the novel does not induce in him an awkward and uncharacteristic ponderousness. The thoughtful games Congreve plays through the interventions of the narrator's voice are balanced by the other major innovation Congreve is determined to explore: the interrelationship of the two genres, novel and drama. The action of *Incognita* owes its matter far more strongly to the traditions of late-seventeeth-century comedy than to anything in the recent development of prose narrative. If, in its brevity and skittishness, the action is in conscious opposition to the extreme length and weighty moralism of French-style prose romance, it clearly also derives its incidents by carefully transposing into the novel the kinds of scenes that fill plays such as Dryden's *An Evening's Love* (1668). Aurelian and Juliana are, admittedly, far more serious lovers than Restoration comedy had been prepared to tolerate, but the formal balance provided by the two couples is reminiscent of the basic structure of countless comedies. Even at this early stage, however, Congreve's perception of drama is a combination of innovation and tradition as well as a predisposition to respect the genre for its emphasis both on action and structure. In an important passage in the preface, Congreve defines the originality of *Incognita* by reference to drama:

> Since all traditions must indisputably give place to the *Drama*, and since there is no possibility of giving that life to the Writing or Repetition of a Story which it has in Action, I resolved in another beauty to imitate *Dramatick* Writing, namely, in the Design, Contexture and Result of the Plot. I have not observed it before in a Novel.

The basic design of *Incognita* has the dramatic form of slow and steady growth, through incidental scenes, toward a climactic scene of discovery and resolution. Everything, as Congreve is at pains to stress, is directed toward that end; all the minor catastrophes combine to make the end both postponed until the required moment of un-

Letter from Congreve to Joseph Keally (28 September 1697), Congreve's Kilkenny College schoolmate and lifelong friend. This letter was written soon after Keally had traveled to Ireland from London, where he had been studying law. The opening sentences refer to French privateers who were seizing English ships and to the soon-to-be-signed Treaty of Ryswick (Henry W. and Albert A. Berg Collection, New York Public Library, Astor, Lenox and Tilden Foundations).

books at that time I have no news of any kind
to send you. I have not seen bottom since I received
yr. Letter but Amory I just now parted with
who is yours. Jerry Marsh is here. as for Luther
I find him tost by yr. account & his own proceeding
unalterable and I hope Champs & you will Come
over together. pray give my hearty service to my
Cosen Congreve. tell the Good Bishop I must have
very good fortune before I am reconciled to the necessity
of my staying in England at a time when I promised
my selfe the Happiness of seeing him at Kilkenny
I would say something very devout to the Dutchesse
but you are a prophane dog & would spoil it. if
the Bishop would sanctifie my Duty to her I would
acquite him in my way. prithee heartily distribute
my service in a most particular manner & make me
popular amongst those acquaintance whom I have forgott
Let me hear when I may expect you & make haste to your

W. Congreve

raveling and at the same time inevitable at that point at which the emotions of the characters and the complications of events have been satisfactorily wound up to an extreme of tension. The "Thread of the Story" is never abandoned, and the digressions are never digressions of narrative, only of circumstantial description. Hence, Congreve is able to claim for his novel what he will repeatedly claim for his plays: "In a Comedy this would be called the Unity of Action; here it may pretend to no more than an Unity of Contrivance." It is appropriate that Congreve should go on in the preface to call attention to his adherence, at least comparatively so, to the other two virtues of neoclassical dramatic theory, the unity of place (Florence) and the unity of time (two or three days). The novelist's skill lies as much in the accomplishment of the action within the terms of such critical orthodoxy as in the local effects of the narrative style: "the difficulty is in bringing it to pass, maugre all apparent obstacles, within the compass of two days."

Congreve's pride in the achievement *Incognita* represents is based, then, on the technical originality of its form. There is a combination here of what Samuel Johnson might have seen in Congreve as a natural inclination to witty dialogue and an obligation to critical awareness; it is perhaps a central part of Congreve's debt to Ben Jonson. It also represents in embryo what would be the recurrent critical problem of responding to Congreve's work: the balance between the celebration of the dazzling local effects of brilliantly polished language and a recognition of the deliberate and innovative peculiarities of Congreve's dramatic forms. In *Incognita*, at least, the harmony between the delightful energy of the one and the provocative sophistication of the other has not received its critical due.

Incognita, published anonymously, made, unsurprisingly, comparatively little impact. Congreve's literary career was immeasurably helped at this time by his remarkably warm friendship with Dryden, still the greatest literary figure in London. Dryden had begun work in 1691 on a translation of Juvenal and Persius, parceling out the satires among different translators. Congreve's translation of Juvenal's Satire XI appeared in the volume when it was published in October 1692 (with 1693 on its title page), together with his poem "To Mr Dryden" prefacing the Persius translations. Dryden's high opinion of Congreve as translator was expressed in the preface to another collection of Dryden's translations, *Examen Poeticum* (1693), in which he wishes Congreve had the leisure and encouragement to produce a complete translation of Homer. By the time *Examen Poeticum* was published, Congreve was on the verge of his triumphant debut as playwright, but the easy stylishness and scholarly worth of his early translations under Dryden's aegis were much more than an adroit use of the skills learned at university for other larger ends. Throughout his life Congreve returned periodically to the art of translation, contributing, for instance, to the translation of Ovid's *Ars Amatoria* in 1709 and his *Metamorphoses* in 1717. Some of his weightiest poetry was written as a series of public and political celebrations of military successes, the victory at Namur, Belgium, in 1695 or John Churchill, first Duke of Marlborough's campaign in 1706, all based on the Pindaric ode. Congreve's essay on the form of the Pindaric ode, published in 1706, was the first attempt in English to define the nature of the apparently formless form, establishing its rules and prescribing its use. It is a typically Congrevean combination of scholarship and contemporary application, of theory and practice.

Congreve began writing *The Old Bachelor* during his stay at his grandfather's home, Stretton Manor in Staffordshire, in 1689, a visit that also resulted in his meeting Katherine Leveson, the dedicatee of *Incognita*. He worked on the play again in the Derbyshire Peaks in 1692. In London he showed it to Thomas Southerne, already an established dramatist and a friend of cousins of Congreve; he was also an Irishman educated, like Congreve, at Trinity College, Dublin. Southerne in turn showed it to Dryden, who, recognizing the play's extraordinary promise, determined to help it along by giving it what Southerne later described as "the fashionable cutt of the town." With help from Dryden, Southerne, and Arthur Mainwaring, the play was polished, Dryden reordering the scenes. Southerne secured its performance at the Theatre Royal in Drury Lane, where it was first produced on 9 March 1693, and Congreve was given the author's privilege of free admission to the playhouse an unprecedented six months before the premiere. Well-worn theatrical clichés about overnight successes are for once fully justified. The theater was full, and the play was, as the earl of Burlington wrote to Congreve's father, "by all the Hearers applauded to bee the best that has been Acted for many yeares."

Congreve in his early twenties (portrait by Henry Tilson; from William Congreve: Letters and Documents, *edited by John C. Hodges, 1964)*

Some part of the success of *The Old Bachelor* must have derived from its brilliant and vital re-creation of familiar, almost conventional, characters and situations from the tradition of Restoration comedy. Most critical judgments of the play have simply been subtle expansions of Johnson's opinion: "it will be found to be one of those comedies which may be made by a mind vigorous and acute, and furnished with comick characters by the perusal of other poets, without much actual commerce with mankind." If much seemed to Johnson to be borrowed material, his praise of the energy in Congreve's handling is crucial. There is a dramatic impetus to the play created by the combination of conventional expectation, stock situations, and a new and dazzling way with words, an impetus largely unprecedented. If the affectations of Belinda, for instance, derive from a character such as Melantha in Dryden's *Marriage A-La-Mode* (1673), there are, in her inventiveness of description and breathlessness of wit, things that had been missed in Restoration drama for many years. When she narrates to Araminta her meeting with a country family shopping at the Exchange, she easily reaches out for an unexpected image to describe the two girls: "fat as Barn-door-Fowl: But so bedeck'd, you would have taken 'em for *Friezland*-Hens, with their Feathers growing the wrong way." In the same way her rejoinder to her lover

Bellmour is crushing as its picks up his image and reshapes it:

> BELLMOUR. . . . Courtship to Marriage, is but as the Musick in the Play-house, till the Curtain's drawn; but that once up, then opens the Scene of Pleasure.
> BELINDA. Oh, foh,—no: Rather, Courtship to Marriage, as a very witty Prologue to a very dull Play.

Congreve's teasing delight in the poise and subtlety of his lovers' wit depends on a remarkable degree of attentiveness on the part of the characters, the actors, and the audience. The image has to be heard, held, and then turned. There are the beginnings, throughout *The Old Bachelor*, of that intensity of shared dialogue that Congreve makes peculiarly his own in his later comedies. It is, above all, a spoken wit, a language sensitively aware and alive to the especial qualities of voice in the theater.

Some of the multiple, interlacing plots of *The Old Bachelor* betray their dramatic ancestry only too clearly. Sharper's gulling of Sir Joseph Wittoll and Captain Bluffe is a neat strand showing Congreve at his most Jonsonian. Captain Bluffe himself is a braggart soldier plainly derived from Bobadill in Ben Jonson's *Every Man In His Humour* (1598), prepared to be cuffed and kicked and to find any possible excuse to avoid drawing his sword. Heartwell, the old bachelor of the title, escapes from his marriage to Sylvia, represented in the play rather unconvincingly as a whore, when the parson who marries them turns out to be Bellmour in disguise, a trick borrowed in part from William Wycherley's *The Country Wife* (1675). But if such moments in the action serve only to corroborate Johnson's criticism, the central action of the play, the relationships of Bellmour and Belinda and of Vainlove and Araminta, is a disturbing reconsideration of the activities of the rake, feeding on a perception of individual anxiety and neurosis that in its peculiarities is both daringly innovative and creatively based on a genuine "commerce with mankind." Restoration comedy thrived on the balance between two men and two women, with one pair embodying the comic and ethical norm of the plays in their greater wit. But both couples conventionally ended the plays with parallel commitments to love and impending matrimony. *The Old Bachelor* cannot simply adopt such a pattern unquestioned. Taking the conventional characteristics of the rake, Congreve redistributes them between Vainlove and Bellmour in an unexpected way.

Vainlove's pleasure lies wholly in the pursuit of an apparently unattainable prey. Using all the rake's wit and charm, he seeks to persuade women to fall for him. But once a woman has committed herself, once she has admitted to being in love with him or being prepared to have sex with him, his interest is immediately terminated. What Vainlove describes as the tedium of the mechanics of sex, frequently covered in the play by the word *business*, is demonstrably a fear both of commitment and of sex itself. Hence, he can assert of Laetitia, the wife of the foolish Alderman Fondlewife, that "I hate Love when 'tis forced upon a Man," though he has evidently been pursuing her for some time. As far as Bellmour is concerned, Vainlove displays extraordinary friendship in his willingness to hand over his victims, once raised to a pitch of sexual readiness:

> BELLMOUR. . . . Dear *Frank* thou art the truest Friend in the World.
> VAINLOVE. Ay, am I not? To be continually starting of Hares for you to Course. We were certainly cut out for one another; for my Temper quits an Amour, just where thine takes it up.

The action of the play, then, is the consequence of the difference between the squeamishness and fastidiousness of Vainlove and Bellmour's readiness to be, as he puts it, "a Cormorant in Love." Hence, Bellmour visits Laetitia in the disguise of Parson Spintext that Laetitia had suggested to Vainlove, while Vainlove's obsessions mean that there is no way his love for Araminta can reach marriage. His refusal to "marry *Araminta* till I merit her" meets an exasperated response from Bellmour:

> BELLMOUR. But how the Devil dost thou expect to get her if she never yield?
> VAINLOVE. That's true; but I would—
> BELLMOUR. Marry her without her Consent; thou'rt a Riddle beyond Woman—

Sylvia need only send Vainlove a letter purporting to come from Araminta and apparently indicating her love for Vainlove for Vainlove to announce "she has miscarried of her Love" and to insult her when they next meet. At the end of the play, as Bellmour and Belinda agree to marry, Vainlove's plea to Araminta for a comparable conclusion, "May I presume to hope so great a Blessing?," secures from her only a nervous withdrawal, frightened at the risk of an end to love that agreeing might produce in him. "We had bet-

Actress Anne Bracegirdle, who created the parts of Araminta in The Old Bachelor, *Cynthia in* The Double Dealer,
Angelica in Love for Love, *Almeria in* The Mourning Bride, *Millamant in* The Way of the World, *Venus in*
The Judgment of Paris, *and Julia in* Squire Trelooby. *According to Colley Cibber, Mellefont's feelings
for Cynthia in* The Double Dealer *reflect Congreve's love for Bracegirdle.*

ter take the Advantage of a little of our Frends Experience first." Vainlove's blindness comes, through Congreve's careful juxtaposition of scenes, to appear dangerously close to the blindness of Fondlewife. It disturbs the action of the play throughout and renders the ending necessarily inconclusive.

Congreve's reading in dramatic theory has one further significant effect on the play, an unusual care in the interaction and interconnection of the scenes within each act. Each entrance and exit is highlighted, marked by a character's observation of others' movements. The result, given how many elements of plot go to making up the play as a whole, is integrated and cohesive in a way that multiple-plot Restoration comedy had rarely managed.

In its quirkily individualist characterization and in its brilliant sense of the possibilities of the theater, *The Old Bachelor* deservedly marked an auspicious debut. But its qualities of dramatic skill and unusually perceptive psychology were placed in a context sufficiently familiar not to trouble the audience.

It was hardly surprising after the success of *The Old Bachelor* that Congreve's next play should have been eagerly anticipated and, as so often in such circumstances, hardly surprising that it should have disappointed. The savagery of the satire in *The Double Dealer*, first produced in Octo-

THE

Old Batchelour,

A

COMEDY.

As it is ACTED at the

Theatre Royal,

BY

Their MAJESTIES Servants.

Written by Mr. *Congreve.*

Quem tulit ad Scenam ventoso gloria Curru,
Exanimat lentus Spectator; sedulus inflat.
Sic leve, sic parvum est, animum quod laudis avarum
Subruit, aut reficit——
Horat. Epist. I. Lib. II.

LONDON,
Printed for *Peter Buck,* at the Sign of the *Temple*
near the *Temple-gate* in *Fleet-street,* 1693.

To the Right Honourable, Charles Lord Clifford
of Lanesborough, &c.

My Lord,

IT is with a great deal of Pleasure, that I lay hold on this first Occasion, which, the Accidents of my Life have given me of writing to your Lordship: For since at the same time I write to all the World, it will be a means of publishing, (what I would have every Body know) the Respect and Duty which I owe and pay to you. I have so much Inclination to be yours, that I need no other Engagement: But the particular Ties, by which I am bound to your Lordship and Family, have put it out of my power to make you any Complement; since all Offers of my self, will amount to no more than an honest Acknowledgment, and only shew a willingness in me to be grateful.

I am very near wishing, That it were not so much my Interest to be your Lordships Servant, that it might be more my Merit; not that I would avoid being obliged to you, but I would have my own Choice to run me into the Debt; that I might have it to boast, I had distinguished a Man, to whom I would be glad to be obliged, even without the hopes of having it in my Power, ever to make him a return.

It is impossible for me to come near your Lordship, in any kind, and not to receive some Favour; and while in appearance I am only making an Acknowledgment (with the usual underhand dealing of the World) I am at the same time, insinuating my own Interest. I cannot give your Lordship your due, without tacking a Bill of my own Priviledges. 'Tis true, if a Man never committed a Folly, he would never stand in need of a Protection: But then Power would have nothing to do, and good Nature no occasion to shew it self; and where those Vertues are, 'tis pity they should want Objects to shine upon. I must confess this is no reason, why a Man should do an idle thing, nor indeed any good Excuse for it, when done; yet it reconciles the uses of such Authority and Goodness, to the necessities of our Follies; and is a sort of Poetical Logick, which, at this time I would make use of, to argue your Lordship into a Protection of this Play. It is the first
A 2   Of-

The Epistle Dedicatory.

Offence I have committed in this kind, or indeed, in any kind of Poetry, tho' not the first made publick; and, therefore, I hope will the more easily be pardoned: But had it been Acted, when it was first written, more might have been said in its behalf; Ignorance of the Town and Stage, would then, have been Excuses in a young Writer, which now, almost four Years experience, will scarce allow of. Yet I must declare my self sensible of the good Nature of the Town, in receiving this Play so kindly, with all its Faults, which I must own were, for the most part, very industriously covered by the care of the Players; for, I think, scarce a Character but receiv'd all the Advantage it would admit of, from the justness of Action.

As for the Criticks, my Lord, I have nothing to say, to, or against any of them of any kind; from those who make just Exceptions, to those who find fault in the wrong place. I will only make this general Answer in behalf of my Play (an Answer, which *Epictetus* advises every Man to make for himself, to his Censurers) viz. *That if they who find some Faults in it, were as intimate with it as I am, they would find a great many more.* This is a Confession, which I need not to have made; but however, I can draw this use from it, to my own Advantage, that I think there are no Faults in it, but what I do know; which, as I take it, is the first step to an amendment.

Thus I may live in hopes (sometime or other) of making the Town amends; but you, my Lord, I never can, tho' I am ever

Your Lordships

most obedient and

most humble Servant,

Will. Congreve.

To

To Mr. CONGREVE.

WHEN Vertue in pursuit of Fame appears,
And forward shoots the growth beyond the Years:
We timely court the rising Hero's Cause;
And on his side, the Poet wisely draws;
Bespeaking him hereafter, by Applause.
The days will come, when we shall all receive,
Returning Interest from what now we give:
Instructed, and supported by that Praise,
And Reputation, which we strive to raise.
Nature so coy, so hardly to be Woo'd
Flies, like a Mistress, but to be pursu'd.
O CONGREVE! boldly follow on the Chase;
She looks behind, and wants thy strong Embrace:
She yields, she yields, surrenders all her Charms,
Do you but force her gently to your Arms:
Such Nerves, such Graces, in your Lines appear,
As you were made to be her Ravisher.
DRYDEN has long extended his Command,
By Right divine, quite through the Muses Land,
Absolute Lord; and holding now from none,
But great Apollo, his undoubted Crown:
(That Empire settled, and grown old in Pow'r)
Can wish for nothing, but a Successor:
Not to enlarge his Limits, but maintain
Those Provinces, which he alone could gain.
His eldest Wicherly, in wise Retreat,
Thought it not worth his quiet to be great.
Loose, wandring, Etherege, in wild Pleasures tost,
And foreign Int'rests, to his hopes long lost:
Poor Lee and Otway dead! CONGREVE appears;
The Darling, and last Comfort of his Years:
May'st thou live long in thy great Masters smiles,
And growing under him, adorn these Isles:
But when——when part of him (be that but late)
His Body yielding must submit to Fate,
Leaving his deathless Works, and thee behind,
(The natural Successor of his Mind)
Then may'st thou finish what he has begun:
Heir to his Merit, be in Fame his Son.
What thou hast done, shews all is in thy Pow'r;
And to Write better, only must Write more.
'Tis something to be willing to commend;
But my best Praise, is, that I am your Friend.
THO. SOUTHERNE.

Title page, dedicatory epistle, and commendatory verse by Thomas Southerne, from the first edition of Congreve's first play. Southerne had helped to polish the play and had convinced the management of the Theatre Royal in Drury Lane to stage it.

To my Dear Friend

Mr. Congreve,

On His COMEDY, call'd,

The Double-Dealer.

WELL then; the promis'd hour is come
     at laſt ;
     The preſent Age of Wit obſcures the paſt :
Strong were our Syres; and as they Fought they Writ,
Conqu'ring with force of Arms, and dint of Wit ;
Theirs was the Gyant Race, before the Flood ;
And thus, when Charles Return'd, our Empire ſtood.
Like Janus he the ſtubborn Soil manur'd,
With Rules of Husbandry the rankneſs cur'd :
Tam'd us to manners, when the Stage was rude ;
And boiſtrous Engliſh Wit, with Art indu'd.
Our Age was cultivated thus at length ;
But what we gain'd in ſkill we loſt in ſtrength.
Our Builders were, with want of Genius, curſt ;
The ſecond Temple was not like the firſt :

       a 2   Till

To Mr. CONGREVE,

Till You, the beſt Vitruvius, come at length;
Our Beauties equal ; but excel our ſtrength.
Firm Dorique Pillars found Your ſolid Baſe :
The Fair Corinthian Crowns the higher Space ;
Thus all below is Strength, and all above is Grace.
In caſie Dialogue is Fletcher's Praiſe :
He mov'd the mind, but had not power to raiſe.
Great Johnſon did by ſtrength of Judgment pleaſe :
Yet doubling Fletcher's Force, he wants his Eaſe.
In differing Tallents both adorn'd their Age ;
One for the Study, t'other for the Stage.
But both to Congreve juſtly ſhall ſubmit,
One match'd in Judgment, both o'er-match'd in Wit.
In Him all Beauties of this Age we ſee ;
Etherege his Courtſhip, Southern's Purity ;
The Satire,Wit,and Strength of Manly Witcherly.
All this in blooming Youth you have Atchiev'd ;
Now are your foil'd Contemporaries griev'd ;
So much the ſweetneſs of your manners move,
We cannot envy you, becauſe we Love.
Fabius might joy in Scipio, when he ſaw
A Beardleſs Conſul made againſt the Law,
And joyn his Suffrage to the Votes of Rome ;
Though He with Hannibal was overcome.
Thus old Romano bow'd to Raphel's Fame ;
And Scholar to the Youth he taught, became.

     Oh that your Brows my Lawrel had ſuſtain'd,
Well had I been Depos'd, if You had reign'd !

                       The

On the Double-Dealer.

The Father had deſcended for the Son ;
For only You are lineal to the Throne.
Thus when the State one Edward did depoſe ;
A Greater Edward in his room aroſe.
But now, not I, but Poetry is curs'd ;
For Tom the Second reigns like Tom the firſt.
But let 'em not miſtake my Patron's part ;
Nor call his Charity their own deſert.
Yet this I Prophecy ; Thou ſhalt be ſeen,
(Tho' with ſome ſhort Parentheſis between :)
High on the Throne of Wit ; and ſeated there,
Not mine (that's little) but thy Lawrel wear.
Thy firſt attempt an early promiſe made ;
That early promiſe this has more than paid.
So bold, yet ſo judiciouſly you dare,
That Your leaſt Praiſe, is to be Regular.
Time, Place, and Action, may with pains be wrought,
But Genius muſt be born ; and never can be taught.
This is Your Portion ; this Your Native Store ;
Heav'n that but once was Prodigal before,
To Shakeſpeare gave as much ; ſhe cou'd not give
     him more.

     Maintain Your Poſt : That's all the Fame You need;
For 'tis impoſſible you ſhou'd proceed.
Already I am worn with Cares and Age ;
And juſt abandoning th' Ungrateful Stage :
Unprofitably kept at Heav'ns expence,
I live a Rent-charge on his Providence :

                But

To Mr. CONGREVE, &c.

But You, whom ev'ry Muſe and Grace adorn,
Whom I foreſee to better Fortune born,
Be kind to my Remains ; and oh defend,
Againſt Your Judgment Your departed Friend !
Let not the Inſulting Foe my Fame purſue ;
But ſhade thoſe Lawrels which deſcend to You :
And take for Tribute what theſe Lines expreſs :
You merit more ; nor cou'd my Love do leſs.

               John Dryden.

               Prologue

John Dryden's response to the public's criticism of Congreve's second play (from the 1694 edition of The Double-Dealer). *As Dryden explained to a friend, "The women think he has exposed their Bitchery too much; and the Gentlemen, are offended with him: for the discovery of their follies; and the way of their Intrigues, under the notion of Friendship to their Ladyes Husbands."*

ber 1693, was unexpected, and, as Dryden noted in a letter to William Walsh on 12 December 1693, it was "much censurd by the greater part of the Town. . . . The women think he has exposed their Bitchery too much; and the Gentlemen, are offended with him: for the discovery of their follies; and the way of their Intrigues, under the notion of Friendship to their Ladyes Husbands." Dryden contributed magnificently to the defense of the play by writing his generous poem "To my dear friend Mr Congreve," printed in the first edition of the play (1694), while Congreve used the preface to defend the play against some of its critics' charges. The town's antagonism or, at best, hesitancy over the play was, however, a natural response to its experimentation both in matter and manner.

The action of love and sex in *The Old Bachelor* is set in the normal urban locales of Restoration comedy. The rooms, streets, and parks of London provide the setting for the flow of the action across the city of the audience. For *The Double Dealer*, Congreve establishes something like a theatrical laboratory in which the action can move precipitately under the vigilant gaze of the audience at its scientific demonstration of human activity. The entire action of the play takes place in Lord Touchwood's house; indeed, every scene takes place in the gallery, except for a single scene set in a bedroom opening off it. The house has a garden into which characters can wander, but, beyond the fact that it must be within moderately easy reach of the town of St. Albans, there are no precise clues to the house's geographical location. It functions both as a perfect example of the neoclassical unity of place that Restoration comedies had consistently ignored and, at the same time, as a dramatic limbo, a dreamlike world into which the characters have been drawn and kept for the duration of the action.

Even the precision of the location in the gallery has its own function, the action unfolding in a space through which characters must pass from one unseen room to another, a space in which chance meetings are paradoxically inevitable as the characters perform their own private routines of courtship and adultery, bumping into others similarly self-obsessed. The stage is simultaneously emphatically real and intensely theatrical, a normal room and a performance space in which the action is played out.

As if to increase the audience's awe at the virtuoso skills needed to contain the action within such a small compass of space, Congreve exacer-

bates the difficulty by demanding a similarly restricted time. Congreve takes the neoclassical notion of the unity of time to its logical extreme, the entire action taking place between "Five a Clock to Eight in the Evening." Not only does the time of performance exactly match the time of the action, but the play insistently watches the clock, reminding the audience more than a dozen times of the interconnection between the time and the action. Even more tightly than its only predecessor in Restoration comedy, Sir Samuel Tuke's *The Adventure of Five Hours* (1663), *The Double Dealer* observes the unity of time to produce a nightmarish, fantastical compression on the action, a nervous and excitable energy onstage—and in the audience—as the plots blossom and wither at breakneck speed. The rapidity of the action in the hours after dinner on the eve of the wedding of Mellefont and Cynthia is both a threat (will the marriage be prevented?) and a promise of release (if the lovers can survive this evening their future happiness will be assured).

This tension is both a fear of the detailed plotting that threatens to stop the match and an equally disturbing fear for the examples of matrimony that cluster around them. Mellefont and Cynthia are innocent, virtuous, passive, and consequently fearful. That Mellefont is not foolish for failing to perceive the plots ranged against him is one of the claims Congreve is at pains to make in the preface: "Is every Man a Gull and a Fool that is deceiv'd? . . . If this Man be deceived by the Treachery of the other; must he of necessity commence Fool immediately, only because the other has proved a Villain?" Cynthia's wry comment in act 2 on the knowledge gained by looking around her at the other married couples was a view Congreve would later have to defend against Jeremy Collier: "I'm thinking, that tho' Marriage makes Man and Wife One Flesh, it leaves 'em still Two Fools"—hence her following question to Mellefont: "What think you of drawing Stakes, and giving over in time?"

The parallel actions of *The Double Dealer* follow three comparable triangles of adultery. The most foolish are Lord and Lady Froth with their attendant cuckolder, the fop Brisk. Mellefont sets his friend Careless to intervene in the marriage of Cynthia's parents, Sir Paul and Lady Plyant, in order to head off the threat posed by Lady Plyant's assumption that Mellefont is really in love with her, not Cynthia, her stepdaughter. Both of these are comic actions of a comfortable form; both contain moments of exuberant oddity that set them apart from their forebears. Lady Froth's endless disquisitions on her verse-epic, *The Sillibub,* or the wonderfully deflating line with which she punctures the hysteria and tension of the end of the play, "You know I told you *Saturn* look'd a little more angry than usual," provide an untroubling comic underpinning of the rest of the play. The Plyants' bizarre bedtime habits are offset by the touching simplicity of Sir Paul's yearning for a son, a son he is unlikely to have when his wife will allow sex only once a year: "But if I had a Son, ah, that's my affliction, and my only affliction; indeed I cannot refrain Tears when it comes in my mind."

The crisscrossing of these plots is contrasted in the play by the rigid separation of the other triangle from the rest of the action. Lord Touchwood may begin as a foolish cuckold, but the intensity of the action that surrounds him leads him to acquire a remarkable and distinctly uncomic dignity. His wife, Lady Touchwood, has a power that in its passionate extremes has much more to do with the angry women of Restoration tragedy. Her outbursts to her lover, Maskwell, her desperation at Mellefont's lack of interest in her, and her fury when her plots are themselves thwarted create a scale of emotion far beyond the compass of the comic world. Where the anger of, for example, Mrs. Loveit in George Etherege's *The Man of Mode* (1676) produces only mockery in response from other characters and audience alike, Lady Touchwood's language has a frightening energy that takes it well beyond ridicule: "Death, do you dally with my Passion? Insolent Devil! But have a care,—provoke me not." Indeed the plotting against Mellefont and Cynthia is finally overcome only because Lady Touchwood *has* been provoked beyond endurance by the discovery of the ramifications of Maskwell's plotting and because her offstage screaming at him is overheard by Cynthia and Lord Touchwood, who happen to be passing through the gallery at the right moment. Most critical attention has been focused on the strange mixture of styles that Congreve has chosen to bring together in the play. The alienness of Lady Touchwood—it is impossible to imagine her as a character in *The Old Bachelor*—seems to upset critics as readers in a way that it never does theater audiences. On stage the grand scope of the play is entirely coherent, and the intrigues that emanate from Maskwell—frequently expounded in soliloquies that in their directness of address to the audience

recall Shakespeare's Iago—generate a fascinated and troubled attentiveness.

For there is no doubt that Maskwell is troubling. His status in the Touchwood household, somewhere between servant and friend, fuels his ambitions. If the three triangles of characters make a pattern that seems to isolate the duo of Mellefont and Cynthia, that is only because as the play develops it becomes clear that Maskwell plans to create a different sort of triangle for them, aiming to marry Cynthia himself, with the help of a tame chaplain, a disguise with the armholes stitched up, and a coach to take him and Cynthia to St. Albans. There is a hideous fascination in Maskwell's brilliant machinations that lures the audience toward a sympathy with the energies and attractiveness of villainous evil. *The Double Dealer* goes far beyond comedy's normal concerns with folly and instead, in Maskwell, presents viciousness and malevolence in its most tempting form. It also makes clear that such evil cannot be controlled by the actions of the good characters. In the end the play relies on Cynthia's agreement in act 4 to an escape clause if Mellefont should fail to defeat his aunt and her accomplices:

> CYNTHIA. Well, if the Devil should assist her, and your Plot miscarry—
> MELLEFONT. Ay, what am I to trust to then?
> CYNTHIA. Why if you give me very clear demonstration that it was the Devil, I'll allow for irresistable odds.

Maskwell's diabolic cunning excuses Mellefont. It is plainly inadequate to argue, as Aubrey L. Williams has, that the play is an orthodox demonstration of the workings of providence. Rather it shows how the power of evil is self-defeating in the intensely theatrical world Congreve has created in which to demonstrate the extent of its threatening power. On a comic stage with its hidings, overhearings, and disguisings, even the devilish ingenuity of a Maskwell is bound to fail.

Love for Love, Congreve's next comedy, was written in 1694 and scheduled for production by the United Company. When the senior actors of the company, led by Thomas Betterton and Mrs. Elizabeth Barry, decided they could no longer put up with the dictatorial mismanagement of the theater by Christopher Rich and petitioned for the right to establish a new company, Congreve had no hesitation in allowing them to take with them his new comedy. *Love for Love* was the opening production for the secessionists in their hastily refurbished theater in Lincoln's Inn

Thomas Doggett, the comedian for whom Congreve wrote the parts of Fondlewife in The Old Bachelor, *Sir Paul Plyant in* The Double Dealer, *Ben in* Love for Love, *and the title role in* Squire Trelooby

Fields, with Congreve supplying a prologue specially written for "the opening of the New House" on 30 April 1695.

After the deliberate experimentation of *The Double Dealer*, *Love for Love* marks a conscious decision to return to the more conventional concerns of Restoration comedy, avoiding the problem of outright evil in favor of a new investigation of generous love. Its title reformulates the concerns of so much of the comedy of the 1690s, epitomized in Thomas D'Urfey's play *Love for Money*, which premiered in 1691. D'Urfey's title—and the action of his play—suggests an undeviatingly satiric

view of the place of love in contemporary society: love, as sexual desire or as marriage, is bought and sold, exchanged for money. In Congreve's comedy the buying and selling of love is a tenet that the central character, Valentine, must learn to revalue, coming in the course of the play to understand that the only commodity for which love can be exchanged is love.

The action opens in a conventional situation, the rake penned up in his room to avoid the demands of his creditors. From Dryden's *The Wild Gallant* (1663) onward, the position of the penniless young man who has run through his in-

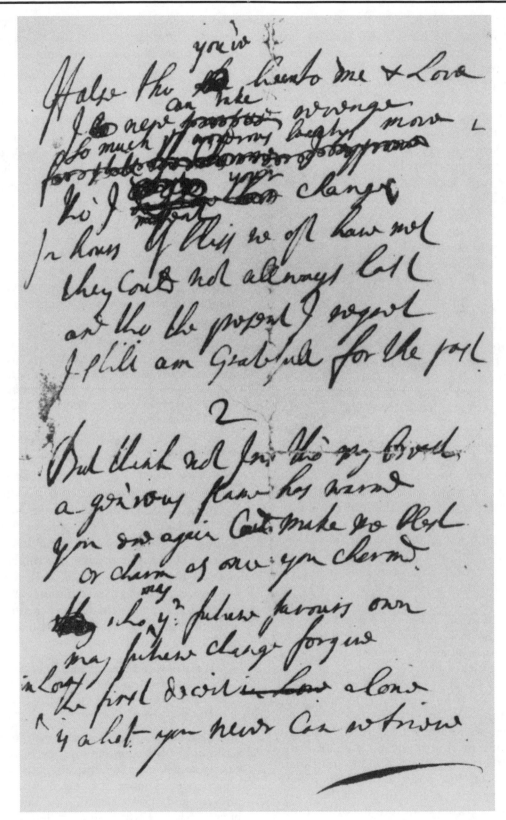

Draft for a poem that Congreve is believed to have addressed to Anne Bracegirdle. A somewhat different version of the first eight lines was published as "A Complaint to Pious Selinda" in 1710 (from John C. Hodges, William Congreve The Man, *1941).*

heritance and now finds himself unable to approach the woman he loves was a familiar starting point for comedy. Valentine's attempts to evade his creditors and to shed his responsibilities, to escape the consequences of his actions, veer between a comic sequence of ploys and a more brutal, more desperate note. At its most vicious, Valentine's attempt to avoid the legacy of his past behavior is seen in his apparently light-hearted exasperation that the wet nurse who appears at the door seeking money for the upkeep of one of his bastards "knows my Condition well enough, and might have overlaid the Child a Fortnight ago, if she had any forecast in her." It is entirely characteristic of the play's continual redefinition of expected reactions that such a suggestion should be stoutly resisted by Valentine's cynical friend Scandal, who sends money to "Bouncing *Margery*, and my Godson."

Margery's lack of "forecast" anticipates the play's multiple consideration of foresight. At its most comic, there is Foresight himself, uncle to Valentine's beloved Angelica, superstitiously unable to act without checking on the omens and prophecies of late-seventeenth-century astrology. Foresight's obsessions with pseudo-scholarship, a sure subject for satire, are contrasted at the opposite end of the scale by the naiveté of Valentine's younger brother Ben, a sailor unable to find his land legs in the play's society, where his forthright honesty is mystified by the indirectness and deviousness of social behavior. Ben and Miss Prue, Foresight's daughter, are the ideal social prey for Mrs. Frail and Tattle, adept in the way of this comic world and pragmatic enough to seize the opportunities for wealthy marriage offered by the two innocents. But their foresight is insufficient, and a series of disguisings and maskings result in Tattle and Mrs. Frail marrying each other, with mockery rather than social success the consequence of their plans.

The play's central concern, however, is with the escape route from financial ruin that is dangled temptingly in front of Valentine, a substantial sum from his father, Sir Sampson Legend, to clear his debts in return for his signature to a deed of disinheritance. The action provides an immediate solution but poses a problem of foresight for him, not only in terms of his future financial prospects but also in terms of his future prospects with Angelica. Much of the action of the play is taken up with Valentine's attempts to avoid the final decision. Having signed a note of intent and received his cash advance, Valentine

feigns madness, since insanity will prevent his executing a binding contract. But Valentine's machinations cannot begin to constitute an adequate response to Angelica. Her response to his feigned madness is to play along with it, to treat his protestations of love as yet more ravings, and to propose, in apparent seriousness, to marry the outrageous and unfatherly Sir Sampson. The play awaits the moment at which Valentine, finally trapped, is forced to act with honesty but also through love. Angelica's forthright statement of her demand for control over her destiny is the final indication of Valentine's need to accept responsibility for his actions; as she sums it up, "you must pardon me, if I think my own Inclinations have a better Right to dispose of my Person, than yours." Valentine's speech of understanding is unlike anything Congreve had written before:

> I have been disappointed of my only Hope; and he that loses hope may part with any thing. I never valu'd Fortune, but as it was subservient to my Pleasure; and my only Pleasure was to please this Lady: I have made many vain Attempts, and find at last, that nothing but my Ruine can effect it: Which, for that Reason, I will sign to—Give me the Paper.

Angelica's response, "Generous *Valentine!*" and her immediate agreement to marry him defines the nature of the love test through which she has put him. Her refusal to be passive in the world, waiting on male decisions about love and marriage, is both a remarkable reformulation of the place of the virtuous woman in Restoration drama and a perceptive recognition on Congreve's part of the extent of male construction of the female. As Angelica says in the last speech of the play,

> You tax us with Injustice, only to cover your own want of Merit. You would have all the Reward of Love; but few have the Constancy to stay till it becomes your due.

Yet Angelica's attempt to act with proper foresight and self-determination, her refusal to be as simply angelic as her name suggests, has puzzled critics. An exchange on the play between Mrs. Mirvan and Lord Orville in Fanny Burney's novel *Evelina* (1778; volume 1, letter 20), typifies later responses:

> "Yet, in a trial so long, . . . there seems rather too much consciousness of her power."

"... I will venture to say, that Angelica bestows her hand rather with the air of a benefactress, than with the tenderness of a mistress. Generosity without delicacy, like wit without judgment, generally gives as much pain as pleasure."

The audiences' and critics' natural sympathies with the comic energies of Valentine are inevitably confused by Angelica's far more subtle perception of the inadequacies of his love. Intelligently, though without recourse to the conventional wit of Restoration heroines, Angelica presents the need for a transparent honesty. When Valentine announces in act 3 that he knows "no effectual Difference between continued Affectation and Reality," he is accurate about everyone else's behavior but wrong in assuming that this is a necessary state of social existence. The flatness of his eventual speech of acceptance is an eschewal of the theatricality that had been the key characteristic of his own and others' language in the play. When he realizes he can choose, he does so without the extravagant heroics or linguistic affectation that such moments had usually summoned forth in earlier plays. A simplicity and purity of language seems in itself almost enough to convince Angelica that he has come to differentiate between affectation and reality.

In February 1696 Trinity College, Dublin, awarded Congreve and his fellow dramatist, Thomas Southerne, honorary M.A.'s. In the summer after the success of *Love for Love*, Congreve received his first government office, being appointed one of the five commissioners for licensing hackney coaches at a salary, recently halved, of one hundred pounds a year. In 1697 he became one of the managers of the Malt Lottery, and from 1700 to 1703 he served as the Customer at Poole, sharing the fees with the deputy who did the work. In 1705 he became a commissioner for wines. But none of these offices provided him with anything like the income of a gentleman, and, while their insignificance meant they survived the changes of party in government, Congreve's search for a lucrative post, sufficient to live on in comfort, was a constant source of anxiety in these years. His friends frequently commented on his poverty.

Encouraged by John Dennis, Congreve took the opportunity in July 1695 of setting down some thoughts on humor in comedy in the form of a letter, "An Essay Concerning Humour in Comedy." This, Congreve's only attempt outside his prefaces and the Collier controversy to outline any theory of comedy, is a remarkably careful and benign attempt to distinguish the types of dramatic character, discriminating between humor, habit, and affectation:

Humour is from Nature, *Habit* from Custom; and *Affectation* from Industry.
Humour, shews us as we *are*.
Habit, shews us, as we appear, under a forcible Impression.
Affectation, shews us what we would be, under a Voluntary Disguise.

For Congreve the comedy in a character is not a product of natural deformity but rather of an untroubling individuality, something "peculiar and Natural to one Man only." While he recognizes that habit and affectation are appropriate forms of characterization for comedy, they are qualitatively less worthwhile than humor, which is prized for its consonance with nature. Like Dryden in *An Essay of Dramatic Poesie*, Congreve singles out for praise Morose in Jonson's *Epicoene* (1609), recognizing how Morose's intolerance for noise is only an exacerbated form of most people's dislike of knives scratched on plates or the sound of a cork being cut. There is, throughout his analysis, a geniality and a genuine fascination with the variety of real people, the only proper study for a writer of comedies.

Congreve was beginning to be sought by new writers as a patron, critic, and adviser. New plays were regularly submitted to him for approval by writers such as Catharine Trotter and Charles Hopkins. When, in 1697, Mary Pix found the plot of her new play had been stolen by George Powell for his *The Imposture Defeated*, Congreve accompanied his protégée to the premiere to hiss the thief.

Catharine Trotter introduced herself to Congreve by writing a poem to him that she hoped he would publish with the text of *The Mourning Bride* (1697). If the twentieth-century history of Congreve's critical and theatrical fortunes has been a steadily increasing valuation of the comedies, little has been found to say in favor of this play, Congreve's only tragedy. The play's initial success and its continued popularity throughout the eighteenth century—it was by far the most often performed of his plays—has seemed to be nothing more than an aberration of previous audiences' taste. Johnson announced authoritatively, "if I were required to select from the whole mass

Elizabeth Barry as Zara in the first production of The Mourning Bride

of English poetry the most poetical paragraph, I know not what I could prefer to an exclamation in *The Mourning Bride*," quoting Almeria's description of a temple in act 2:

No, all is hush'd, and still as Death—'Tis dreadful!
How rev'rend is the Face of this tall Pile,
Whose antient Pillars rear their Marble Heads,
To bear aloft its arch'd and pond'rous Roof,
By its own Weight, made stedfast, and immoveable,
Looking Tranquility.

But Johnson's praise has puzzled Johnson's critics and seems embarrassing hyperbole to anyone who has read *The Mourning Bride*. Even the rapidly growing recent understanding of the considerable merits of other Restoration tragedies, such as Dryden's late plays, has not significantly affected opinions of Congreve's. Recognition that a speech such as the following by Zara in act 2 is deeply affected, or infected, by Congreve's reading of Shakespeare cannot persuade readers that

the language does not collapse into bathetic excess as it strives for effect:

who knows
What racking Cares disease a Monarch's Bed?
Or Love, that late at Night still lights his Camp,
And strikes his Rays thro' dusk, and folded Lids,
Forbidding rest; may stretch his Eyes awake
And force their Balls abroad, at this dead Hour.

Tracing the lineage and descendants of Zara's passion and anger in the rest of Congreve's work back to Lady Touchwood and forward to Mrs. Marwood in *The Way of the World*, both also played by Elizabeth Barry, only reveals the comparative poverty of intelligent characterization here, in the same way that the passivity of the virtuous heroine Almeria is infuriating when located between Anne Bracegirdle's other roles as Angelica in *Love for Love* and Millamant in *The Way of the World*. It is as if the subtlety of Congreve's perception of the social position of women in comic society deserts him under the dead weight of heavy grandeur appropriate to heroic tragedy.

The complexity of plotting, which in the comedies is part both of the indecipherability of social activity and a major part of the moral argument the plays are designed to investigate, here becomes sensationalistic, a pretext for moments of high emotion. Congreve, in a 1703 letter, advised Catharine Trotter that in her new play, *The Revolution in Sweden* (1706),

> One thing would have a very beautiful effect in the catastrophe, if it were possible to manage it thro' the play; and that is to have the audience kept in ignorance, as long as the husband . . . who *Fredage* really is, till her death.

The action of *The Mourning Bride* depends on who knows that Osmyn, captured by Manuel, is really Alphonso, son of Manuel's enemy and husband of his daughter Almeria. Yet the audience is in the know from act 2 onward, and the only moment at which the information is handled with subtlety is when, at the end of act 4, Almeria half reveals Osmyn's identity to her father and his counselor Gonsalez under the misapprehension that they know already. As Gonsalez comments in soliloquy after her exit, "Osmyn Alphonso! no; she over-rates / My Policy, I ne'er suspected it." Not the least of the problems Congreve's plot poses is the essential passivity of both Almeria and Osmyn. Osmyn moves from captivity to freedom and back to captivity, from safety to danger to eventual safety, purely as a result of the everchanging moods and passions of Zara, who loves him and is loved by Manuel. There seems to be virtually nothing an honorable man such as Osmyn can do to affect his own or others' fate. Energy and the handling of the action are at the mercy of those who are passionate without a concomitant virtue. While that has often been problematic for writers of tragedy, in *The Mourning Bride* it becomes a serious hampering of the balance between the good, who, as Oscar Wilde's Miss Prism recommends, "end happily," and the bad, who end "unhappily."

For all its obvious shortcomings the play has a series of moments of fully achieved and highly successful theatricality in which Congreve's inability to find an adequate tragic language is offset by the assuredness with which the stage image is created. Almeria first meets Osmyn, for instance, when she enters the vault to grieve at the grave of Anselmo, Osmyn-Alphonso's father. Kneeling, she calls on her husband, whom she assumes to

have drowned in a shipwreck that Congreve seems to have borrowed from *Twelfth Night* (circa 1601): "To thee, to thee I call, to thee *Alphonso./ O Alphonso.*" Her cry is answered by Osmyn, "ascending from the Tomb": "Who calls that wretched thing, that was *Alphonso*?" The use of "was" is mannered and overweighted, but the effect of Osmyn's calling as he ascends the steps from his father's tomb is self-evidently powerful and effectively dramatic. The echo of *Hamlet* (circa 1600-1601) in Almeria's reply ("Angels, and all the Host of heaven support me!") and the succeeding action, in which each thinks the other is an apparition, with Almeria fainting, inevitably demeans the effect. Zara's death scene, accompanied by her servant Selim and two mutes bearing bowls of poison, has a ritualized solemnity, particularly as the "mutes kneel and mourn over her"; here silence is a valid antidote to the outpouring of poor verse that Congreve feels obliged to give Zara as she dies. Given the number of better Restoration tragedies unrevived, it will be a long time until *The Mourning Bride* receives a professional production, but there are enough signs in the play to suggest that its revival might be more than an act of piety and might reveal a work as dramatically and melodramatically successful as Congreve's comedies.

In April 1698 Jeremy Collier launched his attack on contemporary drama in *A Short View of the Immorality and Profaneness of the English Stage*, and it was inevitable that Congreve should be one of his prime targets, his plays picked apart for details to substantiate Collier's charges. Congreve delayed replying but realized that his work had to be defended. His *Amendments of Mr. Collier's False and Imperfect Citations* was published in July. Congreve's defense was, in its turn, attacked both by Collier himself in the *Defence of the Short View* (published late in 1698) and by anonymous supporters of Collier's campaign in *A Letter to Mr Congreve on his Pretended Amendments, etc of Mr Collier's Short View* and *Animadversions on Mr Congreve's Late Answer to Mr Collier*, both published in the autumn of 1698. The later pamphlets added little to the main charges while finding Congreve's defense, particularly the few places where he was prepared to give ground and admit the justice of Collier's attack on particular words and phrases, vulnerable for its inconsistencies and special pleadings. Congreve outlines four crucial grounds for his defense: that comedy has a moral purpose in laughing the audience out of vice by delighting as well as in-

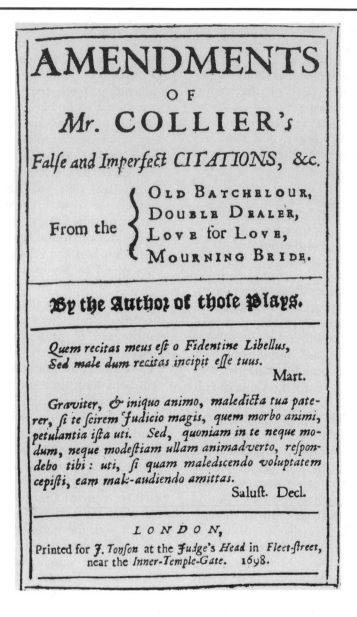

AMENDMENTS

O F

Mr. COLLIER's

False and Imperfect CITATIONS, &c.

From the { OLD BATCHELOUR,
DOUBLE DEALER,
LOVE for LOVE,
MOURNING BRIDE.

By the Author of those Plays.

*Quem recitas meus est o Fidentine Libellus,
Sed male dum recitas incipit esse tuus.*

Mart.

*Graviter, & iniquo animo, maledicta tua pate-
rer, si te scirem Judicio magis, quem morbo animi,
petulantia ista uti. Sed, quoniam in te neque mo-
dum, neque modestiam ullam animadverto, respon-
debo tibi: uti, si quam maledicendo voluptatem
cepisti, eam male-audiendo amittas.*

Salust. Decl.

LONDON,
Printed for *J. Tonson* at the *Judge's Head* in *Fleet-street*,
near the *Inner-Temple-Gate.* 1698.

Title page for Congreve's response to Jeremy Collier's A Short View of the Immorality and Profaneness of the English Stage. *Congreve argues in part that, by taking lines out of context, Collier "first commits a Rape upon my Words, and then arraigns 'em of Immodesty; he has Barbarity enough to accuse the very Virgins that he has deflowr'd. . . ."*

structing; that comedies must contain vicious and foolish characters if they are to achieve this moral aim; that passages must be considered in the scene in which they appear, not wrenched out of context as Collier consistently does; and that words have a "diversity of subject" which gives a "diversity of signification" and, hence, that a word used in one sense in a sacred context need not carry that religious meaning over when "otherwise apply'd." The criteria, except for the last, which deliberately underplays the resonance of biblical usage that Congreve frequently plays on, are, of course, entirely reasonable, however

unlikely they were to satisfy Collier. In carrying them over into the detailed defense of speeches, Congreve concentrates on the third, emphasizing how a speech is placed in a scene, fixed and constricted in its meaning by its surroundings.

While the genuine threat of prosecution and the change in the temper of the times had their local effects in the detailed changes to the dialogue that Congreve introduced in the second edition of *The Double Dealer* in 1706 and in his preparation of the text of all his plays for the edition of his works in 1710, the major response to Collierism that he offered is in the form and mat-

THE

Way of the World,

A

COMEDY.

As it is ACTED

AT THE

Theatre in *Lincoln's-Inn-Fields*,

BY

His Majesty's Servants.

Written by Mr. *CONGREVE.*

Audire est Opera pretium, procedere recte
Qui machis non vultis——   Hor. Sat. 2. l. 1.
——Metuat doti deprensa.——   Ibid.

LONDON:
Printed for *Jacob Tonson*, within *Gray's-Inn-Gate* next
Gray's-Inn-Lane. 1700.

Title page for the first edition of Congreve's most complex comedy. After the unenthusiastic reception accorded its first production, Congreve wrote, "That it succeeded on the stage, was almost beyond my Expectation; for but little of it was prepared for that general Taste which seems now to be predominant in the Palates of our Audience."

ter of the only comedy he wrote after the Collier controversy began, *The Way of the World*.

On 12 March 1700 Lady Marow wrote to a friend, "Congreve's new play, doth not answer expectation, there being no plot in it but many witty things." Lady Marow was the first reviewer of *The Way of the World*; she is also the last one to complain that the play lacked plot. Congreve's statement in the dedication to the published text, "That it succeeded on the Stage, was almost beyond my Expectation," is not simply an author's excuse for a failed play: *The Way of the World* deliberately sets out to make life difficult for the audience. Even the family relationships that bind the characters are both complex and presented in ways that make them virtually impossible for an audience to follow, even a Restoration audience highly attuned to family trees. When Fainall describes Sir Wilfull Witwoud to Mirabell in act 1, he identifies him as "half Brother to this *Witwoud* by a former Wife, who was Sister to my Lady

Wishfort, my Wife's Mother. If you marry *Millamant* you must call Cousins too." Like Shakespeare's history plays, *The Way of the World* seems to need genealogical tables in the program.

The whole action of the play, its series of plots and counterplots in the quest for control of Lady Wishfort's fortune and her control over that of her niece Millamant, moves forward by hint and innuendo. Only at the end of the play, for instance, does the audience discover what on earth Mirabell meant in act 2 when he said to the unhappy Mrs. Fainall about her husband, "When you are weary of him, you know your Remedy." Only then do we learn that Fainall's plots, increasingly violent and vicious as the play proceeds, have been entirely pointless, since, as he reads on a piece of legal parchment handed to him by Mirabell, there is "*A deed of Conveyance of the whole Estate real of* Arabella Languish *Widdow in trust to* Edward Mirabell." If Mirabell controls

Mrs. Fainall's estate, Fainall's activities are foredoomed, though it takes the whole play for this crucial piece of evidence to be revealed.

Congreve, having digested so brilliantly the tenets of neoclassical theory, seems to have decided to ignore its instructions and to create a drama whose plot is mystifyingly opaque. The deed of trust is, as Mirabell tells Fainall, "*the way of the World*, Sir: of the Widdows of the World." It constitutes a solution in itself, by virtue of its immutability and its legality. Such documents, summoned up in *Love for Love* only to be rejected, are necessary in a society deeply affected by the malevolence of Fainall and his mistress, Mrs. Marwood. The deed is an example of Mirabell's prescience, of his combination of virtue, at least in the play's terms, and social cunning. He is, as Mrs. Fainall says in her last words in the play, "a Cautious Friend, to whose advice all is owing."

Yet Mirabell's actions have increasingly troubled the play's critics. Within the time span of the play there is perhaps little to worry us, but the play is uneasy about a crucial piece of its past. Mirabell and Mrs. Fainall (then Arabella Languish) ended their affair when she thought she was pregnant, and Mirabell was instrumental in her marrying Fainall. There is something too coldly rational in Mirabell's answer to her question in act 2: "Why did you make me marry this Man?" As Ian Donaldson has emphasized, the answer is unpalatably evasive for the most part: "A better Man ought not to have been sacrific'd to the Occasion; a worse had not answer'd to the Purpose." The play never contemplates why Mirabell and Mrs. Fainall did not marry. Instead, Mrs. Fainall's extraordinary generosity toward Mirabell, apart from this one moment of complaint, leads her to aid his plans to win Millamant. It is significant and moving that, at the end of the proviso scene, in which Millamant and Mirabell set out the conditions under which they are prepared to marry, Millamant's agreement is only secured when Mrs. Fainall enters and gives her opinion:

> MILLAMANT. *Fainall*, what shall I do? shall I have him? I think I must have him.
> MRS. FAINALL. Ay, ay, take him, take him, what shou'd you do?

While it is never quite clear whether Millamant knows of Mirabell's affair with Mrs. Fainall, there is no comparable example in Restoration comedy of a cast mistress so generously assenting to her former lover's marriage.

The Way of the World is full of such revaluations of apparently stereotypical characters. Indeed, the opening section of the play, a long dialogue between Mirabell and Fainall, establishes a tone in which the two rakes, cautiously and delicately probing each other's motives, are indistinguishable. That the play will go on to show Mirabell's generosity and thoughtfulness and Fainall's passionate viciousness is impossible to predict from their fencing exchanges at the start. Typically, though, where plays such as *The Old Bachelor* open with conversation between two friends, addressing each other as Ned and Frank, *The Way of the World* opens with Mirabell calling the other "Mr. *Fainall*"; the formality of address is disconcerting. No wonder that the "hasty Judges," of whom Congreve complains in the dedication, did not "distinguish betwixt the Character of a *Witwoud* and *Truewit*," since it is no longer simply a matter of identifying the fools in the play but of discriminating between those who are apparently wits.

Even the glib labeling of certain characters as fools proves increasingly inadequate. Sir Wilfull Witwoud, the country cousin arriving in town with mud on his boots and a rustic incomprehension of town manners, comes at the end of the play to be valued for his generosity and his humane compassion, so that Mirabell can say of him without the slightest trace of irony, "Sir *Wilfull* is my Friend." Nothing will make Sir Wilfull more intelligent, but his good nature matters far more. No wit has ever been prepared to consider a man such as Sir Wilfull as his friend before. The moment is the culmination of the play's intense examination of the word "friend," from Mirabell's early description of Mrs. Marwood to Fainall as "your Friend, or your Wife's Friend" (that is, mistress or friend) onward. Friendship, in the ways of this world, is a valuable but also a dangerous commodity, an identification of an individual's perception of value.

In response to a society of such complexity, characters such as Fainall or Mirabell can choose to control it or, at least, to attempt to control it. But for many the only course is to blunder through it with an undeviating belief in themselves. For Lady Wishfort, whose folly in believing herself younger and more attractive than she is leads her to come close to marrying Mirabell's servant Waitwell, disguised as his nonexistent uncle Sir Rowland, the recognition of her own

William Congreve, 1709 (portrait by Sir Godfrey Kneller; National Portrait Gallery, London)

foolishness can lead to its own form of generosity in giving Millamant to Mirabell: "Well Sir, take her, and with her all the Joy I can give you." It is characteristic of the care of Mirabell's plotting, however, that he ensures that Waitwell marries Lady Wishfort's maid Foible before he will allow the plot to go forward.

For Millamant the acuity of perception of the nature of her society leads her to need a defense. Her language, mesmerizing in its profusion and the sheer inventiveness of its wit, is a self-protective device to bemuse others with her surface and keep her inner self hidden. The performance is done with such skill that, as Mirabell says after their first encounter in the play, "To think of a Whirlwind, tho' 'twere in a Whirlwind, were a Case of more steady Contemplation." Her avowal of love to Mirabell at the end of the proviso scene—"Well, you ridiculous thing you, I'll have you"—is as close as she dare come to a direct statement of love to him. Millamant's hesi-

tancy at this point comes about not least because the play is nowhere near its resolution. Where earlier proviso scenes in Restoration comedy had been placed in act 5, Congreve puts his in act 4. Not until the threat by Fainall has been fully revealed and overcome can the lovers actually commit themselves in an exchange that contrasts the fixity of their earlier legalisms with the fluidity that is the hallmark of Millamant:

MILLAMANT. . . . wou'd you have me give my self to you over again?
MIRABELL. Ay, and over and over again; for I wou'd have you as often as possibly I can.

If Mirabell is "sententious," as Millamant calls him, and cautiously analytic, he is still able to find the imaginative and emotional response Millamant needs, a firm recognition of the vulnerability she understands only too well: "Well, heav'n grant I love you not too well, that's all my fear," as he says, adopting her language style for the only time in the play. Millamant is never able to say to Mirabell, only to Mrs. Fainall, that "I find I love him violently."

The Way of the World is not a comforting play. Its society is terrifying in its secrecy and only marginally less threatening when Fainall finally resorts to drawing his sword and tries to run his wife through. Audiences who indulgently enjoy the sophistication of the witty dialogue of Millamant and Mirabell miss the equivalent sophistication in the play's view of a society barely able to contain Fainall's aggression and heavily reliant on trusting Mirabell. Trust, even more than love, comes in the play to be a value society has to have, provided it knows where to place it. Arabella Languish's deed of trust is the play's final symbol of the rules by which society can be effectively and fairly run. *The Way of the World* is a serious and intensely moral comedy, the culmination of Congreve's recurrent fascination with the moral comedy of Terence, and Congreve knew, like Terence's plays, his masterpiece was hardly likely to please most of the audience.

If *The Way of the World* was by no means the failure that tradition would have us believe, it was by no means the success that it deserved to be. In the following few years Congreve wrote three more pieces for the stage but no more full-length plays. His libretto on the subject of the judgment of Paris was written as the text for a music competition. The masque was set by four different composers, John Eccles, Godfrey Finger, Daniel Purcell, and John Weldon, and the four versions were performed successively in the spring of 1701 at Dorset Garden Theatre with eighty-five performers and a specially constructed stage. Finally, all four were given on the same night, and the prize money of two hundred pounds distributed, with Weldon unexpectedly the winner. The text is adequate but unremarkable. Far more substantial is Congreve's opera libretto *Semele*, set by John Eccles but probably not performed, and later set again brilliantly by George Frideric Handel. Congreve's exploration of Juno's revenge on the ambitions of Semele for immortality, a present she seeks from Jupiter, who has set her up in her own palace, veers with great confidence from high heroic seriousness to teasing comedy. Juno's aria of triumph, for instance, sung as she ascends to heaven in a chariot, contrasts the evanescent joys of love with the enduring pleasures of revenge:

With what Joy shall I mount to my Heav'n again,

At once from my Rival and Jealousie freed!
The Sweets of Revenge make it worth while to
    reign,
    And Heav'n will hereafter be Heav'n indeed.

Even Semele, first seen as a virtuous lover of the ruler of heaven, finds when set up as a mistress that love soon palls:

I love and am lov'd, yet more I desire;
Ah, how foolish a Thing is Fruition!
As one Passion cools, some other takes Fire,
And I'm still in a longing Condition.
    Whate'er I possess
    Soon seems an Excess,
For something untry'd I petition;
    Tho' daily I prove
    The Pleasures of Love,
I die for the Joys of Ambition.

At such moments Congreve demonstrates the consequences of applying the virtuosic skills of the songs in his comedies to a subject apparently less amenable to such ironic treatment. *Semele* is the outcome of the embedding of songs into plays: for example, Sylvia's song to Heartwell in act 3 of *The Old Bachelor* or Millamant's use of a song, "Love's but the frailty of the Mind," to seal her triumph over Mrs. Marwood for Mirabell's love in act 3 of *The Way of the World*.

In 1704 Congreve contributed one act to a version of Molière's *Monsieur de Pourceaugnac* (1669), with one act each from John Vanbrugh and William Walsh. The completed play, called *Squire Trelooby*, was performed a few times, beginning on 30 March 1704, but never published. The play was a prelude to the much more substantial collaboration between Congreve and Vanbrugh in the establishment of a new theater in the Haymarket. The company was licensed in December 1704, with the money for the building of the Queen's Theatre coming primarily from a subscription from members of the Kit-Cat Club of one hundred guineas each. The theater opened with an Italian opera in April 1705, but, in spite of Congreve's energetic work, little could compensate for the deficiencies of the theater's design, and by the end of the year Congreve bought his way out of the partnership.

For the rest of his life Congreve lived in comparative retirement, remaining a member of the Kit-Cat Club, writing occasional poems and translations, and seeking cures for the cataracts in his eyes and the gout he suffered because of his taste for good wine. Voltaire, visiting Congreve in

Henrietta, Duchess of Marlborough, the mother of Congreve's daughter, Mary (engraving by F. Kyte, based on a portrait by Sir Godfrey Kneller; National Portrait Gallery, London)

1726, reported angrily (in his *Letters Concerning the English Nation* [1733]) that Congreve spoke disparagingly of his plays as trifles and asked that Voltaire "should visit him upon no other Foot than that of a Gentleman, who led a Life of Plainness and Simplicity." Voltaire found such a notion proof of exceptional vanity, but for Congreve it was the logical outcome of his family and his current status.

It was in the context of gentlemanly retirement that Congreve prepared his works for publication in three octavo volumes in 1710. *The Works* was the greatest product of his long friendship with Jacob Tonson, the finest Restoration publisher and founder of the Kit-Cat Club. Tonson and Congreve had become acquainted soon after Congreve's arrival in London. By 1695 Congreve had lodgings in Tonson's house in Fleet Street, above the publisher's shop, and may have begun living in the Tonson household from as early as

1693. From the publication of *The Double-Dealer* onward, all of Congreve's works were published by Tonson.

The collected edition was one of a series of works of Restoration writers that Tonson published in the first years of the eighteenth century, uniform with Nicholas Rowe's octavo edition of Shakespeare (1709). Without the portentousness and size of the great folio editions of Renaissance dramatists such as Jonson (1616), Shakespeare (1623), or Francis Beaumont and John Fletcher (1647), Tonson's editions were designed to be read by gentlemen, and Congreve responded to the challenge of preparing reading editions. Apart from revising the texts of the plays, Congreve took the chance to present the plays with acts and scenes divided in the neoclassical manner, a new scene being marked with a type ornament and a list of characters onstage at each entrance or exit. With great sensitivity Congreve

Monument to Congreve in Westminster Abbey

and Tonson devised a typographic format that would reflect the plays' structures and Congreve's achievement. As D. F. McKenzie has argued in a preparatory study for his own edition of Congreve, the central volume of *The Works* was designed to state emblematically on its title page the comprehensive nature of Congreve's oeuvre, incorporating one example each of tragedy, comedy, masque, and opera: *The Mourning Bride*, *The Way of the World*, *The Judgment of Paris*, and *Semele*. Throughout his work Congreve thought of a scene as a unit of dialogue altered by the arrival or departure of a character. Only in *The Works* was he able to demonstrate that definition in print, allowing the careful specification of *liaison de scènes*, the linking between characters' movements, to have its full effect. At moments such as Mirabell's soliloquy in act 2 of *The Way of the World*, when Millamant sweeps out while he has "something more" to say, *The Works* creates a combination of dramatic form and typographical layout that is as beautiful as it is effective. The transition of the plays from the theater to the new form of "polite literature" is brilliantly accomplished.

In 1714 Congreve finally secured the government office he needed to give him financial security. Appointed secretary to the Island of Jamaica, he drew a salary of more than seven hundred pounds a year and could begin saving and investing. In 1719 he was at last able to repay Southerne's help with *The Old Bachelor* when he was able to secure production of *The Spartan Dame*, a long-banned tragedy. His friendship with Alexander Pope, mirroring his own friendship with Dryden, resulted in his being the dedicatee of Pope's translation of *The Iliad* in 1715.

Congreve's close friendship with the actress Anne Bracegirdle had begun to dwindle by 1710. His friendship with Francis, second Earl of Godolphin's family, however, resulted in his only true love affair, with Francis's wife, Henrietta, Duchess of Marlborough. When she gave birth to a daughter, Mary, in 1723, nearly twenty years after the birth of her last child, Congreve and Henrietta deflected the town's suspicions. In his will Congreve left her his fortune, then amounting to more than ten thousand pounds, with her husband appointed executor. Henrietta spent more than seven thousand pounds of the money on a diamond necklace and earrings, bequeathing them in turn to their daughter.

Severely ill after an accident in a carriage in Bath, Congreve died in London on 19 January 1729 and was buried in Westminster Abbey. Henrietta erected a monument nearby to "so worthy and Honest a Man, Whose virtue Candour and Witt gained him the love and Esteem of the present Age and whose writings will be the Admiration of the Future."

Letters:

William Congreve: Letters and Documents, edited by John C. Hodges (London: Macmillan, 1964).

Bibliographies:

Albert M. Lyles and John Dobson, *The John C. Hodges Collection of William Congreve in the University of Tennessee Library: A Bibliographical Catalog* (Knoxville: University of Tennessee Libraries, 1970);

Laurence Bartlett, *William Congreve: A Reference Guide* (Boston: G. K. Hall, 1979).

Biographies:

Charles Wilson, *Memoirs of the Life, Writings, and Amours of William Congreve* (London, 1730);

Samuel Johnson, "Congreve," in his *Prefaces, Biographical and Critical, to the Works of the English Poets*, 10 volumes (London: Printed by J. Nichols, for C. Bathurst, etc., 1779-1781); republished in *Lives of Poets*, 3 volumes, edited by G. B. Hill (Oxford: Clarendon Press, 1905), II: 212-234;

John C. Hodges, *William Congreve The Man* (New York: Modern Language Association of America / London: Oxford University Press, 1941);

Kathleen Lynch, *A Congreve Gallery* (Cambridge, Mass.: Harvard University Press, 1951).

References:

E. L. Avery, *Congreve's Plays on the Eighteenth-Century Stage* (New York: Modern Language Association of America, 1951);

F. W. Bateson, "Second Thoughts: II. L. C. Knights and Restoration Comedy," *Essays in Criticism*, 7 (January 1957): 56-67;

Richard Braverman, "Capital Relations and *The Way of the World*," *ELH*, 52 (Spring 1985): 133-158;

H. F. B. Brett-Smith, ed., *William Congreve: Incognita* (Oxford: Blackwell, 1922);

Brian Corman, " 'The Mixed Way of Comedy': Congreve's *The Double Dealer*," *Modern Philology*, 71 (May 1974): 356-365;

Corman, "*The Way of the World* and Morally Serious Comedy," *University of Toronto Quarterly*, 44 (Spring 1975): 199-212;

T. W. Craik, "Congreve as a Shakespearean," in *Poetry and Drama 1570-1700: Essays in Honour of Harold F. Brooks*, edited by Antony Coleman and Antony Hammond (London: Methuen, 1981), pp. 186-199;

Ian Donaldson, " 'Dear Liberty': *The Way of the World*," in his *The World Upside-Down* (Oxford: Clarendon Press, 1970), pp. 119-158;

Jean Gagen, "Congreve's Mirabell and the Ideal of a Gentleman," *PMLA*, 79 (September 1964): 422-427;

Brian Gibbons, ed., *Congreve: The Way of the World* (London: Benn, 1971);

Harriett Hawkins, *Likenesses of Truth in Elizabethan and Restoration Drama* (Oxford: Clarendon Press, 1972);

John C. Hodges, "The Composition of Congreve's First Play," *PMLA*, 58 (December 1943): 971-976;

Hodges, *The Library of William Congreve* (New York: New York Public Library, 1955);

Norman Holland, *The First Modern Comedies* (Cambridge, Mass.: Harvard University Press, 1959);

Peter Holland, *The Ornament of Action* (Cambridge: Cambridge University Press, 1979);

Paul J. Hurley, "Law and Dramatic Rhetoric in *The Way of the World*," *South Atlantic Quarterly*, 70 (Spring 1971): 191-202;

Anthony Kaufman, "Language and Character in Congreve's *The Way of the World*," *Texas Studies in Language and Literature*, 15 (Fall 1973): 411-427;

Malcolm Kelsall, *Congreve: The Way of the World* (London: Arnold, 1981);

Kelsall, ed., *Congreve: Love for Love* (London: Benn, 1969);

L. C. Knights, "Restoration Comedy: The Reality and the Myth," in his *Explorations* (London: Chatto & Windus, 1946);

Clifford Leech, "Congreve and the Century's End," *Philological Quarterly*, 41 (January 1962): 275-293;

John Loftis, *Comedy and Society from Congreve to Fielding* (Stanford: Stanford University Press, 1958);

Harold Love, *Congreve* (Oxford: Blackwell, 1974);

Charles Lyons, "Congreve's Miracle of Love," *Criticism*, 6 (Fall 1964): 331-348;

Patrick Lyons, ed., *Congreve: Comedies: A Casebook* (London: Macmillan, 1982);

David D. Mann, ed., *A Concordance to the Plays of William Congreve* (Ithaca, N.Y. & London: Cornell University Press, 1973);

Mann, "Congreve's Revisions of *The Mourning Bride*," *Papers of the Bibliographical Society of America*, 69 (1975): 526-546;

D. F. McKenzie, "Typography and Meaning: The Case of William Congreve," *Wolfenbütteler Schriften zur Geschichte des Buchwesens*, 4 (1981): 81-126;

McKenzie, "When Congreve Made a Scene," *Transactions of the Cambridge Bibliographical Society*, 7 (1979): 338-342;

Brian Morris, ed., *William Congreve* (London: Benn, 1972);

Paul and Miriam Mueschke, *A New View of Congreve's Way of the World* (Ann Arbor: University of Michigan Press, 1958);

Kenneth Muir, "The Comedies of William Congreve," in *Restoration Theatre*, edited by J. R. Brown and B. Harris (London: Arnold, 1965), pp. 221-237;

Maximillian Novak, *William Congreve* (New York: Twayne, 1971);

Elmer B. Potter, "The Paradox of Congreve's *Mourning Bride*," *PMLA*, 58 (December 1943): 977-1001;

Alan Roper, "Language and Action in *The Way of the World*, *Love's Last Shift* and *The Relapse*," *ELH*, 40 (Spring 1973): 44-69;

J. C. Ross, ed., *Congreve: The Double-Dealer* (London: Benn, 1981);

John Harrington Smith, *The Gay Couple in Restoration Comedy* (Cambridge, Mass.: Harvard University Press, 1948);

H. T. Swedenberg, ed., *Congreve Consider'd* (Los Angeles: William Andrews Clark Memorial Library, 1971);

William Van Voris, *The Cultivated Stance* (Dublin: Dolmen, 1965);

Gerald Weales, "The Shadow on Congreve's Surface," *Educational Theatre Journal*, 19 (March 1967): 30-32;

Aubrey L. Williams, *An Approach to Congreve* (New Haven: Yale University Press, 1974).

Daniel Defoe
(1660 - 24 April 1731)

This entry was written by Maximillian E. Novak (University of California, Los Angeles) for
DLB 39: British Novelists, 1660-1800: Part One.

See also the Defoe entries in DLB 95: *Eighteenth-Century British Poets: First Series and* DLB 101: *British Prose Writers, 1660-1800: First Series.*

SELECTED BOOKS: *A Letter to a Dissenter from His Friend at The Hague* (The Hague [i.e., London]: Printed by Hans Verdraeght [pseud.], [1668]);

Reflections upon the Late Great Revolution (London: Printed for Ric. Chiswell, 1689);

A New Discovery of an Old Intreague: A Satyr Level'd at Treachery and Ambition, Calculated to the Nativity of the Rapparee Plott, and the Modesty of the Jacobite Clergy (London, 1691);

An Essay upon Projects (London: Printed by R. R. for Tho. Cockerill, 1697);

The Character of the Late Dr. Samuel Annesley, by Way of Elegy: with a Preface (London: Printed for E. Whitlock, 1697);

The Poor Man's Plea . . . for a Reformation of Manners, and Suppressing Immorality in the Nation (London, 1698);

The Pacificator: A Poem (London: Printed & sold by J. Nutt, 1700);

The True-Born Englishman: A Satyr (London, 1700);

The Villainy of Stock-Jobbers Detected, and the Causes of the Late Run upon the Bank and Bankers Discovered and Considered (London, 1701);

[Legion's Memorial] ([London, 1701]);

The History of the Kentish Petition (London, 1701);

The Original Power of the Collective Body of the People of England, Examined and Asserted (London, 1702);

An Enquiry into Occasional Conformity (London, 1702);

Reformation of Manners: A Satyr (London, 1702);

The Shortest Way with the Dissenters (London, 1702); republished as *The Shortest Way With the Dissenters. [Taken from Dr. Sach[evere]ll's Sermon, and Others]* (London: Printed & sold by the booksellers, [1703]);

The Opinion of a Known Dissenter on the Bill for Preventing Occasional Conformity (London, 1703);

Frontispiece to the authorized edition of Jure Divino *(engraving by Michael Vandergucht, after a portrait by Jeremiah Taverner)*

A Brief Explanation of a late Pamphlet, Entituled, The Shortest Way with the Dissenters (London, [1703]);

A Hymn to the Pillory (London, 1703);

A True Collection of the Writings of the Author of The True-Born English-Man, Corrected by Himself (London, 1703);

A Review of the Affairs of France: and of all Europe, 9 volumes (London, 19 February 1704 - 11 June 1713)—several name changes, including *A Review of the State of the British Nation* and simply *The Review* for the last volume;

A Serious Inquiry into This Grand Question; Whether a Law to prevent the Occasional Conformity of Dissenters, Would not be Inconsistent with the Act of Toleration (London, 1704);

The Storm: Or, A Collection of the most Remarkable Casualties And Disasters Which happen'd in the Late Dreadful Tempest, Both by Sea and Land (London: Printed for G. Sawbridge & sold by J. Nutt, 1704);

The Double Welcome. A Poem To the Duke of Marlbro' (London: Printed & sold by B. Bragg, 1705);

The Consolidator (London: Printed & sold by Benj. Bragg, 1705);

An Essay at Removing National Prejudices against a Union with Scotland (London, 1706);

Jure Divino: A Satyr in Twelve Books (London, 1706);

Caledonia: A Poem in Honour of Scotland, and the Scots Nation (Edinburgh: Printed by the Heirs and Successors of Andrew Anderson, 1706; London: Printed by J. Mathews & sold by John Morphew, 1707);

A Brief History of the Poor Palatine Refugees (London: Printed & sold by J. Baker, 1709);

The History of the Union of Great Britain (Edinburgh: Printed by the Heirs and Successors of Andrew Anderson, 1709);

A Speech without Doors (London: Printed for A. Baldwin, 1710);

Instructions from Rome (London: Printed & sold by J. Baker, [1710]);

An Essay upon Publick Credit (London: Printed & sold by the Booksellers, 1710);

Reasons Why This Nation Ought to Put a Speedy End to This Expensive War (London: Printed for J. Baker, 1711);

Reasons Why a Party among Us, and also among the Confederates, are Obstinately Bent against a Treaty of Peace ([London]: Printed for John Baker, 1711);

An Essay at a Plain Exposition of that Difficult Phrase a Good Peace ([London]: Printed for J. Baker, 1711);

An Essay on the History of Parties, and Persecution in Britain (London: Printed for J. Baker, 1711);

No Queen; Or, No General (London: Printed & sold by the Booksellers of London & Westminster, 1712);

The Conduct of Parties in England (London, 1712);

Peace, or Poverty (London: Printed & sold by John Morphew, 1712);

The Present State of the Parties in Great Britain (London: Sold by J. Baker, 1712);

An Enquiry into the Danger and Consequences of a War with the Dutch (London: Printed for J. Baker, 1712);

And What if the Pretender Should Come? (London: Sold by J. Baker, 1713);

An Essay on the Treaty of Commerce with France (London: Printed for J. Baker, 1713);

Mercator (26 May 1713 - 20 July 1714);

A General History of Trade, 4 parts (London: Printed for J. Baker, 1713);

Memoirs of Count Tariff (London: Printed for John Morphew, 1713);

Memoirs of John, Duke of Melfort (London: Printed for J. Moor, 1714);

The Secret History of the White Staff: Being an Account of Affairs under the Conduct of Some Late Ministers, 3 parts (London: Printed for J. Baker, 1714-1715);

Advice to the People of Great Britain (London: Printed for J. Baker, 1714);

Hanover or Rome (London: Printed for J. Roberts, 1715);

The Fears of the Pretender Turn'd into the Fears of Debauchery (London: Printed & sold by S. Keimer, 1715);

An Appeal to Honour and Justice (London: Printed for J. Baker, 1715);

The Family Instructor, in Three Parts (London: Sold by Eman. Matthews & Jo. Button, in Newcastle upon Tine, 1715);

An Account of the Conduct of Robert Earl of Oxford (London, 1715);

An Account of the Proceedings against the Rebels (London: Printed for J. Baker & Tho. Warner, 1716);

A True Account of the Proceedings at Perth (London: Printed for J. Baker, 1716);

Fair Payment No Spunge: Or Some Considerations on the Unreasonableness of Refusing to Receive Back Money Lent on Publick Securities (London: Sold by J. Brotherton & W. Meddows, and J. Roberts, 1717);

The Question Fairly Stated, Whether Now is Not the Time to do Justice to the Friends of the Government as well as to its Enemies? (London: Printed for J. Roberts, J. Harrison & A. Dodd, 1717);

Memoirs of the Church of Scotland (London: Printed for Eman. Matthews & T. Warner, 1717);

Considerations on the Present State of Affairs in Great-Britain (London: Printed for J. Roberts, 1718);

Memoirs of the Life and Eminent Conduct of that Learned and Reverend Divine Daniel Williams DD. (London: Printed for E. Curll, 1718);

Memoirs of Publick Transactions in the Life and Ministry of his Grace the D. of Shrewsbury (London: Printed for Tho. Warner, 1718);

The Family Instructor. In Two Parts (London: Printed for Emman. Matthews, 1718);

A Continuation of Letters Written by a Turkish Spy at Paris (London: Printed for W. Taylor, 1718);

The Memoirs of Majr. Alexander Ramkins (London: Printed for R. King & W. Boreham, 1719);

The Life and Strange Surprizing Adventures of Robinson Crusoe (London: Printed for W. Taylor, 1719);

The Anatomy of Exchange-Alley: Or a System of Stock-Jobbing (London: Printed for E. Smith, 1719);

The Farther Adventures of Robinson Crusoe (London: Printed for W. Taylor, 1719);

A Brief State of the Question, between the Printed and Painted Callicoes and the Woollen and Silk Manufacture (London: Printed for W. Boreham, 1719);

Manufacturer (30 October 1719 - 17 February 1720);

The King of Pirates: Being an Account of the Famous Enterprises of Captain Avery (London: Printed for A. Bettesworth, C. King, J. Brotherton & W. Meadows, W. Chetwood, and sold by W. Boreham, 1720);

An Historical Account of the Voyages and Adventures of Sir Walter Raleigh, with the Discoveries and Conquests He Made for the Crown of England (London: Printed & sold by W. Boreham, 1720);

Memoirs of a Cavalier (London: Printed for A. Bell, J. Osborn, W. Taylor & T. Warner, [1720]);

The Life, Adventures and Pyracies of the Famous Captain Singleton (London: Printed for J. Brotherton, J. Graves, A. Dodd & T. Warner, 1720);

Serious Reflections during the Life and Surprising Adventures of Robinson Crusoe (London: Printed for W. Taylor, 1720);

The South-Sea Scheme Examin'd (London: Printed for J. Roberts, 1720);

The Fortunes and Misfortunes of the Famous Moll Flanders (London: Printed for & sold by W. Chetwood & T. Edling, 1722);

Due Preparations for the Plague as Well for Soul as Body (London: Printed for E. Matthews, 1722);

Religious Courtship (London: Printed for E. Matthews & A. Bettesworth, J. Brotherton & W. Meadows, 1722);

A Journal of the Plague Year (London: Printed for E. Nutt, J. Roberts, A. Dodd & J. Graves, 1722);

The History and Remarkable Life of the Truly Honourable Col. Jacque (London: Printed & sold by J. Brotherton, T. Payne, W. Mears, A. Dodd, W. Chetwood, J. Graves, S. Chapman, & J. Stagg, 1722);

The Fortunate Mistress: Or, A History Of The Life and Vast Variety of Fortunes Of Mademoiselle de Beleau. . . . Being the Person known by the Name of the Lady Roxana, in the time of King Charles II (London: Printed for T. Warner, W. Meadows, W. Pepper, S. Harding & T. Edlin, 1724);

The Great Law of Subordination Consider'd (London: Sold by S. Harding, W. Lewis, T. Worrall, A. Bettesworth, W. Meadows & T. Edlin, 1724);

A General History of the Robberies and Murders of the Most Notorious Pyrates, and also Their Policies, Discipline and Government, from Their First Rise and Settlement in the Island of Providence, in 1717, to the Present Year 1824, volume 1 (London: Printed for Ch. Rivington, J. Lacy & J. Stone, 1724); volume 2 published as *The History of the Pyrates* (London: Printed for Ch. Rivington, 1728);

A Tour thro' the Whole Island of Great Britain, 3 volumes (London: Sold by G. Strahan, W. Mears, and others, 1724, 1725, 1727);

The Royal Progress (London: Printed by John Darby & sold by J. Roberts, J. Brotherton & A. Dodd, 1724);

A Narrative of All the Robberies, Escapes &c. of John Sheppard (London: Printed & sold by John Applebee, 1724);

The History of the Remarkable Life of John Sheppard (London: Printed & sold by John Applebee, J. Isted & the Booksellers of London and Westminster, [1724]);

A New Voyage round the World, by a Course Never Sailed Before (London: Printed for A. Bettesworth & W. Mears, 1724);

Every-body's Business, Is No-Body's Business (London: Sold by T. Warner, A. Dodd & E. Nutt, 1725);

A General History of Discoveries and Improvements, in Useful Arts, 4 parts (London: Printed for J. Roberts, 1725-1726);

The Complete English Tradesman, 2 volumes (London: Printed for Charles Rivington, 1726; with supplement, 1727);

A Brief Historical Account of the Lives of the Six Notorious Street-Robbers, Executed at Kingston (London: Printed for A. Moore, 1726);

The Political History of the Devil (London: Printed for T. Warner, 1726);

Some Considerations upon Street-Walkers (London: Printed for A. Moore, [1726]);

The Protestant Monastery: Or, A Complaint against the Brutality of the Present Age (London: Printed for W. Meadows, 1727);

A System of Magick (London: Sold by J. Roberts, 1727);

Conjugal Lewdness: Or, Matrimonial Whoredom (London: Printed for T. Warner, 1727);

A Brief Deduction of the Original, Progress, and Immense Greatness of the British Woollen Manufacture (London: Sold by J. Roberts & A. Dodd, 1727);

An Essay on the History and Reality of Apparitions (London: Printed & sold by J. Roberts, 1727);

A New Family Instructor; In Familiar Discourses between a Father and his Children (London: Printed for T. Warner, 1727);

Parochial Tyranny (London: Printed & sold by J. Roberts, [1727]);

Augusta Triumphans: Or, The Way to Make London the Most Flourishing City in the Universe (London: Printed for J. Roberts & sold by E. Nutt, A. Dodd, N. Blandford & A. Stagg, 1728);

A Plan of the English Commerce (London: Printed for Charles Rivington, 1728);

Atlas Maritimus & Commercialis: Or, A General View of the World, so far as it relates to Trade and Navigation (London: Printed for James & John Knapton; William & John Innys; John Darby; Arthur Bettesworth, John Osborn & Thomas Longman; John Senex; Edward Symon; Andrew Johnston; and the Executors of William Taylor, 1728);

The Unreasonableness and Ill Consequences of Imprisoning the Body for Debt, Prov'd from the Laws of God and Nature, Human Policy and Interest.

Address'd to a Noble Lord (London: Printed & sold by T. Read & J. Purser, 1729);

Second Thoughts are Best (London: Printed for W. Meadows & sold by J. Roberts, 1729);

An Humble Proposal To The People of England, For the Encrease of Their Trade, And Encouragement of their Manufactures (London: Printed for Charles Rivington, 1729);

The Advantages of Peace and Commerce (London: Printed for J. Brotherton & Tho. Cox, and sold by A. Dodd, 1729);

An Effectual Scheme for the Immediate Preventing of Street Robberies (London: Printed for J. Wilford, 1731);

The Compleat English Gentleman, edited by Karl D. Bülbring (London: David Nutt, 1890);

Of Royall Educacion: A Fragmentary Treatise, edited by Bülbring (London: D. Nutt, 1895).

Editions and Collections: *The Novels and Miscellaneous Works of Daniel De Foe*, with prefaces attributed to Sir Walter Scott, 20 volumes (Oxford: Printed by D. A. Talboys for Y. Tegg, 1840-1841);

The Works of Daniel De Foe, 3 volumes, edited by William W. Hazlitt (London: Clements, 1840-1843);

The Novels and Miscellaneous of Daniel De Foe, 7 volumes (London: Bell, 1856-1884);

The Earlier Life and Chief Earlier Works of Daniel Defoe, edited by Henry Morley (London & New York: Routledge, 1889);

Romances and Narratives, 16 volumes, edited by George A. Aitken (London: Dent, 1895);

The Works of Daniel Defoe, 16 volumes, edited by G. H. Maynadier (New York: Sproul, 1903-1904);

A Tour thro' the Whole Island of Great Britain, 2 volumes, introduction by G. D. H. Cole (London: Davies, 1927);

Defoe's Review, 22 volumes, edited by A. W. Secord (New York: Facsimile Text Society, 1938);

Roxana: The Fortunate Mistress, edited by Jane Jack (London: Oxford University Press, 1964);

Colonel Jack, edited by Samuel Monk (London: Oxford University Press, 1965);

Daniel Defoe: Selections from His Writings, edited by James T. Boulton (New York: Schocken, 1965);

A Journal of the Plague Year, edited by Louis Landa (London: Oxford University Press, 1969);

Captain Singleton, edited by Shiv Kurnav (London: Oxford University Press, 1969);

Moll Flanders, edited by G. A. Starr (London: Oxford University Press, 1971);

A General History of the Pyrates, edited by Manuel Schonhorn (London: Dent, 1972);

Memoirs of a Cavalier, edited by Boulton (London: Oxford University Press, 1972);

Robinson Crusoe, edited by J. Donald Crowley (London: Oxford University Press, 1972);

The Versatile Defoe: An Anthology of Uncollected Writings by Daniel Defoe, edited by Laura A. Curtis (London: Prior, 1979; Totowa, N.J.: Rowman & Littlefield, 1979).

Daniel Defoe's modern literary reputation is based almost entirely on the series of prose narratives that he wrote from 1719 to 1724. In April of 1719 *Robinson Crusoe* was published; with the success of that work, he went on to write a sequel that was only slightly less successful. He then produced in rapid succession a series of first-person narratives, the best known of which are *Moll Flanders* (1722), *A Journal of the Plague Year* (1722), and *Roxana* (1724). Within these five years, Defoe single-handedly gave to prose fiction a power and imagination that it had never attained in England before him; if he did not succeed in making prose fiction entirely respectable, in *Robinson Crusoe* he created a work that was to be read throughout the world. It was quickly translated and started a rage for the island tale—the "Robinsonade"—which has yet to show signs of fading. Some biographers and critics have found difficulty in reconciling Defoe's life and ideas with his creation of such fictions, particularly his tales of prostitutes and thieves, but more often than not the problem has lain with some preconceived notion of Defoe's character and milieu.

The year of Defoe's birth, 1660, was a memorable one for England and for those Christians who felt that they could not accept the rules for conformity established by the Church of England. When Charles II landed at Dover in May of that year, he was committed to religious tolerance. The Presbyterians had never had the fierce animosity toward Charles I felt by the Independents and by the various sects associated with Oliver Cromwell's army. But efforts at accommodating those ministers who objected to certain rituals of the Church of England quickly disappeared; and after the failure of the Savoy Conference in 1661, all hope of Christian unity ended. Distinguished members of the Church of England such as Richard Baxter and Samuel Annesley, the preacher of Defoe's family, re-

fused to accept the rules laid down by the bishops of the Church and became "Nonconformists" or "Dissenters." This schism in the Church of England meant that Defoe was brought up among a religious group that experienced persecutions of varying severity for twenty-eight years. Some of the ministers were thrown into jail, and others were heavily fined. Although there is no indication that Defoe's parents, James and Alice Foe, suffered in any extraordinary way, throughout his life Defoe felt the strongest identification with the Dissenters as a religious, social, and political group. If he thought that he suffered a kind of martyrdom at several points in his life, it is also true that he seemed to court such a fate by a daring and defiance peculiar to him. Too often he seems to suggest that he was being punished for what he was rather than for who he was.

Defoe's enemies were fond of reminding him that his real rank—that is, his real worth—was associated with his career as a hosier, or a seller of stockings; but this image of Defoe as a lowly tradesman is belied by what is known of his education and early career. His father was a highly respected member and officeholder of the Butcher's Company. James Foe served an apprenticeship as a butcher, but his occupation likely was always that of a tradesman and merchant. He was prosperous enough to send his son to schools operated by Dissenting ministers, and finally to the distinguished academy operated by Charles Morton at Newington Green. Although Defoe stated that he might have become a minister, and although he went up to London to take careful notes on the sermons of John Collins in the winter and spring of 1681, it is doubtful that Defoe ever seriously contemplated anything but a worldly career. Morton imparted to Defoe a lifelong interest in science and an ability to write English with clarity and what Defoe called "Energy." Defoe was later to describe the kind of class exercise that he and his fellow students had to undergo on a regular basis. They were told to compose a letter written by a certain type of person, say a merchant, to someone in a different station; the letter was to reflect the character of the writer and also suggest the personality of the recipient. It was an exercise in creating a fictional situation and fictional characters. If Defoe was not Morton's prize pupil during his teens, he was certainly to become the master of point of view and character when he came to write his pamphlets and fictions. Defoe may also have imbibed some of Morton's political convictions, for in a debate over the Dissenting academies between Samuel Wesley and Samuel Palmer in 1704, Morton was accused of harboring radical and seditious sympathies and imparting them to his students. Morton's treatise on government has never been located, but Wesley put what he considered to have been a seditious statement by Defoe on the title page of his attack, implying that Morton had produced England's most radical writer.

The earliest writings of Defoe, in the form of two manuscript notebooks, suggest a great deal about the young writer. The first notebook, in addition to Collins's sermons, contains a series of verse "Meditations" in which Defoe explores some of his doubts about his worthiness for a divine calling. Perhaps the most significant of these contains the image of himself as a Jonah fleeing from God's commands, an image he would recall in *Robinson Crusoe*. But the second manuscript is more interesting from the standpoint of studying the nascent novelist, since it not only shows his early involvement with fiction but gives some idea of his youthful reading and daydreams.

"Historical Collections" is partly a gathering of apothegms, or brief maxims, but in Defoe's hands these become short fictions with a particular point. The gathering was made for Defoe's future wife, Mary Tuffley, whom he called "Clarinda," signing himself "Bellmour." Defoe was never to give more than a halfhearted approval to romance, but this does not mean that he did not read romances or know that a young lover, even a city lover, was to show some familiarity with the forms of that genre. Defoe tells stories drawn from one of his favorite writers, Plutarch; but the two most significant elements, perhaps, are the stories taken from Richard Knolles's *History of the Turks* (1604) and the references to King Gustavus II, the Swedish leader of the Protestant forces in the Thirty Years' War and an important character in Defoe's fictional study of that period, *Memoirs of a Cavalier* (1720). From Knolles's work he takes, among other stories, that of the sultan Mahomet, who demonstrated his powers of self-denial by killing Irene, the woman he loved above all things, in front of his troops. It hardly seems the kind of story to tell a woman one is about to marry, but it suggests that in addition to daydreaming about the exotic world of the Turks, Defoe had an admiration for discipline and self-control. His account of Gustavus Adolphus is even more significant in this regard, for the "Swedish Discipline"—the completely controlled military patterns of the Swedish troops—

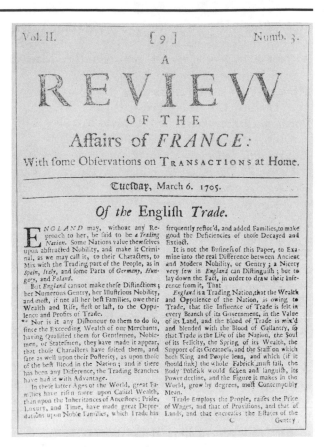

First page of an issue of the journal Defoe put out from 19 February 1704 until 11 June 1713

was one of the ideals of the Puritan "saints" of the first half of the seventeenth century, who saw in such activity a spiritual as well as a military significance.

This is not to say that Defoe was a Puritan, as has occasionally been suggested; indeed, he always refers to that group historically, as "the devout people of the early seventeenth century." But it was one of his daydreams to march with a new Gustavus Adolphus just as surely as his other overpowering fantasy was to voyage with Sir Walter Ralegh to find a new world. Defoe sometimes seems drawn by conflicting images of himself, sometimes rigid and doctrinaire, sometimes expansive and liberal: in one mood he could insist that those Dissenters who occasionally attended services at an Anglican church were possessed of easy consciences; in another mood he could imagine himself exploring the unknown South Seas in *A New Voyage round the World* (1724). The latter daydream was more typical and earned him the reputation of having a wild imagination—of being, as one of his critics remarked, a "Moon Calf." Defoe had many sides:

he was a wit, a projector, an incendiary, a wise counselor; but often these roles were played out as part of a larger fantasy of control and expansiveness.

He started his career as a London tradesman, merchant, and speculator sometime before courting Mary Tuffley, and he must have seemed a promising prospect for the wealthy Tuffley family. Although he received a handsome dowry of thirty-seven hundred pounds when they were married on 1 January 1684 at the Church of St. Botolph, Aldgate, there is no reason to consider the passionate letter prefixed to his present to her a mere formality. Defoe considered marriage without love "legalized prostitution," and there is every reason to believe that his expressions of passionate love were real enough. But if Mary Tuffley ever thought she was marrying a conservative businessman who would provide a calm and prosperous life for her, she was soon to discover her mistake. The chances are, however, that he struck her as a romantic lover and as both a pious and adventurous soul. He was soon to show just how adventurous he could be: in June 1685 he rode out of London to join the forces of James Scott, Duke of Monmouth, who had landed at Lyme Regis on the eleventh of the month to lead a rebellion against the recently crowned king of England, James II.

To the Dissenters, James II seemed destined to lead England away from Protestantism toward the church of Rome; the rebellion failed, in part because that direction did not seem so inevitable to most Englishmen. But to the Dissenters, who had suffered twenty-five years of persecution, the moment must have seemed propitious. Here was Monmouth, the handsome son of Charles II and Lucy Walter, ready to lead England back to the political liberties that had been rapidly fading in the last years of his father's reign. Of course, Monmouth was illegitimate, but the true believers wanted to think that there was a black box hidden somewhere that would reveal a marriage between Charles II and the mother of Monmouth. Although many of those who enlisted under Monmouth's banner were peasants and craftsmen of the area around Taunton, others were the best and brightest of Morton's Academy, Defoe's classmates. Some of them fell in the fighting or became "Western Martyrs," hanged as examples after Monmouth's defeat. Defoe escaped and eventually bought a pardon from the government. Where he lived in the years before 1688, when William III drove out James to the general applause of a nation thoroughly disgusted by James's assault on the Church of England, is not known. He may have traveled, as did many other exiles; he may have gone to Scotland or Holland, made the grand tour of Europe, or even taken ship to other continents. What is known is that his life took on new meaning with William's triumph: Defoe had at last found a hero to match the idol of his youth, Gustav II.

James's attempt to win over the Dissenters by granting toleration may have inspired Defoe's earliest pamphlet, in 1688; but in his autobiographical *An Appeal to Honour and Justice* (1715) he mentions a piece written against the Turks around 1683. Even if he did not have anything published, Defoe was such a compulsive writer that it is hard to believe that he was not filling up notebooks during the 1680s. But the need to defend William's policies brought out a flood of pamphlets in which he denied the importance of a hereditary succession to the crown and argued that the "original power" of government resided with the "people," by which he meant the productive members of the society. In 1691 appeared *A New Discovery of an Old Intreague*, the first work he later acknowledged by including it in his *A True Collection of the Writings of the Author of The True-Born English-Man* (1703), a gathering of poems and pamphlets. He followed this work with "To the Athenian Society," which was published along with one of Jonathan Swift's earliest poems in John Dunton's *Athenian Oracle*, and with a moving elegy on the preacher his family admired so much, *The Character of the Late Dr. Samuel Annesley* (1697).

But as Defoe's claim to fame as a forceful pamphleteer and a poet was emerging, his business career was in trouble. Typical of the speculators of the time, Defoe had many irons in the fire. He had investments in a ship called, appropriately enough, the *Desire*; he had a share in a voyage to America; he put money into a diving engine to recover treasure; he was dealing in wines; he was raising civet cats to make perfume out of their urine. These events are known through a variety of lawsuits: all together, he was sued at least eight times between 1688 and 1694; and before he declared bankruptcy in 1692, he was in prison at least twice. His was no ordinary failure. His indebtedness came to seventeen thousand pounds—an indication, however dismal, of the extraordinary range of his affairs.

After this series of business reversals, Defoe decided to seek patrons in trying to recover his lost fortunes. He dedicated his *Essay upon Projects* to Dalby Thomas, under whom he had worked as a secretary to the commission collecting the glass tax. Although *An Essay upon Projects* was published in 1697, Defoe stated that he had worked on the manuscript from about 1694. That statement may have been an attempt to rescue him from charges of plagiarizing the ideas of others, yet it seems likely that he had been engaged on his book for some time. It was his first major work and typical of him in its ingenuity. *Projector* was a word of abuse during the seventeenth century, but Defoe reshapes the meaning of the term by suggesting that the desperation that often set men upon inventing projects was as good as it was bad: although the projector was not far from being a swindler, the necessity that impelled him to inventiveness often produced genuinely good ideas. For the most part, Defoe was bringing together projects of the seventeenth century: the impulse toward a society in which social institutions managed to protect the aged from poverty and to provide for seamen from cradle to grave was the product of an earlier mercantile vision rather than that of a society moving in the direction of laissez-faire. Similarly, while the idea of an academy for purifying the English tongue was to be debated throughout the eighteenth century, Defoe seemed to have Armand Jean du Plessis, Duc de Richelieu's French model in mind. On the other hand, the humanitarian impulse behind the notion of a humane asylum for the mentally defective ("Fools") seems predictive of a new impulse toward refining the manners of Englishmen; and his argument that women deserve to be educated as well as men was part of the innovative milieu of the 1690s created by writers such as Mary Astell.

An Essay upon Projects is filled with imaginative social engineering and is an early indication of Defoe's inventive mind in action. His argument for a Court Merchant grows out of the horrors of Chancery suits. But his seriousness is always relieved by brief fictions and anecdotes. If his placing the discussion of bankrupts just after the section on the mad shows more exasperation than humor, he could laugh at himself on occasion. And the appeal to William III to establish an academy may not be as impractical as it might seem: he may have known something about William's interest in such an institution, and if an academy were to come into existence, it would have

to be mandated by a monarch, since who else could determine the thirty-six members?

Defoe made many claims to the effect that he was not only a willing agent of William III but a friend. Since so many of his writings between 1697 and William's death on 8 March 1702 were written in defense of William and his policies, it is easy to believe that William used his talents. One may also suspect that Defoe tended to exaggerate the extent of their relationship, even to himself. William tried to keep some forces on foot in the event that Louis XIV returned to his old tricks, and Defoe wrote a series of pamphlets defending the wisdom of a standing army. But the "Classical Republicans" among the Whigs, who believed with Niccolò Machiavelli that a nation such as England needed a militia only, joined with the Tories to reduce William to just seven thousand English troops. William sent home his Dutch troops and considered abdicating, particularly after a series of attacks on the Dutch and the removal of many of the grants he had given his friends. Defoe countered this outburst of xenophobia with one of the most successful political poems of the period, *The True-Born Englishman* (1700). By the end of 1701 it was in its ninth edition, and there were thirty editions before 1750. By showing in a rehearsal of England's history just how many races and nationalities it had taken to produce the Englishman of his time, Defoe reduced arguments about racial and national purity to absurdity. Defoe's rhymes have little of the subtlety of John Dryden's or Alexander Pope's, and his meter is occasionally ragged; but *The True-Born Englishman* is not mere doggerel. It has a power of statement rare among political poetry, as well as some genuinely witty sections. Defoe's verse dominated the volumes of political poetry known as "Poems on Affairs of State" that were published between 1700 and 1710 as a continuation of the volumes of political poems from the Restoration.

Defoe lost the first battle he fought on William's behalf and only gained a moral victory in the second, but he may be said to have won the third. In a series of provocative acts, Louis XIV accepted the will that made his grandson heir to Spain, occupied the barrier fortresses on the border of Holland, and recognized the son of James II as the rightful heir to the throne of England. What was known as "The Kentish Petition," demanding that the nation begin raising forces to stop the growth of French power, was presented to the House of Commons. Defoe was a leading

JURE DIVINO:
A
SATYR.
The Firſt BOOK.
By the Author of the True-born-Engliſhman.
O Sanctas Gentes, quibus hæc naſcuntur in hortis
Numina! ——— Juv. Sat. 15. lin. 11.

FOR·IURE   DIVINO.

THE SHORTEST W

Londŏŵ: Printed by P. Hills in Black-Friers.

Title page for an unauthorized edition of Defoe's 1706 satiric poem, with a caricature of Defoe in the pillory

figure among the Kentish Petitioners, and Parliament began to fear the threat of the London mob, which believed that the realm desperately needed protection. *The Original Power of the Collective Body of the People of England* (1702) pronounced the doctrine that Parliament was merely the servant of the people, and that in times of danger, unresponsive political institutions were invariably swept aside by the mob, a chaotic force whose actions represented the will of the governed. Whereas most contemporaries regarded the mob with horror, Defoe believed that true government could rise from popular turmoil. It was partly through such propaganda efforts that William finally got a Parliament responsive to the need to halt the renewed French aggression. In

what was to become a pattern of action followed by literary production, Defoe participated in the activities of the Kentish Petitioners and then described many of the events of this episode in his *History of the Kentish Petition* (1701).

By 1698 Defoe must have been aware of his ability to command an audience, and in addition to his propaganda efforts for William III, he began to speak out on many of the important issues of his time. He was an active advocate of the Society for Reformation of Manners, and in *The Poor Man's Plea . . . for a Reformation of Manners, and Suppressing Immorality in the Nation* (1698), he adopted the persona of a member of the lower orders to complain that while magistrates were only too willing to punish vice in the poor, the wealthy, who often passed on their vices to the lower ranks, escaped all punishment. In *The Pacificator* (1700), he joined with the Moderns in the "Ancients and Moderns" controversy, attacking some contemporary poets in the process. In *The Villainy of Stock-Jobbers Detected* (1701), he launched an attack upon the kind of deception in dealing in stocks that was to lead to the disastrous South Sea Scandal twenty years later. In 1702, in one of his more effective verse satires, *Reformation of Manners,* he pointed a finger at some of the more blatant corruptions in English society. In *The Pacificator,* Defoe assigned himself mastery of the lampoon—the kind of satire which named names and held people up to public scorn. Defoe may have felt that he was performing the kind of duty that he had called for in *The Poor Man's Plea*; but while he was creating an audience that recognized his particular kind of poem or pamphlet, he was also making enemies. The stage was set for the events that followed publication of *The Shortest Way with the Dissenters* (1702).

The publication of this work marked a dramatic change in Defoe's life. The pamphlet was declared libelous, and a reward of fifty pounds was offered for information that would lead to Defoe's arrest. Defoe wrote to Daniel Finch, Earl of Nottingham, the secretary of state for the Southern Department, who was in charge of the search, explaining that he had no seditious intentions and offering to serve Queen Anne as a "Voluntier" in Flanders as a more useful expiation than imprisonment. In this, the first letter from Defoe extant, dated 9 January 1703, he appealed to Nottingham for mercy: "My Lord a Body Unfit to bear the hardships of a Prison, and a Mind Impatient of Confinement, have been the Onely Reasons of withdrawing My Self: And My Lord The Cries of a Numerous Ruin'd Family, The Prospect of a Long Banishment from my Native country, and the hopes of her Majties Mercy, Moves me to Thro' my Self at her Majties Feet, and to Intreat your Lordships Intercession. . . . But My Lord if after This I Should Still have the Misfortune to Remain Under her Majties Displeasure, I am Then her Most Humble Petitioner, that She will please to Remitt the Rigor of Prosecution, and that Pleading Guilty I may Reciev a Sentence from her Perticular justice, a little More Tolerable to me as a Gentleman, Than Prisons, Pillorys, and Such like, which are worse to me Than Death." But when he was finally caught on 20 May after a four-month search, he received the punishments that he

feared. He was jailed, interrogated, and put in the pillory on 29 July. By this time, however, Defoe had struck a bargain with Robert Harley, the speaker of the House of Commons, who may have been moved by the passage in Defoe's letter to Nottingham in which he wrote, "I am Ready with my hand, my Pen, or my head, to Show her Majtie The Gratitude of a Pardoned Subject." Defoe was not pardoned, but he must have made an agreement with Harley to act as a propagandist and secret agent. The return of his courage is demonstrated by his behavior at the pillory. Instead of being abject, he composed what may be his best poem, *A Hymn to the Pillory* (1703), in which he makes the pillory a sign of honor in a corrupt society. Copies of the poem were sold to the crowd as he was put in the "state machine, / Contrived to punish fancy in," and instead of being stoned to death, he was cheered wildly by the crowd. One newspaper account complained that he was "halloo'd . . . as if he had been a Cicero that had made an excellent oration in it, rather than a Cataline that was exposed and declaimed against there."

The Shortest Way with the Dissenters shows Defoe's ability to create a fictional speaker who can be a convincing character even while he is saying the most outrageous things. After the death of William, High Church officials hoped that they would find in Queen Anne a monarch willing to fulfill their wildest fantasies about persecuting the Dissenters. Defoe decided to imitate the style of such firebrand clergymen as Henry Sacheverell; but as he remarked in defending his work, what they were implying by "Inuendo," he turned into a demand for an immediate program of savage and bloody persecution. The style is so well imitated that critics have sometimes forgotten the distinction between "Inuendo" and a direct demand for a massacre. But Defoe may have been too clever: though a sophisticated reader would detect the irony, Defoe may have wanted to draw in both High Churchmen and Dissenters; he succeeded in his hoax to the extent that both groups were furious with him. He became something of a mob hero at the pillory, but he had lost a degree of favor with many of those who had formerly supported him. The pamphlet brought him fame, but it had its price.

One of the costs involved the suffering of his "Numerous Ruin'd Family." On 24 December 1701 Defoe had had his youngest daughter, Sophia, baptized. She was the last child of whom there is a record, but Mary Defoe gave birth to at least eight children, of whom four daughters—Maria, Hannah, Henrietta, and Sophia—and two sons—Daniel and Benjamin Norton—lived to be adults. Another daughter, Martha, died in 1707. When Defoe became a fugitive, he had a successful tile-work factory at Tilbury. Inevitably, during the seven months in which he was in hiding, the business went to pieces, and Defoe was forced to declare bankruptcy for a second time. In the letter to Nottingham, Defoe also mentions that his "Distress'd Wife" had appealed in vain to Nottingham for a pardon. These must have been difficult times for Mary Defoe, and one can only imagine what she must have thought about his offer to "Raise a Troop of horse" at his own expense and serve "at the head of Them . . . as Long as I Live." But she probably knew that despite this streak of incurable romanticism in Defoe's character, he would somehow manage to take care of her and their children. Although he was to be annoyed by creditors until his dying day, he found a fairly steady income of two hundred pounds a year as a government agent. If the money earned from his writing and various investments is added to this amount, it may be said that Defoe emerged from the possibility of death at the hands of the mob at the pillory in a thriving condition. On the other hand, he probably made a mistake in pleading guilty. Faced with a similar charge, John Tutchin, Defoe's fellow journalist, had managed to escape on legal technicalities. Defoe might have been more his own man had he done likewise; or, if he had agreed to work for the government anyway, he might have received better terms.

The three most important tasks Defoe undertook for Harley were publishing a newspaper in support of the war against France; establishing an information network in all parts of England to report on political activity; and working as a journalist, economic adviser, and spy in Scotland to aid the treaty of union between England and its neighbor to the north. *A Review of the Affairs of France* first appeared on 19 February 1704, and Defoe put out three numbers a week plus various supplements until 11 June 1713. Defoe had been released from Newgate Prison the previous November after receiving a pardon from the queen, and while he was supposed to have remained silent as a condition of that pardon, he was soon writing pamphlets as well as the essays on current politics and economics that constituted the main part of the *Review*. He began a section called "Advice from the Scandal Club" in which he would criticize the style and mannerisms of his fellow journalists and answer letters posing personal problems in the manner of the modern "advice" column. It was the liveliest journal published in England up to that time, and many of the essays still make excellent reading. When readers complained about the repetition of some themes, he pointed out that his aim was to get his ideas across as plainly and as forcefully as possible, and for that a degree of repetition was necessary. As for his style, he laid claim to that "energy" that distinguishes the best writers. When he wrote the final number in 1713, he remarked that the subject about which he enjoyed writing the most was economics or "Trade"; during his defense of the trade treaty with France during 1712 and 1714, he had the opportunity to write on that subject constantly, not only in the *Review* but in a new journal, *Mercator,* and in dozens of pamphlets.

Defoe's work as an agent in England took him around various parts of the country during the summer of 1704. It was during this period that Defoe's remarkable letters to Harley were written. They are political rather than literary, but they must be among the best letters of the eighteenth century in their combination of wit and sharp observation. He continually asks for instructions from Harley and gives advice at great length; he never hesitates to remind Harley of his starving family whenever the secret-service payments have been held up; and in advising Harley about a system of spies, he quotes from that "Meer Romance," Giovanni Paolo Marana's *Letters Writ by a Turkish Spy* (1687-1693), on the value of having a spy at Paris.

Defoe also wanted a "Settl'd Intelligence in Scotland," and he soon saw that such a system was established with himself as the chief of intelligence. He threw himself into the role of master spy, assuming the names Alexander Goldsmith and Claude Guilot for his secret correspondence. Much has been made of Defoe's change of name after 1703 from Foe to Defoe as an indication of his snobbery, but aside from the fact that, as one of his enemies suggested, "foe" was an unfortunate name for someone with so many enemies, Defoe may have liked the idea of changing identities and names. In a 26 November 1706 letter to Harley he wrote: "I Converse with Presbyterian, Episcopall-Dissenter, papist and Non Juror, and I hope with Equall Circumspection. I flatter my Self you will have no Complaints of my Conduct. I have faithfull Emissaries in Every Company

And I Talk to Everybody in their Own way. To the Merchants I am about to Settle here in Trade, Building ships etc. With the Lawyers I want to purchase a House and Land to bring my family & live Upon it (God knows where the Money is to pay for it). To day I am Goeing into Partnership with a Membr of parliamt in a Glass house, to morrow with Another in a Salt work . . . and still at the End of all Discourse the Union is the Essentiall and I am all to Every one that I may Gain some." Defoe's mission was a success. He became friendly with some of Scotland's most influential noble families; he became an adviser to some of the more important committees involved with the Union; he threw himself into the rioting at Glasgow. After the treaty was signed in 1707, he wrote his monumental *History of the Union of Great Britain* (1709).

Defoe retained an interest in Scotland throughout his life, sending his son Benjamin Norton to Edinburgh University and retaining John Russell as his agent there, but his major interest still lay in England. In addition to his pamphlets and newspapers, Defoe produced several full-length treatises during this period. In July 1704 he published a collection of accounts concerning the great storm that struck England at the end of November 1703, an indication of an interest in natural catastrophes that later found a vent in his fictional treatments of storms and plagues. In March 1705 he brought out *The Consolidator,* an allegory about English politics in the form of a voyage to the moon. Though the allegory is thin enough, the work has some interesting elements of fantasy of a kind that Defoe was never again to explore. In May 1706 his long-promised poem on English politics, *Jure Divino,* was published. Defoe had carried on a series of political debates in the *Review of the Affairs of France* with the Jacobite Charles Leslie, and there is something to be said for the notion that Defoe's politics were even closer to some popular Whig notions than those of the eminent John Locke. What emerges from *Jure Divino* is a belief in property, defined broadly as goods and productive labor, as the basis of government. Defoe had less reverence for Parliament than most English writers on politics and was much less afraid of revolution and mob action than almost any of his contemporaries. He dedicated his work to the Goddess Reason, and it represents his fullest and clearest statement on politics.

Defoe was now famous as "Mr. Review," or "The Author of the True-Born Englishman," and it was under the latter name that he brought out collections of his poetry and pamphlets in 1703 and 1705. After the Whigs removed Harley from power in 1708, Defoe had little difficulty transferring his services to Sidney, first Earl of Godolphin; but, following his ill-advised attempt to prosecute Sacheverell for another fiery sermon, the Whigs lost power. When Harley, by then a full-fledged Tory, once more assumed control of the government as lord treasurer, Defoe had to adapt the *Review* and his pamphlets to the views of those wishing a speedy end to the war and a peace treaty with France. This was a severe test of Defoe's beliefs and loyalties. He may have been able to convince himself that the war was dragging on too long, but he always admired England's greatest general, John Churchill, first Duke of Marlborough; and though he defended the economic parts of the treaty with France in the *Mercator,* he later admitted that he was doing as good a job as he could for a difficult cause. He also produced anonymous pamphlets attacking the Tory position. At times he was caught up by the anger of the moment, but he must have been terrified at the possibility of Henry St. John, first Viscount Bolingbroke's taking over power from Harley, who had become Lord Oxford. In 1713 he wrote a series of ironic pamphlets seeming to argue that bringing back the family of James II would not be so bad for the nation. His enemies leapt at the opportunity, and once more Defoe was in jail. Although the irony of the pamphlets is evident, Chief Justice Thomas Parker, first Earl of Macclesfield, noted that men had been hanged for less irony. The prosecution demanded a trial, and Defoe had to be rescued by a pardon from Queen Anne. In 1714 Bolingbroke managed to get the Schism Bill passed; this law prevented the Dissenters from raising their children in schools of their choice, and Defoe was becoming increasingly bitter about the actions of both the Whigs and Tories. Events seemed to be driving the Tories toward the possibility of some kind of reconciliation with the supporters of the family of James II when Queen Anne died on 26 July 1714.

Defoe must have greeted this event with a sigh of relief and a pang of fear. With the first of the Hanoverians, George I, on the throne, the Dissenters would no longer be threatened with extinction. But Defoe had made so many enemies among the Whigs that he could hardly expect to be welcomed back by the party in power. Harley had been snubbed by George I when the mon-

"Daniel De Foe and the Devil at Leap-Frog," a caricature by one of Defoe's contemporaries

arch arrived, and was soon imprisoned in the Tower. How was Defoe, who had been paid five hundred pounds between 16 January and 26 July for his services, to live? He began writing more than ever, and, more significantly, he began exploring some fictional forms. He defended his former patron, Harley, in the three parts of *The Secret History of the White Staff* (1714-1715) and in other "secret histories" related to the events of the time.

While Defoe's writing career was flourishing, in his private life he was having all the difficulties that he might have expected after he lost the protection of Harley. On 19 August 1714 Defoe issued a statement in the *Flying Post*, a paper that he was editing, accusing one of the Lords Regent of being a Jacobite. Defoe was arrested on 28 August, and although he was released on bail, he could not prevent the prosecution from going forward. On 12 July 1715 Defoe was brought to trial in the court of the King's Bench. In this desperate situation, he wrote to Chief Justice Parker. This letter must have been somewhat along the same lines as the one he sent to Nottingham; but this time he may have pulled out all stops, for, mi-

raculously, it succeeded. Defoe gives an account of such a letter in the third volume of *Robinson Crusoe*: "The letter was so strenuous in argument, so pathetic in its eloquence, and so moving and persuasive, that as soon as the judge read it he sent him word he should be easy, for he would endeavour to make that matter light to him; and in a word, never left until he obtained to stop prosecution, and restore him to his liberty and to his family." The result was a "capitulation," and Defoe was once more in the employ of the government—not more or less openly as in the days of the *Review of the Affairs of France*, but secretly as a saboteur of and spy upon the Tory press.

The freedom that this position provided him as well as its peculiar vantage point could not have been entirely displeasing to the man who admired Richelieu and who enjoyed playing Alexander Goldsmith and Claude Guilot. He was never much at home with official Whig ideology, and writing from the Tory standpoint must have held some private pleasures for the author of *The Shortest Way with the Dissenters*. Then in his mid fifties, Defoe was at the height of his powers as a journalist. His specialty had been the editorial essay; working with the daily events of newspapers, he found himself becoming more concrete in his prose style than ever before. In 1715 he began to work for Nathaniel Mist, the publisher of the *Weekly Journal,* and in May 1716 he began editing the monthly summary of the news, *Mercurius Politicus.* In addition to these Tory journals, Defoe began a Whig monthly, *Mercurius Britannicus,* and contributed extensively to the *Whitehall Evening Post* and the *Original Weekly Journal.* He also contributed to publications such as the *Manufacturer,* a journal in support of the wool weavers, and the *Director,* a journal intended to calm the fury of Englishmen embroiled in the South Sea Scandal. To read a journal such as Mist's before and after Defoe added his talents to it is to realize just how brilliant Defoe was compared to most of the writers of his time.

Defoe was also experimenting with various forms of fiction. In *The Memoirs of Majr. Alexander Ramkins* (1719), Defoe finally depicts a fully developed fictional character. Although the work is aimed at showing the delusions of the Jacobites, Ramkins realizes the foolishness of his trust in France and in Jacobite ideals only at the end of the work, which covers his original admiration for James II when he fought for him at the age of seventeen. Ramkin goes to France and experiences wars and adventures. His disillusionment with Louis XIV, as he becomes aware of that monarch's duplicity, comes gradually; but he concludes by recommending to the reader a work that demonstrates how one may be a Roman Catholic and still be loyal to George I. Although Defoe continued to underscore his message, he had just about reached the point of allowing his fiction to speak for itself. *The Life and Strange Surprizing Adventures of Robinson Crusoe* was published some four and a half months later.

Defoe put a great deal of himself into *Robinson Crusoe,* and some critics have taken at face value his claim in *Serious Reflections . . . of Robinson Crusoe* (1720), under the pressure of attacks by Charles Gildon, that the work was an allegory of his life. It should be noted, however, that he also claimed that the work was both a picture of real life and a satire, and that he never drops the identity of Robinson Crusoe. The series of essays in *Serious Reflections . . . of Robinson Crusoe* pontificate on Crusoe's loneliness in a way that— however much one may go along with his request that the work be read symbolically—has little relation to Defoe, the father of a large family and the center of a wide circle of friends. If Defoe occasionally felt a sense of isolation in the midst of crowds, one should credit his creative imagination for transforming such states of feeling into a great fiction rather than search for some obscure allegorical relationship between such events and his life.

Robinson Crusoe has been read as a spiritual autobiography; as a symbolic representation of human development on the level of politics, economics, social life, and education; and as an adventure story. Like a *Vexierbild,* a picture that assumes different shapes depending on how it is viewed, *Robinson Crusoe* tends to appear as only one of these forms at a time and has the power of taking on a wholeness from whichever angle it is considered. The reasons why Defoe turned to this particular fiction are equally complex. In 1718 the Dissenters became embroiled in the "Salters Hall Controversy," which involved a literal belief in the Trinity. Defoe held to his faith in the Trinity, but he also thought that the Dissenters should avoid falling into complete disunity over the issue. Under these circumstances, that he should create a hero whose Christian beliefs are formulated as a series of general doctrines—and that he should have a Catholic priest offer a similarly generalized body of Christian doctrine as the kind of religion he would preach to the dwellers on Crusoe's island—is not entirely surprising.

An event from the beginning of February 1719 that apparently moved his imagination was a plan of the South Sea Company to establish a colony near the mouth of the Orinoco River that would renew the dream of Sir Walter Ralegh; Defoe was to write *An Historical Account of the Voyages and Adventures of Sir Walter Raleigh* (1720) just a year later in support of a settlement in Guiana. (Crusoe's island is in the Caribbean just off the mouth of the Orinoco.) The newspaper story raised images of gold to be discovered and of Indians who would use "a prodigious Consumption of our British Manufactures." Here a new society might flourish free from the corruption of European luxury! The prospect must have started a chain of ideas about a new Eden and an island cut off from civilization where a man might start anew. Defoe was to speculate on the possibility of utopian colonies in his *General History of the . . . Pyrates* (1724, 1728), and his interest in self-sufficient societies within England dates back to 1697 and the *Essay upon Projects. Robinson Crusoe* is a fascinating book in part because Defoe was able to communicate his excitement over the idea

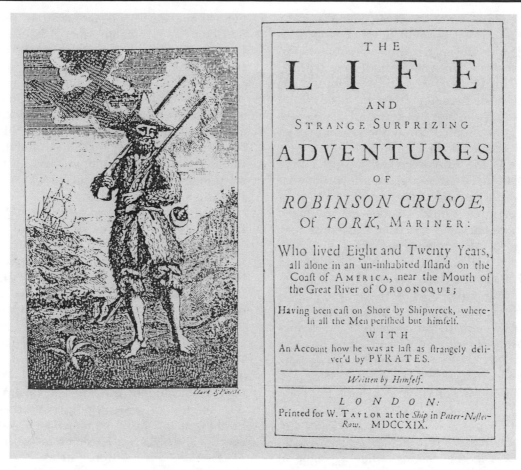

Frontispiece and title page for Defoe's best-known work

of a new colony to the reader. But the real greatness of the work lies in its imaginative re-creation of the life of the solitary Crusoe on his island, and that is explainable only by a sense of Defoe's powers as an artist and thinker.

When, at the end of the eighteenth century and during the beginning of the nineteenth century, *Robinson Crusoe* began to attract critical attention, some writers argued that Defoe had really stolen his work from the account of Alexander Selkirk, the master of a ship that set sail in the expedition of William Dampier to the South Pacific. Selkirk was apparently a difficult man, and after a quarrel with a commander of another ship, he voluntarily agreed to be set ashore on the island of Más a Tierra in the Juan Fernández group, four hundred miles from the coast of Chile. He left his companions in September 1704 and was not rescued from his solitary life until February 1709, when Woodes Rogers, the leader of another expedition, stopped by the island. Accounts of Selkirk's manner of living during his four and a half years of isolation appeared in

Edward Cooke's *Voyage to the South Sea and Round the World* (1712), in Richard Steele's journal *The Englishman* for 3 December 1713, and in Rogers's *A Cruising Voyage round the World* (1718). Poet William Cowper, who wrote a powerful poem about Selkirk beginning "I am the monarch of all I survey," believed that Defoe had merely transcribed what Selkirk told him and deserved no credit for writing *Robinson Crusoe*; but in his survey of critical attitudes toward Crusoe, Pat Rogers discovered that almost no one mentioned Selkirk anymore. Although he attempted to restore the balance by arguing an important role for Selkirk as an inspiration for Defoe's work, Rogers's efforts are unlikely to have a major impact. As has been shown, various economic and religious ideas with little connection to Selkirk lie behind *Robinson Crusoe*, and the story of the survival of an isolato on an island had interested Defoe long before Selkirk's adventures were publicized. Such narratives were common in actual voyage accounts and in various fictional utopias. Since Defoe's fictional method involved the creation of a narrative from various sources, Selkirk's isolation on Más a Tierra would have to be considered along with the many similar accounts upon which Defoe drew. Since many modern interpretations have focused upon the economic implications of Crusoe's career, interest has shifted toward reading the story in terms of a socioeconomic allegory rather than as the adventures of an isolated mariner such as Selkirk.

Once Defoe discovered that his fiction might win him the same acclaim and profit that his poetry and pamphlets had brought him during the reign of Queen Anne, he produced works with remarkable speed and inventiveness. The events of this period furnished him with more than sufficient materials. The period around 1720 saw the development of crime in England on a scale unknown before, and the domestic crime wave was paralleled by an outbreak of piracy that was equally remarkable. The activities of such criminals were often compared to those of the directors of the South Sea Company, who had managed to create a frenzy of stock purchases followed by a fall in prices that left the entire nation chagrined. On the Continent, an outbreak of trouble between Protestants and Catholics in Germany seemed to suggest that a new religious war was in the making, while a plague in the south of France was killing thousands around Toulon and Marseilles.

At the end of 1719, Defoe wrote a narrative of a real pirate, Captain Avery, purportedly told by Avery himself in two letters. He followed this with the story of a fictional pirate in June 1720. *The Life, Adventures and Pyracies of the Famous Captain Singleton* traces Bob Singleton's career from his childhood as an orphan to his going to sea and becoming an adventurer. He crosses Africa after a shipwreck and comes upon an Englishman who has been mining for gold. He stops long enough to enrich himself, but after he returns to Europe, he spends the money rapidly. In his second voyage he acts as a full-fledged pirate, taking ship after ship. What seems to be a series of adventures becomes more complicated and interesting with the introduction of William Walters, a Quaker ship's surgeon, who allows himself to be taken by the pirates provided that he can seem to be coerced and thereby plead innocent to willful wrongdoing. True to his Quaker spirit, he refuses to join in any of the fighting, but he is perfectly willing to share in the booty. Amid a group of almost childlike adventurers, William has the role of reminding everyone that fighting without some profit is a waste of time. When Singleton and William are rich enough, the Quaker, like a good tradesman, persuades his friend to retire, "for no body trades for the sake of Trading, much less do any Men rob for the sake of Thieving." William leads Captain Bob to a quiet life, which includes a religious conversion and marriage to William's sister. In this analogy between the activities of pirates and tradesmen there lies the implicit comparison with the piratical tradesmen and stockbrokers who were to inflate the South Sea Bubble.

Captain Singleton was the first of Defoe's fully developed fictional accounts of criminals; but just a month earlier, in May 1720, the best of his military memoirs, *Memoirs of a Cavalier,* had been published. Instead of focusing entirely on the historical events—the movements of armies, the decisions of kings and generals—Defoe made his Cavalier into a complex, if occasionally sketchy, character who finally concludes—after fighting with Gustav II in Germany during the Thirty Years' War and again under Prince Rupert of Bavaria in the English Civil War—that the horrors of a war pitting brother against brother are too much for him. The Cavalier, however loyal to Charles I, comes to be an admirer of Thomas, third Baron Fairfax, the leader of the parliamentary forces, and a critic of the clergymen who led Charles to commit the errors that eventually led to his execution. The structure of this work—with its balancing of the two scenes of warfare, its creation of a hero with a growing awareness of his own hatred of the Civil War, and its vivid accounts of battles seen through a limited angle of vision—is predictive of Defoe's increasing awareness of the possibilities inherent in the novel form.

In 1722 Defoe still had nine productive years ahead of him; but as a writer of fiction, this was his annus mirabilis. In January, *Moll Flanders* was published, followed in March by *A Journal of the Plague Year* and in December by *Colonel Jack. The Fortunes and Misfortunes of the Famous Moll Flanders,* as E. M. Forster has observed, is a masterpiece of characterization. Moll tells her story to an editor who confesses himself somewhat shocked by her language (he cleans it up) but intrigued by her life. He tells the reader to pay attention to the penitent part of Moll's story, while admitting that she is no longer quite as penitent as she once was. With this warning the reader is taken into the mind and career of an orphan who undergoes an incredible variety of experi-

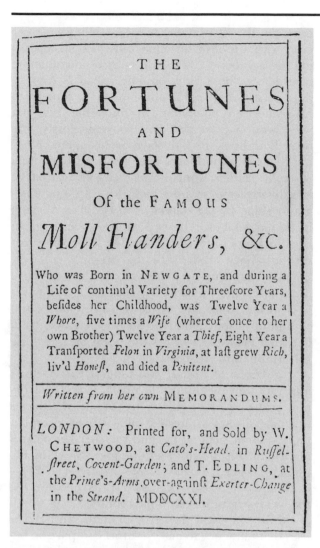

Title page for Defoe's "scandalous" novel

ences. Moll manages through her beauty and cleverness to move from servant to mistress to wife, and then through a series of marriages and affairs that lead her to the poverty she has always feared. Refusing to starve quietly, Moll becomes a thief—not an ordinary thief, but an "Artist" among thieves. She is caught, repents her crimes, manages to be transported to America with the one man she loved almost without qualification, and uses her ill-gotten gains to live the life of an American lady with servants and a plantation. *Moll Flanders* is a lesson in survival, and Defoe must have found this character, who sustains herself in a harsh world by whatever means she can find, an appealing human being; so does the modern reader. Although there were chapbook versions of *Moll Flanders,* it was not the kind of work that was sufficiently "polite" or proper for either the eighteenth or for most of the nineteenth cen-

tury. From this perspective, Samuel Richardson's *Pamela* (1740-1741) was not the first English "novel" but the first novel that was morally acceptable to the middle orders who were to constitute the fiction-reading public. *Moll Flanders* was published in collected editions of Defoe, but for the most part critics who mentioned it at all paused just long enough to express their disapproval of Defoe's subject matter. It awaited an age that was not offended by discussions of sexual seduction to be fully appreciated. Naturalistic novels such as Emile Zola's *Nana* (1880) and Theodore Dreiser's *Sister Carrie* (1900) opened up the possibilities of a critical evaluation of *Moll Flanders,* just as the relaxed moral standards of the 1960s made possible the republication of John Cleland's *Fanny Hill* (1749), a truly pornographic novel influenced by Defoe's work.

A Journal of the Plague Year, a historical novel set in 1665 and 1666, is Defoe's masterpiece of descriptive realism. While he may have written the work to exploit the interest in the plague at Marseilles, he was also intent on arguing against the quarantining of London in case the plague crossed the Channel; and at a time when the South Sea Scandal had turned so many Englishmen against each other and the government, he was plainly eager to depict a period when Englishmen worked together against a common enemy. There is some reason to believe that Defoe had been waiting a long time to write such a book. References to the plague that struck Restoration London abound in his writings. He still recalled a few things about the plague from his childhood and knew the way his family acted at the time. The narrator, H. F., is probably modeled on Henry Foe, his uncle; through H. F., the reader gets a view of the plague from the standpoint of a London tradesman. H. F.'s account includes the story of three artisans who, refusing to obey laws that might cause their destruction, lead a group of Londoners out of the city into the better air of Epsom Forest. It is through this exodus that Defoe makes his political point, but he makes his artistic point with his vivid scenes of death and despair. Along with *Robinson Crusoe, A Journal of the Plague Year* formed a model for the exploitation of dramatic and sublime scenes in the novel genre that Gothic novelists would later borrow to good effect.

Defoe's last novel in this year was *The History and Remarkable Life of the Truly Honourable Col. Jacque. Moll Flanders* was Defoe's portrait of the clever servant girl rising, with various ups and

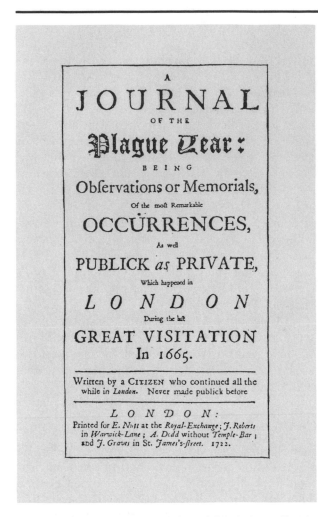

Title page for Defoe's masterpiece of descriptive realism

onel on the Continent, but his military career ends with a foolish flirtation with Jacobitism during the invasion of 1715. He marries a woman he considers to be a lady, but she cuckolds him, as do a series of wives. Disillusioned, he returns to his American plantation to find that his first wife, who had treated him so shamelessly, has been bought as a white slave by his agent. Finding that her experiences have changed her into a wiser, if sadder, woman and discovering that he is still attracted to her, Jack does an ungentlemanly thing by the standards of ordinary society: he remarries her. The end of the novel is given over to Jack's unfortunate scheme to become rich through illicit trade with the Spanish colonies, but the main thrust of the work is clear enough: it questions the values of society through the eyes of a former thief and holds ideals of charity and community above notions of social rank; and, like *Moll Flanders,* it offers the hope of a new life for criminals in America.

Sections of *Colonel Jack* suggest that Defoe's interests were beginning to move away from fiction and toward the direct treatment of subjects that had always interested him—travel, economics, economic geography, and the social problems of Britain. But he still had one great work of fiction to write, *The Fortunate Mistress* (1724)—commonly known as *Roxana* for its heroine. At the very beginning Roxana remarks that she is apt to be "satyrical" in her comments, and Defoe uses that tendency to make a direct comparison between his own age and the luxurious world of Charles II. Nominally, *Roxana* is a historical novel; but while Roxana becomes the mistress of Charles II and is modeled on Louise Renée de Kéroualle, Duchess of Portsmouth, her masquerades belong as much to the world of 1724 as they do to, say, 1678. Roxana is Defoe's first introspective narrator. She has a certain loathing both for herself and for her life, and Defoe delineates her as a woman torn by contradictions—a genuine pleasure in her past sins combined with a horror of her own corruption. She allows herself to become the mistress of a wealthy man when her husband becomes bankrupt and abandons her and her children. Her servant, Amy, puts forth the doctrine of necessity: *"Comply and live; deny and starve,"* and Roxana chooses life. But at the end, at what ought to be the height of her prosperity, she finds herself pursued by one of the children she had been forced to abandon—a daughter whose motives seem to combine a desperate desire to find her mother with the urge to expose

downs, through eighteenth-century society; *Colonel Jack* is his novel of education. Jack begins life as an orphan and a street urchin, raised by a kindly nurse; she reminds him that his father was a gentleman who had urged that the boy should strive to become a gentleman as well. Jack's environment, however, leads him toward becoming a thief, and he takes some pleasure in the "Trade" of picking pockets. But when he graduates to more violent crimes—housebreaking and robbery—he feels considerable reluctance about such acts. Jack only wants the chance to make good through honest work, and after he is spirited to America to slave in the fields, he shows his skill as a manager of slave labor. He becomes a successful plantation owner, but after a former convict gives him a rapid education in history and geography, he longs to return to Europe to become the true gentleman he always wanted to be.

The second half of the novel concerns this downward path to gentility. He becomes a real col-her mother's past. Roxana escapes momentarily, but she states at the end that an unspecified disaster eventually overtook her. Roxana's hysteria and despair are the creation of a writer who might have made further experiments in the psychological novel; but *Roxana* was not as successful as its predecessors, and Defoe decided to go on to other things.

Most of Defoe's writings at this time were published by a consortium of publishers, and there is the distinct possibility that lengthy works such as *Atlas Maritimus & Commercialis* (1728) involved a considerable advance payment. At any rate Defoe apparently abandoned much of his newspaper work, particularly his writing for Mist, to undertake such major works. He still wrote lives of criminals, but they tended to be real criminals such as Jonathan Wild and Jack Sheppard, about whom he wrote in the *Original Weekly Journal,* in separate pamphlets, and in large collections such as the two-volume *General History of the . . . Pyrates,* written under the name Captain Charles Johnson. Not that Defoe was ever to be really through with fiction or fictional structures once he had discovered his genius for narrative: in November 1724 his *A New Voyage round the World,* a west-to-east remake of the voyages of William Dampier and others, was published. The events, including the exploration of a land in the general area of Australia and a march across Argentina, are all fictional, and the narrator remains a shadowy figure whose role is encompassed by his profession as sea captain and explorer. More interesting in their fictional possibilities were the contrasting accounts of the fictional Captain Misson and the real pirate Captain Tew in the second volume of *A General History of the . . . Pyrates.* Although Defoe shows Misson's ideal commonwealth based on equality and liberty as less workable than the practical colony based on slavery set up by Captain Tew, Misson is one of Defoe's more interesting character concepts—a fiery communist whose real counterpart did not appear until the French Revolution.

From the range and excellence of these publications, it should be obvious that though Defoe did not continue the novelistic career that ended so spectacularly with *Roxana,* he was by no means ready to retire. In May 1724 one of his most extraordinary successes—the first volume of *A Tour thro' the Whole Island of Great Britain*—was published. He completed this work—which is, for the most part, a description of the economic life of Britain—with the second volume in 1725 and the final volume in 1727. The work is written in the epistolary form, which gives an informal and personal quality to the narrative of Defoe's wanderings. However useful the *Tour* may be for economic historians, it is also useful as a way of seeing the nation in terms of Defoe's particular views, projects, experiences, and opinions. There are few villages that do not remind Defoe of some experience he had there or of some story about the place. Defoe freely used sources such as William Camden's *Britannia* (1586), but in its focus and interests, the *Tour* reflects his own feelings and ideas. Although it was published anonymously, it was generally known to have been written by Defoe. Interestingly enough, when it came to be revised, the task was undertaken, at least in part, by another great novelist, Samuel Richardson.

Free from the cares of his newspapers and pamphlets, Defoe was able to enjoy his family and take pleasure in his house in Stoke Newington with its pleasant garden and ample library. He had been living in this suburb north of London, with its large population of Dissenters, since 1709. It is at this time that one finally has a firsthand account of his domestic life—through the eyes of Henry Baker, a minor poet with interests in science, who came to Stoke Newington to tutor a deaf-and-dumb child and stayed to court Defoe's youngest daughter, Sophia. Baker obviously approached Defoe as a person of great reputation. He speaks of Defoe's daughters Hannah, Henrietta, and Sophia (Maria was married and living elsewhere) as "admired for their beauty, their education and their prudent conduct." He describes Defoe as dividing his time between his garden and "his studies, which he found means of making very profitable." Although Baker's decision to court Sophia came in 1727, the negotiations over her dowry dragged on interminably. In August 1728 Defoe wrote Baker: "If you desire my daughter, you must take her as I can give her." Although Sophia often expressed her disgust over Baker's insistence on particular terms, his relationship with Defoe was good enough for the veteran writer to contribute the first number to Baker's new journal, the *Universal Spectator,* on 12 October 1728. But on 27 January 1729 Baker wrote to Sophia that if she was his "good genius," her father was "my evil one." Baker's overheated correspondence reached the point in February 1729 that he proposed a double suicide with his beloved "Amanda." Sophia finally became ill, and the marriage took place on 30

April of that year. A month later Baker wrote of his happiness to a friend, and indeed, despite all the contention, the marriage did work out well. The only regret is that of the biographer, who has to wish that Baker had said more about Defoe and less about himself. But there is much to be learned through the picture Baker gives of the relationship between Defoe and his daughter. Defoe called her "the dearest Jewel I possess" and "my best beloved child in whom my Soul delights." Baker depicts Sophia as a woman of sensibility and honesty: "I'll never risque my Happiness but with a Man I love, nor give my Hand but where I can give my Heart," she told him. She demanded absolute sincerity from him: "Use no Disguise nor Flattery, Sincerity is what you will find with me, and what I must expect." These are sentiments that Defoe himself espoused, and if he delighted in disguise in the world of politics, he must have kept his family life free from it.

In 1725 Defoe busied himself with his lives of criminals and with a work that an early biographer, Walter Wilson, considered his masterpiece, *The Complete English Tradesman* (1726-1727). Wilson's opinion may say more about the mercantile mind of a nineteenth-century biographer than about the actual merits of the book, but it is nevertheless a judgment that requires some attention. Defoe's treatment of the life of the tradesman is filled with practical advice: "Let the wise and wary Tradesman take the Hint; keep within the Bounds where Providence has placed him; be content to rise gradually and gently as he has done; and as he is sufficiently rich . . . to softly on, least he comes not softly down." Defoe also launches into an ambiguous discussion of luxury, and defends his theory of the circulation of goods as a means by which the entire nation shared in the wealth. This is by no means Defoe's best work, but it does illustrate some of the best aspects of the working of his mind.

He was also involved with the creation of the persona Andrew Moreton. Moreton is that part of Defoe that felt old and crotchety and fed up with the age. In *Every-body's Business, Is No-Body's Business* (1725), he proposes various social schemes to deal with the insolence of servants. Although this work was popular, the character of Moreton was too pessimistic for Defoe the projector, and he abandoned this persona in his later social tracts. Closer to the real Defoe was the author of *A General History of Discoveries and Improvements, in Useful Arts* (1725-1726), with its ac-

count of progress. In response to the publication by Anthony Collins of a series of skeptical tracts casting doubt upon a literal interpretation of the Bible, Defoe wrote a series of works asserting the validity of the view of sin and redemption in the Bible.

It might be thought that by this time Defoe's prose style would have been so deeply ingrained as to have been part of his very nature, but in *Conjugal Lewdness: Or, Matrimonial Whoredom*, published in January 1727, he revealed a style newly modeled on that of seventeenth-century writer Jeremy Taylor. He used it to add to his indictment of an age that seemed contemptuous of women and of marriage for love. Instead of true passion, the age was offering triviality and occasional perversions; instead of respect for women there was a proliferation of prostitution and the spread of diseases that would turn England into a national hospital ward rather than a nation. There is a certain flavor of Andrew Moreton in *Conjugal Lewdness*, but in his 1728 tracts Defoe turned back to some of his favorite projects. In *Augusta Triumphans: Or, The Way to Make London the Most Flourishing City in the Universe*, published at the beginning of the year, he proposed establishing a London university, a hospital for orphans, and an academy of music. He wanted private madhouses suppressed or controlled, brighter lights installed to reduce robberies, and some regulation of gin to reduce the horrors that would be depicted by William Hogarth in his *Gin Lane* two decades later. In *A Plan of the English Commerce*, published in March, he extolled the virtues of English trade goods and argued against any reduction in the wages of English workmen.

In 1729 Defoe returned to another old subject—the irrationality of laws against debtors and bankrupts—in a pamphlet with the explicit title *The Unreasonableness and Ill Consequences of Imprisoning the Body for Debt*. In this work Defoe tried to show that imprisonment prevented the debtor from earning money to pay off his creditors and support his family. Unlike some of Defoe's other projects, this one had a particular connection with his personal affairs. In 1727 Mary Brooke had opened a proceeding against Defoe in the King's Bench and Exchequer. Defoe filed countersuits in Chancery in 1728 and 1730, but he was not successful. What writing he managed after the summer of 1730 must have been difficult, and the anxiety of having to abandon his

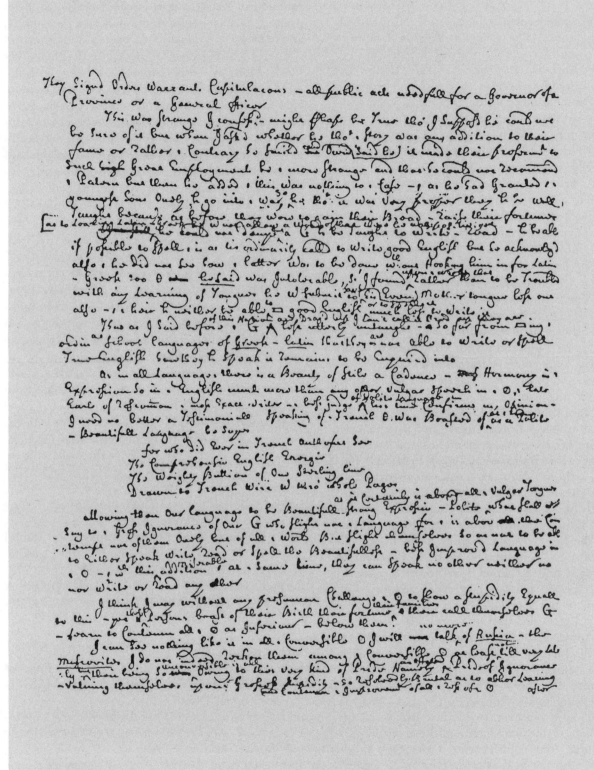

Page from the manuscript for The Compleat English Gentleman, *a work left unfinished by Defoe (British Library)*

home must have made even 1729 an agonizing period.

This may explain why he never finished his last two works, *The Compleat English Gentleman* and *Of Royall Educacion*, both of which were edited by Karl D. Bülbring in the 1890s. *The Compleat English Gentleman* argues that true gentility is a combination of virtue and education achievable by anyone with sufficient leisure. "Instruction only is the fund of knowledge," he advises, and urges those who can afford a tutor to study geography, history, and science in English, without worrying about learning Latin and Greek. He advocates an education similar to that he received at Morton's academy, and he argues that the ancient languages that once constituted almost all of education have become less important. "The knowledge of things, not words, make a schollar," he declares, echoing the view of John Locke. The influence of that philosopher carries over to *Of Royall Educacion*, in which Defoe tries to establish an ideal education for a future English monarch—an education that would make him into a leader like Defoe's hero, Gustav II.

Baker remarks that Defoe suffered from "the Gout and Stone," and that there were several occasions on which he was too ill to see his future son-in-law. Defoe died in Ropemaker's Alley, not far from the area of London where he had lived as a child, on 24 April 1731, still hiding from the creditor who wanted to drag him back to the horrors of Newgate Prison. Before his death he wrote two letters that reveal more of the man than the hundreds he sent to Robert Harley. In the first, to his daughter Sophia, he complains of her "Unkindness" and, after claiming an "Exalted and Sublime" love for her, remarks that he received her letter of reconciliation "with a joy not to be Describ'd, but in the Deepest Silence, or Expressed but in Teares." To Baker, in his last known letter, Defoe speaks of his sorrows and of his longing to see his family, particularly his most beloved daughter: "Kiss my dear Sophy once more for me; and if I must see her no more, tell her this is from a Father that loved her above all his Comforts, to his last Breath." Only in these letters does one have a glimpse of the emotional force that could create Crusoe's solitude and Moll's horror at finding herself in Newgate.

Defoe's literary reputation is probably higher today than it has ever been. Many modern critics look to *Robinson Crusoe*, along with Miguel de Cervantes's *Don Quixote*, as a key work in the formation of the novel; and *Moll Flanders*,

A Journal of the Plague Year, and *Roxana* have been praised as masterpieces. *Colonel Jack* has been praised for its exploration of a new sensibility, and *Memoirs of a Cavalier* has been noted as a forerunner of the historical novel. *A Tour thro' the Whole Island of Great Britain* has been anthologized and has been reedited in a popular edition. New attention has been focused on *A General History of the . . . Pyrates* for its dramatization of an anticapitalist ideology, and the moral conduct books have been used as a basis for providing new insights into domestic life during the eighteenth century. The realism that Sir Walter Scott viewed as Defoe's chief contribution to the development of the novel was attacked by nineteenth-century critics such as Sir Leslie Stephen as a series of cunning devices rather than art, and in the twentieth century F. R. Leavis has attempted to reconfirm this judgment. But more recent critics have demonstrated the complexity of Defoe's techniques and his thought. Defoe the man was both admired and reviled in his own time. He was certainly capable of writing on several sides of an issue, and of a degree of betrayal. Perhaps the kindest judgment would be to allow that if he had not been all too human, he could never have understood the minds and hearts of the thieves and prostitutes who make his fiction so fascinating.

Letters:

Letters of Daniel Defoe, edited by George Healey (Oxford: Clarendon Press, 1955);

Paula R. Backscheider, "John Russell to Daniel Defoe: Fifteen Unpublished Letters," *Philological Quarterly*, 61 (Spring 1982): 161-177;

Backscheider, "Robert Harley to Daniel Defoe: A New Letter," *Modern Language Review*, 83 (October 1988): 817-819.

Bibliographies:

John Robert Moore, *A Checklist of the Writings of Daniel Defoe* (Bloomington: Indiana University Press, 1960);

John A. Stoler, *Daniel Defoe: An Annotated Bibliography of Modern Criticism, 1900-1980* (New York: Garland, 1984);

Spiro Peterson, *Daniel Defoe: A Reference Guide 1731-1924* (Boston: G. K. Hall, 1987).

Biographies:

James Sutherland, *Defoe* (London: Methuen, 1937; revised, 1950);

John Robert Moore, *Daniel Defoe: Citizen of the Modern World* (Bloomington: Indiana University Press, 1958);

Frank Bastian, *The Early Life of Daniel Defoe* (London: Macmillan, 1981);

Paula R. Backscheider, *Daniel Defoe: His Life* (Baltimore: Johns Hopkins University Press, 1989).

References:

Paul Alkon, *Defoe and Fictional Time* (Athens: University of Georgia Press, 1979);

Hans Anderson, "The Paradox of Trade and Morality in Defoe," *Modern Philology*, 39 (August 1941): 23-46;

Paula R. Backscheider, "Cross-Purposes: Defoe's *History of the Union*," *CLIO*, 11 (Winter 1982): 165-186;

Backscheider, *Daniel Defoe: Ambition and Innovation* (Lexington: University Press of Kentucky, 1986);

Backscheider, "Defoe's Prodigal Sons," *Studies in the Literary Imagination*, 15 (Fall 1982): 3-18;

Rodney Baine, *Daniel Defoe and the Supernatural* (Athens: University of Georgia Press, 1979);

G. D. H. Cole, Introduction to *A Tour thro' the Whole Island of Great Britain*, 2 volumes (New York: Kelley, 1968);

J. Alan Downie, *Robert Harley and the Press* (Cambridge: Cambridge University Press, 1979);

Alistair Duckworth, " 'Whig' Landscapes in Defoe's *Tour*," *Philological Quarterly*, 61 (Fall 1982): 453-465;

Peter Earle, *The World of Defoe* (New York: Atheneum, 1977);

John Forster, *Daniel De Foe and Charles Churchill* (London, 1855);

Maximillian E. Novak, *Defoe and the Nature of Man* (Oxford: Clarendon Press, 1963);

Novak, *Economics and the Fiction of Daniel Defoe* (Berkeley: University of California Press, 1983);

Novak, *Realism, Myth, and History in Defoe's Fiction* (Lincoln: Nebraska University Press, 1983);

William Payne, *Mr. Review: Daniel Defoe as the Author of the Review* (New York: King's Crown Press, 1961);

John Richetti, *Defoe's Narratives* (Oxford: Clarendon Press, 1975);

Pat Rogers, "Defoe at Work: The Making of A *Tour thro' Great Britain*, Volume I," *Bulletin of the New York Public Library*, 78 (Summer 1975): 431-450;

Rogers, *Eighteenth-Century Encounters* (Sussex: Harvester, 1985);

Rogers, ed., *Defoe: The Critical Heritage* (London: Routledge, 1972);

Lois Schwoerer, *No Standing Armies!* (Baltimore: Johns Hopkins University Press, 1974);

Arthur Secord, *Studies in the Narrative Method of Defoe* (Urbana: University of Illinois Press, 1968);

Secord, ed., *Defoe's Review, Reproduced from the Original Editions*, 22 volumes (New York: Published by the Facsimile Text Society for Columbia University Press, 1933);

Geoffrey Sill, *Defoe and the Idea of Fiction* (Newark: University of Delaware Press, 1983);

G. A. Starr, *Defoe and Spiritual Autobiography* (Princeton: Princeton University Press, 1965).

Papers:

Manuscripts: *The Compleat English Gentleman* and *Of Royall Educacion* are in the British Library. The Huntington Library, San Marino, California, and the William Andrews Clark Library, Los Angeles, have notebooks and unpublished manuscripts. Locations of letters written by Defoe (most are in the British Library) are given in Healey's edition of the letters.

John Dryden

(9 August 1631 - 1 May 1700)

J. Douglas Canfield
University of Arizona

See also the Dryden entries in DLB 80: Restoration and Eighteenth-Century Dramatists: First Series *and* DLB 101: British Prose Writers, 1660-1800: First Series.

SELECTED BOOKS: *Astraea Redux. A Poem On the Happy Restoration and Return Of His Sacred Majesty Charles the Second* (London: Printed by J. M. for Henry Herringman, 1660);

To His Sacred Majesty, A Panegyrick On His Coronation (London: Printed for Henry Herringman, 1661);

To My Lord Chancellor, Presented on New-years-day (London: Printed for Henry Herringman, 1662);

The Rival Ladies (London: Printed by W. W. for Henry Herringman, 1664);

The Indian Emperour, or The Conquest of Mexico by the Spaniards (London: Printed by J. M. for H. Herringman, 1667); second edition republished with "A Defence of An Essay of Dramatique Poesie" in some copies (London: Printed for H. Herringman, 1668);

Annus Mirabilis: The Year of Wonders, 1666 (London: Printed for Henry Herringman, 1667);

Of Dramatick Poesie: An Essay (London: Printed for Henry Herringman, 1668 [i.e., 1667]);

Secret-Love, or The Maiden-Queen (London: Printed for Henry Herringman, 1668);

Sr Martin Mar-All, or The Feigned Innocence (London: Printed for H. Herringman, 1668);

The Wild Gallant (London: Printed by Tho. Newcomb for H. Herringman, 1669);

The Tempest, or The Enchanted Island, by Dryden and William Davenant (London: Printed for Henry Herringman, 1670);

Tyrannick Love, or The Royal Martyr (London: Printed for H. Herringman, 1670);

An Evening's Love, or The Mock Astrologer (London: Printed by T. N. for Henry Herringman, 1671);

The Conquest of Granada by the Spaniards: In Two Parts (London: Printed by T. N. for Henry Herringman, 1672);

Marriage A-La-Mode (London: Printed by T. N. for Henry Herringman & sold by Joseph Knight & Francis Saunders, 1673);

The Assignation: or, Love in a Nunnery (London: Printed by T. N. for Henry Herringman, 1673);

Amboyna (London: Printed by T. N. for Henry Herringman, 1673);

Notes and Observations on the Empress of Morocco, by Dryden, John Crowne, and Thomas Shadwell (London, 1674);

Aureng-Zebe (London: Printed by T. N. for Henry Herringman, 1676);

The State of Innocence and Fall of Man (London: Printed by T. N. for Henry Herringman, 1677);

All for Love: or, The World Well Lost (London: Printed by Tho. Newcomb for Henry Herringman, 1678);

Oedipus, by Dryden and Nathaniel Lee (London: Printed for R. Bentley and M. Magnes, 1679);

Troilus and Cressida, or, Truth Found too Late (London: Printed for Jacob Tonson and Abel Swall, 1679);

The Kind Keeper; or, Mr. Limberham (London: Printed for R. Bentley and M. Magnes, 1680);

His Majesties Declaration Defended (London: Printed for T. Davies, 1681);

Absalom and Achitophel (London: Printed for J. T. & sold by W. Davis, 1681);

The Spanish Fryar, or The Double Discovery (London: Printed for Richard Tonson & Jacob Tonson, 1681);

The Medall. A Satyre against Sedition (London: Printed for Jacob Tonson, 1682);

Mac Flecknoe, or a Satyr Upon the True-Blew Protestant Poet, T.S. [unauthorized edition] (London: Printed for D. Green, 1682);

An anonymous portrait of Dryden, circa 1662 (Bodleian Library, Oxford University)

Religio Laici or a Laymans Faith (London: Printed for Jacob Tonson, 1682);

The Duke of Guise, by Dryden and Lee (London: Printed by T. H. for R. Bentley and J. Tonson, 1683);

The Vindication [of the Duke of Guise]: or The Parallel of the French Holy-League, and The English League and Covenant (London: Printed for Jacob Tonson, 1683);

Threnodia Augustalis: A Funeral-Pindarique Poem Sacred to the Happy Memory of King Charles II (London: Printed for Jacob Tonson, 1685);

Albion and Albanius, by Dryden, with music by Lewis Grabu (London: Printed for Jacob Tonson, 1685);

A Defence of the Papers Written by the Late King of Blessed Memory and Duchess of York (London: Printed for H. Hills, 1686);

The Hind and the Panther (London: Printed for Jacob Tonson, 1687);

A Song for St Cecilia's Day, 1687, by Dryden, with music by Giovanni Baptista Draghi (London: Printed for T. Dring, 1687);

Britannia Rediviva: A Poem on the Birth of the Prince (London: Printed for J. Tonson, 1688);

Don Sebastian, King of Portugal (London: Printed for Jo. Hindmarsh, 1690);

Amphitryon; or The Two Socia's, by Dryden, with music by Henry Purcell (London: Printed for J. Tonson & M. Tonson, 1690);

King Arthur: or The British Worthy, by Dryden, with music by Purcell (London: Printed for Jacob Tonson, 1691);

Eleonora: A Panegyrical Poem Dedicated to the Memory of the Late Countess of Abingdon (London: Printed for Jacob Tonson, 1692);

Cleomenes, The Spartan Heroe (London: Printed for Jacob Tonson, 1692);

Love Triumphant; or, Nature Will Prevail (London: Printed for Jacob Tonson, 1694);

An Ode, on the Death of Mr. Henry Purcell; Late Servant of his Majesty, and Organist of the Chapel Royal, and of St. Peter's Westminster (London: Printed by J. Heptinstall for Henry Playford, 1696);

Alexander's Feast; Or The Power of Musique. An Ode, In Honour of St. Cecilia's Day (London: Printed for Jacob Tonson, 1697).

Editions: *The Works of John Dryden*, 18 volumes, edited by Walter Scott (London: William

Miller, 1808); revised by George Saintsbury (Edinburgh: William Paterson, 1882-1893);

The Dramatic Works of John Dryden, 6 volumes, edited by Montague Summers (London: Nonesuch Press, 1931);

The Works of John Dryden [The California Dryden], 20 volumes, edited by Edward Niles Hooker, H. T. Swedenberg, and others (Berkeley: University of California Press, 1955-);

The Poems of John Dryden, 4 volumes, edited by James Kinsley (Oxford: Clarendon Press, 1958);

John Dryden: Of Dramatic Poesy and Other Critical Essays, 2 volumes, edited by George Watson (London: J. M. Dent / New York: E. P. Dutton, 1962).

PLAY PRODUCTIONS: *The Wild Gallant*, revised from an older play, possibly by Richard Brome, London, Vere Street Theatre, 5 February 1663;

The Rival Ladies, London, Theatre Royal, Bridges Street, possibly autumn of 1663;

The Indian-Queen, by Dryden and Sir Robert Howard, London, Theatre Royal, Bridges Street, January 1664;

The Indian Emperour, London, Theatre Royal, Bridges Street, early months of 1665;

Secret Love, London, Theatre Royal, Bridges Street, final days of January 1667;

Sir Martin Mar-All, by Dryden and William Cavendish, Duke of Newcastle, London, Lincoln's Inn Fields, 15 August 1667;

The Tempest, revised from William Shakespeare's play by Dryden and William Davenant, London, Lincoln's Inn Fields, 7 November 1667;

An Evening's Love; or, The Mock Astrologer, London, Theatre Royal, Bridges Street, 12 June 1668;

Tyrannic Love, London, Theatre Royal, Bridges Street, 24 June 1669;

The Conquest of Granada, part 1, London, Theatre Royal, Bridges Street, December 1670; part 2, January 1671;

Marriage A-la-Mode, London, Theatre Royal, Bridges Street, probably late November or early December 1671;

The Assignation; or, Love in a Nunnery, London, Lincoln's Inn Fields, not later than early autumn of 1672;

Amboyna, London, Lincoln's Inn Fields, possibly February 1673;

Aureng-Zebe, London, Theatre Royal, Drury Lane, 17 November 1675;

All for Love, London, Theatre Royal, Drury Lane, probably 12 December 1677;

The Kind Keeper; or, Mr. Limberham, London, Dorset Garden Theatre, 11 March 1678;

Oedipus, by Dryden and Nathaniel Lee, London, Dorset Garden Theatre, autumn 1678;

Troilus and Cressida, revised from Shakespeare's play, London, Dorset Garden Theatre, not later than April 1679;

The Spanish Fryar, London, Dorset Garden Theatre, 1 November 1680;

The Duke of Guise, by Dryden and Lee, London, Theatre Royal, Drury Lane, 30 November 1682;

Albion and Albanius, opera with text by Dryden and music by Louis Grabu, London, Dorset Garden Theatre, 3 June 1685;

Don Sebastian, London, Theatre Royal, Drury Lane, 4 December 1689;

Amphitryon, London, Theatre Royal, Drury Lane, probably early October 1690;

King Arthur, opera with text by Dryden and music by Henry Purcell, London, Dorset Garden Theatre, early June 1691;

Cleomenes, by Dryden and Thomas Southerne, London, Theatre Royal, Drury Lane, on or before 16 April 1692;

Love Triumphant, London, Theatre Royal, Drury Lane, probably late January 1694;

"The Secular Masque," inserted into *The Pilgrim*, revised from John Fletcher's play by John Vanbrugh, London, Theatre Royal, Drury Lane, late April or early May 1700.

OTHER: "Upon the Death of the Lord Hastings," in *Lachrymae Musarum: The Tears of the Muses: Exprest in Elegies; Written By divers persons of Nobility and Worth, Upon the death of the most hopefull, Henry Lord Hastings* (London: Printed by Thomas Newcomb, 1649);

"To his friend the Authour on his divine Epigrams," in *Sion and Parnassus*, by John Hoddesdon (London: Printed by R. Daniel for G. Eversden, 1650);

"Heroique Stanzas, Consecrated to the Glorious Memory of his most Serene and renowned Highnesse Oliver Late Lord Protector of this Common-Wealth, &c.," in *Three poems Upon the Death of his late Highnesse Oliver Lord Protector of England, Scotland & Ireland* (London: Printed by William Wilson, 1659);

"To My Honored Friend, Sr Robert Howard, On his Excellent Poems," in *Poems*, by Sir Robert Howard (London: Printed for Henry Herringman, 1660);

"To My Honour'd Friend, Dr Charleton," in *Chorea Gigantum, or The most Famous Antiquity of Great-Britain, Vulgarly called Stone-Heng, Standing on Salisbury Plain, Restored to the Danes*, by Walter Charleton (London: Printed for Henry Herringman, 1663 [i.e., 1662]);

The Indian-Queen, by Dryden and Howard, in *Four New Plays*, by Howard (London: Printed for H. Herringman, 1665);

Ovid's Epistles, Translated by Several Hands, includes a preface, and translations of three epistles, by Dryden (London: Printed for Jacob Tonson, 1680);

Nahum Tate, *The Second Part of Absalom and Achitophel*, includes contributions by Dryden (London: Printed for Jacob Tonson, 1682);

"The Life of Plutarch," in volume 1 of *Plutarchs Lives, Translated from the Greek by Several Hands*, 5 volumes (London: Printed for Jacob Tonson, 1683-1686);

Miscellany Poems, includes the authorized version of *Mac Flecknoe* and twenty-five other contributions by Dryden (London: Printed for Jacob Tonson, 1684);

Louis Maimbourg, *The History of the League*, translated by Dryden (London: Printed by M. Flesher for Jacob Tonson, 1684);

"To the Memory of Mr. Oldham," in *The Remains of Mr. John Oldham in Verse and Prose* (London: Printed for Jo. Hindmarsh, 1684);

Sylvae; or, the Second Part of Poetical Miscellanies, includes a preface and seventeen contributions by Dryden (London: Printed for Jacob Tonson, 1685);

"To the Pious Memory Of the Accomplisht Young Lady Mrs Anne Killigrew, Excellent in the two Sister-Arts of Poësie, and Painting. An Ode," in *Poems By Mrs. Anne Killigrew* (London: Printed for Samuel Lowndes, 1686 [i.e., 1685]);

Dominique Bouhours, *The Life of St. Francis Xavier, of the Society of Jesus*, translated by Dryden (London: Printed for Jacob Tonson, 1688);

The Satires of Decimus Junius Juvenalis Translated into English Verse. By Mr. Dryden, and Several other Eminent Hands. Together with the Satires of Aulus Persius Flaccus Made English by Mr. Dryden . . . To which is Prefix'd a Discourse concerning the Original and Progress of Satire (London: Printed for Jacob Tonson, 1693 [i.e., 1692]);

Examen Poeticum: Being the Third Part of Miscellany Poems, includes fifteen contributions by Dryden (London: Printed by R. E. for Jacob Tonson, 1693);

"A Character of Polybius and His Writings," in *The History of Polybius the Megalopolitan*, translated by Sir Henry Sheeres (London: Printed for S. Briscoe, 1693);

"To my Dear Friend Mr. Congreve, On His Comedy, call'd, The Double-Dealer," in *The Double-Dealer*, by William Congreve (London: Printed for J. Tonson, 1694);

"To Sir Godfrey Kneller," in *The Annual Miscellany: for the Year 1694. Being the Fourth Part of Miscellany Poems* (London: Printed by R. E. for Jacob Tonson, 1694);

Charles Alphonse du Fresnoy, *De Arte Graphica*, Latin text, with prose translation and "A Parallel of Poetry and Painting" by Dryden (London: Printed by J. Heptinstall for W. Rogers, 1695);

The Works of Virgil: Containing His Pastorals, Georgics, and Æneis, translated by Dryden (London: Printed for Jacob Tonson, 1697);

Fables Ancient and Modern; Translated into Verse, from Homer, Ovid, Boccace, & Chaucer; with Original Poems, translated by Dryden (London: Printed for Jacob Tonson, 1700);

"A Dialogue and Secular Masque," in *The Pilgrim*, by John Fletcher, revised by John Vanbrugh (London: Printed for Benjamin Tooke, 1700);

"The Life of Lucian," in volume 1 of *The Works of Lucian, Translated from the Greek by Several Eminent Hands*, 4 volumes (London: Printed for S. Briscoe, 1711);

[Heads of an Answer to Rymer], in volume 1 of *The Works of Mr Francis Beaumont and Mr John Fletcher*, 7 volumes (London: Printed for J. Tonson, 1711).

After John Donne and John Milton, John Dryden was the greatest English poet of the seventeenth century. After William Shakespeare and Ben Jonson, he was the greatest playwright. And he has no peer as a writer of prose, especially literary criticism, and as a translator. Other figures, such as George Herbert or Andrew Marvell or William Wycherley or William Congreve, may figure more prominently in anthologies and literary histories, but Dryden's sustained output in both poetry and drama ranks him higher. After Shakespeare, he wrote the greatest heroic play of the century, *The Conquest of Granada*, (1670-1671), and the greatest tragicomedy, *Marriage A-la-Mode* (1671). He wrote the greatest tragedy of the Restoration, *All for Love* (1677), and one of the greatest comedies, *Amphitryon* (1690). As a writer of prose he developed a lucid professional style, relying essentially on patterns and rhythms of everyday speech. As a critic he developed a combination of methods—historical, analytical, evaluative, dialogic—that proved enabling to neoclassical theory. As a translator he developed an easy manner of what he called paraphrase that produced brilliant versions of Homer, Lucretius, Horace, Ovid, Juvenal, Persius, Giovanni Boccaccio, Geoffrey Chaucer, and above all Virgil. His translation of *The Aeneid* remains the best ever produced in English. As a poet he perfected the heroic couplet, sprinkling it with judicious enjambments, triplets, and metric variations, and bequeathing it to Alexander Pope to work upon it his own magic.

Dryden the poet is best known today as a satirist, although he wrote only two great original satires, *Mac Flecknoe* (1682) and *The Medall* (1682). His most famous poem, *Absalom and Achitophel* (1681), while it contains several brilliant satirical portraits, unlike satire comes to a final resolution, albeit tragic for both David and his son. Dryden's other great poems—*Annus Mirabilis* (1667), *Religio Laici* (1682), *The Hind and the Panther* (1687), and *Alexander's Feast* (1697)—are not satires either. And he contributed a wonderful body of occasional poems: panegyrics, odes, elegies, prologues, and epilogues.

Dryden was born 9 August 1631 into an extended family of rising Puritan gentry in Northamptonshire. But as a teenager he was sent to the King's School at Westminster to be trained as a King's Scholar by the brilliant Royalist headmaster, Richard Busby. Dryden's family sided with the Commonwealth; however, in his first published poem, the elegy "Upon the Death of the Lord Hastings"—included in a commendatory volume (1649) of verses upon this young aristocrat's untimely death from smallpox—Dryden revealed Royalist sympathies in oblique references to rebellion and regicide. In a bold opening for a young (Puritan) poet—and such bold openings were to become characteristic—Dryden hurls a series of theodicean questions about why the good die young. In the middle of the poem he proffers the only answer the poem yields: "The Nations sin." He seems indirectly to identify this sin when

subsequently describing the pustules of Hastings's smallpox: "Who, Rebel-like, with their own Lord at strife, / Thus made an Insurrection 'gainst his Life." What would perhaps have been worse to Dryden's family is his patent refusal to add religious consolation at the end of the elegy. Instead, he suffocates his continuing theodicean challenge—could Heaven choose "no milder way" than the smallpox to recall Hastings?—by the tears of grief instead of the prayers of faith and outrageously suggests that Hastings's disappointed fiancée mate with his soul and engender ideal representations of him. The brash youngster may have been suggesting that she patronize such poets as himself and such ideal "Irradiations" as the current poem.

Aside from two other minor juvenilia (one in a private letter)—and perhaps because of family pressure—Dryden did not go public again until he had left Cambridge, where he was an undergraduate at Trinity College, and had been in the employ of Cromwell's government, probably in the Office of Latin Secretary along with Milton and Marvell. This is perhaps the first evidence of Dryden's trimming his sails to the political winds, as centuries of critics have accused him. His cousin, the prominent Puritan Sir Gilbert Pickering, lord chamberlain to Cromwell, probably procured employment for Dryden, and when the Protector died, Dryden, perhaps out of a sense of duty either internally or externally imposed, published his "Heroique Stanzas, Consecreated to the Glorious Memory . . ." of Cromwell in a commendatory volume (1659). People—especially young people—change their opinions all the time, so we should feel no complusion to make Dryden consistent. But this poem is filled with so many perplexing ambiguities, as especially Steven N. Zwicker has noted, that no coherent republican ideology emerges from it. Dryden skates on perilous ice by outrageously employing in the opening stanzas the metaphor of "treason" to refer to his "best notes": he seems to mean that however good his praise, it cannot properly measure Cromwell's "fame," yet "duty" and "interest" both dictate that he offer such praise as he "can."

Not only does he stumble awkwardly through these early stanzas, Dryden goes on to talk of Cromwell's *"Grandeur"* as if it seemed greater than it really was; to call attention to Cromwell's ambivalence toward being crowned (especially the ambiguity of Cromwell's "Vertue" not being "poyson'd" with *"too early* thoughts of being King"—emphasis added); to a potentially embarrassing implicit reminder of Charles I as one of those "rash *Monarch's* who their youth betray / By Acts their Age too late would wish undone"—surely no cause for beheading. Even when his praise for Cromwell seems unambiguous as he relates Cromwell's series of victories, Dryden raises the general problem of infidelity when he accuses "Treacherous *Scotland*" of being "to no int'rest true." In the light of these and other inappropriate tropes, readers might well have sensed that Dryden's seeming praise of Cromwell's putting an end to the bloodshed "by breathing of the vein" was a grotesque reference to the regicide. But if so, perhaps what Dryden has done is subtly to undercut his apparent praise and therefore to dissociate himself from the mourners. Perhaps his final references to Tarpeia, the traitorous virgin, and to the beached Leviathan leave us with the image of a prodigious monster, who performed great feats, some of them for the good of the empire, but who nonetheless was something of a scourge of God. (Dryden would implicitly portray Cromwell as such in *Annus Mirabilis*). That might make sense of Dryden's strange last stanza:

> His Ashes in a peacefull Urne shall rest,
> His Name a great example stands to show
> How strangely high endeavours may be blest,
> Where *Piety* and *valour* joyntly goe.

The praise sounds unexceptionable, were it not for the troubling adverb "strangely." Maybe at this point we are to reflect back over the poem and wonder at the strangeness of a valor that commits treason and regicide in the name of piety. Are we to remember another "great example" in Western story, another conqueror who pretended to refuse the crown he lusted after, only to be taken off on the verge of it in strangely poetical justice?

If in "Heroique Stanzas" Dryden's ambivalence is expressed in the halting use of the quatrain made fashionable in Sir William Davenant's *Gondibert* (1651), the assuredness of his heroic couplets in *Astraea Redux* (1660), his poem celebrating Charles Stuart's restoration, may perhaps indicate Dryden's comfort with a feudal monarchist rather than a bourgeois republican ideological myth. Moreover, the first twenty-eight lines of *Astraea Redux* can be read as seven quatrains made up of couplets rather than alternating

rhymes—as if to show Dryden could write sophisticated quatrains his own way:

> We sigh'd to hear the fair *Iberian* Bride
> Must grow a Lilie to the Lilies side,
> While Our cross Stars deny'd us *Charles*
>   his Bed
> Whom Our first Flames and Virgin Love did wed.
> For his long absence Church and State did groan;
> Madness the Pulpit, Faction seiz'd the Throne:
> Experienc'd Age in deep despair was lost
> To see the Rebel thrive, the Loyal crost.

The special effects here are manifold: the delightful internal rhyme ("sigh'd . . . Bride"); the image of lily yielding to lily (a play on the Spanish infanta's whiteness and purity being allied to the French fleur-de-lis as metonymy for Louis XIV) subtly underwritten by the collapse of the intervening iamb; the spondees of the last two lines of the first quatrain (the second reinforced by alliteration) underscoring the portrayal of England and Charles as star-crossed lovers; the substitution of initial trochee for iamb to emphasize the irrationality of the "Madness" that has taken over the Puritan "Pulpit"; the assonance that unites and thus equates both "Madness" in the "Church" and "Faction" in the "State"; the enjambment of the last couplet coming to rest in the final caesura, underlining by the rush toward the "Rebel" and the isolation of the "Loyal" the theodicean problem of evil's thriving while the good are star-"crost." Moreover, these images of the monarch as lover and his land as either loyal or disloyal spouse are integral to Dryden's ideological myth throughout the rest of his career. Central to this myth is the ultimate theodicean problem/solution: if power is the essence of government, then God himself can be stormed and "violated"; that is, there is no metaphysical guarantee to enforce the bonds of fidelity between leaders and people. For Dryden, normally absent Astraea (Justice) does return. In this poem "Providence" rules not by sheer power but by law and thus ensures that Charles's "right" is ultimately upheld, that he cannot be "Gods Anointed" in vain.

In many ways *Astraea Redux* anticipates foundational tropes in Dryden's later, greater political poems: the iron law of oligarchy that belies rebellion's rhetoric; the analogy between King Charles and King David; the analogy between the Puritans' Solemn League and Covenant in Charles's England and the Catholics' Holy League in Henri IV's France; the hypocrisy of glozing the "sin" of rebellion with the name of "Religion";

Dryden's brother-in-law and collaborator on The Indian-Queen. *This engraving by R. White is based on a portrait by Sir Godfrey Kneller and was published as the frontispiece to Howard's* Five New Plays *(1692).*

the counseling of mercy over justice; and finally, exhortation of the king to concentrate on England's navy and its trade. What little positive Dryden saw in Cromwell—his contribution to British imperialism—can now be extended exponentially:

> Our Nation with united Int'rest blest
> Not now content to poize, shall sway the rest.
> Abroad your Empire shall no Limits know,
> But like the Sea in boundless Circles flow.

Dryden identifies civilization itself, as opposed to a primitive "lawless salvage Libertie," with the "Arts" of "Empire" from Rome to contemporary England, an empire that is at once patriarchal, hierarchal, monarchal, and commercial.

In between the poems celebrating Cromwell and Charles, Dryden appears to have moved toward his career as a professional writer, his deceased father not having left him a sufficient income to survive where Dryden wanted to live—in the hub of political and cultural activity, London. In the late 1650s he seems to have lived with and written prefaces for the bookseller Henry Herringman, and by the early 1660s he had moved into lodgings with Sir Robert Howard, a younger son of Thomas Howard, first Earl of Berkshire, with impeccable Royalist credentials and a budding literary career. In a system of symbiosis between patrons and poets, Dryden had found himself a patron, and Howard had found himself an editor and collaborator. Dryden helped prepare Howard's first volume of poems for the press in 1660, for which he wrote the first of many panegyrics to prominent individuals, "To My Honored Friend, Sir Robert Howard," and in 1664 they collaborated on *The Indian-Queen*, a drama that contributed significantly to the Restoration fashion of rhymed heroic play (influenced, among other things, by those the exiled court witnessed in France) and that introduced what was to be the staple of Dryden's later contributions, the *noble savage*, whose powerful energy is eventually socialized.

Dryden's relationship with Howard is important in other ways: Dryden married his sister Lady Elizabeth Howard in 1663. Why a member of so prestigious a family would have stooped to a member of the lesser gentry remains a subject for speculation. But the match was certainly advantageous for Dryden, who was now a member of the powerful Howard family, several members of which aside from Sir Robert were playwrights. Along with his brothers-in-law Dryden tried his hand at his own plays. His first, a comedy entitled *The Wild Gallant* (1663), despite being a failure, won the support of another influential aristocrat, Barbara Villiers Palmer, Countess of Castelmaine, to whom Dryden addressed another verse epistle. Indeed, with such encouragement, abetted by his collaboration with Sir Robert (who had become a shareholder in the new Theatre Royal in Bridges Street), Dryden became a stable writer for the King's Company under Sir Thomas Killigrew and began to succeed on his own with his first tragicomedy, *The Rival Ladies* (late 1663?), and with a sequel to *The Indian-Queen*, *The Indian Emperour* (early 1665).

Dryden wrote three other panegyrics during the early 1660s: *To His Sacred Majesty, A*

Panegyrick On His Coronation (1661), *To My Lord Chancellor* (1662), and "To My Honour'd Friend, Dr Charleton" (1663). In them he perfected the witty compliment begun with the poem to Sir Robert. But he also perfected the device of giving advice under cover of compliment, for example reminding the rakish Charles in the Coronation poem that political stability depends on his choosing a bride with all deliberate speed in order to ensure the succession. And the Charleton poem reflects Dryden's interest in the new science, an interest rewarded by invitation in the early 1660s to become a member of the Royal Academy of Science, although he appears not to have participated and was subsequently dropped.

In 1665 the plague was so bad in London that Dryden had to rusticate himself and his wife at her family estate in Charlton, Wiltshire. There he wrote three excellent works: *Of Dramatick Poesie: An Essay* (1668), the first great sustained work in English dramatic theory; *Secret-Love, or The Maiden-Queen* (1668), the tragicomedy that perfected the gay couple motif, complete with proviso scene; and *Annus Mirabilis: The Year of Wonders, 1666* (1667). This "Historical Poem" celebrating English victories at sea during the Second Dutch War and Charles II's conduct during the Great Fire of London won Dryden the poet laureateship in 1668.

Because it was published in 1667, Dryden's heroic poem invites comparison with Milton's great epic *Paradise Lost*, first published in its ten-book format that same year. Ironically, Milton's epic—written by this radical Puritan secretary to Cromwell—despite its bourgeois elements of antimonarchism, emphasis on the individual and the domestic, and celebration of the *paradise within* of the private religious sphere, looks back through its aristocratic mode to classical and medieval times. Dryden's poem, despite its aristocratic elements of monarchism and heroic valor, its classical allusions and epic similes, looks forward through its bourgeois celebration of mercantile expansion, maritime dominance, and homely imagery of laboring citizens to the rule of a capitalist Britannia under a constitutional monarch.

Michael McKeon has brilliantly demonstrated that the poem is essentially political propaganda designed to stifle domestic dissent by rallying the nation around the commmon causes of war abroad and disaster at home. Dryden mythologizes Charles II, his brother James II, and the triumphant admirals and generals as classical and Christian heroes and even gods. The care of the king is portrayed as being analogous to divine providence. The Great Fire of London (1666) is portrayed as a scourge for no particular sins (such as Charles's promiscuity, as his enemies would have it) but for the general sins of the nation and indeed humankind. And the fire's final extinction, having burned temples but not palaces, is portrayed as the result of Jove's melting with ruth upon hearing Charles's humble, pious prayer. This mythologizing seems deployed especially to defuse opposition to Charles and thereby to avert the potential unraveling of the Restoration compromise. Thus Charles is portrayed as the bride of his loyal country, or even more explicitly, of the loyal City of London, and Dryden—from his Dedication to the City through his portrayal of the restored ship *Loyal London* to the restoration of the City itself as a "Maiden Queen" of commerce—exhorts almost desperately a fidelity on the part of the emergent bourgeoisie.

Underneath the mythologizing, Dryden is attempting to placate the growing power of the City as the center of trade and finance by getting it to view the *real* challenge for England as the battle over who controls world trade. Only one nation, one navy can and should control it ("What peace can be where both to one pretend?"). Therefore, the logic of the poem goes, Britain should defeat Holland, eclipse the trade of the rest of Europe, and make the world's waters a "British Ocean." Thus British "Commerce" will make "one City of the Universe." But this universal city will not mark the end of competition in some sort of utopian distribution of the cornucopia. Dryden's model is one of acquisitive crypto-capitalism: "some may gain, and all may be suppli'd." Then as now such a trickle-down theory results in the "some" gaining a disproportionate amount of the world's wealth at the expense and exploitation of the many. Behind Dryden's cornucopia lies an imperialist theory of dominance.

Nevertheless, at his very best Dryden the mythologizer of late feudalism and incipient capitalism descends occasionally from his highly allusive and allegorical mode to portray real people in material situations. Witness the momentary descent in these stanzas:

Night came, but without darkness or repose,
    A dismal picture of the gen'ral doom:

> Where Souls distracted when the Trumpet blows,
>   And half unready with their bodies come.
>
> Those who have homes, when home they do repair
>   To a last lodging call their wand'ring friends.
> Their short uneasie sleeps are broke with care,
>   To look how near their own destruction tends.
>
> Those who have none sit round where once it was,
>   And with full eyes each wonted room require:
> Haunting the yet warm ashes of the place,
>   As murder'd men walk where they did expire.

The opening allegorical yet human image is worthy of Donne. For anyone who has lived through fire, hurricane, tornado, or (in our century) saturation or nuclear bombing, the stanzas painting the near or already homeless are quite poignant. And Dryden's maturity as a poet is evidenced here by his masterful handling of not only image but sound: the reversed iambs and spondees, the frequent alliteration and occasional assonance ("Souls ... blows"), and especially the freeze-frame quality of successive emphasized syllables imitating the eyes' movement from room to room around the absent house.

Dryden also insightfully imagines the contrasting dreams of the English and Dutch sailors during an evening's respite from the battle. But he dares most by his inclusion, in these new heroic stanzas, of indecorously technical and vulgar terms for material work by the laboring force of shipbuilders called upon to repair the British fleet, from picking "bullets" out of planks, to caulking seams with "Okum" and "boiling Pitch," to binding "gall'd ropes" with "dawby Marling," to re-covering masts "with strong Tarpawling coats." Dryden is no democrat; he has no love here as elsewhere in his poetry for "th'ignoble crowd," and he hints at the anarchy unleashed by republican rebels. However, in his image of these industrious laborers demonstrating their loyalty and contributing to the cause, he raises them to the stature of the heroic. However he mythologizes James, then Duke of York, and Prince Rupert and George Monck, Duke of Albemarle, and King Charles himself, the reader experiences the following realistic snapshots within the same poem: Albemarle, his breeches ignominiously blown off, as Dryden's audience would know, "All bare, like some old Oak which tempests beat, / He stands, and sees below his scatter'd leaves"; and while the King harmlessly amuses himself playing with the "new-cast Canons," among the shipworkers "To try new shrouds one mounts into the wind, / And one, below, their

ease or stifness notes." By diminishing heroes and exalting workers Dryden has at least leveled them into a common humanity, united in a bourgeois image of cooperation between government, venture capital, and guild labor in order to subdue the earth.

Dryden's return to London in the winter of 1666-1667 was triumphant. Several of his plays were staged, old (*The Wild Gallant* and *The Indian Emperour*) and new (not just *Secret Love* [1667] but *Sir Martin Mar-All* [1667] and an adaptation of Shakespeare's *The Tempest*, plays he collaborated on with William Cavendish, Duke of Newcastle, and Sir William Davenant, respectively, and which were performed by the rival Duke's Company); the *Essay* was published; the King's Company signed Dryden to a contract in which he became a shareholder and agreed to give them three new plays per year; and he received the laureateship—all before the end of 1668. By the end of 1671 he had produced four more plays, including two masterpieces, *The Conquest of Granada* (1670), a rhymed heroic play in ten acts, and *Marriage A-la-Mode*, a split-plot tragicomedy. Dryden had established himself as the greatest dramatist of his time. And if one can separate out his development as a poet per se—a difficult task when his plays have so much verse, so many songs, and prologues and epilogues in couplets—one would have to conclude that, despite the absence during these years of isolated poems, Dryden achieved a virtuosity of verse and wit unequaled during the Restoration. Palmyra's description of her falling in love with Leonidas in *Marriage A-la-Mode* is lovelily lyrical. The prologue to *An Evening's Love* (1668) concerning poets as worn-out gallants and the songs concerning wet dreams and worn-out marriage vows from *The Conquest of Granada* and *Marriage A-la-Mode* respectively are wickedly witty and wonderfully versified. But Dryden's masterpiece is probably his puckish epilogue to *Tyrannic Love* (1669), spoken by Nell Gwyn, outrageously rakish actress and mistress to Charles II (among others). Having played Valeria, daughter of the Roman emperor Maximin who martyrs St. Catharine, and having herself been a martyr to love, Nell is about to be carried off at the end of the play, when she leaps up—most certainly to the audience's delight in such comic relief—and speaks the epilogue in couplets that rival Alexander Pope's for their colloquial and dramatically conversational style:

> To the Bearer. *Hold, are you mad? you damn'd*
>   *confounded Dog,*

I am to rise, and speak the Epilogue.
To the Audience. *I come, kind Gentlemen, strange news to*
  tell ye,
I am the Ghost of poor departed Nelly. . . .
O Poet, damn'd dull Poet, who could prove
So senselesss! to make Nelly *die for Love;*
Nay, what's yet worse, to kill me in the prime
Of Easter-Term, *in Tart and Cheese-cake time!*
I'le fit the Fopp; for I'le not one word say
T'excuse his godly out-of-fashion Play:
A Play which if you dare but twice sit out,
You'l all be slander'd, and be thought devout.
But farewel, Gentlemen, make haste to me,
I'm sure e're long to have your company.
As for my Epitaph when I am gone,
I'le trust no Poet, but will write my own,

Here *Nelly* lies, who, though she liv'd a
    Slater'n,
Yet dy'd a Princess, acting in S.
    Cathar'n.

The laughter must have brought down the house. Yet twentieth-century critics do not seem to understand that such wit does not *undercut* (their favorite metaphor) the seriousness of such plays as *Tyrannic Love, The Conquest of Granada,* and *Marriage A-la-Mode.* Urbanity does not mean a supercilious, ironic rejection of all values but rather a witty reflexivity and studied insouciance about them.

By 1672, then, Dryden was at the height of his powers and reputation. He had added to the title poet laureate that of historiographer royal. He hobnobbed with the powerful and, despite his increasing family (by then, three sons), appears to have aped the manners of his betters by fashionably taking a mistress, the actress Ann Reeves. But the first hints of the tarnishing of his triumph had also appeared: his feud with his brother-in-law Sir Robert over the aesthetic merit of rhyme in drama escalated through Dryden's *Essay* to Howard's preface to *The Great Favourite; or, The Duke of Lerma* (1668) to Dryden's extremely intemperate "Defence" of the *Essay,* prefixed to the second edition of *The Indian Emperour* in the same year. Because this preface was removed from most copies of this edition, one can speculate that Dryden realized his error in judgment, but his relationship with his brother-in-law may have been permanently damaged. A few years later, perhaps out of pique at Dryden's pride in his success, George Villiers, second Duke of Buckingham, attacked Dryden as a poetaster

in *The Rehearsal* (1671). The era of Dryden's public brawls with his critics had begun.

Things got worse when fire destroyed Dryden's company's theater at the inopportune time of the rival company's moving into an extravagant new theater in Dorset Garden. Furthermore, the Duke's Company was beginning to have the best actors as Thomas Betterton gathered great young talent around him, and it was beginning to attract new and successful playwrights: Thomas Shadwell, Edward Ravenscroft, and Elkanah Settle. Dryden's own new comedy, *The Assignation* (1672), failed, and even his jingoistic propaganda attack against the Dutch during the outbreak of the Third Dutch War, *Amboyna* (1673), did not salvage the fortunes of the King's Company. When their new theater in Drury Lane opened in 1674, Dryden, in an attempt to rival the extravaganzas of the Duke's Company, tried to turn his great admiration for Milton's *Paradise Lost* to account by creating an operatic version, *The State of Innocence.* He appears even to have gone so far as to visit the aged and blind poet, with whom he had once worked, in order to ask his permission. From all his references to Milton's great poems throughout his works, beginning perhaps as early as 1669, one can infer in what respect Dryden held Milton, but unfortunately nothing is known of this meeting. Even more unfortunately, for Dryden and the King's Company at least, the company could not afford to produce the opera, and it was never performed. At this nadir of his career, Dryden sought an appointment at Oxford where he could retire from the stage and write his own epic poem. Neither desideratum was ever to be realized.

Whether caused by Milton's great aesthetic achievements and his attack on rhymed plays, or by Settle's embarrassingly bathetic popular successes in Dryden's erstwhile favorite genre of rhymed heroic play or just by Dryden's own study (perhaps of plays by the great French dramatist Jean Racine), Dryden began his comeback by moving toward a more neoclassical form of drama. In *Notes and Observations on the Empress of Morocco* (1674), he joined in an attack on Settle's extravagance. In 1675, although he gave the King's Company another excellent rhymed heroic play, *Aureng-Zebe,* in the prologue he bade farewell to his "long-lov'd Mistris, Rhyme" (and probably his other mistress, Ann Reeves, as well) as he began to imitate Racine. His next three serious plays were blank-verse neoclassical tragedies, and

one—*All for Love* (1677)—was the greatest tragedy of the Restoration; indeed, it remains the
greatest tragedy in English after Shakespeare,
and it is still performed in England. His theory
of the late 1670s ("Heads of an Answer to
Rymer," "The Grounds of Criticism in Tragedy"), influenced by Thomas Rymer and the
French critics, as well as by Racine, became more
neoclassical. And he turned his attention to the
translation of classics. In his dramatic compositions he was also influenced by the initial successes of two new playwrights, Thomas Otway
and Nathaniel Lee. Dryden entered into a temporary rivalry with Otway, who wrote for the
Duke's Company. Dryden entered into a friendship with Lee, who wrote for the King's, that produced mutual praise (commendatory poems
addressed to each other prefixed to Dryden's *The
State of Innocence and Fall of Man* and Lee's *The
Rival Queens*, both published in 1677) and mutual
work (by 1678 they had both abandoned the
King's Company and moved to the Duke's, for
whom they wrote *Oedipus* in 1678 and *The Duke
of Guise* in 1682). Dryden's severing of ties with
the King's Company had begun as early as 1677,
when he insisted on the third night's profits from
All for Love. It continued with the Duke's
Company's production of *The Kind Keeper* in
1678 (apparently because the King's did not want
it).

In the meantime, however, before Dryden
made the transition from King's to Duke's, from
romance to neoclassical tragedy, from depression
to renewed vigor as dramatist, he had some
scores to settle. When his fortunes were sinking,
he had appealed to John Wilmot, Earl of Rochester, to patronize him, but after some initial flirtation, Rochester proved inconstant, supported
Dryden's rival Thomas Shadwell instead, and lam-
pooned Dryden in "An Allusion to Horace."
Dryden had been feuding with Shadwell over the
theory of comedy for years in various prefaces
and dedications, but the two had remained relatively conciliatory and had collaborated with
John Crowne in the attack on Settle. In early
1676, however, the same year as Rochester's satire was circulating in manuscript, Shadwell broke
the facade of civility and degenerated into lampoon. He pilloried Dryden throughout his comedy *The Virtuoso*, especially in the dedication to
the published text.

Dryden responded with a vengeance probably doubled by displaced anger at Rochester and
compounded by his own poor fortunes, both lit-

eral and figurative, in the first half of the decade. Beginning most likely in the summer of
1676, Dryden wrote one of the two greatest satires in English against rival poets, *Mac Flecknoe* (the other is Pope's *Dunciad*, 1728-1729). He
certainly had finished it by 1678, though it circulated in manuscript until unauthorized publication in 1682. The controlling fiction of the poem
is succession, a daring motif in a country where
the restored monarch had produced no legitimate male heir. Witness the brashness of the opening lines:

> All humane things are subject to decay,
> And, when Fate summons, Monarchs must obey[.]

The phenomenology of the first reading dictates
that the reader's expectations for a heavy, topical
political poem have been aroused. The next couplet provides a crashing diminuendo:

> This *Fleckno* found, who, like *Augustus*, young
> Was call'd to Empire, and had govern'd long.

The poem is a mock panegyric, a paradoxical encomium, complete with parodic procession and
coronation. Dryden the poet laureate destroys his
rival by crowning him anti-poet laureate, king of
"the Realms of *Non-sense*": "from *Ireland* let him
reign / To farr *Barbadoes* on the Western main"—
that is, he reigns over the unpopulated Atlantic
Ocean! By making Richard Flecknoe his poetic
forebear, Dryden denies Shadwell the lineage he
has claimed, to be a new Son of Ben (Jonson) because of his dedication to a comedy of humors. Instead, Flecknoe was a poetaster who paid to have
his plays published, who sometimes changed a
title and added a little window dressing to get
one produced (*Erminia* [1661] to *Emilia* [1672]),
whose plays, whether produced or not were uniformly bad. Yet Flecknoe may also have earned
Dryden's professional envy by having the courage to appeal to Cromwell to reopen the stage in
the dedication to *Love's Dominion* (1654) and by trying his own hand at a history of the English stage
in the preface to that play's revision as *Love's Kingdom* (1664). To make Shadwell Flecknoe's heir
was to put down another upstart, especially by portraying him as impotent, capable of producing
urine and feces and freaks but no legitimate,
manly poetic progeny.

Throughout the poem Dryden combines references to dirt with references to myth. The latter does not "transcend" the former (another
favorite metaphor of critics) but coexists with it,

John Dryden, circa 1683 (portrait by John Riley; from David Piper, The Development of the British Literary Portrait up to Samuel Johnson, *1968)*

cocreates the joke, which is intended to amuse Dryden's friends, antagonize his enemies, and hurt Shadwell himself—as if Dryden were saying, "Don't touch me!" Dryden's technique perhaps can be best illustrated by the following lines:

> The hoary Prince in Majesty appear'd,
> High on a Throne of his own Labours rear'd.

The second line echoes Satan's ascent to his parodic throne in the opening of book 2 of Milton's *Paradise Lost*, and its metaphor of "Labours" alludes to the leitmotiv of labor in Virgil's *Aeneid*, upon which alone can a lasting empire be built. But "Labours" of course refers primarily to a pile of Flecknoe's worthless books. Yet by extension of the repeated references to "Sh——" in the poem—ostensibly *Shadwell* but implicitly *shit* every time, as in "loads of *Sh——* almost chokt the way"—"Labours" refers metaphorically to piles of material more than just books. Dryden

may be portraying Shadwell as an Antichrist of Wit (in anticipation of Pope), but he is also and at the same time debasing him through folk humor as being full of shit. Neither level of meaning supersedes the other.

Another instance of the technique occurs at the end. Playing off the controlling fiction of succession, Dryden's elaborate use of classical and Christian allusions throughout allows him to compare Shadwell to Ascanius, Iulus, Christ himself, or, in the closing lines, Elisha to Flecknoe's Elijah. Flecknoe's last lines of encomium are lost as he disappears through a trapdoor mischievously engineered by a couple of Shadwell's comic characters:

> Sinking he left his Drugget robe behind,
> Born upwards by a subterranean wind.
> The Mantle fell to the young Prophet's part,
> With double portion of his Father's Art.

The *f*, *P*, *p* pattern of the penultimate line begs to be repeated in a *p*, *F*, [*f*] pattern in the last, so that the "subterranean wind" (perhaps an allusion to Milton's wind off the backside of the world that blows hypocrites awry in book 3 of *Paradise Lost*) gets positively identified in the reader's mind sotto voce: this mock-Elisha inherits his mantle upward not downward from his *Father's fart*. Curiously, the Dryden who seems so preoccupied in his prologues and epilogues with establishing a bourgeois community of taste that contemns "low" artistic techniques and types such as slapstick and farce reveals himself to be the master of Rabelaisian humor. In the cruelest cut of all, he has Flecknoe say to Sh——, "With whate'er gall thou sett'st thy self to write, / Thy inoffensive Satyrs never bite." Dryden's satire has bitten so well that he has effectively decapitated Shadwell for three centuries, precisely because he has so masterfully combined high and low. Playing a mock-John the Baptist to Shadwell's mock-Messiah, Flecknoe prepares the way for a mock-Triumphal Entry into Jerusalem-London, where not palm leaves

> But scatter'd Limbs of mangled Poets lay:
> From dusty shops neglected Authors come,
> Martyrs of Pies, and Reliques of the Bum.

This mixing of sacred and scatological is positively medieval in its folk humor. Dryden can pretend that Shadwell has debased Jonson into selling "Bargains, Whip-stitch, kiss my Arse," but this last phrase is exactly what Dryden has commanded Sh—— to do.

After the success of *All for Love* and the growing chances for his security with the Duke's Company, Dryden must have felt emboldened enough to settle his other score by attacking Rochester himself in his preface to the published version of the new play in early 1678. While suggesting that Rochester specifically had bitten off more than he could chew in imitating Horace, that he ought to leave writing to professionals, that his own literary heritage descends from the poetaster translator of the Psalms, Thomas Sternhold, Dryden indicts not just Rochester but his "witty" comrades, such as Buckingham, Rymer, and Charles Sedley, but also his *zanies*, such as Shadwell and Otway. Squire Dryden asserts his talents as a literary professional to be superior to those of the court wits, who properly ought to confine their literary dabbling to being good patrons. Perhaps Dryden was feeling pro-

tected by his new patron, the dedicatee of *All for Love*, Lord Treasurer Thomas Osborne, Earl of Danby. Indeed, shortly after Danby's fall from power in 1679, Dryden was attacked by thugs in Rose Alley and beaten soundly. Did Rochester and his friends finally take their revenge? Or by that time had Dryden offended someone else (suggestions have included the King's mistress, Louise de Kéroualle, Duchess of Portsmouth, and the Whig Opposition)? The point of the beating is that Dryden was considered uppity enough for some group to want to teach him a lesson. But if they thought they would intimidate him, they were mistaken.

In 1678 occurred the infamous Popish Plot. Several witnesses, most notorious among them Titus Oates, offered perjured testimony to the effect that the Jesuits were planning the overthrow of the government and a return of England to the yoke of Catholicism—a threat that Englishmen, in the light of characters in their history since the time of Henry VIII, from Bloody Mary to Guy Fawkes, found credible. (Indeed, they were right to be suspicious, for the Stuarts had made an unholy alliance with France eventually to deliver their nation back into the Catholic fold.) Several Catholic heads rolled, Catholic peers were removed from the House of Lords; James II, then duke of York, and his new Catholic duchess, Maria Beatrice, had to go into exile; and a new Parliament was elected, one that was ready to pass legislation to exclude James from the throne because of his religion: thus the name given to this political turmoil, the Exclusion Crisis. Some of the principals tried to get Charles to declare his bastard son, James Scott, Duke of Monmouth, his legitimate heir. Several playwrights jumped on the anti-Catholic bandwagon as if to say, "we might disagree with the exclusionists, but we are not therefore in favor of a foreign-based Catholic takeover, ultimately by Rome through France." Dryden himself grabbed onto the wagon in his next play, *The Spanish Fryar* (1680), in which he satirizes a priest; nevertheless, in the high plot he strenuously upholds the principle of hereditary, patrilineal monarchal succession. He apparently (his authorship is disputed) even more stridently defended Charles's dissolution of Parliament in a pamphlet entitled *His Majesties Declaration Defended* (1681). And finally he wrote the greatest political poem in the English language, *Absalom and Achitophel* (1681).

Dryden's controlling fiction in this poem is the familiar trope of superimposing scriptural story over current events. He had already availed himself of the David story in *Astraea Redux*. The consequences for propaganda are obvious: Dryden endows his vision of events with sacred authority: the social and the sacred Logos are the same. Thus a theoretical dispute over the mode of political succession gets mythologized and mystified. Parliament's struggle to control succession becomes a blasphemous, ultimately Satanic revolt against "heavens Anointing Oyle." Absalom's sacrilegious revolt against David gets reenacted in contemporary history. The evil counselor Achitophel becomes Anthony Ashley Cooper, third Earl of Shaftesbury, one of the leaders of the Parliamentary party, who was caricatured repeatedly in ways reminiscent of Shakespeare's treatment of Richard III. Dryden adds the further fillip of overlaying Miltonic pattern: Achitophel/Shaftesbury becomes Satan tempting an anti-Messiah to be the people's "*Saviour*."

One of the problems with the biblical parallel is that its arc is tragic. It is as if Dryden wrote Monmouth into a text from which he could not escape. David threatens at the end, "If my Young *Samson* will pretend a Call / To shake the Column, let him share the Fall." David's urge, on the other hand, is to be lenient. But Monmouth never did heed the poet's advice; he led a revolt upon his father's death in 1685 and was executed. Moreover, as with the biblical David, Dryden's David/Charles is trammeled up in the consequences of his adultery. Dryden opens again brilliantly:

> In pious times, e'er Priest-craft did begin,
> Before *Polygamy* was made a sin;
> When man, on many, multiply'd his kind,
> E'r one to one was, cursedly, confin'd:
> When Nature prompted, and no law deny'd
> Promiscuous use of Concubine and Bride;
> Then, *Israel*'s Monarch, after Heaven's
>   own heart,
> His vigorous warmth did, variously, impart
> To Wives and Slaves: And, wide as his Command,
> Scatter'd his Maker's Image through the Land.

However wittily Dryden opens the poem, the ultimate point of its portrayal of David's promiscuity is that "No True Succession" can "attend" the "seed" of David's concubines. Another of Dryden's bold openings has cut to the heart of the matter. When Absalom and David both later complain that Absalom was born too high but not high enough, they may blame "Fate" or "God," but the fault is clearly David's own, as it

was in 2 Samuel when God punished David with Absalom's rebellion for David's adultery with Bathsheba and the murder of her husband, and as Dryden's pointed reference to Bathsheba would remind his audience.

However, the main point of Dryden's poem is neither to recuperate Monmouth nor admonish Charles. It is to thoroughly discredit Charles's enemies and their putative political theory, praise his steadfast friends, and vindicate Charles himself. The first objective Dryden accomplishes with perhaps the most devastating rogues' gallery of satiric portraits ever assembled. The portraits are not devastating solely because of vitriolic lampooning, though there is plenty of that. They are devastating because they at first appear evenhanded, a studied moderation designed to appeal to the common sense of Dryden's contemporary audience. After praising Achitophel/Shaftesbury for being an excellent judge, Dryden breaks out in calculated lamentation:

> Oh, had he been content to serve the Crown,
> With vertues only proper to the Gown; . . .
> *David*, for him his tunefull Harp had strung,
> And Heaven had wanted one Immortal song.

That is, David would not have had to write Psalm 109 attacking Achitophel. "But," Dryden continues with studied sadness:

> wilde Ambition loves to slide, not stand;
> And Fortunes Ice prefers to Vertues Land:
> *Achitophel*, grown weary to possess
> A lawfull Fame, and lazy Happiness;
> Disdain'd the Golden fruit to gather free,
> And lent the Croud his Arm to shake the Tree.
> Now, manifest of Crimes, contriv'd long since,
> He stood at bold Defiance with his Prince:
> Held up the Buckler of the Peoples Cause,
> Against the Crown; and sculk'd behind the Laws.

What could be more temperate, more measured than this cool judgment? After all, Shaftesbury's prince had been lenient with him, forgiven him for supporting Cromwell. Nevertheless, "Restless, unfixt in Principles and Place," Shaftesbury was not content to await the descending benefits of a merciful king but, because of ambition, preferred "Fortunes Ice." Thus Dryden avails himself not only of the posture of fair judgment but also the leitmotiv of inconstancy versus steadfastness. By his very nature or character, Shaftesbury cannot remain fixed; driven by desire, he "loves to slide, not stand." The implication, of course, is that "Fortunes Ice" is perilously thin, that Shaftesbury's use of Parliament and the law is a flimsy ruse.

Dryden's portrait of Absalom also appears balanced. He is like one of Dryden's noble savages. But the difference is that he does not turn out to be the legitimate heir, and he knows it, acknowledging David's "Right" to rule and that of his "Lawfull Issue," if he should have any, or of his "*Collateral* Line," that is, his brother. When through ambition fostered by his noble nature Monmouth succumbs to Achitophel's Satanic temptation, Dryden again assumes the strategy of lamentation:

> Unblam'd of Life (Ambition set aside,)
> Not stain'd with Cruelty, nor puft with Pride;
> How happy had he been, if Destiny
> Had higher plac'd his Birth, or not so high!
> His Kingly Vertues might have claim'd a Throne,
> And blest all other Countries but his own:
> But charming Greatness, since so few refuse;
> 'Tis Juster to Lament him, than Accuse.

The master stroke here is Dryden's sympathy toward Monmouth's ambiguous position in the hierarchy resulting from the circumstances of his birth (not his but Charles's fault) coupled with his insistence (as well as Charles's own) that nevertheless he remains illegitimate. Even if he were legitimate, Dryden implies, he would never be the heir (because he has shown by his character that he could never merit it?); he might have blessed other countries with his noble virtues (through royal intermarriage), but not—and never—his own.

Dryden also portrays the "Best" of the "Malecontents" assembled by Achitophel—that is, primarily, the Country party among the Lords—as being essentially well-meaning but "Seduc'd by Impious Arts" into believing the "power of Monarchy" a threat to "Property." Thus identifying with and appealing to the moderates in the House of Lords, Dryden does not want to seem to be maligning his betters. He saves his nastiness generally for the middle and lower classes, whom he portrays as motivated by "Interest," parsimonious "Husbandry," desire for "Preferment," or, under the hypocritical guise of (dissenting) religion, the sheer desire "all things to Destroy," especially monarchy itself. Dryden portrays the common "herd" as mindless, those "Who think too little, and who talk too much."

Dryden's next justly famous portraits are representatives of the three classes. From the truly rebellious aristocrats (implicitly a mere fringe group) he selects his old enemy Buckingham, whom he portrays as similar to Shaftesbury, too inconstant in his moods, postures, and political positions to remain constant to any one—or, by implication, to the king:

> Some of their Chiefs were Princes of the Land:
> In the first Rank of these did *Zimri* stand:
> A man so various, that he seem'd to be
> Not one, but all Mankinds Epitome.
> Stiff in Opinions, always in the wrong;
> Was every thing by starts, and nothing long:
> But, in the course of one revolving Moon,
> Was Chymist, Fidler, States-Man, and Buffoon:
> Then all for Women, Painting, Rhiming, Drinking;
> Besides ten thousand freaks that dy'd in thinking.

In the whole passage, but especially in the last two couplets, Dryden is at his absolute best at wielding the rhetoric of satire. The zeugma of the antepenultimate line is worthy of Pope's more famous lists, especially when one considers that "States-Man," potentially a pejorative term anyway, gets completely leveled to the status of the concluding "Buffoon." Then the jingle of the participles dances through the feminine ending of the penultimate line, pausing for a moment on the spondee in the middle of "Besides ten thousand freaks" before tripping into the final feminine ending, creating a contemporary mindless marionette.

Dryden's representative of the middle class is the hypocritical Puritan Shimei (Slingsby Bethel, sheriff of London), whose animosity against the office of king itself is so strong he fears not to curse "Heavens Annointed," and whose very religion is simply a means for his personal "Gain." As do modern satirists with televangelists, Dryden turns Shimei's canting rhetoric against him:

> For *Shimei*, though not prodigal of pelf,
> Yet lov'd his wicked Neighbour as himself:
> When two or three were gather'd to declaim
> Against the Monarch of *Jerusalem*,
> *Shimei* was always in the midst of them:
> And, if they Curst the King when he was by,
> Would rather Curse, than break good Company.

In a wonderful marriage of sound, sight, and sense, the middle triplet here inserts a third line into the usual couplet form as if in imitation of the insinuation of Antichrist Shimei into the midst of his disciples.

Dryden's representative of the lower class is Corah, who stands for Titus Oates, the weaver's

son who was the archwitness of the Popish Plot.
Dryden portrays him with dripping sarcasm:

> His Memory, miraculously great,
> Could Plots, exceeding mans belief, repeat;
> Which, therefore cannot be accounted Lies,
> For humane Wit could never such devise.

If Shimei perverts the words of Scripture for his
interest, Corah perverts words in the very citadel
of justice, where oaths are supposed to guarantee
the truth. Indeed, all of Dryden's villains assault
the social logos through disloyalty, hypocrisy, and
perjury, thus challenging the underwriting divine
Logos.

In addition to discrediting his opponents
thus, Dryden discredits their political theory.
Achitophel's articulation of Lockean theory—"the
People have a Right Supreme / To make their
Kings; for Kings are made for them. / All Empire is no more than Pow'r in Trust"—is belied
by his own ambition for power. But Dryden appears to take his theory seriously and to approach the question moderately. Rejecting the
position of absolute monarchy, Dryden equally rejects the position of social-contract theorists who
argue that the people can take their bond back, a
secession resulting, for Dryden, in Hobbist political instability:

> If they may Give and Take when e'r they please,
> Not Kings alone, (the Godheads Images,)
> But Government it self at length must fall
> To Natures state; where all have Right to all.

Purloining Locke's own concept of prudence,
Dryden then asks in his most conciliatory mode,
"Yet, grant our Lords the People Kings can
make, / What Prudent men a setled Throne
woud shake?" While Dryden appears to be adopting a Burkean conservatism based on the weight
of tradition—as is obvious from all the references
to God's involvement in anointing and supporting kings throughout the poem—the grammatical uncertainty of the first line images forth the
political anarchy that would ensue if anyone but
God—lords, commoners, kings themselves, by
tampering with succession—were to make a king.
Dryden then proceeds to portray the king's
friends as a loyal group of peers, bishops, judges,
and even the former speaker of the (now rebellious) House of Commons. Unlike the conspirators, these men kept their words of loyalty and,
like Dryden the poet, used their words to defend
the king and to rebut his attackers—most nota-

bly, perhaps, Jotham, who represents George
Savile, Marquis of Halifax, whose golden tongue
in debate turned the tide against the Exclusion
Bill in the House of Lords.

The greatest wielder of words in the poem
is David himself, who comes forward finally to vindicate his power and position. Weary of abuse despite his wonted clemency and long-suffering,
David insists that even if he has only a part of government, the part belongs to him, cannot be atten-
uated by any other part, and is "to Rule."
Dryden endows his speech with magisterial authority:

> Without my Leave a future King to choose,
> Infers a Right the Present to Depose:
> True, they Petition me t'approve their Choise,
> But *Esau*'s Hands suite ill with *Jacob*'s Voice.

David becomes more aggressive as he progresses:

> What then is left but with a Jealous Eye
> To guard the Small remains of Royalty?
> The Law shall still direct my peacefull Sway,
> And the same Law teach Rebels to Obey.

Thus Dryden stakes out for David/Charles a middle ground between extremes of arbitrary or an-
archic rule. He insists on the king's lawful prerogative granted by the unwritten constitution and
forming part of a balanced system of government. The other parts of that balance have threatened the very Ark of the Covenant, and so David
himself now threatens, "Law they require, let
Law then shew her Face," for "Lawfull Pow'r is
still Superiour found." So David will punish the
transgressors, who will actually devour themselves by turning against each other. Dryden
closes the poem by underwriting David's words
with the Word of God: "He said. Th'Almighty,
nodding, gave Consent: / And Peals of Thunder
shook the Firmament." Dryden's final touch,
then, is a kind of apotheosis: David and God become one: "And willing Nations knew their
Lawfull Lord."

Absalom and Achitophel was a celebration of
Charles's triumph over his foes in the Exclusion
Crisis. As it was published in November of 1681,
Shaftesbury was on trial for treason. But that tri-
umph seemed short-lived, for Shaftesbury, to
Dryden the archconspirator, got off scot-free,
and his supporters cast a medal in his honor.
Early in 1682 Dryden published another attack
on Shaftesbury and his followers, *The Medall. A
Satyre against Sedition*. He relinquished the moder-

ate stance of the earlier poem and wrote a scath-ing Juvenalian satire, prefaced by an equally scath-ing "Epistle to the Whigs." The controlling fiction of the poem is the two sides of the medal, one with a portrait of Shaftesbury, the other with a portrait of the City of London. Again portray-ing Shaftesbury's political inconstancy as a func-tion of inconstancy of character, Dryden says sardonically of the medal, "Cou'd it have form'd his ever-changing Will, / The various Piece had tir'd the Graver's Skill." Dryden traces him through his tortuous twists of allegiance until his final revelation of the "fiend" within.

On the other hand, Dryden addresses *"Lon-don, thou great Emporium of our Isle"* again in a lamentory mode, and one cannot help remember-ing his praise of the city in *Annus Mirabilis* as the emporium of England's imperialist trade. As in *Ab-salom and Achitophel*, Dryden spares the virtuous Londoners from blame, but he stridently attacks the "Fool and Knave" who corruptly misdirect the city's great energies. Here one sees as plainly as anywhere Dryden's fear of and contempt for the rising middle class that couched its political am-bitions in religious rhetoric:

> In Gospel phrase their Chapmen they betray:
> Their Shops are Dens, the Buyer is their Prey.
> The Knack of Trades is living on the Spoyl;
> They boast, ev'n when each other they beguile.
> Customes to steal is such a trivial thing,
> That 'tis their Charter, to defraud their King.

Dryden has perceived the inherent danger of bourgeois individualism and incipient capitalism: the selfish, predatory accumulation of wealth by means of fraud and tax evasion. These are descen-dants of the Commonwealth's men who mur-dered a previous king and who are still bent on the destruction not only of "Kings" but of "Kingly Pow'r" per se.

In both sections of the poem, Dryden sati-rizes (this time he does not pretend to rational de-bate) the political theory of the Whigs. In both he reduces republican theory to a version of might makes right, here applied to the concept of majority rule: "The Most have right, the wrong is in the Few":

> Almighty Crowd, thou shorten'st all dispute;
> Pow'r is thy Essence; Wit thy Attribute!
> Nor Faith nor Reason make thee at a stay,
> Thou leapst o'r all eternal truths, in thy *Pindarique* way!

The wit in these lines resides not only in the bril-liant imitative spillover of the concluding alexan-drine but also in the mock theology: as in the disputes over whether God's will or his reason be his primary essence, Dryden follows his sarcastic reference to the crowd as "Almighty" with a pseudovoluntarist position, reducing reason or "Wit" to a mere "Attribute." But, as he had sug-gested early in his writing,

> If Sovereign Right by Sovereign Pow'r they scan,
> The same bold Maxime holds in God and Man:
> God were not safe, his Thunder cou'd they shun
> He shou'd be forc'd to crown another Son.

The marvelous irony of the last line works espe-cially well when one reads from the caesura of the penultimate line through the enjambment to fall hard upon the reversed iamb of the last line: the implication is that even *He* would be forced, like Charles, to declare another son his legitimate heir. The pun on *crown*, referring to Christ's crown of thorns, is savage.

The best—because, perhaps, the most prophetic—parts of the poem are the early series of analogies to political majority rule and the later series of images of clipping of the royal power until the monarch is purely ceremonial— as indeed he/she became after the revolution Dryden so desperately feared. Dryden mocks the notion that majority rule is stable, citing historical examples of mistakes resulting in the deaths of he-roes, among them Socrates. As he comes closer to his own time, he wickedly asserts, "Crowds err not, though to both extremes they run; / To kill the Father, and recall the Son." His most scathing indictment of this creeping relativism occurs in the following lines:

> Some think the Fools were most, as times went
>   then;
> But now the World's o'r stock'd with prudent men.
> The common Cry is ev'n Religion's Test;
> The *Turk*'s is, at *Constantinople*, best;
> Idols in *India*, Popery at *Rome*;
> And our own Worship onely true at home:
> And true, but for the time; 'tis hard to know
> How long we please it shall continue so.
> This side to day, and that to morrow burns;
> So all are God-a'mighties in their turns.

Instead of mythologizing the political theory he defends, Dryden attempts to justify it on prag-matic grounds, that their British forefathers at-tempted to avoid factional civil war by securing

John Dryden, 1693 (portrait by Sir Godfrey Kneller; National Portrait Gallery, London)

peaceful succession of both power and property through primogeniture. God has already tried us, Dryden argues, by giving the republicans what they wanted during the Commonwealth, and look what happened. And he predicts a similar cannibalistic civil war if Shaftesbury and his cronies succeed, for all will want a piece of the power, and none will be constrained by law. His concluding prophecy seems a bitter wish-fulfillment:

> Thus inborn Broyles the Factions wou'd ingage,
> Or Wars of Exil'd Heirs, or Foreign Rage,
> Till halting Vengeance overtook our Age:
> And our wild Labours, wearied into Rest,
> Reclin'd us on a rightfull Monarch's Breast.

If as at the end of *Absalom and Achitophel* Dryden

is again collapsing both earthly and heavenly monarch together, his vision has progressed from apotheosis to apocalypse, the ultimate curse of the satirist.

In the immediate aftermath of the Exclusion Crisis, Dryden continued to attack the Stuarts' enemies. He contributed satiric portraits of old nemeses now openly Whiggish, Settle and Shadwell, to a sequel to *Absalom and Achitophel*, written mostly by another young protégé, Nahum Tate. He contributed politically satirical prologues and epilogues to several plays. He wrote another play with Nathaniel Lee, *The Duke of Guise* (1682), which exploited the analogy between current events and those in France a century before; he wrote a *Vindication* of that play (1683); and in

1684 he translated Louis Maimbourg's *History of the League*, the source of most of his knowledge of that French analogue. The stridency of Dryden's tone increases proportionally to the growing strength of the Stuart position, especially after the discovery in the summer of 1683 of the Rye House Plot, an alleged plan to assassinate Charles and James and foment a radical revolution based in London.

In the midst of this political activity Dryden published another major poem on an apparently radically different topic, *Religio Laici or a Laymans Faith* (1682). The poem is a response to another French work, recently translated by a friend of his into English as *A Critical History of the Old Testament* (1682). The original was by a French priest, Richard Simon, and employed emerging modern methods of scholarship to examine the biblical text, its errors and contradictions. Dryden's response is essentially a declaration of faith in the few fundamental truths of Christianity that are "uncorrupt, sufficient, clear, intire, / In *all* things which our needfull *Faith* require," among them such doctrines as Original Sin and its consequences, especially death and the loss of heaven; the Incarnation of Christ; His Redemption and the consequent justification for the sin of Adam by means of the imputed righteousness of Christ extended to mankind. Astonishingly, the divinity of Christ is *not* among these essential doctrines, and Dryden is convinced that many, not only heathens but Christians, have been saved without "this Question" even "brought in play." On the other hand, Dryden attacks Deists by insisting that revelation is necessary for those essential truths to be known, that reason cannot discover them by itself, for, as he insists in another bold opening,

> Dim, as the borrow'd beams of Moon and Stars
> To *lonely, weary, wandring* Travellers,
> Is *Reas*on to the *Soul*: And as on high,
> Those rowling Fires *discover* but the Sky
> Not light us *here*; So *Reason*'s glimmering Ray
> Was lent, not to *assure* our *doubtfull* way,
> But *guide* us upward to a *better Day*.
> And as those nightly Tapers disappear
> When Day's bright Lord ascends our Hemisphere;
> So pale grows *Reason* at *Religions* sight;
> So *dyes*, and so *dissolves* in *Supernatural Light*.

Here Dryden perfects a casual epistolary mode of heroic couplets to be later employed by Pope in *An Essay on Man* (1733), among other philosophical poems of the age. The strong medial caesuras, the enjambments, the triplet, and the metric variety lend an air of almost casual conversation. The imagery is worthy of Dante or Donne or Henry Vaughan. At the end Dryden maintains that he has chosen "this unpolish'd, rugged Verse . . . As fittest for Discourse, and nearest Prose." Not even Matthew Arnold could take this quite polished verse for prose. But Dryden had become a master of the philosophical epistle in verse, whose apparent casualness disguises its richly tropic nature.

Dryden had not really made a radical departure from his concurrent political poems, however. His attempt to steer a middle way between what he calls "Extreme[s]" concerning the issue of tradition in biblical interpretation is really a political stance, a proto-Burkean conservatism, indeed, a proto-Swiftian Erastianism:

> 'Tis some Relief, that points not clearly known,
> Without much hazard may be let alone:
> And, after hearing what our Church can say,
> If still our Reason runs another way,
> That private Reason 'tis more Just to curb,
> Than by disputes the publick Peace disturb.
> For points obscure are of small use to learn:
> But *Common quiet* is *Mankind*'s *concern*.

The extremes he attacks in the religious sphere are the same he has been attacking in the political: Catholics and Dissenters, the Catholics especially for their gnostic priesthood, the Dissenters for their pernicious doctrine of individual interpretation, which leads ultimately to the kind of political instability, disturbance of the "Peace," and loss of "Common quiet" detailed above. Dryden would have sided with Edmund Burke against the French Revolution, and he would have been appalled by Thomas Jefferson and Thomas Paine.

By 1685, with the publication of *Sylvae*, a poetical miscellany, Dryden had become a major translator, having turned his hand to Ovid and Virgil as early as 1680 (*Ovid's Epistles*) and adding more Ovid and Theocritus in 1684 (*Miscellany Poems*) and then especially Lucretius and Horace in 1685 (*Sylvae*). Dryden also apparently polished William Soames's translation of Nicolas Boileau-Despréaux's *Art of Poetry* (1684) and contributed a dedication and life of Plutarch to a new edition of *Plutarchs Lives* (1683). While he would return to and memorably refine his versifying of Virgil in the next decade, among these early translations most notable are his deft handling of libertine psychology in Ovid's epistles, especially the incestuous "Canace to Macareus"; his inspired if somber rendition of Lucretius's atheistical arguments against fear of death, and his dextrous attempt at Pindarics in Horace's Ode 3.29. In these poems Dryden engages in some of his most experimental prosody. That Dryden was occupied with issues of translation is evidenced not only by his preface to *Sylvae* but also by his panegyric "To the Earl of Roscomon, on his Excellent Essay on Translated Verse," prefaced to the edition of that essay in 1684. Dryden's poem celebrates translation as an imperialist act whereby Greece, Rome, Italy, France, and now England appropriate the best from the countries they have (ostensibly) superseded.

In 1684 Dryden also published what many consider his best elegiac poem, "To the Memory of Mr. Oldham." Dryden's praise is doubly generous: first, he honors this kindred spirit in satire as having arrived at the goal and won the prize, that is, honor in the field of satire per se, before himself (Oldham's *Satyrs upon the Jesuits* was published in 1681, before *Mac Flecknoe, The Medall,* and, for that matter, *Absalom and Achitophel* were officially published, although it is ironic that Oldham's manuscript copy of *Mac Flecknoe* is dated August 1678—if Oldham was inspired by it, that fact would increase the generosity of Dryden's gesture). Second, Dryden laments Oldham's early death but insists that longer time would have added nothing to Oldham's wit and verse but metrical regularity and "the dull sweets of Rime"—like those of Dryden himself in his satires and indeed in this poem. The poem, like the early elegy to Hastings, closes with no metaphysical consolation, but with these grim, haunting lines:

> Once more, hail and farewel; farewel thou young,
> But ah too short, *Marcellus* of our Tongue;
> Thy Brows with Ivy, and with Laurels bound;
> But Fate and gloomy Night encompass thee around.

Despite the honors garnered by this bright young star (analogous to Augustus's young poet, about whom Virgil sang), he sinks into a "gloomy" land of shades. Dryden achieves a poignant world-weariness in his *ave atque vale* motif.

Dryden's next major poetic task was another unpleasant one, another elegy, this time for Charles II, who died in February 1685. As poet laureate and historiographer royal Dryden had to produce an official, public elegy, one that lamented the deceased king, praised his accomplishments, and underwrote the transition to a new king, around whom swirled such tempests of controversy. For some time Dryden had been preparing an opera to celebrate Charles II, one that was finally produced in late 1685 as *Albion and Albanius*. In it he continued the metric experimentations of his translations. Relying on this metric virtuosity, Dryden produced *Threnodia Augustalis: A Funeral-Pindarique Poem Sacred to the Happy Memory of King Charles II* (1685).

As in *Annus Mirabilis,* Dryden attempts to portray real people in the most material of situations—death—while at the same time mythologizing his subject in the light of the theory of the king's two bodies, public and private. For example, Dryden portrays James's rushing to Charles's bedchamber upon first hearing of his illness in terms that mingle allegorical with realistic details:

> Half unarray'd he ran to his Relief,
> So hasty and so artless was his Grief:
> Approaching Greatness met him with her Charms
>   Of Pow'r and future State;
> But look'd so ghastly in a Brother's fate,
>   He shook her from his Armes.

The rolling alliterative *r*'s in this passage lend force to the tempting "Charms" of Greatness's arms entwining with those of James, who asserts himself by thrusting her and the ambition to which he is susceptible aside.

Dryden draws a scene of pathos designed to extract pity and loyalty from even the most recalcitrant of his audience, especially in the light of his rehearsal of Charles's mild temper, forgiveness, and contributions to an English renascence of both arts and trade after the havoc wreaked by "Rebellion" and "Faction." Dryden portrays Charles's greatest contribution as his intrepid support of the principle of legitimate succession. In imitative rhythms Dryden delineates the progress of this principle down through British history:

> Succession, of a long Descent,
>   Which Chastly in the Channells ran,
>   And from our Demi-gods began,
> Equal almost to Time in its extent,
>   Through Hazzards numberless and great,
> Thou hast deriv'd this mighty Blessing down,
> And fixt the fairest Gemm that decks th'Imperial
>   Crown.

That succession, Dryden insists, falls upon Charles's brother, whether the Opposition likes it or not, and he deserves it because of his—as opposed to their—unswerving devotion to the "plighted vows" of loyalty. In *Annus Mirabilis*, Dryden praised London for its loyalty; in *Absalom and Achitophel* and *The Medall* he blamed Shaftesbury for attempting to effect a divorce, to break "the Bonds she plighted to her Lord"; here Dryden appeals to his countrymen to honor their vows of fealty sworn to their earthly lord in the sight of their heavenly: "Faith is a Christian's, and a Subject's Test." In a desperate wish-fulfillment, Dryden pretends to prophesy, "with a distant view, I see / Th'amended Vows of *English* Loyalty"—a vision that he once again transforms into the prosperity of British imperialism in the wake of its "Conquering Navy," which, under James, will reduce the oceans of the world to acknowledging their rightful "Lord." In the finale of *Albion and Albanius*, Dryden would try again to rally the nation behind this theme. Amidst the final chorus, "Fame *rises out of the middle of the Stage, standing on a Globe; on which is the Arms of* England." The Epilogue concludes a crescendo of appeals to trust with the following version of the myth of human word-as-bond underwritten by the Divine Word:

> He Plights his Faith; and we believe him just;
> His Honour is to Promise, ours to Trust.
> Thus Britain's Basis on a Word is laid,
> As by a Word the World it self was made.

Unlike earlier elegies that omitted theodicean resolutions by means of metaphysical consolations, here (as briefly in the portrait of Young Barzillai in *Absalom and Achitophel*) Dryden in the name of excessive "Grief" stifles the "Impious thought" of his theodicean complaint and acknowledges that Heaven did not take Charles too soon but instead gave him double the dozen years he spent in exile to bring England close to the "Promis'd Land" of political stability.

His next major poem, "To the Pious Memory Of the Accomplisht Young Lady Mrs Anne Killigrew" (1686), also an elegy, is devoid of theodicean complaint and provides the consolation of apotheosis throughout. Even when Dryden, in one of the best images in the poem ("*Destiny* . . . like a hardn'd Fellon," that is, a rapist, refused to finish the "Murder at a Blow, . . . But . . . took a pride / To work more Mischievously slow, / And plunder'd first, and then destroy'd"), laments her premature death from smallpox, he concludes immediately that she, like Katharine Philips, the

matchless "*Orinda*," died only to be "translate[d]" to heaven. Moreover, the person praised is a poet—and a woman to boot. Dryden uses the occasion to apotheosize art itself. Anne is a Beatrice, a descendant of "*Sappho*," whose transmigrating soul now leaves its peregrinations to sing eternally in a heavenly choir and to whom Dryden and other poets can now pray for poetic inspiration:

> Hear then a Mortal Muse thy Praise rehearse,
>   In no ignoble verse;
> But such as thy own voice did practise here,
> When thy first fruits of Poesie were giv'n;
> To make thy self a welcome Inmate there:
>   While yet a young Probationer,
>   And Candidate of Heav'n.

Dryden portrays this "Poetess" as having "Wit . . . more than Man," as being indeed quasi-divine, a second Christ who "attone[s]" for the "Second Fall" of mankind through bad poetry, bad art, and bad drama; a second Noah in her ability to people creation itself through her portraits; and a cocreator who has the power to paint not only James II's "Outward Part" but to "call out" with her very "hand" the "Image of his Heart." Dryden thus portrays Anne's agency on earth as a second Incarnation, one that, like Christ's, raises mankind up to higher status—especially the "Sacred Poets," who, at the sound of the "Golden Trump" on Judgment Day, will, because "they are cover'd with the lightest Ground," spring first from the earth "And streight, with inborn Vigour, on the Wing, / Like mounting Larkes, to the New Morning sing," led by Anne "As Harbinger of Heav'n, the Way to show." Dryden has granted this "Virgin-daughter of the Skies" the status of the Blessed Virgin or Sophia, by implication a coequal member of the Trinity (from which the figure of woman has been conspicuously absent). And one of the main fictions of the poem is that his Pindaric poetry itself participates in the divine emanation. Without music itself, this poem is as wonderfully lyrical as anything the age produced. Witness the last stanza in its entirety:

> When in mid-Aire, the Golden Trump shall sound,
>   To raise the Nations under ground;
>   When in the valley of *Jehosaphat*,
> The Judging God shall close the Book of Fate;
>   And there the last Assizes keep
>   For those who Wake, and those who Sleep;
>   When rattling Bones together fly,

From the four Corners of the Skie,
When Sinews o're the Skeletons are spread,
Those cloath'd with Flesh, and Life inspires the
     Dead;
The Sacred Poets first shall hear the Sound,
     And formost from the Tomb shall bound:
For they are cover'd with the lightest Ground
And streight, with in-born Vigour, on the Wing,
Like mounting Larkes, to the New Morning sing.
There Thou, Sweet Saint, before the Quire shalt
     go,
As Harbinger of Heav'n, the Way to show,
The Way which thou so well hast learn'd below.

The play off the inverted iamb every time the line begins with "When" and then leads, in the first instance—or slams, in the third—into a spondee provides wonderful metric variation, even as the foot-lengths vary, producing, along with the alliterative *f*'s and the collapsed iambs of the second line, these great sound effects: "When ratling Bones together fly, / From the four Corners of the Skie." The use of medial caesuras is masterful especially in the last five lines, including double caesuras that allow the succeeding lines to explode forth in imitation of the mounting larks/resurrected bodies. Even the flirtation with the grotesque in the image of the recreation of those resurrected bodies seems a bold anticipation of the cinematic, cartoonlike process later perfected in Modest Mussorgsky's *Night on Bald Mountain* (1867) in *Fantasia* (1940). Finally, the passage seems reminiscent of Donne, Milton, and Shakespeare—their images respectively of the Last Judgment ("At the round earth's imagin'd corners, blow"), the lady's song "creat[ing] a soul / Under the ribs of Death" (Milton's *Comus*), and the lover's soul "Like to the lark at break of day arising / From sullen earth, sing[ing] hymns at heaven's gate" (Shakespeare's Sonnet 29).

On his deathbed, Charles II declared his conversion to Catholicism, and his Catholic brother James succeeded to the throne, issuing some "Royal Papers" detailing not only Charles's but James's first wife's Catholic faith. Meanwhile, Dryden himself converted, and he was ordered to defend those Royal Papers, which he did in a pamphlet exchange with prominent Anglican bishop Edward Stillingfleet. Apparently Dryden felt obliged to publish another philosophical poem, documenting his own confession of faith and answering his earlier *Religio Laici*. The result was *The Hind and the Panther* (1687), Dryden's longest original poem. Ever since, he has been attacked for insincerity and opportunism. James Anderson Winn, Dryden's modern biographer, argues that from the time of his relationship with the Howards, Dryden was intimately connected with Catholic recusants, one of whom was a prominent cardinal, and one of whom may have been his own wife. His sons were Catholic, and the youngest was studying to be a priest. So his conversion may have taken place over a long period of time. And he himself argues persuasively in the third part of *The Hind and the Panther* that he really stood little to gain and far more to lose by becoming Catholic, mostly because up until that time the aging James had no son, and his new duchess, Maria Beatrice, had lost several babies: the throne would revert to a Protestant upon his death.

Biographers will never ascertain just why Dryden converted, and critics will probably always accuse him of being a trimmer. But there is a logic to his conversion if one studies his works. They are preoccupied with the need for political stability and the concomitant necessity of loyalty to de jure monarchs, whose title is inherited through primogenitive patrilinearity. As Dryden shifted from his early optimism concerning Britain's future as an expansionist imperial power to his defensive posture with regard to the principle of succession amid threats of civil war, his own loyalty to James and to unbroken succession grew stronger. It appears that the more he examined his *Religio Laici* position, the more he came to doubt the Church of England's claim to authority. By the time he wrote *The Hind and the Panther* the analogy between church and state was ironclad. Only Catholicism can trace its origins in unbroken succession back to the primitive church; Anglicanism dates from Henry VIII's break with Rome (a break that occurred for dubious reasons at that, Dryden argues throughout). And without a final arbiter in doctrinal matters, no church can claim authority: "Because no disobedience can ensue, / Where no submission to a Judge is due." Dryden's fears of political anarchy are reflected in his fears of doctrinal anarchy, especially where the Protestant theory of individual interpretation of the Bible pertains. Thus it should come as no surprise that he would finally swear allegiance to Rome. Moreover, Dryden's religious theory of infallibility as residing in both pope *and* General Council can be seen as homologous to his political theory of a government balanced between king and Parliament. And his religious theory of authority based upon histori-

John Dryden, circa 1698 (portrait by Sir Godfrey Kneller; Trinity College, Cambridge University)

cal priority can be seen as homologous to not just a political but an economic theory of succession: "An old possession stands, till Elder quitts the claim" is as true for power and property as it is for the True Church. The problematics of the transmission of the Savior's "Testament" are developed in terms of homology to a contested will, precisely because an unerring guide is needed in both religious and sociopolitical realms. Dryden has the Catholic Hind assert to the Anglican Panther, "For that which must direct the whole, must be / Bound in one bond of faith and unity": both church and state need one leader, to whom his subjects are bound by word-as-bond. In language that expresses Dryden's merged religious and political theory, the Hind concludes triumphantly

that "the mother church . . . with unrivall'd claim ascends the throne."

Not only Dryden's theory but also his very fable mingles political with religious. All along the poem seems to have a dual raison d'etre: to explain Dryden's conversion but also to achieve an alliance between Catholics and Anglicans against the Dissenters. Dryden's antipathy to the latter is essentially political: their theory of individual interpretation leads to religious as well as political anarchy. The heritage of the Presbyterian Wolf may go all the way back to the Old Testament "When the proud *Sanhedrim* [the ancient homologue to Parliament] oppress'd the Prince" or better still, "When *Corah* with his brethren did conspire, / From *Moyses* hand the sov'reign sway to wrest." Even earlier, both the Wolf and the Deistic (read *atheistic*) Fox descend ultimately from "some [postdiluvian] wild currs, who from their masters ran / Abhorring the supremacy of man," and who "In woods and caves the rebel-race began." Passing through "*Wickliff,*" with his "innate antipathy to kings," in their modern manifestation in mid-seventeenth-century England, these radical Protestants (now Roundheads) "fastn'd on the miter'd crown, / And freed from God and monarchy your town"—the City of London. They would draw the nation "to the dreggs of a Democracy," which for Dryden is anarchy. They are the fomenters of "Rebellion" against both "heav'n" and "Prince."

Rebellion is a leitmotiv in the poem, from this early satirical description of the Dissenters through the description of Henry VIII's rebellion, which but teaches others to rebel in part 2, to the final ungrateful rebellion of the Anglican pigeons against their rightful sovereign at the end of part 3. In this last part of the poem Dryden reveals himself as the controversialist he always was, arguing with the bishops Stillingfleet and Gilbert Burnet over not doctrinal but political disputes: why would the Anglicans keep the Test Act, a device introduced in the fright of the Popish Plot to exclude Catholics from power, when the Plot has been shown to be a fraud and when James has shown himself to be tolerant? Of course, Dryden's problem was that he was defending an inept king who kept making matters worse by privileging Catholics. The Panther's fable of the swallows and the martins is a displaced attack on James's policy, which attack, of course, holds his Catholic advisers, especially one Father Edward Petre, primarily responsible. As usual, Dryden is offering advice against potential disaster.

Finally the ending—and perhaps the real import—of Dryden's poem is secular. The Hind finally despairs of an accommodation with the Panther. In vatic style Dryden offers an optimistic, wish-fulfillment prophecy of Catholic hegemony over an Anglican establishment ungrateful ultimately to James's new policy of religious tolerance. But it is as if he could not sustain the optimism. Instead he tacked on a dire prophecy of the advent, at the death of James, of the "Usurper," William of Orange. There is no final apotheosis, no final apocalypse, no final justice. The "Glorious" Revolution that did occur almost immediately forever destroyed Dryden's faith in a fulfillment of his religious/political vision in his

own lifetime. Instead, he moved to the margins of the new order to carry on his critique.

In the meantime, the one event Catholics desired most occurred: James and his queen had a son in June of 1688. Of course, it was the one event most feared by the Protestants. Almost as Dryden had prophesied, the Protestants invited William and Mary to become cosovereigns, and James fled the country. Dryden's celebration of the prince seems strained, almost hysterical. He desperately prays that England be spared another civil war: "Here stop the Current of the sanguine flood, / Require not, Gracious God, thy Martyrs Blood." Yet he cautions the Catholic (potential) martyrs, "Nor yet conclude all fiery *Trials* past, / For Heav'n will exercise us to the last." And all he can praise at the end is no new order but James's "Justice"—darling attribute of God Himself—and James's stoic endurance of whatever "Fortune" and "Fate" will bring.

In a famous passage in *The Hind and the Panther*, Dryden assumes the posture of one who has humbled his ambitious desire for fame. Almost self-pityingly he writes of his (eventual) loss of his offices of poet laureate and historiographer royal, as well as the income that was supposed to go with them:

'Tis nothing thou hast giv'n, then add thy tears
For a long race of unrepenting years:
'Tis nothing yet; yet all thou hast to give,
Then add those *may-be* years thou hast to live.
Yet nothing still: then poor, and naked come,
Thy father will receive his unthrift home,
And thy blest Saviour's bloud discharge the mighty
   sum.

At some level Dryden may have believed that, but immediately after the revolution he began to write again for the stage, partly to make money but also partly to assert himself: his talent, even as his nemesis Shadwell was made the new poet laureate; his spirit amid the storm of political conflict; his worth and thus his justifiable fame. Moreover, though the Hind claims to "discipline" her son, Dryden, "Whose uncheck'd fury to revenge wou'd run," Dryden could not control his Jacobitic rage, which broke out in his later works in various satiric fashions.

Don Sebastian (1689) has as its central theme loyalty to one's king, whatever the circumstances. And when the tragicomic pattern is ruptured by the tragic ending—itself the result of a breach of society's patrilineal codes—Dryden closes with a Christian/Stoical acceptance of the inscrutability of God's ways. But in his next play, *Amphitryon* (1690), Dryden retells the story of Jupiter's seduction of Amphitryon's wife in a witty but ultimately sardonic way, imaging for his audience a world run by a god who is sheer power, without justice as his darling attribute—as if Dryden were Jobishly complaining about the absence of his God's justice in the postrevolutionary world. In *Cleomenes* (1692), Dryden (and Thomas Southerne, who helped him finish the play because he was in poor health) portrayed a king in exile, betrayed and abandoned, who fails to rally a revolution that might result in his restitution in his native land. Several details seem calculated to arouse Jacobite sympathies, especially that of Cleomenes' wife and infant child starving to death, and God finally seems absent, as the play emphasizes Stoic resignation and self-reliance.

In subtler ways Dryden inculcated his Jacobitism into *King Arthur* (1691), an opera that celebrates Britain's resistance to foreign invaders, and *Love Triumphant* (1694), his final play, a tragicomedy featuring a prince who rebels against his father and against the incest taboo, and concluding with a nonresolution to the issues because the prince turns out to be unrelated to either father or sister (by implication, Mary Stuart is still her father's daughter and a usurper). Dryden also inculcated Jacobitism into a series of prologues and epilogues, prose works, and especially brilliant new translations, most notably selected satires of Juvenal and Persius (1693), his Virgil (1697), and *Fables Ancient and Modern* (1700).

Most of the work of his last years was in translation, apparently as a way of achieving a modicum of independence, both political and economic. He returned to favorites, such as Ovid, Virgil, and Homer, and added Giovanni Boccaccio and Geoffrey Chaucer. Especially noteworthy is the malleability of Dryden's heroic couplets. In the *Aeneis*, for example, he occasionally opens up the couplet rather than, like Pope, closing it virtually all the time. He spices couplets with triplets, masculine with feminine endings. He is a past master at the enjambment and particularly of metric variation in the first hemistich. He is also a master weaver of motive, as in the leitmotiv of *labor* in the *Aeneis*, a Virgilian key word and concept he variously translates as *Labour* and *Toyl*—sometimes adding to the Virgilian original and always emphasizng the need to build a kingdom on hard work, as opposed to the easy gains in Carthage. He also embellishes the original with lines such as the following, which emphasize the emerg-

ing theme of self-reliance in his final works: Dryden's Sybil praises Aeneas as being "secure of Soul, unbent with Woes," and advises him, "The more thy Fortune frowns, the more oppose." Dryden's Aeneas answers, in lines that expand on the original:

> no Terror to my view,
> No frightful Face of Danger can be new.
> Inur'd to suffer, and resolv'd to dare,
> The Fates, without my Pow'r, shall be without my
>   Care.

Dryden's Aeneas, then, must learn—like Cleomenes before him and Dryden's "Honour'd Kinsman," John Driden of Chesterton, after him in Dryden's canon—to stand fixed on his own firm center. Aeneas's boast seems Dryden's own.

Meanwhile, Dryden continued to write excellent occasional verse, from prologues and epilogues to elegies to verse epistles. *Eleonora* (1692), a commissioned elegy, was originally to be entitled "The Pattern," and Dryden indeed makes the countess a pattern of Christian piety and charity, as well as of aristocratic wife and motherhood. On the topic of friendship, Dryden achieves one of his best extended similes, one employing his later motive of conveying the fixed self no matter where one goes:

> The Souls of Friends, like Kings in Progress are;
> Still in their own, though from the Pallace far:
> Thus her Friend's Heart her Country Dwelling was,
> A sweet Retirement to a courser place:
> Where Pomp and Ceremonies enter'd not;
> Where Greatness was shut out, and Buis'ness well
>   forgot.

In the midst of this pattern panegyric, however, Dryden's satiric muse once again asserts herself, first in rather misogynistically suggesting that good wives should show "Love and Obedience to [their] Lord": Dryden jibes at his contemporaries, "So Subjects love just Kings, or so they shou'd." At the end Dryden bitterly comments on his own situation:

> Let this suffice: Nor thou, great Saint, refuse
> This humble Tribute of no vulgar Muse:
> Who, not by Cares, or Wants, or Age deprest,
> Stems a wild Deluge with a dauntless brest:
> And dares to sing thy Praises, in a Clime
> Where Vice triumphs, and Vertue is a Crime:
> Where ev'n to draw the Picture of thy Mind,
> Is Satyr on the most of Humane Kind:
> Take it, while yet 'tis Praise; before my rage

Unsafely just, break loose on this bad Age.

In the genre of the verse epistle, sometime around 1686, Dryden wrote a wonderfully witty and wicked letter in Hudibrastics to George Etherege, who had become envoy to Ratisbon, in Bavaria. Again Dryden plays off the Virgilian theme of *labor*, as he addresses the aging libertine as if he were scattering his maker's image through the frozen north of Europe:

> Like mighty Missioner you come
> Ad partes Infidelium.
> A work of wondrous merit sure
> So farr to go so much endure,
> . . . .
> You have made your zeal appear
> Within the Circle of the Bear.
> What region of the Earth so dull
> That is not of your labours full?
> Trioptolemus (so sing the nine)
> Strew'd plenty from his Cart divine
> But spight of all those fable makers
> He never sow'd on Almain Acres.

In "To my Dear Friend Mr. Congreve" (1694), as in his elegy on Oldham, Dryden assumes a magnanimous pose, answering, as it were, his mock-panegyric *Mac Flecknoe* with a genuine panegyric, featuring this time a legitimate succession. Dryden's laurels should descend to Congreve, representative of a new generation of dramatic poets, but they have been intercepted, "For *Tom* the Second reigns like *Tom* the first," that is, Tom Rymer has succeeded Tom Shadwell as historiographer royal (not poet laureate). Nevertheless, Dryden prophesies,

> Thou shalt be seen,
> (Tho' with some short Parenthesis between:)
> High on the Throne of Wit; and seated there,
> Not mine (that's little) but thy Lawrel wear.

Though never actually poet laureate, Congreve certainly rose "high on a throne of his own labors rear'd," for he became for centuries considered the premier Restoration comedy playwright.

Dryden also praises the painter Sir Godfrey Kneller in a miscellany poem of 1694:

> The fair themselves go mended from thy hand:
> Likeness appears in every Lineament;
> But Likeness in thy Work is Eloquent:
> Though Nature, there, her true resemblance bears,
> A nobler Beauty in thy Piece appears.
> So warm thy Work, so glows the gen'rous frame,

Flesh looks less living in the Lovely Dame.

The strong emphasis on the word "Flesh" leads so musically into the lilting alliteration of *l*'s in the last line. But Dryden cannot forbear his satire—and at the expense of women:

> Our Arts are Sisters; though not Twins in Birth:
> For Hymns were sung in *Edens* happy Earth,
> By the first Pair; while *Eve* was yet a Saint;
> Before she fell with Pride, and learn'd to paint.
> Forgive th'allusion; 'twas not meant to bite;
> But Satire will have room, where e're I write.

And at the center of the poem Dryden again has recourse to his emergent theme:

> Thou hadst thy *Charles* a while, and so had I;
> But pass we that unpleasing Image by.
> Rich in thy self; and of thy self Divine,
> All Pilgrims come and offer at thy Shrine.

Self-reliance will compensate for the loss of patrons—and even, perhaps, for the loss of God.

In 1697 Dryden took time out from his other chores to pen one of the greatest odes in the English language, *Alexander's Feast; Or The Power of Musique*. He had written a less remarkable poem on the subject a decade earlier. The original setting by the composer Jeremiah Clarke has been lost, but George Frideric Handel's magnificent setting of 1736 exists, and anyone who has ever heard it must marvel at the incredible virtuosity on the parts of both poet and musician. As has been often noted, the poem is a celebrtion of the power of art. The musician Timotheus modulates Alexander the Great through several moods, manipulating him with sure hand. Not only is Timotheus the real hero, but Alexander is shown, as in Dryden's friend Nathaniel Lee's portrait of him in his *The Rival Queens* (1677), to be the victim of his own reckless passions, from his pride in his quasi-divinity, to his proverbial drunkenness, to his martial vanity followed immediately by pity for the vanquished foe, to his destructive amorousness, and finally to pointless, destructive vengeance. Some critics have seen an implied critique of William III in the poem, and the pitiable portrait of the vanquished Darius, "Deserted at his utmost Need, / By those his former Bounty fed," would certainly have reminded Dryden's audience of the deserted James II. But the poem is a paean to the triumph of art over all military power, over all rulers with delusions of divinity. The sev-

Second page of Dryden's last surviving letter. Writing to a young cousin, Mrs. Elizabeth Steward, Dryden mentions "The Secular Masque" that he has written for John Vanbrugh's revision of John Fletcher's The Pilgrim *and refers to a falling-out with Thomas Betterton's acting company at Lincoln's Inn Fields, perhaps because—as he had written to Mrs. Steward earlier—he felt that the company could have given a better performance of* The Way of the World, *a new play by his friend William Congreve (MA 130, Pierpont Morgan Library).*

enth stanza, expounding the supposed transcendence of St. Cecilia and her organ, calls upon "old *Timotheus*" to "yield the Prize," for "He rais'd a Mortal to the Skies," while "She drew an Angel down" to listen to her. But Dryden qualifies the victory of St. Cecilia by offering an alternative, "Or both divide the Crown": Dryden seems to identify with "old *Timotheus*" himself, and his humility would be false. Proud? He must have been proud to see men not afraid of God for breaking their oaths of loyalty, afraid enough of him and the few others of his courage to restrict further satire on the stage and to enact further punitive laws against Catholics.

In 1698 Dryden published two verse epistles, "To Mr. Granville, on his Excellent Tragedy Call'd *Heroic Love*" and "To My Friend Mr. Motteux." The latter bears some comment, for it includes a response to Jeremy Collier's attack on the supposed immorality and profanity of the English stage:

> 'Tis hard, my Friend, to write in such an Age,
> As damns not only Poets, but the Stage.
> That sacred Art, by Heav'n it self infus'd,
> Which *Moses*, *David*, *Salomon* have us'd,
> Is now to be no more: The Muses Foes
> Wou'd sink their Maker's Praises into Prose.
> Were they content to prune the lavish Vine
> Of straggling Branches, and improve the Wine,
> Who but a mad Man wou'd his Faults defend?
> All wou'd submit; for all but Fools will mend.
> But, when to common sense they give the Lie,
> And turn distorted words to Blasphemy,
> *They* give the Scandal.

Dryden is willing to admit when he has been excessive in his works, provided clerics such as Collier (whom he has made appear a Puritan but who was in fact a nonjuring Anglican, that is, one who refused to take the oaths of loyalty to William and Mary) acknowledge their own faults and grant that "Their Faults and not their Function I arraign" when Dryden attacks corrupt clergy in such plays as *The Spanish Fryar*.

In the last year of his life, though suffering from continual illness, Dryden published his last group of translations, *Fables Ancient and Modern*, along with two last original verse epistles of praise. The first, "To Her Grace the Dutchess of Ormond," contains some of his most graceful compliments. On her recent journey to Ireland, the Ormond's family seat, Dryden writes, "The Land, if not restrain'd, had met Your Way, / Projected out a Neck, and jutted to the Sea." Perhaps influ-

enced by Dante, Edmund Spenser, and the Neoplatonists, Dryden repeatedly praises great beauty in his poems (for example, Maria Beatrice of Modena, James II's second duchess and eventually his queen, whose name is not insignificant). In this poem he maintains that the duchess's beauty is so great that it is capable of obliterating the recent suffering in Ireland, suffering Dryden must have particularly sympathized with, since a great deal of it was in the cause of James and at the hands of William up to the climactic Battle of the Boyne in 1690, which ended the first Jacobite war:

> The Waste of Civil Wars, their Towns destroy'd,
> *Pales* unhonour'd, *Ceres* unemploy'd,
> Were all forgot; and one Triumphant Day
> Wip'd all the Tears of three Campaigns away.
> Blood, Rapines, Massacres, were cheaply bought,
> So mighty Recompence Your Beauty brought.

In "To my Honour'd Kinsman, John Driden," Dryden praises a relative of different political and religious persuasion—perhaps because Driden had sent money and goods to his cousin in an act of familial friendship and Christian charity that transcended partisan politics and religion, but also because Driden provides the poet with an opportunity to portray the emergent hero. One of the dominant images in the poem is the circle, as in this famous passage about the hare:

> The Hare, in Pastures or in Plains is found,
> Emblem of Humane Life, who runs the Round;
> And, after all his wand'ring Ways are done,
> His Circle fills, and ends where he begun,
> Just as the Setting meets the Rising Sun.

The circle is traditionally an emblem of perfection, of the human soul, which ends where it began, as Dryden's poem does, referring to the blessedness Driden will finally attain in "Heav'n." Moreover, the circle is an emblem for the "Integrity" Dryden praises in his cousin, for the man with such integrity stands fixed on his own firm center, no matter what the strife. Dryden portrays Driden "void of Strife" in his country retirement and as "composing Strife" in his role of justice of the peace. He is "Lord" of him "self" and, Dryden adds in one of his increasingly misogynistic portraits of women, "uncumber'd with a Wife," who, by her nature, farther removed from God (Dryden exaggerates even Milton's misogynistic hierarchy), would only drag him down. Perhaps Dryden intended this as a witty compliment to an aging bachelor in a family with an increasing number of childless patriarchs. And he certainly wanted the iconography of the One Just Man standing alone. But the misogyny is an unwelcome alloy.

Dryden also avails himself of another emerging motive, the Younger Brother. Driden is not the heir to his father's fortunes but to his mother's. Yet unlike his older brother, whom Dryden did not like, Driden made the best of his more limited means by being charitable to the poor and by being a generous host.

Driden thus becomes the figure for the new "Patriot," a word usually appropriated by the Whiggish Country party. It is a figure appropriated by the rebels in the American Revolution: not the eldest, but nevertheless an equal citizen. Furthermore, Dryden portrays his cousin as unselfishly willing to serve his turn in Parliament if elected, where he, fixed on his own center, will help to balance contending elements:

> Betwixt the Prince and Parliament we stand;
> The Barriers of the State on either Hand:
> May neither overflow, for then they drown the
>   Land.

Note that Dryden has employed the first-person plural pronoun "we." By doing so he identifies himself with his cousin as a patriot, one who helps the politician teach England to avoid disastrous foreign wars (the poem is full of criticisms of William III and his military policies, from war to a standing army). When Dryden reminds his cousin of his ancestor, Erasmus Dryden, who bravely refused in an earlier Parliament "to lend the King against his Laws," he of course implies their common heritage. And by his praise of Erasmus, who "in a lothsom Dungeon doom'd to lie, / In Bonds retain'd his Birthright Liberty, / And sham'd Oppression, till it set him free," Dryden obviously intends his own portrait as one who, though in exile, retained his liberty. Dryden closes by asking Driden to accept this portrait, for poets also serve: "Praise-worthy Actions are by thee embrac'd; / And 'tis my Praise, to make thy Praises last." Dryden has drawn the portrait of his cousin round and, as the portrait maker, shares the praise.

Dryden ended his life in squabbles with his publisher and in bitterness over his own fate and that of not only his king but the principle of succession he had fought so hard to defend. He con-

cluded his career with a contribution to a revision of John Fletcher's *Pilgrim* by his new friend, Sir John Vanbrugh. His prologue continues his attack, begun in "To my Honour'd Kinsman, John Driden" on the latest of his detractors, Sir Richard Blackmore and Luke Milbourne, poetaster and quack doctor, and the epilogue continues his ongoing attack against self-righteous Puritans who attack the stage and the age in general. But his best contribution is a fitting epitaph, both for himself and his century. In "The Secular Masque," (1700), Dryden portrays Momus, the god of mockery, showing up at a celebration of the century. Momus's comments are devastating, as he attacks the god or goddess associated with each third of the century. To Diana, patroness of the early Stuarts, Momus comments, "Thy Chase had a Beast in View"; to Mars, patron of the Interregnum, "Thy Wars brought nothing about"; to Venus, patroness of the later Stuarts, "Thy Lovers were all untrue." This last is perhaps his most devastating statement, for it refers not only to the licentious loves of Charles's time but to James's subjects' infidelity. No wonder the expiring poet would with his last breath sing, " 'Tis well an Old Age is out, / And time to begin a New." Dryden meant not only the century itself but his own old age. As a frustrated but nevertheless believing Catholic, he could only hope that he was on his way to a new life, one free from the strife and disappointment of this life, one appreciative of the celestial strains of his great poetry.

Letters:

The Letters of John Dryden: With Letters Addressed to Him, edited by Charles E. Ward (Durham, N.C.: Duke University Press, 1942).

Bibliographies:

Hugh McDonald, *John Dryden: A Bibliography of Early Editions and Drydeniana* (Oxford: Oxford University Press, 1939);

John A. Zamonski, *An Annotated Bibliography of John Dryden: Texts and Studies, 1949-1973* (New York: Garland, 1975);

David J. Latt and Samuel Holt Monk, *John Dryden: A Survey and Bibliography of Critical Studies, 1895-1974* (Minneapolis: University of Minnesota Press, 1976);

James M. Hall, *John Dryden: A Reference Guide* (Boston: G. K. Hall, 1984).

Biographies:

Samuel Johnson, "John Dryden," in *The Works of*

the English Poets, With Prefaces, Biographical and Critical, 68 volumes (London: Printed by H. Hughes for C. Bathurst and others, 1779-1781); in volume 1 of the standard edition, Lives of the English Poets, 3 volumes, edited by George Birkbeck Hill (Oxford: Clarendon Press, 1905);

Walter Scott, The Life of John Dryden, volume 1 of Scott's edition of The Works of John Dryden (London: William Miller, 1808); published separately in 1826;

Charles E. Ward, The Life of John Dryden (Chapel Hill: University of North Carolina Press, 1961);

George McFadden, Dryden: The Public Writer, 1660-1685 (Princeton: Princeton University Press, 1978);

James Anderson Winn, John Dryden and His World (New Haven & London: Yale University Press, 1987);

Paul Hammond, John Dryden: A Literary Life (New York: St. Martin's Press, 1991).

References:

Donald R. Benson, "Dryden's The Hind and the Panther: Transubstantiation and Figurative Language," Journal of the History of Ideas, 43 (April-June 1982): 195-208;

Benson, "Space, Time, and the Language of Transcendence in Dryden's Later Poetry," Restoration, 8 (Spring 1984): 10-16;

Benson, "Theology and Politics in Dryden's Conversion," Studies in English Literature, 1500-1900, 4 (Summer 1964): 393-412;

Louis I. Bredvold, The Intellectual Milieu of John Dryden (Ann Arbor: University of Michigan Press, 1934);

Sanford Budick, Dryden and the Abyss of Light: A Study of "Religio Laici" and "The Hind and the Panther" (New Haven: Yale University Press, 1970);

David Bywaters, Dryden in Revolutionary England (Berkeley: University of California Press, 1991);

J. Douglas Canfield, "Anarchy and Style: What Dryden 'Grants' in Absalom and Achitophel," Papers on Language and Literature, 14 (Winter 1978): 83-87;

Canfield, "The Authorship of Emilia: Richard Flecknoe's Revision of Erminia," Restoration, 3 (1979): 3-7;

Canfield, "Flecknoe's Early Defence of the Stage: An Appeal to Cromwell," Restoration and 18th-Century Theatre Research, second series 2 (Winter 1987): 1-7;

Canfield, "The Image of the Circle in Dryden's To My Honour'd Kinsman," PLL, 11 (Spring 1975): 168-176;

Canfield, "Poetical Injustice in Some Neglected Masterpieces of Restoration Drama," in Rhetorics of Order / Ordering Rhetorics in English Neoclassical Literature, edited by Canfield and J. Paul Hunter (Newark: University of Delaware Press, 1989), pp. 23-45;

Canfield, "Regulus and Cleomenes and 1688," Eighteenth-Century Life, 12 (November 1988): 67-75;

Canfield, "Royalism's Last Dramatic Stand: English Political Tragedy, 1679-89," Studies in Philology, 82 (Spring 1985): 234-263;

Canfield, Word as Bond in English Literature from the Middle Ages to the Restoration (Philadelphia: University of Pennsylvania Press, 1989);

Michael J. Conlon, "The Passage on Government in Dryden's Absalom and Achitophel," Journal of English and Germanic Philogy, 78 (January 1979): 17-32;

Conlon, "The Rhetoric of Kairos in Dryden's Absalom and Achitophel," in Rhetorics of Order / Ordering Rhetorics in English Neoclassical Literature;

Elizabeth Duthie, " 'A Memorial of My Own Principles': Dryden's To My Honour'd Kinsman," Journal of English Literary History, 47 (Winter 1980): 682-704;

Mother M. Eleanor, "Anne Killigrew and Mac Flecknoe," Philological Quarterly, 43 (January 1964): 47-54;

T. S. Eliot, John Dryden: The Poet, the Dramatist, the Critic (New York: Holliday, 1932);

William Empson, "A Deist Tract by Dryden," Essays in Criticism, 25 (January 1975): 74-100;

Empson, "Dryden's Apparent Scepticism," EIC, 20 (April 1970): 172-181;

William Frost, Dryden and the Art of Translation (New Haven: Yale University Press, 1955);

Paul H. Fry, The Poet's Calling in the English Ode (New Haven: Yale University Press, 1980);

Thomas H. Fujimura, "Dryden's Changing Political Views," Restoration, 10 (Fall 1986): 93-104;

Fujimura, "The Personal Drama of Dryden's The Hind and the Panther," PMLA, 87 (May 1972): 406-416;

James D. Garrison, *Dryden and the Tradition of Panegyric* (Berkeley: University of California Press, 1975);

Dustin Griffin, "Dryden's Charles: The Ending of *Absalom and Achitophel*," *Philological Quarterly*, 57 (Summer 1978): 359-382;

Griffin, "Dryden's *Oldham* and the Perils of Writing," *Modern Language Quarterly*, 37 (June 1976): 133-150;

Phillip Harth, *Contexts of Dryden's Thought* (Chicago: University of Chicago Press, 1968);

Harth, Alan Fisher, and Ralph Cohen, *New Homage to John Dryden* (Los Angeles: William Andrews Clark Memorial Library, 1983);

Arthur W. Hoffman, *John Dryden's Imagery* (Gainesville: University of Florida Press, 1962);

D. W. Jefferson, "The Poetry of *The Hind and the Panther*," *Modern Language Review*, 79 (January 1984): 32-44;

Oscar Kenshur, "Scriptural Deism and the Politics of Dryden's *Religio Laici*," *ELH*, 54 (Winter 1987): 869-892;

Bruce King, ed., *Dryden's Mind and Art* (Edinburgh: Oliver & Boyd, 1969);

James and Helen Kinsley, eds., *Dryden: The Critical Heritage* (New York: Barnes & Noble, 1971);

Jay Arnold Levine, "John Dryden's Epistle to John Driden," *JEGP*, 63 (July 1964): 450-474;

Thomas E. Maresca, "The Context of Dryden's *Absalom and Achitophel*," *JELH*, 41 (Fall 1974): 340-358;

Michael McKeon, "Historicizing *Absalom and Achitophel*," in *The New 18th Century: Theory, Politics, Literature*, edited by Felicity Nussbaum and Laura Brown (New York: Methuen, 1987), pp. 23-40;

McKeon, *Politics and Poetry in Restoration England: The Case of Dryden's 'Annus Mirabilis'* (Cambridge, Mass.: Harvard University Press, 1975);

Earl Miner, *Dryden's Poetry* (Bloomington: Indiana University Press, 1967);

Miner, ed., *John Dryden* (Athens: Ohio University Press, 1972);

Douglas Murray, "The Musical Structure of Dryden's *Song for St. Cecilia's Day*," *Eighteenth-Century Studies*, 10 (Spring 1977): 326-334;

Murray, "The Royal Harmony: Music and Politics in Dryden's Poetry," *Restoration*, 11 (Spring 1987): 38-47;

William Myers, "Politics in *The Hind and the Panther*," *Essays in Criticism*, 19 (January 1969): 19-34;

Maximilian E. Novak, "Shaping the Augustan Myth: John Dryden and the Politics of Restoration Augustanism," in *Greene Centennial Studies*, edited by Paul J. Korshin and Robert R. Allen (Charlottesville: University of Virginia Press, 1984), pp. 1-20;

Richard L. Oden, ed., *Dryden and Shadwell: The Literary Controversy and Mac Flecknoe (1668-1679): Facsimile Reproductions* (Delmar, NY: Scholars' Facsimiles & Reprints, 1977);

H. J. Oliver, *Sir Robert Howard, 1626-1698: A Critical Biography* (Durham, N.C.: Duke University Press, 1963);

Cedric D. Reverand, *Dryden's Final Poetic Mode: The "Fables"* (Philadelphia: University of Pennsylvania Press, 1988);

Reverand, "Patterns of Imagery and Metaphor in Dryden's *The Medall*," *Yearbook of English Studies*, 2 (1972): 103-114;

Alan Roper, *Dryden's Poetic Kingdoms* (London: Routledge & Kegan Paul, 1965);

Roper, "Dryden's *Secular Masque*," *Modern Language Quarterly*, 23 (March 1962): 29-40;

Bernard N. Schilling, *Dryden and the Conservative Myth: A Reading of "Absalom and Achitophel"* (New Haven: Yale University Press, 1961);

Judith Sloman, *Dryden: The Poetics of Translation* (Toronto: University of Toronto Press, 1985);

Ruth Smith, "The Argument and Contexts of Dryden's *Alexander's Feast*," *Studies in English Literature, 1500-1900*, 18 (Summer 1978): 465-490;

Peter Stallybrass and Allon White, *The Politics and Poetics of Transgression* (London: Methuen, 1986);

Donna Elliot Swaim, "Milton's Immediate Influence on Dryden," Ph.d. dissertation, University of Arizona, 1978;

H. T. Swedenberg, ed., *Essential Articles for the Study of John Dryden* (Hamden, Conn.: Archon, 1966);

David M. Vieth, "The Discovery of the Date of *Mac Flecknoe*," in *Evidence in Literary Scholarship: Essays in Memory of James Marshall Osborn*, edited by René Wellek and Alvaro Ribeiro (Oxford: Clarendon Press, 1979), pp. 63-87;

David Wykes, *A Preface to Dryden* (London & New York: Longman, 1977);

Steven N. Zwicker, *Dryden's Political Poetry: The Typology of King and Nation* (Providence: Brown University Press, 1972);

Zwicker, *Politics and Language in Dryden's Poetry: The Arts of Disguise* (Princeton: Princeton University Press, 1984).

Papers:

Few Dryden manuscripts remain. The only poetic manuscript extant, the fair copy of the elegy for Cromwell, is on display at the British Library. The primary collection of Dryden materials is at the William Andrews Clark Memorial Library, University of California at Los Angeles; letters can be found in several collections, including those at the British Library, the Bodleian Library, and the libraries at Harvard and Yale Universities.

Henry Fielding

(22 April 1707 - 8 October 1754)

*This entry was updated by Martin C. Battestin (University of Virginia) from his entry in
DLB 39: British Novelists, 1660-1800: Part One.*

See also the Fielding entries in DLB 84: Restoration and Eighteenth-Century Dramatists: Second Series *and* DLB 101: British Prose Writers: 1660-1800: First Series.

BOOKS: *The Masquerade: A Poem, Inscribed to C—t H—d—g—r, by Lemuel Gulliver, Poet Laureat to the King of Lilliput* (London: Printed & sold by J. Roberts & A. Dodd, 1728);

Love in Several Masques: A Comedy (London: Printed for John Watts, 1728);

The Temple Beau: A Comedy (London: Printed for J. Watts, 1730);

The Author's Farce; and The Pleasures of the Town, as Scriblerus Secundus (London: Printed for J. Roberts, 1730; revised edition, London: Printed for Watts, 1750);

Tom Thumb: A Tragedy (London: Printed & sold by J. Roberts, 1730);

Rape upon Rape; or, The Justice Caught in His Own Trap: A Comedy (London: Printed for J. Watts, 1730); republished as *The Coffee-House Politician; or, The Justice Caught in His Own Trap* (London: Printed for J. Watts, 1730);

The Letter-Writers; or, A New Way to Keep a Wife at Home: A Farce, as Scriblerus Secundus (London: Printed & sold by J. Roberts, 1731);

The Tragedy of Tragedies; or, The Life and Death of Tom Thumb the Great (London: Printed & sold by J. Roberts, 1731);

The Welsh Opera; or, The Grey Mare the Better Horse, as Scriblerus Secundus (London: Printed for E. Rayner, 1731); republished as *The Genuine Grub-Street Opera* (London: Printed & sold for the benefit of the Haymarket Comedians, 1731); republished as *The Grub-Street Opera* (London: Roberts, 1731 [most likely printed for Andrew Millar in 1755]);

The Lottery: A Farce (London: Printed for J. Watts, 1732);

The Modern Husband: A Comedy (London: Printed for J. Watts, 1732);

The Old Debauchees: A Comedy (London: Printed for J. Watts & sold by J. Roberts, 1732); republished as *The Debauchees* (London: J. Watts, 1745);

The Covent-Garden Tragedy (London: Printed for J. Watts & sold by J. Roberts, 1732);

The Mock Doctor; or, The Dumb Lady Cur'd: A Comedy done from Molière (London: Printed for J. Watts, 1732);

The Miser: A Comedy Taken from Plautus and Molière (London: Printed for J. Watts, 1733);

Henry Fielding (engraving by James Basire, after a drawing by William Hogarth). This portrait, done from memory nearly eight years after Fielding's death, served as the frontispiece to the 1762 edition of Fielding's works.

The Intriguing Chambermaid: A Comedy of Two Acts, Taken from the French of Regnard (London: Printed for J. Watts, 1734);

Don Quixote in England: A Comedy (London: Printed for J. Watts, 1734);

An Old Man Taught Wisdom; or, The Virgin Unmask'd: A Farce (London: Printed for John Watts, 1735);

The Universal Gallant; or, The Different Husbands: A Comedy (London: Printed for John Watts, 1735);

Pasquin, a Dramatick Satire on the Times: Being the Rehearsal of Two Plays, viz. a Comedy Call'd The Election; and a Tragedy Call'd The Life and Death of Common-Sense (London: Printed for J. Watts, 1736);

Tumble-Down Dick; or, Phaeton in the Suds: A Dramatick Entertainment of Walking, in Serious and Foolish Characters, interlarded with Burlesque, Grotesque, Comick Interludes Call'd Harlequin a Pick-Pocket, Invented by the Ingenious Monsieur Sans Esprit; the Musick Compos'd by the Harmonious Signior Warblerini, and the Scenes Painted by the Prodigious Mynheer Van Bottom-Flat (London: Printed for J. Watts, 1736);

The Historical Register for the Year 1736; to Which Is Added a Very Merry Tragedy Call'd Eurydice

Hiss'd; or, A Word to the Wise (London: Printed & sold by J. Roberts, 1737);

The Champion: or, British Mercury, by Capt. Hercules Vinegar, nos. 1-158, by Fielding and James Ralph (London, 15 November 1739 - 15 November 1740); essays of nos. 1-94 (15 November 1739 - 19 June 1740) republished in 2 volumes (London: Printed for J. Huggonson, 1741);

Of True Greatness: An Epistle to the Right Honourable George Dodington Esq. (London: Printed for C. Corbett, 1741);

The Vernon-iad, Done into English from the Original Greek of Homer (London: Printed for Charles Corbett, 1741);

An Apology for the Life of Mrs. Shamela Andrews, as Conny Keyber (London: Printed for A. Dodd, 1741);

The Crisis: A Sermon, on Revel. XIV. 9, 10, 11 (London: Printed for A. Dodd, E. Nutt & H. Chappelle, 1741);

The Opposition: A Vision (London: Printed for T. Cooper, 1741);

The History of the Adventures of Joseph Andrews and of His Friend Mr. Abraham Adams, Written in Imitation of the Manner of Cervantes, Author of Don Quixote, 2 volumes (London: Printed for A. Millar, 1742);

A Full Vindication of the Dutchess Dowager of Marlborough, both with Regard to the Account Lately Published by Her Grace and to Her Character in General (London: Printed for J. Roberts, 1742);

Miss Lucy in Town, a Sequel to the Virgin Unmask'd: A Farce, with Songs (London: Printed for A. Millar, 1742);

Some Papers Proper to Be Read before the Royal Society Concerning the Terrestrial Chrysipus, Golden-Foot or Guinea, Collected by Petrus Gualterus, but Not Published till after His Death (London: Printed for J. Roberts, 1743);

The Wedding-Day: A Comedy (London: Printed for A. Millar, 1743);

Miscellanies, 3 volumes (London: Printed for the author & sold by A. Millar, 1743);

An Attempt towards a Natural History of the Hanover Rat (London: Printed for M. Cooper, 1744);

The Charge to the Jury; or, The Sum of the Evidence on the Trial of A.B.C.D. and E.F. All M.D. for the Death of One Robert at Orfud before Sir Asculapius Dosem (London: Printed for M. Cooper, 1745);

The History of the Present Rebellion in Scotland, Taken from the Relation of James Macpherson,

Who Was an Eyewitness of the Whole (London: Printed for M. Cooper, 1745);

A Serious Address to the People of Great Britain, in Which the Certain Consequences of the Present Rebellion Are Fully Demonstrated (London: Printed for M. Cooper, 1745);

A Dialogue between the Devil, the Pope and the Pretender (London: Printed for M. Cooper, 1745);

The True Patriot; and, The History of Our Own Times, nos. 1-33 (London: Printed for M. Cooper, 5 November 1745 - 17 June 1746);

The Female Husband; or, The Surprising History of Mrs. Mary, Alias Mr. George Hamilton, Taken from Her Own Mouth since Her Confinement (London: Printed for M. Cooper, 1746);

Ovid's Art of Love Paraphrased, and Adapted to the Present Time, with Notes and a Most Correct Edition of the Original, Book I (London: Printed for M. Cooper, A. Dodd & G. Woodfall, 1747);

A Dialogue between a Gentleman of London, Agent for Two Court Candidates, and an Honest Alderman of the Country Party. Wherein the Grievances under Which the Nation at Present Groans Are Fairly and Impartially Laid Open and Considered. Earnestly Address'd to the Electors of Great Britain (London: Printed for M. Cooper, 1747);

A Proper Answer to a Late Scurrilous Libel, Entitled, An Apology for the Conduct of a Late Celebrated Second-Rate Minister, by the Author of the Jacobite's Journal (London: Printed for M. Cooper, 1747);

The Jacobite's Journal, by John Trott-Plaid, Esq., nos. 1-49 (London: Printed for M. Cooper, 5 December 1747 - 5 November 1748);

The History of Tom Jones, a Foundling, 6 volumes (London: Printed for A. Millar, 1749);

A Charge Delivered to the Grand Jury, at the Sessions of the Peace Held for the City and Liberty of Westminster, &c. On Thursday the 29th of June 1749 (London: Printed for A. Millar, 1749);

A True State of the Case of Bosavern Penlez, Who Suffered on Account of the Late Riot in the Strand (London: Printed for A. Millar, 1749);

An Enquiry into the Causes of the Late Increase of Robbers etc. with Some Proposals for Remedying this Growing Evil (London: Printed for A. Millar, 1751);

A Plan of the Universal Register Office (London, 1751);

Amelia, 4 volumes (London: Printed for A. Millar, 1751);

The Covent-Garden Journal, by Sir Alexander Drawcansir, Knt. Censor of Great Britain, nos. 1-72 (London: Printed for Mrs. Dodd, 4 January - 25 November 1752);

Examples of the Interposition of Providence in the Detection and Punishment of Murder (London: Printed for A. Millar, 1752);

A Proposal for Making an Effectual Provision for the Poor, for Amending Their Morals and for Rendering Them Useful Members of the Society (London: Printed for A. Millar, 1753);

A Clear State of the Case of Elizabeth Canning, Who Hath Sworn That She Was Robbed and Almost Starved to Death by a Gang of Gipsies and Other Villains in January Last, for Which One Mary Squires Now Lies under Sentence of Death (London: Printed for A. Millar, 1753);

The Life of Mr. Jonathan Wild the Great. A New Edition with Considerable Corrections and Additions. (London: Printed for A. Millar, 1754);

The Journal of a Voyage to Lisbon (London: Printed for A. Millar, 1755)—in two versions;

The Fathers; or, The Good-Natur'd Man: A Comedy (London: Printed for T. Cadell, 1778).

Editions and Collections: *The Works of Henry Fielding, Esq.; with the Life of the Author*, 4 volumes, edited by Arthur Murphy (London: Printed for A. Millar, 1762);

The Works of Henry Fielding, 12 volumes, edited by Edmund Gosse (Westminster: Constable, 1899; New York: Scribner, 1899);

The Complete Works of Henry Fielding, Esq., 16 volumes, edited by W. E. Henley (London: Heinemann, 1903; New York: Barnes & Noble, 1967);

The Covent-Garden Journal, 2 volumes, edited by Gerard Edward Jensen (New Haven: Yale University Press, 1915);

The Shakespeare Head Edition of Fielding's Novels, 10 volumes (Oxford: Blackwell, 1926);

The Female Husband, and Other Writings, edited by Claude E. Jones (Liverpool: Liverpool University Press, 1960);

Joseph Andrews and Shamela, edited by Martin C. Battestin (Boston: Houghton Mifflin, 1961; London: Methuen, 1965);

The History of Tom Jones, edited by A. R. Humphreys (London: Dent, 1962);

Amelia, edited by Humphreys (London: Dent, 1962);

The Journal of a Voyage to Lisbon, edited by Harold Pagliaro (New York: Nardon, 1963);

The History of Tom Jones, edited by R. P. C. Mutter (Harmondsworth, U.K.: Penguin, 1966);

The Author's Farce (Original Version), edited by Charles B. Woods (Lincoln: Nebraska University Press, 1966; London: Edward Arnold, 1967);

The Wesleyan Edition of the Works of Henry Fielding, edited by W. B. Coley and others (Oxford: Clarendon Press / Middletown, Conn.: Wesleyan University Press, 1967-), the standard edition, volumes published to date as follows:

The History of the Adventures of Joseph Andrews and of His Friend Mr. Abraham Adams, edited by Battestin (1967);

Miscellanies, Volume One, edited by Henry Knight Miller (1972);

The History of Tom Jones, a Foundling, 2 volumes, edited by Battestin and Fredson Bowers (1974);

The Jacobite's Journal and Related Writings, edited by Coley (1975);

Amelia, edited by Battestin (1983);

The True Patriot and Related Writings, edited by Coley (1987);

The Covent-Garden Journal and A Plan of the Universal Register Office, edited by Bertrand A. Goldgar (1988);

An Enquiry into the Causes of the Late Increase of Robbers and Related Writings, edited by Malvin R. Zirker (1988);

The Historical Register for the Year 1736; and Eurydice Hissed, edited by William W. Appleton (Lincoln: Nebraska University Press, 1967; London: Edward Arnold, 1968);

The Grub-Street Opera, edited by Edgar V. Roberts (Lincoln: Nebraska University Press, 1968; London: Edward Arnold, 1969);

The True Patriot, edited by Miriam A. Locke (University: University of Alabama Press, 1969);

Tom Thumb and The Tragedy of Tragedies, edited by L. J. Morrissey (Edinburgh: Oliver & Boyd, 1970);

Joseph Andrews and Shamela, edited by Douglas Brooks (London: Oxford University Press, 1970);

Jonathan Wild and The Journal of a Voyage to Lisbon, edited by Humphreys and Brooks (London: Dent / New York: Dutton, 1973);

A Journey from This World to the Next, edited by Claude Rawson (London: Dent / New York: Dutton, 1973);

The History of Tom Jones, edited by Sheridan Baker (New York: Norton, 1973);

The Grub-Street Opera, edited by Morrissey (Edinburgh: Oliver & Boyd, 1973);

Pasquin, edited by O. M. Brack, Jr., William Kupersmith, and Curt A. Zimansky (Iowa City: University of Iowa Press, [1973]);

Joseph Andrews, edited by R. F. Brissenden (Harmondsworth, U.K.: Penguin, 1977);

The History of Tom Jones, a Foundling, edited by Battestin and Bowers (Middletown, Conn.: Wesleyan University Press, 1978);

The History of Tom Jones, a Foundling, edited by Battestin and Bowers, illustrated by Warren Chappell (Middletown, Conn.: Wesleyan University Press, 1982);

Jonathan Wild, edited by David Nokes (Harmondsworth, U.K.: Penguin, 1982);

Amelia, edited by David Blewett (Harmondsworth, U.K.: Penguin, 1987);

Joseph Andrews, edited by Stephen Copley (London: Methuen, 1987);

Joseph Andrews, Shamela, and Related Writings, edited by Homer Goldberg (New York: Norton, 1987).

TRANSLATIONS: *The Military History of Charles XII, King of Sweden, by M. Gustavus Adlerfeld, Translated into English*, 3 volumes (London: Printed for J. & P. Knapton, J. Hodges, A. Millar & J. Nourse, 1740);

Plutus, the God of Riches: A Comedy Translated from the Original Greek of Aristophanes, with Large Notes Explanatory and Critical, translated by Fielding and William Young (London: Printed for T. Waller, 1742).

OTHER: *The History of Our Own Times, by a Society of Gentlemen*, edited and partly written by Fielding, nos. 1-4 (15 January - 5 March 1741); edited by Thomas Lockwood (Delmar, N.Y.: Scholars Facsimile & Reprints, 1985);

Sarah Fielding, *The Adventures of David Simple*, second edition, preface by Henry Fielding (London: Printed for A. Millar, 1744); edited by Malcolm Kelsall (Oxford: Oxford University Press, 1969);

Sarah Fielding, *Familiar Letters between the Principal Characters in David Simple, and Some Others*, preface and letters 40-44 by Henry Fielding (London: Printed for S. Fielding & sold by A. Millar, 1747);

Martin C. Battestin, *New Essays by Henry Fielding: His Contributions to the Craftsman (1734-1739) and Other Early Journalism*, with a Stylometric

Analysis by Michael G. Farringdon (Charlottesville: University Press of Virginia, 1989).

There are many ways, many forms, in which novelists attempt to give their readers what Henry Fielding in *Tom Jones* (1749) refers to as "a Representation, or, as *Aristotle* calls it, an Imitation of what really exists. . . ." Fielding is best remembered today as the author of four such works, which he preferred to call not novels (a term associated in his day with mere catchpenny romances) but "histories," "biographies," or "comic epic-poems in prose." Three of these works, each differing in form and spirit from the others, have become classics of our literature—*Joseph Andrews* (1742), *Jonathan Wild* (in *Miscellanies*, 1743), and *Amelia* (1751); the fourth, *Tom Jones*, is justly ranked among the dozen or so greatest novels ever written.

Borrowing E. M. Forster's metaphor representing the novel as a sort of sprawling and richly variegated country, one can say that Fielding was a pioneer in uncharted regions. He was the first English novelist to beat the genre's ample fields, as Alexander Pope might have put it, and to explore its cheerier heights, where he discovered veins of truest ore. Before him, Daniel Defoe in *Robinson Crusoe* (1719) had in his irrepressibly pragmatic way settled other coasts and marked out clear boundaries; in so doing, he was also preparing the way for another of Fielding's precursors, Samuel Richardson, who in *Pamela* (1740-1741) began his disturbing, claustrophobic descent into subterranean regions, carrying his torch—as the French critic Denis Diderot would later say of Richardson's masterpiece *Clarissa* (1747-1748)—into the depths of the cavern.

From the beginning there have been critics—Samuel Johnson, for instance—who preferred the more introspective and circumstantial fiction of Richardson to Fielding's expansive comedies of manners; Richardson, declared Johnson, "knew how a watch was made," whereas Fielding could merely "tell the hour by looking on the dialplate." But there have been others, such as Samuel Taylor Coleridge, who have redressed the balance in Fielding's favor: for Coleridge, coming to Fielding from a reading of Richardson was like throwing open the windows of a sickroom, letting in the sunshine and fresh air and revealing the panorama of England's pleasant countryside. As recently as the middle of the twentieth century, influential critics have tried to restrict the proper provinces of prose fiction to those claimed first by Defoe and Richardson. It was by reference to their common method of "formal realism" and their common emphasis on the individuality of character that Ian Watt, for example, accounted for "the rise of the novel"; and F. R. Leavis, still less sympathetic to Fielding's theory and practice of his art, allowed him no place at all in "the great tradition" of British fiction, in which Leavis could more easily accommodate the morbid libidinal fantasies of the Puritan Richardson and the sexual evangelicism of D. H. Lawrence. Fielding's reputation suffered in Victorian drawing rooms because his subjects, chiefly the adventures of footmen and foundlings, were too "low" and his recognition of human sexual appetites too frank; critics of Leavis's temper are offended because Fielding, seeing these matters as part of the human comedy, made them funny. Certain feminist critics, too, have heard in the ironic, manly narrator of *Tom Jones* "the voice of the Oppressor." But this must now seem an odd complaint in light of Angela J. Smallwood's recent study, *Fielding and the Woman Question* (1989), which places Fielding in the very vanguard of the "rationalist feminism" of his day.

Already at midcentury the "Fielding revival" had begun, to which Kingsley Amis referred in the *New York Times Book Review* in 1957. Amis observed that Fielding's humor was "closer to our own than that of any writer before the present century," and that in rejecting "the novel of consistent tone," contemporary authors had followed Fielding in attempting "to combine the violent and the absurd, the grotesque and the romantic, the farcical and the horrific within a single novel." One thinks, for example, of Saul Bellow's *Adventures of Augie March* (1953), of John Barth's *The Sot-Weed Factor* (1960), and of Amis's own *Lucky Jim* (1954). More recently, in reviewing the Battestins' biography in the London *Observer* (1989), no less a master of the form than Anthony Burgess paid Fielding the handsomest tribute of all: he was, declared Burgess, "conceivably, England's greatest novelist." Yet another sign of the renewed freshness of Fielding's appeal was the brilliant success of Tony Richardson's film of *Tom Jones* (1963), and the same director's adaptation of *Joseph Andrews* (1977).

While novelists and film directors were finding in Fielding's fiction a tone and form congenial to their own interests, his novels were also becoming the focus of searching, sympathetic analyses by critics from within the academy. It seems safe to say that despite the spasm of feminist complaints in the 1980s, Fielding's reputation remains high. Indeed, in 1985 Leopold Damrosch concluded his incisive 1985 study of the fictional imagination from Milton to Fielding by asserting that *Tom Jones* was "the greatest single literary work of the eighteenth century." It is certainly true that the nature and motives of Fielding's art have never been so well understood. Critics such as Andrew Wright have eloquently paid tribute to Fielding's most enduring quality, his genius for comedy, by analyzing the artful ways in which, with such apparent spontaneity, he goes about celebrating the feast of life; others, such as Martin C. Battestin and Henry Knight Miller, have emphasized what is no less essential in his fiction, the ultimate seriousness—which is not to say gravity!—of the moral dramas he enacts against a background of universal Order, a worldview reminiscent of Pope's cautious optimism in the greatest philosophical poem of the age, *An Essay on Man* (1733-1734). The so-called "Chicago Aristotelians" (R. S. Crane and Sheldon Sacks, in particular) have clarified what Coleridge must have meant when he declared that Sophocles' *Oedipus Rex*, Ben Jonson's *The Alchemist* (1610), and *Tom Jones* evinced the three most nearly perfect plots in all of literature. In the best general introduction to Fielding's fiction, Robert Alter points out (*pace* Dr. Leavis) that there are other "great traditions" of fiction, and that in one of the most delightful of these, extending from Cervantes' *Don Quixote* (1605, 1615) through Laurence Sterne's *Tristram Shandy* (1759-1767) to James Joyce and Vladimir Nabokov and John Barth, Fielding's place is secure: this is the tradition of what Robert Alter calls the "Architechtonic Novel," the novel with a certain "self-reflexive" quality as the narrator explores the ways in which pure fiction, the flaunting of a deliberate and self-conscious artificiality, can enhance one's awareness of dimensions of "reality" beyond those reflected, perhaps too faithfully, in the mirror of "formal realism." This interest in the functions of Fielding's self-conscious narrator—who continually reminds the reader that he is telling and fashioning a story and who comments on the moral that story implies—has led critics of the "reader-response" school, such as Wolfgang Iser and John Preston, to observe that the reader is being manipulated by the narrator's masterly control over language and plot, that in the process of reading the text the reader does not merely discover but creates its meanings.

Although these qualities of Fielding's fiction have been fully explored and articulated only since the middle of the twentieth century, his virtues as a novelist have always existed in the novels themselves, where they have influenced some of the greatest masters of the form—from Tobias Smollett (who, though he slandered Fielding, paid him the compliment of imitating him) to Charles Dickens (who even gave a favorite son Fielding's name) to William Makepeace Thackeray (who admired Fielding's "literary providence") to George Eliot (who envied the easy rapport Fielding achieved with his readers, bringing his armchair to the proscenium and chatting with them "in all the lusty ease of his fine English"). Authors and critics alike have understood that the modern British novel, in many ways, may be said to begin with Fielding. He was the first novelist to realize the possibilities of the so-called "omniscient narrator," and the first to master the aesthetic principle of a unified and significant form. But it is impossible to enumerate the whole range of his innovations. Perhaps they can best be summed up in the statement that he was the first novelist to grasp an essential truth that separates authors in the realistic mode, such as Defoe and Richardson, from those in the tradition of the "Architectonic Novel." This is the perception that the distinction between life as it is lived and life as it can be represented artificially in a narrative is absolute; but that, when exploited by a writer who knows his craft, the resources of artifice—whether in the invention and interaction of the characters, the unfolding of an intricate plot, or the construction of English sentences as well and as wittily as the language allows—can more than bridge the gap between life and art by helping to make the reader a wiser and better human being.

Though Fielding is remembered today chiefly for his novels, he had many talents and many sides to his character. It is probably not too much to say that in some ways he was the most representative Englishman of the second quarter of the eighteenth century. He was, for example, the most prolific and popular dramatist of the 1730s, whose satiric farces against the government caused Parliament to pass a law that shut down his theater. Since he could not make a living as a barrister, the profession he entered when he could no longer write plays, he perfected another skill he had practiced surreptitiously during his theatrical period and joined the ranks of the political journalists, eventually mastering yet another

literary form, the periodical essay. During this same decade of the 1740s, he began his career as a novelist. As that career was culminating in 1748 with the imminent publication of his masterpiece *Tom Jones*, he was rewarded for his services as apologist for the government by being appointed to the magistracy—an arduous post at which he labored so conscientiously that he shortened his life. In the effort to remedy the twin diseases afflicting the social order at midcentury—an increase in violent crime and the spreading blight of poverty—he organized London's first effective police force and became, both in his legal tracts and in his final novel, *Amelia*, the most articulate advocate of basic social reforms.

In broadest outline Fielding's own life resembles that of his foundling hero, Tom Jones, who learned to tame his wild nature before he could win the girl he loved, Sophia, whose name signifies wisdom. No one would have predicted from Fielding's unruly and impudent behavior as a youth that he would end his life as a sagacious and indefatigable defender of the social order. Born on 22 April 1707 at Sharpham Park, near Glastonbury, Somerset, Fielding was the eldest son of Edmund and Sarah Gould Fielding. Edmund Fielding was a charming, wholly improvident military man who had fought gallantly with John Churchill, first Duke of Marlborough, at Blenheim and who would eventually rise to become one of the dozen or so ranking officers in the army. From his father, Fielding had noble blood in his veins: Edmund's father, John, a respected member of the Church of England who held the offices of canon residenciary of Salisbury Cathedral and archdeacon of Dorset, was the youngest brother of William Feilding, third Earl of Denbigh. The Goulds, on the other hand, included distinguished lawyers, notably Fielding's grandfather Sir Henry Gould, a judge of the Queen's Bench. Unlike any of those who seriously took up novel writing before him, Fielding was by birth a gentleman; he took a certain pride in the fact, signing "Esquire" after his name.

The marriage between Sarah and Edmund was apparently a love match, not at first approved by Sarah's family. But Sir Henry was eventually reconciled to his son-in-law and by the terms of his will made it possible for the couple to move in 1710 from Sharpham Park, the Gould family seat, to a sizable farm at East Stour, Dorset. Situated amid some of the most beautiful country in England, the house was just a few steps away from the parish church that, in due

The house at East Stour, Dorset, where Fielding spent his childhood

time, would become the cure of the Reverend William Young, a distinguished classical scholar and the original of Fielding's most memorable character, Parson Adams. Meanwhile, the Reverend John Oliver, curate of nearby Motcomb parish, tutored Fielding in Latin and laid the necessary foundation of his deep love of the classical authors; Oliver surely was the model for the judicious clergyman of the same name who in *Shamela* (1741), Fielding's hilarious parody of *Pamela*, reveals the "true" character of Richardson's heroine.

By the time the Fieldings came to East Stour, Sarah had given birth to Henry's sisters Catharine in 1708 and Ursula in 1709. Once they were settled on the farm, the family continued to grow: another sister, Sarah—Fielding's favorite, who would herself achieve fame as a novelist and classical scholar—was born in 1710; Anne followed in 1713 (though she would live only three years); Beatrice was born in 1714; and in 1716 they were joined by a brother, Edmund, who would eventually emulate his father by joining the army. Since their father was often posted overseas in Ireland and Portugal, Fielding grew up in a family of women and girls who appear to have indulged his every whim. When his mother died in

April 1718, shortly before Fielding's eleventh birthday, Edmund ensured his estrangement from his son by leaving the children in the care of their maternal grandmother and her sister, and going off to London to court a new wife—a widow of the Roman Catholic faith with daughters of her own being educated in convents on the Continent. Edmund compounded this insult to Sarah's memory by selling off part of the farm, which Sir Henry had bequeathed to his daughter and her children, and by applying the income from what remained of the estate to his own uses.

In 1720, angered at Edmund's precipitate second marriage and eager to preserve her grandchildren's inheritance, as well as their continued adherence to the Church of England, his mother-in-law brought suit in Chancery to gain legal custody of the children from their father and "Papist" stepmother. The records of these proceedings provide a rare and disturbing glimpse into the most intimate circumstances of Fielding's childhood. Even after Fielding's death, his closest friend, James Harris, remembered him as a man of violent passions. As a child—his mother dead, his father having abandoned him and his sisters to the influence of a stepmother whom they feared—Fielding was emotionally beyond all control: he insulted the servants, spoke disrespectfully to his grandmother and great-aunt, and defied anyone who attempted to check his behavior. According to the testimony of Edmund's housekeeper, he did not stop at some sort of erotic dalliance with his sister Beatrice—a circumstance that, taken together with other evidence, may help to explain the curious fascination with narrowly averted incestuous relationships in his plays and novels, a fascination found in few other authors of the decades preceding the vogue of "Gothic" fiction after 1765—the most notable exception being, interestingly enough, the fiction of his sister Sarah.

By the time his mother-in-law was awarded custody of the children in 1722, Edmund had packed Henry off to Eton to be educated as the son of a Whig gentleman and, he no doubt hoped, to be soundly thrashed into better manners. In *Tom Jones*, Fielding would pay sarcastic homage to Eton's "birchen Altar" at which he sacrificed his blood, and his opinion of the rod-wielding pedagogues who enforced such lessons upon him is preserved in the character of Thwackum. At Eton, however, he learned more than the advantage of greater self-discipline; he learned Latin and Greek, as well as the classic works written in those languages, and his knowledge of the Scriptures and the doctrines of Low Church Anglicanism was deepened. Though he wore his erudition lightly in the pages of his fiction, Fielding was a man of wide and impressive learning. At Eton—and later at the University of Leyden in Holland, though his sojourns there were brief—he was thoroughly initiated into the great tradition of Western thought known as Christian humanism, a tradition centered on the appreciation of the classical poets, philosophers, and historians, but informed throughout by an enlightened acceptance of the Christian faith. At Eton, too, he made the acquaintance of friends who, in the lean years ahead, would become his patrons and benefactors: among these were William Pitt, later the first earl of Chatham, and, most especially, George Lyttelton, to whom he dedicated *Tom Jones*.

Not much else is known with certainty about his years at Eton, where he remained during the school terms from 1719 to about 1724—except for a brief period in the spring of 1721, when he ran away from the school's stern disciplinarians and sought refuge, not with his father and stepmother in London, but with his grandmother at Salisbury. The anecdote that a fellow Etonian later told about Fielding's school days may well be true: that he once neglected his studies to write a comedy about his father and family. How much this earliest offspring of his satiric muse might reveal about Fielding's deepest feelings during a turbulent, formative period of his adolescence! Again and again the glimpses one catches of him reveal a headstrong young man of violent passions given to defying figures of authority, to brawling, and, in more amiable moods, to romancing a variety of young women. One of these, Sarah Andrew—a beautiful fifteen-year-old heiress who was his cousin by marriage—he attempted to abduct one Sunday morning in the autumn of 1725 at Lyme Regis. The young lady's guardians prevented the rape, and for their trouble they were immortalized in the defiant declaration Fielding, before he fled town, affixed prominently to the customhouse door: "This is to give notice to all the World that Andrew Tucker and his Son John Tucker are Clowns, and Cowards." This document, amusingly enough, is the earliest of Fielding's writings to have been preserved.

While yet a schoolboy, it appears, Fielding dreamed of becoming a playwright—and, to judge from his earliest productions, he took as his models the great comic dramatists of the preceding generation, William Congreve and George Farquhar. Assisted by his influential cousin Lady Mary Wortley Montagu, to whom he dedicated the piece, Fielding had his first play, *Love in Several Masques,* produced at Drury Lane in February 1728, in his twentieth year. The comedy, which had to compete against the prodigious run of John Gay's *Beggar's Opera,* ran for four nights. The winter of 1728 also saw Fielding's debut as a satiric poet, for late in January—in obvious homage to two of his favorite authors, Jonathan Swift and the poet Samuel Butler—he had a poem published entitled *The Masquerade,* purporting to have come from the pen of "Lemuel Gulliver, Poet Laureat to the King of Lilliput." Focusing as they do on "masques"—on the ideas of affectation and hypocrisy, of concealing one's true nature behind false appearances—both the play and the poem sound the first notes in what would be a recurrent theme of Fielding's comic writings, a theme most clearly articulated some years later in the theory of "the true Ridiculous" set forth in the famous preface to *Joseph Andrews.* In August of the same year, his first piece as a humorist in prose, an essay "On the Benefit of Laughing," was published anonymously in *Mist's Weekly Journal*. The essay's thesis of the therapeutic effects of laughter anticipates the theory of comic catharsis also later expounded in the preface to *Joseph Andrews*.

In April 1728 Fielding attained his majority, but he had no fortune to inherit. A gentleman born and bred, he would nevertheless have to earn a living by his wits: he had the choice, he once told Lady Mary, of becoming a hackney writer or a hackney coachman. Before he settled down in earnest to forge a career in the theater, he was sent abroad by his father to continue his education. In March 1728 he registered at the University of Leyden, Holland, as a student of literature. He returned home for the summer, but in February 1729, a few weeks after his father had married for the third time, he set off again for Leyden, perhaps intending to extend his travels to other parts of the Continent, the tour of Europe being the customary way by which gentlemen of the time finished their education. In any case, it is clear from recently discovered documents that by the end of April he had left Leyden permanently, leaving behind his belongings and the unpaid bills of his landlord, his bookseller, and his Italian tutor. Improvidence with money and a chronic inability to pay his debts were among the traits Fielding shared with his father.

When he returned from his travels, Fielding brought with him several plays that he had sketched out abroad. With the theatrical season of 1729-1730 he was ready to enter seriously upon a career as a dramatist. After the cool reception accorded *Love in Several Masques*, however, the managers at Drury Lane were no longer interested in producing his pieces. *The Temple Beau*, another five-act comedy in the manner of Congreve, had to be staged in the City at the much less fashionable theater in Goodman's Fields, the haunt not of the beau monde but of tasteless "cits." Though the play ran for nine nights in January and February 1730 and was thereafter revived from time to time, it was not the success Fielding needed. That would come a month later on yet a third stage—one that in due course he would make, quite notoriously, his own: the Little Theatre in the Haymarket. With *The Author's Farce*, which opened on 30 March, Fielding had at last found his true element as a dramatist. His first experiment in the "irregular" modes of farce and burlesque, the ballad opera and the rehearsal play, it enjoyed the most spectacular run of any new play since *The Beggar's Opera*—a run assisted, to be sure, by the strategy of pairing it after 24 April with his uproariously funny travesty of heroic tragedy, *Tom Thumb*.

Fielding did not move eagerly in these new directions. Before the year was out he had returned to the more prestigious form of the five-act comedy, and had completed his two most interesting and ambitious works in this genre: *Rape upon Rape; or, The Justice Caught in His Own Trap* (soon renamed *The Coffee-House Politician*) and *The Modern Husband*. Though employing the conventional five-act structure of "regular" drama, these plays were in fact experiments in a new kind of comedy: they are more earnest in manner and their subjects more daring. They aim not at the innocuous foibles of the upper classes but at "vice" that "hath grown too great to be abus'd; / By power defended from the piercing dart. . . ." Invoking, therefore, not the comic but "the heroic Muse," Fielding in *Rape upon Rape* exposes corruption in the magistracy; in *The Modern Husband*, his target is what he represents as the peculiarly contemporary evil of calculated adultery, in which husband and wife connive at entrapping and blackmailing her powerful lover. These two plays comprise a kind of manifesto of Fielding's deeper intent as a satirist: he would not be content with the role he claimed for himself in his essay "On the Benefit of Laughing," where he appears as a sort of benign doctor of mirth prescribing laughter as a cure for the vapours or the spleen; instead, in the analogy he later used in his periodical the *Champion* (27 March 1740), he would serve as a "physician" who does not flinch from applying caustic remedies to purge the mind of vice and the body politic itself of corruption. These plays proved far too strong a dose for London audiences, however. The English stage would see nothing quite like them for more than 150 years, when Bernard Shaw would attempt, with a greater genius, such subjects as that of *Mrs. Warren's Profession* (1902).

But Fielding continued to entertain audiences in the lesser modes of burlesque and ballad opera, and in the winter of 1731-1732 he was cordially welcomed back to Drury Lane. It was there that he staged *The Modern Husband* (dedicating the play, surprisingly it has always seemed to some of his critics, to the prime minister Sir Robert Walpole), and it was there a year later that he achieved, with a splendid version of Molière's *The Miser* (1668), his only popular success in the five-act form. For two years he remained at Drury Lane, generally recognized as the "house" author of the Establishment's own theater.

Early in 1734, however, an internal dispute between the managers and some of the principal actors at the theater, as well as the indifference of Walpole to his appeals for patronage, moved him into the camp of the political Opposition, whose leaders included Philip Dormer Stanhope, fourth Earl of Chesterfield, and Fielding's friends from school days at Eton, Pitt and Lyttelton. To Chesterfield he dedicated *Don Quixote in England* (April 1734), a ballad opera he had sketched out some years earlier at Leyden and to which, in this election year, he added scenes satiric of the bribery and corruption that kept Walpole in power. At this time he also began supporting the Opposition's cause in a series of witty articles published anonymously in the *Craftsman*. For five years (1734 to 1738) Fielding maintained this clandestine association with the principal organ of his political friends, the so-called "Patriots"; it is not too much to say that during this period he was chiefly responsible for the reputation the *Craftsman* enjoyed as the cleverest and most impudent of contemporary periodicals.

Fielding would have ranked another event of this year as more precious than any of his literary activities, for in November 1734 he married Charlotte Cradock of Salisbury, a woman admired for her beauty and loved by those who knew her for the qualities Fielding would later embody in his fiction in the characters of Sophia Western and Amelia Booth. It was she, he declared shortly before her untimely death in 1744, "from whom I draw all the solid Comfort of my Life."

In 1736 Fielding's career in the theater reached the very pinnacle of popular success. The doors of both the principal theaters having been firmly shut against him, Fielding early in 1736 leased the Little Theatre in the Haymarket and, as manager of "the Great Mogul's Company of English Comedians," staged *Pasquin: A Dramatick Satire on the Times*—an unusual farce in five acts, comprising the "rehearsal" of two plays: a comedy called "The Election" and a tragedy called "The Life and Death of Common Sense." Its uproarious satire, though directed at the Opposition's favorite targets—the venality and moral debilitation of England in the Age of Walpole—was nevertheless dealt out with some show of impartiality. The play ran to packed houses for more than sixty performances. Walpole fretted but took no action until the following season, when, in *The His-*

torical Register (1737), another wildly successful satire in the same vein, Fielding dared too much, bringing the prime minister himself and his brother Horatio, easily recognizable through the most transparent of disguises, upon the stage. The result—made inevitable by Walpole's convenient discovery of a certain indecent manuscript farce ridiculing not only the ministry but the royal family—was the speedy passage in June 1737 of the Theatrical Licensing Act that shut down Fielding's theater and ended his career as a dramatist. In November he entered the Middle Temple to begin studying for the bar.

For seven years Fielding had been England's most inventive and most popular living playwright. In that short time he produced more than a score of plays—comedies, farces, ballad operas—experimenting with new forms and testing new theories of the didactic function of the drama in his "heroic" comedies and his political satires. Indeed, though the praise may seem extravagant, no less astute a judge than Bernard Shaw declared Fielding to be "the greatest dramatist, with the single exception of Shakespeare, produced by England between the Middle Ages and the nineteenth century." The best of his plays can still be read with pleasure, and they deserve to be revived.

Though in 1737 the idea that he should one day be reduced to scribbling novels for a living had never occurred to him, Fielding would soon be applying to the art of prose fiction some important skills and strategies he had learned while mastering the dramatist's craft. The distancing device of the rehearsal plays, in which the "author" comments upon a drama more "emblematical" than realistic—a drama which in *The Author's Farce* is indeed no other than a satiric puppet show performed by live actors; the conception of characters as representative "types"; the accuracy of his ear for dialogue that rings true while it also reveals the essential nature and motives of the characters; and the ability to control and shape an action, to give it a coherent form— these are only some of the features of Fielding's practice as a play wright that illuminate his practice as a novelist. Indeed, in his last novel, *Amelia*, which is set in 1733, he not only literally returns to the period of his play writing, but his subject strongly recalls the thematic program of his "heroic" comedies, especially *The Modern Husband*; and his de-emphasis of the role of the intrusive narrator, together with his greater reliance on unmediated scene and dialogue for his effects, seems to bring his fiction closer to the literary mode he first loved—the drama.

With the passage of the Theatrical Licensing Act, Fielding, so recently the center of public attention, disappeared entirely from view. His energies—and his appetite for learning and the great strength of his intellect, qualities he scarcely required while writing for the stage—he now applied with the utmost diligence to the study of the law. Indeed, so assiduously did he devote himself to his studies that he was admitted to the bar in June 1740, less than three years after he entered the Temple. To eke out a meager livelihood during this period, he intensified his activities for the Opposition press—at first by increasing the number of his anonymous contributions to the *Craftsman* (a role he played in the campaign to bring down Walpole that ranks among the best-kept secrets of the century), and then, in November 1739, by launching with his friend and collaborator James Ralph a new journal called the *Champion*. Conceived after the example of Joseph Addison and Richard Steele in the *Spectator* and the *Tatler*, Fielding's periodical far outshone its numerous rivals in those rarest of literary qualities, wit and humor; its style was at once vigorous, yet easy and elegant. His subjects, moreover, ranged well beyond the narrow interests of party politics (a topic he generally left to Ralph) to include humorous essays on the taste and manners of the age, as well as more earnest discourses on moral and religious themes. Like his mastery of the dramatist's craft, Fielding's mastery of this literary mode, the familiar essay, was preparing him to succeed as a novelist: as an essayist he was perfecting that singular narrative voice and method that none of his many imitators ever quite got right. For, as Wayne Booth has observed, in Fielding's greatest novels it is the narrator himself who becomes the most important "character" of all as he addresses the reader formally in those wise and amusing essays prefixed to each book of the novel, and as he accompanies the reader throughout, telling the story, interrupting it to comment on its general truths, presiding over his "great Creation" with good-humored "omniscience." These are talents—an ease and familiarity of manner and a habit of wise reflection—that Fielding refined during his years as a periodical essayist.

Always improvident with money, and now with no lucrative "benefit" nights to replenish his supply, Fielding was sinking deeper into debt. In 1738 he had to sell what his father had left of the farm at East Stour; but the money, according to the terms of his grandfather's will, was divided equally among Fielding, his four sisters, and his brother. In the following year he began to be hounded by his creditors and on at least one occasion cooled his heels in a bailiff's sponging house—experiences he would vividly re-create in *Amelia*. Like Mr. Wilson in *Joseph Andrews* he tried to supplement his income from the *Champion* by translating and by other Grub Street employments.

In November 1740, however, at a time when he was about to discontinue his authorship of the *Champion*, there occurred one of the most momentous literary events of the century: the publication of Samuel Richardson's *Pamela; or, Virtue Rewarded*. Richardson's novel, at once edifying and sexually titillating, took the form of a series of private letters written "to the moment" by the chaste but oh-so-sorely-tested servant girl whose story they recorded in the most circumstantial detail; Richardson himself, then a well-established master printer in his early fifties, pretended to be merely the editor of this "authentic" correspondence. Few literary works have achieved such instantaneous fame: from the simple villagers of Slough, who are said to have gathered regularly at the smithy to hear the story read aloud and to have celebrated the heroine's marriage by ringing the church bells, to readers of the most sophisticated tastes—such as the Reverend Benjamin Slocock, who recommended the book from the pulpit of St. Saviour's, Southwark, and Alexander Pope, who was reported as saying that the novel would do more good than many volumes of sermons—*Pamela*, it seemed, had wholly captured the hearts and imaginations of the public.

It was this event that started Fielding on the career that has assured his own lasting fame. For Fielding thought *Pamela* a bad book, crude and pretentious in the writing and pernicious in the mercenary morality it so piously inculcated: that Providence would reward with pounds and social position the virtue of shrewdly chaste servant girls by marrying them to their randy masters. In April 1741 appeared the first of the so-called "anti-*Pamela*'s," Fielding's *An Apology for the Life of Mrs. Shamela Andrews*. A devastating travesty of Richardson's novel, the essence of which it hilariously distills into a few pages, *Shamela* purports to be the "true" story of the young woman whose odd name the "editor" of her doctored papers had got wrong. Richardson's "Mr. B" is revealed as "Squire Booby," hopelessly incompetent in his

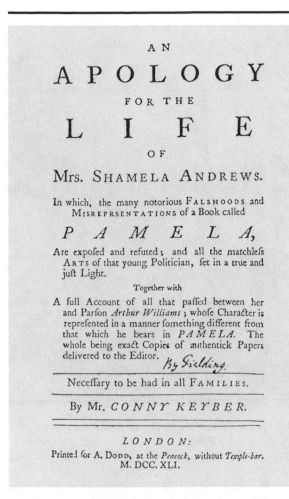

A N

APOLOGY

FOR THE

LIFE

OF

Mrs. SHAMELA ANDREWS.

In which, the many notorious FALSHOODS and
MISREPRSENTATIONS of a Book called

PAMELA,

Are expofed and refuted; and all the matchlefs
ARTS of that young Politician, fet in a true and
juft Light.

Together with

A full Account of all that paffed between her
and Parfon *Arthur Williams*; whofe Character is
reprefented in a manner fomething different from
that which he bears in *PAMELA.* The
whole being exact Copies of authentick Papers
delivered to the Editor. *By Fielding.*

Neceffary to be had in all FAMILIES.

By Mr. *CONNY KEYBER.*

LONDON:

Printed for A, DODD, at the *Peacock*, without *Temple-bar*.
M. DCC. XLI.

Title page for Fielding's travesty of Samuel Richardson's
Pamela. *The inscription "By Fielding" was written by
Horace Walpole in his copy of the book.*

lust, while the heroine is an artful minx who
knows her man, cunningly using her "vartue"
to make her fortune. Fielding's parody is complete—a comic abridgment of the original work,
including not only its epistolary form, its circumstantial "writing to the moment," and its inter-
jected pieties, but also its pages of prefatory
"puffs" so flattering to Richardson's vanity. When
he wrote *Shamela,* Fielding probably did not
know the identity of the author of *Pamela.* But
the author of *Shamela* was later known to Richardson, whose enmity was unremitting toward the
man who produced what Richardson called this
"lewd and ungenerous engraftment" on his work
and who was about to become Richardson's chief
rival in the art of the novel.

Fielding had long since abandoned hope
that as the eldest son of a general he might enjoy
a measure of financial security upon his father's
death. Edmund, in fact, died in June 1741, irretrievably in debt, having spent the last few

months of his life confined in the Fleet Prison.
Fielding's enemies would later accuse him of having reviled his father, during Edmund's humiliation, for wasting his patrimony; and indeed some
such bitterness can be read between the lines of
The Crisis, an electioneering pamphlet published
in April 1741, a month after Edmund had married for the fourth time. The fact is that Fielding
was himself dangerously in debt and deeply troubled at the suffering his impecuniousness was causing Charlotte and his children.

Sometime during the year he proposed to
put out by subscription a three-volume collection
of his unpublished works, to be called *Miscellanies*
(1743), and was gratified at the response from
his noble patrons and his newfound friends
among the lawyers. It is especially curious to find
prominently listed among the most generous of
the subscribers the name of his old antagonist Walpole, who, when he fell from power in February
1742, was elevated to the peerage as earl of
Orford. It is clear from Fielding's satire *The Opposition: A Vision* (December 1741) that by the time Parliament met to settle Walpole's fate, Fielding had become disenchanted with his former
friends. One other sign that he had mended relations with Walpole is the fact that the major work
of the *Miscellanies,* his ironic fable of "Greatness,"
The Life of Mr. Jonathan Wild the Great, was probably sketched out earlier, during Fielding's editorship of the *Champion,* and held back from
publication until it was no longer timely. The
novel was no doubt originally intended as a stinging satire of "the Great Man" himself, Walpole;
for the figure of Wild, a notorious rogue hanged
in 1725, had been so thoroughly associated with
Walpole in the Opposition press that any reference to him would inevitably have conjured up
the prime minister. There is indeed some reason
to suspect that Fielding had taken Walpole's
money to suppress the piece, or at least to with-
hold it from publication until after the critical election of 1741, when—carefully revised and its
ridicule generalized to include the rogues of both
parties—it would be politically harmless.

In autumn of 1741 Fielding was hard at
work on an even better book—a book prompted,
like *Shamela,* by the extraordinary success of *Pamela.* Unlike his parody, however, this would be
much more than a ludicrous "engraftment" on
Richardson's story; it would be in its own right a
masterly example of the novelist's art. Fielding declared his allegiance boldly on the title page: *The
History of the Adventures of Joseph Andrews and of*

In this 1741 engraving by an unknown artist, The Funeral of Faction, *Fielding carries the banner of* The Champion *in the procession mourning the defeat of an attempt to impeach Sir Robert Walpole on 13 February 1741. By the end of the year Fielding had changed his mind about Walpole.*

His Friend Mr. Abraham Adams, Written in Imitation of the Manner of Cervantes, Author of Don Quixote. Published on 22 February 1742, it is the splendid realization of a theory of fiction diametrically opposed to Richardson's, and one for which there had been no precedent in English. In his famous preface—itself an important document in the history of criticism—and in the introductory chapter to Book III of the narrative, Fielding attempted to define the kind of work he had written. Carefully distinguishing it from the most popular forms of prose fiction—from, on the one hand, those voluminous French romances of the preceding century, featuring exotic settings and improbably idealized characters; and on the other hand, from the scandalmongering *romans à clef* of Mary de la Rivière Manley and her followers—Fielding called *Joseph Andrews* "a comic Epic-Poem in Prose," or, alternatively, a special form of "History" or "Biography," truer than the works usually associated with those terms because its subject was timeless and universal. Like its great model *Don Quixote,* then, though set firmly in the England of George II, *Joseph Andrews* would be "the History of the World in general." In relating that history, Fielding meant to repre-

sent nothing less than the essential and unchanging truths of the human comedy: "I describe," he declared, "not Men, but Manners; not an Individual, but a Species."

Such a conception of the way in which an artist imitates "what really exists" places Fielding squarely in the tradition of neoclassicism—the tradition out of which Imlac speaks in Samuel Johnson's *Rasselas* (1759) when he states that the poet's proper function is not to "number the streaks of the tulip"—not, in other words, to offer accurate photographic images of individual objects in real life, which will invariably be idiosyncratic, deviating from the general type—but rather to represent the truly essential qualities that define the species in general: the nature, as it were, of Tulipness. This view of the novelist's art distinguishes Fielding's kind of fiction from that of Defoe and Richardson, the authors to whom Ian Watt attributes "the rise of the novel": for their attempt is—by using the techniques of circumstantial realism to produce a narrative full of particulars in which every streak of the tulip is numbered—to create an illusion, a counterfeit, of actuality. Fielding gives his reader only those few particulars—the gold coin Joseph wears around his neck, Parson Adams's threadbare cassock or his manuscript of Aeschylus—which, though of course helping the reader to visualize a character, function primarily to reveal the values that define the character's true nature.

Implicit in these opposing theories of fiction is the distinction between classical and modern worldviews. The circumstantial manner in which Defoe and Richardson go about imitating "what really exists" is part and parcel of that new, empirical sense of reality to which the scientists of the Royal Society subscribed, whose approach to truth was through the amassing, weighing, and measuring of particulars. Sir Francis Bacon had founded the New Science a century earlier. Fielding, however, like his contemporaries Swift and Pope, remained loyal to the old values of the Christian humanist tradition that the Baconian empiricism was gradually displacing. In this tradition, represented preeminently by the philosophies of Plato and Aristotle, the highest reality transcends the realm of shifting particulars in which life is actually lived: it is found instead in the essential forms of things and in generalized types—in, to return to Johnson's example, the idea of Tulipness; in the species, not the individual. The aim of the artist in this tradition—whether novelist, poet, or painter—will always be to penetrate through multiplicity to unity, through the particular to the general, through what is merely local and idiosyncratic to what is universal and representative.

This is Fielding's aim. But as any good novelist must do, he achieves it by presenting believable characters involved in interesting predicaments, whose stories are set at a particular moment in time and in a particular place: the time in *Joseph Andrews* is the autumn of 1741; the place, chiefly the highways, inns, and villages of the western counties of England. The protagonists are a manly young footman and his elderly friend, a country parson, who encounter a plentiful cast of characters drawn from the whole range of English society—upper-class ladies and beaus, chambermaids and stewards, coachmen and postilions, constables and thieves, clergymen and peddlers, and of course—since the story unfolds along the road westward from London to Dorset—the masters and mistresses of a good many inns and alehouses. Indeed, though *Joseph Andrews*, like its great model *Don Quixote*, satisfies the requirements of the neoclassical theory of art, it is also, as the nineteenth-century critic William Hazlitt observed, the most vivid re-creation imaginable of England in the Age of George II.

Joseph Andrews is also a great comic novel, and to prepare his readers for the kind of story they would be reading, Fielding wrote his famous preface. The theory of comedy he there sets forth also informs his masterpiece, *Tom Jones*. To his first readers it would have been clear at once that Fielding was making the highest possible claims for his "new species of writing," for he opens the essay by defining his work in the terms critics of the day usually reserved for discussions of epic poetry—and in this period the epic was considered, as John Dryden and Pope had declared, "the greatest work human nature is capable of." Fielding methodically takes up the questions of genre, fable, action, characters, sentiments, and diction, and concludes that the book he is about to offer the public is no mere romance or novel, but something more—"a comic Epic-Poem in Prose." Fielding includes his theory of the therapeutic effects of comedy that he first proposed facetiously in his early essay "On the Benefit of Laughing"—"Mirth and Laughter" being "more wholesome Physic for the Mind, and . . . better to purge away Spleen, Melancholy and ill Affections, than is generally imagined."

Since he no doubt feared that some readers would dismiss his work as merely another travesty of *Pamela* (which, indeed, many readers, including Richardson, were inclined to do), Fielding warns that he has not written a parody or burlesque—except occasionally in the diction, "as in the Descriptions of the Battles," which he has included for the entertainment of "the Classical Reader." What he has written, he maintains, is truest *comedy*, in which "we should ever confine ourselves strictly to Nature from the just Imitation of which, will flow all the Pleasure we can this way convey to a sensible Reader." To illustrate the distinction between burlesque and comedy, he looks to painting, the so-called "Sister Art" of poetry, for an analogy, and pays a handsome compliment to his close friend William Hogarth, whom he calls "a Comic History-Painter" in reference to Hogarth's celebrated series *The Harlot's Progress* (1732) and *The Rake's Progress* (1735). Like Hogarth, Fielding would be no mere caricaturist, but a skillful delineator of "character"— the former deliberately distorts and exaggerates the original, while the latter concerns himself with "the exactest copying of Nature." (Hogarth playfully returned this compliment a year later in his celebrated study *Characters and Caricaturas.*) Fielding's province is, he declares, "the true Ridiculous," which, though it has its "only Source" in affectation, reveals itself ultimately as either vanity or hypocrisy. It was Ben Jonson, the great English dramatist, who "of all Men understood the *Ridiculous* the best. . . ."

Essentially, Fielding's theory of "the true Ridiculous" attributes laughter to a sudden perceived incongruity between what an individual pretends to be and what he in fact is in his nature. Examples in *Joseph Andrews* would be the lecherous Lady Booby affecting a reputation for modesty; the self-proclaimed man of courage fleeing in fear of his life at the first hint of real danger; or the rich Parson Trulliber, so proud of his knowledge of Scripture, refusing to part with a shilling in charity. But in all Fielding's fiction the scene that most vividly serves as a paradigm of this comic theory is the one in Molly Seagrim's bedroom in *Tom Jones* when, the curtain concealing him having fallen, the lofty philosopher Square, who has made a career of denouncing the body, is revealed squatting ignominiously in the corner, clad in nothing but a nightcap; here, rendered in a quite literal way, is the hidden metaphor informing Fielding's theory of "the true Ridiculous"— the naked truth behind the drapery of pretension. Obviously, this is a theory of satiric laughter only, reminiscent of Thomas Hobbes's notion in the *Leviathan* (1651) that laughter is an expression of the "sudden glory" we feel when we sense our superiority over another. In his actual practice, the sources of Fielding's humor are more varied, stemming from a more sympathetic apprehension of the human comedy in all its aspects, cheerful as well as sardonic. Parson Adams, for example, perhaps Fielding's most delightful character, excites mirth, but not contempt. The reader laughs at his unworldliness and absence of mind, at his bookishness and his little vanities—and of course at the ludicrous figure he makes with his long beard and torn cassock, his crabstick or tobacco pipe or manuscript of Aeschylus ever at hand, outpacing coaches with his long legs or knocking down ruffians with his great fists. But in Adams what provokes mirth also prompts love, reminding the reader that there is something of the feckless pilgrim in us all.

It was once a commonplace among historians of the novel that Fielding began *Joseph Andrews* as a second travesty of *Pamela,* but then, by a lucky stroke, stumbled upon the character of Parson Adams and thus was able to transform what would have been merely another literary bagatelle into a comic masterpiece in "the manner of

THE

HISTORY

OF THE

ADVENTURES

OF

JOSEPH ANDREWS,

And of his FRIEND

Mr. *ABRAHAM ADAMS.*

Written in Imitation of

The *Manner* of CERVANTES,

Author of *Don Quixote.*

IN TWO VOLUMES.

VOL. I.

LONDON:

Printed for A. MILLAR, over-against
St. Clement's Church, in the *Strand.*
M.DCC.XLII.

Title page for Fielding's "comic Epic-Poem in Prose"

Cervantes." What encouraged this unlikely notion is the joke with which the novel begins: the hero is none other than Pamela's brother, a young footman irresistibly handsome yet no less chaste than his illustrious sister; his virtue, however, is in danger of being sacrificed to the lust of his mistress, Lady Booby, who happens to be the aunt of Pamela's Mr. B. "How ought Man to rejoice," exclaims Fielding after Joseph, later in the novel, has beaten off the still more passionate advances of Betty the Chambermaid, "that his Chastity is always in his own power, that if he hath sufficient Strength of Mind, he hath always a competent Strength of Body, to defend himself: and cannot, like a poor weak Woman, be ravished against his Will." Clearly, Fielding meant to continue his sport with Richardson's novel; in the final chapter he actually introduces Pamela and Squire Booby into his own story.

But from the beginning of the novel it is clear that Fielding is up to something different, something much more ambitious than poking fun at *Pamela:* he is offering nothing less than his own alternative conception of the art of fiction. For one thing (and most essentially), it is his own "voice" that is heard from the opening sentence.

Except for some incidental missives Joseph writes Pamela in chapters 6 and 10, the mocking of Richardson's epistolary form has been wholly abandoned; in its place is the narrative manner— easy and clear, witty yet with just the right note of urbane familiarity, elegant yet without a trace of studied affectation—which is the peculiar glory of Fielding's prose style. Moreover, though the satire of *Pamela* is plainly intended, Pamela's supposed brother's story has a function all its own within Fielding's thematic design for his novel. Fielding's declared model, *Don Quixote,* obviously suggested several of the distinctive features of *Joseph Andrews*. Parson Adams, in his innocence and unworldliness, is indebted to Cervantes' hero—though Adams's idealism and his muscular Christianity are owing to his own goodness of heart, and to his reading of the classics and the Scriptures rather than of the romances of knight errantry. The basic structure of the novel, furthermore—which consists of the heroes' journey from London to Adams's parish in Dorset—is borrowed from the tradition of the picaresque novel, those panoramic stories of the road to which *Don Quixote* is related.

For the most part, however, Fielding's novel is an original creation. In accord with the theory of the epic to which he subscribed, his story, for all its great good humor, is designed to inculcate a moral: the complementary lessons of chastity in the broadest sense, that control over our passions and appetites which is the duty we owe to ourselves, and of charity, the duty we owe to our fellowmen. Again in accord with contemporary theory of the epic, Fielding chose his characters and shaped his action to embody these twin themes: his hero is named Joseph, Fielding says, "for a good Reason"—to recall the example of his biblical namesake, whose chastity was strong enough to withstand the seductive blandishments of Potiphar's wife; similarly, his friend Parson Adams is called Abraham in order to recall the patriarch who, according to St. James, proved his faith through the performance of good works. In *Joseph Andrews*, Fielding thus gave to the loose form of the picaresque novel a coherence and significance of design it had never had. After sounding the theme of chastity in the opening chapters by using the trials of Pamela's "brother" as a comic redaction of the story of Joseph and Potiphar's wife, Fielding takes to the road to involve his heroes—and particularly Parson Adams—in a series of adventures that ring changes on the theme of charity. The central

movement of the novel (extending from Book I, chapter 12, through the final chapter of Book III) opens with the parable of the Good Samaritan reenacted on an English country road, and it closes with Parson Adams debating the nature of true charity with the miser Peter Pounce; along the way, episode after episode enforces this same lesson, which was for Fielding the sum of morality and of true religion. Placed precisely at the center of the novel, even the digression of Mr. Wilson, whose story is a version of Hogarth's *Rake's Progress* but with a happier ending, enacts in little the movement of the novel as a whole, as he retires from the vanities of London to live with the woman he loves a simple, useful life in the country.

Despite every threat to the happiness of Joseph and his beloved Fanny Goodwill—the jealousy of Lady Booby; the snobbery of Pamela; the lechery of "Beau" Didapper, whose designs on Fanny's virtue precipitate the hilarious "Night-Adventures" at Booby Hall—despite even the interference of Fate itself, when it appears that the young lovers are in fact brother and sister, whose marriage would have involved them unwittingly in, as Parson Adams exclaims, "the dreadful Sin of Incest!"—the novel nevertheless ends as comedies traditionally must, with every obstacle overcome and all complexities resolved. The true identities of Joseph and Fanny are providentially revealed—he is Mr. Wilson's lost son; she is the sister of Pamela—and the lovers, united by Parson Adams, retire to the country to emulate Mr. Wilson's wise and loving way of life.

With *Joseph Andrews*, his comic prose epic, Fielding had invented a "new species of writing" in which his true genius as a literary artist could find fullest expression. Just as important to him was the fact that the novel was well received. Why, then, did it happen that his next works of prose fiction—*The Life of Mr. Jonathan Wild the Great* and *A Journey from This World to the Next,* both of which were included in his *Miscellanies* (April 1743)—should be so completely different in kind? Critics have worried over this apparent aberration in his development as a novelist, in which *Joseph Andrews* ought logically to have led to *Tom Jones.* The most likely answer is that both *The Life of Mr. Jonathan Wild the Great* and *A Journey from This World to the Next* were substantially sketched out sometime *before* November 1740, when the publication of *Pamela* provided the inspiration he needed to experiment with a new formula; *Shamela,* the negative response of parody, was the logical first step leading, in a more positive and creative way, to the realization of a kind of fiction completely different from Richardson's. The *Miscellanies* were originally projected well before the winter of 1741-1742, though, because of his own "Indisposition . . . and a Train of melancholy Accidents scarce to be parallell'd" (as Fielding later explained to the subscribers), the volumes were not actually brought out until some fourteen months after the publication of *Joseph Andrews*. Also, it is likely that Fielding would have begun *Jonathan Wild,* an obvious satire of Walpole, before he disassociated himself from the *Champion* in the winter of 1740-1741. It is far easier to surmise that the allusions in *Jonathan Wild* to events of 1742 are the result of Fielding's efforts thoroughly to revise the narrative and to generalize the political satire than it is to suppose that he first thought of writing the novel after those two crucial occurrences of February 1742: the first being the demise of Walpole as prime minister, which rendered less than timely the ironic analogy between Wild and "the Great Man" that is the basic jest of the novel; the second being the publication of *Joseph Andrews*. *A Journey from This World to the Next,* enjoyable as it certainly is, also represents a distinctly inferior conception of the possibilities of the art of fiction that Fielding had begun to explore in *Joseph Andrews.* The *Journey,* like *Jonathan Wild,* contains allusions to events of 1742; and though Fielding has his spirit author begin his narrative on 1 December 1741, it is probably safe to assume that this work "existed in embryo," as Henry Knight Miller puts it, well before the composition of *Joseph Andrews.* Perhaps, as Miller speculates, December 1741 represents the time when Fielding expected to publish the *Miscellanies,* which he had promised to deliver to his subscribers that winter.

Fielding may have taken his hint for at least one prominent feature of the *Journey*—the numerous transmigrations of the soul of Julian the Apostate—from the Myth of Er in Plato's *Republic*; but he also had his eye on the works of Lucian, his favorite among the Greek satirists—particularly on Lucian's *Dialogues of the Dead.* Resorting to the familiar convention of pretending to have discovered this fragmentary work—a curious manuscript that his stationer was using to wrap bundles of pens—Fielding produces it for his reader's edification. It is for a while an entertaining performance, though certainly the oddest and, finally, the least effective of Fielding's fictions. The narrative falls into three distinct parts. The first part (chapters 1-9), easily the best, recounts the spirit narrator's untimely death, his descent into the underworld, and his entrance into Elysium; there are vivid descriptions of the City of Diseases and the Palace of Death and some delightful satire of contemporary types and manners, and in Elysium the fun continues as the reader is introduced to the shades of such departed worthies as Homer and Virgil, Addison and Steele, Shakespeare and Milton—not forgetting the "very small spirit" whom Fielding had himself immortalized, Tom Thumb. The second part of the narrative (chapters 10-25) is less successful, being given over to Julian the Apostate's relation of the lives he lived in his numerous reincarnations—a series of adventures told in a perfunctory manner as Fielding seems, understandably, to have wearied of the device. In the final section, probably contributed by his sister Sarah, Anne Boleyn relates the history of her life.

Far livelier, and much better sustained (despite the thorough recasting it presumably received), is *The Life of Mr. Jonathan Wild the Great*—a work unique among Fielding's major novels both in its form and in the nature of its irony. Indeed, some critics have preferred to call it a "moral fable" or an "apologue," because it is not a novel in the conventional sense at all. Jonathan Wild in real life was both a receiver of stolen goods and a thief-taker, an unscrupulous master criminal whose coldly calculated treachery even to members of his own gang caused him to be hated by the entire populace; he was hanged in 1725, insulted and pelted with missiles by the mob—an event that Fielding elsewhere says he witnessed. Defoe wrote what purports to be an authentic biography of Wild, which served Fielding as a source; and in his "Newgate pastoral" *The Beggar's Opera,* John Gay based the character of Peachum upon Wild, plainly hinting at the similarity between his roguery and that of Prime Minister Walpole. This was the analogy Fielding wished to exploit—an analogy that originated in the Opposition press soon after Wild's execution and that had been kept fresh in the public mind ever since. In Fielding's fiction, then, Jonathan Wild the Great becomes a figure, first of all, of "the Great Man" Sir Robert Walpole. But he is also, more generally, the personification of that false "Greatness"—the characteristic of ruthlessly ambitious "heroes" from Alexander the Great and Julius Caesar to Charles XII of Sweden—which Fielding attacked throughout his career.

Also included in the *Miscellanies,* for example, is a poem whose purpose is to distinguish "True Greatness" from false. Indeed, as Glenn W. Hatfield has observed, one of Fielding's chief motives as a writer is the attempt to purify the moral vocabulary: in *Joseph Andrews* he aimed to define the true nature of chastity and charity; in *Tom Jones* he would similarly explore the meanings of love and prudence.

The story of Wild, then, became for Fielding a parable of knavery, and to intensify the force of the lesson he for the only time in his fiction experimented with a kind of irony more nearly reminiscent of Swift, another of his literary models, than of the Horatian manner of *Joseph Andrews* and *Tom Jones*—a manner at once witty and urbane, yet cheerful and benign. In *Jonathan Wild* the narrator expects the reader to admire the consummate villainy of his hero, who is so well skilled in what Fielding elsewhere calls "the Art of Thriving," and to despise as weaknesses the compassion and generosity that impede a man from rising in the world by climbing on the necks of his fellow human beings. The necessary foil to Wild's greatness—for there must be fools for knaves to victimize—is the kindly and unsuspecting Heartfree, Wild's former schoolmate, now happily married to a virtuous woman and prospering in his business as a jeweler. Though probably modeled on Fielding's good friend, the dramatist George Lillo, Heartfree in this parable serves as the personification of "Good-Nature," a quality central to Fielding's ethical system and the attribute of all the admirable characters of his fiction. In his poem on the subject, also published in the *Miscellanies,* he calls it "the glorious Lust of Doing Good"; in his "Essay on the Knowledge of the Characters of Men," included in the same collection, he is more explicit: "Good-Nature is that benevolent and amiable Temper of Mind which disposes us to feel the Misfortunes, and enjoy the Happiness of Others; and consequently pushes us on to promote the latter, and prevent the former; and that without any abstract Contemplation on the Beauty of Virtue, and without the Allurements or Terrors of Religion."

Possessing this virtue in the highest degree, Heartfree in his innocence is the easiest of marks. Through a series of malevolent contrivances Wild reduces him from happiness to the most abject misery: he is stripped of his jewels, imprisoned for debt, deprived of his wife, and sentenced to hang on a trumped-up charge. Of course the contrivances of Fielding's authorial providence are, in the end, more than a match for Wild's own, and, as Heartfree is at a stroke restored to his liberty, his fortune, and his wife, the "hero" achieves another sort of fitting exaltation at Tyburn gallows.

F. Homes Dudden plausibly speculated that the addition of the story of Heartfree was the principal way by which Fielding recast his original narrative, which had been a "mock-heroic" biography of Wild comprising a transparent satiric allegory of Walpole. Traces of such an intent clearly remain in the novel, even after Fielding subjected it to a further revision in the final year of his life (in the final version, for example, sardonic references to "prime ministers" have become more neutral observations about "statesmen"). For the version of 1743, however, Fielding had already tried to generalize the political satire to include scoundrels of all parties. The keys to his new attitude are to be found especially in two chapters. In Book II, chapter 6 ("Of Hats"), the reader finds, much like Gulliver in Lilliput, that the political principles dividing Whigs and Tories are no more substantial than the differences in the hats they wear: "Viz.: those who wore hats *fiercely* cocked, and those who preferred the *nab* or trencher hat, with the brim flapping over their eyes. The former were called *cavaliers* and *tory rory ranter boys,* etc.; the latter went by the several names of *wags,* roundheads, shakebags, oldnolls, and several others." In Book IV, chapter 3 ("Curious Anecdotes relating to the History of Newgate"), the world is imaged as a prison containing two classes of convicts, the debtors (common people) and the "*prigs*" or felons (Wild and his kind). Now, however, it is not Wild, but another notorious criminal, Roger Johnson, who represents Walpole, Wild having come to stand for those former leaders of the Opposition who dragged "the Great Man" down in order to seize power themselves. The lesson Fielding means to teach is spoken by the "very grave man" to his fellow debtors: "It is better to shake the plunder off than to exchange the plunderer."

The three volumes of *Miscellanies* no doubt satisfied what Fielding called his most "urgent Motive" in publishing them, for—after the charges of his bookseller, Andrew Millar, had been met— the proceeds from more than 425 subscribers netted him about £650—by no means an inconsiderable sum in those days. In his preface Fielding most particularly thanked his fellow lawyers, declaring his "Sense of the Friendship shewn me by a Profession of which I am a late and unworthy Member, and from whose Assistance I derive more than half the Names which appear to this Subscription." For more than a year after this, he appears to have ceased his literary activities in an attempt to establish himself as a lawyer. For example, drawing on a manuscript left by his distinguished grandfather Judge Gould, he tried to compose an ambitious work on Crown Law; though never printed, this was sufficiently far advanced by February 1745 for Fielding to announce that its publication was imminent.

Whatever may have happened to prevent his completing this treatise, it was at about this time that Fielding began work on his masterpiece, *Tom Jones*—which, until its actual publication four years later, his friends invariably called by its original title, "The Foundling." Another important development was the formation in December 1744 of the so-called Broad Bottom government, a coalition in which the "Old Whigs"—who represented such former associates of Walpole as Henry Pelham; his brother Thomas Pelham-Holles, Duke of Newcastle; and Lord Chancellor Philip Yorke, first Earl of Hardwicke—joined forces with the "Patriots," the Chesterfield-Cobham faction that included Fielding's good friend George Lyttelton. It had been the "Patriots" whose interests Fielding had served in his writing, whether plays or verse or journalism, throughout the period 1734 to 1741. In November 1744, while they were still in opposition, he had promoted their cause with *An Attempt towards a Natural History of the Hanover Rat,* a stinging satire against the ministry.

By the autumn of 1745, his friends now at the head of the government, there would be a far more urgent need of his services—the need not merely to promote the cause of his friends in power but to preserve the nation itself from destruction. By then news had reached London that Charles Edward Stuart, son of the pretender to the throne of Great Britain, had landed in Scotland and, at the head of thousands of highlanders who had rallied to his standard, was in full march toward London—intending to reestablish the Stuart monarchy with its absolutist principles of government and to institute Roman Catholicism as the national religion. For Fielding, as for all those who supported the House of Hanover, a monarchy sworn to defend the constitution and the Church of England, the Jacobite Rebellion of 1745 was a dark and ominous moment when the nation was poised at "the very Brink of Ruin." It

THE
HISTORY
OF
TOM JONES,
A
FOUNDLING.

In SIX VOLUMES.

By HENRY FIELDING, Esq;

——*Mores hominum multorum vidit.*——

LONDON:
Printed for A. MILLAR, over-against
Catharine-street in the *Strand.*
MDCCXLIX.

Title page for Fielding's best-known work, admired by many modern novelists

was a time, Fielding later recalled, "far more terrible to all the Lovers of Liberty and the Protestant Religion, than this Age had ever seen before, or is, I hope, in any Danger of seeing again."

In such a crisis he set aside the great novel he was writing, having completed about a third of the work, and devoted his talents to rallying his countrymen to put down the rebellion. Within two weeks in October 1745 he produced three hortatory pamphlets calculated to arouse the nation in defense of its constitution and religion. The same motives prompted him to undertake the *True Patriot,* a weekly paper he conducted from 5 November 1745 until 17 June 1746. When he resumed work on *Tom Jones* after the issues of the rebellion had been settled in blood at the Battle of Culloden, he gave his novel a new time scheme, setting the central narrative in November 1745, "the very Time when the late Rebellion was at the highest." Having been expelled from his home at "Paradise Hall," Fielding's hero was now provided with the opportunity to prove himself "a hearty Well-wisher to the glorious Cause of Liberty, and of the Protestant Religion," and he joins a company of the king's soldiers marching north to meet the Jacobite enemy.

As a reward for Fielding's efforts as the government's chief apologist and the champion of the Hanoverian Establishment, John Russell, fourth Duke of Bedford, in April 1746 appointed him high steward of the New Forest, Hampshire, a post in which he was required to prosecute poachers and other trespassers on the royal preserve. He had at last become—in a quite official, if very modest, way—a pensioner of the ministry; and, though his office and function would change with his later appointment to the magistracy, he would remain the Establishment's man for the rest of his life. Accordingly, in June 1747 he was again employed to argue the ministry's cause in an electioneering pamphlet entitled *A Dialogue between a Gentleman of London, Agent for Two Court Candidates, and an Honest Alderman of the Country Party;* and on 5 December he launched another periodical in behalf of Pelham and his friends in power. This was the *Jacobite's Journal,* in which, though the scurrility of the Opposition journalists eventually caused him to abandon the joke, Fielding assumed the ironic pose of "John Trott-plaid," an inane and unshakable supporter of the Pretender.

During the period immediately preceding the publication of *Tom Jones,* Fielding was engaged in a variety of other activities as an author, two of which are particularly noteworthy. In April 1747 his sister Sarah's *Familiar Letters between the Principal Characters in David Simple,* a sequel to her first successful novel, was published; to this work Fielding contributed the preface and letters 40 through 44. A year later, in the spring of 1748, Fielding took time off from conducting the *Jacobite's Journal* to become involved in what must have been one of the most amusing enterprises of his public life—one that would briefly revive for him, in a droll sort of way, the excitement of his days as theatrical manager and author of such expressionistic dramas as *The Author's Farce.* From 28 March to 2 June 1748, under the name of "Madame de la Nash," he ran a puppet theater in Panton Street, improbably delighting the most fashionable audiences with the antics of Punch and Joan in a series of sketches satirizing "the Comical Humours of the Town"— among them such topics as "Drums . . . Hoops, Plaid Wastecoats, Criticizing, Whisk-Learning, Muffle-Boxing," all of which would receive due attention in the latter books of *Tom Jones.* Indeed, with Fielding's recent experiment as author and

impresario of a puppet show in mind, one can better understand that curious episode in the novel in which his hero defends his "old Acquaintance Master Punch" against the genteel aspersions of a traveling puppet-master.

In this final theatrical fling—which, in order to evade the restrictions of the Licensing Act, he had to stage as a free entertainment in a chocolate house—Fielding was assisted by his former cookmaid Mary Daniel, whom he had married in November 1747, three years after the death of his beloved Charlotte. The reason for this unlikely union is clear from the fact that their first child, William, was born just three months later in February 1748. As his cousin Lady Mary Wortley Montagu would later observe, Fielding's "natural spirits gave him rapture with his cookmaid"; and of course his enemies would not lose such an opportunity for sniggering and derision for some years to come. But it must be said that eighteenth-century gentlemen rarely felt obliged to make honest women of the servants they got with child, preferring to pay them off and settle money on their bastards. That Fielding should choose to legitimize his relationship with this plain, good woman—marrying her in the church of St. Benet's, Paul's Wharf, with his friend Lyttelton in attendance—reveals at least as much about his character as does the passionate affair itself.

The winter of 1748-1749 will stand as one of the memorable moments in the history of the English novel: on 6 December the final volumes of *Clarissa* were published; by 10 February, the announced date of publication, the entire first edition of *The History of Tom Jones, a Foundling,* had been sold out. Within the space of two months had appeared the masterpieces of Richardson and his archrival in the new art of novel writing: the greatest tragic novel of the century, and the crowning achievement of a matchless genius in the comic mode. Both novels were instantaneous successes. Even Fielding, who had ridiculed *Pamela,* was so moved by Richardson's second novel that he wrote him a remarkable letter praising the work. As for *Tom Jones,* a second edition was published before the month was out, and two others would appear by September—a total of ten thousand copies.

As Richardson once observed, there is a marked autobiographical dimension in the best of Fielding's fiction, and in a certain sense the story of Tom Jones is his author's own story— romanticized, to be sure, even made to serve the didactic purposes of a kind of allegory; but recognizable nonetheless in its essential form. Like his author, Tom Jones begins life in Glastonbury, Somerset (the specific place is never named in the novel, but the location is plain enough from the coordinates Fielding coyly supplies). Indeed, Sharpham Park would have been for Fielding almost literally "Paradise Hall," for "Paradise" is the name of that part of the estate that bordered on the church where he was baptized. Squire Allworthy, Tom's foster father, is a composite portrait of George Lyttelton and Ralph Allen, the benevolent patrons who served Fielding as his own prodigal father never did. Sophia Western is the woman whom Fielding knew and loved as Charlotte Cradock. And surely Fielding would have seen his own unsteady progress from a passionate and unruly youth to a more judicious maturity reflected in Tom's nature and his pursuit of the young woman whose name signifies wisdom.

But whatever personal meanings the novel may have had for Fielding, *Tom Jones* is ultimately the fulfillment of that theory of fiction he had earlier experimented with in *Joseph Andrews*—in which he set out to write "the History of the World in general," to represent not individuals but the human species. Announced in the opening chapter, the subject of *Tom Jones* is nothing less than "Human Nature"—not only the passions and foibles, virtues and vices, shared by men and women of every social class, but the characteristics of society itself in all its ranks and degrees: Black George the gamekeeper and his willing daughter Molly, the squires Allworthy and Western and their irrepressible sisters, Thwackum the divine and Square the deist philosopher, Partridge the barber and Jenny Jones, the lawyer Dowling and the soldier Northerton, Mrs. Honour the maid and Mrs. Miller the landlady, Lady Bellaston and Lord Fellamar—and so many others: innkeepers, coachmen, gypsies, puppetmasters and their merry-andrews. As Fielding declares in his opening chapter, he means to offer the feast of life itself. Few books in any literature have managed to be so entertaining and so wise: the characters live (who can forget Sophia's father, the hare-hunting, hard-drinking Jacobite, Squire Western?); the famous plot draws the reader irresistibly on; and for nearly a thousand pages Fielding sustains the reader's delight and confidence in his narrator.

The compliment Hazlitt paid to *Joseph Andrews* holds as well for *Tom Jones:* Fielding has captured the entire panorama of mid-Georgian England. But he means his book to transcend the particularities of time and place by implying universal matters. His story may be read not only as an accurate imitation, but also as an interpretation of life. In this sense *Tom Jones* is the consummate expression of the ethos of England's Augustan Age, the embodiment in narrative form of the optimistic worldview set forth discursively by Pope in *An Essay on Man* (1733-1734). The theme of that poem—which, Fielding once remarked, "taught me a System of Philosophy in English Numbers"—is succinctly stated in these famous lines:

All Nature is but Art, unknown to thee,
All Chance, Direction, which thou canst not see;
All Discord, Harmony, not understood;
All partial Evil, universal Good....

The middle of the eighteenth century marks what Leo Spitzer called "the great caesura" in the history of Western thought: the break between the intellectual tradition of Christian humanism, which had nourished faith in a world divinely ordered and presided over by Providence, and the skepticism and solipsism that have increasingly come to characterize modern thought. Fielding meant *Tom Jones* as a model or paradigm of the Christian humanist worldview. In a passage echoing Pope's *Essay on Man*, he refers to the novel as his "great Creation," and even the form he gave the work expresses the Augustan faith in order. In a brilliant essay, R. S. Crane analyzed the "intricate scheme of probabilities" by which Fielding organically developed his plot; yet even more fundamental to the narrative (because it is the matrix that contains it) is a quite amazing design not at all organic or probable, but as artificial as the pure geometrical shapes of a building by Andrea Palladio, in which the principles of symmetry and balance, the harmonious relationship of part to part, are strictly observed. Fielding conceived of his "great Creation" as a structure of eighteen books, each beginning with a prefatory essay, and the whole divided into three equal parts of six books each: Part I is set in the country at "Paradise Hall" in Somerset; Part II takes place along the road; Part III presents the great city itself, London. At the mathematical center of this structure, in Books IX-X, are the adventures at the inn at Upton, in which the threads of the plot come together and then separate again; and flanking this central section on either side are the two major digressions of the novel, the narratives of the Old Man of the Hill in Book VIII and of Mrs. Fitzpatrick in Book XI, whose stories serve as negative analogues to those of Tom and Sophia, respectively. Fielding's delight in such symmetries extends to other instances of the arrangement of his characters: in each of the novel's three parts, for example, Tom is seduced by a woman from a different social class—Molly Seagrim, Mrs. Waters, Lady Bellaston; then there is Fielding's inclination to people the novel with contrasting characters who stand as foils to one another—Tom and Blifil, Allworthy and Western, Thwackum and Square.

Why would an author go to such lengths (and such immense trouble!) to impose this abstract and highly artificial form on a narrative? Except perhaps for James Joyce's system of symmetries in *Ulysses* (1922), it is hard to think of another novelist from any period whose form is so gratuitously complex. What is all the more curious about this feature of Fielding's novel is that he cannot have expected his readers even to have been aware of it, caught up as they must be in the detail of the story and the unfolding of the plot, and in responding to the continual observations of the narrator—those essential aspects of Fielding's fiction that have been so well illuminated by critics such as R. S. Crane and Wolfgang Iser. The answer may again be found in the *Essay on Man*, in which Pope points out that restricted as we are to our private experience of life and limited in our perspective, it is only "the Part we see and not the Whole"; the enigmatic set of paradoxes in that poem is comprehensible only from the divine perspective—where the apparent confusion and multiplicity of nature can be seen to be the intricacies of an elegant work of art. So the "little Reptile of a Critic" who contemplates Fielding's own "great Creation" is chided that "to presume to find Fault with any of its Parts, without knowing the Manner in which the Whole is connected, and before he comes to the final Catastrophe, is a most presumptuous Absurdity."

Just as nature is art, so chance is direction in the worldview Fielding shared with Pope. As Crane noted, one curious feature of that "intricate scheme of probabilities" that is Fielding's plot is that it often turns upon such improbable coincidences. Tom's lucky encounter at the crossroads with the illiterate beggar who has found the pocketbook that Sophia accidentally dropped is only the most glaring of many examples. This element in life—what Pope calls "Chance" and Field-

ing usually refers to as "Fortune"—is in the Christian humanist tradition ultimately subsumed under the idea of Providence. "Certain it is," Fielding observes, "there are some Incidents in Life so very strange and unaccountable, that it seems to require more than human Skill and Foresight in producing them." "Good Heavens!" exclaims Allworthy upon the lucky discovery of Tom's true identity, "well, the Lord disposeth all Things. . . ."

The form of the novel, therefore, embodies the faith of Fielding and his age in Order. The analogy is grand indeed, but it was deliberate: Fielding is to his own "great Creation" as the Deity is to His. As he undertook *Tom Jones*, Fielding saw himself as producing a kind of timeless model of human life, which was, in the very precise sense expounded by Pope in the *Essay on Man*, ultimately conceived as a comedy, all partial evil being universal good, all chance being direction. The symmetrical design of the novel, its famous "omniscient" author, the unfolding of its plot both through the probable interactions of the characters and through highly improbable coincidences, sometimes apparently unlucky in the extreme (Mrs. Waters appears to be Tom's mother!) but eventually very fortunate indeed— all these features are the perfect expression of Fielding's theme.

Most of Fielding's work as a novelist, or earlier as a dramatist, has the kind of schematic or "emblematical" dimension so clearly evident in the form of *Tom Jones*. The story, too—though it is of course first and foremost a *story*, a tale concerning likable and despicable people whose adventures entertain the reader—may also be seen to have broadly allegorical implications that give it a more universal significance. Tom Jones is a kind of Everyman, his name one of the commonest possible, his status as a foundling (emphasized in the full title of the book) serving as a metaphor of the human condition, for, as children of erring parents in Eden, we are foundlings all: such is the import of that curious passage in which Captain Blifil and Squire Allworthy debate the consequences of Tom's bastardy in language echoing arguments for and against the theological doctrine of absolute reprobation. We will be judged, Allworthy and his author imply, not for any taint in our blood, but according to our own success or failure in the pursuit of virtue. Lest the reader miss the point of Tom's expulsion from his home at "Paradise Hall," Fielding underscores it as his hero begins his journey: "*The*

World, as *Milton* phrases it, *lay all before him;* and *Jones,* no more than *Adam,* had any Man to whom he might resort for Comfort or Assistance." Hounded by Blifil, the envious marplot of his lost Eden, and plunged ever deeper into misfortune by his own impetuous actions, Fielding's good-natured hero reaches the very nadir of despair when he finds himself in prison, the improbably comic analogue of that archetype of all tragic heroes, Sophocles' Oedipus: for not only is he about to be hanged for murder, but it appears that he has committed incest with his mother.

It is at this moment that he proves he has learned the lesson toward which the narrative has been taking him—the lesson of self-knowledge that is the highest pitch of wisdom: " 'Sure,' cries *Jones,* 'Fortune will never have done with me, till she hath driven me to Distraction. But why do I blame Fortune? I am myself the Cause of all my Misery. All the dreadful Mischiefs which have befallen me, are the Consequences only of my own Folly and Vice.' " This confession signals Tom's acquisition of true "Prudence," the chief of the four cardinal virtues of antiquity. Prudence in this sense is that practical wisdom that enables a person to distinguish what is truly good from that which only appears to be good, and which also, by helping him to learn from his past experiences, enables him to act in the present in full awareness of the probable consequences of his actions. Once Jones has mastered this lesson, the doors of his symbolic prison fly open, and he is ready to marry the lovely girl whose name signifies wisdom.

The anatomy of "Prudence" is one of the major themes of *Tom Jones:* it is, Allworthy advises Tom, "the Duty which we owe to ourselves." It was also the virtue that Tom's author had so notoriously lacked in his youth, and that, since it was generally regarded as the indispensable attribute of a good magistrate, he had to acquire. "Prudentissimi" is the superlative compliment carved in stone on the funerary tablet commemorating Fielding's distinguished grandfather, Sir Henry Gould, justice of the Queen's Bench. In this context, the new career that Fielding was entering upon as he brought Tom Jones's story to a close was particularly appropriate.

As early as November 1748, when he discontinued the *Jacobite's Journal,* Fielding began to serve the government as a magistrate—at first only for the City of Westminster but in January 1749, when his patron John Russell, fourth Duke of Bedford, enabled him to qualify for the post, also for the County of Middlesex. It was a decidedly dubious honor his friends had conferred upon him; the so-called trading justices of Westminster, more than eighty in number, were chiefly known for their venality, bias, and ignorance of the law. But almost immediately upon establishing himself at Bow Street, Covent Garden— in the heart of one of the most disreputable districts in town—Fielding applied all his formidable energy and power of mind toward reforming this despised office. Not only did he take no bribes or otherwise make a living by gouging fees from those accused of petty offenses; he gathered evidence against magistrates who were guilty of such practices, and lodged a complaint against a certain Henry Broadhead, magistrate of St. Giles, Cripplegate. Concerned, moreover, at the mounting incidence of violent crime and the closely related problem of increasing unemployment among the poor, he searched diligently for a solution. As early as July 1749 he submitted to the lord chancellor an elaborate plan for reorganizing the constabulary, drafting it in the form of a bill to be presented to Parliament. Though his scheme was ignored, it was a first step toward one of the major practical achievements of his five brief years on the bench: the establishment of London's first organized police force, a band of intrepid thief-takers known as "the Bow Street Runners." For this accomplishment, requiring imagination and a selfless industry that no previous officer of the law had shown, Fielding's memory is honored even today at New Scotland Yard. He also worked assiduously and with some success to introduce reforms into the penal system, in part by recommending able and honest men to serve as keepers of the prisons. He carried on these activities in addition to the usual daily drudgery of "justice business," as he called it, which he often allowed to occupy him far into the night. It is hardly an exaggeration to say that there was something heroic about the manner in which Fielding, almost single-handedly, attempted to realize literally in his new office the role he had often performed metaphorically as satirist in his journals—that of "Champion" or "Censor" of Great Britain.

Not only did he serve the public actively in such ways with a diligence that shortened his life; he also applied his talents as an author knowledgeable in the law to publicizing the gravity of these social problems and recommending solutions. In his *Charge Delivered to the Grand Jury* (July 1749)—

written on the occasion of his being elected chairman of the Westminster Sessions just six months after he had received his commission—he called attention to the debilitating and demoralizing effects on the social order of the licentiousness that had spread downward from the upper classes to infect those who ought to be the most useful members of society; he was particularly critical of gaming-houses, brothels, masquerades, and evil-speaking against God and the king. In his *Enquiry into the Causes of the Late Increase of Robbers* (January 1751) he stressed the manifestations among the lower classes of a newly acquired taste for luxuries—idleness and indulgence in expensive diversions, drunkenness (particularly the curse of cheap gin), and gaming. He examined as well the inadequacy of the laws designed to punish receivers of stolen goods and to curb vagabonds, and the difficulties, both in the laws themselves and in the reluctance of victims to prosecute, of apprehending and punishing criminals. Two years later he returned to a more fundamental problem, first sketchily addressed in this pamphlet. Some of the solutions put forward in Fielding's *Proposal for Making an Effectual Provision for the Poor* (January 1753), as well as in the *Enquiry*, will strike a modern reader as harsh: he recommends, for example, that the able-bodied poor, identified by badges, be collected together in huge county workhouses and made to earn a modest living. These measures, however, are in fact relatively humane in the context of contemporary social thought. Indeed, of the many similar works written in the period, these three tracts are the most judicious, learned, and articulate discussions of contemporary social disorders that have been preserved.

Fielding regarded the social order in terms of the traditional metaphor of the body politic, which, as he could now see more clearly from his vantage point in Bow Street, had become diseased, infected with luxury and infidelity. What was needed was a thoroughgoing reform of England's "Constitution"—the reform not merely of certain statutes that had proven ineffectual or unjust, but of the "constitution" of the social organism itself, the "customs, manners, and habits of the people," to use his own definition in the preface to the *Enquiry*. In his last great work as a novelist he would attempt to use the affective resources of fiction to just such an ameliorative purpose. The result was not entirely successful; readers who expected another *Tom Jones* were disappointed when he offered them a different

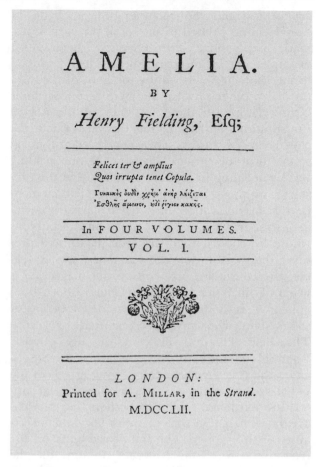

Title page for Fielding's final novel, which he considered his "favourite Child"

kind of novel altogether—a work monitory rather than amiable in tone, not celebrating the feast of life or affirming the reassuring harmonies of the world of Sir Isaac Newton and Pope but rather, as Fielding declares in dedicating the book to his friend and benefactor Ralph Allen, exposing "some of the most glaring Evils, as well public as private, which at present infest the Country. . . ." Though it was not another *Tom Jones,* and was not meant to be, *Amelia,* published in December 1751, is a fascinating and quite remarkable work in its own right. In it Fielding returns to the themes that inform his darker "heroic" comedies of the early 1730s, *Rape upon Rape* and *The Modern Husband*; and because he now writes from a deeper experience of the causes of corruption, his satire has the true ring of authority.

Begun in the autumn of 1749, toward the end of his first year as a Bow Street magistrate, *Amelia* is ostensibly the story of a marriage; but it had from the start a more public purpose. It deserves to be distinguished as the first novel of social protest and reform in English. In it the issues Fielding probed in his social tracts find dramatic expression. The narrative begins, for example, not by directing the reader's attention to the character who will be the hero of the story (as in his other novels), but by offering sardonic "Observations on the Excellency of the *English* Constitution" and by taking the reader into the courtroom of Justice Thrasher, a magistrate as venal, incompetent, and cruel as the one Fielding was prosecuting in real life. The focus at the very start is on those glaring public evils Fielding mentions in his dedication, most particularly the outrageous inadequacies of the agents and institutions whose function it is to dispense justice and preserve the social order: the watchmen are too feeble, the constables take bribes, the magistrate is worst of all. When the hero, Captain Booth, does appear, it is as the last in a parade of victims of the system who have been abused by Justice Thrasher. Though innocent of any offense, Booth is committed to Newgate, where he experiences the ruinous and demoralizing effects of the penal system: some of the prisoners he encounters are hardened felons, but others, like himself, are the wretched victims of unjust laws and the tyranny of the keeper. The first three books of the narrative are set in Newgate, though for the most part they are given over to the stories of Booth and his ardent admirer Miss Mathews. Later in the novel Fielding twice takes the reader inside one of the notorious sponging houses of London, where bailiffs charge the imprisoned debtors extortionate fees for every amenity, while the desperate prisoners try to raise the money to satisfy their creditors. Failing to do so, they are committed to the noisome dungeons of Newgate to rot in the company of felons.

Other scenes in the novel are calculated to expose disorders of a less statutory kind in the "Constitution" of the body politic—moral and spiritual disorders in the "customs, manners, and habits of the people." These scenes, revealing the rage for luxury, the hedonism, and the irreligion of the upper classes, locate the source of corruption where Fielding in his social tracts had declared it to be: in the rich and powerful, who, because they were beyond the reach of the institutions of justice, could be punished only by ridicule and satire. One after another the complaints Fielding specified in his *Charge Delivered to the Grand Jury* and the *Enquiry* are rendered in dramatic form, revealing their consequences in the damaged lives of the characters of the novel: gaming, lewdness

and adultery, the licentious pleasures of masquerades, and atheism.

This last theme is one of the most important in the novel, reflecting Fielding's conviction that a growing spirit of infidelity—manifested, for example, in the deism of Anthony Collins and the skepticism of David Hume—was undermining the only sure foundation either of private morality or of the social order. Thus his spokesman in the novel is the exemplary clergyman Dr. Harrison—a man of charity, learning, and good judgment, the strongest of all of Fielding's good men; his goodness, however, is made more palatable by a certain inclination to satire, which he shares with his author. Fielding's concern over the pernicious consequences of infidelity is also evident in the fact that his hero, Captain Booth, is a skeptic who very much resembles Hume in doubting not only the Providence of God but the freedom of the will: like Hume, Booth believes that reason is the slave of the passions and that a person acts according to whichever of his passions is uppermost. This necessitarian doctrine logically relieves the individual of any sense of responsibility for his actions, and it has debilitating consequences for Booth's moral character: though at bottom a good-natured and amiable man, Booth succumbs to every temptation. As Fielding made room at the end of *Tom Jones* for the conversion of the deist philosopher Square to Christianity, so, in an episode much more important to the central concerns of *Amelia*, he here makes a convert of his hero: while once again incarcerated in a sponging house, Booth reads the sermons of Isaac Barrow "in Proof of the Christian Religion," and the scales fall from his eyes.

These, in brief, are the larger themes of Fielding's powerful final work of fiction. But the novel also had a personal significance for him, for, as readers such as his rival Richardson and his cousin Lady Mary immediately saw, there is a prominent autobiographical dimension to *Amelia*, which is to some degree (but where fact ends and fiction begins will never be determined) the story of Fielding's relationship with his beloved first wife. Even to her damaged nose, Amelia is modeled on Charlotte Cradock, just as Booth, her good-natured but weak and feckless husband, is recognizable as a self-portrait. But why, then, should Fielding have made his hero a gallant officer in the army? Might it be that he did so with Edmund in mind, a man who resembled his son in his improvidence with money and his fondness

Fielding circa 1753 (drawing attributed to Sir Joshua Reynolds; British Museum)

for women? Might it be that by so doing Fielding meant to admit this deeper kinship and to reconcile himself to his father's memory? It is pleasant to think so.

Though Fielding considered *Amelia* his "favourite Child," few readers have shared his fondness for the novel. His publisher, Andrew Millar, printed a first edition of five thousand copies, expecting a run on the booksellers comparable to what happened with *Tom Jones*; but no second edition was called for until 1762, when Arthur Murphy incorporated Fielding's revisions into the version included in Fielding's *Works*. These revisions were meant to correct or to mitigate the faults emphasized by the first readers of the novel: Amelia's nose, crushed in the overturn of a carriage, had never been repaired in the first edition—the noselessness of Fielding's heroine became the joke of the town for many months; other readers were either offended by the "lowness" of the prison scenes or put off by Fielding's

inability to equal Richardson in the sentimental passages. The novel certainly has its faults, but from many points of view it is an original, even a daring, work of considerable power, representing in form, spirit, and its boldly conceived ameliorative intent a radical departure from the proven, successful formula of *Tom Jones*. Indeed, in its satire of social institutions it looks far forward—as far forward as the novels of Dickens. Perhaps Lady Mary's estimate of *Amelia*, written in her personal copy, is the most just verdict: "Inferior to himself, superior to most others."

With *Amelia* already eliciting this mixture of derision and disdain from its first readers, Fielding began on 4 January 1752 to publish a new periodical, the *Covent-Garden Journal*. In the early numbers he responded to his critics with obviously hurt pride, declaring that, though *Amelia* was his "favourite Child" whom he had raised on no less great a model than Virgil's *Aeneid*, he would "trouble the World no more with any Chil-

Fielding's monument in the English cemetery in Lisbon

dren of mine by the same Muse." He was as good as his word. Though he would devote a few hours to revising *Amelia* and *Jonathan Wild*, he never again attempted the thankless business of writing novels. The *Covent-Garden Journal*, which ran until 25 November 1752, was the last of his literary productions, and perhaps, on balance, the very best of his periodicals (though several of the essays in the *Champion* are written with more zest and humor). This time he had no political ax to grind. Adopting the persona of "Sir Alexander Drawcansir, Knight Censor of Great Britain," he ranged freely over a variety of subjects, correcting the taste, the manners, and the morals of the public. Though it was the product of what he liked to call his "gayer Muses," the journal may be seen as an extension of that energetic program of social reform that encompassed virtually every activity of his public life during his magistracy. Indeed, the journal is uniquely valuable to those interested in Fielding's activities as a magistrate because in it he regularly reported on the proceedings at Bow Street.

Except for his *Proposal for Making an Effectual Provision for the Poor* and his hasty defense of his role in the mysterious case of Elizabeth Canning, a young servant girl who claimed to have been abducted by a band of gypsies (Fielding believed her story, but she was convicted of perjury and transported to America), nothing else of importance by Fielding was published during his lifetime. Indeed, he did not have long to live. He had lived hard as a young man, and for many years suffered the torments of the gout. The fatigues of his office would have taxed the constitution even of a man in better health, and instead of sparing himself, Fielding continued to apply every talent he possessed to serve the public. In the winter of 1753, as his plan for suppressing the huge and merciless gangs of robbers was beginning to have dramatic results, his health worsened. He had contracted what in his day was known as dropsy (actually cirrhosis of the liver), a hideous and debilitating disease that bloated his belly and left him discolored by jaundice. As the English weather refused to improve with the spring, his only hope of recovering his health seemed to be a change of climate. Entrusting his "justice business" to his blind half brother John, who had recently been commissioned a magistrate, he left his country house at Ealing on 26 June 1754 to begin a prolonged and tedious journey to Lisbon.

"On this day the most melancholy sun I had ever beheld arose, and found me awake at my house at Fordhook. By the light of this sun I was, in my own opinion, last to behold and take leave of some of those creatures on whom I doated with a motherlike fondness, guided by nature and passion, and uncured and unhardened by all the doctrine of that philosophical school where I had learned to bear pains and to despise death." These are the words that begin his account of that journey, *The Journal of a Voyage to Lisbon,* published posthumously in 1755. Even though he must have known that death was approaching, in his preface he considers how he might use this opportunity to realize the best potentials of the genre of voyage writing. More surprisingly, perhaps, he repudiates the art of fiction, preferring the "true histories" of Herodotus, Thucydides, and Xenophon to the "romances" of Homer. In this respect, and in what it reveals of a once great and generous spirit in sad decline, those who cherish Fielding's novels and admire the man who wrote them will find this final testament of his life a disturbing work. On 7 August 1754 this most English of authors, completing what must have seemed to him his own "journey from this world to the next," disembarked at Lisbon, a city he saw as ruinous and inhospitable, alien in every aspect. There, on 8 October, he died at the age of forty-seven.

For many years Fielding's grave in the English cemetery in Lisbon was shamefully neglected. In 1830 a handsome monument was erected there to mark his resting place with suitable dignity. It bears a fine inscription in Latin commemorating his many achievements. But just as eloquent in expressing what his fiction has meant to later readers and novelists is the tribute paid by Bowen, the young writer in Kingsley Amis's *I Like It Here* (1958), who, standing before the stone sarcophagus in which the author of *Tom Jones* rests, reflects on the significance of the master:

> Bowen thought about Fielding. Perhaps it was worth dying in your forties if two hundred years later you were the only noncontemporary novelist who could be read with unaffected and wholehearted interest, the only one who never had to be apologized for or excused on the grounds of changing taste. And how enviable to live in the world of his novels, where duty was plain, evil

arose out of malevolence and a starving wayfarer could be invited indoors without hesitation and without fear. Did that make it a simplified world? Perhaps, but that hardly mattered beside the existence of a moral seriousness that could be made apparent without the aid of evangelical puffing and blowing.

Letters:

The Correspondence of Henry and Sarah Fielding, edited by Martin C. Battestin and Clive T. Probyn (Oxford: Clarendon Press, 1992).

Bibliographies:

Martin C. Battestin, "Henry Fielding," in *New Cambridge Bibliography of English Literature,* volume 2, edited by George Watson (Cambridge: Cambridge University Press, 1971);

Battestin, "Fielding," in *The English Novel: Selected Bibliographical Guides,* edited by A. E. Dyson (London: Oxford University Press, 1974), pp. 71-89;

H. George Hahn, *Henry Fielding: An Annotated Bibliography* (Metuchen, N.J.: Scarecrow Press, 1979);

John A. Stoler and Richard D. Fulton, *Henry Fielding: An Annotated Bibliography of Twentieth-Century Criticism, 1900-1977* (New York: Garland, 1980).

Biographies:

Austin Dobson, *Henry Fielding: A Memoir* (New York: Dodd, Mead, 1900);

Gertrude M. Godden, *Henry Fielding: A Memoir* (London: Low, Marston, 1910; New York: Barse & Hopkins, 1910);

Wilbur L. Cross, *The History of Henry Fielding,* 3 volumes (New Haven: Yale University Press, 1918);

F. Homes Dudden, *Henry Fielding: His Life, Works, and Times,* 2 volumes (Oxford: Clarendon Press, 1952);

Pat Rogers, *Henry Fielding: A Biography* (New York: Scribners, 1979);

Martin C. Battestin, with Ruthe R. Battestin, *Henry Fielding: A Life* (London & New York: Routledge, 1989).

References:

Robert Alter, *Fielding and the Nature of the Novel* (Cambridge, Mass.: Harvard University Press, 1968);

Hugh Amory, ed., *Poets and Men of Letters,* volume 7 of *Sale Catalogues of Libraries of Emi-*

nent Persons, general editor A. N. L. Munby (London: Mansell & Sotheby Parke Bernet, 1973);

Martin C. Battestin, *The Moral Basis of Fielding's Art: A Study of Joseph Andrews* (Middletown, Conn.: Wesleyan University Press, 1959);

Battestin, "Pictures of Fielding," *Eighteenth-Century Studies*, 17 (Fall 1983): 1-13;

Battestin, *The Providence of Wit: Aspects of Form in Augustan Literature and the Arts* (Oxford: Clarendon Press, 1974);

Battestin, ed., *Twentieth-Century Interpretations of Tom Jones* (Englewood Cliffs, N.J.: Prentice-Hall, 1968);

Jerry C. Beasley, *Novels of the 1740s* (Athens: University of Georgia Press, 1982);

John Bender, *Imagining the Penitentiary: Fiction and the Architecture of Mind in Eighteenth-Century England* (Chicago & London: University of Chicago Press, 1987);

Frederic T. Blanchard, *Fielding the Novelist: A Study in Historical Criticism* (New Haven: Yale University Press, 1926);

Harold Bloom, ed., *Henry Fielding* (New York: Chelsea House, 1987);

Bloom, ed., *Henry Fielding's "Tom Jones"* (New York: Chelsea House, 1987);

Wayne C. Booth, *The Rhetoric of Fiction* (Chicago: University of Chicago Press, 1961);

Leo Braudy, *Narrative Form in History and Fiction: Hume, Fielding, and Gibbon* (Princeton, N.J.: Princeton University Press, 1970);

Douglas Brooks, *Number and Pattern in the Eighteenth-Century Novel: Defoe, Fielding, Smollett and Sterne* (London: Routledge & Kegan Paul, 1973);

Terry Castle, *Masquerade and Civilization: The Carnivalesque in Eighteenth-Century English Culture and Fiction* (London: Methuen, 1986);

Thomas R. Cleary, *Henry Fielding: Political Writer* (Waterloo, Ont.: Wilfrid Laurier University Press, 1984);

R. S. Crane, "The Concept of Plot and the Plot of *Tom Jones*," in *Critics and Criticism: Ancient and Modern*, edited by Crane (Chicago: University of Chicago Press, 1952);

Leopold Damrosch, Jr., *God's Plot & Man's Stories: Studies in the Fictional Imagination from Milton to Fielding* (Chicago & London: University of Chicago Press, 1985);

Peter Jan De Voogd, *Henry Fielding and William Hogarth: The Correspondences of the Arts* (Amsterdam: Rodopi, 1981);

Aurélien Digeon, *The Novels of Fielding* (London: Routledge, 1925);

Irvin Ehrenpreis, *Fielding: Tom Jones* (London: Arnold, 1964);

E. M. Forster, *Aspects of the Novel* (London: Edward Arnold, 1927);

Homer Goldberg, *The Art of Joseph Andrews* (Chicago: University of Chicago Press, 1969);

Morris Golden, *Fielding's Moral Psychology* (Amherst: University of Massachusetts Press, 1966);

Bertrand A. Goldgar, *Walpole and the Wits: The Relation of Politics to Literature: 1722-1742* (Lincoln: University of Nebraska Press, 1976);

Bernard Harrison, *Henry Fielding's Tom Jones: The Novelist as Moral Philosopher* (London: Sussex University Press, 1975);

Anthony J. Hassall, *Henry Fielding's Tom Jones* (Parramatta, Australia: Sydney University Press, 1979);

Glenn W. Hatfield, *Henry Fielding and the Language of Irony* (Chicago: University of Chicago Press, 1968);

William Hazlitt, *Lectures on the English Comic Writers* (London, 1819);

Robert D. Hume, *Henry Fielding and the London Theatre, 1728-1737* (Oxford: Clarendon Press, 1988);

J. Paul Hunter, *Occasional Form: Henry Fielding and the Chains of Circumstance* (Baltimore: Johns Hopkins University Press, 1975);

Eleanor Newman Hutchens, *Irony in Tom Jones* (University: University of Alabama Press, 1965);

Michael Irwin, *Henry Fielding: The Tentative Realist* (Oxford: Clarendon Press, 1967);

Robert William Irwin, *The Making of Jonathan Wild* (New York: Columbia University Press, 1941);

Wolfgang Iser, *The Implied Reader: Patterns of Communication in Prose Fiction from Bunyan to Beckett* (Baltimore: Johns Hopkins University Press, 1974);

Maurice Johnson, *Fielding's Art of Fiction* (Philadelphia: University of Pennsylvania Press / London: Oxford University Press, 1961);

Benjamin Maelor Jones, *Henry Fielding: Novelist and Magistrate* (London: Allen & Unwin, 1933);

Mitchell Kalpakgian, *The Marvellous in Fielding's Novels* (Washington, D.C.: University Press of America, 1981);

Frederick R. Karl, *A Reader's Guide to the Eighteenth-Century Novel* (New York: Noonday, 1974);

Donald Kay, ed., *A Provision of Human Nature: Essays on Fielding and Others in Honor of Miriam Austin Locke* (University: University of Alabama Press, 1977);

Richard Simon Keller, *The Labyrinth of the Comic: Theory and Practice from Fielding to Freud* (Tallahassee: University Presses of Florida, 1985);

Arnold Kettle, *An Introduction to the English Novel* (London: Hutchinson University Library, 1951);

Bernard Kreissman, *Pamela-Shamela: A Study of the Criticisms, Burlesques, Parodies, and Adaptations of Richardson's Pamela* (Lincoln: University of Nebraska Press, 1960);

F. R. Leavis, *The Great Tradition* (London: Chatto & Windus, 1948);

George R. Levine, *Henry Fielding and the Dry Mock: A Study of the Techniques of Irony in His Early Works* (The Hague: Mouton, 1967);

Peter J. Lewis, *Fielding's Burlesque Drama* (Edinburgh: Edinburgh University Press, 1987);

John Loftis, *Comedy and Society from Congreve to Fielding* (Stanford: Stanford University Press, 1959);

James J. Lynch, *Henry Fielding and the Heliodoran Novel: Romance Epic and Fielding's New Province of Writing* (Rutherford, N.J.: Fairleigh Dickinson University Press, 1986);

Thomas E. Maresca, *Epic to Novel* (Columbus: Ohio State University Press, 1974);

Brian McCrea, *Henry Fielding and the Politics of Mid-Eighteenth-Century England* (Athens: University of Georgia Press, 1981);

Michael McKeon, *The Origins of the English Novel, 1600-1740* (Baltimore: Johns Hopkins University Press, 1987);

Alan D. McKillop, *The Early Masters of English Fiction* (Lawrence: University of Kansas Press, 1956);

Henry Knight Miller, *Essays on Fielding's Miscellanies: A Commentary on Volume One* (Princeton, N.J.: Princeton University Press, 1961);

Miller, *Henry Fielding's Tom Jones and the Romance Tradition* (Victoria, B.C.: University of Victoria, 1976);

Robert Etheridge Moore, *Hogarth's Literary Relationships* (Minneapolis: University of Minnesota Press, 1948);

Ronald Paulson, *Popular and Polite Art in the Age of Hogarth and Fielding* (Notre Dame, Ind.: University of Notre Dame Press, 1979);

Paulson, *Satire and the Novel in Eighteenth-Century England* (New Haven: Yale University Press, 1967);

Paulson, ed., *Fielding: A Collection of Critical Essays* (Englewood Cliffs, N.J.: Prentice-Hall, 1962);

Paulson and Thomas Lockwood, *Henry Fielding: The Critical Heritage* (London: Routledge & Kegan Paul / New York: Barnes & Noble, 1969);

John Preston, *The Created Self: The Reader's Role in Eighteenth-Century Fiction* (London: Heinemann, 1970);

Martin Price, *To the Palace of Wisdom: Studies in Order and Energy from Dryden to Blake* (Garden City, N.Y.: Doubleday, 1964);

Clive T. Probyn, *English Fiction of the Eighteenth Century, 1700-1789* (London: Longman, 1987);

Probyn, *The Sociable Humanist: The Life and Works of James Harris 1709-1780* (Oxford: Clarendon Press, 1991);

C. J. Rawson, *Henry Fielding and the Augustan Ideal under Stress* (London: Routledge & Kegan Paul, 1972);

Rawson, ed., *Henry Fielding: A Critical Anthology* (Harmondsworth, U.K.: Penguin, 1973);

Albert J. Rivero, *The Plays of Henry Fielding: A Critical Study of His Dramatic Career* (Charlottesville: University Press of Virginia, 1989);

Eric Rothstein, *Systems of Order and Inquiry in Later Eighteenth-Century Fiction* (Berkeley & Los Angeles: University of California Press, 1975);

Sheldon Sacks, *Fiction and the Shape of Belief: A Study of Henry Fielding, With Glances at Swift, Johnson, and Richardson* (Berkeley & Los Angeles: University of California Press, 1964);

Sean Shesgreen, *Literary Portraits in the Novels of Henry Fielding* (De Kalb: Northern Illinois University Press, 1972);

Angela J. Smallwood, *Fielding and the Woman Question: The Novels of Henry Fielding and Feminist Debate, 1700-1750* (Hemel Hempstead, U.K.: Harvester Wheatsheaf / New York: St. Martin's Press, 1989);

Patricia Meyer Spacks, *Desire and Truth: Functions of Plot in Eighteenth-Century English Novels* (Chicago & London: University of Chicago Press, 1990);

Spacks, *Imagining a Self: Autobiography and Novel in Eighteenth Century England* (Cambridge, Mass.: Harvard University Press, 1976);

William Makepeace Thackeray, *English Humourists of the Eighteenth Century* (London: Smith, Elder, 1853);

Simon Varey, *Henry Fielding* (Cambridge: Cambridge University Press, 1986);

Ian Watt, *The Rise of the Novel: Studies in Defoe, Richardson, and Fielding* (Berkeley & Los Angeles: University of California Press, 1957; London: Chatto & Windus, 1957);

Ioan Williams, ed., *The Criticism of Henry Fielding* (London: Routledge & Kegan Paul, 1970; New York: Barnes & Noble, 1970);

Murial Brittain Williams, *Marriage: Fielding's Mirror of Morality* (University: University of Alabama Press, 1973);

Andrew Wright, *Henry Fielding: Mask and Feast* (Berkeley & Los Angeles: University of California Press, 1965; London: Chatto & Windus, 1965);

Malvin R. Zirker, Jr., *Fielding's Social Pamphlets* (Berkeley & Los Angeles: University of California Press, 1966).

Papers:

The only extant literary manuscripts by Fielding are the poems (circa 1729 to 1733) in the collection of the Harrowby MSS Trust, Sandon Hall, Stafford; and the printer's copy for an essay he contributed to the periodical *Common Sense* (1738) at the Public Record Office, Chancery Lane, London. The largest collection of his letters available to the public is the correspondence addressed to the duke of Bedford and his agent on deposit at the Bedford Office, London, and at the Hampshire Record Office, Winchester. Miscellaneous documents and letters listed by Battestin in his biography and his edition of the correspondence are dispersed among several private and institutional collections, including the British Library, Harvard University, the Huntington Library, the Hyde Collection, the Morgan Library, Princeton University, and the Victoria and Albert Museum.

Oliver Goldsmith

(10 November 1730 or 1731 - 4 April 1774)

This entry was updated by Samuel H. Woods, Jr. (Oklahoma State University) from his entry in
DLB 104: British Prose Writers, 1660-1800: Second Series.

See also the Goldsmith entries in DLB 39: British Novelists, 1660-1800: Part One; DLB 89: Restoration and Eighteenth-Century Dramatists: Third Series; *and* DLB 109: Eighteenth-Century British Poets: Second Series.

BOOKS: *An Enquiry into the Present State of Polite Learning in Europe* (London: Printed for R. & J. Dodsley, 1759);

The Bee, nos. 1-8 (London, 6 October - 24 November 1759); republished as *The Bee. Being Essays on the Most Interesting Subjects* (London: Printed for J. Wilkie, 1759);

The Mystery Revealed: Containing a Series of Transactions and Authentic Testimonials Respecting the Supposed Cock-Lane Ghost (London: Printed for W. Bristow, 1762);

The Citizen of the World; or, Letters from a Chinese Philosopher, Residing in London, to His Friends in the East, 2 volumes (London: Printed for the author & sold by J. Newbery & W. Bristow, J. Leake & W. Frederick, Bath; B. Collins, Salisbury; and A. M. Smart & Co., Reading, 1762; Albany, N.Y.: Printed by Barber & Southwick for Thomas Spencer, 1794);

Plutarch's Lives, Abridged from the Original Greek, Illustrated with Notes and Reflections, 7 volumes (London: Printed for J. Newbery, 1762);

The Life of Richard Nash, of Bath, Esq., Extracted Principally from His Original Papers (London: Printed for J. Newbery and W. Frederick, Bath, 1762);

An History of England in a Series of Letters from a Nobleman to His Son, 2 volumes (London: Printed for J. Newbery, 1764);

The Traveller; or, a Prospect of Society (London: Printed for J. Newbery, 1764; enlarged, 1765; Philadelphia: Printed by Robert Bell, 1768);

Essays. By Mr. Goldsmith (London: Printed for W. Griffin, 1765; enlarged, 1766);

Edwin and Angelina: A Ballad by Mr. Goldsmith, Printed for the Amusement of the Countess of

Oliver Goldsmith (National Portrait Gallery, London). This painting is a copy, probably by Sir Joshua Reynolds or one of his students, of the portrait Reynolds painted for Henry and Hester Thrale.

Northumberland (London: Privately printed, 1765);

The Vicar of Wakefield: A Tale, 2 volumes (Salisbury: Printed by B. Collins for F. Newbery, London, 1766; second edition, revised, London: Printed for F. Newbery, 1766; Philadelphia: Printed for William Mentz, 1772);

The Good Natur'd Man: A Comedy (London: Printed for W. Griffin, 1768);

The Roman History, from the Foundation of the City of Rome, to the Destruction of the Western Empire, 2 volumes (London: Printed for S. Baker & G. Leigh, T. Davies & L. Davis, 1769);

The Deserted Village: A Poem (London: Printed for W. Griffin, 1770; Philadelphia: Printed by William & Thomas Bradford, 1771);

The Life of Thomas Parnell, D.D. (London: Printed for T. Davies, 1770);

The Life of Henry St. John, Lord Viscount Bolingbroke (London: Printed for T. Davies, 1770);

The History of England, from the Earliest Times to the Death of George II, 4 volumes (London: Printed for T. Davies, Becket & De Hondt & T. Cadell, 1771);

Threnodia Augustalis: Sacred to the Memory of the Princess Dowager of Wales (London: Printed for W. Woodfall, 1772);

Dr. Goldsmith's Roman History, Abridged by Himself for the Use of Schools (London: Printed for S. Baker & G. Leitch, T. Davies & L. Davis, 1772; Philadelphia: Printed for Robert Campbell, 1795);

She Stoops to Conquer; or, The Mistakes of a Night: A Comedy (London: Printed for F. Newbery, 1773; Philadelphia: Printed & sold by John Dunlap, 1773);

Retaliation: A Poem (London: Printed for G. Kearsly, 1774);

The Grecian History, from the Earliest State to the Death of Alexander the Great (2 volumes, London: Printed for J. & F. Rivington, T. Longman, G. Kearsly, W. Griffin, G. Robinson, R. Baldwin, W. Goldsmith, T. Cadell & T. Evans, 1774; 1 volume, Philadelphia: Printed for Mathew Carey, 1800);

An History of the Earth, and Animated Nature (8 volumes, London: Printed for J. Nourse, 1774; 4 volumes, Philadelphia: Printed for Mathew Carey, 1795);

An Abridgement of the History of England from the Invasion of Julius Caesar to the Death of George II (London: Printed for B. Law, G. Robinson, G. Kearsly, T. Davies, T. Becket, T. Cadell & T. Evans, 1774; Philadelphia: Printed for R. Campbell, 1795);

The Haunch of Venison: A Poetical Epistle to Lord Clare (London: Printed for J. Ridley & G. Kearsly, 1776);

A Survey of Experimental Philosophy, Considered in Its Present State of Improvement, 2 volumes (London: Printed for T. Carnan & F. Newbery jun., 1776);

The Grumbler: A Farce, adapted by Goldsmith from Sir Charles Sedley's translation of David Augustin de Brueys's *Le Grondeur*, edited by Alice I. Perry Wood (Cambridge, Mass.: Harvard University Press, 1931).

Editions: *The Miscellaneous Works of Oliver Goldsmith, M.B.*, 4 volumes, edited by Thomas Percy (London: Printed for J. Johnson and others, 1801);

Collected Works of Oliver Goldsmith, 5 volumes, edited by Arthur Friedman (Oxford: Clarendon Press, 1966).

OTHER: Jean Marteilhe, *The Memoirs of a Protestant, Condemned to the Galleys of France for His Religion*, translated by Goldsmith as James Willington, 2 volumes (London: Printed for R. Griffiths & E. Dilly, 1758);

Richard Brookes, *A New and Accurate System of Natural History*, 6 volumes, preface and introductions to volumes 1-4 by Goldsmith (London: Printed for J. Newbery, 1763-1764);

William Guthrie, John Gray, and others, *A General History of the World from the Creation to the Present Time*, 13 volumes, preface to volume 1 by Goldsmith (London: Printed for J. Newbery, R. Baldwin, S. Crowder, J. Coote, R. Withy, J. Wilkie, J. Wilson & J. Fell, W. Nicoll, B. Collins & R. Raikes, 1764);

C. Wiseman, *A Complete English Grammar on a New Plan*, preface by Goldsmith (London: Printed for W. Nicoll, 1764);

M. Formey, *A Concise History of Philosophy and Philosophers*, translated anonymously by Goldsmith (London: Printed for F. Newbery, 1766);

Poems for Young Ladies. In Three Parts. Devotional, Moral and Entertaining, edited by Goldsmith (London: Printed for J. Payne, 1767);

The Beauties of English Poesy, 2 volumes, edited by Goldsmith (London: Printed for William Griffin, 1767);

Charlotte Lennox, *The Sister: A Comedy*, epilogue by Goldsmith (London: Printed for J. Dodsley & T. Davis, 1769);

Thomas Parnell, *Poems on Several Occasions*, includes Goldsmith's biography of Parnell (London: Printed for T. Davies, 1770);

Henry St. John, Lord Viscount Bolingbroke, *A Dissertation upon Parties*, includes Goldsmith's biography of Bolingbroke (London: Printed for T. Davies, 1770);

Joseph Cradock, *Zobeide: A Tragedy*, prologue by Goldsmith (London: Printed for T. Davies, 1770);

The Comic Romance of Monsieur Scarron, translated by Goldsmith, 2 volumes (London: Printed for W. Griffin, 1775).

During his short but remarkable literary career of only fifteen years, Oliver Goldsmith wrote individual essays, a pseudoletter essay series, biographies, poems, a novel, and plays—every literary genre practiced in mid-eighteenth-century England. In all, his style showed such grace and charm that, when his friend Samuel Johnson wrote the epitaph for Joseph Nollekens's monument to Goldsmith in Westminster Abbey, he made special note of Goldsmith's versatility, adding that he had touched virtually every literary form, and he had touched none that he did not adorn. In one way or another Goldsmith commented on almost every social change that he and his contemporaries were living through: greater social mobility, the beginnings of the Agricultural and Industrial Revolutions, increasing urban growth and economic development, changing sexual customs, and even the early effects of British imperialism at home and abroad. Through the years since, his literary reputation has rested chiefly on *The Vicar of Wakefield* (1766), a novel both comic and romantic; *The Deserted Village* (1770), a pastoral poem nostalgic for a simpler, more innocent time; and *She Stoops to Conquer* (1773), now a classic comedy in the English dramatic repertory.

Goldsmith was born, probably in 1730, on 10 November at Pallas, County Longford, Ireland. His life falls into two almost equal periods, from his birth until his arrival in London in 1756 and then from 1756 until his premature death in 1774, the second covering his whole career as a professional writer. Considerable knowledge about the second half of his life survives, and, of course, it demands our primary interest; reliable information about his early life is sketchy, although extremely important, because during his early years in Ireland, his personality and character received their definitive shape. He was the fourth child and second son of Charles Goldsmith, himself a younger son and a none too energetic Church of Ireland clergyman, and of Ann Jones, who also had several relatives that were clergymen. Her uncle was curate-in-charge of the parish of Kilkenny West in eastern County Longford and took Charles on as his assistant. The uncle died a short time after Oliver's birth, and Charles Goldsmith succeeded as curate-in-charge, moving to Lissoy, a few miles from the church. His income of about two hundred pounds a year meant relative prosperity for the family, and he lived the life of both priest and gentleman farmer.

Goldsmith's childhood in Lissoy was a happy one. Memories of it almost certainly helped him create the strong nostalgia that permeates *The Deserted Village* and appears in his other works as well. Though the family was financially secure after Charles was installed in Kilkenny West and could count themselves as members of the Anglo-Irish Establishment, or at least of its fringes, they lived with a family skeleton: a Goldsmith ancestor had been a Franciscan friar in the seventeenth century; he was converted to the established Church of Ireland and married, apparently in all sincerity. The family lived with this unpleasant secret at the same time that they followed the free and easy ways of the Protestant Ascendancy, and, if anything, the secret strengthened their identification with the Anglo-Irish, although unlike many of his contemporaries, Goldsmith never attacked the Roman Catholic church or its members in his writings. He could remember with pleasure and homesickness the family dairymaid singing "Johnny Armstrong's Last Good Night" at the family hearth, as he wrote his brother-in-law Daniel Hodson from London in 1757. His descriptions of the warm, cozy life that the Primroses lead in *The Vicar of Wakefield* almost certainly come more from memories of the simple pleasures of hospitality, country walks, tea parties, and picnics and from his knowledge of English country life rather than from the grim poverty of Ireland, but the Primroses' sense of family closeness surely recalls Goldsmith's own memories of his happy childhood. The relaxed easiness of the Anglo-Irish Ascendancy that permeated Goldsmith's childhood had a lasting effect on his own personality, and many of the traits his English friends later in life found bizarre and peculiar had their origin in the easy-going informality that dominated Ascendancy manners, all the more relaxed by the family's remoteness in the country, away from Dublin's more polished life. Both conversation and behavior continued to reflect the less constrained standards of the late seventeenth century rather than the creeping gentility that *The Spectator* (1711-1712, 1714) and books such as Daniel Defoe's *Family Instructor* (1715) were beginning to impose on middle-class English society.

Goldsmith's first teacher, his relative Mrs. Elizabeth Delap, found little promise of future talent in her three-year-old charge. When he was six, his father sent him to the village school, where Thomas Byrne was master. A retired soldier from the Marlborough wars, Byrne was easily diverted by his pupils into tales of his soldier-ing days, but Byrne could also extemporaneously translate Virgil's *Eclogues* into Irish verse. Gold-smith had almost certainly learned some Irish from playing with the children of his father's Celtic Irish tenants and may well have improved his knowledge of the language while Byrne was his teacher. Certainly, in some of his early newspa-per essays, he discussed the native Celtic Irish cul-ture and could well have heard some of the performances of Carolan, the last of the Irish bards, during his boyhood or adolescence. His ma-ternal uncle and later patron, the Reverend Thomas Contarine, showed considerable interest in the old native culture and may well have taken his nephew along on some of his investigations.

Perhaps because of Byrne's interest in po-etry, Goldsmith increased his own interest in Latin verse and built up his own confidence in himself enough so that he became a leader in schoolboy sports. He also had a severe case of smallpox that left his face severely scarred for life. After his early years with Byrne, his father sent him to three successive schools in the area—the diocesan school in Elphin, where he could live with relatives, then briefly to a school in Athlone, and finally to one in Edgeworthstown di-rected by a friend of his father's, who treated him with great kindness and stimulated his inter-est in Latin poetry even further. As his school days were ending, his future career worried the family. His father had originally intended him for a career in business since the family was al-ready paying the expenses of his older brother, Henry, then studying at Trinity College, Dublin, intending him for a career in the established church. A college education for Oliver would strain their finances severely, but his mother be-lieved his talents justified university study. His Uncle Contarine agreed and offered to pay some of his expenses, though Oliver would still have to go as a sizar, serving as a waiter at the Fellows' table, not as a gentleman commoner like Henry. He strongly resisted what he considered an indig-nity, but finally agreed and entered Trinity on 11 June 1745.

Both Oxford and Cambridge had fallen into intellectual doldrums during the eighteenth century, but Trinity had somehow escaped. Gold-smith was not a distinguished student. He thought the emphasis on logic dull, as Jonathan Swift had, and he was never fully reconciled to being a sizar and having to wear the red cap that marked his inferior rank. In his academic work

Statue of Goldsmith, by Foley, at the gate of Trinity College, Dublin

he found his tutor, Dr. Theaker Wilder, difficult to get along with. Unfortunately his father had arranged for him to have Wilder, a violent-tempered, sarcastic man, because his family lived near the Goldsmiths. Goldsmith seems to have spent more time playing his flute than studying, and he reportedly increased his slender pocket money by selling ballads about events of the day, which he composed instead of preparing his les-sons. Like most of his fellow students, he sam-pled much of the entertainment available in Dublin, then the second largest city in the British Isles, especially the theater and concerts. He prob-ably began to gamble during his years at Trinity, an activity at which he never developed any real skill (throughout his life he was more often loser than winner). Accordingly, even in his later years when he earned very considerable sums of money, he was almost always short of ready cash and usually heavily in debt. During his second year at Trinity his father died, making his money troubles even more difficult. In May 1747 Goldsmith became involved in a serious riot, though he was not a ringleader, and was lucky to escape with a public reprimand rather than expulsion. A month later he won a small prize and celebrated his good fortune with a party in his college rooms that became noisy and disorderly enough to disturb his tutor, Wilder, who stopped the party abruptly, berating Goldsmith thoroughly and boxing his ears soundly. Goldsmith was so upset by the incident that he ran away from college, and only his brother Henry's persuasion convinced him to return. Finally, nearly five years after he entered Trinity, he met his degree requirements and received his B.A. in February 1750.

When Goldsmith returned to his family after his graduation, they had no doubts about his future career. On both sides of the family, tradition and influence virtually demanded that he find his future in the established church. He appears to have done some reading in theology as halfhearted preparation for holy orders, but very wisely Bishop Edward Synge of Elphin rejected his candidacy on the ground that he had not yet reached the canonical age. The legend that he presented himself for the interview in scarlet breeches seems apocryphal, but there is no evidence that the bishop urged him to return once he had reached the proper age, and he may well have believed that Oliver was not temperamentally suited to the clerical life, a belief that seems well founded. After his rejection he seemed to have no real plans and surely tried his mother's patience greatly with his idleness. Finally, his Uncle Contarine helped him find a job as tutor with a family in nearby County Roscommon, though a disagreement over cheating at cards soon ended that. He had saved some money and set out for Cork with America as his ultimate goal. Five weeks later he was back home with a sorry horse named Fiddleback and an elaborate but fanciful explanation. His mother's patience was now exhausted, and he moved in with the Daniel Hodsons, his brother-in-law and sister. Another family council convened to discuss his future, and Uncle Contarine put up fifty pounds for his passage money to London and first expenses in studying the law at the Temple. He gambled away the money in Dublin, completely destroying his mother's faith in his talent.

Of the learned professions only medicine remained for him to try, and the family gathered again to start him in this last remaining possibility. Once again, the family, mainly Uncle Contarine, provided his support. In September 1752 he sailed for Edinburgh and enrolled in several courses of lectures, including those of Alexander Munro, the well-known professor of anatomy. On 8 May 1753 he wrote his uncle about his progress in his studies, praising Munro as the best of his teachers, and his name appears as a member of the Medical Society, then chiefly a student group, in January 1753. On 26 September 1753 he wrote his cousin Robert Bryanton to describe the dances he attended. Because Elizabeth, Duchess of Hamilton, was a famous Irish beauty, he enjoyed frequent dinners at the ducal table, although once he realized he was welcomed mainly as a kind of court jester, a role he found unworthy of his calling as a physician, he stopped going. In December 1753 he wrote his uncle, proposing to move on to Leyden the following year, and in May 1754 he wrote him again, proposing to finish his medical training and then return home. His letters to his uncle all seem calculated to present himself as a hardworking student, though their complete accuracy seems rather doubtful. Even so, when he did move on to Leyden in early 1754, he at least went through the motions of continuing his medical studies and praised the lectures of Gaubius, though he complained that except for those lectures, the quality of the teaching was vastly inferior to that in Edinburgh. His May 1754 letter to his uncle contains a long description of the Dutch and their country. The people he found stolid, dull, and fat, whether male or female, though he did admire the beauty of the country's towns: "Whenever I turn my Eye fine houses elegant gardens statues grottoes vistas present themselves but enter their towns and you are charmed beyond description. Nothing can be more clean or beautiful." He limited himself to these lovely features, even though, when he came to write *The Traveller* ten years later, he presented the country as one in which the love of riches has almost destroyed liberty:

> At gold's superior charms all freedom lies,
> The needy sell it, and the rich man buys
> A Land of tyrants, and a den of slaves
> Here wretches seek dishonourable graves,
> And calmly bent, to servitude conform
> Dull as their lakes that slumber in the storm.

Though in the first stages of decline as an imperial power and destined to yield its primacy to Britain, Holland very likely impressed Goldsmith as a society out of balance, in which the huge riches amassed by those engaged in commerce and trading upset the social equilibrium with the landed interest, with which Goldsmith's traditionalist sympathies naturally lay because of his own Irish rural experience. He repeatedly warned his English readers of the destruction of liberty that luxury had brought to those who had succumbed to its "silken sloth," contrasted with the moral magnificence of the uncorrupted English farmers:

> Pride in their port, defiance in their eye,
> I see the lords of human kind pass by.
> ....
> Fierce in their native hardiness of soul,
> True to imagin'd right, above control[.]

The probability that these ideas formed themselves fully in his mind while he was dividing his time between medical lectures and compulsive gambling is slight, but if we think of these as germs of future ideas incubating in the seedbed of his mind, blooming in their definitive form during his all-too-brief creative life of fourteen years, we shall not be far wrong.

A year after he had mentioned (to his uncle) leaving Edinburgh, he left Leyden, writing his uncle that he would finish up his study of medicine soon. (In May 1754, as he had begun his studies in Leyden, he had written his uncle that he was not sure how long he would stay there, but he hoped to be back in Ireland by the following March.) Goldsmith's travels through Europe may have covered much the same route as lordlings followed on their Grand Tours, but he performed them on foot, often depending on his flute to get him bed and board, in somewhat the same way that George Primrose describes his travels in *The Vicar of Wakefield*. His tour took him through Antwerp, Brussels, and Maestrecht, then on to Paris, Strasbourg, and Switzerland, where he saw a good bit of the Alps that summer. He then walked south through the Piedmont as far as Padua, where he spent six months, much of it in nearly total poverty. He wrote Daniel Hodson, begging for money to see him back to Ireland, money that Hodson collected as he could, though it never reached Goldsmith. Nearly destitute as he was, he made his way back through the principal north Italian cities and then turned northwest into France. How many of George Primrose's experiences we can accept as fact or near fact must remain uncertain, and especially doubtful is George's account of disputing theses at uni-

versities along the way in return for bed and board. By February 1756 Goldsmith had reached Calais and took the packetboat to Dover, landing there virtually penniless, still unprepared for any vocation at age twenty-five. Goldsmith's travels had shown him much of the practical side of life, even if at the lower end of the social scale rather than at the higher. His pride kept him from going back to Ireland and admitting his failure. Like Samuel Johnson and many others, he tried teaching school, and then he worked for an apothecary. One of his friends from Edinburgh days found him in the apothecary's shop and did what he could to help financially. Goldsmith briefly tried to establish a medical practice on London's Bankside in Southwark, but gave it up because his patients were, if anything, poorer than he was. After he had established himself as a writer, he was generally known as "Dr. Goldsmith," and the title pages of most of his signed work describe him as a bachelor of medicine. When or if he may have been granted any such degree remains an unsolved problem, and some have argued that he may have been granted an M.B. from Trinity College, Dublin, about 1756; but Bishop Thomas Percy, his friend from 1759 until his death and his first reliable biographer, expressed doubts that Goldsmith had ever received any medical degree.

Like Tobias Smollett and Johnson, Goldsmith had written a tragedy, now lost even in name, and he sought the help and influence of Samuel Richardson, but with no success. Richardson did, however, offer him work correcting proofs in his printing shop. In late 1756 one of Goldsmith's Edinburgh friends, named Milner, whose Presbyterian father, Dr. John Milner, kept a school in Peckham, was looking for a deputy to look after the school while his father was too sick to do so, and he invited Goldsmith to take charge of the school during his father's sickness. Goldsmith's management was haphazard at best since his pupils easily diverted him into singing songs and telling stories. He indulged in such practical jokes as tricking a servant boy into eating a candle by convincing him it was cheese. Except for his inability to manage his money, a lifelong problem, his time at Dr. Milner's school seems to have been reasonably happy, unlike his first experience as school usher immediately after his return from Europe, unhappiness almost certainly reflected by George Primrose's cousin in *The Vicar of Wakefield*, who described the tyranny of the headmaster, his wife's dislike of his ugly face, the schoolboys' obstreperousness, and his own lack of freedom for any social life of his own.

Dr. Milner, his ailing headmaster, did have a wide acquaintance, including influential friends who promised to help Goldsmith secure a physician's post with the East India Company at one of their stations near Coromandel in South India. Much more important, though, Milner introduced Goldsmith to Ralph Griffiths, the owner and publisher of the *Monthly Review,* founded in 1749, and then the only periodical in London exclusively devoted to reviewing books. Shortly afterward, Griffiths offered Goldsmith board and lodging at his house in Paternoster Row and one hundred pounds a year, which Goldsmith gladly accepted, though he lived with the Griffithses only about seven or eight months. Although he still clung to his scheme of going to India to make his fortune, Goldsmith had, without fully realizing it, found his niche. He gave Griffiths good value for his money: his long and largely favorable review (May 1757) of Edmund Burke's *Philosophical Enquiry into the Origin of Our Ideas of the Sublime and Beautiful* remains perhaps the best contemporary comment on that book. More important for his own future career, in his review (August 1757) of *Letters from an Armenian, to his Friends at Trebisonde*, he showed a clear understanding of this particular literary form, the pseudoletter series:

> The Writer who would inform, or improve, his countrymen, under the assumed character of an Eastern Traveller, should be careful to let nothing escape him which might betray the imposture. If his aim be satirical, his remarks should be collected from the more striking follies abounding in the country he describes, and from those prevailing absurdities which commonly usurp the softer name of fashions. His accounts should be of such a nature, as we may fancy his Asiatic friend would wish to know,—such as we ourselves would expect from a Correspondent in Asia.

He faulted the supposed Armenian for his failure to maintain his pretended identity (though Goldsmith would change his mind about this point when he came to write his own *Citizen of the World* [1762]) and for devoting entirely too much space to trivial matters such as the doings of the wife of the lord mayor of Dublin. In September 1757 he confidently attacked Thomas Gray's *Odes* as directed to a coterie rather than the larger, general public he believed Gray had the

ability to reach. He further attacked Gray's choice of unfamiliar Celtic subjects and unclear imagery, implicitly preferring the heroic couplet tradition and expository manner he would choose for his own *Traveller* in 1764.

Griffiths and Goldsmith quarreled in late 1758, and in January 1759 Goldsmith started contributing to Smollett's *Critical Review*, founded in 1756. He also translated Jean Marteilhe's *Mémoires d'un Protestant* (1758), signing it "James Willington," the name of one of his Trinity contemporaries. To finance his outfit for his Indian scheme, he contracted with Robert and James Dodsley to write a survey of belles lettres in Europe and England. In 1758 the East India Company confirmed his appointment, though he still had not found the money for his outfit and passage. Since the profit from his book for the Dodsleys remained uncertain, in December he underwent, but failed, an examination by the College of Surgeons that would have qualified him as a surgeon's mate, a post that would have paid his passage. With no more resources than his pen he found his financial affairs with Griffiths tangled. He avoided arrest for debt only by making over to Griffiths the copyright to a short life of Voltaire. His reviews had attracted the attention of the Reverend Thomas Percy, then chaplain to Hugh Smithson Percy, Earl (later Duke) of Northumberland, and Percy hunted him down in the slum of Green Arbour Court, where his room had only one broken chair and his bed. During their conversation, a neighbor's daughter interrupted them to ask for a chamberpot of coals. But the friendship thus begun with Percy lasted until Goldsmith's death in 1774. When the Dodsleys published his *Enquiry into the Present State of Polite Learning in Europe* in April 1759, he described from firsthand experience the difficult life of professional writers and their troubles with hard-hearted, greedy publishers, unsympathetic critics, and an uninterested public.

Goldsmith still held to his dream of making his fortune in India, but his writing skill and something like fate seemed to be pushing him toward a writing career. In March 1759 long-delayed news from India destroyed his dream of making his fortune there: the French had captured Coromandel a year before. Even though the British had recaptured it, fighting in the area continued and no assurances came of when normal life in the region could resume. Goldsmith saw that any future for him in India was far too uncertain to rely on and that he had best channel his energies into his developing career as a writer. Most of his reviews for Smollett's *Critical Review* show the same confident self-assurance of the reviews he wrote for Griffiths and concentrate on the merit or, more usually, the demerit of the books he was considering, now largely forgotten with the possible exception of his fellow Irishman Arthur Murphy's adaptation of Voltaire's play *The Orphan of China*. In his May 1759 review Goldsmith found far more faults than virtues, though he praised and republished one scene he did admire, concluding with praise of Voltaire as the first European who had praised English poetry, a point he had stressed in his "Memoirs of M. de Voltaire," written about this time but not published until two years later when it appeared in the February-November 1761 issues of the *Lady's Magazine*.

Even though Goldsmith's reviews for both Griffiths's *Monthly Review* and Smollett's *Critical Review* show little if any political bias, these two proprietors certainly did, with Griffiths showing strong Whig leanings and Smollett a strong Tory bias. In addition Griffiths had no reason to love Goldsmith since they had quarreled over money matters, and he almost certainly looked on Goldsmith as a turncoat for writing for Smollett's rival magazine. Thus, when the Dodsleys published Goldsmith's *Enquiry into the Present State of Polite Learning in Europe* on 2 April 1759, even though the book appeared anonymously, Griffiths, like most insiders in the book trade, almost certainly knew Goldsmith was the author. He assigned the review to William Kenrick, who was fast gaining a reputation as a shrewd and partisan hack, able and willing to savage any book Griffiths wanted attacked. Kenrick went after Goldsmith with vigor, shrewdly snapping at one of Goldsmith's important strategies in the book: adopting the persona of a well-educated gentleman of leisure who was giving the reader his personal reflections. *An Enquiry into the Present State of Polite Learning in Europe* does not always reflect the self-confident air that Goldsmith had adopted in his reviews; at times it seems somewhat strained and inflated, lacking the easily informal, relaxed style he was to make his own. Though in no sense profound or original, the book does show many of Goldsmith's preoccupations that crop up again and again in his discursive writing: the sad plight of the author when the patronage system was dying and the modern system of royalty payments had not yet emerged, the importance of literature as an index to a society's cultural health, and the dan-

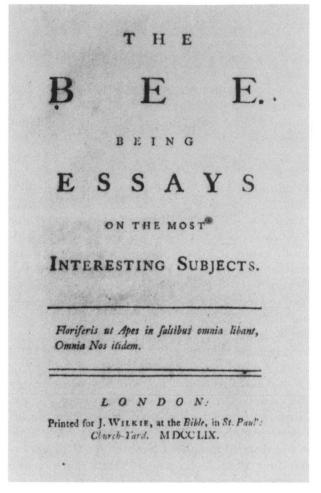

Title page for the collected edition of the weekly periodical Goldsmith wrote in 1759

gers of novelty for the sake of novelty at the expense of traditional literary forms.

With the publication of *An Enquiry into the Present State of Polite Learning in Europe* Goldsmith's reputation as a more than usually promising writer was growing, as was his circle of friendships. Because of his continuing reviews for the *Critical Review*, his friendship with his editor Smollett deepened; Percy had sought him out, and their friendship ripened; and probably about this time he met Johnson, very much a major figure in literary circles because of his monumental *Dictionary* (1755) and also his *Rambler* (1750-1752). In addition, as throughout his life, Goldsmith made close friends among his poor neighbors, especially with their children, and among the many Irishmen who, like him, had come to England dreaming of finding fame and fortune.

He slacked off work for the *Critical Review* because he had a new, promising project. He hoped to capitalize on the current popularity of the relatively new magazine format. Edward Cave's *Gentleman's Magazine* dated from 1731, but in the late 1750s a spate of magazines flowed from the publishers, most of them destined to die after only a few issues. The publisher John Wilkie hired Goldsmith to edit and provide almost all the copy for a new weekly, to be called *The Bee.* For Goldsmith the move from reviewer to editor-contributor was a step up the literary ladder. In the first number, Goldsmith presents a variation of the persona he had already used in his reviews and in *An Enquiry into the Present State of Polite Learning in Europe.* No longer purporting to be the cultivated gentleman of leisure, he describes his shyness and social awkwardness but announces his intention, like the bee, to flit from subject to subject as his pleasure leads him; yet he promises also pleasant instruction, recalling for his contemporaries Swift's bee that provides sweetness and light. The first issue provides a reliable example of his typical subjects: the introduction establishing his persona; an essay on the theater praising French actors over their English contemporaries; a fable titled "Septimus and Alcander, taken from a Byzantine Historian," complete with a moral illustrating poetic justice; a translation from Voltaire; a pseudoletter from a traveler in Poland praising English freedom over the wretched life of the Poles; an essay on the French *philosophe* Pierre-Louis Moreau de Maupertius, who had died the preceding July; and two verse epigrams, one imitated from the Spanish and another Latin one in the same manner. By the fourth number, he wrote in his introductory essay that he had almost certainly aimed at too limited and cultivated an audience and should have sought the larger, less discriminating reading public. In all, he wrote eight numbers; all contain a great deal of material either adapted or translated from sources in French, especially the *Encyclopédie*; however, the seventh and eighth numbers include more material drawing on English sources. Even though *The Bee* failed, not surprisingly since Goldsmith wrote virtually everything printed in each thirty-two-page issue, he thought well enough of his effort to republish in his collected *Essays. By Mr. Goldsmith* (1765), with considerable revisions, eight of the forty-one pieces, and one reappeared with minor changes in *The Citizen of the World* (1762), even though Goldsmith did not use it as one of the Citizen of the

World letters printed in the *Public Ledger.* Wilkie collected the unsold copies of *The Bee* and bound them up for sale in volume form (1759), but with no marked success. Enough copies remained unsold that after Goldsmith's death these were republished with a new, undated title page by the publisher W. Lane.

If Goldsmith was disappointed by the failure of *The Bee,* he hardly had time to mourn, since as he wound up *The Bee,* he was also writing for the *Busy Body,* the *Weekly Magazine,* the *Royal Magazine,* and Smollett's *British Magazine,* as well as the *Lady's Magazine,* published by Wilkie and edited for a time by Goldsmith. As he established a reputation for versatility and hard work, his standing among the booksellers rose vastly, though to the public he remained just one more anonymous Grub Street writer, unknown and hence unrecognized.

The bulk of the pieces Goldsmith contributed to these newspapers and magazines are straightforward expository essays setting forth his opinions on various subjects, some of general and topical interest, such as "On the Present State of Our Theaters," published in the *Weekly Magazine* for 12 January 1760, attacking the theater managers for presenting more pantomimes than plays, especially plays by new authors; and "Some Remarks on the Modern Manner of Preaching," written for the *Lady's Magazine* for December 1760, urging preachers to show more liveliness and emotion in their sermons. However, in Goldsmith's collection of his anonymously published pieces, *Essays. By Mr. Goldsmith* (1765), discursive essays predominate, but nearly one-third, eight of the twenty-seven pieces, use some kind of fictional device to make their discursive points. None of them is a short story in the modern sense of the term, but they are short fictions just as much as *Gulliver's Travels* is a fiction, even if it is not usually considered a novel in today's very elastic generic vocabulary. Goldsmith was, as usual, breaking no new literary ground here, since Addison had often resorted to allegories such as *Spectator* no. 159, "The Vision of Mirza," and Johnson frequently used fictional correspondents in *The Rambler.* Some of Goldsmith's fictive essays are little more than anecdotes, such as no. 15 in *Essays* (1765)—none of the pieces in the volume have titles—revised from the second number of *The Bee,* where it had the title "On Dress," in which an old bachelor pursues a fashionably dressed woman in St. James's Park, hoping for a romantic conquest. The lady, unfortunately, turns out to be his slightly older Cousin Hannah, and they spend the remainder of their time together criticizing the fashions of the day, as well as illustrating Goldsmith's main point that people often dress to conceal their faults and flaws, that clothing reveals appearances only, not reality, a point both Swift and Thomas Carlyle make at much greater length and far more elaborately.

Two of the best-known pieces Goldsmith chose to revise and reprint in *Essays* (1765) are no. 16, called "The Proceedings of Providence Vindicated. An Eastern Tale" when originally published in the *Royal Magazine* for December 1759, but also often called "Asem the Man-hater"; and no. 19, entitled "A Reverie at the Boar's-Head-Tavern in Eastcheap" when it appeared in the *British Magazine* for February, March, and April 1760. In the first Goldsmith burlesques the Oriental sublime allegory that had become a literary cliché by 1759, using the comic techniques of an overly inflated style, reductive and absurd illustrations, and a hurried, mechanical ending to attack the complacent optimism of contemporaries, such as Soame Jenyns, who argued that most human misery was divinely ordained. Using mock-sublime diction, Goldsmith relates how Asem, a wealthy young man from Segestan, has withdrawn into a life of solitary misanthropy near Mount Tauris. On the point of suicide he is stopped by a spirit later identified as the Genius of Conviction. Conviction tells him that Mohammed had once experienced a similar depression and that Allah had formed a world without vice or cruelty to show him that the ordinary world of men is really preferable. Conviction conducts him to a nearby lake and takes him below the surface to show him this alternate world, leading him through various stages of life in the Great Chain of Being: predatory animals are still predatory so that the land will not be overrun with noncarnivores. When Asem and Conviction encounter human beings, they find men fleeing from an army of squirrels, and dogs chasing another man. To answer Asem's objections Conviction replies that the men have no rational justification for attacking the animals, who have lately grown very powerful and troublesome. When they find a sick, starving man by the roadside, Conviction explains to Asem that in a perfectly rational world no one has more than just enough, so that no one practices charity without harming himself or his family. Asem then admits he showed only his own ignorance, praying that

in the future he can avoid vice and pity it in others, and he finds himself back on the lake shore. He quickly abandons his retreat, returns to his native Segestan, where his frugality brings wealth, and he ends his days surrounded by friends in affluence and ease. Thus, Goldsmith shows the sensitive reader his sturdy distrust of abstract philosophical systems that provide overly easy answers to the problem of evil. He uses the fiction of the Oriental allegory to set forth one of his chief themes, warning of the folly and danger in allowing generous impulses to outweigh prudence.

In the second, "A Reverie," Goldsmith's persona falls into a daydream induced by the Gothic architecture of the room, memories of Falstaff and Prince Hal, and a good bit of the landlord's wine. These influences all transform the landlord into Dame Quickly, who then tells him of the various purposes the tavern has served—a brothel, then a monastery in which the friars seduced maidens come for confession; then during the Reformation the monks were burned as schismatics, after which the building became a tavern once again, run by one of the king's cast-off mistresses, and in her hands the tavern once again became a lively, if none too decorous, place. Unfortunately she was ruined by courtiers who failed to pay their bills, and adventurers, pimps, and gamesters took over the place. The last landlady was burned for a witch, and since then the tavern has served by turns as a brothel, a meetinghouse for Dissenters, now a meeting place for Whigs, then a center for Tories. The persona interrupts her to complain: "you have really deceived me; I expected a romance and here you have been this half hour giving me only a description of the spirit of the times: if you have nothing more to communicate, seek some other hearer: I am determined to hearken only to stories." He awakens only to hear the landlord telling him about repairs he has made to the old inn. Though "A Reverie" is cast as a narrative, Goldsmith's point here, that human nature has changed very little over the centuries, is one commonly found among the conservative humanists of the time and is probably set forth most eloquently by Samuel Johnson in his *Preface to Shakespeare* (1765).

John Newbery, one of the most enterprising and innovative publishers of the time, had moved to London from publishing a successful newspaper in Reading and almost overnight established himself as a major force in the book trade. Along with Benjamin Collins of Salisbury, Newbery planned a new daily newspaper, the *Public Ledger*, a prototype of the London *Financial Times* and the *New York Wall Street Journal*, aimed primarily at the City merchants and traders. He signed Goldsmith on as a regular contributor at one hundred pounds a year, and Goldsmith's first trial effort consisted of two letters, the first to a London merchant from a Dutch trader introducing a Chinese traveling to observe Western manners and the second a letter from the Chinese himself, Lien Chi Altangi, to the Dutch merchant after his arrival in London. When these letters appeared together in the issue of 24 January 1760, they almost immediately found admiring readers. Very quickly, the letters took over the leading position on the first page and continued to hold it until the series of 119 ended on 14 August 1761. Goldsmith collected the series, adding four to the original number, and Newbery with five other publishers, among them Benjamin Collins of Salisbury, published them in two volumes on 1 May 1762 with the title *The Citizen of the World*.

The *Citizen of the World* has always found admirers among Goldsmith's readers, some singling out individual letters as among the examples of Goldsmith's best writing. Wayne Booth considers the collection the best of all Goldsmith's achievements, surpassing *The Vicar of Wakefield*, *The Deserted Village*, and *She Stoops to Conquer*. Beyond any doubt *The Citizen of the World* is Goldsmith's first important literary work, but its popularity with twentieth-century readers—because its particular literary form, the pseudoletter series, no longer exists—has never been great. Only excerpted letters appear in anthologies, and the complete series exists only in older editions and in Arthur Friedman's magnificent *Collected Works* (1966), generally available only in research libraries. To appreciate Goldsmith's achievement fully, a reader must read the entire series.

As in all the literary forms that Goldsmith used, he adapted an already existing form, one quite popular among the readers of his time. The use of an Oriental observing and commenting on Western customs had existed at least since Giovanni Paolo Marana's *L'Espion turc* (1684-1686) and was most widely known in Montesquieu's *Lettres persanes* (1721), which Goldsmith drew upon occasionally. He was much more heavily indebted to the 1755 English translation of Jean-Baptiste, Marquis d'Argens's *Lettres chinoises*, from which he took long passages, although none of his borrowings from d'Argens show that minor philosophe's almost obsessive attacks on

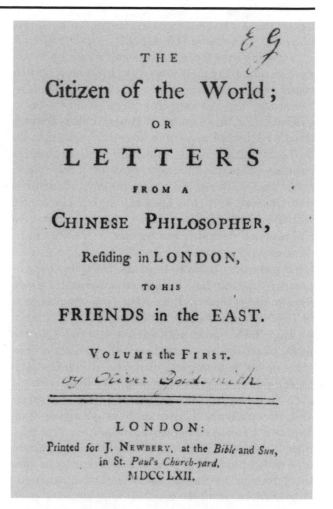

Title page for the collected edition of the essay series Goldsmith wrote for the Public Ledger *in 1760-1761*

the absolute monarchy of the Bourbons or on the corruptions of the monastic system for the very obvious reason that the English monarchy has always been a limited monarchy, at least in theory and certainly in practice since the Revolution of 1688. Henry VIII abolished the monastic foundations, and few of Goldsmith's readers had ever seen a monk or a nun unless they had traveled to France or Italy. As a result, Goldsmith used d'Argens's work chiefly for local color and avoided the Frenchman's militant atheism. His principal sources for Chinese matters were the two volumes of J. B. Du Halde's *Description of the Empire of China* (English translation, 1738) and Louis Le Comte's *Nouveaux Mémories sur l'état présent de la Chine* (third edition, 1697); he frequently acknowledged his use of these two works by Jesuit missionaries in his footnotes to his collected edition. He took his main Chinese character's name from Horace Walpole's pamphlet *A*

Letter from Xo Ho, a Chinese Philosopher at London to his friend, Lien Chi at Pekin (1757).

By the time Goldsmith began writing his Chinese letters, the tide of taste for chinoiserie had already reached its highwater mark in the 1750s in literature, and the taste for pagodas and such in gardens and in Thomas Chippendale's adaptations of Chinese motifs in furniture was already well established. Thus Goldsmith realized that his primary audience of City merchants and traders knew and understood a fair amount about matters Chinese and that his Chinese traveler could ridicule many of the grosser deviations from real Chinese art, customs, and manners. He was confident enough of his own powers to realize that he need not worry too much about "betraying the imposture," as he had earlier described the problem in his review of the *Letters from An Armenian in Ireland, to his Friends at Trebisonde* (1757). As it pleased him, Goldsmith did keep his Chinese mask in place for gently satirical accounts of English social behavior and for serious matters such as religion and politics, as well as in reports of such leisure activities as the theater, the races, and the pleasure places such as Vauxhall Gardens. In letter 8, a prostitute robs Lien Chi, who mistakes her for one of the "well disposed daughters of hospitality," an experience that leads him to comment on the de facto polygamy of many Englishmen, though English law permits each man only one wife. Likewise, when he finds that Englishwomen lack the black teeth and tiny feet he so admires in Chinese women, we recognize Goldsmith's mocking his protagonist and raising the general question of the relativity of some cultural standards. As satirist, Lien Chi ridicules the prevalence of English hypochondria—the spleen and vapors so commonly mentioned by his contemporaries, and likewise notices in letter 69 the absurd fear of mad dogs, a short-lived epidemic terror in the 1760s—and the English love of strange sights and sideshow monsters. He can also praise Englishwomen for showing more restraint in gambling than his own countrywomen. In some letters Lien Chi's Chinese traits hardly figure, as Goldsmith uses him to speak out on some of the subjects dear to his heart: the booksellers' exploitation of poor authors; the advantages and, more important, the disadvantages of luxury; the benefits of the English limited monarchy in contrast to the absolutism in the Chinese empire; and the dangers of acquiring a colonial empire. Several letters comment on quite topical events: letter 43 eulogizes Voltaire, always one of Gold-

smith's intellectual heroes, after a false report of his death in May 1760, and letter 53 severely attacks the first two volumes of *Tristram Shandy* as a work in which "Bawdry is often helped on by another figure, called Pertness." Even though Lien Chi never mentions Laurence Sterne's novel by name, the letter heading supplied in *The Citizen of the World* makes the identification clear.

One of the principal differences between such essay serials as *The Spectator* and *The Rambler* and the pseudoletter series is that while *The Spectator* and *Rambler* have little or no unity except for that provided by the central persona who purports to conduct the series, pseudoletter series such as the *Lettres persanes* and *The Citizen of the World* have some narrative element. Montesquieu's Persians, for example, inquire about life in Isfahan and hear reports of troubles among the women of the harem. Some literary critics have devoted discussions to the narrative elements in Goldsmith's series, but such discussions are brief, even fragmentary.

The narrative elements in *The Citizen of the World* play such an important role in the series that they may almost be called a frame story. Lien Chi has departed from China without imperial permission, so that the emperor has proscribed his entire family, all of whom die, except for his son Hingpo, whom his old friend and principal correspondent in China, Fum Hoam, hides and smuggles out of the empire. Hingpo determines to join his father in the West, but as he makes his way, Tartars capture him and sell him as a slave to a wealthy Persian. In the Persian's household he falls head over heels in love with a fellow slave, the beautiful Zelis, a European who returns his love. They escape from the Persian, who had determined to make Zelis one of his wives, when Tartars sack the Persian's palace. Both of them intend to make their way west via Moscow, though in the manner of the best romances they must endure separation before they eventually meet once more. Again, in the best romantic manner, Zelis turns out to be the niece of the Man in Black, Lien Chi's closest English friend.

Almost immediately after receiving Hingpo's series of letters about his enslavement and love for Zelis, Lien Chi writes his son, first giving him some rather heavy-handed fatherly advice about the conduct proper for a youth entering the world and then sending another extremely fatherly letter about how Catherina Alexowna won the heart of the Tsar Peter the Great by her humility, beauty, and virtue—qualities he makes quite clear Hingpo should look for in Zelis. These exchanges show Lien Chi's all-too-human doubts and fears over what he believes may be his son's infatuation with a woman of whom he knows virtually nothing and his, to us, amusing efforts to counsel prudence and caution, to help Hingpo see the difference between love and gratitude and the need to learn wisdom from living with other people. Besides these moralizing letters written to his son, Lien Chi's concern as a parent appears in letters to Fum Hoam. These touch more than incidentally on the need for prudence in life and on various aspects of marriage, such as the attack in letter 72 on the Marriage Act of 1753, which rumor reported might be revised and which Goldsmith criticized as making marriages across class lines too difficult. Thus, several letters not overtly related to Lien Chi's relationship with Hingpo show Lien Chi's mind is very full of his concerns about his son.

Lien Chi met the Man in Black on his visit to Westminster Abbey in letter 13, in which he shows Lien Chi splendid monuments erected to insignificant, but wealthy people; the collection of monuments in Poet's Corner, which includes no tablet to Alexander Pope; and the battered Coronation Chair with the legendary Stone of Scone. All these comments by the Man in Black reflect Goldsmith's rather acid views on the lottery of fame. The Man in Black, Mr. Drybone, who reappears in letters 26 and 27, tells Lien Chi his story, some elements of which have often been accepted as barely disguised autobiography, chiefly on the authority of Goldsmith's sister, Mrs. Daniel Hodson, a not always reliable source, especially when she recalled events in Goldsmith's London life for Bishop Percy shortly after Goldsmith's death in 1774. In letter 26 Lien Chi describes his friend as "an humourist in a nation of humourists," generously giving money to a beggar whose story he only half believes, just after he has railed against the poor: "imposters, every one of them; and rather merit a prison than relief." The Man in Black undoubtedly shares some traits with his creator, especially his willingness to give money to individual beggars, a trait Goldsmith shared with Samuel Johnson, even though he half knew his compassion was exploited. As the Man in Black explains, his father "told [his children] that universal benevolence was what first cemented society." Throughout his life Goldsmith was exceedingly skeptical about "universal benevolence" because it could not distinguish between

the genuinely needy and those too lazy to work, and he also believed it could reduce anyone who practiced it to poverty too, as Mr. Drybone tells Lien Chi in his story of his own life, an account remarkably similar to Mr. Wilson's in Henry Fielding's *Joseph Andrews* (1742). Though personal appeals often overcame his theoretical objections, Goldsmith repeatedly advocated worldly prudence, the need to recognize the deceitful and dishonest, an insight which the Man in Black possesses but almost never practices, as Lien Chi describes his helping an old beggar, then a one-legged former naval officer, and finally a poor ragged woman ballad singer with two children. The Chinese clearly notes the inconsistency between his friend's theory and practice. Only when he came to write of Sir William Thornhill in *The Vicar of Wakefield* did Goldsmith present a character who has learned from experience, like Fielding's Mr. Wilson, to live prudently in a world filled with imposture—though Sir William's own behavior is eccentric by any standard as he wanders about his estates disguised as Mr. Burchell.

Through the Man in Black, Lien Chi acquires a circle of London friends, such as Beau Tibbs and his wife, who pathetically burlesque the manners and language of the nobility, and the letters about these characters form the second narrative element in the series. Tibbs pesters both Lien Chi and the Man in Black with his transparently invented accounts of dinners with the Duchess of Picadilly and Lady Grogram and coach rides with Lord Muddler, though the Man in Black acutely but gloomily foretells Tibbs's future: "Condemned in the decline of life to hang upon some rich family whom he once despised, there to undergo all the ingenuity of studied contempt, to be employed only as a spy upon the servants, or a bugbear to fright the children into duty." In letter 55 Tibbs blithely invites Lien Chi and Drybone to the squalor of his garret, where his coy but slatternly wife orders them a dinner of ox cheek and bottled beer to be served two hours hence. Lien Chi pleads a prior engagement and escapes to satisfy his hunger elsewhere. Somewhat later on, in letter 73, the Man in Black invites Lien Chi to a supper at Vauxhall Gardens, together with the Tibbses and a pawnbroker's widow, whom Mr. Drybone is courting and for whom he turns out in superlative finery. The party marks one of the comic high points of the series, since the widow pines to see the waterworks display and Mrs. Tibbs is determined they shall

The Preface

In whatever light we regard the present war which has disturbed all Europe, we shall find it the most important of any recorded in modern history. Whether we consider the power of the nations at variance, the number of the forces employ'd, the skill of the generals conducting, we shall equally find matter for improvement or admiration. We shall see small kingdoms forced by the prudence of one man into an astonishing degree of power, and extensive countries scarce able to support their own rights or repel the invaders.

But whatever these contentions may be thought of by others, they will never be regarded by Britons but as instances of her power, her bravery, and her freedom. In this war England will appear in greater splendour than in any period of the most boasted antiquity, it will be seen to poize the fates of Europe and bring its most potent and most ambitious states into the lowest degree of humiliation. This is a glory which should excite every lover of his country to celebrate as well as to share in.

The desolation of war, the insolent severity of victors, and the servitude of those who happen to be overcome have been often the topics of Declamation and employ'd the reasoner as well as the Rhetorician; but still I would doubt whether even wars have not their benefits, whether they do not serve as motion to water, desperate states of all that a great number of vices contracted by long habits of peace. If we attentively examine the records of history we shall ever find that long indolence in any country was only productive of mischief, and that those very arts which were brought to perfection in peace often proved to introduce new vices with new luxury. The Roman state stood firm until Italy had no longer any enemies to fear, contented with enjoying the fruits of victory they no more desired to obtain it, their wars were carried on by mercenary soldiers, their armies were levied in distant provinces, and those very provinces at length became their masters.

But to what purpose to cite ancient History when we have so recent and so near an instance in the Dutch. That people once brave, Enthusiasts in the cause of freedom, and able to make their state formidable to their neighbours, is by a long continuance of peace, divided into faction, set upon private interest, and neither able, nor willing to usurp its rights or revenge oppression. This may serve as a memorable instance of what may be the result of a total inattention to war, and an utter extirpation of martial ardour. Insulted by the French, threatened by the English, and almost universally despised by the rest of Europe. How unlike the brave peasants their ancestors, who spread terror into either India, and always declared themselves the allies

Pages from the preface to "The Political View of the Result of the Present War with America upon Great Britain, France, Prussia, Germany, and Holland," a history of the Seven Years' War that Goldsmith compiled in 1761 from articles that had appeared in the Lady's Magazine *during 1756-1758 (HM176, Henry E. Huntington Library and Art Gallery). The history was published for the first time in 1837, as* Preface and Introduction to the History of the Seven Years's War.

of those who drew the sword in defence of freedom!

The friendship between the English and the Dutch was at first conceived to be inseparable, they were termed in the stile of Politicians faithful friends, natural allies Protestant confederates, and by many other names of national endearment. Both had the same interest as opposed to France, and some resemblance of religion or opposd to popery, yet these were but slight ties with a nation whose only views were comerce, a rivalry in that will serve to destroy with themever connected. No merely mercantile man, or mercantile nation has any friendship but for money, and an alliance between them will last no longer than their common safety or common profit is endangered, no longer than they have an enemy ready to deprive them of more, than they can be able to steal from each other.

A long continuance of property in the same channel is also very prejudicial to a nation, in such a state emulation is in some measure destroyed fortune seems to stand still with those who are already in possession of it. they who are rich have no need of an exertion of their abilities in order to ~~every~~ preserve their wealth, and the poor must rest in hopeless indigence, but war gives a circulation to the wealth of a nation, the poor have many opportunities of bettering their fortune, and the rich must labour in order to support the necesasary expences required in defraying it. Thus all are in action, and emulative industry is the parent of every national virtue.

A long continuance of peace in England was never productive of advantageous consequences, upon such occasions, we have ever seen her divided into factions, her senates becoming venal, and her ministers even avowing corruption. But when a foreign enemy appears, private animosities cease, factions are forgotten, and party rage is united against the common foe. I am not an advocate for war, but it were happy if mankind did not require such a scourge to keep them within those bounds which they ought to observe with respect to their country and themselves. It is not likely however that the English should relax into the abject state of debility of a neighbouring nation, they will have ever cause of distrust while France continues to cherish views of ambition. A Nation that seems the enemy of Britain by nature. Different in religion, government and disposition it is almost impossible they can ever be thoroughly reconciled, and perhaps this rivalry will continue to preserve them both in circumstances of vigour and power longer than any other nations recorded in history, since from the situation of each country it does not seem easy to conceive how the one will ever be able entirely to oppress the other.

The System of Politicks at present pursued by the English may properly be said to have taken rise in the reign of Queen Elizabeth, at this time the protestant religion was established, which then allied us to those countries who embraced the have a genteel box for their supper, away from the view of the waterworks. After much prevailing from the company, most of it patently insincere, Mrs. Tibbs favors them with an almost interminable song, singing until the waterworks display is over, and the poor widow fails in her dearest wish and leaves in great displeasure, though the Tibbses assure everyone else the most fashionable hours are just beginning.

When Goldsmith wrote the letters for the *Public Ledger*, in the letter collected as number 116 in *The Citizen of the World* Lien Chi joins the Man in Black to argue with his unnamed niece that love is a fictitious passion. She had first appeared in London in what is collected as letter 99 (letter 97 in the *Public Ledger*), in which Lien Chi praises her exquisite beauty, manners, and intelligence. In the *Public Ledger* only two letters intervened between the debate between Lien Chi and the Man in Black's niece over the nature of love, and the letter collected as number 123, in which Hingpo is reunited with his father and recognizes the Man in Black's niece as Zelis, his beloved, and the various loose ends are tied into a happy ending for the major characters. The two intervening letters discuss the willingness of the Dutch to undergo any indignity to secure trading rights with Japan (letter collected as number 118) and the absurdity of some English titles (letter collected as number 120).

Goldsmith appears to have thought, or perhaps heard criticism, that the conclusion he gave the series of letters in the *Public Ledger* was hurried. At any rate, when he collected the letters for publication as *The Citizen of the World*, he added four letters to stretch his material between the debate over love and Hingpo's presentation of his beloved to his father. None of these letters touches upon the approaching resolution, and his dealing with other matters may help make the conclusion somewhat more credible. Letter 117 in *The Citizen of the World*, "A City Night-Piece," was originally published in the fourth number of *The Bee* (27 October 1759); letter 119, on the distresses of the poor, as shown by the career of a sentinel, was originally published in the *British Magazine* for June 1760; letter 121, written especially for *The Citizen of the World*, compares the political fluctuation in Britain favorably with the stable tyranny of China; and letter 122, also written especially for *The Citizen of the World*, satirizes the overly minute, dull detail of recent travel books. Only then did Goldsmith use the letter which concludes the series in the *Public Ledger*.

The material that appears in these insertions is not nearly so important as the fact that Goldsmith apparently realized that he needed several more letters before springing the grossly coincidental reunion between Zelis and Hingpo on his readers. His conclusion in *The Citizen of the World* still violates the most elementary canons of probability, but not nearly so strongly as the arrangement in the *Public Ledger* does. The sensible reader knows Goldsmith is pulling his leg in resorting to the conventions of romance, but after all, just as Goldsmith does not expect the reader to take Lien Chi seriously as a Chinese philosopher, so he does not expect the reader to take seriously, either, the frame story in which Lien Chi acts. Both are parts of Goldsmith's tongue-in-cheek Irish humor.

Most critics and literary historians have underrated or ignored the two fictional threads that run throughout *The Citizen of the World*, usually dismissing the Hingpo-Zelis thread as romantic claptrap, though such romantic improbability is surely one of Goldsmith's objects of attack. The letters about Lien Chi's family, by Hingpo or by Lien Chi addressed to Hingpo, total twenty-three, although some of Lien Chi's to his son may seem to be completely discursive. However, most of Lien Chi's letters of this sort are actually fatherly advice, such as letter 66, distinguishing love and gratitude, clearly an appropriate subject for a father writing to a son newly enamored of a young woman about whom the father knows nothing. This letter is not primarily a discursive essay, but one written by a particularly concerned parent to a faraway son lacking parental guidance. In addition, whenever Goldsmith has Lien Chi or Hingpo write, shortly following is a letter, or even letters, treating the themes of love, marriage, parents and children, or similar topics, showing Lien Chi's concern for his son and his affairs, even if he may be writing to Fum Hoam in Pekin, his most usual correspondent. At least seven such letters show Lien Chi with the Man in Black or the other members of his circle. Clearly, in some of these, such as letter 28—Lien Chi's observation of the great number of old bachelors and maiden ladies—the Man in Black serves chiefly as a foil, explaining that neither the bachelors nor the old maids will surrender their independence. However, we can also see that this letter, not unreasonably, to some degree points to the romantic affairs of Hingpo and Zelis.

Some critics have seen *The Citizen of the World* as a work showing some elements of the novel and even moving toward the novel form. While forty-six letters, more than a third of the total number, do involve either the Hingpo-Zelis romance or Lien Chi's London circle, this view of the work as novelistic but not a full-blown novel seems influenced by the fact that Goldsmith's next prose work of any length is his novel *The Vicar of Wakefield*. Such discussions concentrate on The Man in Black, and the Tibbses, and hardly discuss the Hingpo-Zelis love affair and its intimate connection with the London circle letters. The view that in *The Citizen of the World* Goldsmith was developing skills such as characterization necessary for a novelist is partly true at best, and at worst mistaken. In Goldsmith's day there were several well-accepted forms of fiction, works not necessarily novels in the modern sense of the word. *Gulliver's Travels* is, of course, the best-known example. But the pseudoletter genre was also a common and lively form, and the fact that we have no exact modern equivalent is no reason we should try to fit this, one of Goldsmith's finest works, on the procrustean bed of the novel, which it clearly is not, or on the equally unsuitable bed of the miscellaneous essay series exemplified by *The Spectator* or *The Rambler*, where it clearly will not fit, either, without losing essential characteristics of its form. We must take it for what it is, a pseudoletter series, easily the best in English literature, with more than a third of the letters devoted to one narrative strand or another, though many of these make important discursive points as well, and slightly more than half the letters discursively treat English follies in comparison with Chinese virtues but also celebrate English virtues in comparison with Chinese failings. Unfortunately, many of the best things in the series disappear when anthologists excerpt what they consider representative letters. The very real merits of *The Citizen of the World* reveal themselves best to readers of all the letters.

For six months after he collected the letters and Newbery published them in two volumes, Goldsmith continued writing for the *British Magazine* and various other publications controlled by Newbery. That summer he spent some time in Bath, though not vacationing. He gained access to Beau Nash's papers from Nash's literary executor, absorbed the flavor of the society Nash had done so much to establish there, and collected anecdotes from those who had known him before his death in February 1761. His *Life of Richard Nash* (1762), published by Newbery and W. Frederick of Bath, follows the model of Johnson's *Life*

of *Richard Savage* (1744) in presenting the life of a man of middle social rank, avoiding excessive praise but showing the relative insignificance of Nash's position as "King of Bath" through its ironic, mock-heroic tone.

Back in London, Goldsmith found himself in money troubles, and his landlady had him arrested for his unpaid rent. Goldsmith sent word to Johnson for help. Johnson sent him a guinea and came to Wine Office Court as soon as he could. There he found Goldsmith beginning to console himself with a bottle of Madeira bought with part of the guinea, but otherwise taking no steps to solve his problem. Johnson promptly corked the wine, calmed Goldsmith as best he could, and asked if he had any unpublished manuscripts. Goldsmith gave him the manuscript for a novel he had been working on, and, after scanning it, Johnson set off for a publisher, almost certainly John Newbery, returning with sixty pounds cash, more than enough both to settle the demands of the landlady, whom Goldsmith berated for her incivility, and to give him some pocket money. On 28 October 1762 Newbery sold a one-third share of the copyright to Benjamin Collins of Salisbury, his partner in the *Public Ledger*. The novel, of course, was *The Vicar of Wakefield*, though it would not be published for four more years.

After this embarrassment, Goldsmith very willingly put Newbery, his principal employer over the past three years, in charge of his financial affairs. Newbery promptly moved him from Wine Office Court, with its easy access to tavern life and gambling tables, to Islington, where the bookseller used Canonbury House as his own weekend and summer retreat. In the Canonbury Tower, he also housed and managed the affairs of his talented but unstable son-in-law, Christopher Smart, as well as Goldsmith's. Goldsmith was to write what Newbery directed, and Newbery in turn would keep him in pocket money but hold back most of his earnings to pay Goldsmith's bills, including his bed and board. Here in Islington, Goldsmith renewed work on the poem that would become *The Traveller*. For almost a year he was removed from the temptations of London, yet close enough to town that he could enjoy Christmas dinner with Thomas Davies, the actor turned bookseller, and Davies's other guests, Robert Dodsley, the publisher of Goldsmith's *Enquiry into the Present State of Polite Learning in Europe*, and the flighty young Scot James Boswell, then on his first visit to London.

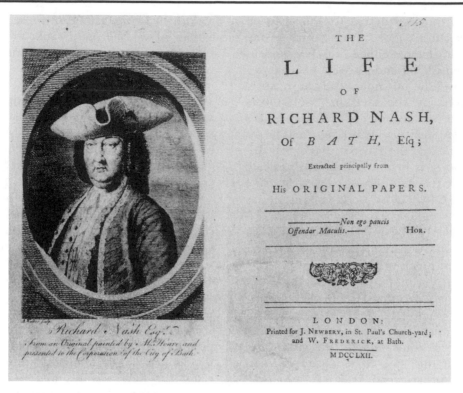

Frontispiece and title page for Goldsmith's biography of the supreme arbiter of Bath society, who, Goldsmith said,
"had too much merit not to become remarkable, yet too much folly to arrive at greatness"

In the late fall of 1764, Sir Joshua Reynolds, finding Johnson's company and often melancholy conversation something of a burden, began sounding out their mutual friends with the idea of a dining club that would meet every Monday evening at the Turk's Head Tavern in Soho. Besides Johnson and Reynolds, there were Edmund Burke; Sir John Hawkins, a lawyer with a strong interest in music; two young aristocrats, Bennet Langton and Topham Beauclerk; and two others interested in literary and cultural matters. Goldsmith was also chosen as a charter member, probably at Johnson's suggestion, though Reynolds knew him well too. Hawkins thought him little better than another Grub Street hack, but *The Citizen of the World*, if not a runaway best-seller, had been well received in 1762, as had his *Life of Nash* in the fall of the same year. Another anonymous work had appeared in June, *An History of England in a Series of Letters from a Nobleman to His Son*, credited by some to Philip Dormer Stanhope, Lord Chesterfield, and by others to George, Lord Lyttelton, ascriptions that must have provided Goldsmith wry amusement. Indeed, he never acknowledged his authorship in any of the several editions published during his lifetime. Though all his work had so far been published anonymously and praised by literary insiders such as Johnson, Goldsmith was only then finishing up the first work that would bear his name on its title page, his discursive poem *The Traveller*, to be published in December 1764. Johnson not only read the poem in manuscript but helped Goldsmith by providing several couplets, including the final one. Thus, he was certainly convinced of Goldsmith's talent, and when the poem did appear Johnson described it in the *Critical Review* for December 1764 as "a production to which, since the death of Pope, it will not be easy to find anything equal." Though Goldsmith's fellow members might often treat him as a clown and make him the butt of their jokes, to those who knew, his literary talents amply justified his membership, and, during the ten years following, his literary works were ranked, by common consent, as the best for that decade.

In the tradition of the French *philosophes*, *The Traveller* surveys Italy, Switzerland, Holland, France, and England, relating the effects of climate to national traits but arguing that each country has lost its power and glory, usually through the baleful influence of luxury, which has overwhelmed national virtues. England appears as a country whose fate still remains undetermined and which may yet escape decline by maintaining the careful balance of a strong but limited monarchy, checking the influence of a power-hungry oligarchy, and balancing a healthy agriculture against the mercantile and trading interests that, like the magnates, endanger the social equilibrium by promoting luxury. Goldsmith's couplets show slightly more run-on lines than Pope's and avoid the Latinate diction of Johnson's couplet poems, but mainly they achieve their individuality through repeated words and phrases, a device he would exploit to achieve almost lyric effects in *The Deserted Village* six years later. He dedicated the poem to his brother Henry, a poor parish priest in Ireland, rather than seeking out some lord who would have gladly paid a good, round sum for the honor.

The Traveller confirmed Johnson's high opinion of Goldsmith's literary talent, and, as was customary in the period, the publication of his widely praised poem established him overnight as a major figure among contemporary writers, just as a strikingly successful novel would for a twentieth-century writer. Newbery and Goldsmith seized the opportunity to publish, in June 1765, *Essays. By Mr. Goldsmith*, a collection of twenty-seven pieces previously published anonymously in newspapers, nine from *The Bee*, nine from *The Citizen of the World*, and the rest from various other places. This collection received wide praise for showing that his talent as an essayist was equal to his skill as a poet. He had emerged from general obscurity to become the leading literary lion of the time, flooded with dinner invitations from his fellow club members as well as from other major literary and social figures on the London scene, and he gloried in this new attention.

Despite his literary success, money troubles dogged him; he had received twenty guineas for *The Traveller* and a lesser sum for his *Essays*. Hoping to capitalize on his literary fame, he made his last, unsuccessful attempt to set up a medical practice. A second edition of *The Traveller*, with new lines (363-380) added, appeared in August 1765, with third and fourth editions of the enlarged poem also appearing in 1765. In 1766 a second edition of his *Essays* appeared, with two additional pieces. While Goldsmith received little money from these revised versions, they did keep his name before the public.

In the fall of 1764, Goldsmith had moved from Islington back to London, this time to 3 King's Bench Walk in the Temple. Apparently

the revision Newbery wanted kept him busy and out of major difficulties. Newbery had plans for the manuscript of the novel he had bought in 1762, realizing no doubt that Goldsmith's name on it would guarantee a lively sale. The book appeared in two volumes in March 1766, printed by Benjamin Collins of Salisbury, who had bought one-third of the copyright back in 1762, for Francis Newbery, John Newbery's nephew. The original reviewers were mainly favorable but did not quite know what to make of it. Goldsmith's old enemies at the *Monthly Review* commented: "Through the whole course of our travels in the wild regions of romance, we never met with anything more difficult to characterize than the Vicar of Wakefield. . . ." But the *Critical Review* was more enthusiastic: "Genuine touches of nature, easy strokes of humor, pathetic pictures of domestic happiness and domestic distress (a happiness proceeding from innocence and obscurity, and a distress supported with resignation and cheerfulness) are some of the methods here made use of to interest and move us." The reviewer deplored the piling up of Dr. Primrose's calamities in the second half and the hurried conclusion. Johnson disliked it, describing it to Fanny Burney as showing nothing of real life and little of nature. Excerpts appeared in several newspapers, and three London editions followed swiftly, the second of which contained extensive revisions by Goldsmith. A Dublin edition appeared in 1767 as well as French and German translations. The novel's great popularity really came only after Goldsmith's death in 1774, with more than twenty editions published in London before the end of the century.

Throughout the nineteenth century at least two editions appeared almost every year, and additional translations into French, German, Italian, and Spanish continued. Johann Wolfgang von Goethe was heavily influenced by it during his youth and in his old age came to admire its wise irony. Both Sir Walter Scott and Washington Irving admired it, as did Leigh Hunt, Charles Dickens, William Makepeace Thackeray, George Eliot, and Henry James. Something of the novel's appeal to nineteenth-century audiences can almost certainly be attributed to Goldsmith's avoiding the racier and coarser pictures of eighteenth-century life in both Fielding and Smollett.

More recently, as academic critics have freed themselves from the blinders of Romantic assumptions about literature, several critics have argued that the book, like much of Goldsmith's other writing, contains considerably more laughing irony and comic satire than most Romantic readers and critics—except Goethe—found, just as modern criticism of Swift and Pope differs radically from that of the nineteenth century. Modern critics have come to understand and stress the heavily rhetorical nature of virtually all writing before the Romantic period, and several have emphasized that Goldsmith's personas are not writing unalloyed autobiography. While Goldsmith the man becomes a less clearly defined figure, his literary creations become more sharply focused. As yet, critics have reached no consensus about many quite basic features of *The Vicar of Wakefield*, such as its prevailing tone—is it prevailingly comic, or comic and then sentimental?—or Goldsmith's attitude toward his narrator-protagonist—is he a wise and admirable religious man or an egotistical, imprudent erring human, perhaps still lovable or perhaps self-deceived and materialistic?

From the beginning, readers have noticed that the book falls into two almost equal parts, the first an almost unrelieved pastoral idyll and the second an almost equally unrelieved series of disasters that are finally reversed to present a happy ending. More-recent critics have argued that the novel's construction shows considerable care. The first three chapters serve as a prologue and are balanced by the final three chapters, in which the loose ends are tied up. The central part does fall into two roughly equal parts. In the first, we see the Primroses living an almost ideal life, their Eden threatened only by the villainous Squire Thornhill, though his evil nature is balanced by the virtue of Mr. Burchell, a wanderer with little or no fortune, whom Dr. Primrose charitably receives into the family circle. The second half plunges the Primroses into the sordid realities of the actual world, with George's tale of his misfortunes after leaving home, Olivia's apparent seduction, the burning of their house, the Vicar's dispossession and imprisonment, rumors of Olivia's death, Sophia's apparent abduction, and George's impending execution. Throughout, however, Goldsmith leaves clues for the observant reader: Mr. Burchell's slip of the tongue hints strongly that he may be someone other than the humble wanderer he seems; his ballad of Edwin and Angelina presents a happy ending and foreshadows the conclusion of the novel; and in the latter half a sharp reversal undoes the violence, cruelty, and wretchedness in the interpolated tale of Mathilda. Though the humor that dominates

Caricature of Goldsmith by Henry Bunbury
(British Museum)

the first half dims during the second part, we recognize Goldsmith's reliance on the swift changes of fortune typical of romance conventions.

Goldsmith's most memorable character in the novel is certainly his narrator, the Vicar, Dr. Charles Primrose, who is sublimely convinced of his ability to govern his family according to traditional customs and received wisdom, though he patronizes his wife and daughters shamelessly for their social pretentions and homemade cosmetics. When faced with the very real evil of Squire Thornhill, the Vicar is easily duped, and Goldsmith shows his skill in handling his familiar theme of innocence undone by worldly wisdom, as Fielding often does too. Dr. Primrose, like Tom Jones, needs to temper his benevolence with worldly prudence, just as Sir William Thornhill has learned from his youthful experiences in a self-education strongly reminiscent of Mr. Wilson's in *Joseph Andrews*. Dr. Primrose's experiences in prison move him beyond Fielding's world, where Tom Jones could expect worldly happiness once he had learned to act prudently. The Vicar's almost unbelievable succession of disasters and his apparently hopeless position in prison lead him to abandon thoughts of relief in this world to prepare himself for eternity. His powerful sermon to the prisoners stresses faith over hope, that rewards and punishments belong to man's future state, not necessarily to this world. In the sermon, Dr. Primrose shows a radical change in his values, abjuring worldly prudence for Christian faith.

Just how lasting the Vicar's conversion is may well seem uncertain in the last three chapters, where a series of reversals occurs almost as incredibly as the series of disasters that overtook him, and the family happiness and prosperity are restored. Olivia has not died a fallen woman after all. The squire's minion Jenkinson could not bring himself to ruin Olivia in a mock marriage and secured a genuine priest—though Olivia shows enough sense to live apart from the squire. Sir William Thornhill, abandoning his disguise as Mr. Burchell the lowly vagrant, reclaims the powers he had delegated to his rascally nephew. Sir William has also had ample opportunity to observe Sophia and to realize that she loves him for himself alone, not for his fortune. By happy chance, the embezzler who stole the Vicar's fortune is captured with the money largely intact.

Beginning with the reviewer for the *Critical Review*, critics have found these almost incredible disasters and reversals troublesome, but in more recent years, some have seen them as Goldsmith's reliance on the conventions of romance as a way of giving his book a happy ending. Virtually all these critics see Sir William, finally revealed in his true identity after his long disguise as Mr. Burchell the penniless wanderer, as a character type also drawn from romance conventions.

Most recent critical disagreement lies in establishing Goldsmith's attitude toward Dr. Primrose: is he a self-deceived and often foolish man or is he Goldsmith's portrait of a clerical ideal, as the village preacher in *The Deserted Village* certainly is? These and other apparent problems in the novel depend on when Goldsmith finished work on it. Clearly the manuscript that Johnson sold was sufficiently finished that John Newbery, certainly no fool in money matters, was willing to purchase it, though that is not clear proof that the novel was ready for the press, however clearly Goldsmith had laid out the major framework. The advertisement to the novel, which argues that "the hero of this piece unites in himself the three greatest characters upon earth; he is a priest, a husbandman, and the father of a family," has usually been taken as a clear statement of Goldsmith's intention to portray his central character as an ideal type, but more than one episode in the book clearly shows him as a dupe, ill-equipped to cope with his adversary Squire Thornhill, and, without Sir William's intervention at the end, the Vicar's ability to cope with worldly problems seems improbable at best. The advertisement raises almost as many questions as it seems to answer. Primarily, we do not know when Goldsmith wrote the advertisement—in 1762 when fresh from writing *The Life of Richard Nash*, having just finished his mock-heroic celebration of the "King of Bath," or shortly before the novel's publication in 1766. Ever since *The Traveller* had appeared in 1764, Newbery had Goldsmith working almost incessantly revising the poem, then collecting the pieces that make up *Essays* (1765), and then enlarging that work by two for *Essays* (1766). Presumably, Newbery had physical possession of the manuscript for *The Vicar of Wakefield* from 1762 onward, so that even if Goldsmith had had time in his new fame after the publication of *The Traveller*, he could not have devoted considered thought and time to the kinds of problems that have bothered so many critics, such as the improbability that Sir William Thornhill and his nephew are approximately the same age. Thus, the published novel may very well represent two stages of composition: the first and most carefully constructed part written about 1761-1762, and a second, later part, how long we shall never know, but probably including the advertisement, written hastily to meet Newbery's 1766 deadline. How carefully Goldsmith reconsidered what he had composed around 1762, when most of the writing he had been doing was comic, remains a matter of speculation, but certainly the works he had done since 1764, especially *The Traveller* and his *History of England in a Series of Letters from a Nobleman to His Son* (June 1764), are both predominantly serious. Only his *Essays*, 1765 and 1766, contain more comic than serious writing, some of it the result of fairly careful revision.

Goldsmith was not entirely satisfied with the first edition of *The Vicar of Wakefield* and made extensive revisions for the second edition of May 1766, among them substituting the "Whistonean Controversy," a figment of Dr. Primrose's imagination, for the very real Bangorian Controversy of the first edition, although the latter had been largely a dead issue for nearly fifty years. If Goldsmith did intend to satirize Dr. Primrose, however gently, he did not apparently have time to insert additional signals, like the change to the "Whistonean Controversy," to suggest to the reader his own amiably ironic view of his protagonist. Undoubtedly Newbery pushed him hard for the revised copy, since the book sold only moderately well and both Newbery and Collins wanted to garner all possible profits from it. Whether or not Goldsmith would have corrected the improbabilities, objected to by critics who believe the novel is realistic, will remain forever moot, but, given the many conventions derived from romances of the time appearing in both halves of the book, such changes seem rather improbable. Though Johnson thought the book salable when he took it to Newbery, his later opinion that it contains little of real life and nothing of nature only shows his own misunderstanding of Goldsmith's probable intention, to burlesque romance so broadly that even lovers of that form could not fail to see that he was gently and amiably satirizing not only romantic type-characters but also implausible romantic plots. It would not be the first time an Englishman has failed to see the point of an Irishman's joke. That Johnson was not the only reader confused is amply shown by the way few nineteenth-century readers perceived this dimension of the book—Goethe almost alone seems to have grasped it—but also by the present disagreement among critics over interpreting the book. Whether or not a critical consensus will eventually emerge seems most uncertain at present, but even with some decline in its popularity, it remains, with *Gulliver's Travels* (1726), *Robinson Crusoe* (1719), and *Tristram Shandy* (1759-1767), one of the very few examples of eighteenth-century fiction to attract the attention of Johnson's common reader and enjoy some life outside the classroom.

Goldsmith was heartened by the success of the novel, even if the success were a modest one, but it brought him no money, and so he began to work on a play, since a successful play meant almost instant fortune. He offered David Garrick *The Good Natur'd Man*, written during 1767, for Drury Lane, but Garrick put him off repeatedly, still remembering Goldsmith's sharp criticism of the theater managers in *An Enquiry into the Present State of Polite Learning in Europe* in 1759. He then turned to George Colman the Elder at Covent Garden, who accepted the play but delayed opening it until after Garrick presented Hugh Kelly's *False Delicacy*, a prime example of sentimental comedy. Goldsmith's play did open on 29 January 1768, bringing with it an author's share of

four hundred pounds, and had a moderately successful run.

Goldsmith's success as a playwright reverses the pattern Henry Fielding had followed, since Fielding had learned from writing plays how to plot a story and to present believable characters who speak believable dialogue. For his plays Goldsmith drew on the character types he had used successfully in *The Citizen of the World* and *The Vicar of Wakefield*. In *The Good Natur'd Man*, Sir William Honeywood, the disguised manager of the other characters' lives, clearly derives from Sir William Thornhill; Lofty, the snobbish name dropper, comes from Beau Tibbs; and Miss Richland, the wise and patient heroine, develops from Sophia in *The Vicar of Wakefield*, though this character-type would not reach full flower until Kate Hardcastle in *She Stoops to Conquer*. Honeywood, the "Good Natur'd Man," is another of Goldsmith's universal benevolists like the Man in Black and Sir William Thornhill. Though Honeywood loses almost his entire fortune and also Miss Richland's through his rash imprudence, his worldly wise uncle saves him from utter destruction, though not from arrest for debt. He has to disguise, not very successfully, the bailiffs as his butler and footmen, but Miss Richland's loving compassion and wisdom bring about her happy marriage to the now responsible Honeywood. Many of the audience must have been confused by the play, since it burlesques sentimental comedy so subtly that at times it seems an example of that form, and almost certainly some of the audience failed to see the burlesque, while some understood Goldsmith's intent.

With the money from his play Goldsmith bought the lease on his last London home, rooms at no. 2 Brick Court, in the Temple. About this time, together with a Temple neighbor, he secured a country cottage out the Edgeward Road for a weekend and working retreat from the bustle of London. He also received word of his brother Henry's death in Lissoy, and perhaps out of his grief came the spark for *The Deserted Village* (1770). The last forty-six lines of *The Traveller* (1764) contain in embryo much of Goldsmith's best-known poem, and, as early as 1762, Goldsmith had written for *Lloyd's Evening Post* a scathing account of the disastrous effect the enclosure laws were having on English agricultural life, further upsetting the precarious traditional balance between agriculture and trade in English society. He put the blame on the increase in luxury, largely the result of enormous growth in the mer-

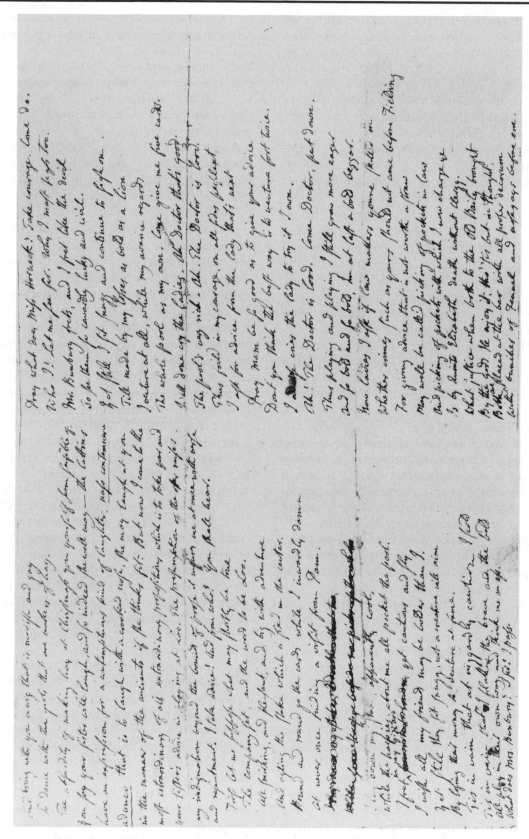

Pages from Goldsmith's circa 25 December 1773 response to Catherine Horneck Bunbury's verse epistle inviting him to Barton, Suffolk, her brother-in-law's home, for New Year's festivities (MA 1297, Pierpont Morgan Library)

cantile and trading interests. By the spring of 1769, he had finished the poem, and Griffin, who had also published *The Good Natur'd Man*, published the poem on 16 May 1770, with a dignified but somber dedication to Reynolds.

The poem took the town by storm, with six editions printed by the end of the year and admiring reviews in both the *Monthly* and *Critical* reviews as well as praise in the *Gentleman's Magazine*. Then, as now, most readers have responded to the poem's nostalgia for a simpler time and place, an appeal made all the stronger by the social mobility the Industrial Revolution was bringing on. Its early readers sometimes saw Goldsmith's descriptions of the now-vanished village life and the portraits of the preacher, the blacksmith, the schoolmaster, and the surviving widow as almost unchanged autobiographical memories of his father and brother and boyhood friends, a view strong in that part of County Longford, Ireland, even today. Blended with this strongly emotional nostalgia, Goldsmith preaches his favorite social doctrine, that the peasants were being driven from ancestral holdings by merchants who, enriched by their trade in luxuries, wanted to create imposing country seats with lavish gardens and noble landscape prospects, driving their former tenants to starve in the cities or to the wild and savage semitropical jungles of such colonies as Georgia. Several reviewers attacked Goldsmith's social protests as extreme and exaggerated, but certainly many old villages were being destroyed to make room for Georgian pleasure domes, though some were destroyed in the name of progress, as the English Agricultural Revolution moved relentlessly ahead.

Goldsmith's criticism that the traditional combination of small farms and villages was being eliminated and that many of the country's best people were immigrating to the colonies is merely a highly memorable expression of social and political views he had long held and had shared with other conservatives, such as Samuel Johnson, another anti-imperialist. As far back as the 1730s, the decade of Goldsmith's birth, Jonathan Swift had bitterly criticized the Irish landlords who were replacing their farming tenants in the fertile central Irish plain with sheep and cattle herders. Today, the poem's continuing popularity owes less to its political and social ideas, though we may recall contemporary arguments over the American family farm, than to the strongly and skillfully evoked emotion of nostalgia and the belief that a largely rural past was better, especially among readers who find themselves living in a society in which traditional values, even those of the two-parent family, are badly shaken and seem to many to be at severe risk. *The Deserted Village* anglicizes the conventions of the classical pastoral and infuses them with new power, and Goldsmith convinces his readers of personal loss, as well as a whole community's irreparable loss. His repetition of words and phrases gives his heroic couplets a remarkable lyric strain. After more than two centuries the poem still marks its readers with its power and indelible effect.

From 1767, when *The Good Natur'd Man* brought him prosperity for the first time in his life, until a year or so before his death, Goldsmith's writing assured him a handsome income, usually around four hundred pounds a year, but his expensive habits—his generosity to the poor, especially poor Irishmen in London; his taste for expensive clothes; his hospitality in entertaining his friends; and especially his gambling losses—kept him always in debt to his publishers. His friendship with Reynolds had deepened profoundly, as his dedication of *The Deserted Village* shows, and through Reynolds he had met Mrs. Kane Horneck, a widow, and her two daughters, with whom he vacationed in Paris during the summer of 1770. He also met Robert Nugent, Viscount Clare, later Earl Nugent, an Irish peer who entertained him frequently in London, in Bath, and at his Essex country estate. Lord Clare once sent him a haunch of venison, and in return Goldsmith dashed off a thank-you poem, posthumously published in 1776, showing his talent for humorous anapestics that foreshadow his much finer and wiser, but unfinished, *Retaliation*, published posthumously in 1774, a group of incisive character sketches of friends in the guise of imaginary epitaphs.

His life in the fashionable world was expensive, but he was working hard. During 1768 he compiled for 250 guineas his two-volume *Roman History, from the Foundation of the City of Rome, to the Destruction of the Western Empire*, published in May 1769 by Tom Davies. Davies had been much impressed by the sales of Goldsmith's epistolary *History of England* (1764) and believed correctly that there was a ready market among general readers for shorter, plainer histories than the far longer multivolume works of Smollett and David Hume. In June 1769 Goldsmith contracted with Davies to write a four-volume history of England for five hundred pounds, and the preceding Feb-

Oliver Goldsmith (portrait by Benjamin West; from Temple Scott, Oliver Goldsmith Bibliographically and Biographically Considered, *1928)*

ruary he had contracted with William Griffin to write an eight-volume natural history of animals at a hundred guineas a volume. As long as booksellers such as Griffin and Davies would offer him contracts, he apparently was willing to sign them and produce what they wanted. However, during the last two years before his death, the stress brought on by the need to fill these contracts undoubtedly affected his health.

In April 1769 Reynolds had been knighted following his appointment as president of the Royal Academy, and in December he appointed Goldsmith Professor of Ancient History and Johnson Professor of Ancient Poetry in the Royal Academy, both unpaid, honorary positions, though for Goldsmith the appointment reflected his new importance in the contemporary cultural world. His lives of Thomas Parnell and of Henry St. John, Viscount Bolingbroke, both appeared in 1770, and the following year he did produce the four-volume history of England for which he had contracted with Davies in June 1769.

By 1773 Goldsmith had finished his second play, *She Stoops to Conquer,* and encountered the same problems with Colman and Garrick he had had with *The Good Natur'd Man,* but with the firm intervention of Johnson and other friends,

Colman reluctantly presented the play on 15 March 1773, very late in the season for Goldsmith to expect a decent return. However, the play was an overwhelming success, and Goldsmith's share came to £502. As in his first play, he attacked the sentimental drama of the time, although instead of burlesquing that fashionable form, he presented more directly laughing comedy. Before the play's production, Goldsmith had anonymously published "An Essay on the Theatre; or, a Comparison between Laughing and Sentimental Comedy" in the *Westminster Magazine* for January 1773. Arguing that the aim of comedy is to provoke laughter by showing the "Frailties of the Lower Part of Mankind" and invoking Aristotle by name, he clearly hoped to prepare the ground for his soon-to-be produced play. Tony Lumpkin, a boorish, hard-drinking young country squire with an eye for the wenches, fulfills Goldsmith's and Aristotle's requirements, but the play belongs to Kate Hardcastle, Goldsmith's finest heroine, who exploits a misunderstanding created by Tony, and through her own skill and wit, ingeniously leads Marlow, her reluctant suitor—by her pretended roles as a barmaid and then as a poor relation—to what promises to be a triumphantly happy marriage. With a skill reminiscent of Viola in *Twelfth Night,* she conquers Marlow's shyness with fine ladies so skillfully he hardly knows what is happening to him. Probably Goldsmith's best single work, the play remains a solid and frequently revived part of the standard English dramatic repertory.

Following the custom that had worked so well for him in writing *She Stoops to Conquer,* Goldsmith spent his summers in the country, working on the two-volume *Grecian History, from the Earliest State to the Death of Alexander the Great,* and resumed work on his eight-volume natural history, both published posthumously in 1774, the latter as *An History of the Earth, and Animated Nature.* But his literary fame and livelier social life left him discontented, perhaps because of the pressure under which he was working. He physically attacked a newspaper editor who implied in print he was romantically involved with one of the Horneck sisters, but he was able to settle the matter out of court by contributing to the editor's favorite charity. His earlier friendship with Hugh Kelly had collapsed over the greater popularity of Kelly's *False Delicacy* and *School for Wives,* both of which Garrick had produced in competition with Goldsmith's two plays. He quarreled seriously with Reynolds over Reynolds's flattering

portrait of James Beattie, a minor Scottish clergyman, who had been given a royal pension for his
Essay on Truth (1770), which Goldsmith considered mere claptrap. Beattie's pension especially,
and perhaps Johnson's earlier one, seemed to
Goldsmith unfair, since he had certainly contributed to literature far more than Beattie had or
was ever likely to contribute.

Boswell's *Life of Johnson* for the years 1773
and 1774, the last year and a half of Goldsmith's
life, shows Johnson often overpowering him, and
most others, in conversation, never Goldsmith's
strong suit. However, even when Boswell uses
Goldsmith as a foil to Johnson in his generally
unflattering presentation of Goldsmith, he
does record Goldsmith's incisive comments on
Johnson—namely, that he had only the bear's
rough skin and that in any fable Johnson might
write, his fishes would all talk like whales. Johnson had proved a true and valuable friend to Goldsmith, at least from the time Johnson had sold
the manuscript for *The Vicar of Wakefield* and extri-
cated him from the clutches of his landlady. He
had helped him by contributing key lines to both
The Traveller and *The Deserted Village*; he brow-
beat Colman into producing *She Stoops to Conquer*;
and, of course, he composed the inscription for
the memorial table to Goldsmith in Poets' Corner, Westminster Abbey.

Goldsmith's hard work over the last several
years had left him in precarious health, and after
a relatively short illness he died in his Temple
rooms on 4 April 1774, almost certainly of a kidney infection, complicated by his own stubborn insistence in taking large doses of Dr. James's Fever
Powders, against the professional advice and
strong objections of his doctors. Partly because of
his relative youth—he was only forty-three—and
his position as arguably the leading active writer
of the time, his death produced almost universal
shock and grief. In Reynolds's character sketch,
discovered among Boswell's papers and published in 1952, Reynolds notes that "The literary
world deplored his death more than could be expected, when it is considered how small a part of
his works were wrote for fame, yet epigrams, epitaphs and monodies to his memory were without
end." Johnson described him as "a very great
man." But Goldsmith knew his own flaws, since
with modest irony in *Retaliation* (1774) he describes himself as "Magnanimous Goldsmith, a
goosbery fool," the pleasantly light dessert to the
literary banquet in the poem. In this posthumously published, unfinished poem, he provides

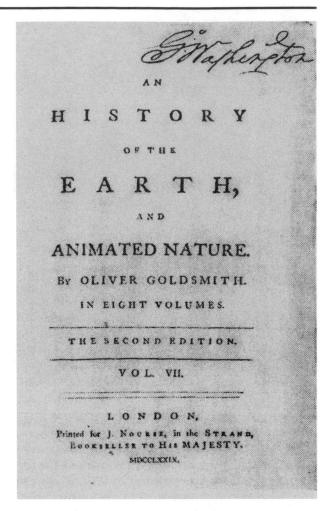

AN

HISTORY

OF THE

EARTH,

AND

ANIMATED NATURE.

By OLIVER GOLDSMITH.

IN EIGHT VOLUMES.

THE SECOND EDITION.

VOL. VII.

LONDON,

Printed for J. Nourse, in the Strand,
Bookseller to His MAJESTY.

MDCCLXXIX.

*Title page for a volume of Goldsmith's natural history that
once belonged to George Washington (Sotheby's auction catalogue, 27 March 1985)*

splendidly incisive but balanced character
sketches in the form of imaginary epitaphs for
such friends as Edmund Burke, Richard Cumberland, and David Garrick. Boswell's generally unflattering portrait in *The Life of Johnson* presents
Goldsmith as a foolish man who wrote extremely
well, ironically, a view very like Thomas Babington Macaulay's opinion of Boswell, and has, unfortunately, established what has remained the general opinion of Goldsmith's personality. However, Reynolds's prose character sketch presents
Goldsmith in a far more sympathetic light, arguing that he often behaved like a fool on principle
and more often than not may have mocked his
sobersided English friends.

The most striking feature of Goldsmith's
writing is his versatility: he produced memorable,
even first-rate work in every literary form practiced in his lifetime—the individual essay, the pseudoletter series, the novel, poetry, history, and biog-

raphy. Repeatedly, both in conversation and in his tributary Latin epitaph, Johnson showed that he believed Goldsmith was a first-rate writer who adorned all the forms in which he wrote. Running throughout all Goldsmith's writing is a strong moral strain, attacking cruelty and injustice, while allowing amply for flawed humanity's frailties and errors. Like Fielding, who heavily influenced his writing, Goldsmith strongly attacked perversions of the law that serve selfish, powerful interests. His conservative social and political ideas, formed as he grew up in Ireland, ally him with the Augustan humanists, such as Swift and Pope, as well as Johnson, with whom he also shared a largely rhetorical conception of literature, far more than with any of those whose ideas would coalesce into Romanticism. His sentiment remains sentiment, sometimes quite powerful, as in *The Deserted Village*. He strongly and consistently attacked the emerging sentimental ethos, just as his rural settings always show man as nature's steward, following the Christian humanist position. When Goldsmith satirizes human folly, he does so in a comic spirit; to use John Dryden's broad classifications, Goldsmith's approach is Horatian, not Juvenalian like Swift's or Pope's, though his social and political ideas are as close to theirs as they are to Johnson's. He may have learned something from the manner of Addison and Steele, but he despised and strongly condemned the Whiggery and sentimentality that figure so largely in their works.

His literary reputation was higher in the nineteenth century, among writers such as Dickens and Thackeray, than it probably is today, though *The Vicar of Wakefield* appears to have some life with the general reading public, and *She Stoops to Conquer* lives in the repertories of many community theaters as well as enjoying reasonably frequent professional revivals, most recently in London in 1984-1985. Most readers encounter *The Deserted Village* in classrooms, but many of them find that its nostalgia has a powerful appeal in an industrial society with few roots and virtually no traditional life. In a world where prose fiction is the overwhelmingly dominant form, Goldsmith's writings strongly attract students of literature. Students of narrative art find much to interest them in *The Citizen of the World* because of the way widely varied social comment relates to the narrative frame story. Because *The Vicar of Wakefield* consolidates many of the social, moral, religious positions common in the eighteenth century as well as most of the literary tech-

niques used by Richardson, Fielding, Smollett, and even Sterne, the novel has aroused spirited debate in recent years. But, for those who would truly understand Goldsmith's beliefs in matters social, moral, and religious, his essays will always be the necessary beginning point.

Letters:

The Collected Letters of Oliver Goldsmith, edited by Katharine C. Balderston (Cambridge: Cambridge University Press, 1928).

Bibliography:

Temple Scott, *Oliver Goldsmith Bibliographically and Biographically Considered* (New York: Bowling Green Press, 1928).

Biographies:

Thomas Percy, Memoir of Goldsmith in volume 1 of *The Miscellaneous Works of Oliver Goldsmith, M.B.* (London: Printed for J. Johnson by H. Baldwin & Sons, 1801); modern edition of the memoir: *Thomas Percy's Life of Dr. Oliver Goldsmith*, edited by Richard L. Harp (Salzburg: Institut für Englische Sprache und Literatur, 1976);

Ralph M. Wardle, *Oliver Goldsmith* (Lawrence: University of Kansas Press, 1957);

Peter Dixon, *Oliver Goldsmith Revisited*, Twayne's English Authors Series, no. 487 (Boston: G. K. Hall, 1991).

References:

Sven Bäckman, *"This Singular Tale": A Study of "The Vicar of Wakefield" and Its Literary Background* (Lund, Sweden: Gleerup, 1971);

Martin C. Battestin, "Goldsmith: The Comedy of Job," in his *The Providence of Wit: Aspects of Form in Augustan Literature and the Arts* (Oxford: Clarendon Press, 1974), pp. 193-214;

Howard Bell, Jr., *"The Deserted Village* and Goldsmith's Social Doctrines," *PMLA*, 59 (September 1944): 747-772;

Wayne C. Booth, "Preconceptions about a Proper Structure: *The Citizen of the World*," in his *Critical Understanding: The Powers and Limits of Pluralism* (Chicago: University of Chicago Press, 1979), pp. 301-316;

Ronald S. Crane and Hamilton J. Smith, "A French Influence on Goldsmith's *Citizen of the World*," *Modern Philology*, 19 (August 1921): 83-92;

Curtis Dahl, "Patterns of Disguise in *The Vicar of Wakefield*," *English Literary History*, 25 (March 1958): 90-104;

Oliver W. Ferguson, "Oliver Goldsmith: The Personality of the Essayist," *Philological Quarterly*, 61 (Spring 1982): 179-191;

Morris Golden, "The Family-Wanderer Theme in Goldsmith," *English Literary History*, 25 (September 1958): 181-193;

Golden, "Goldsmith's Reputation in His Day," *Papers on Language and Literature*, 16 (Spring 1980): 213-238;

Robert H. Hopkins, *The True Genius of Oliver Goldsmith* (Baltimore: Johns Hopkins Press, 1969);

D. W. Jefferson, "Observations on *The Vicar of Wakefield*," *Cambridge Journal*, 3 (1949-1950): 621-628;

Charles A. Knight, "Ironic Loneliness: The Case of Goldsmith's Chinaman," *Journal of English and Germanic Philology*, 82 (July 1983): 347-364;

Roger Lonsdale, " 'A Garden and a Grave': The Poetry of Oliver Goldsmith," in *The Author in His Work*, edited by Louis L. Martz and Aubrey Williams (New Haven & London: Yale University Press, 1978), pp. 3-30;

Patrick Murray, "The Riddle of Goldsmith's Ancestry," *Studies* (Dublin), 63 (Summer 1974): 177-190;

William Bowman Piper, "The Musical Quality of Goldsmith's *The Deserted Village*," *Studies in Eighteenth-Century Culture*, 14 (1984): 259-274;

Ricardo Quintana, *Oliver Goldsmith: A Georgian Study* (New York: Macmillan, 1967);

Joshua Reynolds, *Portraits by Sir Joshua Reynolds. Character Sketches of Oliver Goldsmith, Samuel Johnson, and David Garrick, together with Other Manuscripts of Reynolds Discovered among the Boswell Papers and now First Published*, edited by Frederick W. Hilles (New York: McGraw-Hill, 1952), pp. 44-59;

G. S. Rousseau, ed., *Goldsmith; The Critical Heritage* (London & Boston: Routledge & Kegan Paul, 1974);

Samuel H. Woods, Jr., "Images of the Orient: Goldsmith and the *Philosophes*," *Studies in Eighteenth-Century Culture*, 16 (1985): 257-270;

Virginia Woolf, "Oliver Goldsmith," in her *The Captain's Death Bed and Other Essays* (New York: Harcourt, Brace, 1950), pp. 3-14.

Papers:
Literary manuscripts in Goldsmith's own hand are extremely rare, that of *The Haunch of Venison* in the New York Public Library being one of the few that survive. The largest concentration of Goldsmith manuscripts is in the British Library (Add. MSS 42515-42517). Margaret M. Smith has compiled a careful list of the surviving autograph manuscripts, giving their present ownership and location, for the eighteenth-century volume of *The Index of English Literary Manuscripts*.

Thomas Gray

(26 December 1716 - 30 July 1771)

This entry was written by Wallace Jackson (Duke University) for
DLB 109: Eighteenth-Century British Poets: Second Series.

BOOKS: *An Ode on a Distant Prospect of Eton College* (London: Printed for R. Dodsley and sold by M. Cooper, 1747);

An Elegy Wrote in a Country Church Yard (London: Printed for R. Dodsley and sold by M. Cooper, 1751);

Designs by Mr. R. Bentley, for Six Poems by Mr. T. Gray (London: Printed for R. Dodsley, 1753);

Odes, by Mr. Gray (London: Printed at Strawberry-Hill for R. & J. Dodsley, 1757);

Poems by Mr. Gray (London: Printed for J. Dodsley, 1768);

The Poems of Mr. Gray: To Which Are Prefixed Memoirs of His Life and Writings by W. Mason, M.A. (York: Printed by A. Ward; and sold by J. Dodsley, London; and J. Todd, York, 1775);

The Works of Thomas Gray, in Prose and Verse, 4 volumes, edited by Edmund Gosse (London: Macmillan, 1884);

Gray's English Poems, Original, and Translated from the Norse and Welsh, edited by D. C. Tovey (Cambridge: University Press, 1898);

The Complete Poems of Thomas Gray: English, Latin and Greek, edited by H. W. Starr and J. R. Hendrickson (Oxford: Clarendon Press, 1966);

The Poems of Thomas Gray, William Collins, Oliver Goldsmith, edited by Roger Lonsdale (London & Harlow: Longmans, Green, 1969).

OTHER: Robert Dodsley, ed., *A Collection of Poems: By Several Hands,* volume 2, includes Gray's "Ode on the Spring," "Ode on the Death of a Favourite Cat," and "Ode on a Distant Prospect of Eton College" (London: Printed for R. Dodsley, 1748).

Thomas Gray is generally considered the second most important poet of the eighteenth century (following the dominant figure of Alexander Pope) and the most disappointing. It was generally assumed by friends and readers that he was the most talented poet of his generation, but the relatively small and even reluctantly published body of his works has left generations of scholars puzzling over the reasons for his limited production and meditating on the general reclusiveness and timidity that characterized his life. Samuel Johnson was the first of many critics to put forward the view that Gray spoke in two languages, one public and the other private, and that the private language—that of his best-known and most-loved poem, "Elegy Written in a Country Churchyard" (published in 1751 as *An Elegy Wrote in a Country Church Yard*)—was too seldom heard. William Wordsworth decided in his preface to *Lyrical Ballads* (1798), using Gray's "Sonnet on the Death of Richard West" (1775) as his example, that Gray, governed by a false idea of poetic diction, spoke in the wrong language; and Matthew Arnold, in an equally well-known judgment, remarked that the age was wrong for a poetry of high seriousness, that Gray was blighted by his age and never spoke out at all. Such judgments sum up the major critical history of Gray's reception and reputation as a poet. He has always attracted attentive critics precisely because of the extraordinary continuing importance of the "Elegy," which, measured against his other performances, has seemed indisputably superior.

Born in Cornhill on 26 December 1716, Gray was the fifth of twelve children of Philip and Dorothy Antrobus Gray and the only one to survive infancy. His father, a scrivener given to fits of insanity, abused his wife. She left him at one point; but Philip Gray threatened to pursue her and wreak vengeance on her, and she returned to him. From 1725 to 1734 Thomas Gray attended Eton, where he met Richard West and Horace Walpole, son of the powerful Whig minister, Sir Robert Walpole.

In 1734 Gray entered Peterhouse College, Cambridge University. Four years later he left Cambridge without a degree, intending to read law at the Inner Temple in London. Instead, he

Thomas Gray (portrait by John Giles Eccardt, 1747-1748; National Portrait Gallery, London)

and Horace Walpole sailed from Dover on 29 March 1739 for a Continental tour. The two quarreled at Reggio, Italy, in May 1741; Gray continued the tour alone, returning to London in September. In November 1741 Gray's father died; Gray's extant letters contain no mention of this event.

Except for his mother, West was the person most dear to Gray; and his death from consumption on 1 June 1742 was a grievous loss to the poet. West died in the year of Gray's greatest productivity, though not all of the work of that year was inspired either by West's death or by Gray's anticipation of it.

West's death did inspire the well-known (largely because of Wordsworth's use of it) "Sonnet on the Death of Richard West," yet it is the shortest and least significant work of the year. The "Ode on the Spring" (1748) owes something

to an ode West sent Gray on 5 May, and *An Ode on a Distant Prospect of Eton College* (1747) may owe something to West's "Ode to Mary Magdelene." The "Hymn to Adversity" (1753) and the unfinished "Hymn to Ignorance" (1768) complete the work of the year, which, together with 1741, may comprise Gray's most critical emotional period.

Gray's poetry is concerned with the rejection of sexual desire. The figure of the poet in his poems is often a lonely, alienated, and marginal one, and various muses or surrogate-mother figures are invoked—in a manner somewhat anticipatory of John Keats's employment of similar figures—for aid or guidance. The typical "plot" of the four longer poems of 1742 has to do with engaging some figure of desire to repudiate it, as in the "Ode on the Spring," or, as in the Eton College ode, to la-

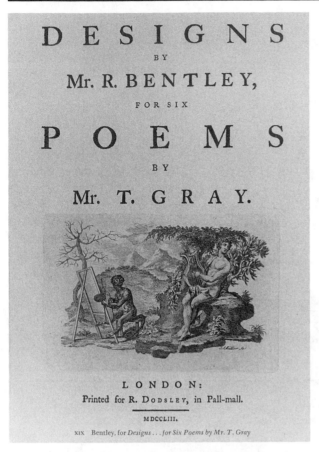

XIX   Bentley, for *Designs . . . for Six Poems by Mr. T. Gray*

*Title page for the volume in which Gray's
"Hymn to Adversity" was first published*

ment lost innocence. Sometimes, as in the "Hymn to Adversity," a harsh and repressive figure is conjured to rebuke excessive desire and to aid in the formation of a modest and humane fellowship, the transposed and social form of sexual desire. In the "Hymn to Ignorance" a goddess clearly modeled on Pope's Dulness in *The Dunciad* (1728) is used to rebuke the "I" who longs for the maternal and demonic presence. In different but related ways these four poems enact the poet's quest for his tutelary spirit, for the muse who will preside over the making of poetic and personal identity.

The "Ode on the Spring" was written while West was still alive and is to some extent a response to the ode he sent Gray on 5 May. In West's poem "the tardy May" is asked, as "fairest nymph," to resume her reign, to "Bring all the Graces in [her] train" and preside over a seasonally reviving world. Gray's "Ode on the Spring" was sent to West at just about the time of his death and was returned unopened ("Sent to Fav: not knowing he was then Dead," Gray noted on

the manuscript in his commonplace book; Favonius was Gray's affectionate name for West). The ode takes the implicit form of elegy, displacing spring from the context of renewal to that of death, and is consistent with a 27 May 1742 letter to West in which Gray explains that he is the frequent victim of "a white Melancholy, or rather Leucocholy" but is also occasionally host to "another sort, black indeed, which I have now and then felt, that has somewhat in it like Tertullian's rule of faith, Credo quia impossible est [I believe because it is impossible]; for it believes, nay, is sure of every thing that is unlikely, so it be but frightful; and, on the other hand, excludes and shuts its eyes to the most possible hopes." Already characteristic of Gray is the view advocated in the "Ode on the Spring" by a tutelary figure:

> Beside some water's rushy brink
> With me the Muse shall sit, and think
> (At ease reclin'd in rustic state)
> How vain the ardour of the Crowd,
> How low, how little are the Proud,
> How indigent the Great!

The lines preview Gray's appreciation in the "Elegy" of rustic simplicity against the claims of the proud and the great and reveal the inception of a poetic persona that will be adapted and modified during the coming years. The poem therefore offers a model for reading Gray's early poetry, in which the various rejections of desire are the major adventure of the speaker of the poems.

In *An Ode on a Distant Prospect of Eton College*, which is "about" the return of a disillusioned adult to the site of his schoolboy years, desire is represented by "grateful Science [who] still adores / Her HENRY'S holy Shade" (Henry VI was the founder of the college). The ode's opening implies the persistence of desire within the trope of loss and mourning. Science and Henry are icons of desire and loss that signify the import of the speaker's return to Eton: the apprehension of yearning and loss. What arises from the Etonian landscape are more shades, prefiguring future loss: "Ministers of human fate," Anger, Fear, Shame, images of desire defeated: "Or pineing Love shall waste their youth, / Or Jealousy with rankling tooth. . . ." Father Thames authorizes the speaker's vision; he is a silent confirmatory figure, another version of the tutelary muse.

Muse, Contemplation (in the "Ode on the Spring"), and Father Thames are evoked for the

On the Death of a favourite Cat
drown'd in a China-Tub of
Gold-Fishes.

'Twas on a lofty Vase's Side,
Where China's gayest Art had dyed
The azure Flow'rs that blow,
Demurest of the tabby Kind,
The pensive Selima reclined
Gazed on the Lake below.

Her conscious Tail her Joy declared,
Her fair round Face, her snowy Beard,
The Velvet of her Paws,
Her Coat, that with the Tortoise vies
Her Ears of Jet, & Emerald Eyes,
She saw & purr'd Applause.

Still had she gazed, but midst the Tide
Two angel Forms were seen to glide,
The Genii of the Stream:
Their scaly Armour's Tyrian Hue
Thro' richest Purple to the View
Betray'd a golden Gleam.

The hapless Nymph with Wonder saw,
A Whisker first, & then a Claw,
With many an ardent Wish,
She stretch'd in vain to reach the Prize:
What Female-Heart can Gold despise?
What Cat's averse to Fish?

Presumptuous Maid! with Eyes intent
Again she stretch'd, again she bent,
Nor knew the Gulph between.
Malignant Fate sat by, & smiled.
The slippery Verge her Feet beguiled:
She tumbled headlong in.

Eight times emerging from the Flood
She mew'd to ev'ry watry God
Some speedy Aid to send.
No Dolphin came, no Nereid stir'd,
Nor cruel John, nor Susan heard;
A Fav'rite has no Friend!

Volti sub

First page of one of three known manuscripts for Gray's playful tribute to Horace Walpole's cat Selima, which drowned in a goldfish bowl in February 1747 (Pierpont Morgan Library)

First page of one of three known drafts for Gray's "Elegy Wrote in a Country Church Yard" (Eton College)

Title page for the first edition of Gray's "Elegy"

prophetic wisdom they possess. One function of prophecy is to transform desire into "pineing Love" or the "fury Passions." The imagination's habit of personification exposes the debased forms assumed by desire ("Envy wan, and faded Care"), just as the "race of man" in the "Ode on the Spring" is revealed as insect life to "Contemplation's sober eye." Vision always serves to reveal form, and in Gray what is revealed is diminished, repudiated, or forbidden. The strategy of reductive acknowledgment in the "Ode on the Spring" dismisses the dream of desire; the strategy of creating giant spectral forms in the Eton College ode encourages bad dreams, translating desire into the demonic. Northrop Frye describes something similar to this action in his discussion of quest-romance: "Translated into dream terms, the quest-romance is the search of the libido or desiring self for a fulfillment that will deliver it from the anxieties of reality but still contain that reality." Fulfillment may require, as with Gray,

that a protective maternal figure displace a threatening female judicial figure; guilt is thereby dissipated in the approval received by the obedient actor who has rejected desire. This summary also describes the "Hymn to Adversity."

Adversity and Virtue are both daughters of Jove; the former is older than and tutor to the latter. Adversity is equipped with "iron scourge and torturing hour" but also has an alternative "form benign," a "milder influence." Virtue needs Adversity "to form her [Virtue's] infant mind"; the function of the tutelary spirit here is to engender pity ("she learn'd to melt at others' woe"). The instruction is absorbed by Virtue (the "rigid lore / With patience many a year she bore"). Virtue, subdued by Adversity, is enabled to recognize grief ("What sorrow was, thou bad'st her know") and is preserved from desire ("Scared at thy frown terrific, fly / Self-pleasing Folly's idle brood, / Wild Laughter, Noise, and thoughtless Joy, / And leave us leisure to be good"). Adversity, implored to "lay thy chast'ning hand" on her "Suppliant's head" and to appear "Not in thy Gorgon terrors clad, / Nor circled with the vengeful band / (As by the Impious thou art seen)," suggests the threatening form of Adversity seen by those who are not "good." Desire is converted into the antithetical form of horror. The speaker who experiences Adversity's "milder influence," her "philosophic Train," undergoes a transformation in which guilt is changed into the generous emotions of love and forgiveness. Adversity here joins Muse, Contemplation, and Thames as figures authorizing the rejection of desire. At the end of the Eton College ode the reader is reminded that the suffering "all are men." At the end of the "Hymn to Adversity" the speaker asks to be taught "to love and to forgive," to be led to "know myself a Man."

Gray's poems indicate a radical sexual distress. In the "Hymn to Adversity" Gray has arrived at the first clear castrative symbolism in the progress of his imagination (though one might argue that the reduction of humanity to insect life in the "Ode on the Spring" is a significant form of sexual loss), the replacement of Virtue by the poet. The threat of castration is transposed into an acceptance of it. The threatening figure of Adversity is pacified but requires a surrender of sexual identity.

In the "Hymn to Ignorance" Gray returns to Cambridge, invoking its "gothic fanes, and antiquated towers" as he had Eton's "distant spires" and "antique towers." Whereas in the Eton College ode "ignorance [small *i*] is bliss," in the "Hymn to Ignorance" Ignorance [large *I*] is a "soft salutary power." Ignorance is a maternal presence ("Prostrate with filial reverence I adore") possessed of a "peaceful shade"; its "influence breathed from high / Augments the native darkness of the sky." Ignorance is ambivalently represented as undesirable within the terms of desire ("Thrice hath Hyperion rolled his annual race, / Since weeping I forsook thy fond embrace"). The oedipal actors include mother/muse (Ignorance), father (Hyperion), and the returning son/poet, Gray.

On 15 October 1742 Gray returned to Peterhouse as a fellow-commoner to read for a law degree. After 1742 he wrote poetry only sporadically. He received an LL.B. degree in November 1743. He and Walpole were reconciled in 1745, though the friendship was never again quite as intimate.

When Gray returned to writing poetry, he composed two poems that rebuke desire in different ways. Selima, Walpole's cat in "Ode on the Death of a Favourite Cat, Drowned in a Tub of Gold Fishes" (1748), is tempted beyond "lawful prize" into a watery grave. The "Ode on the Death of a Favourite Cat" is a cautionary tale; its purpose is to deaden desire by revealing its effect on the "Presumptuous Maid!" Selima's desire to apprehend "Two angel forms . . . / The Genii of the stream," is an investment in death. Implicit in the scene of desire are the unattainability of the object and the abandonment of the desiring figure to her fate: "Eight times emerging from the flood / She mew'd to ev'ry watery god." Selima's fate appears in the concluding stanza as if to Contemplation's sober eye. Her plunge into the goldfish bowl is another vain dream of the desiring self. Selima wishes to possess what is taboo; it requires her engagement with a medium in which she cannot survive. Her fate is a variation on the fate of those who would appropriate that which is beyond their proper sphere. The poem might be read as pertinent to Gray's sense of his poetic vocation: his poetic output was small, and his poems were generally short and often unfinished.

In "A Long Story" (1753), composed in 1750, the Peeress whose judgment the poet fears invites him to dinner instead of rebuking him. Brought before her authority the poet disavows himself:

"He once or twice had pen'd a sonnet;
"Yet hoped, that he might save his bacon:
"Numbers would give their oaths upon it,
"He ne'er was for a conj'rer taken.["]

"A Long Story" involves a flight from the figures of desire, the "heroines" who attempt to lure the poet into polite country pleasures, leaving a note ("a spell") on the table. This self-representation points toward the poet of the "Elegy": the poet who is there heard by the hoary-headed swain, " 'Muttering his wayward fancies,' " is here "something . . . heard to mutter, / 'How in the park beneath an old-tree / '(Without design to hurt the butter, / 'Or any malice to the poultry,). . . .' " The old tree of "A Long Story" is the transplanted "nodding beech" of the "Elegy," under which the poet " 'His listless length at noontide would . . . stretch.' " The poet of "A Long Story" is the parodic form of the poet of the "Elegy." The shift in the "Elegy" from "I" to "thee" is pre-

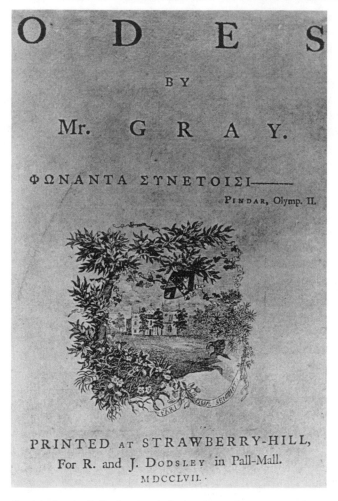

Title page for the collection that includes Gray's Pindaric odes, "The Progress of Poesy" and "The Bard."
The volume was the first book published by Horace Walpole's press at Strawberry Hill.

figured in "A Long Story" in an unidentified voice which suddenly breaks in to rebuke the speaker for his tedium: "Your Hist'ry whither you are spinning? / Can you do nothing but describe?" "A Long Story" is actually a short one (145 lines) of identity mocked, function abused ("Whither are you spinning?"), and voice lost. What here dominates Gray's imagination is a vision of prophecy reduced to absurdity, of the seer as merely a bothersome miscreant

> Who prowl'd the country far and near,
> Bewitch'd the children of the peasants,
> Dried up the cows and lam'd the deer,
> And suck'd the eggs, and kill'd the pheasants.

If it were only for the "Elegy" Gray's reputation would endure, for it is surely the finest elegiac poem of the age and one of the half-dozen or so great English elegies. As was usual with Gray the poem's progress was hesitant and de-layed (two distinctly different versions of the poem exist), and its publication was imposed on him when the poem was pirated from privately circulated copies and printed by the *Magazine of Magazines*. Its publication in 1751 places it more than halfway in Gray's poetic career, between the highly productive year of 1742 and the publication of the two Pindaric odes in 1757.

Almost everyone who reads poetry is familiar with the opening of the poem: "The curfew tolls the knell of parting day, / The lowing herd wind slowly o'er the lea, / The plowman homeward plods his weary way, / And leaves the world to darkness and to me." It echoes lines from John Milton and William Shakespeare (and is echoed later by James Beattie and Wordsworth); it reflects a melancholic evening mood that has probably never found better expression. The eye of the speaker moves along the periphery of vision and returns to its center, the churchyard where "The rude Forefathers of the hamlet sleep." As the legacy of day is the night, the legacy of the past is death, an inheritance of mortality bequeathed equally by the rich and by the poor. Everyone awaits the inevitable hour. Within the poem the brooding churchyard stands as an abiding memento mori, a powerful eschatological symbol appropriately heralded by the "droning" beetle, the "mopeing owl," the "yew-tree's shade." Against such an initial vision, as its contrary, are set the emblems of Christian eschatology: the "incense-breathing Morn," "the swallow," "the cock's shrill clarion," "the echoing horn"—none of which shall ever again rouse the slumberers. The vast negative absolute of death informs the poem, and Gray confronts the omnipresent fact of mortality, letting the confrontation arise implicitly from the opposition of the two major symbols within the poem: the chronicle and the grave, the epitaph and the churchyard.

One of the abiding paradoxes of the poem resides in the idea of satisfactory unfulfillment: village-Hampdens; mute, inglorious Miltons; guiltless Cromwells of the rural life. The paradox is spawned by Gray's vision of human life as dominated by the only inevitability it contains, that of death. Before this inevitability the triumphs of man pass into insignificance, for "The paths of glory," like all paths, "lead but to the grave." Against the grave is posed the chronicle or epitaph, and the latter is of considerable complexity in the poem. It develops through various modalities before it emerges finally as the poet's own epitaph, with which the work concludes. The specific manifestations of the chronicle include the "annals of the poor," the "storied urn," the "boast of heraldry," the "animated bust," the "frail memorial." In each case the objects of remembrance are diminished by the qualifying context: the annals of the poor are "short and simple," the boast of heraldry "awaits . . . th' inevitable hour," the storied urn and animated bust cannot "Back to its mansion call the fleeting breath," the memorial is "frail." Such images bespeak futility. Yet what emerges as truly valuable is human relationship. Gray's reading of epitaphs is a coming-to-know: he did not know these people as they lived; he knows them by the imaginative re-creation of their lives through a meditation on the surviving memorials.

So, too, the reader is given to understand, will the "kindred Spirit" know the narrator through his own epitaph. If in the end everyone is alone, solitude is qualified by shared mortality, and further qualified by the presence of a kindred sensibility. Mortality is not submitted to some scheme of personal salvation or redemption. The "Elegy" is not in this respect a conventional pastoral elegy; it does not provide the consolation of, say, Milton's Lycidas (1637). Gray's poem suggests that the elegist is himself powerless in the face of death, unable to refer it to a religious belief by which it can be made comprehensible. What are justified are the unrealized lives, of which the poet's life is one example. The "Elegy" is perhaps most of all an exercise in the varieties of feeling: the speaker feels for the unhonored dead and for the honored dead; he imagines particular persons for whom he can feel; he employs the pathetic fallacy to feel for the flower "born to blush unseen"; he feels for "mankind"; and through the "kindred Spirit" he feels for himself. The poem is an exercise in sensibility. The darkness in which the narrator stands is the night of mortality illuminated only by varieties of feeling. This common denominator of sympathy, as everything in the poem evidences, is all that binds man to man, and, along with the fact of death that occasions this sympathy, is the single principle of unity within life perceived by the poet.

The inception of "The Progress of Poesy: A Pindaric Ode" followed directly on the publication of the "Elegy." It presents a further, yet concealed, rendering of the self-image found especially at the end of the "Elegy." "The Progress of Poesy" associates the solitary poet with his mother-muse, the female goddess to whom he owes his capacity to perceive "forms" illuminated by "the Muse's ray," a light that is "unborrow'd of the Sun." Ceres ("Ceres' golden reign") embodies the generative power of nature. "Helicon's harmonious springs" are associated with generation ("The laughing flowers . . . / Drink life and fragrance as they flow"). The lyre is the "Parent of sweet and solemn-breathing airs." These three elements dominate the opening of the poem. The first ternary closes with Aphrodite ("Cytherea's day"), a figure of generative force mingling the union of water and music ("brisk notes in cadence beating"; "arms sublime, that float upon the air"). She is the reemergent Venus of the "Ode on the Spring," attended, as was Venus in that poem, by a train of celebrants: "O'er her warm cheek, and rising bosom, move / The bloom of young Desire, and purple light of Love." In the "Ode on the Spring," the "rosy-

Pembroke College, Cambridge University, Gray's principal residence from March 1756 until his death in 1771

bosom'd Hours, / . . . Disclose the long-expected flowers, / And wake the purple year!"

The familiar Etonian demons recur in this poem: "Man's feeble race what Ills await, / Labour, and Penury, the racks of Pain." In the second ternary the recognition of loss rises against the figures of desire, opposing them with "Night, and all her sickly dews." Night, a "mighty Mother" of sorts, will hold sway "Till down the eastern cliffs afar / Hyperion's march they spy, and glitt'ring shafts of war." Hyperion is an idealized figure associated through the "eastern cliffs" with Milton's Raphael, and more vaguely with Christ as he disposes half his might against Satan's legions. But the ode relegates his progress to an indefinite future, to an apocalyptic dawn that will "justify the laws of Jove." Hyperion departs from the poem at the close of the first strophe of the second ternary. Thus the defeat of Night, the graveyard goddess whose "Spectres wan, and Birds of boding cry" are the antithesis to the "rosy-crowned Loves" attending Aphrodite, is deferred.

The "Muse" who appears at this point is a variation on the pastoral-maternal female, one who "deigns to hear the savage Youth repeat / In loose numbers wildly sweet / Their feather-cinctured Chiefs, and dusky Loves." She is a "soft salutary power" ("Hymn to Ignorance"), "form benign" ("Hymn to Adversity").

The oedipal fantasy is played out in pastoral surroundings: "In thy green lap was Nature's Darling [Shakespeare] laid, / What time, where lucid Avon Stray'd, / To Him the mighty Mother did unveil / Her aweful face. . . ." The anticipation of unveiling led the voyeur Milton to ride "sublime / Upon the seraph-wings of Extasy, / The secrets of th' Abyss to spy." Yet the laws of Jove are preserved: the primal scene is never viewed. The Hyperionic march is rendered irrelevant by "Such forms, as glitter in the Muse's ray"; these forms that tease Gray's own "infant eyes," bringing him into proximity to Shakespeare, the "immortal Boy." The "orient hues" that dazzled the child Gray were "unborrow'd of the sun"— another rejection of the sublime poetic (Hyperionic) principle. Between oedipal desire (the desire for the "mighty Mother") and the lonely sublime passion of the middle poet there is no adequate middle ground (though Gray hopes to find one). The "distant way" chosen by the poet at the end of the poem is necessitated by the refusal to be the poet of sublime vision (Milton) and by the impossibility of possessing the mother-muse who appears to the child of nature (Shakespeare). Much of the ode is occupied with the scene of

Letter from Gray to his friend William Mason (Collection of A. T. Lloyd, Esq., of Lockinge)

desire—Milton's and Shakespeare's—and is thus concerned, however covertly, with the relation between sexual power and poetic vision. Gray's modest announcement at the end of the poem shows a recognition of his distance from the great figures of English literature and from the power with which their visions were informed: he is "Beneath the Good . . . but far above the Great"—in any event, alone.

"The Bard: A Pindaric Ode" (1757) is a companion piece to "The Progress of Poesy." It presents another identity, a solitary prophet who can more readily justify the laws of Jove than can any agent in the "The Progress of Poesy." At the beginning of the ode he is "Robed in the sable garb of woe," the insignia of his office. At the end he "plung[es] to endless night," another entrance into darkness. The plunge into the abyss seems to be a wish-fulfillment fantasy; the mighty Mother is darkness itself, the unshaped figure of desire. The poet who strikes "the deep sorrows of his lyre" in "The Bard" produces not the

"sweet and solemn-breathing airs" of "The Progress of Poesy" but the harmonies of loss and consolation.

The Eton College ode identifies the progress of human life in terms of absolute separation between youth and age. The "Ode on the Pleasure Arising from Vicissitude," written around 1754-1755 and published in 1775, recreates, through the language of kindredness, the law of succession and cycle: "Still, where rosy Pleasure leads, / See a kindred Grief pursue." "Rosy Pleasure" is joined here to an opposite that follows it in an endless alternation. The "blended form" composed by the two figures unifies the figures of desire and authority in what is apparently Gray's version of the marriage of heaven and hell. The principle of authority (and desire) is found in Vicissitude, a figure who imposes an Adversity-like "chastening":

The hues of Bliss more brightly glow,
Chastised by sabler tints of woe. . . .

219

The ode negates its initial figure of desire, "the golden Morn aloft" who

> . . . woo's the tardy spring:
> Till April starts, and calls around
> The sleeping fragrance from the ground;
> And lightly o'er the living scene
> Scatters his freshest, tenderest green.

Morn and April give way to tableaux in which the kindred activities of mourning and consolation are enacted: "Smiles on past Misfortune's brow / Soft Reflection's hand can trace; / And o'er the cheek of Sorrow throw / A melancholy grace." The initial act of wooing becomes another sort of engagement, Grief pursuing rosy Pleasure, Comfort approaching Misery. The "blended form" is a sublimation of the sexual ardor between Morn and April, transformed into a depersonalized aesthetic in which "artful strife" and "strength and harmony" displace the seductive Morn who "With vermeil cheek and whisper soft / . . . woo's the tardy spring." Courtship is metamorphosed into consolation, and Vicissitude becomes another figure like Contemplation or Adversity, under whose aegis desire is eliminated. Vicissitude, unlike Adversity, is a genderless figure, representing no threatening sexual image The ode revisits another place, as Eton is revisited by the disillusioned speaker in *An Ode on a Distant Prospect of Eton College* or as Gray returns to Cambridge in the "Hymn to Ignorance." Here the return is to the beginning of the "Elegy," to "darkness" and to the landscape over which the "plowman homeward plods his weary way." All of Gray's poems are poems of progress, journeys in which the challenge lies in discovering something other than the circularity of ends that are constituted of beginnings ("And they that creep, and they that fly, / Shall end where they began" ["Ode on the Spring"]).

Gray's mother died on 11 March 1753. On 5 March 1756 he moved from Peterhouse College across the street to Pembroke College, reportedly as a consequence of a prank played on him by some students who, knowing of his fear of fire, raised a false alarm. When the master of Peterhouse, Dr. Law, failed to take Gray's complaint about the prank seriously, Gray "migrated" to Pembroke. When the poet laureate, Colley Cibber, died in 1757, Gray was offered the position; but he declined it. In July 1759 he moved to London to study at the British Museum, which had been opened to the public in January. In December 1761 he returned to Cambridge; except for frequent trips to London, other parts of England, Scotland, and Wales, he remained in Cambridge for the rest of his life.

Poems by Mr. Gray (1768) includes two translations from the Norse. "The Fatal Sisters" and "The Descent of Odin" are poems of prophecy. The first is dominated by what Gray in the preface calls "twelve gigantic figures resembling women" whose purpose is to weave the web of futurity and whose way leads through another field of the dead ("As the paths of fate we tread, / Wading thro' th' ensanguin'd field. . . ." The easily identifiable figure of desire in the early verse has been replaced by vast terrifying forms, "*Mista* black, terrific Maid, / *Sangrida,* and *Hilda,*" "*Gondula,* and *Geira.*" Such women appeared first as Contemplation or Adversity. They represent the combined identities of muse-mother-death, the unified form of desire and authority toward which Gray's imagination has been traveling.

"The Descent of Odin" concerns Odin's visit to the underworld—the kingdom of Hela, Goddess of Death—to discover his son Balder's fate; he learns from the prophetess that Hoder will murder Balder and that Vali, the son of Odin and Rinda, will avenge the crime. The " prophetic Maid" is revealed as the "Mother of the giant-brood." Odin wakes her with "runic rhyme; / Thrice pronounc'd, in accents dread." The poem with the maid denying prophetic knowledge to any future "enquirer . . . / . . . till substantial Night / Has reassum'd her ancient right." The maid's last oracular utterance is a vision of ultimate closure, when "wrap'd in flames, in ruin hurl'd, / Sinks the fabric of the world."

In July 1768 Gray was made professor of modern history at Cambridge, though he never lectured or published on the subject. The most significant personal event of his last years was a brief, intense friendship with a young Swiss student, Karl Victor von Bonstetten. The friendship was apparently complicated by physical desire on Gray's part, though no sexual relation is believed to have occurred between them. In July 1771 Gray became ill while dining at Pembroke College; a week later, on 30 July, he died. In his *Souvenirs* (1832) Bonstetten reflected on the poet: "Je crois que Gray n'avait jamais aimé, c'était le mot de l'énigme, il en était résulté une misère de coeur qui faisait contraste avec son imagination, ardente et profond qui, au lieu de faire le bonheur de sa vie, n'en était que le tourment" (I think the key to the mystery is that Gray never loved; the result was a poverty of heart contrast-

Gray's tomb in the churchyard at Stoke Poges

ing with his ardent and profound imagination, which, instead of comprising the happiness of his life, was only its torment).

Gray remains an important poet in the context of generally disappointing poets in the second half of the eighteenth century. In this sense he is one of a group, including William Collins, James Macpherson, Thomas Chatterton, William Cowper, Christopher Smart, and Joseph and Thomas Warton, who largely failed to provide English poetry with any especially distinctive period identity and whose achievements were shortly to be overshadowed by the emergence in the 1780s and 1790s of Wordsworth, Coleridge, and the quickly succeeding second generation of Romantic writers.

Three aspects of Gray's prose remain of value to modern students of the later eighteenth century. His extensive correspondence reveals his various interests and displays his intelligence and character in ways that the poetry cannot. Gray

was an amateur entomologist, an enthusiastic traveler, and a discerning admirer of the sublime in nature. A well-known passage in his correspondence (16 November 1739) describes his journey to the Grande Chartreuse during his Continental tour: "Not a precipice, not a torrent, not a cliff, but is pregnant with religion and poetry. There are certain scenes that would awe an atheist into belief, without the help of other argument. One need not have a very fantastic imagination to see spirits there at noonday. You have death perpetually before your eyes, only so far removed, as to compose the mind without frightening it." His journal of his tour of the English Lakes was published in *The Poems of Mr. Gray* (1775); it is the work by him that most favorably influenced Wordsworth and is said to be the best of his prose compositions. Finally, Gray proposed a history of English literature which came to little more than some sketches and a few literary essays revealing his interest in meter, rhyme, unity

Detail of the monument to Gray, by John Bacon the Elder, in Westminster Abbey

of poetic effect, and older English poets. With the important exception of the correspondence, the prose remains largely unread today and occupies the sort of place in his oeuvre accorded the Latin compositions in prose and verse that he occasionally produced. Much of his career is marked by an unsettling tendency toward the occasional, the random, and the unsustained; his poetry may be the best indication of the difficulties in writing a new public poetry in the age following Alexander Pope.

Letters:

The Correspondence of Thomas Gray, 3 volumes, edited by Paget Toynbee and Leonard Whibley (Oxford: Clarendon Press, 1935; reprinted, with additions and corrections by Herbert W. Starr, Oxford: Clarendon Press, 1971).

Bibliographies:

Clark S. Northrup, *A Bibliography of Thomas Gray* (New Haven: Yale University Press, 1917);

Herbert W. Starr, *A Bibliography of Thomas Gray, 1917-1951* (Philadelphia: University of Pennsylvania Press, 1953);

Alan T. McKenzie, *Thomas Gray: A Reference Guide* (Boston: Hall, 1982);

Donald C. Mell, Jr., *English Poetry, 1660-1800* (Detroit: Gale Research, 1982), pp. 238-251.

Biographies:

Roger Martin, *Essai sur Thomas Gray* (London: Oxford University Press / Paris: Les Presses Universitaires de France, 1934);

William Powell Jones, *Thomas Gray, Scholar: The True Tragedy of an Eighteenth-Century Gentleman* (Cambridge, Mass.: Harvard University Press, 1937);

Robert W. Ketton-Cremer, *Thomas Gray: A Biography* (Cambridge: Cambridge University Press, 1955).

References:

Matthew Arnold, "Thomas Gray," in his *Essays in Criticism: Second Series* (London: Macmillan, 1889), pp. 69-99;

Karl Victor von Bonstetten, *Souvenirs de Ch. Victor de Bonstetten, écrits en 1831* (Paris: Cherbuliez, 1832);

Frank Brady, "Structure and Meaning in Gray's *Elegy*," in *From Sensibility to Romanticism: Essays Presented to Frederick A. Pottle*, edited by Frederick W. Hilles and Harold Bloom (New York: Oxford University Press, 1965), pp. 177-189;

Lord David Cecil, "The Poetry of Thomas Gray," in *Eighteenth Century English Literature: Modern Essays in Criticism*, edited by James L. Clifford (New York: Oxford University Press, 1959), pp. 233-250;

Albert S. Cook, *Concordance to the English Poems of Thomas Gray* (Boston & New York: Houghton, Mifflin, 1908; reprinted, Gloucester, Mass.: Smith, 1967);

Francis Doherty, "The Two Voices of Gray," *Essays in Criticism*, 13 (July 1963): 222-230;

Frank H. Ellis, "Gray's *Elegy*: The Biographical Problem in Literary Criticism," *PMLA*, 66 (December 1951): 971-1008;

Northrop Frye, *Anatomy of Criticism* (Princeton: Princeton University Press, 1957), p. 193;

Morris Golden, *Thomas Gray* (New York: Twayne, 1964);

Donald Green, "The Proper Language of Poetry: Gray, Johnson, and Others," in *Fearful Joy: Papers from the Thomas Gray Bicentenary Conference at Carleton University*, edited by James Downey and Ben Jones (Montreal: McGill-Queen's University Press, 1974), pp. 85-102;

Leon Guilhamet, "Imitation and Originality in the Poems of Thomas Gray," in *Proceedings of the Modern Language Association: Neoclassicism Conferences, 1967-1968*, edited by Paul J. Korshin (New York: AMS, 1970), pp. 33-52;

Wallace Jackson, "Thomas Gray and the Dedicatory Muse," *ELH*, 54 (Summer 1987): 277-298;

Jackson, "Thomas Gray: Drowning in Human Voices," *Criticism*, 28 (Fall 1986): 361-379;

Jackson and Paul Yoder, "Wordsworth Reimagines Thomas Gray: Notations on Begetting a Kindred Spirit," *Criticism*, 31 (Summer 1989): 287-301;

Samuel Johnson, "Life of Thomas Gray," in his *The Lives of the English Poets*, 3 volumes, edited by George Birkbeck Hill (London: Clarendon Press, 1905), III: 421-445;

Roger Lonsdale, "The Poetry of Thomas Gray: Versions of Self," *Proceedings of the British Academy*, 59 (1973): 105-123;

Patricia Meyer Spacks, " 'Artful Strife': Conflict in Gray's Poetry," *PMLA*, 81 (March 1966): 63-69;

Spacks, "Statement and Artifice in Thomas Gray," *Studies in English Literature*, 5 (Summer 1965): 519-532;

Howard D. Weinbrot, "Gray's *Elegy*: A Poem of Moral Choice and Resolution," *Studies in English Literature*, 18 (Summer 1978): 537-551;

Henry Weinfeld. *The Poet without a Name: Gray's Elegy and the Problem of History* (Carbondale & Edwardsville: Southern Illinois University Press, 1991);

William Wordsworth, Preface to *Lyrical Ballads, with a Few Other Poems*, second edition, 2 volumes, by Wordsworth and Samuel Taylor Coleridge (London: Printed for T. N. Longman and O. Rees by Briggs & Co., Bristol, 1800; Philadelphia: Printed and sold by James Humphreys, 1802).

Papers:

A commonplace book, in three volumes, at Pembroke College, Cambridge, contains Thomas Gray's transcripts of many of his poems and transcripts of other of Gray's poems made by William Mason after Gray's death.

Samuel Johnson

(18 September 1709 - 13 December 1784)

This entry was updated by Donald Greene (University of Southern California) from his entry in
DLB 104: British Prose Writers: 1660-1800: Second Series.

See also the Johnson entries in DLB 39: British Novelists, 1660-1800: Part One *and* DLB 95: Eighteenth-Century British Poets: First Series.

BOOKS: *A Voyage to Abyssinia by Father Jerome Lobo . . . and Fifteen Dissertations . . . by Mr. Le Grand. From the French* (London: Printed for A. Bettesworth & C. Hitch, 1735);

London: A Poem, in Imitation of the Third Satire of Juvenal (London: Printed for R. Doddesley, 1738);

Marmor Norfolciense: or an Essay on an Ancient Prophetical Inscription, In Monkish Rhyme, Lately Discover'd near Lynn in Norfolk. By Probus Britanicus (London: Printed for J. Brett, 1739);

A Compleat Vindication of the Licensers of the Stage, from the Malicious and Scandalous Aspersions of Mr. Brooke, Author of Gustavus Vasa . . . By an Impartial Hand (London: Printed for C. Corbett, 1739);

A Commentary on Mr. Pope's Principles of Morality, or Essay on Man. By Mons. Crousaz (London: Printed for A. Dodd, 1739);

An Account of the Life of Mr. Richard Savage, Son of the Earl Rivers (London: Printed for J. Roberts, 1744);

Miscellaneous Observations on the Tragedy of Macbeth: with Remarks on Sir T. H.'s Edition of Shakespear. To which is affix'd, Proposals for a New Edition of Shakeshear [sic] (London: Printed for E. Cave & sold by J. Roberts, 1745);

A Sermon Preached at the Cathedral Church of St. Paul, before the Sons of the Clergy, on Thursday the Second of May, 1745. by the Honourable and Reverend Henry Hervey Aston (London: Printed for J. Brindley & sold by M. Cooper, 1745);

Prologue and Epilogue, Spoken at the Opening of the Theatre in Drury-Lane 1747 (London: Printed by E. Cave, sold by M. Cooper & R Dodsley, 1747);

The Plan of a Dictionary of the English Language; Addressed to the Right Honourable Philip Dormer, Earl of Chesterfield (London: Printed for J. & P. Knapton, T. Longman & T. Shewell, C. Hitch, A. Millar and R. Dodsley, 1747);

The Vanity of Human Wishes. The Tenth Satire of Juvenal, Imitated (London: Printed for R. Dodsley & sold by M. Cooper, 1749);

Irene: A Tragedy. As it is Acted at the Theatre Royal in Drury-Lane (London: Printed for R. Dodsley & sold by M. Cooper, 1749);

The Rambler, nos. 1-208 (London: Printed for J. Payne & L. Bouquet, (20 March 1750 - 14 March 1752); republished in 2 volumes (London: Printed for J. Payne, 1753);

A New Prologue Spoken by Mr. Garrick, Thursday, April 5, 1750. At the Representation of Comus, for the Benefit of Mrs Elizabeth Foster, Milton's Grand-Daughter, and only surviving Descendant (London: Printed for J. Payne & J. Bouquet, 1750);

A Dictionary of the English Language, 2 volumes (London: Printed by W. Strahan for J. & P. Knapton, T. & T. Longman, C. Hitch & L. Hawes, A. Millar, and R. & J. Dodsley, 1755);

An Account of an Attempt to Ascertain the Longitude at Sea. . . . By Zachariah Williams (London: Printed for R. Dodsley & J. Jeffries & sold by J. Bouquet, 1755);

Proposals for Printing, by Subscription, the Dramatick Works of William Shakespeare (London, 1756);

The Prince of Abissinia. A Tale, 2 volumes (London: Printed for R. & J. Dodsley and W. Johnston, 1759); American edition: *The History of Rasselas, Prince of Abissinia,* 1 volume (Philadelphia: Printed by Robert Bell, 1768);

The Idler, collected edition, 2 volumes (London: Printed for J. Newbery, 1761)—first published in the *Universal Chronicle, or Weekly Gazette* (15 April 1758 - 5 April 1760);

The Plays of William Shakespeare, in Eight Volumes, with the Corrections and Illustrations of Various

Samuel Johnson, 1756 (portrait by Sir Joshua Reynolds; National Portrait Gallery, London)

Commentators; to which are added Notes by Sam. Johnson (London: Printed for J. & R. Tonson and ten others, 1765); revised by Johnson and George Steevens (London, 1773);

The False Alarm (London: Printed for T. Cadell, 1770);

Thoughts on the Late Transactions Respecting Falkland's Islands (London: Printed for T. Cadell, 1771);

The Patriot. Addressed to the Electors of Great Britain (London: Printed for T. Cadell, 1774);

A Journey to the Western Islands of Scotland (London: Printed for W. Strahan & T. Cadell, 1775);

Taxation No Tyranny; an Answer to the Resolutions and Address of the American Congress (London: Printed for T. Cadell, 1775);

Prefaces, Biographical and Critical, to the Works of the English Poets, 10 volumes (London: Printed by J. Nichols for C. Bathurst and thirty-five others, 1779 [volumes 1-4]; 1781 [volumes 5-10]).

Editions: *Prayers and Meditations, composed by Samuel Johnson*, edited by George Strahan (London: Printed for T. Cadell, 1785);

The Works of Samuel Johnson, LL.D. volumes 1-11, with *Life* by Sir John Hawkins (London: Printed for J. Buckland and forty others, 1787); volumes 12 and 13, *Debates in Parliament* (London: Printed for John Buckland, 1787); volume 14 (London: Printed for John Stockdale and G. G. J. & J. Robinson, 1788); "volume 15" (London: Printed for Elliot & Kay and C. Elliot, 1789);

The Lives of the English Poets [Prefaces, Biographical and Critical, to the Works of the English Poets], 3 volumes, edited by G. B. Hill (Oxford: Clarendon Press, 1905);

Samuel Johnson's Prefaces and Dedications, edited by Allen T. Hazen (New Haven: Yale University Press, 1937);

The Yale Edition of the Works of Samuel Johnson (13 volumes to date):

Volume 1: *Diaries, Prayers, and Annals*, edited by E. L. McAdam, Jr., with Donald and Mary Hyde (New Haven: Yale University Press / London: Oxford University Press, 1958);

Volume 2: *The Idler and The Adventurer*, edited by W. J. Bate, John M. Bullitt, L. F. Powell (New Haven & London: Yale University Press, 1963);

Volumes 3-5: *The Rambler*, edited by Bate and Albrecht B. Strauss (New Haven & London: Yale University Press, 1969);

Volume 6: *Poems*, edited by McAdam with George Milne (New Haven & London: Yale University Press, 1964);

Volumes 7 & 8: *Johnson on Shakespeare*, edited by Arthur Sherbo (New Haven & London: Yale University Press, 1968);

Volume 9: *A Journey to the Western Islands of Scotland*, edited by Mary Lascelles (New Haven & London: Yale University Press, 1971);

Volume 10: *Political Writings*, edited by Donald J. Greene (New Haven & London: Yale University Press, 1977);

Volume 14: *Sermons*, edited by Jean H. Hagstrum and James Gray (New Haven & London: Yale University Press, 1978);

Volume 15: *A Voyage to Abyssinia*, edited by Joel J. Gold (New Haven & London: Yale University Press, 1985);

Volume 16: *Rasselas and Other Tales*, edited by Gwin J. Kolb (New Haven & London: Yale University Press, 1990);

The Life of Savage, edited by Clarence Tracy (Oxford: Clarendon Press, 1971);

Samuel Johnson, edited by Donald Greene, The Oxford Authors (Oxford & New York: Oxford University Press, 1984).

OTHER: *A Miscellany of Poems by Several Hands. Publish'd by J. Husbands*, includes Johnson's Latin verse translation of Alexander Pope's *Messiah* (Oxford: Printed by Leon. Lichfield, 1731);

Catalogus Bibliothecae Harleianae, 5 volumes, catalogue of the Harleian library, includes contributions by Johnson (London: Apud Thomas Osborne, 1743-1745);

Robert James, M.D., *A Medicinal Dictionary*, 3 volumes, written with the assistance of Johnson (London: Printed for T. Osborne & J. Roberts, 1743-1745);

The Harleian Miscellany, or a Collection of . . . Pamphlets and Tracts, 8 volumes, includes an introduction and annotations by Johnson (London: Printed for T. Osborne, 1744-1746);

Preface and "The Vision of Theodore, the Hermit of Teneriffe," in *The Preceptor: Containing a Course of General Education* (London: Printed for R. Dodsley, 1748);

William Lauder, *An Essay on Milton's Use and Imitation of the Moderns in His Paradise Lost*, includes a preface and a postscript by Johnson (London: Printed for J. Payne & J. Bouquet, 1750);

Charlotte Lennox, *The Female Quixote; or, the Adventures of Arabella*, includes a dedication by Johnson, who may also have written part of book 9, chapter 11 (London: Printed for A. Millar, 1752);

The Adventurer (London: Printed for J. Payne, nos. 1-140 (London, 7 November 1752 - 9 March 1754)—includes twenty-nine essays by Johnson;

Lennox, *Shakespear Illustrated: or the Novels and Histories on Which the Plays of Shakespear Are Founded*, includes a dedication by Johnson (London: Printed for A. Millar, 1753);

Sir Thomas Browne, *Christian Morals. . . . The Second Edition. With a Life of the Author by Samuel Johnson*, edited, with biography and annotations, by Johnson (London: Printed by Richard Hett for J. Payne, 1756);

Richard Rolt, *A New Dictionary of Trade and Commerce*, includes a preface by Johnson (London: Printed for T. Osborne & J. Shipton and four others, 1756);

The Greek Theatre of Father [Pierre] Brumoy. Translated by Mrs. Charlotte Lennox, includes a dedication and translations of two essays by Johnson (London: Printed for Mess. Millar, Vaillant, and six others, 1759);

Introduction on the history of early Portuguese exploration, in *The World Displayed; or a Curious Collection of Voyages and Travels*, 20 volumes (London: Printed for J. Newbery, 1759-1761), I: iii-xxxii;

Proceedings of the Committee Appointed to Manage the Contributions begun at London Dec. xviii, MDCCLVIIII, for Cloathing French Prisoners of War, includes an introduction by Johnson (London: Printed by Order of the Committee, 1760);

John Gwynne, *Thoughts on the Coronation of His Present Majesty King George the Third, or, Reasons of-*

The marketplace at Lichfield in 1785 (engraving after a drawing by Stringer). Johnson was born in the building on the far right, which housed his father's bookshop on the ground floor.

fered against confining the procession to the usual track, and pointing out others more commodious and proper, much of the text written by Johnson (London: Printed for the Proprietor, and sold by F. Noble and three others, 1761);

"Author's Life" and dedication, in *The English Works of Roger Ascham . . . With Notes and Observations, and the Author's Life. By James Bennet*, edited in large part by Johnson (London: Printed for R. & J. Dodsley and J. Newbery, 1761);

Thomas Percy, ed., *Reliques of Ancient English Poetry*, includes a dedication by Johnson, who also provided general assistance (London: Printed for J. Dodsley, 1765);

Anna Williams, *Miscellanies in Prose and Verse* (London: Printed for T. Davies, 1766)—Johnson contributed the Advertisement, a short poem, "The Ant," possibly revisions to Miss Williams's poems, and *The Fountains: A Fairy Tale*;

The Convict's Address to His Unhappy Brethren. Delivered in the Chapel of Newgate, on Friday, June 6, 1777. By William Dodd, largely written by Johnson (London: Printed for G. Kearsley, 1777);

Poems and Miscellaneous Pieces, with a Free Translation of the Oedipus Tyrannus of Sophocles. By the Rev. Thomas Maurice, includes a preface and possibly a dedication by Johnson (London: Printed for the Author and Sold by J. Dodsley and three others, 1779);

Dedication to the King, in *An Account of the Musical Performances in Westminster-Abbey and the Pantheon . . . in Commemoration of Handel. By Charles Burney* (London: Printed for the Benefit of the Musical Fund and sold by T. Payne and Son and G. Robinson, 1785);

Sir Robert Chambers, *A Course of Lectures on the English Law Delivered at the University of Oxford 1767-1773 by Sir Robert Chambers and Composed in Association with Samuel Johnson*, edited by Thomas M. Curley (Madison: University of Wisconsin Press, 1986; Oxford: Clarendon Press, 1986).

Samuel Johnson—poet, dramatist, journalist, satirist, biographer, essayist, lexicographer, editor, translator, critic, parliamentary reporter, political writer, story writer, sermon writer, travel writer and social anthropologist, prose stylist, conversationalist, Christian—dominates the eighteenth-century English literary scene as his contemporary, the equally versatile and prolific Voltaire, dominates that of France. Perhaps more: Voltaire had redoubtable rivals during his lifetime, Jean-Jacques Rousseau and Denis Diderot; Johnson had none. Alexander Pope, a greater poet (though Johnson was a fine one), and Jonathan Swift, a greater satirist (though Johnson's skill as a satirist has been underestimated), had died in the 1740s; Joseph Addison and Richard Steele, Johnson's precursors as popular essayists, still earlier. When Johnson's name began to be known, not long after the deaths of Swift and Pope, no challenger arose during the next forty years for the title of preeminent English man of letters.

That period has often been called the Age of Johnson. To be sure, he had notable contemporaries—Edmund Burke, David Hume, Edward Gibbon—but their literary abilities, formidable as they were, moved in a narrower circle of concerns. Henry Fielding, Samuel Richardson, and Laurence Sterne received and deserve great acclaim as the founding fathers of the English novel, but their contributions to other areas of writing are less noteworthy. Almost as prolific as Johnson and as varied in his interests was Horace Walpole, who sometimes expressed aristocratic disdain for the lowborn Johnson, though he never seems to have impinged greatly on Johnson's consciousness. Walpole might be argued to have made a greater impact than Johnson on the following century, in the form of those somewhat dubious legacies the "Gothic" romance and Victorian pseudo-Gothic architecture. But no one has ever suggested calling the later eighteenth century "the Age of Horace Walpole." It is not surprising that the standard bibliographies of studies in eighteenth-century English literature show Johnson to have been their most popular subject, followed at some distance by Swift and Pope, and at a longer one by Fielding, Daniel Defoe, John Dryden, and William Blake, with Walpole an also-ran.

Johnson's origins were humble, and much of his life was spent in not so genteel poverty. He once boasted, in reply to a complaint that he advocated preserving class distinctions, that he could hardly tell who his grandfather was. That grandfather seems to have been a small tenant farmer or day laborer, one William Johnson. William's son Michael, Samuel's father, was assisted by a charitable society to become apprenticed as a stationer. After serving his time he set up as a bookseller and, in a small way, publisher in the Midlands cathedral city of Lichfield. For a time he prospered, and attained minor civic office. In the poignant small fragment of an autobiography that has survived, Samuel recorded Michael's joy at his birth: "When he [the obstetrician] had me in his arms, he said, 'Here is a brave boy.' . . . My father being that year Sheriff of Lichfield, and to ride the circuit of the County the next day, he was asked by my mother, 'Whom he would invite to the Riding?' and answered 'All the town now.' "

Michael had married late. He was fifty-two and his wife forty when their first son was born on 18 September 1709. She was Sarah Ford, of a family of tradesmen and small landholders who thought themselves socially superior to the lowly Johnsons. "My father and mother had not much happiness from each other," Samuel recorded. "They seldom conversed, for my father could not bear to talk of his affairs, and my mother, being unacquainted with books, cared not to talk of any thing else." In spite of her no doubt strongly expressed advice, Michael's business deteriorated, and he died in the poverty from which he had briefly risen. Sarah then took over the bookshop and ran it competently for the rest of her life. It was not a happy family. Sarah's bourgeois values were at odds with Michael's and Samuel's more intellectual interests, and recent scholars have attributed some of Samuel's later psychological problems to her lack of understanding or affection for the boy. A younger brother, Nathanael, seems to have suffered also; almost all that is known of him is a pathetic letter to Sarah written when he was twenty-four, accusing Samuel of turning his mother against him and giving a most gloomy picture of his own prospects. He died shortly afterward, and suicide has been suspected.

From childhood Samuel suffered from various physical ailments that plagued him throughout his life—near blindness in one eye, the tubercular infection scrofula (the "King's Evil," which even the royal touch of Queen Anne failed to cure), a persistent uncontrollable tic. But he grew up to be a strong, muscular man: his height of six feet was unusual in the eighteenth century, and, when he first sought employment in London as a writer, he was once advised rather to hire himself out as a public porter. He received the standard classical education in Latin and

A

VOYAGE

TO

ABYSSINIA.

BY

Father *Jerome Lobo,*

A PORTUGUESE JESUIT.

CONTAINING,

A Narrative of the Dangers he underwent in his first Attempt to pass from the *Indies* into *Abyssinia*; with a Description of the Coasts of the *Red-Sea.* An Account of the History, Laws, Customs, Religion, Habits, and Buildings of the *Abyssins*; with the Rivers, Air, Soil, Birds, Beasts, Fruits and other natural Productions of	that remote and unfrequented Country. A Relation of the Admission of the Jesuits into *Abyssinia* in 1625, and their Expulsion from thence in 1634. An exact Description of the *Nile*, its Head, its Branches, the Course of its Waters, and the Cause of its Inundations.

With a Continuation of the History of *Abyssinia* down to the Beginning of the Eighteenth Century, and Fifteen Dissertations on various Subjects relating to the History, Antiquities, Government, Religion, Manners, and natural History of *Abyssinia*, and other Countries mention'd by Father *JEROME LOBO.*

By MR. *LE GRAND.*

From the *FRENCH.*

LONDON.

Printed for A. BETTESWORTH, and C. HITCH at the *Red-Lyon* in *Paternoster-Row.*

MDCCXXXV.

Title page for Johnson's first book, a translation and adaptation of a book he had read at Oxford

Greek at Lichfield grammar school, where he was regarded as something of a prodigy. He said that he caught his first enthusiasm for literature when, as a boy, searching for a cache of apples he thought Nathanael had hidden behind a shelf of books in their father's shop, he came across a volume of Petrarch (no doubt in Latin), and became so absorbed in it that he forgot about the apples. When he was sixteen, he transferred to the grammar school in nearby Stourbridge, where some of his Ford relations lived, and later paid tribute to the influence of his cousin Cornelius Ford, a polished intellectual, who encouraged the boy's love of books and ambition to write. While there, he began to compose boyish poetry—translations of Horace's odes, conventional love poems to young ladies, even one, the earliest that has survived, "On a Daffodil."

When he was seventeen, he returned to Lichfield and put in two no doubt reluctant years working in the bookshop, where, however, he had the opportunity to devour much of its contents; he later said that he knew almost as much at eigh-

teen as he did when he was in his fifties. The lad's learning and promise caused him to be taken up by the cultured Gilbert Walmesley, an official of the ecclesiastical court of the diocese, who used to invite Johnson and another younger Lichfield lad, the lively David Garrick, to dine with him and who encouraged Johnson's intellectual interests. Two years later a small legacy from a relation of Mrs. Johnson's enabled Samuel to enroll in Oxford University, where many of his less brilliant but more affluent schoolmates had already gone. When he entered Pembroke College, the breadth of the young man's reading is said to have made an impression on the dons. But the thirteen months he spent there before the money ran out were hardly successful ones. He found his tutors incompetent, and instead of attending lectures spent his time in such amusements as sliding on the ice and encouraging his fellow undergraduates in rebellious indiscipline. "I was rude and violent," he later said. "It was bitterness which they mistook for frolic. I was miserably poor, and I thought to fight my way by my literature and wit." Nevertheless it was at Oxford that he composed his first published work, a translation into Latin verse of Pope's long poem *Messiah* that appeared in a collection edited by an Oxford don (1731). Pope said it was so well done that it would be hard to tell whether his or the anonymous translator's was the original—a great compliment from the greatest poet of his time.

Leaving without a degree, Johnson returned to Lichfield for another two years, doing just what, no one knows—probably reading further in the bookshop and quarreling with the rest of his uncongenial family. Michael died in 1731, and presumably Samuel was told that he no longer need expect to be supported by the small income from the shop. He held one miserable teaching job for a few months and applied unsuccessfully for others where he was rejected because it was thought his strange appearance would cause him to be laughed at by the pupils. He went to live with a former schoolfellow in Birmingham, where he found occasional employment on the local newspaper, and published a set of proposals (1734, nonextant) for an edition of the poetry of the Italian Renaissance writer Politian, with a life of Politian, and a history of Renaissance Latin poetry from Petrarch to Politian. Nothing came of this, but a windfall of sorts was a commission to translate from the French *A Voyage to Abyssinia* by the Portuguese Jesuit Jerónimo Lobo, with additional essays on the geography and customs of the country by Joachim Le Grand.

Published in 1735, this first book of Johnson's is of considerable interest. In the early seventeenth century, Portugal, in order to make its trade routes to India more secure, sponsored a Jesuit missionary expedition to Ethiopia, in the hope of converting its rulers from their ancient and, as the Jesuits thought, corrupt form of Christianity to Roman Catholicism and hence to bring the country more firmly under Portuguese influence. Lobo and Le Grand give a vivid account of this nearly unknown part of the world, supposedly the land of Prester John and the mysterious source of the Nile. Johnson's preface dwells on two themes that were to recur in his later work: he compliments Lobo on the honesty with which he, unlike other travel writers, has "described things as he saw them . . . copied nature from the life . . . consulted his senses, not his imagination," and he condemns the Portuguese and the Jesuits for trying to impose by force European domination on indigenous peoples, and justifying that force in the name of Christianity. The book had stirred up a heated controversy in Europe: Protestants maintained that the Ethiopian church was as legitimate a branch of Christianity as Roman Catholicism, perhaps even a purer one. Johnson makes it clear that he is on the Protestant side. His work is "by no means a translation, but an epitome": he does much skillful condensation and adaptation, often toning down the Catholic expressions in the text. His version runs to four hundred pages; for it young Johnson received five guineas (around two hundred dollars in present United States currency).

While living in Birmingham, Johnson met the merchant Henry Porter and his wife Elizabeth, née Jervis. Harry Porter died in September 1734, and on 9 July 1735 Johnson married his widow. Many eyebrows have been raised at this marriage between a penniless youth of twenty-five and a widow of forty-five with three fatherless children (after the wedding the children went to live with other relatives). But Johnson always praised her intellect and her beauty, and she was evidently intelligent enough to recognize the quality of Johnson's mind; at her death eighteen years later, he was devastated. She brought with her some six hundred pounds from her marriage settlement, and with it Johnson opened a boarding school at Edial, close to Lichfield. It attracted only a few pupils, one of them being David Garrick. It soon closed, and Johnson, hav-

ing tried in vain to earn a living in the Midlands by the use of his pen and his brains, decided to try his fate in the larger arena of London.

On 2 March 1737, Johnson, accompanied by young Garrick, set out to cover the hundred miles or so to London. They could afford only one horse and used the old method of "riding and tying." For the next twenty-five years Johnson was to earn a precarious living in London with his pen. Earlier he had written to Edward Cave, the enterprising publisher who had founded the first periodical to use the title "Magazine," the monthly *Gentleman's Magazine*. The word means simply a storehouse, and at first Cave's periodical consisted mostly of reprinted pieces from other London journals. It was to continue publication from 1731 to 1907, an astonishingly long life. Johnson suggested that there were numerous improvements that could be made to it if he were to contribute. Cave did not reply to this cheeky letter, but, after Johnson approached him in London, he began to use Johnson's services as a writer and used them more and more as time went on; there are times when Johnson seems to have been virtually in editorial control of the journal.

Johnson's long involvement with journalism is the most undeservedly neglected part of his career. He was one of its pioneers; after he joined Cave's staff, the *Gentleman's* was transformed into the prototype of the modern intellectual magazine, providing for the educated but not specialist reader a broad and thoughtful overview of events of current intellectual interest, reviewing important new books and printing original articles on the political scene, new literature, advances in science, religious controversy, and much else. Johnson contributed to its regular feature "Foreign History," reporting news from European capitals, battles in the War of the Austrian Succession, a massacre in Java, a coup d'état in Persia. He initiated a "Foreign Books" feature, reporting literary events in Europe. He did some "investigative reporting," uncovering the literary frauds of William Lauder, as he was later to do with "the Cock Lane ghost" affair and James Macpherson's "Ossian" imposture. In time he came to be regarded as the pundit of journalism, and was called on to write the opening manifestos for many new periodicals, in which he had wise things to say about the journalist's responsibility for the education of the thinking public, the need for truth in news reporting, the importance of timely correction or retraction of reports that have proved erroneous, and the dangers from fraudulent advertising.

The 1738 numbers of the *Gentleman's* carried, as well as some short pieces of verse by Johnson, his "Life of Sarpi." Paolo Sarpi's great *History of the Council of Trent* (1619), a classic of historiography, recounts, from an antipapal point of view, the events of this famous "ecumenical" council of the Roman Catholic church which, from 1545 to 1563, attempted to meet the growing challenge of Protestantism by tightening discipline and doctrine in the church. Sarpi was one of many Catholics who opposed the increase in centralized control. His much admired history had been translated into French, and Cave published a prospectus for a translation of this work into English by Johnson, who in fact completed a sizable portion of it. But a competing translation was announced, and Cave's project was abandoned. Johnson's succinct "Life" is presumably an attempt to salvage something from the project. Johnson's involvement with the *History of the Council of Trent* contradicts two legends about him, that he despised history and that his intellectual interests were the narrow ones of a "Little Englander," an archetypal John Bull. On the contrary, as his early dealings with Petrarch and Politian indicate, he was deeply interested in what happened in the rest of the world, and throughout his life was concerned to encourage his fellow countrymen to expand their intellectual horizons beyond the English Channel.

But the outstanding publishing event in the *Gentleman's Magazine* after Johnson arrived there in 1738 was the inauguration of a feature that was to continue for seven years and was greatly to increase its circulation and establish its lasting prosperity and authority. This was no less than the project of publishing reports of the debates in the British Parliament. Their publication had long been forbidden, politicians then as later being reluctant to have their doings scrutinized too closely, and in the spring of 1738 the House of Commons passed a resolution threatening offenders with "the utmost severity" if they attempted to do so. This was a blow to Cave. The prime minister, Sir Robert Walpole, had held office for sixteen years, and was now beleaguered by opponents intent on ousting him. For four more years the attacks on him in Parliament reached a pitch of violence seldom equaled in that always outspoken assembly, until Walpole was finally overthrown. The general public was keenly interested in the contest, and any periodi-

cal able to report the debates would see a great increase in its sales. Cave and his staff—some said primarily young Johnson—thought of a way around the ban. An article appeared in which the grandson of Lemuel Gulliver described a voyage he had recently made to the land of Lilliput, once visited by his famous grandfather. He discovered that the Lilliputian Parliament was debating issues very similar to those in London, and that opposition members such as the Urgol Ptit were hurling blistering attacks against Sir Retrob Walelop. He had brought back a shipload of reports of the debates of the Senate of Lilliput, which the *Gentleman's Magazine* thought might interest its readers during the unfortunate absence of reports of the debates in their own Parliament.

Throughout his life, Johnson was no friend to the preservation of official secrets. "The time is now come," he was later to write, "in which every Englishman expects to be informed of the national affairs, and in which he has a right to have that expectation gratified." For instance, one burning issue of the time was the charge that Walpole was weakly allowing Spain to maintain its embargo against English maritime trade with its South American possessions, a conflict which was presently to erupt in the so-called War of Jenkins's Ear. This gives the writer of the introduction to the Lilliputian debates the opportunity to reflect on the history of European exploitation of the New World: the Europeans "have made conquests and settled colonies in very distant regions, the inhabitants of which they look upon as barbarous, though in simplicity of manners, probity, and temperance superior to themselves; and seem to think they have a right to treat them as passion, interest, or caprice shall direct, without much regard to the rule of justice or humanity; they have carried this imaginary sovereignty so far that they have sometimes proceeded to rapine, bloodshed, and desolation."

The British record in North America is not spared: "When any of their people have forfeited the rights of society, by robberies, seditions, or other crimes," they are transported to America, "undoubtedly very much to the propagation of knowledge and virtue." These indictments Johnson was to repeat many times in his later writings. He concludes his account with a hair-raising description of how the Lilliputians, enraged by the corruptions of government in the time of Lemuel senior, "set fire to the palace" of the emperor, "and buried the whole royal family in its ruins," together with the evil ministers who had

St. John's Gate, London, where the office of the Gentleman's Magazine *was located*

fled there for protection. This was fifty years before the storming of the Bastille, and it is noteworthy that the implied threat is not only against Walpole and his associates but against the king he served, George II.

The Lilliputian debates occupied much of the *Gentleman's* space from 1738 to 1745 (Walpole was forced to resign in 1742, but an unsuccessful attempt to impeach him continued beyond that time). All the debates that appeared between July 1741 and March 1744, totaling around half a million words, are usually attributed to Johnson. Earlier and later debates are said to have been composed by others, perhaps with assistance or revision by Johnson, but there is no way of determining this. It used to be thought that they were entirely fictional compositions, but recent study shows, by comparing them with other extant reports, that their substance corresponds fairly well to what the speakers are supposed actually to have said, though the prose has undoubtedly been polished, as printed reports of parliamentary or congressional speeches still are. The quasi-official *Parliamentary History*, the predecessor of the official record, "Hansard," reprints them, and they are still sometimes quoted by historians unaware of Johnson's share in them as examples of the rhetorical ability of their supposed speakers. Johnson is once supposed to have said, "I took care not to let the Whig dogs have the best of it," but most of those who ranted against Wal-

pole were also Whigs. In fact, a careful reading of the debates will show that the honors for effectiveness are fairly equally divided between Walpole's supporters and his enemies, and on one occasion, the great debate in the House of Commons on 13 February 1741, on a motion calling for the removal of Walpole from office, Walpole is given a masterly final speech in reply. Other topics than the conduct of the Walpole administration are the subjects of extended debate: the state of the armed forces, foreign affairs, trade, the control of the sale of spirits, "urban renewal" (a bill for paving the streets of Westminster). Three or more years of reporting detailed discussion of such matters were a splendid apprenticeship for the general commentator on human affairs that Johnson was to become.

During these early years, Johnson published a good deal elsewhere than in the columns of the *Gentleman's*, publications with which Cave was also connected. In May 1738 a nineteen-page booklet appeared, containing a poem of 263 lines in heroic couplets (and one triplet) entitled *London*. It caused a mild stir and reached a second edition within a week. Pope, whose long poem *One Thousand Seven Hundred and Thirty Eight*, likewise a denunciation of life at that time and in that place, was published the same day, gave high praise to his unknown rival's work. *London* is subtitled *A Poem, in Imitation of the Third Satire of Juvenal*, which was a diatribe against life in contemporary Rome. It is important to understand that an "imitation" is not a translation or even paraphrase of an original work, but rather what might be called a set of variations on a theme. Juvenal satirizes aspects of life in Rome which displease him, Johnson does the same with life in London; for instance, Juvenal condemns the baneful influence of Greek immigrants, Johnson of French. Both cities suffer from things that still plague metropolises—street hoodlums, jerry-built structures, corrupt politicians:

> Their ambush here relentless ruffians lay,
> And here the fell attorney prowls for prey;
> Here falling houses thunder on your head,
> And here a female atheist talks you dead.

There is enough humor in lines such as these to make one wonder just how serious much of the poem is in its denunciations. But the key line in the poem, which Johnson puts in capital letters, is serious enough: "SLOW RISES WORTH BY POVERTY DEPRESSED." The speaker in the poem is one Thales, whose talents and integrity the city has not recognized, and who is about to abandon it for the peaceful and virtuous life of the country. This has raised difficulties for those who recall Johnson's supposed saying that the man who is tired of London is tired of life. But that saying did not come until much later in Johnson's life—if he said it at all, and there is considerable doubt that he did—when he no longer suffered from poverty and obscurity. In 1738, like many another young man fresh from the provinces, he could well have been dismayed by the hectic confusion of the capital. Indeed, in the following year he returned to Lichfield for some months and once again tried to find a teaching position—and was once again turned down: worth rose no faster in the country than in the city. Then it was back to London's Grub Street once more, this time permanently.

London is heavily laced with the standard opposition propaganda of the time. The woes and the degeneracy of life in the capital are all due to the nefarious regime of Walpole and his minions; even his nominal master, King George, is lambasted for his frequent trips to visit his mistress in Hannover. The next year saw two long and violent prose pamphlets on the same theme—pseudonymously signed, of course, though even so, it was said that Johnson had to go into hiding for a time to avoid arrest. *Marmor Norfolciense* (The Norfolk Stone) relates the discovery in

Walpole's home county of an ancient boulder carved with a mysterious prophetic inscription, which a bumbling pedant, a Walpolian hanger-on, has great difficulty in explicating, though the reader has no trouble in seeing it as a rousing tirade against the many sins of the administration. Its satire is perhaps too heavily laid on for it to be very effective: Johnson seems to be trying to do what Swift had done in *The Windsor Prophecy* (1711), but he lacks Swift's control. In *A Compleat Vindication of the Licensers of the Stage*, the satire is more skillfully handled. What is being "vindicated" is the action of the lord chamberlain's censors, appointed under the recently passed Stage Licensing Act, in refusing permission for a public performance of Henry Brooke's play *Gustavus Vasa*. It was a transparent piece of opposition propaganda, in which a noble "patriot" leads a revolt that liberates his country from the tyranny of a usurping king and his despicable prime minister. The act, the provisions of which remained in force until, incredibly, 1968, provided that no play could be publicly performed in London without the prior approval of the script by the lord chamberlain; it was of course designed to protect the administration from such criticism as Brooke's. Johnson's biting satire takes the form of a defense of the licensers by a stupid authoritarian government official, who goes on to propose that books too should be subjected to similar censorship, and, even better, that elementary schools should be abolished so that no one will be taught to read and so run the danger of being exposed to antigovernment views: "The nation will rest at length in ignorance and peace." It is as brilliant a piece of condemnation as has ever been written of the obscurantism fostered by dictatorial governments, a kind of prelude to George Orwell's *1984* (1949). Johnson's political thinking had, in fact, a good deal in common with Orwell's.

Another publication of Johnson's in 1739, which until recently has been little studied, is his annotated translation, from the French, of Jean-Pierre Crousaz's *Commentary* on Pope's recently published *Essay on Man* (1733-1734). Crousaz, a Swiss clergyman and critic of some prominence, was much disturbed by Pope's poem, which seemed to him—as indeed it did to others—to deny Christian moral teaching and instead to advocate a form of deism. In the three-hundred-page work, Johnson stalwartly defends Pope's poem (with the exception of his theory of a "ruling passion"), and has no trouble showing that Crousaz, who, as he points out, knew no English, was misled by the many errors in the French translation that he used. Johnson makes his points by careful scrutiny of short passages of the poem and Crousaz's interpretation of them—the kind of "close reading" which was to be characteristic of Johnson's later literary criticism. As with Lobo and Sarpi, Johnson again demonstrates his concern with cultural events elsewhere than in Britain.

The *Gentleman's Magazine* between 1739 and 1744 contains much else by Johnson besides what has already been mentioned. Indeed there may be still more to be found; most journalism at that time was unsigned. Many of these pieces are short biographies, for the most part derived from earlier sources but enhanced by vivid and lucid prose and including frequent interpolations of pungent comment by Johnson. The lives of Sir Francis Drake, who in the reign of Elizabeth I circumnavigated the world and terrorized the Spanish fleet, and Robert Blake, Oliver Cromwell's admiral who defeated the Dutch, were no doubt inspired by the opposition line of castigating Walpole for Britain's failures in naval actions against the Spanish. The life of Hermann Boerhaave praises the great Dutch medical scientist's championship of scientific empiricism against dogmatic theorizing, and his adherence to simple and pious Christianity. The sketches of the Dutch scholar Pieter Burman and the scholarly prodigy Jean-Philippe Barretier are, like the Boerhaave life, extended obituaries—all three had only recently died. The life of Thomas Sydenham, a famous medical innovator of the seventeenth century, and a translation of a eulogy of the French botanist Louis Morin by Bernard Le Bovier de Fontenelle, secretary of the French Académie des Sciences, further demonstrate Johnson's interest in the sciences, as his translation of a long excerpt from the Frenchman J.-B. Du Halde's account of China indicates his interest in distant lands and cultures. A penetrating review of the memoirs of Sarah, Duchess of Marlborough, widow of the great duke and herself the close confidante and adviser—some said dominator—of Queen Anne, passes incisive judgments on the still controversial political events of the reigns of the last Stuarts and considers the problems of the historian: "Distrust is a necessary qualification of a student in history. Distrust quickens his discernment of different degrees of probability, animates his search after evidence, and perhaps heightens his pleasure at the discovery

of truth; for truth, though not always obvious, is generally discoverable."

In the later years of his connection with the *Gentleman's*, Johnson was also involved in the immense task of preparing a multivolumed catalogue of the great library of the Harleys, Earls of Oxford, an experience which gave him intimate familiarity with a huge number of pamphlets emanating from the political and religious controversies of sixteenth- and seventeenth-century England, some of which he annotated in the *Harleian Miscellany* (1744-1746), an eight-volume collection of reprints of some of them, and insight into the scholarly techniques needed to make proper use of them. His introduction to this miscellany is a splendid essay, "On the Origin and Importance of Small Tracts and Fugitive Pieces," which contains a rousing paragraph in praise of them as a manifestation of a free press in a free country:

> The form of our government, which gives every man that has leisure, or curiosity, or vanity the right of inquiring into the propriety of public measures, and, by consequence, obliges those who are entrusted with the administration of national affairs to give an account of their conduct to almost every man who demands it, may be reasonably supposed to have occasioned innumerable pamphlets which would never have appeared under arbitrary governments, where every man lulls himself in indolence under calamities of which he cannot promote the redress, or thinks it prudent to conceal the uneasiness of which he cannot complain without danger.

These early writings of Johnson have sometimes been disparaged as "hackwork." They were written to earn a living, to be sure, as a great deal of his later work was. But they are indispensable in showing us the foundations of the intellectual concerns and attitudes that persisted throughout his life, and the reader cannot neglect them without putting himself in danger of too shallow an understanding of Johnson's later writings.

Around 1744 Johnson's connection with the *Gentleman's Magazine* began to be more tenuous, but he and Cave collaborated on other projects. One of them was Johnson's most substantial piece of biography. In 1743 the writer who called himself Richard Savage died in a debtor's prison in Bristol. For many years he had made himself notorious in London by his ability to ingratiate himself with one patron after another, then to al-

A N

A C C O U N T

O F   T H E

L I F E

O F

Mr *Richard Savage,*

Son of the Earl R I V E R S.

LONDON:

Printed for J. ROBERTS in *Warwick-Lane.*
M.DCC.XLIV.

Title page for Johnson's biography of the poet who claimed to be the illegitimate son of Anne, Countess of Macclesfield, and Richard Savage, Earl Rivers

ienate him by extravagant antics, and to publish satiric denunciations and complaints of the way so talented an individual as himself was ill-used by society—the paradigm of an "injustice collector" as one psychiatric critic calls him. At some time or other Johnson had known him and, like others, been attracted by his charismatic personality: Johnson related how, having not even the few pence needed for a bed in the meanest flophouse, they roamed the London streets together at night, inveighing against the crimes of the Walpole government, "reforming the world, dethroning princes, establishing new forms of government, and giving laws to the several states of Europe." Savage was thought to have provided the model for Thales in *London,* who, like Savage, went into exile in Wales.

On Savage's death Cave and Johnson saw that a biography of this well-known figure could be popular. Moreover, his strange career and personality offered Johnson a compelling challenge. Savage made much of the story he told very plausibly of his origin. According to him, he was the son of Anne, Countess of Macclesfield, by an adulterous affair with Richard Savage, Earl Rivers, and she freely proclaimed this to facilitate her divorce by her husband. After the divorce, Lady Macclesfield displayed the greatest hostility toward the child, would have nothing to do with him, and arranged to have him brought up in ignorance of his identity and in the humblest circumstances, even trying to have him shipped off to America. He went on to tell a pathetic story of how, after he learned his true identity, he used to haunt the street before her house hoping for a glimpse of her, and once, when the door was left open, ventured to enter and present himself to her, hoping for some token of affection. Instead, she screamed and ordered the servants to eject this intruder who had planned to murder her. Later, after Savage had been convicted of killing a man in a tavern brawl—he maintained that it was in self-defense—and sentenced to death, she intervened with the queen to try to prevent his being pardoned, though she was unsuccessful in doing so.

All this Lady Macclesfield denied, and indeed there is not a scrap of evidence of its truth other than Savage's assertions. History is full of impostors who have maintained that they were the long-lost and ill-used children of some celebrity. Johnson took this story from an earlier anonymous biography of Savage, the details of which were probably supplied by Savage himself, embellished them and obviously relished them: his dramatic prose makes his book a classic tearjerker. It has been suggested that his doing so throws some light on his suppressed feelings toward his own mother. Throughout the rest of the book, Johnson relates Savage's later ups and inevitable downs. He is fully aware of Savage's self-destructive and self-pitying nature. His account of Savage's furious indignation when some friends took up a collection to buy him a much needed suit of clothes and prudently gave the money to the tailor instead of to Savage himself, is reminiscent of an incident when Johnson was an undergraduate at Oxford, and his friends, noticing that his shoes were so dilapidated that he could not attend lectures, quietly placed a new pair before his door. As they stole away, the door

Gough Square, London, where Johnson lived during the years he worked on his Dictionary *(ceiling painting by Felix Kelly, in the Donald Hyde Rooms at the Houghton Library, Harvard University)*

opened and the shoes were hurled after them.

The *Life of Mr. Richard Savage* (1744) is an astonishing work, perhaps the first "psychobiography" ever written. It alternates between passages of sympathetic description of Savage's woes, and analyses of the causes of them—Savage's irresponsibility and high opinion of his own importance, which Johnson clearly discerns and condemns. Yet it ends with this memorable apologia (though a paragraph was added, perhaps at Cave's insistence, emphasizing Savage's "want of prudence . . . negligence, and irregularity"): "Those are no proper judges of his conduct who have slumbered away their time on the down of plenty, nor will a wise man easily presume to say, 'Had I been in Savage's condition, I should have lived, or written, better than Savage.'" Perhaps this is also an apologia for the rebellious violence of some of young Johnson's early writings against "the establishment," and perhaps the writing of his friend's life had some kind of cathartic effect on his own bitterness about the world's neglect of his talents. At any rate he was later to retract his

earlier denunciations of Walpole as the source of all the evil in his world: "He was a fine fellow. . . . He honoured his memory for having kept his country in peace many years, as also for his goodness and placability of his temper."

"Ambition is a noble passion," when properly directed, Johnson once declared, and wrote of Pope, "Self-confidence is the first requisite to great undertakings." Johnson was now in his mid thirties, and it became evident that he was intent on greater undertakings than those he had so far tried his hand on. The greatest challenge to an eighteenth-century man of letters was to edit Shakespeare, as Pope himself had done, with less than notable success. In 1745 Cave published a sheet of "Proposals for Printing"—by subscription—"a New Edition of the Plays of William Shakespeare," in ten volumes. The editor was to be "the Author of the Miscellaneous Observations on the Tragedy of Macbeth," a sixty-four-page pamphlet to which the proposals were appended. These "notes critical and explanatory" on *Macbeth* were intended as a sample of what might be expected in the edition, and were praised by William Warburton, who in his own edition of Shakespeare in 1747, said they were written by "a man of parts and genius"—a compliment for which the unknown Johnson was grateful, and which caused him to mitigate some of the very harsh criticism he bestowed on Warburton's edition when his own at last came out, twenty years later.

The 1745 proposals proved abortive; the rival bookseller Jacob Tonson declared that he was the sole proprietor of the copyright of Shakespeare's works, and threatened Cave with a lawsuit. The intervention turned out to be a blessing in disguise, for it deflected Johnson into another "great undertaking," which was to prove essential for the success of his own eventual edition. This was the first scholarly historical dictionary of the English language. The idea of preparing scholarly dictionaries of the new vernacular tongues that had replaced the Latin of the Roman Empire and the older Germanic tongues of its barbarian conquerors arose in the Renaissance. In Italy one of the recently founded scholarly academies, the Accademia della Crusca, had in 1612 published its *Vocabolario* of the new tongue of that country. In 1694 there appeared the *Dictionnaire* of the Académie Française, founded in emulation of the Italian academies.

These were not, like the ordinary "desk dictionary," intended merely for the casual user to check spelling and look up the meaning of "hard words," but were minutely detailed historical records of how the words in their language had hitherto been used, like the successor to Johnson's dictionary, the great *Oxford English Dictionary*. The function of his, Johnson wrote, was to facilitate "exactness of criticism and elegance of style." Johnson was also keenly aware that Britain in the eighteenth century was in the process of becoming a world power instead of the insignificant little island on the fringes of Europe that it had been, and that English would eventually become a world language. In his *Plan of a Dictionary* (1747) he expressed his hope that it would "fix" the language. But after he had completed his work on it, he confessed in its preface that this goal had been impossible—that language would inevitably suffer a process of change, and that his duty was not to "form, but register the language," not to "teach men how they should think, but relate how they have hitherto expressed their thoughts." At the same time the existence of such a record would inevitably result in

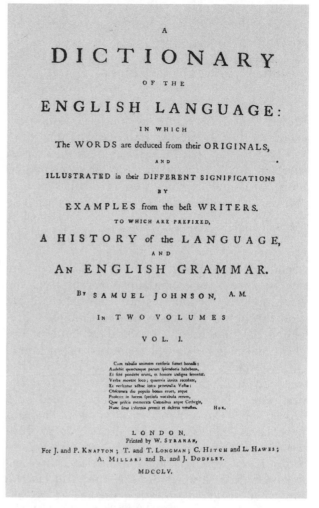

A

DICTIONARY

OF THE

ENGLISH LANGUAGE:

IN WHICH

The WORDS are deduced from their ORIGINALS,

AND

ILLUSTRATED in their DIFFERENT SIGNIFICATIONS

BY

EXAMPLES from the beſt WRITERS.

TO WHICH ARE PREFIXED,

A HISTORY of the LANGUAGE,

AND

AN ENGLISH GRAMMAR.

BY SAMUEL JOHNSON, A. M.

IN TWO VOLUMES

VOL. I.

Cum tabulis animum cenſoris ſumet honeſti :
Audebit quæcunque parum ſplendoris habebunt,
Et ſine pondere erunt, et honore indigna ferentur,
Verba movere loco; quamvis invita recedant,
Et verſentur adhuc intra penetralia Veſtæ:
Obſcurata diu populo bonus eruet, atque
Proferet in lucem ſpecioſa vocabula rerum,
Quæ priſcis memorata Catonibus atque Cethegis,
Nunc ſitus informis premit et deſerta vetuſtas.   HOR.

LONDON.
Printed by W. STRAHAN,
For J. and P. KNAPTON; T. and T. LONGMAN; C. HITCH and L. HAWES;
A. MILLAR; and R. and J. DODSLEY.
MDCCLV.

Title page for the first scholarly historical dictionary of the English language

a degree of stability, desirable in a language which was to become the means of communication among peoples in many parts of the world. The existence of Johnson's *Dictionary* and its successors did undoubtedly slow the rate of change of the language.

"Such as Chaucer is, shall Dryden be," Pope had lamented. Three hundred years after Chaucer wrote, his English was almost unintelligible except to the specially trained student; Dryden's, after the same period of three hundred years, remains perfectly lucid, virtually indistinguishable from that written in the twentieth century. It is presumably advantageous to be able to read Dryden as easily as a modern newspaper editorial, and for this we have Johnson and later lexicographers to thank.

Johnson acknowledged the great Italian and French dictionaries as his inspiration. They were produced over many years by teams of learned scholars, that of France being sponsored by the government itself. Johnson's was the result of private enterprise—that of a consortium of London publishers, with whom Johnson contracted in 1746 to produce it in three years, though in fact it took nine. The publishers agreed to pay him fifteen hundred guineas—modern equivalent around fifty thousand dollars. Out of this Johnson had to pay for the services of six assistants, who sat at tables in the attic of Johnson's rented house in Gough Square, London—still shown to visitors—taking dictation or assembling slips. The account given in James Boswell's *Life of Johnson* of how it was compiled is completely mistaken and was corrected not long afterward by Johnson's friend Thomas Percy. Johnson went about the task in a way not essentially different from the way modern dictionaries are constructed. He read through the books which he thought represented the best writing in standard modern English, marking words which seemed to exemplify various shades of meaning. The books so marked were given to the amanuenses, who noted the first letter of the marked word and copied on a slip of paper the sentence containing it. The slips were later assembled under the words so illustrated, and eventually arranged in alphabetical order (later lexicographers would use three-by-five-inch cards instead of slips, and still later, a computer program would do the recording and sorting). When this work had been done, Johnson would study the slips for a certain word, sort them out according to the different significations they seemed to convey in various contexts, formulate a definition to suit each of them, select quotations that supported that definition, arrange the definitions, along with the protocol quotations for each in an order that usually runs, roughly, from the more concrete to the more abstract or figurative, and send the result to the printer.

When the work was at last complete in 1755, it was at once recognized as England's greatest contribution to lexicography. Presentation copies were sent to the Italian and French academies and received with high compliment: "It was a very noble work, would be a perpetual monument of fame to the author, an honor to his own country in particular, and a general benefit to the republic of letters," said the president of the Accademia della Crusca. They sent presentation copies of their own dictionaries to Johnson in return. The two heavy folio volumes, priced at four pounds, ten shillings—around $150, about

what a publication of that size would cost today—contained some 40,000 word entries, with a total of around 115,000 supporting quotations; it was estimated that these were chosen from a total of twice that number collected for the purpose. The subtle discriminations between shades of meaning are impressive—the verb *to fall* is given 69 different significations, *to set* 88, *to take* 134; the *Oxford English Dictionary* has more, but it drew from a further century and a half of widespread use of English. Johnson, in his splendid preface, had named Francis Bacon, Richard Hooker, John Milton, and Robert Boyle, representing respectively philosophy, theology, poetry, and science, as models of the sources from which he had worked, but more mundane sources were also heavily drawn on, manuals of gardening, husbandry, military terminology, and other practical matters.

There was to be criticism of various definitions, some of it misplaced. The fact that *oats* were consumed by humans as well as by horses in Scotland had been noted by earlier commentators as an unusual phenomenon worth recording; the definition of *excise*—"a hateful tax levied upon commodities . . . "—a subject of much political controversy at the time, is no more hostile than the remarks on the subject in Sir William Blackstone's *Commentaries* (1765-1769), the great legal textbook of the century; the entry for *Whig*, which has been faulted for its tendentiously brief definition ("the name of a faction") contains a long and sympathetic description of Whig principles by Bishop Gilbert Burnet, a leading Whig. To be sure, Johnson very occasionally indulged his prejudices and his wit, as in the entry for *irony*, "A mode of speech in which the meaning is contrary to the words, as, *Bolingbroke* was a holy man"—the libertine Henry St. John, Viscount Bolingbroke, was one of Johnson's pet hates. The dictionary did not exclude down-to-earth words: *piss*, "To make water"—not even stigmatized as "low" as Johnson did some less than elegant words—is wittily illustrated by a quotation from Sir Roger L'Estrange, "One ass pisses, the rest piss for company," an observation which Johnson as well as its author no doubt thought had some relevance to human as well as quadruped behavior. Four editions of the complete work were published in Johnson's lifetime, the last, in 1773, being extensively revised by Johnson himself. There were numerous later editions and abridgments; it was superseded as the standard authority on English vocabulary only by the *Oxford*

English Dictionary, published between 1884 and 1928.

It might be thought that Johnson's work on this vast project, extending over nearly a decade, would have consumed all his available time and energy. But the fifteen hundred guineas advanced by his publishers by no means covered all his expenses, and had to be supplemented. Philip Dormer Stanhope, Earl of Chesterfield, the *grand seigneur* of the intellectual world at the time, had allowed Johnson to dedicate the *Plan of a Dictionary* to him in 1747; he gave Johnson ten pounds and then ignored him. When at last the work was ready for publication in 1755, Chesterfield hastened to get on the bandwagon by publishing two condescending essays praising it. He received a letter from Johnson that contained the most famous snub in the history of literature; Thomas Carlyle called it "the death-knell of patronage."

Meanwhile David Garrick, Johnson's pupil and companion on the road to London, had quickly made a name for himself in the theater, and was soon to become the most celebrated English actor of the century—perhaps of any century. In 1747 he was appointed manager of the Theatre Royal, Drury Lane, and called on his old teacher to write a prologue to be recited at its opening, one of Johnson's finest short poems, briefly surveying the history of English drama and calling on it to use its capacity for "useful mirth and salutary woe" in the service of truth and virtue. When Johnson and Garrick had traveled to London ten years before, Johnson brought with him a draft of a piece he had been working on in the Midlands, a tragedy in blank verse called *Irene* (three syllables—"I-rē-nē"). The then standard way for an ambitious young writer to make a name for himself was to have a successful play performed on the London stage. Johnson's tragedy at first received no encouragement from producers, but at last, in 1749, Garrick put it on at Drury Lane, doing all he could to make it succeed, with a galaxy of leading actors in the cast, and himself playing the principal male role. It ran for nine nights, a moderate success at the time, and brought Johnson three hundred pounds (around twelve thousand dollars).

The play was not, however, revived and has received some harsh criticism, not all of it deserved. The plot, which is based on a historical incident, deals with the classic conflict between duty and inclination; it more closely resembles works such as Pierre Corneille's *Cid* (1637) and Jean Racine's *Bérénice* (1670) than it does most English attempts at tragic drama. The story had been used by earlier dramatists. Irene, a beautiful young Greek, captured at the fall of Constantinople to the Turks in 1453, is passionately loved by the victorious Sultan Mohammed. He wishes to make her his sultana, but she must renounce her Christianity and become a convert to Islam. She is strongly tempted by the grandeur of the position and the power it will give her to do good to the vanquished Greeks. Her friend Aspasia, another Greek maiden, pleads with her not to abandon her religion. In the end, after much inward struggle, she succumbs and agrees to the marriage. But she is unwittingly caught up in an intrigue involving disaffected Turkish officers and Greek captives planning to overthrow Mohammed, and is accused of taking part in a plot to assassinate him. This is a lie, but Mohammed believes it and orders her to be put to death. Too late a messenger comes with proof that Irene has been loyal and indeed tried to prevent the attempt to murder Mohammed. It is conceivable that, with brilliant acting and direction, *Irene* might still succeed on the stage. It is handicapped, however, by the somewhat monotonous rhythm of the blank verse traditionally used for English verse tragedy; Johnson would have been more at home writing in heroic couplets, which he always preferred. The stories of Johnson's later mourning, "I thought it had been better" and saying, when a Mr. Pot was reported as having praised it highly, "If Pot says so, Pot lies" are of dubious authenticity.

A month before the first performance of *Irene*, Johnson published his greatest poem, *The Vanity of Human Wishes. The Tenth Satire of Juvenal, Imitated*. Of it and *London*, T. S. Eliot was to write, "Both of them seem to me to be among the greatest verse satires of the English or any other language," and "If lines 189-220 of *The Vanity of Human Wishes*"—the passage on Charles XII of Sweden—"are not poetry, I do not know what is." As used in connection with the Roman poets Juvenal, Persius, and Horace, who inaugurated the genre, "verse satire" was an informally organized address in verse, very often to an intimate friend. Horace's were labeled *sermones*, which means not "sermons" but something like a one-sided conversation, on some subject of contemporary interest, for instance, as in *London*, the current problems of life in that city. *Satura* or *satira* means a mixture, a hodgepodge—things that strike the speaker's mind, in no particular order. It is almost identical with "dramatic mono-

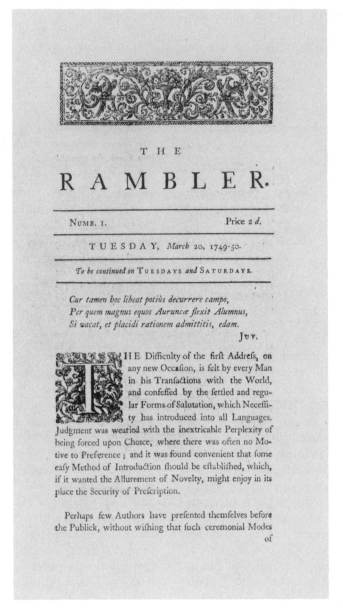

THE

RAMBLER.

NUMB. 1.   Price 2 *d.*

TUESDAY, *March* 20, 1749-50.

To be continued on TUESDAYS *and* SATURDAYS.

Cur tamen hoc libeat potiùs decurrere campo,
Per quem magnus equos Auruncæ flexit Alumnus,
Si vacat, et placidi rationem admittitis, edam.

JUV.

THE Difficulty of the firſt Addreſs, on any new Occaſion, is felt by every Man in his Tranſactions with the World, and confeſſed by the ſettled and regular Forms of Salutation, which Neceſſity has introduced into all Languages. Judgment was wearied with the inextricable Perplexity of being forced upon Choice, where there was often no Motive to Preference ; and it was found convenient that ſome eaſy Method of Introduction ſhould be eſtabliſhed, which, if it wanted the Allurement of Novelty, might enjoy in its place the Security of Preſcription.

Perhaps few Authors have preſented themſelves before the Publick, without wiſhing that ſuch ceremonial Modes of

The first number of Johnson's first series of periodical essays, through which he hoped to give "ardour to virtue and confidence to truth"

logue," popular with Robert Browning and T. S. Eliot ("Prufrock," "Gerontion," much of *The Waste Land*). It gives the impression of being casual and haphazard, but when successful, it will have a careful though inconspicuous dramatic organization.

The speaker in Johnson's poem begins with the exhortation to his listener to "Let Observation, with extensive view, / Survey mankind from China to Peru," and discover how much needless unhappiness is caused the human race by pursuing fallacious objects of desire that are thought to lead to happiness, but do not. The opening couplet does not, as has been asserted, say, "Let observation with extensive observation observe mankind extensively." As the critic George Saintsbury pointed out, observation (here personified) may be intensive or extensive; Johnson specifies the latter. It may observe various things, nature, governments, mankind; Johnson specifies the last. China, in the northeast corner of a map of the world with Britain at its center, was regarded in the eighteenth century as the home of a peaceful and enlightened civilization, superior to that of war-torn Europe. Peru, in the diagonally opposite corner, had been not long before the scene of the massacres and oppression inflicted on the native population by Francisco Pizarro and his Spanish invaders. The two places represent the two contrasting poles of potential human activity, from the best to the worst.

The poem continues with accounts of how the pursuit of merely human values leads in the end not to the expected happiness but to misery; how desire for political power destroyed Thomas Wolsey; George Villiers, first Duke of Buckingham; Thomas Wentworth, Earl of Strafford; and Edward Hyde, Earl of Clarendon; how the reward of ambition for scholarly fame may be "Toil, envy, want, the garret, and the jail"—after Johnson's encounter with Chesterfield, "garret" was changed to "patron"; for military glory, the inglorious end of the young King Charles XII of Sweden and the humiliations of Xerxes of Persia and Charles Albert of Bavaria; how he who yearns for a long life may end it in senile impotence; how the young woman who thinks physical beauty and desirability the be-all and end-all at last finds only contempt and infamy. Or, as it has been more succinctly put, "Be careful of what you wish for when you are young, for you may get it."

Does this gloomy recital mean, as some have thought, that human life is inevitably destined to be miserable? Not at all: the poem asserts not the vanity of human *life* but the vanity of merely human *wishes*; if one wants to avoid self-inflicted misery, adopt another set of values than those of wealth, power, glory, and the rest. Perhaps one should start reading the poem with its final twenty-five lines. If the pursuit of the objects described has resulted only in disillusion and grief, "Where then *shall* hope and fear their objects find?" Is the answer the Stoic and fatalist one, "Hope and fear nothing: refuse to get emotionally involved with anything"? "Must dull Suspense corrupt the stagnant mind? / Must helpless man, in ignorance sedate, / Roll darkling down the torrent of his fate?" "Enquirer, cease," the listener is abruptly told: there *are* things to be hoped and ceaselessly sought for which will not in the end produce such sterile and frustrated lives as those that have been described—not the "human" wishes for power, wealth, beauty, but those derived from a more than human source, the heavenly values of love, patience, faith ("faith, hope, charity"). "With these celestial Wisdom calms the mind," the poem ends, "And *makes* the happiness she does not *find*." This is an optimistic, not a pessimistic, view of life.

The plan of the poem is curiously close to that of *The Waste Land* ("waste" and "vanity" come from the same Latin root, *vanus*, empty). The first four sections of Eliot's poem (1922) give a most depressing picture of life in an emotionally sterile world; the last presents the remedy, "give, sympathize, control," and ends with an evocation of "the peace which passeth understanding." Like Eliot's, Johnson's poem is a difficult one. Garrick said rightly that when Johnson was younger, and "saw a good deal of what was passing in life, he wrote his *London*, which is lively and easy"—so much so that its exuberance gives the impression that, however many faults may be found with the London of the 1730s, life in it was at least exciting. "When he had become more retired"—as he must have done when beginning work on the *Dictionary*—"he gave us his *Vanity of Human Wishes*, which is as hard as Greek." Anyone who wishes to test this assertion might try a close reading of lines 135-156, sorting out the close-packed and bewilderingly varied imagery in the description of the young scholar's "quest."

After 1755 Johnson became widely known as "Dictionary Johnson." But before that time, and indeed after it, he was often referred to as "the Author of *The Rambler*," the great series of essays he published every Tuesday and Saturday from March 1750 to March 1752. The periodical essay is a form almost exclusively to be found in eighteenth-century Britain. It was made immensely popular by *The Tatler* and *The Spectator* of Steele and Addison from 1709 to 1714. It looked like something easy to write, and hundreds of imitations were begun by ambitious young authors during the following decades. But to turn out without interruption six carefully written essays a week, as with *The Spectator*, or twice a week, as with *The Rambler*, or even once a week, as with Johnson's *The Idler*, was a grueling task, and the great majority of them ceased after a few numbers. The genre demands different abilities from the "occasional essay," such as Montaigne, Francis Bacon, and Charles Lamb wrote when some subject took their fancy. Perhaps the closest modern analogy is with the work of the popular syndicated newspaper columnist, who also is required to produce his copy at stated times, and has certain topics and points of view his readers come to expect. The columnist signs his actual name, or sometimes an easily penetrated pseudonym. The author—or authors, for they were sometimes jointly written—of the periodical essay adopted the name of a persona, "Mr. Tatler,"

THE

NUMB. 2.

UNIVERSAL CHRONICLE,

OR

WEEKLY GAZETTE.

To be Published every SATURDAY, Price Two-PENCE HALF-PENNY.

From SATURDAY, APRIL 8, to SATURDAY, APRIL 15, 1758.

The IDLER. No. I.

Vacui sub umbra

Lusimus. HOR.

THOSE who attempt periodical Essays seem to be often stopped in the beginning, by the difficulty of finding a proper Title for their Work. Two Writers since the time of the Spectator, have assumed his Name, without any Pretensions to lawful Inheritance; an Effort was once made to revive the Tatler; and the strange appellations, by which Papers have been called, sufficiently show that the Authors were distressed, like the Natives of America, who sometimes come to the Europeans to beg a Name.

It will be easily believed of the *Idler*, that if his Title had required any search, he never would have found it. Every mode of life has its conveniencies. The *Idler*, who habituates himself to be satisfied with what he can most easily obtain, not only escapes labours which are often fruitless, but sometimes succeeds better than those who despise whatever is within their reach, and think every thing more valuable as it is harder to be acquired.

If similitude of manners be a motive to kindness, the *Idler* may flatter himself with universal Patronage. There is no single character under which such numbers are comprised. Every man is, or hopes to be, an *Idler*. Even those who seem to differ most from us are hastening to encrease our Fraternity; as Peace is the end of war, to be idle is the ultimate purpose of the Busy.

There is perhaps no Appellation by which a Writer can better denote his Kindred to the human Species. It has been found hard to describe Man by an adequate Definition. Some Philosophers have called him a reasonable Animal, but others have considered Reason as a Quality of which many Animals partake. He has been termed likewise a laughing Animal; but it is said that some Men have never laughed. Perhaps Man may be more properly distinguished as an Idle Animal; for there is no Man who is not sometimes Idle. It is at least a Definition from which none that shall find it in this Paper can be excepted; for who can be more idle than the Reader of the *Idler*?

That the Definition may be complete, Idleness must be not only the general, but the peculiar characteristic of Man; and perhaps

he is the only Being that can properly be called Idle, that does by others what he might do himself, or sacrifices Duty or Pleasure to the Love of Ease.

Scarcely any Name can be imagined from which less envy or competition is to be dreaded. The *Idler* has no Rivals or Enemies. The Man of Business forgets him; the Man of Enterprize despises him; and though such as tread the same track of Life, fall commonly into jealousy and discord, *Idlers* are always found to associate in Peace, and he who is most famed for doing Nothing, is glad to meet another as Idle as himself.

What is to be expected from this paper, whether it will be uniform or various, learned or familiar, serious or gay, political or moral, continued or interrupted, it is hoped that no Reader will enquire. That the *Idler* has some scheme, cannot be doubted; for to form schemes is the *Idler's* privilege. But tho' he has many projects in his head, he is sparing of communication, having observed, that his hearers are apt to remember what he forgets himself; that his tardiness of execution exposes him to the encroachments of those who catch a hint and fall to work, and that very specious Plans, after long contrivance and pompous displays, have subsided in weariness without a trial, and without miscarriage been blasted by derision.

Something the *Idler's* Character may be supposed to promise. Those that are curious after diminutive History, who watch the Revolutions of Families, and the Rise and Fall of Characters either Male or Female, will hope to be gratified by this Paper; for the *Idler* is always inquisitive and seldom retentive. He that delights in Obloquy and Satire, and wishes to see Clouds gathering over every Reputation that dazzles him with its Brightness, will snatch up the *Idler's* Essays with a beating Heart. The *Idler* is naturally censorious; those who attempt nothing themselves suppose every thing easily performed, and consider the unsuccessful always as criminal.

I think it necessary to give notice, that I make no contract, nor incur any obligation. If those who depend on the *Idler* for intelligence and entertainment, should suffer the disappointment which commonly follows such ill-placed expectations, they are to lay the blame only on themselves.

Yet Hope is not wholly to be cast away. The *Idler*, tho' sluggish, is yet alive, and may sometimes be stimulated to vigour and activity. He may then descend into profoundness, or tower into sublimity; for the diligence of an *Idler* is

rapid and impetuous; as ponderous bodies forced into velocity move with violence proportionate to their weight.

But these violent exertions of intellect cannot be very frequent, and he will therefore gladly receive help from any Correspondent, who shall enable him to please without his own labour. He excludes no style, he prohibits no subject; only let him that writes to the *Idler* remember, that his letters must not be long; no words ought to be squandered in declarations of esteem, or confessions of inability; conscious dulness has little right to be prolix, and praise is not so welcome to the *Idler* as quiet.

✷✷✷✷✷✷✷✷✷✷✷✷✷✷✷✷✷✷

Monday, APRIL 10.

Landshut, March 22.

THE King of Prussia, who arrived here the 17th, set out the 19th for Crossau, where the head quarters of his army will be established tomorrow. 30,000 Prussians are actually encamped between Breslau and the frontiers of Poland, in order to observe the motions of the Russians, who are marching towards this province.

Dantzick, March 21. In all probability some bloody scenes will be disclosed on the banks of the Vistula, where both the Russians and Prussians seem as if they designed to assemble considerable forces. The 24th instant a numerous corps of the former advanced as far as Thorn, under the Command of Prince Galliczin. On the other hand, a strong detachment of Marshal Lehwald's army has already made its appearance in the environs of Stolpe, where it seized on several posts, and seems to expect only a few regiments to form a grand enterprize.

Prague, March 29. The head quarters of the army were not moved the 23d, on account of the great quantity of snow that fell the preceding day, which retarded its operations. A body of 10,000 Prussians, commanded by General Fouquet, have driven the troops under General Jahnus out of the county of Glatz; and it is thought their view is to seize our magazine at Leutomyssel. The King of Prussia's motions in Silesia seem to indicate a design to attack our main army, and that he concerns himself very little about the progress of the Russians.

The body of troops under General Nadasti is to assemble in the Upper Silesia.

By letters which came to hand the 26th inst. we learn, that Marshal Count Daun's army has advanced towards Silesia, and that General Laudon is dead of a fever.

Berlin, March 30. We have received advice, that a detachment of five hundred Austrian hussars, being part of a body of troops posted in the Upper Lusatia, came a few days ago to Cottbus, and seized all the money they found there

The first number of Johnson's second essay series, which includes far more political commentary than The Rambler

"Mr. Spectator," "Mr. Rambler," which he sometimes but by no means always paid lip service to in his writing; but, as with the columnist, the author of the periodical essay gave his reader some assurance of a certain amount of consistency in the subjects he might expect to read about and the views about them he might expect to encounter.

Johnson closed his last *Rambler* with the assertion that his intention in the series had been to give "ardour to virtue and confidence to truth." The subjects of the essays, as in other such series,

are highly diverse, and the same rich variety is to be found in his later essay series, *The Adventurer* (1752-1754), a collaboration of four authors, and *The Idler* (1758-1760). There is much on writing itself—journalism, biography, diction, versification, translation. There are a large number about social evils: denunciation of imprisonment of debtors, the harshness of the criminal law (Johnson's plea that capital punishment be restricted to cases of murder is far ahead of his time), vivisection, the social conditions that give rise to prostitution, the tyranny of country squires—attitudes that nowadays would cause him to be considered a thoroughgoing "liberal." Many—using a familiar device of the genre—consisted of letters supposedly written to Mr. Rambler or Mr. Idler asking for his advice about personal problems. There are memorable satires of would-be literary critics and fanatically partisan politicians.

Contemporary (and later) readers sometimes complained about the "heavy" prose style of *The Rambler*, and compared it unfavorably with the lighter touch of *The Spectator*. It is true that the papers—like *The Vanity of Human Wishes*—are closely written and require careful and sensitive reading in order to follow their sometimes intricate exposition of an abstract moral question. It was reported, although no concrete evidence was cited, that they had a circulation of only five hundred, compared with that of *The Spectator*, at its height, of ten thousand. But it has also been shown that of the current series of periodical essays *The Rambler* was the most frequently reprinted by the provincial press. *The Idler*, printed, unlike *The Rambler*, as a "column" in a weekly journal, the *Universal Chronicle*, generally has a lighter touch in its prose, but it contains some of Johnson's most blistering comments on political matters—the tremendous denunciation in *Idler* 81 of the history of European oppression of the native population of the Americas, and *Idler* 22 (in the original numbering—it was omitted from the collected editions, perhaps because of its bitterness), in which a family of vultures observes the scene of gore left on a human battlefield and speculates what motives these strange creatures can have for slaughtering each other to provide a feast for vultures.

The presence of such political commentary in *The Idler* is accounted for by the fact that a great international war—a world war—had broken out in 1756, between Britain and Prussia on one side and France and Austria, later joined by Spain, on the other. This, the Seven Years' War, was to lead to the acquisition by Britain of Canada and India, and, indirectly, to the American Revolution. When the *Dictionary* was at last published in 1755, the fifteen hundred guineas from its publishers had long gone, and Johnson had at once to turn to other projects to earn a living. In the spring of 1756 he became editor of a new monthly, the *Literary Magazine*, which, in spite of its title, was largely devoted, under Johnson's editorship, to foreign affairs and, in particular, the course of the new war, the official declaration of which he printed in full in its first number. He

was not inexperienced in such matters. His involvement in the "Foreign History" feature in the *Gentleman's* had familiarized him with the events of the War of the Austrian Succession and helped him with the background for a long biographical account in the *Literary Magazine* of Frederick "the Great" of Prussia, Britain's ally in the later war.

That war was very popular in Britain, especially when it became clear, after some early reverses, that the British were on the winning side, and that their success in it would lead to the establishment of a worldwide empire, with greatly increased opportunities for British trade. From the beginning Johnson expressed the strongest hostility to this enterprise, and published in his new journal what was planned to be a series of long articles giving a most uncomplimentary history of British involvement in colonization and consequent embroilment with foreign powers. Why shed blood for the possession of Canada, "a cold, uncomfortable, uninviting region, from which nothing but furs and fish were to be had"? In North America his sympathies are all with the natives, whom the European invaders have robbed of their lands: "The American dispute between the French and us is . . . only the quarrel of two robbers for the spoils of a passenger." When the French capture the island of Minorca, Johnson's attitude is "good riddance"; it would be well to get rid of Gibraltar as well. When Admiral John Byng was court-martialed and executed for the loss of Minorca, an action which Johnson maintained was only a cover-up for the administration's incompetence, he is as vociferous as his French counterpart Voltaire in its condemnation. That Johnson had been put in charge of the journal may have been due only to the fact that its proprietors were supporters of William Pitt, who at the time was in opposition to the administration. When, after five numbers of the journal had been published, Pitt was returned to power and took over the running of the war, Johnson's antiwar and antiadministration efforts were no longer in demand. The magazine adopted a stridently "patriotic" position, and, except for a few later articles, there is no further sign of Johnson's hand in it.

The *Literary Magazine*, however, contains some brilliant journalism by Johnson. There is close coverage of the war and foreign relations, including the printing in full of public documents concerned with them, and much incisive book reviewing. One long review is superb. A wealthy dilettantish dabbler in politics, literature, and theology, Soame Jenyns, had published *A Free Enquiry into the Nature and Origin of Evil*, purporting to answer the age-old question, how, given a God who is both omnipotent and benevolent, can we account for the presence of evil in the world which He has created? Jenyns explains this by use of the well-worn device of "the great chain of being": if one takes the long view, what appears to be evil to the individual who suffers pain or loss or poverty is really for the overall good of the whole of creation. In any case, God has mercifully provided alleviation for these evils by keeping the poor ignorant: there are some who would foolishly bestow education on the poor, but this would only increase their sensitivity to the ills they are exposed to. Ignorance is the opiate of the poor, Jenyns asserts. Johnson, who had had firsthand experience of poverty in a way Jenyns had not, has no difficulty demolishing such arguments.

Johnson's wife had died in 1752, and he poignantly records the loss and his loneliness at the end of his preface to the *Dictionary*. A year later he hoped to marry a second time; the lady who was apparently his choice, the learned and pious Hill Boothby, was already ill and died shortly afterward. Johnson's mother followed in 1759. For all that she had lived almost ninety years and that Johnson's relations with her may not always have been satisfactory—he did not see her during the last twenty years of her life—her death was another blow. To pay for the expenses of her last illness, he wrote, "in the evenings of a week," *The History of Rasselas, Prince of Abissinia*, a *conte philosophique* like Voltaire's *Candide* (which appeared at almost the same time), rather than a romance or a novel. It opens in "The Happy Valley," surrounded by high mountains, where the younger relations of the Emperor of Abyssinia are immured for life so they can offer no danger to his rule. (This had been a historical custom in Ethiopia, except that the place of imprisonment was a mountain rather than a valley; Johnson had read many travelers' accounts of that distant land as well as that of Father Lobo.) Among its inmates is the fourth son of the emperor, Rasselas—"Ras" is an Ethiopian title meaning "prince" or "chief."

Although the Happy Valley is provided with everything to satisfy the physical wants of its inhabitants—the ultimate "welfare state"—the young prince is not happy (nor, it transpires, are its other dwellers, in spite of all the sensual gratifi-

cation they receive). Why? Because he has nothing to hope and long for, nothing to feed "that hunger of imagination which preys incessantly upon life, and must be always appeased by some employment." Man's nature is such that he must always strive for something beyond his reach; to rest content with what he has is to deny that nature. The theme is remarkably close to that of Johann Wolfgang von Goethe's *Faust* (1808), where Faust agrees that his soul will be forfeit to Mephistopheles if, no matter how his human wishes are gratified—Johnson had written a poem about them—the day should come when he can say, "I am content." It never does. An old teacher of Rasselas reproaches him: if he knew the miseries of the outside world, he would appreciate life in the Happy Valley. Now at last Rasselas has something to desire—to see that outside world. He tunnels through the rocks, and is joined by an older man, the poet Imlac, who tells the story of his eventful life in the outside world, where, like Candide, he has constantly met with disillusion—and yet he is bored by the stultification of the Happy Valley. They are unexpectedly joined at the last moment by Rasselas's highly intelligent sister, the Princess Nekayah, and her lady companion Pekuah.

They emerge from the tunnel and set out on their search for a solution to the problem of "the choice of life," as Johnson originally entitled the tale. They sample the busy life of Cairo and the solitary life of a hermit, the pastoral life and the life of the rich and powerful, none of which leads to happiness. Nekayah makes a special study of married life, and comes to the conclusion "Marriage has many pains, but celibacy has no pleasures." Rasselas attends the lectures of learned philosophers, one of whom informs him that the answer lies in Stoic detachment—never allow yourself to be emotionally involved with anything outside yourself—and then breaks down at the news of his daughter's death. Another informs him that the secret is "to live according to Nature," but when Rasselas asks him, cannot explain how to go about this. While the others explore the Great Pyramid and wonder what can have possessed its builders to erect so enormous and useless a structure—it was the incessant human hunger of imagination, Imlac explains—Pekuah is carried off by a handsome Arab sheik, who bears her away to his harem. This turns out to be another Happy Valley: the women have no outlets for *their* imagination and live frivolous and discontented lives; Pekuah wonders how the sheik can endure these bored and boring creatures. It is of course Pekuah's lively intelligence that attracts him; he too is an intelligent and honorable person and at length returns Pekuah to her companions. But intelligence in itself is not enough to ensure happiness. They visit a famous astronomer, who, after many years of studying the heavenly bodies in solitude, becomes paranoid and convinces himself that it is he who controls their movements. The astronomer is eventually cured of his "dangerous prevalence of imagination"—the dangerous condition when fantasy prevails over contact with reality—by being gradually weaned away from his solitary existence and brought into contact with his fellow human beings, especially—a nice touch—with the feminine charms of Nekayah and Pekuah.

They discuss death and the arguments for the immortality of the soul. At last they feel they have come to the end of their searches, and it is time to make their choices of life. They decide to return to their native Abyssinia—though not to the Happy Valley, where the one thing guaranteed is unhappiness—and to enter on the occupations which most attract their imaginations: for Rasselas, government; for Nekayah, education; for Pekuah, the administration of a convent of pious young women (perhaps a reaction to her observation of the life of the harem). They set high ideals for themselves in these, though knowing that those ideals will never be fully realized. As Johnson put it at the end of *Adventurer* 84, "Some deficiency must be forgiven all, for all are men. . . . It is, however, reasonable to have perfection in our eye, that we may always advance towards it, though we know it never can be reached." *Rasselas* has always been popular: hundreds of editions and dozens of translations have been and continue to be published.

The death in 1760 of George II, aged seventy-seven, whom Johnson had so often denounced along with the Whig ministries the king had supported, and the accession to the throne of his grandson George III, aged twenty-two, seemed to many, including Johnson, to give hope of a "new deal" in British politics. The new king was a conscientious and idealistic youth, as suspicious as Johnson of the old Whig oligarchy. George II and Walpole had been much condemned for failing to encourage literature and the arts; George III's first administration seemed to give notice of a change by awarding Johnson in 1762 an annual government pension of three hundred pounds. Such pensions to impecunious

writers and scholars were not uncommon, but Johnson's came at an unfortunate time, when George was evidently intent on freeing himself from the old Whig ascendancy and bringing in new ministers unconnected with it, such as the Scottish John Stuart, third Earl of Bute. Johnson's powerful blasts against the old political regime were well known; moreover, the practice of rewarding minor political hangers-on of the administration with pensions had impelled him to define *pension* in the *Dictionary* as "pay given to a state hireling for treason to his country." Hitherto most published comment on Johnson's work had been laudatory or at least respectful. Now he was subjected by those hostile to the political innovations of the new regime to a furious tirade of condemnation as a hireling lackey of the tyrannical administration of George III, and for the rest of his life abuse continued not only of his alleged political stance, but of his physical appearance, his personality, his prose style, his *Dictionary*, and almost everything else he wrote. Much of this abuse was repeated in the next century by that dedicated Whig propagandist Thomas Babington Macaulay, and traces of it still linger in modern comment on Johnson.

Johnson paid little heed; for the first time in his life he was free of pressing financial need. His way of life continued to be modest, but to assuage his loneliness he maintained a household of individuals whom his more fashionable friends tended to look down their noses at: the blind, but cultured, Anna Williams, a close friend of his dead wife; Elizabeth Desmoulins, daughter of his godfather Samuel Swynfen of Lichfield; an unqualified medical practitioner, Robert Levett, who worked with London slum dwellers too poor to pay the fee for regular medical attendance; his black servant, Frank Barber, born a slave in Jamaica, whom Johnson tried without great success to educate and was to make the residuary legatee of his estate. He could now become less "retired" than when he was slaving at journalism or lexicography. He paid his first visit in twenty years to his native Lichfield, finding "the streets much narrower and shorter than I had left them, inhabited by a new race of people to whom I was very little known." In the following years he made extended visits to Oxford and the Midlands to see old friends, his stepdaughter Lucy Porter and his old schoolfellow John Taylor, and others from time to time; to Cambridge, Devonshire, Lincolnshire, and Northamptonshire; and, in the 1770s, long trips to Scotland, Wales, and France.

Pages from a letter to Hester Thrale, including a report on a Club meeting—attended by Charles James Fox and Edmund Burke, among others—where actress Sarah Siddons and Fanny Burney's novel Cecilia *were discussed (MA 204, Pierpont Morgan Library). The letter also mentions Sir Joshua Reynolds's most recent prize-day discourse at the Royal Academy.*

In London he engaged in an active social life, dining out often with such friends as the artist Sir Joshua Reynolds, the musician Charles Burney, the scholar and future bishop Thomas Percy, and above all with his new friends Henry Thrale, a wealthy brewer and member of Parliament, and his vivacious wife, Hester, whose country home, Streatham Place, south of London, became a second home for him. The young Scot, James Boswell, in search of famous men with whom to claim acquaintance, sought him out and from time to time, on trips from his home in Edinburgh, called on him and made copious notes of his conversation. Johnson gained a reputation for conversational wit and sometimes rather rough repartee, though, as with other celebrities, many jests floating around in the public domain were illicitly fathered on him. The role in his life of the famous Club, founded by Reynolds and Johnson, has perhaps been exaggerated. It was not, as some readers think, a modern men's club, with a clubhouse to which members regularly resort in the evenings for casual chat. It was a small group, only nine to begin with, which met for dinner at a tavern twice a month when Parliament was in session, around November to May, and, in the years for which records have been preserved, often had a very small attendance, with Johnson himself averaging only about three or four attendances a year.

Johnson's first obligation, after the award of the pension, was to finish his long delayed edition of Shakespeare. The 1745 proposals, we have seen, were withdrawn. But in 1756, after the *Dictionary* had been completed, new proposals were published. Tonson, who had blocked the earlier project, now agreed to print eight octavo volumes of the plays by subscription, with one guinea, half the subscription, to be paid in advance. Johnson dawdled and is even said to have lost the list of subscribers. He was twitted in satiric verse—"He for subscribers baits his hook, / And takes your cash; but where's the book?" The book finally appeared in 1765.

Like everything else of his after the pension, it received some violent attacks, but there is no question that it was by far the best edition of Shakespeare yet published. In the noble preface, as well as much memorable general literary criticism, Johnson states his principles of textual editing, so important in dealing with the difficult text of the early printings of the plays. Earlier editors, such as Pope and Warburton, when confronted by some word or expression unfamiliar

Johnson in 1769 (mezzotint by James Watson, after a portrait by Sir Joshua Reynolds)

to them, simply asserted that it must be a silly printer's mistake, and changed it to something closer to their own vocabulary. Not only was Johnson the first editor of Shakespeare to have access to a historical dictionary of the English of Shakespeare's time, he had compiled it himself. Thus when he sees that some word whose meaning had been forgotten in the eighteenth century makes sense in the signification it had in the sixteenth, he retains it, with an explanatory note. Johnson's is the first "variorum" edition of the plays—that is, it not only includes the present editor's comment on a passage, but republishes the notes of earlier editors which he finds helpful or which contain a misreading that he thinks should be corrected. It has been said that in modern variorum editions, when one wants the clearest and most convincing explanation of an obscure passage, one turns first to Johnson's note on it.

At the end of each play, Johnson makes a general observation on its effectiveness. As always, his criticism begins with his own personal reaction: those reactions are often strong and he has no false modesty about describing them: at the end of *King Lear*, "I was many years ago so shocked by Cordelia's death that I know not whether I ever endured to read again the last scenes of the play till I undertook to revise them as an editor," and of *Julius Caesar*, though many passages in it have been praised, "I have never been strongly agitated in perusing it and think it somewhat cold and unaffecting." Such frankness shocked the bardolaters of the nineteenth century, for whom Shakespeare could do nothing wrong. "Others abide our question; thou art free," wrote Matthew Arnold. To Johnson, Shakespeare was a supremely great writer, nevertheless one not superhuman and immune to questioning. In 1773 Johnson published an extensively revised edition of his work in which he was assisted by George Steevens, who played a greater role in the edition of 1778. Nearly all later editions of Shakespeare owe something to these.

For three or four years from 1766 onward, Johnson was involved in another major work, the full details of which have only recently become known. This was his secret collaboration with Sir Robert Chambers, Vinerian Professor of English Law at Oxford University, on a series of lectures introducing undergraduates to the fundamentals of the common law—secret apparently to all Johnson's friends except Mrs. Thrale. Johnson had met Chambers in 1754 when Chambers was only seventeen and had just arrived from his native Newcastle to enroll as a law student at the Middle Temple in London, where Johnson was living at the time, and to matriculate at Lincoln College, Oxford. All who knew Chambers testified to his modesty and amiable disposition, and Johnson seems to have become a kind of surrogate father to him, advising him on his studies, getting him to write an article for his *Literary Magazine*, writing a recommendation when Chambers applied for one of the fellowships endowed by Charles Viner for the advancement of the study of English law, a new subject at Oxford. This fellowship brought Chambers into contact with the first Vinerian Professor, Sir William Blackstone, whose lectures were published as his famous *Commentaries on the Law of England*, throughout the eighteenth and nineteenth centuries the standard textbook for beginning law students in Britain and America.

When Blackstone resigned his chair in 1766, Chambers, only twenty-nine, was appointed to succeed him. He was understandably nervous about having to prepare a lecture series to compete with that of his eminent predecessor, so much so that he found it hard even to begin, and he forfeited a good deal of his stipend for fail-

ing to deliver the required number of lectures. He called on Johnson for assistance, and Johnson spent much time in Oxford and London working with him. Eventually a full series was completed, running to some 450,000 words, which has only recently been published in its entirety. How much of this series comes from Johnson's own hand awaits further study. But certainly there are passages in it which sound very much like Johnson's prose and convey views on history, government, and political morality with which Johnson would certainly have agreed. It was another "great enterprise" almost in the class of the *Dictionary* and the edition of Shakespeare, and its potential for influencing British (and American) legal and political thinking was great.

The early 1770s found Johnson's style of political controversy as vigorous as it had been in the days of Walpole and his cohorts. John Wilkes, a witty and unscrupulous demagogue, after being elected Member of Parliament for the county of Middlesex, had been convicted on a charge of seditious libel and obscene publishing, and sentenced to a fine and imprisonment, whereupon the House of Commons expelled him from its membership. Wilkes was then twice reelected by the voters of Middlesex. The House then passed a resolution declaring him ineligible to sit, and instead seated his opponent, who had obtained only a minority of the votes, as the only qualified candidate in the election. Elected legislative bodies, including the American House of Representatives, still jealously guard their right to expel members whose conduct they disapprove, but the seating of Wilkes's opponent caused a nationwide hullabaloo by the opposition, who trumpeted that democracy was imperiled by this "alarming crisis," and raised the cry of "Wilkes and liberty." Early in 1770 Johnson, who, with his friend Henry Thrale M.P., was on the side of the administration in this, published *The False Alarm*, arguing the case for the House of Commons and sarcastically denouncing Wilkes's supporters as self-seeking rabble-rousers. It is worth noticing that, though Johnson has been denominated an undeviatingly partisan Tory, he denounces the "frigid neutrality" of "the Tories" in this affair.

The next year saw a preview of the struggle over the Falkland Islands that broke out again in 1982. Since the sixteenth century, Spain and Britain had squabbled about which, through early exploration and settlement, had the prior claim to sovereignty of this bleak archipelago in the south Atlantic. In 1770 the governor of Buenos Aires,

A

J O U R N E Y

TO THE

WESTERN ISLANDS

OF

S C O T L A N D.

LONDON:
Printed for W. STRAHAN; and T. CADELL in the Strand.
MDCCLXXV.

*Title page for Johnson's book about his 1773 visit
to the Hebrides with James Boswell*

then a Spanish colony, sent a naval expedition to the islands, which captured the small English settlement there. The British government protested to Madrid against this violation of its sovereignty, and it seemed that a war might be imminent. The ministry, however, now headed by the young Frederick, Lord North, skillfully used diplomatic negotiations to avert a conflict, and the Spanish eventually agreed to withdraw their forces from the islands, though without prejudice to their claim of sovereignty over them. The opposition in Britain was furious: they had seen in the incident an opportunity to oust North and his ministry, and they accused it of cowardice and of sullying Britain's honor in not making war on Spain. Johnson's *Thoughts on the Late Transactions Respecting Falkland's Islands* (1771) gives a most lucid account of the early history of the islands and the sequence of events that led up to the incident—he had been given access by the government to the official documents concerning it—and has no difficulty in defending the ministry's actions, accusing the opposition of warmongering in order to fill the pockets of their supporters, the defense contractors.

The Patriot (1774) is a short but hard-hitting pamphlet designed to help reelect Thrale as M.P. in the general election of 1774. It recapitulates the matters discussed in the two earlier pamphlets, and sharply distinguishes between true patriotism and that of the self-proclaimed "patriots" of the opposition: "Patriotism," Johnson was to say in a memorable remark, "is the last refuge of a scoundrel." It introduced a subject which Johnson enlarged on the next year in *Taxation No Tyranny*, a formal answer to the resolutions and address to the British people promulgated by the first Continental Congress, which had met in Philadelphia a few months earlier. Probably the movement for independence in the Thirteen Colonies had by this time gone too far for any attempt at appeasement to be successful. Johnson makes no such attempt. He controverts the American arguments so forcefully that the North ministry, which had more or less sponsored the pamphlet, toned it down considerably at the printer's, much to Johnson's disgust. The main thrust is stated in its title: for a government to collect taxes from a people in order to finance the benefits which that people are receiving from it is not tyranny—in the case of the Americans, the benefits, especially of the defense afforded them by the British army and navy, at great expense to the British taxpayer, had freed them from the French threat to their north. Yet much of Johnson's lack of sympathy for the American settlers came from the fact that their land had been taken by force from its Indian possessors. As for the lack of American representation in the taxing body, the House of Commons, a large number of British taxpayers had no representation there either. The cry that the British government is planning further oppression by permitting the inhabitants of Quebec to practice their traditional Roman Catholicism, he says, comes oddly from those who are agitating for "freedom of conscience." He gets in another bitter jibe at southern American patriots in "How is it that we hear the loudest yelps for liberty among the drivers of Negroes?" On the right of secession of the Thirteen Colonies from the British empire, Johnson takes the position that Abraham Lincoln was to take eighty-six years later and was to result in a far bloodier war than that of 1775 to 1783: no such right exists. The pamphlet was highly controversial at the time, and still is. But it is vividly written and clearly argued, and cannot be casually dismissed without an attempt to counter those arguments.

An incidental result of Johnson's writing *Taxation No Tyranny* was the award to Johnson by Oxford University, of which Prime Minister Lord North was the chancellor, of the honorary degree of Doctor of Civil Law (D.C.L.). Ten years earlier, the University of Dublin (Trinity College) had made him Doctor in Utroque Jure (J.U.D.: doctor of both canon and civil law). When the *Dictionary* was published in 1755, strings were pulled to have him awarded an honorary master of arts degree; it was thought that the appearance of "A.M." on the title page would enhance the work's respectability and sales. It is ironic that later writers, though not so many as there once were, have insisted on referring to him as "Doctor Johnson" or "the Doctor," for he thought very little of this title; like most sensible writers holding an honorary doctorate, he never used it, and scolded Boswell for arguing that it ought to be used. Sir John Hawkins reported that, after receiving the degree from Dublin, he resented being called "Doctor." Nor was there great distinction in having received the Oxford degree. Two years before, North had on a single occasion conferred sixty-eight honorary doctorates, many of them on minor political hangers-on of his, such as Henry Thrale, M.P., whom no one ever seems to have thought of calling "Doctor Thrale." In his *Journey to the Western Islands of Scotland* (1775), after describing his visit to Aberdeen University, Johnson gives a scathing criticism of the proliferation of doctorates: Aberdeen had given one to William Kenrick, a scurrilous hack writer who had published a violent attack on Johnson's edition of Shakespeare. In the manuscript of his journal of the Scottish tour, which Johnson had read and praised, Boswell always refers to his companion as "Mr. Johnson," but when, after Johnson's death, he put it into print as *The Journal of a Tour to the Hebrides with Samuel Johnson, LL.D.* (1785), he changed all the "Mr.'s" to "Dr.'s" and, in the title of the work, added to Johnson's name the inaccurate "LL.D." One wonders why. At any rate, there seems no more point in a modern reader referring to "Doctor Johnson" than to "Doctor Wordsworth" or "Doctor Einstein," who also held honorary doctorates from Oxford. All three had earned enough distinction by their achievements not to need any more identification than their surnames.

It might seem that by his sixty-sixth year, Johnson had dealt with almost every possible

genre of writing. His readers were to be surprised in 1775 to find him dealing successfully with a new one, that of the "travel book"—*A Journey to the Western Islands of Scotland*. "I had desired to visit the Hebrides, or Western Islands of Scotland, so long that I scarcely remember how the wish was originally excited," it begins. The notion of Johnson's being an insular and bigoted John Bull, uninterested in any place beyond his constricted London parish, is entirely mistaken. When he was only twenty, discontented with Oxford, he was overheard muttering to himself, "Well, I have a mind to see how they go on in other places of learning. I'll go see the universities abroad. I'll go to France and Italy. I'll go to Padua. . . . For an Athenian"—read "Oxonian"—"blockhead is the worst of all blockheads." He eventually got to France, with Mr. and Mrs. Thrale, in the same year his *Journey to the Western Islands of Scotland* was published. Most of this two-month tour was spent in or near Paris, where he saw all the most famous sights, including young King Louis XVI and Marie Antoinette at dinner. In 1774 he had made, with the Thrales, a three-month tour of the English Midlands and north Wales, in which they visited such great country houses as Chatsworth, Blenheim, and Kedleston, and Mrs. Thrale's native Welsh haunts. For the next year, 1775, an extended tour of Italy with the Thrales was planned, but at the last minute young Harry Thrale, their only son, died, and in their distress they did not feel like going. Johnson was deeply disappointed: more than any other place, he had longed to visit Italy, the cradle of the Renaissance, where his early heroes Petrarch and Politian had played their part in "the revival of learning." In the last year of his life, it was thought that the warmth of Italy might help him live through the winter, and plans were made for him to go there, but by that time he was too ill to travel.

Johnson's records of the trips to Wales and France remained in the form of brief diary notes. But those of the tour of Scotland provided the material for a substantial and readable book. From various places on the route he jotted down his observations in long letters to Mrs. Thrale, which he later used when putting the book together. His companion on the tour was James Boswell, who left his own record of it in *The Journal of a Tour to the Hebrides with Samuel Johnson, LL.D.* It has often been remarked that, whereas Johnson's book is about Scotland, Boswell's is about Johnson. Johnson's is much more than the

Page from the manuscript for Johnson's "Preface to Pope," written in 1780 and published the next year
(MA 205, Pierpont Morgan Library)

bare record of an itinerary: it has been called a pioneering work of social anthropology. The rugged hills of the Highlands and the life lived there by the clansmen, not long removed from a feudal existence and speaking a tongue of their own, were almost as much a mystery to the English and the Lowland Scots as those of Ethiopia, and Johnson wanted to explore that mystery.

The travelers set out from Edinburgh on 18 August 1773. For the first ten days their route lay along the North Sea coast, still part of the "civilized" Lowland culture, where Johnson was received and honored at the Universities of St. Andrews and Aberdeen and where they were welcomed at the homes of Scottish nobles and gentry. At Inverness they bade farewell to roads and wheeled vehicles and continued across the rugged terrain on horseback, accompanied by a sturdy servant and local guides. Johnson talked to the natives he met, questioning them closely about their way of life, and noting details of their occupations, their dwellings, their language, and their food. They crossed the water to Skye, the largest and most settled of the Hebrides, where they were entertained by various Macdonalds and Macleods, the two great clans of the island, with Highland dancing and song and bagpipe music. They clambered among the rocks in the rain, and Johnson had his first and probably only drink of Scotch whisky.

Three matters particularly concerned Johnson. One was the breakdown of the old clan system, and, connected with this, the widespread emigration from the Hebrides to America. He was ambivalent about this change: the orderliness of the clan organization, and the loyalty of the clansmen to their chiefs, appealed to him; yet at the same time he could understand why a Highlander should be willing to endure the hardships of starting a new life in a distant and largely unsettled land in order to have land of his own rather that to hold it at the pleasure of the chief. The other matter was the authenticity of the "Ossian" poems, a best-seller of the time, which James Macpherson proclaimed were translated from orally transmitted poems in Gaelic. After much inquiry, Johnson could find no evidence of the existence of such originals, and denounced them as a hoax, to Macpherson's anger. The travelers experienced some hair-raising journeys by boat to other islands during the stormy autumn season. They reverently visited Iona, where Christianity had first come to Great Britain after the barbarian invasions, and eventually made their way

back to Edinburgh on 9 November. Forty years earlier Johnson had written in the dedication of his version of Lobo's *Voyage to Abyssinia*, "A generous and elevated mind is distinguished by nothing more certainly than an eminent degree of curiosity, nor is that curiosity more agreeably or usefully employed than in examining the laws and customs of foreign nations." *A Journey to the Western Islands* shows how agreeably and usefully such a mind can be employed.

Considering how frequently Johnson complained in his letters and diaries of ill health, one is surprised by all this activity in his mid sixties. He never seems to have suffered any incapacitating illness on his strenuous journeys, and one feels strongly tempted to conclude that, like his similarly energetic contemporary Voltaire, he was a considerable hypochondriac. Even more surprising is to find him, on his seventieth birthday in 1779, busily engaged in his last "great undertaking," begun two years before and to continue for another two years. This project was initiated by the London booksellers, a group for which Johnson, himself a bookseller's son, usually had high praise. Alarmed at the rumor that an Edinburgh publisher was bringing out a collection of works of English poets, and wishing to establish what they thought their copyright in these, they projected a multivolume anthology of the works of fifty-two English poets, most of them published between 1650 and 1750. They asked Johnson to write prefaces to the works of each poet. Johnson gladly agreed, asking only two hundred pounds; the delighted publishers at once raised this to three hundred, and later added another hundred.

Probably they expected no more than the perfunctory few pages a modern publisher envisions when he engages a celebrity to provide some desultory comments to be prefaced to a republication of a familiar work, to help publicity and sales; and indeed Johnson's prefaces to the poems of the many minor and forgettable versifiers included among the fifty-two *are* short and perfunctory. But when faced with such challenges as Milton, Dryden, and Pope, Johnson could not resist giving free rein to his pen, and the result was long, pamphlet-length essays. Possibly because of scheduling difficulties in printing so vast a work— it ran to sixty-eight volumes in all—Johnson's contributions did not at first precede the poetry they are supposed to introduce, but were printed separately, four volumes in 1779 and a further six volumes in 1781, although in later editions of the

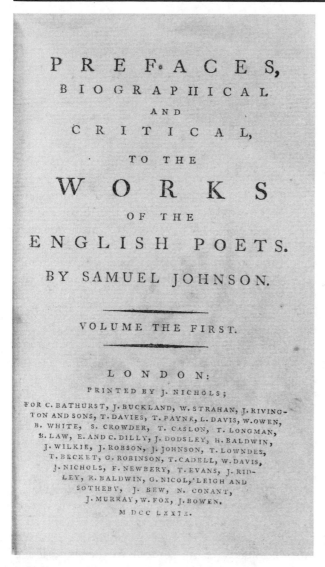

PREFACES,

BIOGRAPHICAL

AND

CRITICAL,

TO THE

WORKS

OF THE

ENGLISH POETS.

BY SAMUEL JOHNSON.

VOLUME THE FIRST.

LONDON:

PRINTED BY J. NICHOLS;

FOR C. BATHURST, J. BUCKLAND, W. STRAHAN, J. RIVING-
TON AND SONS, T. DAVIES, T. PAYNE, L. DAVIS, W. OWEN,
B. WHITE, S. CROWDER, T. CASLON, T. LONGMAN,
B. LAW, E. AND C. DILLY, J. DODSLEY, H. BALDWIN,
J. WILKIE, J. ROBSON, J. JOHNSON, T. LOWNDES,
T. BECKET, G. ROBINSON, T. CADELL, W. DAVIS,
J. NICHOLS, F. NEWBERY, T. EVANS, J. RID-
LEY, R. BALDWIN, G. NICOL, LEIGH AND
SOTHEBY, J. BEW, N. CONANT,
J. MURRAY, W. FOX, J. BOWEN.

M DCC LXXIX.

Title page for the first volume of essays that Johnson wrote as prefaces to a multivolume anthology of the works of fifty-two English poets. Because of delays in printing the anthology, Johnson's prefaces were first published separately.

collection, edited by Alexander Chalmers and Robert Anderson, the works were so prefaced. It is important to remember that their original title, *Prefaces, Biographical and Critical, to the Works of the English Poets*, accurately describes their intended function. The later popular title, *The Lives of the Poets*, which was not devised by Johnson, is misleading. They are not biographies, and their organization makes this clear: there is first a sketch of the life of the author, and then a critical essay on his writings. In the longer prefaces, there intervenes between these two sections what was called a "character" of the writer—an attempt to sum up and comment on what are perceived as the most important traits in his psychology and behavior.

The biographical parts of the *Prefaces* make delightful reading, at least for those who do not demand a hero-worshiping approach to famous writers, as some of their early readers did, expressing their outrage that Johnson should approach such celebrities as fallible human beings. Johnson treats them much more in the vein of Lytton Strachey than of Thomas Carlyle. Johnson detests Milton's egocentricity and "left-wing" politics, remarking of his dictatorial treatment of his family, "It has been observed that they who most loudly clamour for liberty do not most liberally grant it" (the observer having been Samuel Johnson, who four years earlier had written, "How is it that we hear the loudest yelps for liberty among the drivers of Negroes?"). His distaste for Swift has puzzled many; after all, it is argued, they were both strong Tories. Perhaps; but there may be different kinds of Tories, and moreover, Swift called himself a Whig. Johnson's disrespect in referring to George, Lord Lyttelton, as "poor Lyttelton" nearly ruptured his friendship with the magnificent Mrs. Elizabeth Montagu, who admired Lyttelton. There is considerable dry irony at the expense of the somewhat ostentatiously pious Addison (Johnson's irony, for which he had a considerable talent, is often so subtle that casual readers tend not to notice it). Even Pope, to whom he devoted the longest of the biographical sketches and whose poetry he so greatly admired, is not spared, and his numerous human failings are not glossed over.

But in recording the foibles of his subjects, Johnson never becomes indignant. He fully appreciates, to quote the great modern biographer of James Joyce, that artistic grandeur can live with human weakness. In his *Rambler* 60, almost a manifesto of modern biographical theory, he firmly rejects the older view, that the function of biography is to teach morality by presenting either saintly and heroic figures to be imitated or deplorable ones whose vices are to be avoided. Like Strachey after him, he believed, "Human beings are too important to be treated as mere symptoms of the past. They have a value which . . . must be felt for its own sake." "I have often thought," he wrote, "that there has rarely passed a life of which a judicious and faithful narrative would not be useful." And the most telling parts of such a narrative are not of how the subject achieved worldly fame, "not how any man became great, but how he was made happy; not how he lost the favour of his prince, but how he became discontented with himself." Such a narrative will record the small, concrete details of how a life was lived: "Nothing is too little for so little a creature as man." And so we are given such details as the poignant account of Pope's having to be helped by a maid to dress because of his physical weakness, and that he wore three pairs of stockings to make his shrunken legs look more presentable; that Swift used to attend church daily, but as early as possible in the morning so that no one would see him and think him ostentatiously devout; that when Addison "suffered from vexation" by his wife, the haughty Charlotte, Countess of Warwick, he would escape to a tavern and console himself by drinking too much. Sometimes the *Prefaces* are enlivened by personal reminiscences by Johnson himself: how his father reported that Dryden's *Absalom and Achitophel* (1681) had been the second-best-selling item in the history of his bookshop; how the boys of Lichfield grammar school, which Addison had attended, used to engage in the practice of "barring out" the master from admission. The short life of the minor poet Edmund "Rag" Smith—so named from his shabby dress—gives Johnson an opportunity to express his grateful memory of Walmesley's courteously entertaining Lichfield boys such as himself and David Garrick, whose recent death, he laments, "has eclipsed the gaiety of nations, and impoverished the public stock of harmless pleasure."

Thoughtful and readable as the biographical sketches are, so much more scholarly investigation of the lives of figures such as Milton, Dryden, Swift, and Pope has taken place since Johnson's time that the serious student would be foolish to rely on them as definitive. Indeed, some of their most memorable stories have been discredited, such as the one that Swift's animosity toward Dryden can be accounted for by Dryden's having remarked, after reading Swift's early poems, "You will never be a poet, cousin Swift." But the massive body of literary criticism contained in the *Prefaces* remains as valid and thought provoking as ever. Like most other great critics—Dryden, Samuel Taylor Coleridge, Matthew Arnold, T. S. Eliot—Johnson never attempted to construct some all-embracing critical theory: he has little use for those who "judge by principles rather than perception." To try to confine his wide-ranging talent for critical perception in some pigeonhole labeled "neoclassicism" or the like is a waste of time. But certain generalizations about it can be made. Horace had said that poetry—that is, imaginative literature—should ei-

ther please or instruct. Johnson corrects this prescription to "The end of poetry is to instruct *by* pleasing." "Works of imagination excel by their allurement and delight; by their power of attracting and detaining the attention. That book is good in vain which the reader throws away." *Imagination* and *imagery* are among the terms Johnson most frequently uses in the *Prefaces*; he is always concerned to assess the skill of the poet in the use of effective images, which called up "pictures to the mind."

The starting point for Johnson's judgment of a work of literature is always the impression it makes on himself. We have seen that his never having been "strongly agitated" by *Julius Caesar* cancels out praise that others have given it. Similarly, *Lycidas* fails to please him: its use of the hackneyed pastoral genre, its blasphemous introduction of pagan mythology into a Christian setting, and, above all, what seems to him the callousness of using the death of a friend as a stage on which to exhibit technical virtuosity makes it impossible for him to respond to the work with anything but repulsion. The language of poetry, he believes (as William Wordsworth was to do), should be contemporary, "a selection of the language really spoken by men," if contemporary readers are to be able to respond to it emotionally. He despises the pedantic and affected use of archaic diction and convoluted sentence order in Thomas Gray and William Collins. The "generality" in literature that he praises, through the mouth of Imlac in chapter 10 of *Rasselas*, means the accessibility of its content to the experience of its readers; it does not mean "abstract," a word Johnson never uses as a critical term. Again, the "instruction" the reader receives through the pleasure a work gives him does not mean the inculcation of moral precepts. A modern interpretation of literature's "instructing by pleasing" might be "by involving the reader emotionally—by 'attracting and detaining his attention'—literature effects desirable changes in the patterns in his nervous system." It is a concept close to Aristotle's *katharsis*, or to Lionel Trilling's description of the function of the modern novel, "the most effective agent of the moral imagination in our time; its greatness and its practical usefulness [lie] in its unremitting work of involving the reader himself in the moral life, inviting him to put his own motives under examination, suggesting that reality is not as his conventional education has led him to see." And literature is and must be "practical" in that sense; it has to do

Johnson in 1783 (portrait by John Opie; National Galleries of Scotland)

with real human experience or it is nothing. "The only end of reading," Johnson tells Soame Jenyns, "is to enable the readers better to enjoy life, or better to endure it."

The last few years of Johnson's life were marked by the death of old friends—Garrick, Anna Williams, his companion of so many years, and Robert Levett, whom, in 1783, he mourned in an exquisite elegiac poem. Most disturbing of all were the death of Henry Thrale and the decision of his widow, on whom he had so long depended for sympathy and care—he was surely more than a little in love with her—to marry again, this time the Italian musician Gabriel Piozzi, younger and more attractive than the stolid Henry, whose unfaithfulness to Hester was notorious. Johnson wrote her a letter of terrible

denunciation; she replied with an equally spirited one, and communication between them ceased.

A few months before Johnson's death on 13 December 1784, of cardiovascular deterioration, he had undergone what, in his last prayer, asking God to forgive its lateness, he called his "conversion." A full discussion of Johnson's religious life would be impossible in a short space, and what has been published on it by modern scholars has not been very helpful. But it may be affirmed that, theologically, he was a sincere and orthodox Anglican, displaying an ecumenical tolerance to the theology of other branches of Christianity; he gives, for example, the highest praise to the *Paradise Lost* of the arch-Puritan Milton, and asserts that he appears "to have been untainted by any heretical peculiarity of opinion." The episode of the conversion is related in detail by his old friend and biographer Sir John Hawkins. Hawkins called on Johnson one day, and found him in deep depression. He was suffering from severe edema (dropsy; accumulation of fluid in the tissues), which no medical attention seemed to be able to relieve, and knew that death was near. What concerned him was his spiritual state; he was in agony because he had no confidence of his salvation. Hawkins tried to reassure him by calling attention to the purity of his life and to all that his writings had done for the cause of human virtue. These were of no value, Johnson replied; all that counted was wholehearted faith in God, and this, he felt, he was without. He proposed to spend the next day in seclusion and in prayer and meditation.

On the following day Hawkins called again, and found Johnson now at peace with himself; he reported that after prolonged prayer and deep meditation, there had been a sudden copious evacuation of fluid, and he believed that this was a sign of his acceptability to God. From then until his death, his prayers reflect this new confidence. This incident has puzzled some scholars, but it is perfectly in accordance with the Anglican and general Protestant doctrine of justification by faith alone; mere "good works" in themselves can contribute nothing to an individual's salvation. The doctrine is clearly stated not only in the Anglican Book of Common Prayer, but in one of Johnson's sermons, in which he remarks that, although one may practice the outward forms and ceremonies of a religious life, "To give the heart to God, and to give the whole heart, is very difficult; the last, the great effort of long labour, fervent prayer, and diligent meditation." A recent medical study argues that the diuretic medication Johnson was taking for his dropsy, when accompanied by a state of intense emotion, may result in such a discharge as he experienced.

No doubt because of general concern with psychological matters in recent decades, a good deal has been written attempting to associate Johnson's religious beliefs with the periods of depression which he suffered throughout much of his adult life. The extent of these may have been exaggerated: most literary and other artists have so suffered, many of them to a worse degree than Johnson and with more serious consequences. It is well to keep in mind the opening sentence of one classic biography. "Samuel Johnson was a pessimist with an enormous zest for living,"

and that pessimism, as his greatest poem makes clear, was directed not toward life itself but toward false values in life. Taking the teachings of Christianity seriously may of course involve the Christian in psychological struggle, in "mental fight," as very many "spiritual autobiographies," such as Bunyan's, demonstrate. Johnson followed the practice which for many centuries was recommended to Christians, of periodically making a close examination of his spiritual state. He did so each New Year's Day, during Easter week, and on his birthday, vehemently condemning himself for his sloth and other failures to live up to the Christian ideal, asking God's pardon for them, and praying for divine help in self-improvement. Sometimes he reproached himself for laxity in churchgoing, though he once excused himself on the grounds that his partial deafness made it difficult to hear the sermons, and, on one occasion, that when he could hear them, the mouthings of "ignorant and affected" preachers detracted from a religious frame of mind.

The mention of Johnson as a sermon writer is a reminder of what a great deal of his writing even so long an article as this lacks the space to deal with adequately. Twenty-six of a reported forty sermons which he composed (for an honorarium of five pounds each) for clerical friends to deliver have survived. They deal lucidly and forcefully with familiar religious topics, and are in the straightforward and somewhat austere style of Anglican homiletics of the time. Johnson was also a skilled letter writer: more than fifteen hundred of his survive, in a great variety of tones, from the charming ones he wrote to Mrs. Thrale's little daughters, the intimate and humorous ones to Mrs. Thrale herself, formal ones to the somewhat intimidating Mrs. Montagu, informal and sometimes ironic ones to James Boswell, to masterpieces of denunciation such as those to Chesterfield and Macpherson and the unforgivable one to Mrs. Thrale on her marriage to Piozzi. There have been collected some fifty anonymous prefaces and dedications he wrote, often to help the sales of works by friends. He polished and added lines to poems by his friend Oliver Goldsmith, by George Crabbe, and by others. A good deal of his own best poetry is in Latin, at the time a more frequent medium for poetry of personal reflection and introspection than English. He wrote many more short biographies, reviews, essays, journalistic features and published more editorial work and translation than there has been room to describe here.

After his death, Johnson received many honors. He was buried in Westminster Abbey, near the memorial to Shakespeare, and a fine larger-than-life statue stands prominently in St. Paul's Cathedral, its Roman costume displaying his muscular frame; it gives a very different impression from the most often reproduced portrait of him by Reynolds, which gives him puffy cheeks and a decided pout. A general admiration of Johnson's achievement was the rule until the mid nineteenth century, when the historian Macaulay, in two widely circulated essays, picked up the themes of detraction of the partisans of Johnson's own time and improved on them. Many traits of this caricature were still current in the late twentieth century: Macaulay's account continued to be published in the *Encyclopaedia Britannica* until the 1960s.

Probably no major writer has ever been the subject of more misrepresentation than Johnson. It may be useful to list, in order that the student may avoid them, some of the most widespread errors about Johnson, errors that have long been exploded by serious scholars and careful readers of Johnson's writings. He was not a pigheaded adherent to "Toryism," whatever "Toryism" in the eighteenth century may have been. He was not an authoritarian or a blind devotee of monarchs and monarchism; few of his contemporaries were more devastating in their criticism of the monarchs under whom he lived and the ministries which they appointed. He was not an insular "John Bull"; he loved travel and was an enthusiastic student of foreign cultures. He did not despise history; he did not distrust modern science, but was a dedicated student of it. His *Dictionary* was a landmark in the study of the English language, as his *Shakespeare* was a landmark in the history of the editing of that writer. He was a fine poet, as T. S. Eliot has testified. He was a superb critic, as Edmund Wilson and other modern critics have insisted. He was a magnificent prose stylist: Macaulay's attack on what he called "Johnsonese" is based on an untrue story told by Boswell that once, after saying, "It has not wit enough to keep it sweet," Johnson immediately "translated" it into "It has not vitality enough to preserve it from putrefaction"; there is no record of his ever having done anything of the kind. He was in fact capable of an immense range of stylistic effects. He could use long and erudite Latinate words when it suited his artistic purpose; he could also effectively use short "Anglo-Saxon" ones. One scholar, praising a lovely sentence in *Rasselas*—"No man can taste the fruits of autumn while he is delighting his scent with the flowers of the spring: no man can, at the same time, fill his cup from the source and the mouth of the Nile"—pointed out that of its forty words, thirty-seven are monosyllables. The sentence also gives the lie to the myth that Johnson was addicted to generalities and abstractions: in two beautiful images he has vividly concretized the abstract generalization "One must choose between two mutually exclusive sources of happiness." It is no doubt true, as Macaulay is fond of pointing out, that Johnson's physical appearance and such traits as his nervous tics were unattractive, that his clothing was shabby, and that his table manners and tastes in food were often bizarre—to which one can only reply, "So what?" His conversational wit could sometimes be acerbic; but many of the best-known insults and wisecracks attributed to him, by Boswell and others, are apocryphal, derived from popular joke books and in the public domain. He was not a literary dictator, a "Great Cham"; he affirmed his reluctance to pass judgment on contemporary literary productions, and the evidence supports him.

Despite the longevity of the mythical construct of Macaulay, the real Johnson continues to attract more students than any other English writer of his time. Why? Perhaps two Latin tags contain the answer, one applicable to the immense variety of Johnson's concerns, the other to his skill as a writer. One is Terence's "Homo sum; humani nil a me alienum est"—"I am a man; nothing human is irrelevant to me." The other is the splendid epitaph that Johnson composed for his friend Goldsmith and could justly serve as his own: "Nullum fere scribendi genus non tetigit, nullum quod tetigit non ornavit"—"Almost no form of writing was not touched by his pen, and he touched nothing that he did not adorn."

Letters:

The Letters of Samuel Johnson, with Mrs. Thrale's Genuine Letters to Him, 3 volumes, edited by R. W. Chapman (Oxford: Clarendon Press, 1952).

Bibliographies:

William P. Courtney and D. Nichol Smith, *A Bibliography of Samuel Johnson* (Oxford: Clarendon Press, 1915);

R. W. Chapman and Allen T. Hazen, "Johnsonian Bibliography: A Supplement to Courtney," *Proceedings of the Oxford Bibliographical Society*, 5 (1939): 119-166;

Donald Greene, "The Development of the Johnson Canon," in *Restoration and Eighteenth-Century Literature*, edited by Carroll Camden (Chicago: University of Chicago Press, 1963), pp. 407-427;

James L. Clifford and Donald J. Greene, *Samuel Johnson: A Survey and Bibliography of Critical Studies* (Minneapolis: University of Minnesota Press, 1970);

Donald Greene and John A. Vance, *A Bibliography of Johnsonian Studies, 1970-1985*, University of Victoria English Literary Studies, no. 39 (Victoria, B.C., 1987).

Biographies:

Hester Lynch Piozzi (Mrs. Thrale), *Anecdotes of the Late Samuel Johnson, LL.D. During the Last Twenty Years of His Life* (London: Printed for T. Cadell, 1786); republished in *Memoirs of the Life and Writings of the Late Dr. Samuel Johnson* [by William Shaw]. *Anecdotes of the Late Samuel Johnson* [by Mrs. Piozzi], edited by Arthur Sherbo, Oxford English Memoirs and Travels (Oxford: Oxford University Press, 1974);

Sir John Hawkins, *The Life of Samuel Johnson, LL.D.*, volume 1, of *The Works of Samuel Johnson, LL.D.* (London: Printed for J. Buckland and forty others, 1787); republished (slightly abridged), edited by Bertram H. Davis (New York: Macmillan, 1961);

James Boswell, *The Life of Samuel Johnson, LL.D.*, 2 volumes (London: Printed by Henry Baldwin for Charles Dilly, 1791); republished in *Boswell's Life of Johnson, Together with Boswell's Journal of a Tour to the Hebrides and Johnson's Diary of a Journey into North Wales*, 6 volumes, edited by G. B. Hill, revised and enlarged by L. F. Powell (Oxford: Clarendon Press, 1934-1964);

G. B. Hill, ed. *Johnsonian Miscellanies*, 2 volumes (Oxford: Clarendon Press, 1897);

Aleyn Lyell Reade, *Johnsonian Gleanings*, 11 volumes (London: Privately printed for the author, 1909-1952);

Joseph Wood Krutch, *Samuel Johnson* (New York: Holt, 1944);

James L. Clifford, *Young Sam Johnson* (New York: McGraw-Hill, 1965);

John Wain, *Samuel Johnson* (London: Macmillan, 1974; New York: Viking, 1975);

The Early Biographies of Samuel Johnson, edited by O M Brack, Jr., and Robert E. Kelley (Iowa City: University of Iowa Press, 1974);

W. Jackson Bate, *Samuel Johnson* (New York: Harcourt Brace Jovanovich, 1977; London: Chatto & Windus, 1978);

Clifford, *Dictionary Johnson: Samuel Johnson's Middle Years* (New York: McGraw-Hill, 1979; London: Heinemann, 1979).

References:

The Age of Johnson [annual], edited by Paul J. Korshin (New York: AMS Press, 1987-   );

Paul K. Alkon, *Samuel Johnson and Moral Discipline* (Evanston, Ill.: Northwestern University Press, 1967);

Bertrand H. Bronson, "The Double Tradition of Dr. Johnson," *ELH: A Journal of English Literary History*, 18 (June 1951): 90-106;

Bronson, "Johnson Agonistes," in his *Johnson and Boswell: Three Essays* (Berkeley & Los Angeles: University of California Press, 1944);

Joseph Epes Brown, *The Critical Opinions of Samuel Johnson* (Princeton: Princeton University Press, 1925);

Morris R. Brownell, *Samuel Johnson's Attitude Toward the Arts* (Oxford: Clarendon, 1989);

John J. Burke, Jr., and Donald Kay, eds. *The Unknown Samuel Johnson* (Madison: University of Wisconsin Press, 1983);

Chester F. Chapin, *The Religious Thought of Samuel Johnson* (Ann Arbor: University of Michigan Press, 1968);

Thomas M. Curley, *Samuel Johnson and the Age of Travel* (Athens: University of Georgia Press, 1975);

T. S. Eliot, Introduction to *London and the Vanity of Human Wishes* (London: Etchells & Macdonald, 1930);

J. D. Fleeman, ed., *The Sale Catalogue of Samuel Johnson's Library: A Facsimile Edition*, University of Victoria English Literary Studies, no. 2 (Victoria, B.C., 1975);

Robert Folkenflik, *Samuel Johnson, Biographer* (Ithaca, N.Y.: Cornell University Press, 1978);

James Gray, *Johnson's Sermons: A Study* (Oxford: Clarendon Press, 1972);

Donald Greene, *The Politics of Samuel Johnson* (New Haven: Yale University Press, 1960; revised edition, Athens: University of Georgia Press, 1990);

Greene, *Samuel Johnson* (New York: Twayne, 1970; revised edition, Boston: Twayne, 1989);

Greene, *Samuel Johnson's Library: An Annotated Guide*, University of Victoria English Literary Studies, no. 1 (Victoria, B.C., 1975);

Greene, ed., *Samuel Johnson: A Collection of Critical Essays* (Englewood Cliffs, N.J.: Prentice-Hall, 1965);

Jean H. Hagstrum, *Samuel Johnson's Literary Criticism* (Minneapolis: University of Minnesota Press, 1952);

F. W. Hilles, ed., *The Age of Johnson: Essays Presented to C. B. Tinker* (New Haven: Yale University Press, 1949);

Hilles, ed., *New Light on Dr. Johnson* (New Haven: Yale University Press, 1959);

Benjamin B. Hoover, *Samuel Johnson's Parliamentary Reporting* (Berkeley & Los Angeles: University of California Press, 1953);

George Irwin, *Samuel Johnson: A Personality in Conflict* (Auckland, N.Z.: Auckland University Press / New York: Oxford University Press, 1971);

Johnsonian News Letter [quarterly] (New York: Department of English, Columbia University, 1940-   );

Thomas Kaminski, *The Early Career of Samuel Johnson* (New York: Oxford University Press, 1987);

Paul J. Korshin ed., *Johnson After Two Hundred Years* (Philadelphia: University of Pennsylvania Press, 1986);

Mary Lascelles, James L. Clifford, and others, eds., *Johnson, Boswell, and Their Circle: Essays Presented to L. F. Powell* (Oxford: Clarendon Press, 1965);

E. L. McAdam, Jr., *Dr. Johnson and the English Law* (Syracuse, N.Y.: Syracuse University Press, 1951);

Richard B. Schwartz, *Samuel Johnson and the New Science* (Madison: University of Wisconsin Press, 1971);

Schwartz, *Samuel Johnson and the Problem of Evil* (Madison: University of Wisconsin Press, 1975);

Arthur Sherbo, *Samuel Johnson, Editor of Shakespeare, with an Essay on The Adventurer* (Urbana: University of Illinois Press, 1956);

James H. Sledd and Gwin J. Kolb, *Dr. Johnson's Dictionary: Essays in the Biography of a Book* (Chicago: University of Chicago Press, 1955);

John A. Vance, *Samuel Johnson and the Sense of History* (Athens: University of Georgia Press, 1984);

Robert Voitle, *Samuel Johnson the Moralist* (Cambridge, Mass.: Harvard University Press, 1961);

W. K. Wimsatt, Jr., *Philosophic Words: A Study of Style and Meaning in the Rambler and Dictionary of Samuel Johnson* (New Haven: Yale University Press, 1948);

Wimsatt, *The Prose Style of Samuel Johnson* (New Haven: Yale University Press, 1941).

Papers:

Although Johnson's output of writing was enormous, only a relatively small amount of manuscript material has survived. The largest holding is in the Hyde Collection, Four Oaks Farm, Somerville, New Jersey, which incorporates the collection of R. B. Adam, described in four volumes (*The R. B. Adam Library Relating to Dr. Samuel Johnson and His Era*, 1929-1930); important holdings are in other private collections. The Yale University Library, the British Library, the Bodleian Library, the library of Pembroke College, Oxford, the Pierpont Morgan Library, and the Johnson Birthplace Museum, Lichfield, have important manuscripts. A useful guide is J. D. Fleeman's *A Preliminary Handlist of Documents and Manuscripts of Samuel Johnson* (Oxford Bibliographical Society Occasional Publications, no. 7, 1967). A longer, though not always accurate, list is Margaret M. Smith's in *Index of English Literary Manuscripts*, volume 3 (London & New York: Mansell, 1987), pp. 121-178. They do not include the locations of manuscripts of Johnson's letters, which are listed in R. W. Chapman's edition of the letters (1952). A forthcoming new edition of the letters, in five volumes, will include newly discovered letters and new locations of previously known ones.

Andrew Marvell
(31 March 1621 - 16 August 1678)

R. V. Young
Franciscan University of Steubenville

BOOKS: *The First Anniversary of the Government Under His Highness the Lord Protector* (London: Printed by Thomas Newcomb & sold by Samuel Gellibrand, 1655);

The Rehearsal Transpros'd: Or, Animadversions Upon a late Book, Intituled, A Preface Shewing What Grounds there are of Fears and Jealousies of Popery (London: Printed by A. B. for the assigns of John Calvin & Theodore Beza, 1672);

The Rehearsal Transpros'd: The Second Part (London: Printed for Nathaniel Ponder, 1673);

Mr. Smirke; or The Divine in Mode (N.p., 1676);

An Account of the Growth of Popery, and Arbitrary Government in England (Amsterdam, 1677);

Remarks Upon a Late Disingenuous Discourse, Writ by one T. D. Under the pretense De Causa Dei (London: Printed & sold by Christopher Hussey, 1678);

Miscellaneous Poems. By Andrew Marvell, Esq. (London: Printed for Robert Boulter, 1681).

Editions: *The Complete Works in Prose and Verse of Andrew Marvell*, 4 volumes, edited by Reverend Alexander B. Grosart (London: Robson & sons, printers, 1872-1875);

The Poems and Letters of Andrew Marvell, 2 volumes, edited by H. M. Margoliouth (Oxford: Clarendon Press, 1927); third edition, revised by Pierre Legouis with E. E. Duncan-Jones (Oxford: Clarendon Press, 1971);

Andrew Marvell: The Complete Poetry, edited by George deF. Lord (London: Dent, 1968; New York: Random House, 1968);

The Rehearsal Transpros'd and The Rehearsal Transpros'd: The Second Part, edited by D. I. B. Smith (Oxford: Clarendon Press, 1971);

Andrew Marvell: The Complete Poems, edited by Elizabeth Story Donno (Harmondsworth, U.K.: Penguin, 1972);

Andrew Marvell, edited by Frank Kermode and Keith Walker, Oxford Authors Series (Oxford & New York: Oxford University Press, 1990).

Andrew Marvell, circa 1655-1660 (artist unknown; National Portrait Gallery, London)

OTHER: "Ad Regem Carolum Parodia" and Πρὸς Κάρολον τὸν βασιλέα , in Συνωδία sive Musarum Cantabrigiensium Concentus et Congratulatio ad Serenissimum Britanniarum Regem Carolum (Cambridge, 1637);

"To his Noble Friend Mr. Richard Lovelace, upon his Poems," in Richard Lovelace, *Lucasta* (London: Printed by Tho. Harper & sold by Tho. Ewster, 1649);

"Upon the death of Lord Hastings," in *Lachrymæ Musarum; The Tears of the Muses. . . . Collected and set forth by R. B.* (London: Printed by Tho. Newcomb, 1649);

"Dignissimo suo Amico Doctori Wittie. De Translatione Vulgi Errorum D. Primrosii" and "To his worthy Friend Doctor Witty upon his Translation of the Popular Errors," in *Popular Errours. Or the Errours of the People in Physick*, by James Primrose, translated by Robert Wittie (London: Printed by W. Nelson for Nicholas Bourne, 1651);

"A Dialogue ᴜᴄᴛween Thyrsis and Dorinda," in John Gamble, *Ayres and Dialogues, . . . The Second Book* (London: Printed by Godbid for Nathaniel Ekin, 1659);

"The Character of Holland," lines 1-100, in *Harleian Miscellany*, volume 613 (London: Printed by T. Mabb for Robert Horn, 1665);

"Clarindon's House-Warming," in *Directions To A Painter. For Describing our Naval Business: In Imitation of Mr. Waller. Being The Last Works of Sir John Denham. Whereunto is annexed* Clarindons *House-Warming. By an Unknown Author* (London: 1667);

"On the Victory Obtained by Blake over the Spaniards in the Bay of Santacruze, in the Island of Teneriff. 1657," in *A New Collection of Poems and Songs. Written by several Persons* (London: Printed by J. C. for William Crook, 1674);

"On Mr. Milton's *Paradise lost*," in *Paradise Lost*, second edition (London: Printed by S. Simmons, 1674).

In an era that makes a better claim than most upon the familiar term *transitional*, Andrew Marvell is surely the single most compelling embodiment of the change that came over English society and letters in the course of the seventeenth century. Author of a varied array of exquisite lyrics that blend Cavalier grace with Metaphysical wit and complexity, Marvell turned, first, into a panegyrist for the Lord Protector and his regime and then into an increasingly bitter satirist and polemicist, attacking the royal court and the established church in both prose and verse. It is as if the most delicate and elusive of butterflies somehow metamorphosed into a caterpillar.

To be sure, the judgment of Marvell's contemporaries and the next few generations would not have been such. The style of the lyrics that have been so prized in the twentieth century was already out of fashion by the time of his death, but he was a pioneer in the kind of political

verse satire that would be perfected by his younger contemporary John Dryden and in the next generation by Alexander Pope (both writing for the other side)—even as his satirical prose anticipated the achievement of Jonathan Swift in that vein. Marvell's satires won him a reputation in his own day and preserved his memory beyond the eighteenth century as a patriotic political writer—a clever and courageous enemy of court corruption and a defender of religious and political liberty and the rights of Parliament. It was only in the nineteenth century that his lyrical poems began to attract serious attention, and it was not until T. S. Eliot's classic essay (first published in the *Times Literary Supplement*, 31 March 1921), marking the tercentenary of Marvell's birth, that Marvell attained recognition as one of the major lyric poets of his age.

In recent years postmodernist theory has once again focused on Marvell as a political writer, but with as much attention to the politics of the lyric poems as in the overtly partisan satires. Doubtless what sustains critical interest in Marvell and accommodates the enormous quantity of interpretive commentary attracted by his work is the extraordinary range and ambiguity of theme and tone among a comparatively small number of poems. Equally uncertain are the nature and timing of his personal involvement and his commitments in the great national events that occurred during his lifetime. Nevertheless, despite the equivocal status of many of the details of Marvell's life and career, the overall direction is clear enough: he is a fitting symbol for England's transformation in the seventeenth century from what was still largely a medieval, Christian culture into a modern, secular society. In his subtle, ironic, and sometimes mysterious lyrics, apparently written just at the middle of the century, we have one of our finest records of an acute, sensitive mind confronting the myriad implications of that transformation.

The son of the Reverend Andrew Marvell and Anne (Pease) Marvell, Andrew Marvell spent his boyhood in the Yorkshire town of Hull, where his father, a clergyman of Calvinist inclination, was appointed lecturer at Holy Trinity Church and master of the Charterhouse when the poet was three years old. His father was, Marvell wrote years later in the second part of *The Rehearsal Transpros'd*, "a Conformist to the established Rites of the Church of *England*, though I confess none of the most over-running or eager in them." Not surprisingly then, at the age of twelve in 1633, Marvell was sent up to Trinity College, Cambridge. This was the very year that William Laud became archbishop of Canterbury. If not such a stronghold of Puritanism as Emmanuel College (alma mater of Marvell's father), Trinity was characterized by a moderation that sharply contrasted with a college such as Peterhouse (Richard Crashaw's college), which ardently embraced the Arminianism and ritualism of the Laudian program. Indeed, the liberal, rationalistic tenor of Marvell's religious utterances in later life may owe something to the influence of Benjamin Whichcote, who in 1636 as lecturer at Trinity Church began to lay the foundation for the latitudinarian strain that was so important in the Church of England after the Restoration. Such tenuous evidence as exists, however, does not suggest Puritan enthusiasm on the part of the youthful poet. The story that Marvell, converted by Jesuits, ran away from Cambridge and was persuaded to return by his father, who found him in a London bookshop, has never been properly verified (although embarrassment over such a youthful indiscretion might go far to explain the virulent anti-Catholicism of his later years). More provocative is the lack of any evidence that he participated in the English Civil War, which broke out a few months after his twenty-first birthday, and the Royalist tone of his poems before 1650.

Marvell's earliest surviving verses lead to no conclusions about his religion and politics as a student. In 1637 two pieces of his, one in Latin and one in Greek, were published in a collection of verses by Cambridge poets in honor of the birth of a fifth child to Charles I. Other contributors were as diverse as Richard Crashaw, who would later be a Catholic priest, and Edward King, whose death by drowning that same year was the occasion for John Milton's *Lycidas* (1638). Marvell's Latin poem, "Ad Regem Carolum Parodia," is a "parody" in the sense that it is a close imitation—in meter, structure, and language—of Horace, *Odes* I.2. While the Roman poet hails Caesar Augustus as a savior of the state in the wake of violent weather and the flooding of the Tiber, Marvell celebrates the fertility of the reigning sovereign and his queen on the heels of the plague that struck Cambridge at the end of 1636. Marvell's contribution in Greek asserts that the birth of the king's fifth child had redeemed the number five, of ill omen since attempts had been made on the life of James I on 5 August 1600 and 5 November 1605. It

would be easy enough to condemn the poem's frigid ingenuity but for a reluctance to be harsh with the work of a sixteen year old capable of writing Latin and Greek verse.

If little can be made of these student exercises, the poems written in the 1640s that imply a close association between Marvell and certain Royalists furnish intriguing (if meager) grounds for speculation. The mystery is further complicated by a lack of evidence regarding Marvell's whereabouts and activities during most of the decade. In 1639 he took his B.A. degree and stayed on at the university, evidently to pursue the M.A. In 1641, however, his father drowned in "the Tide of *Humber*"—the estuary at Hull made famous by "To his Coy Mistress." Shortly afterward Marvell left Cambridge, and there is plausible speculation that he might have worked for a time in the shipping business of his well-to-do brother-in-law, Edmund Popple. We are on firmer ground in the knowledge that sometime during the 1640s Marvell undertook an extended tour of the Continent. In a letter of 21 February 1653 recommending Marvell for a place in his own department in Cromwell's government, Milton credits Marvell with four years' travel in Holland, France, Italy, and Spain, where he acquired the languages of all four countries. Regrettably, Milton casts no light upon the motives and circumstances of this journey. Modern scholarship has generally assumed that Marvell served as the companion/tutor of a wealthy and perhaps noble youth, but all the candidates brought forward for this role have been eliminated by one consideration or another. Some have suggested that Marvell was merely avoiding the war, others that he was some kind of government agent. Although the explanation that he was a tutor seems most plausible, there is no certainty about what he was doing.

Whatever the purpose of his travel, its lasting effects turn up at various points in Marvell's writings. The burlesque "Character of Holland," for example, draws on reminiscences of the dikes of the Netherlands: "How did they rivet, with Gigantick Piles, / Thorough the Center their new-catched Miles." "Upon Appleton House" describes a drained meadow by evoking a Spanish arena "Ere the Bulls enter at Madril," and a letter "To a Friend in Persia" recalls fencing lessons in Spain (9 August 1671). The circumstantial detail of "Fleckno, an English Priest at Rome," a satire very much in the manner of John Donne's efforts in that genre, suggests that Marvell actu-

Miniature of Marvell, possibly by Samuel Cooper (Harry Ransom Humanities Research Center, University of Texas, Austin)

ally met the victim of his poem in Rome when Richard Flecknoe was there in 1645-1647. Flecknoe is, of course, the man immortalized as Thomas Shadwell's predecessor as king of dullness in John Dryden's *Mac Flecknoe* (1682). Marvell mercilessly ridicules both the poverty of Flecknoe's wit and his literal poverty and consequent leanness. The jokes at the expense of Catholic doctrine seem almost incidental to the abuse of Flecknoe's undernourished penury:

> Nothing now Dinner stay'd
> But till he had himself a Body made.
> I mean till he were drest: for else so thin
> He stands, as if he only fed had been
> With consecrated Wafers: and the *Host*
> Hath sure more flesh and blood than he can boast.

Doubtless these lines play irreverently with the Thomist teaching that the Body and Blood of Christ are both totally contained under each of the eucharistic species, as well as with accounts of the life of Saint Catherine of Siena, who is said to have subsisted for several years with no other nourishment than daily Communion. But the real object of this quasi-Scholastic wit (again, much in the style of Donne) is the absurdity of Flecknoe, and it lacks the virulent loathing that characterizes Marvell's attack on the doctrine of Transubstantiation years later in *An Account of the Growth of Popery* (1677). His mockery of the narrowness of Flecknoe's room makes a similar joke with the doctrine of the Trinity, which was accepted by virtually all Protestants at the time:

> there can no Body pass
> Except by penetration hither, where

Two make a crowd, nor can three Person here
Consist but in one substance.

While the jocular anti-Catholicism of "Fleckno" hardly implies militant Puritanism, by placing Marvell in Rome between 1645 and 1647, it raises the possibility that he met Lord Francis Villiers, who was also in Rome in 1645 and 1646. This would strengthen the case for Marvell's authorship of "An Elegy upon the Death of my Lord Francis Villiers" and bring to three the number of Royalist poems that he wrote. Two poems published in 1649, "To his Noble Friend Mr. Richard Lovelace, upon his Poems" and "Upon the death of Lord Hastings," are both indisputably by Marvell and indisputably Royalist in sentiment. It is not simply that both poems celebrate known adherents of the king's failed cause, but that they do so with pungent references to the triumphant side in the civil war. The death of Henry, Lord Hastings, in 1649 at the age of nineteen may have resulted immediately from smallpox, but the ultimate source of his fate is that "the *Democratick* Stars did rise, / And all that Worth from hence did *Ostracize*." The poem to Lovelace is one of the commendatory pieces in the first edition of *Lucasta* (1649). Marvell observes how "Our Civill Wars have lost the Civicke crowne" and refers with explicit scorn to the difficulty encountered in acquiring a printing license for the volume:

> The barbed Censurers begin to looke
> Like the grim consistory on thy Booke;
> And on each line cast a reforming eye,
> Severer then the yong Presbytery.

In subsequent lines Marvell refers to Lovelace's legal difficulties with Parliament, especially his imprisonment for presenting the Kentish petition requesting control of the militia and the use of the Book of Common Prayer.

"An Elegy upon the Death of my Lord Francis Villiers" was first published in the Margoliouth edition from an apparently unique pamphlet left to the Worcester College Library by George Clarke (1660-1736) with an ascription of the poem to Marvell in Clarke's hand. Villiers (1629-1648), posthumous son of the assassinated royal favorite George Villiers, first Duke of Buckingham, died in a skirmish against Parliamentary forces. Here the poet celebrates not just a Royalist, but a Royalist killed in military action against the revolutionary government. "Fame" had "Much rather" told "How heavy *Cromwell* gnasht the earth and fell. / Or how slow Death farre from the sight of day / The long-deceived *Fairfax* bore away." Villiers is credited with erecting "A whole Pyramid / Of Vulgar bodies," and the poet recommends that those who lament him turn to military rather than literary "Obsequies":

> And we hereafter to his honour will
> Not write so many, but so many kill.
> Till the whole Army by just vengeance come
> To be at once his Trophee and his Tombe.

All the evidence suggests that Clarke was a reliable witness; there is nothing in the style of the poem that rules out Marvell as the author; and, though more extreme politically, it is certainly compatible in sentiment and tone with the Hastings elegy and the commendatory poem for *Lucasta*, which Marvell is known to have written about the same time. If the Villiers elegy is in fact Marvell's, then it casts a rather eerie light on the man who would the following year write "An Horatian Ode upon Cromwel's Return from Ireland" and in 1651 become tutor to the daughter of Thomas, third Baron Fairfax.

The "Horatian Ode" is undoubtedly one of the most provocatively equivocal poems in English literature. It has been read both as a straightforward encomium of Cromwell and as an ironic deprecation. There is plentiful evidence for both extremes as well as for intermediate positions. Interpretations are only more confused by the fact that the poem can be narrowly dated. Its occasion is the return of Oliver Cromwell from one of the more brutally successful of the many British efforts to "pacify" the Irish, at the end of May 1650. It anticipates his invasion of Scotland, which occurred on 22 July 1650. These dates furnish a reasonable terminus a quo and terminus ad quem. During the interval Thomas, Lord Fairfax, already unhappy about the execution of King Charles, resigned his position as commander in chief of the Parliamentary army because he disapproved of striking the first blow against the Scots. His lieutenant general, Cromwell, was appointed in his place and proceeded with the attack. Little is known about Marvell's footing with the Royalists whom he honored with poems in 1649 or with his Puritan employers, Fairfax beginning in 1651 and later Cromwell himself; hence it is futile to infer the attitude of the 1650 ode from the sketchy biographical facts.

Whatever was in Marvell's mind at the time, the "Horatian Ode" succeeds in expressing with surpassing finesse and subtlety a studied ambivalence of feeling sharply bridled by the decisive grasping of a particular point of view. Written near the exact midpoint of the century and very nearly in the middle of the poet's fifty-seven years, the ode on Cromwell establishes its portentous subject as a paradigmatic figure of the great transformation of English culture then unfolding—as both a cause and effect of the final dissolution of the feudal order of medieval Christendom. The *argument* of the ode, which shares something of the driving energy of the "forward Youth" and of "restless *Cromwel*" himself, is almost completely devoted to the exaltation of the victorious general as a man in whom a relentless individual will to power and an inevitable historical necessity have converged to refashion the world. Cromwell is described both as a conscious, deliberating agent and as an ineluctable force of nature:

> So restless *Cromwel* could not cease
> In the inglorious Arts of Peace,
>   But through adventrous War
>   Urged his active Star.
> And, like the three-fork'd Lightning, first
> Breaking the Clouds where it was nurst,
>   Did thorough his own Side
>   His fiery way divide.

He is exonerated for the violence and destruction of his campaigns because he is the instrument of divine wrath, but he is also given credit for character, courage, and craftiness:

> 'Tis Madness to resist or blame
> The force of angry Heavens flame:
>   And, if we would speak true,
>   Much to the Man is due.

Marvell accepts the contemporary rumor that Cromwell deliberately engineered Charles's flight from Hampton Court, by "twining subtile fears with hope," so that after the king's recapture his loss of crown and head was more likely; but the device is adduced not to exemplify Cromwell's malice, but his "wiser Art." Cromwell is thus the rehabilitation of Niccolò Machiavelli. Even the closing stanzas, while asserting the continued necessity of military force to maintain the regime, in no way condemn it. Writing in the year before Thomas Hobbes published *Leviathan* (1651) Marvell has come independently to the same conclusion, that power is essentially its own justification:

> But thou the Wars and Fortunes Son
> March indefatigably on;
> And for the last effect
> Still keep thy Sword erect:
> Besides the force it has to fright
> The Spirits of the shady Night,
> The same *Arts* that did *gain*
> A *Pow'r* must it *maintain*.

Undoubtedly Marvell means that Cromwell is to keep his "Sword erect" by keeping the blade up, ready to strike; but the assertion that it would thus "fright / The Spirits of the shady Night," notwithstanding precedents in Homer's *Odyssey* and Virgil's *Aeneid*, still calls to mind the opposite procedure: holding up the hilt as a representation of the cross. By implicitly rejecting the cross as an instrument of political power, Marvell obliquely indicates that one effect of the vast cultural revolution set in motion by the civil war was the banishing of religion from political life, just one aspect of the general secularization of Western civilization already under way at the time.

Of course what distinguishes the "Horatian Ode" is the emotional shudder that pervades it, acknowledging the wrenching destructiveness of massive social change. Marvell concedes that Charles I, in some sense, has *right* on his side, but he will not concede that the right, or justice, is an inviolable absolute to which a man must remain unshakably committed. A terrible exhilaration marks the stanza in which the "ruine" of "the great Work of Time" is regretted but unblinkingly accepted:

> Though Justice against Fate complain,
> And plead the antient Rights in vain:
> But those do hold or break
> As Men are strong or weak.

There is a finely calculated irony in the way "the *Royal Actor*" on the "*Tragick Scaffold*" occupies the very center of an ode dedicated to Cromwell's victories and furnishes the poem's most memorable lines:

> *He* nothing common did or mean
> Upon that memorable Scene:
> But with his keener Eye
> The Axes edge did try:
> Nor call'd the *Gods* with vulgar spight
> To vindicate his helpless Right,
> But bow'd his comely Head,
> Down as upon a Bed.

These lines are moving, and they seem to reflect Marvell's genuine admiration for the king as well as a vivid realization that some ineffable cultural value was lost irrecoverably with Charles's head, but nostalgia for what was passing away is subsumed in the excited awareness of the advent of what was new: "This was that memorable Hour / Which first assur'd the forced Pow'r." The word *forced* is not pejorative here; force is, finally, the hero of the poem even more than the individual Cromwell.

The brilliant ambivalence of feeling is enhanced by Marvell's deft deployment of classical precedents. The obvious Horatian model is *Odes* I.37, a celebration of Augustus's naval victory at Actium that closes with a tribute to Cleopatra's courage in committing suicide rather than facing the humiliation of a Roman triumph. In addition, Marvell has drawn upon the language and imagery of Lucan's *Pharsalia*, both in the original and in Thomas May's English translation. That Marvell's language describing Cromwell is mainly borrowed from Lucan's descriptions of Caesar (whom Lucan detested) is not an encoded condemnation of the English general; it is an aspect of Marvell's strategy for praising Cromwell not merely in spite of, but because of, qualities that are conventionally condemned. The point of the "Horatian Ode" is that Cromwell has ushered in a new era that renders "the antient Rights" obsolete.

Given the radical character of the "Horatian Ode," it is actually easier to account for the apparent anomaly of Marvell's poem "Tom May's Death." May, who died on 13 November 1650 and whose translation of Lucan seems to have influenced some passages of the "Horatian Ode," had made his reputation as a poet at the court of Charles I and apparently hoped to succeed Ben Jonson as poet laureate upon Jonson's death in 1637. According to his enemies—including the author of "Tom May's Death"—it was chagrin at having been passed over in favor of William Davenant that led May to switch sides and became a propagandist for Parliament. In the major action of the poem the shade of Ben Jonson, in "supream command" of the Elysian Fields of poets, expels May from their number for "Apostatizing from our Arts and us, / To turn the Chronicler of *Spartacus*." Critics have wondered how the same man who celebrated Cromwell in the "Horatian Ode" could only a few months later scornfully equate the Parliamentary rebellion against the king with the revolt of Roman slaves under

Spartacus, or depict the two best-known regicides of the classical world thus: "But how a double headed Vulture Eats, / *Brutus* and *Cassius* the Peoples cheats." What Marvell may well be doing in this poem is simply distancing himself from May, who seems to have been a loutish individual (according to contemporary accounts he died in a drunken stupor) and whose political choices seemed to have been determined by sheer expediency as well as personal pique. His death perhaps afforded Marvell an opportunity to deal with residual Royalist sentiment in conflict with his judgment and even to assure himself that his own changing allegiances were not motivated by venality. Given the ambiguity of Marvell's politics in 1650, it is not reasonable to exclude a poem from the canon because it seems politically incompatible with another poem. It is also difficult to deny Marvell lines such as these:

> When the Sword glitters ore the Judges head,
> And fear has Coward Churchmen silenced,
> Then is the Poets time, 'tis then he drawes,
> And single fights forsaken Vertues cause.
> He, when the wheel of Empire, whirleth back,
> And though the World's disjointed Axel crack,
> Sings still of ancient Rights and better Times,
> Seeks wretched good, arraigns successful Crimes.

It is by no means displeasing to think that Marvell had second thoughts about his dismissal of the "antient Rights" in the "Horatian Ode."

Perhaps before the end of 1650, but certainly by 1651, Marvell was employed as tutor in languages to the twelve-year-old daughter of Thomas, Lord Fairfax, who had returned to his Yorkshire estates after resigning his military command. It is not known who recommended Marvell for the post, but doubtless his own Yorkshire background was a factor. Marvell remained with Fairfax until early 1653 when he sought employment in the Cromwell government with John Milton's recommendation. Instead Cromwell procured Marvell a position as tutor to William Dutton, who was being considered as a husband for Cromwell's youngest daughter, Frances. Marvell served as Dutton's tutor until 1657, living in the house of John Oxenbridge, a Puritan divine who had spent time in Bermuda to escape Laud's reign over the Church of England. In 1657 Marvell did receive a government post with Milton as his supervisor. The period of the poet's employment as a tutor is generally thought to be the time when his greatest lyrics and topographical poems—the works on which his twentieth-century reputation is founded—were written.

Undoubtedly having their source in Marvell's sojourn with Fairfax are three poems on the general's properties at Bilbrough and Nun Appleton: "Epigramma in Duos montes Amosclivum Et Bilboreum. Farfacio," "Upon the Hill and Grove at Bill-borow To the Lord Fairfax," and "Upon Appleton House, to my Lord Fairfax." The first two of these poems, the Latin epigram and its English companion piece, allegorize topographical features in and around the Fairfax manor at Bilbrough to praise the character of Marvell's patron. The Latin poem attributes to Fairfax both the forbidding ruggedness of Almscliff and the gentleness of the hill at Bilbrough: "Asper in adversos, facilis cedentibus idem" (the same man is harsh to enemies, easy on those who yield); while the English poem elaborates upon the agreeable qualities of Bilbrough as an emblem of the man who modestly withdrew from "his own Brightness" as a military leader to a life of rural retirement. "Upon Appleton House" takes up the theme and develops it through nearly eight hundred lines into a subtle and complex meditation on the moral implications of choosing a life of private introspection over action, of withdrawal from the world rather than involvement in its affairs. Beginning as a country-house poem in the mode of Jonson's "To Penshurst," Marvell's poem expands into a leisurely survey of the entire landscape that moves with an ease that is the antithesis of the urgency of the "Horation Ode."

"Upon Appleton House" covers an array of topics with an extraordinary range of wit and tone, but its central preoccupation is the identical theme of the ode on Cromwell, only in reverse: while that poem gives an exhilarating account of the career of Cromwell's "active Star," moderated by a keen sense of the violence of "the three-fork'd Lightning," the poem on Fairfax expresses a deep affection as well as respect for its hero, tempered by just a hint that Fairfax's scruples and modesty may have been excessive and detrimental to his country. Marvell comments on the incongruity between the floral ordinance of Nun Appleton's fort-shaped flower beds and the actual warfare that had laid England waste; then he suggests that, had Fairfax's conscience been less tender, it might have been within his power to set England right:

> And yet their walks one on the Sod
> Who, had it pleased him and *God*,

Might once have made our Gardens spring
Fresh as his own and flourishing.
But he preferr'd to the *Cinque Ports*
These five imaginary Forts:
And, in those half-dry Trenches, spann'd
Pow'r which the Ocean might command.

The fine discrimination of these lines defies comment: Is there an intimation, however slight, that preference for "imaginary Forts" is not worthy of a man of Fairfax's gifts during a national crisis? But even to suggest this much is to suggest too much: it is never put in doubt that Fairfax is listening to his conscience; that is, to God. While there is regret that the best man is impeded by his very goodness from assuming the position for which he is fitted, there is no recrimination; the sorrow is, finally, a result of the inherent condition of fallen mankind:

Oh Thou, that dear and happy Isle
The Garden of the World ere while,
Thou *Paradise* of four Seas,
Which *Heaven* planted us to please,
But, to exclude the World, did guard
With watry if not flaming Sword;
What luckless Apple did we tast,
To make us Mortal, and The Wast?

If Fairfax himself has succeeded in withdrawing from the world—now become "a rude heap together hurled"—into the "lesser *World*" of Nun Appleton, "*Heaven's Center, Nature's Lap. / And Paradice's only Map*," his daughter must go out into that world in marriage to carry on "beyond her *Sex* the *line*." Always the individual hope of happy retirement is threatened by the historical necessity of society:

Whence, for some universal good,
The *Priest* shall cut the sacred Bud;
While her *glad Parents* most rejoice,
And make their *Destiny* their *Choice*.

We can only wonder how Marvell responded to the marriage of his former pupil when it came in 1657, and Maria Fairfax was joined with George Villiers, second Duke of Buckingham, elder brother of Lord Francis Villiers, and one of the most notorious rakes of the notorious Restoration era. Such a "destiny" may have shaken even the poet's cool detachment.

Many of Marvell's best-known lyrics are associated with his tenure as Maria Fairfax's tutor be-cause they deploy language and themes that appear in "Upon Appleton House." The Mower poems, for example, provide a particular focus on the undifferentiated figures of the mowing section of "Upon Appleton House" (lines 385-440). Four in number, the Mower poems are a variant of the pastoral mode, substituting a mower for the familiar figure of the shepherd (as Jacopo Sannazaro's *Piscatorial Eclogues* [1526] substitutes fishermen). "The Mower against Gardens" is the complaint of a mower against the very idea of the formal enclosed garden planted with exotic hybrids—an increasingly fashionable feature of English country estates in the seventeenth century, condemned by the mower as a perverted and "luxurious" tampering with nature at her "most plain and pure." The theme is unusual, if not unprecedented, with the most familiar treatment coming in Perdita's argument with Polixenes in *The Winter's Tale* (IV.4). As is so often the case in Marvell's poems, the point is stated in its most extreme form by his censorious mower: it is not just excess that offends him, the "Onion root [tulip bulb] they then so high did hold, / That one was for a Meadow sold"; but the very notion of the luxuriant, ornamental garden as an improvement over nature: " 'Tis all enforc'd; the Fountain and the Grot; / While the sweet Fields do lye forgot." The poem is thus pervaded by hints of timely references to the revolutionary situation of England at midcentury: the mower's strictures against formal gardens recall the Puritan's suspicion of religious images and courtly extravagance, the laboring man's bitter disdain for the self-indulgent idleness of his social "betters," and the whole vexed issue of land enclosures. Yet these are overtones not arguments, and the single-minded moralizing of the mower is certainly not in the poet's own style, although a part of his nature would doubtless sympathize with the mower's "root-and-branch" viewpoint.

The other three Mower poems, "Damon the Mower," "The Mower to the Glo-Worms," and "The Mower's Song," all express Damon's frustration at his rejection by a certain "fair Shepheardess," Juliana. It cannot be determined whether Damon is to be identified with the speaker of "The Mower against Gardens," but the voice in all the Mower poems displays the belligerent intensity of wounded self-righteousness. "Damon the Mower" is in a line of pastoral figures beginning with the Polyphemus of Theocritus, *Idylls* 11, and Ovid, *Metamorphoses* 13, and the Corydon of Virgil, *Eclogues* 2, all of whom enumer-

66.

May it please your Excellence,

It might perhaps seem fit for me to seek out words to give your Excellence thanks for my selfe. But indeed the honely Civility which it is proper for me to practise with so eminent a Person is to obey you; and to performe honestly the worke that you haue set me about. Therefore I shall use the time that your Lordship is pleas'd to allow me for writing, onely to that purpose for which you haue giuen me it; That is to render you some account of M.r Dutton. I haue taken care to examine him seuerall times in the presence of M.r Oxenbridge, as those who weigh and tell ouer mony before some witnesse ere they take charge of it. For I thought that there might possibly be some lightnesse in the Coyn, or errour in the telling, which hereafter I should be bound to make goods. Therefore M.r Oxenbridge is the best to make your Excellence an impartiall relation thereof. I shall onely say that I shall striue according to my best understanding (that is according to those Rules your Lordship hath giuen me) to increase whatsoeuer Talent he may haue already. Truly he is of a gentle and waxen disposition; and, God be praised, I can not say that he hath brought with him any euill Impression, and I shall hope to set nothing upon his Spirit but what may be of a good Sculpture. He hath in him two things which make Youth most easy to be managed, Modesty which is the bridle to Vice, and Emulation which is the spurr to Virtue. And the care which your Excellence is pleas'd to take of him is no small incouragement and shall be so represented to him. But aboue all I shall labour to make him sensible of his Duty to God. For then we begin to serue faithfully, when we consider that he is our Master. And in this both he and I ow infinitely to your Lordship, for hauing placed us in so godly a family as that of M.r Oxenbridge whose Doctrine and Example are like a Book and a Map, not onely instructing the Eare but demonstrating to the Ey which way we ought to trauell. And M.rs Oxenbridge.

Letter to Oliver Cromwell written soon after Marvell began tutoring William Dutton (Society of Antiquaries)

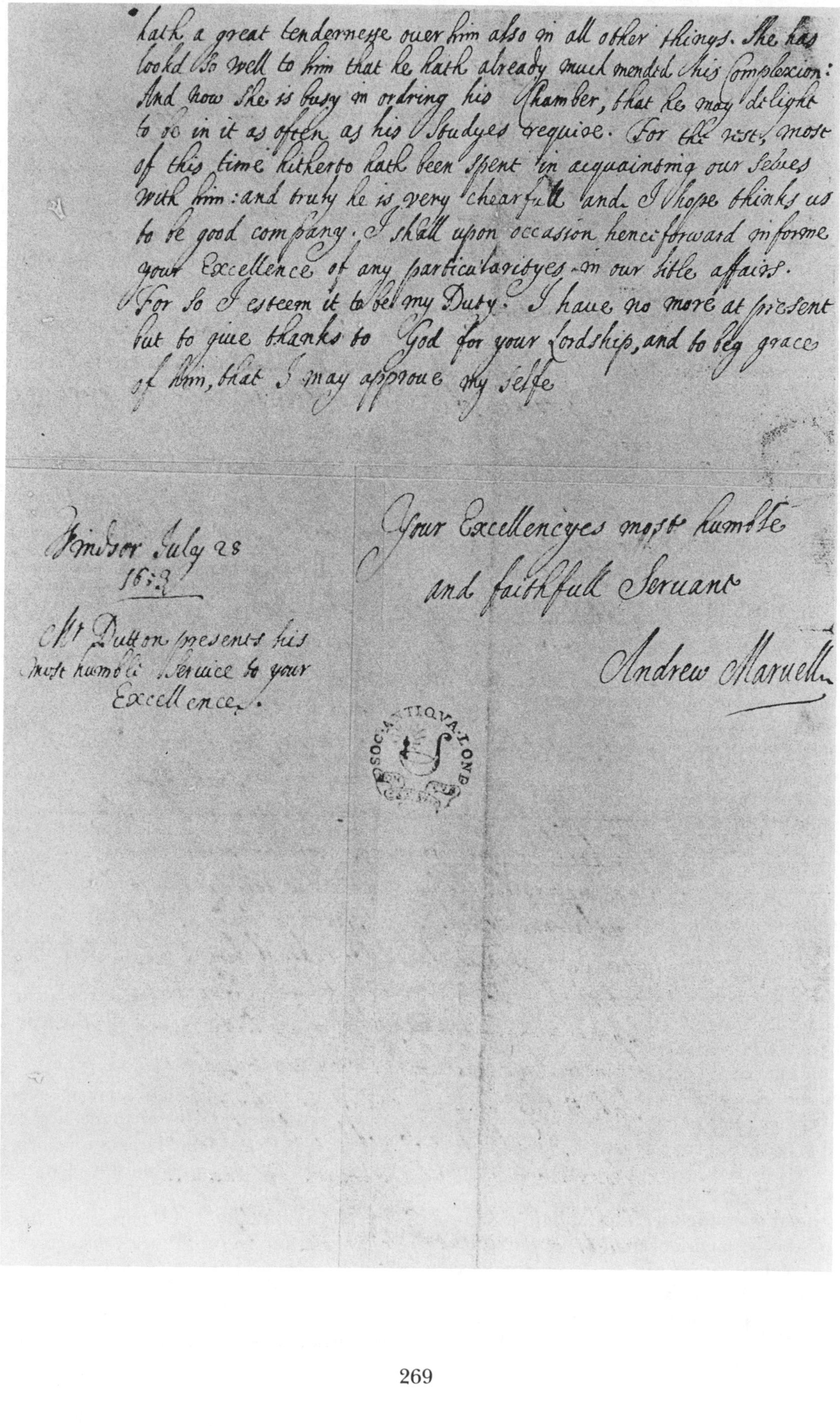

hath a great tendernesse ouer him also in all other things. She has
lookd so well to him that he hath already much mended his complexion:
And now she is busy in ordring his Chamber, that he may delight
to be in it as often as his Studyes require. For the rest, most
of this time hitherto hath been spent in acquainting our Selues
with him: and truly he is very chearfull and. I hope thinks us
to be good company. I shall upon occasion henceforward informe
your Excellence of any particularityes in our litle affairs.
For so I esteem it to be my Duty. I haue no more at present
but to giue thanks to God for your Lordship, and to beg grace
of him, that I may approue my selfe

Windsor July 28
1653

Mr Dutton presents his
most humble Seruice to your
Excellence.

Your Excellencyes most humble
and faithfull Seruant

Andrew Maruell

ate their clownishly rustic wealth and personal attributes with incredulous frustration at the beloved's refusal to respond favorably to their advances. In keeping with the classical precedents, Marvell tempers the lugubriousness of his unhappy mower by endowing him with a certain threatening aura. In "Damon the Mower" the frantic activity of the lovesick laborer results in "Depopulating all the Ground" as he "does cut / Each stroke between the Earth and Root." When he inadvertently cuts his own ankle, he is solemnly mocked with the line "By his own Sythe, the Mower mown"; but Damon dismisses this wound as inconsequential compared to that given by "*Julianas* Eyes," and the poem closes with a sinister reminder of the symbolism of the Mower: " 'Tis death alone that this must do: / For Death thou art a Mower too." Similarly, in "The Mower's Song" his obsessive fixation on desire disdained is expressed in a grim refrain, the only one in Marvell's verse, closing out all five stanzas: "For *Juliana* comes, and She / What I do to the Grass, does to my Thoughts and Me." Even "The Mower to the Glo-Worms" leaves its disconsolate speaker benighted despite the friendly efforts of the fireflies, "For She my Mind hath so displac'd / That I shall never find my home." There are undoubtedly political resonances in the vociferous mower—sprung out of the soil, brandishing his scythe, and denouncing wealthy gardeners and shepherds and scornful shepherdesses—but his menacing air is blended with a larger measure of absurd pathos. The Mower poems are thus characteristic of Marvell's aloof irony.

"The Garden" shares in this equivocal detachment, as the endless debates about its sources (in classical antiquity, the Church Fathers, the Middle Ages, hermeticism, and so on), its relation to contemporary poetry, and its own ultimate significance show. The poem has been regarded as an account of mystical ecstasy by some commentators, of Horatian Epicureanism by others; some find in it an antilibertine version of the poetry of rural retirement, while others interpret it in terms of "the politics of landscape." What seems indisputable is its congruence with the vision of reality proposed by the "Horatian Ode" and "Upon Appleton House": a virtually unbridgeable chasm is seen between contented withdrawal into contemplation and the actual life of man in the world. Ostensibly a celebration of the contemplative garden, hinting equally at the Garden of Eden and the garden enclosed of the Song of Songs, and the garden of the mind of classical philoso-

phy, "The Garden" subverts the solemnity of the meditative theme by engulfing it in irony. The dismissal of the active life, of ambition or love, in the first four stanzas is stated in terms of absurd hyperbole: the strenuous efforts of politicians, soldiers, and even poets are disparaged because they result, at best, in only the "short and narrow verged Shade" of a single wreath, "While all Flow'rs and all Trees do close / To weave the Garlands of repose." Similarly, the "lovely green" of "am'rous" plants is preferred to the conventional red and white of the Petrarchan mistress's complexion; and Apollo and Pan are supposed to have pursued Daphne and Syrinx not for the sake of their feminine charms, but for the laurel and reed into which the nymphs were transformed. The wit of these first four stanzas is highlighted by the labored elaboration of the same conceits in the Latin version of the poem, "Hortus," which lacks any lines corresponding to stanzas 5-8 of "The Garden." Sharply contrasted to, but never wholly free of, this foolery is the stunning depiction of "The Mind" and its transcendent activity, "Annihilating all that's made / To a green Thought in a green Shade." But this introspective solitude can be known only as a longed-for impossibility by the self-conscious intelligence that defines itself in relation to the Other:

> Such was that happy Garden-state,
> While Man there walk'd without a Mate:
> After a Place so pure, and sweet,
> What other Help could yet be meet!
> But 'twas beyond a Mortal's share
> To wander solitary there:
> Two Paradises 'twere in one
> To live in Paradise alone.

The speaker's petulant misogyny expresses at a deeper level a loathing for the social nature of the human condition, which creates the longing for total withdrawal into contemplative solitude and also renders it impossible.

"The Nymph complaining for the death of her Faun" posits the dichotomy in even starker terms: retirement into the innocence of nature, epitomized by a sublimely exquisite beast, is disrupted by warfare, that most violent manifestation of social conflict. Whether the "wanton Troopers riding by," who have slain the fawn belong to Prince Rupert's Royalist forces, to the Scotch covenanting army of 1640, or to Cromwell's New Model Army is finally irrelevant to their significance in the poem. They personify the turbulent strife of the world outside the garden of contemplative withdrawal that, on this occasion, they have invaded. The casual indifference with which they kill the fawn aligns them with the Cromwell of the "Horatian Ode" who, as "The force of angry Heavens flame," wreaks indiscriminate havoc. Similarly, the Nymph and the fawn are attractive but ineffectual figures, much like the King Charles of the "Ode." The Nymph, in contrast to Isabel Thwaites and Maria Fairfax of "Upon Appleton House," attempts to maintain a life of perpetual virginity and solitude, already disillusioned by "Unconstant *Sylvio*" before the advent of the "Ungentle men" who kill the fawn. At the center of the poem is the dying fawn itself. Swathed in a web of allusions to the Song of Songs and Virgil, as well as to other scriptural and classical passages, the fawn has been regarded as a symbol for Christ or the Church of England, or a *surrogatus amoris* for the deceived Nymph. The ambiguity of the fawn's significance does not, however, obscure the meaning of the poem; it *is* the meaning of the poem. In the seventy years since, it has not been better expressed than in T. S. Eliot's tercentenary essay: "Marvell takes a slight affair, the feeling of a girl for her pet, and gives it a connection with that inexhaustible and terrible nebula of emotion which surrounds all our exact and practical passions and mingles with them." Of course, in surrounding the "slight affair" of personal emotion with a panoply of traditional references with mystical overtones, Marvell anticipated the enhanced role of subjective experience in the modern world and manifested a poignant awareness of the alienation of the private individual from the public objective realm.

Alienation is likewise the keynote of Marvell's love poems, which frequently elaborate the treatment of love in "Upon Appleton House," where William Fairfax wins Isabel Thwaites by force, wresting her away from the nuns, and Maria Fairfax's marriage is anticipated as a ritual sacrifice. "Young Love" and "The Picture of little T.C. in a Prospect of Flowers" both take up a theme which originates in the Greek Anthology and proceeds through Horace to several seventeenth-century poets, including Thomas Randolph and Thomas Carew, before Marvell; that is, love for an unripe girl before or just at the threshold of nubility. What is striking in Marvell's poems is a certain ominousness: both girls are reminded that they may perish prematurely before their mature charms become threatening to men, and it is the threat of their

Marvell in 1662 (artist unknown; Wilberforce House Museum, Hull)

growing beauty that leads the poet to seek peace before he is stricken. The application to a little girl of the full Petrarchan topos of the woman who murders by a combination of beauty and disdain, as in these lines from "The Picture of little T.C.," borders on grotesquery:

O then let me in time compound,
And parly with those conquering Eyes;
Ere they have try'd their force to wound,
Ere, with their glancing wheels, they drive
In Triumph over Hearts that strive,
And them that yield but more despise.

The war of the sexes is similarly depicted in "The Fair Singer"; here the object of the poet's desire adds to the advantage of her captivating eyes the charms of an exquisite singing voice, which combine to defeat all his resistance conceived in martial terms: "And all my Forces needs must be undone, / She having gained both the Wind and Sun." "The Match" portrays the beauties of one Celia as the storehouse of Nature's vitality, the poet as the conflagration of Love's powder magazine in her presence; and in "The Gallery" the poet's soul is a portrait gallery containing pictures only of Clora in an endless variety of guises and poses. She is both "Enchantress" and "Murtheress," both Aurora and Venus. The poet confesses that he prefers the painting "at the Entrance" where she appears as a shepherdess, "with which I first was took"; but of course the point is that this "Posture," like all the rest, is just a pose, a disguise—the real "Clora" cannot be finally identified, and certainly not relied upon.

The negative view of love suggested by these heightened Petrarchan conceits is intensified by two poems which blend tragic despair with an ingenious baroque extravagance. "The unfortunate Lover" deploys a series of emblematic images of the lover as a gallantly embattled knight of despair, born by "a *Cesarian Section*" to a woman shipwrecked on rocky shoals. The state of the lover is likened to the torment of Tityrus in hell (in Lucretius's *De rerum natura*). Cormorants "fed him up with Hopes and Air, / Which soon digested to Despair." Hence the birds both nurture and consume him: "And as one Corm'rant fed him, still / Another on his Heart did bill." The lover thus exists in a condition of endlessly frustrated hope. The heraldic image at the poem's close suggests that the lover's tormented dissatisfaction makes him *only* the hero of romantic stories, but that such hopeless love is valuable not in reality, but *only* in romance:

> Yet dying leaves a Perfume here,
> And Musick within every Ear:
> And he in Story only rules,
> In a Field *Sable* a Lover *Gules*.

These lines are reminiscent of the Charles I of the "Horatian Ode," who is a "*Royal Actor*" upon the "*Tragick Scaffold*" but not really fit to rule.

"The Definition of Love" depicts the hopelessness of love in geometric terms. The lovers are like opposite poles of the globe, enviously separated by Fate's "Decrees of Steel"; to consummate this love would require the destruction of the world: "And, us to joyn, the World should all / Be cramp'd into a *Planisphere*." It is the very perfection of such love that renders impossible its temporal and physical realization:

> As Lines so Loves *oblique* may well
> Themselves in every Angle greet:
> But ours so truly *Paralel*,
> Though infinite can never meet.

The alternative to fateful, despairing passion

would seem to be cynicism. In "Daphnis and Chloe" the latter, whom nature "long had taught . . . to be coy," offers to yield when Daphnis announces that he has given over his suit and will depart forever. Daphnis refuses this desperate offer for several high-sounding reasons, but the penultimate stanza reveals that his real motive is casual cruelty: "Last night he with *Phlogis* slept; / This night for *Dorinda* kept; / And but rid to take the Air."

The masculine assault upon the reluctance of the "coy" woman lies at the heart of Marvell's best-known love poem—perhaps the most famous "persuasion to love" or carpe diem poem in English—"To his Coy Mistress." Everything we know about Marvell's poetry should warn us to beware of taking its exhortation to carnality at face value. Critics from T. S. Eliot on took note of the poem's "logical" structure, but then it began to be noticed that the conditional syllogism in that structure is invalid—a textbook case of affirming the consequent or the fallacy of the converse. Has Marvell made an error? Or does he attribute an error to the speaking persona of the poem? Or is the fallacy part of the sophistry that a seducer uses on an ingenuous young woman? Or is it a supersubtle compliment to a woman expected to recognize and laugh at the fallacy? These alternatives must be judged in the light of the abrupt shifts in tone among the three verse paragraphs. In the opening lines the seducer assumes a pose of disdainful insouciance with his extravagant parody of the Petrarchan blason:

> An hundred years should go to praise
> Thine Eyes, and on thy Forehead Gaze.
> Two hundred to adore each Breast:
> But thirty thousand to the rest.
> An Age at least to every part,
> And the last Age should show your Heart.

Although the Lady is said to "deserve this State," the compliment is more than a little diminished when the speaker adds that he simply lacks the time for such elaborate wooing. It is also likely that most women would be put off rather than tempted by the charnel-house imagery of the poem's middle section where the seducer, sounding like a fire-and-brimstone preacher, warns that "Worms shall try / That long preserv'd Virginity." Finally, the depiction of sexual intimacy at the poem's close, with its vision of the lovers as "am'rous birds of prey" who will "tear our Pleasures with rough strife," is again a disconcerting image in an ostensible seduction poem. The perso na's desire for the reluctant Lady is mingled with revulsion at the prospect of mortality and fleshly decay, and he manifests an ambivalence toward sexual love that is pervasive in Marvell's poetry.

Marvell's poems of religious inclination are few in number and so equivocal in status that one critic, J. B. Leishman, puts "religious" in quotation marks. The first problem is to decide which pieces in the Marvell canon count as religious poems. "Clorinda and Damon" and "A Dialogue between Thyrsis and Dorinda" are both pastorals with quasi-religious overtones. In the first of these Damon has met "Pan" (pastoral jargon for Jesus, as Good Shepherd) and loftily informs Clorinda that he will no longer wanton with her in "that unfrequented Cave," which she calls "Loves Shrine" but which to him is now "Virtue's Grave." Clorinda is easily (too easily?) convinced to join Damon in praising "Pan" in place of wanton frolic. In "A Dialogue between Thyrsis and Dorinda," Dorinda is so enraptured by her religious vision (of "Elizium") that she persuades Thyrsis to enter into a suicide pact with her so they can reach "Elizium" as quickly as possible. Insofar as these dialogues touch on religious themes, they might be taken as sardonic parodies of Richard Crashaw's pastoral Nativity hymn, which also includes a shepherd named Thyrsis and concludes with the shepherds offering to burn as a sacrifice in the fiery eyes of the Christ Child. "Eyes and Tears" could similarly be taken as a not altogether pious imitation of Crashaw's "The Weeper." Only the eighth stanza of Marvell's poem, a translation of his own Latin epigram on Mary Magdalene, makes an explicitly Christian reference. "Eyes and Tears" employs the baroque extravagance of "The Weeper" without Crashaw's devotional intensity.

"A Dialogue, Between The Resolved Soul, and Created Pleasure" and "A Dialogue between the Soul and Body" are essentially philosophical in tone and substance although the former does make glancing allusion to the Pauline "whole armor of God" (Ephesians 6.13-17) and the delight of "Heaven" in the soul's triumphant resistance to the temptation of worldly pleasure. The soul/body dialogue makes no expressly Christian references and, contrary to the usual fashion of such poems, shows the body getting the better of the argument and undercutting the aloof smugness of the "Resolved Soul":

What but a Soul could have the wit
To build me up for Sin so fit?

So Architects do square and hew,
Green Trees that in the Forest grew.

By the same token "On a Drop of Dew," for all its perfect meditative form, is more Neoplatonic than Christian in mood, and this is equally true of its Latin companion piece, "Ros." Both poems deploy the similitude of an evaporating drop of dew for the soul "dissolving" back into its natural home, "the Glories of th'Almighty Sun," and only a further comparison to evaporating manna provides a scriptural reference.

"Bermudas" and "The Coronet" of all Marvell's poems most resolutely develop Christian themes. The former doubtless dates from the time Marvell spent as a tutor to William Dutton in the Eton home of John Oxenbridge, who had sought refuge in Bermuda during Laud's persecution of Puritans. In part the poem is polemical: in Bermuda the psalm-singing English boatmen are "Safe from the Storms, and Prelat's rage"; but mainly it develops a vision of an earthly paradise as symbol for that withdrawal from the workaday world that is Marvell's constant preoccupation. The remote island is a garden spot of contemplative retirement, and its imagery is reminiscent of "The Garden": "He hangs in shades the Orange bright, / Like golden Lamps in a green Night." "The Coronet" is perhaps the most witheringly self-conscious poem of a poet of studied self-consciousness. Written in the tradition of John Donne's "La Corona" and George Herbert's "A Wreath," Marvell's effort at repentance by weaving "So rich a Chaplet . . . / As never yet the king of Glory wore" can be said almost to "deconstruct" the devotional tradition that it invokes. "Dismantling all the fragrant Towers / That once adorn'd my Shepherdesses head" in order to weave a garland for Christ is clearly a figure for sacred parody—application of the tropes and themes of profane love poetry to devotional poetry. Marvell finds the whole procedure, central to the religious verse of the seventeenth century, flawed by an inevitable lack of purity of intention or of sincerity. The result is implicitly idolatry, the worship of our own devices and desires:

Alas I find the Serpent old
That, twining in his speckled breast,
About the flow'rs disguis'd does fold,
With wreaths of Fame and Interest.

Letter to the "Commissioners of the Militia for the town & Country of Kingston upon Hull," written on 29 May 1660, the day on which Charles II arrived in London to assume the British throne (Pierpont Morgan Library)

Hence in a sophisticated manner, Marvell shares the Puritan suspicion of any ritual worship as not only inadequate but unworthy to express true devotion to God. Religious gesture and image (and perhaps the religious poem) must be destroyed to destroy the devil lurking within: "Or shatter too with him my curious frame: / And let these wither, so that he may die, / Though set with Skill and chosen out with Care." Thus is Puritanism a recipe for secularization: since there can be no fitting or innocent expression of religious feeling, religion must remain silent; and art and culture are left to what is profane.

During the years that Marvell served as tutor to Dutton, Cromwell's virtual ward, the poet evidently came to be on intimate footing with the Lord Protector. Toward the end of 1654 Marvell commemorated *The First Anniversary of the Government under O.C.* in more than two hundred heroic couplets. The poem was published in quarto early in the following year by Thomas Newcomb, the government printer. The praise here is considerably less equivocal than in the "Horatian Ode," but even so scholars have debated the ultimate intention of *The First Anniversary*. Is it a simple panegyric, a deliberative poem urging Cromwell to legitimate and solidify his power by having himself crowned king (the thesis of John M. Wallace), or an apocalyptic poem that celebrates Cromwell as the herald and architect of a new order of things? The last seems by far most probable, since Marvell pointedly contrasts Cromwell with "Unhappy Princes, ignorantly bred, / By Malice some, by Errour more misled," who fail to recognize "Angelique *Cromwell*" as the "Captain" under whom they might pursue "The Great Designes kept for the latter Dayes!" The greatest design in which the subordinate monarchs should join the Protector is, evidently, the destruction of the Catholic church, "Which shrinking to her *Roman* Den impure, / Gnashes her Goary teeth; nor there secure." Indeed, this poem, with its apocalyptic overtones, is the first sample of the virulent anti-Catholicism which will become central to Marvell's post-Restoration politics. He approaches the prophecy that Cromwell is the harbinger of the Millenium, but draws back into a cautious uncertainty: "That 'tis the most which we determine can, / If these the Times, then this must be the Man." What *The First Anniversary* leaves us with, finally, is a sense of the fragility of the regime that depended so much on one man, whose mortality was so pointedly signaled by his potentially fatal Hyde Park coach accident in September 1654, a central incident in the poem.

In 1657 Marvell was appointed Latin secretary, the post for which Milton had recommended him four years earlier, and wrote two different though equally public poems: "On the Victory Obtained by Blake over the Spaniards in the Bay of Sanctacruze, in the Island of Teneriff. 1657" and "Two Songs at the Marriage of the Lord Fauconberg and the Lady Mary Cromwell." The following year Cromwell died, and Marvell celebrated the late Lord Protector in *A Poem upon the Death of O.C.* Although the closing lines of this poem seem to proffer allegiance to Oliver's son, Richard Cromwell, who succeeded to his father's place, when Richard's government failed and he fled the country, the poet was a member of the Parliament that restored Charles II to the throne his father had lost. Elected M.P. for Hull in 1659, a position he held until the end of his life, Marvell was safe himself in the wake of the Restoration and well placed to help other members of the Interregnum government, including Milton, whose life he may well have saved.

Apart from two diplomatic journeys in the service of Charles Howard, Earl of Carlisle, in Holland (1662-1663) and in Russia, Sweden, and Denmark (1663-1665), Marvell remained generally in London, faithfully and energetically representing his Hull constituency of middle-class merchants. Naturally he became increasingly disenchanted with and alienated from the court of Charles II, who resorted to secret subsidies from Louis XIV and high-handed taxation measures to circumvent Parliament's reluctance to support his pro-French foreign policy and toleration of Catholicism. The most charming of Marvell's poems of this period is "On Mr. Milton's *Paradise lost*," first published in the second edition of Milton's great epic (1674). Better than anyone else, Marvell expresses the wonder that most readers have felt upon perusing Milton's work: "Where couldst thou Words of such a compass find? / Whence furnish such a vast expense of Mind?" Otherwise, Marvell's Restoration poetry is almost exclusively confined to political satire of an extremely topical bent. With these poems questions of text and authenticity of attribution are extremely vexed. During an age of severe censorship, such fierce attacks upon the government could be published or circulated only anonymously; while still alive Marvell could not safely claim authorship, and after his death a poem gained immediate currency if attributed to the re-

The cottage in Highgate where Marvell lived from 1673 until his death in 1678. This photograph was taken by John Haynes before the house was demolished in 1868 (Heal Collection, Camden Borough Libraries).

nowned patriot, whether he actually wrote it or not. Among the satires that Marvell certainly wrote, the most important are *Clarindon's House-Warming, The last Instructions to a Painter,* and *The Loyall Scot.* Reasonable arguments can also be made for *The Kings Vowes, The Statue in the Stocks-Market, The Statue at Charing Cross, A Dialogue between the Two Horses,* and one or two other minor satires. George deF. Lord argues vigorously for the inclusion in the Marvell canon of the second and third "Advice to a Painter" poems, but his contention has not been widely accepted.

Clarindon's House-Warming reverses the architectural symbolism of "Upon Appleton House" by attacking the character of Henry Hyde, Earl of Clarendon, the king's chief minister, through ridicule of the ostentatious and very expensive house he built between 1664 and 1667, a time when London was suffering from the combined effects of fire, plague, and unsuccessful war with the Dutch. *The last Instructions to a Painter* is one of several satirical burlesques of Edmund Waller's panegyric on a naval victory commanded by the king's brother, James, Duke of York, titled *Instructions to a Painter, For the Drawing of the Posture and Progress of His Majesties Forces at Sea*

(1666). Running to almost one thousand lines, *The last Instructions to a Painter* is the longest poem Marvell wrote. Although not infrequently enlivened by flashes of wit and intensity that anticipate the satires of Dryden and Pope, on the whole it lacks the clarity and universal appeal of Dryden's *Absalom and Achitophel* (1681) or Pope's *Dunciad* (1728, 1742). Perhaps the most effective of Marvell's satires is *The Loyall Scot,* which purports to be a recantation by the ghost of John Cleveland of his Royalist anti-Presbyterian satire, *The Rebel Scot* (1644). Marvell's satire on the ineptitude of the Royal Navy in an encounter with the Dutch under Michel Adriaanszoon de Ruyter (1667) is highlighted by contrast with the heroic death of the Scottish Captain Archibald Douglas. In lines that also appear in *The last Instructions to a Painter,* Marvell captures the young Scot's fiery death with the baroque intensity of his earlier manner:

> Like a glad lover the fierce Flames he meets
> And tries his first Imbraces in their sheets.
> His shape Exact which the bright flames enfold
> Like the sun's Statue stands of burnisht Gold:
> Round the Transparent fire about him Glowes
> As the Clear Amber on the bee doth Close;

And as on Angells head their Glories shine
His burning Locks Adorn his face divine.

Marvell also wrote satires in prose, which are generally more successful in themselves while providing a model, in this case, for the prose of Jonathan Swift. Of these the best are surely the two parts of *The Rehearsal Transpros'd* (1672, 1673), in which Marvell takes on the Reverend Samuel Parker, an erstwhile Puritan turned intolerant Tory Anglican, who recommended severe persecution of Protestant dissenters from the established church. The title of Marvell's work comes from George Villiers, second Duke of Buckingham's farcical mockery of Dryden's poetry, *The Rehearsal* (1672), and it engages in the same sort of high-spirited, if scurrilous, mockery in religious controversy that Buckingham had introduced into a literary quarrel. For once Marvell found himself, superficially at least, in agreement with the king, who had just issued the short-lived Declaration of Indulgence, which removed criminal penalties against Protestant dissenters and Catholic recusants alike. Charles, however, was mainly interested in protecting the recusants, and Marvell had sympathy only for the dissenters, so the marriage of convenience did not last long. Marvell continued his attack on Anglican intolerance in *Mr. Smirke; or The Divine in Mode*, which was published with his *Historical Essay on General Councils* (1676), and he is probably the author of *Remarks Upon a Late Disingenuous Discourse* (1678), which defends the independent nonconformist John Howe from the strictures of a severe Calvinist dissenter, Thomas Danson. Finally, just before his death, Marvell produced *An Account of the Growth of Popery, and Arbitrary Government in England* (1677), which blends shrewd insights into the devious machinations of the government of Charles II in circumventing Parliament with Marvell's own brand of furiously anti-Catholic intolerance.

By the time of Marvell's death, generally attributed to a fever, on 16 August 1678, there was a reward offered by the government for the identity of the author of *An Account of the Growth of Popery*, though there was little doubt who the author was. Popular rumor attributed Marvell's death to poisoning by the Jesuits. Whatever the event, the ensuing decades would see Marvell remembered essentially as a patriot, and a great many political satires, most of which he could not have written, were attributed to him. In 1681 the folio edition of *Miscellaneous Poems. By Andrew Marvell, Esq.*, including the lyrics that made the poet's twentieth-century reputation, was published under mysterious circumstances. Although there is no record that Marvell ever married, the volume is prefaced by a short note by a woman claiming to be the poet's widow and calling herself "Mary Marvell." She was in fact his housekeeper, Mary Palmer, and no one except William Empson believes that the marriage ever took place. Instead it is generally regarded as a ruse to protect Marvell's small estate from the depredations of his business partners' creditors. Whatever their motivations, the editors of the *Miscellaneous Poems* have earned the gratitude of modern readers, and it seems fitting that a certain ambiguity should surround the posthumous publication of such ambiguous poetry.

Letters:
Volume 2 of *The Complete Works in Prose and Verse of Andrew Marvell*, 4 volumes, edited by Reverend Alexander B. Grosart (London: Robson & sons, printers, 1872-1875);
Volume 2 of *The Poems and Letters of Andrew Marvell*, third edition, 2 volumes, edited by H. M. Margoliouth, revised by Pierre Legouis with E. E. Duncan-Jones (Oxford: Clarendon Press, 1971).

Bibliographies:
Gillian R. Szanto, "Recent Studies in Marvell," *English Literary Renaissance*, 5 (Spring 1975): 273-286;
Dan S. Collins, *Andrew Marvell: A Reference Guide* (Boston: G. K. Hall, 1981).

Biography:
Pierre Legouis, *Andrew Marvell: Poet, Puritan, Patriot*, second edition (Oxford: Clarendon Press, 1968).

References:
Don Cameron Allen, "Andrew Marvell: 'The Nymph Complaining for the Death of her Faun'" and "Andrew Marvell: 'Upon Appleton House,'" in his *Image and Meaning: Metaphoric Traditions in the Renaissance*, revised edition (Baltimore: Johns Hopkins Press, 1968), pp. 165-186, 187-225;
Anne E. Berthoff, *The Resolved Soul: A Study of Marvell's Major Poems* (Princeton, N.J.: Princeton University Press, 1970);
Harold Bloom, ed., *Andrew Marvell: Modern Critical Views* (New York: Chelsea House, 1989);

M. C. Bradbrook and M. G. Lloyd-Thomas, *Andrew Marvell* (Cambridge: Cambridge University Press, 1940);

R. L. Brett, ed., *Andrew Marvell: Essays on the Tercentenary of his Death* (Oxford & New York: Published for the University of Hull by Oxford University Press, 1979);

John Carey, ed., *Andrew Marvell: A Critical Anthology* (Baltimore: Penguin, 1969);

Warren L. Chernaik, *The Poet's Time: Politics and Religion in the Work of Andrew Marvell* (Cambridge: Cambridge University Press, 1983);

Rosalie L. Colie, *"My Ecchoing Song": Andrew Marvell's Poetry of Criticism* (Princeton, N.J.: Princeton University Press, 1970);

Michael Craze, *The Life and Lyrics of Andrew Marvell* (London: Macmillan, 1979);

Patrick Cullen, *Spenser, Marvell, and Renaissance Pastoral* (Cambridge, Mass.: Harvard University Press, 1970);

T. S. Eliot, "Andrew Marvell," in his *Homage to John Dryden: Three Essays on Poetry of the Seventeenth Century* (London: Hogarth Press, 1924);

William Empson, "Marvell's Garden," in his *Some Versions of Pastoral* (London: Chatto & Windus, 1935), pp. 117-145;

Empson, "Natural Magic and Populism in Marvell's Poetry," in Brett, pp. 36-61;

Kenneth Friedenreich, ed., *Tercentenary Essays in Honor of Andrew Marvell* (Hamden, Conn.: Shoestring Press, 1977);

Donald F. Friedman, *Marvell's Pastoral Art* (Berkeley: University of California Press, 1970);

George R. Guffey, *A Concordance to the English Poems of Andrew Marvell* (Chapel Hill: University of North Carolina Press, 1974);

John Dixon Hunt, *Andrew Marvell: His Life and Writings* (Ithaca, N.Y.: Cornell University Press, 1978);

Lawrence Hyman, *Andrew Marvell* (New York: Twayne, 1964);

J. B. Leishman, *The Art of Marvell's Poetry* (London: Hutchinson, 1966);

George deF. Lord, ed., *Andrew Marvell: A Collection of Critical Essays* (Englewood Cliffs, N.J.: Prentice-Hall, 1968);

Louis L. Martz, "Andrew Marvell: The Mind's Happiness," in his *The Wit of Love* (Notre Dame, Ind.: Notre Dame University Press, 1969), pp. 151-190;

C. A. Patrides, ed., *Approaches to Andrew Marvell: the York Tercentenary Essays* (London: Routledge & Kegan Paul, 1978);

Annabel M. Patterson, *Marvell and the Civic Crown* (Princeton, N.J.: Princeton University Press, 1978);

Maren-Sofie Rostvig, *The Happy Man: Studies in the Metamorphosis of a Classical Idea*, 2 volumes (Oslo: Akademisk forlag, 1954, 1958);

Kitty W. Scoular, *Natural Magic: Studies in the Presentation of Nature from Spenser to Marvell* (Oxford: Clarendon Press, 1965);

Phoebe S. Spinrad, "Death, Loss, and Marvell's Nymph," *PMLA*, 97 (January 1982): 50-59;

Spinrad, "Marvell and Mystic Laughter," *Papers on Language and Literature*, 20 (1984): 259-272;

Harold E. Toliver, *Marvell's Ironic Vision* (New Haven: Yale University Press, 1965);

James Turner, *The Politics of Landscape: Rural Scenery and Society in English Poetry 1630-1660* (Cambridge, Mass.: Harvard University Press, 1979);

John M. Wallace, *Destiny His Choice: The Loyalism of Andrew Marvell* (Cambridge: Cambridge University Press, 1968);

Ruth Wallerstein, "Marvell and the Various Light," in her *Studies in Seventeenth-Century Poetic* (Madison: University of Wisconsin Press, 1950), pp. 149-342;

Michael Wilding, ed., *Marvell: Modern Judgments* (London: Macmillan, 1969);

R. V. Young, "Andrew Marvell and the Devotional Tradition," *Renascence*, 38 (Summer 1986): 204-227.

Papers:

There are Marvell manuscripts in the collections of the British Library; the Bodleian Library, Oxford; the Public Record Office, London; and the Codrington Library, All Souls College, Oxford.

John Milton

(9 December 1608 - 8? November 1674)

Albert C. Labriola
Duquesne University

SELECTED BOOKS: *A Maske Presented at Ludlow Castle, 1634 [Comus]* (London: Printed for Humphrey Robinson, 1637);

Epitaphivm Damonis. Argvmentvm (London: Printed by Augustine Mathewes?, 1640?);

Of Reformation Touching Chvrch-Discipline in England: And the Cavses that hitherto have hindered it (London: Printed for Thomas Underhill, 1641);

Of Prelatical Episcopacy, and Whether it may be deduc'd from the Apostolical times by vertue of those Testimonies which are alledg'd to that purpose in some late Treatises: One whereof goes under the Name of Iames' Archbishop of Armagh (London: Printed by R. O. & G. D. for Thomas Underhill, 1641);

Animadversions upon the Remonstrants Defence, against Smectymnvvs (London: Printed for Thomas Underhill, 1641);

The Reason of Church-governement Urg'd against Prelaty (London: Printed by E. G. for Iohn Rothwell, 1641 [i.e., 1642]);

An Apology Against a Pamphlet Call'd A Modest Confutation of the Animadversions upon the Remonstrant against Smectymnuus (London: Printed by E. G. for Iohn Rothwell, 1642);

The Doctrine and Discipline of Divorce: Restor'd to the Good of Both Sexes, From the bondage of Canon Law, and other mistakes, to Christian freedom, guided by the Rule of Charity (London: Printed by Thomas Payne & Matthew Simmons, 1643; second edition, "revis'd and much augmented," London, 1644);

Of Education: To Master Samuel Hartlib (London: Printed for Thomas Johnson, 1644);

The Ivdgment of Martin Bucer, Concerning Divorce. Writt'n to Edward the sixt, in his second Book of the Kingdom of Christ. And now Englisht (London: Printed by Matthew Simmons, 1644);

Areopagitica: A Speech of Mr. John Milton For the Liberty of Vnlicenc'd Printing, To the Parlament of England (London, 1644);

John Milton, circa 1670 (pastel by William Faithorne; Princeton University Library)

Colasterion: A Reply to A Nameless Answer Against the Doctrine and Discipline of Divorce (London: Printed by Matthew Simmons, 1645);

Tetrachordon: Expositions Upon The foure chief places in Scripture, which treat of Mariage, or nullities in Mariage (London: Printed by Thomas Payne & Matthew Simmons, 1645);

Poems of Mr. John Milton, Both English and Latin, Compos'd at Several Times. Printed by His True Copies. The Songs were Set in Musick by Mr. Henry Lawes (London: Printed by Ruth Raworth for Humphrey Moseley, 1645);

The Tenure of Kings and Magistrates (London: Printed by Matthew Simmons, 1649; second edition, enlarged, 1650);

ΈΙΚΟΝΟΚΛΑ'ΣΤΗΣ. *in Answer to a Book Intitl'd* ΈΙΚΩ'Ν ΒΑΣΙΛΙΚΗ, *The Portraiture of his Sacred Majesty in His Solitudes and Sufferings* (London: Printed by Matthew Simmons, 1649; second edition, enlarged, London: Printed by T. N. & sold by Tho. Brewster & G. Moule, 1650);

Joannis Miltoni Angli Pro Populo Anglicano Defensio Contra Claudii Anonymi, alias Salmasii, Defensionem Regiam (Londini: Typis DuGardianis, 1651);

Joannis Miltoni Angli Pro Populo Anglicano Defensio Secunda. Contra infamen libellum anonymum cui titulus, Regii sanguinis clamor ad cœlum adversus parricidas Anglicanos (Londini: Typis Neucomianis, 1654);

Joannis Miltoni Angli pro se Defensio contra Alexandrum Morum Ecclesiasten, Libelli famosi, cui titulus, Regii sanguinis clamor ad cœlum adversùs Parricidas Anglicanos, authoren rectè dictum (Londini: Typis Neucomianis, 1655);

Considerations Touching The likeliest means to remove Hirelings out of the church. Wherein is also discourc'd of Tithes, Church-fees, Church-revenues; and whether any maintenance of ministers can be settl'd by law (London: Printed by T. N. for L. Chapman, 1659);

A Treatise of Civil Power in Ecclesiastical Causes: Shewing That it is not lawfull for any power on earth to compell in matters of Religion (London: Printed by Tho. Newcomb, 1659);

The Readie & Easie Way to Establish a Free Commonwealth, and the Excellence thereof Compar'd with The inconveniences and dangers of readmitting kingship in this nation (London: Printed by T. N. & sold by Livewell Chapman, 1660; second edition, "revis'd and augmented," London: Printed for the author, 1660);

Brief Notes Upon a late Sermon, titl'd, The Fear of God and the King; Preachd, and since Publishd, By Matthew Griffith, D. D. And Chaplain to the late King (London, 1660);

Paradise lost. A Poem Written in Ten Books by John Milton (London: Printed & sold by Peter Parker, Robert Boulter, and Matthias Walker, 1667);

Accedence Commenc't Grammar, Supply'd with Sufficient Rules, For the use of such as, Younger or Elder, are desirous, without more trouble then needs, to attain the Latin Tongue; the elder sort es-pecially, with little teaching, and their own industry (London: Printed by S. Simmons, 1669);

The History of Britain, That part especially now call'd England. From the first Traditional Beginning, continu'd to the Norman Conquest (London: Printed by J. M. for James Allestry, 1670);

Paradise Regain'd. A Poem In IV Books. To Which Is Added Samson Agonistes. The Author John Milton (London: Printed by J. M. for John Starkey, 1671);

Joannis Miltoni Angli, Artis Logicæ Plenior Institutio, Ad Petri Rami Methodum concinnata (Londini: Impensis Spencer Hickman, 1672);

Of True Religion, Hæresie, Schism, Toleration, and what best means may be us'd against the growth of Popery (London, 1673);

Poems, &c. upon Several Occasions. By Mr. John Milton: Both English and Latin, &c. Composed at several times. With a small Tractate of Education To Mr. Hartlib (London: Printed for Tho. Dring, 1673);

Joannis Miltoni Angli, Epistolarum Familiarum Liber Unus: Quibus Accesserunt, Ejusdem, jam olim in Collegio Adolescentis, Prolusiones Quædam Oratoriae (Londini: Impensis Brabazoni Aylmeri, 1674);

A Declaration, or Letters Patents of the Election of this present King of Poland John the Third, Elected on the 22d of May last past, Anno Dom. 1674, translated by Milton (London: Printed for Brabazon Aylmer, 1674);

Paradise Lost. A Poem in Twelve Books. The Author John Milton. The Second Edition Revised and Augmented by the Same Author (London: Printed by S. Simmons, 1674);

Literæ Pseudo-Senatûs Anglicani, Cromwellii, Reliquorumque Perduellium nomine ac jussu conscriptæ (Amsterdam: Printed by Peter & John Blaeu, 1676);

A Brief History of Moscovia: and of Other Less-Known Countries Lying Eastward of Russia as far as Cathay. Gather'd from the Writings of Several Eye-witnesses (London: Printed by M. Flesher for Brabazon Aylmer, 1682);

Letters of State, Written by Mr. John Milton, to most of the Sovereign Princes and Republicks of Europe. From the Year 1649. Till the Year 1659. To Which Is Added, an Account of His Life. Together with Several of His Poems (London, 1694);

Joannis Miltoni Angli De Doctrina Christiana libri duo posthumi, quos ex schedis mauscripts deprompsit et typis mandari primus curavit C. R. Sumner

(Cantabrigiae: Typis Academicis excudit Joannes Smith, 1825);

A Common-place Book of John Milton, and a Latin Essay and Latin Verses Presumed To Be by Milton, edited by A. J. Horwood, Camden Society Publications, new series 16 (Westminster: Printed for the Camden Society, 1876; revised, 1877);

A Common-Place Book of John Milton. Reproduced by the Autotype Process from the Original Manuscript in the Possession of Sir Frederick J. U. Graham.... With an Introduction by A. J. Horwood (London: Privately printed at the Chiswick Press, 1876).

Editions: *The Poetical Works of Mr. John Milton. Containing Paradise Lost, Paradise Regain'd, Sampson Agonistes, and His Poems on Several Occasions. Together with Explanatory Notes on Each Book of the Paradise Lost and a Table Never before Printed*, with notes to *Paradise Lost* by David Hume (London: Printed for Jacob Tonson, 1695);

The Works of Mr. John Milton (London, 1697);

A Complete Collection of the Historical, Political, and Miscellaneous Works of John Milton, both English and Latin; with som Papers Never Before Publish'd, 3 volumes (Amsterdam [i.e. London], 1698);

The Poetical Works of Mr. John Milton, 2 volumes (London: Printed for Jacob Tonson, 1705);

Paradise Regain'd. A Poem in Four Books. To Which is Added Samson Agonistes: and Poems on Several Occasions.... From the text of Thomas Newton, D.D. (Birmingham: Printed by John Baskerville for J. & R. Tonson, London, 1758);

Paradise Lost. A Poem, in Twelve Books.... From the Text of Thomas Newton D.D. (Birmingham: Printed by John Baskerville for J. & R. Tonson, London, 1758);

Poems upon Several Occasions, English, Italian and Latin, With Translations by John Milton.... With Notes Critical and Explanatory and Other Illustrations, edited by Thomas Warton (London: Printed for J. Dodsley, 1785);

The Poetical Works of John Milton. With a Life of the Author, by William Hayley, 3 volumes (London: Printed by W. Bulmer for John & Josiah Boydell and George Nicol, 1794-1797);

Latin and Italian Poems of Milton Translated into English Verse, and a Fragment of a Commentary on Paradise Lost, translated by William Cowper, edited by William Hayley (London: Printed by J. Seagrave for J. Johnson & R. H. Evans, 1808);

The Poetical Works of John Milton, with Notes of Various Authors. To Which are added Illustrations, and Some Account of the Life and Writings of Milton.... Second edition, with considerable additions and with a Verbal Index to the whole of Milton's poetry, 7 volumes, edited by H. J. Todd (London: Printed for J. Johnson by Law & Gilbert, 1809);

Milton's Life and Poetical Works with Notes by William Cowper.... With Adam, a Sacred Drama, 4 volumes, edited by Hayley (Chichester: Printed by W. Mason for J. Johnson, London, 1810);

The Poetical Works of John Milton.... with Imaginative Illustrations by J. M. W. Turner, 6 volumes, edited by Sir Egerton Brydges (London: J. Macrone, 1835);

The Prose Works of John Milton, 5 volumes, edited by J. A. St. John, Bohn's Standard Library (London: Bell, 1848-1881);

The Works of John Milton in Verse and Prose, Printed from the Original Editions with a Life of the Author, 8 volumes, edited by John Mitford (London: Pickering, 1851);

The Poems of John Milton, 2 volumes, edited by Thomas Keightley (London: Chapman & Hall, 1859);

English Poems by John Milton, 2 volumes, edited by R. C. Browne (Oxford: Clarendon Press, 1870; revised, 1873);

The Poetical Works of John Milton, 3 volumes, edited by David Masson (London: Macmillan, 1874; revised, 1890);

The Poetical Works of John Milton, Edited after the Original Texts, edited by H. C. Beeching (Oxford: Clarendon Press, 1900);

The Poetical Works of John Milton, edited by William Aldis Wright (Cambridge: Cambridge University Press, 1903);

The Cambridge Milton for Schools, 10 volumes, edited by A. Wilson Verity, Pitt Press series (Cambridge: Cambridge University Press, 1891-1896; revised edition of *Comus*, 1909; revised edition of *Paradise Lost*, 1910);

The Poems of John Milton, 2 volumes, edited by H. J. C. Grierson (London: Chatto & Windus, 1925);

Milton's Prose, edited by Malcolm W. Wallace (London: Oxford University Press, 1925);

Areopagitica and Other Prose Works (London: Dent, 1927; New York: Dutton, 1927);

The Student's Milton, Being the Complete Poems of John Milton, with the Greater Part of His Prose Works, Now Printed in One Volume, Together with New Translations into English of His Italian, Latin and Greek Poems, edited by Frank Allen Patterson (New York: Crofts, 1930; revised, 1933);

The Works of John Milton, 18 volumes in 21, edited by Patterson (New York: Columbia University Press, 1931-1938);

Paradise Regained, the Minor Poems and Samson Agonistes, Complete and Arranged Chronologically, edited by Merritt Y. Hughes (New York: Odyssey Press, 1937);

The English Poems of John Milton, from the Edition of H. C. Beeching Together with an Introduction by Charles Williams, and a Reader's Guide to Milton Compiled by Walter Skeat (London: Oxford University Press, 1940);

The Complete Poetical Works of John Milton, edited by Harris Francis Fletcher (Boston: Houghton Mifflin, 1941);

John Milton's Complete Poetical Works, Reproduced in Photographic Facsimile, 4 volumes, edited by Fletcher (Urbana: University of Illinois Press, 1943-1948);

John Milton: Prose Selections, edited by Hughes (New York: Odyssey Press, 1947);

The Poetical Works of John Milton, 2 volumes, edited by Helen Darbishire (Oxford: Clarendon Press, 1952-1955); republished with Latin poems edited by H. W. Garrod and Italian poems edited by John Purves (London & New York: Oxford University Press, 1958);

Complete Prose Works of John Milton, 8 volumes in 10, edited by Don M. Wolfe and others (New Haven: Yale University Press, 1953-1982);

Poems, edited by B. A. Wright (London: Dent/ New York: Dutton, 1956);

Complete Poems and Major Prose, edited by Hughes (New York: Odyssey Press, 1957);

The Complete Poetical Works of John Milton, edited by Douglas Bush (Boston: Houghton Mifflin, 1965; London: Oxford University Press, 1966);

The Prose of John Milton, edited by J. Max Patrick (Garden City, N.Y.: Doubleday, 1967);

The Poems of John Milton, edited by John Carey and Alastair Fowler (London: Longmans, Green, 1968);

The Complete Poetry of John Milton, revised edition, edited by John T. Shawcross (Garden City, N.Y.: Doubleday, 1971);

Selected Prose of John Milton, edited by C. A. Patrides (Harmondsworth, U.K.: Penguin, 1974);

John Milton: The Complete Poems, edited by Wright, with an introduction by Gordon Campbell (London: Dent / New York, Dutton, 1980);

John Milton, edited by Stephen Orgel and Jonathan Goldberg (Oxford & New York: Oxford University Press, 1991).

OTHER: "An Epitaph on the admirable Dramaticke Poet, W. SHAKESPEARE," in Mr. William Shakespeares Comedies, Histories, and Tragedies, Second Folio (London: Printed by Tho. Cotes for Robert Allot, 1632);

"Lycidas," in Justa Edovardo King, naufrago, ab Amicis moerentibus, amoris & μνείας χάριν (Cantabrigiæ: Apud Thomam Buck & Rogerum Daniel, 1638); part 2: Obsequies to the Memorie of Mr. Edward King, Anno Dom. 1638 (Cambridge: Printed by Th. Buck & R. Daniel, 1638), pp. 20-25;

Sonnet to Henry Lawes, in Choice Psalmes, Put into Musick for Three Voices, by Henry and William Lawes (London: Printed by James Young for Humphrey Moseley, 1648);

"Observations on the Articles of Peace," in Articles of Peace, made and concluded with the Irish Rebels, and Papists, by James Earle of Ormond, for and in behalfe of the late King, and by vertue of his Autoritie (London: Printed by Matthew Simmons, 1649);

The Cabinet-Council: Containing the Chief Arts of Empire, and Mysteries of State . . . By . . . Sir Walter Raleigh, published by Milton from a manuscript (London: Printed by Thomas Newcomb for Thomas Johnson, 1658).

John Milton's career as a writer of prose and poetry spans three distinct eras: Stuart England; the Civil War (1642-1648) and Interregnum, including the Commonwealth (1649-1653) and Protectorate (1654-1660); and the Restoration. When Elizabeth I, the so-called Virgin Queen and the last of the Tudors, died, James VI, King of Scots, was enthroned as Britain's king. Titled James I, he inaugurated the House of Stuart. His son and successor, Charles I, continued as monarch until he lost the Civil War to the Parliamentarians, was tried on charges of high treason, and was beheaded on 30 January 1649. For eleven years thereafter England was governed by the military commander and later Lord Protector, Oliver Cromwell, who was succeeded by his son, Richard. By 1660 the people, no longer supportive of the Protectorate, welcomed the Restoration, the return of the House of Stuart in the person of Charles II, son of the late king.

Milton's chief polemical prose was written in the decades of the 1640s and 1650s, during the strife between the Church of England and various reformist groups such as the Puritans and between the monarch and Parliament. Designated the antiepiscopal or antiprelatical tracts and the antimonarchical or political tracts, these works advocate a freedom of conscience and a high degree of civil liberty for humankind against the various forms of tyranny and oppression, both ecclesiastical and governmental. In line with his libertarian outlook, Milton wrote *Areopagitica* (1644), often cited as one of the most compelling arguments on the freedom of the press. In March 1649 Milton was appointed secretary for foreign tongues to the Council of State. In that capacity his service to the government, chiefly in the field of foreign policy, is documented by official correspondence, the *Letters of State*, first published in 1694. In that capacity, moreover, he was a vigorous defender of Cromwell's government. One of his assignments was to counteract the erosion of public support of the Commonwealth, a situation caused by the publication of the *Eikon Basilike* (1649) or King's Book, which had widespread distribution after Charles I's execution. Believed to have been written by the king himself—though composed chiefly by an episcopal divine, Dr. John Gauden, who later became a bishop—the work sought to win public sympathy by creating the image of the monarch as a martyred saint. *Eikonoklastes* (1649), or Imagebreaker, is Milton's refutation, a personal attack on Charles I, which likened him to Shakespeare's duke of Gloucester (afterward Richard III), a consummate hypocrite. As a result Milton entered into controversy with Claude de Saumaise, a French scholar residing in Holland and the polemicist who wrote on behalf of Charles I's son in exile in France.

The symptoms of failing eyesight did not deter Milton, who from an early age read by candlelight until midnight or later, even while experiencing severe headaches. By 1652 he was totally blind. The exact cause is unknown. Up to the Restoration he continued to write in defense of the Protectorate. After Charles II was crowned Milton was dismissed from governmental service, apprehended, and imprisoned. Payment of fines and the intercession of friends and family, including Andrew Marvell, Sir William Davenant, and perhaps Christopher Milton, his younger brother

Milton at age ten (portrait attributed to Cornelius Janssen; Pierpont Morgan Library)

and a Royalist lawyer, brought about Milton's release. In the troubled period at and after the Restoration he was forced to depart his home in Petty-France, Westminster, which he had occupied for eight years. He took up residence elsewhere, including the house of a friend in Bartholomew Close; eventually, he settled into a home at Artillery Walk toward Bunhill Fields. On or about 8 November 1674, when he was almost sixty-six years old, Milton died of complications from gout.

While Milton's impact as a prose writer was profound, of equal or greater importance is his poetry. He referred to his prose works as the achievements of his "left hand." In 1645 he published his first volume of poetry, *Poems of Mr. John Milton, Both English and Latin*, many of which were written before he was twenty years old. The volume manifests a rising poet, one who has planned his emergence and projected his development in numerous ways: mastery of ancient and modern languages—Greek, Latin, Hebrew, Italian; awareness of various traditions in literature; and avowed inclination toward the vocation of poet. The poems in the 1645 edition run the gamut of various genres: psalm paraphrase, sonnet, canzone, masque, pastoral elegy, verse letter, English ode, epigram, obituary poem, companion poem, and occasional verse. Ranging from religious to political in subject matter, serious to mock-serious in tone, and traditional to innovative in the use of verse forms, the poems in this volume disclose a self-conscious author whose maturation is undertaken with certain models in mind, notably Virgil from classical antiquity and Edmund Spenser in the English Renaissance.

Like the illustrious literary forebears with whom he invites comparison, Milton used his poetry to address issues of religion and politics, the central concerns also of his prose. Placing himself in a line of poets whose art was an outlet for their public voice and using, like them, the pastoral poem to present an outlook on politics, Milton aimed to promote an enlightened commonwealth, not unlike the *polis* of Greek antiquity or the cultured city-states in Renaissance Italy. When one considers that the 1645 volume was published when Milton was approximately thirty-seven years old, though some of the poems were written as early as his fifteenth year, it is evident that he sought to draw attention to his unfolding poetic career despite its interruption by governmental service. Perhaps he also sought to highlight the relationship of his poetry to his prose and to call attention to his aspiration, evident in several works in the 1645 volume, to become an epic poet. Thus, the poems in the volume were composed in Stuart England but published after the onset of the English Civil War. Furthermore, Milton may have begun to compose one or more of his mature works—*Paradise Lost*, *Paradise Regained*, and *Samson Agonistes*—in the 1640s, but they were completed and revised much later and not published until after the Restoration.

This literary genius whose fame and influence are second to none, and on whose life and works more commentary is written than on any author except William Shakespeare, was born at 6:30 in the morning on 9 December 1608. His parents were John Milton, Sr., and Sara Jeffrey Milton, and the place of birth was the family home, marked with the sign of the spread eagle, on Bread Street, London. Three days later, at the parish church of All Hallows, also on Bread Street, he was baptized into the Protestant faith of the Church of England. Other children of John and Sara who survived infancy included Anne, their oldest child, and Christopher, seven years

younger than John. At least three others died shortly after birth, in infancy, or in early childhood. Edward Phillips, Anne's son by her first husband, was tutored by Milton and later wrote a biography of his renowned uncle, which was published in Milton's *Letters of State* (1694). Christopher, in contrast to his older brother on all counts, became a Roman Catholic, a Royalist, and a lawyer.

Milton's father was born in 1562 in Oxfordshire; his father, Richard, was a Catholic who decried the Reformation. When John Milton, Sr., expressed sympathy for what his father viewed as Protestant heresy, their disagreements resulted in the son's disinheritance. He left home and traveled to London, where he became a scrivener and a professional composer responsible for more than twenty musical pieces. As a scrivener he performed services comparable to a present-day attorney's assistant, law stationer, and notary. Among the documents that a scrivener executed were wills, leases, deeds, and marriage agreements. Through such endeavors and by his practice of moneylending, the elder Milton accumulated a handsome estate, which enabled him to provide a splendid formal education for his son John and to maintain him during several years of private study. In "Ad Patrem" (To His Father), a Latin poem composed probably in 1637-1638, Milton celebrated his "revered father." He compares his father's talent at musical composition, harmonizing sounds to numbers and modulating the voices of singers, to his own dedication to the muses and to his developing artistry as a poet. The father's "generosities" and "kindnesses" enabled the young man to study Greek, Latin, Hebrew, French, and Italian.

Little is known of Sara Jeffrey, but in *Pro Populo Anglicano Defensio Secunda* (The Second Defense of the People of England, 1654) Milton refers to the "esteem" in which his mother was held and to her reputation for almsgiving in their neighborhood. John Aubrey, in biographical notes made in 1681-1682, recorded that she had weak eyesight, which may have contributed to her son's similar problems. She died on 3 April 1637, not long before her son John departed for his European journey. Her husband died on 14 March 1647.

In the years 1618-1620 Milton was tutored in the family home. One of his tutors was Thomas Young, who became chaplain to the English merchants in Hamburg during the 1620s. Though he departed England when Milton was approximately eleven years old, Young's impression on the young pupil was longstanding. Two of Milton's familiar letters, as well as "Elegia quarta" (Elegy IV), are addressed to Young. (The term *elegy* in the titles of seven of Milton's Latin poems designates the classical prosody in which they were written, couplets consisting of a verse of dactylic hexameter followed by a verse of pentameter; *elegy*, when used to describe poems of sorrow or lamentation, refers to Milton's meditations on the deaths of particular persons.) Also dedicated to Young is *Of Reformation* (1641), a prose tract; and the "TY" of the acronym SMECTYMNUUS in the title of Milton's antiprelatical tract of 1641 identifies Young as one of the five ministers whose stand against church government by bishops was admired by Milton.

From 1620 until 1625 Milton attended St. Paul's School, within close walking distance of his home and within view of the cathedral, where almost certainly he heard the sermons of Dr. John Donne, who served as dean from 1621 until 1631. The school had been founded in the preceding century by John Colet, and the chief master when Milton attended was Alexander Gill the Elder. His son, also named Alexander and an instructor at the school, did not teach Milton. Some of Milton's familiar letters are addressed to the elder and the younger Gills, with whom he maintained contact, chiefly to express gratitude for their commitment to learning and to communicate to them his unfolding plans and aspirations. During his years at St. Paul's, Milton befriended Charles Diodati, who became his closest companion in boyhood and to whom he wrote "Elegia prima" (Elegy I) and "Elegia sexta" (Elegy VI). They maintained their friendship even though Diodati attended Oxford, while Milton was at Cambridge.

On 9 April 1625, Milton, then sixteen years of age, matriculated at Christ's College, Cambridge, evidently in preparation for the ministry. For seven years he studied assiduously to receive the bachelor of arts degree (1629) and the master of arts degree (1632). With his first tutor at Cambridge, the logician William Chappell, Milton had some sort of disagreement, after which he may have been whipped. Thereafter, in the Lent term of 1626, Milton was rusticated or suspended, a circumstance to which he refers in "Elegia prima." After his return to Cambridge later that year and for the remainder of his years there, he was tutored by Nathaniel Tovey. At Cam-

Milton circa 1629 (artist unknown; National Portrait Gallery, London)

bridge Milton was known as "The Lady of Christ's," to which he refers in his sixth prolusion, an oratorical performance and academic exercise that he presented in 1628. While the reasons for the sobriquet are uncertain, one suspects that Milton's appearance seemed feminine to some onlookers. In fact, this theory is supported by a portrait of Milton commissioned by his father when the future poet was ten years old. The delicate features, pink-and-white complexion, and auburn hair, not to mention the black doublet with gold braid and the collar with lace frills, project a somewhat feminine image. Another portrait, painted while he was a student at Cambridge, shows a handsome youth, appearing somewhat younger than his twenty-one years. His long hair falls to the white ruff collar that he wears over a black doublet. His dark brown hair has a reddish cast to it, and his complexion is fair. Apart from his appearance, Milton may have been called "The Lady of Christ's" because his commitment to study caused him to withdraw from the more typical male activities of athletics and socializing.

By 1632 Milton had completed a sizable body of poetry. At St. Paul's he had translated and paraphrased Psalms 114 and 136 from Greek into English. Throughout his Cambridge years he composed many of the poems in the 1645 volume: the seven Latin elegies (three verse letters, two funeral tributes, a celebration of spring, and an acknowledgment of the power of Cupid), other Latin verse, seven prolusions, six or seven sonnets (some in Italian), and numerous poems in English. The works in English include "On the Morning of Christ's Nativity," "The Passion," "On Shakespeare," the Hobson poems, "L'Allegro," and "Il Penseroso."

The circumstances of composition of Milton's Nativity poem, classified as an ode, are recounted in "Elegia sexta," a verse letter written to Charles Diodati in early 1630. To his close friend Milton confided that the poem was composed at dawn on Christmas day in December 1629. In "Elegia sexta" Milton summarizes the poem, which, he says, sings of the "heaven-descended King, the bringer of peace, and the blessed times promised in the sacred books." Likewise, the Christ child "and his stabling under a mean roof" are contrasted with the "gods that were suddenly destroyed in their own shrines" (translation by Merritt Y. Hughes). "On the Morning of Christ's Nativity" is divided into two sections, the induction and the hymn. The induction is composed of four stanzas in rime royal, a seven-line stanza of iambic pentameter; the hymn consists of twenty-seven stanzas, each eight lines long, combining features of rime royal and the Spenserian stanza. The poem develops thematic opposition between the pagan gods—associated with darkness, dissonance, and bestiality—and Christ—associated with light, harmony, and the union of divine and human natures.

In addition to the contrasting themes, the poem addresses two of the major paradoxes or mysteries of Christianity: the Virgin Birth and the two natures of Christ. By using oxymoron or succinct paradox—"wedded Maid, and Virgin Mother"—to describe Mary, the poet suggests the mystery of the Virgin Birth, whereby Mary retains her purity and chastity despite impregnation by the godhead. To describe the combination of two natures in Christ, the poet resorts to biblical allusion, particularly Paul's letter to the Philippians (2:6-11), which recounts how the Son emptied himself of his godhead in order to take on humanity. Paul states that the Son having assumed the form of a servant or slave was obedient unto death on the cross. In the Nativity poem Milton indicates that the Son, while custom-

arily enthroned "in Trinal Unity," has "laid aside" his majesty to undergo suffering. By such biblical allusion Milton interrelates the Incarnation and Redemption. Paradoxically, Milton affirms that the heroism of the Son is attributable to his voluntary humiliation, so that, in effect, his triumph over the pagan gods is anticlimactic. Significantly, in a poem about the birth of the Savior, Milton foreshadows the death of Jesus, the consummate gesture of voluntary humiliation. The manger is described as a place of self-sacrifice, where the light from the star overhead and the metaphoric reference to the fires of immolation converge: "secret altar touched with hallowed fire."

Not to be overlooked is Milton's use of mythological allusions to dramatize the effect of Christ's coming. Thus, the Christ child is characterized as triumphant over his pagan adversaries, one of whom, Typhon, is "huge ending in snaky twine." Typhon, the hundred-headed serpent and a leader of the Titans, rebelled against Zeus, who cast a thunderbolt against him. After his downfall he was incarcerated under Mount Aetna and tormented by the active volcano. Such myths were typically related to the Hebraic-Christian tradition in numerous ways: in illustrated Renaissance dictionaries and encyclopedias, editions of Ovid's *Metamorphoses*, and other lexicons known to Milton. Indeed, early biographers report that Milton himself was planning a similar compilation and interpretation of myths, though this work was never completed. Traditionally, Typhon, his revolt against Zeus, and his subsequent punishment are analogues of Satan's rivalry of the godhead, of his downfall thereafter, and of his everlasting torment in the fires of Hell. Thus, the triumph in the Nativity poem looks backward to the War in Heaven while anticipating the final conquest over Satan foretold in the Apocalypse. The appearance of Typhon as a multiheaded serpent is further correlated by Renaissance commentators with the biblical figure of Leviathan, the dragonlike monster associated with Satan in interpretations of the Hebraic and Christian scriptures. At the same time, the Christ child is likened to the infant Hercules, who overcame the serpent that attacked him in his cradle. The foregoing examples typify how Milton's erudition and literary imagination enable him to pursue and synthesize a wide range of mythological and biblical allusions.

Illustrated Renaissance lexicons, along with manuals of painting, which guided artists and au-

*Title page for the volume in which Milton collected his early
poems, many written before he was twenty*

thors in the use and significance of visual details,
may be employed to interpret other allegorical figures in the Nativity poem. Thus, at the birth of
the Savior, the poem recounts how "meek-eyed
Peace" descends, "crowned with Olive green,"
moved by "Turtle wing," and "waving wide her
myrtle wand." Such visual details suggest the
peace and harmony between the godhead and humankind when the dove returned with the olive
branch after the Deluge and when the Holy
Spirit, figured as a dove, descended at the baptism of the Lord.

A dominant feature of the Nativity poem is
the frequent reference to pagan gods, many of
whom are included in the epic catalogue in book
1 of *Paradise Lost*. One such figure is Osiris,
whose shrine in the Nativity poem is described:
"with Timbrel'd Anthems dark / the sable-stoled
Sorcerers bear his worshipt Ark." This descrip-

tion suggests a funeral procession, thereby dramatizing the causal relationship between the birth of
Christ and the death of the pagan gods. Additionally, the phrase "worshipt Ark" calls attention to
the ark of the Covenant, associated with the tab-
lets of law from the Old Dispensation. Christ,
however, rewrites the law in the hearts of humankind, a process to which Milton's poem alludes.
The Chosen People of the Old Dispensation
thus anticipate the faithful Christian community centered on Jesus. The poem presents
the first such community when the holy family,
shepherds, angels, and narrator unite in their ado-
ration of the Christ child. The narrator endeavors to join his voice to the chorus of angels so
that his sacred song and devotional lyrics are har-
monized with theirs. He also informs us of the imminent arrival of the Magi, who will enlarge the
community of worshipers and chorus of praise.
Characteristically, the poem highlights unity and
harmony between humankind and the godhead,
earth and Heaven, the Old and New Dispensa-
tions.

What also emerges from the Nativity poem
is an overriding awareness of Christian history,
which is both linear and cyclical. As time unfolded, Old Testament events were fulfilled in
Christ's temporal ministry. Thereafter, the faithful community looks toward the Second Coming.
Along this linear disposition of time there are recurrent foreshadowings and cyclical enactments
of triumphs over God's adversaries. Like the Apocalypse, the Nativity poem foresees that the ultimate defeat of Satan, having been prefigured in
numerous ways, will be one of the climactic
events of Christian or providential history.

Despite its early date of composition, the Nativity poem foreshadows many features of
Milton's major works: the allusions to mythology
and their assimilation to the Hebraic-Christian tradition, the conflict between the godhead and numerous adversaries, the emphasis on voluntary
humiliation as a form of Christian heroism, the
paramount importance of the redemptive ministry of the Son, and the Christian view of history.

Probably intended as a companion piece to
the Nativity poem, "The Passion" was written at
Easter in 1630. Only eight stanzas in rime royal
were composed, presumably as the induction. Appended to the unfinished work is a note indicating that the author found the subject "to be
above the years he had, when he wrote it, and
nothing satisfied with what was begun, left it unfinished." The eight stanzas clarify Milton's unful-

filled intent: to dramatize more fully the humiliation of the Son, "sovereign Priest" who "Poor fleshly Tabernacle entered."

"On Shakespeare," Milton's first published poem, was composed in 1630 and printed in the Second Folio (1632) of Shakespeare's plays, where it was included with other eulogies and commendatory verses. Milton's poem, a sixteen-line epigram in heroic couplets, was included perhaps because of the intercession of his friend and eventual collaborator Henry Lawes, a musician and composer, who wrote the music for Milton's *Comus* (1637) and probably for the songs of "Arcades" in Milton's 1645 *Poems*. Milton celebrates his friend's musical talent in Sonnet XIII. Lawes's patron was William Herbert, third Earl of Southampton, to whom the Second and Third Folios of Shakespeare's plays were dedicated. Milton's poem echoes a prevalent opinion evident in other commendatory verses—that Shakespeare, the untutored genius with only a grammar-school education, was a natural poet whose "easy numbers flow" in contrast to "slow-endeavoring art." Perhaps the implied contrast is between the spontaneity of Shakespeare and the more deliberate and learned composition of Ben Jonson. The foregoing contrast is explicit in "L'Allegro," where Shakespeare's plays, the products of "fancy's child" who composes his "native Wood-notes wild," are contrasted with Jonson's "learned Sock." The reference to Jonson calls attention to the sock or low shoe worn by actors during comedy, as well as to the learned imitation of classical dramaturgy practiced by Jonson, who had a university education. Ironically, Jonson's commendatory poem on Shakespeare, included in the First Folio (1623) and republished in the folios thereafter, is the most renowned of the lot. It cites the excellence and popularity of Shakespeare as a dramatist despite his "small Latin, and less Greek," an allusion, no doubt, to his lack of education beyond grammar school. More to the point, Jonson used the metonymy of the sock to appraise Shakespearean comedy as nonpareil: "when thy socks were on / Leave thee alone." Therefore, Milton may have appropriated but adapted the allusion in order to contrast the learned and spontaneous playwrights, respectively Jonson and Shakespeare.

Central to the poem is Milton's recognition that an erected monument, possibly even the Stratford burial site with its bust of Shakespeare, is unsuitable to memorialize the playwright's unique genius. Ultimately, Milton argues that Shakespeare alone can and does create a "livelong Monument": his readers transfixed by wonder and awe. So long as his works are read, his readers will be immobilized when confronting his transcendent genius. To be sure, the inadequacy of stone or marble monuments to perpetuate one's memory is one major theme in Shakespeare's sonnets; a complementary theme is the permanence of literary art despite the mutability and upheaval in the human condition. Milton integrates both themes from Shakespeare's sonnets into his poem, perhaps to emphasize that the unique achievement of Shakespeare must be memorialized by the words and ideas of none other than the master poet and dramatist himself. Despite his admiration for Shakespeare, Milton in his prose and poetry explicitly referred to the playwright only three times: in "On Shakespeare," "L'Allegro," and *Eikonoklastes*. Despite the paucity of explicit reference, commentators have, nonetheless, sought to identify verbal parallels between the works of Shakespeare and Milton. Though such parallels or apparent echoes abound, they are inadequate to establish source or influence. Virtually identical similarities may be adduced between the works of Milton and the writings of other Elizabethans. It seems unlikely that Milton, having prepared himself to be an author of religious and biblical poetry, relied heavily on Shakespeare, whose dramatic works are vastly different in conception and subject matter.

Two of the most amusing poems of the Cambridge years were written about Thomas Hobson, the coachman who drove the circuit between London and Cambridge from 1564 until shortly before his death on 1 January 1631. Several of Milton's fellow students also wrote witty verses. In Milton's first poem, "On the University Carrier," Death is personified; his attempts to claim Hobson have been thwarted in various ways. Hobson, for instance, is described as a "shifter," one who has dodged Death. In effect, his perpetual motion made him an evasive adversary until he was forced to discontinue his trips because of the plague; then Death "got him down." The allusion is to a wrestling match, Hobson having been overthrown. Death is personified, in turn, as a chamberlain, who perceives Hobson as having completed a day's journey. He escorts the coachman to a sleeping room, then takes away the light. The second poem, "Another on the Same," is more witty as it elaborates a series of paradoxes. Thus, "an engine moved with wheel and weight" refers at once to Hobson's coach—the means of his livelihood—and to a timepiece. The circuit of the coachman is likened to movement around the face of a timepiece, motion being equated with time. The assertion that "too much breathing put him out of breath" refers to the interruption of his travel caused by the plague. While idle, in other words, he himself took ill and died. Furthermore, the poem likens his former travel to the waxing and waning of the moon, a reciprocal course of coming and going. These playful poems that treat the topic of death may be contrasted with Milton's lamentations, such as his funeral tributes, "Elegia secunda" (Elegy II) and "Elegia tertia" (Elegy III), and the later renowned pastoral elegies: "Lycidas," which memorializes Edward King, and "Epitaphium Damonis" (Damon's Epitaph), which mourns the loss of Charles Diodati.

Probably in 1631, toward the end of his stay at Cambridge, Milton composed "L'Allegro" and "Il Penseroso," companion poems. They may have been intended as poetic versions or parodies of the prolusions, the academic exercises at Cambridge that sometimes involved oppositional thinking. Clearcut examples include Milton's Prolusion I ("Whether Day or Night Is the More Excellent") and Prolusion VII ("Learning Makes Men Happier than Does Ignorance"). The correspondences and contrasts between "L'Allegro" and "Il Penseroso"—in themes, images, structures, and even sounds—are innumerable. Essentially, Milton compares and contrasts two impulses in human nature: the active and contemplative, the social and solitary, the mirthful and melancholic, the cheerful and meditative, the erotic and Platonic. Some commentators have identified Milton with the personality type of "Il Penseroso," and Charles Diodati with that of "L'Allegro." Though the poems anatomize each personality type and corresponding life-style apart from the other, the overall effect may be to foster the outlook that a binary unit, which achieves a wholesome interaction of opposites, is to be preferred. While it is difficult to assess the autobiographical significance of the companion poems or to develop a serious outlook when Milton himself may have composed them playfully, "L'Allegro" and "Il Penseroso" graphically demonstrate the dialectic that distinguishes much of Milton's poetry, particularly the dialogues and debates between different characters in various works, including the Lady and Comus in *Comus*, the younger and elder brothers in the same work, Satan and Abdiel in *Paradise Lost*, Adam and Eve, Samson and his visitors, and the Christ and the tempter in the wilderness of *Paradise Regained*.

Having spent seven years at Cambridge, Milton entered into studious leisure at his parents' home in Hammersmith (1632-1635) and then at Horton (1635-1638). Perhaps he was caring for his parents in their old age because his sister and brother were unable to do so. Anne had become a widow in 1631 and had two young children. Probably in 1632 she married Thomas Agar, a widower who had one young child. Milton's younger brother, Christopher, was a student at Christ's College. The situation with his parents may explain why Milton, after Cambridge, did not accept or seek a preferment in the church. Although he may still have intended to become a minister, it seems likely that the prevailing influence of William Laud, Archbishop of Canterbury, who established and enforced ecclesiastical and religious regulations, deeply affected Milton's outlook. The most concise but cryptic explanation for his eventual rejection of the ministry as a career is provided by Milton himself, who in one of his prose treatises, *The Reason of Church-governement* (1642), comments that he was "church-outed." An undated letter to an unidentified friend, a document surviving in manuscript in the Trinity College Library at Cambridge, sheds further light on Milton's view of the ministry as a career. Some commentators speculate that Thomas Young is the addressee. Another influential factor in Milton's decision may have been his longstanding inclination to become a poet, evident in poems written in his Cambridge years and published in the 1645 edition. One of the most self-conscious, though ambiguous, statements concerning Milton's sense of vocation is Sonnet VII ("How soon hath time"). Unfortunately, it cannot be accurately dated, though 1631-1632 seems likely. In the poem he refers to the rapid passing of time toward his "three and twentieth year." His "hastening days fly on with full career," though the direction of movement, toward the ministry or poetry, goes unidentified. In any case, he contends that his process of development toward "inward ripeness" continues under the allseeing eye of Providence.

Milton's course of study in his leisure is outlined in Prolusion VII, which was influenced by Francis Bacon's *Advancement of Learning* (1605). History, poetry, and philosophy (which included natural science) are celebrated as important to individual growth and to civic service. Milton's *Of Education* (1644), an eight-page pamphlet written in

Manuscript for Sonnet VII, probably written in 1631 or 1632 (MS R.3.4, Trinity College Library, Cambridge)

the early 1640s, elaborates on many of the ideas in Prolusion VII and cites specific authors to be read. Autobiographical statements in various forms emerge from Milton's period of private study, which enabled him to supplement extensively his education at Cambridge and to read numerous authors of different eras and various cultures. In a 23 November 1637 letter to Charles Diodati, Milton indicated the progress of his study, particularly in the field of classical and medieval history, involving the Greeks, Italians, Franks, and Germans. At this time, moreover, Milton kept two important records of his reading and writing. The "Trinity Manuscript" or "Cambridge Manuscript," so called because it is kept in the Library of Trinity College, Cambridge, includes works such as "Arcades," *Comus*, the English odes, "Lycidas," "At a Solemn Music," and other later, but short, poems. Also in the manuscript are sketchy plans and brief outlines of dramas, some of which were eventually transformed and assimilated to *Paradise Lost*. For some of the poems, the "Trinity Manuscript" includes various drafts and states of revision. The second record kept during this period is the commonplace book (now in the British Library), which lists topics under the threefold Aristotelian framework of ethics, economics, and political life, topics that aroused Milton's interest and that were later incorporated into his prose works. The entries include direct quotations or summaries, with sources cited, so that one learns not simply what books Milton read but also what editions he used.

Two important works that Milton wrote during the years of studious leisure include *A Maske Presented at Ludlow Castle* and "Lycidas." The masque was first performed on 29 September 1634, as a formal entertainment to celebrate the installation of John Egerton, Earl of Bridgewater, as lord president of Wales. The performance was held in the Great Hall of Ludlow Castle in Shropshire, close to the border of Wales. The composer of the music was Henry Lawes, also the music tutor of the Egerton children. The three children—Alice (fifteen), John (eleven), and Thomas (nine)—enacted the parts of the Lady, the elder brother, and the younger brother. Lawes himself was the Attendant Spirit, named Thyrsis. Other characters include Comus, a tempter, by whose name the masque has been more commonly known, at least since the eighteenth century, and Sabrina, a nymph of the Severn River. Because the earl of Bridgewater had taken up his viceregal position without his family having accompanied him, a reunion was planned. To honor the earl of Bridgewater and to use the occasion of family reunion so that his children could act, sing, and dance under his approving eye are other purposes of the masque.

While *Comus* may be examined in relation to masques of the same era, most notably the collaborations of Ben Jonson and Inigo Jones, the remoteness of Ludlow prevented Milton and Lawes from mounting the sort of spectacle with elaborate scenery, complicated machinery, and astounding special effects that Jones and Jonson produced. Nor were trained dancers and singers transported from London. Nevertheless, *Comus* does have scenery, chiefly for its allegorical significance; singing, especially by individuals, such as the Lady, Sabrina, and Thyrsis; and dancing, both the riotous antimasque of Comus and his revellers and the concluding song and dance of triumph featuring the three children and others referred to as "Country-Dancers," all under the direction of Lawes in his role as the Attendant Spirit. The three major settings of the masque are the "wild Wood" at the outset, actually a location indoors decorated with some foliage (more imaginatively depicted by vivid language); the palace of Comus, in which the tables are "spread with all dainties"; and the outdoors, near the lord president's castle and within view of the town of Ludlow. These elements of spectacle are incorporated into a plot severely limited by the circumstances of the celebration and by the fact that only six notable players, three of them children of the earl of Bridgewater, participated.

Within these limitations Milton wrote a masque—actually, it is more a dramatic entertainment—that develops the theme of temperance and its manifestation in chastity. The theme evolves against the three major settings and by reference to the character of the Lady. From the outset of the masque, the Lady is separated from her two brothers in the "wild Wood," which suggests the mazes and snares that confuse and entrap unwary humankind. Allegorically, the topography signifies the vulnerability of humankind to misdirection, the result of having pursued intemperate appetites rather than the dictates of right reason, or the consequence of having been deceived by an evil character who professes "friendly ends," the phrase used by Comus in his plans to entrap the Lady. Misled by Comus, who appears to be a "gentle Shepherd" and innocent villager, the Lady travels to his "stately Palace set out with all manner of deliciousness," where she, while "set in an enchanted chair," resists the offer to drink from the tempter's cup. Thereafter, she sits "in stony fetters fixed and motionless" though continuing to denounce the tempter and his blandishments. Despite her immobility, she affirms the "freedom of my mind." Her brothers "rush in with Swords drawn," so that Comus is put to flight; and Sabrina, "a Virgin pure" and "Goddess" of the Severn River, sprinkles drops of water on the breast of the Lady to undo the spell of the enchanter. When liberated, the Lady and her brothers "tri-

umph in victorious dance / Over sensual folly and Intemperance."

The suspense, adventure, and dramatic rescue enhance the conflict between the tempter and his prospective victim. Typically, Milton uses classical analogues to cast light on the situation. The Lady is likened to the goddess of chastity, Diana, who frowned at suggestions of lasciviousness and whose role as huntress made her a formidable adversary, one whose virtue was militant, not passive. The Lady is also likened to Minerva, the goddess of wisdom, on whose shield is pictured one of the Gorgons, whose look would turn one to stone. By analogy the Lady's disapproving glance casts dread into lustful men. The classical analogues of the enchanter are best explained by his parentage, Bacchus and Circe. His father is the god of wine and revelry; his mother is the sorceress who turned Ulysses' mariners into swine when they imbibed the drink that she proffered. In fact, the journey of Ulysses and the temptations encountered by him and his men provide a context in which to understand the travel of the Lady through adversity, her endeavor to withstand temptation, and the reunion that she anticipates.

These classical analogues and others like them call attention to a moral philosophy that contrasts the lower and higher natures of humankind. Degradation or sublimation, respective inclinations toward vice or virtue, are the opposite impulses adumbrated in the masque. Accordingly, Comus's followers, having yielded to the vice of intemperance, are degraded, so that they appear "headed like sundry sorts of wild Beasts." They were imbruted when, "through fond intemperate thirst," they drank from Comus's cup. Their "foul disfigurement" is a defacement of the "express resemblance of the gods" in the human countenance. With his charming rod in the one hand and the glass containing the drink in the other, Comus is indeed akin to his mother, Circe. Like her, he has attracted a rout of followers, whose antimasque revelry, both in song and dance, suggests a Bacchanal, the sensualistic frenzy associated with his father. Before, during, and after her encounter with Comus the Lady has a "virtuous mind," and she is accompanied by "a strong siding champion Conscience," enabling her to see "pure-eyed Faith," "white-handed Hope," and the "unblemished form of Chastity." In this series of three virtues chastity is substituted for charity, which typically appears along with faith and hope. Milton therefore suggests

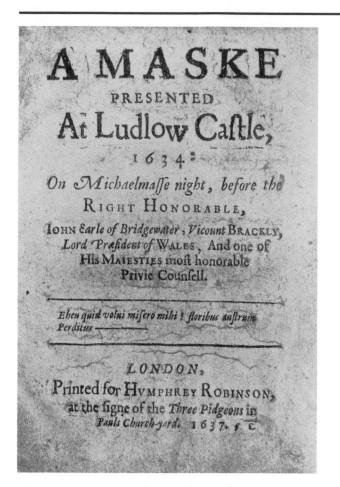

Title page for the first edition of Comus, *written for performance by the three children of John Egerton, Earl of Bridgewater, and their music tutor, Henry Lawes*

that chastity and charity are interrelated. Chastity is a form of self-love, not vanity but a wholesome sense of self-worth that enables one to value the spirit over the flesh and to affirm the primacy of one's higher nature. When viewed from this perspective, chastity is the necessary prerequisite to one's love of God, not to mention one's neighbor.

The moral philosophy of *Comus* reflects the imprint of Neoplatonism. In the Renaissance, particularly between 1450 and 1600, the works of Plato were reinterpreted and the central ideas emphasized. Beginning in Italy at the Platonic Academy of Florence, Renaissance Neoplatonism eventually spread throughout the Continent and entered the intellectual climate of England. The Renaissance version of Platonism synthesized the ideas of Plato and Plotinus with elements of ancient mysticism, all of which were assimilated, in turn, to Christianity. The fundamental tenet of Renaissance Neoplatonism asserted by Marsilio Ficino (1433-1499), one of the foremost intellectu-

als of the Florentine Academy, is that "the soul is always miserable in its mortal body." The soul, having descended from the realm of light, strives to return homeward. While on earth, the soul is immersed in the darkness of the human condition and imprisoned in the human body. In effect, the soul and the body are in a state of tension, the one thriving at the other's expense. When the appetites are denied virtue prevails, and the soul is enriched. When, on the other hand, the appetites of the flesh are indulged vice predominates, and the soul suffers. The term *psychomachia*, which means "soul struggle," designates the inner conflict that one experiences as virtue and vice contend for dominance. The foregoing paradigm is typical of certain Renaissance paintings of the fifteenth and sixteenth centuries. Several works of Perugino and Andrea Mantegna, having been influenced by Neoplatonic philosophy, depict the contention between *ratio* and *libido*, or reason and desire. These paintings show classical gods and goddesses whose allegorical significance was established. Venus and Cupid embody desire and its attendant vices; Diana and Minerva, to whom the Lady of *Comus* is likened, signify reason and its accompanying virtues.

Another tradition that may have contributed to *Comus* is the morality drama of the late Middle Ages, which uses allegorical characters to present the conflict between the virtues and vices. Furthermore, Edmund Spenser's allegorical treatment of temperance and chastity in *The Faerie Queene* (1590, 1596) is pertinent to an understanding of Milton's work. After all, Milton in *Areopagitica* refers to the "sage and serious poet Spenser," whom he calls "a better teacher than Scotus and Aquinas, describing true temperance under the person of Guyon." Much as Sir Guyon's temperance in book 2 of Spenser's epic anticipates the Lady's virtue in *Comus*, so too Britomart, the female knight in book 3, by her chastity foreshadows the Lady's heroism. While the depiction of the natural setting in *Comus*, such as the maze of woods in which the Lady is lost, resembles at times the topography in *The Faerie Queene*, both English and Continental pastoral dramas of the Renaissance also provide analogues, including John Fletcher's *Faithful Shepherdess* (1610) and Torquato Tasso's *Aminta* (1573).

Within the dynamic conflict between the virtues and vices, the role of reason, particularly in maintaining one's inner liberty, is crucial. If right reason, or *recta ratio*, enables one to see the light of virtue, then the Lady has a rational and imaginative vision of the Platonic ideals of faith, hope, and chastity, for which she is the earthly embodiment. But when reason is misled by the appetites, it is no longer effective. Upstart appetites gain control of a person in whom the legitimate predominance of reason has been subverted. Such a person in whom right reason no longer functions is enslaved by vice. Inward servitude having been permitted, enslavement by an external captor becomes a sign of one's loss of self-government. The congruence of inner and outer thralldom is emphasized by Milton in various works, ranging from *The Tenure of Kings and Magistrates* (1649), an antimonarchical tract in which he argues that "bad men" are "all naturally servile," to *Paradise Lost*, where in book 12 the archangel Michael explains to Adam that Nimrod has tyrannized others under the sufferance of God, who permits "outward freedom" to be enthralled as a sign and consequence that one is enslaved by "inordinate desires" and "upstart Passions," which create a condition of effeminacy. Thus, Neoplatonism may be combined with moral philosophy and Christian theology in order to contrast the rational or virtuous freedom of the Lady in *Comus* with the enslaved state of the enchanter's followers. Renaissance faculty psychology is also involved because it highlights the interaction of sensory perception, the appetites or passions, reason, and the will.

Milton himself may be used as a commentator on the contest between virtue and vice in *Comus*. His private exposition of Christian theology, *De Doctrina Christiana* (The Christian Doctrine), which was discovered in the nineteenth century and published in 1825, includes a section in which he defines and classifies virtues and vices, then cites scriptural passages, called proof-texts, to substantiate his views. Temperance is "the virtue which prescribes bounds to the desire of bodily gratification." Under it are "comprehended sobriety and chastity, modesty and decency." Chastity "consists in temperance as regards the unlawful lusts of the flesh." Opposed to chastity is effeminacy, which licenses the appetites and promotes sensual indulgence. *De Doctrina Christiana* may also be used to distinguish the two kinds of temptation at work in *Comus*: evil and good. In *De Doctrina Christiana* Milton explains that a temptation is evil "in respect of him who is tempted." Having yielded to temptation, one suffers the evil effects, enslavement to upstart passions and at times external thralldom, pre-

cisely what befall the enchanter's victims in *Comus*. A good temptation, on the other hand, is directed at the righteous "for the purpose of exercising or manifesting their faith or patience," a definition that aptly pertains to the Lady in *Comus*. Biblical examples, particularly Abraham and Job, are cited in *De Doctrina Christiana*. The results of good temptation are described as "happy issue," an assertion supported by a biblical proof-text, James 1:12: "Blessed is the man that endureth temptation; for when he is tried, he shall receive the crown of life." In *Comus*, phrases such as "happy trial" and "crown of deathless praise" are succinct references to the good temptation undergone by the Lady and the heavenly reward for her Christian heroism.

When the rich and diverse contexts surrounding *Comus* are thus recognized, Milton's composition becomes more meaningful. Seemingly minor details, including references to birds, fit into the overall design. Snares are mentioned, such as "lime-twigs," which result from the application of a glutinous substance that prevents a bird from flying away. A bird thus trapped signifies a foolish person enslaved to his or her passions. The virtuous Lady, on the other hand, is described by her elder brother in another way: "She plumes her feathers, and lets grow her wings." Her freedom to elude Comus's temptations is signified by her readiness to fly. Flight also connotes her sublimated and rarefied ascent from the human condition. Other verbal images are auditory but at times may involve actual music. Comus and his followers when performing the antimasque revelry create "barbarous dissonance," whereas verbal imagery suggests that the Lady's "Saintly chastity" causes "Angels" to communicate with her: "in clear dream and solemn vision" she learns "of things that no gross ear can hear."

The characterization of the Lady as an exemplar of temperance and chastity and the definition of her Christian heroism acquire focus in two debates, the one between the two brothers, the other between the Lady and Comus. The younger brother stresses the pathos of his sister's situation: she is helplessly and hopelessly lost in the woods and vulnerable to threats from beasts and mankind alike. The elder brother counters his younger brother's anxieties, arguing that their "sister is not defenceless left" but armed with "a hidden strength," chastity. In his unfolding exposition of the strength afforded by chastity, the elder brother alludes to Neoplatonism,

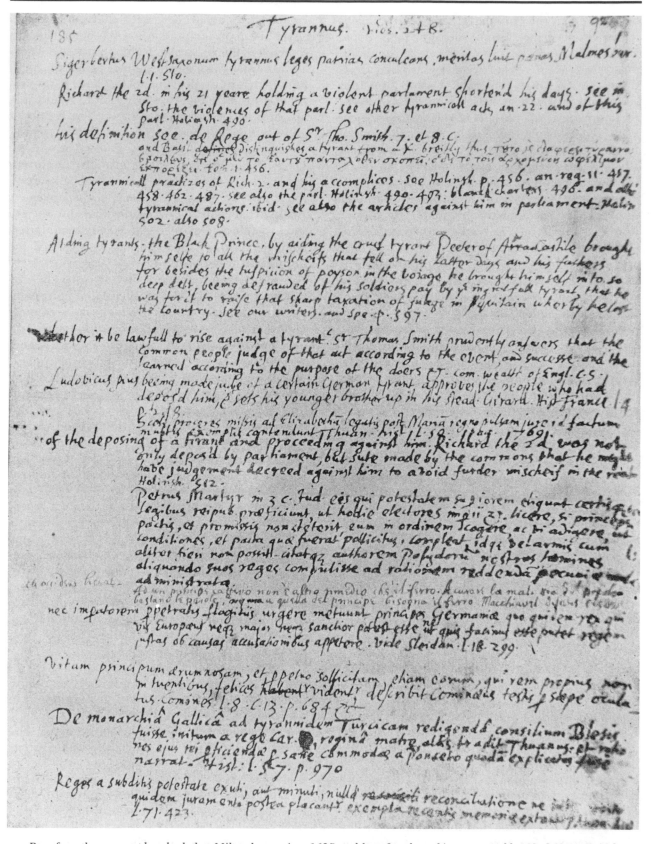

Page from the commonplace book that Milton began circa 1635 and kept for about thirty years (Add. MS. 36354, British Library) These notes probably date from 1639-1641.

moral philosophy, Christian theology, faculty psychology, and the other contexts in which the Lady's defense against the wiles of Comus is more clearly understood.

In the Lady's debate with the enchanter the theoretical exposition of the elder brother is translated into action. The debate, reminiscent of Milton's prolusions at Cambridge, pits the sophistry of Comus against the Lady's enlightened reasoning, which is informed by her commitment to virtue, specifically temperance and chastity. Comus's palace, with "all manner of deliciousness" and "Tables spread with all dainties," is intended to arouse the Lady's appetites. The intricacies of the debate are manifold, but the essence of Comus's argument is simply stated: that appetites are naturally licit and innocent when gratified. Having exhibited "all the pleasures" in his palace, Comus alleges that such plenitude or bounty was provided by Nature for the use and consumption of humankind—in particular, to "sate the curious taste." The Lady, on the other hand, perceives that overindulgence or even exquisite indulgence is unnatural. To pursue one's appetites without rational self-control is to degrade human nature. Such rebuttal is accompanied by the Lady's external rejection of the "treasonous offer" of the cup, which signifies licensed passions that would overthrow the predominance of reason. As the debate intensifies, Comus resorts to a form of sophistry in which he reasons by analogy, likening the Lady's beauty to a coin or comparing her to a "neglected rose." Much as coins are to be used, so also the Lady's beauty should be put into circulation. A rose is to be admired, and the Lady likewise is to be appreciated. A corollary of Comus's argument is that the Lady's beauty, comparable to a rose, is ephemeral, an allusion to a prevalent theme—*carpe diem*, or seize the day—in seventeenth-century poetry. Comus strives to engender a sense of urgency in the Lady so that she will respond affirmatively and immediately to his overture.

While Comus's sophistical arguments and the Lady's compelling counterarguments are more subtle than the foregoing account suggests, the upshot is that the Lady's virtue, right reason, and wariness enable her to affirm her "well-governed and wise appetite" while she refutes and debunks the "false rules pranked in reason's garb" and "dear Wit and gay Rhetoric" of her would-be seducer. The Lady's "freedom" of mind is manifested while she is physically restrained in the enchanted seat, where she re-

mains immobilized even after her brothers enter with drawn swords to disperse Comus and his followers. When Sabrina, the nymph who is invoked by the Attendant Spirit, emerges from the Severn River and sprinkles drops on the breast of the Lady, the Attendant Spirit's comment—"Heaven lends us grace"—interprets Sabrina's presence and gesture as divine assistance, which may be explained theologically. In *De Doctrina Christiana* Milton comments that natural virtue is elevated to supernatural status only with an infusion of grace from above. Such, indeed, may be the case with the Lady, whose heroism is rewarded by divine approval and whose joyous reunion with her father at the end of the masque anticipates the relationship of the sanctified soul and the Lord in the heavenly hereafter.

In *Areopagitica* Milton comments that he "cannot praise a fugitive and cloistered virtue, unexercised and unbreathed, that never sallies out and sees her adversary." Rather, he extols virtue that has undergone "trial . . . by what is contrary," then triumphed. In line with this view, *Comus*, a theatrical presentation in the Marches or border region between England and Wales, may advance the Lady as an exemplar of the virtue and moral rectitude, not to mention civility, that the lord president seeks to establish in his jurisdiction. As the seat of both the council and the court of the Marches, Ludlow Castle was the central location from which administrative and judicial policy and decisions were issued. Accordingly, the corruptions among the people in the border region—drunkenness, gambling, sexual immorality, witchcraft, and occultism—may suggest the sociopolitical context in which Milton's masque was composed and the relation of the work to the local populace.

Despite the early date of composition, *Comus* is a sophisticated foreshadowing of Milton's later poetry. The contention between virtue and vice is reenacted in "Lycidas," *Paradise Lost*, *Samson Agonistes*, and *Paradise Regained*. Though each poem presents the archetypal conflict somewhat differently, long expositions and debates, or certainly meditations, are crucial in all the works, especially the later ones.

The second important work written during Milton's studious leisure is "Lycidas," a pastoral elegy commemorating Edward King, a fellow student of Milton's at Christ's College, Cambridge, who died on 10 August 1637 when a vessel on which he was traveling capsized in the Irish Sea. King, like Milton, was a poet who intended to enter the ministry. Milton's poem was included in a collection of thirty-five obsequies, *Justa Edouardo King* (1638), mostly in Latin but some in Greek and English. *Justa* refers to justments or the due ceremonies and rites for the dead. By writing a pastoral elegy that is heavily allegorical, Milton taps into an inveterate tradition of lament, one that dates back at least to the third century B.C., when poets in Greek Sicily, like Theocritus, Bion, and Moschus, presumably initiated the genre. From the pre-Christian era through the Renaissance in Italy, France, and England, pastoral elegies were written by notable authors, including Virgil, Petrarch, Mantuan, Baldassare Castiglione, Pierre de Ronsard, and Spenser. Of the works by these poets, the fifth and tenth eclogues of Virgil's *Bucolics* and Spenser's *Shepheardes Calender* (1579) were exceptionally influential. As the literary tradition of the pastoral elegy unfolded certain conventions were established, creating a sense of artificiality that amuses or antagonizes, rather than edifies, some readers, including Samuel Johnson in the eighteenth century. Some of the major conventions include the lament by a shepherd for the death of a fellow shepherd, the invocation of the muse, a procession of mourners, flower symbolism, satire against certain abuses or corruptions in society and its institutions, a statement of belief in immortality, and the attribution of human emotions to Nature, which, in effect, also mourns the loss of the shepherd.

Through the use of such conventions Milton recounts his association with Edward King at Cambridge, likening himself and his friend to fellow shepherds together from early morning, through the afternoon, and into nightfall. Because of their friendship Milton, through the narrator, expresses an urgency, if not compulsion, to memorialize his friend. As a simple shepherd, he will fashion a garland of foliage and flowers to be placed at the site of burial. Allegorically, the garland signifies the flowers of rhetoric woven together into a pastoral elegy. The narrator also expresses modesty and humility concerning his talent to memorialize his friend: "with forced fingers rude" he may "shatter" the leaves of the foliage that he strives to fashion into a garland. The allegorical significance relates to the daunting challenge of crafting a pastoral elegy. The three kinds of foliage cited by the narrator—laurels, myrtles, and ivy—are evergreens, which symbolically affirm life after death. At the same time they are associated with different mythologi-

cal divinities. The laurel crown of poetry was awarded by Apollo; the love of Venus was reflected in the myrtle; and Bacchus wore a garland of ivy. Signified thereby is the poetry written at Cambridge by King and Milton in imitation of classical Greek and Latin literature. Later in "Lycidas," when the narrator mentions the "oaten flute" and its "glad sound," to which "rough satyrs danced" while accompanied by "fauns with cloven heel," he is alluding to the erotic and festive poetry, perhaps Ovidian, that King and Milton composed as students under the supervision of a tutor at Cambridge.

Despite the conventions that Milton assimilates to his poem and the artificiality of his pose as a naive shepherd, "Lycidas" is still an outlet for earnest sentiment. The poem is Milton's endeavor to write a pastoral elegy in order to test his talent, to manifest his proficiency in a genre associated with the most reputable poets, and to signal his readiness to progress to other challenges. But King, who died before he fulfilled his potential as a poet and priest, no doubt reminds Milton of his own mortality. By implication in "Lycidas" and explicitly in other poems, Milton registered concern that his unfolding career as a poet might be interrupted not only by early death but by the failure to progress in his development as a poet or because of failed inspiration. Milton, in short, may be alluding to himself when he complains that Lycidas, who equipped himself "to scorn delights, and live laborious days," died without having achieved the fame as a poet to which he aspired. While the allusions recount King's abstemiousness and strict regimen of study, they glance, as well, at Milton's similar habits. But lament turns to bitterness, so that the narrator in the allegorical framework of the poem impugns God's justice: "the blind Fury with th'aborred shears" cuts "the thin spun life." Some critics suggest that Milton erred in his reference to the Furies, whose keen sight—they are by no means "blind"—enables them to serve as agents of divine vengeance. From this vantage point, Milton should have alluded to the Fates—Clotho, Lachesis, and Atropos—who spin the thread of life. In particular, Atropos, whose name means "inflexible," is equipped with shears to cut the thread. The more likely explanation is that Milton conflates the Furies and Fates into one allusion in order to heighten the narrator's bitterness, which emerges from his misperception that vengeance was misdirected and, therefore, that justice is blind. The narrator's bitterness is

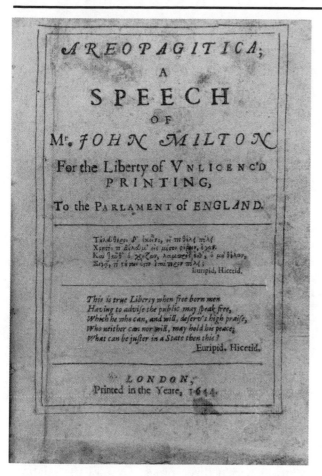

Title page for the work that Milton wrote "in order to deliver the press from the restraints with which it was encumbered"

also aroused because he associates the death of Lycidas with that of Orpheus, who was dismembered by the Thracian women. The mythological figure's remains scattered on the Hebrus River and in the Aegean Sea suggest the route of King's travel from the River Deva to the Irish Sea.

Appropriately, Apollo, the classical patron of poetry who intervenes to rectify the shortsightedness of the narrator, distinguishes "broad rumor" from "fame." Although Lycidas did not achieve earthly renown through "broad rumor," he was elevated much earlier into the hereafter, where an eternal reward, "fame," will be conferred on him under the eyes of the godhead. Apollo's speech, which some critics perceive as a digression, is integral to the poem because it affirms that the godhead is both clearsighted and just.

Balancing Apollo's commentary on the role and reward of the poet is Saint Peter's perspective on the priesthood. For Milton, King was the ideal clergyman, whose pastoral ministry would have been exemplary. King's premature death at first appears to be another example of injustice, for the corrupt clergymen and bishops of the Church of England continue to prosper. Against the clergy and most notably the bishops, Milton issues a virtual diatribe, a poetic counterpart of his enraged denunciation of them in the antiprelatical or antiepiscopal tracts. The speaker of the diatribe is "the pilot of the Galilean lake," Saint Peter. As the principal Apostle, Saint Peter is perceived, in effect, as the first bishop. As the one who wields the keys—"The golden opes, the iron shuts amain," images that signify, respectively, access to Heaven and incarceration in Hell—Saint Peter functions as the sharpsighted judge. Inveighing against the bishops as "Blind Mouths!," Saint Peter thus likens them to tapeworms that infest the sheep. Later they are equated with infectious diseases tainting the flock. Saint Peter's stern tone anticipates his eventual use of the "two-handed engine at the door," an instrument of divine justice that he wields in judgment against reprobates. His message, in sum, is that corrupt clergy and bishops may thrive in the present life, but justice will be exacted in the hereafter. In his prose treatises Milton uses the odious term "hireling," derived from the Gospel of John, to describe a venal clergyman. In John's Gospel the "hireling" is contrasted with the Good Shepherd, whose faithful service would have been reembodied in King.

Across the panorama of the poem, the narrator undergoes a change in outlook. At first sorrowful and depressed, he projects his mood onto the landscape. The flowers that he enumerates in a virtual catalogue manifest the human emotion of grief, as well as the ritualistic appearance and gestures of mourning—"Cowslips . . . hang the pensive head"; "every flower . . . sad embroidery wears"; and "Daffadillies fill their cups with tears." Later in the poem, when the narrator comes to recognize that Lycidas has been elevated into the heavenly hereafter, his outlook and tone change noticeably. Whereas Lycidas's "drooping head" has sunk into the waves, the narrator likens this downfall to the sunset, followed by sunrise. Lycidas, like the sun, "tricks his beams" and "flames in the forehead of the morning sky," enhanced by the sheen of the water. Both fire and water bring about baptismal cleansing so that Lycidas enters Heaven, where he "hears the unexpressive nuptial song," the intimate union of the sanctified soul and the Lord celebrated in the Book of Revelation. Like the resurrected Christ, Lycidas is finally triumphant and glorified. At the end of the poem most of the biblical allusions that celebrate joy after sorrow are from Revelation.

Despite its brevity (only 193 lines), "Lycidas" anticipates a recurrent theme in Milton's major poems: the justification of God's ways to humankind. In *Paradise Lost*, for example, the downfall of Adam and Eve and the introduction of sin and death into the human condition are interpreted from a providential perspective. From this vantage point, the deity is not vengeful but merciful, not misguided or blind but instrumental in humankind's ultimate triumph. In *Samson Agonistes* (1671), the downfall of the protagonist results in bitterness toward God. Samson, having been chosen by God to liberate the Israelites from the tyranny of the Philistines, is himself enslaved. By the end of the dramatic poem Samson and others who have impugned God's justice come to recognize that the "unsearchable dispose" or Providential intent is very different from what they had alleged.

As a capstone to his education at Cambridge and to the years of private study, the twenty-nine-year-old Milton, with an attendant, traveled abroad for fifteen months in 1638-1639 to France but chiefly through Italy. The principal source of information about the Grand Tour is Milton's *Defensio Secunda*. Despite his vocal opposition to Roman Catholicism, while he was abroad Milton fraternized with numerous Catholics, including Lucas Holstenius, the Vatican librarian; presumably Cardinal Francesco Barberini; and Giovanni Battista Manso, the patron of both Giambattista Marini and Tasso. In his poem "Mansus," Milton, who recognizes the importance of patrons such as Manso, yearns for such friendship and support in order to write a poem about King Arthur. Milton did not compose an Arthuriad, probably because his concept of heroism was very different by the time that he wrote *Paradise Lost*. In Italy, moreover, Milton viewed numerous works of art that depicted biblical episodes central to his later works—*Paradise Lost*, *Samson Agonistes*, and *Paradise Regained*. The relationship of the works of art to the visual imagery in the major poems is the subject of much critical commentary. During his stay in Florence, Milton visited the aged and blind Galileo. Having suffered through the Inquisition, Galileo was under virtual house arrest in his later years. In *Paradise Lost* Milton refers to Galileo's telescope and to the view of the heavens that it provided. As a victim of persecution, Galileo became for Milton a symbol of the adversity that a spokesperson of the truth underwent. Also in Florence, Milton read his Italian poetry at the academies, where he elicited the plaudits of the humanists for his command of their language. Milton corresponded with his Florentine friends, such as Carlo Dati, after his return to England. Years later, Milton continued to remember his friends at the Florentine academies with intense affection. Before his departure from Italy he shipped home numerous books, including musical compositions by Claudio Monteverdi. From Venice, Milton headed to Geneva. In Italy or in Switzerland, he learned of the deaths of his sister, Anne, and of Charles Diodati. To memorialize Diodati, Milton wrote a pastoral elegy, "Epitaphium Damonis," in Latin.

After his return to England, Milton assisted in the education and upbringing of Anne's children, John and Edward Phillips. He also became embroiled in the controversies against the Church of England and the growing absolutism of Charles I. The freedom of conscience and civil liberty that he advocated in his prose tracts were pursued at a personal level in the divorce tracts. Milton married three times; none of the relationships ended in divorce. His first wife, Mary Powell, left Milton shortly after their marriage in summer 1642 in order to return to her parents. This separation evidently motivated the composition of *The Doctrine and Discipline of Divorce* (1643). By 1645 they were reunited. Mary died in 1652. His second wife, Katherine Woodcock, whom he married on 12 November 1656, died in 1658. Milton's third wife, Elizabeth Minshull, whom he married on 24 February 1663, survived him. In addition to his marital woes Milton faced the deaths of his infant son, John, in 1651 and of an infant daughter in 1658. In the same period Milton's relationship with his three daughters by Mary Powell—Anne, Mary, and Deborah, all of whom survived their father—was troublesome, especially because they did not inherit their father's interest in and aptitude for learning. Further adversity resulted from his failing eyesight and total blindness by 1652. These adversities, along with Milton's involvement in politics, may have delayed the composition of the major poetry, and *Paradise Lost*, *Samson Agonistes*, and *Paradise Regained* surely bear the imprint of Milton's personal experience and public service.

Engraving by William Marshall that was published as the frontispiece to Milton's 1645 Poems. *Milton wrote the Greek caption, which says: "That an unskillful hand had carved this print / You would say at once, seeing that living face; / But, finding here no jot of me, my friends, / Laugh at the botching artist's misattempt."*

Milton's major work, *Paradise Lost*, was first published in ten books in 1667, then slightly revised and restructured as twelve books for the second edition in 1674, which also includes prose arguments or summaries at the outset of each book. *Paradise Lost*, almost eleven thousand lines long, was initially conceived as a drama to have been titled "Adam Unparadised," but after further deliberation Milton wrote a biblical epic that strives to "assert Eternal Providence, / And justify the ways of God to men." To vindicate Providence, Milton attempts to make its workings understandable to humankind. In accordance with epic conventions, he begins his work in medias res. An overview of major characters and their involvement in the action are the prerequisites to

further critical analysis. In the first two books the aftermath of the War in Heaven is viewed, with Satan and his defeated legions of angels having been cast down into Hell, a place of incarceration where they are tormented by a tumultuous lake of liquid fire. By the end of the first book they have been revived by Satan, under whose leadership they regroup in order to pursue their war against God either by force or guile. Most of the second book depicts the convocation of the fallen angels in Hell. Rather than continue their warfare directly against God and his loyal angels, they choose to reconnoiter on the earth, the dwelling place of God's newly created human beings, whose lesser nature would make them more vulnerable to onslaught or subversion. Satan, who volunteers to scout the earth and its inhabitants, departs through the gates of Hell, which are guarded by two figures, Sin and Death. He travels through Chaos, alights on the convex exterior of the universe, then descends through an opening therein to travel to earth. While Satan is traveling, God the Father and the Son, enthroned in Heaven at the outset of book 3, oversee the progress of their adversary. Foreknowing that Adam and Eve will suffer downfall, the Father and the Son discuss the conflicting claims of Justice and Mercy. The Son volunteers to become incarnate, then to undergo the further humiliation of death in order to satisfy divine justice. At the same time his self-sacrifice on behalf of humankind is a consummate act of mercy, one by which his merits through imputation will make salvation possible.

In a soliloquy at the beginning of book 4, a vestige of the dramatic origin of the epic, Satan, having arrived in the Garden of Eden, laments his downfall from Heaven and his hypocritical role in instilling false hope in his followers, whom he misleads into believing that they will ultimately triumph against God. Satan's first view of Eden and of Adam and Eve arouses his admiration, which is rapidly replaced by his malice and hate for the creator and his creatures. Overhearing the conversation of Adam and Eve, Satan learns that God has forbidden them to partake of the fruit of a certain tree in the Garden of Eden. By the end of book 4 Satan has entered the innermost bower of Adam and Eve while they are asleep. In the shape of a toad at Eve's ear, he influences her dream. When detected by the good angels entrusted with the security of Eden, Satan reacquires his angelic form, confronts Gabriel, but departs Eden. At the outset of book 5, Eve recounts her dream to Adam. In the dream Satan, who appears as a good angel, leads Eve to the interdicted tree, partakes of the fruit, and invites her to do likewise. Adam counsels Eve that her conduct in the dream is blameless because she was not alert or rational. He concludes his admonition by urging Eve to avoid such conduct when she is awake. Also in book 5 God sends the angel Raphael to visit Adam and Eve, chiefly to forewarn them that Satan is plotting their downfall. Midway through book 5, in response to a question from Adam, Raphael gives an account of the events that led to the War in Heaven.

Book 6 describes the war in detail as the rival armies of good and evil angels clash. Personal combat between Satan and certain good angels, such as Michael, is colorfully rendered; but a virtual stalemate between the armies is the occasion for intervention by the godhead. God the Father empowers the Son to drive the evil angels from Heaven. Mounting his chariot, the Son, armed with thunderbolts, accelerates toward the evil angels and discharges his weaponry. To avoid the onrushing chariot and the wrathful Son, the evil angels, in effect, leap from the precipice of Heaven and plummet into Hell. Also in response to a question from Adam, Raphael provides an account of the seven days of Creation, highlighting the role of the Son, who is empowered by the Father to perform the acts by which the cosmos comes into being, including the earth and its various creatures, most notably humankind. This account takes up all of book 7. In book 8 Adam recalls his first moments of consciousness after creation, his meeting with Eve, and their marriage under God's direction. Using that account as a frame of reference, Raphael admonishes Adam to maintain a relationship with Eve in which reason, not passion, prevails.

Book 9 dramatizes the downfall of Eve, then Adam. Working apart from Adam, Eve is approached by Satan, who had inhabited the form of a serpent. Led by him to the interdicted tree, Eve yields to the blandishments of the serpent and partakes of the fruit, and the serpent rapidly departs. Eve, having rejoined Adam, gives him some fruit. His emotional state affects his power of reasoning, so that he eats the fruit. Book 10 begins with the Son having descended from Heaven to judge Adam and Eve. Though they are expelled from Eden, his merciful judgment, their contrition, and the onset of grace will eventually convert sinfulness to regeneration. Satan, who retraces his earthward journey to return to

Hell, encounters Sin and Death, who had followed him. He urges them to travel to the earth and to prey on humankind. For the last two books of the epic, Adam, having been escorted to a mountaintop by the angel Michael, has a vision of the future. Narrated by Michael, the vision presents biblical history of the Old and New Testaments, with emphasis on the redemptive ministry of Jesus and the availability of salvation to humankind. The vision concludes with a glimpse of the general conflagration at Doomsday, the Final Judgment, and the separation of the saved from the damned in the hereafter.

Milton's work differs significantly from the epic traditon of Greco-Roman antiquity, the Middle Ages, and the Renaissance. Earlier epics developed ideas of heroism that celebrate martial valor, intense passions such as wrath or revenge, and cunning resourcefulness. If indeed such traits of epic heroism are retained by Milton, they tend to be embodied in Satan. In other words, Milton uses the epic form simultaneously as a critique of an earlier tradition of heroism and as a means of advancing a new idea of Christian heroism for which the crucial virtues are faith, patience, and fortitude. Undoubtedly, this idea of heroism was influenced by Milton's personal experience with adversity and by his public service as a polemicist and an opponent of Stuart absolutism and the episcopacy of the Church of England. Under attack from his adversaries, Milton, from his perspective, was the advocate of a righteous cause that failed. The triumph of his adversaries, his solitude after the Restoration, and his struggle to understand how and why, under the sufferance of Providence, evil seemingly prevailed—and other questions—presumably impelled him to modify an earlier plan to compose a British epic on Arthur. At the same time, however, one may acknowledge that some traditional traits of epic heroism are embodied in characters such as the Son. Surely wrath and martial effectiveness are manifested in the War in Heaven, but Milton more emphatically affirms that the greater triumph of the Son is his voluntary humiliation on behalf of humankind. Accordingly, faith, patience, and fortitude are the crucial virtues to be exercised by the Son in his redemptive ministry, which he has agreed to undertake because of meekness, filial obedience, and boundless love for humankind.

Heroism is simply one of a series of epic conventions used but adapted by Milton. Another is the invocation of the muse, who is not precisely

John Milton was born the 9th of December
1608 die Veneris half an howr after 6 in the
morning

Christofer Milton was born on Friday about
a month before Christmass at 5 in the morning
1615

Edward Phillips was 15 year old August 1645
John Phillips is a year younger about Octob.

My daughter Anne was born July the 29th
on the fast at eebning about half an howre
after six 1646.
My daughter Mary was born on Wedensday
Octob. 25th on the fast day in the morning about
6 a clock 1648.
My son John was born on Sunday March the
16th about half an hower past nine at night 1650
My daughter Deborah was born the 2d of May
being Sunday somwhat before 3 of the clock in the
morning. 1652.
my wife hir mother dyed about 3 days after. And my
son about 6 weeks after his mother
Katherin my daughter, by Katherin my second wife, was
borne ye 19th of October, between 5 and 6 in ye morning,
and dyed ye 17th of March following, 6 weeks after hir
mother, who dyed ye 3rd of Feb. 1657

Flyleaf in Milton's Bible, with entries in the handwriting of Milton and his amaneunsis Jeremy Picard (Add. MS. 32310, British Library)

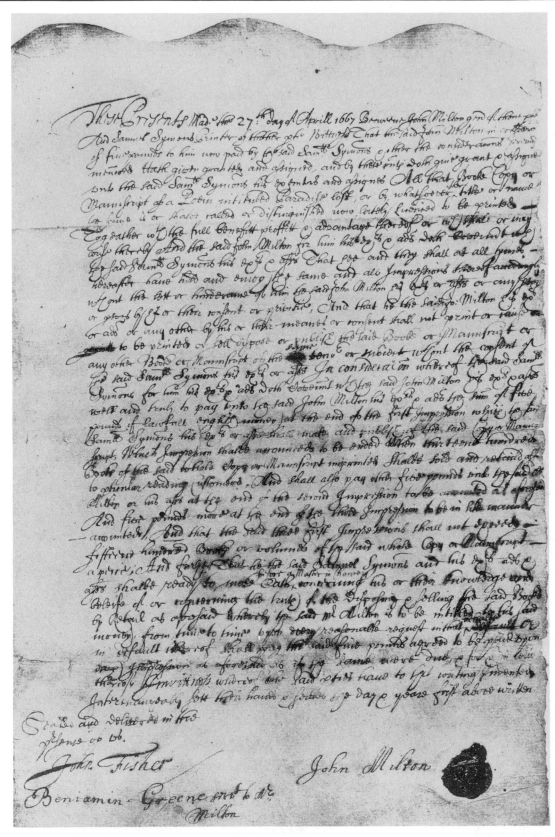

Contract between Milton and Samuel Simmons for the printing of Paradise Lost, *signed for Milton by his amaneunsis Jeremy Picard and witnessed by one John Fisher and Milton's servant Benjamin Greene (Add. MS. 5016, British Library)*

identified—whether the Holy Spirit or, more generally, the spirit of the godhead. At times, Milton alludes to the classical muse of epic poetry, Urania. The intent, however, is to identify her not as the source of inspiration but as a symbol or imperfect type of the Hebraic-Christian muse through which the divine word was communicated to prophets or embodied in Jesus for dissemination to humankind. A third convention is intrusion by supernatural beings, action that takes place throughout the epic—when, for example, the godhead sends Raphael to forewarn Adam and Eve of the dangers of Satan or when the Son descends to Eden as the judge of humankind after the fall. In Adam's vision of the future, the Son's role as the Incarnate Christ and the unfolding of his redemptive ministry are highlights. The descent into the underworld, a fourth epic convention, occurs in *Paradise Lost* as early as book 1, which shows the punishment of the fallen angels in Hell. A fifth convention is the interrelation of love and war. The love of Adam and Eve before and after their expulsion from Eden is central to the epic, but the self-sacrifice of the Son on behalf of fallen humankind is the most magnanimous example of love. Warfare in *Paradise Lost* is sensational when the good and evil angels clash and as the Son expels Satan and his followers from Heaven; but the epic develops another form of struggle, humankind's experience of temptation after Satan conceals his malice behind external friendliness and solicitude. Finally, the style of *Paradise Lost*, including the extended similes and catalogues, is a sixth epic convention. In book 1 Satan, who had plummeted from Heaven into Hell, is prone on the fiery lake. Across several lines, the narrator compares Satan's enormous size with that of the Titans. Later in book 1, as the fallen angels file from the burning lake, an epic catalogue is used to cite their names as false gods whose idols were worshiped in infidel cultures, particularly in Asia Minor. Both the similes and catalogues, when examined closely, provide insight into other, but related, aspects of style, such as the Latinate diction and periodic sentence structure, which when accommodated to blank verse create a majestic rhythm, a sense of grandeur, and at times sublimity.

While contributing to Milton's grand design, each book in the epic has distinctive features. The first book begins with an invocation, and three other books—three, seven, and nine—have similar openings. In all four instances the narrator invokes divine assistance or inspiration

to begin or continue his epic poem. Furthermore, the invocations enable the narrator periodically to characterize himself, to announce his aspirations, and to assess his progress in composing the epic. Thus, in the invocation of book 1, the narrator pleads for inspiration comparable to what Moses experienced in his relationship with the Lord. Topography is mentioned, including Horeb and Sinai, the mountains, respectively, where God announced his presence to Moses and gave him the Commandments, and Siloa's brook, where Christ healed the blind man. By implication the narrator interrelates Hebraic-Christian landscapes with the haunts of the classical muses. With his vision thus illuminated, he hopes to describe events of biblical history. At the same time, he invites comparison with epic writers of classical antiquity; but his work, which treats the higher truth of biblical history and interpretation, will supersede theirs.

After the invocation to book 1, the narrator's description of Hell incorporates accounts of the volcanic fury of Mt. Aetna, where the leaders of the Titans, Typhon and Briareos, were incarcerated when cast down by Jove's thunderbolts. Coupled with this analogue and others, including classical descriptions of Hades, is Milton's adaptation of details from Dante's *Inferno*. When, for example, the narrator describes how the fires of Hell inflict pain but do not provide light, the allusion is to Dante. And the lines "Hope never comes / That comes to all," which describe the plight of the fallen angels, paraphrase the inscription on the gate to Hell in the *Inferno*: "Abandon all hope, ye who enter here." In reviving the fallen angels Satan, upright and with wings outstretched over the fiery lake, resembles the dove brooding on the abyss (book 1) or the Son (book 7) standing above Chaos to utter the words that result in Creation. Satan also parodically resembles Moses, who led his followers away from the threat of destruction. His speeches instill false hope in the angels, who are gulled by his public posturing; but the narrator alerts the reader to Satan's duplicity. Privately the archfiend is in a state of despair. By the end of book 1 the fallen angels assemble in a palace called Pandemonium to deliberate on a course of action: to pursue the war against God by force or guile. As this convocation begins, Satan is not only the ruler in the underworld but its virtual deity.

Book 2 opens with Satan enthroned above the other angels. The first of the speakers to address the topic of ongoing warfare with God is Moloch, the warrior angel who urges his cohorts to ascend heavenward and to use black fire and thunder as weaponry. Despite his call to action, he recognizes that force will not prevail against God. To disrupt Heaven and to threaten its security, though not military triumphs, are nevertheless vengeful. The second speaker, Belial, debunks the argument of Moloch. Not to endure one's lot in defeat is a sign of cowardice, rather than courage, Belial argues. Moreover, he says, the fiery deluge is not as tumultuous as it was immediately after the expulsion of the fallen angels from Heaven, thus suggesting that God's ire is remitting. Under these circumstances the fallen angels may become more acclimated to the underworld. By diverting attention from the stated premise of ongoing war against God and by urging the fallen angels to orient themselves toward their present habitat, Belial lays the groundwork for the third speaker, Mammon, who advocates the creation of a kingdom in Hell. To redirect the debate to its fundamental premise of ongoing war, Beëlzebub, Satan's chief lieutenant, intervenes. He mocks the fallen angels, particularly Belial and Mammon, by calling them "Princes of Hell" to indicate where their attention and energies are presently focused. At the same time he knows implicitly that if Moloch, the warrior angel, despairs of military success, then no one will be eager to pursue open war against God. Accordingly, he revives Satan's earlier suggestion—that the earth and its newly created inhabitants should be assessed and then overcome by force or seduced by guile. After the hazards of travel to the newly created world are described, the fallen angels become silent until Satan agrees to undertake the mission. Seemingly voluntary, the decision is virtually constrained. Recognizing that an antagonistic relationship with God is essential to the pretense that the fallen angels are hopeful rivals, not vanquished foes, Satan revives the possibility of victory on the middle ground of earth. Having agreed to scout the earth, he emphasizes that he will travel alone. By preventing others emboldened by his lead from accompanying him, he reserves the glory for himself.

At the gates of Hell, Satan accosts Death, a wraithlike figure who challenges him. Nearby is Sin, a beautiful woman above the waist but a serpent below, tipped with a deadly sting. Her transmogrification prefigures Satan's own degradation. As an allegorical figure, she synthesizes Homer's Circe and Spenser's Error. In her appearance and interactions with Satan and Death, she dramatizes the scriptural account that uses an image of monstrous birth to describe how Sin and Death emerge from lustful urges, which include both pride and concupiscence (James 1: 15). Having recalled that she emerged from Satan's forehead, an allusion to the birth of Athena from the head of Zeus, Sin incestuously consorts with the archfiend, a relationship that begets Death. What results is an infernal trinity, in which the offspring, Death, even copulates with his mother, Sin. The remainder of the book follows Satan's journey through Chaos.

The invocation of book 2, like that of book 1, is a petition by the narrator for light or illumination, so that he may report events that occur in Heaven. Having ascended from Hell, through Chaos, to the convex exterior of the universe, the blind narrator likens himself to a bird, particularly the nightingale, which sings in the midst of darkness. He mentions many of the same topographic features—the mountains and waters associated with classical and Hebraic-Christian inspiration—cited in the invocation of book 1. Building on the earlier invocation, in which he courts comparison with earlier epic authors, he acknowledges a desire for fame comparable to that of Homer and Thamyris, a blind Thracian poet. Like the blind prophets of classical antiquity, Tiresias and Phineus, the narrator affirms that his physical affliction is offset by the gift of inward illumination. As he reports the dialogue in Heaven, the narrator develops structural and thematic contrasts between books 2 and 3, not to mention differences between Satan and the Son. The infernal consult, which aimed to bring about the downfall of humankind, is balanced against the celestial dialogue, which outlines the plan of redemption. If Satan is impelled by capital sins, such as hate, envy, revenge, and vainglory, then the opposite virtues are the Son's meekness, obedience, love, and humility. The interaction of Justice and Mercy is also a central topic of the dialogue, which is interrupted by the Father's question: Who among the angels "will be mortal" to redeem humankind? The question and the silence that ensues are contrasted structurally and thematically with book 2, when Satan, amid the hushed fallen angels, agrees to risk the threats of Chaos to travel to earth. As the Son volunteers to die on behalf of humankind the dialogue resumes, with emphasis on the imputation of his merits and the theology of atonement. In the meantime Satan, having traveled to the opening in the cosmos, alongside the point at which the world is connected to Heaven by a golden chain, descends. He flies first to the sun, where, by posing as a lesser angel, he acquires directions from Uriel to earth, where he arrives at the top of Mount Niphates in Eden.

Book 4 begins with a soliloquy by Satan, the speech that was to have opened the drama "Adam Unparadised." At this point the so-called heroic nature of Satan as the archetypal rebel is offset by his candid awareness that downfall was caused by his own ambition; that his repentance is prevented by vainglory, which impelled him to boast to the fallen angels that they would overcome God; and that reconciliation with God, if possible, would lead inevitably to another downfall because of ambition. Satan thus becomes the prototype of the obdurate sinner. As he takes on the shapes of various animals—a cormorant, other predators, a toad, and finally a serpent— Satan's degradation contrasts markedly with his earlier vainglorious posturing. Satan observes the resemblance of Adam and Eve to their maker, assesses the complementary relationship of male and female, learns of the divine prohibition concerning the Tree of Knowledge, and overhears Eve's account of her creation, especially her attraction to her self-image reflected from the surface of a pool of water. Led from her reflected image by the voice of God, Eve encountered Adam, to whom she is wed. From the first, she acknowledges her hierarchical relationship with Adam, wherein "beauty is excelled by manly grace." Appellations that she applies to him, such as "Author" and "Disposer," reaffirm the relationship, along with her other assessments: "God is thy law, thou mine." Satan, who becomes a toad at Eve's ear, influences her dream while she and Adam are asleep in their bower of roses. He regains his shape as an angel when accosted by Gabriel and the other attendants in Eden.

When Eve at the outset of book 5 recounts her dream, it is evident that Satan has appealed to her potential for vainglory, the narcissistic inclinations toward self-love, which when magnified disproportionately would elevate her above Adam. Thus, the appellations that the tempter applies to Eve during her dream—"Angelic Eve" and "Goddess"—may engender in her the psychology of self-love and pride, precisely what brought about Satan's downfall. Much as Satan challenged his hierarchical relationship with God, so too Eve is tempted to question her subordination to Adam. Dividing Book 5 in half is the visit

by Raphael, who descends to earth at the behest of God to forewarn Adam and Eve of the wiles of the tempter. In his account of hierarchy, which is a discourse on the great chain of being, Raphael emphasizes how "by gradual scale sublimed" humankind, through continuing obedience, will ascend heavenward. His discourse, an apt commentary on Eve's dream, particularly the temptation to disobedience, prepares for the account of Satan's rebelliousness, the occasion for the emergence of Sin from the archfiend. The context for Satan's rebellion is the so-called begetting of the Son, which does not refer to his origin as such but to his newly designated status as "Head" of the angels or to his first appearance in the form and nature of an angel. The latter possibility is the more likely because Satan's hate and envy would emerge from his subordination to a being like himself, at least in external appearance. Having summoned numerous angels to a location in the northern region of Heaven, ostensibly to celebrate the begetting of the Son, Satan argues that God's action is an affront to the dignity of the angels. One of the angels, Abdiel, refutes Satan's argument. He contends that the manifestation of the Son as an angel is a humiliation of the godhead but an exaltation of the angelic nature. Such an argument anticipates the eventual Incarnation of the Son, who unites his deific nature with the human nature. In both instances, with the Son having manifested himself in lesser natures, the solicitude of the deity for angels and humankind alike is paramount.

Approximately one-third of the angels rally behind Satan, who leads them in the three-day War in Heaven, the subject of book 6. Typical epic encounters include the personal combat of Satan and Abdiel, then Satan and Michael, not to mention the large-scale clashes of angels. On the dawn of the third day, a situation that prefigures the glorification of Christ at the Resurrection, the Son as the agent of the Father's wrath speeds in his chariot toward the evil angels. His onrush, accompanied by lightning and a whirlwind, suggests the chariot of Ezekiel. Having described the the wrathful godhead in the War in Heaven, Raphael balances this terrifying example by presenting a picture of the benevolent and bountiful deity in book 7. First, however, the narrator in the invocation alludes to his work's half-finished state, expressing anxiety that his inspiration may be interrupted or that his personal safety is threatened. Through the narrator, Milton perhaps alludes to his own situation at the Restoration, his

13

First Book

Hung on his shoulders like the moon whose orb
Through optick glasse the Tuscan Artist views
At evening from the top of Fesole,
290 Or in Valdarno, to descry new lands,
Rivers or Mountaines in her spotty globe.
His Speare, to equall which the tallest pine
Hewn on Norwegian hills, to be the mast
Of some great Ammirall, were but a wand,
He walkt with, to support uneasy steps
Over the burning Marle, not like those steps
On Heavens azure; and the torrid clime
Smote on him sore besides, vaulted with fire;
Nathlesse hee so endur'd, till on the beach
Of that inflamed sea, hee stood and call'd
300 His legions, Angell forms, who lay intranst
Thick as Autumnall leaves that strow the brooks
In Vallombrosa, where th' Etrurian shades
High overarcht imbowr: or scatterd sedge
Afloat when with fierce winds Orion arm'd
Hath vext the red-sea coast, whose waves o'rethrew
Busiris and his Memphian chivalry
While with perfidious hatred they pursu'd
The sojourners of Goshen, who beheld
310 From the safe shore thir floating carcases

Page from the setting copy for the 1667 edition of Paradise Lost *(Pierpont Morgan Library), dictated by Milton
to an amaneunsis circa 1665*

intercessors presumably having negotiated an agreement that spared his life, so long as he observed certain conditions. After the invocation, book 7 includes an account of Creation, which elaborates on the catalogues of Genesis to highlight how the plenitude, continuity, and gradation are manifestations of God's benevolence. Most significant is the interactive relationship of male and female principles in Nature—for example, the sun's rays against the earth—a model for the union of Adam and Eve.

Across books 5-7, the begetting of the Son, Satan's sinfulness, the War in Heaven, and Creation are episodes that build toward a pointed commentary by Raphael on the relationship of Adam and Eve. Adam, however, first gives an account of his creation, the first moments of his consciousness, and his marriage to Eve. Whereas Eve was led shortly after her creation by the voice, not by the visible presence, of the Lord, Adam at his creation first experiences the warmth of sunlight, falls asleep, and in a dream is led by a "shape Divine" toward the summit of the Garden of Eden. When he awakens, he views among the trees his "Guide" or "Presence Divine," who speaks to Adam: "Whom thou sought'st, I am." This disclosure is comparable to what the Lord from the bush on Horeb uttered to Moses. Adam's recognition of "single imperfection" moves him to request a helpmate, who is created from his side. At once in his relationship with Eve, Adam experiences "passion" and "commotion strange," which cause Raphael to warn him not to abandon rational control. Discoursing on the hierarchy of reason and passion, the distinction between love and lust, and the scale or ladder along which humankind is to ascend heavenward, Raphael, by conflating Neoplatonic philosophy and traditional Christian theology, amplifies the context in which to understand obedience and disobedience.

The invocation of book 9 recapitulates Milton's earlier plans to write an epic on "hitherto the only argument / Heroic deemed": the exploits of "fabled knights," like Arthur. As an index of his departure from epic tradition, Milton, through his narrator, argues that "the better fortitude / Of patience and heroic martyrdom," previously "Unsung," will distinguish his work. After the invocation the narrator describes how Satan, who enters a serpent, utters a soliloquy ("O foul descent!") which laments his degradation, an outlook that contrasts with the Son's willingness to inhabit the nature and form of humankind. Because he is implementing a strategy of deception, Satan conceals his true nature behind a disguise; whereas the Son by becoming human intends to reveal and implement the divine plan of salvation.

In her first speech to Adam in book 9 Eve proposes that she and Adam "divide" their "labors" because their mutual affection has diverted them from their duties of gardening. Adam counters her proposal by affirming that he and Eve when together are "More wise, more watchful, stronger." Despite the cogency of his argument, Adam twice urges Eve to "Go," thereby forfeiting his responsibility to issue a lawful command for Eve to remain with him, a command that she would be free to obey or disobey. The topic of a lawful command recurs at the end of book 9, when during their mutual recrimination Eve faults Adam: "why didst not thou, the head, / Command me absolutely not to go . . . ?" Agreeing to reunite with Adam by noon, Eve works alone among the roses, propping up the flowers with myrtle bands. Ironically, the very duty of gardening that she performs should bring to mind her relationship with Adam, from whom she is separated. Satan is pleased to have found her alone. Eve's beauty momentarily awes Satan, who is rendered "stupidly good," a phrase suggesting that he is disarmed of his enmity. In his approach to Eve the serpent-tempter seeks to recreate in her the psychology of transcendence, which he had engendered during her dream. Feigning submissiveness and awe because of her beauty, Satan deceives Eve into believing that his power of reasoning derives from the forbidden fruit. Characterizing God as a "Threatener" and "Forbidder" who denies the fruit to others to prevent them from becoming his equals, the serpent-tempter capitalizes on Eve's unwariness, influences her perception, and thus affects her will. Having engorged the forbidden fruit, Eve for a time contemplates possible superiority over Adam; but fearful that death may overtake her and that Adam would be "wedded to another Eve," she resolves to share the fruit with him. As he was awaiting the return of Eve, Adam fashioned a garland of roses. Astonished to learn at their reunion that Eve violated the divine prohibition, he drops the wreath, which withers. This dramatic event foreshadows the process of dying that will be introduced into the human condition as a consequence of the downfall of Adam and Eve. Whereas Eve was deceived by the tempter, Adam is "overcome with Female charm," a reaction whereby judgment gives way to passion, precisely the concern that Raphael had expressed at the end of book 8. Not unlike the phantasmic experience of Eve's dream, Adam and Eve undergo illusory ascent, then sudden decline. With the onset of concupiscence, moreover, their lustful relationship contrasts with the previous expression of love in their innermost bower. Besieged by turbulent passions, Adam and Eve become involved in mutual recrimination, each faulting the other for their downfall, both denying culpability.

At the outset of book 10 the Father sends the Son to earth as "the mild Judge and Intercessor both," as one who will temper justice with mercy. Despite the retribution meted out to Adam and Eve, the greater emphasis of the Son's ministry is to encourage an awareness of sinfulness and the onset of sorrow and contrition as steps in the process of regeneration. Satan, who has begun to return to Hell, where with the fallen angels he plans to revel in his triumph over humankind, meets Sin and Death, who traveled earthward in the wake of his earlier journey. He urges them to prey on Adam and Eve and all their progeny. Though Adam and Eve have continued their mutual recrimination, each eventually acknowledges responsibility for sinfulness. Despite their evident frailties and imperfections, Adam and Eve are neither victims nor victors. Having been created "Sufficient to have stood, though free to fall," they are endowed with the capability to withstand temptation; but when they suffer downfall, they cannot undergo regeneration without divine assistance. Their predicament, which typifies the human condition, provides the context for the Christian heroism of Milton's epic. When measured in relation to humankind, heroism is manifested as one resists temptation in the manner of the Lady of *Comus* or when one, having yielded to temptation, experiences regeneration.

Books 11 and 12 include Adam's dream-vision of the future, which is narrated by the angel Michael, who presents a panoramic overview of the implementation of the divine will in human history. As Adam views Hebraic and Christian biblical history, the prophets and patriarchs of the Old Testament, such as Noah, Abraham, Isaac, Jacob, Moses, and Joshua, are presented as "shadowy Types," prefiguring the Son's incarnate ministry of redemption. Interspersed with descriptions of the Old Testament types are accounts of evildoers, such as the tyrant Nimrod. The cyclical interaction of goodness and evil, which contin-

ues under the sufferance of Providence, is the context wherein obedience and heroism are manifested, for which Christ is the perfect exemplar. Indeed, the Pauline view that Jesus was obedient even unto death on the cross is the Christian heroism at the center of Adam's dream-vision. In addition to its typological emphasis, the vision of human history in books 11 and 12 is also apocalyptic, with focus on the Second Coming, when the final victory over Satan will occur and the union of sanctified souls with the godhead will take place in the heavenly hereafter. More immediate for Adam and Eve, however, is their expulsion from Eden and the change in their perception of Paradise—from an external garden to "A paradise within," which results from the indwelling of the godhead in one's heart.

Because of its length, complexity, and consummate artistry, *Paradise Lost* is deemed Milton's magnum opus, the great work for which he had prepared himself since youth and toward which, in his view, the godhead guided him. As a biblical epic, *Paradise Lost* is an interpretation of Scripture: a selection of biblical events, their design and integration according to dominant spiritual themes—downfall and regeneration, the presentation of a Christ-centered view of human history, a virtual dramatization of the phenomenon of temptation to create psychological verisimilitude, and final affirmation about personal triumph over adversity and ultimate victory over evil. Imprinted in the epic are Milton's personal and political circumstances: his blindness, on the one hand, and the dissolution of the Protectorate, on the other. Thus, Milton may have identified himself with intrepid spokespersons who advocated a righteous cause despite the adversity confronting them. Such figures include Abdiel, whose "testimony of Truth" is the single refutation of Satan and the fallen angels in book 5, and Noah, the "one just man" who, while surrounded by reprobates, continues to advocate the cause of goodness. Though evil may be ascendant for a time, including the Stuart monarchy at the Restoration, goodness in the cyclical panorama of history will have its spokesperson and, ultimately, will prevail.

After *Paradise Lost* Milton's two major works are *Paradise Regained* and *Samson Agonistes*, published in the same volume in 1671. As such, the works may be perceived as complementary, if not companion, pieces on the topic of temptation. The Christ of *Paradise Regained* successfully withstands the temptations of Satan in the desert,

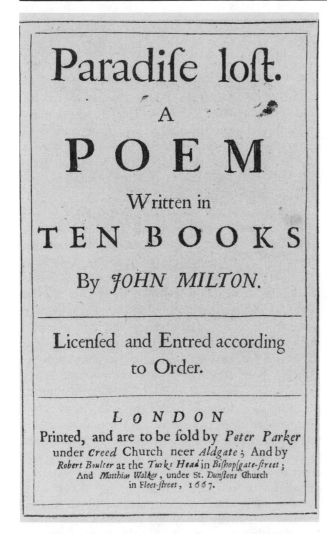
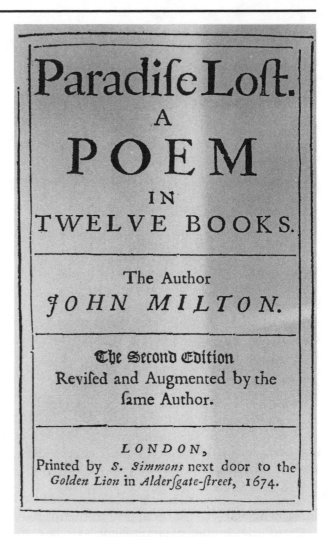

Title pages for the first and revised editions of the Christian epic in which Milton hoped to "assert Eternal Providence, / And justify the ways of God to men"

whereas Samson, who yields to temptation earlier in his career, undergoes the cycle of spiritual regeneration. Like the Lady in *Comus*, the Christ of *Paradise Regained* heroically refutes his tempter. Like Adam in *Paradise Lost*, Samson manifests his heroism in recovery after downfall.

If *Paradise Lost* treats "man's disobedience," then *Paradise Regained* presents Christ, whose human nature is emphasized, as the example of consummate obedience. The work, approximately one-fifth the length of *Paradise Lost*, is divided into four books. In the first book, after the Holy Spirit is invoked, Satan overhears the announcement by the Father, "the great proclaimer," that Christ is his "beloved Son." At Satan's command a convocation of the fallen angels is held in "mid air," after which the tempter travels earthward to use his wiles in order to

learn the identity of Christ. His fear is that Christ fulfills the prophecy that "Woman's seed" will inflict the "fatal wound" on him. Christ enters the desert, where he cogitates on the Old Testament prophecies of his coming, the earlier events of his life, and his role in the divine plan of redemption. After Christ has been in the wilderness for forty days the tempter, disguised as an old man, accosts him. Urging him to convert stones into bread so that the two of them can alleviate their hunger, Satan is refuted by Christ, who acknowledges that he is being tempted to "distrust" God. In book 2 the absence of Christ troubles especially his mother. Satan in the meantime has convoked the fallen spirits in order to plan a more subtle seduction, which will begin with a temptation of food, then proceed to an appeal to one's desire for "honor, glory, and popular praise." Christ, who experiences hunger, dreams of food; when he awakens, he beholds "A table richly spread." Rejecting the "guiles" of the tempter, Jesus also dismisses materialism and worldly power, symbolized by the scepter: "who reigns within himself, and rules / Passions, Desires, and Fears, is more a King."

By the third book Satan is focusing on fame and glory, but Christ rejects earthly fame as false, decrying military heroes and extolling spiritual heroism. From a high mountain Christ views ancient kingdoms, over which he could become the ruler by commanding the numberless troops that he also sees. Christ remains unmoved by "ostentation." Continuing the temptation in book 4, Satan shows Christ the Roman Empire, of which he could become the benevolent sovereign. Jesus, however, notes that "grandeur and majestic show" are transitory, whereas "there shall be no end" to his kingdom. Thereafter Satan presents him with a view of the whole world, a temptation that Jesus rejects outright. Still endeavoring to tempt Jesus with glory, Satan offers him the total learning of Greek antiquity—art, philosophy, and eloquence. By such gifts he would be equipped to rule the world. Christ dismisses Greek learning because his own direct knowledge of the Lord is the higher truth. While Jesus sleeps, Satan strives unsuccessfully to trouble him with dreams and a storm. The climax of the work occurs when Satan, having brought Christ to the pinnacle of the temple of Jerusalem, tells him to stand or to cast himself down so that angels will rescue him. Christ's rebuke causes the tempter to flee. Angels then minister to Jesus, who by resisting temptation has begun the liberation of humankind from the wiles of the devil to which Adam had succumbed.

Milton follows the order of the temptations outlined in the Gospel of Luke, rather than in Matthew. Despite the focus on the trial in the desert, Milton interrelates this experience of the Son to earlier and later biblical history. Thus, Christ meditates on the events of his childhood and youth but also remembers Old Testament biblical prophecy that anticipates the coming of the Messiah. Furthermore, God the Father announces his intention to "exercise" Christ in the desert, where "he shall first lay down the rudiments / Of his great warfare" in preparation for his conquest over "Sin and Death" at the Crucifixion and Resurrection. At the same time the patience, faith, and fortitude that Christ manifests in the desert perfect the previous exercise of similar virtues by Old Tes-

tament precursors, notably Job, who is cited by Christ in one of his refutations of Satan. From this perspective the Book of Job is another biblical source of Milton's so-called brief epic. Perhaps Milton was also modeling the trials and triumphs of Jesus after Spenser's account of Sir Guyon in book 2 of *The Faerie Queene*, where a demonic figure tests the knight with temptations of materialism, worldly power, and glory. *Christs Victorie and Triumph in Heaven and Earth* (1610) by Giles Fletcher the Younger is another model possibly adapted by Milton.

When one considers the grand scale across which the action of *Paradise Lost* takes place—in Hell, Chaos, Heaven, the Cosmos, and Earth—*Paradise Regained* seems both limited and limiting in its outlook. When one recalls the grand events of *Paradise Lost*—from the War in Heaven to the Creation—what occurs in *Paradise Regained* appears to be static. Furthermore, the dramatic elements of *Paradise Lost*, such as motives for action, suspense, and conflict, excite the reader and encourage both intellectual and psychological responses. In *Paradise Regained*, on the other hand, the tempter is doomed to failure from the start because Christ does not heed the temptations at all but rejects them outright, with little or no internal conflict. Probably Milton is depending on the contrast between Christ's wholesale dismissal of the temptations and the more engaged response by the reader, who is perhaps allured by the attractiveness of earthly glory. In his exercise of perfect obedience and of virtues such as faith, patience, and fortitude, Christ is the exemplar after whom we model our own conduct.

Though *Paradise Regained* lacks the grand and spectacular events of Milton's longer epic, its purpose is vastly different. Milton's plan is to provide a context for philosophical meditation and debate by Christ, who, at the outset of his public ministry, is being equipped for his role as the Savior. As such, Christ meditates on the significance of the two natures, divine and human, united in him. The drama of the brief epic derives in part from the tension in Christ between these two natures and the questions that emerge therefrom—how divine omniscience is balanced against human reasoning, why suffering is the prelude to triumph, and when Providence should rectify the misperceptions of the people, who expect the Messiah to be an earthly conqueror. While it is a foregone conclusion that Satan will not succeed with his wiles, the meditations of Christ and the debates with his adversary enable him to reconcile his two natures, to develop his message to the people, and to prepare for public service as a preacher and exemplar. Related to these perspectives is the tension between the ongoing relationship of Christ with the other divine persons and his disengagement from them after he becomes incarnate. Though the Father and the Spirit manifest themselves at the baptism of the Son in order to affirm his divinity in spite of his humanity, afterward the Son enters the human condition as fully as possible to enact his role as the suffering servant. This role, which becomes evident to him in the wilderness, culminates with his death on the cross.

If suffering, temptation, and heightened self-perception are characteristic of *Paradise Regained*, they are equally significant in *Samson Agonistes*, a dramatic poem not intended for stage performance. Using the Book of Judges as his chief source, Milton refocuses the saga of Samson in order to emphasize regeneration after downfall, rather than sensational feats of physical strength. Beginning the work with Samson's degradation as a prisoner in a common workhouse in Gaza, Milton portrays a psychologically tormented character, confused about his downfall and at times antagonistic toward the godhead. Throughout the work a chorus of Danites from Samson's tribe both observe his plight and speak with him. Three successive visitors also converse with Samson: Manoa, his father; Dalila, his wife; and Harapha, a Philistine giant. In the course of these three visits Samson acquires gradual, not complete, understanding of himself and of his relationship with the godhead. With the departure of Harapha, the change in Samson is noticeable to the chorus, which praises his psychological resurgence from a state of acute depression and his faith in the higher, though obscure, workings of Providence. The poem concludes with Samson in the theater of Dagon, collapsing its pillars of support so that the falling structure kills more of his adversaries than he has slain cumulatively in the past. He himself is killed in the process.

One of the chief ironies of Milton's rendition is that Samson, though physically strong, is spiritually weak. After he becomes a captive of the Philistines, a consequence and manifestation of his having yielded to temptation, he gradually undergoes spiritual regeneration, which culminates in his renewed role as God's faithful champion against the Philistines. Within the framework of temptation and regeneration Milton recasts the concept of heroism, debunking or at

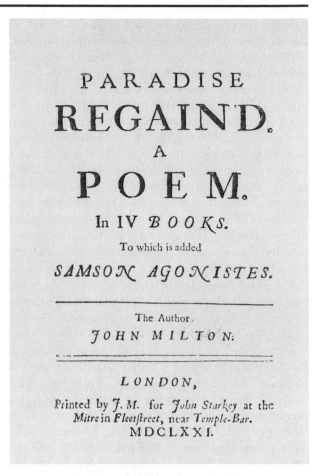

PARADISE
REGAIN'D.
A
POEM.
In IV *BOOKS*.
To which is added
SAMSON AGONISTES.

The Author,
JOHN MILTON.

LONDON,
Printed by *J. M.* for *John Starkey* at the
Mitre in *Fleetstreet*, near *Temple-Bar.*
MDCLXXI.

Title page for the book that includes Milton's epic of "Recover'd Paradise to all mankind" and his attempt to write a tragedy "after the ancient manner" that incorporates the Christian concept of redemption

least subordinating feats of strength to the heroism of spiritual readiness, the state in which one awaits God's call to service. In line with this outlook the structure of the work and the developing characterization of Samson are discernible. At the outset Samson is tormented by the irony of his captivity. The would-be liberator is himself enslaved. He questions the prophecy to his parents that they would beget an extraordinary son "Designed for great exploits." At first Samson laments the contrast between his former, seemingly heroic, status and his present state of captivity and degradation. He and others recall his past feats: slaying a lion, dislodging and transporting the gates of Gaza, and slaughtering vast numbers of Philistines with only the jawbone of an ass.

As the poem progresses Samson's self-knowledge increases, and he comes to realize that "like a petty God" he "walked about admired of all," until "swollen with pride into the snare" he fell. This realization, as it gradually develops in

Samson, is crucial to his self-knowledge and to the understanding of his relationship with God. Samson and others, such as the chorus and Manoa, have questioned, indeed impugned, Providence, likening God's justice to the wheel of fortune, which is turned blindly. They allege that God, after having chosen Samson to be his champion, inexplicably rejected him. Samson believes that he is alienated from God. As the poem unfolds it first becomes evident to the reader, rather than to the characters, that God had guided Samson into an encounter with the woman of Timna in order to warn his champion of the dangers of pride. In particular, Samson married the woman of Timna, a Philistine, who cajoled him until he disclosed the secret of a riddle that he had posed to the thirty groomsmen at his wedding. When he yields the secret of the riddle to her, she divulges it to the groomsmen. Despite God's plan to use this episode as a warning, Samson continues to be blinded by pride so that he falls into the snare of Dalila. Thus, his external blinding by the Philistines aptly signifies Samson's benighted spiritual state. In Milton's poem, moreover, Dalila is not simply a concubine, her role in Scripture, but Samson's wife. This point emphasizes the parallel between the woman of Timna and Dalila, though the essential difference is that Samson violates divine prohibition when he reveals the secret of his strength to Dalila. The marital relationship of Samson and Dalila also enables Milton to suggest contrasts with the conjugal union of Adam and Eve. Whereas Samson rejects Dalila, Adam and Eve pursue their regeneration cooperatively.

After his downfall, therefore, Samson must clarify his perception in order to begin the process of regeneration. By recognizing that pride was the cause of his downfall, Samson becomes contrite. In the course of his trials, which involve both physical affliction and psychological torment, Samson exercises patience, faith, and fortitude until he regains the state of spiritual readiness that will enable him to serve as an instrument of God. Ironically, no one, not even Samson, believes that he will again be called to service by God.

The three visitors Manoa, Dalila, and Harapha function unwittingly—another source of irony—to assist Samson in the process of regeneration. Paternal solicitude impels Manoa to negotiate with the Philistines for his son's liberation. If their desire for revenge against Samson is satisfied, Manoa believes, the Philistines may release his son. He does not recognize that enslavement by the Philistines is simply a sign of Samson's inward thralldom to sinful passions. Nor does he recognize that God's justice, rather than Philistine revenge, is to be satisfied and that Samson's suffering is both a means of divine retribution and a source of wisdom. Dalila, who seeks by various arguments to elicit Samson's forgiveness and to persuade him to be reunited with her, is rejected wholesale. In short, a measure of his progress is that Samson, who previously yielded to Dalila, resists her wiles.

Of all three visitors, Dalila is perhaps the most important because of past and present relationships with Samson. In his earlier relationship with Dalila, Samson recalls, he was "unwary" so that her "gins and toils" ensnared him. He likens her to a "bosom snake," suggesting that she had gained access to, and influence over, his innermost being. Though it has been anticipated by the woman of Timna, Samson calls Dalila's betrayal of him both "Matrimonial treason" and "wedlock-treachery." To describe his present rejection of Dalila, Samson resorts to classical allusions. He shuns her "fair enchanted cup" and remains impervious to her "warbling charms," thereby likening her to Circe and the Sirens, respectively. In his encounter with Dalila, Samson for the first time is gratified, rather than displeased, by the contrast between his past status and his present self. Another way of perceiving Samson's relationships with Dalila is by reference to Milton's *De Doctrina Christiana*. When Samson yielded to Dalila, he experienced evil temptation; as he resists her, he exercises virtue in the course of good temptation. Additionally, the rage that Dalila elicits in Samson carries over to his encounter with Harapha, who expects to see a crestfallen captive. Instead, Samson challenges the Philistine giant, who retreats.

The climax of the poem occurs when Samson, at first unwilling to attend the activities at the theater of Dagon, the Philistine idol, is impelled by "rousing motions" to go there. Initially, Samson feared that he would be publicly humiliated when performing feats of strength to entertain the Philistines; but his faith in the higher, but obscure, plan of Providence is rewarded not simply by the impulsion to attend the Dagonalia but by the inner light. "With inward eyes illuminated," Samson, who becomes aware of the divine will, exercises his volition in concert with it by collapsing the pillars that support the theater of Dagon. Significantly, Samson's death is described more as a resurrection, whereby he is likened to the phoenix that emerges from the conflagration at its funeral pyre. Finally, the fame that Samson achieves by his renewed spiritual readiness and service as God's agent transcends his previous glory from feats of strength and slaughter of the Philistines. After all, he is included among the heroes of faith celebrated in the Epistle to the Hebrews.

Not to be overlooked are the political dimensions of the poem, at times counteracting the more traditional outlook on Samson. The saga of Samson may allegorize the heroic ambitions and failings of the Puritan revolution, and his demise, rather than a sign of heroism, may be the product of self-delusion. *Samson Agonistes* may also emerge from Milton's personal and political circumstances—his blindness and his role during the rise and fall of a political movement in Britain toward which Providential intent was obscure.

If Milton conceived of his dramatic poem after the manner of Greek tragedy, the resemblance is clearcut. The unities of time, place, and action are observed. The poem begins at dawn and ends at noon on the same day. The single place for the action is the workhouse, where, after the destruction of the Philistines, a messenger gives an account of the catastrophe. The action centers on Samson's spiritual regeneration, culminating in his heroism. Because of Samson's death and victory, the poem combines features of classical tragedy and Christian drama of regeneration, for which the saga of Samson is a Hebraic prefiguration. When *Paradise Lost*, *Paradise Regained*, and *Samson Agonistes* are juxtaposed in their probable order of composition, the threefold arrangement, a virtual triptych, depicts Old Testament types—Adam and Samson—yielding to temptation, then undergoing regeneration; Christ's triumph over the tempter is the New Testament antitype at the center.

Milton's influence in later eras derives from his prose and his poetry. His treatises against various forms of oppression and tyranny have elicited admiration in many quarters and in different eras. In fact, his influence as a political writer was felt in the American, French, and Russian revolutions, when he was cited to justify the opposition to monarchs and absolutists. Among the English Romantics, Milton was extolled as a libertarian and political revolutionary. His refusal to compromise on matters of principle, his blindness, and his punishment after the Restoration have caused many admirers to cite Milton as a model of the spokesperson of truth and of someone who pursues idealism despite adversity.

Milton's reputation as one of the finest English poets was widespread soon after his death in 1674. While most of the critical attention was directed at *Paradise Lost*, it is essential to realize that his other works drew extensive commentary. In 1712 Joseph Addison devoted eighteen *Spectator* papers to *Paradise Lost*—six general essays and twelve others, one on each book of the epic. At times the outlook on Milton as a poet reflected the biases of the commentators. In the eighteenth century, for example, Tories and Anglicans had little admiration for him, but the Whigs were laudatory. Interestingly, *Paradise Lost* was cited for its contributions to the teaching of traditional Christianity because most interpreters were inattentive to possible implications in the epic that the Son might be subordinate to the Father. Also at the center of attention in the eighteenth century were the grandeur and sublimity of the poem. By the nineteenth century the critical outlook shifted to technical and stylistic features of the verse; but the Romantic admirers of the figure of Satan in *Paradise Lost*, including William Blake and Percy Bysshe Shelley, implicitly attacked the traditional theological and philosophical ideas in the work. Through the nineteenth and twentieth centuries Milton's reputation as a poet becomes quite complex. For a time, in fact, Milton fell into disrepute because of T. S. Eliot's adverse comments decrying the artificiality of his verse.

More recently, *Paradise Lost*, in particular, has been at the center of rich and diverse critical commentary. The theology of the epic, its indebtedness to works of classical antiquity, its adaptation of Scripture and the Genesis tradition, its Christian humanism, its political overtones, and its varied perspectives on gender relations—these and other topics are explored and debated. Even Milton's reputation as a misogynist has been challenged by feminists, who perceive tension in the Genesis tradition and in *Paradise Lost* between the orthodox hierarchical relationship of Adam and Eve and their reciprocal or complementary interaction, especially after their downfall and through their regeneration. Such commentary and the controversies that it ignites demonstrate that Milton's poetry, like his prose, has durability and applicability beyond the era in which it was composed. It is not simply of an age but for all time.

Bibliographies:

David H. Stevens, *A Reference Guide to Milton from 1800 to the Present Day* (Chicago: University of Chicago Press, 1930);

Harris F. Fletcher, *Contributions to a Milton Bibliography, 1800-1930* (Urbana: University of Illinois Press, 1931);

Calvin Huckabay, *John Milton: An Annotated Bibliography, 1929-1968*, revised edition (Pittsburgh: Duquesne University Press, 1969);

James Holly Hanford and William A. McQueen, *Milton*, second edition, Goldentree Bibliographies (Arlington Heights, Ill.: AHM, 1979);

John T. Shawcross, *Milton: A Bibliography for the Years 1624-1700* (Binghamton, N.Y.: Medieval & Renaissance Texts & Studies, 1984).

Biographies:

David Masson, *The Life of John Milton: Narrated in Connexion with the Political, Ecclesiastical, and Literary History of His Time*, 7 volumes (Cambridge & London: Macmillan, 1859-1894; volume 1 revised, 1881; index, 1894);

Helen Darbishire, ed., *The Early Lives of Milton* (London: Constable, 1932);

James Holly Hanford, *John Milton, Englishman* (New York: Crown, 1949);

Joseph Milton French, ed., *The Life Records of John Milton*, 5 volumes (New Brunswick, N.J.: Rutgers University Press, 1949-1958);

William Riley Parker, *Milton: A Biography*, 2 volumes (Oxford: Clarendon Press, 1968);

A. N. Wilson, *The Life of John Milton* (New York: Oxford University Press, 1983).

References:

Robert M. Adams, *Ikon: John Milton and the Modern Critics* (Ithaca, N.Y.: Cornell University Press, 1966);

Arthur Barker, ed., *Milton: Modern Essays in Criticism* (New York: Oxford University Press, 1965);

Joan S. Bennett, *Reviving Liberty: Radical Christian Humanism in Milton's Great Poems* (Cambridge, Mass.: Harvard University Press, 1989);

Boyd M. Berry, *Process of Speech: Puritan Religious Writing and Paradise Lost* (Baltimore: Johns Hopkins University Press, 1976);

Harry Blamires, *Milton's Creation: A Guide Through Paradise Lost* (London: Methuen, 1971);

Francis C. Blessington, *Paradise Lost and the Classical Epic* (London: Routledge, 1979);

C. M. Bowra, *From Virgil to Milton* (London: Macmillan, 1945);

John B. Broadbent, *Some Graver Subject: An Essay on Paradise Lost* (London: Schocken, 1967);

Archie Burnett, *Milton's Style* (London: Longman, 1981);

Douglas Bush, *Paradise Lost in Our Time: Some Comments* (New York: P. Smith, 1957);

Jackson I. Cope, *The Metaphoric Structure of Paradise Lost* (Baltimore: Johns Hopkins University Press, 1962);

Roy Daniells, *Milton, Mannerism, and Baroque* (Toronto: University of Toronto Press, 1963);

Dennis Danielson, ed., *The Cambridge Companion to Milton* (Cambridge: Cambridge University Press, 1989);

Helen Darbishire, *Milton's Paradise Lost* (Oxford: Clarendon Press, 1951);

Stevie Davies, *Images of Kingship in Paradise Lost* (Columbia: University of Missouri Press, 1983);

John G. Demaray, *Milton and the Masque Tradition* (Cambridge, Mass.: Harvard University Press, 1968);

Demaray, *Milton's Theatrical Epic: The Invention and Design of Paradise Lost* (Cambridge, Mass.: Harvard University Press, 1980);

John S. Diekhoff, *Milton's Paradise Lost: A Commentary on the Argument* (New York: Humanities Press, 1958);

T. S. Eliot, "Milton I," in his *On Poetry and Poets* (London: Faber & Faber, 1957);

William Empson, *Milton's God*, revised edition (London: Chatto & Windus, 1965);

J. M. Evans, *Paradise Lost and the Genesis Tradition* (London: Oxford University Press, 1968);

Anne Davidson Ferry, *Milton's Epic Voice: The Narrator in Paradise Lost* (Cambridge, Mass.: Harvard University Press, 1963);

Stanley Fish, *Surprised by Sin: The Reader in Paradise Lost* (New York: Macmillan, 1967);

Michael Fixler, *Milton and the Kingdoms of God* (Evanston, Ill.: Northwestern University Press, 1964);

Harris F. Fletcher, *The Intellectual Development of John Milton*, 2 volumes (Urbana: University of Illinois Press, 1956, 1962);

Northrop Frye, *The Return of Eden: Five Essays on Milton's Epics* (Toronto: University of Toronto Press, 1965);

Roland Mushat Frye, *Milton's Imagery and the Visual Arts: Iconographic Tradition in the Epic Poems* (Princeton, N.J.: Princeton University Press, 1978);

Helen Gardner, *A Reading of Paradise Lost* (Oxford: Oxford University Press, 1965);

Christopher Grose, *Milton's Epic Process: Paradise Lost and Its Miltonic Background* (New Haven: Yale University Press, 1973);

Christopher Hill, *Milton and the English Revolution* (New York: Viking, 1977);

John Spencer Hill, *John Milton, Poet, Prophet, Priest* (London: Macmillan, 1979);

E. A. J. Honigmann, *Milton's Sonnets* (New York: St. Martin's, 1966);

Merritt Y. Hughes, *Ten Perspectives on Milton* (New Haven: Yale University Press, 1965);

G. K. Hunter, *Paradise Lost* (London: Allen & Unwin, 1980);

William B. Hunter, Jr., C. A. Patrides, and J. H. Adamson, *Bright Essence: Studies in Milton's Theology* (Salt Lake City: University of Utah Press, 1971);

Hunter, gen. ed., *A Milton Encyclopedia*, 9 volumes (Lewisburg, Pa.: Bucknell University Press, 1978-1983);

John R. Knott, Jr., *Milton's Pastoral Vision: An Approach to Paradise Lost* (Chicago: University of Chicago Press, 1971);

Burton O. Kurth, *Milton and Christian Heroism: Biblical Epic Themes and Forms in Seventeenth-Century England* (Hamden, Conn.: Shoe String Press, 1966);

Jon S. Lawry, *The Shadow of Heaven: Matter and Stance in Milton's Poetry* (Ithaca, N.Y.: Cornell University Press, 1968);

Edward S. Le Comte, *Milton and Sex* (New York: Columbia University Press, 1978);

J. B. Leishman, *Milton's Minor Poems* (London: Hutchinson, 1969);

Barbara Kiefer Lewalski, *Milton's Brief Epic: The Genre, Meaning, and Art of Paradise Regained* (Providence, R.I.: Brown University Press, 1966);

C. S. Lewis, *A Preface to Paradise Lost*, revised edition (London & New York: Oxford University Press, 1960);

Michael Lieb, *Poetics of the Holy: A Reading of Paradise Lost* (Chapel Hill: University of North Carolina Press, 1981);

Lieb, *The Sinews of Ulysses: Form and Convention in Milton's Works* (Pittsburgh: Duquesne University Press, 1989);

Anthony Low, *The Blaze of Noon: A Reading of Samson Agonistes* (New York: Columbia University Press, 1974);

Isabel G. MacCaffrey, *Paradise Lost as Myth* (Cambridge, Mass.: Harvard University Press, 1959);

William G. Madsen, *From Shadowy Types to Truth: Studies in Milton's Symbolism* (New Haven: Yale University Press, 1968);

Louis L. Martz, *Poet of Exile: A Study of Milton's Poetry* (New Haven: Yale University Press, 1980);

Diane McColley, *Milton's Eve* (Urbana: University of Illinois Press, 1983);

Anna K. Nardo, *Milton's Sonnets and the Ideal Community* (Lincoln: University of Nebraska Press, 1979);

C. A. Patrides, *Milton and the Christian Tradition* (Oxford: Clarendon Press, 1966);

Patrides, ed., *Milton's Lycidas: The Tradition & the Poem*, second edition (Columbia: University of Missouri Press, 1983);

Elizabeth M. Pope, *Paradise Regained: The Tradition and the Poem* (Baltimore: Johns Hopkins University Press, 1947);

Mary Ann Radzinowicz, *Toward Samson Agonistes: The Growth of Milton's Mind* (Princeton, N.J.: Princeton University Press, 1978);

Balachandra Rajan, *The Lofty Rhyme: A Study of Milton's Major Poetry* (London: Routledge, 1970);

Rajan, *Paradise Lost and the Seventeenth-Century Reader* (London: Chatto & Windus, 1947);

Stella P. Revard, *The War in Heaven: Paradise Lost and the Tradition of Satan's Rebellion* (Ithaca, N.Y.: Cornell University Press, 1980);

Christopher Ricks, *Milton's Grand Style* (Oxford: Clarendon Press, 1963);

William G. Riggs, *The Christian Poet in Paradise Lost* (Berkeley: University of California Press, 1972);

Murray Roston, *Milton and the Baroque* (Pittsburgh: University of Pittsburgh Press, 1980);

John T. Shawcross, *Paradise Regain'd: Worthy T'Have Not Remain'd So Long Unsung* (Pittsburgh: Duquesne University Press, 1988);

Shawcross, *With Mortal Voice: The Creation of Paradise Lost* (Lexington: University of Kentucky Press, 1982);

Shawcross, ed., *Milton 1732-1801: The Critical Heritage* (London: Routledge, 1972);

John M. Steadman, *Epic and Tragic Structure in Paradise Lost* (Chicago: University of Chicago Press, 1976);

Steadman, *Milton and the Renaissance Hero* (Oxford: Clarendon Press, 1967);

Arnold Stein, *Answerable Style: Essays on Paradise Lost* (Seattle: University of Washington Press, 1953);

Stein, *The Art of Presence: The Poet and Paradise Lost* (Berkeley: University of California Press, 1977);

Joseph H. Summers, *The Muse's Method: An Introduction to Paradise Lost* (Cambridge, Mass.: Harvard University Press, 1962);

Edward Tayler, *Milton's Poetry: Its Development in Time* (Pittsburgh: Duquesne University Press, 1980);

James Thorpe, *John Milton: The Inner Life* (San Marino, Cal.: Huntington Library, 1983);

E. M. W. Tillyard, *Milton*, revised edition (London: Chatto & Windus, 1966);

James Grantham Turner, *One Flesh: Paradisal Marriage and Sexual Relations in the Age of Milton* (Oxford: Clarendon Press, 1987);

Rosemond Tuve, *Images and Themes in Five Poems by Milton* (Cambridge, Mass.: Harvard University Press, 1957);

A. J. A. Waldock, *Paradise Lost and Its Critics* (Cambridge: Cambridge University Press, 1947);

Joan M. Webber, *Milton and the Epic Tradition* (Seattle: University of Washington Press, 1979);

Joseph A. Wittreich, Jr., *Feminist Milton* (Ithaca, N.Y.: Cornell University Press, 1987);

Wittreich, *Visionary Poetics: Milton's Tradition and His Legacy* (San Marino, Cal.: Huntington Library, 1979);

Don M. Wolfe, *Milton in the Puritan Revolution* (New York: Humanities Press, 1963).

Papers:
Milton materials are scattered around the world, but most of the important collections of manuscripts and early printed editions are in Britain and the United States. In Britain, the important depositories are the British Library in London, the Bodleian Library in Oxford, and the Trinity College Library in Cambridge. In the United States the important depositories are the New York Public Library, the Folger Shakespeare Library, the Henry E. Huntington Library, the Yale University Libraries, the University of Kentucky Libraries, Columbia University Library, the Union Theological Seminary Library, the University of Illinois Library, and the Princeton University Library.

Samuel Pepys

(23 February 1633 - 26 May 1703)

This entry was updated by E. Pearlman (University of Colorado at Denver) from his entry in
DLB 101: British Prose Writers, 1660-1800: First Series

BOOKS: *Memoirs Relating to the State of the Royal Navy in England, for Ten Years, determin'd December 1688* (London: Printed for R. Griffin, 1690); facsimile, edited by J. R. Tanner as *Pepys' Memoires of the Royal Navy, 1679-1688* (Oxford: Clarendon Press, 1906);

An Account of the Preservation of King Charles after the Battle of Worcester, edited by Sir David Dalrymple (London: Printed for William Sandby, 1766);

Memoirs of Samuel Pepys, Esq., F. R. S., Secretary to the Admiralty in the Reigns of Charles II. and James II., Comprising His Diary from 1659 to 1669, Deciphered by the Rev. John Smith, 2 volumes, edited by Richard, Lord Braybrooke (London: Colburn, 1825);

Diary and Correspondence of Samuel Pepys, F. R. S., Secretary to the Admiralty in the Reigns of Charles II. and James II. . . . 3rd Edition, Considerably Enlarged, 5 volumes, edited by Braybrooke (London: Colburn, 1848, 1849);

Diary and Correspondence of Samuel Pepys, Esq., F. R. S., from His Manuscript Cypher in the Pepysian Library, 6 volumes, deciphered and edited by Rev. Mynors Bright (London: Bickers, 1875-1879);

The Diary of Samuel Pepys, 10 volumes, edited by Henry B. Wheatley (London & New York: Bell, 1893-1899);

Samuel Pepys's Naval Minutes, edited by J. R. Tanner (London: Printed for the Navy Records, 1926);

The Tangier Papers of Samuel Pepys, edited by Edwin Chappell (London: Printed for the Navy Records Society, 1935);

Mr. Pepys upon the State of Christ-Hospital, edited by Rudolf Kirk (Philadelphia: University of Pennsylvania Press / London; Oxford University Press, 1935);

Charles II's Escape from Worcester: A Collection of Narratives Assembled by Samuel Pepys, edited by William Matthews (Berkeley & Los Angeles: University of California Press, 1966);

The Diary of Samuel Pepys: A new and complete transcription, 11 volumes, edited by Robert Latham and William Matthews (Berkeley & Los Angeles: University of California Press, 1970-1983).

Samuel Pepys, author of the finest and best-known diary in English, was born in Salisbury Court near Fleet Street in London on 23 February 1633. He was the fifth of eleven children, of whom only three (Pepys the eldest) survived to adulthood. His father, John Pepys, was a tailor, his mother, Margaret Kite Pepys, the sister of a butcher. Pepys attended Huntingdon Grammar School, whose best-known graduate was Oliver Cromwell. From about 1646 Pepys studied at St. Paul's School, at that time adjacent to the great London cathedral. The curriculum was weak in mathematics, strong enough in classical languages and Hebrew to have well served John Milton, who had preceded Pepys by a generation. In his diary Pepys confessed to being "a great round-head when . . . a boy." After 1660, when royalty had been restored, Pepys repented of his youthful radicalism. He met an old classmate and was "much afeared that he would have remembered the words that I said the day that the King was beheaded (that were I to preach upon him, my text should be: 'The memory of the wicked shall rot')." From St. Paul's Pepys proceeded in 1650 to Magdalene College, Cambridge. Among his fellow students at Magdalene was John Dryden (a remote relation), with whom he maintained a lifelong acquaintanceship. At Cambridge Pepys composed a romance called "Love a Cheat," which he destroyed ten years later: "I wondered a little at myself at my vein at the time when I wrote it, doubting that I cannot do so well now if I would try." From about the age of twenty, Pepys suffered from kidney stones. On 26 March 1658, with "the pain growing insupportable," Pepys underwent major surgery and was relieved of a stone about the size of a tennis ball. He hon-

Samuel Pepys (portrait by Sir Godfrey Kneller; Sotheby's auction catalogue, 1 April 1931)

ored the date of his delivery with an annual feast.

Pepys was distantly connected to the powerful and wealthy Mountagu family. During the late 1650s, sometime after he took his bachelor's degree in March 1654, and while also employed as a clerk to George Downing in the Exchequer, Pepys served as secretary and man of business to Edward Mountagu (later first earl of Sandwich). On 1 December 1655 Pepys married Elizabeth St. Michel, who was fifteen years old, unconnected, and penniless. He later recalled that he had been "really sick" for love of her and compared his emotions to the feeling of being "ravished" by music.

Despite the youthful passion, the couple lived apart for a short period during 1657—a separation caused, Pepys says cryptically, by "differences" (possibly an attack of his recurrent jealousy). The separation was a harbinger of a generally stormy marriage. On the first day of 1660, Pepys began the shorthand diary which he kept so assiduously until the last day of May 1669:

Blessed be God, at the end of the last year I was in very good health, without any sense of my old pain but upon taking of cold.

I lived in Axe-yard, having my wife and servant Jane, and no more in family then us three.

Elizabeth Pepys (engraving by James Thomson after a portrait by John Hayls)

My wife, after the absence of her terms for seven weeks, gave me hopes of her being with child, but on the last day of the year she hath them again.

Pepys's patron Mountagu, once a strong parliamentarian, had become, with George Monck, one of the architects of Charles II's return from exile. In May 1660 Mountagu arranged for Pepys to accompany his fleet to Holland for the purpose of bringing Charles back to England, and it was Mountagu who in June procured Pepys's appointment as Clerk of the Acts to the Navy Board. Although Pepys was honest enough to admit that "chance without merit brought me in," he made the most of his opportunity. Public

service became his life's work and earned him a niche in administrative as well as naval history. As clerk he was one of the four senior officers on the Navy Board. Pepys was appointed to a navy that was totally chaotic by today's standards: ships might or might not be owned by the state; seamen were not regularly employed, and as a result there was no clear distinction between civilian and military; no regular systems were in place for supplying the ships or paying the men; officers were likely to be courtiers appointed without experience at sea; many administrators seem regularly to have jumbled their public and private accounts; the taking of gifts—bribes in modern terminology—was a standard procedure and

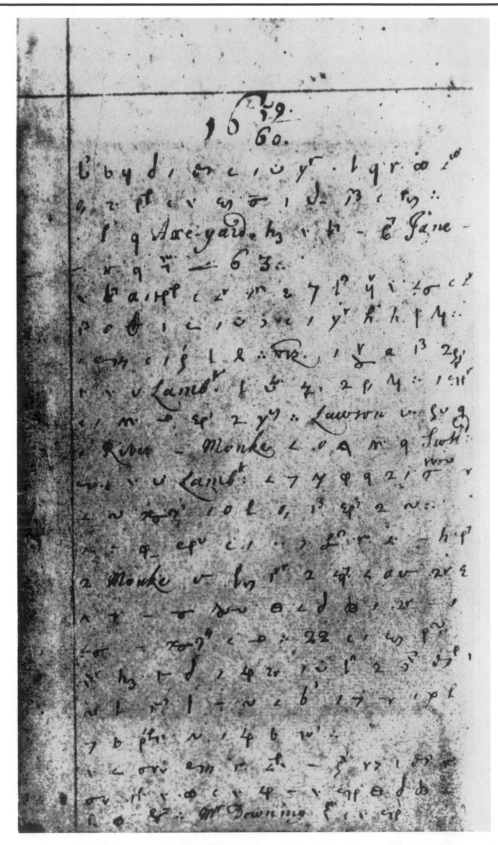

First and last pages from Pepys's shorthand diary (Magdalene College, Cambridge)

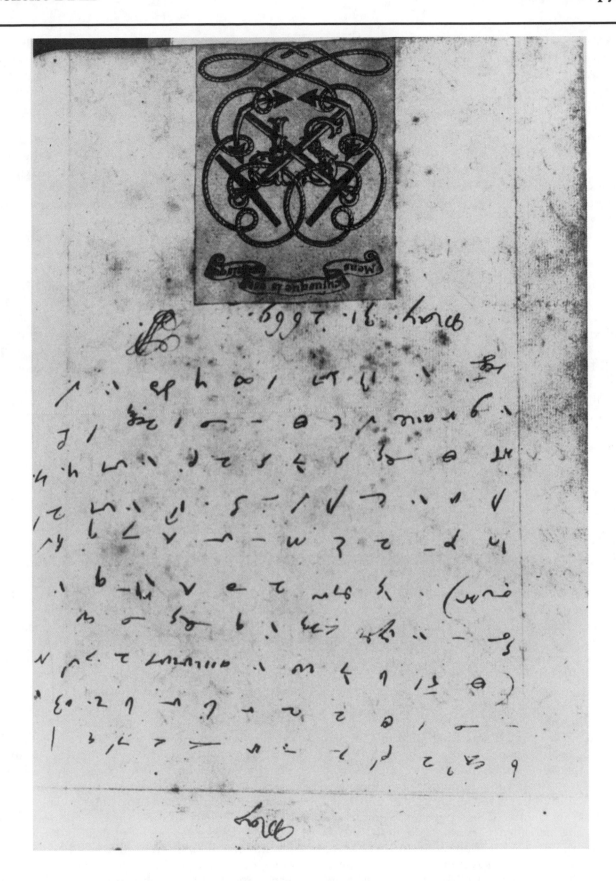

considered one of the perquisites of office. Pepys pioneered thousands of small changes that would eventually transform this chaos into an orderly and professional navy.

Pepys established his reputation as a knowledgeable and skilled public servant during the disastrous Second Dutch War (1665-1667). The failures of the navy, which were especially evident in Michel Adriaanszoon de Ruyter's courageous and daring Medway raid, were under investigation by angry committees of the Commons. Pepys took the lead in defending the management of the war, following the advice of his mentor Sir William Coventry "to be as short as I can, and obscure, saving in things fully plain," and he conducted himself so that "all the world that was within hearing, did congratulate me, and cry up my speech as the best thing they ever heard."

Pepys's marriage was under strain in 1668 and 1669 after Elizabeth discovered him with his "main" in his pubescent maid Deb Willet's "cunny." On 31 May 1669, troubled by severe pain in his eyes and convinced that he was going blind, he drew his diary to a poignant close: "and therefore resolve from this time forward to have it kept by my people in longhand, and must therefore be contented to set down no more then is fit for them and all the world to know. . . . And so I betake myself to the course, which is almost as much as to see myself go into my grave—for which, and all the discomforts that will accompany my being blind, the good God prepare me."

A few months later, on a holiday in the Low Countries and France, Elizabeth Pepys contracted a fever. She died on 10 November shortly after returning to England. Pepys never remarried; his intimate relationship with Mary Skinner began shortly after 1669 and continued to his death in 1703.

In June of 1673 Pepys left his clerkship for the Admiralty (to which the Navy Board reported). The admiral was King Charles's Roman Catholic brother James, whose exclusion from office at that time under the terms of the Test Act gave Pepys scope for administrative initiative. Pepys was able to prosecute a series of important reforms in shipbuilding, pensions, and what would now be called personnel practices. Pepys's seat in the House of Commons in 1673-1678, 1679, and 1685-1687 gave him a forum to speak on behalf of the navy. In 1678-1679, during the anti-Catholic hysteria associated with the Popish

Plot, Pepys was accused of being a secret Papist. He was imprisoned for six weeks under suspicion of espionage; the charges were ultimately dropped but not until he had spent an enormous amount of time and effort developing an elaborate defense. Pepys was out of office until 1683-1684, when he served as secretary to an expedition to supervise the abandonment of the Tangier Mole, a massive and expensive breakwater built to create an artificial harbor, which was perhaps the century's greatest military folly. His so-called second diary covers these events. In 1683 Pepys was suddenly returned to the Admiralty with a great deal more authority than he had previously enjoyed, but with the revolution of 1688, he left office never to return. He devoted his retirement years to expanding and cataloguing his collections and corresponding with some of the great men of his time. (He had served as President of the Royal Society in the 1680s.) On 26 May 1703 his great friend John Evelyn wrote in his own diary: "This day dyed Mr. Sam: Pepys, a very worthy, Industrious & curious person, none in England exceeding him in the Knowledge of the Navy. . . . [He] was universally beloved, Hospitable, Generous, Learned in many things, skill'd in Musick, a very great Cherisher of Learned men." It is difficult to discover the raffish young man of Pepys's diary in so respectable an epitaph.

The diary itself is an acute record not only of Pepys's life but of the public events of the first decade of the Restoration. It was kept with admirable diligence: in the 113 months from the beginning of January 1660 to the end of May 1669, there are only a handful of days for which Pepys made no entry. Altogether the diary is a massive work of about one and a quarter million words. Some years are more extensively chronicled than others: eighty-four thousand words in 1661, more than two hundred thousand in 1667. The diary was kept in a shorthand code based on Thomas Shelton's well-known *Short Writing* (1626, twenty-one subsequent editions before 1710). The system provided Pepys with the security which allowed him to write frankly and without fear of discovery. Pepys did not advertise the existence of his diary. He records mentioning it only to "the lieutenant of the *Swiftsure*" and to Coventry, and there is no reason to believe that during his lifetime it was ever glimpsed by any eyes other than his own. Erotic passages were kept in a macaronic cryptograph which, although not especially difficult to decipher, provided further protection from intrusion. But Pepys seems to have intended to bequeath the diary to posterity. It was carefully bound in six volumes, each labeled "IOVRNAL," and displayed publicly among the collections he willed to Magdalene College. The diary was decoded and printed, but only in part, in 1825. Successive editions added more material, but the whole—including the passages which Leslie Stephen announced in his *Dictionary of National Biography* entry "could not possibly be printed"—did not appear until the monumental and scrupulous edition of Robert Latham and William Matthews (1970-1983), which is an invaluable repository of information not only about Pepys but of almost everything and everyone he encountered or mentioned during the diary years. It is the principal resource for students of the diary or the diarist.

The diary is engaging both for content and style. It is best known and admired for two great anthology pieces—the accounts of the plague and fire of 1666. Now that it is available in unexpurgated form, Pepys's tormented affair with Deb Willet will become equally notorious. But the diary can be best appreciated by wide reading, especially of the later volumes, when the texture of experience deepens and Pepys reveals more and more about himself.

A reader of the diary becomes acquainted with a man of great verve and wide interests. Pepys was a virtuoso—a "learned and ingenious person"—curious about whatever was new and exciting, whether it was shipbuilding, the new sciences, music, languages, prints, ballads, mathematics, or the theater. He was also a Baconian who seemed never to be without his copy of *Faber Fortunae*. He was enthusiastic about beauty, especially the beauty of music and women; yet he labored constantly to resist the temptations of drink, of the theater, and of the numerous "Mrs. Bagwells" whom he pawed in closet, kitchen, or coach. He remained the tailor's son who admired clothes, both his own and others. He was extravagant about his own pleasures but kept his wife on a short financial leash. Pepys was a connoisseur of the ephemeral who preferred Sir Samuel Tuke's *Adventure of the Five Hours* to *Othello*, and *Sir Martin Mar-all* to *A Midsummer Night's Dream*. He was an eminently clubbable man and counted among his friends such distinguished individuals as Robert Hooke, Robert Boyle, John Wilkins, William Petty, and of course John Evelyn. He was an extraordinarily acquisitive and patient collector of ship models, scientific instruments, portraits,

ballads, money, and women. Pepys's diary may well be thought of as the most sophisticated expression of his instinct to collect and possess.

Pepys's prose style is worthy of the closest inspection. Here are two representative sentences drawn from his account of the days when the great fire was finally burning itself out: "At home did go with Sir W. Batten and our neighbor Knightly (who, with one more, was the only man of any fashion left in all the neighborhood hereabouts, they all removing their goods and leaving their houses to the mercy of the fire) to Sir R. Ford's and there dined, in an earthen platter a fried breast of mutton, a great many of us. But very merry; and endeed as good a meal, though as ugly a one, as ever I had in my life." Even so small a sample reveals a great deal about Pepys, including the fact that he was resilient enough to make sure that the disaster to the city would not compromise the pleasure of the table. The buoyant and heightened emotion that marks the diary is present in the superlatives which come so easily to his pen—"a great many," "very merry," "as ever I had in my life." Pepys has the eye for detail of a great novelist. Whenever possible, the general is supplanted by the particular: "an *earthen* platter"; "a *fried* breast of mutton." Pepys's world is specific, material, diverse, and a mingled yarn of the superlatively ugly and extraordinarily good.

The illusion of realism is created by the heaping of details, while the diary's immediacy is contrived by unobtrusive but effective tricks of style. The most obvious of these is ellipsis: "At home did go" omits the subject "I"; "But very merry" leaves out "we were." The elisions create the appearance of haste, spontaneity, even breathlessness. Spontanteity is also generated by Pepys's fluid grammar. In the first sentence above, for example, there are four successive grammatical subjects: first the elided "I"; next the first person plural which joins Pepys to his companions; third, the men "of fashion" of the neighborhood who are mentioned in the parenthetical insertion; and finally, the principal grammatical subject of the sentence—"a great many of us"—which makes its appearance as an enclitic tacked on to the end of the sentence, almost as afterthought. The suspended subject mimics the rhythms of informal conversation and generates the intimacy which make Pepys as much a companion as a figure out of the past. Added to these qualities is the wonderful appearance of verisimilitude. Neighbor Knightly, Pepys affirms, is the only "man of any fashion" who has not abandoned the blighted area. But the attentive reader must be subtly influenced by unemphatic modifiers ("with one more"; "hereabouts"). Pepys is content to allow a little vagueness; either he knows or thinks he may remember some other gentleman who also stayed on, or perhaps he waffles on the definition of "neighborhood." The modifiers reassure us that Pepys strives for exactness and accuracy, and they help to establish confidence and trust between diarist and reader.

In these two representative sentences, in fact, there is only one flaccid phrase: the gesture toward piety in the formulaic "*to the mercy* of the fire." On the whole Pepys artistically creates that sense of spontaneity, immediacy, trust, and verisimilitude which makes sustained reading of the Diary so easy and pleasurable. The passage sounds as if it were written "to the moment." But it is an illusion. Further reading in the diary tells us that Pepys did not compose this entry until 18 January 1667, or about three months after the events took place; rather, he kept notes on "loose papers," as seems to have been his general practice, and wrote in the diary when time permitted. Pepys is not a naive genius but an artist.

It is frequently asserted that Pepys is a modern person, recognizable as a member of our own civilization rather than of the late medieval world that we have lost. Pepys has been described as an individualist in an age of emerging individualism and a protocapitalist in a period marked by burgeoning entrepreneurship. Certainly, Pepys was a member of the first cohort of Englishmen for whom experience was organized not primarily around theology or faith, but around secular experience. Pepys was Christian in ceremonial terms, but indifferent to ideology. When Daniel Mills, the rector of St. Olave's, delivered "an unnecessary sermon upon Originall Sin, neither understood by himself nor the people," Pepys dismissed him as a "lazy fat priest." But on another occasion the same Mills distinguished himself, in Pepys's eyes at least, with "a very excellent and persuasive, good and moral sermon. Shewed like a wise man, that righteousness is a surer moral way of being rich, than sin and villainy." Mills's welcome and reassuring sermon was clearly part of the mysterious process by which Calvinist introspection was transformed into the Protestant ethic and became the servant rather than the antagonist of capitalism. Pepys's religion was tepid (though he was secretly attracted to the forms of Catholic worship), and his religious excla-

mations unselfconsciously comic; casting his accounts, "I did find myself really worth 1900 1., for which the Great God of Heaven and Earth be praised." Church attendance too had its consolations: "I did entertain myself with my perspective glass up and down the church, by which I had the great pleasure of seeing and gazing a great many very fine women. . . ."

The genuine modernity of Pepys is implicit in his attitude toward religion and can best be illustrated by comparing him with another diarist of his generation. Pepys's exact contemporary, Philip Henry, also recorded his reaction to the fire of London, but in very different terms. Henry confined his description of the event itself to a few general sentences, and then turned immediately to find a "use" for this "sad providence." Henry drew a series of lessons: that he should "get [his] heart deeply affected with . . . sin the cause of it, the nations sin . . ."; that he should distrust worldly success "seeing in one moment it makes to itself wings and flies away"; that the fire is a warning of that "terrible day . . . when all the world shall be of fire." Henry's diary entry is ingenious, allegorical, exotic, and stakes a claim to universality; Pepys's entry is richly detailed, concrete, and while indifferent to transcendent truth, is nevertheless convincing and human. A second example: when Philip Henry's son died, his diary entry paid only the scantest attention to the child and explored instead Henry's spiritual relationships: "Lord wherefore is it that thou contendest, show mee, show mee. Have I overboasted, over-loved, over-prized?" Pepys's response to the death of his brother Tom is egocentric in the modern sense. Its appeal is not to the supernatural but to the self, and Pepys is frank about his amusement with both human frailty and his own nature: "But Lord, to see how the world makes nothing of the memory of a man an hour after he is dead. And indeed, I must blame myself; for though at the sight of him, dead and dying, I had real grief for a while, while he was in my sight, yet presently after and ever since, I have had very little grief indeed for him." It is in these forthright sentences rather than in Philip Henry's allegorizing that we recognize ourselves.

The changes in his own personality that Pepys records also contribute to the sense of the modernity of his own person. Learning self-discipline and learning how to keep to business are the principal themes of the diary. In the beginning, Pepys regularly suffered the chagrin of the

Pepys's library in York Buildings, King Street, where he went to live in 1679. The book presses are now in the Pepys Library at Magdalene College, Cambridge (drawing by Nichols, circa 1693; Magdalene College, Cambridge).

chronically dissolute: "at night to Sir W. Battens and there very merry with a good barrell of oysters; and this is the present life I lead." The conflict between the desire for pleasure and the need for industry constitutes the comic backdrop of the diary: "But Lord, to consider how my natural desire is to pleasure, which God be praised that he hath given me the power by my late oaths to curb so well as I have done, and will do again after two or three plays more." Indeed, the diary records in full the contention between industry and idleness: "Against my nature and will (yet such is the power of the Devil over me I could not refuse it) to the Theatre and saw *The Merry Wives of Windsor*, ill done. . . . And after supper to prayers." Pepys struggled mightily to gain control of his hedonistic impulses, even to devising an elaborate scheme of oaths and monetary penalties to keep himself out of harm's way: "So I . . . to the office, where I did with great content faire a vow to mind my business and laisser aller les femmes for a month." Though the battle remained unresolved, there is ample evidence that Pepys had become productive and efficient.

In sum, several qualities combine to make Pepys's diary so wonderful. Pepys was curious about all things and at the center of important events. He was both passionate and honest. His prose style is uniquely suited to its purpose. In addition, the diary reveals almost novelistic themes—the secularization of theology, the struggle between idleness and diligence, the pleasures and pains of marriage and infidelity. One final set of traits also contributes mightily to the success of the diary. The same Pepys who was so frank about the achievement of discipline was also very vain of his orderliness. Even Edward Hyde, Earl of Clarendon congratulated him saying, according to Pepys, that "no man in England was of more method. . . than myself." Pepys was sometimes amazed at his own passion for order: "my delight is in the neatness of everything, and so cannot be pleased with anything unless it be very neat, which is a strange folly." He was also a fanatic about secrecy, and once attacked his brother John, calling him "Asse and Coxcomb, for which I am sorry" for leaving a door unlocked. "One thing that I hate in others and more in myself, to be careless of keys." Verve alone would have resulted in a marvelous life, but verve allied to secrecy and orderliness produced the marvelous diary.

Letters:

Private Correspondence and miscellaneous papers of Samuel Pepys, 1679-1703, 2 volumes, edited by J. R. Tanner (London: Bell, 1926; New York: Harcourt, Brace, 1926);

Further Correspondence of Samuel Pepys, 1662-1679, edited by Tanner (London: Bell, 1929; New York: Harcourt, Brace, 1929);

Letters and the Second Diary of Samuel Pepys, edited by E. G. Howarth (London: J. M. Dent / New York: Dutton, 1932);

Shorthand Letters of Samuel Pepys, edited by Edwin Chappell (Cambridge: Cambridge University Press, 1933);

Letters of Samuel Pepys and His Family Circle, edited by Helen Truesdell Heath (Oxford: Clarendon Press, 1955).

Bibliography:

Dennis G. Donovan, *Elizabethan Bibliographies Supplements XVIII John Evelyn (1920-1968) Samuel Pepys, 1933-1968* (London: Nether Press, 1970).

Biographies:

Arthur Bryant, *Samuel Pepys*, 3 volumes (Cam-

bridge: Cambridge University Press / New York: Macmillan, 1933);

John Harold Wilson, *The Private Life of Mr. Pepys* (New York: Farrar, Straus & Cudahy, 1959);

Richard Ollard, *Pepys: A Biography* (London: Hodder & Stoughton, 1974).

References:

Marjorie Hope Nicolson, *Pepys' Diary and the New Science* (Charlottesville: University Press of Virginia, 1965);

E. Pearlman, "Pepys and Lady Castlemaine," *Restoration*, 7 (Fall 1983): 43-53;

Ivan E. Taylor, *Samuel Pepys* (New York: Twayne, 1967).

Papers:

Pepys's books and papers, including the manuscript for his diary, are in the Pepys Library at Magdalene College, Cambridge.

Alexander Pope

(21 May 1688 - 30 May 1744)

The entry was written by Aubrey L. Williams (University of Florida) for DLB 95: Eighteenth-Century British Poets: First Series.

See also the Pope entry in DLB 101: British Prose Writers, 1660-1800: First Series.

SELECTED BOOKS: *An Essay On Criticism* (London: Printed for W. Lewis & sold by W. Taylor, T. Osborn & J. Graves, 1711);

The Critical Specimen (London, 1711);

Windsor-Forest. To the Right Honourable George Lord Lansdown (London: Printed for Bernard Lintott, 1713);

The Narrative of Dr. Robert Norris, Concerning the strange and deplorable Frenzy of Mr. John Denn-- (London: Printed for J. Morphew, 1713);

The Rape of the Lock. An Heroi-Comical Poem. In Five Canto's (London: Printed for Bernard Lintott, 1714; revised, 1718);

The Temple of Fame: A Vision (London: Printed for Bernard Lintott, 1715);

A Key to the Lock. Or, A Treatise proving, beyond all Contradiction, the dangerous Tendency of a late Poem, entituled, The Rape of the Lock, to Government and Religion. By Esdras Barnivelt, Apoth. (London: Printed for J. Roberts, 1715);

The Dignity, Use and Abuse of Glass-Bottles. Set forth in A Sermon Preach'd to an Illustrious Assembly, And now Publish'd for the Use of the Inferiour Clergy, sometimes attributed to Pope (London: Printed & sold by the Booksellers of London & Westminster, 1715);

The Iliad of Homer, Translated by Mr. Pope, 6 volumes (London: Printed by W. Bowyer for Bernard Lintott, 1715-1720);

A Full and True Account of a Horrid and Barbarous Revenge by Poison, On the Body of Mr. Edmund Curll, Bookseller (London: Sold by J. Roberts, J. Morphew, R. Burleigh, J. Baker & S. Popping, 1716);

God's Revenge Against Punning [single sheet] (London: Printed for J. Roberts, 1716);

A Further Account of the most Deplorable Condition of Mr. Edmund Curll, Bookseller (London: Printed & sold by all the Publishers, Mercu-

Alexander Pope in 1716 (painting by Godfrey Kneller; Collection of Baron Barnard, Raby Castle, Durham)

ries, and Hawkers within the Bills of Mortality, 1716);

The Works of Mr. Alexander Pope (London: Printed by W. Bowyer for Bernard Lintot, 1717; enlarged edition, Dublin: Printed by & for George Grierson, 1727);

A Clue To the Comedy of the Non-Juror. With some Hints of Consequence Relating to that Play. In a Letter to N. Rowe, Esq; Poet Laureat to His Majesty (London: Printed for E. Curll, 1718);

The Odyssey of Homer, 5 volumes, translated by Pope (London: Printed for Bernard Lintot, 1725-1726);

*Miscellanea. In Two Volumes.—Never before Published.
—Viz. I. Familiar Letters Written to Henry Cromwell Esq. by Mr. Pope. II. Occasional Poems by
Mr. Pope, Mr. Cromwell, Dean Swift, &c. III.
Letters from Mr. Dryden to a Lady* (London,
1727 [i.e., 1726]);

The Dunciad. An Heroic Poem. In Three Books
(Dublin, Printed, London Reprinted for A.
Dodd [i.e., London: Printed for A. Dodd],
1728);

*The Dunciad, Variorum. With the Prolegmena of
Scriblerus* (London: Printed for A. Dod,
1729);

*An Epistle To The Right Honourable Richard Earl
of Burlington. Occasion'd by his Publishing
Palladio's Designs of the Baths, Arches, Theatres,
&c. of Ancient Rome* (London: Printed for L.
Gilliver, 1731); enlarged as *Of False Taste . . .*
(London: Printed for L. Gilliver, 1731 [i.e.,
1732]);

Of The Use of Riches, An Epistle To the Right Honorable Allen Lord Bathurst (London: Printed by
J. Wright for Lawton Gilliver, 1732 [i.e.,
1733]);

*The First Satire Of The Second Book of Horace, Imitated in a Dialogue between Alexander Pope of
Twickenham in Comm. Midd. Esq.; on the one
Part, and his Learned Council on the other* (London: Printed by L. G. & sold by A. Dodd, E.
Nutt & the Booksellers of London & Westminster, 1733);

An Essay On Man. Address'd to a Friend.—Part I (London: Printed for J. Wilford, 1733);

An Essay On Man. In Epistles to a Friend.—Epistle II
(London: Printed for J. Wilford, 1733);

*An Essay On Man. In Epistles to a Friend.—Epistle
III* (London: Printed for J. Wilford, 1733);

The Impertinent, Or A Visit to the Court. A Satyr (London: Printed for John Wileord [Wilford],
1733);

*An Epistle To The Right Honourable Richard Lord
Visct. Cobham* (London: Printed for Lawton
Gilliver, 1733 [i.e., 1734]);

*An Essay On Man. In Epistles to a Friend.—Epistle
IV* (London: Printed for J. Wilford, 1734);

An Essay on Man, Being the First Book of Ethic Epistles. To Henry St. John, L. Bolingbroke [Epistles
I-IV] (London: Printed by John Wright for
Lawton Gilliver, 1734; Philadelphia: Printed
by William Bradford, 1747);

A Most Proper Reply to the Nobleman's Epistle to a Doctor of Divinity (London: Printed & sold by J.
Huggonson, 1734);

*The First Satire Of The Second Book of Horace, Imitated in Dialogue Between Alexander Pope of
Twickenham in Com' Mid' Esq; and his Learned
Council.—To which is added, The Second Satire
of the same Book* (London: Printed for L. G.,
1734);

*Sober Advice From Horace, To The Young Gentlemen
about Town. As deliver'd in his Second Sermon*
(London: Printed for T. Boreman, 1734); republished as *A Sermon against Adultery* (London: Printed for T. Cooper, 1738);

An Epistle From Mr. Pope, To Dr. Arbuthnot (London: Printed for Lawton Gilliver, 1735);

The Works of Mr. Alexander Pope, Volume II (London: Printed for L. Gilliver, 1735);

Of The Characters of Women: An Epistle To A Lady (London: Printed for Lawton Gilliver,
1735);

Letters of Mr. Pope, and Several Eminent Persons (London: Printed & sold by the Booksellers of
London & Westminster, 1735);

*A Narrative of the Method by which Mr. Pope's Private Letters were procured and published by
Edmund Curll, Bookseller* (London, 1735);

*The Second Epistle Of The Second Book of Horace,
Imitated* (London: Printed for R. Dodsley,
1737);

*The First Epistle Of The Second Book of Horace,
Imitated* (London: Printed for T. Cooper,
1737);

*Letters of Mr. Alexander Pope, and Several of his
Friends* (London: Printed by J. Wright for
J. Knapton, L. Gilliver, J. Brindley & R.
Dodsley, 1737);

The Sixth Epistle Of The First Book of Horace Imitated (London: Printed for L. Gilliver, 1737
[i.e., 1738]);

*The First Epistle Of The First Book Of Horace
Imitated* (London: Printed for R. Dodsley,
1738);

One Thousand Seven Hundred and Thirty Eight. A Dialogue Something like Horace (London: Printed
for T. Cooper, 1738);

One Thousand Seven Hundred and Thirty Eight. Dialogue II (London: Printed for R. Dodsley,
1738);

Letters between Dr. Swift, Mr. Pope, &c. (London:
Printed for T. Cooper, 1741);

The Works of Mr. Alexander Pope, In Prose. Vol. II
(London: Printed for J. & P. Knapton, C.
Bathurst & R. Dodsley, 1741);

The New Dunciad: As it was Found In the Year 1741
(London: Printed for T. Cooper, 1742);

The Dunciad, in Four Books. Printed according to the complete Copy found in the Year 1742 (London: Printed for M. Cooper, 1743);

The Last Will and Testament of Alexander Pope, of Twickenham, Esq. (London: Printed for A. Dodd, 1744);

The Works of Alexander Pope Esq. In Nine Volumes Complete. With His Last Corrections, Additions, And Improvements; As they were delivered to the Editor a little before his Death; Together With the Commentaries and Notes of Mr. Warburton (London: Printed for J. & P. Knapton, 1751).

Editions: *The Prose Works of Alexander Pope*, volume 1, edited by Norman Ault (Oxford: Blackwell, 1936); volume 2, edited by Rosemary Cowler (Hamden, Conn: Archon Books, 1986);

Memoirs of the Extraordinary Life, Works, and Discoveries of Martinus Scriblerus, by Pope, Jonathan Swift, John Arbuthnot, John Gay, Thomas Parnell, and Robert Harley, Earl of Oxford; edited by Charles Kerby-Miller (New Haven: Yale University Press, 1950);

Literary Criticism of Alexander Pope, edited by Bertrand A. Goldgar (Lincoln: University of Nebraska Press, 1965);

Selected Prose of Alexander Pope, edited by Paul Hammond (Cambridge: Cambridge University Press, 1987).

OTHER: *The Works of Shakespear*, 6 volumes, edited, with a preface, by Pope (London: Printed for Jacob Tonson, 1725);

Preface to *Miscellanies in Prose and Verse. The First Volume*, edited by Pope and Jonathan Swift (London: Printed for Benjamin Motte, 1727);

"Memoirs of P. P. Clerk of This Parish," "Stradling versus Stiles," and "Thoughts on Various Subjects," in *Miscellanies. The Second Volume*, edited by Pope and Swift (London: Printed for Benjamin Motte, 1727);

Peri Bathous: or, Martinus Scriblerus. His Treatise of the Art of Sinking in Poetry, in *Miscellanies. The Last Volume*, edited by Pope and Swift (London: Printed for B. Motte, 1727);

"To The Reader" and letters, in *The Posthumous Works of William Wycherley, Esq; In Prose and Verse. The Second Volume*, edited by Pope (London: Printed for J. Roberts, 1729);

"A Strange but True Relation How Edmund Curll of Fleetstreet, Stationer, Out of an extraordinary Desire of Lucre, went into Change-Alley, and was converted from the Christian Religion by certain Eminent Jews: And how he was circumcis'd and initia-ted into their Mysteries" and "An Essay Of the Learned Martinus Scriblerus, Concerning the Origine of Science," in *Miscellanies. The Third Volume*, edited by Pope and Swift (London: Printed for Benj. Motte, 1732).

There was a time when scholars, and educated people in general, tended to think of the first half of the eighteenth century as the "Age of Pope." Now the period is more commonly termed the Augustan Age or the Neoclassical period. Yet the earlier denomination, no matter its simplistic emphasis on the poetic art of one man at the expense of great achievements by others in prose fiction, accurately reflects the fact that Alexander Pope, both in his superbly crafted verse and in his equally crafted public persona, seemed, in the eyes of many gifted literary contemporaries if not of everyone else, to be the presiding artistic genius of his time.

Some degree of the esteem, and even awe, aroused by his poetic powers and by his reputation for an exalted ethical rectitude is reflected in the words of two of his most eminent contemporaries. Jonathan Swift, one of Pope's dearest friends, in a fit of poetic petulance perhaps not altogether feigned, wrote, in *Verses on the Death of Dr. Swift* (1739):

> In Pope, I cannot read a Line,
> But with a Sigh, I wish it mine:
> When he can in one Couplet fix
> More Sense than I can do in Six:
> It gives me such a jealous Fit,
> I cry, Pox take him, and his Wit.

The second testimony comes from David Garrick, the most esteemed actor of the eighteenth century, who in later life recalled the occasion in the winter of 1742 when Pope, who had less than two years to live, attended a triumphant appearance of Garrick in the title role of Shakespeare's *Richard III*. "When I was told . . . that POPE was in the house," Garrick said, "I instantaneously felt a palpitation at my heart; a tumultuous, not a disagreeable emotion in my mind. I was then in the prime of youth; and in the zenith of my theatrical ambition. It gave me a particular pleasure that RICHARD was my character, when POPE was to see, and hear me. As I opened my part; I saw our little poetical hero; dressed in black; seated in a side box, near the stage; and viewing me with a serious, and earnest attention. His look

Edith Turner Pope, the poet's mother (etching by C. Carter, based on a drawing by Jonathan Richardson)

shot, and thrilled, like lightning, through my frame; and I had some hesitation in proceeding, from anxiety, and from joy. As RICHARD gradually blazed forth, the house was in a roar of applause; and the conspiring hand of Pope shadowed me with laurels." The character Garrick was playing before the diminutive hunchback Pope was ironically that of the legendary "crookback" Richard III.

Tributes such as these, while serving to recall the genuine esteem in which Pope was regarded by some of the best talents of his time, obviously give a lopsided impression of the character and art of a man whose actual existence, to use his own words about the life of any so-called wit (in the preface to the 1717 edition of his collected works), was for the most part "a warfare upon earth." Throughout his life Pope struggled not only with the extreme infirmities of a congenitally frail constitution but also against various establishments—religious, political, and critical—

of his time. And as much as it is possible to see him as the very glass and mold of his age (master of a shimmering poetic mode and self-conscious avatar of certain traditional and putatively classical values, private as well as public), it is well to keep in mind that he was also a spokesman for values and visions soon to be almost totally forsaken and for which he was to suffer reprobation in the oncoming Romantic and Victorian climates of sensibility. Though he became, in the eyes of many, *arbiter morum* as well as *arbiter elegantiarum* to his own age, he himself was guilty of enough bellicosity, petty intrigue, and self-aggrandizement to forfeit, for many nineteenth-century readers, the high and special regard he received through most of the eighteenth century. In the twentieth century, with the publication of a definitive edition of all his works, a five-volume edition of his letters, and a substantive and sympathetic biography, as well as the arrival of a critical sensibility willing to engage his art in more understanding and more historical terms, Pope once again, with all his many personal shortcomings, seems securely positioned as the greatest English poet between John Milton and William Wordsworth.

The year of Pope's birth, 1688, was also the year of the "Glorious Revolution," when the Roman Catholic monarch James II, having alienated most of the overwhelmingly Protestant population of England by his foolish endeavors to impose Romish policies and appointees on church and state, was forced to abdicate his throne. Fleeing to France, James was replaced by William of Orange, a Protestant Dutch prince who had married James's Protestant daughter Mary and who had been invited to assume the throne by a coalition of Whigs and Tories, Anglicans, and Dissenters. The major group disadvantaged by this relatively peaceful revolution was the Roman Catholics; for repressive measures soon prohibited them from openly practicing their religion or holding public office, from inheriting and purchasing land or owning a horse valued at more than five pounds (an animal worth five pounds or less would presumably be of little military value), from living within ten miles of London, and from attending "public schools" (such as Eton, Rugby, and Westminster) or the Universities of Oxford and Cambridge. Such strictures, while not always rigorously enforced, necessarily circumscribed and influenced the daily life and upbringing of the young Pope, the child of Catholic parents, requiring that he be educated in private schools of uneven quality or tutored at home, determining to some extent how and where he lived, instilling in him and other Catholics even from childhood a sense that, no matter how patriotic and loyal they might feel as Englishmen, they were regarded by most of their fellow countrymen as alien, perhaps even subversive. Pope's own resentment at such status surfaces frequently in his mature verse, as in *The Second Epistle Of The Second Book of Horace, Imitated* (1737), when he writes of "certain Laws, by Suff'rers thought unjust," which not only deprived his own family of their "paternal Cell" but denied to any Roman Catholic "all Hopes of Profit or of Trust"; or when he alludes to the London Monument—erected in memory of the Great Fire of 1666 and bearing an inscription blaming Catholics for that catastrophe—as a "tall bully" who "lifts the head, and lyes" (*Of The Use of Riches*, 1732).

Pope's father, also named Alexander, was a London linen merchant; the poet was the only child of his second marriage, to Edith Turner, of a Yorkshire family. In an edition of Virgil he later possessed, Pope recorded the exact time of his birth as follows: "Natus Maji 21, 1688, Hora Post Merid. 6 3/4." In his early childhood Pope lived in London or its environs, but in 1700 his father, who apparently retired from business about the time of his son's birth, moved his family, perhaps to comply with the ten-mile exclusionary law, to the village of Binfield, in the royal forest of Windsor. Before the move the young Pope had received some more or less formal schooling at two small Catholic academies, at one of which he was "whipped and ill-used," according to Joseph Spence, for a "satire on his master, and taken from thence on that account." Until he was about twelve, therefore, Pope's educational experience was sporadic, frequently tutorial, certainly haphazard, and foreshortened, as is apparent when he speaks of his first teacher, a priest named Bannister who started him in "Latin and Greek together": "I was then about eight years old, had learnt to read of an old aunt, and to write by copying printed books. After having been under that priest about a year I was sent to the seminary at Twyford, and then to a school by Hyde Park Corner [in London]—and with the two latter masters lost what little I had got under my first. [When] about twelve, I went with my father into the Forest [to Binfield] and there learned for a few months under a fourth priest. This was all the teaching I ever had, and God knows, it extended a very little way." In effect, Pope's education was largely the result of his own intense energy and assiduity: "He set to learning Latin and Greek by himself [at] about twelve," reported a cousin (who was also a Catholic priest), "and when he was about fifteen would go up to London [by himself] and learn French and Italian. We in the family looked upon it as a wildish sort of resolution, for as his ill health would not let him travel we could not see any reason for it. He stuck to it, went thither, and mastered both those languages with a surprising dispatch. Almost everything of this kind was of his own acquiring. He had had masters indeed, but they were very indifferent ones, and what he got was almost wholly owing to his own unassisted industry." Irregular and autodidactic as it was, Pope's learning was eventually such that he could move at ease among many of the best and most formally trained minds of his age.

Pope at age seven (anonymous portrait; collection of James M. Osborn, New Haven)

It was not only by a restrictive religious segregation and civil disfranchisement that Pope was early set apart. Although as a child he was described, according to Spence, as having a "particularly sweet temper" and a face that was "round, plump, pretty, and of a fresh complexion," at some time during his twelfth year, having already survived a trampling by a "wild cow" when he was about three, his outward form began to exhibit the ruinous consequences of Pott's disease (tuberculosis of the spine), which he must have contracted during infancy, possibly from his nurse's breast-feeding. For Pope the infection meant a crooking of chest and humping of back, along with a devastation of constitution so severe that for the rest of his life he seemed, in the solicitous words of one of his later friends, Allen, Lord Bathurst, "to have the headache four days in a week, and to be as sick as a breeding woman the other three" (in a 20 July 1732 letter to Pope). A description of Pope by the painter Sir

Joshua Reynolds, who must have scrutinized him with an eye trained better than most, gives us a vivid image of his appearance in his early fifties. He stood, wrote Reynolds, "about four feet six high; very humpbacked and deformed; he wore a black coat; and according to the fashion of that time, had on a little sword; he had a large and very fine eye, and a long handsome nose; his mouth had those peculiar marks which always are found in the mouths of crooked persons; and the muscles which run across the cheek were so strongly marked as to appear like small cords. [Louis François] Roubilliac, the statuary, who made a bust of him from life, observed that his countenance was that of a person who had been much afflicted with headache, and he should have known the fact from the contracted appearance of the skin between his eyebrows, though he had not otherwise been apprised of it."

While Pope's friends might have regarded his deformation and infirmities with fond and so-

The house at Binfield in Windsor Forest, where Pope spent his boyhood. Windsor-Forest *and the* Pastorals *were inspired by this idyllic setting.*

licitous eyes, he early in life got a taste of how harsh and pitiless the gaze of others could be. In his precocious *Essay On Criticism* (1711), begun in his teens and published just before his twenty-third birthday, Pope was so rash and impudent as to deride the critical dicta, as well as the mien and mannerisms, of John Dennis, a leading critic but mediocre playwright, under the sobriquet of "Appius," who "reddens at each Word you speak, / And *stares, Tremendous!* with a *threatning Eye,* / Like some *fierce Tyrant* in *Old Tapestry!*" Dennis *had* written a failed tragedy entitled *Appius and Virginia,* his favorite adjective (as everyone knew) *was* "tremendous," and he *was* famed for his overbearing manner. But in return for the effrontery of this caricature, no matter its basic accuracy (or because of it), the youthful Pope was subjected not only to a savage attack on the content and style of *An Essay On Criticism,* his Roman Catholicism, and his supposed Jacobite sympathies for the exiled James II, but to the following brutal words: "As there is no Creature in Nature so ven-

omous, there is nothing so stupid and so impotent as a hunch-back'd Toad'; a "young, squab, short Gentleman," marked by "the very Bow of the God of Love"; let his person "be never so contemptible, his inward Man is ten times more ridiculous; it being impossible that his outward Form, tho' it should be that of downright Monkey, should differ so much from human Shape, as his immaterial unthinking part does from human Understanding."

Baptized, indeed drenched, so early by so wrathful and so caustic an assault on his personal figure, Pope acquired, outwardly at least, the fortitude and the witty and deprecatory regard of self that would enable him to face, with at least an appearance of sangfroid and nonchalance, a lifetime of personal abuse from hostile quarters. Only a year after Dennis's onslaught, in a letter to Sir Richard Steele printed in the *Guardian,* 12 August 1713, Pope wrote: "When a smart fit of sickness tells me this scurvy tenement of my body will fall in a little time, I am e'en as

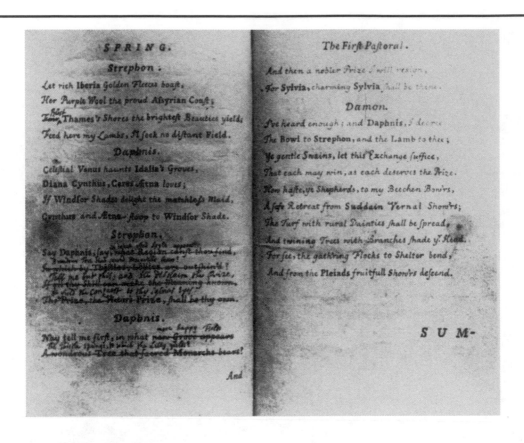

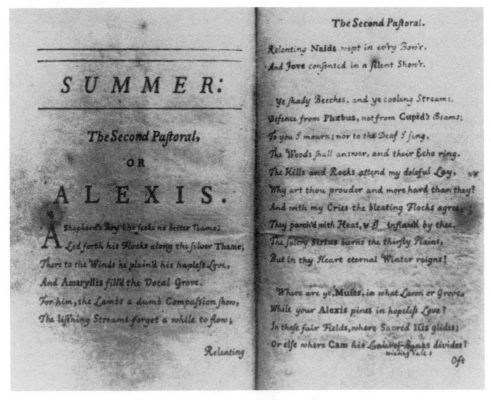

Last two pages of "Spring" and first two pages of "Summer" in the earliest extant manuscript (circa 1704) for Pope's Pastorals, *in the hand Pope used to imitate printing (Christie, Manson & Woods, Ltd., auction catalogue, 11-12 June 1980)*

unconcern'd as was that honest *Hibernian,* who being in bed in the great storm some years ago [the terrible "great storm" of 1703], and told the house would tumble over his head, made answer, What care I for the house? I am only a lodger." Years later this same cast of mind enabled him to regard with scornful amusement those who, in their efforts to flatter favors out of him, made attempts to transmute his obvious physical defects into the physiognomical traits and signs of genius. In his *Epistle to Dr. Arbuthnot* (1735) he writes: "There are, who to my Person pay their court, / I cough like *Horace,* and tho' lean, am short, / *Ammon*'s great Son [Alexander the Great] one shoulder had too high, / Such *Ovid*'s nose, and 'Sir! you have an *Eye*'— / Go on, obliging Creatures, make me see / All that disgrac'd my Betters, met in me." A mind of such mettle may make itself the stuff of poetry, as when Pope reminds himself (and his readers) of his deportment in spite of a harrowing personal disfigurement: "What is't to me (a Passenger God wot) / Whether my Vessel be first-rate or not? / The Ship it self may make a better figure, / But I that sail, am neither less nor bigger" (*The Second Epistle Of The Second Book of Horace, Imitated*). As a twentieth-century writer has said about a twentieth-century poet: "If poems can teach one anything, [Philip] Larkin's teach that there is no desolation so bleak it cannot be made habitable by style. If we live inside a bad joke, it is up to us to learn, at best and worst, to tell it well" (Jonathan Raban, *Coasting,* 1987).

The move to Binfield was a propitious one for Pope, for there, among a circle of Roman Catholic neighbors, he established some of his most enduring friendships. Among others, he came to know John Caryll, through whom he probably met such notable literary figures as the playwright William Wycherley and the celebrated actor Thomas Betterton. He became friendly also with the two young sisters Martha and Teresa Blount, both of whom were later to appear in some of his finest verse, and one of whom, Martha, was to be his lifelong friend (supposed by some, who were probably mistaken, to be his mistress). The warm, and affectionate regard Pope received from this group was powerfully supplemented by the attention and favor he gained from Sir William Trumbull, a statesman who had served three English monarchs and who, now retired to his estate near Binfield, acted as verderer, or overseer, of the Windsor Forest district. With Trumbull, Pope was later to say, he used

"to take a ride" on horseback in the forest "three or four days in the week, and at last, almost every day." Trumbull's affection for Pope was intense. He wrote his nephew in 1707 that "the little creature is my darling more and more." It was he, furthermore, who urged Pope to write a poem on Windsor Forest and to attempt translations of Homer. By this time Pope also apparently had come to the attention of William Walsh, member of Parliament and a minor poet and critic, and William Congreve, the best dramatist of the late seventeenth century. The results of the encouragement and fostering given to Pope by such eminent early admirers are evident in the following letter which he, a lad of seventeen, received on 20 April 1706 from Jacob Tonson, the leading publisher of the time: "Sir, —I have lately seen a pastoral of yours in mr. Walsh's and mr. Congreves hands, which is extreamly ffine & is generally approv'd off by the best Judges in poetry. I Remember I have formerly seen you at my shop & am sorry I did not Improve my Acquaintance with you. If you design your Poem for the Press no person shall be more Carefull in the printing of it, nor no one can give you a greater Incouragment to it; than Sir Your Most Obedient Humble Servant."

The four poems of the *Pastorals,* along with Pope's *Episode of Sarpedon, Translated from the Twelfth and Sixteenth Books of Homer's Iliads,* and *January and May,* his redoing in modern English of Chaucer's *Merchant's Tale,* appeared in 1709 in Tonson's *Poetical Miscellanies: The Sixth Part.* "A Discourse on Pastoral Poetry," which later prefaced the *Pastorals* in other editions, was not published until 1717 (in the collected works), but Pope always maintained that both the poems and their introductory essay were substantially in shape by 1704. If this claim is true, the works are only slightly less remarkable for their precocity than they are for their introduction of a couplet style more refined and musical than any before in English versification. In content the four poems, named after the four seasons, may appear today as rather bland and conventional, largely because Pope chose to write in a pastoral tradition that idealized shepherd life. According to this tradition, pastoral poetry should be an "imitation" of shepherd life in a putative golden age, reflective of a state of innocence and simplicity, and devoid of any such intrusions of real life as human venality and betrayal, much less war and homicide. Such a mode of pastoral, in contrast to Virgil's *Eclogues* (37 B.C.) or Edmund Spenser's *Shepheardes Calen-*

Pope circa 1715-1720 (painting by Charles Jervas; National Portrait Gallery, London)

der (1579), is drastically limited in depth, complexity, and imaginative range. Yet the judgment of Samuel Johnson, in his *Life of Pope* (1781), may be invoked in defense of these youthful poems: "To charge these Pastorals with want of invention, is to require what was never intended. . . . It is surely sufficient for an author of sixteen . . . to have obtained sufficient power of language, and skill in metre, to exhibit a series of versification, which had in English poetry no precedent, nor has since had an imitation." Tame in subject though the *Pastorals* may be, they nevertheless augur truly that supple couplet instrument that later would so cunningly "Eye Nature's walks, shoot Folly as it flies, / And catch the Manners living as they rise" (*An Essay On Man*, 1733-1734). Even in themselves, as in the following lines later used in George Frideric Handel's oratorio *Semele* (1744), they have given a delicate pleasure to many who may never have known their source in Pope's "Summer": "Where-e'er you walk, cool Gales shall fan the Glade, / Trees, where you sit, shall crowd into a Shade, / Where-e'er you tread, the blushing Flow'rs shall rise, / And all things flourish where you turn your Eyes."

Prophetic, in their small way, as the *Pastorals* were of things to come, it was Pope's next publication, *An Essay On Criticism*, which established him, in spite of Dennis's wrathful onslaught, as a major poetic figure. The manuscript for the poem says it was "Written in the Year 1709," but the evidence for an exact date of composition is vague. In all probability the poem was assembled from fragments written when Pope was in what, according to Spence, he called his "great reading period," the time between his thirteenth and twentieth years, when he "went through all the best critics, almost all the English, French, and Latin poets of any name, the minor poets, Homer and some other of the greater Greek poets in the original, and Tasso and Ariosto in translations"; to this he added: "I wrote the *Essay on Criticism* fast, for I had digested all the matter in prose before I began upon it in verse." In any event, the poem appeared, anonymously, in mid May 1711, only a week before Pope turned twenty-three, and the following December it received high praise from the reigning critic of the day, Joseph Addison, in the *Spectator*. Terming it a "Masterpiece in its Kind," Addison particularly praised Pope's demonstration of the ways "*Sound* must seem an *Eccho* to the *Sense*" (as Pope writes in line 365 of the poem). Addison also admired how Pope, like Longinus, the Greek philosopher and critic, "exemplified several of his Precepts in the very Precepts themselves." Johnson, in his biography of Pope, seconded Addison's estimation of the poem, declaring that if Pope "had written nothing else," it "would have placed him among the first criticks and the first poets, as it exhibits every mode of excellence that can embellish or dignify didactick composition, selection of matter, novelty of arrangement, justness of precept, splendour of illustration, and propriety of digression."

An *Essay On Criticism* is in three parts, in a design reflective of a pattern to be discovered as far back as the Old Testament and pagan classics: successive stages representative of an Edenic or golden age; a fall or decay into sin and disorder; and finally a restoration to some semblance of the original state (though not the original purity itself). In another context, in his treatise *Of Education* (1644), John Milton had written that "The end then of learning is to repair the ruins of our first parents by regaining to know God aright," a proposition reaffirmed and transferred to the secular context of poetry by, ironically enough, John Dennis, who asserted that "The great Design of Arts is to restore the Decays that happen'd to human Nature by the Fall, by restoring Order."

The relevance of this traditional scheme to Pope's poem can be seen when one considers how, in part one, he creates a vision of a golden era in art and criticism, when the ancients, in a kind of springtime of the world, and with a clearer and purer perception of reality, could better follow "Nature" and the "light of Nature," that "Unerring Nature," which, "still divinely bright, / One *clear, unchang'd*, and *Universal Light*, / Life, Force, and Beauty, must to all impart, / At

Arabella Fermor, on whom Pope based the character Belinda in his Rape of the Lock *(painting by W. Sykes, circa 1714; Collection of the Roch family, Llanarth Court, Raglan)*

once the *Source*, and *End* and *Test* of Art." Nature, while not quite divine herself, yet stands as a correlative entity to that Divine Being supposed to lie behind and within all other beings—order and the source of order within the creation, mysterious yet apprehensible. The ancients, the patriarchs (such as Homer), in the secularized terms of Pope's poem but rather like Adam in paradise, were able to see more clearly than their descendants this "Nature" and reflect it in their art, to the extent that modern writers may find, even as Virgil did, that "*Nature* and *Homer* were . . . the same." In celebration of such a glorious past state, the first part ends: "Still green with Bays each *ancient* Altar stands, / Above the reach of *Sacrilegious* Hands. . . . / Hail *Bards Triumphant*! born in *happier Days*; / *Immortal* Heirs of *Universal* Praise!"

The second part of the poem creates a vision of the decay and disorder into which literary criticism has fallen, specifically because of pride, the original sin and source of all other sin: "Of all the Causes which conspire to blind / Man's erring Judgment, and misguide the Mind, / What the weak Head with strongest Byass rules, / Is *Pride*, the *never-failing Vice of Fools*." Other eyes than Pope's saw early-eighteenth-century literary criticism as having fallen into a degenerate state. Swift, for example, in *The Battle of the Books* (1704), describes a "malignant Deity, call'd *Criticism*": "At her right hand sat *Ignorance*, her Father and Husband, blind with Age; at her left, *Pride* her Mother, dressing her up in the Scraps of Paper herself had torn. . . . About her play'd her Children, *Noise* and *Impudence, Dullness* and *Vanity, Positiveness, Pedantry*, and *Ill-Manners*." In agreement was Samuel Cobb, who in *A Discourse of Criticism* (1707) declared: "Criticism, which was formerly the Art of Judging well, is now become the pure Effect of Spleen, Passion, and Self-conceit." In such a climate it was not difficult for Pope to parallel the enervating dissensions within literary criticism to those that had characterized the history of Christianity: "Some *foreign* Writers, some our *own* despise; / The *Ancients* only, or the *Moderns* prize; / (Thus *Wit*, like *Faith*, by each Man is apply'd / To *one small Sect*, and All are *damn'd beside*)."

Having documented the divisions, failings, and egoisms that pervaded the critical establishment, Pope in the third part of the poem turns to the means of reformation, reconciliation, and restoration, making clear in his opening lines that what is needed is not simply more learning or even more acumen, but rather more personal virtue: "Learn then what MORALS Criticks ought to show, / For 'tis but *half a Judge's Task*, to Know. / 'Tis not enough, Taste, Judgment, Learning, join; / In all you speak, let Truth and Candor shine." The hortatory tenor of these lines rounds off and makes more explicit an ethical dimension and intent present throughout the poem: a concern with matters of morality amid matters of criticism; a concern with humility ("So *vast* is Art, so *narrow* Human Wit"; "A *little Learning* is a dang'rous Thing"); with charity ("In ev'ry Work regard the *Writer's End*"; "To Err is *Humane*; to Forgive, *Divine*"); and with prudence ("Let such teach others who themselves excell"; "*Fools* rush in where *Angels* fear to tread").

Within the poem's large, conciliatory, imaginative design and embrace, one finds Pope attempting also to accommodate apparently conflicting and even contradictory artistic principles and values. The accommodations are usually made in the most appropriate, albeit teasing, rhetorical terms, those of oxymoron and paradox.

Illustration of a scene in the fourth canto of The Rape of the Lock *(engraving, circa 1717, attributed by Horace Walpole to William Hogarth)*

On the claims of authority and the rules versus individual freedom and spontaneity, he writes: "Great Wits sometimes may *gloriously offend*, / And *rise* to *Faults* true Criticks *dare not mend*; / From *vulgar Bounds* with *brave Disorder* part, / And *snatch* a *Grace* beyond the Reach of Art"; on the serendipitous stroke versus painstaking application: "Some Beauties yet, no Precepts can declare, / For there's a *Happiness* as well as *Care*"; on, most puzzling of all, the idea that unrestricted Nature is no more productive of the "natural" than unrestricted Liberty is productive of total "freedom": "*Nature*, like *Liberty*, is but restrain'd / By the same Laws which first *herself* ordain'd." If *An Essay On Criticism* is to be taken as a neoclassical critical "platform," that platform must be seen as an attempt to pull together an array of diverse, often almost mutually exclusive premises and precepts. It is certainly not expressive of a narrow rationalistic or highly prescribed literary ideal; for as the language of the poem repeatedly makes clear, the art it endorses is an art comprehending "*nameless Graces*," "*brave Disorder*," "*gen'rous Pleasure*," and an imaginative energy "Which, without passing thro' the *Judgment*, gains / The *Heart*, and all its End *at once* attains."

The next five or six years completed the first third of Pope's career, with the publication of a variety of works scarcely anticipatory of the preeminent satirist he was to become in the last phase of his life. In 1712, in *Miscellaneous Poems and Translations. By Several Hands*, there appeared the *Fable of Vertumnus and Pomona*, a translation from Ovid, and also Pope's translation of the first book of the *Thebais*, an epic poem by the Latin poet Statius. In 1712 Pope also published another, very loose, translation from Ovid, *Sappho to Phaon*, as well as his last experiment in the pastoral mode, *Messiah: A Sacred Eclogue*, an adjustment of certain prophetic, messianic passages of the Old Testament Book of Isaiah to Virgil's fourth Eclogue, the "Pollio," which had predicted the birth of an infant whose reign would inaugurate a new golden age. In 1713, with the appearance of *Windsor-Forest*, Pope exchanged the pastoral mode for the georgic, etymologically suggestive of farming and the rural life, which Virgil (in his *Georgics*) had employed to celebrate the blessings of peace brought to Italy by Caesar Augustus. In his poem, Pope draws upon a variety of resources—classical, continental, and English—to celebrate the peace and prosperity England seemed to be enjoying under Queen Anne, the last of the Stuart line. In particular the poem commemorates the Treaty of Utrecht (1713), which brought an end to the War of the Spanish Succession and which ceded to Great Britain both Gibraltar and Minorca, as well as Nova Scotia, Newfoundland, and the Hudson Bay region in North America. One of Pope's predecessors in the georgic mode had been Sir John Denham, whose *Cooper's Hill* (1642), in its versification and its topographical subject matter, became one of the most admired poems of the seventeenth century. In one of Pope's comments on this work may be seen his own intentions and strategies in *Windsor-Forest*. In a note to Book XVI in his later translation of the entire *Iliad*, he speaks of Homer's "indirect and oblique manner of introducing moral Sentences and Intentions . . . even in Descriptions and poetical Parts, where one naturally expects only Painting and Amusement." Pope continues: "I must do a noble *English* Poet the justice to observe, that it is this particular Art that is the very distinguishing Excellence of *Cooper's-Hill*: throughout which, the Descriptions of Places, and Images rais'd by the Poet, are still tending to some Hint, or leading into some Reflection, upon moral Life or political Institution: Much in the same manner as the real Sight of such Scenes and Prospects is apt to give the Mind a compos'd Turn, and induce it to Thoughts and Contemplations that have a Relation to the Object."

During this period Pope produced his most celebrated work, *The Rape of the Lock*: "the most airy, the most ingenious, and the most delightful of all his compositions," in the opinion of Johnson (*Life of Pope*). First published in 1712, in two cantos of only 334 lines, the poem appeared two years later in five cantos (comprising 794 lines)

and included for the first time its brilliantly conceived "machinery" (the "supernatural" personages: sylphs and gnomes, nymphs and salamanders); the heroine's ominous prophetic dream; the card game of Ombre (literally, "man"); the Cave of Spleen episode; and much more. Pope's poem is supposedly based on a real-life incident: during a social occasion in 1711, a young peer, Robert, Lord Petre (the "Baron" of the poem), snipped a lock of hair from the head of a young, beauteous, and distant relation, Arabella Fermor (the poem's "Belinda"); the poem was reportedly written at the request of Pope's friend John Caryll to heal a consequent estrangement between the two families. *The Rape of the Lock* fuses classical and Christian resources in a mock-heroic manner both satirical and playfully tender. The classical background is omnipresent, from the opening invocation through the descent into the "underworld" of Belinda's bowels to the closing grandiose battle of the sexes; but the main structural design of the poem seems to depend on its sequences of allusions and parallels to Milton's *Paradise Lost*: the "Morning-Dream" summoned to the sleeping Belinda by Ariel, her "Guardian Sylph," which not only warns her of some impending "dread Event" and encourages her to know her "own Importance," but also recalls the dream, similarly encouraging of excessive self-esteem, insinuated into Eve's mind by Milton's Satan; the scene at Belinda's dressing table, where she appears to worship her own image in her mirror, is reminiscent of the newly created Eve's narcissistic admiration of herself as reflected in the Edenic pool; and most crucially, just before the Baron's cutting of Belinda's lock, the moment when Ariel seeks out the "close Recesses of the Virgin's Thought" and finds an "Earthly Lover lurking at her Heart" clearly recalls the scene in *Paradise Lost* when, after Adam's fall of his own free will, his angelic guardians, "mute and sad," depart from him, as powerless as Ariel finds himself to be before Belinda's own free choice of an earthly rather than a sylphic lover.

Belinda's fall, in one sense, appears merely to be part of the normal human process of "falling" in love, or a maiden's innermost and private decision not to spurn so attractive and eligible a suitor as the Baron. From this point of view the state of her heart at her moment of choice deserves sympathy more than censure: neither she nor the world in general would wish her to remain a virgin forever (as the poem later says,

Belinda's Toilet *(circa 1795), a drawing by Benjamin West of a scene from* The Rape of the Lock
(from Edmund Gosse, English Literature: An Illustrated Record, *1903)*

"she who scorns a Man, must die a Maid"). But if she secretly acquiesces to the Baron's courtship (leaving aside for the moment the incivility of his approach), she has no right to consider the cutting of her lock equivalent to a "rape" of her person: it is a desired rather than a forced "deflowering." In light of Belinda's apparent compliance in the Baron's act, her immediate response to the loss of a lock seems utterly prudish and hypocritical, particularly since her outraged and tearful denial of any complicity in the event is made in defense of an "Honour" at whose "unrival'd Shrine," in the words of her friend Thalestris, "Ease, Pleasure, Virtue, All, our Sex resign." Amid this ugly situation, an alternative to Thalestris's viragolike indignation is offered by Clarissa (the "clarifier") in a passage added to the poem by Pope in 1717, in order, he says, "*to open more clearly the MORAL of the Poem.*" Based on a Ho-

meric speech by the Trojan warrior Sarpedon, which Pope had earlier translated and published, Clarissa's words offer Belinda a course of candor and equanimity in the face of her loss (however she may define that loss). But, as one might expect in a poem so reflective of moral disarray in a society's values and priorities (a disarray succinctly established by the articles on Belinda's dressing table: "Puffs, Powders, Patches, Bibles, Billet-doux"), Ariel's sylphic tutelage of Belinda is replaced by that of Umbriel, under whose gnomish influence she chooses the path of prudery (allied in the poem with "*Ill-nature*" and "*Affectation*") and demands an impossible "restoration" of the virginity symbolized by her stolen curl. And though the lock is actually lost for good (as her virginity, if defined as a state of psychic chastity, has been), in the tumultuous melee of the sexes in the last canto, Pope assures the reader that it has been "translated" (in the theological sense) to the heavens and metamorphosed into a star, "consecrate to Fame." The pattern of the poem, and of Belinda's day, resembles the tripartite pattern in *An Essay On Criticism*: a state of "innocence," its loss, and a kind of "restoration."

Published in *The Works of Mr. Alexander Pope* (1717), *Eloisa to Aberlard* is another poem of extraordinary warmth and empathy for female character. Sometimes described as an example of a "pre-Romantic" trend in English letters, the poem is more properly perceived as "post-metaphysical" in character. Again based on an actual sexual relationship, though a far more illustrious one than that of a belle and a beau, the poem may have been inspired by the publication in 1713 of an English translation of letters exchanged between Pierre Abelard, the renowned French philosopher and theologian, and his most famous pupil, Héloïse, who became celebrated as a nun, abbess, and thinker in her own right. Falling in love when he was thirty-eight and she was seventeen, they had a son and were subsequently married, though secretly. Héloïse's uncle, a canon at Notre Dame in Paris, outraged at Abelard's seduction of his niece and unaware of their marriage, hired a gang of thugs to trap and emasculate him. Héloïse retreated to a convent, and later, when Abelard became a Benedictine monk, she, at his desire, became a Benedictine nun. Some time later Abelard founded a monastic school, which he called the Paraclete and which, after he had become abbot of a monastery in Brittany, he turned over to Héloïse and a group of sisters. Pope's poem, a kind of dramatic monologue in the form of a verse epistle from Eloisa to Abelard, was provided with a headnote by the poet in which he recalls some of their history and states the "Argument" of his own fictional re-creation of it: "*It was many years after* [their] *separation, that a letter of* Abelard's *to a Friend which contain'd the history of his misfortune, fell into the hands of* Eloisa. *This awakening all her tenderness, occasion'd those celebrated letters (out of which the following is partly abstracted) which give so lively a picture of the struggles of grace and nature, virtue and passion.*"

Struggles of "grace and nature" are scarcely Romantic or even pre-Romantic themes, so one must look backward to understand the shape, content, and tone of Pope's poem. One relevant precursor is the Ovidian verse epistle, in Ovid's so-called *Heroides*, whose common theme is female love, frequently of a despairing kind. Pope,

Frontispiece for The Works of Mr. Alexander Pope, *1717*

of course, had translated and published in 1712 one of these epistles, *Sappho to Phaon*. The Ovidian format and subject had also been acclimated to the English scene by earlier poets (John Donne and Michael Drayton among them), but *Eloisa to Abelard* derives special flavor from Pope's incorporation of specifically Roman Catholic devotional practices and theological sanctions in a highly charged erotic dilemma for Eloisa: love of God is apparently opposed to love of man. The dilemma may be seen as resolved by the end of the poem but probably only by understanding the way Pope's epistle is shaped and slanted by such specifically Catholic devotional usages as the "spiritual exercise" (a disciplined meditation on the events in Christ's life, most especially when one is saying the Rosary); by earlier devotional literature (the autobiography of St. Teresa, for example) that had vividly combined the mystical and the erotic; and by the fact that ultimately, in the Roman Catholic vision of the totality of human experience, there really need be no essential conflict between "grace" and "nature."

As noted, Pope, from boyhood, had tried his hand at translating various classical writers, but he seems to have been especially attracted to Homer. Late in life he told Spence that the translation of Homer by John Ogilby was "one of the first large poems" he read; "he still," Spence added, "spoke of the pleasure it then gave him, with a sort of rapture only on reflecting on it." And more poetically, in one of his imitations of Horace (*The Second Epistle*), Pope writes: "Bred up at home, full early I begun / To read in Greek, the Wrath of Peleus' Son [Achilles]." During his early years Pope must also have been meditating on William Trumbull's suggestion that he translate the entire *Iliad*.

At any rate, in 1713, in his twenty-fifth year, he announced a proposal to undertake, by subscription, just such a staggering task, one that would dominate his life for the next seven years or so. This period, followed by the years from 1720 to 1725, when he was additionally busied with the translation of Homer's *Odyssey*, may be said to constitute the second phase of Pope's literary career, when little original work appeared. Not that the *Iliad* translation should be depreciated for not being "original" work, for as Johnson unequivocally asserted in his *Life of Pope*: "It is certainly the noblest version [translation] of poetry which the world has ever seen; and its publication must therefore be considered as one of the great events in the annals of Learning."

Some idea of the magnitude of the undertaking, at least Pope's idea of it, may be gathered from his comments to Spence in 1743, years later: "What terrible moments does one feel after one has engaged for a large work! In the beginning of my translating the *Iliad* I wished any body would hang me, a hundred times"; the *Iliad* "took me up six years, and during that time, and particularly the first part of it, I was often under great pain and apprehensions. Though I conquered the thoughts of it in the day, they would frighten me in the night. I dreamed often of being engaged in a long journey and that I should never get to the end of it. This made so strong an impression upon me that I sometimes dream of it still."

Pope's "pain and apprehensions" intensified when rumors began to circulate that Thomas Tickell, a minor poet, university trained, and a protégé of Joseph Addison, was being egged on by Addison (even as he feigned support for Pope's venture) and his coterie at Button's Coffee

Frontispiece for the 1719 edition of Pope's poem inspired by the love letters of French philosopher Pierre Abelard and his student Héloïse

House to undertake a rival translation that supposedly would reveal, by contrast, just how deficient any effort by such an upstart as Pope must be. By now, however, Pope's standing was such that, whatever his personal trepidations may have been, he was able to attract as subscribers to his translation many of the most powerful and prestigious figures of his day. And when his first volume appeared in 1715, it not only completely overshadowed Tickell's effort (which had been timed to appear simultaneously) but immediately established him in the public consciousness as the predominant literary figure of his age. In a gesture declaring his independence from any personal patronage by the rich, aristocratic, or politically powerful, he dedicated his translation

Godfrey Kneller's 1721 portrait of Pope, employing numismatic motifs (Collection of Lord Home of the Hirsel K.T., Coldstream, Berwickshire)

to a fellow writer, William Congreve. Proceeds from the undertaking, indeed, helped found the fortune that would make Pope the first English man of letters to become financially independent by means of his own work. Specifically, he received two hundred guineas for each of the edition's six volumes from the publisher, plus 750 sets printed in a noble and limited edition for which the subscribers each paid six guineas. Now, "thanks to *Homer*," he writes in *The Second Epistle*, he could "live and thrive, / Indebted to no Prince or Peer alive." As for Addison and the part he played in the scheme to denigrate and imperil Pope's arduous task, his reward would be Pope's masterly portrayal of him as "Atticus," "Willing to wound, and yet afraid to strike," and "so obliging that he ne'er oblig'd," in *An Epistle to Dr. Arbuthnot.*

The last of the *Iliad* volumes appeared in 1720. For a time afterward, Pope was preoccupied with editing the work of two deceased friends: a collection of poems by Thomas Parnell, and the writings of John Sheffield, Duke of Buckinghamshire. But he was also apparently

contemplating, and even making progress on, a translation of the *Odyssey*. This time, however, he solicited, covertly, the collaboration of two friends: a cleric, William Broome, and Elijah Fenton, a minor poet. The arrangement was obviously muffled so as not to deter potential subscribers, who, if they had known that Pope was to be fully responsible for translating only twelve of the original's twenty-four books, might well have backed off; but such was the division of labor, with Fenton responsible for four books and Broome for eight others plus all of the prose commentary. And even though Pope rigorously supervised and revised the work of his partners, when the duplicitous nature of the whole business leaked out, as it inevitably did, it not only gave Pope much personal embarrassment; it also gave ammunition of fairly heavy caliber to all those whose animosity he had stirred for whatever reasons.

The *Odyssey* translation, appearing in five volumes in 1725 and 1726, did turn out to be, in spite of the taint it gave to Pope's reputation, a financial success, for both him and his collabora-

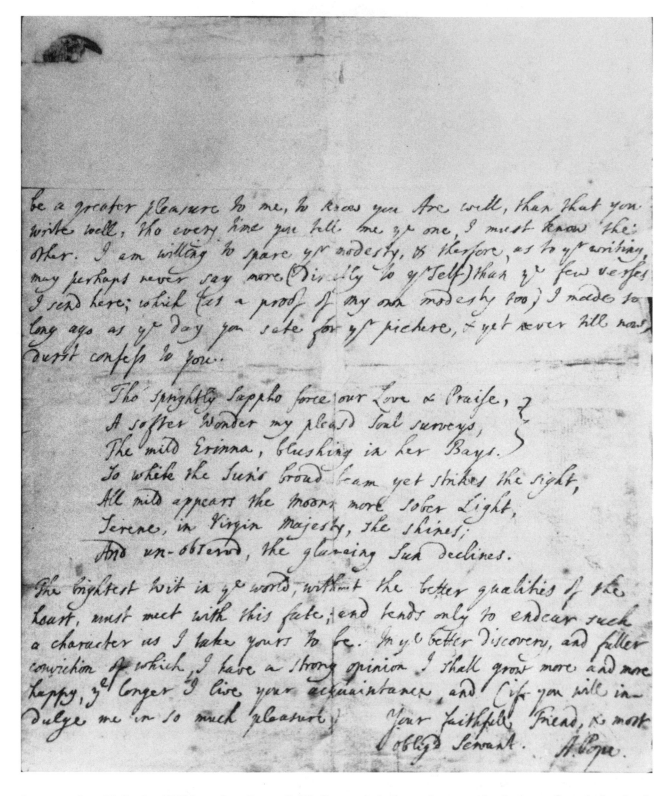

Last page of an 18 October 1722 letter from Pope to Judith Cowper, including a short poem that he eventually revised and published in Of The Characters of Women, *1735 (Christie, Manson & Woods, Ltd., auction catalogue, 11-12 June 1980)*

tors. But adding to Pope's discomfiture over the revelations that accompanied it were the consequences of two other projects undertaken during these years. The first, the editing of Sheffield's works, must have seemed innocent enough at the time, but when the two volumes of the duke's writings appeared in January 1723, they were almost immediately seized by the government for allegedly containing Jacobite and therefore seditious leanings. The ban against the edition was soon enough lifted, but there can be little doubt that Pope suffered some alarm at the possible government mistrust of his own loyalties, as well as some chagrin over scurrilous insinuations in the public press about his role in getting the edition published. The second project with an unpleasant sequel was his agreement, for a flat fee of one hundred pounds, to act as editor of a six-volume edition of Shakespeare, a task for which he cannot be said to have been even minimally qualified—though given the general state of textual scholarship at the time his performance is more understandable. Not that he failed to enable the educated public better to "appreciate" Shakespeare; that he did, not only by singling out passages that seemed to him especially admirable but also by providing an evaluative preface, which ends with this remarkable comment: "I will conclude by saying of *Shakespear*, that with all his faults, and with all the irregularity of his *Drama*, one may look upon his works, in comparison of those that are more finish'd and regular, as upon an ancient majestick piece of *Gothic* Architecture, compar'd with a neat Modern building: The latter is more elegant and glaring, but the former is more strong and solemn. It must be allow'd, that in one of these there are materials enough to make many of the other. It has much the greater variety, and much the nobler apartments; tho' we are often conducted to them by dark, odd, and uncouth passages."

But whatever virtues Pope's edition of Shakespeare may be said to have, its flagrant shortcomings were disdainfully exposed barely a year after its publication, when Lewis Theobald, an attorney and poetaster with pretensions to scholarship, in 1726 published a work the title of which alone makes its animus apparent: *SHAKESPEARE restored: OR, A SPECIMEN OF THE Many ERRORS, AS WELL Committed, as Unamended, by Mr. POPE In his Late EDITION of this POET. DESIGNED Not only to correct the said EDITION, but to restore the True READING of SHAKESPEARE in all the Editions ever yet publish'd.*

Theobald's work, often heavy-handed, nitpickingly pedantic, and self-glorifying, nonetheless scored many valid points against Pope's inadequacies and made some real contributions to Shakespearean interpretation as well. Coming when it did, when Pope had been smarting for some time from allegations of his deficiency in the Greek necessary to translate Homer, and more recently from rumors of his Jacobite sympathies and from public disapproval of his actual disingenuous dealings in the *Odyssey* translation, it must have rankled the more. Leaving aside the steady drumbeat of snide and brutal comment on his physical deformities, from 1711—with the attack on his person, character, and talent by Dennis—until 1727, over fifty printed assaults had appeared, in pamphlets, books, plays, novels, and miscellanies, most of them written by literary hacks or out of personal envy and spite. They charged Pope variously with blasphemy, obscenity, plagiarism, and libel, and damned him as venal, vain, seditious, malicious, and faithless as a friend.

For two decades Pope held his peace amid such calumnies. If he had died before his fortieth birthday there would be little, except for a few derisive squibs and pieces of mockery, to presage the preeminent satirist he was to become. But during this period he must have been meditating his revenge, and when it came it was on a scale as massive as it was devastating: in May 1728 appeared the first version of *The Dunciad*, in three books, with Pope's Shakespearean adversary Theobald (always spelled "Tibbald" by Pope, to belittle him and to rhyme with such words as "ribald") crowned as king of duncery, supreme embodiment of everything tasteless, inept, and depraved in art and criticism—as well as in those who fostered and patronized such art. In Pope's usage, duncery is not so much mere stupidity of mind as it is a perverse misapplication of one's reason and talents; its implications may be somewhat better understood if we recall that etymologically the word stems from the name of Duns Scotus, the medieval theologian whose disciples, because of their specious and hairsplitting habits of reasoning, became known contemptuously as "duns men." The broad pejorative implications of duncery were such, moreover, that Pope could use the word to stigmatize a wide range of individual types and institutions, from obtuse royalty to hack writers, from degenerate theatrical performances to unscrupulous publishers, from the schools and universities to mendacious politicians

Pope's home at Twickenham (engraving by J. Michael Rysbrach, based on a painting by Augustin Heckell)

A Perspective View of Mr. Pope's Grotto *(engraving based on a drawing by J. Serle)*

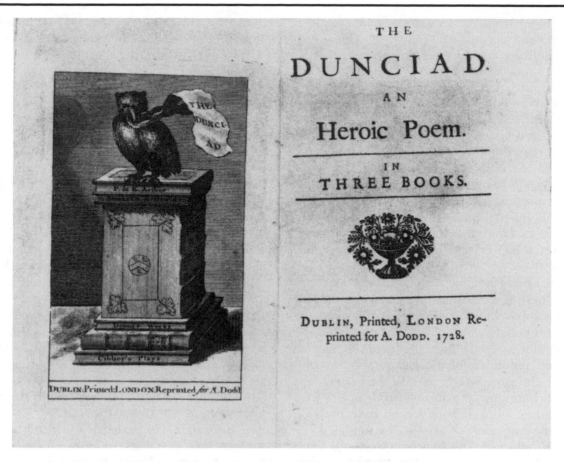

Frontispiece and title page for the second printing of Pope's notorious satire

and the current poet laureate, Laurence Eusden, a clergyman known at the time more for his drunkenness than for any other attributes, priestly or poetic. The poem's impact was instantaneous and explosive, if we may believe the contemporary account by Richard Savage of the immediate uproar and outrage among Pope's victims: "On the Day the Book was first vended, a Crowd of Authors besieg'd the Shop [of the publisher]; Entreaties, Advices, Threats of Law, and Battery, nay Cries of Treason were all employ'd to hinder the coming out of the *Dunciad*: On the other Side, the Booksellers and Hawkers made as great Efforts to procure it."

While *The Dunciad* certainly enabled Pope to settle personal scores, the poem is also formed on a larger template incised to convey breathtakingly larger alterations in Western culture. The opening lines—"The Mighty Mother, and her Son who brings / The Smithfield Muses to the ear of Kings"—suggest the upheavals and transformations Pope has in mind: the displacement of traditional classical and Christian values, ideally embodied in the crown, by the crass and debased tastes associated with the fairs and rabble of Smithfield—puppet shows, prizefights, bearbaitings, and so on. As Pope says through his editorial mouthpiece, the duncely pedant Martinus Scriblerus, the poem was written at a time when paper "became so cheap, and Printers so numerous, that a deluge of Authors covered the land." Before this authorial flood, swollen in part by a suddenly enlarged reading public with an apparently insatiable appetite for the most heterogeneous (as well as cheap and vulgar) reading matter, the more traditional (and aristocratic) strongholds of learning and literature might well have seemed, from one point of view, in danger of being totally swept away. That such a concern is at the heart of Pope's poem seems clearly indicated by alternative but reciprocal descriptions of its *"one, great,* and *remarkable action"*: in 1729 that action is said by Scriblerus to be "the introduction of the lowest diversions of the rabble in *Smithfield* to be the entertainment of the court and town; or in other words, the Action of the Dunciad is the Removal of the Imperial seat of Dulness [the presiding deity or 'Mighty Mother' of the poem] from the City to the polite world"; in the revised version of 1743, the "action" has been redefined and given a cosmic range: it is "the restoration of the reign of Chaos and Night, by the ministry of Dulness their daughter, in the removal of her imperial seat from the City to the polite World."

Art, and taste in art, and even the topography of Greater London thus become metaphors expressive of the poem's import. When the goddess Dulness, having "annointed" Theobald as her son and earthly "king," leads him and the rest of his fellow dunces, her "chosen," through the streets of London from the City (that part of London that had become associated with mercantile values) on an invasion of the "polite world" (the West End of London with its cluster of aristocratic values), the cultural upheaval Pope aims to portray is apparent: the overrunning and smothering of traditional values by low, cheap, and modern substitutes. And since the poem is also a mock-epic, reminders of the gigantic figures and events of the past, in one parodic analogue after another, continuously make scornful and ridiculous all those who, in Pope's eyes, have contributed to the degrading of art and learning.

Publication of *The Dunciad* effectually confirmed Pope's posture as an antiestablishment figure. As early as 1713, although he apparently tried to avoid a partisan political stance in *Windsor-Forest*, he betrayed in that poem a deep sympathy for Queen Anne, last of the Stuarts. At about the same time, he became intimate with a select group of Anne's Tory ministers and adherents who were to become abiding friends: Robert Harley, Earl of Oxford, the lord treasurer and "prime" minister; Dr. John Arbuthnot, the queen's personal physician, himself an ingenious writer; Swift, at the time a polemical writer on behalf of the queen and her ministry; and the poets John Gay, later to write *The Beggar's Opera* (1728), and Parnell, mentioned earlier. This group established the famed Scriblerus Club, named after an imaginary blockhead of a pedant (the one Pope put to such comical use in *The Dunciad*), in whose name they met and planned to satirize abuses in learning and art wherever they might be found. The group met as an entity for only six months or so (the death of Queen Anne inevitably caused its disintegration), but in their association were planted the seeds that would later bear such fruit as *Gulliver's Travels* (1726) and Gay's ballad opera, as well as the collaborative *Memoirs of the Extraordinary Life, Works, and*

Discoveries of Martinus Scriblerus (1741) and Pope's own *Peri Bathous: Or, Of the Art of Sinking in Poetry* (1727), a hilarious prose satire on bad writers and bad writing. Pope's intimacy and empathy with this alliance almost certainly prohibited fraternal relationships with the writers and hangers-on at Button's, the circle around Addison, whose Whig ties and loyalties were such that he became secretary of state under Anne's successor, George I. For a variety of reasons, then (Pope's Roman Catholic background and the insults and prejudices it inspired, his membership in the Scriblerian group and the loyalties formed there, the envy and animosity shown him by Addison and his cronies in the matter of the Homer translation, and his growing sense that neither he nor his friends could expect royal or ministerial favor under the first two Georges and their powerful prime minister, Robert Walpole), Pope henceforth became an unrelenting hounder of the monarchy and its minions, a role enunciated when, in *The Dunciad*, glancing at George II's succession to his father's throne, he inquires: "Say from what cause, in vain decry'd and curst, / Still Dunce the second reigns like Dunce the first?"

Back in 1716, perhaps as a result of more stringent tax penalties recently enacted against Roman Catholics, Pope's father had disposed of his property at Binfield, and for a time the family had lived at Chiswick, nearer to London. There, in 1717, the elder Pope died. His life and his death were commemorated by his son in *An Epistle to Dr. Arbuthnot*:

> Born to no Pride, inheriting no Strife,
> Nor marrying Discord in a Noble Wife,
> Stranger to Civil and Religious Rage,
> The good Man walk'd innoxious thro' his Age.
> No Courts he saw, no Suits would ever try,
> Nor dar'd an Oath, nor hazarded a Lye:
> Un-learn'd, he knew no Schoolman's subtle Art,
> No Language, but the Language of the Heart.
> By Nature honest, by Experience wise,
> Healthy by Temp'rance and by Exercise:
> His Life, tho' long, to sickness past unknown,
> His Death was instant, and without a groan.
> Oh grant me thus to live, and thus to die!
> Who sprung from Kings shall know less joy than I.

A year or so after his father's death Pope leased a villa at Twickenham, which he was to make celebrated for the elegance of the house and the variegated pleasures and graces of its grounds. Twelve miles outside London (and therefore outside the ten-mile limit), and facing the Thames, the two-

The Distressed Poet, a 1736 engraving by Hogarth, with a quotation from The Dunciad *as its caption*

story edifice and its front lawn were separated from five acres in the rear by the London Road. Pope had a subterranean passageway made to connect the two areas, explaining to his friends that "What we cannot *overcome*, we must *undergo*." This underground passageway, with its various recesses, became the famous grotto in which he delighted to entertain his most intimate friends and which he once described in a 2 June 1725 letter to Edward Blunt: "it is finished with Shells interspersed with Pieces of Looking-glass in angular forms; and in the Ceiling is a Star of the same Material, at which when a Lamp (of an orbicular Figure of thin Alabaster) is hung in the Middle, a thousand pointed Rays glitter and are reflected over the Place."

At Twickenham (or "Twit' nam," as he affectionately dubbed it) Pope could indulge a passion he apparently inherited from his father—gardening. Small as the space was at his command, he managed to fill it with an astonishing variety of features: a bowling green and a kitchen garden, a shell temple and a vineyard, an orangery and, after his mother's death, an obelisk in her memory. In a facetious October 1725 letter to the earl of Stafford, he described his landscaping activities: "I am as busy in three inches of Gardening, as any man can be in threescore acres. I fancy myself like the fellow that spent his life in cutting the twelve apostles in one cherry-stone. I have a Theatre, an Arcade, a Bowling-Green, a Grove, & what not? in a bitt of ground that

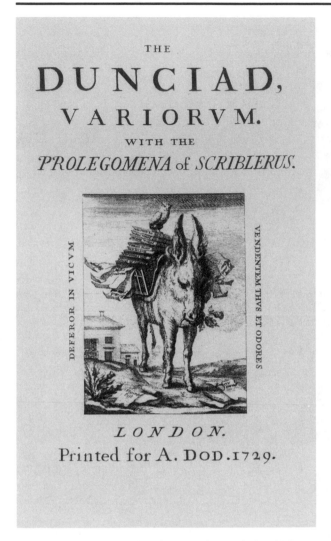

THE
DUNCIAD,
VARIORVM.
WITH THE
PROLEGOMENA of SCRIBLERUS.

DEFEROR IN VICVM

VENDENTEM THVS ET ODORES

LONDON.
Printed for A. DOD. 1729.

Title page for the revised and enlarged Dunciad, *which was to be expanded again in 1743*

would have been but a plate of Sallet to Nebuchadnezzar, the first day he was turn'd to graze." He was fond of reminding his friends that, in Cicero's words, "*Agricultura proxima Sapientiae*" (agriculture is nearest to wisdom) and that gardening was a most "innocent Employment, & the same that God appointed for his First Man." A "true relish of the beauties of nature," he wrote, "is the most easy preparation and gentlest transition to an enjoyment of those of heaven; as on the contrary a true town life of hurry, confusion, noise, slander, and dissension, is a sort of apprenticeship to hell and its furies."

In his letters, Pope remarked several times that "*Mihi & Amicis* [for me and my friends] would be the proper Motto" over his garden gate; or "indeed, Plus Amicis quam Meipsi" (more for my friends than for myself). Several

years later he referred to his "Grotto of Friendship & Liberty" and even mentioned a Latin version of this same phrase ("Libertati & Amicitiae"), which he was "putting over [his] Door at Twitnam." Friendship seems to have been the first of secular pieties for Pope, and whatever asperity of temper is exhibited in his published work finds its counterpoise in the warm affection he lavished privately on his remarkable number of friends from all ranks. During the 1730s especially, as his opposition to Walpole and the establishment stiffened, his villa and its grotto became a center in which "friendship" and its twin virtue "liberty" found a quiet and hospitable harbor; there, among a few cherished companions, including others also out of ministerial favor, he could share a "Feast of Reason" and a "Flow of Soul" (as he says in *The Second Satire*). There also he could enjoy alone a place of retreat and meditation, away from what he increasingly regarded as the corrupt, and corrupting, world of London, the world of what he called the "Money-headed & Mony-hearted Citizen" (the mercantile "Cits" within the old City walls). In the sanctuary provided by "Twit' nam," as he says in *The Second Epistle*, he could meet with and catechize his very heart:

> Soon as I enter at my Country door,
> My Mind resumes the thread it dropt before;
> Thoughts, which at Hyde-Park-Corner I forgot,
> Meet and rejoin me, in the pensive Grott.
> There all alone, and Compliments apart,
> I ask these sober questions of my Heart.
> > If, when the more you drink, the more you
> > crave,
> You tell the Doctor; when the more you have,
> The more you want, why not with equal ease
> Confess as well your Folly, as Disease?

Shortly before *The Dunciad* appeared, Pope too confidently wrote to Swift that the poem would "rid" him of "those insects," the "fools and scoundrels" who had pestered him for so many years. If anything, of course, the poem simply inflamed the dunces the more. And so they attempted a kind of revenge, of the shoddiest sort to be sure, in 1731 when the first of Pope's "Epistles to Several Persons" appeared. Entitled *An Epistle To The Right Honourable Richard Earl of Burlington. Occasion'd by his Publishing Palladio's Designs of the Baths, Arches, Theatres, &c. of Ancient Rome*, the poem is informed throughout by Pope's proficiency, empirical as well as conceptual, in landscape gardening, as well as in the

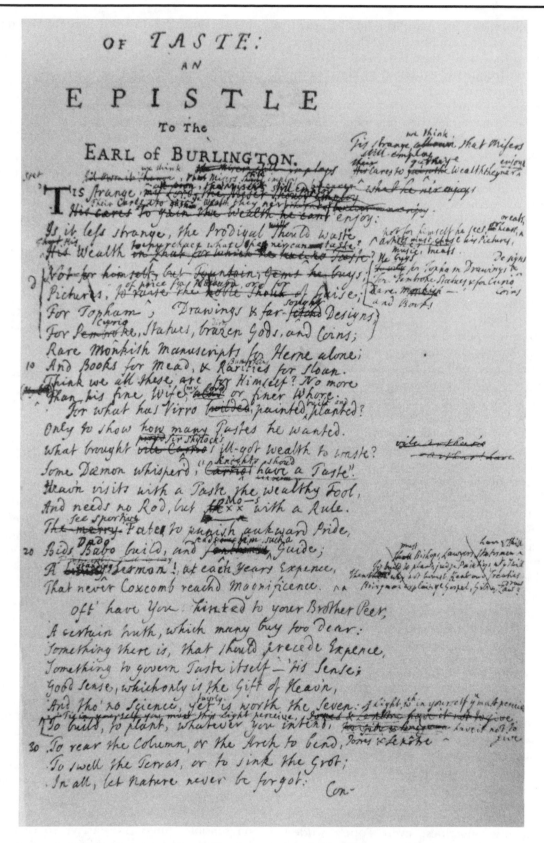

First page of an early draft for the poem Pope published as An Epistle To The Right Honourable Richard Earl of Burlington, *1731 (MA 352, Pierpont Morgan Library)*

ways the gardener's art may offer analogues to the art of poetry. In addition, the work is a withering satire on the vanity, false taste, and misuse of riches all too frequently exhibited by the wealthy in their creation of vast and opulent estates. There seems absolutely no reason to think Pope had any particular estate, or nobleman, in view; the particular example he gives of follies and monstrosities—the "Timon's Villa" of the poem—is obviously a fictional amalgam of common excesses and deficiencies. But the dunces, in a campaign as malicious as unjustified, spread rumor and gossip, in lampoon and pamphlets, that the poem was aimed mainly at the estate of one particular nobleman, James Brydges, Duke of Chandos, a person to whom Pope had reason to be grateful and who was, furthermore, a friend of the very earl to whom he had addressed the epistle.

During this period Pope had been planning a major poem on the human condition in general, a work more philosophical than satirical, as he told Spence, which would serve as both a *"general Map of MAN"* and as an introduction to a larger poetic scheme including the "Epistles to Several Persons" as well as other poems on such subjects as "knowledge and its limits," "government, both ecclesiastical and civil," and "morality, in eight or nine of the most concerning branches of it." Such a grand design was never to be realized, but with the furor raised by *The Dunciad* and the *Epistle to Burlington* in mind, and to ensure an unbiased reception of the introductory poem, Pope devised an elaborate stratagem to persuade the public, including the dunces, that *An Essay On Man* was the work of a new and unknown author. To this end he had his regular publisher issue, in early 1733, two poems under his own name: in January there appeared *Of The Use of Riches, An Epistle To the Right Honorable Allen Lord Bathurst* (dated 1732), followed in February by Pope's first "Imitation" of Horace, *The First Satire Of The Second Book of Horace*. Having thus signaled himself as busied with such satiric pieces, Pope in late February had a publisher previously unassociated with his work issue the first epistle of *An Essay On Man*, with the second and third epistles following in the next several weeks (a fourth and final epistle was published in early 1734).

The scheme was enormously successful, exceeding, one imagines, even Pope's wildest dreams, for not only did the general public hail the poem as the work of a newly risen genius, but some of his most inveterate detractors and tra-

ducers were hoodwinked into according it the most adulatory praise—and in print. As perhaps no protest or appeal could have done, the entrapment of his enemies in their own acclaiming words made it utterly clear how personally prejudiced their incessant hounding of him had been. In later editions of *The Dunciad* Pope, no doubt with considerable gleefulness of spirit, reprinted, among other "testimonies" to himself, some of the choicer specimens of praise the dunces of that very poem had accorded him, including these verses by Bezaleel Morris:

Auspicious bard! while all admire thy strain,
All but the selfish, ignorant, and vain;
I, whom no bribe to servile flatt'ry drew,
Must pay the tribute to thy merit due:
Thy Muse, sublime, significant, and clear,
Alike informs the Soul, and charms the Ear.

This was a gratifying salute indeed, especially considering its authorship.

As for the poem itself, *An Essay On Man* probably has an ancestry as ancient as Psalm 19, the opening lines of which are: "The heavens declare the glory of God; and the firmament sheweth his handiwork. Day unto day uttereth speech, and night unto night sheweth knowledge." The psalm is in two parts, the first six verses presenting the argument for God's creation of the universe in the very "talk" of the natural world itself, while the second half refers us to the testimony of the "law," that is, the revelations to man found in the Pentateuch, the first five books of the Old Testament. Pope follows the mode of the first half of the psalm in his poetic "theodicy"—his investigation, that is—of the evils and deficiencies to be found in the creation, and his "vindication" or "justification" of the "ways of God to Man" in man's earthly experience of such evils. Choosing to exclude from his poem any appeal to revelation, Old Testament or New, Pope proceeds by way of "physico-theology"—the examination of Nature (including, in Pope's case, "human" nature) for evidence of God's existence and purposes. Such a procedure can in part be understood and justified by Milton's view (in *Of Education*) that "our understanding cannot in this body found itself but on sensible things, nor arrive so clearly to the knowledge of God and things invisible, as by orderly conning over the visible and inferior creature." Pope's consonance with Milton may be

First page of the manuscript for Pope's poem to Lord Bathurst (HM 6007, Henry E. Huntington Library and Art Gallery) seen in the second paragraph of *An Essay On Man*:

> Say first, of God above, or Man below,
> What can we reason, but from what we know?
> Of Man what see we, but his station here,
> From which to reason, or to which refer?
> Thro' worlds unnumber'd tho' the God be known,
> 'Tis ours to trace him only in our own.

Pope's deliberate eschewing of matters of faith and revelation in his argument (however ancient and honorable his method) was liable to misinterpretation from certain quarters, and it is not surprising that after several years of acclaim, both in England and on the Continent, the poem was suddenly attacked for supposedly unorthodox tendencies, particularly some of a fatalistic tenor, by a Swiss theologian, Jean-Pierre de Crousaz. Crousaz's attack was based primarily on two faulty French translations of *An Essay On Man*, one in prose and one in verse, the last a hopeless battering and hacking of both Pope's words and intentions. The charges nevertheless disturbed Pope deeply and once again provided his enemies with new opportunities for detraction. Amid this commotion, the poet unexpectedly acquired a potent, even commanding, champion in Rev. William Warburton, an Anglican clergyman (later bishop of Gloucester) who took it upon himself to come to Pope's defense with a vigorous rebuttal to Crousaz's accusations. Pope's relief and gratitude were such that he immediately established a friendship with his new ally, one that would lead to Warburton's becoming a close literary confidant for the last four years of Pope's life as well as one of his chief legatees after his death.

In *An Essay On Man* Pope expounds the premises of philosophic "optimism," not the optimism of a cheery or evolutionary view of things but rather the view that this world is the "best" or "optimum" world that God could create (to suppose that he could have done better but did not is to impugn his goodness and benevolence). Such a world has both physical and moral evil in it: "There deviates Nature, and here deviates Will." Nevertheless, there is a grand and general order in the cosmos, usually only dimly or incorrectly perceived by man, mainly because of a prideful disposition it is his duty to overcome: "From pride, from pride, our very reas'ning springs; / Account for moral as for nat'ral things: / Why charge we Heav'n in those, in these acquit? / In both, to reason right is to submit." Evoking the immensities of the universe, full of its multitudes of creatures with multiple claims and appetites of their own, Pope's "vindication" of what he calls the universe's "disposing Pow'r" is clear and unequivocal (and not lacking in reminiscences of the Book of Job, chapters 38-41):

> Cease then, nor ORDER Imperfection name:
> Our proper Bliss depends on what we blame.
> Know thy own point: This kind, this due degree
> Of blindness, weakness, Heav'n bestows on thee.
> Submit—In this, or any other sphere,
> Secure to be as blest as thou canst bear;
> Safe in the hand of one disposing Pow'r,
> Or in the natal, or the mortal hour.
> All Nature is but Art, unknown to thee;
> All Chance, Direction, which thou canst not see;
> All Discord, Harmony, not understood;
> All partial Evil, universal Good:
> And, spite of Pride, in erring Reason's spite,
> One truth is clear, "Whatever IS, is RIGHT."

Sometime in May 1730 Spence recorded that Pope had formed a "new hypothesis, that a prevailing passion in the mind is brought with it into the world, and continues till death (illustrated by the seeds of the illness that is at last to destroy us being planted in the body at our births"). This hypothesis of a "ruling Passion" found its poetic enunciation three years later in Epistle II of *An Essay On Man*:

> As Man, perhaps, the moment of his breath,
> Receives the lurking principle of death;
> The young disease, that must subdue at length,
> Grows with his growth, and strengthens with his
>   strength:
> So, cast and mingled with his very frame,
> The Mind's disease, its ruling Passion came;
> Each vital humour which should feed the whole,
> Soon flows to this, in body and in soul.

A year later, in the third of his "Epistles to Several Persons," addressed to Richard Temple, Viscount Cobham, Pope adverted to the same idea with the following injunction and comment:

> Search then the Ruling Passion: There, alone,
> The Wild are constant, and the Cunning known;
> The Fool consistent, and the False sincere;
> Priests, Princes, Women, no dissemblers here.
> This clue once found, unravels all the rest. . . .
>
> Time, that on all things lays his lenient hand,
> Yet tames not this; it sticks to our last sand.
> Consistent in our follies and our sins,
> Here honest Nature ends as she begins.

The idea that a person's entire life and character (no matter how various, contradictory, and fl-

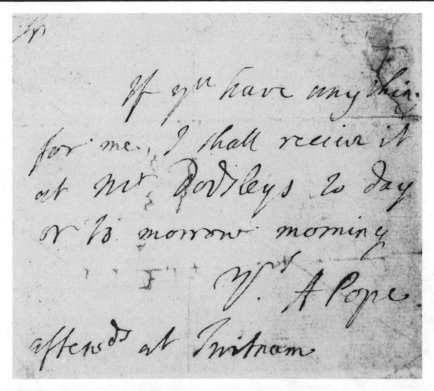

Note by Pope written in a copy of the first edition of his Essay on Man, *during a visit to Robert Dodsley (RB 106530, Henry E. Huntington Library and Art Gallery)*

nally mysterious) might be explained by such a "passion" has appeared to most to be crude and simplistic, and possibly Pope himself came to such a realization, for there is scant appeal to it in the poems of the last decade of his life (1734-1744). For one thing, in the Christian view of life (and Pope, no matter how vague or free his religious beliefs, never seemed to write in opposition to Christian doctrine) the concept would seem an obvious encroachment on the doctrine of free will; for another it would seem to preclude any kind of conversionary experience.

The hypothesis of a ruling passion does appear as a significant element once more in one of Pope's best pieces, the last of his "Epistles to Several Persons," *Of The Characters of Women: An Epistle To A Lady* (1735). The lady of the title was Martha Blount. The imaginary setting for part of the poem is an art gallery, with the speaker a cicerone who conducts the reader past portraits of various female characters exemplifying the notion that, "good as well as ill, / Woman's at best a Contradiction still." There is the flirtatious Rufa (a redhead), who studies the philosopher John Locke; the timid Silia (snub-nosed?), who flies into a rage over a pimple; Papillia (butterfly), who longs for a country estate but cannot stand the "odious, odious Trees"; and Narcissa—"A very Heathen in the carnal Part, / Yet still a sad, good Christian at her heart." Five or six more portraits are also designed to enforce Pope's thesis that women in general, and in contrast to men, are governed by only two "Ruling Passions": the "Love of Pleasure, and the Love of Sway." The poem's conclusion, in contrast to the unflattering female characterizations and the highly suspect maxim just quoted, offers a tender, affectionate, admiring portrayal of Blount (never mentioned in the poem by name), to whom Phoebus Apollo, the god of poetry, has given "good Sense, Good-Humour, and a Poet."

In several poems written during the 1730s Pope conducts an on-and-off defense of his life and art, but *An Epistle to Dr. Arbuthnot* provides the major apologia of these years. The poem appeared in January 1735, a month before the *Epistle To A Lady* and only a few weeks before the death of Arbuthnot, the witty physician who had been a kindly adviser to Pope since the days of Queen Anne and the Scriblerus Club. In a headnote to the poem Pope explained that it was "*a Sort of Bill of Complaint, begun many years since, and drawn up by snatches, as the several Occasions offer'd,*" and that he had "*no thoughts of publishing*

Sepia drawing by Pope later engraved as the frontispiece for a 1745 edition of An Essay On Man *(Collection of W. S. Lewis, Farmington, Connecticut)*

duce *Verses addressed to the Imitator of Horace* (1733), one of the most malicious attacks ever directed at Pope—and the more disgraceful, considering the aristocratic status of the authors. An unpleasant taste of their addresses to Pope may be absorbed from lines that tell him that his "crabbed Numbers" (rough verses) are as "Hard as [his] Heart, and as [his] Birth obscure"; that question how he could "by Beauty's Force be mov'd, / No more for loving made, than to be lov'd"; and that conclude with this malediction:

> Like the first bold Assassin's be thy Lot,
> Ne'er be thy Fault forgiven, or forgot;
> But as thou hat'st, be hated by Mankind,
> And with the Emblem of thy crooked Mind,
> Mark'd on thy Back, like *Cain*, by God's own Hand;
> Wander like him, accursed through the Land.

The second of the two poems cited in Pope's headnote, *An Epistle to a Doctor of Divinity from a Nobleman at Hampton Court* (1733), apparently by Hervey alone (unlike the first, which Pope called his "Witty Fornication" with Montagu), was comparatively tame. But for their pains, both virulent and doggerel, the pair of attackers achieved a kind of surpassing notoriety, Montagu living on in Pope's verse as a venal and slovenly poetess called Sappho, and Hervey destined to endure in the Proteus-like shape-shifting nastiness of his portrayal in *An Epistle to Dr. Arbuthnot* as Sporus, the name of the young catamite who was gelded and taken in "marriage" by the Emperor Nero:

>   this Bug with gilded wings,
> This painted Child of Dirt that stinks and stings;
> Whose Buzz the Witty and the Fair annoys,
> Yet Wit ne'er tastes, and Beauty ne'er enjoys,
> So well-bred Spaniels civilly delight
> In mumbling of the Game they dare not bite.
> Eternal Smiles his Emptiness betray,
> As shallow streams run dimpling all the way.
> Whether in florid Impotence he speaks,
> And, as the Prompter breathes, the
>   Puppet squeaks;
> Or at the Ear of *Eve*, familiar Toad,
> Half Froth, half Venom, spits himself abroad,
> In Puns, or Politicks, or Tales, or Lyes,
> Or Spite, or Smut, or Rymes, or Blasphemies.
> His Wit all see-saw, between *that* and *this*,
> Now high, now low, now Master up, now Miss,
> And he himself one vile Antithesis.
> Amphibious Thing! that acting either Part,
> The trifling Head, or the corrupted Heart!
> Fop at the Toilet, Flatt'rer at the Board,

it, till it pleas'd some Persons of Rank and Fortune [the Authors of Verses to the Imitator of Horace, and of an Epistle to a Doctor of Divinity from a Nobleman at Hampton Court,] to attack in a very extraordinary manner, not only my Writings (of which being publick the Publick judge) but my Person, Morals, and Family, whereof to those who know me not, a truer Information may be requisite." The "Persons of Rank and Fortune," and authors of the two poems cited within Pope's brackets, were Lady Mary Wortley Montagu, a minor poet later famous for, among other things, her early advocacy of inoculations against smallpox, and John, Lord Hervey, a courtier and confidant of Caroline, George II's queen, and notorious for his profligacy and effeminate manner. Miffed by what they took as slighting allusions to themselves in Pope's first "Imitation" of Horace, Montagu (with whom Pope had been deeply infatuated before they were estranged by some obscure quarrel) and Hervey joined such talents as they possessed, along with an inordinate supply of spleen, to pro-

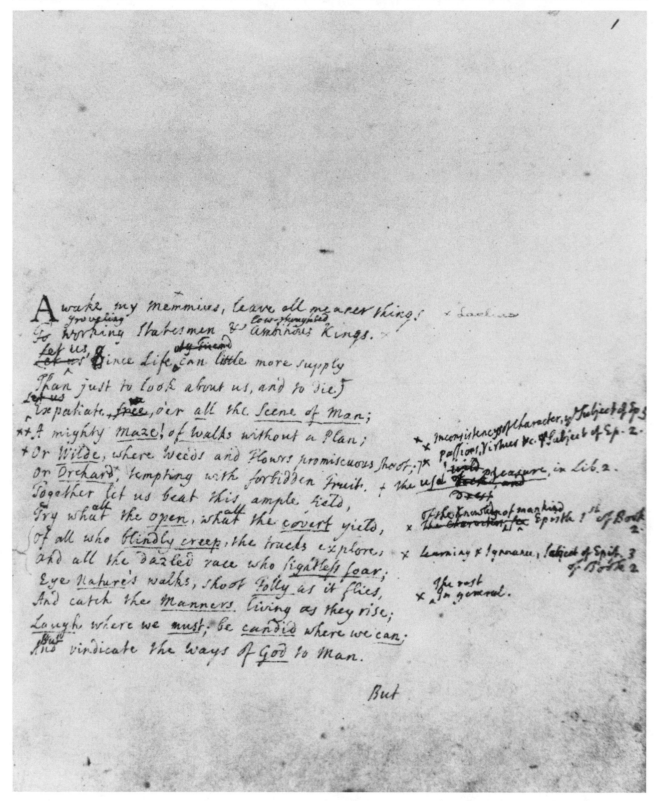

On this and the next two pages: opening pages from the earliest extant draft, written circa 1731, for Pope's Essay on Man
(MA 348, Pierpont Morgan Library)

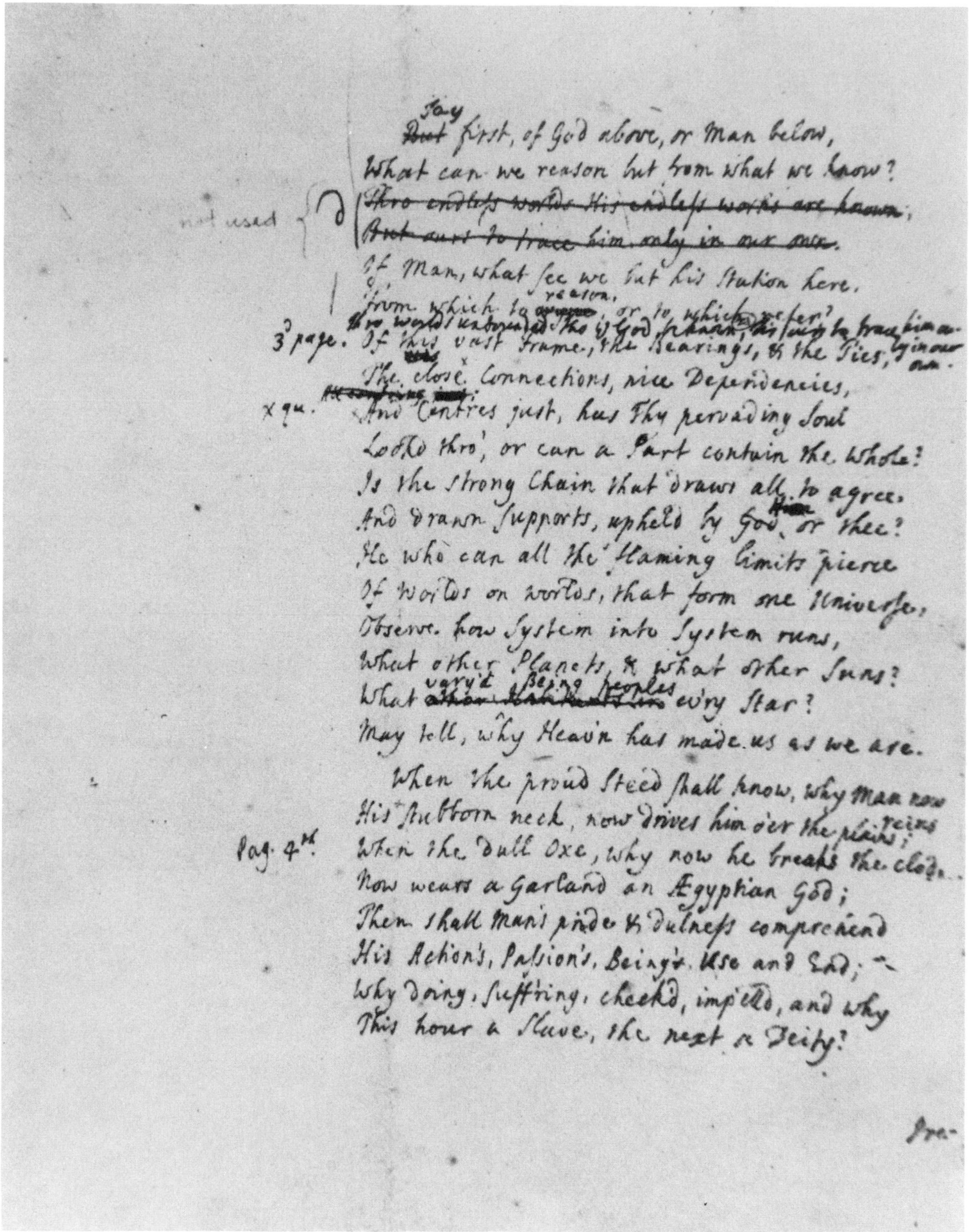

Say
~~But~~ first, of God above, or Man below,
What can we reason but from what we know?
~~Thro endless worlds His endless works are known;~~
~~But sure to trace him only in our own.~~

not used

Of Man, what see we but his Station here,
From which to ~~argue~~ reason, or to which ~~refer?~~
3 page.   ~~thro world unbounded~~ Tho if God ~~reason~~ this ~~seep to trace him in our own~~
If this vast Frame, the Bearings, & the Ties,
The close Connections, nice Dependencies,
x qu.   ~~His works~~ And Centres just, has Thy pervading Soul
Looked thro', or can a Part contain the Whole?
Is the strong Chain that draws all to agree,
And drawn supports, upheld by God, or thee?
He who can all the' flaming limits pierce
Of worlds on worlds, that form one Universe,
Observe, how System into System runs,
What other Planets, & what other Suns?
What varry'd Being peoples ~~other~~ ~~ev'ry Star?~~
May tell, why Heav'n has made us as we are.

When the proud Steed shall know, why Man now
His Stubborn neck, now drives him o'er the plains;   reins
Pag. 4th.   When the dull Oxe, why now he breaks the clod,
Now wears a Garland an Egyptian God;
Then shall Man's pride & dulness comprehend
His Action's, Passion's, Being's Use and End; ~
Why doing, suffring, check'd, impell'd, and why
This hour a Slave, the next a Deity!

Dra-

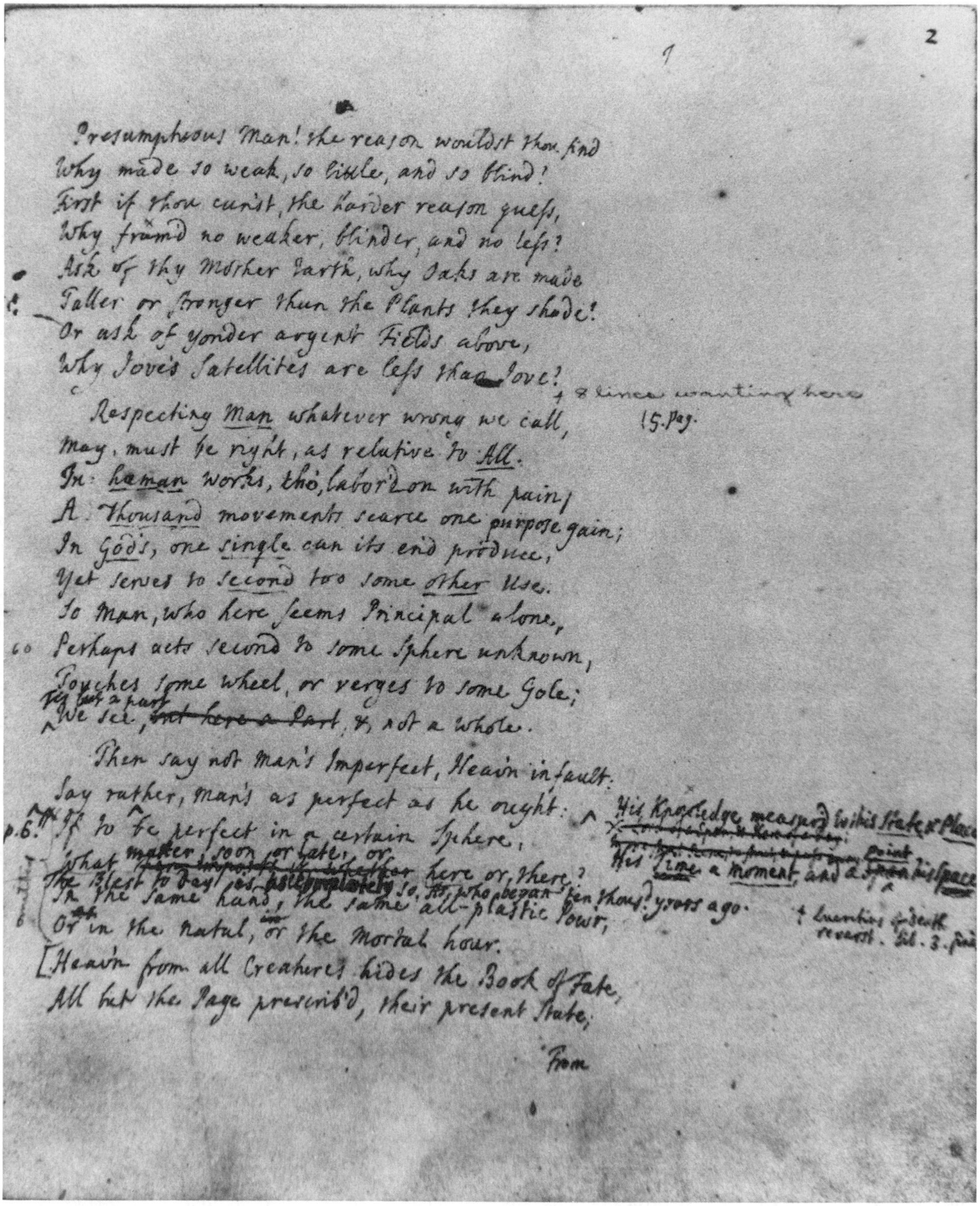

Presumptuous Man! the reason wouldst thou find
Why made so weak, so little, and so blind!
First if thou canst, the harder reason guess,
Why fram'd no weaker, blinder, and no less?
Ask of thy Mother Earth, why Oaks are made
Taller or stronger than the Plants they shade?
Or ask of yonder argent Fields above,
Why Jove's Satellites are less than Jove?
+ 8 lines wanting here 15. Pag.

Respecting Man whatever wrong we call,
May, must be right, as relative to All.
In human works, tho' labor'd on with pain,
A thousand movements scarce one purpose gain;
In God's, one single can its end produce,
Yet serves to second too some other use.
So Man, who here seems Principal alone,
Perhaps acts second to some Sphere unknown,
Touches some wheel, or verges to some Gole;
'Tis but a part we see, ~~not here a Part~~, & not a Whole.

Then say not Man's Imperfect, Heav'n in fault;
Say rather, Man's as perfect as he ought:
His Knowledge measur'd to his State & Place,
His Time a moment, and a point his space.
If to be perfect in a certain Sphere,
What matter, soon or late, or here or there?
The Blest to day is as completely so,
As who began ten thous^d years ago.
In the same hand, the same all-plastic Powr,
Or at the natal, or the mortal hour.
[Heav'n from all Creatures hides the Book of Fate,
All but the Page prescrib'd, their present State;
From

Engraving based on a portrait of Pope by William Hoare

Now trips a Lady, and now struts a Lord.
Eve's Tempter thus the Rabbins have exprest,
A Cherub's face, a Reptile all the rest;
Beauty that shocks you, Parts that none will trust,
Wit that can creep, and Pride that licks the dust.

In *An Epistle to Dr. Arbuthnot* Pope so arranged and tinted autobiographical materials as to distinguish the motivations and values of his own poetic art from those of a dreary horde of scribblers and hirelings: the hacks of Grub Street with their prostitutions of self as well as the "witlings" of the beau monde with their tripping insipidities. Unquestionably, amid the poem's carefully crafted defense of his own works and its equally artful construction of an authorial ethos favorable to Pope himself, the poet achieved retaliations for personal injuries, some new, as with Montagu and Hervey, some of an elder date, harking back to the Buttonian conspiracy against his Homer. Here Addison is transfigured into Atticus, a man "Blest with each Talent and each Art to please," but also a critic whose habit it was to "Damn with faint praise, assent with civil leer, / And without sneering, teach the rest to sneer." But above all, *An Epistle to Dr. Arbuthnot*, along

with the four "Epistles to Several Persons," may be seen as inaugurating, if not fully incorporating, the more introspective, even pensive and self-examining tone that characterizes Pope's work during what remained of the 1730s—in spite of his unremitting inveighings against King George II, his ministry, and their political and poetical spawnings.

It is the "Imitations of Horace," however, which appear to represent Pope, amid his self-examining moments, at his most relaxed, assured, and mature, still pressing his embarrassing charges against royal and ministerial fatuity and corruption, but also seeking out, defining, and defending the qualities of mind and spirit essential to good poetry and the good life. Leaving aside some relatively minor pieces in this mode, there appeared during a five-year span seven major "imitations" of Horace, plus "versifyings" of two satires by John Donne. In order of appearance, these nine works are: *The First Satire Of The Second Book of Horace, Imitated* (1733); *The Impertinent, Or A Visit to the Court. A Satyr* (1733), the initially anonymous redoing of a Donne poem later given the title *The Fourth Satire of Dr. John Donne, Dean of St. Paul's, Versifyed,* and included in Pope's *Works* of 1735; *The Second Satire Of The Second Book of Horace Paraphrased* (1734); *Sober Advice From Horace,* published anonymously in 1734, then twice republished in 1738 as, first, *A Sermon against Adultery,* and then as *The Second Satire of the First Book of Horace*; *The Second Satire of Dr. John Donne, Dean of St. Paul's, Versifyed* (1735); *The Second Epistle Of The Second Book of Horace, Imitated* (1737); *The First Epistle Of The Second Book of Horace, Imitated* (1737); *The Sixth Epistle Of The First Book of Horace Imitated* (1738); and *The First Epistle Of The First Book Of Horace Imitated* (1738).

The attraction of the Horatian originals and the allusive advantages he gained in adapting them to his own time and situation were given in part by Pope himself in two "Advertisements." In the 1735 *Works* version of *The First Satire* he wrote: "*The Occasion of publishing these* Imitations *was the Clamour raised on some of my* Epistles [to Several Persons]. *An Answer from* Horace *was both more full, and of more Dignity, than any I cou'd have made in my own person; and the Example of much greater Freedom in so eminent a Divine as Dr.* Donne, *seem'd a proof with what Indignation and Contempt a Christian may treat Vice or Folly, in ever so low, or ever so high, a Station.*" Then, in 1737, in the "Advertisement" to *The First Epistle Of The Second Book of Horace* (his ironic adaptation of

Horace's complimentary address to Caesar Augustus to the character of his own English monarch, christened George Augustus), Pope says:

> The Reflections of Horace, and the Judgments past in his Epistle to Augustus, seem'd so seasonable to the present Times, that I could not help applying them to the use of my own Country. . . .
>
> We may farther learn from this Epistle, that Horace made his Court to this Great Prince, by writing with a decent Freedom toward him, with a just Contempt of his low Flatterers, and with a manly Regard to his own Character.

Although entitled "Imitations," and originally published with the Latin texts on facing pages, the Horatian poems (and the "versifications" of Donne as well) must be respected as poems having a new and distinct entity of their own, susceptible to interpretations quite at variance with their forebears. With Horace's and his own text printed side by side, Pope invited reference to the original so that both his adherence to and departure from it could be assessed: the accommodations of the Roman to the English scene leading to a new artifact, one whose paternal lineaments are everywhere evident but whose independence, filial though it be, is continually affirmed. With the possible exception of *Sober Advice From Horace*, a bawdy "sermon" against adultery that argues that a "tight, neat Girl" will serve one's needs much more safely than "thy Neighbour's Wife," the "Imitations" have a variety and complexity not easily summarized. Nevertheless, one is steadily aware of three themes or emphases: corruptions in poetry as well as in politics; Pope's own intense preoccupation with satire and the role of the satirist in society; and his striving for a personal *ars vivendi*, an art of living, grounded in virtue of mind, engendering both strength and tranquillity of spirit.

These emphases are not easily distinguished one from the other. In *The First Satire*, for example, Pope early disavows any seeking of royal favor from George II (a monarch who despised poetry and indeed most learning but preened himself on his martial bent), refusing to cram his verse with "ARMS, and GEORGE, and BRUNSWICK" (German origin of the Georges), in order to rend "with tremendous Sound your ears asunder, / With Guns, Drum, Trumpet, Blunderbuss & Thunder." The declaration not only distances Pope from the sycophancy so widespread among George's courtiers and hireling poets but asserts a sturdy independence of spirit, poetic as well as

personal. And when, some lines later, he further declares that, while he lives, "no rich or noble knave / Shall walk the World, in credit to his grave," and that he will be "To VIRTUE ONLY and HER FRIENDS, A FRIEND," he stakes out the moral high ground from which he henceforth will challenge the establishment and its hangers-on.

The most daring of Pope's challenges to the crown as being itself the center and source of political corruption and cultural flaccidity is doubtless *The First Epistle Of The Second Book*, the poem so mockingly addressed to George Augustus, the first six lines of which are the sliest and most impertinent possible disclosure of the king's hollow monarchal pretentions:

> WHILE YOU, great Patron of Mankind, sustain
> The balanc'd World, and open all the Main;
> Your Country, chief, in Arms abroad defend,
> At home, with Morals, Arts, and Laws amend;
> How shall the Muse, from such a Monarch steal
> An hour, and not defraud the Publick Weal?

Any sophisticated reader of the day would have known that while George II, of the German house of Hanover, delighted in military affairs, much of his time in "Arms," whether at "home" or "abroad," was in the arms of one or another of his mistresses, and that any interest he had in "amending" the "Morals, Arts, and Laws" of his English subjects was negligible. The word *Patron*, by which he is addressed in line one, is in all probability a pun. Sometimes pronounced in the period like "pattern," it may have been designed to recall an ancient Latin maxim: *qualis rex, talis grex* (like king, like people). The likelihood that Pope had such a concept in mind while composing his poem is further suggested by a later passage that centers on the line, "All, by the King's Example, liv'd and lov'd." In this passage the principal allusion is to the atmosphere of luxury and debauchery imparted to the English court by King Charles II on his restoration to the throne in 1660; but the passage at the same time reinforces the idea, pervasive in the epistle, that kingdoms generally take on the distinguishing characteristics of their rulers, for good or bad. As Pope presents George II's reign, the throne, traditional embodiment of a nation's moral, intellectual, and artistic ideals, has become a contaminant of such ideals, much in accord with Swift's observation (in *A Project for the Advancement of Religion and the Reformation of Manners*, 1709) that "human nature seems to lie under this disadvantage, that the ex-

A copy of the only full-length portrait of Pope, drawn without his knowledge by William Hoare, as Pope was in conversation with Ralph Allen at Prior Park, Allen's estate (Edmund Gosse, English Literature: An Illustrated Record, *1903)*

ample alone of a vicious prince, will, in time, corrupt an age."

But *The First Epistle*, known as "To Augustus," was not merely a caustic attack on the monarchy and what it represented—difficult if not impossible legally to refute or chastise because of its ironies and ambiguities. It also offered an appraising survey of English literary history, from Chaucer and John Skelton, through Shakespeare, Philip Sidney, and Cowley, even up to Addison, to whom, in spite of their earlier antipathies, Pope pays a compliment: if we "excuse some Courtly stains," he says, "No whiter page than Addison remains. / He, from the taste obscene reclaims our Youth, / And sets the Passions on the side of Truth; / Forms the soft bosom with the gentlest art, / And pours each human Virtue in the

heart." The history also extends to Colley Cibber, the buffoonish playwright and actor whom George II was to make poet laureate and who would succeed Theobald as king of the dunces in the revised 1743 edition of *The Dunciad*: Pope gives even him a mite of applause for at least one of his plays (*The Careless Husband*, 1704). Much of the point of Pope's evaluative literary history is that antiquity alone neither guarantees nor measures excellence: "I lose my patience, and I own it too, / When works are censur'd, not as bad, but new; / While if our Elders break all Reason's laws, / These Fools demand not Pardon, but Applause."

As he comes to the close of his critique of the English literary scene, past and present, Pope suddenly intrudes with a personal poetic manifesto, vibrant in its emotional surge, and utterly in-

Marble bust of Pope by L. F. Roubiliac, 1741 (Shipley Art Gallery, Gateshead)

consistent with any view of him as the personification of a cold and formal "neoclassicism":

Yet lest you think I railly more than teach,
Or praise malignly Arts I cannot reach,
Let me presume for once t'instruct the times,
To know the Poet from the Man of Rymes:
'Tis He, who gives my breast a thousand pains,
Can make me feel each Passion that he feigns,
Inrage, compose, with more than magic Art,
With Pity, and with Terror, tear my heart;
And snatch me, o'er the earth, or thro' the air,
To Thebes, to Athens, when he will, and where.

The last two lines, it is obvious, repudiate the so-called classical or neoclassical unities of time and place. But the preceding lines, with their insistence on the "magic" in art, and on the poet's capacity to arouse pain, even "a thousand pains," to re-create "Passion," to "Inrage, compose," to "tear" the heart with "Terror" or with "Pity," declare clearly the primacy of the passional (rather than the rational) in great art. From *An*

Essay On Criticism—when as a mere youth he had praised those "Great Wits" who

> may *gloriously offend*,
> And *rise to Faults* true Criticks *dare not mend*;
> From *vulgar Bounds* with *brave Disorder* part,
> And *snatch a Grace* beyond the Reach of Art,
> Which, without passing thro' the *Judgment*, gains
> The *Heart*, and all its End *at once* attains—

to the Horatian imitations, Pope was never the advocate of a cold poetic "correctness." His verse may be honed to a fine edge and polish, coiled for lithe and ready strike, but the seeming ease and inevitability of his match of form and sense in his couplets is the product of a genius racked by the effort to discipline its own imaginative energies; as his epigraph to *The First Epistle* has it, *Ludentis speciem dabit & torquebatur* (He will give the appearance of playing, and yet be tortured with effort). The severity he believed practiced by great poets, the severity he imposed on himself, and the severity he would have all poets emulate, is the theme of this passage, also from *The First Epistle*:

> But how severely with themselves proceed
> The Men, who write such Verse as we can read?
> Their own strict Judges, not a word they spare
> That wants of Force, or Light, or Weight, or Care,
>
> Prune the luxuriant, the uncouth refine,
> But show no mercy to an empty line;
> Then polish all, with so much life and ease,
> You think 'tis Nature, and a knack to please.

These lines, from the poem of 1737, are then rounded off with lines only barely modified from a couplet of 1711 (in *An Essay On Criticism*): "But Ease in writing flows from Art, not Chance, / As those move easiest who have learn'd to dance." The severity Pope preached and practiced from the beginning to the end of his career prompted these words from Johnson in the *Life of Pope*: "he did not court the candour, but dared the judgement of his reader, and expecting no indulgence from others, he shewed none to himself. He examined lines and words with minute and punctilious observation, and retouched every part with indefatigable diligence, till he had left nothing to be forgiven."

These poems of the 1730s are not often far from an autumnal contemplative self-appraisal. In 1738, when Pope was forty-nine and in what he calls the "Sabbath" of his days (seven times

Pope in 1742 (painting by J. B. Van Loo; Collection of W. S. Lewis, Farmington, Connecticut)

seven), he wrote in *The First Epistle Of The First Book Of Horace*: "A Voice there is, that whispers in my ear, / ('Tis Reason's voice, which sometimes one can hear) / 'Friend Pope! be prudent, let your Muse take breath, / And never gallop Pegasus to death' "; and so he resolves:

> Farewell then Verse, and Love, and ev'ry Toy,
> The rhymes and rattles of the Man or Boy:
> What right, what true, what fit, we justly call,
> Let this be all my care—for this is All:
> To lay this harvest up, and hoard with haste
> What ev'ry day will want, and most, the last.

Though he is still unwavering in his determination to "Brand the bold Front of shameless, worthless Men" (*The First Satire*), he also yearns for "the Virtue and the Art / To live on little with a chearful heart" (*The Second Satire*). And (as a Catholic) unable legally to own his villa and grounds at Twickenham, he nonetheless recommends a freehold within anyone's power (in *The Second Sat-*

ire): "Let Lands and Houses have what Lords they will, / Let US be fix'd, and our own Masters still." Time's annual erosions, even those imperceptible ones of the self, are traced in these haunting lines from *The Second Epistle*:

> Years foll'wing Years, steal something ev'ry day,
> At last they steal us from our selves away;
> In one our Frolicks, one Amusements end,
> In one a Mistress drops, in one a Friend:
> This subtle Thief of Life, this paltry Time,
> What will it leave me, if it snatch my Rhime?
> If ev'ry Wheel of that unweary'd Mill
> That turn'd ten thousand Verses, now stands still.

There comes a time, however, when even the tuning of verses must give way to a tuning of self, for

> Wisdom (curse on it) will come soon or late.
> There is a time when Poets will grow dull:
> I'll e'en leave Verses to the Boys at school:

To Rules of Poetry no more confin'd,
I learn to smooth and harmonize my Mind,
Teach ev'ry Thought within its bounds to roll,
And keep the equal Measure of the Soul.

As the 1730s drew to a close, Pope called attention to governmental corruption and mendacity with two final poems in the "manner," though not in "imitation," of Horace. Following upon passage of the Licensing Act of 1737, a measure designed to stifle criticism of the government in stage plays but perceived as threatening wider literary sanctions, and following also a steady stream of usually anonymous but also, at times, apparently government-sponsored attacks on Pope, the two poems were originally entitled *One Thousand Seven Hundred and Thirty Eight. A Dialogue Something like Horace,* and *One Thousand Seven Hundred and Thirty Eight. Dialogue II.* In 1740 the two poems were subsumed under the title *Epilogue to the Satires, Written in 1738, Dialogues I and II.* Some feel of the menacing climate in which they appeared may be gathered from a footnote to the last line of *Dialogue II,* presumably written by Pope (though possibly by Warburton), but not printed until an edition (1751) after his death:

> This was the last poem of the kind printed by our author, with a resolution to publish no more; but to enter thus, in the most plain and solemn manner he could, a sort of PROTEST against that insuperable corruption and depravity of manners, which he had been so unhappy as to live to see. Could he have hoped to have amended any, he had continued those attacks; but bad men were grown so shameless and powerful, that Ridicule was become as unsafe as it was ineffectual. The Poem raised him, as he knew it would, some enemies; but he had reason to be satisfied with the approbation of good men, and the testimony of his own conscience.

The "dialogue" of the two poems is carried on between a "Friend" (identified as "Fr." or "F." in the texts) and a character identified only as "P." (either for "Pope" or the "Poet"). The friend's cautionary voice nervously urges P. to play it safe, as stated in the first poem, not to offend those in power, and, if he must "lash the Greatest," to do so only when they are "in Disgrace." The voice of P. is stubbornly, though deviously, recalcitrant, scoring points even while seeming to back off, and, at the close of the first dialogue, hardening to a scathing indictment of a divine "Vice" worshipped with a "reverential Awe" by all classes of English society, but particularly by those in positions of "Greatness." The indictment, and the poem, are concluded with this restrained but scornful couplet: "Yet may this Verse (if such a Verse remain) / Show there was one who held it ["Vice"] in disdain."

Dialogue II opens on a renewed note of urgency, with "P." declaring that "Vice with such Giant-strides comes on amain, / Invention strives to be before in vain; / Feign what I will, and paint it e'er so strong, / Some rising Genius sins up to my Song." The "Friend's" remonstrances continue, objecting when P.'s attacks become either too particular or too general, too "high" or too "low," and finally accusing P., because of his judgmental terms and attitudes, of being "strangely proud," provoking P. to this rejoinder:

> So proud, I am no Slave:
> So impudent, I own myself no Knave:
> So odd, my Country's Ruin makes me grave.
> Yes, I am proud; I must be proud to see
> Men not afraid of God, afraid of me:
> Safe from the Bar, the Pulpit, and the Throne,
> Yet touch'd and sham'd by *Ridicule* alone.

In the closing passages of *Dialogue II* Pope dramatizes, perhaps to the point of histrionics, the figurative stance of the lonely satirist, sole surviving and knightly champion of truth and freedom, beset on all sides by a host of fools, knaves, and coxcombs, but armed with the customary weapons, consecrate to virtue. First the lance:

> O sacred Weapon! left for Truth's defence,
> Sole Dread of Folly, Vice, and Insolence!
> To all but Heav'n-directed hands deny'd,
> The Muse may give thee, but the Gods must guide.

Then the sword:

> Yes, the last Pen for Freedom let me draw,
> When Truth stands trembling on the Edge of
> Law. . . .

The sound of Roland's horn, however distant, is not without an echo in these lines.

One last great poetic enterprise emerges from the remaining three or four years of Pope's life. In 1743, more than fourteen years after the original appearance of *The Dunciad,* with Theobald crowned king of the dunces, Pope published a fourth book in which the satiric targets are vastly multiplied, and Theobald is not even mentioned. A year later, after he had revised all four books in an attempt (not altogether successful) to give them new coherence, the "greater" *Dunciad* appeared, with Theobald deposed and Cibber, the bumptious but talented actor and playwright who had been created poet laureate by George II, crowned in his stead. To name Cibber monarch of duncery, however much a matter of personal animus on Pope's part, was inspired; for the king's choice of so vile a poet and so boorish and immodest a man as poet laureate itself glaringly indicted the royal grossness of taste and judgment imputed by Pope to George II in "To Augustus." The appointment also supported the other charges Pope had made about the contemporary state of letters and the hireling and sycophantic writers who "served" that state.

The fourth, and by far the longest, book of *The Dunciad* is something of a satiric avalanche, picking up and overwhelming in its path a multitude of human types and vocations not even hinted at in the original three-book version: logicians and rhetoricians, opera singers, schoolmasters and university professors, antiquarians and scientific dilettantes, clergy and philosophers. The scene is supposedly that of a royal levee, or formal court reception, where the Goddess Dulness (with her "Laureate son" in repose on her lap) "mounts the Throne." Before her appear all those other "sons" and suitors who will be blessed and encouraged in the great undertaking of making "ONE MIGHTY DUNCIAD OF THE LAND!" Grand, hilarious, sweeping as the progress of this new book is, it does not seem to be smoothly integrated into the "action" or vision of the original version. Yet complaining about the four-book version's congruity of parts ultimately seems, in the face of its satiric energy and scope, merely captious. And the magnificent close, seemingly testifying to the expiration of civilization (and indeed Pope did witness the close of one particular epoch of Western culture), elevates to apocalyptic intensity all of those threats, insidious as well as brutally overt, by which, as Pope saw it, his particular era of civilization was being undermined and overthrown. Here is Pope's dramatic evocation of the "black hole" into which he sees the "world" he inherited being sucked and out of which he sees another "world" being born:

> She comes! she comes! the sable Throne behold
> Of *Night* Primaeval, and of *Chaos* old!

> See skulking *Truth* to her old Cavern fled,
> Mountains of Casuistry heap'd o'er her head!
> *Philosophy*, that lean'd on Heav'n before,
> Shrinks to her second cause, and is no more.

> *Physic* of *Metaphysic* begs defence,
> And *Metaphysic* calls for aid on *Sense*!
> See *Mystery* to *Mathematics* fly!
> In vain! they gaze, turn giddy, rave, and die.
> *Religion* blushing veils her sacred fires,
> And unawares *Morality* expires.
> Nor *public* Flame, nor *private*, dares to shine;
> Nor *human* Spark is left, nor *Glimpse* divine!
> Lo! thy dread Empire, CHAOS! is restor'd;
> Light dies before thy uncreating word;
> Thy hand, great Anarch! lets the curtain fall;
> And Universal Darkness buries All.

During the final months of 1743 and the early months of 1744, Pope's physical condition deteriorated rapidly, and he endured periods of amnesia and delusion. On 12 December 1743 his friend Spence "was asked to witness Pope's signature on his will," which specified among other things that he was to be buried near the monument to his "dear parents" in "Twit'nam" church, and that his body "be carried to the grave by six of the poorest men of the parish," for each of whom he ordered "a suit of grey coarse cloth, as mourning." On 10 May 1744 he said to Spence: "One of the things I have always most wondered at is that there should be any such thing as human vanity. If I had any, I had enough to mortify it a few days ago, for I lost my mind for a whole day." And "on the fourteenth he complained of seeing false colours on objects." When "a friend asked him whether he would not die as his father and mother had done, and whether he should send for a priest," Pope replied: "I do not suppose that is essential, but it will be right, and I heartily thank you for putting me in mind of it." The next morning, "after the priest had given him the last sacraments," Pope commented: "There is nothing that is meritorious but virtue and friendship, and indeed friendship is only a part of virtue." His last hours were thus recorded by Spence: "Mr. Pope died the thirtieth of May, in the evening, but they [including Spence himself] did not know the exact time, for his departure was so easy that it was imperceptible to the standers-by. May our end be like his!"

Letters:
The Correspondence of Alexander Pope, 5 volumes, edited by George Sherburn (Oxford: Clarendon Press, 1956).

Bibliography:
R. H. Griffith, *Alexander Pope: A Bibliography*, 1 vol-

ume in two parts (Austin: University of Texas Press, 1922, 1927);

J. V. Guerinot, *Pamphlet Attacks on Alexander Pope: 1711-1744. A Descriptive Bibliography* (London: Methuen, 1969).

Biographies:

Owen Ruffhead, *The Life of Alexander Pope* (London: Printed for C. Bathurst, 1769);

George Sherburn, *The Early Career of Alexander Pope* (Oxford: Clarendon Press, 1934);

Maynard Mack, *Alexander Pope: A Life* (New Haven: Yale University Press, 1985).

References:

John M. Aden, *Pope's Once and Future Kings: Satire and Politics in the Early Career* (Knoxville: University of Tennessee Press, 1978);

Aden, *Something Like Horace: Studies in the Art and Allusion of Pope's Horatian Satires* (Nashville: Vanderbilt University Press, 1969);

Emmett G. Bedford and Robert J. Dilligan, *A Concordance to the Poems of Alexander Pope* (Detroit: Gale, 1974);

Frederic V. Bogel, *Acts of Knowledge: Pope's Later Poems* (Lewisburg, Pa.: Bucknell University Press, 1981);

Benjamin Boyce, *The Character-Sketches in Pope's Poems* (Durham: Duke University Press, 1962);

Douglas Brooks-Davies, *Pope's Dunciad and the Queen of Night: A Study in Emotional Jacobitism* (Manchester: Manchester University Press, 1985);

Reuben Arthur Brower, *Alexander Pope: The Poetry of Allusion* (Oxford: Clarendon Press, 1959);

Laura Brown, *Alexander Pope* (Oxford: Blackwell, 1985);

Morris Brownell, *Alexander Pope and the Arts of Georgian England* (Oxford: Clarendon Press, 1978);

Leopold Damrosch, *The Imaginative World of Alexander Pope* (Berkeley: University of California Press, 1987);

Thomas R. Edwards, *This Dark Estate: A Reading of Pope* (Berkeley: University of California Press, 1963);

H. H. Erskine-Hill, *The Social Milieu of Alexander Pope* (New Haven: Yale University Press, 1975);

David Fairer, *Pope's Imagination* (Manchester: Manchester University Press, 1984);

Rebecca Ferguson, *The Unbalanced Mind: Pope and the Rule of Passion* (Philadelphia: University of Pennsylvania Press, 1986);

Dustin M. Griffin, *Alexander Pope: The Poet in the Poems* (Princeton: Princeton University Press, 1978);

Joseph V. Guerinot, *Pamphlet Attacks on Alexander Pope, 1711-1744* (New York: New York University Press, 1969);

Brean Hammond, *Pope and Bolingbroke: A Study of Friendship and Influence* (Columbia: University of Missouri Press, 1984);

Wallace Jackson, *Vision and Re-vision in Alexander Pope* (Detroit: Wayne State University Press, 1983);

John A. Jones, *Pope's Couplet Art* (Athens: Ohio University Press, 1969);

Douglas M. Knight, *Pope and the Heroic Tradition: A Critical Study of His Iliad* (New Haven: Yale University Press, 1951);

Maynard Mack, *Collected in Himself: Essays Critical, Biographical, and Bibliographical on Pope and Some of His Contemporaries* (Newark: University of Delaware Press, 1982);

Mack, *The Garden and the City: Retirement and Politics in the Later Poetry of Pope, 1731-1743* (Toronto: University of Toronto Press, 1969);

Mack, *The Last and Greatest Art: Some Unpublished Poetical Manuscripts of Alexander Pope* (Newark: University of Delaware Press, 1984);

Mack, " 'Wit and Poetry and Pope': Some Observations on His Imagery," in *Pope and His Contemporaries*, edited by James L. Clifford and Louis A. Landa (Oxford: Clarendon Press, 1949);

Mack, ed., *Essential Articles for the Study of Alexander Pope* (Hamden, Conn.: Archon, 1968);

Mack and James A. Winn, eds., *Pope: Recent Essays* (Hamden, Conn.: Archon, 1980);

Thomas E. Maresca, *Pope's Horatian Poems* (Columbus: Ohio State University Press, 1966);

A. D. Nuttal, *Pope's Essay on Man* (London: Allen & Unwin, 1984);

Robert W. Rogers, *The Major Satires of Alexander Pope* (Urbana, Ill.: University of Illinois Press, 1955);

John Paul Russo, *Alexander Pope: Tradition and Identity* (Cambridge, Mass.: Harvard University Press, 1972);

Robert M. Schmitz, *Pope's Essay on Criticism: 1709: A Study of the Bodleian Manuscript Text with Facsimiles, Transcripts, and Variants* (St. Louis: Washington University Press, 1962);

Schmitz, *Pope's Windsor Forest: 1712: A Study of the Washington University Holograph* (St. Louis: Washington University Press, 1952);

John Sitter, *The Poetry of Pope's Dunciad* (Minneapolis: University of Minnesota Press, 1971);

Patricia Ann Spacks, *An Argument of Images: The Poetry of Alexander Pope* (Cambridge, Mass.: Harvard University Press, 1971);

Joseph Spence, *Observations, Anecdotes, and Characters of Books and Men*, 2 volumes, edited by James M. Osborn (Oxford: Clarendon Press, 1966);

Frank Stack, *Pope and Horace: Studies in Imitation* (Cambridge: Cambridge University Press, 1985);

Geoffrey Tillotson, *On the Poetry of Pope* (Oxford: Clarendon Press, 1950);

Tillotson, *Pope and Human Nature* (Oxford: Clarendon Press, 1958);

Joseph Warton, *An Essay on the Writings and Genius of Pope* (London: Printed for M. Cooper, 1756);

Earl R. Wasserman, *Pope's Epistle to Bathurst: A Critical Reading with an Edition of the Manuscripts* (Baltimore: Johns Hopkins University Press, 1960);

Howard Weinbrot, *Alexander Pope and the Traditions of Formal Verse Satire* (Princeton: Princeton University Press, 1982);

Douglas H. White, *Pope and the Context of Controversy: The Manipulation of Ideas in An Essay on Man* (Chicago: University of Chicago Press, 1970);

Aubrey L. Williams, *Pope's Dunciad: A Study of Its Meaning* (London: Methuen, 1955);

William K. Wimsatt, *The Portraits of Alexander Pope* (New Haven: Yale University Press, 1965).

Papers:
The British Library has the largest collection of Pope's papers. Houghton Library, Harvard University, also has an important collection.

Samuel Richardson

(July 1689 - 4 July 1761)

This entry was written by Margaret Anne Doody (Princeton University) for
DLB 39: British Novelists, 1660-1800: Part Two.

BOOKS: *The Apprentice's Vade Mecum; or, Young Man's Pocket Companion* (London: Printed for J. Roberts & sold by J. Leake, 1734 [i.e., 1733]);

A Seasonable Examination of the Pleas and Pretensions of the Proprietors of, and Subscribers to, Play-houses, Erected in Defiance of the Royal Licence (London: Printed for T. Cooper, 1735);

Aesop's Fables, with Instructive Morals and Reflections, Abstracted from All Party Considerations, Adapted to All Capacities; and Design'd to Promote Religion, Morality, and Universal Benevolence (London: Printed for J. Osborn, Jr., 1739);

Pamela; or, Virtue Rewarded. In a Series of Familiar Letters from a Beautiful Young Damsel, to Her Parents. Now First Published in Order to Cultivate the Principles of Virtue and Religion in the Minds of the Youth of Both Sexes (2 volumes, London: C. Rivington & J. Osborn, 1740; 1 volume, Philadelphia: Reprinted & sold by B. Franklin, 1742-1743);

Letters Written to and for Particular Friends, on the More Important Occasions. Directing Not Only the Requisite Style and Forms to Be Observed in Writing Familiar Letters; but How to Think and Act Justly and Prudently, in the Common Concerns of Human Life (London: Printed for C. Rivington, J. Osborn & J. Leake, 1741);

Pamela; or, Virtue Rewarded. In a Series of Familiar Letters from a Beautiful Young Damsel to Her Parents: And Afterwards, in Her Exalted Condition, between Her, and Persons of Figure and Quality, upon the Most Important and Entertaining Subjects, in Genteel Life. The Third and Fourth Volumes. Published in Order to Cultivate the Principles of Virtue and Religion in the Minds of the Youth of Both Sexes, 2 volumes (London: Printed for Samuel Richardson & sold by C. Rivington & J. Osborn, 1741);

Clarissa; or, The History of a Young Lady: Comprehending the Most Important Concerns of Private Life. And Particularly Shewing the Distresses That May Attend the Misconduct Both of Parents and Children in Relation to Marriage, 7 volumes (London: Printed for S. Richardson & sold by A. Millar, J. & J. Rivington, John Osborn & J. Leake, 1747-1748; New Haven: From the press of William W. Morse, 1800);

Answer to the Letter of a Very Reverend and Worthy Gentleman Objecting to the Warmth of a Particular Scene in the History of Clarissa (London: Samuel Richardson, 1749);

Meditations Collected from the Sacred Books; and Adapted to the Different Stages of a Deep Distress; Gloriously Surmounted by Patience, Piety, and Resignation. Being Those Mentioned in the History of Clarissa as Drawn Up by Her for Her Own Use (London: J. Osborn, A. Millar, J. & J. Rivington & James Leake, 1750);

Letters and Passages Restored from the Original Manuscripts of the History of Clarissa (London: Printed for S. Richardson & sold by John Osborn, Andrew Millar, J. & J. Rivington & J. Leake, 1751);

The Case of Samuel Richardson of London, Printer; with Regard to the Invasion of His Property in The History of Sir Charles Grandison, by Publication, by Certain Booksellers in Dublin (London: Samuel Richardson, 1753);

The History of Sir Charles Grandison. In a Series of Letters. Publish'd from the Originals, by the Editor of Pamela and Clarissa, 7 volumes (London: Printed for S. Richardson & sold by C. Hitch & L. Hawes, J. & J. Rivington, Andrew Millar, R. & J. Dodsley & J. Leake, 1753-1754);

Copy of a Letter to a Lady. Who Was Solicitous for an Additional Volume to the History of Sir Charles Grandison (London: S. Richardson, 1754);

Answer to a Letter from a Friend, Who Had Objected to Sir Charles Grandison's Offer to Allow His Daughters by Lady Clementina to Be Educated Roman Catholics (London: S. Richardson, 1754);

An Address to the Public, on the Treatment Which the Editor of the History of Sir Charles Grandison

Richardson in 1750, portrait by Joseph Highmore (National Portrait Gallery, London)

Has Met with, from Certain Booksellers and Printers in Dublin (London: Samuel Richardson,
1754);
A Collection of the Moral and Instructive Sentiments,
Maxims, Cautions, and Reflections, Contained in
the Histories of Pamela, Clarissa and Sir Charles
Grandison (London: Printed for Samuel Richardson, 1755).

Editions and Collections: *The Novels of Samuel
Richardson*, 20 volumes, edited by Ethel
M. M. McKenna (Philadelphia: Lippincott,
1902);
The Complete Novels of Mr. Samuel Richardson, 20 vol-
umes, edited by Austin Dobson, with a life
and introduction by William Lyon Phelps
(London: Heinemann, 1902);

Familiar Letters on Important Occasions, edited by Brian W. Downs (London: Routledge, 1928; New York: Dutton, 1928);

The Shakespeare Head Edition of the Novels of Samuel Richardson, 18 volumes (Oxford: Blackwell, 1929-1931);

Samuel Richardson's Introduction to Pamela, edited by Sheridan W. Baker (Los Angeles: William Andrews Clark Memorial Library, 1954);

Pamela or Virtue Rewarded, edited by William M. Sale, Jr. (New York: Norton, 1958);

Pamela, 2 volumes, edited by George Saintsbury, introduction by Mark Kinkead-Weekes (London: Dent, 1962);

Clarissa; or, The History of a Young Lady, 4 volumes, introduction by John Butt (London: Dent, 1962);

Pamela, edited by T. C. Duncan Eaves and Ben D. Kempel (Boston: Houghton Mifflin, 1971);

The History of Sir Charles Grandison, 3 volumes, edited by Jocelyn Harris (London: Oxford University Press, 1972);

Pamela; or, Virtue Rewarded, 4 volumes, edited by M. F. Shugrue (New York: Garland, 1974);

Pamela, edited by Peter Sabor, introduction by Margaret Doody (Harmondsworth, U.K.: Penguin, 1980);

Clarissa; or, The History of a Young Lady, edited by Angus Ross (Harmondsworth, U.K.: Penguin, 1985).

OTHER: Daniel Defoe, *A Tour thro' the Whole Island of Great Britain,* second edition, revised and edited by Richardson (London: S. Richardson, 1738);

Penelope Aubin, *A Collection of Entertaining Histories and Novels,* preface attributed to Richardson, 3 volumes (London: D. Midwinter, 1739);

Sir Thomas Roe, *The Negotiations of Sir Thomas Roe, in His Embassy to the Ottoman Porte 1621 to 1628,* edited, with dedication and preface, by Richardson (London: Printed by Samuel Richardson for the Society for the Encouragement of Learning; sold by G. Strahan, C. Rivington, P. Vailland & J. Osborn, Jr., 1740);

Edward Young, *Conjectures on Original Composition, in a Letter to the Author of Sir Charles Grandison,* with suggestions and revisions by Richardson (London: A. Millar & R. & J. Dodsley, 1759).

Samuel Richardson, often in his own time compared to Shakespeare for universality, originality, and emotional truth, is generally acknowledged as the founder of a new school of novel writing in England. The new novel had its origins partly in English domestic fiction, particularly fiction by women; in Richardson's work the story of rape or courtship acquired massive force and philosophical complexity. The origins of the new fiction are also partly to be found in seventeenth-century works of religious self-examination, both Catholic and Protestant. Richardson's novels, all epistolary, concentrate on the inner thoughts and states of the individual. The individual is, however, always involved in social relationships, and many scenes are presented dramatically; Richardson makes references to tragic and comic drama of the seventeenth and eighteenth centuries. There is, even in his tragic or pathetic work, a range of comic devices and insights, sometimes even a wild humor, as well as a strong sense of the numinous or fantastic potential of commonplace things. Samuel Johnson notably preferred Richardson to Henry Fielding, not only for morality but for subject and perception: "Characters of manners are very entertaining, but they are to be understood by a more superficial observer, than characters of nature, where a man must dive into the recesses of the human heart." Johnson told Boswell that "there was as great a difference between them as between a man who knew how a watch was made and a man who could tell the hour by looking on the dial-plate." Richardson's study of "nature" was honored in an era philosophically concerned with the discovery of the nature of man.

The Richardsonian novel, observing at once the tempo of outer life and the flux of inner consciousness, begins a new tradition in English and Continental fiction. From it sprang the novels of Jean-Jacques Rousseau, Pierre Choderlos de Laclos, and Johann Wolfgang von Goethe, as well as the works of Jane Austen, George Eliot, Henry James, and Virginia Woolf. Richardson's own novels are not superseded by those of his followers; he is one of the great novelists of the world. He might be called "the novelist's novelist"; his appeal to fellow writers of fiction can be attested in the twentieth century, in which André Gide and Angus Wilson have been among his admirers.

Samuel Richardson was born in Mackworth, Derbyshire, where he was baptized on 19 August 1689. Biographers have surmised that he was born on 31 July, but his own birthday may well be the one he gave to his heroine Clarissa: 24 July. Richardson's ancestors on his father's side were yeomen of Byfleet in Surrey. According to the novelist, "My Father was . . . descended of a Family of middling Note in the County of Surrey; but which having for several generations a large Number of Children, the *not* large Possessions were split and divided; so that He and his Brothers were put to Trades. . . ." The novelist's father, whose name was also Samuel, was sent to London in 1667 to be apprenticed to Thomas Turner, a joiner. This Samuel "understood Architecture" and did well enough as a joiner (a woodworker chiefly engaged in construction and ornament) to become a freeman both of the Joiners' Company and of the City of London, where he lived and worked on Aldersgate Street. His first wife died in 1680, and he married again in 1682. Richardson's mother's name was Elizabeth; her son said that she was "of a Family not ungenteel; but whose Father and Mother died in her Infancy within half an Hour of each other in the London Pestilence of 1665."

In his major piece of autobiography, a long letter to his Dutch translator Johannes Stinstra on 2 June 1753, Richardson says that his father was involved with James Scott, Duke of Monmouth, whom he knew personally, and "thought proper, on the Decollation of the . . . unhappy Nobleman, to quit his London Business and to retire to Derbyshire." But Monmouth was beheaded in July 1685; and Richardson's biographers T. C. Duncan Eaves and Ben D. Kimpel have discovered that the elder Richardson had London connections after that date, while the house on Aldersgate Street remained registered in his name until 1693. Perhaps Richardson's father maintained two establishments, even after the Glorious Revolution of 1688 ensured safety for any supporter of the Protestant cause against James II; or it may be that Richardson the joiner contracted for work in Derbyshire that took some while to complete. The Richardsons were still in Mackworth, the village outside Derby where Richardson was born and baptized, in 1693, when a daughter was baptized; Richardson says that he and three other children out of nine were born in Derbyshire.

In 1699, however, the records of St. Botolph, Aldgate, London, show that the Richardsons had their son Benjamin baptized there, and in January 1703 Thomas was also baptized there. By 1699 the Richardsons were living in Mouse Alley, Tower Hill; by 1703 the family had moved to Rosemary Lane near the Minories. The novelist's early years may have been spent in the country, but the formative years of his childhood and youth were spent in urban circumstances, in a world of docks and warehouses, small shops and stinking lanes. Richardson's childhood had something in common with those of William Hogarth and Charles Dickens; none of these could escape knowing the more brutal facts of existence.

The novelist says that his father "designed me for the Cloth." He appears to have been given some formal education: a Samuel Richardson is on the records of the Merchant Taylors' School for 1701-1702; when he left he was in the third form. The first rudiments of Latin would have been acquired, but Richardson was evidently only beginning the education of a gentleman when poverty forced him to cease. His family could certainly not afford the university education he would have needed to be a clergyman of the Church of England. Little is known of Richardson's school days except that other students called him "*Serious* and *Gravity*" and yet turned to him as an entertainer: "And five of them particularly delighted to single me out . . . to tell them Stories, as they phrased it. Some I told them from my Reading as true; others from my Head, as mere Invention; of which they would be most fond. . . ." Looking back, Richardson saw the seeds of the novelist in these stories—and an audience of children is not an undemanding one.

Between the ages of twelve and seventeen Richardson may have assisted his father. In this period the "bashful and not forward Boy" was a favorite "with all the young Women of Taste and Reading in the Neighbourhood"; he read aloud to them while they did their needlework. He says that three young women revealed "their Love-Secrets" to him when he was "not more than Thirteen," as they wished him to write the answers to their lovers' letters. The young scribe noticed the difference between what went into the epistle and what went on in the heart.

Richardson's love of books and of writing helped him to choose a profession, but he was apprenticed very late; perhaps the family had been waiting for some patronage, which did not materialize, to support his education, or perhaps they simply could not afford the premium until 1706. Richardson said that, left by his father to choose a business, "I chose that of a Printer, tho' a Stranger to it, as what I thought would gratify my Thirst after Reading." There was an irony in this choice, as he noted later in letters to friends: his business filled his days with compulsory mechanical reading, leaving him much less time than he wanted for reading for recreation. The seventeen-year-old apprentice found the work hard, serving "a Master who grudged every Hour to me, that tended not to his Profit, even of those times of Leisure and Diversion, which the Refractoriness of my Fellow-Servants *obliged* him to allow them, and were usually allowed by other Masters to their Apprentices." This account exhibits a lingering bitterness toward John Wilde, who did not reward the virtue of the young apprentice who was too proud to break any rules, even though he had other pressing interests: "I stole from the Hours of Rest and Relaxation, my Reading Times for Improvement of my Mind; and being engaged in a Correspondence with a Gentleman greatly my Superior in Degree . . . these were all the Opportunities I had . . . to carry it on." Yet, he adds, he took care "that even my Candle was of my own purchasing," and was careful "not to disable my self by Watching . . . to perform my Duty . . . in the Day-time." The scrupulousness reflects the pride of an independent person who can never be truly happy under the command of another. Fortunately, Richardson was well suited to the late-night private work he enjoyed; all his life he was one of the enviable few who require little sleep. This gift of nature, which he regarded merely as a good habit, he bestowed on his most intellectually lively characters.

In 1713 Richardson's apprenticeship expired, and on 13 June 1715 he became a freeman of the Stationers' Company and a citizen of London. He worked for some years as a compositor and press corrector. He appears still to have had expectation of some patronage from the mysterious "Gentleman" who was his "Superior in Degree," the "Master of the Epistolary Style" who wrote him letters from abroad. This person has been speculatively identified (first by Richardson's daughters) with the wild young man whose story appears in a passage in the first edition of the *Pamela* sequel (1741), a passage deleted in later editions. Whatever were Richardson's hopes of patronage or even a change of career, this "better Expectation" finally vanished: "*That* failing, I began for myself, married, and pursued Business."

He was given some timely assistance. Richardson had evidently been helping the widowed Mrs. John Leake to run her printing business; on

her death in April 1721 Richardson was one of her executors, and he inherited a small legacy. He may already have been living in the house he soon leased, on the corner of Salisbury Court, off Fleet Street, that had formerly been rented by James Leake, printer and stationer. It is likely that he was able to purchase the printing presses and forms of Mrs. Leake's business at an advantageous rate, for soon after her death he was able to set up for himself. In November 1721 Richardson married Martha Wilde, the twenty-three-year-old daughter of his former master. He had his own business and household at the age of thirty-two.

Precisely what he had been doing between the ages of twenty-four and thirty-two remains mysterious. These are Richardson's "lost years," for which no biographer has yet been able to account. It is a pity that nothing is known, for the twenties are an important era in anyone's life and of major significance in the life of a writer. There are indications that Richardson in that period wished for some other career. The decisions of 1721 meant that there was to be no escape from the printing house. There were, however, to be many compensations. Being master even of a struggling business is better than being an apprentice. Richardson's income and influence rose steadily. He was admitted to the livery of the Stationers' Company in 1722 and held his first elected office in the company in 1727. His peers respected him.

Richardson's first years as a printer were marked by an interest in politics. He printed works by Tory authors such as Archibald Hutcheson, to whom he refers with approval in *Clarissa* (1747-1748); Francis Atterbury; George Kelly; and Philip, Duke of Wharton. Atterbury and Kelly were arrested and tried for participation in an alleged Jacobite plot in 1722; Atterbury was banished for treason, and Kelly was imprisoned in the Tower of London. Richardson printed a book defending Atterbury, as well as an edition of Kelly's speech in his own defense before the House of Lords. In 1722 Samuel Negus, a printer, gave Charles Townshend, secretary of state, a list of disaffected printers, including Richardson and his brother-in-law Allington Wilde among those "Said to be High Flyers" (that is, High Tories). Richardson printed the duke of Wharton's *True Briton,* a periodical extremely critical of Prime Minister Robert Walpole's government, written by a Tory who was in fact a Jacobite—though this may not have been known by all his associates at the time. (John Duncombe was later to tell John Nichols that Richardson himself wrote the sixth paper of the *True Briton,* though Richardson's recent biographers believe this to be untrue.) The title page of the periodical states that it was "printed for T. Payne," and Thomas Payne took the blame as publisher and printer. When he was arrested in June 1723, bail was offered by two sureties, one of whom was Richardson; Richardson offered bail again when Payne was arrested a second time. Payne was tried for seditious libel in February 1724, found guilty, and sentenced to a fine and a year's imprisonment. Richardson saw how those in power could treat dissent.

The government, however, had found it difficult to penetrate the close world of the printing trade. Informers were in danger of complete loss of livelihood; members stuck by each other. There were occasional traitors, such as Negus, and the notorious bookseller Edmund Curll, who tried to convince the government that although he had been prosecuted for obscenity his political heart was in the right place. Curll offered in 1728 to help detect the author of a pointed essay against George I, George II, and Walpole that had appeared in *Mist's Weekly Journal.* Curll named Richardson as one of the printers of this Tory journal. Nathaniel Mist's press was broken, and those involved with the publication were arrested, tried, and sentenced to prison and pillory. Richardson was not among those arrested, but he was being accused behind the scenes and cannot have been free of danger. There is a certain daring, and certainly imprudence, in beginning one's business by affronting the powers that be. Though in his later career Richardson seemed less hostile to the Walpole government, he never reneged on his earlier principles or denied his Tory associates. Many years later, in 1737, he printed (and perhaps even wrote) a favorable obituary of Mist.

In the testing times of the 1720s, Richardson experienced the real strength of the printing fraternity. The phrase "family of love" is used several times of the Grandison family in Richardson's novel *Sir Charles Grandison* (1753-1754), but the phrase in its origin refers, interestingly, to a secret international sect centering upon the Antwerp printer Christopher Plantin. The early Familists were printers; their beliefs were the inception of Rosicrucianism, Freemasonry, and other elements of Enlightenment thought. Richardson did not need to be a Freema-

son (though it is uncertain whether he was not) or a Rosicrucian or a Familist to appreciate his inheritance. The sense of solidarity under persecution and the high sense of calling that marked Renaissance printers survived into the eighteenth century. For Richardson the first "family of love" was the association of printers, of which the Stationers' Company was only a partial reflection. Richardson's major characters all seek a "family of love," including but transcending the family of the blood tie, offering fraternal and sororal support and encouragement to each member. Richardson was set up in business through the kindness of the Leakes; he chose both his wives from the families of printers; and he was buried at last in St. Bride's Church—the church of William Caxton—which has been called "the Cathedral Church of English Printing."

Richardson's occupation made him a contributor to the Enlightenment. The printing press was, as Elizabeth Eisenstein has shown, an agent of change. Ideas and information, as disseminated by printed matter and through centers of printing, invited commentary and addition; knowledge was seen as progressive rather than as static. In the eighteenth century, as in the Renaissance, booksellers and printers were consciously adding to the body of knowledge and provoking debate. Printers stood at the center of a continuous exchange of ideas. Richardson, at the crossroads of change, contributed to political debate and controversy at the very outset in his involvement with the *True Briton*; from the beginning he was also a contributor to the public store of knowledge.

Richardson added to the common knowledge of English geographical and economic conditions with the printing of Defoe's *Tour thro' the Whole Island of Great Britain* (1724-1727). That he took the subject seriously is shown in his work as an editor and reviser in the second edition (1738) and subsequent editions. (Some images in *Clarissa* seem to be drawn from recollection of this work—for example, the reference to Elden Hole.) Richardson was also the printer of *A Complete Collection of State Trials* (1729), a six-volume work edited by Thomas Salmon and Sollom Emlyn. The printer needed commissions from booksellers, but this collection might have been Richardson's own choice, for a constant interest in the idea and image of "trial" can be seen in his fictional works. Certainly the manner in which trials were presented in print, with dialogue in stageplay format, interpolations, and descriptions,

North End, the country retreat where Richardson wrote his novels

resembles Richardson's method of setting out extensive passages of his fiction.

Richardson's desire to make a truly original contribution to learning can clearly be seen in his persistent endeavors to publish *The Negotiations of Sir Thomas Roe, in His Embassy to the Ottoman Porte 1621 to 1628.* Richardson had come into possession of the letters of the seventeenth-century English ambassador to Constantinople and tried to publish an edition of these by subscription in 1730-1731. There were too few subscribers; eventually he was able to interest the Society for the Encouragement of Learning (whose printer he was) in publishing the material. Richardson, as editor, prepared a preface and a table of contents. *The Negotiations of Sir Thomas Roe* was published in March 1740; a respectable contribution to historical knowledge, the work found its way into libraries, but the whole edition was never sold, and the promised further volumes could not be produced. This venture into the world of historical scholarship was not unrelated to the interests of the novelist; the Roe papers are letters and describe, like the first part of *Clarissa,* the endeavors of an individual to negotiate with an arbitrary power.

Richardson was evidently interested in acquiring a degree of control over what he printed, though, particularly at the outset, he had to rely on work given him by individual booksellers or associations of booksellers (called "congers"). Under such arrangements a printer ran off only part of a large work and acted as a subordinate and indeed a hireling of the bookseller. The biography of Richardson published in the *Universal Magazine* in 1786 states that the "parliamentary branch of his business enabled Mr. Richardson to be more independent of the booksellers than printers usually are." The source of this article's information is Richardson's daughters, who can surely be heard here echoing the novelist's opinion. When he was made printer to the House of Commons in 1733, Richardson found a means to a cherished independence. The job meant steady work and pay, without reliance on a middleman; but it also involved considerable labor and inconvenience, as the printer had personally to collect the bills, orders, and reports. He was, however, thus in a good position to know precisely what issues were exercising the members of Parliament and what were the issues of debate and the manners and attitudes of legislators. A knowledge of the crosscurrents of the contemporary world, and of the views of those who had the power to change that world through legislation and influence, was invaluable to a novelist who was to depict not only the middle classes but the gentry and the aristocracy in processes of change and in relation to a whole society. Robert Lovelace and Sir Charles Grandison are expected to take seats in the legislature, and there are references in the novels to lawmaking and to the state of the law, as well as to existing ordinances and to real or projected acts of Parliament.

In his work for the House of Commons, Richardson came to know Arthur Onslow, Speaker of the House, who became a firm friend. It may have been through Onslow's influence that Richardson in 1742 was given the important contract to print all the past journals of the House of Commons, a responsible and remunerative assignment that assured Richardson's financial prosperity independent of booksellers' whims. Onslow thought highly of Richardson; later it was said that Onslow had wished to obtain a station at court for Richardson, and that Richardson had refused to consider accepting such an employment.

Richardson formed other important friendships. His work introduced him to a variety of literary men. Little is known about his association with Defoe, although they must certainly have been acquainted. He printed Aaron Hill's periodicals, the *Plain Dealer* (1723-1724) and the *Prompter* (1734-1736), and other of Hill's works. Through Hill he became acquainted with the Scots poets James Thomson and David Mallet, whose works he printed. As Thomson's *Britannia* (1729) was a covert attack on Walpole's policy, Richardson was still evidently not averse to expressing some hostility to Walpole's government. He was also the first printer of Thomson's complete *Seasons* (1730). Richardson made the acquaintance of another young and struggling writer, presumably in the first half of the next decade. Samuel Johnson, who boasted that he "never sought much after any body," admitted to Boswell that he had sought after Richardson, paying him frequent visits until he had overcome the printer's shyness and confirmed a friendship.

Richardson's career as a printer was just getting under way in the adventurous and uncertain 1720s. In the 1730s he was established, relatively independent, with varied work and new acquaintances. He had begun to hold offices in the Stationers' Company. The one real reference to his conviviality is to be found in a series of comic verses (one of these by Richardson) in the *Gentleman's Magazine* of 1736. It is pleasant to know that his friends had seen his "rosy face" when "flush'd with wine." Yet, if the 1730s seem to have been a time of sociability and prosperity, they were also largely a desolate time for Richardson. The previous decade had been clouded by the loss of children. His first baby, a son, died

within a month of birth, in 1722; the second child, another son, survived less than four months. A young Samuel born in 1725 died early in 1726. A little Martha was born and died in 1728. The fourth son, William, born in 1727, survived infancy and must have promised consolation, but he died in May 1730. The last of Martha Richardson's children, another Samuel, was christened in April 1730. His mother did not live to see this child die in 1732; Martha died in January 1731. Richardson later wrote that the loss of William, "a most delightful Child, carried away his most worthy Mother, at least contributed to her Death." Richardson remarked in 1748 that "I cherish the memory of my lost Wife to this Hour."

Richardson, a childless widower of forty-three, married again in February 1733. His new wife was Elizabeth Leake, daughter of the printer with whose family Richardson had long been connected. She was thirty-five—rather elderly in that period for childbearing. Yet her children fared better than Martha's. Their first infant, a girl, died within a month, but the four girls who followed, Mary (1734 or 1735), Martha (1736), Anne (1737), and Sarah (1740), lived to adulthood. Yet another Samuel was born in 1739 and was buried a year later. By the time he wrote his first novel, Richardson must have known that it was unlikely that he would ever have a son and heir.

There were other bereavements during this period. Richardson's father died, lingeringly and in pain as the result of an accident (the date is unknown); Richardson attended him in his last illness. Two brothers and a friend also died. Richardson spoke seldom, but movingly, of a period of physical and moral crisis resulting from the stress of all these wrenching losses: "No less than Eleven concerning Deaths attacked me in Two years." He became ill, suffering from digestive afflictions, nervousness, and dizziness. He may have feared privately that he was going mad. Hill recommended strong coffee to drive away the humors; Dr. George Cheyne prescribed a vegetable diet, exercise, and purges. Richardson's malady, a constant in his life after the mid 1730s, "the Distemper that common Curatives would not subdue," may have been Parkinson's disease. He was so shaky that sometimes he could walk only by supporting himself heavily on his stick. Yet he continued with tremendous energy to build up his printing establishment and in late middle age was to take on an exhausting second career as a writer of long novels.

Richardson was writing during his years as a printer. In addition to the preface to the Roe book and the additions to Defoe's *Tour*, he contributed unsigned comments and prefaces to printed books, not all of which have been identified. Cave's note on Richardson in the *Gentleman's Magazine* of January 1736, which says that "the Publick is often agreeably entertain'd with his Elegant Disquisitions in Prose," hints at work more extensive even than the "Indexes, Prefaces, & sometimes . . . *honest* Dedications" that Richardson briefly sums up for Stinstra.

The first complete and identifiable work by Richardson is *The Apprentice's Vade Mecum; or, Young Man's Pocket Companion* (published in 1733, though 1734 appears on the title page). The date is significant. The pamphlet was written after the long stream of losses that left Richardson childless. Two years earlier, he had written a letter of advice to his nephew Thomas Verren Richardson, eldest son of his brother William. In August 1732 the fifteen-year-old Thomas was apprenticed to Richardson; he died in November of that year. Richardson had thus been deprived of a substitute son, a potential successor.

Amplifying his earlier letter of advice into a booklet for the benefit of numerous young men seems to have been Richardson's way of dealing with his loss. In his instructional work he could make rational and assert control over a harsh world. He could act as a father, giving advice to young men who would themselves rise to the position of master. Richardson is not really addressing inferiors, but passing along social, moral, and practical wisdom to his own kind.

The pamphlet, he explains in his preface, is intentionally written in a plain style. If any of the *"Directions"* seems *"to descend too low,"* the reader must consider *"that they are calculated for all Sorts of Capacities."* His instructions are *"principally designed for Youth of tender years, who are to be dictated to in a plain and easy manner, and consider'd as Persons just stepping out into Life, and who, like tender Plants, being removed into a new Soil and climate, require the gentlest Management. . . ."* There is an attractive gentleness in that last image, though Richardson's notion of what is demanded of an apprentice is very strict. The lad is to be invariably industrious and sober, always mindful of his master's welfare, never criticizing his master and never wasting time, particularly not in a tavern or a playhouse. The style of the stern *Apprentice's*

THE

APPRENTICE's

VADE MECUM:

OR,

Young Man's Pocket-Companion.

In THREE PARTS.

PART I. Containing useful Comments and Observations on the Covenants entered into between Master and Servant, by way of *Indenture*; wherein that wise Obligation is considered Article by Article. With some occasional Remarks on *Play-houses*; and particularly on one lately erected.

PART II. Containing general Rules and Directions for a young Man's Behaviour in his Apprenticeship. Familiarly address'd to the Youth himself.

PART III. Some brief Cautions to a young Man against the Scepticism and Infidelity of the present Age, which insnare the Minds, and debauch the Morals of the Youth of this Kingdom: Wherein the essential Principles of Christianity are laid down and vindicated in so intelligent and forcible a Manner, as may serve for a Preservative against the contagious Infidelity of the present Age, and enable a young Man to give a *Reason* for his *Faith*.

Addressed to the Right Worshipful the Chamberlain of *London*.

The Whole calculated for the mutual Ease and Benefit both of Master and Servant; and recommended to the serious Consideration of all Parents, &c. who have Children that they design to put out Apprentice.

LONDON:

Printed for J ROBERTS in *Warwick-Lane*; and Sold by J. LEAKE at *Bath*. 1734.

Title page for the first complete work that can be attributed with certainty to Richardson. The pamphlet grew out of a letter of advice that Richardson wrote to his nephew, Thomas Verren Richardson, and seems to have been written as a means of dealing with the death of the young man, whom Richardson had hoped to make his successor.

Vade Mecum can, however, sometimes slip into exuberance or playfulness, as in the description of the City apprentice who tries to be a fop, wearing a new-fashioned wig *"plaister'd* rather than *powder'd,* and appearing like the *Twigs* of a *Gooseberry-Bush* in a *deep Snow*; his Shoulders also crusted or iced over with White, as thick as a *Twelf-Cake. . . ."*

The Apprentice's *Vade Mecum* has attracted most attention because of its apparently hostile attitude to theater. The hostility is reinforced in a later pamphlet attributed to Richardson, *A Seasonable Examination of the Pleas and Pretensions of the Proprietors of, and Subscribers to, Play-houses, Erected in Defiance of the Royal Licence* (1735). This pamphlet quotes several passages of *The Apprentice's Vade Mecum* on the corrupting effect of drama on middle-class and working-class youths. But the *Sea-*

sonable Examination is essentially a specific response to a specific issue, the endeavor to set up a theater in Goodman's Fields in defiance of the City and its inhabitants. *The Apprentice's Vade Mecum,* which is more theoretical, sets out social and aesthetic arguments against the contemporary theater.

Theaters, it states, are improper resorts not only for apprentices but for tradesmen, who there see themselves insulted and degraded: "To make a Cuckold of a rich Citizen, is a masterly Part of the Plot; and such Persons are always introduced under the meanest and most contemptible Characters." The plays also inculcate sexual depravity, and the recent drama has merely increased bawdiness and immorality while decreasing the level of wit. At least the dramatist of Charles II's reign had something intelligent to offer: "Most of our most taking Performances are such, as our Progenitors even of *Charles the Second*'s Reign, would have been asham'd of. Genteel Comedy . . . has long left the Stage, as well as the nobler Tragic Muse: And all our late Heroes and Heroines of the Drama, have been fetch'd from *Newgate* and *Bridewell*. The celebrated *Congreve*'s *Niky, Horner,* and others that I might name, were odious and detestable Characters . . . but then there was so much Wit mingled with the Immorality, as made it pass when we could get no better. But now the horrid Pantomime and wicked Dumb Shew, the infamous Harlequin Mimicry . . . These are . . . the edifying Subjects that have given Delight to crouded Audiences, to the Disgrace both of the *British* Taste and Stage." Richardson cannot sustain an antitheatrical prejudice; he moves to a condemnation of particular aspects of the contemporary stage, and he was far from being the only critic who objected to the wordless shows. His critique has several bases—in class loyalty, in moral right, and in "Taste." It should also be noted that Richardson shows some real knowledge of the Restoration comedies. Though he is careless in naming dramatists, he remembers the Nykin scenes from William Congreve's *The Old Batchelour* (1693) as well as William Wycherley's Horner. Also, in instructing his apprentice he gives a convincing—and revealing—account of how the mind becomes "too much ingag'd" by representation. He describes the addiction of the theatergoer: "If he has any Taste for those Diversions, the Musick will always play upon his Ears, the Dancers will constantly swim before his Eyes. This or that Part of an applauded Actor will perpetually

take up his Attention, and he will be desirous of seeing him shine in others, and so will want to trace one Player or other thro' every Scene, and every Season." The addiction seems to be described from firsthand knowledge. It seems evident that during Richardson's "lost years," when he was out of his apprenticeship and before he took on a business of his own and family responsibilities, he permitted himself the pleasures of theatergoing, and knew what it was to wish to see a favorite actor or actress in different roles. The point is worth stressing if only because of a traditional critical notion that Richardson was too "middle-class" and "Puritan" to know anything of live theater, a notion that looks for backing to a superficial reading of *The Apprentice's Vade Mecum.* The number and nature of dramatic and theatrical allusions in Richardson's novels could scarcely have been introduced by someone who took no interest in the theater. Some of his characterizations would seem to owe something to characters represented on stage (with telling gestures and stage business) by celebrated actors.

Richardson never denied that he had attended the theater. In later years he regretted that his malady and a phobia about crowded places prevented him from attending either church or theater. His sustained friendships with Hill, Colley Cibber, and David Garrick argue a continuing interest in the dramatic world. In 1748 he not only read Hill's *The Art of Acting* (1746), which he had printed, but tried to follow the expressions of the "ten Dramatic Passions": "I endeavoured to follow you in your wonderful Description of the Force of Acting, in the Passions of Joy, Sorrow, Fear, Anger, &c. And my whole Frame, so nervously affected before, was shaken by it. . . ." His attempt to read Hill's manual "not as a Printer" but as an apprentice actor hints that he had, like most novelists, a buried actor hidden within himself.

After *The Apprentice's Vade Mecum* and the *Seasonable Examination* there were doubtless other small works not yet traced. It has been convincingly argued that the preface to the posthumous collected works of Penelope Aubin, *A Collection of Entertaining Histories and Novels* (1739), is by Richardson. It represents his first public discussion of the nature and qualities of the modern novel. He offers five "Rules" (including the reward of Virtue "either *here* or *hereafter*" and the enforcement of "an universal *Benevolence* to Mankind") and discusses the idea of the novel as a universally appealing form: "Amusements of this Kind have always been highly approved of in the most polite nations, both of Europe and Asia." But Richardson's first piece of signed, published fiction was not a novel but a relatively unadventurous work, a revision of Roger L'Estrange's 1692 version of *Aesop's Fables*.

Richardson's work had been commissioned to compete with the version of the Whig Samuel Croxall. While removing L'Estrange's old Tory bias, Richardson, in a preface "Abstracted from all Party Considerations," makes a smart retort upon the Whig writer and praises the old Restoration loyalist L'Estrange. The "High-Flyer" in Richardson was not quite dead. He is, however, careful to make the "Moral" and the "Reflection" that appear after each fable apply to personal or social behavior rather than to politics. Richardson's *Aesop's Fables* (1739) was put out in a format and style designed for the use of children and is a pioneer work in children's literature. The poet William Shenstone was later to approve both the fables and the "Reflections" but regretted that Richardson had "admitted, through an extravagant and mistaken love of drollery that vulgarity of phrase" which was really L'Estrange's "vulgarity." L'Estrange was a master of colloquial phrase and common imagery; rewriting his *The Fables of Aesop* was an education in the powers of lively common English. One can hear the influence of this work in the voice of Pamela and other characters in all of Richardson's novels who allude to Aesop.

Also in 1739, Richardson was asked by the bookseller Charles Rivington to write "a little Volume of Letters, in a common Style, on such Subjects as might be of Use to those Country Readers who were unable to indite for themselves." Such compilations of sample letters had been common since the Renaissance. In this unpretentious project, Richardson had the opportunity to create modern characters, to suggest different voices through epistolary styles, and to capture the shifts and surges of change in English social life, the conflicts between classes and generations. It was in writing this "letter-writer" that Richardson discovered that he was a novelist. While writing letters "giving one or two as cautions to young folk circumstanced as Pamela was," he recollected an anecdote from real life he had once heard, and "gave way to enlargement." (Evidently the letters in question are number 138, "A Father to a Daughter in Service, on hearing of her Master's attempting her Virtue," and number 139, "The Daughter's Answer.") *Letters*

Title page for the novel in which Richardson examined the conflicts of male against female, class against class, and society against the individual, creating one of the most radical statements of the early Enlightenment

Written to and for Particular Friends, on the Most Important Occasions, begun in September or October 1739, was interrupted in November by *Pamela* and not completed until January 1741.

The letters in *Familiar Letters*, as the work is generally known, deal largely with love and courtship. Though the subjects allow Richardson to air what are evidently authorial opinions, all opinions are expressed by a character in a particular situation, and few statements are not counterbalanced by a reply from someone with another point of view. Sometimes the less orthodox view, coming from someone not in a position of authority, is rhetorically the best one. "A facetious young Lady to her Aunt, ridiculing her serious Lover" gives a vivid description of her Sunday visitor, Mr. Leadbeater, standing pompously in front of the fire and discoursing on the sermon, or giving "an account of all the Religious Societies, unask'd" over tea. Such a passage gives early indication of what might be called the Dickensian elements in Richardson's imagination: "After he had pretty well rubbed heat into his hands he stood up with his back to the fire, and, with his hand behind him, held up his coat, that he might be warm all over.... And then he twang'd his nose, and lifted up his eyes, as if in an ejaculation."

Familiar Letters gives advice not only on marriage and giving in marriage, but also on general social behavior. The reader is advised not to keep repeating in adult company the tales and sayings of his children, "dragging out an unwilling *Ay, very pretty indeed, sir! A charming boy! ...* Which kind of *yawning applause* is sometimes ... mistaken for approbation." There are vivid comic glimpses of common life, as in the narrative of the poor man living in modest lodgings who is suddenly reputed to be rich; his landlady is acquainted with the false secret: "The very next morning, I had a clean towel hung over my water-bottle, tho' I never before had more than one a week during the twenty years I have lodg'd here." The comedy in *Familiar Letters* is quite varied. There is even a mild approach to indecency, in play with a Restoration trope that always interested Richardson, the comparison of men to monkeys. A gentleman, in a humorous epistle to a lady, resents her fondness for a monkey: "What valuable qualification is Mr. Pug endowed with, which I am destitute of? What can he do, which I cannot perform, tho' with less agility, to full as good purpose? Is it a recommendation in him, that he wears no breeches? For my part, I will most willingly surrender mine at your feet." The writing of *Familiar Letters* prepared Richardson for his work as a novelist by eliciting his pleasure in comic play with language as well as his interest in creating characters and points of view.

It has been pointed out that Richardson became a novelist only after assured fortunes allowed him to turn his energies to new purposes. The success of his printing business was well established. In 1736 he had been able to move to a large house on the west side of Salisbury Court, the upper part of which accommodated the printing press. In the same year, probably in response to Dr. Cheyne's advice, he spent part of his time in the country. In 1738 he was able to lease a country retreat; The Grange, North End, Fulham, his second home for many years, had handsome gardens and a grotto. Yet it should be remembered that while the 1730s had ended in financial success, the story of Richardson's emotional life is harsher and sadder. Richardson had experienced

great sorrow; his health had been unsettled into a lifelong malady. In the novel that he unexpectedly found himself writing, the youthful heroine, unlike those mourned and missing children who did not live to grow up, is endowed with splendid health and a vitality capable of reforming the world. Tempted by suicide, she rejects death as she rejects sin, and her affirmation of life is rewarded. Richardson began the novel, he told Hill, on 10 November 1739 and finished it on 10 January 1740. *Pamela; or, Virtue Rewarded* (or at least the first complete draft of it) was written in two months, at a heat, with the kind of energy the heroine herself represents.

Pamela is a fifteen-year-old servant girl whose master, Mr. B., tries to seduce her. When the girl resists his advances and leaves her employment in his house in Bedfordshire, he has her abducted to his other estate in Lincolnshire. There, narrowly guarded by his housekeeper, Mrs. Jewkes, Pamela tries to plot her freedom, at first with the inefficient aid of the poor local curate, Parson Williams. After an abortive attempt at escape, she considers suicide. When her master comes and finds her unwilling to accept his propositions, he attempts rape, but, overcome by the sincerity of her resistance, he gives over such attempts. Mr. B. begins at last to admit the depth of his feeling for the servant girl, a feeling that grows as he reads her letters and journals. At last he allows her to go free; but then he calls her back and decides to marry her. Their marriage is accepted by his family and friends, though not without initial hostility on the part of Mr. B.'s sister, the hot-tempered Lady Davers. Pamela rules over the households where she was once a servant, even a prisoner.

The novel itself is largely Pamela, the indefatigable narrator who tells her story in letters to her poor and helpless parents or in journal-letters in her captivity. It is a story of considerable erotic tension. Pamela, as her emotional experience grows, advances into emotional territory where her well-meaning and limited parents cannot follow, as when she wonders, "Is it not strange, that Love borders so much upon Hate?" The psychological nuances and the subtleties of erotic suffering owe something to the romance tradition from the Greeks onward; Pamela's name points to Sir Philip Sidney's *Arcadia* (1590) as one of the novel's precursors. The erotic analysis is also related to the domestic fiction dealing with love that had developed from the late seventeenth century through the early eighteenth cen-

Illustration by Joseph Highmore for Pamela *(National Portrait Gallery, London)*

tury, particularly in the work of women writers such as Eliza Haywood. But Richardson's novel presents something entirely new, a story grounded in a realism until then associated only with satires of low life or stories of rogues. Pamela is not a fine lady masquerading as a servant; she is a servant and thinks like one, as seen in her concern over her wages and keeping her job even while she mourns the death of Mr. B.'s mother in her first letter. She uses the language of the low. When Mr. B. makes his first attempt on her in the summerhouse, as she describes it, "He kissed me two or three times, as if he would have eaten me," and she thinks, idiomatically, "I would have given my Life for a Farthing." Mr. B., when flustered, also commands low language, as in the same scene: "What a foolish Hussy you are. . . . Cease your blubbering!"

Pamela and Mr. B. are a pair of unorthodox lovers. They create something startlingly new in their endeavor to come together in a relationship ultimately their own invention, a relationship that will transcend the limitations of class and the assumptions with which they start out. Through its presentation of sexual conflict, Richardson's novel shows the conflict of male against female, class against class, Establishment against individual. The novel is one of the most radical statements of the early Enlightenment.

Pamela learns that the church and the state do not care about her, that according to the prevailing ethos Mr. B. is entitled to seduce his mother's servant-maid, and that only ladies (whose chastity is connected with their value as conduits of property) are permitted to make any ado about sexual integrity. Pamela questions all such hierarchical values, as the novel itself does in inducing the reader to take an interest in someone so unimportant and so politically helpless. Pamela asks furiously, "How came I to be his Property?" She will not be anyone's property.

The attraction of Pamela's fierce integrity and power to resist, however, lies in the characterization of a complex and growing personality, which is at the outset believably crude or unformed in impulses and judgment. Pamela is sometimes vain and often self-dramatizing, even self-pitying. Her letters reflect her, tell more about her than she is aware. She has to fight off a recognition of her increasing attraction to Mr. B.; there are clues to which she cannot afford to attend, though the reader must: "What is the Matter, with all his ill Usage of me, that I cannot hate him? To be sure, I am not like other People!" At length, when she is free to decide for herself, she can realize that "all the time, this Heart is *Pamela*." The development of a character through time to firmer integration and deeper self-recognition is one of Richardson's contributions to the Western novel.

Mr. B. is a secondary character, a comic character who struggles unsuccessfully for primacy over the text, remaining "B" to Pamela Andrews's "A." He is not the hero to the reader that he is to Pamela; the reader recognizes that this young man, spoiled by his mama, has mundane moments of unease and private motivations for swaggering in false manliness. The story is both comic and serious, a mock-pastoral set in a world of homely sunflowers, cucumbers, and cows. The vulgar Mrs. Jewkes, standing in for the grosser aspect of the reader, desires, as the narrative appears to do, to come to the climax. She urges Mr. B. on: "What you do, Sir, do; don't stand dilly-dallying." Like all good Augustan works, the novel contains parodies of its own procedures. "Let the worst happen that can," teases Mr. B., "you'll have the Merit, and I the Blame; and it will be a good Subject for Letters to your Father and Mother . . . we shall make out between us, before we have done, a pretty Story in Romance, I warrant ye." At one point, when Pamela thinks (erroneously) that she will soon be free, she refers to her own recent letters as "a most tedious Parcel of Stuff, of my *Oppressions*, my *Distresses*, my *Fears*."

Pamela's "Parcel of Stuff," her papers that constitute the text, play a physical part in the story they narrate. The novel proceeds in a textual manner. Mr. B. is converted by reading Pamela's account of her story, a narrative that he (unlike the reader) has to peruse out of chronological order. His collation at last of the complete text constitutes his recognition of her. Pamela as author has (like a printer) disseminated a complete and authenticated text that creates social alteration and reform. Within that roomy text itself, however, there is constant interplay of narrative and commentary; there are choices, interpretations, parallel texts, forged texts, and re-readings.

Richardson was accused of exhibiting "leveling" tendencies in portraying his successful rebel, his lower-class heroine who, though an uneducated girl, claims and creates the authority of an author. Indeed, a struggle is started in the claims of woman against the authority of man, the claims of the working class against the authority of the landowner—a struggle that cannot be totally resolved by closing the novel with the happy ending of "Virtue Rewarded." The independence Pamela has exhibited and the equal affection Mr.

B. has learned to express must, in some degree, be rescinded in fitting the pair back into the model of marriage. The disobedient servant girl will have to be the obedient wife. One feels at times that Pamela and Mr. B. have walked into an institution a size too small for them, but there are still some rumbles of discontent and questioning. Lady Davers's prolonged hostility to the marriage, in the name of her class and family, provides a still-needed conflict after marital happiness sets in, and there is a peculiar (and Richardsonian) endorsement of family life as the arena of healthy fighting.

Pamela made its first appearance in two duodecimo volumes on 6 November 1740. A second edition followed in February 1741 and a third edition the following month, with a fourth edition in May and a fifth in October. This novel has been called the first modern best-seller. Everybody, high and low, read it. Its scenes furnished decorations for fashionable objects, from fans and teapots to the boxes at Vauxhall. *Pamela* was also read on the Continent, and it was dramatized there by Voltaire and Carlo Goldoni as it was at home by Henry Giffard and others. The egalitarianism in the novel had to be altered somewhat for export. The French objected to the vulgarity of the heroine's language, and Goldoni turned to time-honored tradition in making the heroine of his *Pamela Nubile* (1751) discover her true rank as the daughter of a count. Goldoni explained that the Italian nobility would never accept such a misalliance, whereas in England a gentleman need not lose all social position in marrying a servant.

Even in England, there were protests as well as acclamations. An anonymous pamphlet, *Pamela Censured*, complained that the novel contained offensive scenes and ribald passages. Charles Povey, who wrote the allegorical fable *The Virgin in Eden* (1741) as an antidote to *Pamela,* was even more shocked: "Can amourous Embraces delineated in these Images tend to inculcate Religion in the Minds of Youth, when the Blood is hot, and runs quick in every Vein?" The most notable of the attacks on *Pamela* is Fielding's *An Apology for the Life of Mrs. Shamela Andrews* (1741), a work soon picked up and imitated in *Anti-Pamela: or, Feign'd Innocence Detected* (1741)—probably by Eliza Haywood—and James Parry's *True Anti-Pamela* (1741), though these latter are really only seizing on what their authors see to be a vogue in warm novels. In Fielding's pseudonymous *Shamela*, the servant-maid Shamela is a prostitute, daughter of an Irish prostitute; she has already borne a bastard to lewd Parson Williams, with whom she continues a liaison while plotting to get Squire Booby to marry her, though she despises him. In this degradation both of the central situation of Richardson's story and of its heroine, Fielding is making an upper-class, old-Etonian protest not only against *Pamela*'s "low" style but also against its tendency toward equalizing sexes and classes.

Fielding probably did not know that Richardson was the author of *Pamela,* nor did the printer-novelist evidently know at first that Fielding, with whom Richardson had some slight acquaintance, was the author of *Shamela.* Richardson seems to have accepted without excessive resentment the parody of *Pamela* in *Joseph Andrews* (1742), of which Fielding was the acknowledged author. Fielding was one of the early readers to whom Richardson showed the volumes of *Clarissa* in progress before publication. The rift between the two men comes puzzlingly late. It is possible that *Shamela* was the cause and that Richardson discovered only in late 1748 or early 1749 that Fielding was the author of the earlier attack; all his known references to Fielding's authorship of *Shamela* were made in 1749 or later. A sense of having been deceived would exacerbate Richardson's pride. Although all his references to Fielding and Fielding's works after the late 1740s are uncharitable, Richardson seems to have assisted Fielding financially, and he helped to make arrangements for Fielding's dying journey to Lisbon. Fielding never publicly acknowledged *Shamela* as his own, and its omission in the posthumous collection of Fielding's works edited by his friend Arthur Murphy may indicate that Fielding himself had intended to suppress it.

The success of *Pamela* led not only to such "lewd and ungenerous engraftment," as Richardson called Fielding's parodies, but also to false sequels written by Grub Street hacks exploiting the novel's popularity. Richardson reclaimed his own creation and his characters in producing a sequel, the third and fourth volumes of *Pamela,* which appeared in a new edition of the whole in December 1741. To friends who read drafts of the sequel and complained of want of incident, Richardson protested that he did not want "the French Marvellous," and desired no "Plots, Stratagem and Intrigue"; the original two volumes included "the Storms, the Stratagems, and all that could indanger Virtue and ingage the Attention of the Reader, for its Distresses—The succeeding

of course were to be more calm, serene, and instructive." The new piece should have only "such a Variety, as should be consistent with Probability, and the general Tenor of a genteel married Life." "When the four Volumes shall appear together, it will then be a piece of natural Life, wth. the *ups* and *downs,* the *Stormy* and the *Sedate,* that we generally find it, or (as to *Sedate*) hope to find it."

Richardson's new novel, now generally referred to as *Pamela II,* was thus an experiment in capturing the rhythms and recognitions of ordinary daily life instead of heightened sensations in moments of great stress. The novel suffers from a lack of structural plan. Johnson was later to say to Boswell about all of Richardson's fiction, "Why, Sir, if you were to read Richardson for the story, your impatience would be so much fretted that you would hang yourself. But you must read him for the sentiment. . . ." But despite this famous dictum, one does read Richardson for the story, and the novelist works best when he has an intense and prolonged conflict, involving plots and counterplots, with which to deal. Here he is concerned (after the attacks on the "leveling" tendencies of the first novel with its "low" heroine) to make Pamela an exemplary upper-class matron, and she may at first seem too complacent in her newfound happiness. She is, however, in the position of Don Quixote in part two of Miguel de Cervantes' novel. Pamela, like the Spanish don, knows that her own story has been read and commented upon. She has her own previous self to live up to, and this is a cause of occasional anxiety, as she has secret doubts of her own worth or lovableness. The novel gains strength and momentum when Mr. B. seems to be straying into an affair with a beautiful countess. Pamela, at first absorbed in her new baby, eventually has to notice what is going on. For a time she follows the approved rules and suffers in silence. Finally she breaks through the rules of genteel married life and the limitations of a good woman's place and confronts Mr. B. with their problem. In arranging her "Trial," Pamela is willing to face the possibility that their marriage has in effect come to an end; Mr. B., however, has been trying madly to gain his wife's attention, feeling threatened by her absorption into her own nursery world and her love of baby Billy. Jealousy, uncertainty, and the domestic fluctuations of a daily relationship are powerfully and intelligently rendered. The novel sketches a gallery of characters, drawing on old ones such as Lady Davers and her silly nephew-

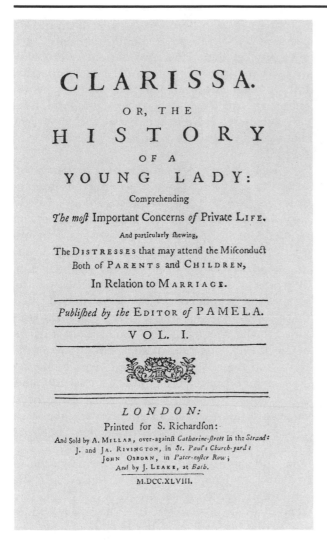

CLARISSA.

OR, THE

HISTORY

OF A

YOUNG LADY:

Comprehending

The most Important Concerns of Private LIFE.

And particularly shewing,

The DISTRESSES that may attend the Misconduct
Both of PARENTS and CHILDREN,

In Relation to MARRIAGE.

Published by the EDITOR of PAMELA.

VOL. I.

LONDON:

Printed for S. Richardson:

And Sold by A. MILLAR, over-against *Catharine-street* in the *Strand*:
J. and JA. RIVINGTON, in *St. Paul's Church-yard*:
JOHN OSBORN, in *Pater-noster Row*;
And by J. LEAKE, at *Bath*.

M.DCC.XLVIII.

Title page for the longest novel written in English, which Richardson continued to revise for most of his life

by-marriage Jacky and creating new types, especially the lively, argumentative Polly Darnford, the first of a memorable series of witty and undocile young ladies.

Pamela II is in some respects a philosophical treatment of the quotidian. It is one of the many eighteenth-century documents treating the search for happiness, and specific doctrines sometimes appear. Richardson's interest in Locke's theories of education and in what might be called progressive methods of teaching the young emerge strongly in the book. The exemplary aspect of Pamela's management of her household and servants, and her education of her children, appealed to Rousseau, who learned through *Pamela II* that the novel could be a vehicle of philosophy. The influence of *Pamela II* is specifically evi-

dent in both his *Julie, ou la Nouvelle Héloïse* (1761) and *Emile* (1762).

Richardson suffered prolonged illness in the spring of 1742, an attack that he attributed to the shock of the death of his friend Rivington but that may also have been related to his finishing his novel. He visited Bath in 1742 in search of relief for his maladies and received elaborate directions as to regimen from his physician friend Cheyne, who was himself to die in April 1743. Richardson's illness did not impede his progress in business, and he seems also to have returned to novel writing as soon as possible.

When *Clarissa; or, The History of a Young Lady* was first conceived is unknown, but the whole plan seems to have been well developed by June 1744 when Edward Young discussed with the author the nature of Lovelace—the novel's hero-villain—and the proposed ending. Hill refers to reading the "design" in June; by November he was able to read an extensive manuscript. Other readers also perused the first draft of the novel in installments. By June 1745 Laetitia Pilkington and Colley Cibber were discussing the novel's central event, the rape by Lovelace of Clarissa, and by November 1745 they were discussing the approaching death of the heroine. In early 1746 Richardson undertook a thorough revision of his completed novel. He had an extensive list of readers, but as he told Hill in January 1746, "none of these have seen it . . . as it now stands. And they would think it a new Thing were they to see it." Richardson, rather like Dickens, needed a current audience reacting to a work in progress, and select readers knew *Clarissa* as a work in progress over a period of three or four years. Richardson valued response—though, like most authors, he found well-meaning advice on particulars usually irrelevant.

The revised *Clarissa* was itself revised and considerably shortened. None of the drafts has survived. By November 1747 Richardson was ready to begin publication; the first two volumes were advertised in December 1747. These volumes were successful and immediately gave rise to controversy over the behavior of Clarissa Harlowe and her family. The third and fourth volumes appeared in April 1748. Richardson wondered whether the novel "has not suffer'd too much by the Catastrophe's being too much known and talked of." Richardson's design had been bruited about, and new readers interested in Clarissa and her fate wrote to the author begging for "what they call, an Happy Ending."

Some readers got advance copies of the new volumes; Edward Moore and Fielding were reading volume five by mid October 1748. Fielding, who praised the novel highly, was one of the readers who pleaded that Clarissa's life should be spared. The fifth, sixth, and seventh volumes were published in December 1748.

Publication did not end revision. The second edition of 1749 is substantially different, containing material Richardson claimed to be restoring from the original manuscript, as well as new material intended to sharpen the reader's apprehension of certain points, particularly the machinations of Lovelace. The third edition of 1751, appearing in duodecimo and octavo, contained even more extensive revisions, restorations, and prefatory matter. The table of contents supplied with the second edition (evidently based on an index compiled by Solomon Lowe but perhaps owing something to Richardson's experience of indexing Roe's *Negotiations*) was in the third edition broken up and allocated to individual volumes, in order to enable "the less attentive Reader, in a work of such Length, to carry on the Thread of the Story." Richardson carefully distinguishes material added to the printed novel since the first edition by a pointing of dots in the margin, thus in effect creating his own variorum *Clarissa*. He also published separately a pamphlet, *Letters and Passages Restored from the Original Manuscripts of the History of Clarissa* (1751), so that purchasers of the first edition would not suffer for having bought the novel on its first appearance; they could read the new material without having to purchase an expensive new edition. The third edition should be the basic copy-text of any modern edition of *Clarissa*, as it most decidedly represents the author's full intention. There are later minor revisions, up to and including the edition of 1790, which claims to represent the author's last corrections.

Clarissa is a long novel, the longest novel in English—though not too long for those who love it: Dr. Johnson was glad of the expansion in 1751 and rejoiced that Richardson "was now got above all fears of prolixity." Like the works of James Joyce and Marcel Proust, *Clarissa* is meant for those who like reading, and it is also a work that demands rereading. The characters themselves reread, both metaphorically and literally, their own experience. Angus Wilson says of the pace of the work, "The journey before the reader will be, for three quarters of the book . . .

drawn out and long, but what he is reading at any given moment is sharply felt and quick." The novel's effects are complex and cumulative; the reader encounters extraordinary flashes of mind, the friction of self against other. The plot is designed with a peculiar capacity to generate acute suspense through the leisurely, but never slack, accretion of material.

The central story is a tale of entrapment and violence. Clarissa Harlowe, a beautiful young girl who is the pet and pride of her ambitious family, is willed an estate by her grandfather, disturbing the Harlowe family's notions of ownership and progress. She is wooed by an aristocratic suitor, Robert Lovelace, who has first to contrive to make her plain elder sister Arabella refuse him. The family is flattered, but Clarissa's brother James is determined that Clarissa must not be the victor in the race to fortune and noble name. He picks a quarrel with Lovelace, making the aristocrat wound the heir of the Harlowes; the Harlowe uncles beat Lovelace from their doors. Clarissa's brother then punishes her by inducing the family to force her into a marriage with Mr. Solmes, a wealthy miser. James is assisted in this unkind plan by the jealous Arabella; but James's views, unlike the plain sister's, will be forwarded as much by Clarissa's disgracing herself and running away with Lovelace as by her forced marriage to Solmes. Clarissa, resisting Solmes, is for a time locked up in her room. Threatened by a forced marriage, she agrees to meet Lovelace, even planning to escape with his help, a plan from which she has withdrawn when she meets him. He tricks her, however, into running off with him.

Soothing the girl with assurances that he respects her and her wishes to be reconciled with her family before they marry, Lovelace takes Clarissa to London, where he places her in handsome lodgings; this is really a brothel well known to him, run by the fat bawd "Mrs. Sinclair," who masquerades as a respectable widow of an army officer. Her "daughters" Sally and Polly, really young prostitutes and part-owners of the brothel, secretly egg on Lovelace to make Clarissa one of them. Lovelace, though never utterly insincere in his references to marrying Clarissa, is determined to test her chastity by attempting to seduce her, hoping to lead her to cohabitation with him. She resists, and, after Lovelace bursts into her bedroom on the pretense of a fire, she suspects his plotting and flees the house.

Lovelace follows Clarissa to lodgings in Hampstead and wins over the women of the neighborhood by his story of an eloped virgin wife. He persuades Clarissa to go into the protection of his aunt and cousin, but these "Ladies" who come to the girl are really prostitutes. Clarissa is conveyed to the brothel, where she is drugged and raped by Lovelace. Clarissa will not, however, succumb to his forced claim on her or acquiesce in a prostituted and helpless condition. After a period of insanity she grows in strength of resistance. Lovelace cannot make her submit to a repetition of the sexual act, a repetition that would entail the assent of her will and bring her to the position of whore. "But who would have thought there had been such a woman in the world?" he wonders. "Of all the Sex I have hitherto known, or heard, or read of, it was *once subdued, and always subdued*. The *first* struggle was generally the *last.* . . ." Lovelace cannot even make the amends he was sure would always be in his power. Clarissa will not marry him: *"The man who has been the villain to me you have been, shall never make me his wife."*

Clarissa escapes from the brothel and finds lodgings with the kindly, practical Smiths, glove makers who own a small shop in Covent Garden. But she is arrested for debt in front of St. Paul's Church at the instigation of Sinclair and her partners, who have her thrown into the sponging-house. Lovelace himself is horrified at her imprisonment. Belford, his best friend, finds her and sees to her release; he begins a friendship with her that estranges him from Lovelace. Clarissa, restored to her freedom but in broken health, has already deciphered the progress of Lovelace's plots against her and the range of his deceit. Forbidding him to come near her, she makes her preparations for death in her own way, given at last the independence she craved in vain from Lovelace and from her own family. The Harlowes, grudging and suspicious, postpone going to see their youngest child until it is too late. Clarissa returns to Harlowe Place in her coffin. Lovelace undergoes a period of illness and insanity at Clarissa's death. Recovered, he takes a tour to the Continent, where Clarissa's cousin Morden—against her express wish—pursues him and kills him in a duel.

The novel is epistolary, and complex in its telling. The two major characters each have a confidant; Clarissa writes to the saucy, skeptical, and heartfree Anna Howe, and Lovelace to his admiring follower, the more awkwardly rakish and fun-

Lady Dorothy Bradshaigh, who begged Richardson to allow Clarissa to live

damentally serious Jack Belford. These characters have their own stories and developments: Anna in the course of her courtship by honest, unglamorous Mr. Hickman, and Belford in his movement toward a more independent personality. Anna and Belford, always articulate, have their own views of what is going on. The narratives of the major characters are thus furnished with commentary, reactions, and questions, while in the correspondence that the reader can see whole—unlike the letter writers, who at the time of writing are involved in only one side of the narrative—the reader can observe the war between the sexes and the operation of quite different individual views of reality. The same scenes are depicted differently in the letters of different characters.

The personages are all fully characterized and endowed with complexity and psychological motivation. Clarissa and Lovelace are among the first modern fictional characters, characters with a modern capacity for change and self-analysis. Clarissa, like Pamela, is one of the first characters in English prose fiction to develop, rather than to undergo a change through a sudden conversion experience. The catastrophic events make their impact on a character already changing. In the first part of the novel Clarissa has to emerge from the dreamy childhood state of loved and petted youngest child to realize that her relationship with her family is not what she thought. She has to reinterpret her past as well as the present. She is vitally good but no plaster saint, as is seen when she turns sarcastically on her elder sister: "It is not my fault, Bella, the *opportune* gentleman don't come!" Clarissa is conditioned by her place in a family suffering long-felt unease and already strained by its continuous attempt to rise.

Richardson's social observation is acute. *Clarissa* exhibits not only representatives of every class but also the class dynamics of Georgian Britain. One sees the new conflict between the middle-class gentry, rising by colonial trade and coal mining, and the old nobility. Lovelace, inheritor (the last of his line) of the nobility he exploits but does not value, has a contempt for the Harlowes' upstart ostentation. The Harlowes are tellingly depicted in their remnants of vulgarity, their awkward self-consciousness, and their sensitivity to slight. Only the hero and the heroine transcend, however perversely, the limitations of their class and time. Both brilliant, both independent, both capable of analyzing the world in which they live, Clarissa and Lovelace are obviously meant for each other. This is a love story of a couple destined to destroy each other, yet each is without equal save for the other. The battle between them is a heroic battle of wills.

Lovelace, who thinks often in dramatic terms, sees himself as author or director of a drama in real life. His is the sensibility of a dramatist—or novelist—turned perverse. He sees himself as the rake in Restoration and eighteenth-century comedy. Tragedy is for and about women, but what he imagines and creates must be, as he dictates, perpetual comedy: "The devil's in it, if a confided-in Rake does not give a girl enough of Tragedy in his Comedy." He is unprepared to admit that the drama of life may not be under his control, that Clarissa can transform his comedy into a tragedy that involves him. Clarissa, he claims, is merely being put to a test, to see if her chastity is real and she is worthy to be his wife—but of course she was never meant to pass this test. "Abhorred be *force*. . . . There is no triumph in *force*—No conquest over the will!" he exclaims, for triumph over Clarissa's will is what he desires. But at last he feels compelled to turn to force: "Have I not tried every other method? And have I any other recourse left me?"

The rape is meant to be an unmistakable act of possession, a total triumph over Clarissa that will leave her without a will. Clarissa refuses to read the event in the way Lovelace supposed she must. Her strength is shown in her willingness to cast away or let go of all the things the Harlowes value—wealth, comfort, position in the world—in order to save her own soul. Common respectability becomes less important to her, as one hears in her tired, ironic tones during the prison conversation with the mocking prostitutes who try to tempt her back to the brothel: "We two will bail you, *Miss,* if you will go back with us to Mrs. Sinclair's. . . . Hers are very handsome apartments." "The fitter for those who own them!" "These are very sad ones." "The fitter for *me!*" "You may be very happy yet, *Miss,* if you will." "I hope I shall."

The novel is, at one level, realistic and socially observant. At another level it is dreamlike and expressionistic; the characters' own dreams furnish some of the imagery of the novel, and in their waking moments characters produce images with subconscious symbolic force—as when the mocking Arabella, trying patterns of rich materials on her sister, suggests that Clarissa marry Solmes in a black velvet wedding gown. Sexual codes hint at other meanings, as in the mock-objective description of Mrs. Sinclair's two good houses, "only joined by a *large handsome passage,*" of which "the *inner-house* is the genteelest" with its "little garden" displaying "a true female fancy." The house image runs through the novel to its end; when Clarissa sells her clothes to purchase "a house," she buys a coffin. Lovelace tends to pick up common images in order to create a private phantasm, as in his play upon the idea of Vanity Fair, or his description to the earnest Hickman of the new wooer Clarissa is receiving in preference to himself: "A bald-pated villain, yet grudges to buy a peruke to hide his baldness: For he is as covetous as hell, never satisfied, yet plaguy rich . . . the rascal has estates in every county. . . ." When Hickman protests that if this is the case "we must surely have heard of him," Lovelace responds, "Heard of him! Ay, Sir, we have all heard of him—. . . . His name, in short, is DEATH!—DEATH, Sir, stamping, and speaking loud, and full in his ear; which made him jump half a yard high."

Clarissa uses all the resources of print, including typographical degeneration representing

Clarissa's degeneration in her page of fragmented quotations. The novel is a textual work. The reader is subjected to a full and often disconcerting experience of reactions, estimations, readings of matters fraught with ambiguities and subject to rereading and fresh interpretation. He sees the text being made, catches ironies of which the various writers are not aware, and collates statements, noting diverse variations of meanings that can never be fully expressed at any moment. The novel swallows one up in a world of its own like, Angus Wilson suggests, "an enveloping, inescapable boa constrictor." As Denis Diderot notes in his "Eloge de Richardson" (1762), one can pick up the novel looking for appropriate quotations and become absorbed yet again in the reading.

Richardson's novel was translated into French in an abridgement that Diderot criticized as cutting into the web of tight meaning and injuring the poetic quality. Many French writers, such as Diderot, Mme Anne de Staël, and Rousseau, read the novel in the original. *Clarissa* was translated into German, attaining its second German edition in 1749. The Dutch translation (1755) by the Mennonite clergyman Johannes Stinstra gave rise to the correspondence and Stinstra's request for biographical detail that supplies Richardson's only continuous piece of autobiography. Richardson did not realize that his favorite translator had fudged the whole issue of his novel. Stinstra was too modest to use the Dutch word for rape, and his translation allows readers to believe that Clarissa was seduced.

Clarissa is a masterpiece not only of the epistolary mode but of Richardson's own discovery, the technique of "writing to the moment." As one of the characters comments, *"Much more lively and affecting . . . must be the Style of those who write in the height of a present distress; the mind tortured by the pangs of uncertainty (the Events then hidden in the womb of Fate); than the dry, narrative, unanimated Style of a person relating difficulties and dangers surmounted . . . ,"* a remark Richardson quotes in his preface. The novelist points out the fluid, temporary nature of each letter: "All the Letters are written while the hearts of the writers must be supposed to be wholly engaged in their subjects (The events at the time generally dubious): So that they abound not only with critical Situations, but with what may be called *instantaneous* Descriptions and Reflections . . . " Instants are modified by new instants, and the meaning of any experience cannot stay stable. *Clarissa* is a great Christian novel, but the moral and spiritual truths are always realized here through experience that is not static but living and changing. Moral principle has to be known and felt in the middle of the disturbing, insistent present moment, subject to the *"instantaneous."* Clarissa, Richardson's exemplary character, must revise and reread herself, passing from one present time to another.

The novel's appearance in installments meant that its first readers shared the characters' experience of not knowing for many months the events "hidden in the womb of Fate." Some readers offered their suggestions to a work that appeared still open, like a life; they did not choose to acknowledge that the artist, unlike his characters, had an inescapable design. Cibber and Fielding all begged Richardson to let Clarissa live and to provide a happy ending. People unknown to the author wrote him to the same purpose. The most important of these new correspondents was Lady Dorothy Bradshaigh, wife of the baronet Roger Bradshaigh of Haigh, Lancashire. Lady Bradshaigh first wrote to Richardson in 1748 under the pseudonym "Belfour," begging for Clarissa's life and worldly happiness. In 1749 the Bradshaighs visited Joseph Highmore's London studio and admired the paintings illustrating *Pamela* and the two new illustrations of *Clarissa*, one (now at Yale) showing the Harlowe family, the other (now lost) Clarissa's portrait "in the Van Dyck taste" as referred to in the novel. But Lady Bradshaigh did not then have the courage to seek out Richardson personally, and their first meeting did not take place until March 1750. She remained a lifelong friend, an eager reader of Richardson's work in progress, and one of his most frequent correspondents.

Lady Bradshaigh's sister, Lady Elizabeth Echlin, wife of a baronet residing mainly in Ireland, also became a correspondent. She objected strongly to the ending of the novel and proposed another, going so far as to write an extensive new version in which Clarissa dies unviolated, James and Arabella are heartily punished, and Lovelace is reformed. Richardson was amused by this attempt and carried the game even further: "Lovelace, by his own Interest and that of his Uncle, might have been made the Governour of some of the American Colonies, and there shone, as a Man you had reformed, by giving an Example of Piety. . . ." But Lady Echlin's main point was that Clarissa's story should be told "without a vile, unlikely rape," and she objected to parts of the story that "serve only to wound good minds." *Her* Clarissa would not have been deceived for a moment more by Lovelace after the fire scene, and she makes the girl apologize to Anna for "supine stupidity" and weak credulity. Lady Echlin's endeavor to spare Clarissa the worst is in some ways in keeping with criticisms made by modern feminists who object to Clarissa's humiliations. On the other hand, Richardson sometimes had reason to fear that he had made Lovelace too attractive; in revisions of the novel he pointedly clarified the hero-villain's machinations, partly because readers had not been reading attentively. When Edward Moore thought of dramatizing *Clarissa*, David Garrick wanted to play the part of Lovelace; it is a pity that the piece never came into existence. Nineteenth-century dramatizations are largely based on Jules Janin's *Clarisse Harlowe* (1846), a novel in French loosely related to Richardson's work. There has not yet been a full dramatization of Richardson's real story, though part one of a dramatization by Florian Stuber and Margaret Doody, *Clarissa: A Theater Work,* was presented in an off-off-Broadway production in New York City in the fall of 1984.

Clarissa brought the novelist new friends, not only Lady Bradshaigh and Lady Echlin but Mrs. Mary Delany, her friend Anne Donellan, Sarah Chapone, and her son John. With his new acquaintances Richardson was able to observe closely the manners and attitudes of upper-class people, real-life "fine ladies," material valuable to him in his new work. He had also acquired young friends, including Susanna Highmore (daughter of the artist), her fiancé John Duncombe, and Hester Mulso (later to marry John Chapone). Susanna Highmore drew a picture of Richardson in the grotto at North End reading *Sir Charles Grandison* to this circle of young friends. The composition of this novel was carried on in a social and expansive manner, in an atmosphere of young love and love-debate.

Richardson began *The History of Sir Charles Grandison* around 1750. It would seem that he had thought of writing the story hinted at in *Pamela II,* the story of the rake who loved two women. But his new novel became, as soon as it was formulated, the story of a good man in love with two women. It had been pointed out to Richardson that his earlier novels both glorified women and gave them exemplary models; it was high time that the novelist should speak out for his own sex's qualities and offer a pattern of masculinity and masculine behavior. Richardson saw

in advance that such a program posed problems: "To avoid leading him into difficulties, such as challenges, &c. that a good man . . . would be . . . subject to, because I might not know how to extricate him from them, consistent with his character . . . would be doing nothing. And then, to make *sport* for the *tender-hearted* reader . . . must we not give him great distresses? only taking care to make him happy at last, as it is called . . . ," he wrote to Anne Donellan on 20 July 1750. Dueling became an important masculine moral issue in the novel, and Richardson showed his hero, though an expert swordsman, coolly daring to quell hostile opponents without drawing upon them—if not always without some violence, yet almost always gaining the victory by moral force and the power of reason. The dueling question may have been on Richardson's mind since the time of the *Familar Letters.* "Six Original Letters upon Duelling," published posthumously in the *Candid Review* in 1765, letters in which Thomas Gilles by epistolary persuasion induces his two friends Andrew Crisp and John Orme to give up a planned duel, may have been among the material Richardson omitted from the *Familiar Letters* as "too high for the Design."

The new novel had a high "Design." Sir Charles was to be the magnificent Christian hero, a model for his sex; yet he had to be believable. Richardson acknowledged to Hester Mulso in July 1751, "I shall want a few unpremeditated faults . . . to sprinkle into this man's character, lest I should draw a *faultless monster.*" But, given the ethos of the time, it was difficult to imagine either faults or distresses to which a good man who was well born and well-to-do could be subject. In the Georgian era, men were supposed to be rational, independent, self-reliant. In giving the title role to a male, Richardson, at least on the surface, abandoned the underclass and the unenfranchised, who had formerly been his central characters, in favor of embodying and authorizing privilege and power. Sir Charles, already at twenty-six visibly a patriarch in the making, fulfills the English dream-image of the country gentleman on his estate. Inordinately handsome, learned without pedantry, and utterly self-assured, Sir Charles organizes the world around him with a ruthlessness that terrifies some of the objects of his unstoppable benevolence. When he rescues the heroine Harriet Byron from her villainous abductor Sir Hargrave Pollexfen, Sir Charles is strong enough and contemptuous enough to throw the sword-wielding Pollexfen to

Richardson in the grotto at North End reading the manuscript of Sir Charles Grandison *to his friends; drawing by Susanna Highmore (Pierpont Morgan Library)*

the ground: "I seized him by the collar . . . and with a jerk, and a kind of twist, laid him under the hind-wheel of his chariot." No wonder would-be challengers quail and never accuse the duel-refusing hero of cowardice.

The dominating Sir Charles has many of the energies and talents of Lovelace, but directed into socially acceptable channels. The force of Richardson's writing is such that Sir Charles is a credible, if not appealing, character. The author provides him with psychological motives in his determination both to vindicate and to counteract (in a way, to erase) his father, the selfish rake Sir Thomas Grandison, who caused so much suffering to his wife and female children. Though the reader hears about the parents and about the children's early lives in flashback, as it were, the Grandison family as a whole is as believable as the Harlowes. Richardson is good at family dynamics. Sir Charles's sisters Caroline and Charlotte both react to family position and unhappy family life. Caroline, the elder, is timid and slightly indolent. Charlotte, the youngest child, is witty, aggressive, and daring; since her youthful angry relationship with her now-dead father she

has both feared men and desired a relationship with a man, but she cannot accept any arrangement in which she might be overwhelmed by her partner. The three form a credible and interesting group of siblings; their similarity of name suggests that they are three aspects of the same entity. (The root name *Charles*, repeated with variations, might also be taken as the last flourish of Richardson's sympathies with Stuarts and Tories.)

The hero's only real distress is to find himself beloved by—and possibly in love with—two women at once. Indeed, there are more women than the story's central two heroines in love with him; other lady suitors approach, including the violent Italian Olivia, with her flashing eyes, diamonds, and poniard, who makes propositions to Sir Charles. Harriet Byron, the English girl whose letters open the novel, is vivacious and confident. Richardson wanted Harriet to be what Clarissa might have been had her life been happy, but Harriet is a different character, a personality in her own right. At the beginning of the novel, Harriet has just left adoring relatives in the country and taken a trip to London. Unlike Clarissa, Harriet is an orphan, free of the enormous pressures exerted by immediate family. She is carefree, even flippant, critically discovering the world and not afraid of voicing her own opinion. Yet her lack of parents or siblings makes natural her response to the close-knit and mutually confidential Grandison family, and her delight at being part of it.

Harriet falls in love with Sir Charles before he betrays any symptoms of a reciprocal feeling. In February 1751 Richardson contributed a paper to Johnson's *Rambler* as a kind of Valentine Day issue; the unnamed writer is introduced by Johnson as "an author who has enlarged the knowledge of human nature, and taught the passions to move at the command of virtue." In *Rambler* number 97 Richardson (or, rather, the old man who once courted his Laetitia, the *character* who writes to the *Rambler*) laments the forwardness of modern women and firmly dictates female reserve: "That a young lady should be in love, and the love of the young gentleman undeclared, is an heterodoxy which prudence, and even policy, must not allow." It is a trifle perverse and teasing of Richardson to write thus solemnly at the very time he was constructing a novel whose central interest depends on the reader's sympathy with an attractive young heroine, a warmhearted woman of twenty-one who is "in love, and the love of the young gentleman undeclared." Imprudently falling in love, the heterodox Harriet tries to maintain a reserve as to the embarrassing fact, but Sir Charles's sisters discover her secret and hope to promote the marriage. All, however, are stunned by the revelation of Sir Charles's commitment to an Italian girl, Clementina.

Sir Charles, during his years abroad, had befriended young Jeronymo della Porretta and had been received into the household of the della Porrettas, proud Italian aristocrats of Bologna. Their youngest child and only daughter, Clementina, fell in love with him. At first concealing her love (and behaving very strangely), Clementina had been taught by her family to renounce Sir Charles, since the della Porrettas could not bear that their daughter should marry a Protestant foreigner. But now, Clementina, under the stress of trying to deny and suppress her feelings, has gone mad. Sir Charles, to the surprise of his family and the dismay of Harriet, is summoned to Italy; if his presence can cure Clementina's derangement, her family will think him entitled to marry her. The narrative then moves between England and Italy. Harriet waits

tensely at home for bulletins and learns to admire the younger rival, thinking the Italian girl in some ways the more worthy contender for Sir Charles's hand. Clementina begins to recover (after several "mad scenes") once she is given more emotional room and freedom of choice. Clementina at last decides for herself that she will renounce Grandison, as she is fearful that either living as his wife might cause her to swerve from the true faith, or she would be wretched as to the ultimate destiny of her Protestant husband. It is only her Catholicism, not her affections, that prevents the match, and her cure takes a long time to complete.

Sir Charles returns to England. Now free, he proposes to Harriet; they marry in an elaborate and prolonged festivity that in some sense makes up for the absent wedding in *Clarissa*. Unlike Clarissa, whose last "house" is her coffin, Harriet is translated to Grandison Hall, the most splendid of mansions on the most spacious of estates. When Clementina, having run away from home, comes to them there, Sir Charles and his lady are able to mediate with her family and to offer her peace of mind. The novel ends with the promise of "a little Temple" to be erected on the grounds "consecrated to our triple friendship."

The world of *Sir Charles Grandison* is a widening circle, in keeping with Sir Charles's benevolence. The Grandison family, that "family of love," extend their affections throughout Britain, Europe, and the world, counteracting bigotry and narrowness of mind. Friends bring in new friends; new characters enter; weddings are performed; babies are born. The ending emphasizes expansion and harmony, values present all along in the only eighteenth-century novel to have a leitmotiv (George Frideric Handel's *Alexander's Feast*). The scenes are leisurely, and letters are often shared by numerous readers within the novel. The epistolary method is used without the tensions and ironies that directed *Clarissa*. Scenes are also richly comic, varied, and absorbing. "How shall a man obscurely situated," Richardson had wondered to Lady Bradshaigh on 24 March 1751, "pretend to describe and enter into characters in upper life? How shall such a one draw scenes of busy and yet elegant trifling?" But if the "upper life" he created was partly imagined, the domestic world he created was vividly realized.

Despite its titular hero, Richardson's last completed novel is still essentially a story about hero-

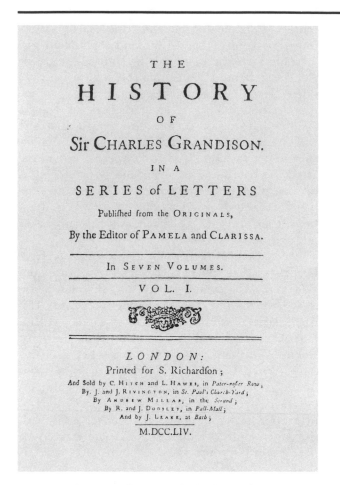

Title page for Richardson's novel about a good man in love with two women, written in response to the criticism that his earlier novels had provided exemplary role models for women but none for men

ines. The rivals each have their own attractions; various readers favored Harriet or Clementina, but Clementina is observed by others rather than being a narrating intelligence. Richardson was praised for his drawing of her madness, which was compared to Shakespeare's depictions of Ophelia and Lear. Clementina is a credible picture of a confused young woman who has been severely repressed while being overpetted by her family. Her mad scenes are psychologically believable as she finds a way to punish her family and, at moments, to exhibit her own sexuality in a manner for which she cannot be punished. She runs away from the doctors to Sir Charles; holding out "her lovely arm a little bloody" she begs not to be bled, and presses him, "Do *you* wish to see me wounded? ... For *your* sake, Chevalier?— Well, will it do you good to see me bleed?" Harriet, more accustomed to self-expression and to grappling with her own problems, is attractive in an honesty that constantly refutes the doc-

trines of *Rambler* number 97: "And why should you deny, that you *were* susceptible of a natural passion? You must not be prudish, Lucy."

There are other attractive female characters; some readers have liked Charlotte Grandison best. Charlotte is an independent-minded woman of twenty-five; formerly entangled (in an effort to escape from her home) with an army officer from whose courtship her brother extricates her, she is doomed by Charles's tyrannical benevolence to marry Lord G., certainly her inferior in wit, talent, and attractiveness. Charlotte's adjustment to her marriage is an important part of the story; her wedding is one of its best comic episodes: "I overheard the naughty one say, as Lord G. led her up to the altar, You don't know what you are about, man. I expect to have all my way: Remember that's one of my articles before marriage." Being married does not annihilate Charlotte's sharpness in jest, nor her glee in observation even during matrimonial quarrels: "He attempted to hum a tune of contempt, upon my warbling an Italian air. An opera couple, we! Is it not charming to sing *at* (I cannot say *to*) each other, when we have a mind to be spiteful?" But Charlotte's disharmony is only part of the larger harmony that *Sir Charles Grandison* endorses, as the novel seeks its fulfillment through diverse characters and different experiences of love. Another attractive female character is young Emily Jervois, Sir Charles's ward, whose dawning love for her guardian has to endure frustration as part of her growing up. Lady Bradshaigh was upset that such a young girl (age fourteen) should be shown as in love, saying that it made her "Ashamed for her Sex." Richardson retorted on 8 December 1753: "O dear! Ashamed of human Nature! Do all fruits ripen alike? Ask this Question in your Orangery, Madam." *Sir Charles Grandison* is a novel that countenances, encourages, female sexuality and emotional warmth; these women are in circumstances where it is allowable for them to love, to say yes in their hearts to sex. It is also a novel that endeavors to portray the richness of human nature, the variety of styles of goodness and liveliness to be encountered within the human family, of which the Grandisons are a microcosm.

Sir Charles Grandison is, like *Clarissa*, one of the first of the great Romantic novels as well as an English Augustan work. Romantic writers as diverse as Mme de Staël, Sir Walter Scott, William Hazlitt, and François René de Chateaubriand were to enter heatedly into preferences for

Clementina or for Harriet, and to be moved by both. Stendhal was to weep over *Sir Charles Grandison*, and the characters in Aleksander Pushkin's *Evgeni Onegin* (1832) know it almost by heart. In terms of English literary history, however, *Sir Charles Grandison* has been important for its position as the first of a new kind of domestic comedy. It is the ancestor of Jane Austen's novels, and of Anthony Trollope's. George Eliot admired this novel and its morality ("There is nothing for the new lights to correct," she declared); *Sir Charles Grandison* may have influenced Eliot's *Daniel Deronda* (1876), whose hero is a Grandisonian type. In George Meredith's *The Egoist* (1879), Sir Willoughby Patterne is a Grandison mocked; so, rather differently, is the John Graham Bretton of Charlotte Brontë's *Villette* (1853), whose heroine Lucy Snowe, suffering from unrequited love for this piece of perfection, combines qualities of Harriet and Clementina. There seems to be a tribute to the novel in Barbara Pym's *An Unsuitable Attachment* (1982), whose likable mock-Grandisonian hero Rupert Stonebird is caught between two women, one of whom is named Penelope Grandison.

Richardson had made, or pretended to make, the writing of *Sir Charles Grandison* a communal activity. He did some correspondents the favor of letting them contribute touches, or took points from their own descriptions of people they knew. Hester Mulso seems to have been not unaware that she was, in part, functioning as an epistolary model for Harriet Byron. More generously, Richardson always encouraged women writers in their seeking publication. With Samuel Johnson, he assisted Charlotte Lennox with the publication of *The Female Quixote* (1752), which Richardson printed. He praised Frances Sheridan for the romance she had written in her youth, encouraged her to think of herself as a novelist, and was her confidant in the writing of her *Memoirs of Miss Sidney Bidulph* (1761). He encouraged and assisted Sarah Fielding, sister of the better-known Henry, in her novel writing, and printed works by her and by her friend Jane Collier. He and Mrs. Richardson subscribed for six copies of Sarah Fielding's *The Lives of Cleopatra and Octavia* (1757). He seems often to have acted as an agent for women writers, dealing for them with the booksellers. Future women novelists such as Fanny Burney and Austen were to profit by the examples of the predecessors whom Richardson had helped, and by the high place given

to women in his novels, in which female characters function as commentators, narrators, *writers*.

Sir Charles Grandison was, like its predecessor, published in installments, though it came out in the cheaper duodecimo and more expensive octavo editions at the same time. The first four volumes were published in November 1753; volumes five and six (only volume five of the octavo) appeared in December; the last volume (seven of duodecimo, six of octavo) appeared in March 1754. Richardson had labored to shorten the work; he cut out about two volumes' worth before printing the novel. Publication was marred by the activity of Irish pirates, who had gotten copy from workmen in Richardson's shop. In September 1753 Richardson published a statement of his grievances, *The Case of Samuel Richardson of London, Printer; with Regard to the Invasion of His Property*, which he distributed. The English newspapers took up his cause. Soon Richardson's sense of betrayal extended to his Irish bookseller, George Faulkner. In February 1754 he published *An Address to the Public*, a statement of his case against Faulkner, which was also inserted in the last volume of *Sir Charles Grandison*. The piracy cost Richardson money, but it could have been much more damaging had the pirates, as they threatened, sold their copy of the novel to European publishing houses.

While fighting off pirates, Richardson enjoyed a lighter game of teasing his readers. The staggered appearance of the novel allowed for reader suspense and suggestions, and gave Richardson the opportunity to hint at possible dire catastrophes: Sir Charles might be murdered; he might propose polygamy; Harriet might die in childbirth, leaving her child to the care of Sir Charles and Clementina. Such teasing depended on reader interest. But the same reader interest made piracy tempting to those who saw their own chance of exploiting the novel.

In September 1752 Richardson's printing shop, just below his dwelling area, caught fire. The author was apprised of it by feeling the heat through the floor as he sat drinking tea in the room above. Fortunately, the building was insured. He bought a new home in Salisbury Court and in 1755 built a new "Printing Office"; for the first time, his business premises were separate from his home, and the considerable cost involved in knocking down a row of houses and building a new plant shows that Richardson's business was doing very well. The new landlord of North End raised the rent in 1754, so in August

[3]

[Handwritten autobiographical letter by Samuel Richardson. Opening lines read:]

And now, Sir, give me Leave to attend to the Questions, which your Partiality for me, makes you think it worth your while to ask.

My Father was a very honest Man, descended of a Family of middling Note in the County of Surrey; but which having for several Generations a large Number of Children, the not large Possessions were split and divided: So that He and his Brothers were put to Trades; and the Sisters were married to Tradesmen. My Mother was also a good Woman, of a Family not ungenteel; but whose Father and Mother died in her Infancy within half an Hour of each other in the London Pestilence of 1665.

My Father's Business was that of a Joiner, then more distinct from that of a Carpenter, than now it is with us. He was a good Draughtsman, and understood Architecture. His Skill and Ingenuity, and an Understanding superior to his Business, with his remarkable Integrity of Heart and Manners, made him personally beloved by several Persons of Rank, among whom were the Duke of Monmouth and the first Earl of Shaftesbury; both so noted in our English History. Their known Favour for him having, on the Duke's Attempt on the Crown, suggested him to be looked upon with a jealous Eye, notwithstanding he was noted for a quiet and inoffensive Man, he thought proper, on the Decollation of the first-named unhappy Nobleman, to quit his London Business, and to retire to Derbyshire; tho' to his great Detriment; and there I, and three other Children out of Nine, were born.

He designed me for the Cloth. I was fond of his Choice: But while I was very young, some heavy Losses having disabled him from supporting me as genteelly as he wished in an Education proper for the Function, he left me to chuse at the Age of Fifteen or Sixteen, a Business; having been able to give me only common School-Learning. I chose that of a Printer, tho' a Stranger to it, as what I thought would gratify my Thirst after Reading. I served a diligent Seven Years to it, to a Master who grudged every Hour to me, that tended not to his Profit, even of those times of Leisure and Diversion, which the Refractoriness of my Fellow-Servants obliged him to allow them, and were usually allowed by other Masters to their Apprentices. I stole from the Hours of Rest and Relaxation, my Reading Times for Improvement of my Mind; and being engaged in a Correspondence with a Gentleman greatly my Superior in Degree, and of ample Fortunes, who, had he lived, intended high things for me; those were all the Opportunities I had in my Apprenticeship to carry it on. But this little Incident I may mention, I took Care, that even my Candle was of my own purchasing, that I might not in the most trifling Instance make my Master a Sufferer (and who used to call me the Pillar of his House) and not to disable myself by Watching or Sitting-up, to perform my Duty to him in the Day-time.

Part of Richardson's autobiographical letter of 2 June 1753 to his Dutch translator, Johannes Stinstra (Gemeenteliike Archiefdienst, Amsterdam) of that year Richardson leased another house, at Parson's Green on King's Road between Fulham and Chelsea, and the family moved in the autumn. North End, the place so intimately associated with the writing of novels, was gone.

There were family problems of a more serious nature. In 1750 the novelist's brother Benjamin had died; Richardson helped support the family he left and took Benjamin's daughter Susanna to live with him. Early in the decade Richardson feared he was to lose another of his children: Anne (Nancy) was very ill in 1751-1752. Sarah (Sally) suffered from rheumatism, and had an alarming affliction of the lungs in 1758. Mary (Polly) was courted by Philip Ditcher, a surgeon of Bath, who had decided views about the dowry to which he was entitled. Richardson thought Ditcher undervalued his daughter and criticized Mrs. Richardson for falling in too readily with Ditcher's wishes. Mary and Ditcher were married in September 1757; Richardson's first grandchild was baptized in October 1758. The other Richardson children were not to marry until after Richardson's death. Martha (Patty) married Edward Bridgen and had no children; Sarah married Richard Crowther, a surgeon, in 1763, and died in 1773, leaving two sons and a daughter. Anne Richardson outlived her sisters and died, unmarried, in 1803.

During the 1750s Richardson was still active in the printing shop, where he employed thirty to forty men. He was a master of the Stationers' Company in 1754-1755. He was still working on publication of the *Universal History*; he had owned a sixth share but had sold half of it in 1753 to the Rivingtons. His work on the *Universal History* brought him into contact with Tobias Smollett, who was editing it, and their relations were always civil, if not profoundly friendly.

The novelist's health continued to trouble him, with an ominous increase in trembling and dizziness. Friends thought he was more healthy and cheerful when he was writing. Catherine Talbot suggested to Elizabeth Carter that she think of "subjects for plays" and "notify them to Mr. Richardson; for . . . a play must be his next undertaking." Richardson had found himself his own task in collecting the sentiments in his novels. In March 1755 he published *A Collection of the Moral and Instructive Sentiments, Maxims, Cautions, and Reflections, Contained in the Histories of Pamela, Clarissa and Sir Charles Grandison*. It was an age that valued maxims and reflections; Benjamin Franklin borrowed more than twenty of

Richardson's sentiments for *Poor Richard's Almanack* (1732-1757). But, as Richardson himself knew, such a collection was "a dry Performance." He thought of ideas for novels, toying briefly with writing the history of a good widow. More seriously, he wished to attempt the history of Mrs. Hortensia Beaumont, a story that seems to have its roots in Richardson's personal recollection of a woman he had known, perhaps loved, in his youth. Mrs. Beaumont appears briefly in *Sir Charles Grandison* as a middle-aged Englishwoman sympathetic to Clementina. Among Richardson's papers at his death was part of a fiction, which was published by Anna Laetitia Barbauld as "History of Mrs. Beaumont, A Fragment. In a Letter from Dr. Bartlett to Miss Byron." It is likely that this "Fragment" was part of *Sir Charles Grandison* that had been cut out. Richardson may have hoped to build a new story upon it, and hence kept that narrative piece separate from the rest. It is odd that other rejected portions of both *Clarissa* and *Sir Charles Grandison* have not come to light. It seems unlikely that Richardson would have destroyed parts of his novels that were not yet published, particularly as the option of altering and adding was open to him.

By the end of 1755 Richardson seems to have given up the idea of writing any more novels, referring to "an unconquerable Aversion to the Pen." He told Lady Echlin, "I think the little Spirit I once had, of that Kind, is departed from me." His shaky handwriting at the end of the decade betrays increased ill health. (It also makes it easy to trace his own revisions during that period of his and his correspondents' letters, which he was apparently preparing for publication either by himself or by posterity.) He was not so ill as to refuse help to the persistent Anna Meades, assisting the twenty-three-year-old author with revisions and corrections to the manuscript of her novel *Sir William Harrington* (1771).

The old Richardsonian spirit flares out most strongly, however, in his contributions to what was to become in effect the joint work of himself and Edward Young. Young's draft of *Conjectures on Original Composition*, first couched in the form of a letter to the author of *Sir Charles Grandison*, was sent to Richardson in 1756. Richardson's suggestions and revisions were detailed and considerable; the publication of the work was delayed until 1759 while the two friends discussed moral and aesthetic principles. Richardson was anxious that creative genius not be set above spiritual wisdom or moral virtue, but at the same time he em-

Frontispiece portrait of Richardson for an 1811 edition of his works; engraving by E. Scriven from a picture by M. Chamberlin

phatically supported the value of originality. An original work, he wrote to Young on 14 January 1757, "is not the laboured improvement of a modern cultivator . . . but the touch of Armida's wand, that calls forth blooming spring out of the shapeless waste, and presents in a moment objects new and various, which his genius only could have formed in that peculiar manner. . . ."

Conjectures on Original Composition (1759) pleased William Warburton, Ralph Allen, and Johnson. Johnson promised to send Young some observations on it, though he was later to tell Boswell that "he was surprised to find the Doctor [Young] receive as novelties, what Mr. Johnson thought very common thoughts." *Conjectures on Original Composition* has sometimes been treated as a manifesto of the new Romantic age; actually, it represents the critical views and attitudes of Richardson's own age, though much of what is called "romantic" is inherent in Augustan thought. Richardson himself, always an original, had an interest in a high value being placed on originality; he could boast to Stinstra on 2 June

1753 that his last novel was "entirely new & unborrowed, even of myself."

Richardson's best criticism is to be found in discussions of his own work in letters to his readers, especially to Lady Bradshaigh. In these he raises the issues of fiction making, examines subtle intentions in his novels, and treats the ambiguities of his characters. He clearly values complexity and movement over stasis and fixed meanings: "I have lost a great Part of my Aim, if I do not occasion many Debates upon different Parts of my Management," he wrote on 8 December 1753. The godlike, forming novelist absents himself or becomes fragmented, diffused. Richardson's dramatic concept of characterization has something in common with John Keats's Negative Capability: "I am all the while absorbed in the character. It is not fair to say—I, identically I, am any-where, while I keep within the character," he wrote on 17 February 1754. In such statements by a novelist at once so present in and so absent from his works can be heard the precedents for Henry James and James Joyce.

By 1760 Richardson was having great difficulty in keeping up any of the correspondence that had once been so pleasant a part of his life. "Paralytic Fits" affected his writing. While drinking tea with Joseph Highmore on 28 June 1761, Richardson suffered a stroke. He died on 4 July and was buried in St. Bride's Church beside his first wife and his children. His second wife was laid to rest there also, in 1773, when she failed to survive the shock of Sally's death. Richardson's will shows the solid financial status he had achieved: he left about fourteen thousand pounds.

For Richardson's funeral oration one must look abroad, to Diderot's impassioned "Eloge de Richardson." It is an extensive and loving critique: "This author ceaselessly brings you back to the important concerns of life." Here is fitting praise from another man of the Enlightenment, a fellow philosopher and novelist. Diderot concludes with the trumpet of a prophecy: "O Richardson! if thou hast not enjoyed in thy lifetime all the reputation which thou merited, how great wilt thou appear to our posterity, when they shall see thee at the distance from which we now regard Homer! Then, who is it who will dare to wrest away one line from your sublime works? . . . Centuries, make haste to run and bring with you the honors which are due to Richardson!" This tribute by a man of another country shows the extent to which Richardson had succeeded in reaching out to the wider world, extending universal benevolence and creating across frontiers the "family of love."

Letters:

The Correspondence of Samuel Richardson, 6 volumes, edited by Anna Laetitia Barbauld (London: Phillips, 1804; New York: AMS Press, 1966);

Selected Letters of Samuel Richardson, edited by John Carroll (Oxford: Clarendon Press, 1964).

Bibliographies:

William Merritt Sale, Jr., *Samuel Richardson: A Bibliographical Record of His Literary Career with Historical Notes* (New Haven: Yale University Press, 1936; London: Oxford University Press, 1936);

Sarah W. R. Smith, *Samuel Richardson: A Reference Guide* (Boston: G. K. Hall, 1984).

Biographies:

William Merritt Sale, Jr., *Samuel Richardson: Master Printer* (Ithaca, N.Y.: Cornell University Press, 1950);

T. C. Duncan Eaves and Ben D. Kimpel, *Samuel Richardson: A Biography* (Oxford: Clarendon Press, 1971);

Carol Houlihan Flynn, *Samuel Richardson: A Man of Letters* (Princeton: Princeton University Press, 1982);

Jocelyn Harris, *Samuel Richardson* (Cambridge: Cambridge University Press, 1987).

References:

Sheridan W. Baker, "The Idea of Romance in the Eighteenth-Century Novel," *PMASAL,* 49 (1964): 507-522;

Anna Laetitia Barbauld, "Richardson," in *The British Novelists,* 50 volumes (London: Rivington, 1810): i-xlvi;

Leo Braudy, "Penetration and Impenetrability in *Clarissa,*" in *New Approaches to Eighteenth-Century Literature: Selected Papers from the English Institute,* edited by Phillip Harth (New York & London: Columbia University Press, 1974), pp. 177-206;

R. F. Brissenden, *Virtue in Distress: Studies in the Novel of Sentiment from Richardson to Sade* (London: Macmillan, 1974);

Elizabeth Bergen Brophy, *Samuel Richardson: The Triumph of Craft* (Knoxville: University of Tennessee Press, 1974);

Rachel M. Brownstein, *Becoming a Heroine: Reading about Women in Novels* (New York: Viking Press, 1982);

John Carroll, "Lovelace as Tragic Hero," *UTQ,* 42 (1972): 14-25;

Carroll, "On Annotating *Clarissa,*" in *Editing Eighteenth-Century Novels: Papers on Fielding, Le Sage, Richardson . . . Given at the Conference on Editorial Problems, University of Toronto, November, 1973,* edited by Gerald E. Bentley, Jr. (Toronto: Hakkert, 1975);

Terry Castle, *Clarissa's Ciphers: Meaning and Disruption in Richardson's "Clarissa"* (Ithaca, N.Y. & London: Cornell University Press, 1982);

Robert Adams Day, *Told in Letters: Epistolary Fiction before Richardson* (Ann Arbor: University of Michigan Press, 1966);

Denis Diderot, "Eloge de Richardson," *Journal Étranger,* 8 (1762): 5-38;

Austin Dobson, *Samuel Richardson,* English Men of Letters series (London: Macmillan, 1902);

Margaret Anne Doody, "Deserts, Ruins and Troubled Waters: Female Dreams in Fiction and the Development of the Gothic Novel," *Genre,* 10 (1977): 529-572;

Doody, *A Natural Passion: A Study of the Novels of Samuel Richardson* (Oxford: Clarendon Press, 1974);

Brian W. Downs, *Richardson* (London: Routledge, 1928; New York: Dutton, 1928);

John A. Dussinger, "Conscience and the Pattern of Christian Perfection in *Clarissa,*" *PMLA,* 81 (1966): 236-245;

Dussinger, "Richardson's Tragic Muse," *Philological Quarterly,* 46 (1967): 18-33;

Terry Eagleton, *The Rape of Clarissa: Writing, Sexuality and Class Struggle in Samuel Richardson* (Oxford: Blackwell, 1982; Minneapolis: University of Minnesota Press, 1982);

Lady Elizabeth Echlin, *An Alternative Ending to Richardson's "Clarissa,"* edited by Dimiter Daphinoff, Swiss Studies in English No. 107 (Bern: Francke Verlag, 1982);

Leslie Fiedler, *Love and Death in the American Novel* (New York: Criterion, 1960);

Henry Fielding, *The Covent-Garden Journal,* 10 (4 February 1752);

Fielding, *The Jacobite's Journal and Other Writings,* edited by W. B. Coley (Oxford: Wesleyan University Press, 1975), pp. 119-120;

Sarah Fielding, *Remarks on Clarissa, Addressed to the Author* (London: J. Robinson, 1749);

Robert Folkenflik, "A Room of Pamela's Own," *ELH,* 39 (1972): 14-25;

Christina Marsden Gillis, *The Paradox of Privacy: Epistolary Form in "Clarissa"* (Gainesville: University Presses of Florida, 1984);

Rita Goldberg, *Sex and Enlightenment: Women in Richardson and Diderot* (Cambridge: Cambridge University Press, 1984);

Morris Golden, *Richardson's Characters* (Ann Arbor: University of Michigan Press, 1963);

Irwin Gopnik, *A Theory of Style and Richardson's "Clarissa"* (The Hague & Paris: Mouton, 1970);

Edmund Gosse, "The Novelists," in his *A History of Eighteenth-Century Literature* (London: Macmillan, 1889), pp. 245-251;

Jean Hagstrum, *Sex and Sensibility: Idea and Erotic Love from Milton to Mozart* (Chicago: University of Chicago Press, 1980), pp. 186-218;

Richard Gordon Hannaford, *Samuel Richardson: An Annotated Bibliography of Critical Studies* (New York & London: Garland, 1980);

Thomas Hardy, "The Profitable Reading of Fiction," in *Life and Art by Thomas Hardy: Essays, Notes, and Letters,* edited by Ernest Brennecke, Jr. (New York: Greenberg, 1925);

Jocelyn M. Harris, " 'As if they had been living friends': *Sir Charles Grandison* into *Mansfield Park,*" *Bulletin of Research in the Humanities,* 83 (1980): 360-405;

Harris, "The Reviser Observed: The Last Volume of *Sir Charles Grandison,*" *Studies in Bibliography,* 29 (1976): 1-31;

William Hazlitt, *Lectures on the English Comic Writers* (London: Taylor & Hessey, 1819), pp. 233-239;

Christopher Hill, "Clarissa Harlowe and her Times," in his *Puritanism and Revolution* (London: Secker & Warburg, 1958), pp. 367-394;

F. W. Hilles, "The Plan of *Clarissa,*" *Philological Quarterly,* 45 (1966): 236-248;

Katherine Gee Hornbeak, "The Complete Letter Writer in English," *Smith College Studies in Modern Languages,* no. 15, parts 3-4 (Northampton, Mass.: Smith College, 1934);

Hornbeak, "Richardson's 'Familiar Letters,' and the Domestic Conduct Books; Richardson's 'Aesop'," *Smith College Studies in Modern Languages,* no. 19, parts 1-2 (Northampton, Mass.: Smith College, 1938);

Francis Jeffrey (Lord Jeffrey), review of A. L. Barbauld, ed., *Richardson's Life and Correspondence, Edinburgh Review,* 5 (1804): 23-44;

Anthony M. Kearney, *Samuel Richardson* (London: Routledge & Kegan Paul, 1968; New York: Humanities Press, 1968);

Frank Kermode, "Richardson and Fielding," *Cambridge Journal,* 4 (1950): 106-114;

Arnold Kettle, *An Introduction to the English Novel,* 2 volumes (London: Hutchinson, 1951), I: 65-71;

Mark Kinkead-Weekes, "*Clarissa* Restored?," *Review of English Studies,* new series 10 (1959): 156-171;

Kinkead-Weekes, *Samuel Richardson: Dramatic Novelist* (Ithaca, N.Y.: Cornell University Press / London: Methuen, 1973);

Ira Konigsberg, *Samuel Richardson and the Dramatic Novel* (Lexington: University of Kentucky Press, 1968);

Bernard Kreissman, *Pamela-Shamela: A Study of Burlesques, Parodies, and Adaptations of Richardson's "Pamela"* (Lincoln: University of Nebraska Press, 1960);

David Masson, *British Novelists and their Styles* (Cambridge & London: Macmillan, 1859);

Alan Dugald McKillop, *The Early Masters of English Fiction* (Lawrence: University of Kansas Press, 1956);

McKillop, *Samuel Richardson, Printer and Novelist* (Chapel Hill: University of North Carolina Press, 1936);

McKillop, "Samuel Richardson's *Advice to an Apprentice,*" *JEGP,* 42 (1943): 40-54;

Charles Mullett, ed., *The Letters of Dr. George Cheyne to Samuel Richardson (1733-1743)* (Columbia: University of Missouri Press, 1943);

John Preston, *The Created Self: The Reader's Role in Eighteenth-Century Fiction* (London: Heinemann, 1970);

Norman Rabkin, "*Clarissa:* A Study in the Nature of Convention," *ELH,* 23 (1956): 204-217;

John J. Richetti, *Popular Fiction before Richardson: Narrative Patterns 1700-1739* (Oxford: Clarendon Press, 1969);

Pat Rogers, "Richardson," in his *The Augustan Vision* (London: Weidenfeld & Nicolson, 1974; New York: Harper & Row, 1974), pp. 267-274;

Marijke Rudnik-Smalbraak, *Samuel Richardson: Minute Particulars within the Large Design* (Leiden: Leiden University Press, 1983);

Peter Sabor, "The Cooke-Everyman Edition of *Pamela,*" *Library,* 32 (1977): 360-366;

George Saintsbury, *The English Novel* (London: Dent, 1913; New York: Dutton, 1913), pp. 82-103;

William Merritt Sale, Jr., "From *Pamela* to *Clarissa,*" in *The Age of Johnson: Essays Presented to Chauncey Brewster Tinker,* edited by F. W. Hilles (New Haven: Yale University Press, 1949), pp. 127-138;

Sir Walter Scott, "Prefatory Memoir of Richardson," *Ballantyne's Novelists Library,* 10 volumes (London: Hurst, Robinson, 1824), VI: i-xlviii;

Roger Sharrock, "Richardson's *Pamela:* the Gospel and the Novel," *Durham University Journal,* 57 (1964): 67-74;

Arthur Sherbo, "Time and Place in Richardson's *Clarissa,*" *Boston University Studies in English,* 3 (1957): 139-146;

Patricia Meyer Spacks, "The Sense of an Audience: Samuel Richardson, Colley Cibber," in her *Imagining a Self* (Cambridge, Mass.: Harvard University Press, 1976), pp. 193-226;

Leslie Stephen, "Richardson's Novels," *Cornhill Magazine,* 17 (1868): 48-69;

Florian Stuber, "Clarissa and Her World," Ph.D. dissertation, Columbia University, 1980;

Clara Linklater Thomson, *Samuel Richardson: A Biographical and Critical Study* (London: Marshall, 1900);

Janet Todd, *Women's Friendship in Literature* (New York: Columbia University Press, 1980);

John Traugott, "*Clarissa's* Richardson: An Essay to Find the Reader," in *English Literature in the Age of Disguise,* edited by Maximillian E. Novak (Berkeley: University of California Press, 1977), pp. 157-208;

Dorothy Van Ghent, "On *Clarissa Harlowe,*" in her *The English Novel: Form and Function* (New York: Rinehart, 1953), pp. 45-64;

William Beatty Warner, *Reading "Clarissa": The Struggles of Interpretation* (New Haven & London: Yale University Press, 1979);

Ian Watt, "The Naming of Characters in Defoe, Richardson, and Fielding," *Review of English Studies,* 25 (1949): 322-338;

Watt, "The Novelist as Innovator: Samuel Richardson," *Listener,* 73 (1965): 177-180;

Watt, *The Rise of the Novel: Studies in Defoe, Richardson and Fielding* (Berkeley: University of California Press, 1957);

Alan Wendt, "Clarissa's Coffin," *Philological Quarterly,* 39 (1960): 481-495;

Angus Wilson, "An Interview with Angus Wilson," by Frederick F. P. McDowell, *Iowa Review,* 3 (1972): 77-105;

Wilson, "Richardson's *Clarissa,*" *Horizon,* 17 (1975): 103-106;

Judith Wilt, "He Could Go No Farther: A Modest Proposal about Lovelace," *PMLA,* 92 (1977): 19-32;

Cynthia Griffin Wolff, *Samuel Richardson and the Eighteenth-Century Puritan Character* (Hamden, Conn.: Shoe String Press, 1972);

Wolfgang Zach, "Mrs. Aubin and Richardson's Earliest Literary Manifesto (1739)," *English Studies,* 62 (1981): 271-285.

Papers:

The largest deposit of Richardson manuscripts is in the Forster Collection of the Victoria and Albert Museum in London. Other important material can be found in the Henry W. and Albert A. Berg Collection of the New York Public Library; the James Marshall and Marie-Louise Osborn Collection of the Beinecke Library, Yale University; the British Library; the Bodleian Library, Oxford; the Library of the University of Edinburgh; the Henry E. Huntington Library, San Marino, California; and the Pierpont Morgan Library, New York.

Richard Brinsley Sheridan

(1751 - 7 July 1816)

*This entry was written by Mark S. Auburn (Indiana University-Purdue University at Fort Wayne) for
DLB 89: Restoration and Eighteenth-Century Dramatists: Third Series.*

SELECTED BOOKS: *The Rivals, A Comedy. As it is
Acted at the Theatre-Royal in Covent-Garden*
(London: Printed for John Wilkie, 1775); re-
vised as *The Rivals, A Comedy. As it is Acted at
the Theatre-Royal in Covent Garden. Written by
Richard Brinsley Sheridan, Esq. The Third Edi-
tion Corrected.* (London: Printed for John
Wilkie, 1776);

*Songs Duets, Trios, &c. in The Duenna; or, The Dou-
ble Elopement. As Performed at the Theatre-
Royal in Covent-Garden* (London: Printed for
J. Wilkie, 1775);

*Verses To the Memory of Garrick. Spoken as A Mon-
ody, at the Theatre Royal in Drury-Lane* (London: Published by T. Evans, J. Wilkie, E. &
C. Dilly, A. Portal, and J. Almon, 1779);

The School for Scandal. A Comedy [pirated edition]
(Dublin, 1780);

*The Critic or A Tragedy Rehearsed. A Dramatic Piece
in three Acts as it is performed at the Theatre
Royal in Drury Lane. By Richard Brinsley Sheridan Esqr.* (London: Printed for T. Becket,
1781);

*A Trip to Scarborough. A Comedy. As Performed at the
Theatre Royal in Drury Lane. Altered from
Vanbrugh's Relapse; or, Virtue in Danger. By
Richard Brinsley Sheridan Esq.* (London:
Printed for G. Wilkie, 1781);

*St. Patrick's Day; or, the Scheming Lieutenant. A
Comic Opera: As It is Acted at the Theatre-
Royal, Smoke-Alley* [pirated edition] (Dublin:
Printed for the booksellers, 1788);

*The Duenna: A Comic Opera. In Three Acts. As Per-
formed at the Theatre Royal, Covent Garden:
With Universal Applause. By R. B. Sheridan,
Esq* (London: Printed for T. N. Longman,
1794);

*The Camp, A Musical Entertainment. As Performed at
the Theatre Royal, Drury Lane. By R. B. Sheridan, Esq.* [pirated edition] (London, 1795);

*Pizarro; A Tragedy, In Five Acts; As Performed at the
Theatre Royal in Drury-Lane: Taken from the German Drama of Kotzebue; and Adapted to the English Stage by Richard Brinsley Sheridan* (London: Printed for James Ridgway, 1799).

Collections: *Sheridan's Plays Now Printed as He
Wrote Them and His Mother's Unpublished Com-
edy 'A Journey to Bath,'* edited by W. Fraser
Rae (London: David Nutt, 1902);

The Plays and Poems of Richard Brinsley Sheridan, 3
volumes, edited by R. Crompton Rhodes (Oxford: Blackwell, 1928);

The Dramatic Works of Richard Brinsley Sheridan, 2
volumes, edited by Cecil Price (Oxford: Clarendon Press, 1973).

SELECTED PLAY PRODUCTIONS: *The Rivals*,
London, Theatre Royal, Covent Garden,
17 January 1775; revised version, London,
Theatre Royal, Covent Garden, 28 January
1775;

St. Patrick's Day, London, Theatre Royal, Covent
Garden, 2 May 1775;

Prelude on Opening Covent Garden next Season, London, Theatre Royal, Covent Garden, 20 September 1775;

The Duenna, London, Theatre Royal, Covent Garden, 21 November 1775;

A Trip to Scarborough, London, Theatre Royal in
Drury Lane, 24 February 1777;

The School for Scandal, London, Theatre Royal in
Drury Lane, 8 May 1777;

The Camp, London, Theatre Royal in Drury
Lane, 15 October 1778;

Verses to the Memory of Garrick, London, Theatre
Royal in Drury Lane, 11 March 1779;

The Critic, London, Theatre Royal in Drury Lane,
30 October 1779;

Pizarro, London, Theatre Royal, Drury Lane, 24
May 1799.

Richard Brinsley Sheridan wrote and produced three plays that have been performed
more frequently than the works of any other playwright between William Shakespeare and Bernard Shaw. *The Rivals, The School for Scandal,* and
The Critic entered the performing repertoire im-

Richard Brinsley Sheridan (portrait by Thomas Gainsborough)

mediately upon their first appearance in the 1770s, and one or more of them is still performed every year. They are both timely and timeless pieces of art: timely because they reflect not only the concerns and mores but also the literary and theatrical style of late-eighteenth-century England; timeless because they speak to the human condition and to the nature of artistic creation in the theater. As the basis for a major artistic reputation, three plays seem thin, particularly in comparison to the creations of Dr. Samuel Johnson, Oliver Goldsmith, Laurence Sterne, and even Tobias Smollett. Yet, because Sheridan exploited a late neoclassical style, tempered exuberant spirits with knowledge of the exigencies of theatrical production, and infused comic attack with the charitable spirit of good nature, his plays are still produced around the world.

Sheridan's pedigree forecast literary and theatrical achievement. His mother, Frances Cham-

berlain Sheridan, who died while he was an adolescent student at Harrow, wrote one fairly successful play and one respected novel. His father, Thomas, was a playwright, actor, theater manager, orator, and also a scholar of English elocution who published a dictionary. His paternal grandfather, Thomas Sheridan, spent many intimate years with Jonathan Swift. Sheridan met and exceeded the gifts of this heritage and the expectations loaded upon his shoulders as the second son, the one sent to the famous boarding school Harrow in 1762 while his favored elder brother and his two younger sisters remained with the family, the one who was to learn to shift for himself. He rose from genteel Irish poverty to become holder of the royal patent for Drury Lane theater, a member of Parliament, a minister of government (on three occasions), and finally a landowner. His time as an active playwright covered about five years; his career as a politician

Elizabeth Linley Sheridan, circa 1785 (portrait by Thomas Gainsborough; Andrew W. Mellon Collection, National Gallery of Art, Washington, D.C.)

spanned three decades. During all of his mature life, even the last few years, he knew material success that far exceeded anything his parents had ever experienced; he enjoyed the respect and affection of the greatest people of his day; and he served his country on a broader stage than Smock Alley (the Dublin theater his father managed) or Drury Lane (the London theater he owned). At the same time, as witnessed by his election to Johnson's Literary Club in March 1777, he became a man of letters who conversed as an equal with the principal male artists of his own generation and of the next—George Gordon, Lord Byron; William Wordsworth; Samuel Taylor Coleridge; Robert Southey; Thomas Moore.

Sheridan's brief burst of literary and theatrical activity from 1775 to 1779 still commands attention and respect, while three decades of public service garner rich footnotes in histories of the stuttering growth of the British Empire. His literary and theatrical activity occurred in a context that has bequeathed to us only one other immortal play, Oliver Goldsmith's *She Stoops to Conquer* (1773); his political contributions issued forth during a tumultuous period of European history when wars and revolutions, caused by new ideas about the citizen's relationship with the social fabric and fueled by technological advances in manufacture and transportation, signaled the growth of empire. If he was only a supporting actor in the world of power, he was the star comic playwright of the Age of Garrick.

Theater in Sheridan's time appealed to the upper and middle and even lower classes, though fewer of the last could afford so little as one shilling for the upper gallery than could gentry and aristocrats the two, three, and five shillings for the first gallery, pit, and boxes. Nevertheless, the appeal encompassed all classes, and the repertoire reflected all tastes. Plays appeared in London during the winter season (September through May) mostly upon the stages of the two royal patent houses, Covent Garden and Drury Lane. Their two splendid auditoriums welcomed thousands of visitors nightly to a world more brightly lit (both by candles and by oil-fed stage devices) than anyone could see in almost any other enclosed public structure. During about 180 nights a season audiences watched versions of Shakespeare and Ben Jonson and John Fletcher, plays by George Farquhar, Richard Steele, Colley Cibber, and Susanna Centlivre, and recent comedies by Isaac Bickerstaffe, George Colman the Elder, Richard Cumberland, David Garrick, and Hugh Kelly. They did not often see plays by George Etherege, William Wycherley, Thomas Shadwell, John Dryden, or William Congreve: these century-old writers of the Restoration failed to hold a place in the British repertoire much beyond the second decade of the eighteenth century. Auditors seemed to want not only comedies, melodramas, and tragedies to their own tastes but also such entr'acte entertainments as rope dancing (tightrope walking), harlequinades, singing, monologues, and other variety pieces. And the theatrical evening had to conclude with a farce or comic operetta of an hour or so, stretching the theatrical experience into five hours or longer, from prologue, mainpiece, epilogue, entr'actes, through afterpiece.

Within its repertoire, high Georgian theater included the most stageworthy of its forebears from the early seventeenth century, the better productions of its early-eighteenth-century fellow-technicians, and the recent plays of its contemporaries. High Georgian theater, especially under David Garrick's management, ignored most of the comedies and tragedies of the Caroline period (1670-1710), the plays of Farquhar and Centlivre excepted. It offered a lot of Shakespeare, though usually Shakespeare revised. A small portion of what it presented, and almost nothing of what it originated, has earned a place in literary history.

As artisans for the Georgian stage, in their published plays both Frances Sheridan and Thomas Sheridan reflect a comedic bias toward their more remote past and toward their present, just like this repertoire. Their second son, "Dick," as they called him, worked within this tradition. And when he sought subjects for his first fully developed stage works, he turned to his own experience.

While living with his father, brother, and sisters in Bath in the early 1770s, Sheridan met Elizabeth Ann Linley, the most admired singer of the period, called a "lark," a "saint," the "siren of Bath." Sheridan's father, Thomas, had made the acquaintance of the Linley family (famous musicians all) in order to expand his "Attic Entertainment," an evening of theatrical oratory and declamation which required music for balance. This presentation was Thomas Sheridan's principal means of support at Bath, and money was always tight for his growing family; Dick complained of being mocked as the "poor player's son" at Harrow. The Linleys were far more comfortable than the Sheridans; but Thomas Sheridan privately denigrated Elizabeth's father, Thomas Linley, as a mere musician, and even later he would denigrate Dick's alliance with a musician's daughter—his son was the son of a scholar, not the son of a player; his son should not marry the daughter of a "music maker."

At the start of their acquaintance, Dick seemed to have had no such pretensions. Eliza, after all, was engaged to Sir Walter Long, an older baronet of substantial revenue. Even when this alliance was broken, with much public notice, including a farce by Samuel Foote, Sheridan's part could only be advisory, particularly since Dick's older brother, Charles, was a rival for Elizabeth's affections. History has not made clear how Dick became the favored suitor, but it has left us titillating romantic hints in the form of indisputable events: a Captain Mathews addressed Eliza; the younger "Mr. S------n" assisted Miss Linley in an elopement to France; there were paragraphs in the Bath newspapers, two duels between Mathews and Sheridan (during the second of which Dick suffered severe wounds), a six-month exile for Dick at Waltham Abbey, where he was supposed to prepare himself for the bar, and at last on 13 April 1773 a clandestine wedding of the eldest Linley and the second Sheridan son. Thomas Sheridan refused to countenance the marriage for many months: he told Charles in a burst of self-indulgent affection, "I consider myself now as having no son but you," and he prevented his daughters, Lissy and Betsy, from seeing Dick and Eliza for three years. But Thomas Linley recognized the alliance immediately and even provided his daughter a small dowry.

And so it was that Richard Brinsley Sheridan found himself married and living in London during the 1773-1774 season without an income and soon with a growing family, for on 17 November 1775, the couple's son, Thomas, was born. Richard Sheridan would not permit Eliza to sing

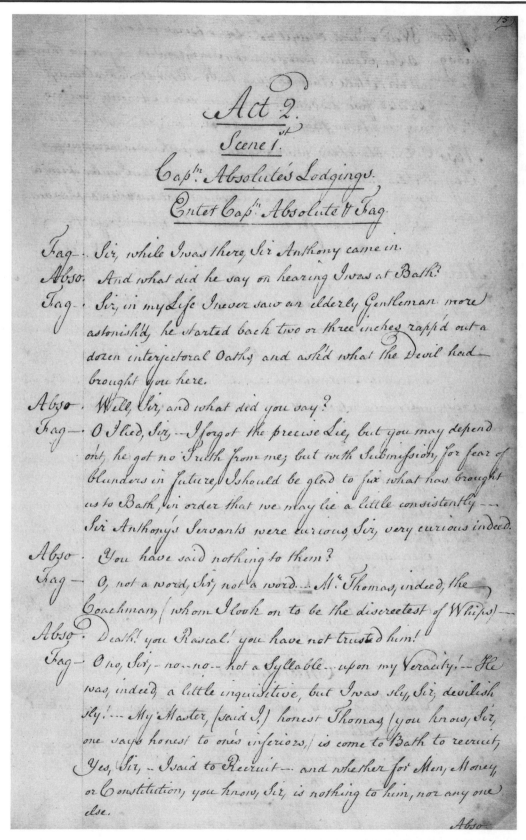

Page from the playhouse copy of the original version of The Rivals, *submitted to the Examiner of Plays for licensing prior to its performance on 17 January 1775 (Larpent Collection, LA 383; Henry E. Huntington Library and Art Gallery). The play was revised extensively before it was staged again, on 28 January 1775.*

for money, even though she could command as much as fifteen hundred pounds for a series of concerts. James Boswell tells of Dr. Johnson's applauding the decision:

> We talked of a young gentleman's marriage with an eminent singer, and his determination that she should no longer sing in publick. . . . It was questioned whether the young gentleman, who had not a shilling in the world, but was blest with very uncommon talents, was not foolishly delicate, or foolishly proud. . . . Johnson, with all the high spirit of a Roman senator, exclaimed, "He resolved wisely and nobly to be sure. He is a brave man. Would not a gentleman be disgraced by having his wife singing publickly for hire? No, Sir, there can be no doubt here. I know not if I should not *prepare* myself for a publick singer, as readily as let my wife be one."

And so Dick turned to his "very uncommon talents," and to his mother's unpublished work, to produce his first play.

The Rivals appeared on 17 January 1775. It represents a lively if confusing imbroglio of young love triumphing over parental disapproval in the way of Roman New Comedy, with this important difference: the old parents in fact desire the marriage of the young people, and the young people create their own difficulties. Romantic Lydia Languish wants to elope rather than marry anyone with her "friends' consent." To humor her, Captain Jack Absolute has disguised himself as penniless Ensign Beverley. Lydia's aunt, Mrs. Malaprop, is negotiating with Sir Anthony Absolute about an alliance of Lydia with his son Jack Absolute. Complicating the picture are two other rivals for Lydia's affections: the foppish country booby Bob Acres and the pugnacious fortune-hunting Sir Lucius O'Trigger. Neither of these rivals ever crosses Lydia's mind, and Sir Lucius's pretensions are particularly absurd since Mrs. Malaprop herself is attracted to him. Both Mrs. Malaprop and Sir Lucius are betrayed by the scheming maidservant Lucy in the correspondence which the aunt thinks she is carrying on with Sir Lucius and which Sir Lucius thinks he is carrying on with Lydia. In a subplot which Sheridan meant to be comic but which rarely plays as such, overly delicate and emotionally insecure Faulkland tests the affections of his orphaned fiancée, Julia Melville (Sir Anthony's niece and Lydia's best friend). The difficulties are good-naturedly resolved at the scene of a six-way duel: Acres to fight "Beverley," Jack to fight Sir Lucius

(either for Jack to defend his pretensions to Sir Lucius's Lydia or for Sir Lucius to avenge a slight upon Ireland which he alleges Jack made—the text gives both reasons and thereby indicates the subservience of plot to characterization), and Faulkland to fight anyone who is willing. Sir Anthony and Mrs. Malaprop arrive in time to prevent the rivals from dueling and to sort out the marriages. The keys to the amiable tone of the play are Acres's resignation of any interest, Sir Lucius's offer to hold a party for everyone assembled even though he has been disappointed of a fortune and a bride, and Sir Anthony's sage advice to bring the correct couples together.

In its first performance, *The Rivals* was too long by an hour, too indelicate by a half-dozen oaths and several bawdy references, and too ill acted, especially by favorite Ned Shuter, to win the audience's approbation. Covent Garden manager Thomas Harris immediately withdrew it, and Sheridan's theatrical career might have ended then (as Eliza thought it had) except for Harris's prudent assessment of Sheridan's powers of revision. Eleven nights later, on 28 January 1775, a new version appeared, earned applause, and played steadily in the repertoire for the rest of the season and into every season thereafter. In its original performances, the play featured the best Covent Garden comedians, five of whom had created roles in Goldsmith's *She Stoops to Conquer*: Jane Green was Mrs. Malaprop as well as Mrs. Hardcastle; Mary Bulkley portrayed Julia Melville as well as Kate Hardcastle; Ned Shuter, now "perfect" in his lines (that is, he knew them this time), took Sir Anthony Absolute after having created Mr. Hardcastle; perhaps John Quick as Acres incorporated features of his portrayal of Tony Lumpkin; and Lee Lewes as Jack's pompous servant, Fag, found a small but worthy successor to his formal young Marlowe. Joined by veterans such as Henry Woodward (at sixty-five still acceptable in young romantic roles such as Jack Absolute) and newcomers such as Jane Barsanti as Lydia and Lawrence Clinch as Sir Lucius O'Trigger (in the second opening, taking the part in which John Lee had failed on 17 January), the cast represented Covent Garden's strongest comic ensemble.

Thomas Moore, Sheridan's biographer and first systematic critic, wrote that "The characters of *The Rivals* . . . are *not* such as occur very commonly in the world; and, instead of producing striking effects with natural and obvious materials, which is the great art and difficulty of a

Richard Brinsley Sheridan, 1788 (portrait by John Russell; National Portrait Gallery, London)

painter of human life, [Sheridan] has here overcharged most of his persons with whims and absurdities, for which the circumstances they are engaged in afford but a very disproportionate vent." Moore correctly assesses the artificial nature of these characters' idiosyncrasies, and by focusing on the characters he points as well to the essence of the play: it is a comedy of character, not a comedy of plot, and our satisfaction derives more from the exposures of foibles and absurdities for their own sakes than from a probable and necessary resolution of the difficulties in which the characters are involved or from the capacity of the artistic fabric to weave colorfully and consistently strands of truth about human existence.

Subsequent critics have attributed the comedy's greatness to its exuberant play with language and with language's power to obfuscate reality, but this language emanates from, as well as serves to form, distinctly drawn, wonderfully absurd characters, stage types as ancient as Menander's (the old father, the miles gloriosus, the amorous dowager) and as fresh as George Colman the Elder's Polly Honeycombe (1760). Sheridan's instinctive artistry took the types and complicated them—not just a country booby but also a fop, not just a romantic ingenue but a girl whose fantasies are formed by novels, not just an amorous dowager but an abuser of words so strongly portrayed that her name gave our language a new word, *malaprop-*

ism. Yet every character proves an amiable humorist, good-natured at base, a perfect stage representative of the fundamentally warm and sentimental Georgian theater.

One of Sheridan's recent critics argues persuasively that the twenty-three-year-old playwright, who denied plagiarism in the preface to the first edition of *The Rivals,* depended heavily upon Shakespeare, whether consciously or unconsciously. And both Sheridan's contemporaries and his latter-day admirers have found convincing correspondences linking his works with William Congreve's as well as with the comedies of the Garrick era. That Mrs. Malaprop's origin is Mrs. Tryfort, a character in Frances Sheridan's unpublished "A Journey to Bath," seems indisputable. But if "faded ideas float in the fancy like half-forgotten dreams," as Sheridan argued in that preface, their recombination created a stage-worthy fantasy never long off the boards. Throughout the nineteenth century and into the twentieth, in Britain and America, *The Rivals* played steadily and became by turns a starring vehicle for Mrs. Malaprop, Sir Anthony, and even Bob Acres, depending upon the acting company's resources.

Though Sheridan the fledgling playwright proved brilliant in drawing quickly and surely a range of stage characters from many walks of life and showed that he could combine them in bouncing scenes comic for their wit, their characterization, and their manifest absurdity, it is the Sheridan of comically ironic situation who proves himself more than a brilliant apprentice in *The Rivals.* His technique of empowering the audience as spectators more knowledgeable than any one of the characters permits full appreciation of every imposture and self-deception. In the third scene of the third act, for instance, Jack appears in his real character to Mrs. Malaprop but as "Beverley" to Lydia, permits thereby each woman to appear absurdly overmatched with him but foolishly pleased in her deception of the other, yet augurs his own downfall as overreaching knave. Thus, the audience anticipates the reversal that very nearly does not occur: in the second scene of the fourth act, Sir Anthony drags Jack back to Mrs. Malaprop's for the confrontation during which both niece and aunt discover the impostures played upon them, and even Sir Anthony learns how he too has been duped. Rather than surprise the audience with the probable but unexpected, Sheridan makes us coconspirators who know what must happen, who relish our more

complete understanding, and who look forward to the characters' learning the truth. The only surprise arises from the artist's gratifying verbal brilliancies and unusual arrangement of familiar materials—the pleasure of the classical sonata form rather than of the tone poem.

The success of *The Rivals* led immediately to other opportunities for Sheridan. At Covent Garden on 2 May 1775 his two-act farce, *St. Patrick's Day; or, the Scheming Lieutenant,* appeared and earned for itself a minor place in the afterpiece repertoire. Written for Lawrence Clinch's benefit performance in gratitude for his having taken over Sir Lucius O'Trigger, the farce contains many of the elements of *The Rivals:* idiosyncratic but essentially good-natured characters, scenes of disguise and of revelation, amiable humorists of broad, quick, verbal strokes, and a farcical starring role rich in numerous assumed disguises for the principal male actor. Sheridan is said to have written it in forty-eight hours, but a contemporary testified that Sheridan had made a thorough review of the farcical afterpiece literature before embarking on the project, and certainly the many similarities to a variety of comedies and farces popular in the Georgian repertoire suggests ideas hardly faded in the fancy. Similarly, *Prelude on Opening Covent Garden next Season* (Covent Garden, 20 September 1775), surviving only through newspaper accounts, demonstrates the same competence as comic dramatist writing for the occasion.

In *The Duenna* (Covent Garden, 21 November 1775), however, Sheridan once more rose beyond competence to brilliance. Like *The Rivals* and *St. Patrick's Day,* the book of this comic opera reflects Sheridan's youthful experience and the typical situations of Roman New Comedy. Donna Louisa wishes to marry Antonio, but her crusty old father, Don Jerome, plans to marry her to the rich (converted) Jew Isaac Mendoza. Louisa's jealous brother, Ferdinand, wants to marry Louisa's best friend, the somewhat grave Donna Clara. Margaret, Donna Louisa's old, ugly, and clever duenna, plays upon Don Jerome's credulity and Isaac's cupidity to pass herself off as Donna Louisa, marry Isaac secretly, and permit both young couples to wed. The characters possess the same idiosyncratic artificiality as those of Sheridan's two earlier comedies, and they appear even more artificial because the setting this time is Seville, the conventional never-never land of a variety of older comedies (by Fletcher and Centlivre) and newer comic operas (by Isaac

First page of "The Slanderers" (above), one of Sheridan's early drafts for part of The School for Scandal, *and the corresponding page in the Frampton Court manuscript (right), the earliest surviving complete draft (Princeton University Library)*

13   1.

Act 1:st — Scene 1:st —

— Lady — Sneerwell's House —
— Lady — Sneerwell at her dressing Toilette with Lappet —

Lady Sneerwell. The Paragraphs you say were all inserted?

Verj. — — — — They were Madam — and as I copied them myself
in a feign'd Hand there can be no suspicion whence
they came. —

Lady Sneer. Did you circulate the Report of Lady Brittle's
Intrigue with Captain Boastall?

Verj. Madam by this Time Lady Brittle is the Talk
of half the Town — and I doubt not but in a
Week the Men will toast her as a Demirep.

Lady Su. What have you done as to the insinuation
of a certain Baronet's Lady & a certain Cook.

Verj. — That is in as fine a Train as your Ladyship
could wish. — I told the story yesterday to
my own maid with directions to communicate it im-
-mediately to my Hairdresser. He I am informed
has a Brother who courts a milleners Prentice
in Pallmell whose mistress has a first
cousin whose sister is Fame de Chambre
to Lady Clackit — so that in the common
course of Things it must reach Lady Clackit's
Ears within four & twenty Hours & then
you know the Business is as good as done

Bickerstaffe) in the Georgian repertoire. But more important, the music lends a sweet poignancy to the action, cutting down thereby the manifest absurdity of character and situation.

The Duenna played an unprecedented seventy-five nights that first season and was praised by audience and critics alike. A little more than a year later, in March 1777, Johnson proposed Sheridan for membership in The Literary Club, calling him the author of "the two best comedies of his age," and Johnson meant *The Rivals* and *The Duenna*. Forty years later even William Hazlitt praised it effusively:

> The "Duenna" is a perfect work of art. It has the utmost sweetness and point. The plot, the characters, the dialogue, are all complete in themselves, and they are all [Sheridan's] own; and the songs are the best that ever were written, except those in the "Beggar's Opera." They have a joyous spirit of intoxication in them, and a strain of the most melting tenderness.

For the music, Sheridan was indebted to his father-in-law and brother-in-law, the elder and younger Thomas Linleys, though to the latter more than the former. By using in the decorative part of Don Carlos the tenor Meyer Leon, he helped guarantee a splendid musical presentation while foregoing the profits of a score of Friday performances when Leon (a Jew in real life but not in the comic opera) insisted upon retiring to his synagogue.

The Duenna was the greatest hit of many seasons, outplaying for many years even John Gay's perennially popular *Beggar's Opera* (1728), but it did not survive much beyond the early nineteenth century. Later critics have found it too slight, even putting aside the frivolity of the genre. In our century, perhaps the ridicule of Isaac because he was born a Jew offends modern sensibilities, though today we can still be amused by Louisa's comparisons of Isaac's incomplete conversion—he "stands like a dead wall between church and synagogue, or like the blank leaves between the Old and New Testament." And if Margaret's dependent position and deformed visage strike us as no subjects for comedy, her wit and cleverness earn her right to the title. Moreover, in the last decade revivals have begun to occur.

Sheridan, the "poor player's son," earned a small fortune in this first year and a half of dramatic penmanship and directing, though how much he actually earned we cannot be sure. Proba-

bly dismayed to see the money-making talents of his daughter unemployed and anxious for Eliza and Dick to find financial security, Thomas Linley had for some time urged his son-in-law to form an alliance with David Garrick, actor-manager-patentee of Drury Lane, the more profitable of the two winter Theatres Royal. But Sheridan had seen his chance after *The Rivals* to capitalize upon his growing familiarity with the talents of the Covent Garden company and gave *The Duenna* to Thomas Harris, though he also took care to cultivate Garrick's friendship. (Indeed, at that March 1777 election meeting of The Literary Club, Garrick was present along with Johnson, Edmund Burke, Adam Smith, Joshua Reynolds, and Sheridan's future political ally Charles James Fox, who was in the chair.) As the 1775-1776 season wore on, Garrick complained that "the Devil of a Duenna has laid hold upon the Town," and he even tried a revival of Frances Sheridan's *The Discovery* (1763), with himself as Sir Anthony Branville, to bring audiences home to Drury Lane. One wag remarked that "the old woman would be the death of the old man." Ill from a variety of then-incurable ailments, most particularly renal-urinary tract malfunctions, Garrick determined to make the 1775-1776 season his last as an actor and to sell his half-share of the Drury Lane patent, which he valued at thirty-five thousand pounds. Sheridan, in concert with Thomas Linley, Sr., and the wealthy, fashionable physician James Ford, purchased it. In 1778 Sheridan sold his one-seventh interest to Linley and Ford and purchased the other half-interest held by Willoughby Lacy, thus becoming half-owner of the patent, with Linley and Ford controlling the other half. But in order to accomplish these financial transactions, Sheridan had to borrow heavily (probably twenty-five thousand pounds) and stand surety to a thousand-pound lifetime annuity to Lacy. Thus began a pattern of leveraged finance (Sheridan put down only thirteen hundred pounds for all these transactions) that left Sheridan socially comfortable but chronically in debt. His son Tom once said that his father had changed the family name to "O'Sheridan": after all, he *owed* most of the world. Once in Tom's company Sheridan bragged to a friend that he had permitted Tom a generous allowance at college; "yes," said Tom, "you *allowed* it, but you never paid it." On another occasion, when Sheridan threatened to cut Tom off with a shilling, Tom replied, "Then, Sir, you must borrow it."

Garrick and all of London's theatergoers expected much of the twenty-four-year-old playwright when by June 1776 his accession of the Drury Lane patent was assured. Linley would be in charge of the music; Thomas Sheridan (after three years reconciled temporarily with his son and daughter-in-law) would manage the actors; Dick would keep the books and—everyone expected—write plays for his new company. Until late in the winter, however, the public must have thought that having Sheridan was small compensation for the loss of Garrick, its favorite actor. First, there was an actors' strike in which a dominant pro-Sheridan faction chaffed against Willoughby Lacy's attempts to interfere with Sheridan's management. (Thomas Sheridan had refused his son's terms and fled to Ireland; he would return as acting manager in 1778-1779 and 1779-1780, but during his fretful management profits dropped four thousand pounds from 1777-1778 and another three thousand the second year.) Next, there was no new play from Sheridan. Only one new tragedy and seven new short pieces by other hands appeared.

But Sheridan was busy, and indeed all the principal changes to the Drury Lane repertoire sprang from his creative activity. He directed Congreve's *Old Bachelor* (1693) and *Love for Love* (1695), advertising them "with alterations," even if the scripts were only purged of bawdry and suggestion. He took Garrick's popular *A Christmas Tale* and cut it for afterpiece format, garnering thirty-two performances. He refurbished the popular pantomime *Harlequin's Invasion* and earned twenty-seven presentations. He redirected *The Rivals* with a Drury Lane cast. By the time the 187 nights of the 1776-1777 season expired, 84 had featured something directly or indirectly from Sheridan's pen; and since as the principal acting manager (or artistic director) he helped to shape every new prelude, mainpiece, afterpiece, and every redirected or refurbished piece, fully 179 of the 187 nights featured some product of his creative talents.

In offering two Congreve revivals, Sheridan attempted what he would laugh at in *The Critic* as a "bungling reformation." Congreve was a greatly respected if no longer produced literary playwright, and Drury Lane was the home of high comedy. Audiences perceived Covent Garden as the home of low comedy. The distinctions were nice even in 1775, but (generally) low comedy portrayed old-fashioned "humours" characters and encompassed more farcical and possibly more sexually suggestive situations, whereas high comedy signified the witty, elegant, satiric, and even genteel. Sheridan of Covent Garden correctly gauged the company's talents with *The Rivals* and *The Duenna;* Sheridan of Drury Lane sputtered in his attempts to exploit his actors' best skills with revisions of literary giants such as Congreve and Sir John Vanbrugh.

The first major step after Congreve was an adaptation of Vanbrugh's *The Relapse* (1696). Appearing on 24 February 1777, *A Trip to Scarborough,* Sheridan's version, shows both how greatly theatrical tastes had changed in the eighty years since Vanbrugh's comedy had appeared and how skillful Sheridan could be as a crafter of plots. Tom Moore thought Vanbrugh's original to be "luminous" only from "putrescence": to remove the "immoral" "taint" of *The Relapse* is "to extinguish" its "light." Portrayals of heterosexual libertinism and homosexual lust would offend Georgian audiences. But if Sheridan excised these, he also recrafted the plot to stand alone, divorced from its reliance upon the comedy to which Vanbrugh pretended his play to be a sequel, Colley Cibber's *Love's Last Shift* (1696); and he gave to the story an internal coherence lacking in the original. In Sheridan's version there are both probable and necessary connections among the characters of Vanbrugh's two plots, even if those connections are somewhat thin. Still, the new unified setting in a fashionable watering place remains unexploited, and the opportunity to flesh out the milieu, so brilliantly handled with servants in the Bath of *The Rivals,* passes without notice. Moore doubted that Vanbrugh's subject, even in Sheridan's hands, could "bear a second crop of wit"; and Sheridan did not sow the field he had weeded. Indeed, he did not even cast the adaptation well, for as the mildly saucy Berinthia he put forward Mrs. Mary Ann Yates, a tragic actress who was hissed off the stage at one point, prompting a noble friend from the boxes and Sheridan himself from the wings to implore her to retake the scene.

If Sheridan "spoiled" Vanbrugh's comedy (as one contemporary reported him to confess), the reason for paying less than full attention to the project became public ten weeks later, on 8 May 1777, when appeared *The School for Scandal,* the best-playing comedy of manners in the English language.

Three strands of action intertwine to make the plot of *The School for Scandal.* One might be called punitive comedy of exposure, the process

Robert Baddeley as Moses in the first production of The
School for Scandal *(portrait by Johann Zoffany; Lady
Lever Collection)*

Act 4, scene 3, of The School for Scandal: *Thomas King as Sir Peter Teazle, Frances Abington as Lady Teazle, William Smith
as Charles Surface, and John Palmer as Joseph Surface in the original production (painting by James Roberts; Garrick Club)*

by which the villainous Lady Sneerwell and her scandalmongering friends and the hypocritical Joseph Surface are revealed to testy old Sir Peter Teazle, honest Sir Oliver Surface, bluff steward-manager Rowley, and lively, naive, fashion-seeking Lady Teazle as the malicious manipulators that they have been. The strand most problematic is a comedy of self-adjustment, in which the old bachelor Sir Peter and the country-bred Lady Teazle learn how to respect one another; many critics believe that their rapprochement is only a product of self-interest, but evidence in the text and what we know about the original performances suggest mutual affection to be the means of resolution. The third strand, a comedy of merit rewarded, shows how mildly libertine Charles Surface reveals himself as valuing openness, honesty, and family affection above his spendthrift habits, thereby meriting the continued support of his returning "nabob" uncle Sir Oliver and the hand of the sober, virtuous Maria, Sir Peter's orphaned ward.

If the broad, rollicking humor and sweet, touching music of *The Duenna* eighteen months before had brought all London's attention to the home of low comedy, the witty repartee of fashionable society, the Cain-and-Abel motif, and the delightful recitation of the May-and-December theme in *The School for Scandal* now brought the town's acclamation to the house of high comedy. Sheridan had been more than customarily tardy in completing the comedy, and long-held tradition reports that the play was actually in rehearsal days before a complete final draft was in the hands of William Hopkins, prompter at Drury Lane and hence responsible for copying out parts for the actors. Sheridan scrawled out at the end of the manuscript:

> —finis—
> Thank God!
> R B S—

Then he added, again in his own hand,

> Amen!
> W. Hopkins

But even so late in the season (indeed, the actors' benefits had concluded), the play engendered wildly enthusiastic support. Passing by the outer walls of Drury Lane just as the famous screen fell and the audience exploded in laughter and applause, a journalist of the day claimed to have run for his life in fear that the building was collapsing. Twenty performances came before Drury Lane closed for the year, and in the next season forty-five were offered for a total of sixty-five in its first full year—short of the seventy-five *The Duenna* received in its first season, but grossing thirty percent more in 1777-1778 than the average evening of Sheridan's first season as manager. Intellectual observers began calling Sheridan "the modern Congreve," a sobriquet which stuck with some and which led several generations of critics beginning a century later to assess the achievement of the play not in the context of Sheridan's time but in the context of the Restoration.

We have the evidence of Sheridan's "bungling reformation" of Congreve and Vanbrugh to guide our search for literary forebears, but we find in his works few if any verbal correspondences or convincing structural similarities to Restoration comedy. Further, Sheridan never wrote (or was quoted) about his literary debts. Yet, he was a conscious artist who, despite his oft-repeated claim that he never sat through the whole performance of any play, his own included, left us evidence especially in the cases of *The Critic* and *The School for Scandal* that he worked and reworked his own materials. These early materials themselves reflect literary and theatrical debts of a general nature and demonstrate not anxiety of influence but pride of craftsmanship. In the plays, as in the early jottings which were incorporated, reside situations and conventions of comedy from all times.

Schoolboy notebooks containing sketches of scenes which were shaped into the final version of *The School for Scandal* survive to this day. (Tom Moore printed generous portions in 1825, Cecil Price these and others in 1973.) In "The Slanderers" and "The Teazles" (as the two most developed portions have been called) Sheridan outlined characters and exchanges of a score or more lines which, reworked, became Joseph and Charles and Lady Sneerwell and the meetings of the Scandalous College and Sir Peter and Lady Teazle's "daily jangles." Probably composed in Sheridan's Bath years (before August 1772), the sketches are as unlike the final as "the block to the statue, or the grub to the butterfly," to quote Moore about one characterization. But in these sketches is the cynicism of the Restoration and the convolution of Jonson and Fletcher as well as a generous imagination and a faltering but occasionally firm comic touch. When he came to amalgamate the sketches into *The School for Scandal*,

John Philip Kemble as Rolla in the first production of Pizarro

Sheridan sacrificed coarseness, uncertainty, melodrama, cynicism, and diffuseness to satiric focus, wit, and sure-handed portrayal of good nature.

For the first time in his play-writing career, Sheridan focused his satire on palpable social institutions as well as general human frailties. Witty abuse of those present or absent has characterized comedy of all eras and reached brilliance in the Restoration, but the Georgian period joined the love of gossip and ridicule to print publication. Journalism, whose birth many place in 1702 with the commencement of the first daily newspaper in England, was now in its adolescence and like a mischievous teenager had discovered the public's voracious appetite for scandalmongering. "The Paragraphs you say, Mr. Snake, were all inserted?" asks Lady Sneerwell in the first line of the play. In the 1760s and 1770s, unsubstantiated rumors and malicious surmise occupied the columns of British journals in the form of brief paragraphs, the names of the individuals masquerading with first and last initials interspersed by asterisks or dashes; the younger "Mr. S******n,"

"Miss L****y," and "Captain M*****s" had thus appeared in Bath newspapers during the eventful courtship. One monthly featured a particularly vicious column in which facing silhouette portraits of a man and a woman, identified by pseudonyms or initials, preceded a description of their presumed relationship. Mrs. Clackit, says Snake, has caused more than one "Tête-à Tête in the Town and Country Magazine—when the Parties perhaps have never seen each other's Faces before in the course of their Lives." Sheridan's was not the first satiric attack on these practices; references to "paragraphs" form large and small parts of a half dozen Georgian comedies before *The School for Scandal,* and scurrilous journalists like Snake appear in several, most particularly Colman's Spatter in *The English Merchant* (1767), who bears the same name as Sheridan's early version of Snake in "The Slanderers."

Sheridan's originality was to dramatize the agents of scandal and slander more vividly than any purely decorative comic wits or would-be wits had been represented since the time of Congreve. Sir Benjamin Backbite, "the prince of pink heels" in his first portrayal, Mr. Crabtree, and Mrs. Candour appear only together and only in three scenes; but these appearances provide the badinage upon which much of Sheridan's playwriting reputation for wit is based. What is curious about their roles as the principal agents of the comedy's satire is the process through which the audience is put by them. Lady Teazle's head (if not her heart) is turned by her misunderstanding of the social fashion of London. Like her, the audience is attracted to the quick-paced malice of the Scandal School on its first appearance, to the inventiveness of sneer, the imputation of weakness, and the innuendo of sexual frailty. When the Scandalous College meets a second time and Lady Teazle participates so gaily and maliciously, the audience may not note how her wit exceeds theirs or how Sir Peter's sly ripostes provide increasing distance and hence some objectivity. But by their third and last appearance—at Sir Peter's house following the fall of the screen—they have become more the objects than the agents of satire. Possessed of misinformation and inclined (like Fag in *The Rivals*) to fabricating elaborately circumstantial accounts rather than presenting simple forged bills, the Scandalous College now appears ridiculous in itself and a principal cause of the misunderstandings among people for whom we have come to care. The audience undergoes the same process of learning by which Lady Teazle is changed: attraction to fashionable vice, doubt, and finally enlightened, experiential rejection. Maria's wish to be granted a "double Portion of Dullness" rather than participate in slander and Sir Peter's sarcastic cautions about Lady Teazle's "charming set of acquaintance" cannot effect the profound change in attitude toward gossip and malice that the slanderers themselves bring about.

This delicate dramatic problem challenged the young playwright even more than the eternal May-and-December story of Sir Peter and Lady Teazle. In the early version he toyed with a harsh cuckolding story like Geoffrey Chaucer's "Miller's Tale" and Wycherley's *Country Wife* (1675), but in the final version he sought and achieved the amiable tone of Georgian comedy. Lady Teazle learns to trust her heart, not the fashion, and Sir Peter learns to be less the father and more the husband of his young bride. To effect their mutual adjustments they must suffer considerable embarrassment, it is true, but they are no Pinchwife and Margery. As late as 1804, when he read the role of Sir Peter to an actor taking over from Thomas King, Sheridan still rejected a picture of Sir Peter as an "old fretful dotard" to be harshly chastened.

The greatest dramatic challenge, however, lay in handling the Cain-and-Abel story. Here there were three problems: how to make Joseph Surface evil but still entertaining; how to make Charles Surface culpable yet charming, essentially virtuous but not dull; and how to maximize satisfaction in the long-expected and desired reversal of fortune. Two of these problems Henry Fielding faced and overcame in *Tom Jones* (1749), the eighteenth century's greatest story of sibling rivalry. But Fielding did not face in his novel the dramatist's difficulty of portraying evil palpably before an audience without slipping into melodrama. (It is useful to know that Fielding's unperformed stage comedy on a similar theme, *The Fathers*, may have been in Sheridan's hands before the appearance of *The School for Scandal*. Sheridan would produce the play at Drury Lane on 30 November 1778, and his autograph corrections may be found in the manuscript sent to the lord chamberlain for licensing before its performance.)

Sheridan solved the first problem with the same techniques he had used in *The Rivals* and *St. Patrick's Day*; he chose a verbal characterizing device, in this case the "sentiment," not only to make Joseph entertaining but to expose him simultaneously. When Joseph utters such epigrams as "to smile at the jest which plants a Thorn in another's Breast is to become a principal in the Mischief," he expresses what he never practices and calls into doubt the motives of others who speak such "scraps of morality" and pretend to such elevation of thought and feeling. Thus, he too becomes object as well as agent of attack. And his "sentiments" join with false logic, and the dramatic soliloquy (allowed to no other character in the comedy but Sir Peter) amplifies the falseness of sentiment to maximize the contrast between Joseph's surface appearance and his real motives. Joseph becomes a comic Iago; and, like the other comic villains Mosca, Volpone, and Tartuffe, because he is complex and intelligent he is curiously attractive, even though his eventual downfall brings long-awaited pleasure.

The second problem—making Charles attractive yet mildly culpable—Sheridan solved in two ways: by keeping Charles off the stage for the first half of the representation and by characterizing him quickly but deftly, if flatly, by means

"Pizarro Contemplating over the Product of His New Peruvian Mine," caricature of Sheridan by James Gilray, 4 June 1799. By drawing an analogy between the playwright and the title character in his new, highly successful play, Gilray was not only commenting on Sheridan's reaction to the proceeds from it but also suggesting that his political attitudes were more like Pizarro's than those of the play's patriotic Peruvian general, Rolla.

of the very virtues constantly opposed to the vices of the schemers and of the Scandal School. For two-and-a-half acts we see Joseph, the calumniator, and Sir Peter, Joseph's dupe, brand Charles as spendthrift and prodigal, and though we mistrust Joseph's reports and discount Sir Peter's blind acceptance, we cannot make the final judgment ourselves. In this choice to keep Charles offstage lay peril lest he seem helpless or deserving of blame when he finally did appear. (Contrast Goldsmith's portrayal of Honeywood in *The Good-Natured Man* [1768] to see mismanagement of a somewhat similar dramatic problem.) When Charles does take the stage, in the eighth and ninth scenes of this fourteen-scene comedy, he immediately establishes himself as a hearty, vital, honest, plain-dealing young fellow, one who likes his wine but does not get drunk or abusive, one who gambles with money (offstage) but not with others' reputations, one who would sell the family silver and portraits but not the image of his

benefactor. If sentimentality is a failure of feeling, then the lines in which Charles bluffly refuses to sell "that ill looking little fellow over the settee" because "hang it, I'll not part with poor Noll—The Old Fellow has been very good to me, and Egad I'll keep his Picture, while I've a Room to put it in" show that feeling supersedes rationality. Yet, they provide one means of maximizing the contrasts of dissimulation, prudential hypocrisy, avarice, and casuistry with plain dealing, honesty, familial affection, generous benevolence, and gratitude. Joseph is one pole, Lady Teazle through her affectation of fashion an intermediate latitude, and Charles is the other and true pole, the lodestar. Like Tom Jones he has faults; but unlike Tom's, his are not sexual. Like Tom and Blifil, Charles and Joseph work two sides of a sentimental street.

And through this contrast, Sheridan solved his third dramatic problem: how to maximize pleasure in the inevitable comic reversal of fortune. By keeping the terms of his equation focused solely upon truth in conduct and generosity of spirit he kept from view the unknowns of self-deceit and sexual promiscuity. By bringing together both recognition and reversal at one place, the screen scene, four-fifths of the way through his play, he found a comic solution discovered as elegantly only by Molière in *Tartuffe* (1664) and Oscar Wilde in *The Importance of Being Earnest* (1895).

Dramatically, the two most important things about the long third scene of the fourth act of *The School for Scandal* are its placement within the three strands of plot and its joining of the reversal of fortunes with the revelation of essential character. In the plot, this "screen scene" comes early, though it clearly anticipates the working out of the comedy of self-adjustment (most of which occurs offstage) and the comedy of merit rewarded (much of which involves only five or six lines of affirmation) while foreshadowing the final scenes of the punitive comedy of exposure in the twelfth and fourteenth segments. As drama, the screen scene reflects three separate movements: Joseph's casuistry and Lady Teazle's temptation; Sir Peter's further duping by Joseph; and Charles's insistence upon open and honest disclosure of the truth, even to the "little milliner" supposedly behind the screen. When Charles's desire for openness and plain dealing leads to the exposure of Lady Teazle and hence of Joseph, all dramatic questions have been answered. The audience knows that Sir Oliver will be confirmed in his assessment of both nephews; that Charles will probably be rewarded with Maria; that Sir Peter will become comfortable with his decision to permit his young wife a separate maintenance (that is, an allowance, not a divorce); and that Joseph's scandalmongering friends will lose their capacity to do damage to the relationships of the Teazle and Surface families. Sheridan keeps the story going with three or four minireversals; but all significant terms of the equation have been identified, and the rest is mere ciphering.

Few disputed the artistry of *The School for Scandal* in its time. It has been presented on stage to paying audiences every year since its premiere. Henry James and Bernard Shaw, a century after its first appearance, found fault with its sentimentality. Henry Fielding's is the greater and more serious exploration of one aspect of the comedy's subject, and one cannot dispute the essentially uncomplicated view of human nature and human relationships presented by *The School*

for Scandal. But a century after James and Shaw, critics have rediscovered Sheridan's greatest play and found it worthy of serious attention.

With *The School for Scandal* Sheridan answered the expectations many had for his management of Drury Lane after Garrick. There were detractors, including his irascible and intemperate father, Thomas Sheridan, who remarked: "Talk about the merit of Dick's comedy, there's nothing to it. He had but to dip in his own heart and find there the characters both of Joseph and Charles." But most welcomed Sheridan's greatest comedy and hoped for more. In the 1777-1778 season there was nothing except Thomas Sheridan's inept direction. In the 1778-1779 season came two minor pieces: an entertainment called *The Camp* (15 October 1778) and the dramatic *Verses to the Memory of Garrick* (11 March 1779). *The Camp* exploited fears of a French invasion consequent upon that nation's recognizing the American rebels as the legitimate government of England's North American colonies. Home guards had mobilized, fashionable ladies joined them in their safe camps, and stories could be told. Garrick had discovered one Philippe de Loutherbourg, a scene painter and stage designer of great talent, and Sheridan used that talent to popular effect, particularly in this pastiche on military mobilization. Four months later Sheridan rose to the unhappy occasion offered by Garrick's death at sixty-one to produce at Drury Lane *Verses to the Memory of Garrick,* an elegy performed by the tragic actress Mrs. Yates. Sheridan himself headed Garrick's bier as the chief mourner.

A pastiche and a monody might carry one season during which Sheridan wrestled to gain full control of Drury Lane. But something more substantial must answer the expectations of the London audiences: hence, *The Critic* (30 September 1779), a long afterpiece first performed following a representation of *Hamlet* and destined to replace George Villiers, second Duke of Buckingham's *The Rehearsal* (1671) in the repertoire.

The Critic has no plot. Instead, it blends a variety of briefly drawn situations to burlesque the theater, theatrical literature, and the audience itself. In the first act, theatrical hangers-on Mr. and Mrs. Dangle discuss news of the Theatres Royal, receive critic Sneer, thin-skinned author Sir Fretful Plagiary (played as a caricature of Georgian dramatist Richard Cumberland in the original performances), a troupe of Italian singers for audition, and Mr. Puff, author of "The Spanish Armada," a tragedy then supposed to be in rehearsal. This first act, set in the Dangles' lodgings, recalls the opening scenes of *The School for Scandal* and *Love for Love* as a mannered presentation of interesting characters who, in Sheridan's and in Congreve's comedies, would become involved in increasingly complicated situations to be unraveled only by a startling and satisfying denouement. But the flavor of this appetizer bears little relationship to the main course of the farce, acts 2 and 3, in which Mr. Dangle and Mr. Sneer observe a rehearsal of Puff's play, comment upon it sardonically, and serve only to direct the audience's attention to the most egregious of its absurdities. (Why Puff is the author of "The Spanish Armada" rather than Sir Fretful Plagiary, presented so brilliantly in the first act and then excused, cannot be satisfactorily explained. But Puff's original portrayer, Thomas King, had in real life presented a grand entertainment on the same topic during the preceding summer of 1779 at Sadler's Wells, where he was the manager-impresario.)

Theatrical self-reflection—drama which calls attention to itself as drama—intrigued Sheridan. Five years or so before *The Rivals* he and school friend Nathaniel Brassey Halhed had projected a farce on the Amphitryon myth using a rehearsal format, and among Sheridan's papers Moore found and reprinted numerous scenes and sketches about the theater and theatrical craftsmanship. Georgian audiences, too, evidently relished this inversion of dramatic convention, given the record of plays about the theater in the repertoire. Four entertainments and burlesques from the 1770s probably influenced Sheridan's final design, most particularly Garrick's *A Peep behind the Curtain* (1767). But his design surpassed all other examples in the repertoire, including Buckingham's perennially popular (and constantly updated) *The Rehearsal*, and two centuries passed before *The Critic* itself would be replaced as the quintessential play about the theater by the comedies of Tom Stoppard.

That *The Critic* endured so long surprises in light of its topicality, for it is every bit as timely as *The Camp*. On 18 June 1779 Spain declared war on England; by 16 August 1779 reports circulated that French and Spanish fleets had slipped by a British squadron into the Channel. Newspapers reprinted Queen Elizabeth's 1588 speech to the army at Tilbury Fort as fears of a new Span-ish armada mounted. If invasion anxiety lessened as autumn approached, the memory was still fresh in late October.

Moreover, Sheridan tied *The Critic* to numerous other local phenomena. The manager who "writes himself" is Sheridan, of course, and Mrs. Dangle resembles Eliza Sheridan, who was probably aiding her husband in the management of the King's Opera House, which Dick and Covent Garden manager Thomas Harris had recently acquired. The actors took occasion to mimic their peers: Dangle was recognized as Thomas Vaughan, author of a Sheridan-directed farce, theatrical amateur, and "dangler" about the greenroom; Miss Pope's rendition of Tilburina took off Mrs. Ann Crawford's tragic acting; and young Bannister as Don Ferolo Whiskerandos mimicked William Smith in the role of Richard III. Sheridan had gained a reputation for writing "puffs" for Drury Lane, and Puff's "puff direct" may be a "puff preliminary" for Elizabeth Griffith's *The Times*, a comedy then in rehearsal. And everyone recognized in William Parsons's portrayal of Sir Fretful Plagiary a caricature of the sentimental dramatist, Richard Cumberland, whose tragedy *The Battle of Hastings* Sheridan had produced 24 January 1778.

A favorite but probably apocryphal story places Cumberland with his children at a performance of *The Critic*. As the audience laughs at Sir Fretful, so do the younger Cumberlands. "Keep still, you little dunces, there is nothing to laugh at!" says the father, pinching them soundly. Hearing a report of Cumberland's response, Sheridan remarked that he could not understand why Cumberland would not laugh at his comedy: after all, said Sheridan, I laughed a great deal at his tragedy.

But if *The Critic* is time bound because of its local and domestic references, its art arises from its timelessness. Unlike its predecessors, *The Critic* burlesques not specific examples of theatrical literature but serious drama in general. Few if any lines in "The Spanish Armada" echo stage tragedies of the Georgian period. Instead, Sheridan focuses on ineptitude in dramatic craftsmanship divorced from any time or place. And not content merely to attack poor plotting, characterization, and dialogue, Sheridan includes inception, production, and reception as well as theatrical literature. This comprehensiveness is why the first act, so different in tone and focus, is an integral part of the farce. It is why Dangle is the amateur of dubious influence, unsure tastes, and uncer-

Hester Ogle Sheridan with her son, Charles Brinsley Sheridan (engraving based on a painting by John Hoppner)

tain loyalties; why Sneer is the cynical, self-interested critic; why Sir Fretful every thin-skinned playwright and Puff every spectacle monger.

One key to the informing principle of *The Critic,* to burlesque the theater in all aspects, is to be found in its grand finale, full of "magnificence! battle! noise! and procession!" The presentation of the defeat of the Spanish Armada by the English fleet, chorused by the patriotic song "Britons Strike Home" and the procession of *"all the English rivers and their tributaries,"* evoked surprised delight. And early critics lavishly praised de Loutherbourg's scenes and effects for their realism, not their mockery of theatrical effect. Thus the audience, with its appetite for spectacle, becomes the unspoken object of satire, satisfied with noise, battle, and claptrap. What better conclusion to five years of building a theatrical ca-

reer dependent upon the fickle tastes of theater-goers?

When *The Critic* appeared on 30 October 1779 Sheridan was just twenty-eight years old. It would be his last comedy and his last important dramatic work. On 12 September 1780 he was elected member of Parliament for Stafford. Horace Walpole remarked in October 1781 that "Sheridan has the opera and all the nation to regulate, and some plays to write." He would be a legislator for thirty-two years, representing Stafford and other constituencies, until in 1812 when Stafford at last turned him out of Parliament. Sheridan, M.P., was the Sheridan of his own devising, his own ambition. He returned once to dramatic literature with an adaptation of the translation of a translation—August von Kotzebue's *Die Spanier in Peru* (1796), based on Jean-François Marmontel's *Les Incas* (1777)—for *Pizarro; A Tragedy*

(1799). The major interest of *Pizarro* is not literary but theatrical and political—and it was a crowd-pleasing, money-generating success. John Loftis (1977) has written convincingly about the oratorical extravaganza.

Throughout his busy career as politician and his distracted management of Drury Lane, Sheridan was constantly projecting a new play, particularly when money was tight. Fragments and titles survive—"Affectation," "The Statesman." There is a grand entertainment or two like *The Camp,* one from 1794, two years after the death of Elizabeth on 28 June 1792 and shortly before his marriage to Hester Jane Ogle on 27 April 1795. Michael Kelly, a talented musician in Sheridan's employ at Drury Lane, who for thirty-five years maintained his friendship, tells of the king and queen chatting with Sheridan after a performance of *The School for Scandal,* probably sometime in the late 1780s or early 1790s. King George III praised the comedy but professed greater affection for *The Rivals.* The queen asked when they could expect another comic work from Sheridan's pen, to which he replied that he "expected very shortly to finish" one. Kelly took the occasion later to rehearse the conversation; you will not write another comedy because you are afraid. Afraid of whom? asked Sheridan. "You are afraid of the author of the 'School for Scandal,'" said the musician.

During the last four decades of his life, Sheridan was no further from the theater than his literary friends were from their publishers and his aristocratic friends were from their landed estates. Drury Lane was, after all, *his* estate. It provided him with income and with capital upon which to borrow. It was a great investment of which nearly every financier wanted a piece, until Sheridan's inability to manage it made clear how very overextended was the investment. Still, Drury Lane permitted Sheridan to buy several expensive elections, according to the practices of his day, and it provided him the capital (twelve thousand pounds) to purchase Polesden Lacey, a 341-acre estate with a seventeenth-century mansion, after his marriage to Hester in 1795, thus bringing into his life the "dirty acres" his chronically poor parents had never enjoyed. Polesden was settled upon his and "Hecca's" child, Charles Brinsley, born 14 January 1796, and although Sheridan died a man beset by bailiffs, he always had the small profits of Polesden to supplement his other schemes.

Many stories are told about the later years—his sexual adventures, his excessive drinking, his financial profligacy. Each tendency was clear even in his younger days. Eliza complained to her closest confidants of Dick's philandering and probably took the only revenge in her power by having an affair with Lord Edward Fitzgerald a year or two before her death. Sheridan's complicated financial transactions rode an erratic course from the heights of extravagance to the valleys of penury. And though stories of Sheridan's drunkenness multiplied as he aged, his behavior was not uncharacteristic of his age. But, always, even in his later years, we hear of a Sheridan who was charming and witty, who at forty-three with a red nose and ravaged countenance could still win the hand of the young daughter of the dean of Winchester, become in their mutual baby talk her "poor Dan," and enjoy a second twenty-year marriage. It is a Sheridan who brushes off his creditors with humor. Hazlitt reports on one contrivance: a dun brings him a bill, often presented before, and complains of its soiled and tattered condition. "I tell you what I'd advise you to do, my friend," said Sheridan. "Take it home and write it on parchment." In another story an agent demands interest for a long overdue bill. Sheridan responds, "My dear sir, you know it is not my *interest* to pay the *principal;* nor is it my *principle* to pay the *interest.*"

It is Sheridan the member of Parliament about whom most stories are told. The famous "Begum Speech" (1787), his exhaustive and exhausting attack upon Warren Hastings, administrator of the British East India Company, excited his contemporaries. In that two-day speech, Sheridan, M.P., praised historian Edward Gibbon, then recanted later—"Did I say 'luminous'? I meant 'voluminous.' " On another occasion Sheridan, M.P., said on the floor about a fellow that "the gentleman owes his facts to his imagination and his jests to his commonplace book." Sheridan, M.P., told Charles James Fox that while it was good to take the bull of opportunity by the horns, "you need not have drove him into the room" first. Sheridan, M.P., extemporaneously put Lord Belgrave to rights on an exact quotation of Demosthenes, but there is reason to think that he imitated the sounds of Greek without the substance, thereby silencing every member who could not understand the language—that is, the whole house. Sheridan, M.P., it was who on the night of 24 February 1809 sat in the Piazza Coffee House watching the Drury Lane theater burn

A contemporary engraving of the fire that destroyed Sheridan's Drury Lane theater

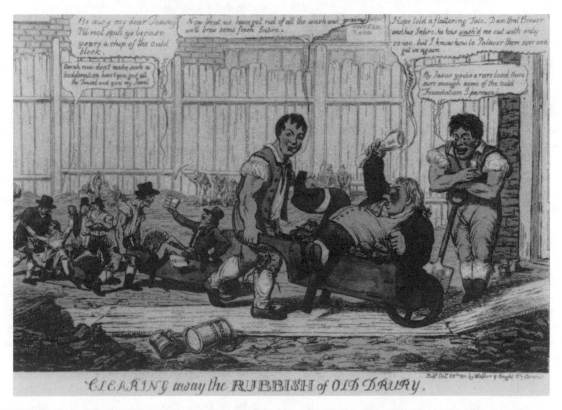

Samuel Whitbread, who rebuilt the Drury Lane theater and bought out the Sheridan family's interest, set out to convince potential investors not to associate his enterprise with the Sheridans'. Charles Williams's 1811 caricature shows Sheridan in a wheelbarrow of rubbish pushed by Whitbread, whose assistant follows with the playwright's son Thomas.

to the ground and remarked to a meddling inter-locutor, "A man may surely take a glass of wine by his own fireside."

And while Sheridan, M.P., Under-Secretary of State (1782), Secretary of the Treasury (1783), Navy Treasurer (1806) in the "Ministry of All Talents," lover of Lady Duncannon and others of the most beautiful women of his day, and doting father to his elder son, Tom, and his young son, Charles, may seem a queer candidate for elevation to the peerage of great writers, his production as a young man of the theater beggars comparison with any of his contemporaries and with most of his successors. Byron put it well:

> Whatever Sheridan has done or chosen to do has been, *par excellence,* always the *best* of its kind. He has written the *best* comedy (*School for Scandal*) [,] the *best* drama [*The Duenna*] (in my mind, far before that St. Giles's lampoon, the Beggar's Opera), the best farce (the *Critic*—it is only too good for a farce), and the best Address (Monologue on Garrick), and, to crown it all, delivered the very best Oration (the famous Begum Speech) ever conceived or heard in this country.

Byron wrote these words in his journal only three years before Sheridan died in London on 7 July 1816 in the sixty-fifth year of his life. Sheridan expired in poverty, according to many accounts with bailiffs around him to protect their clients' interests should some money or goods be sent to succor the fading playwright-politician. Six days after his death his remains were interred at Westminster Abbey, in the Poets' Corner, the bier followed by numerous noble acquaintances and friends including two princes of the blood royal. Byron's appreciation of Sheridan's contribution to English cultural history was shared by most of their contemporaries.

But Byron could not have our perspective, which rates Sheridan as the finest British playwright between Shakespeare and Shaw. Sheridan eschewed the didactic, the melodramatic, the coldly cynical, and the violently satiric, choosing instead the middle, good-natured course of his time. He strove for original characterization, tight construction, and brilliant dialogue. He never achieved the poetic unity or intellectual penetration of Congreve, but he never sought them. He boosted the fresh boisterousness of Farquhar and avoided the cold cynicism of Vanbrugh, the tears of Steele in his decline, and the coincidences of Goldsmith.

Always Sheridan's subject matter reflected his own experience: young love, the battle of youth with age, the natural conflicts of the sexes, and (after he became a member of it) high society. In the five brief years of his active involvement as playwright he seems to have mellowed a bit as he moved from low comedy to high. But he always found self-deception to be central to the human condition.

Sheridan's plots are often so complex that readers find them hard to follow, but they work wonderfully in the theater. In that five-year burst of comic creativity Sheridan eschewed the bifurcated plot forms of his contemporaries, avoided simple coincidence, put aside duels and elopements as resolution devices, and chose instead (in *The School for Scandal*) the full unification of plot lines that point toward a single comic catastrophe in which recognition and reversal are one. Character for its own sake—as in *The Rivals* and *The Duenna*—yields to character for the drama's sake in *The School for Scandal.*

Yet Sheridan was a sentimentalist. Beneath all his comic excoriations of folly there flows a tolerance of a human nature which he believes, finally, will support social good rather than individual self-interest. Well-intentioned folks, aided by a benevolent providence, will expel the vicious from society.

Sheridan's characters are complicated psychologically only in *The School for Scandal.* Before that play, and sometimes in that play, he created stage types whose characteristics we can all recognize as part of the theatrical context rather than as natural human beings. And his dialogue for these characters represents his greatest achievement. On the one hand it marks each person as unique: it is "characteristic," to cite his contemporaries' praise. On the other it is complex and original—not just epigrammatic like Congreve but brilliantly different—witness Malaprop, Acres, Joseph Surface. We remember these characters more than the comedies in which they appear.

Sheridan's comic theatrical achievement everywhere relies upon the technique of drawing the audience in as a part of the unfolding presentation. As auditors we do not sit upon the sidelines; instead, we are privileged to know much more than the players and the cheerleaders. We understand the "comedy of situation" of which we have been partners. We revel in the "how" of reaching agreement more than the "what" of the action. We pride ourselves upon the knowledge that resolution will occur because of what we know.

William Hazlitt understood Sheridan's achievement well: "Whatever he touched he adorned with all the ease, grace, and brilliancy of his style.... He was assuredly a man of first-rate talents."

Letters:

The Letters of Richard Brinsley Sheridan, 3 volumes, edited by C. J. L. Price (Oxford: Clarendon Press, 1966).

Bibliography:

Jack D. Durant, *Richard Brinsley Sheridan: A Reference Guide* (Boston: G. K. Hall, 1981).

Biographies:

Thomas Moore, *Memoirs of the Life of the Right Honourable Richard Brinsley Sheridan* (London: Longman, Hurst, Rees, Orme, Brown & Green, 1825);

W. Fraser Rae, *Sheridan, A Biography* (London: Richard Bentley, 1896);

Walter Sichel, *Sheridan* (London: Constable, 1909);

R. Crompton Rhodes, *Harlequin Sheridan* (Oxford: Blackwell, 1933);

Stanley Ayling, *A Portrait of Sheridan* (London: Constable, 1985);

James Morwood, *The Life and Works of Richard Brinsley Sheridan* (Edinburgh: Scottish Academic Press, 1985).

References:

Mark S. Auburn, "The Pleasures of Sheridan's *The Rivals*: A Critical Study in the Light of Stage History," *Modern Philology,* 72 (February 1975): 256-271;

Auburn, *Sheridan's Comedies: Their Contexts and Achievements* (Lincoln: University of Nebraska Press, 1977);

F. W. Bateson, "The Application of Thought to an Eighteenth-Century Text: *The School for Scandal,*" in *Evidence in Literary Scholarship. Essays in Memory of James Marshall Osborn,* edited by René Wellek and Alvaro Ribeiro (Oxford: Clarendon Press, 1979), pp. 321-335;

Peter Davidson, ed., *Sheridan: Comedies* (London: Macmillan, 1986);

Christian Deelman, "The Original Cast of *The School for Scandal,*" *Review of English Studies,* new series 13 (1962): 257-266;

Joseph W. Donohue, Jr., "Sheridan's *Pizarro:* Natural Religion and the Artificial Hero," in his *Dramatic Character in the English Romantic Age* (Princeton: Princeton University Press, 1970), pp. 125-156;

Jean Dulck, *Les Comédies de R. B. Sheridan: Etude Littéraire* (Paris: Didier, 1962);

Jack D. Durant, "The Moral Focus of *The School for Scandal,*" *South Atlantic Bulletin,* 31 (November 1972): 44-53;

Durant, "Prudence, Providence, and the Direct Road of Wrong: *The School for Scandal* and Sheridan's Westminster Hall Speech," *Studies in Burke and His Time,* 15 (Spring 1974): 241-251;

Durant, *Richard Brinsley Sheridan* (Boston: G. K. Hall, 1975);

Durant, "Sheridan's 'Royal Sanctuary': A Key to *The Rivals,*" *Ball State University Forum,* 14 (Winter 1973): 23-30;

Durant, "Truth for Sheridan: The Biographical Dilemma," in *A Fair Day in the Affections: Literary Essays in Honor of Robert B. White,* edited by Durant and Thomas Hester (Raleigh, N.C.: Winston, 1980), pp. 119-130;

Roger Fiske, "The Linleys 1775-1780," in his *English Theatre Music in the Eighteenth Century* (Oxford: Oxford University Press, 1973), pp. 413-421;

Fiske, "A Score for *The Duenna,*" *Music and Letters,* 42 (April 1961): 132-141;

Arthur Friedman, "Aspects of Sentimentalism in Eighteenth-Century Literature," in *The Augustan Milieu: Essays Presented to Louis A. Landa,* edited by Henry Knight Miller, Eric Rothstein, and G. S. Rousseau (Oxford: Clarendon Press, 1970), pp. 247-261;

Robert D. Hume, "Goldsmith and Sheridan and the Supposed Revolution of 'Laughing' against 'Sentimental' Comedy," in *Studies in Change and Revolution,* edited by Paul J. Korshin (Menston, U.K.: Scolar Press, 1972), pp. 237-276;

J. R. De J. Jackson, "The Importance of Witty Dialogue in *The School for Scandal,*" *Modern Language Notes,* 76 (November 1961): 601-607;

Henry James, "*The School for Scandal* at the Boston Museum," *Atlantic Monthly,* 34 (December 1874): 754-757;

Philip K. Jason, "A Twentieth-Century Response to *The Critic,*" *Theatre Survey,* 15 (May 1974): 51-58;

A. N. Kaul, "A Note on Sheridan," in his *The Action of English Comedy: Studies in the Encounter of Abstraction and Experience from Shakespeare to Shaw* (New Haven: Yale University Press, 1970), pp. 131-149;

Louis Kronenberger, "Sheridan," in his *The Thread of Laughter: Chapters on English Stage Comedy from Jonson to Maugham* (New York: Knopf, 1952), pp. 191-202;

Leonard J. Leff, "The Disguise Motif in Sheridan's *The School for Scandal*," *Educational Theatre Journal*, 22 (December 1970): 350-360;

Leff, "Sheridan and Sentimentalism," *Restoration and 18th Century Theatre Research*, 12 (May 1973): 36-48;

John Loftis, *Sheridan and the Drama of Georgian England* (Cambridge, Mass.: Harvard University Press, 1977);

Oliver Lutaud, "Des acharniens d'Aristophane au critique de Sheridan," *Les Langues Modernes*, 60 (1966): 433-438;

Samuel L. Macey, "Sheridan: The Last of the Great Theatrical Satirists," *Restoration and 18th Century Theatre Research*, 9 (November 1970): 35-45;

R. D. Nussbaum, "Poetry and Music in *The Duenna*," *Westerly* (June 1963): 58-63;

Cecil Price, "Pursuing Sheridan," in *Evidence in Literary Scholarship. Essays in Memory of James Marshall Osborn*, edited by René Wellek and Alvaro Ribeiro (Oxford: Clarendon Press, 1979), pp. 309-320;

Richard Little Purdy, Introduction to *The Rivals, A Comedy. As it was first Acted at the Theatre-Royal in Covent-Garden. Written by Richard Brinsley Sheridan, Esq. Edited from the Larpent MS.* (Oxford: Clarendon Press, 1935), pp. xi-lii;

Allan Rodway, "Goldsmith and Sheridan: Satirists of Sentiment," *Renaissance and Modern Essays Presented to Vivian de Sola Pinto*, edited by G. R. Hibbard (New York: Barnes & Noble, 1966), pp. 65-72;

Andrew Schiller, "*The School for Scandal:* The Restoration Unrestored," *PMLA*, 71 (September 1956): 694-704;

George Bernard Shaw, "The Second Dating of Sheridan," *Saturday Review*, 81 (1896): 648-650;

Dane Farnsworth Smith, "*The Critic*, Its Sources, and Its Satire," in *The Critics in the Audience of the London Theatres from Buckingham to Sheridan: A Study of Neoclassicism in the Playhouse, 1671-1779* (Albuquerque: University of New Mexico Press, 1953), pp. 115-143;

Arthur C. Sprague, "In Defence of a Masterpiece: *The School for Scandal* Reexamined," *English Studies Today*, third series, edited by G. E. Duthie (Edinburgh, 1964), pp. 125-135;

Garland F. Taylor, "Richard Brinsley Sheridan's *The Duenna*," Ph.D. dissertation, Yale University, 1940;

Linda V. Troost, "The Characterizing Power of Song in Sheridan's *The Duenna*," *Eighteenth-Century Studies*, 20 (Winter 1986-1987): 153-172.

Papers:
Sheridan materials are scattered throughout England and the United States, both at research libraries and in private hands. Yale, Georgetown, Harvard, and Princeton University libraries house particularly rich collections. Cecil Price in *Letters* and in *Dramatic Works* details holdings known to him through 1973.

Tobias Smollett

(March 1721 - 17 September 1771)

This entry was updated by Jerry C. Beasley (University of Delaware) from his entry in
DLB 39: British Novelists, 1660-1800: Part Two.

See also the Smollett entry in DLB 104: British Prose Writers, 1660-1800: Second Series.

BOOKS: *The Tears of Scotland* (London, 1746?);

Advice: A Satire (London: Printed for M. Cooper, 1746);

Reproof: A Satire. The Sequel to Advice (London: Printed for W. Owen & M. Cooper, 1747);

The Adventures of Roderick Random, 2 volumes (London: Printed for J. Osborn, 1748; Philadelphia: Mathew Carey, 1794);

The Regicide; or, James the First, of Scotland: A Tragedy, anonymous (London: J. Osborn & A. Millar, 1749);

The Adventures of Peregrine Pickle, in Which Are Included Memoirs of a Lady of Quality, 4 volumes (London: Printed for the author & sold by D. Wilson, 1751; New York: R. M'Dermut & D. D. Arden, 1813);

An Essay on the External Use of Water in a Letter to Dr. ****, with Particular Remarks upon the Present Method of Using the Mineral Waters at Bath in Somersetshire, and a Plan for Rendering Them More Safe, Agreeable and Efficacious (London: Printed for M. Cooper & sold by D. Wilson & Leake, 1752);

A FAITHFUL NARRATIVE of the base and inhuman Arts That were lately practised upon the Brain of Habbakkuk Hilding, Justice, Who Now Lies at His House in Covent-Garden, in a Deplorable State of Lunacy: A Dreadful Monument of False Friendship and Delusion, as Drawcansir Alexander, Fencing Master and Philomath (London: Printed for J. Sharp, 1752);

The Adventures of Ferdinand Count Fathom, 2 volumes (London: Printed for W. Johnston, 1753; New York: By A. Paul for D. Huntington, 1816);

The Reprisal; or, The Tars of Old England: A Comedy of Two Acts (London: R. Baldwin, 1757);

A Complete History of England, Deduced from the Descent of Julius Caesar to the Treaty of Aix la Chapelle, 1748: Containing the Transactions of One Thousand Eight Hundred and Three Years, 4 volumes (London: James Rivington & James Fletcher, 1757-1758);

Continuation of the Complete History of England, 5 volumes (London: R. Baldwin, 1760-1765);

The Adventures of Sir Launcelot Greaves (2 volumes, London: Printed for J. Coote, 1762; 1 volume, Baltimore: Published by F. Lucas & A. Miltenberger, 1811);

Travels through France and Italy: Containing Observations on Character, Customs, Religion, Government, Police, Commerce, Arts and Antiquities, with a Particular Description of the Town, Territory and Climate of Nice; to which Is Added a Register of the Weather, kept during a Residence of Eighteen Months in that City, 2 volumes (London: Printed for R. Baldwin, 1766);

The History and Adventures of an Atom, 2 volumes (London: Printed for J. Almon, 1769);

The Expedition of Humphry Clinker (3 volumes, London: Printed for W. Johnston & B. Collins, 1771; 2 volumes, Boston: Published by Watson & Bangs, 1813);

Ode to Independence (Glasgow: Printed by Robert & Andrew Foulis, 1773).

Editions and Collections: *The Works of Tobias Smollett, M.D., with Memoirs of His Life*, 8 volumes, edited by John Moore (London: Printed for B. Law, J. Johnson, C. Dilly, G. G. & J. Robinson, R. Baldwin, A. Strahan, R. Faulder, W. Richardson, W. Lane, W. Lowndes, S. Hayes, G. & T. Wilkie, Ogilvy & Son, T. N. Longman, and Cadell, jun. & Davies, 1797);

The Works of Tobias Smollett, 12 volumes, edited by George Saintsbury (London: Gibbings, 1895-1903; Philadelphia: Lippincott, 1895-1903);

The Works of Tobias Smollett, 12 volumes, edited by W. E. Henley and Thomas Seccombe (London: Constable, 1899-1901; New York: Scribners, 1899-1901);

The Novels of Tobias Smollett, Shakespeare Head Edition, 11 volumes (Oxford: Blackwell, 1925-1926; Boston: Houghton Mifflin, 1925-1926);

Tobias Smollett, circa 1770 (portrait by an unknown Italian artist; National Portrait Gallery, London)

An Essay on the External Use of Water, edited by Claude E. Jones (Baltimore: Johns Hopkins Press, 1935);

Travels through France and Italy, introduction by Seccombe (London & New York: Oxford University Press, 1935);

The Adventures of Peregrine Pickle, edited by James L. Clifford (London: Oxford University Press, 1964); revised by Paul-Gabriel Boucé (Oxford: Oxford University Press, 1983);

The Expedition of Humphry Clinker, edited by Lewis M. Knapp (London: Oxford University Press, 1966); revised by Boucé (Oxford: Oxford University Press, 1984);

The Expedition of Humphry Clinker, edited by Angus Ross (Harmondsworth, U.K.: Penguin, 1967);

The Adventures of Ferdinand Count Fathom, edited by Damian Grant (London: Oxford University Press, 1971);

The Life and Adventures of Sir Launcelot Greaves, edited by David Evans (London: Oxford University Press, 1973);

Travels through France and Italy, edited by Frank Felsenstein (Oxford: Oxford University Press, 1979);

The Adventures of Roderick Random, edited by Boucé (London: Oxford University Press, 1979; revised edition, Oxford: Oxford University Press, 1981);

The Works of Tobias Smollett, Jerry C. Beasley, general editor (Athens: University of Georgia Press, 1988-);

The Life and Adventures of Sir Launcelot Greaves, edited by Peter Wagner (Harmondsworth, U.K.: Penguin, 1988);

The Adventures of Ferdinand Count Fathom, edited by Boucé (Harmondsworth, U.K.: Penguin, 1990).

OTHER: William Smellie, *A Treatise on the Theory and Practice of Midwifery,* edited by Smollett (London: Printed for D. Wilson & T. Durham, 1751);

Smellie, *A Collection of Cases and Observations in Midwifery,* edited by Smollett (London: Printed for D. Wilson & T. Durham, 1754);

Alexander Drummond, *Travels through Different Cities of Germany, Italy, Greece and Several Parts of Asia, as Far as the Banks of the Euphrates: In a Series of Letters,* edited by Smollett (London: Printed by W. Strahan for the author, 1754);

A Compendium of Authentic and Entertaining Voyages, Digested in a Chronological Series, 7 volumes, edited by Smollett (London: R. & J. Dodsley, 1756);

The Modern Part of an Universal History, by the Authors of the Ancient Part, 44 volumes, edited by Smollett (London: T. Osborn [etc.], 1759-1765);

Smellie, *A Collection of Preternatural Cases and Other Observations in Midwifery,* edited by Smollett (London: Printed for D. Wilson & T. Durham, 1764);

The Present State of All Nations: Containing a Geographical, Natural, Commercial, and Political History of All the Countries in the Known World, 8 volumes, edited by Smollett (London: Printed for R. Baldwin, W. Johnston, and Robinson & Roberts, 1768-1769).

TRANSLATIONS: Alain René Lesage, *The Adventures of Gil Blas of Santillane,* 4 volumes, translated by Smollett (London: J. Osborn, 1748; Baltimore: Published by Fielding Lucas, Jun., J. Cushing & J. & T. Vance, 1814);

Lesage, *The Devil upon Crutches,* 2 volumes, translated by Smollett (London: Printed by William Strahan for Osborn, 1750);

Select Essays on Commerce, Agriculture, Mines, Fisheries and Other Useful Subjects (London: Printed for D. Wilson & T. Durham, 1754; Philadelphia: Printed for Robert Bell, 1777);

The History and Adventures of the Renowned Don Quixote, Translated from the Spanish of Miguel de Cervantes Saavedra (2 volumes, London: T. Osborn, T. & T. Longman, R. Miller, C. Hitch & L. Hawes, J. Hodges, and J. & J. Rivington, 1755; 4 volumes, Philadelphia: John Conrad / Baltimore: M. & J. Conrad / Washington, D.C.: Rapin, Conrad, 1803);

The Works of M. de Voltaire, Translated from the French, with Notes, Historical and Critical, by Dr. Smollett and Others, translated by Smollett and Thomas Francklin (35 volumes, London: Printed for J. Newberry, R. Baldwin [etc.], 1761-1770; 6 volumes, New York: Derby & Jackson, 1859);

The Adventures of Telemachus, the Son of Ulysses, Translated from the French of Messire François Salignac de la Mothe Fénelon (London: S. Crowder, 1776).

Tobias Smollett has always been recognized as one of the truly great English novelists of the eighteenth century, the period during which the novel as it is known today emerged and was established as a significant new form of literary expression. But Smollett and his achievement—five ambitious and popular works of fiction published within a span of twenty-four years—have also been overshadowed by his most celebrated contemporaries and their masterpieces of storytelling. *Robinson Crusoe* (1719), *Clarissa* (1747-1748), *Tom Jones* (1749), and *Tristram Shandy* (1760-1767) have all enjoyed, almost without interruption, both critical acclaim and a devoted audience from the moment of their initial appearance in print; and Daniel Defoe, Samuel Richardson, Henry Fielding, and Laurence Sterne have been praised by important members of every generation since their own as men of huge talent, admirable accomplishment, and broad appeal to a variety of intelligent readers. Smollett has received the applause of many over the years, and critics have singled out his first and last novels— *Roderick Random* (1748) and *Humphry Clinker* (1771)—as particularly fine contributions to the early history of English prose fiction. But, since the height of his popularity in his own day, he has been less widely read than Defoe, Fielding, and the rest of his major contemporaries; and scholars, who have by no means entirely ne-

glected him, have until recently given him less attention than he has deserved.

Eminent Victorians condemned Smollett's coarseness, which they found far more objectionable than the bawdy earthiness of the authors of *Tom Jones* and *Tristram Shandy*. As late as the 1920s, critics who ought to have known better were still remarking that Smollett's books were unfit for young minds and should be kept out of schoolrooms. Never mind that a very respectable Charles Dickens read them as a boy, and not only grew up uncorrupted but actually learned from them some of his own most important novelistic attitudes and techniques. The critical Grundyism of the last century seriously undermined Smollett's just position as a writer, and its effects were long felt. Since the 1950s, however, thanks largely to the loving efforts of Lewis M. Knapp, Smollett and his novels have enjoyed a considerable revival of interest and enthusiasm. Following Knapp's definitive biography of 1949, other scholars and critics have produced many articles and books devoted to Smollett's life and works. Nearly half of the more than three hundred pages of entries in Robert Donald Spector's comprehensive 1980 bibliography of writings about Smollett since 1746 are given over to the period from 1950 to 1978. Spector's range of coverage is worldwide, as his subject's reputation increasingly is. After so many years of being acknowledged as great by literary historians and read by very few others, Smollett appears at last to be on the threshold of acceptance as the equal of any of his contemporaries in the art of novel writing.

It is his novels that are justly of greatest interest now, but in his own time Smollett was known for many other achievements as well. He was, with varying degrees of popular and critical success, a poet, playwright, controversial pamphleteer, translator, editor, compiler, journalist, historian, and travel writer—in short, a professional author who worked with proficiency and extraordinary industry in many forms. Since his writings of all kinds are frequently autobiographical, any study or account of them must keep the important facts of his life in view. Tobias George Smollett was born into a distinguished Scottish family, probably in early March 1721. His parents, Archibald and Barbara Cunningham Smollett, presented their third child for baptism at the parish church of Cardross, Dumbartonshire, on the nineteenth of that month. Archibald Smollett, chronically ill at the time of Tobias's birth, had married without the consent of his father, Sir

James, who objected to Barbara Cunningham on the grounds that she was penniless. When Archibald died, his wife and young children were left with no money and were forced into humiliating dependency upon wealthy cousins, chiefly (it appears) James Smollett of Bonhill. The bitterness of Smollett's portrait of the tyrannical old grandfather in the opening chapters of *Roderick Random* surely derives in part from his memories of childhood hardships caused by the severity of his own parents' treatment by Sir James, who was in other respects, however, a much better man than the mean-spirited, ancient Random.

Relatively few details of Smollett's earliest years are known. He grew up in the then-idyllic environs of Loch Lomond and Leven-Water, and his lifelong passionate affection for the Scottish countryside—as so often reflected in his novels—may be traced to his boyish wide-eyed delight in the romantic scenery of what he later called the "Arcadia of Scotland." In 1727 or 1728 Smollett entered the Dumbarton grammar school, where he first encountered the world of books and learning, another lifelong source of delight and admiration. John Love, the headmaster at the school, was an outstanding teacher who seems to have conveyed to his young charge a deep enthusiasm for the classical languages and the great English writers. Smollett was an apt pupil, and his studies inspired him at an early age to begin writing verses. These youthful literary efforts have been lost, but it is likely that Smollett's dreams of authorship first came to him when he was only a boy.

Life was hard at school. Discipline was severe, the diet was sparse, the regimen was Spartan; attendance at church was mandatory, and the young scholars were closely examined on the sermons. The accounts in *Roderick Random* of rough-and-tumble games, frequent fights, and violent pranks very likely reflect with accuracy the means by which the strictly confined schoolboys found a release for their energies and an outlet for their anger over the regular floggings and other harsh punishments inflicted for infractions of rules or indolence at their books. But the five or so years Smollett spent studying under Love seem to have been happy ones; and they were certainly formative in many ways, as were the months or years he afterward spent at Glasgow University and the experiences gained during his apprenticeship to the distinguished surgeons William Stirling and John Gordon. Smollett never matriculated at Glasgow, and so it is impossible to determine exactly when or for how long he was

there. He must have attended, as many students did at the time, with no plans of earning a degree. Knapp has speculated that his second-class status at the university, of which he was daily made conscious by the elegantly gowned degree candidates as they strolled about the courts and gardens of the campus, intensified in Smollett a sense of personal alienation and inferiority—something he had already lived with from childhood as a consequence of his father's disinheritance and the subsequent misfortunes of his family.

While at Glasgow the young Smollett probably improved his knowledge of the classics, heard lectures in moral and natural philosophy, and certainly (as *Roderick Random* openly hints) pursued his love of poetry and belles lettres. He apparently continued to write as well as read, thus nursing along his early aspirations to authorship. But he could hardly afford the luxury of such indulgence. Smollett was essentially on his own during this period, and he had to think of making a living. He may have attended the anatomical and medical lectures at the university, and if he did, these would have helped qualify him to serve as apprentice to Stirling and Gordon, who formally took him on for a five-year period beginning in the spring of 1736.

Gordon appears to have known members of Smollett's family, which may partially account for the generosity of the arrangement he and his partner struck for the apprenticeship. But both were kindly men who had given tirelessly of themselves to provide medical care for the poor; and they were no doubt glad of the opportunity to assist a bright, talented young man whose services would lighten the burden of their busy practice. Stirling and Gordon treated Smollett well and trained him carefully. The time he spent with them gave him the knowledge and experience he needed to enter their profession, and likewise furnished him with a store of observations about the medical trade that he was later to use with such effect in his novels. The world of eighteenth-century medical practice, especially in England, was largely populated by charlatans and quacks; and Smollett, who took the profession seriously even after he left it to turn full-time author, made those who abused it the continual objects of his mockery.

In 1739, partly because of a persistent cough that interfered with his work, Smollett gained a release from his apprenticeship and undertook fulfillment of a dream he had long indulged. In spare hours he had been writing a tragedy, *The Regicide,* and he now set off for London with high hopes of seeing his play acted to great applause. When he arrived, a raw young man of proud Scottish ancestry in a bustling, dirty, disorderly city that responded to such outsiders with little tenderness, he was nearly penniless and almost entirely alone. His only real contacts were a well-connected distant relative and the group of Scottish medical men to whom he carried letters of introduction. Almost immediately he met with disappointment at the hands of those whose assistance he needed in order to have his play produced. His failure with *The Regicide* embarrassed and embittered the young author, who indeed never—despite years of intermittent efforts to do so—succeeded in getting the work upon the stage. Nor did he soon (if ever) for get the mistreatment he felt he had received.

Shortly after Smollett's arrival in London, England declared war against Spain (the so-called War of Jenkins' Ear), and the young Scotsman deflected his attention away from the theatrical world, turned again to medicine, and successfully sat for examinations that qualifie͏ͤ him to join the naval service as a surgeon's mate aboard a British man-of-war. He sailed on the eighty-gun *Chichester* (the model for Roderick Random's *Thunder*), which left Blackstakes on 3 April 1740 as part of the fleet that later participated in the disastrous Cartagena expedition of 1741. Smollett's account of this inglorious defeat for the British and his powerfully authentic pictures of the hardships, filth, disease, cruelty, and hunger that eighteenth-century enlisted sailors had to endure occupy some fourteen chapters of *Roderick Random.* Here Smollett vents what was surely a personal rage against the incompetence, stupidity, and even viciousness of the naval administration and the officers who served it.

From early 1742 until he set up his surgical practice in Downing Street, London, sometime during the spring of 1744, Smollett's trail is nearly impossible to follow. He was in the West Indies for a while; perhaps after leaving the navy he had signed on as medical officer aboard a merchant ship that took him there. In any case he fell in love with and married Anne Lassells, daughter of a wealthy Jamaican planter, and brought her home to England. Back in London, his new career as a surgeon did not flourish. In fact, Smollett never gained any recognition as a man of real importance among the physicians practicing in the English capital. He was, after all, a Scots-

man, and the London medical establishment was generally hostile to outsiders. Paradoxically, some of the best and most widely respected doctors and surgeons in mid-eighteenth-century London were Scots—Dr. James Douglas and his brother Dr. John Douglas (in whose Downing Street house Smollett lived for a time), Dr. William Hunter, Dr. William Smellie, and Dr. John Armstrong. Smollett appears to have known all of these distinguished men, but their friendship was insufficient to guarantee the easy reception of their young countryman, despite his talent and enthusiasm. Smollett, alienated by the accident of birth from the center of things in his chosen profession, labored under a considerable additional difficulty: he owned no medical degree. In fact, he did not earn the right to call himself "Doctor" until June 1750, when he followed a common practice of his time and purchased his M.D. from Aberdeen University for twenty-eight pounds Scots, just as he was about to give over medicine almost entirely in favor of a career as professional author.

By 1750, of course, Smollett had already enjoyed his first real taste of literary success with *Roderick Random.* This triumph in a domain he had always preferred to that of surgery, where he had never met with any signal success anyway, most certainly made it easier for him to undertake a permanent change of vocation. Smollett never lost interest in medicine; he made a genuinely important contribution to medical practice and controversy with his *Essay on the External Use of Water,* which appeared in 1752—well after he had all but ceased practicing as a surgeon. This pamphlet is an energetic, skillfully developed attack on the commonplaces concerning the benefits of the Bath waters, which Smollett judged to be unsafe, unclean, and nearly always useless to relieve the many afflictions for which they were routinely prescribed. But from the beginning of his London medical career in 1744, Smollett may have helped to determine his own less-than-happy prospects in the profession by dividing his attention between surgery and literature. At that time he renewed his attempts to have *The Regicide* accepted for production and was continually frustrated and angered by the coolness of his reception among the managers, actors, and patrons of the London theatrical establishment—James Lacy, John Rich, David Garrick, James Quin, George Lyttelton, and Philip Dormer Stanhope, fourth Earl of Chesterfield. In 1744 or 1745, however, Smollett did succeed in having his first work published, a lyric called *A New Song,* with music by the Scottish composer James Oswald. From this time forward he appears always to have devoted his emotional and creative energies more to the art of writing than to the business of medicine.

Smollett's life seems to have rushed along at a breakneck pace, and during the mid 1740s he moved from residence to residence—Downing Street to Chapel Street to Beaufort Street—trying to find a clientele that would make his surgical practice thrive, and no doubt looking for the stability that would afford him the leisure to write. He wrote even without the stability he sought. The Battle of Culloden, which brought the Jacobite Rebellion of 1745-1746 to such a bloody end, prompted from him a lovely ballad, *The Tears of Scotland,* which first appeared in the spring (probably) of 1746 and was reprinted many times. Smollett was no Jacobite, but his poem movingly represents the sufferings of his countrymen as a consequence of their loyalty to the failed cause of the Young Pretender, Charles Edward Stuart. *The Tears of Scotland* was widely read, sung (to Oswald's melody), and admired by those who shared its author's horror at the atrocities committed by William Augustus, Duke of Cumberland's "butchers" as they mercilessly pursued the ragtag Highland rebels back into the wilds of their homeland.

Smollett's poem was by no means a great success, but the attention it aroused surely emboldened him to write more. *Advice,* a verse satire in the manner of Alexander Pope, appeared in September 1746, followed in January 1747 by a companion work called *Reproof.* Derivative and rather pedestrian, neither of these satires deserved or received much notice from the public, but in writing them Smollett appears to have discovered his real literary talent, which was for sharp-eyed satiric observation, precise character portraiture, and unhesitating exposure of the seamy corruptions of contemporary life. During most of the remaining months of 1747 he would put this talent to much better use in composing his first novel, *The Adventures of Roderick Random.*

Smollett worked furiously on his new book, which was, he wrote to his friend Alexander Carlyle, "begun and finished in the Compass of Eight months, during which time several Intervals happened of one, two, three and four Weeks, wherein I did not set pen to paper." He acknowledged a "little Incorrectness," owing to his haste, and hoped that it might "be excused." The

novel was published in two duodecimo volumes on 21 January 1748, and Smollett continued to revise it through the fourth edition of 1754 (dated 1755), so that he himself must have had difficulty excusing its occasional awkwardness. Despite his hurry, Smollett knew what he was about as he wrote. *Roderick Random* was, he explained to Carlyle, "intended as a Satire on Mankind." "Of all kinds of satire," he observed in the opening lines of his preface to the work, "there is none so entertaining, and universally improving, as that which is introduced, as it were, occasionally, in the course of an interesting story."

Smollett's satire in the novel is often savage; it is developed with relentless intensity in a fiercely energetic style; and it is both generalized and particular. The mercurial adventures of his young hero, a "friendless orphan" of "modest merit," as the preface describes him, begin with an unhappy childhood in Scotland. There he is brutalized by the cruelties of the grandfather who causes his mother's death and the disappearance of his father, by the taunts of the cousin who assumes his birthright, and by the floggings and assorted tortures of an incompetent schoolmaster. Later, as a young man, he is thrown into encounters with a wide variety of character types along the road to London, where much of the story takes place. Roderick, like his author before him, is an outsider in the disordered, teeming city, where violence, cruelty, lust, avarice, hypocrisy, lying, social pretentiousness, and all the many other forms of moral rottenness almost overwhelm his native decency and threaten his moral survival. Smollett spares no class and no institution; the graphic picture of British society he develops in *Roderick Random* gives the illusion of comprehensiveness, and it is a dark picture of nearly universal depravity revealed for all to see, with its many disguises ruthlessly stripped away. Scattered throughout the novel are references to real people; among these are the actual commanders under whom Smollett had served—as Roderick does—during the naval expedition to Cartagena, and the leaders of the theatrical world whose supposed abuses of the author's feelings and merit are exposed in the interpolated story of the melancholy poet Melopoyn.

Roderick himself is the narrator of the work, and his voice is an angry one. He is repeatedly "confounded" and enraged by the "artifice and wickedness of mankind." His sufferings are so acute that he is occasionally driven near to madness, as when he lies chained to the poop deck of

Illustrations by Thomas Rowlandson for an 1805 British edition of Roderick Random; *top: Roderick's battle with the midshipman on the* Thunder; *bottom: Roderick discovers his Uncle Bowling in distress*

the *Thunder* during a battle, enduring punishment for a crime that exists only in the fiendishly twisted imaginations of his superior officers. Roderick is almost blinded by the brains of an officer of marines whose head is blown off within inches of his face. The world the reader sees through Roderick's troubled eyes, which so often dart fury and indignation, frequently takes on the qualities of a nightmare. The people the reader meets are often precisely represented as bestial grotesques, lacking in the human attributes of thought and compassion. Even the names of Smollett's characters, particularly the villainous ones, suggest something of the dehumanizing power of a society that gives small quarter to moral principle and less encouragement to the ideals of love and Christian virtue. People with names such as Potion, Weazel, Cringer, Oakum, Whiffle, Thicket, Chatter, Quiverwit, and Straddle seem to dominate the world as Roderick's pained imagination renders it; and even when they are merely types of human folly or stupidity, they participate in a texturing that makes reality appear sinister and at times almost terrifyingly menacing. Roderick's progress is through an environment of "terrible apparitions," as he so regularly characterizes it. It is no wonder that his own anger and indignation nearly overcome him, allowing the world to draw him with what seems an irresistible power into the vortex of its sordid meanness and moral anarchy.

The shipboard scenes of *Roderick Random*, in addition to providing an authentic account of eighteenth-century navy life, accumulate to become an almost emblematic microcosm of the nightmarish horrors of the world at large. Roderick is alternately confused, frightened, infuriated, and sickened by what he witnesses while serving as surgeon's mate on board the *Thunder*. There disease, putridness, filth, hunger, violence, and the officers' mindless indifference to suffering and death in all their many horrid forms add up to a hellish picture that gives concentrated definition to the entire novel's representation of man's inhumanity to man. It is Roderick's capacity to convey his vision of such scenery so convincingly, with an intensity almost too great to be borne by himself or the reader, that gives Smollett's novel much of its power. Later episodes, which leave the hero shipwrecked, beaten, naked, and alone on a barren English shore where it seems that no one will take him in, are similarly horrifying and compelling; and the prison chapters of the last quarter of the novel,

which find Roderick sinking irretrievably (it appears) into squalor and despair, are only slightly less dark and troubling.

If Smollett's striking projection of his hero's suffering and fury is a great strength of his novel, it has also been viewed as a liability. From the beginning, at least some readers have complained that *Roderick Random* fails as a work of art because its author lacked sufficient distance from his creation. The style, so this line of argument goes, is too energetic and intense, the indignation too fierce and complete and destructive to permit any meaningful understanding of Roderick by the reader. The providential ending of the book—which rescues the hero from the consequences of his own violent outbursts at a world that has victimized him but likewise entrapped him by teaching him to scourge and hate it—is preposterous. Such characters as Roderick's good-natured traveling companion Hugh Strap, the kindhearted seafaring eccentrics Bowling and Morgan, the beauteous heroine Narcissa—these are all little more than absurdly theoretical moral abstractions, disruptions of the narrative's natural consistency, though Bowling and Morgan are recognized as entertainingly comic, but authentic, portraits of eighteenth-century sailors.

Objections such as these have become commonplaces among some modern critics, who characterize *Roderick Random* as an aborted version of the conventional picaresque tale or as an ill-fated attempt to re-create the vision and devices of verse satire in the form of a fictional prose narrative. The novel's origins in the picaresque and in the traditions of verse satire, say these critics, account for its inorganic, chaotic structure of accumulating episodes and for its unintentional confusion of vision. There is some merit in such views. Smollett was doubtless conscious of the conventions of satiric poetry as he wrote *Roderick Random*, whose proud, vengeful first-person narrator certainly possesses some of the attributes of a typical satiric persona. Smollett makes plain his indebtedness to the picaresque tradition in the preface to his novel, where he acknowledges Alain René Lesage's *Gil Blas* (1715-1735), a work he knew well and admired, as one of his important models. Indeed, he may have been planning his own translation (published in October 1748) of *Gil Blas* while he was finishing *Roderick Random*.

But Smollett also announces, in the same preface, that he is attempting something new in his first novel, a moralized picaresque tale that will project its central personage as an instrument of satire against the world while seeking to compel the reader's sympathetic identification with him. Roderick, like the conventional picaro, is an outsider in the world through which he moves, but he is no merely resourceful rogue, mindlessly indifferent to moral idealism and neutral to the meaning of his own character. Nor is he simply a vehicle of private rage, the product of his author's failure to separate himself from his imagined character. What Smollett's most insistent detractors miss is the apparent deliberateness with which he constructed the narrative of *Roderick Random* in identifiable patterns. These patterns precisely reflect the disorder of experience as it threatens to demolish human goodness by brutalizing it, meanwhile obscuring the transcendent moral reality by which, according to Christian orthodoxy, providence governs and will ultimately redeem the world.

As the good-natured hero is flung about from episode to episode in the course of his adventures, he is confronted time and again by clustered types of human villainy, until at last he almost helplessly submits to the supposed rule of fortune—he goes in desperation to the gaming tables—and descends inevitably into misery and wretchedness. He is the world's victim, but his own as well. Upon this pattern of empirical reality, which to the suffering but misguided Roderick is increasingly the only meaningful one, Smollett superimposes a moral pattern defined by the presence of Bowling, Narcissa, and the several other representations of benevolence and Christian love.

Narcissa, an idealized portrait of perfect virtue whom Roderick learns to adore and finally marries, is of particular importance. Her role in the novel resembles that of Sophia Western in Fielding's *Tom Jones*. She is an "amiable apparition" when Roderick first meets her about halfway through the story; but, as he sinks progressively into the darkness of anger, cynicism, and despair, he clings lovingly to his vision of her exalted beauty and goodness. Finally, when his good nature has suffered enough as victim of the world and himself, his author intervenes to rescue him and remove him from scenes of hopelessness. Smollett gives Roderick a father and the emotional stability he has always desired and blesses him with happy marriage and tranquil retirement to the paradisal retreat of his ancestral estate in Scotland. The wrenching of the fictional world that occurs in the end is anticipated both directly and (more often) indirectly throughout the

novel, but still it is undeniably violent and even a bit awkward. It is not merely gratuitous, however, for it registers and defines Smollett's sense of the degradation that threatens to separate forever failed humanity from the realm of divine love and truth. The Christian promise of redemption, in his view, can be fulfilled only by a merciful act of radical transformation.

The structure of *Roderick Random,* when seen in this light, may be understood as inherently comic, but without diminishing the importance of the novel's insistently throbbing satiric content. A comic structure is appropriate to Smollett's moral and artistic purposes, though his management of the overlay of providential design lacks the sure touch of Fielding's comparable maneuverings in *Tom Jones*. The confusion of vision some readers have complained about is not Smollett's but Roderick's; his self-destructive rage and cynicism are understandable given the sufferings he must endure, but they necessarily lead to the near collapse of his personal integrity, and they threaten the annihilation of his moral character. Smollett punishes his hero severely and justly before relieving him.

No doubt the portrait of Roderick is a reflection upon the author's own character. It is in this important sense, and not in the repetition of details from his personal experience, that Smollett made his first novel an exercise in fictionalized autobiography. In the mock dedication (to himself) with which he began *Ferdinand Count Fathom,* published five years after *Roderick Random,* Smollett commented quite directly upon his own tendencies to respond to hard experience with incorrigible irascibility, rage, and cynicism, and upon his lifelong efforts to keep those impulses in check so as to avoid their costs in suffering and self-destruction. *Roderick Random* brings the vision of the artist and moralist to bear on this personal struggle, dramatizing it, demonstrating the disastrous consequences of failure, and manipulating it toward a hopeful and happy conclusion.

Roderick Random answered Smollett's fondest hopes for success with his mid-eighteenth-century audience. Three editions reaching the unusually large total of sixty-five hundred copies came from the presses of William Strahan between January 1748 and November 1749, and by the time of Smollett's death in 1771 the work was in its eighth edition; four others followed before the end of the century. There were, in addition, many piracies in London, Dublin, and Edinburgh, and there were translations into German

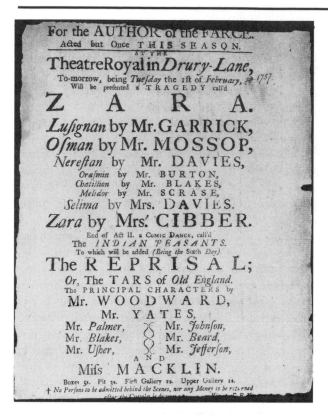

For the AUTHOR of the FARCE.
Acted but Once THIS SEASON.
AT THE
Theatre Royal in *Drury-Lane*,
To-morrow, being *Tuesday* the 1st of *February*, 1757,
Will be presented a T R A G E D Y call'd
Z A R A.
Lusignan by Mr. GARRICK,
Osman by Mr. MOSSOP,
Nereftan by Mr. DAVIES,
Orasmin by Mr. BURTON,
Chatillon by Mr. BLAKES,
Melidor by Mr. SCRASE,
Selima by Mrs. DAVIES.
Zara by Mrs. CIBBER.
End of Act II. a COMIC DANCE, call'd
The INDIAN PEASANTS.
To which will be added (Being the Sixth Day)
The REPRISAL;
Or, The TARS of *Old England.*
The PRINCIPAL CHARACTERS by
Mr. WOODWARD,
Mr. YATES,
Mr. *Palmer*, Mr. *Johnson*,
Mr. *Blakes*, Mr. *Beard*,
Mr. *Usher*, Mr. *Jefferson*,
AND
Miss MACKLIN.
Boxes 5s. Pit 3s. First Gallery 2s. Upper Gallery 1s.
† No Persons to be admitted behind the Scenes, nor any Money to be returned

Playbill for the only play by Smollett to be produced. The Reprisal *was modestly successful with the public, but was reviled
by the critics (Harvard University Library,
Theater Collection).*

(1754), French (1761), and later Russian (1788), Danish (1802), Dutch (1805), and Swedish (1824). A London edition of 1792 was adorned with the fine illustrations of Thomas Rowlandson, whose splendid comic talent was exactly suited to the task of drawing Smollett's characters and scenes. While still enjoying its first rush of popularity, *Roderick Random* received belated and brief but favorable notice in the *Gentleman's Magazine* (March 1749) and the *Monthly Review* (May 1749). It was in subsequent years many times adapted in jestbooks, dramatic interludes, and comic operas. A famous racehorse of 1750 bore the name of Smollett's hero. Influential readers, from Richardson's friend Miss Catherine Talbot to Samuel Johnson's crony Thomas Birch, applauded Smollett's novel for its exuberance, humor, and variety.

The work did not escape criticism, however. Miss Talbot, like many other readers of her century, was irritated and embarrassed by its lowness of subject matter. Henry Fielding, a more important judge, found almost nothing praiseworthy about it. In the *Covent-Garden Journal* (7 January 1752) he blasted both *Roderick Random* and

Smollett's second novel, *Peregrine Pickle* (1751), for their complete want of merit, an assessment that may have been prompted in part by some unkind references to his own work and character in the latter story. Smollett was not amused. One week later appeared a pamphlet almost certainly his, a mean-spirited personal attack on Fielding called *A FAITHFUL NARRATIVE of the base and inhuman Arts That were lately practised upon the Brain of Habbakkuk Hilding.* Among his other grievances, Smollett suspected his rival of plagiarizing the characters of Partridge in *Tom Jones* and Miss Matthews in *Amelia* (1751) from his own Strap and Nancy Williams of *Roderick Random.* Smollett's admirers have always preferred to believe that the scurrilous *Habbakkuk Hilding* was by someone else, for it does its writer little credit. But there seems no sufficient reason to doubt Smollett's authorship, and indeed this ephemeral work is a good indication of the anger that sometimes racked his mind and heart.

With the publication of *Roderick Random,* Smollett caused the London world of letters to take notice of a new and significant talent in its midst. Such success and celebrity as his novel enjoyed must have encouraged him to give more and more of his attention to literary interests at considerable detriment to his surgical practice. Certainly he bloomed into a busy and productive writer during the years 1748 and 1749. Following the appearance of his translation of *Gil Blas* in October 1748, he completed the subscription arrangements for getting *The Regicide* into print in May 1749, meanwhile occupying himself with what must have been an extraordinary work: *Alceste,* a combination of opera, tragedy, and masque supposedly prepared in collaboration with George Frideric Handel. For some reason this play, now lost, was never produced, despite John Rich's promise to bring it on at Covent Garden. A comedy called *The Absent Man,* also lost, suffered the same fate during the theatrical season of 1749-1750. Smollett must have thought himself doomed to be excluded forever from the stage. If so, he was very nearly right. Not until January 1757, when his farce *The Reprisal; or, The Tars of Old England* was acted at Drury Lane, did he manage to fulfill what was actually his earliest ambition as a writer. *The Reprisal* enjoyed a modest success with the theatergoing public and was regularly revived during the next several decades. But the critics reviled it. Their taunts may have discouraged Smollett from undertaking further attempts upon the fickle world of the theater. He wrote no more plays after *The Reprisal.*

Doubtless it was not just discouragement but also his frenzied involvement with other, more rewarding projects that deflected Smollett away from his old dreams of fame as a playwright. His fine English version of *Gil Blas* was an instantaneous success, and even today it is counted the best translation of that work. He appears to have followed it in the spring of 1750 with another translation from Lesage, *The Devil upon Crutches,* and thereafter made the business of rendering foreign works into English a major part of his literary activity. While preparing *Gil Blas* for the press, he probably began work on *Don Quixote,* a slow and difficult task for him, as his Spanish was not fluent. This translation was not published until February 1755, and Smollett appears to have been quite willing to allow his progress with it to be interrupted by less demanding or more congenial enterprises.

The most important such interruption was the composition of his second novel, *The Adventures of Peregrine Pickle,* parts of which were likely written before or during a brief summer trip to Paris in 1750. Smollett was in his later years an enthusiastic traveler, and he was also a devoted reader and active compiler of travel narratives. His love for the idea of motion itself, which figures so crucially in all of his novels, possibly began with his journey from Glasgow to London in 1739 and was surely deepened during his naval voyages of the early 1740s. A tour of France, Flanders, and Holland in the summer of 1749 gave him his first real opportunity to view European culture with his own eyes. What he saw then, together with his experiences in Paris a year later, provided him with a range of subject matter for his new story far broader than that represented in *Roderick Random.*

Peregrine Pickle is nearly twice as long as Smollett's first work of fiction. Vast, mammoth, even sprawling in its treatment of a roguish, scoundrelly hero whose adventures take him through much of England and all over the European Continent, the narrative actually represents an ambitious experiment toward using the new form of the novel to anatomize virtually the whole of Western society. It is at times more savagely satirical than anything Smollett had written previously, and it lacks restraint and discipline. *The Adventures of Ferdinand Count Fathom,* another experimental story of roguery in motion that Smollett completed in 1753, two years after *Peregrine*

Pickle, is much more thoughtfully conceived and more carefully and tightly crafted. But *Peregrine Pickle,* while it does not deserve its usual estimation as the best of Smollett's novels after *Humphry Clinker* and *Roderick Random,* has much to recommend it, not least its delightful portraits of eccentric character types and its energetic laughing (or mocking) glances at some of the real people, places, events, and institutions of its author's period in history.

The acerbity of Smollett's allusions to contemporaries such as Garrick, Quin, Lyttelton, the earl of Chesterfield, Mark Akenside, and Fielding made enemies for his new book, but no doubt also stirred interest in it. His introduction in chapter 88 of the lengthy, scandalous "Memoirs of a Lady of Quality," presumably by Lady Frances Vane with revisions by Smollett, was eagerly anticipated prior to the novel's publication because it was played up in the press. In chapter 106 Smollett paused over an extended reference to the celebrated James Annesley, the self-proclaimed "young nobleman" whose many years of legal struggle to regain his supposedly stolen birthright from a greedy uncle had already generated a quantity of sensational writing.

The appeal of such ingredients as these was immediate but ephemeral. Certainly they have little to do with the literary integrity of *Peregrine Pickle,* and in fact undermine it. But, oddly, they also contribute to the texture of the novel as a reflection of its age and as a particularly revealing body of evidence concerning the author's sensibilities. Through his references to members of the literary establishment Smollett expressed his scorn for those who succeeded without talent, and he also continued to pay off old debts of animosity against those who had frustrated his youthful aspirations as a playwright or—in the case of Fielding—had mocked his achievement, so Smollett thought, by plagiarizing it. His inclusion of the interpolated story of Lady Vane, a kind of female picaro, created a parallel with the main plot and its account of the rascally sexual adventures of Peregrine, while it also helped Smollett to expand upon his novel's general exposure of the vicious debasements of English high society. The melancholy Annesley, so long deprived of what was his by the power of a corrupt aristocracy, provided yet another opportunity for emphasizing a meaningful connection between the imaginary world and the actual. Both of these lengthy intrusions upon his narrative, and the many glimpses of other recognizable people as well, made it easier for the author of *Peregrine Pickle* to define his work as an unvarnished satiric representation of life as it is lived in all its meanness, deviousness, promiscuity, and moral stupidity.

Smollett's mockery of powerful figures in the literary circles of London, besides deepening old antagonisms, may have caused his book's comparative failure with the critics and the public. John Cleland praised *Peregrine Pickle* in the *Monthly Review* (March 1751), but few others added to his endorsement. Most of the attention given to the work in the press centered on the "Lady of Quality" and her "Memoirs," to the exclusion of its other attractions. Smollett appears to have believed that his enemies wrecked the novel's chances for popular success by discouraging reviewers from dealing with it and by preventing publication of a second edition. It is impossible to say whether his suspicions were justified, but it is certainly true that after the initial appearance of *Peregrine Pickle* in four volumes on 25 February 1751, no further edition was called for until seven years later.

By that time a good many of Smollett's long-nursed wounds had healed. Garrick had helped with production of *The Reprisal,* Fielding was dead, and the memories of affronts from other people had faded. In preparing the text of the new edition of *Peregrine Pickle,* which appeared in March 1758, Smollett eliminated or muted most of the personal references that, in his more mature judgment, had disfigured his work in its original form. He also excised several of the "lowest" and crudest passages, polished some of the prose, and shortened the novel by almost eighty pages. The result was a more graceful work but one that, as many critics have justly observed, lacks much of the energy, the caustic satire, the raw violence of incident so typical of the early Smollett. Such modern scholarly editions as exist have generally returned to the first edition of *Peregrine Pickle* as the best text with which to represent the real nature of its achievement.

Peregrine Pickle is rich in its variety of episodes, settings, and characters. Peregrine (or Perry), whose birth must await the conclusion of a long opening account of his father's retreat from active city life and marriage to a shrewish wife, suffers in his childhood some of the same misfortunes that befall his predecessor Roderick Random. But he is surrounded by a remarkable collection of comic eccentrics, whose portrayal is one of the genuine glories of this novel: Gamaliel Pickle, Perry's father and a type of the

henpecked husband; Grizzle, Perry's ancient, gnarled, spinster aunt; the curmudgeonly but good-hearted and quixotic former sailor, Commodore Trunnion; and Trunnion's similarly quixotic protégés in his house or "Garrison," Tom Pipes and Jack Hatchway. There are others, and the loving but sharp-eyed manner in which Smollett draws them in all their oddity makes the early chapters of his novel the most memorable part of any reader's encounter with it. In the three works of fiction that followed *Peregrine Pickle,* Smollett never exceeded, and perhaps never equaled, his achievement in these comic portraits, which actually make a significant contribution to the structure and meaning of his novel as a whole, since most of them recur and serve to illuminate the moral content of Peregrine's erratic adventures.

The boy Perry, mistreated by his family but educated with the assistance of the kindly Trunnion, eventually sets off for the university at Oxford, where he studies for a time with some success before moving on to London. In the city he encounters a new gallery of character types, almost universally wicked and foolish. Like Roderick Random, Perry had been brutalized by early experience, but this time Smollett's protagonist is no outsider reluctantly drawn in by the world's villainies. He is an Englishman by birth, and he possesses little of that "modest merit" by which the character of the Scottish Roderick had maintained at least a modicum of the reader's sympathy. A violent and cruel prankster as a lad, he continues as a young man to humiliate, vilify, or thrash those who provoke his scorn or his wrath. He is the embodiment of a fierce Juvenalian satirist in action against the targets of his ingenuity or his meanness. The emptiness and corruption of English society, and particularly high society, he leaves exposed for all to see.

Perry's continental adventures continue in the same vein, substituting the manners and characters of other European cultures—and especially the French—as the recipients of his coarse, rambunctious mockery. The resemblances to the *Satyricon* of Petronius are obvious, and they are certified in an extended parodic version of Trimalchio's feast. In France, Perry is joined by Tom Pipes, who becomes his faithful, affectionate traveling companion and often the butt of his cruel jokes and the victim of his anger. Pipes plays Strap to Perry's Roderick Random, and his good-natured presence serves to underscore the frequent viciousness of his master. Later in the course of his French adventures Perry meets the stupid, pretentious English painter Pallet, along with a nameless physician (he is probably a portrait of Akenside) whose chief distinction is his pompous incompetence. Pallet and the doctor are the most effectively drawn among the many eccentric characters introduced into this long portion of the narrative, which is actually a severe satire on the tradition of the Grand Tour. Eventually the scene shifts to Holland and then to England once again, and, following the moving episode of Commodore Trunnion's death, Perry renews his roguish ways on his native soil. He joins with the remarkable misanthrope Cadwallader Crabtree in a mischievous scheme to expose the vices of fashionable society; he sinks into the sordid world of London political intrigue, is ruined by a pack of gamesters, turns author and fails at it, and ultimately finds himself confined for debt in the Fleet Prison, where he is overcome by a hopeless melancholy as he contemplates the cell that surrounds him.

Desperation leads to self-knowledge and redemption, as it had for Roderick Random, and in the end Smollett restores his miscreant hero and makes him happy. Perry's happiness consists chiefly in the reward of marriage to the beauteous, virginal Emilia, on whom he had previously used all the arts of seduction at his command, but without success. The idealized Emilia echoes Narcissa, though she enters the story much earlier than her counterpart in *Roderick Random*. Emilia continually gives her love to Perry even when he least deserves it, which is most of the time. This wayward youth's roguish instincts run much deeper than those of Roderick, whose sexual exploits and efforts at fortune hunting pale by comparison with those of his fictional descendant. Perry has thoughtlessly left a long trail of ravished or seduced or persecuted women behind him, and his redemption in the end seems even less justified than Roderick's, despite the continued affection of Emilia, Trunnion, Pipes, and Hatchway. The presence of these important representations of good nature and benevolence actually serves to remind the reader constantly of Perry's failings as a proud, self-absorbed, vindictive man who only reflects the evils of the very world that he condemns and scourges. Meanwhile, such eccentrics as Grizzle Pickle and Cadwallader Crabtree help to underscore, in a comic way, the grotesque and quite destructive absurdity of the qualities of pride and meanspiritedness they share with the hero.

Smollett displays his portrait of Peregrine against a background of dark and teeming sordidness that is brightened and relieved only by the images of those few he should esteem but cannot until the final episode. The structure thus depends upon a rhetorical pattern of satiric contrasts. The realities of depravity and villainy are juxtaposed to the ideals of goodness, and the hero is seen in motion between these two extremes. The motion is the plot of the novel, which, like that of *Roderick Random* and all of Smollett's other narratives, is conducted by the accumulation of episodes, each episode containing its comic or satiric or sentimental drama as acted out by an assemblage of various character types. The progress is only superficially linear or chronological. Smollett became an accomplished historian during his career, but when he was writing as a novelist he cared little for the laws of causality or process. He was much more interested in creating a whole "picture," with a center located in the moral conflict played out in his protagonist's experience.

His casual uses of historical facts in *Peregrine Pickle* (the Annesley story, among other instances), without precise reference to their places in actual historical sequence, only confirm Smollett's understanding of the novel as a form of verbal art closely paralleling the visual art of the painter. It is the crucial detail of history or experience, the individual moment deeply felt and deeply understood, that matters most to Smollett the artist, who does not simply mirror the surfaces of reality as a historian would do but instead attempts to record the way the process of living actually feels. Life is, for this writer, essentially an extended encounter with scattered fragments of reality, which always threatens chaos. "I am old enough," he remarked to Garrick in a letter of 1761, "to have seen and observed that we are all playthings of fortune." The episodic, often apparently erratic structures of his novels typically reflect this personal vision, but they impose a design that collects together wildly assorted "episodes" or "facts" (whether invented or borrowed from history), reveals the meaning of each by visualizing and dramatizing it, and then shapes the whole into an original configuration or "picture."

A Smollett novel arrives at resolution only when its process of accumulation is complete, and the center of interest or conflict, to which the reader's eye is inevitably drawn, is fully defined. In *Peregrine Pickle*, as in *Roderick Random*, such final definition occurs when the despairing hero recognizes the nature of the moral failure that has divided him in his aimless roguery from all that is worth having in moral life: love, beauty, tranquillity. "I desire," Smollett continued in his letter to Garrick, "to live quietly with all mankind, and if possible to be upon good terms with all those who have distinguished themselves by their extraordinary merit." At the moment when Peregrine Pickle is able to interpret his own wayward experience as leading inevitably, through conflict, to this same desire, he is transformed and made happy.

Peregrine Pickle was Smollett's first attempt with third-person narration, and no doubt that method of telling his story made its satiric purposes easier to clarify and sustain. This novel generally avoids the blurring of vision that threatens to undermine the satiric effectiveness and comic resolution of *Roderick Random*. But Smollett's method in his new book may also have cost him something in the way of restraint and control of his fictional material. *Roderick Random* is more tightly structured precisely because its focus is limited by the singleness, even the obsessiveness, of the hero's voice as it records what his eye sees and his body and mind feel during the progress of his remarkable adventures. *Peregrine Pickle* sprawls because it lacks such singleness of emphasis. Indeed, Smollett seems never to have been comfortable with third-person narration. He tried the technique again in his third novel, *Ferdinand Count Fathom*, where he sought to impose restraint by keeping the relationship between the villainous protagonist and his principal victim always at or near the exact center of the story's definition of moral conflict. The greater economy of structure in *Ferdinand Count Fathom* measures his considerable success in the attempt at restraint, but at the sacrifice of some exuberance and variety and the loss of such lovingly detailed character portraits as Trunnion and Hatchway in *Peregrine Pickle*.

In *The Adventures of Sir Launcelot Greaves* (serialized in 1760-1761; published in two volumes, 1762), Smollett once more employed a third-person narrator, and while this novel may be called an exercise in structural economy, it was an experiment unsuited to the author's real talent. Greaves, an idealized quixotic figure, dominates the work as the center of moral attention, and his failure to see the world as it really is inhibits the story, depriving it for the most part of those great virtues of energetic bustle and

shrewd satiric observation that so distinguish Smollett's earlier fiction. Smollett, like Defoe, was at his best when projecting from his imagination a consciousness that became its own vehicle for registering the disordered appearances of experience, completely disguising the author behind the mask of his invention. Not until he returned to the illusion of the personal voice in the letters that pass among the characters in *Humphry Clinker* did Smollett achieve another triumph to equal—or, as many of his readers would have it, to surpass—his original success with *Roderick Random*.

Smollett's first three novels, all written while he was a young man still in the process of discovering his talent, may certainly be read as important experiments in novelistic composition. But, as interestingly—often brilliantly—told stories reflecting their author's reactions to life in mid-eighteenth-century England, they are sources of continual delight. Their strength and their appeal derive in part from their preoccupation with the subject matter of roguery. *Roderick Random, Peregrine Pickle,* and *Ferdinand Count Fathom* are all adaptations from the picaresque, and they tell much about Smollett's simultaneous fascination and revulsion at the daily eighteenth-century spectacle of violence, horrid cruelty, and criminality. He shared this complexity of response with many others of his day, including writers such as Fielding (one has only to think of *Jonathan Wild*, 1743), a fact that is underscored by the continual popularity of rogue and criminal biography. But his awareness of the impatient irascibility of his own temperament, which so often drove him to anger and tempted him into the scourging of enemies real and imaginary, must have sharpened his sensitivity to the stark reality of impetuous aggressiveness and evil impulses in human character.

During the year following the publication of *Peregrine Pickle*, Smollett became embroiled in a most unpleasant legal battle that cost him money he did not have and very nearly got him thrown into prison under a judgment of attempted murder. At this time Smollett's surgery business was failing, though he had moved to Chelsea to be nearer the center of the London medical establishment. His work as a writer was earning him too little to provide any comfort or security, though it kept him busy. He was now writing for the *Monthly Review*, and his *Essay on the External Use of Water* had been published. Neither these efforts nor *Peregrine Pickle* had brought him much

Illustrations by Rowlandson for an 1805 British edition of Peregrine Pickle; *top: Commodore Trunnion and Jack Hatchway on a fox hunt; bottom: the "Feast after the manner of the Antients" in France*

money, and he had made the mistake of lending a sizable sum to a hack writer named Peter Gordon, who took advantage of Smollett's generosity and refused to pay him back. Enraged, Smollett thrashed this miscreant and his landlord Edward Groom, who accused him of homicidal assault and filed suit against him. He was tried in the King's Bench, acquitted of the criminal charge, and forced to pay more than twenty pounds in damages and costs.

While all of these assorted troubles were plaguing him, Smollett somehow managed to write the two volumes of *Ferdinand Count Fathom,* which appeared in mid February 1753, just at the time of his trial. That he was able to complete the book at all while under such stress is at least mildly remarkable. It is a substantial and thoughtfully conceived work, though much shorter than either of his previous novels. *Peregrine Pickle* is twice its bulk, and *Roderick Random* is longer by some fifty thousand words. In certain respects, however, *Ferdinand Count Fathom* is a more ambitious undertaking. Its scenery ranges over much of Europe and England, yet the motions of its protagonist are more directed and purposeful (on the part of both character and author) than those of the energetic drifter Peregrine, his nearest counterpart in calculated roguery. Fathom is even more the initiator of action than Pickle, his villainy is more complete, and he is in fact a deliberate study in the type of the single-minded, aberrant, inherently criminal character. As such, he is something of a new departure for his author.

In the parodic dedication to *Ferdinand Count Fathom,* besides commenting on his own private personality, Smollett defends the storyteller's prerogative to delineate wickedness in all its sinister attractiveness—as Shakespeare had done, the reader is reminded, with the dramatic portrait of Richard III. He also introduces his only extended theoretical statement on the subject of the novel as a form of literary expression. This statement has been routinely dismissed by critics and historians of early fiction as merely conventional and as a forgettable observation that has little to do with its author's own work. But it actually contains extremely important clues to Smollett's understanding of the nature of his peculiar talent; and it points directly to the meaning of his characteristic approach to the writing of fiction. "A Novel," he says, "is a large diffused picture, comprehending the characters of life, disposed in different groupes and exhibited in various attitudes, for the purposes of an uniform plan, and gen-

eral occurrence [that is, concurrence], to which every individual figure is subservient." For this "uniform plan" to be apparent and effective, he goes on, there must be "a principal personage to attract the attention, unite the incidents, unwind the clue of the labyrinth, and at last close the scene by virtue of his own importance."

The dramatic analogy hinted at here was always important to Smollett the novelist. His narratives are richly punctuated by allusions, sometimes brief and fleeting and sometimes long and elaborated, to Shakespeare and other playwrights whose works he admired. As a writer whose first hope was for success in the theater, he is naturally alert to the value of effective dramatic scenes within the context of a prose narrative. The individual episodes of his stories may almost always be read as playlets, self-contained and self-defined. It is the analogy of painting, however, that should most interest the student of Smollett's fiction. The terms *groups* and *attitudes* were important to the eighteenth-century aesthetic of history painting. By the analogy he evokes through explicit use of those terms, Smollett accounts for the seemingly inorganic structure of his episodic narratives, which multiply dramatic episodes, juxtaposing assorted events and characters until the center of moral interest— Roderick, Peregrine, Fathom—is fully lined out in its relation to the rest of the imaginary world. A Smollett composition, as the author plainly hints, may be best understood through application of the same principles by which one might "read" a series of dramatic paintings, such as the *Rake's Progress* of William Hogarth.

Ferdinand Count Fathom represents Smollett's most serious and most rigorous attempt to work according to the principles of pictorial composition he had been developing through the process of writing *Roderick Random* and *Peregrine Pickle.* When read with an eye to his new experimentation with these principles, Smollett's third novel seems a much better narrative than its many detractors over the years have allowed it to be. The story line itself involves no particularly new departure, except for the centrality of its emphasis on the thoroughgoing, innate villainy of its titular character. Fathom is a traveler, an instrument of satire, and the overall pattern of his progress from episode to episode does not differ markedly from what one finds in Smollett's first two novels. Born a nobody, he is the illegitimate son of a whoring camp follower during the War of the Spanish Succession. He first sees the light of day in a wagon as it crosses the border from Holland to Flanders. When his mother dies violently while committing an act of plunder upon a fallen soldier, the little Fathom is kindly taken in by a Hungarian colonel, Count de Melvile, who rears him along with his own boy, Renaldo, at his home in Pressburg. There the clever young reprobate perfects his inherited arts of swindling, thieving, gulling, and seduction on members of the household, meanwhile cultivating the affection and loyalty of his foster brother. Ferdinand and Renaldo are separated following some youthful military exploits, during which Ferdinand proves his cowardice and Renaldo his bravery, and from this point Smollett temporarily turns his story's attention almost exclusively upon his hero-villain.

Fathom's adventures take him to Paris and then, by his own design, to England. There he falsely assumes the title of count and proceeds to victimize everyone he can by exercising the brilliance of his charlatan's manner upon the naiveté and stupidity he finds all about him in the assorted persons of pretentious leaders of fashion, greedy and gullible merchants, virginal girls and sexually deprived middle-aged women, and incompetent sharpers and gamesters. He is himself gulled from time to time, but he learns quickly. When his noble lineage is questioned, he is able to shift his identity from bogus count to quack physician and then to musician as a means of continuing to feed his rapacious appetites for money, admiration, and female flesh. Exposed and imprisoned in consequence of a momentary lapse of vigilance, he is relieved by the sudden reappearance of Renaldo, who spends nearly all of his pocket money to secure his old friend's release. Renaldo and his beloved Monimia—a character drawn and named after the melancholy heroine of Thomas Otway's tragedy *The Orphan* (1680)—become Fathom's new prey. His lust for Monimia nearly destroys her and her devoted Renaldo as well. Fathom succeeds in separating them, but when Monimia appears to have died of grief, he finds other objects for his schemes. At last he is undone and is thrown into prison a second time, where he languishes in misery until Renaldo returns once more, finally recognizes Fathom for what he is, hears his groans of penitence and confession, and kindly rescues him. Monimia, it turns out, was not dead after all, and she and Renaldo now may look forward to a future of wedded bliss. Fathom, meanwhile, is redeemed but displaced, only to turn up again as the apothecary Grieve encountered along the road by the travelers in *Humphry Clinker*.

Ferdinand Count Fathom contains some interesting character portraits—the English bumpkin Sir Stentor Stile; Sir Mungo Barebones and the other eccentrics Fathom meets when he is in prison for the first time; the benevolent old Jew Joshua Manasseh, who lends Renaldo money after he has rendered himself penniless by coming to Fathom's assistance. The satiric exposure of the follies and vices of European and English society at Vienna, Paris, London, Bath, Bristol Springs, Tunbridge Wells, and elsewhere is in the best manner of *Roderick Random* and *Peregrine Pickle*. But in some ways Smollett's satire in *Ferdinand Count Fathom* is more complexly effective because it is carried out by a character who so darkly victimizes those upon whose failings he preys. The novel also contains what are usually cited as the earliest instances of Gothic horror and melodrama in English fiction, the scenes in which Fathom is terrorized by the events of a nighttime journey through a forest and the later episode of Monimia's reappearance to Renaldo in the midnight gloom of a graveyard.

But it is the purposeful scoundrel Fathom, his character illuminated by the presence of the two virtuous figures who eventually triumph over him, that defines the center of this novel. His motion is incessant, his resourcefulness nearly inexhaustible, and the whole design of Smollett's narrative seems contrived to reveal the full range of evil possibilities in human character, so that they may be recognized, enjoyed for the perversely vicarious but cathartic pleasure their representation affords, and finally controlled. In the drama of each of his rascally escapades, Fathom's depravity is graphically displayed in all of its deceptive brilliance; and as he prowls over the landscape of the novel, his encounters bring him into direct interaction with characters and circumstances both fictional and real. Some of the "facts" of Smollett's fiction are drawn from the real world; and it is in his explicit and quite unusual manner of referring to topical subjects that Smollett most provocatively affirms his artistic notion of the importance of the individual moment of historical or fictional experience as it participates in, contributes to, and helps to define a larger configuration that is finally timeless in its moral significance.

Smollett begins the novel by locating its protagonist in the context of specific historical circumstance. Fathom is born in 1711, the "last year of the renowned Marlborough's command," and the experiences of his youth coincide exactly with the dates of important European military conflicts: the War of the Spanish Succession, which ended with the Treaty of Utrecht in 1713; the bloody Austrian campaign against the Turks from 1716 to 1718; and the War of the Polish Succession between 1733 and 1735. But suddenly the author introduces the first of a series of anachronisms that disrupt the illusion of exact historical sequence. Fathom arrives in England at the age of twenty-four or twenty-five; the fictional "date" could hardly be later than 1735 or 1736. But he is promptly mistaken for the Young Pretender, whose mysterious escape from his pursuers following the Jacobite Rebellion of 1745-1746 had caused such a stir that it was still remembered vividly in 1753. Later, when Fathom finds himself in a London prison, he meets several recognizable characters whose experiences refer to events of the late 1740s and early 1750s. A fellow inmate, the eccentric Captain Minikin, offers him a library of books, all published within a year or two of Smollett's own. The appearance in later chapters of the kindly old Jew, Joshua, alludes directly to the controversy over the Jewish Naturalization Act that was raging at the very time when *Ferdinand Count Fathom* went to the bookstalls.

Such anachronisms as these—and there are many others besides—could not have been the result of mere accident or carelessness. Certainly they represent more than the author's opportunistic exploitation of topical subjects to captivate his readers. Fathom's character is continually highlighted by the framing of his experience within a context of history, and the same process of framing illuminates the meaningful connections that exist between the fictional world and the real one. The ignobility of Smollett's villain is made starkly apparent when seen in an implied comparison with John Churchill, first Duke of Marlborough, and Prince Eugene of Savoy, the two brave generals whose brilliant triumphs figure in the background of the novel's early chapters. In the first of the anachronistic episodes, Fathom's criminal dreams of himself as a second conquering Caesar destined to plunder the luxurious isle of England and pocket its riches are given an undeniable depth of definition by the joining of his character with that of Prince Charles Edward Stuart; the two characters, imaginary and historical, are both talented adventurers pursuing ugly and destructive fantasies of power and glory, though in

different spheres. The virtue and generosity of Joshua Manasseh, one of the "descendants of Judah" and a supposed inheritor of the so-called curse of Antichrist, create an irony that deepens the reader's understanding of Fathom as a despicable, avaricious fraud, a sinister enemy to moral idealism and a dangerous force against the practice of charity and love.

For Smollett the novelist, the lessons of history were cumulative; villainy was villainy, as goodness was goodness, wherever they might be located in the busy and relentless sequence of mankind's experience. It was a matter of the artist's choice to appropriate a relevant historical fact, abstract it from its place in chronological process, and make it part of his novelistic configuration. Since a work of fiction is an interpretation of life, and not its mirror reflection, the writer is free to re-create the materials of his knowledge and observation, whatever their source, and make them answer his moral and artistic purposes. This is precisely what Smollett does in *Ferdinand Count Fathom*, and to a lesser extreme in his other novels as well. The "plot" of history, which Smollett records so faithfully and so capably in his later historical writing, was for him only superficially linear—like the "plot" of a fictional narrative, whose real interest and meaning reside in intensely felt moments as they gather themselves toward a center to complete the "uniform plan," or design, of the novelist's timeless picture of human life and society.

Smollett's experiment in *Ferdinand Count Fathom* was only a partial success. His readers have never found it a particularly rewarding book. Modern critics have on the whole judged it a dismal failure, though few of them appear to have read it carefully enough on its own terms. Whatever its merit, and despite its failure ever to find an audience, the novel tells much about its author's understanding of his art. Smollett may have been discouraged by the less-than-enthusiastic reception of this third novel. It was not popular enough to justify a second edition during his lifetime, and the one reviewer who bothered to notice it was hardly ecstatic. The "history of count *Fathom*," wrote Ralph Griffiths in the *Monthly Review* for March 1753, "is a work of a mixed character, compounded of various and unequal parts." Griffiths admired some of the work's "affecting incidents" and "animated descriptions," and he praised its author for "great proficiency in the study of mankind"; but he found the principal personage morally objection-

Letter from Smollett to the printer William Strahan in 1759, in which Smollett attempts to patch up a misunderstanding caused by Strahan's printing pamphlets by Smollett's "inveterate enemies" (MA 1229, Pierpont Morgan Library) able and the composition as a whole marred by a profusion of regrettable "incongruities" and "crudities." With *Ferdinand Count Fathom,* Smollett had failed for the second time to renew the early success of *Roderick Random,* and he published no more fiction for seven years.

He did, however, keep frantically busy with his pen, meanwhile struggling against the symptoms of an asthmatic condition that began to plague him in 1753 and that would eventually cause a serious decline in his health. The next few years found him engaged in all kinds of journeyman work, doubtless undertaken to bring him an income. In 1754 his editions of Alexander Drummond's *Travels through Different Cities* and Dr. William Smellie's *Cases in Midwifery* were published. His *Don Quixote* came out at last in 1755, and on 1 March 1756 he began his *Critical Review,* which he edited until 1763 and to which he regularly contributed reviews that were intelligent, predictably cantankerous, and often controversial. The *Critical Review* quickly rivaled Griffiths's *Monthly Review* as a reviewing organ, and it gave Smollett a position of power in literary circles that he had never before enjoyed. A seven-volume *Compendium of Authentic and Entertaining Voyages,* prepared under Smollett's editorial supervision, appeared one month after the first number of the *Critical Review.* At the same time he was continuing the huge task, probably begun in 1755, of writing his *Complete History of England.* This work, the first three volumes of which were published in April 1757, brought him financial security for the first time in his life.

The *Complete History of England,* as revised and then concluded in 1758 with the appearance of its fourth volume, is a very capable work of its kind. It chronicles the story of England through 1748 and is gracefully written, reliable in its synthesis of facts, and still worthy of being read and consulted. Its Tory bias angered some prominent Whigs, who attacked it in the press, but the work was popular enough to rival David Hume's prestigious *History of Great Britain* (1754-1763). The *Complete History of England* was widely reprinted and widely read, and, following as it did his modest success with *The Reprisal* in 1757, it must have left Smollett feeling less burdened by life and work. Late in 1757 he prepared his revised edition of *Peregrine Pickle.* In May 1758 the old irascibility that had enlivened the original version of that novel manifested itself once more, with painful results, in a pulverizing blast at Admiral Charles Knowles in the *Critical Review.* Knowles,

who was possibly one of Smollett's models for Captain Oakum, the stupid and heartless commander of the *Thunder* in *Roderick Random,* had written a pamphlet defending his conduct in the failed expedition to Rochefort, France, in 1757. Smollett attacked him mercilessly in a review, was successfully sued for libel, and spent the last months of 1760 and possibly the early months of 1761 in prison.

His health was continuing to deteriorate at this time, and Smollett had spent the period from June to October 1758 resting on the Continent, where he hoped the more congenial climate might help him to improve his strength. A compulsive worker, he returned to England and commenced with his editorial participation in *The Modern Part of an Universal History,* which continued from 1759 until 1765. The year 1760 witnessed the beginning of a period of extraordinarily frenetic activity that may have cost Smollett all hope of ever feeling physically well again. He started a new periodical venture, a six-penny monthly miscellany called the *British Magazine,* and continued his connection with it until 1763, writing much of its contents himself and arranging for contributions from other important people such as Oliver Goldsmith, Samuel Derrick, and Samuel Richardson. In this magazine Smollett printed some of his own poems, and, in monthly installments running from January 1760 to December 1761, he presented to the public his fourth novel, *The Adventures of Sir Launcelot Greaves.*

No doubt *Sir Launcelot Greaves* was introduced into the *British Magazine* to support its sales, and there is evidence to suggest that it did just that. In any case this novel was the first by an important English writer to be thus serialized. Goldsmith and others noticed the new story favorably elsewhere in the London press, and Smollett was emboldened to have the work published separately in 1762. It failed in that form. Neither the *Monthly Review* (May 1762) nor Smollett's own *Critical Review* (May 1762) found much to praise in it, though the writer for the *Critical Review* did express admiration for the characters. There was no second edition of the novel during the author's lifetime, unless one counts the piracies that appeared in Dublin (1762) and Cork (1767). Later generations have been no more enthusiastic about *Sir Launcelot Greaves* than Smollett's own, and today it is justly counted the weakest of his five works of fiction.

Still, the narrative does contain some interesting strokes of satire and some noteworthy indications of shifts in Smollett's fictional subject matter. *Sir Launcelot Greaves* is one of many eighteenth-century adaptations from the enormously popular and influential *Don Quixote* (1615), and it introduces what was for Smollett a new strain of sentimental idealism, which he treats both mockingly and seriously. The adventures of the hero follow an episodic pattern resembling that of the author's other novels, showing that his major principles of composition had not changed. The work uses current and also anachronistic references to historical fact in the manner of *Ferdinand Count Fathom,* and the method is still that of juxtaposing separate episodes and disposing "groups" of characters into their "various attitudes" until the entire fictionalized picture of the society represented is complete. But the scale of Smollett's conception in *Sir Launcelot Greaves* is much less ambitious than that of any other novel he had yet written. His canvas is smaller, his range of observation less panoramic. There is, in other words, the suggestion of a certain restraint in the composition of the work. The use of third-person narration with the subject matter of this novel, while limited in its effectiveness, does represent a careful artistic choice. Smollett thoughtfully allows the reader sufficient distance from which to witness and enjoy the confrontations between Greaves's idealism and the quirky world in which he seeks to practice it.

Greaves, unlike his predecessors among Smollett's fictional heroes, possesses not the least hint of roguery in his character. He is, instead, a champion of goodness whose head has been turned following the disappointment of his hopes of marriage to a beautiful young woman whom he loves profoundly. He is decidedly quixotic, but no lunatic; the world through which he moves, however, often looks crazy enough. Indeed, the issue of moral sanity is at the heart of Greaves's quest to restore honor and virtue among the people he meets. Smollett's gallery of eccentric characters is smaller and the pictures less memorably drawn than in earlier novels, but there are some minor triumphs: Timothy Crabshaw, who plays Sancho Panza to the knight; Captain Crowe, the old sea veteran and something of a Quixote figure himself; Justice Gobble, the avaricious country magistrate whom Greaves reforms; and Ferret, the misanthropic pamphleteering mountebank whose character is no doubt modeled upon one of Smollett's old ene-

mies, the novelist and political controversialist John Shebbeare. Greaves's adventures take him through some finely executed scenes in madhouses and prisons, whose horrors Smollett mercilessly exposes as the products of a heartless society. But the vision of the work is unmistakably festive and comic. Smollett brings his ebullient hero into repeated triumphant encounters with the follies and corruptions of the worlds of contemporary fashion, legal and medical practice, and politics. The satiric and moral purpose is, once again, to create the illusion of a comprehensive representation, pictorially and interpretively rendered, of life as it is actually lived among men and women.

Sir Launcelot knows the difference between a windmill and a giant, though he is decidedly naive as he begins his quest. He further diverges from Cervantes' original in that he seeks to transform not the entire world, but the individual characters he meets—Justice Gobble, for instance. This he regularly succeeds in doing by the force of his example and by the exercise of his bravery. No wonder, then, that he never turns cynic, as Roderick Random had done. When Sir Launcelot finally is convinced of his beloved Aurelia's affection, which he thought he had lost to the world's evil machinations against them both, he concludes his adventures and settles into a life of ease and happiness, confident of the goodness of his own life and the benefits bestowed by his energetic Christianity.

The new sentimentality of *Sir Launcelot Greaves* will be obvious to anyone familiar with its author's earlier works. Many readers have seen the story as a transitional effort anticipating the still more pronounced mellowness of *Humphry Clinker.* The events and the writings of the years intervening between the two novels would seem to discredit such a view. But there can be no doubt of the altered mood of Smollett's fourth novel, which allows human feeling and benevolent impulses to express themselves freely and even to prosper and conquer in an imaginary world that threatens to be, but never really is, very dark. The collision between moral idealism and sordid reality is often violent in the novel, but it is productive instead of always portending a descent into chaos, and the hero requires no sudden intervention from his author to rescue him from despair and transplant him into a blissful paradisal retreat.

The sometimes excessive sentimental posturing and language of Greaves and other examples

Illustrations by Anthony Walker for the British Magazine *serialization of* The Adventures of Sir Launcelot Greaves.
*These are said to be the first known magazine illustrations for a fictional work. Left: Sir Launcelot Greaves and his squire,
Timothy Crabshaw; right: Greaves and Crabshaw at a country election.*

of idealism in the novel suggest that Smollett was mocking the new fashion in novels of sensibility, as Laurence Sterne was to do some years later in *Sentimental Journey* (1768). Indeed, Smollett was never very good at writing the language of sentiment unless he was ridiculing it, as he does in this novel with considerable success. Besides the sentimental theme, Smollett also introduced into *Sir Launcelot Greaves* some new Gothic effects, renewing the gestures in this direction already made in *Ferdinand Count Fathom*. The opening chapter describes a stormy night, full of "darkness," "uproar," and "divers loud screams" that drive a group of travelers—Ferret, Captain Crowe, the country surgeon Fillet, and several others—inside an inn. There Smollett quickly captures them visually in a miniature comic picture of terrified humanity, thus signifying both the tone and the compositional method that his novel is to develop throughout.

As it happens, most of the scary "uproar" and all of the "divers screams" are the blustering work of an "apparition" who proves to be no other than Sir Launcelot Greaves. This hero is approaching the shelter of the inn bearing the soaked carcass of his nearly drowned squire Crabshaw. The comic effects of the scene undermine its Gothic possibilities, as happens elsewhere in the story, suggesting that Smollett was deliberately parodying his own contrivance. But Gothic terror is simply another manifestation of the power of human feeling, and Smollett's treatment of it involves a mixture of affirmation and ridicule. The darkness of the Gothic night bears an important relation to the spiritual darkness that might overtake the fictional world if characters such as Greaves were not on hand to lend it the brightness of their wholesome virtue and their sentimental idealism.

Smollett naturally mistrusted the unrestrained Gothic sensibility, but he was obviously not above using the devices of terror for comic or moral purposes. Such maneuvers were insufficient to make *Sir Launcelot Greaves* seem fresh or interesting to more than a few readers of his day, despite the popularity of graveyard poetry and the vigorous antiquarianism that was at the time promoting widespread enthusiasm for medieval ruins and the aesthetics of the sublime. The Gothic had not yet become a fashion in fiction; Horace Walpole's *Castle of Otranto* (1765), the so-called first Gothic novel, was still some years away, and the popular obsession with this kind of romantic story would not set in until the mid 1770s. Smollett's novel was unable to find an audience because it lacked the virile satiric energy of his best early work and because, having departed from the manner of *Roderick Random* and *Peregrine Pickle* to become another eighteenth-century adaptation from *Don Quixote*, it really offered nothing beyond what writers such as Fielding, in *Joseph Andrews* (1742), and Charlotte Lennox, in *The Female Quixote* (1752), had already accomplished in the same vein.

After *Sir Launcelot Greaves,* Smollett avoided novel writing for another long period, this time nearly a decade, until *The Expedition of Humphry Clinker* was published in the last year of his life. He continued with his efforts as a journalist, historian, and translator. While *Sir Launcelot Greaves* was still appearing in serial form, he commenced publication, in weekly parts, of his massive *Continuation of the Complete History of England,* the fifth volume of which finally went to press in the fall of 1765. He almost simultaneously initiated, in collaboration with Thomas Francklin, a multivolume translation of the works of Voltaire that was not completed until 1769. In May 1762 Prime Minister John Stuart, third Earl of Bute, persuaded Smollett to launch a new periodical called the *Briton,* whose sole purpose was to defend the Tory government against a vigorous Opposition press. As is shown by some of the topical references in *Sir Launcelot Greaves,* Smollett had earlier supported the policies of William Pitt, first Earl of Chatham, and the Whigs in their efforts to conclude the Seven Years' War; but he had become disillusioned with Whig factionalism and with the ineptitude of many of Pitt's subordinate ministers. Smollett was by temperament a Tory anyway, or at least he was a political conservative who objected to the increasing democratization of English culture under the Whig oligarchy that

A 1764 portrait of Smollett, by Sir Nathaniel Dance-Holland (Lew David Feldman, House of El Dieff, Fortieth Anniversary Catalogue, 1975)

had dominated court and Parliament since the Hanoverian Succession in 1714. Thus he was not difficult to attract into the Tory camp of controversialists, especially since Bute was a fellow Scot.

But Smollett was not suited for the brutal and often bloody skirmishes of political warfare as it was carried on in the eighteenth-century press. His manner was abrasive and caustic enough, yet he was transparently honest and refused to descend to the rhetorical devices of hysterical name-calling and violent character assassination that distinguished the pages of the chief Opposition organ, the *North Briton.* Smollett was also vulnerable to personal attack. His old friend John Wilkes, together with Charles Churchill, flayed him mercilessly in the rival paper. The entire experience was a miserable and frustrating one for Smollett, and though the *Briton* was as good as other papers of its kind in the period, it did not succeed either in its appeals to a skeptical public or in its assaults against the Opposition. Smollett gave up his editorship on 12 February 1763, less than a year after he had undertaken it. Just weeks later, on 3 April, his only child, Elizabeth, died at the age of fifteen, leaving him almost prostrate with grief. His health now troubled him more seriously than ever, and he began a two-year stay in France and Italy, spending most of his time rather comfortably in the warm climate near Nice.

Upon his return to England in 1765 Smollett's health was only a little improved, and he wandered from Bath to Bristol Springs to Scotland and back to Bath again, hoping for medical and spiritual relief. The trip to Scotland in the spring of 1766 provided something of the latter, but there was no permanent help for his physical condition. He was seriously ill with a recurring asthma, cough, and fever, probably the result of some form of tuberculosis. These symptoms so weakened his constitution that at last he was unable to fight off the acute intestinal infection that killed him in 1771. In the meantime, and despite these troubles, he completed his splendid *Travels through France and Italy,* which was published in May 1766, distinguishing himself as a travel writer by the shrewdness and originality of his painstaking observations on Continental scenery, customs, people, religion, and art. This book clearly anticipates *Humphry Clinker,* and it is no ordinary work of its kind. In a series of forty-one artfully composed letters, it mixes precise description liberally with geniality and honesty—its author did not admire the *Venus de Medicis,* for example, and he says so. Criticism and satire enliven Smollett's *Travels through France and Italy,* but there are few signs of the "Dr. Smelfungus" that Sterne said (in *Sentimental Journey*) he had met in its pages.

The year 1767 brought Smollett a new disappointment in the form of his third rejection for a consulship in Italy, where he hoped to return permanently for his health. He made plans to go there anyway, but in the interim before his move he sent the first installments of his *Present State of All Nations* to the press in June 1768 and continued to provide weekly copy through the completion of the project in the next year. From the dignified historical and political essays of *The Present State of All Nations* he turned to the fierce historical and political satire of *The History and Adventures of an Atom,* which appeared in print in early April 1769. Long thought of as a doubtful attribution, *The History and Adventures of an Atom* has now been unmistakably identified as Smollett's work, partly because of the parallels between its topical references and his experiences in partisan controversy early in the 1760s. *The History and Adventures of an Atom* was Smollett's last such burst of angry satire. By October 1769 he

had settled at Leghorn in Italy where, before he died, he completed the novel that many have called his masterpiece, *The Expedition of Humphry Clinker.*

This work has often been cited, and justly so, as its author's most mature and balanced reflection upon himself and his age. The references to real people and circumstances, both current and from times recently past, nevertheless put one in mind of the textures of his earliest novels. *Humphry Clinker* is a mellowed, yet still sharp, satiric, and comic study of personal and social conflict, of charlatanism in all the professions, of social pretentiousness and hypocrisy, and of incompetence, rivalry, and fraud in literature and the arts. Once again, Smollett's imaginary world seems almost entirely populated by quirky, eccentric, often grotesquely silly and even deformed manifestations of human oddity, perverseness, and folly. But the view of mankind in *Humphry Clinker* is on the whole loving and tolerant, focused upon the ideal of reconciliation rather than the evil of fragmentation and the thrill of Juvenalian scourging.

The irascible but good-natured Matthew Bramble, Smollett's biographers have convincingly shown, is an amused and quite touching self-portrait. Matt's progress from irritated valetudinarianism to tranquillity and sweetness, like the passage of his entourage from Wales, through England and Scotland, and back to Wales again, is a pilgrimage leading toward wholeness and away from both worldly and internal conflict and divisiveness. This pilgrimage is completed only when Bramble has been able to "unclog" the "wheels of life" and has learned to enjoy the movements of his bowels and his heart as well as those of his mind. Bramble is a splendidly created character whose presence provides a comic and moral center to the book, but he is surrounded by an assemblage of family members and servants who join him, with differing degrees of success, in a progress that parallels his own: the worldly Oxonian Jery Melford, Matt's nephew; Jery's sister Lydia, a type of the languishing sentimental heroine; the comic grotesque Tabitha Bramble, Matt's bitter, grizzled spinster sister, who mutilates the English language in her attempts at refined discourse in her letters; and the sweet-natured servant Win Jenkins, another malapropist whose language often slips into unwitting sexual jokes. The methodistical innocent, Humphry Clinker, joins the party along the way; and if any reader has doubted the earthiness of this very funny novel,

THE

EXPEDITION

OF

HUMPHRY CLINKER.

By the AUTHOR of

RODERICK RANDOM.

IN THREE VOLUMES.

VOL. I.

——Quorſum hæc tam putida tendunt,
Furcifer? ad te, inquam——— HOR.

LONDON,
Printed for W. JOHNSTON, in Ludgate-Street;
and B. COLLINS, in Saliſbury.
MDCLXXI.

Title page for the novel that has been widely regarded as Smollett's masterpiece, a comic study of personal and social conflict, charlatanism, hypocrisy, incompetence, and fraud

the appearance of Clinker in rags insufficient to cover his alabaster posterior sets the matter straight. The introduction of the quixotic grotesque Lismahago, a battered and broken old Scottish half-pay lieutenant, completes the gallery of assorted comic travelers.

Smollett's method of structuring *Humphry Clinker* is familiar, with the important exception that he employs the epistolary mode and introduces multiple letter-writing protagonists, who, because they are so varied as character types, effectively represent collective humanity drawn in a comic miniature. Samuel Richardson, of course, had brilliantly projected a largish group of carefully differentiated correspondents in his tragic story of Clarissa Harlowe (1747-1748). But Smollett was the first important novelist to attempt such a display of virtuosity in a comic fiction. The attempt was a complete success, and Smollett's brilliance equals Richardson's. The manner in which the characters of *Humphry Clinker* are "disposed" into their various "attitudes" is intensely visual, the peculiar language of each correspondent enforcing the reader's sense of his or her physical characteristics. The verbal technique represents a reversal upon the pictorial devices of a Hogarth or Rowlandson, who so completely capture their figures in self-revealing postures that one almost expects to hear them speak.

The journey of the Bramble party is superficially linear, or rather circular—suggesting, of course, a pattern for their progress toward wholeness. But the pattern proceeds by a strategy of interruptions. Each place visited—Gloucester, Clifton, Bath, London, Harrogate, Edinburgh, the Scottish countryside—creates an episodic pause in the narrative that allows the letter writers, singly and collectively, to observe and anatomize the people and the society on display. Among the most famous passages in all of *Humphry Clinker* are Matt Bramble's energetic descriptions of the fashionable city of Bath, with its putrid waters and the social pretentiousness of the "noisome crowd" that they attract. Matt's representations of the "vitriolic scum," spoiled food, filth, racket, and violence of London are similarly graphic and equally memorable. By contrast, the scenes of rural Scotland, where Bramble effectually completes his quest for health and tranquillity, occasion some of the most lyrical writing to be found anywhere in Smollett's novels.

Such multiplicity as *Humphry Clinker* offers might threaten narrative chaos in the work of a lesser writer, but Smollett uses it toward creation of a series of comprehensive pictures, each structured by its internal contrasts between good sense or good feeling on the one hand and stupidity, falseness, or even wickedness on the other. The episodes in the series gradually accumulate to become a panoramic representation of the entirety of English and Scottish society. Inevitably the travelers who register the facts of the world and transcribe them in their letters are, like the reader, drawn toward recognition of and participation in the story's moral and comic center. That center resides in the ideal of reconciliation and balance in life that everyone adopts in the end—except Tabitha Bramble and possibly Lieutenant Lismahago, whose obsessive but ineffectual misanthropy becomes a comic commentary upon the progress of the others. The "uniform plan" of *Humphry Clinker* was carefully conceived according to the principles laid down many years before in the dedication to *Ferdinand Count Fathom,* and in his last novel Smollett finally brought those principles into perfect execution.

Humphry Clinker has been properly called a comic romance. The titular hero of the novel, who can boast no noble lineage and indeed turns out to be Bramble's illegitimate son, does not even arrive on the scene until the story is many pages along, suggesting a spoof of the typical beginning to a romance. The "expedition" is hardly his. Humphry's name, which draws upon the stock of heroic conventions but adds a punning reference to a blacksmith's cinder and a human turd, further underscores the appropriateness of the label "comic romance." Repeatedly in his novel, Smollett deflates foolish idealism or sentimental nonsense—Lydia's excessive grieving and swooning over her affairs of love, for example, or her raptures at the wonders of Bath and London. He typically does it by a rhetoric of reduction, which often works through some pointed reminder of bodily functions analogous to the clever contrivance of the title.

But *Humphry Clinker* is more than the term "comic romance" implies. It is a remarkably eclectic work that actually unites many familiar conventions of eighteenth-century fiction writing within a single text, re-creating them and making them part of the wholeness of its own coherent form. One is tempted to suppose that in his last work of fiction, Smollett tried to bring together in an intricate, complete, and culminating expression all of the scattered devices, techniques, themes, and modes of narrative with which he and his fellow storytellers had been experimenting as they brought the new species of the novel through the period of its birth and infancy.

Humphry Clinker is all about a journey or "expedition"; in the characters of Humphry and Lismahago it offers new versions of the Quixote figure; it is a "biographical" or "historical" work that focuses upon individual lives in the manner of Richardson's *Pamela* (1740-1742) or Fielding's *Joseph Andrews* or Smollett's own earlier stories. *Humphry Clinker* even echoes the conventions of such popular "spy-letter" fictions as Charles de Secondat Montesquieu's *Persian Letters* (1721) and Goldsmith's *Citizen of the World* (1762), for it introduces alien characters into contemporary society and causes them to report their satiric or moral observations in letters addressed to confidential friends at home or, in the case of Jery Melford, at that supposed seat of learning and cultivation called Oxford. Smollett's comic tale is, besides, as complete a spoof of the popular novel of sensibility as Sterne's *Sentimental Journey,* which had preceded it by only three years and which had

similarly mixed ridicule of excess with a genuine reverence for the beneficial effects of wisdom and balance in the expressions of the feeling heart. Smollett himself had anticipated this same mixture a decade earlier in *Sir Launcelot Greaves.* It is one of those truly odd coincidences of literary history that *Humphry Clinker,* a masterly comic study of sentimentalism in action, should have appeared in print simultaneously with that most celebrated and most effusive of all novels of sensibility, Henry Mackenzie's *The Man of Feeling* (1771).

Smollett's eclecticism surely improved his book's chances of success with the public. But it was the warm exuberance of his humor in *Humphry Clinker,* the amazing stylistic virtuosity with which he developed the personal voice of each of his traveling correspondents, and the genial but still compelling power of his satiric representation of society that most impressed his earliest reviewers. These same qualities have delighted his critics and his readers ever since. Writers for the *Town and Country Magazine* (June 1771), the *Court and City Magazine* (July 1771), the *Gentleman's Magazine* (July 1771), the *Critical Review* (August 1771), and the *Universal Magazine* (November 1771) expressed nearly unqualified enthusiasm for *Humphry Clinker*—in some instances immoderately, and at great length. Only the reviewer for the *Monthly Review* (August 1771), who wrote a single paragraph of irritated commentary upon the novel's supposed coarseness, raised any serious objection to what his counterparts almost universally admired as the finest achievement of Smollett's literary career.

The work was a popular as well as a critical success. Following its initial appearance in three volumes on or about 15 June 1771, it was twice reprinted (with new typesettings) in the same year and then brought out again in 1772. Among Smollett's novels only *Roderick Random,* published more than two decades earlier, exceeded *Humphry Clinker* in the number of editions printed before the eighteenth century had drawn to an end. There were early translations into German (1772), Dutch (1779), and Danish (1796-1798), so that the fame of the book spread over much of Europe within only a few years. In the following century that fame would extend ever farther, with new translations into Swedish (1855) and Russian (1861) as well as French (1826). Illustrations by Rowlandson were added to a London edition of 1790, and in 1831 George Cruikshank, Dickens's earliest illustrator, provided a new set

Illustrations by Rowlandson for an 1805 British edition of The Expedition of Humphry Clinker;
top: The first appearance of Lieutenant Lismahago; bottom: Clinker preaching in prison

of drawings to accompany the text of Smollett's still-popular story.

The author of *Humphry Clinker,* who had struggled through all of his literary life to have his work accepted and applauded for its merit, did not survive to enjoy any of the adulation his fifth and last novel called forth from its many admirers. On 17 September 1771, just three months after the publication of his book in London, Smollett died at his home in faraway Leghorn. The feverish infection that laid him in his grave had made his last days a torment. But the manner of his death was only the painful conclusion to a long period of intense suffering that had so ravaged him as to make the final stages of the composition of *Humphry Clinker* a daily agony. On 19 September, Smollett was buried in the English cemetery at Leghorn, and when the news of his passing reached England, he was widely mourned in printed obituaries, panegyrics, and generous assessments of his many contributions to English letters.

His contemporaries' final estimate of Smollett's achievement persisted for about a generation, but not much longer. Sir Walter Scott, Dickens, Edward George Bulwer-Lytton, Frederick Marryat, Charles Lever, and even William Makepeace Thackeray were admiring readers of his books, though the praise that Scott and Thackeray gave to them was somewhat qualified by reservations concerning their morality. Readers and critics of the high Victorian period initiated the wrongheaded revisionist view of Smollett's lowness, his crudeness, and his inferiority to Henry Fielding that prevailed well into the twentieth century. The renewal of interest in Smollett that has recently occurred among scholars and critics, together with their gradually more favorable estimate of his work, has been long delayed, but it seems certain to restore him to his proper place among the great eighteenth-century originators of the English novel. Perhaps it will also help to swell his modern audience. New and carefully prepared paperback reprints of *Roderick Random, Peregrine Pickle, Ferdinand Count Fathom, Sir Launcelot Greaves,* and the *Travels through France and Italy* have recently been published. These books may now be as conveniently picked up and read as the perennially popular *Humphry Clinker.* The first serious scholarly edition of Smollett's works ever to be undertaken is now in progress at the University of Georgia Press. As the many volumes of this edition appear, all serious students of the texts they contain will gain access to new in-

formation about them that should lead to new critical insights and new reading pleasures.

Smollett was a writer of extraordinarily versatile talent, richly inventive imagination, and unusually abundant energy and resourcefulness. If he was too long underestimated it was in some part because his genius was just unorthodox enough to deflect readers and critics away from the real centers of interest and originality in his work. He was misunderstood because those who observed him in his performances did not pause to contemplate or study him closely enough. The inscription written in 1773 for the monument erected in his memory by his cousin, James Smollett of Bonhill, on the banks of the Leven seems to have anticipated this lapse of critical attention, which it addresses directly. There is a fine appropriateness in the fact that the lines were composed with the assistance of that greatest of eighteenth-century English critics, Samuel Johnson. The words of the inscription speak for themselves, and they may still be heard as a fitting tribute to their subject and an invitation to enjoy and to value his achievement as it deserves. "Stay, traveller!" wrote Johnson and his collaborators,

> If elegance of taste and wit,
> If fertility of genius,
> And an unrivalled talent
> In delineating the characters of mankind,
> Have ever attracted thy admiration,
> Pause a while
> On the memory of TOBIAS SMOLLETT, M.D.

Letters:

The Letters of Tobias Smollett, M.D., edited by Edward S. Noyes (Cambridge, Mass.: Harvard University Press, 1926);

The Letters of Tobias Smollett, edited by Lewis M. Knapp (Oxford: Clarendon Press, 1970).

Bibliographies:

Robert Donald Spector, *Tobias Smollett: A Reference Guide* (Boston: G. K. Hall, 1980);

Mary Wagoner, *Tobias Smollett: A Checklist of Editions of His Works and an Annotated Secondary Bibliography* (New York: Garland, 1984).

Biographies:

David Hannay, *Life of Tobias George Smollett,* with bibliography by John P. Anderson (London: Walter Scott, 1887);

Louis L. Martz, *The Later Career of Tobias Smollett* (New Haven: Yale University Press, 1942);

Lewis M. Knapp, *Tobias Smollett: Doctor of Men and Manners* (Princeton: Princeton University Press, 1949).

References:

Robert Alter, "The Picaroon as Fortune's Plaything," in his *Rogue's Progress: Studies in the Picaresque Novel* (Cambridge, Mass.: Harvard University Press, 1964), pp. 58-79;

Jerry C. Beasley, *Novels of the 1740s* (Athens: University of Georgia Press, 1982), pp. 85-125;

Beasley, "Smollett's Novels: *Ferdinand Count Fathom* for the Defense," *Papers on Language and Literature*, 20 (Spring 1984): 165-184;

Fred W. Boege, *Smollett's Reputation as a Novelist* (Princeton: Princeton University Press, 1947);

Alan Bold, ed., *Smollett: Author of the First Distinction* (London: Vision Press, 1982);

Paul-Gabriel Boucé, *The Novels of Tobias Smollett* (London: Longmans, 1976);

Howard Swazey Buck, *A Study in Smollett, Chiefly Peregrine Pickle, with a Complete Collation of the First and Second Editions* (New Haven: Yale University Press, 1925);

Robert Giddings, *The Tradition of Smollett* (London: Methuen, 1967);

M. A. Goldberg, *Smollett and the Scottish School: Studies in Eighteenth-Century Thought* (Albuquerque: University of New Mexico Press, 1959);

Damian Grant, *Tobias Smollett: A Study in Style* (Manchester, U.K.: Manchester University Press, 1977);

Eugène Joliat, *Smollett et la France* (Paris: Champion, 1935);

George M. Kahrl, *Tobias Smollett: Traveler-Novelist* (Chicago: University of Chicago Press, 1945);

Alan Dugald McKillop, "Tobias Smollett," in his *The Early Masters of English Fiction* (Lawrence: University of Kansas Press, 1956), pp. 147-181;

Ronald Paulson, "Satire in the Early Novels of Smollett," *Journal of English and Germanic Philology*, 59 (July 1960): 381-402;

William B. Piper, "The Large Diffused Picture of Life in Smollett's Early Novels," *Studies in Philology*, 60 (January 1963): 45-56;

Thomas R. Preston, "Smollett and the Benevolent Misanthrope Type," *PMLA*, 79 (1964): 51-57;

Rufus Putney, "The Plan of *Peregrine Pickle*," *PMLA*, 60 (December 1945): 1051-1065;

George S. Rousseau and Boucé, eds., *Tobias Smollett: Bicentennial Essays Presented to Lewis M. Knapp* (New York: Oxford University Press, 1971);

John Sekora, *Luxury: The Concept in Western Thought, Eden to Smollett* (Baltimore, Md.: Johns Hopkins University Press, 1977);

Robert Donald Spector, *Tobias Smollett* (New York: Twayne, 1968);

Philip Stevick, "Stylistic Energy in the Early Smollett," *Philological Quarterly*, 64 (October 1967): 712-719;

Albrecht B. Strauss, "On Smollett's Language: A Paragraph in *Ferdinand Count Fathom*," in *Style in Prose Fiction: English Institute Essays 1958*, edited by Harold C. Martin (New York: Columbia University Press, 1959), pp. 25-54.

Papers:

Relatively few documents and letters in Smollett's hand have survived, and a good many of these are privately owned. The manuscripts of his novels have all been lost. The following libraries hold small collections of Smollett papers, mostly letters: the National Library of Scotland; the University of Glasgow Library; the British Library; the Library of the Royal College of Surgeons; the Pierpont Morgan Library in New York; the Huntington Library in San Marino, California; and Harvard University Library.

Richard Steele

(March 1672 - 1 September 1729)

This entry was written by Calhoun Winton (University of Maryland, College Park) for
DLB 101: British Prose Writers, 1660-1800: First Series.

See also the Steele entry in DLB 84: Restoration and Eighteenth-Century Dramatists: Second Series.

BOOKS: *The Procession. A Poem on Her Majesties Funeral. By a Gentleman of the Army* (London: Printed for Thomas Bennet, 1695);

The Christian Hero: An Argument Proving that no Principles but Those of Religion Are Sufficient to make a Great Man (London: Printed for J. Tonson, 1701);

The Funeral: or, Grief a-la-Mode. A Comedy. As it is Acted at The Theatre Royal in Drury-Lane, By His Majesty's Servants (London: Printed for Jacob Tonson, 1702);

The Lying Lover, or, The Ladies Friendship. A Comedy. As it is acted at the Theatre Royal *By Her Majesty's Servants* (London: Printed for Bernard Lintott, 1704);

The Tender Husband, or The Accomplish'd Fools. A Comedy. As it is Acted at the Theatre-Royal in Drury-Lane. By Her Majesty's Servants (London: Printed for Jacob Tonson, 1705);

Prologue to the University of Oxford. Written by Mr. Steel, and spoken by Mr. Wilks [broadside] (London: Printed for B. Lintott, 1706);

The Tatler. By Isaac Bickerstaff, Esq., nos. 1-271 (London: Printed by John Nutt for John Morphew, 12 April 1709 - 2 January 1711);

The Spectator, nos. 1-555, by Steele and Joseph Addison (London: Printed for Samuel Buckley & J. Tonson, 1 March 1711 - 6 December 1712);

The Englishman's Thanks to the Duke of Marlborough (London: Printed for A. Baldwin, 1712);

The Guardian, by Steele, Addison, and others, nos. 1-175 (London: Printed for J. Tonson, 12 March - 1 October 1713);

The Englishman: Being the Sequel of the Guardian, first series nos. 1-56 (London: Printed for Sam. Buckley, 6 October 1713 - 11 February 1714);

The Importance of Dunkirk Consider'd: In Defence of the Guardian of August the 7th. In a Letter to the Bailiff of Stockbridge (London: Printed for A. Baldwin, 1713);

The Crisis: Or, A Discourse Representing, from the most Authentick Records, the just Causes of the late Happy Revolution: and the several Settlements of the Crowns of England and Scotland on Her Majesty; and on the Demise of Her Majesty without Issue, upon the Most Illustrious Princess Sophia, Electress and Dutchess Dowager of Hanover, and The Heirs of Her Body Being Protestants . . . With Some Seasonable Remarks on the Danger of a Popish Successor (London: Printed by S. Buckley & sold by F. Burleigh, 1714);

The Englishman: Being the Close of the Paper so called, no. 57 (London: Printed for Ferd. Burleigh, 15 February 1714);

A Letter to a Member of Parliament Concerning the Bill for Preventing the Growth of Schism (London: Printed & sold by Ferd. Burleigh, 1714);

The French Faith Represented in the Present State of Dunkirk. A Letter to the Examiner, In Defense of Mr. S——le (London: Printed & sold by Ferd. Burleigh, 1714);

The Lover. Written in Imitation of the Tatler. By Marmaduke Myrtle, Gent., nos. 1-40 (London: Printed & sold by Ferd. Burleigh, 25 February - 27 March 1714);

The Reader, nos. 1-9 (London: Printed by Sam. Buckley, 22 April - 10 May 1714);

The Romish Ecclesiastical History of Late Years (London: Printed for J. Roberts, 1714);

Mr. Steele's Apology for Himself and His Writings; Occasioned by his Expulsion from the House of Commons (London: Printed & sold by R. Burleigh, 1714);

The Englishman, second series nos. 1-38 (London: Printed & sold by R. Burleigh, 11 July 1715 - 21 November 1715);

A Letter from the Earl of Mar to the King, Before His Majesty's Arrival in England. With some Remarks on my Lord's subsequent Conduct (London: Printed for Jacob Tonson, 1715);

Richard Steele, 1711 (portrait by Sir Godfrey Kneller; National Portrait Gallery, London)

Town-Talk. In a Letter to a Lady in the Country, nos. 1-9 (London: Printed by R. Burleigh & sold by Burleigh, Anne Dodd, James Roberts & J. Graves, 17 December 1715 - 15 February 1716);

A Letter to a Member, &c. concerning the Condemn'd Lords, in Vindication of Gentlemen Calumniated in the St. James's Post *of Friday* March *the 2d* (London: Printed & sold by J. Roberts, J. Graves & A. Dodd, 1716);

Chit-Chat. In a Letter to a Lady in the Country. By Humphrey Philroye, nos. 1-3 (London: Printed & sold by R. Burleigh, March 1716);

An Account of the Fish-Pool, by Steele and Joseph Gillmore (London: Printed & sold by H. Meere, J. Pemberton & J. Roberts, 1718);

The Plebeian. . . . By a Member of the House of Commons, nos. 1-4 (London, 14 March - 6 April 1719);

The Antidote, in a Letter to the Free-Thinker (London: Printed for J. Roberts, 1719);

The Antidote. Number II. In a Letter to the Free-Thinker (London: Printed for J. Roberts, 1719);

A Letter to the Earl of O——d, Concerning the Bill of Peerage (London: Printed for J. Roberts, 1719);

The Spinster: In Defence of the Woolen Manufactures (London: Printed for J. Roberts, 1719);

The Crisis of Property (London: Printed for W. Chetwood, J. Roberts, J. Brotherton & Charles Lillie, 1720);

A Nation a Family: Being the Sequel of the Crisis of Property (London: Printed for W. Chetwood, J. Roberts, J. Brotherton & Charles Lillie, 1720);

The State of the Case Between the Lord-Chamberlain of His Majesty's Household, and the Governor of the Royal Company of Comedians. With the Opinions of Pemberton, Northey, and Parker, concerning the Theatre (London: Printed for W. Chetwood, J. Roberts, J. Graves & Charles Lillie, 1720);

The Theatre. By Sir John Edgar (London: Printed for W. Chetwood, J. Roberts & C. Lillie, 2 January - 5 April 1720);

A Prologue to the Town, as it was spoken at the theatre in Little Lincoln's Inn Fields. Written by Mr. Welstead. With an Epilogue on the same occasion, by Sir Richard Steele (London: Printed & sold by J. Brotherton & W. Meadows, J. Roberts, A. Dodd, W. Lewis & J. Graves, 1721);

The Conscious Lovers. A Comedy. As it is Acted at the Theatre Royal in Drury-Lane, By His Majesty's Servants (London: Printed for Jacob Tonson, 1723 [i.e., 1722]);

Pasquin, nos. 46 and 51 (London: Sold by J. Peele, 9 and 26 July 1723).

Editions: *Richard Steele,* edited, with an introduction and notes, by G. A. Aitken, Mermaid Series (London: Unwin / New York: Scribners, 1894)—includes notes and fragments of "The School of Action" from the Blenheim manuscripts, apparently since lost;

Tracts and Pamphlets by Richard Steele, edited by Rae Blanchard (Baltimore: Johns Hopkins Press, 1944);

Steele's The Englishman, edited by Blanchard (Oxford: Clarendon Press, 1955);

Steele's Political Journalism, 1714-16, edited by Blanchard (Oxford: Clarendon Press, 1959);

The Theatre, edited by John Loftis (Oxford: Clarendon Press, 1962);

The Spectator, 5 volumes, edited by Donald F. Bond (London: Oxford University Press, 1965);

The Plays of Richard Steele, edited by Shirley Strum Kenny (Oxford: Clarendon Press, 1971);

The Guardian, edited by John Calhoun Stephens (Lexington: University Press of Kentucky, 1982);

The Tatler, 2 volumes, edited by Bond (London: Oxford University Press, 1987).

PLAY PRODUCTIONS: *The Funeral,* London, Theatre Royal, Drury Lane, between 9 October and 11 December 1701;

The Lying Lover, Theatre Royal, Drury Lane, 2 December 1703;

The Tender Husband, Theatre Royal, Drury Lane, 23 April 1705;

The Conscious Lovers, Theatre Royal, Drury Lane, 7 November 1722.

Richard Steele was recognized, was indeed famous, in his own time as an innovative essayist, edi-

tor, and pamphleteer. No doubt the principal reasons for his being remembered today have to do with his activities as a writer of prose. His entry into the world of writing and publishing coincided exactly with the great explosion of printing after the Licensing Act expired in 1695, when government control over printing in the English-speaking world came to an abrupt end.

Steele was one of the first, it might be argued *the* first, to appreciate fully the consequences of this explosion, to understand the positive possibilities of the coming of print culture, when some of his most perceptive contemporaries saw only the dangers. Mass audiences for the first time in human history became theoretically available, and Richard Steele set about devising means of communicating with those audiences.

He was also a dramatist; he achieved his earliest recognition in London as a writer of popular comedies, and this should be remembered in assessing him as a prose writer. Dramatic concerns made their way into his prose writings. He was, for example, the virtual inventor of theater reviewing, which he introduced into the first issue of his *Tatler,* and his essay periodicals are a rich primary source of information about theatrical literature, personnel, and practices, as well as the locus of dramalike fictional scenes.

Richard Steele was born in Dublin in 1672, probably sometime in late February or early March because he was christened in St. Bride's parish church on 12 March of that year. His father, Richard Steele, an attorney, was a member of the Church of Ireland; he was, that is, a Protestant. Steele's mother was born Elinor Sheyles Symes; she was therefore a member of the ancient Irish family of O'Sheills; no doubt she was born a Roman Catholic. Steele came from divided ways; that may be one of the reasons the print medium, that great leveler of class and condition, appealed to him.

He did not spend his entire boyhood in Ireland, as did his contemporary Jonathan Swift; the elder Richard Steele died young and Richard his son was adopted, formally or informally, by his father's aunt Katherine and her second husband, Henry Gascoigne. As private secretary to James Butler, Duke of Ormonde, who was lord lieutenant of Ireland, Gascoigne was in a position to know that severe times were ahead for Ireland, and some time in the early 1680s he moved his household to London. Richard Steele was enrolled in the Charterhouse in November 1684, through Ormonde's influence. This was the beginning of his formal education as far as anyone knows. Charterhouse was, and still is, a demanding school, and Steele was forced into a curriculum rich with Latin and Greek, a late educational heritage of Renaissance humanism. In 1686 Joseph Addison, son of an Anglican priest, enrolled at the Charterhouse. London was an interesting and instructive place to be in the late 1680s, as the Catholic King James II attempted to recast British institutions in the old mold. London, by and large, resisted; so did the family circle in which Steele lived, a circle dominated by the presence of the duke of Ormonde; so of course did Addison's family connections. In 1688, with the coming of King William and Queen Mary in the revolution of that year, prospects looked better for Richard Steele than they ever had before.

On its social side the Charterhouse school was one of those winnowing institutions that English society has maintained for centuries, designed to educate to a passable extent the children of the aristocracy but also designed with places reserved for young men of unusual ability and not much in the way of financial resources who could be singled out and put on the road to education, leadership, and success. If one had inherited wealth and position, of course, one did not have to go to school at all and thus avoided the tiresome process of learning to translate Catullus and Horace. But for boys of intelligence and little money, boys such as Addison and Steele—or John Dryden, or Matthew Prior, or Samuel Johnson—schools such as the Charterhouse were steps up the social ladder. Influence helped, too. When Steele was ready for university in 1689, his foster father, Henry Gascoigne, was ready to help him: Gascoigne now had a place in King William's household, and he saw to it that young Richard was admitted to Christ Church, Oxford, the duke of Ormonde's old college. Aunt Katherine, who knew something about the value of appearances if not much about spelling, wrote Gascoigne, "[P]ray give him a pare of gloves, and Send him a Sord and Show him how to put it one, That he may be like The young Lads nex doer."

Oxford, unlike London, provided little food for Steele's aesthetic imagination. Years later he looked back to his university days with an alumnus's fondness, but he never settled into the academic track. His friend Addison, who had preceded him there by two years, was already recognized as being on the way to a brilliant career.

Lack of money probably made Steele restless, especially in a fashionable college such as Christ Church. In 1691 he migrated to Merton College as a portionista or postmaster, the name Merton has used over the centuries for its endowed scholarships. Legend has it that Steele wrote a comedy while he was at Merton but destroyed it on the advice of one of his fellow postmasters; nothing is known of what other writing, if any, he did at Oxford.

In the spring of 1692 King William was recruiting a larger army to pursue his campaign on the Continent against the French; in May of that year Steele went down from Merton, not to return as a student. At some time, presumably that spring, he enlisted as a trooper in the second troop of Life Guards, the royal bodyguard, then commanded by the young second duke of Ormonde, who had in 1688 succeeded his grandfather, Gascoigne's patron. Like their successors at Buckingham Palace today, the Life Guards were both a ceremonial and a fighting outfit. The second troop was on active service in Flanders for the campaigns of 1692 and 1693. Though the muster rolls do not exist to prove it, there seems no reason to doubt Steele's statement that he was there with them, as he reminisced years later, with a "broad Sword, Jack-Boots, and Shoulder-Belt, under the Command of the unfortunate Duke of *Ormond*."

Back in London, on guard duty in Whitehall and at St. James's Palace, Steele had plenty of time to pursue the advancement of his career, whatever that might turn out to be. Troopers of the Life Guards were officially referred to as "private gentlemen" and addressed as "Mister." With the Gascoignes living in London, providing a convenient address, Steele could see and be seen. In 1695 he left the Life Guards and joined the Coldstreamers, the second foot guards, commanded by John, Baron Cutts, to whom Steele, not coincidentally, dedicated *The Procession*, a poem published in April. In April 1697 he was commissioned ensign in Lord Cutts's own company, with the brevet rank of captain. Hence, hereafter, Captain Steele.

Just at this time London was experiencing, more or less without recognizing it, the liberating effect brought about by the failure of King William to renew the Licensing Act in 1695. This act had severely limited the number of presses in the British Isles. When William had come ashore from Holland, in Exeter in 1688, he had been unable to find a printing press in the west of England on which to print his manifesto. None existed. Whatever the motives for William's action—whether he recognized the value of print for a sovereign or whether he sought some other means than the Licensing Act to control press and printing—the practical effect was to encourage the spread of printing throughout the English-speaking world.

The expansion of printing came in good time for Richard Steele. By 1700 his life and career seemed to have stalled: the Treaty of Ryswick had brought peace to Europe and unemployment to soldiers, though not to Steele himself. Much of what little money he had had literally gone up in smoke in alchemical experiments. He had fathered an illegitimate daughter and was financing her support; he had fought and won a duel in Hyde Park. Everything was in the past tense; at twenty-eight he had no prospects.

Then, suddenly, matters turned around. Like his fellow officers John Vanbrugh and George Farquhar, Steele turned to writing, producing in April 1701 his first major published work, a religious self-help book entitled *The Christian Hero*, and in December of that year his first play, *The Funeral*. Both were successes.

It was typical of Steele that he tried more than one road to fulfillment; for the rest of his active life, until his retirement to Wales, he would be mixing modes: writing poetry, prose, drama; living the soldier's life, the politician's life, the writer's life. This variety of experience contributed substantially to the success of what he wrote; several years later when he began his first, and in some ways his best, periodical, *The Tatler*, he took for it this motto from Juvenal's First Satire: "*Quicquid agunt homines . . . nostri farrago libelli*" (Whatever mankind does is grist for our mill).

Certainly the contrast in mode and manner between *The Christian Hero* and *The Funeral* is striking. *The Funeral* is a good-natured comedy about family relationships, with satiric touches and effective farcical episodes; *The Christian Hero* is a serious, even solemn work of popularized piety, which, as Richard Dammers has shown, represents a response to the recent Stoic revival and an affirmation of ethical Christianity. The Christian heroes include Christ himself, Saint Paul, and, most significantly, King William III. From the point of view of his later career, perhaps the most interesting aspect of *The Christian Hero* is his inclusion of women and women's concerns. *The Christian Hero* was no masterpiece of prose: an early critic complained that he must have written

it "on the Butt-end of a Musquet," but readers seem not to have minded: the book ran to some eight editions in his lifetime and was reprinted for many years. It is not farfetched to see *The Christian Hero* as part of William's effort to establish his presence in British, especially English, society, though Steele of course was sincere in his praise of the dour soldier-king.

Steele was given a commission as captain in the Thirty-Fourth Foot in 1702, probably partly because his book had attracted the right kind of attention, from the court's point of view. William's death in 1702, however, precluded any more royal favor, and Steele spent the next several years assigned to Landguard Fort in Suffolk, looking at the ships coming into and out of Harwich, and working on stage comedies in his spare time, which was plentiful. Two were actually produced: *The Lying Lover* in 1703, with indifferent success, and *The Tender Husband*, perhaps his best play, in 1705. *The Tender Husband* became a staple of the repertory theater, was revived every season except three for the next forty years, and was acted in the provinces and the American colonies for decades. With it Steele became an established figure in the London theater world.

He was feeling secure enough to sell his commission, probably in the spring of 1705, and to marry a widow, Margaret Stretch, who possessed a considerable estate in Barbados. By the end of 1706 she had died, but Steele, whether through charm, influence, or a combination of these, had received his first civil preferment—which was worth one hundred pounds a year, tax free—as gentleman waiter to Queen Anne's husband, Prince George of Denmark. At Margaret's funeral Steele met a young woman from Wales, Mary Scurlock—possibly a family friend—and on 9 September 1707 they were married, after a waiting period just within the bounds of social decorum. During the courtship Steele commenced a correspondence which continued until the death of Mary, or "Dear Prue" as Steele addressed her, in pregnancy in 1718. Preserved with meticulous care by Mary, who evidently had a keener sense of literary merit than she has been given credit for, these hundreds of notes and letters written at all hours of the day and night and in every variety of emotional state constitute one of the great archives of the personal letter. Produced in an era when letter writing evolved from mere communication to an art form, Steele's letters to Dear Prue are comparable in quality with those of

The first issue of Steele's first periodical, in which he promised to tell male readers "what to think" while also providing "Entertainment to the Fair Sex"

Swift or Horace Walpole or Fanny Burney, but entirely different in their character.

About the time he got married, in 1707, Steele received more preferment, this time a post in which, he fondly imagined, he could use his literary talents. He was appointed writer of the *London Gazette*, the official government news medium. His friends in the circle of Whig leaders known as the Junto recognized that theirs was becoming an age of political pamphleteering and that party leaders needed writers to help them get into office and to defend them when they were there. Steele received the appointment

for political reasons, though the post was ostensibly nonpartisan, and lost it for the same reasons a few years later when the tide of politics turned against the Whigs, but the experience he gained in putting a newspaper out twice a week was invaluable. He was forced to learn about printer's deadlines, about distribution networks, about readership, even if he did not use those terms which were yet to be coined. This was beginning journalism when journalism itself was in the course of being invented. It paid well, too: three hundred pounds a year, which together with the hundred from his position as gentleman waiter totaled four hundred, a sum sufficient to keep a couple of modest tastes in considerable comfort.

But Steele's tastes were never modest. By 1708 he was involved in a lawsuit having to do with the estate of his first wife, and about that time he must have been meditating on ways to increase the family income. As it happened, that year Jonathan Swift was in London, casting his keen eye about for satiric targets. One target of opportunity was John Partridge, a former shoe repairman, now a quack doctor and astrologer, who was making a fortune by publishing an annual almanac full of vague predictions. Swift published his own *Predictions for the Year 1708*, writing under the name of one Isaac Bickerstaff, in which Bickerstaff, also an astrologer, predicted precisely the death of Partridge. In his next almanac Partridge, incredibly, denied that he was dead. London wits joined the chase; Swift himself produced an anonymous, richly ironic *Vindication of Isaac Bickerstaff, Esq.* (1709). A year after the publication of Swift's *Predictions for the Year 1708* everyone in literary London knew about John Partridge and his rival, Isaac Bickerstaff.

Steele and Swift were still enjoying amicable relations—political differences would soon change that—and, when Steele decided to publish a periodical paper on his own time (he was also editing the *Gazette*), he chose "Isaac Bickerstaff" as the name of the putative editor for *The Tatler*. On 12 April 1709 Bickerstaff produced the first number of his new paper, "By *Isaac Bickerstaff*, Esq.," a folio half sheet printed on both sides and resembling to twentieth-century eyes an oversized handbill, about eight inches by thirteen and a half. In the first issue Bickerstaff announced that he would tell his male readers "what to think," and that he would provide something of "Entertainment to the Fair Sex." Steele gave away the first four issues, then charged a penny each. The paper was to be published three times a week, to coincide with the mails posted to provincial towns. *The Tatler* proved to be a runaway success, without question the most successful periodical in any language to that time.

This was not solely, or even principally, because of the Partridge-Bickerstaff controversy. Success was a result of Steele's own experience, judgment, and acumen. Even with the Licensing Act serving as a rein on press activity before 1695, many newspapers and periodicals of various kinds had been published earlier than 1709—public newspapers such as the *Gazette* and privately owned papers such as the *Daily Courant*. Some periodicals, such as the *Athenian Mercury*, were devoted entirely to questions and answers. Defoe was in the fifth year of his *Review*, which carried both news and editorial opinion. Steele identified and combined the appeals of various periodicals into one. The question-and-answer and the hoax letter appeared, for example—sometimes separate, sometimes combined—transfigured as the letter to the editor; shrewd editors have exploited the same device ever since. News was included at first to attract readers; Steele felt that as gazetteer he would have access to the freshest foreign news in the form of diplomatic reports. For various reasons this stratagem did not work out, and news as such gradually disappeared from *The Tatler*, though matters of topical interest continued to appear in differing forms.

The principal appeals, however, were just those Bickerstaff had announced in the first issue: variety, entertainment for the women and information for the men, and actually both for both. This is Horace's *prodesse aut delectare*, instruction and entertainment, in a new format attractive to the widest possible audience. Horace he had read at Charterhouse and Oxford; the possibility of a mass audience was a product of his observing the oncoming print culture. Ostensibly the audience addressed was the inner circle of wit and learning, those who knew of and laughed at the Partridge-Bickerstaff hoax. But Steele was speaking over the heads of these to the vastly larger circle of readers in London and the provinces and even the colonies who wanted to be told how to act, what to read, what—as Bickerstaff had put it in the first issue—to think; who wanted to learn these things outside of church or chapel and yet who were suspicious of the libertinism associated with the literary life since Charles II's reign. From our perspective in the twentieth century we see Steele's activities as an early aspect of the British Enlightenment.

On the practical side Steele had to contend with the triweekly demand for copy, with the restrictions of space which the half-sheet format imposed on him, and with the expenses of running a periodical. He had to fill his paper three times a week; it was a small paper but every copy cost money. How to balance these demands he had to learn on the job. No one had ever run a paper like this one, and so there was no one to tell him. In the first number he set up various departments: one for news, one for "poetry" (that is, literary and theatrical matters), another for "accounts

Frontispiece to The Lucubrations of Isaac Bickerstaff Esq. *(1710-1711), the first collected edition of* The Tatler

of learning," and a fourth for "gallantry, pleasure, and entertainment." This gave him enough scope for variety, but since the maximum number of words that could be set on both sides of the half sheet was about three thousand, using all four departments each issue would make for short entries. In addition advertisements had to be accommodated. Advertisements, which were placed at the end of the editorial matter, meant income, but they also absorbed precious space. Furthermore, as the popularity of the paper increased so did the demand for advertising space. Editorial and business decisions had to be made by Steele, three times a week, every week. Modern journalism was born.

His decisions had consequences, but readers

of *The Tatler* did not, it goes without saying, concern themselves with consequences; their response was simply to read or not read the paper. Steele developed a spectrum of strategies to keep them reading, introducing, for example, theatrical criticism in *Tatler* number 1 and continuing it regularly thereafter. This was an important development: for the first time actors and dramatic authors could look forward to seeing in print regular comment on the plays they had appeared in or written. Within a few weeks Bickerstaff was beginning to receive letters to the editor, and in *Tatler* number 9 he reported that he had received a communication from his "ingenious Kinsman" Humphrey Wagstaff, a poem written "in a Way

461

perfectly new." Wagstaff was Jonathan Swift, and the poem was his "Description of the Morning," printed for the first time. From this point on Steele would be soliciting contributions from his friends and acquaintances for *The Tatler* and for its successors. These were always printed anonymously; when he wound up the papers Steele would sometimes identify the authors, and sometimes he would not, presumably according to the desires of the writers themselves. As far as one knows, there was no direct compensation for the contributions at first, but the prestige and wide readership of the papers made them good places in which to be published. Over the next three years Steele would publish more of Swift's work and contributions from, among many others, John Gay, Alexander Pope, and most important, Joseph Addison. In 1713 he printed several essays by the young philosopher George Berkeley in *The Guardian*. A legend has it that Berkeley was rewarded with a dinner at Steele's elegant new house and a guinea gold coin for each essay; if so, this would be perhaps the earliest example of direct payment for a journalistic contribution. Twenty-five years later Samuel Johnson would be making his living in London by this means.

In the early days of *The Tatler* Steele used the "departments" which he had set up in the first issue; this made for short entries of a few hundred words under each by- (or, more properly, from-) line. Fairly soon the paper evolved toward the single essay of some fifteen hundred or two thousand words that would take up both sides of the half sheet, less the advertising. This was the informal essay, derived ultimately from Montaigne, which became in *Tatler* form the periodical essay and gave the name to its vehicle, the essay periodical. Use of the essay form in periodicals was not new: Defoe had been writing them in his *Review* since 1704. It never became the exclusive form in *The Tatler* partly because the narrative persona, Isaac Bickerstaff, was inflexible. Defoe could write his essays more or less in his own voice, whereas Steele was constrained by the narrative mediation of Bickerstaff the astrologer, who was at the same time both an impediment and a benefit.

The persona of Isaac Bickerstaff had provided a starting point for the paper and an apparently convenient mask behind which Richard Steele could exercise his editorial authority. As the paper continued Bickerstaff took on a life of his own, attracted other kinspeople, including Humphrey Wagstaff and Jenny Distaff, who

wrote him letters, and eventually achieved celebrity status by having his "portrait" drawn, from which prints were made and sold to the public. Bickerstaff was invited to a performance at the Drury Lane theater and someone—Steele in disguise?—attended and was applauded. By this time he had adopted the mock-heroic but half-serious title "Censor of Great Britain," bestowed on him by a correspondent in number 140.

Mock-heroic because Isaac Bickerstaff was no Marcus Porcius Cato, the stern Censor of the Roman republic; but also half-serious because one of the principal themes of *The Tatler*, and *The Spectator*, was the reform of manners. This subject is difficult to treat without appearing either pedantic or obvious. The virtues Steele, and Addison after him, advocated in this reform are the ordinary, homely ones: good sense, decency, kindness, simple generosity. Their reform is in the direction of tolerance and accommodation rather than stiffer laws and regulated conduct. Steele, for example, opposed dueling, with its strict code of "honor." He knew about dueling's cruelty because in June 1700 he had wounded Captain Henry or Harry Kelly with his sword in Hyde Park, and watched the blood run out of his body. There must be better ways, he might have thought then, to settle these things; later, in his periodicals, he would suggest some.

In the summer of 1709 Steele was fully employed: he had a new member of his family, his daughter Elizabeth, born in March, and he was meeting five deadlines a week, two for the *Gazette* and three for *The Tatler*. "Don't be displeased that I do not come home till eleven o'clock," he wrote Prue. Still, he had reason for satisfaction; he received another sinecure, a commissionership of the Stamp Office, at three hundred pounds a year. Better yet, his new paper was succeeding. The *British Apollo*, a question-and-answer journal, complained that it had lost "near two thousand Subscribers" to Bickerstaff but then went on to "recommend him to the Reading of all our Subscribers." Here is journalistic generosity indeed! Imitators appeared: *The Tatling Harlot, Titt for Tatt, The Grouler,* and the longest-lived and best, "Mrs. Crackenthorpe's" *Female Tatler*.

This imitation may have gratified Steele's sensibility; nevertheless, a deadline was a deadline, and he desperately needed help. In the autumn of 1709, he received some. In September his friend and schoolmate Joseph Addison returned from Ireland, where he had been serving as secretary to the lord lieutenant, Thomas, Lord

Joseph Addison and Richard Steele at the time they were collaborating on The Tatler

Wharton. From time to time he began contributing a department or an entire essay to *The Tatler*. It was still very much Steele's paper, however—he probably wrote three-quarters of the total wordage—and he did not scruple to take it into political areas where the more cautious Addison would hesitate to venture. In the fourth number and again in number 130, he heaped praise on members of the government, who were mostly his patrons the Junto Whigs. The new Tory paper, *The Examiner*, which was secretly supported by Robert Harley in his bid for political power, advised Bickerstaff, "Give me leave to tell you, you mistake your talent, whenever you meddle with matters of state . . ." (31 August 1710).

By the summer of 1710 the political balance of power was shifting visibly. In June the queen, with Harley's approval, dismissed Steele's immediate supervisor, Charles Spencer, Earl of Sunderland, from his post as secretary of state. Steele chose to fly his colors by publishing a series of partisan political *Tatlers* in June and July; in August Henry St. John, a leader of the resurgent Tories, associated Bickerstaff with a "Factious Cabal" in *A Letter to the Examiner*. In the middle of October Steele resigned the editorship of the *London Gazette*, as Harley consolidated his position. Steele's principles would not let him support a ministry which would, he knew, be hostile to his hero, John Churchill, Duke of Marlborough. Toward the end of 1710 Steele decided to wind *The Tatler* up; possibly it was the price Harley exacted from him for keeping the commissionership of stamps. He and his paper had become identified with the Whigs.

It had been an exciting time for Steele: in a year and a half *The Tatler* had established itself as far and away the outstanding periodical in English. In that same period of time Steele's image had been transformed in the London mind from that of a minor playwright and Junto Whig follower to that of Isaac Bickerstaff, Censor of Great Britain, editor of the best-known paper in the land. When he published the last *Tatler* on 2 January 1711, and signed it with his own name rather than Bickerstaff's, Steele must have realized that he possessed handsome resources; he was not yet forty years old and full of plans.

Addison was back in London, permanently, and as a Whig out of office he had time on his hands. He and Steele were able to plan a new periodical with some care; it was probably Addison's prudential counsel that led them to adopt a nonpartisan stance for it. The immediate political future was rather clear: the now-dominant Tories would attempt to discredit the duke of Marlborough and displace him from his position as commander-in-chief of the allied armies battling France. If Steele wished to write Whig propaganda, he could do so over his own signature. Both editors now had general experience in journalism and particular experience in essay periodicals. Steele was especially familiar with the business side of publishing. He would be the general editorial supervisor, responsible for seeing the paper through the press. Because a six-day-a-week publishing schedule was envisioned, two printing shops were signed on to take care of the anticipated volume, to be assisted at various times in the distribution by at least a dozen other establishments. On 1 March 1711, two months after the final *Tatler* appeared, Addison and Steele brought out the first issue of their new periodical, *The Spectator*. Like *The Tatler*, it found a waiting reading public and prospered from the first, as Steele, at least, devoutly hoped because he was being sued for debt at the time. It appeared daily except Sunday until 6 December 1712, a total of five hundred and fifty-five issues. As regards style, content, method, *The Spectator* is Addison's as *The Tatler* was Steele's. In the first number, for example, the narrator, self-described as "a Spectator of Mankind," declares that he has "never espoused any Party with violence, and am resolved to observe an exact Neutrality between the Whigs and Tories, unless I shall be forced to declare my self by the Hostilities of either Side."

In the second number he describes the Club of which he is a member: Sir Roger de Coverley, the country squire; an unnamed attorney; Sir Andrew Freeport, the eminent merchant; Captain Sentry, the retired army officer; Will Honeycomb, the aging fop; and the anonymous philosophic clergyman. These are intended to replace in a sense the various departments of *The Tatler*, offering Addison and Steele the opportunity to move in various directions as far as subject matter is concerned and at the same time separating the authors from their materials.

Although the various departments of *The Tatler* are abandoned and *The Spectator* moves toward a single-essay format (always with advertisements, however), considerable variety could be achieved even within that more restrictive format. Steele's number 11, for example, begins with the satiric presentation of a male-chauvinist fop who is put down by Mr. Spectator's learned friend Arietta, first as she reapplies one of Aesop's fables to him and then as she recites the story of Inkle and Yarico. Inkle is an English merchant who is left ashore in America by his companions but rescued and sheltered by the Indian maiden Yarico. They fall in love, and when a ship appears several months later bound for Barbados, the couple board it. In Barbados, Inkle sells the pregnant Yarico into slavery, making "use of that Information [that she is pregnant], to rise in his Demands upon the Purchaser." This single "essay" thus proceeds from casual fictional comedy, presented in dramatic terms, to a pointed satire on male hypocrisy, to a poignant narrative depicting man's—and mankind's—inhumanity to mankind. The exuberant variety of *The Spectator*, like that of *The Tatler*, is one of the ingredients of its popular appeal, but the variety also renders formal literary criticism difficult; in fact, Michael Ketcham's *Transparent Designs* (1985) is, perhaps surprisingly, the first book-length essay in criticism on it ever published.

On the other hand, some aspects of the paper contribute to unity rather than variety: among others, the Club motif itself, of course; the various essay series; and the editorial tone. The Club, as Ketcham has pointed out, has the inward, unifying quality of such an organization, but is also infinitely extensible, so as to include all the periodicals' readers in its membership. The series, such as the twelve essays on "The Pleasures of the Imagination" or the eighteen on *Paradise Lost*, are largely the work of Addison, but Steele's many essays on the theater and drama also have a unity of attitude if not of focus. Editorial tone is the great unifying principle—and the great triumph of the editors: learned, witty, affable, faintly pedantic, slightly patronizing, it spoke to readers who were in the midst of the Enlightenment without realizing it.

Richard Steele, 1712 (portrait by Jonathan Richardson; National Portrait Gallery, London)

Although *The Spectator* steered clear for the most part of direct political involvement, Steele and Addison discreetly arranged the paper's presentation so that the Whigs and commercial interests would at least not be depreciated. Sir Roger de Coverley, the Tory squire, is depicted as lovable but ineffectual, in sharp contrast to Sir Andrew Freeport, the merchant of broad vision who "will tell you that it is a stupid and barbarous Way to extend Dominion by Arms; for true Power is to be got by Arts and Industry." Still, it behooved the authors to tread cautiously: 1711 and 1712 were turbulent years in British politics, and Steele needed the money the paper was garnering, in large amounts. Swift meanwhile had taken over, anonymously, editorial direction of the Tory periodical *The Examiner*, and in November 1711 published his brilliant pamphlet *The Conduct of the Allies*, which sought to discredit not

only the departed Whig government, Steele's friends and patrons, but also the series of campaigns on the Continent directed by the much-admired duke of Marlborough. Marlborough was dismissed from all offices in December, and in January 1712 Steele published in reply to Swift a short pamphlet over the pseudonym "Scoto-Britannus," *The Englishman's Thanks to the Duke of Marlborough*. Although undistinguished in itself, it represents the first of many political pamphlets written by Steele over the succeeding ten years. Swift's and Steele's differing opinions about the great duke would result in the end of their friendship. As 1712 progressed, the Tories tightened their control of the government and pursued the peace treaty their political strategy called for.

By the end of the year 1712 Addison and Steele were ready to close out their paper, perhaps because both wanted to move on to something new, to end the game while they were ahead. With number 555 of 6 December 1712 the original series ended, Steele acknowledging over his signature some of those who had helped. In number 550 Addison, as Mr. Spectator, had remarked on his taciturnity, adding that he has "Thoughts of being very loquacious in the Club which I now have under Consideration." It was to begin "on the twenty-fifth of March next."

By that time Addison was involved with completing his tragedy *Cato* and seeing about its production at Drury Lane. Steele, therefore, began the new paper, *The Guardian*, on 12 March 1713, precisely as Mr. Spectator had predicted. He continued to edit it except for a month's relief by Addison in August until he brought it to a close on 1 October of that year. A folio half sheet in format, *The Guardian* continued the demanding six-issues-a-week schedule of *The Spectator*. Obviously Steele could not write it all himself, and he sought assistance from his acquaintances. Addison's 53 *Guardians* represent almost a third of the final total of 175 numbers. Alexander Pope was an important—and controversial—contributor. Steele entertained the young philosopher George Berkeley, just in from Dublin, at his fine new house in Bloomsbury Square and, as noted above, eventually printed about a dozen of his essays in the paper.

The persona of *The Guardian* was one Nestor Ironside, whose name bespeaks elderly wisdom and toughness; in the first number he declares his resolve to "make the Pulpit, the Bar, and the Stage, all act in Concert in the Care of Piety, Justice, and Virtue." Reform and entertainment as usual; the mixture of enlightenment and chitchat which had been proven in *The Spectator* were to remain the staple of *The Guardian*. Ironside has friends, a numerous Northamptonshire family named Lizard, who reside at Lizard Hall. Steele evidently expected them to take over some of the functions of Mr. Spectator's Club; in the seventh *Guardian*, for example, Nestor visits Lady Lizard at her tea table and participates in a discussion about the proper age for marriage. Mary Lizard writes in number 43 of her attendance at Addison's *Cato*, with her brother Tom. Steele appears to have wearied of the idea: the Lizards never achieve the reality of Sir Roger de Coverley and his crew.

In number 98 Nestor describes his intention to set up a lion's mouth at Button's Coffeehouse, like the legendary receptacle in Venice, where communications could be deposited for the paper. A "lion" he had earlier identified as a "great Man's Spy." Some of the amusing letters he received did come by way of Button's lion; many were perhaps commissioned, such as that on sacred poetry by Steele's friend Edward Young, fellow of All Souls, Oxford. Steele wrote letters to the editor, to himself, as he had been doing ever since the days of *The Tatler*. Steele was busy. He had four children at home now, and was still supporting his illegitimate daughter. Perhaps he was so busy that he did not take in Alexander Pope's ploy in number 40, when he received copy for the paper from Pope. Pope been irritated by the praise of Ambrose Philips's pastorals in number 22; he felt his own work in the genre had been overlooked. *Guardian* number 40 is a straightfaced demonstration that Philips's pastorals are after all very like the Grub Street ballads of Tom D'Urfey. Philips was furious—he is said to have kept a switch on the bar at Button's, for use if Pope happened by. Steele presumably was embarrassed—but the controversy sold papers. Theatrical criticism, which Steele had virtually invented in *The Tatler*, continued as a popular feature in the new paper. John Gay's new comedy, *The Wife of Bath*, is handsomely puffed by Nestor Ironside in number 50.

Politics kept Swift from contributing to Steele's paper: they were entirely on opposite sides of the political fence now, with Swift providing hints for the Tory *Examiner* in its attacks on Marlborough, and on Steele himself. During the summer of 1713 Steele decided to sever all remaining ties with the Tory Ministry and run for Parliament in the general elections which were approaching in the fall. He resigned his preferments, including his earliest, the pension as gentleman waiter to Queen Anne's late husband. In early August Steele published a fiery political paper, *Guardian* number 128, in which he arraigned the government's conduct in certain aspects of the recently concluded Treaty of Utrecht. Fortifications for the port of Dunkirk, which the treaty had specified for removal, were still there, Steele complained. Propagandists on Robert Harley's payroll, including Daniel Defoe, chose to interpret this as an attack on the queen; *The Examiner* (21 August 1713) called Steele's paper a "scandalous libel." In spite of the government's opposition, Steele was elected a member of Parliament for the borough of Stockbridge in Hampshire.

Elated no doubt by his election, Steele turned *The Guardian* over to Addison in Septem-

Richard Steele circa 1713 (perhaps a copy of a portrait by Sir James Thornhill; from Willard Connely, Sir Richard Steele, *1934)*

ber and on 22 September published a pamphlet called *The Importance of Dunkirk Consider'd,* which marked his full-time entry into the propaganda wars. The pamphlet sold well, going to a third edition within a week, and the Tories determined to strike back at Steele, along two lines of attack. The first was to find ways of expelling him from his seat in Parliament; the second was by direct answers to his pamphlet. Defoe published an anonymous reply in September and Swift his masterly ad hominem attack on Steele, *The Importance of the Guardian Considered,* also anonymous, in October.

By then, Steele had ended *The Guardian,* on 1 October, without notice or explanation. It had been a fine periodical, second in quality only to *The Tatler* and *The Spectator,* but its reputation has suffered because Steele was caught up in the political battle. Even contributors such as Addison felt constrained to distance themselves somewhat

from Steele and thus from the paper he had started and seen through to the end. On 6 October Steele began still another periodical, this one styled *The Englishman,* the narrator of which related that he had "purchased the Lion, Desk, Pen, Ink, and Paper, and all other Goods of NESTOR IRONSIDE, Esq." This was going to be a political paper; in the first issue Steele addressed a letter to Harley over his own name in which he announced his independence as a member of Parliament: "I am accountable to no Man, but the greatest Man in *England* is accountable to me."

We'll see about that, said Harley and the Tories in effect: *The Examiner* began to track Steele's paper closely; behind the scenes, preparations continued for his expulsion from Parliament when the new session opened. At first Steele tried to make at least a gesture toward matters of general interest, including, for example, a discussion of the formation of literary taste in number 7, and, importantly, an account in number 26 of Alexander Selkirk's marooning on Más a Tierra in the Juan Fernández group, in a paper that has often been cited as a source for Daniel Defoe's *Robinson Crusoe* (1719). Sometime in late 1713 Steele had business in Oxford; after a sentimental tour of his old haunts he wrote a celebration of the university in number 34 for 22 December. It was a turning point; henceforth the pages of the journal were closed to everything but politics. He was at the same time preparing a pamphlet on the present situation, as the Whigs saw it, to be titled *The Crisis* (1714).

The crisis in question was that of royal succession: Queen Anne's health, never hearty, had worsened, and worries were widespread that the Catholic Pretender might be introduced on her death. The Tories took the position that there was no such thing as a crisis, and that Steele's allegations about a crisis constituted sedition. When Steele's pamphlet was published with his name on the title page as author, it had a sensational sale: a hostile writer estimated that forty thousand copies were sold by subscription. No masterpiece of prose, *The Crisis* nevertheless made its point as Whig propaganda. In retrospect, one can see its importance as a landmark of propaganda, the earliest use of mass printing, advertising, and distribution techniques in a political context. Steele lent his encyclopedic knowledge of printing and distribution to the Whig cause: the employment of coordinated multiple printing presses and distribution networks, which had been invented to manufacture and circulate his periodicals, both within London and to provincial towns, was here devoted to political rather than literary ends. What the twentieth century would term mass-media techniques had come to politics. The example of *The Crisis* was not lost on politicians.

It demanded an answer by the Tories. Jonathan Swift's reply, published anonymously as usual with Swift, is one of his best pieces of political rhetoric, *The Publick Spirit of the Whigs* (1714). Swift met Steele's arguments by blandly denying that the Hanoverian succession was in danger at all and proceeding against the Whig author himself, branding his doubts about the situation "seditious."

This was a key word: Harley's ministry intended to punish Steele by charging him with sedition. Unlike most political writers of the day, he had signed his name to his propaganda, giving a convenient handle to his enemies. The result was

a foregone conclusion: the Tories had the votes in the House of Commons and could make the charge stick. Although ably defended by Robert Walpole, Steele was expelled on 18 March 1714, by a vote of 245 to 152. It was only a paper defeat, however; within the year the Tories were out, after Queen Anne's death, and Steele was back in Parliament. No one could foresee this outcome, of course, and Steele returned to journalism, to help pay his many creditors.

Perhaps anticipating his expulsion, he had started a new periodical in February: *The Lover*, edited by one "Marmaduke Myrtle, Gent." As its name implies, love was its theme, or, as Marmaduke describes it in the first number, its purpose was "to trace the Passion or Affection of Love, through all its Joys and Inquietudes. . . ." This was a topic on which Richard Steele could pronounce with some authority. He had occasional assistance for this three-a-week publication, but *The Lover* was essentially his own. That spring the Scriblerus Club was meeting: Pope, Gay, Swift, John Arbuthnot, and Harley, literary Tories. Steele was on the other side of the fence politically, but he used a quotation from the newly expanded *Rape of the Lock* in his paper. *The Rape of the Lock* clearly fit the paper's organizing motif, being concerned with love, but the quotation was also intended as a friendly gesture on Steele's part. On 27 May, with issue number 40, Steele wound the paper up. Although *The Lover* is almost forgotten now, it was highly regarded in Steele's day: five collected editions appeared in his lifetime and four more before the end of the century. It contains some of his most effective writing.

He started a new political paper in April, *The Reader*, but it lacked distinction and survived for only nine numbers, expiring without warning on 10 May. The political situation had seemingly been almost talked out. However, in that same month he published *The Romish Ecclesiastical History of Late Years*, ostensibly an account of the canonization of several saints by Pope Clement XI. Interspersed with descriptions of the ceremony are speeches by Cardinal Gualterio that present political conditions in England to the pope. These fictitious creations by Steele are intended to associate the English Jacobites, supporters of the Roman Catholic Pretender, with the Church of Rome, and of course, the Tories with the Jacobites. It was a propaganda line possessing special urgency in the spring of 1714, when the queen's health was deteriorating, but it proved to have en-

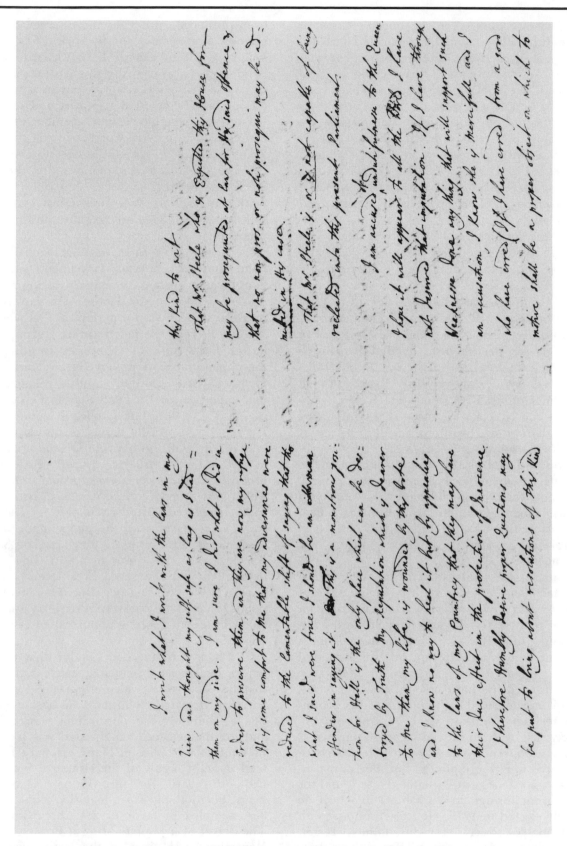

Pages from Steele's 19 March 1714 letter to Sir Thomas Hanmer, Speaker of the House of Commons, written the day after
Steele was expelled from Parliament (Pierpont Morgan Library)

during vitality even after the queen's death: if the English public could be persuaded that Tories were really Catholic Jacobites, or Jacobite sympathizers in disguise, the Tories could be (and were) kept out of office for decades. This turned out to be a potent argument, however specious in fact it might be—the English Catholics were a tiny, almost powerless, minority. Echoes appear more than thirty years later, in Henry Fielding's *Tom Jones* (1749), where Fielding portrays Tom's servant Partridge as a crypto-Jacobite. If Steele did not invent the line, he certainly implemented its circulation.

In the spring of 1714 the threat of the Pretender's return seemed real enough to Steele and his Whig associates, and in fact the Tory ministry was engaged in secret negotiations with the Pretender, looking toward his possible return. The queen, however, still possessed some power of her own; after dismissing Robert Harley, Earl of Oxford, on her deathbed she handed the treasurer's white staff of office to Charles Talbot, Duke of Shrewsbury, a Hanover Tory. Queen Anne's death on 1 August 1714 signaled a change of momentous consequence for most of the important writers of the time: Swift and his Tory associates would be in opposition for the rest of their lives— and would produce satire of enduring brilliance, from their point of view as outsiders. Addison, Steele, and their Whig colleagues now made up the government; their literary output dwindled. Politics came first—*had* to come first if one was in the governing majority as both Addison and Steele now were.

Paradoxically, and sadly, the literary partnership which had been so fruitful in the days of *The Tatler* and *The Spectator* was nearing an end. Addison revived *The Spectator*, but Steele did not contribute. In a few years the former partners found themselves on different sides of a political dispute, and at Addison's death, in 1719, they were estranged, perhaps not on speaking terms. Addison had achieved high political office, becoming a secretary of state in 1717, and was immensely rich, with an official income estimated at about ten thousand pounds a year. Steele's political rewards were more modest but they were considerable: a safe seat in Parliament was found for him, Boroughbridge in Yorkshire, to which he was duly elected in 1715. He leased a house with a fashionable address for his family, 26 St. James's Street, just up the hill from the palace. In October 1714 he was named governor of the theater in Drury Lane, where his comedies had

been produced, with a stipend of seven hundred pounds a year, and on 9 April 1715 he was knighted by King George I. Sir Richard's knighthood, pleasing as it was to this Irish orphan, was of course a political reward, and he knew it. It was bestowed not on the essayist and dramatist but on the pamphleteer and member of Parliament. As such, he was expected by the governing Whig coalition to render support to their policies, in the House of Commons and in the press. Steele was willing to do so, but only up to a point, the point at which their policies conflicted with his beliefs. This was to cause him plenty of problems.

He was active in the management of Drury Lane, and very busy in Parliament, sitting on more than a dozen committees during his first year of service in the House. The government called on him to start a periodical that would be used to discredit the fallen Tories, a group which included the duke of Ormonde. In June 1715 the impeachment of Robert Harley, Earl of Oxford, was moved, and on 11 July Steele began his new paper, called *The Englishman* like his periodical of 1713-1714, but published anonymously. He was not especially happy in his assignment; he had, after all, ridden with Ormonde and had worked for and respected Harley. He dutifully ground out the twice-a-week propaganda sheet, which sold a few hundred copies an issue, a flyspeck compared to the circulation of *The Tatler* and *The Spectator*. Still, the paper made money. Steele and his printer, the veteran Samuel Buckley, now knew how to adjust their operations so that the theoretical break-even point was a mere 240 copies sold per issue. Low break-even points, Steele had discovered, were an important factor in the burgeoning popularity of essay periodicals.

When word reached London that the Pretender had invaded Scotland, Steele had a topic that he could treat with enthusiasm. Instead of harrying defeated politicians, his task was now that of sounding the alarm. This was civil war, and the theme Steele emphasized was James the Pretender's Catholicism. Many ordinary Englishmen thought highly of the House of Stuart and had no regard for the German Hanoverian kings, but nothing like a majority could possibly be assembled in favor of a Catholic sovereign. The defeat of a Jacobite army at Preston in early November 1715 signaled the beginning of the end for the rebels. With the prospect of another session of Parliament and a new season at Drury

Lane before him, Steele ended the life of the second *Englishman* with number 38 on 21 November.

He was working about this time on a biography of his hero—and Swift's archvillain—the duke of Marlborough, apparently being supplied biographical materials by the duke and duchess, but it was a project he never finished. More to his style of the literary life was an essay periodical, and he started another one in December, *Town-Talk. In a Letter to a Lady in the Country*. Drury Lane was experiencing a disappointing season, and it may be that Steele's fellow actor-managers persuaded him to begin the new paper, which would supply that lady in the country and her counterparts in London with news of what was going on in the metropolis, especially at the theater. Steele writes about the importance of producing plays of merit, and Drury Lane was in fact mounting a total of eight plays by Shakespeare during the season. He discusses Addison's new comedy, *The Drummer* (but does not mention the author's name), as an example of the encouragement of good living writers. *Town-Talk*, as Steele conceived it, was essentially theatrical criticism, which he had virtually invented in *The Tatler*. This was the time to support the theater, for the patent was his major source of income, and he was desperately short of money. He was writing political pamphlets, which would sell in those troubled times, and in the ninth, and as it proved, the last *Town-Talk*, he quit theatrical matters to talk of the sentencing of the six noblemen who had pleaded guilty to participation in the Pretender's rebellion. A few months later, in June 1716, he was named to the commission which would administer and sell the estates of those noblemen forfeited to the Crown.

His stipend as commissioner was a handsome thousand pounds a year and with the income from Drury Lane should have made life on St. James's Street easy. But then, in the spring of 1716, his health gave way. He was stricken with a severe attack of what his physician, Dr. John Woodward, diagnosed as gout, a condition that left him helpless and immobile. Woodward administered purgatives and clysters, in accordance with his theories of medicine, but Steele recovered anyway. Still, it was an ominous event. He was investing effort and money in a scheme, called the Fish Pool, which sought to deliver fish alive to the London market. His duties on the commission of course entailed his going to Scotland, and Drury Lane required at least token attention. Not much

time and strength were left over for writing, though he did grind out what amounted to an advertising pamphlet for the Fish Pool.

In late 1718 his wife died, probably from complications in pregnancy, and in the following year he was involved in a bruising pamphlet war with his old collaborator and friend, Joseph Addison. The issue was a complicated one involving representation in the House of Lords, the so-called Peerage Bill. Steele was in opposition, while Addison represented the government's position in a periodical called *The Old Whig*. Steele, in his new periodical, *The Plebeian*, alleged that Addison was only masquerading as a Whig: "I am afraid he is so *old a Whig* that he has quite *forgot his Principles*." The famous friendship ended in this wretched political wrangle. Addison named James Craggs his literary executor—a pointed affront to Steele, of course—and died on 17 June 1719.

In retribution for his part in opposing them, the government, represented by Thomas Pelham-Holles, Duke of Newcastle, as lord chamberlain, moved to revoke Steele's license as manager of Drury Lane. Steele began what was to be the last of his periodicals, *The Theatre*, on 2 January 1720. He intended to, and did, plead his side of the case in his new paper, but he also called on the expertise derived from years in the editor's chair to produce a lively publication, mingling comment and anecdote in the manner he knew best, of all living men. The new paper succeeded beyond the printer's expectations; the first impression of several numbers sold out, and more had to be printed to meet the demand. His arguments did not prevail, however; he was effectively excluded from the Drury Lane enterprise. When he ended *The Theatre* with number 28 on 5 April 1720 and began preparing to go to Scotland for the commission meetings, it seemed that his career in the theater might be over. But then in 1721, in the aftermath of the South Sea scandal, Steele's friend Sir Robert Walpole took control of the government and called on Newcastle to restore Steele to his place in the management of Drury Lane. There he was able to see produced his last play, *The Conscious Lovers*, in November 1722. It was his greatest success in the theater, though not his best play, and the last extended piece of writing which he was able to complete. His health was declining steadily; in 1724 he chose to retire to Wales, to preserve what money he had for his children's inheritance. He lived on an estate his late wife had left him, until

Sir Richard Steele circa 1722 (miniature on ivory, attributed to Christian Richter;
National Portrait Gallery, London)

his death on 1 September 1729. He was buried in St. Peter's Church, Carmarthen.

Steele's literary reputation, high in his own day and indeed throughout the next century as well, has declined drastically in the twentieth century. The New Criticism was unable to deal effectively with periodical journalism; under its terms Addison was judged, correctly, to be the more discriminating prose stylist, and Steele was scarcely judged at all. Recent interest in the concept of print culture, in rhetorical practice, and in the history of printing and journalism, however, has made Steele once more a subject of study. His mark was set principally as a literary innovator. After having made all the necessary allowances for anticipation, influence, and assistance, one returns to the judgment that the essay periodical was effectively his idea. He invented *The Tatler*

and the rest followed. Better than anyone else of his time, except perhaps Defoe, he understood the possibilities of using the medium of print to communicate with mass audiences. Later in the century the truly revolutionary implications of his discovery would be worked out in America and France.

Letters:

The Correspondence of Richard Steele, edited by Rae Blanchard (London: Oxford University Press, 1941).

Biographies:

George A. Aitken, *The Life of Richard Steele*, 2 volumes (London: Wm. Isbister, 1889);

Calhoun Winton, *Captain Steele* (Baltimore: Johns Hopkins Press, 1964);

Winton, *Sir Richard Steele, M.P.* (Baltimore & London: Johns Hopkins Press, 1970).

References:

Rae Blanchard, Introduction to *Steele's The Englishman*, edited by Blanchard (Oxford: Clarendon Press, 1955);

Blanchard, Introduction to *Steele's Periodical Journalism 1714-16*, edited by Blanchard (Oxford: Clarendon Press, 1959);

Donald F. Bond, Introduction to *The Spectator*, 5 volumes, edited by Bond (London: Oxford University Press, 1965);

Bond, Introduction to *The Tatler*, 2 volumes, edited by Bond (London: Oxford University Press, 1987);

Richmond P. Bond, *The Tatler: The Making of a Literary Journal* (Cambridge, Mass.: Harvard University Press, 1971);

Richard H. Dammers, *Richard Steele* (Boston: Twayne, 1982);

Michael G. Ketcham, *Transparent Designs* (Athens: University of Georgia Press, 1985);

Brian McCrea, *Addison and Steele Are Dead* (Newark: University of Delaware Press, 1989);

Louis T. Milic, "The Reputation of Richard Steele: What Happened?," *Eighteenth-Century Life*, 1 (June 1975): 81-87;

Fritz Rau, *Zur Verbreitung und Nachahmung des Tatler und Spectator* (Heidelberg: Carl Winter, 1980);

Peter Smithers, *The Life of Joseph Addison* (Oxford: Clarendon Press, 1954);

John Calhoun Stephens, Introduction to *The Guardian*, edited by Stephens (Lexington: University Press of Kentucky, 1982);

William B. Todd, "Early Editions of *The Tatler*," *Studies in Bibliography*, 15 (1962): 121-133;

Calhoun Winton, "Addison and Steele in the English Enlightenment," *Studies on Voltaire and the eighteenth century*, 27 (1963): 1901-1918;

Winton, "Richard Steele, Journalist—and Journalism," in *Newsletters to Newspapers: Eighteenth-Century Journalism*, edited by Donovan Bond and W. R. McLeod (Morgantown: West Virginia University School of Journalism, 1977), pp. 21-31.

Papers:

The British Library holds the most important collection of Steele's papers, mostly correspondence. The collection at Blenheim Palace, seat of the dukes of Marlborough, which was consulted by Aitken and others earlier in this century, has apparently been dispersed in recent years, presumably by private sale. Yale University has some of Steele's letters.

Laurence Sterne

(24 November 1713 - 18 March 1768)

This entry was updated by Melvyn New (University of Florida) from his entry in
DLB 39: British Novelists, 1660-1800: Part Two.

BOOKS: *The Case of Elijah and the Widow of Zerephath* (York: Printed for J. Hildyard Bookseller, 1747);

The Abuses of Conscience (York: Printed by Caesar Ward, 1750);

A Political Romance, Addressed to——Esq. of York (York, 1759);

The Life and Opinions of Tristram Shandy, Gentleman, volumes 1 and 2 ([York], 1760); volumes 3 and 4 (London: R. & J. Dodsley, 1761); volumes 5 and 6 (London: Printed for T. Becket & P. A. De Hondt, 1762 [i.e. 1761]); volumes 7 and 8 (London: T. Becket & P. A. De Hondt, 1765); volume 9 (London: T. Becket & P. A. De Hondt, 1767);

The Sermons of Mr. Yorick, volumes 1 and 2 (London: R. & J. Dodsley, 1760); volumes 3 and 4 (London: Printed for T. Becket & P. A. De Hondt, 1766); volumes 5, 6, and 7 published as *Sermons by the Late Rev. Mr. Sterne* (London: Printed for W. Strahan, T. Cadell & T. Becket, 1769);

A Sentimental Journey through France and Italy, by Mr. Yorick, 2 volumes (London: Printed for T. Becket & P. A. De Hondt, 1768).

Editions and Collections: *The Works of Laurence Sterne*, 10 volumes (London: Printed for W. Strahan, J. Rivington [etc.], 1780);

The Complete Works and Life of Laurence Sterne, 12 volumes, edited by Wilbur L. Cross (New York: Taylor, 1904);

The Works of Laurence Sterne, Shakespeare Head Edition, 7 volumes (Oxford: Blackwell, 1926-1927; Boston: Houghton Mifflin, 1926-1927);

A Sentimental Journey through France and Italy, introduction by Virginia Woolf (London: H. Milford, Oxford University Press, 1928);

A Sentimental Journey through France and Italy, edited by Herbert Read (London: Scholartis Press, 1929);

Laurence Sterne in the 1760s. The artist is unknown though the head may have been painted by William Hogarth (National Portrait Gallery, London).

The Life and Opinions of Tristram Shandy, Gentleman, edited by James A. Work (New York: Odyssey Press, 1940);

The Life and Opinions of Tristram Shandy, Gentleman, edited by Ian Watt (Boston: Houghton Mifflin, 1965);

The Life and Opinions of Tristram Shandy, Gentleman, edited by Graham Petrie (Baltimore: Penguin, 1967);

A Sentimental Journey through France and Italy, edited by Gardner D. Stout, Jr. (Berkeley: University of California Press, 1967);

A Sentimental Journey through France and Italy, edited by Petrie (Baltimore: Penguin, 1967);

A Sentimental Journey through France and Italy, with *A Political Romance* and "Journal to Eliza," edited by Ian Jack (London: Oxford University Press, 1968);

A Political Romance (Menston, U.K.: Scolar Press, 1971);

"The Rabelaisian Fragment," edited by Melvyn New, *PMLA*, 87 (1972): 1083-1092;

The Florida Edition of the Works of Laurence Sterne, Melvyn New, general editor; volumes 1 and 2, *The Text of Tristram Shandy*, edited by Melvyn New and Joan New (Gainesville: University Presses of Florida, 1978); volume 3, *The Notes to Tristram Shandy*, edited by Melvyn New with Richard A. Davies and W. G. Day (Gainesville: University Presses of Florida, 1984);

The Life and Opinions of Tristram Shandy, Gentleman, edited by Howard Anderson (New York: Norton, 1980);

The Life and Opinions of Tristram Shandy, Gentleman, edited by Ian Campbell Ross (Oxford: Oxford University Press, 1983).

Laurence Sterne's enduring reputation as an author rests upon two works, *The Life and Opinions of Tristram Shandy, Gentleman* (1760-1767) and *A Sentimental Journey through France and Italy* (1768), both of which were written and published during the last nine years of his life. During that time he was the recipient of excessive praise and the target of vituperative criticism, heralded as a second François Rabelais, Miguel de Cervantes, or Jonathan Swift, and condemned as an immoral hypocrite. Controversy continues about the precise nature of Sterne's contribution to English literature, but no one any longer denies him a place among the most important of eighteenth-century writers. It is Sterne more than any other author of the century whose work has seemed, time and again, of especial interest to modern fiction writers, as they experiment with realism, psychology, and "metacommentary" as the organizing principles of narrative.

Sterne was born on 24 November 1713 in Clonmel, Ireland. His father, Roger Sterne, was an ensign in the army, the middle son of a family that in the seventeenth century had included the archbishop of York; his mother, the former Agnes Nuttall, was the daughter of an army provisioner. Sterne's early childhood was spent traveling between Ireland and England as his father's fortunes dictated; not until he was ten years old

did Sterne finally settle in Yorkshire, where he would spend almost his entire adult life.

Sterne attended school near Halifax, close to the home of his uncle, Richard Sterne. In the brief memoirs of his life that he wrote for his daughter in 1756 he recounted one schoolboy experience: "He [the schoolmaster] had had the cieling [*sic*] of the school-room new white-washed—the ladder remained there—I one unlucky day mounted it, and wrote with a brush . . . LAU. STERNE, for which the usher severely whipped me. My master was very much hurt at this, and said, before me, that never should that name be effaced, for I was a boy of genius. . . ." During this time, Sterne lived either at school or with Richard's family; when his father died in Jamaica in 1731, he was briefly reunited with his mother; but she returned to Ireland while he remained in Yorkshire until 1733, at which time he entered Jesus College, Cambridge. It is noteworthy that a writer so often praised for one of the most carefully drawn family circles in English literature should have lived away from his parents after the age of ten.

Sterne left Cambridge in 1737 with his bachelor's degree and a license to fill the assistant curacy of St. Ives in Huntingdon. The decision to enter the ministry may have depended upon social and economic considerations, but evidence also suggests that Sterne was very good at his vocation, and indeed for the next twenty-two years his most serious attentions seem to have remained focused on his church career. By 1738 he had assumed the vicarage of Sutton-on-the-Forest, a village some eight miles north of York, which was to remain his home until 1759. Indeed, no one point is more important to keep in mind about Sterne's biography than this, that almost his entire adult life was spent as a rural clergyman.

In 1740 Sterne received his master's degree from Cambridge, and a year later, after a one-year courtship, he married Elizabeth Lumley. Sterne's most thorough biographer, Arthur H. Cash, quotes a characterization of Elizabeth by her cousin, the famous Bluestocking Elizabeth Montagu: "Mrs. Sterne is a Woman of great integrity & has many virtues, but they stand like quills upon the fretfull porcupine. . . ." Sterne and Elizabeth, Cash concludes, "would not have a happy life together." The couple had a daughter, Lydia, who was born on 1 December 1747.

During the 1740s and 1750s Sterne barely emerged from the obscurity of domesticity and a

Sterne's wife, Elizabeth Lumley Sterne (pastel by Francis Cotes; from Wilbur L. Cross, The Life and Times of Laurence Sterne, *1925)*

rural parish. There was, however, a brief flurry of political writing at the beginning of this period, and some of his pieces have been identified in surviving issues of the *York Gazetteer*, a paper representing Whig interests. But perhaps the only noteworthy result of Sterne's brief participation in eighteenth-century provincial politics was a letter he wrote in 1742 to the rival *York Courant*, one that suggests his capacity for finding the proper perspective from which to view the passions of the moment:

> Sir,
> I find by some late Preferments, that it may not be improper to change Sides; therefore I beg the Favour of you to inform the Publick, that I sincerely beg Pardon for the abusive Gazetteers I wrote during the late contested Election....

Years later in *Tristram Shandy*, Sterne would have Tristram affirm:

> I have no
> > Zeal or Anger——or
> > Anger or Zeal——

And till gods and men agree together to call it by the same name—the errantest TARTUFFE, in

science—in politics—or in religion, shall never kindle a spark within me....

Sterne maintained throughout his life this level-headed refusal to become involved in the pressing issues of his own day, as well as a concomitant toleration of the opinions and foibles of others. However, this posture exists in constant tension with an opposing characteristic, a persistent awareness that human values and conduct could—and should—be measured by a set of standards readily available in the eighteenth century.

The standards were, of course, those of Christianity, and Sterne's second area of public activity during these years was the separate publication of two sermons, one in 1747 and the other in 1750. The latter, *The Abuses of Conscience*, is noteworthy because ten years later Sterne included it verbatim in *Tristram Shandy*. The sermon's point is that the conscience is inadequate and untrustworthy as a moral guide; it tends to be easily swayed by the passions and interests of the individual, a fallen creature whose self-judgment is too susceptible to negligence, self-deception, and corruption. The solution: "Call in religion and morality ... What is written in the law of God?" Sterne's argument is traditional, and indeed several key passages are borrowed from Swift's sermon on the same subject. But Swift's and Sterne's version of the conscience had lost many adherents among philosophers and moralists by the middle of the century, a casualty of the "moral sense" school, which maintained the infallible judgment of the conscience and the perfectibility of the moral sense, independent of religion and revelation.

Sterne's political writings did not prevent the victory of the Opposition, and his two published sermons did not change the course of theology. Had Sterne died in his forty-fifth year, he would have done so unnoticed by the world then—and certainly unrecognized by the world today. Hence, the year 1759 was truly an annus mirabilis, a year of sudden and surprising achievement that carried Sterne from his country pulpit to the center of London's literary life. How did it happen?

In January 1759 a pamphlet entitled *A Political Romance* was being readied for publication in York. It was a local satire, based upon incidents in an ongoing dispute over prerogatives within the York church establishment, but unlike the several dull pamphlets that had previously appeared on the subject, this was an imaginative, witty reduction of the issues and personalities; and it was a clear indication that its author, Sterne, who had earlier helped one party in the quarrel argue his case, had now been stirred by that desire for proper perspective he had exhibited in his 1742 letter to the *York Courant* and had found a way to shame *all* the participants for their pettiness and venality. Here was the archbishop of York reduced to the parson of the parish, the dean of York portrayed as a parish clerk, and the main adversary, a church lawyer named Francis Topham, reduced to a "sexton and dog-whipper."

Sterne's satire brought the entire conflict to a halt. Its publication was suppressed (only six copies survive), as both sides concluded that their quarrel, seen in the light cast by *A Political Romance*, was indeed a sad commentary on their behavior. For Sterne, however, *A Political Romance* was the beginning, not the end; within the year he was able to offer to Robert Dodsley, the most famous publisher in London, a manuscript of *Tristram Shandy*. In *A Political Romance* itself one does not find overwhelming evidence of heretofore hidden genius, but one certainly can identify interests that persist in Sterne's subsequent work. One notes, for example, the motto of *A Political Romance*, lines from Horace that may be translated, "Ridicule often cuts hard knots more forcefully and effectively than gravity." One notes also that Sterne had been reading the great French satirist Rabelais, to whom he alludes at one point. Equally important is the presence in *A Political Romance* of Swift, the unrivaled master in English prose of the technique of satiric reduction. Surely Swift's kingdom of Lilliput must have been in Sterne's mind as he reduced to a proper perspective the follies of the York churchmen.

Yet another interest evident in *A Political Romance* is Sterne's minute observation of human action and interaction, including the first sign of the "hobby-horse," an idea he was to exploit fully in *Tristram Shandy*. In the "Key" each character offers an interpretation of the "Romance" based upon an obvious prior interest; the tailor is fascinated by the shape of trousers, the lawyer by legalisms. Each character, Sterne writes, "turn'd the story to what was swimming uppermost in his own Brain"—an insight concerning human behavior that lies at the center of everything Sterne would subsequently write.

What happened next is conjecture, but it might be argued that Sterne's subsequent effort was to be another satire, perhaps in imitation of

Alexander Pope's *Peri Bathous* (1727). The first two chapters of such a work, the "Fragment in the Manner of Rabelais," are extant. The idea of a Pope-like parody of Longinus's *Peri Hupsous (On the Sublime)*, designed as an "Art of Sermon-Writing," is combined with the tone and diction of the piece in the aptly named Longinus Rabelaicus, one of the two main characters. The other main character is the erstwhile preacher Homenas, and surrounding the two is a genial group of Rabelaisian namesakes, Panurge, Gymnast, Triboulet, Epistemon. Sterne's headnote to chapter 2 promises that "the Reader will begin to form a Judgment, of what an Historical, Dramaticcal, Anecdotical, Allegorical and Comical Kind of a Work He has got hold of "; the chapter itself tells of Homenas's attempts to write his weekly sermon, his seeking help by raiding his library shelves, and his fall from the library balcony: "*Alass* poor *Homenas*," Sterne writes.

And so one enters the world of *Tristram Shandy*, in which one certain guise for the author is the village parson Yorick, a name with which Sterne felt extremely comfortable, since he used it again when his sermons were published under the title *The Sermons of Mr. Yorick* (1760-1766), and yet again when he named the protagonist of *A Sentimental Journey*. On the one hand, the figure is clearly the king's jester; on the other, it is a jester whose appearance in *Hamlet* occurs only as a skull to be contemplated in the famous gravediggers' scene: "Alas, poor Yorick! I knew him, Horatio. A fellow of infinite jest, of most excellent fancy." In *Tristram Shandy* the death of Yorick occurs early in volume one and is marked, dramatically, by a black page; but because the chronology of the work moves backward as well as forward, Yorick reappears in several episodes, always as the jester's embodiment of shrewd observation and good sense in a world gone mad. Somewhere between *A Political Romance* and the "Rabelaisian Fragment" Sterne had found not only a comfortable identity as the jester/memento mori, but had discovered as well his need to "bury" that identity in order to bring to life a voice that would sustain him for eight years and nine volumes, the voice of Tristram Shandy himself.

Some version of *Tristram Shandy* was ready by 23 May 1759, when Sterne sent a volume to Dodsley. "The plan," he wrote, "is a most extensive one,—taking in, not only, the Weak part of the Sciences, in which the true point of Ridicule lies—but every Thing else, which I find laugh-at-able in my way." Dodsley responded negatively a month later; and Sterne seems to have spent the summer rewriting, still with Dodsley in mind, for in October he wrote to the publisher again: "I propose . . . to print a lean edition, in two small volumes . . . at my own expense, merely to feel the pulse of the world. . . . The book shall be printed here, and the impression sent up to you. . . ." Two months later, at the end of December, the first edition of volumes one and two was printed in York. The title page nowhere indicates the place of publication because Sterne wanted to conceal the provincial origins of his work. Indeed, he was busy orchestrating a reception in London that in a very short time answered his fondest hopes. *Tristram Shandy* was an immediate success, as can be deduced from Dodsley's willingness in early March to pay Sterne £250 for the copyright in order to publish a second edition, as well as £380 for the next installment. A friend reported that when Sterne returned from the bargaining he "came skipping into the room, and said that he was the richest man in Europe."

The second edition appeared in early April with the additions of a dedication to William Pitt, then prime minister, and an illustration by William Hogarth of Trim's reading the sermon; two more editions were required during the year to meet the demand. In May, Dodsley published two volumes of the *Sermons of Mr. Yorick*, having paid Sterne well for that privilege. Meanwhile, Sterne spent the winter and spring in London, basking in his success in the company of David Garrick, who introduced him into London society, and Joshua Reynolds, who painted a fine portrait of him; and Bishop William Warburton, supposedly in response to the rumor that Sterne intended to include the bishop in later volumes as a tutor for Tristram, gave him a purse of gold in order to forestall such an eventuality. James Boswell was also in London at this time, and wrote for Sterne a "Poetical Epistle": "Who has not 'Tristram Shandy' read? / Is any mortal so ill-bred?" But perhaps Sterne most cherished a meeting he had with Allen, Lord Bathurst, seventy-five years old in 1760; years later Sterne recalled the meeting with pride: "He came up to me, one day, as I was at the Princess of Wales's court. I want to know you, Mr. Sterne; but it is fit you should know, also, who it is that wishes this pleasure. You have heard, continued he, of an old Lord Bathurst, of whom your Popes, and Swifts, have sung and spoken so much: I have lived my life with geniuses of that cast; but have

survived them; and, despairing ever to find their equals, it is some years since I have closed my accounts, and shut up my books, with thoughts of never opening them again: but you have kindled a desire in me of opening them once more before I die; which I now do; so go home and dine with me."

Finally, at the end of May 1760, Sterne returned to Yorkshire, to a new home in Coxwold, the gift of an admirer; Shandy Hall still stands in this beautiful village fifteen miles north of York. By August, Sterne had finished the third volume and by November, the fourth, and he again departed for London to see them through the press—a practice he assiduously followed. This installment of *Tristram Shandy* appeared at the end of January 1761, again with a frontispiece by Hogarth, illustrating Tristram's christening. A second edition was called for within the year, but as knowledge spread that the author was a clergyman, the reception of Sterne's work was being influenced more and more by a sense of outrage. Sterne seems to acknowledge this when he writes to a friend: "One half of the town abuse my book as bitterly as the other half cry it up to the skies. . . ." Moreover, the stream of insipid, often lascivious imitations that had started after the first two volumes was becoming a flood. So annoying did this flood of bad imitations become that Sterne personally signed "L. Sterne" on the top of the first page of text of every copy of volumes five, seven, and nine as a validation of their authenticity.

By June 1761 Sterne was back in Coxwold, and he worked on the next installment throughout the summer. "These two volumes are, I think, the best.—I shall write as long as I live, 'tis, in fact, my hobby-horse . . . ," he wrote in September. Volumes five and six appeared in December 1761 but are dated 1762; the title pages indicated that Sterne had cut his ties with Dodsley and was now working with T. Becket and P. A. De Hondt, a less established firm. Why Sterne changed publishers is not known; but one suspects that he was able to make a more profitable arrangement, and money had become a serious concern. Two weeks after publication, Sterne left England for France in pursuit of better health: "Indeed, I am very ill, having broke a vessel in my lungs—hard writing in the summer, together with preaching, which I have not strength for, is ever fatal to me. . . ."

Sterne's illness was tubercular; it had been with him, intermittently, since college days, and al-

From this representation
we are led to this demony ... Truth.
of Things, ~~it seems plain then~~
that God never intended to
debar Man of Pleasure, under
certain Limitations —

Travellers on a Business
of the last & most important
Concern, may be allowed to
please their Eyes with the
natural and artificial Beau-
-ties of the Country they are
passing thro' without reproach
of forgetting the main Errand
They are sent upon: And if
They are not led out of their
Road by variety of Prospects —
Edifices & Ruins, would it
not be a senseless Piece of
severity to shut their Eyes,
ag.t such Gratifications —

Page from the manuscript for a sermon on penances, preached by Sterne on 8 April 1750 (Pierpont Morgan Library) though he would experience some periods of relief during the remaining six years of his life, there seems little question but that his health was steadily deteriorating. It is an important part of understanding Sterne's life and writing to be aware that, like Tristram in volume seven, he might well have considered himself in a perpetual "flight" from death.

Had Sterne kept to the schedule he had set for himself, volumes seven and eight would have appeared in January 1763; but the journey to France took its toll, and by May he had reached a low point: "I had the same accident I had at Cambridge," he wrote to a friend, "of breaking a vessel in my lungs. It happen'd in the night, and I bled the bed full. . . ." He spent the summer recuperating in Toulouse, but in October he had yet another setback. Typically, he announced his recovery with great spirit: "I am now stout and foolish again as a happy man can wish to be—and am busy playing the fool with my uncle Toby, who I have got soused over head and ears in love." Clearly this remark alludes to the contents of volume eight, but January passed without his having written enough to fill two volumes. Indeed, the next January (1764) passed as well, and still the Sternes stayed in France, Laurence continuing to have intervals of high spirits between dreadful bouts of illness. He was losing his patience, however, with France and French doctors, and in February he began the journey back to England, leaving his wife and daughter behind; he arrived in Coxwold in June. The writing was clearly a struggle, and in September he was still at work on Toby's amours. At last, in a letter dated 11 November 1764, he makes evident for the first time his solution to the problems that had delayed his progress for two years: "I will contrive to send you these 2 new Vols of Tristram, as soon as ever I get them from the press—You will read as odd a Tour thro' france, as ever was projected or executed by traveller or travell Writer, since the world began——." Volumes seven and eight were published at the end of January 1765, volume seven containing the heteroclite tour that Sterne's motto insists is not a digression but the work itself; and volume eight, the amours of Toby he had begun three years earlier.

Sterne's letters during 1765 suggest a frantic pace in London, in Bath, and in Coxwold. He prepared two more volumes of sermons for the press, and carried on (or gave every impression of carrying on) flirtations that belied his married state, his age, and his cloth—but not, perhaps,

his encounter with death. It was the period of his life that most shocked Victorians such as Thackeray.

In October 1765 Sterne again departed England, not only to visit Elizabeth in France, but to undertake a tour of Italy as well. By July 1766 he was back in Coxwold—still without his family—with a clear plan in mind to write one more volume of *Tristram Shandy* and then begin "a new work of four volumes. . . ." The final volume of *Tristram Shandy* appeared at the end of January 1767. While the nature of Sterne's narrative method would have allowed him to develop a sequel with no difficulty, it does seem, as Wayne Booth has cogently argued, that volume nine brings to a conclusion the several premises, concerns, and themes of the work as it had appeared in eight volumes during the previous seven years. It may safely be affirmed that for Sterne, *Tristram Shandy* was a finished work.

The "new work" Sterne now turned to had actually been in his mind since his first sojourn in France. Some of its contents, certainly, had been used in volume seven of *Tristram Shandy*, but Sterne's travels had opened to him scenes and personages not available to the rural parson who had created the Shandy family, and a new vehicle was required. In addition, the initial popularity of *Tristram Shandy* had waned considerably. Even if Sterne had been willing to withstand the criticisms of the Tartuffes who found his work (and life) reprehensible, he was far from willing to withstand a return to obscurity—or poverty. His letters to Becket from France are filled with inquiries concerning the slow sales of volumes five and six; and although volumes seven and eight had better success, the critics were now responding in a significantly uniform chorus: the redeeming value of Sterne's writings was to be found in sentimental episodes like that of the death of Le Fever. The editor of the *Monthly Review* spoke for many: "Give up your Long Noses . . . try your strength another way. One of our gentlemen once remarked . . . that he thought your excellence lay in the PATHETIC. I think so too." Sterne never did abandon that bawdy aspect of his writing epitomized in the phrase "Long Noses"; but he did find a new voice for his final work, the voice of yet another Yorick, in whom good sense has become sensibility, and frankness has become ambiguity—the narrative voice of *A Sentimental Journey*.

Sterne did not start writing until his return to Coxwold in June; the preceding six months were spent gathering subscriptions among the great for the book and paying attention to a young married woman, Elizabeth Draper. Mrs. Draper had been born in India in 1744 and had married Daniel Draper at the age of fourteen. In 1767 she was visiting in London with her two children, while her husband, a government official in Bombay, remained abroad. She was twenty-two years old when she met Sterne near the end of January, and Sterne's first letter to her typifies the "language of the heart" that became the idiom of their relationship: "I know not how it comes in—but I'm half in love with You.—I ought to be *wholy so*—for I never valued, (or saw more good Qualities to value,)—or thought more of one of yr Sex than of You.—" Mrs. Draper returned to India in early April, a departure that occasioned Sterne's "Journal to Eliza," written while he was working on *A Sentimental Journey* and certainly an important clue to the nature of that work. *A Sentimental Journey* was published in late February 1768; once again illness had slowed his progress, and indeed the projected four volumes of a tour through France and Italy appeared as only two volumes, located almost solely in France. Three weeks later Sterne died of pleurisy in London.

Early in *Tristram Shandy*, Sterne chides the reader ("Madam" in this instance) for her failure to grasp his meaning and sends her back to reread a chapter as penance. It is an appropriate warning to every reader of Sterne's fictions, both because his works lack the structural clues provided by an orderly, sequential plot and because his language is replete with the ambiguities and allusions, ironies and ambivalences more usually associated with poetry than with prose.

It will help the reader to keep in mind three distinct categories into which to divide the various episodes of *Tristram Shandy*. First, there are the events surrounding the conception, birth, and upbringing of Tristram, events that take place between 1718 and 1723 at Shandy Hall. Second, there are the events on the bowling green and those relating to the courtship of Uncle Toby and the widow Wadman, which take place between 1695 and 1714; given Sterne's digressive structure, however, these earlier events can be—and are—chronicled by Tristram simultaneously with his own life. Finally, there is the adult Tristram as author-in-his-study, the self-conscious narrator who comments upon his book as he writes it, and upon himself in the act of writing. These events take place between 1759 and 1766, the ac-

tual years of composition. Sterne is always quite aware of the games he is playing with the interweaving of these three time schemes, and he is always capable of complicating issues still further by introducing, digressively, an episode quite distinct from any of the three categories.

A second aid to reading *Tristram Shandy* is to have in mind some of the authors Sterne was responding to (imitating, parodying, copying) as he wrote. Rabelais and Miguel de Cervantes head any such list, and Sterne often calls attention to his debts to both. Sterne knew Rabelais in the English translation by Thomas Urquhart and Peter Motteux, with extensive notes by John Ozell (1737), and Cervantes in a translation by Motteux and Ozell (1719). Naturally enough, these translations tended to bring the two works closer than might otherwise have been the case. But these authors were also pulling Sterne in opposite directions. Rabelais was the model of the bold, sharp-tongued, satyr-like satirist, whose bawdy and irreverent attitude was intended to reflect upon the hypocrisies of the church, the state, the professions, and, most importantly perhaps, human nature itself. Sterne's contemporaries almost immediately compared him to Rabelais, and Sterne, far from rejecting the association, has Yorick carry *Gargantua* (1534) in his "right-hand coat pocket." Cervantes, on the other hand, provided Sterne with a model of intrusive narration (a narrator who allows—indeed invites—the reader to observe him at work); with the posture of ironic gravity that the entire century identified with Cervantes; and with, in Sterne's own words, the "GENTLE Spirit of sweetest humour," that the century more and more came to discover in the character of Don Quixote.

Another of Sterne's favorite authors was Michel de Montaigne, whose *Essays* (1580) gave him an example of unabashed self-examination ranging over the widest possible sweep of subjects. In addition, Sterne certainly learned from Montaigne a reverence for the minute detail, the close observation of human behavior. The same tastes led him also to Robert Burton's *Anatomy of Melancholy* (1621) and John Locke's *Essay Concerning Human Understanding* (1690), both of which share Montaigne's minuteness of detail and encyclopedic nature. Sterne never mentions Burton's work, although he borrows heavily from it for portions of *Tristram Shandy*, particularly at the opening of volume five. Locke offers a far more difficult problem for readers of Sterne, and indeed the influence of his *Essay Concerning Human*

Chap. 2ᵈ

In which the Reader will begin to form a Judgment, of what an Historical, Dramatical, Anecdotical, Allegorical and Comical Kind of a Work, He has got hold of. ——

Homenas who had to preach next Sunday [before God knows whom] — knowing Nothing at all of the Matter —— was all this while ~~beating~~ ^at^ it as hard as He could drive in the very next Room: for having

Page from the manuscript for Sterne's "Fragment in the Manner of Rabelais," in which a preacher named Homenas writes his weekly sermons by cribbing from the works of others (Pierpont Morgan Library)

Understanding on *Tristram Shandy* has been a vexing problem for modern readers. Sterne mentions Locke in his discussion of the difficulty of definition, in his discussion of duration versus clock time, in his discussion of wit and judgment—subjects upon which scarcely anyone in the century spoke without allusion to Locke. Precisely this sense of the commonplace makes Sterne's interest in him problematic; Locke's position in the eighteenth century is comparable to Freud's in the twentieth, and in both instances allusions to their insights need not represent a profound study of their works.

Sterne certainly liked to read, but even more, one suspects, he liked to be considered well-read—and indeed, following in the footsteps of Rabelais, Montaigne, and Burton, he must have felt obliged to appear to be as diversely learned, indeed encyclopedic, as were these authors. It is no wonder, then, that when we list his favorite authors, the name of Ephraim Chambers appears, for Chambers's *Cyclopaedia* (1738) was one of his most often consulted sources. When Sterne wanted to appear knowledgeable on fortifications, he did not read treatises on the subject, but rather Chambers's entry on fortification—and he borrowed among other things the names of the authorities he should have read. Over and over again, a piece of esoteric knowledge in *Tristram Shandy* can be traced to Chambers, or to other similar compilations of knowledge. Sterne's "learned wit" almost always has more "wit" and less "learning" than his readers are encouraged to believe. This is not to disparage Sterne; he makes no claim to being a scholar, but every claim to being a "wit"—a writer of exuberant fancy with an inexhaustible capacity for inventiveness.

Of course another influence on Sterne was that of his immediate predecessors in England. These were not, interestingly enough, Daniel Defoe, Henry Fielding, Samuel Richardson, and Tobias Smollett, the major novelists who appeared before Sterne; indeed, with the exception of Smollett's *Travels through France and Italy* (1766), Sterne gives no concrete indication that he read these writers. Rather, one must look to the Scriblerian tradition, to Swift's *Tale of a Tub* (1704) and Pope's *Peri Bathous* and the collective *Memoirs of the Extraordinary Life, Works, and Discoveries of Martinus Scriblerus* (1741) for those works that seem most to have been in Sterne's mind as he wrote *Tristram Shandy*. Once again, as with Locke, one enters into often-debated territory. Few questions in reading Sterne are more diffi-

cult, because even when one feels comfortable in identifying an image or character as Scriblerian, the debate over "tone" and "intention" remains. There is a Scriblerian presence in *Tristram Shandy*, but what one makes of it seems open to an infinite variety of coherent readings.

Certainly the opening situation of *Tristram Shandy* is Scriblerian. Walter Shandy, like Cornelius Scriblerus, is the traditional figure of the *philosophus gloriosus*, with roots in the satires of Aristophanes and Lucian. Both characters display their comic reliance upon theory in their efforts to propagate and raise a male child; both become satiric victims because reality consistently undercuts their a priori reasoning. Walter offers a barrage of theories: that the future of his child can be secured by an intense concentration on the imparting of his seed; that a cesarean or podal (feetfirst) delivery is vastly preferable to the natural headfirst birth; that a goodly nose is required for worldly success; that a person's name determines his future. The first five volumes, insofar as they deal with the Shandy household, tell of the events surrounding Walter's attempts to impose these theories and the disappointments he encounters. Thus, the magnificent opening scene at the same time both defies Horace's dictum against beginning a story ab ovo (from the egg, that is, the beginning) and follows his advice to begin instead in the middle of things (in medias res). *Tristram Shandy* opens in the Shandy bed; Walter Shandy is hard at work concentrating his efforts when Mrs. Shandy interrupts him with a question; the beginning of the work and the beginning of Tristram, the ab ovo of literary creation and of procreation, are made to reinforce one another, just as the interruption by Mrs. Shandy will be echoed over and over in the digressive meanderings of Tristram in his study.

For Walter Shandy this opening episode explains why *"Tristram's misfortunes began nine months before ever he came into the world."* Tristram, however, then goes on to demonstrate that his birth came eight months after this night, a teasing suggestion of illegitimacy that Sterne neither develops nor abandons. This is typical of Sterne's sexual suggestiveness; the burden is shifted to the reader to complete the joke, but when it is complete, he discovers that the author has no use for the insight—that the innuendo is, if not entirely superfluous, then a trap into which his own concupiscent imagination has fallen.

Almost immediately, the reader also hears the voice of Tristram-in-his-study, the author who, in 1759, is writing about these events that took place forty-one years earlier. Tristram interrupts his narrative to mention his authority for it (Uncle Toby), to inform the reader that he expects his book to be as popular as *Pilgrim's Progress* (1678, 1684), to argue with Horace, and, most important, to offer his theory of the hobbyhorse. The voice here is that which Wayne Booth identifies as the self-conscious narrator of much eighteenth-century fiction: self-confident, modernistic, pandering, ambitious. But it is also a voice sufficiently aware of its own ironies: "[If I] should sometimes put on a fool's cap with a bell to it, for a moment or two as we pass along,—don't fly off,—but rather courteously give me credit for a little more wisdom than appears upon my outside. . . ." Indeed, the Shandean voice is a most difficult one to define and certainly a major crux for the critics. One can see this difficulty at once in the idea of the hobbyhorse. Many readers have taken it as an endorsement of toleration for the foibles and follies of men—"there is no disputing against HOBBY-HORSES." Others, however, have suggested that Tristram's tolerance is not shared by Sterne—that the essential problem of finding a proper perspective upon one's own behavior is rendered impossible when one is mounted and galloping.

Another aspect of Tristram-in-his-study is his digressive urge, a deliberate refusal to tell his story in a straightforward way. As with other characteristics of the authorial voice, this too is something of a commonplace in eighteenth-century narratives, but in Sterne digression carries at least two considerable burdens of meaning. On the one hand, digressiveness enables him to mimic the fertility of his favorite authors, Rabelais, Cervantes, Burton, and Montaigne. The opportunity to display arcane learning, to involve the reader in intricate mazes of related ideas, is made available through the digressions, the pursuit of paths away from the narrative line. Indeed, as the work progresses, the tension between progression and digression becomes more and more pronounced, and one may see the anxiety of Tristram to tell his story straightforwardly as a displacement of Sterne's real anxiety that he will be unable to sustain the imagination, wit, and learning demonstrated by his Renaissance forebears. But digressiveness is also a way for Sterne to build into the form of his work his primary insight about communication, namely, that it takes place best by indirection; that the surest way toward comprehension is not the straight

line of reason, but rather the parabolas and zigzags and roundabouts of feeling.

Chapter 10 begins one such digression, the account of Yorick, the Shandy family's village parson and alter ego for Sterne. Surely the account of Yorick's Cervantic character, his inability to be grave or quiet in the face of folly—even when laughter endangers his career—is a barely disguised version of Sterne's own life in the church. At the same time, this account is also not far removed from William Shakespeare's Yorick in *Hamlet*, for it is an account of death, and the dramatic black page mourning Yorick's death is Sterne's own "death's head." Since Yorick's death takes place *after* the events of the narrative, he is able to participate in them, always as a normative voice of reasonableness and common sense.

Volume one continues to be dominated by Walter's theories. Tristram explains, for example, his father's faith in the outmoded theory of the divine right of kings; and he touches upon Walter's sympathy with male physicians in their running battle with midwives. Significantly, Sterne suggests that the essence of a midwife's approach to the delivery of a child was to let nature take its course; the physicians, on the other hand, were beginning to suggest ways to "improve" upon nature, through instruments and superior anatomical knowledge. It is hardly surprising that Walter is on the side of science in this battle—or that science is represented by Dr. Slop, Sterne's portrayal of a Yorkshire physician, Dr. John Burton. Many of the obstetrical details of the first two volumes of *Tristram Shandy* are borrowed directly from Burton's writings; Sterne's penchant for both pillaging and parodying a work of learning is nowhere more evident than in this instance.

Tristram also explains Walter's theory of names, and while doing so explains one aspect of the hobbyhorse: Walter "was systematical, and, like all systematick reasoners, he would move both heaven and earth . . . to support his hypothesis." The reader is not yet told how it happens, but he is prepared for the worst when he compares the title page with the observation that "of all the names in the universe, [Walter] had the most unconquerable aversion for TRISTRAM."

In many examples of self-conscious narration, one is not only made aware of the author-as-author, but also of the reader-as-reader. Constantly, Tristram observes the reader reading his book, cajoles him as reader, or, in the in stance of volume one, chapter 20, chastises the reader for missing the point through inattention. Tristram had said that he had to be "born before [he] was christened"; this, he now informs the reader, is a clear indication that his mother *"was not a papist."* Obviously, no reader could be expected, beforehand, to understand Tristram's chain of reasoning, but when he presents the full text (in French) of a deliberation by three learned doctors concerning intrauterine baptism, the reader begins to see his point. What is worth noting in this episode is, first, Sterne's desire to display, and at the same time parody, a bit of esoteric learning; and second, that the entire chapter is carefully arranged around one final joke, that it would be even more effective to baptize the sperm than the child in the womb, assuming that it could be done with the same small injection tube and without pain to the father—*"sans faire aucun tort à le pere."* This punch line is indicative of Sterne's common procedure, the construction of an elaborate joke, often based on an exuberant display of learning and told always in a serious, grave manner, up to that last moment when Sterne deflates the gravity and undercuts the learning with a sentence that causes both to implode. It is a procedure perhaps best epitomized by the discussion of prodigies of learning in volume six. Sterne, borrowing from a learned source, has Walter list some famous prodigies of the Renaissance, concluding with the "great *Lipsius* . . . who composed a work the day he was born." Toby delivers the punch line: "They should have wiped it up . . . and said no more about it." The deflation of human pretentiousness, the triumph of common sense—surely that is one of the primary strategies of *Tristram Shandy*.

Volume one concludes with an account of Uncle Toby's hobbyhorse, although, typically, the approach is roundabout. It begins in chapter 21 when Toby is interrupted in midsentence (a sentence he will not complete until chapter 6 of volume two), and Tristram sets out to explain his uncle's "unparallel'd modesty of nature." To do so, he must begin with the wound in the groin that Toby received at the siege of Namur (1695), the origin of his hobbyhorse. The actual connection between this wound and Toby's modesty (his estrangement from women) will not be fully explained to the reader, however, until the final pages of the last volume. At this point, Tristram loses track of his initial intention and describes rather how Toby's efforts to explain to his visi-

tors exactly how and where he was wounded involve him in greater and greater complexities, until his orderly, Corporal Trim, offers him the solution: play out the siege in miniature on the bowling green of his country home. Tristram had earlier warned the reader about how such suggestions become hobbyhorses; the hobbyhorse, he writes, works something like yeast, "but more generally after the manner of the gentle passion, beginning in jest,—but ending in downright earnest." It is no accident, then, that when Toby leaves London to retire to the country, the language is romantic: "Never did lover post down to a belov'd mistress with more heat and expectation, than my uncle *Toby* did. . . ." Nor is it an accident that this language parallels closely a later description of Walter's enjoyment of one of his favorite theories: "When my father got home, he solaced himself with *Bruscambille* after the manner, in which, 'tis ten to one, your worship solaced yourself with your first mistress. . . ." Walter is consistently critical of and impatient with Toby's hobbyhorse; Toby's argument against Walter's theories is to whistle "Lillabullero," a patriotic nonsense song of Irish Protestants. But while each recognizes the absurdity of the other mounted and galloping, they do not see themselves with equal clarity; and that, Sterne seems to be saying, is a fundamental characteristic of the hobbyhorse—or, more broadly, of human nature.

In a book where the characters are all mounted on hobbyhorses, it is no accident that the reader is introduced to Dr. Slop at a moment when, trotting toward Shandy Hall, he is upset by the galloping servant Obadiah, who has been sent to fetch him. It is, in miniature, an emblem of *Tristram Shandy*, a book of cross-purposes and collisions. In addition, it is worth noting, as part of the work's most serious undercurrent, that Slop's bag of "instruments of salvation" really contains instruments of death. The *tire tête* (head-puller), for example, was a hook with which the skull was cracked and drawn out of the womb when a live birth was deemed impossible. These opening volumes are about the procreation and birth of Tristram (and the parallel creation of his *Life and Opinions*), but it is important to remain aware of the many hints of death (and impotence) that recur—the wasting away of Yorick, the black page of his end, the baptism of a doomed infant in the womb, the wound in Toby's groin and Walter's sciatical hip, the presence of warfare, and now, Slop's "green bays [baize]

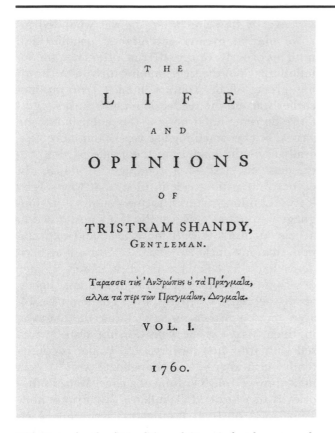

T H E

L I F E

A N D

O P I N I O N S

O F

TRISTRAM SHANDY,
GENTLEMAN.

Ταρασσει τὰς Ἀνθρώπες ὰ τὰ Πράγμαλα,
αλλα τὰ περι τῶν Πραγμάλων, Δογμαλα.

V O L. I.

1 7 6 0.

*Title page for the first edition of Sterne's best-known work,
with the place of publication—York—deliberately omitted in
order to conceal the provincial origins of the work*

bag." These hints of mortality become more and more dominant in the course of the work.

One of Sterne's boldest digressions now takes place: the introduction into the text, as part of its narrative, of a sermon he had written and that had been published almost ten years earlier. The scene was illustrated, at Sterne's specific request, by the great eighteenth-century artist William Hogarth, and it is important to see how brilliantly the two altered a public occasion into a private one. The usual view would be that of the preacher as the cynosure of all eyes; here, the viewer stands behind the angular, comic figure of Corporal Trim, looking at his auditors, Toby and Walter, who sit close together on a bench in the corner, mirror images of one another, as they smoke their pipes and look in opposite directions away from Trim. In the foreground Dr. Slop is presented in profile and asleep. It is a memorable visual rendition of a carefully imagined literary scene.

Sterne did not make a single significant change in his 1750 sermon when he included it in *Tristram Shandy*. On the one hand, as with the Sorbonne Memoire in volume one, he obviously

delighted in his capacity to absorb such digressive material into his work without alteration. On the other hand, and equally important, it suggests that Sterne considered his sermon compatible with the work he was now writing, despite the sermon's substantial orthodoxy concerning self-evaluation and self-deception. Sterne's lesson is that an individual's moral innocence is not determined by his conscience, as many in the eighteenth century argued, but is worked out with great difficulty between the individual and his religion. When a man's conscience does not accuse him, he is not "therefore innocent." Self-deception is too easy, is indeed the natural condition of the human mind that seeks justification rather than self-examination. Thus conscience cannot be trusted to work without assistance. Rather, Sterne argues, it must be joined to religion, to the "law of God." In this sermon Sterne joins issue with the dominant moral theorist of the early part of the century, Anthony Ashley Cooper, third Earl of Shaftesbury, and his theory of the moral sense. Shaftesbury and his followers argued for the innate love of virtue in man, a moral system set free from the church, the clergy, and the Scriptures. Sterne's sermon, almost reactionary in 1759, argues to the contrary that neither religion nor moral sense could act independently from the other. Religion without morality is the history of the Inquisition; morality without religion is self-interested, self-absorbed self-deception. By juxtaposing the sermon with the Shandy household, Sterne invites a weighing of the hobbyhorse by the values of his pulpit; if nothing else, the reader might be more hesitant than otherwise before declaring all hobbyhorses to be innocent bagatelles.

Volume two ends with another of Walter's theories, this time concerning headfirst delivery. In a discussion that touches upon the nature and location of the soul, Walter explains his notion that headfirst delivery can damage the soul (thus demonstrating his materialism) and hence that a cesarean birth would be far better. That Mrs. Shandy turns pale at the suggestion is explained by the fact that the operation always proved fatal to the mother before the nineteenth century. Again Sterne's obvious sympathies are with the midwives and their insistence that nature be allowed to take its course. More broadly, in that Tristram's discussion about the soul involve him with Cartesian theories (borrowed from Chambers's *Cyclopaedia*), Sterne is parodying all learning that seems to him devoid of common sense.

Sterne opens volume three with the same deflating remark Toby had already made in response to Walter's and Slop's theories: *"I wish . . . you had seen what prodigious armies we had in Flanders."* As usual, Toby is able to pierce immediately to the normative statement that will dismount his brother from his hobbyhorse; he is not, however, able to remain dismounted himself, and Walter's reaching for his handkerchief brings to mind the "transverse zig-zaggery" of the trenches before Namur. Some critics stress this constant collision of hobbyhorses, while others are interested in the reconciliation that always takes place, often a nonverbal reconciliation, by which the two brothers express affection for one another despite their differences. Certainly both brothers can unite in their persecution of Dr. Slop, and they take the opportunity to do so when the doctor curses Obadiah for tying knots in his obstetrical bag. The image is suggestive of Sterne's usual mode: the long folk tradition of untying the knots in a household to ensure an easy birth is here transformed into a dramatic scene; and at the same time, Sterne plays with the analogy between delivering Tristram into the world and delivering the "instruments" from Slop's bag. In addition, Sterne is preparing another joke, one that finally explodes in the last line of chapter 15: " 'Good God!' cried my uncle *Toby*, *'are children brought into the world with a squirt?'* " But before that, Slop's curse of a Shandy servant must be atoned for, and the brothers succeed in tricking Slop into reading aloud the excommunication of a twelfth-century bishop. Once again, Sterne takes a text apparently quite foreign to anything he is writing and incorporates it verbatim into his ongoing text. While he is clearly shocked, as a good Protestant, by the malevolence of the Roman Catholic Church as exhibited in such documents, he is also, perhaps, more than slightly entertained by the exuberance of the curse, its absolute thoroughness and richness. It has a fecundity that undercuts its sterile meaning; the interplay between the creative and destructive urges of man is beautifully exhibited.

With the birth of Tristram upstairs going slowly indeed, the two brothers fall asleep in the parlor; and Tristram, in chapter 20 of his third volume, finally offers his "Preface." Once again it is a text seemingly inapropos—a preface should be at the beginning of a work. This "Preface," however, Sterne could not have written a year

earlier: it is concerned primarily with the relationship between wit and judgment, and seems designed to answer those critics who objected to the bawdiness of the first two volumes, most especially because they were written by a clergyman. Sterne's task is to justify his wit, and he does so by attacking the notion, promulgated especially by Thomas Hobbes and Locke, that wit and judgment are mutually exclusive. Sterne, on the contrary, argues that they are mutually supportive faculties—a view that many, including Pope and Fielding, had argued before him. For Sterne, the attack on his wit was an attack by Tartuffes and "grave folks," people who had confused judgment with gravity; his response tries to balance wit and judgment, avoiding the sharpness of biting satiric wit and the dullness of long-faced judgment. But while it is clear that Sterne's public struggle is with those who were accusing him of being deficient in judgment, it is also possible that the "Preface" begins an interior monologue in which Sterne as author wrestles with the deficiency of wit that always threatens a writer committed to *not* telling his story, but rather to embellishing and ornamenting the spaces within the narrative. Or, to put it another way, Sterne had chosen as his models writers such as Rabelais and Montaigne; to follow them he had to have what must have seemed an inexhaustible capacity to heap wit upon wit. It was not an easy task he had set for himself.

What Sterne would not do was surrender to those voices urging him to bridle his wit—by which "bawdy wit" was most often meant. Hence, from this point in *Tristram Shandy* until the middle of volume four, the major subject is the length of the nose as an indicator of male potency. Dr. Slop has crushed Tristram's nose with his forceps, crushing as well Walter's hopes for Shandy potency. But rather than proceeding with this story, Tristram regresses to the origins of his father's theory. The allusions are primarily to Rabelais, and when the reader is asked to unravel the "many opinions, transactions and truths" of a marbled page that Sterne inserted into his text, he is being asked, in Rabelais's own language, to read *Tristram Shandy* with an eye upon Sterne's great predecessor.

Tristram, however, directs the reader to another antecedent, the fictional text of Hafen Slawkenbergius (loosely, a pile of manure), the source of Walter's preoccupation with noses. Here Sterne breaks somewhat with his previous practice of incorporating a preexistent text into

Sterne in 1760 (portrait by Sir Joshua Reynolds; Collection of the Marquess of Lansdowne)

his own; rather, he invents a new text and then interrupts his ongoing text in order to provide a sample—and he does so in both Latin and English (on facing pages), so that the relationship of texts becomes even further complicated. Tristram would have the reader believe that he is copying and translating a Latin text, but actually one can be certain that Sterne wrote the tale in English and then translated the opening section into Latin. The tale is, of course, not a found text at all, but yet one further invention of a fertile imagination, a tale that sounds much like Giovanni Boccaccio, although Cervantes also lends a hand. As with so many episodes of *Tristram Shandy*, this too reverberates with common motifs, especially the idea that sexual curiosity is a major human drive; a town is lost, the reader learns, because its citizens were all outside the gates awaiting the return of the hero with his enormous "nose."

At the same time, the town, particularly identified as Strasbourg, is useful to Sterne because it was a city clearly divided between Protestants and Catholics, a natural division for the Rabelaisian satire on Scholasticism that is another aspect of the tale. The basic quarrel repeats, indeed, an earlier discussion between Walter and Toby upon the cause of large noses. Walter seeks answers in sci-

ence, while Toby offers the answer of religion—large noses exist because God wants them. Similarly, in Strasbourg the learned clergy debate the possibility of a nose "575 geometrical feet in length," with the Catholics declaring that anything is possible for God and the Protestants that God will only work within natural causes and effects. The argument was an extremely important one to Thomas Aquinas, but for Sterne it seems primarily a means to demonstrate the futility of theory divorced from practical application. What Sterne seeks from religion is an "ounce of practical divinity," as he says about sermon writing; and what he seeks from man is a recognition of the limits of human reason, a favorite subject among eighteenth-century authors.

Having failed to control Tristram's conception or his birth with his theories, Walter plays his next card: he will christen the child Trismegistus. Of course, the reader already knows that this scheme is also doomed to failure—what remains is to discover what new accident will interfere with Walter's carefully laid plans. For indeed the "plot" of the opening volumes of *Tristram Shandy* is finally becoming apparent, although only at a point in the work at which Sterne will soon change direction. The action thus far has been intended to discredit Walter's theorizing, to place in opposition to his cerebral hypothesizing the realities of chance, interruption, misdirection, and, above all, natural process. It is no accident that when Walter receives the bad news, Sterne thrusts into his story an older text from one of his sermons: "But mark, madam, we live amongst riddles and mysteries—the most obvious things, which come in our way, have dark sides, which the quickest sight cannot penetrate into; and even the clearest and most exalted understandings amongst us find ourselves puzzled and at a loss. . . ." Whatever the answer might be for living among these riddles of human life, quite clearly a total reliance upon the mind of man is not it. Walter is not quite finished with his attempts to impose his own mind on the reality of Tristram, but the reader is beginning to look elsewhere.

At this point a word must be said about Tristram-in-his-study, where certain confusions are beginning to accumulate. For one, Tristram is becoming more strident in his defiance of "rules." Hence, in a discussion of the rationale for making chapter divisions he admits that it is all done by sudden "impulse": "A pretty story! is a man to follow rules—or rules to follow him?"

At the same time, he is also beginning to show an awareness, if not of the cause, at least of the effect of ignoring all rules. He is in his fourth volume and has just been born, and his first day is not yet over—"'tis demonstrative," he writes, "that I have three hundred and sixty-four days more life to write just now, than when I first set out; so that instead of advancing . . . in my work . . . I am just thrown so many volumes back. . . ." Tristram is, of course, delighted by the prospect of never catching up with himself, with a program of infinite continuity. But the nature of art and of life work against such a plan; art requires selectivity at every turn, and one cannot usually call in an outsider, as Tristram does, to drop a curtain on scenes that must be ended by the author himself. Similarly, art requires proportion, an awareness Tristram parodies when he omits ten pages from his text, ten pages that would have made everything else in the chapter flat and disappointing. The insight, however, is a real one—the process of selection is part of art's demand for proportion, and Tristram's failure to be selective is becoming more and more troublesome to him. His book has become his hobbyhorse, a fact made clear by the metaphorical description of it at the opening of chapter 20; and like all riders, he seems impervious to the collisions he experiences and the chaos he leaves in his path. The lack of selectivity involves subject matter the inclusion of which angered many people; and it also has left Tristram 364 days behind himself. To be sure, Sterne is quite in control of those comments he includes in his work that might offend, and of those digressions and regressions that put his "story" further and further behind. The point is that Sterne's book and Tristram's book are not the same thing, and thus, that Tristram-in-his-study encounters concerns *created* by Sterne rather than *confronted* by him. Indeed, it is particularly appropriate to note at this point that Sterne's own characteristic as an author is not a lack of judgment or control, but the opposite: Sterne manifests a growing anxiety that he will not be able to continue his work with the energy and the élan of his masters. Tristram frets about getting his story told; Sterne's concern is to continue to find a sufficient store of diverse materials to prevent his book from becoming a narrative.

Certainly the visitation dinner is one such digression, since it resolves nothing in the narrative, nor is it intended to. What it does do is reestablish Yorick's normative presence in *Tristram Shandy*, while once again laughing at the pomp and pedantry of the clergy. The argument concerning the legitimacy of a baptism using the wrong Latin forms is borrowed directly from a footnote in Rabelais, and the final joke, the *Argumentum commune*, comes from John Selden's *Table Talk* (1689). Sterne was beginning to raid his library for more and more material, a gesture of which he seems fully cognizant as he begins volume five with an attack on plagiarists—in sentences taken directly from Burton's *Anatomy of Melancholy*.

Also from the very beginning of volume five he makes clear that he has not surrendered his bawdy wit to the outraged demands of some critics and most clergymen. The digression "Upon Whiskers" is perhaps the most gratuitous piece of bawdiness in the entire work, serving only the already established fact that Sterne can charge any word (*nose, button-hole, crevice, thing*) with sexual implications. Like that of many satirical writers before him, Sterne's patience with prudery was wearing thin—or at least he pretended that it was, in a gesture reminiscent of Swift or Pope. Having used the proverbial expression "to bridle one's ass at the tail," meaning to take something the wrong way, he then adds: "And when the *extreams* of DELICACY, and the *beginnings* of CONCUPISCENCE, hold their next provincial chapter together, they may decree that bawdy also."

Walter's funeral oration provides perhaps the best example in *Tristram Shandy* of Sterne's desire to weave his fabric with many, many threads. The fragments that Walter shores against his ruin are borrowed from Joseph Hall, Francis Bacon, Montaigne, and, primarily, Burton. Sterne did not go to the classical sources, but picked up his citations as well as his sentences from these Renaissance writers. His aims, as usual, are many. He wants, of course, to ridicule once again Walter's substitution of rhetoric for thought; as Walter orates, he absolutely forgets his subject. He wants to reestablish his capacity to dazzle the reader with a fund of learning, the hallmark of the writers he is imitating. Finally, he wants, in a most traditional manner, to denigrate the classical consolations for death by contrasting them with Corporal Trim's parallel oration in the kitchen. The device is a standard trope in Christian apologetics, but Sterne brings new life to it by dramatizing Trim's mastery over his audience—and his subject. It is no accident that Trim's words are also echoes, but echoes of biblical—not classical—consolations. It is also no accident that his appeal is directed to the emotions. We "are men cloathed with bodies, and governed by our imaginations," Sterne writes, and quite clearly his argument is that Christianity, alone among the received systems of thought, addresses this reality, teaches us how to deal with the riddles and mysteries of this world. Walter, on the contrary, never can accept the world as anything but what his mind would make it out to be, so that reality constantly eludes him.

This is nowhere more apparent than in the *Tristrapaedia*, Walter's belated guide to the rearing of his son, and most specifically in that section advocating the use of auxiliary verbs as a Northwest Passage to logical discussion and demonstration. This system was seriously discussed at the end of the seventeenth century in Obadiah Walker's *Of Education* (1673), from which Sterne borrowed many passages verbatim; Sterne's use is rendered comic not only by his centering the discussion upon the inane subject of a white bear, but more broadly by his having it represent for Walter so definite a compensation for the defeat of all his other systems. This last demonstration of the folly of Walter Shandy leaves the reader with a sense of finality and futility. As with many great comic moments, it is heavily tinged with a tragic awareness of the fragility of human reason and the inadequacy of human solutions. In Sterne's own terms (eighteenth-century terms), the "head" has been found wanting as a means by which to govern our lives; in volume six, Sterne turns toward the "heart." He begins in earnest the story of the amours of Uncle Toby.

As usual, the story he actually tells, the story of Le Fever, is both a digression from Toby's story, and a way of telling it as well. What Sterne needs to establish in volume six is the shift of emphasis from Walter's head to Toby's heart as a center of moral attention, and it is the story of Le Fever that dramatizes the new direction. Sterne would seem to be following advice some readers had been giving him from the beginning, that his forte was in the pathetic and the sentimental. Sentimentalism was, without doubt, the major fictional market of the second half of the eighteenth century—one might observe that it dominated the intellectual marketplace as well. Whatever other reaction Sterne's severest critics had to his book, almost to a person they had kind words for Toby. If the human head could not be counted on to solve our problems, Toby's heart might well be the answer.

Most precisely in chapter 20 of volume six, Tristram announces his own change of direction: "WE are now going to enter upon a new scene of events." The Treaty of Utrecht has put an end to the enactments on the bowling green, and Toby's attention shifts, at long last, to the widow Wadman. The promise of the first volume, that the reader would be told the story of Toby's amours and the source of his modesty, is finally to be fulfilled. It will take Sterne the rest of *Tristram Shandy* to do so, but quite clearly these later volumes—excepting, of course, volume seven—are concentrated on telling one particular episode.

Toby's "apologetical oration" concerning war is made up of passages from Don Quixote's defense of knight-errantry over the profession of scholar, and from Burton's fierce diatribe against war in the opening pages of *Anatomy of Melancholy*. Both sources tend to suggest that Toby's defense has ironic undercurrents, that Sterne is more aware than Toby of the clash between his sentimental nature and his battlefield games—and that this clash is, for Sterne, a commentary on the nature of Toby Shandy. Like Walter forgetting why he is delivering his funeral oration, Toby too, mounted and galloping, forgets where he is (chapter 34), and, more tellingly, he forgets the true nature of military endeavors. One need not be a moralist to note that at the battle for which Toby dresses with special care, the Siege of Lille, during which he tries his water-pipe cannons for the first time, some twenty-three thousand men were killed or wounded. As Sterne was writing these volumes, England and Europe were engaged in the even more deadly Seven Years' War; if nothing else, this fact cautions one to read with care Toby's justifications of his bowling-green activities.

Sterne's game with straight lines, wavy lines, and the devils of John della Casa's "theory" of creation (namely, that fecundity is the temptation of the devil) is not only a complicated one, but quite possibly the central game of the work. Tristram's posture is that his digressions require discipline and that his efforts should now be directed toward telling the story of Toby in as straight a line as possible. Under the weight of his own incompleteness, of the accumulation of fragments, promises, and confusions, Tristram seems ready to abandon the freedom he so readily embraced at the outset and to opt instead for the imposed control of narrative—the rule of the straight line. But for Sterne the straight line remains precisely

Shandy Hall, the house in Coxwold given to Sterne in 1760 by an admirer

that indication of sterility and failure—the failure to equal his models—that he most dreads. Sterne's gesture here is one of simple displacement. That which as a writer he most fears—the drying up of his digressive strain, the inability to continue to find matter to embellish and sidetrack whatever story he is intent upon *not* telling—he makes his narrator's desideratum. But it is volume seven that indicates most clearly Sterne's thoughts about straight lines.

"This is not a digression, but the work itself," one may translate the motto to volume seven, in which Tristram quite abandons the story of Toby to describe his own flight from death. It was a volume that took Sterne almost three years to write, not because he did not have success in moving forward with the story of Toby, but rather, one may suspect, because the story of Toby was moving too rapidly forward, while the ornamentation lagged behind. Sterne's solution to this flagging energy was finally solved when he cast aside Toby altogether for volume seven and allowed Tristram's travels to occupy the volume. It was a bold stroke, a solution to

two years of impasse. In the sense that the book Sterne was writing required a constant flow of heterogeneous matter, volume seven is indeed "the work itself."

Tristram's flight to the Continent to repair his health is a flight from death, an inversion of the traditional medieval icon of the *danse macabre*. Tristram flees and Death follows; for those who have read *Tristram Shandy* with care, the presence of death is hardly unexpected. From Yorick's death to Bobby's death to Le Fever's death, from the "instruments of salvation" to the games of war to the images of sterility, illness, and injury, the work has constantly referred to death. Indeed, one might best see volume seven as the emergence of this theme into a dominant position, overcoming finally whatever hopes one might have had that birth and fecundity might overbalance the theme of mortality.

And yet, of course, Tristram does outrace death. *Tristram Shandy* as his own act of creation is itself one indication of his triumph. The sheer momentum of his effort is another: "So much of motion, is so much of life, and so much of joy," he writes, and the exuberance of his comic dash through France might well induce the reader to feel that he is right. Tristram sees very little, traveling at night and at breakneck speed; his travelogue is in fact a tour through the clichéd observations of contemporary travel books. It is also a series of rapid flirtations with young women in an attempt to flee death and in a search for life-giving energy. Hence it is with some dismay that the reader notes Tristram's admission of sexual failure with Jenny in chapter 29; and again that when his pace slows measurably after the journey down the "rapid Rhone" and he crosses the plains of Languedoc at a leisurely pace, he finally dances *away* from Nannette and the inviting slit in her petticoat. When Sterne returns to his travels as a basis for his fiction in *A Sentimental Journey*, precisely the same pattern recurs.

Once again in volume seven, Sterne answers those readers still critical of his bawdiness, this time with the ludicrous story of the abbess of *Andoüillets* (little sausages). It has been argued that Sterne began to conform to his critics by shifting from the intellectual satire surrounding Walter Shandy to a more sentimental mode as he moved to Uncle Toby. Yet in these two volumes Sterne deliberately continues his bawdy games; perhaps no passage in the entire work is as blatantly suggestive as chapter 11 of volume eight. Over and over again, Sterne seems to be talking directly to his critics; the abbess's attempt to avoid the "sin" of the words she uses is one reflection he makes on human priggishness; Tristram's " 'Not touch it for the world' did I say" is another. Whatever else Sterne does in *Tristram Shandy*, he insists upon the human necessity to "touch it" again and again. It is neither stubbornness nor bawdiness that motivates this theme; rather, central to Sterne's vision—moral, social, and religious—is a view of man that comprehends his body as well as his soul, his loins as well as his head and his heart. To consider man as anything else, Sterne seems to say, is to fail to address sufficiently the human condition. Despite the outcries of certain churchmen, Sterne persisted in his vision, perhaps because he recognized that Christianity itself was a system designed not for saints but for "men cloathed with bodies, and governed by . . . imaginations."

Corporal Trim is the character who most clearly understands the role of the body in human affairs. His liaisons with Susannah and Bridget are chronicled, and his falling in love with the "fair beguine" serves as a measure both of Toby's amours and of sentimentalism more generally. What is evident in all these epsiodes is the physicality of Trim, his "corporeality" in a world where the other characters seem bent upon denying their bodily existence—with the notable exception, of course, of the widow Wadman. For the essence of the story of Toby's courtship is her curiosity over the extent of his groin injury. The entire movement of the last two volumes is directed toward that final moment when Uncle Toby naively suggests to Trim that Mrs. Wadman's concern over his wound shows her moral superiority over Bridget, whose concern for Trim's knee wound is negligible:

> ——God bless your honour! cried the Corporal—
> —what has a woman's compassion to do with a wound upon the cap of a man's knee? . . .
> "The knee is such a distance from the main body—whereas the groin, your honour knows, is upon the very *curtin* of the *place*."

Toby's disillusionment, the source of his estrangement from women, is traced to this very moment, and Sterne's work is completed. In that Toby so often highlighted the follies of Walter, with his innocent comments or whistling, it is only fitting that Walter, borrowing directly from Pierre Charron's *Of Wisdome* (1612), should point the moral of Toby's tale: "Wherefore, when we go about to make and plant a man, do we put out the candle? and for what reason is it, that all the parts thereof—the congredients—the preparations—the instruments, and whatever serves thereto, are so held as to be conveyed to a cleanly mind by no language, translation, or periphrasis whatever?" It is with this series of pointed questions that Sterne seems to end his exploration of the Shandy family.

A word remains to be said about the figure of Tristram-in-his-study in these final volumes. Most noticeably, the story of Toby's amours is a more straightforward narrative than any the reader has encountered thus far; the story moves with some rapidity toward its conclusion, and the reader reacts with expectation and curiosity, if only to share Mrs. Wadman's emotions. For Tristram this narrative regularity is in keeping with the ruled line he drew at the end of volume six, and for Sterne it does bring his "cock-and-bull" story to its conclusion. But such regularity is a flagging of narrative imagination, an inability to diversify the text in a manner worthy of his great predecessors. That Sterne's attention is focused

Watercolor illustrations of scenes from Tristram Shandy *painted in 1786 by John Nixon (Collection of J. C. T. Oates)*

on this problem is perhaps indicated most apparently by "The Story of the king of Bohemia and his seven castles," where, rather obviously, there is no story to tell but only constant interruptions to record. It is precisely this obviousness that suggests that Tristram is in trouble, for the essence of *copia* (elaboration, variation, abundance), as thus far practiced in *Tristram Shandy*, has been its spontaneity, its overflow. Sterne's artistry created this sense of abundance, just as now it creates a sense of authorial exhaustion in the face of a book that Tristram will not be able to continue for forty more volumes, forty more years. However much he tries to revive his digressive energies, the story of Toby's amours carries him straightforward toward its impotent conclusion.

Tristram's desperation breaks into the open in volume nine: "UPON looking back from the end of the last chapter and surveying the texture of what has been wrote, it is necessary, that upon this page and the five following, a good quantity of heterogeneous matter be inserted.... The only difficulty, is raising powers suitable to the nature of the service...." *Tristram Shandy* is no less brilliant in its closing volumes than in its initial ones seven years earlier. Indeed, Sterne nowhere shows more skill and humor than in the portrait of Toby's disillusionment at the hands of Mrs. Wadman. But at the same time Sterne tells that story, he is also telling Tristram's story, one of human limitations, proper perspectives, a story of the hopes of time and desire and the disappointments of impotence and death. It is, indeed, a story of very large subjects—Christian subjects—that occupied Sterne's entire writing career. In one of the most beautiful passages in *Tristram Shandy*, one replete with biblical echoes, Tristram is made to turn toward death rather than away from it, toward judgment and last things: "I will not argue the matter: Time wastes too fast: every letter I trace tells me with what rapidity Life follows my pen; the days and hours of it, more precious, my dear Jenny! than the rubies about thy neck, are flying over our heads like light clouds of a windy day, never to return more....——Heaven have mercy upon us both." No message from the pulpit could be more commonplace. In *Tristram Shandy*, however, it achieves the full intensity of its initial desperation and the full pathos of its final resignation. As Sterne entered the final year of his life, he once again concentrated all his attention on this one simple truth: Man is a creature surrounded by mysteries and riddles,

and the final mystery is the interweaving of desire and death.

Sterne's *A Sentimental Journey* must be read with volumes seven through nine of *Tristram Shandy* in mind, and also with the awareness that its chapters were interleaved, so to speak, with Sterne's entries in the "Journal to Eliza." What the three texts have in common is the flight away from self—the death-burdened male—toward the other—the death-defying female. Sterne conducts this flight along the twin paths of language and desire, both of which alternately reveal and conceal their direction and intention. The final episode of *A Sentimental Journey* is a paradigm for much that concerned him during the period. Traveling alone, Yorick finds himself required to share a room with a woman at the inn. For both, the sexual nature of the encounter is uppermost in mind, but the treaty they make puts Yorick on his honor to ignore desire; it is, as the chapter title has it, a "Case of Delicacy." But when in the course of a restless night Yorick exclaims "O my God," the treaty breaks down. The lady, who has also not slept, accuses him of breaking their agreement; Yorick, choosing an unfortunate word, protests it was only an "ejaculation"; and, in one of the most famous of fictional endings, he reaches across the space between the beds just as madame's maid comes running into the room: "So that when I stretch'd out my hand, I caught hold of the Fille de Chambre's/END OF VOL. II." This final ambiguous gesture, along with the verbal ambiguity of *ejaculation*, and indeed of *case*—a longstanding pun for the pudendum—in the title, encapsulate the persistence of desire in *A Sentimental Journey* and, as well, our persistent evasions of it as we communicate with one another—and indeed, with ourselves.

A Sentimental Journey opens with an episode in which Yorick, newly arrived in France, refuses charity to a begging monk and retreats, significantly, into a *desobligéant*, a one-person carriage, in order to write a preface. The episode deals with isolation and communication, approached, as is Sterne's usual practice, within a variety of tropes, the act of writing—creation—being never very far removed from the language of desire—procreation. Hence, modern readers quickly understand that *communication* and *commerce* in Yorick's vocabulary have connotations similar to *intercourse* in their own—and that *conversation* is also not innocent.

Yorick's isolation is broken by contact with a woman, and through her, by the charitable act to-

The christening of Tristram Shandy (illustration by William Hogarth, published in the first edition of Tristram Shandy, *volumes three and four)*

ward the monk that earlier he had refused. The entire encounter is magnificently self-conscious; indeed, the woman tells Yorick as much: "Who but an English philosopher," she chides him, "would have sent notices of [our holding hands] to the brain to reverse the judgment?" As everywhere in *A Sentimental Journey*, Yorick attempts to move outside himself, to connect with the feminine, always with a gesture covertly sexual. Sensibility masks sexuality, but for Yorick sexuality is particularly characterized by acute sensibility: "The pulsations of the arteries along my fingers pressing across hers, told her what was passing within me. . . ." It is this communion that allows Yorick to return to the monk with charity, and, in a scene that became the touchstone of romantic sensibility on the Continent, he exchanges snuffboxes with him. When he recounts his later return to Calais and to the monk's grave, Yorick writes that he "burst into a flood of tears—but I am as weak as a woman. . . ." The significance of Sterne's portrayal of human sexuality is his awareness, shared by his contemporary Richardson, and in the twentieth century by Marcel Proust, that male aggressiveness is internalized self-

destructiveness, while female passivity is the powerful fuel of appetite, the energy by which we convert ourselves into another; it is an insight not far away from what Sterne preached from his pulpit concerning the true nature of Christian love.

Sterne explores the interrelationship between love and language in Yorick's inability to write to Madame de L**** when they meet at Amiens; and more precisely in the neat turn of La Fleur's all-occasion love letter:

L'amour n'est *rien* sans sentiment.
Et le sentiment est encore *moins* sans amour.

Quite clearly, Le Fleur's *amour* suggests physical love, while *sentiment* suggests an idealized love. In an age of sexual freedom, the first sentence is obviously most apropos: love is *nothing* without sentiment. But in a sentimental age, when the "language of the heart" has become the measure of man, then the second sentence is the moralist's stern reminder: sentiment is even *less* without love. As Sterne had earlier brought Toby toward a realization of human sexuality, so also in *A Sentimental Journey* he confronts his character with the reality of desire, glimpsed intermittently through a language that masks as often as it provides communication.

Yorick's arrival in Paris once again manifests his isolation:

> I own my first sensations, as soon as I was left solitary and alone in my own chamber in the hotel were far from being so flattering as I had prefigured them. I walked gravely to the window in my dusty black coat, and looking through the glass, saw all the world in yellow, blue, and green, running at the ring of pleasure.—The old with broken lances, and in helmets which had lost their vizards—the young in armour bright. . . .
>
> Alas, poor Yorick! cried I, what art thou doing here?

The passage is typical of Sterne's most mature writing—a virtuoso mingling of heretofore incompatible intentions, most obviously the pathetic and the bawdy. The sad redundancy of *solitary and alone*, the elevation of *prefigured*, the touching contrast that begins with *gravely*, moves to the *dusty black coat* (*grave*, *dust*, and *black* playing out another trope) and concludes with the prismatic colors through the glass—all this is the work of a masterly craftsman earning an emotional response. But then comes the ring of pleasure, a bawdy image borrowed from Rabelais, and a sudden series of jokes—"broken lances," "lost vizards" (the ravages caused by mercury in the treatment of venereal disease), and the young "in armour," the contemporary term for condoms. The accumulation of pathos is too rich to be unintentional, but so is the accumulation of bawdiness. Watching over Yorick's struggle to escape from language into desire and, conversely, from desire back into language, Sterne seems to posit sexual union as an elusive peace that passes understanding. Even when the union is achieved—and it is achieved several times in *A Sentimental Journey*—Yorick is unable or unwilling to sustain the moment and, like Tristram before him, moves away from the "cursed slit" in the petticoat. Herein lies the full pathos of man, whose fulfillment both begins and ends in language and hence, at the very moment of harmony and oneness, begins again to separate, divaricate.

In the next episode, Yorick feels the pulse of a shopgirl, a scene of the utmost delicacy—and sexuality, insofar as the fitting of a glove is yet one more trope for sexual union. But this time Sterne gives the reader a strong hint of union, significantly one that sets language aside:

> There are certain combined looks of simple subtlety . . . that all the languages of Babel set loose together could not express them—they are communicated and caught so instantaneously, that you can scarce say which party is the infecter.
> . . . she had a quick black eye, and shot through two such long and silken eye-lashes with such penetration, that she look'd into my very heart and reins. . . .

The nonverbal gesture, which Sterne had used successfully to allow Walter and Toby to bridge their mental and emotional gaps, is here made a viable path between the baffling conflicts of the self and the elusive intentions of the other. Most significantly, this movement from self to other is imaged as a silent sexual exchange ("which party is the infecter?"), perhaps Sterne's major insight into the nature of human desire, where union is achieved when the female penetrates and the male receives.

Sterne reinforces his insight about nonverbal communication and sexual exchange in the following chapter, "The Translation," in which once again the sexual union begins with nonverbal stasis, as Yorick and the marquesina attempt to sidestep one another; here, however, the balance is

beautifully maintained, while again the aggressor and recipient roles are reversed: "Upon my word, Madame . . . I made six different efforts to let you go out—And I made six efforts, replied she, to let you enter. . . ." The passage is, of course, bawdy, but unlike earlier passages where the bawdiness held pathos in check, here it releases it. A union with the marquesina is strongly indicated, and the "connection" is a moment of fulfillment quite alone in *A Sentimental Journey* in its implicit unfettered actualization. It is noteworthy that it takes place in the portion of Yorick's journey that remained unwritten, namely, the journey to Italy. Perhaps it is a projection of the fulfillment to be achieved at journey's end, after all has been learned and experienced; or perhaps, more subtly, it suggests that "connection" must always be that portion of our journey that remains unverbalized, unwritten.

The problem of penetrating the other holds Sterne's attention throughout the middle of *A Sentimental Journey*. Each episode suggests the value of nonverbal communication and, at the same time, explores the failure of language in the search for "connection." Of particular significance for understanding Sterne's commentary on the Age of Sensibility are the chapters concerned with the caged starling. Yorick "translates" the bird's song as "I can't get out," but for Sterne the exercise of translation, no matter how energetically pursued, is often nothing more than "sentiment . . . sans amour." Significantly, Yorick replays the encounter with the marquesina; the bird cannot "get out," and Yorick, try as he might imaginatively to enter into the bird's captivity, cannot "get in": "I could not sustain the picture of confinement which my fancy had drawn." Indeed, the bird is passed from hand to hand but is never freed, for the roles remain always the same: "All these [the owners] wanted to *get in*—and my bird wanted *to get out*. . . ." This failure is not merely a failure of the imagination. Insofar as Yorick's efforts to identify with the starling are conscious and aggressive (filled as they are with English Francophobia), they are diametrically opposed to the reversal of roles that Sterne finds necessary for true penetration and connection. Until the bird is allowed to leave the cage and Yorick can enter it, Sterne sees no communication taking place, despite the emphasis his contemporaries placed on moral sensibility and empathic understanding.

Yorick's quest for his passport is a final search for identity, which begins in earnest when

A

SENTIMENTAL JOURNEY

THROUGH

FRANCE AND ITALY.

BY

MR. YORICK.

VOL. I.

LONDON:

Printed for T. BECKET and P. A. DE HONDT,
in the Strand. MDCCLXVIII.

Title page for Sterne's last work, a fiction about the never-ending quest for human contact

the conversation with the count, who is to secure the passport, turns to women. Yorick proclaims his view: one must love womankind in order to love a particular woman, he "being firmly persuaded that a man who has not a sort of an affection for the whole sex, is incapable of ever loving a single one. . . ." Yorick returns to a similar equation a paragraph later when in response to the count's bawdy innuendo, he tells the reader that he "cannot bear the shock of the least indecent [sexual] insinuation." But Yorick acknowledges that this "modesty" is no particular virtue; indeed, trying to overcome it, he has "hazarded a thousand things [in conversation] to a dozen of the sex together—the least of which I could not venture to a single one, to gain heaven." One is reminded of Swift's famous comment that he detested "that animal called man, although I heartily love John, Peter, Thomas and so forth." Yorick comes at the question of love from the other direction, loving all women, but unable to say to one woman what is required to "gain heaven."

It is no accident, given this admission that Yorick "can't get in," that the count's next question forces upon him the question of identity, or that Yorick's first response is that there "is not a more perplexing affair in life to me. . . ." The problem of identity is the problem of appetites, what Yorick calls "bad sensations," and the human tendency to ignore, or mask, or argue them down. Yorick's evasion, for example, is to counterbalance the "bad" with "some kindly and gentle sensation." We cannot, however, understand the nature of desire by counterpoising sensibility, which, Sterne argues, is an evasion of desire, a refusal to acknowledge that desire must be defined on its own terms, and its value acknowledged in its own right. We can only identify ourselves, in short, if we know ourselves.

In one of his finest passages, Sterne has Yorick grasp this truth: "But there is nothing unmixt in this world; and some of the gravest of our divines have carried it so far as to affirm, that . . . the greatest [enjoyment] *they knew of*, terminated *in a general way*, in little better than a convulsion." Yorick cites one such grave authority, a Dutch physician named Bevoriskius, whose attention was caught by sparrows copulating on his window ledge: "How merciful," Bevoriskius exclaims, "is heaven to his creatures!" Here is Yorick's real identity, and his "passport" to connection, fulfillment, "heaven": Man is a creature born to the puzzlement of his sexual appetite and his desperate need for connection with the other. To acknowledge him as such is to begin to unravel the puzzle; Yorick's response, however, suggests his refusal even to take this first step:

> Ill fated Yorick! that the gravest of thy brethren should be able to write that to the world, which stains thy face with crimson, to copy in even thy study.
>
> But this is nothing to my travels. . . .

On the contrary, Bevoriskius's sparrows embody the thematic core of *A Sentimental Journey*.

Sterne's short novel, which might better be called a fable or apologue, since it is organized by a series of episodes designed to sustain a viewpoint rather than a situation or person, concludes with several further encounters between Yorick and women. The episode with the *fille de chambre* is purposely ambivalent. In their earlier meeting, Yorick had talked about "virtuous convention," and the "fine-spun threads" that draw an affection—and in the language of sensibility he had dismissed the girl. Now, however, he admits to something in him "not in strict unison with the lesson of virtue I had given her . . . the devil was in me." Earlier, despite the sensibility, Yorick's desires were clearly revealed by bawdy undercurrents. In the second meeting, the bawdy innuendos remain, but Yorick confronts his desires not masked by the posturing of sentiment but with an open assault on the puzzle of man's constitution. When he and the girl tumble on the bed together, the chapter abruptly ends; and the next, "The Conquest," begins with a challenge to "clay-cold heads and luke-warm hearts" who are able to argue down or mask their passions: "Tell me, what trespass is it that man should have them? . . . If nature has so wove her web of kindness, that some threads of love and desire are entangled with the piece—must the whole web be rent in drawing them out?" Bevoriskius's sparrows suggest that it need not be, and Yorick's impassioned apostrophe and question seem to be leading toward a frank avowal of desire and connection. But Yorick retreats again from sexuality, choosing instead a "virtue," the ambivalence of which is in his language: "Wherever thy providence shall place me for the trials of my virtue . . . let me feel the movements which rise out of it, and which belong to me as a man—and if I govern them as a good one—I will trust the issues to thy justice. . . ." Yorick suggests a masculine victory, a triumph over desire by firm governance—a conquest over himself. *A Sentimental Journey*, however, contains a search not for moral triumph, but for the more difficult victory of self-understanding and human love, and that remains out of Yorick's reach.

Yorick's penultimate encounter is with Maria, the same mad girl that Tristram had met during his tour. In Sterne's day, and for a century after, Maria was an emblem of sentimental fiction, the melancholy distressed maiden of romantic literature and art. Indeed, nowhere in *A Sentimental Journey* does Yorick seem closer to an honest union of desire and language. As he weeps with Maria, he discovers in a convincing manner the strongest sense of identity, not simply with her but with himself; he discovers the existence of his soul: "I felt such undescribable emotions within me, as I am sure could not be accounted for from any combinations of matter and motion. I am positive I have a soul. . . ." The feeling, significantly, is not free from sexual desire. Yorick's description of Maria is really the first time he "sees" the woman he is with as a physical being rather than merely a sentimental idea:

"Maria, tho' not tall, was nevertheless of the first order of fine forms—affliction had touch'd her looks with something that was scarce earthly—still she was feminine—and so much was there about her of all that the heart wishes, or the eye looks for in woman, that could the traces be ever worn out of her brain . . . she should *not only eat of my bread and drink of my own cup*, but Maria should lay in my bosom, and be unto me as a daughter." The last phrases paraphrase Nathan's parable of the poor man's ewe lamb (2 Samuel 12:3), which is cared for as Yorick vows to care for Maria. Nathan uses the parable to recall to David his sin of taking Bathsheba from Uriah, David being Sterne's favorite example of the strict moralist who is severe on other sinners but blind to his own transgressions. As such, the biblical allusion reminds one again of the question of identity; as David is forced to acknowledge his desire (and his sinfulness), so Yorick, finally, comes to an honest awareness of his own desires—free from deception, from innuendo, from repression.

It is within this context of a hard-won embrace of the complex nature of man that Yorick's famous apostrophe to sensibility in the next chapter must be understood. It has often marked Sterne as the foremost sentimentalist of a sentimental age. Its context, however, is the exploration of sensibility's relation to desire and to language that precedes it; and in this context "sensibility" must be understood as that particular capacity that makes love possible: the awareness of the wholeness of human experience and the knowledge that sensibility is not limited to those stirrings we can accept with clean hands and uplifted hearts: "—Dear sensibility! source inexhausted of all that's precious in our joys, or costly in our sorrows! . . . all comes from thee, great—great SENSORIUM of the world! which vibrates, if a hair of our heads but falls upon the ground, in the remotest desert of thy creation." Yorick's prayer is an assertion of Providence (Matthew 10:29-31), God's continuing hand in human affairs despite the Fall and the intricate web of good and evil that life had become. It is, in short, a statement of faith.

Faith is answered by "Grace," the penultimate chapter of *A Sentimental Journey*. Tristram found a similar moment of communion in the peasant dance at the end of his tour through France, although the moment was tainted by repressed desire, Nanette's "cursed slit" in her petticoat. However, nothing interferes with Yorick's appreciation of the moment. In harmony with himself at last, he is able to be in harmony with others. The beautiful assertion that he beholds *"Religion* mixing in the dance" is an insight gained through travel and loneliness—and, perhaps, the impending threat of death, which renders the need for connection all the more necessary. Importantly, the "grace" is not spoken but acted out; equally important, Yorick is able to find the words to express the joy of the dance without equivocation or innuendo. The distance between Tristram and Yorick at this point is the measure of the wisdom of *A Sentimental Journey,* Sterne's final effort to bring his readers to his own understanding of the nature of language and of desire.

Yet, as Pope writes: "Man never Is, but always To be blest." The moment of "grace," of insight, is ultimately only a moment in the stream of life. Tristram flees from insight; Yorick is simply unable to sustain it, which, in a fallen world, is man's natural relationship to grace. And so the "Case of Delicacy" is the final chapter, reminding the reader that the quest is as long as life itself, that however else Yorick may be remembered, he is also the man endlessly reaching across the void for the woman on the other side. Insight, love, wholeness, grace, all are possible for the human being, but none of them permanently. What is permanent is desire, and the language by which we conceal it from ourselves and reveal it to others. "Vive l'amour! et vive la bagatelle!"—this was La Fleur's motto and might well have been Sterne's.

Critical theory at the end of the twentieth century has suggested that at least as much can be discovered about an age and its critics by reading its criticism as about the works being criticized—and in all likelihood, rather more. For example, the eighteenth century and the Romantics—whether in England or on the Continent—found the heart of *Tristram Shandy* in such episodes as when Toby gently catches a fly and sets it free at the window. But surely the predilection for this scene is a comment primarily on the Age of Sensibility in which Sterne wrote, and the Age of Romanticism that followed. Similarly, if in the middle and late nineteenth century Sterne underwent a period of public hostility, this says at least as much about Victorian England as about Sterne. The twentieth century has also shaped Sterne to its own liking, and his great popularity among critics and scholars—as an innovator in fictional forms, a liberator of classical restraints and moral rigidities, a philosopher of time, language, and the nature of self—has its

Sterne confronted by death, a 1766 painting by Thomas Patch (Jesus College, Cambridge)

origin in the modern love of innovation, liberalism, and "high seriousness," even in comic writers. If the Romantics loved Toby and the fly, twentieth-century critics love Tristram's "most puzzled skein of all," when he tries to unravel the three journeys he has taken to Auxerre, a splendid confusion of spatial sameness and chronological difference. The point worth bearing in mind is that the above discussion of *Tristram Shandy* mentions neither passage, deliberate omissions designed to suggest that thirty years from now a passage perhaps quite unsuspected at this time will be the key that unlocks Sterne's works for readers of the twenty-first century.

This being the case, the question of critical reception and reputation should be approached in the broadest possible terms. Despite Samuel Johnson's dictum that "Nothing odd will do long. 'Tristram Shandy' did not last," the fact is that it has endured, has—to use Johnson's own criteria—pleased many and pleased long, and hence has an assured place within the English literary tradition. Sterne has had his critics, to be sure, the

Tartuffes of one age, the "high culturists" of another: F. R. Leavis accused Sterne of "nasty trifling" and dismissed him in a footnote in his *The Great Tradition* (1948). But Sterne has also been admired from the outset by great authors such as James Boswell, Voltaire, and Denis Diderot; and indeed, the list of major critics and writers who have praised him forms a veritable who's who in the Western literary tradition: Samuel Taylor Coleridge, William Hazlitt, Thomas Carlyle, Johann Wolfgang von Goethe ("I still have not met his equal in the broad field of literature"), Honoré de Balzac, Aleksander Pushkin, and Count Lev Nikolayevich Tolstoy, to name a handful. In the twentieth century, Virginia Woolf, James Joyce, Thomas Mann, and Samuel Beckett have all found something to admire and to imitate in Sterne, although the nature of his influence is as various as the authors named.

The complexity of literary influence is nowhere better displayed than in the relationship of Marcel Proust to Sterne. Earlier twentieth-century critics would have found an influence in the fictional reconstruction of the working mind of Tristram and of Marcel in *Remembrance of Things Past* (1913-1927). It seems just as likely, however, that Proust could easily have shaped Marcel without reading a word of *Tristram Shandy*. But it might also be suggested that the three thousand pages of *Remembrance of Things Past* could not have been written had not Sterne first explored as honestly as he did the intricacies of desire and language in the 150 pages of *A Sentimental Journey*; or perhaps that the reading of *A Sentimental Journey* provided above would not have been possible without Proust. In this way, modernist critics are able to make paradoxical statements such as the assertion that Proust influenced Sterne and not be too far from an essential truth. The modern reader wanting to understand and appreciate Sterne's achievements needs to read Proust and Joyce and Mann. The reader must also know Rabelais and Montaigne, Cervantes' *Don Quixote* and Burton's *Anatomy of Melancholy*. Finally, Sterne's great contemporaries, Pope and Swift, Fielding and Richardson, must be read. In short, Sterne is a major author comprehensible only in relation to other major authors, to that tradition that he both uses and helps to create. Readers who come to *Tristram Shandy* or *A Sentimental Journey* before reading anything else in the tradition will find themselves perplexed. However, one must begin somewhere, and if it is with *Tristram Shandy*, one should consider Sterne's own warning to the

reader to "have a little patience," to bear with him and let him go on and tell his story his own way. Sterne is a difficult and complex author; he is also a most rewarding author for those willing to let him work his magic. One would like to be living at the end of the twenty-first century if only to be able to see what readers then will be making of him.

Letters:
Letters of Laurence Sterne, edited by Lewis Perry Curtis (Oxford: Clarendon Press, 1935).

Bibliographies:
Lodwick Hartley, *Laurence Sterne in the Twentieth Century: An Essay and a Bibliography of Sternean Studies, 1900-1965* (Chapel Hill: University of North Carolina Press, 1966);

Hartley, *Laurence Sterne: An Annotated Bibliography, 1965-1977* (Boston: G. K. Hall, 1978).

Biographies:
Percy Fitzgerald, *The Life of Laurence Sterne*, 2 volumes (London: Chapman & Hall, 1864);

Wilber L. Cross, *The Life and Times of Laurence Sterne*, third edition (New Haven: Yale University Press, 1929);

Arthur H. Cash, *Laurence Sterne: The Early and Middle Years* (London: Methuen, 1975);

Cash, *Laurence Sterne: The Later Years* (London: Methuen, 1986).

References:
Robert Alter, "*Tristram Shandy* and the Game of Love," *American Scholar*, 37 (1968): 316-323;

Theodore Baird, "The Time-Scheme of *Tristram Shandy* and A Source," *PMLA*, 51 (1936): 803-820;

Martin C. Battestin, *The Providence of Wit: Aspects of Form in Augustan Literature and the Arts* (Oxford: Clarendon Press, 1974);

Battestin, "*A Sentimental Journey* and the Syntax of Things," in *Augustan Worlds*, edited by J. C. Hilson, M. M. B. Jones, and J. R. Watson (Leicester: University of Leicester Press, 1978), pp. 223-239;

Wayne Booth, "Did Sterne Complete *Tristram Shandy*?," *Modern Philology*, 48 (1951): 172-183;

Booth, "The Self-Conscious Narrator in Comic Fiction before *Tristram Shandy*," *PMLA*, 67 (1952): 163-185;

Frank Brady, *"Tristram Shandy:* Sexuality, Morality, and Sensibility," *Eighteenth-Century Studies,* 4 (1970): 41-56;

R. F. Brissenden, "The Sentimental Comedy: *Tristram Shandy,"* in *Virtue in Distress: Studies in the Novel of Sentiment from Richardson to Sade* (London: Macmillan, 1974);

Brissenden, "Sterne and Painting," in *Of Books and Humankind: Essays Presented to Bonamy Dobre* (London: Routledge & Kegan Paul, 1964), pp. 93-108;

Sigurd Burckhardt, *"Tristram Shandy's* Law of Gravity," *ELH,* 28 (1961): 70-88;

Arthur H. Cash, "The Lockean Psychology of *Tristram Shandy,"* *ELH,* 22 (1955): 125-135;

Cash, *Sterne's Comedy of Moral Sentiments: The Ethical Dimension of the "Journey"* (Pittsburgh, Pa.: Duquesne Studies Philological Series, 6, 1966);

Cash and John M. Stedmond, eds., *The Winged Skull: Papers from the Laurence Sterne Bicentenary Conference* (Kent, Ohio: Kent State University Press, 1971);

John A. Dussinger, "Yorick and the 'Eternal Fountain of our Feelings'," in *Psychology and Literature in the Eighteenth Century,* edited by Christopher Fox (New York: AMS Press, 1987), pp. 259-276;

Patricia Hogan Graves, "A Computer-Generated Concordance to Sterne's *Tristram Shandy,"* 4 volumes, Ph.d. dissertation, Emory University, 1974;

William V. Holtz, *Image and Immortality: A Study of* Tristram Shandy (Providence, R.I.: Brown University Press, 1970);

Alan B. Howes, ed., *Sterne: The Critical Heritage* (London: Routledge & Kegan Paul, 1974);

D. W. Jefferson, *"Tristram Shandy* and the Tradition of Learned Wit," *Essays in Criticism,* 1 (1951): 225-248;

Richard Lanham, Tristram Shandy: *The Games of Pleasure* (Berkeley: University of California Press, 1973);

Kenneth MacLean, "Imagination and Sympathy: Sterne and Adam Smith," *Journal of the History of Ideas,* 10 (1949): 399-410;

Alan Dugald McKillop, *Early Masters of English Fiction* (Lawrence: University Press of Kansas, 1956), pp. 182-219;

Helene Moglen, *The Philosophical Irony of Laurence Sterne* (Gainesville: University Presses of Florida, 1975);

Kenneth Monkman, "The Bibliography of the Early Edition of *Tristram Shandy,"* *Library,* 25 (1970): 11-39;

Valerie Grosvenor Myer, ed., *Laurence Sterne: Riddles and Mysteries* (London: Vision Press / Totowa, N.J.: Barnes & Noble, 1984);

Melvyn New, *Laurence Sterne as Satirist: A Reading of Tristram Shandy* (Gainesville: University of Florida Press, 1969);

New, "Sterne, Warburton, and the Burden of Exuberant Wit," *Eighteenth-Century Studies,* 15 (1982): 245-274;

Betty Pasta, David J. Pasta, and John Pasta, "A Concordance to Laurence Sterne's *A Sentimental Journey,"* 2 volumes (Urbana: University of Illinois Department of Computer Science, 1974);

Ronald Paulson, *Satire and the Novel in Eighteenth-Century England* (New Haven: Yale University Press, 1967), pp. 248-265;

Graham Petrie, "Rhetoric as Fictional Technique in *Tristram Shandy,"* *Philological Quarterly,* 48 (1969): 479-494;

Rufus D. S. Putney, "The Evolution of *A Sentimental Journey,"* *Philological Quarterly,* 19 (1940): 349-369;

Putney, "Laurence Sterne: Apostle of Laughter," in *The Age of Johnson: Essays Presented to Chauncey Brewster Tinker* (New Haven: Yale University Press, 1949);

Herbert Read, "Sterne," in his *The Sense of Glory* (New York: Harcourt Brace, 1930), pp. 123-151;

Michael Rosenblum, "The Sermon, the King of Bohemia, and the Art of Interpolation in *Tristram Shandy,"* Studies in Philology, 75 (1978): 472-491;

Eric Rothstein, *"Tristram Shandy,"* in his *Systems of Order and Inquiry in Later Eighteenth-Century Fiction* (Berkeley: University of California Press, 1975), pp. 62-108;

John M. Stedmond, *The Comic Art of Laurence Sterne: Convention and Innovation in Tristram Shandy and A Sentimental Journey* (Toronto: University of Toronto Press, 1967);

James E. Swearingen, *Reflexivity in Tristram Shandy: An Essay in Phenomenological Criticism* (New Haven: Yale University Press, 1977);

John Traugott, *Tristram Shandy's World: Sterne's Philosophical Rhetoric* (Berkeley: University of California Press, 1954);

Ernest Tuveson, "Locke and Sterne," in his *Reason and the Imagination: Studies in the History of Ideas, 1600-1800* (New York: Columbia University Press, 1962);

Leland E. Warren, "The Constant Speaker: Aspects of Conversation in *Tristram Shandy*," University of Toronto Quarterly, 46 (1976): 50-67;

W. B. C. Watkins, *Perilous Balance: The Tragic Genius of Swift, Johnson & Sterne* (Princeton: Princeton University Press, 1939).

Papers:

The only portion of *Tristram Shandy* that survives in manuscript, arguably in the hand of a copyist rather than of Sterne himself, is a version of the Le Fever episode in volume six that Sterne presented to Lady Spencer, wife of his patron (see the dedicatory letter to Lord Spencer prefacing volumes five and six). This manuscript of twenty-seven pages disappeared in 1898 but resurfaced in the British Library in 1989. Manuscript versions of *A Sentimental Journey* are in the British Library and the J. Pierpont Morgan Library. Some forty letters and the manuscript of the "Rabelaisian Fragment" are also in the Morgan Library. The manuscript of the "Journal to Eliza" and some additional letters are in the British Library.

Jonathan Swift

(30 November 1667 - 19 October 1745)

This entry was updated by Roger D. Lund (LeMoyne College) from his entry in
DLB 39: British Novelists, 1660-1800: Part Two.

See also the Swift entries in DLB 95: Eighteenth-Century British Poets: First Series *and* DLB 101: British Prose Writers, 1660-1800: First Series.

SELECTED BOOKS: *A Discourse of the Contests and Dissensions between the Nobles and the Commons in Athens and Rome* (London: Printed for John Nutt, 1701; Boston, 1728);

A Tale of a Tub, Written for the Universal Improvement of Mankind. Diu multumque desideratum. To Which Is Added, An Account of a Battel between the Antient and Modern Books in St. James's Library (London: Printed for John Nutt, 1704); expanded as *A Tale of a Tub: The Fifth Edition, with the Author's Apology and Explanatory Notes by W. W—tt—n B. D. and Others* (London: Printed for John Nutt, 1710);

Predictions for the Year 1708. Wherein the Month and Day of the Month Are Set Down, the Persons Named, and the Great Actions and Events of Next Year Particularly Related, as They Will Come to Pass. Written to Prevent the People of England from Being Further Impos'd on by Vulgar Almanack-Makers. By Isaac Bickerstaff, Esq. (London: Sold by John Morphew, 1708);

The Accomplishment of the First of Mr. Bickerstaff's Predictions: Being an Account of the Death of Mr. Partrige, the Almanack-Maker, upon the

Jonathan Swift circa 1718 (portrait by Charles Jervas;
National Portrait Gallery, London)

29th Inst., in A Letter to a Person of Honour (London, 1708);

An Elegy on Mr. Partrige, the Almanack-Maker, Who Died on the 29th of this Instant March, 1708 (London, 1708);

A Vindication of Isaac Bickerstaff Esq; Against What Is Objected to Him by Mr. Partrige, in His Almanack for the Present Year 1709. By the Said Isaac Bickerstaff, Esq (London, 1709);

A Letter from a Member of the House of Commons in Ireland to a Member of the House of Commons in England, Concerning the Sacramental Test (London: Printed for John Morphew, 1709);

A Famous Prediction of Merlin, the British Wizard; Written above a Thousand Years ago, and Relating to this Present Year. With Explanatory Notes. By T. N. Philomath (London: Printed & sold by A. Baldwin, 1709);

A Project for the Advancement of Religion, and the Reformation of Manners. By a Person of Quality (London: Printed for Benj. Tooke, 1709);

Baucis and Philemon, Imitated from Ovid (N.p., 1709);

A Meditation upon a Broom-stick, and somewhat Beside; of the Same Author's (London: Printed for E. Curll, 1710);

The Virtues of Sid Hamet the Magician's Rod (London: Printed for John Morphew, 1710);

A Short Character of His Ex. T. E. of W. L. L. of I—. With an Account of Some Smaller Facts, during His Government, Which Will Not Be Put into the Articles of Impeachment (London: Printed for William Coryton, 1711);

Some Remarks upon a Pamphlet, Entitl'd, A Letter to the Seven Lords of the Committee, Appointed to Examine Gregg. By the Author of the Examiner (London: Printed for John Morphew, 1711);

The Conduct of the Allies, and of the Late Ministry, in Beginning and Carrying on the Present War (London: Printed for John Morphew, 1711);

An Excellent New Song: Being the Intended Speech of a Famous Orator against Peace (N.p., 1711);

Miscellanies in Prose and Verse (London: Printed for John Morphew, 1711);

The W—ds—r Prophecy (London, 1711);

Some Advice Humbly Offer'd to the Members of the October Club, in a Letter from a Person of Honour (London: Printed for John Morphew, 1712);

The Fable of Midas (London: Printed for John Morphew, 1712);

Some Remarks on the Barrier Treaty, between Her Majesty and the States-General. By the Author of the Conduct of the Allies (London: Printed for John Morphew, 1712);

A Proposal for Correcting, Improving and Ascertaining the English Tongue; In a Letter to the Most Honourable Robert Earl of Oxford and Mortimer, Lord High Treasurer of Great Britain (London: Printed for Benj. Tooke, 1712);

Some Reasons to Prove, That No Person Is Obliged by His Principles, as a Whig, to Oppose Her Majesty or Her Present Ministry. In a Letter to a Whig-Lord (London: Printed for John Morphew, 1712);

A Hue and Cry after Dismal: Being a Full and True Account, How a Whig L--d Was Taken at Dunkirk, in the Habit of a Chimney-Sweeper, and Carryed before General Hill (London, 1712);

Peace and Dunkirk; Being an Excellent New Song upon the Surrender of Dunkirk to General Hill (London, 1712);

*A Letter of Thanks from My Lord W****n to the Lord Bp of S. Asaph, in the Name of the Kit-Cat-Club* (London, 1712);

Mr. C—n's Discourse of Free-Thinking, Put into Plain English, by Way of Abstract, for the Use of the Poor. By a Friend of the Author (London: Printed for John Morphew, 1713);

Part of the Seventh Epistle of the First Book of Horace Imitated: And Address'd to a Noble Peer (London: Printed for A. Dodd, 1713);

The Importance of the Guardian Considered, in a Second Letter to the Bailiff of Stockbridge. By a Friend of Mr. St- - - (London: Printed for John Morphew, 1713);

A Preface to the B- - - -p of S- -r- -m's Introduction to the Third Volume of the History of the Reformation of the Church of England. By Gregory Misosàrum (London: Printed for John Morphew, 1713);

The First Ode of the Second Book of Horace Paraphras'd: and Address'd to Richard St- -le, Esq (London: Printed for A. Dodd, 1713);

The Publick Spirit of the Whigs: Set Forth in Their Generous Encouragement of the Author of the Crisis: With Some Observations on the Seasonableness, Candor, Erudition, and Style of that Treatise (London: Printed for John Morphew, 1714);

A Letter from a Lay-Patron to a Gentleman, Designing for Holy Orders (Dublin: Printed by E. Waters, 1720); republished as *A Letter to a Young Gentleman, Lately Enter'd into Holy Orders, By a Person of Quality* (London: Printed for J. Roberts, 1721);

A Proposal for the Universal Use of Irish Manufacture, in Cloaths and Furniture of Houses, &c., Uterly Rejecting and Renouncing Every Thing

Wearable That Comes from England (Dublin: Printed & sold by E. Waters, 1720);

Epilogue, to be Spoke at the Theatre-Royal this Present Saturday Being April the 1st. In the Behalf of the Distressed Weavers (Dublin: Printed by J. W., 1721);

The Bubble: A Poem (London: Printed for Benj. Tooke, 1721);

The Bank Thrown Down. To an Excellent New Tune (Dublin: Printed by John Harding, 1721);

The Last Speech and Dying Words of Ebenezor Elliston, Who Is to Be Executed This Second Day of May, 1722. Publish'd at His Desire for the Common Good (Dublin: Printed by John Harding, 1722);

Some Arguments against Enlarging the Power of Bishops, in Letting of Leases. With Remarks on Some Queries Lately Published (Dublin: Printed for J. Hyde, 1723);

A Letter to the Shop-Keepers, Tradesmen, Farmers, and Common People of Ireland, Concerning the Brass Half-Pence Coined by Mr. Woods, with a Design to Have Them Pass in this Kingdom. By M. B. Drapier (Dublin: Printed by John Harding, 1724);

A Letter to Mr. Harding the Printer, upon Occasion of a Paragraph in His News-Paper of Aug. 1st. Relating to Mr. Wood's Half-Pence, By M. B. Drapier (Dublin, 1724);

To His Grace the Arch-Bishop of Dublin, A Poem (Dublin: Printed by John Harding, 1724);

His Grace's Answer to Jonathan (Dublin, 1724);

An Excellent New Song upon His Grace our Good Lord Archbishop of Dublin. By Honest JO, One of His Grace's Farmers in Fingel (Dublin: Printed by John Harding, 1724);

Prometheus, A Poem (Dublin, 1724);

A Letter to the Right Honourable the Lord Viscount Molesworth. By M. B. Drapier, Author of the Letter to the Shop-keepers, &c. (Dublin: Printed by John Harding, 1724);

A Serious Poem upon William Wood, Brasier, Tinker, Hard-Ware-Man, Coiner, Counterfeiter, Founder and Esquire (Dublin: Printed by John Harding, 1724);

Fraud Detected; or, The Hibernian Patriot. Containing, All the Drapier's Letters to the People of Ireland, on Wood's Coinage, &c. (Dublin: Reprinted & sold by George Faulkner, 1725);

The Birth of Manly Virtue from Callimachus (Dublin: Printed by & for George Grierson, 1725);

Cadenus and Vanessa. A Poem (Dublin, 1726);

Travels into Several Remote Nations of the World. In Four Parts. By Lemuel Gulliver, First a Surgeon, and Then a Captain of Several Ships, 2 volumes (London: Printed for Benj. Motte, 1726);

A Short View of the State of Ireland (Dublin: Printed by S. Harding, 1728);

An Answer to a Paper, Called A Memorial of the Poor Inhabitants, Tradesmen and Labourers of the Kingdom of Ireland. By the Author of the Short View of the State of Ireland (Dublin: Printed by S. Harding, 1728);

The Journal of a Dublin Lady; In a Letter to a Person of Quality (Dublin: Printed by S. Harding, 1729); republished as *The Journal of a Gaming Lady of Quality, in a Letter to a Friend* (New York: Printed & sold by J. Parker & W. Weyman, 1758);

A Modest Proposal for Preventing the Children of Poor People from Being a Burthen to Their Parents, or the Country, and for Making Them Beneficial to the Publick (Dublin: Printed by S. Harding, 1729);

An Epistle upon an Epistle from a Certain Doctor to a Certain Great Lord: Being a Christmas-Box for D. D– – –y (Dublin, 1730);

An Epistle to His Excellency John Lord Carteret, Lord Lieutenant of Ireland (Dublin, 1730);

A Vindication of His Excellency the Lord C– – – –T, from the Charge of Favouring None but Tories, High-Churchmen, and Jacobites. By the Reverend Dr. S–T (London: Printed for T. Warner, 1730);

A Soldier and a Scholar: or The Lady's Judgment upon Those Two Characters in the Persons of Captain – – and D–n S–T (London: Printed for J. Roberts, 1732);

*Considerations upon Two Bills Sent down from the R– H– the H—of L— to the H–ble H— of C—— Relating to the Clergy of I*****D* (London: Printed for A. Moore, 1732);

An Examination of Certain Abuses, Corruptions, and Enormities in the City of Dublin (Dublin, 1732);

The Lady's Dressing Room. To Which Is Added, A Poem on Cutting Down the Old Thorn at Market Hill. By the Rev. Dr. S–T (London: Printed for J. Roberts, 1732);

The Advantages Propos'd by Repealing the Sacramental Test, Impartially Considered (Dublin: Printed by George Faulkner, 1732);

The Life and Genuine Character of Doctor Swift, Written by Himself (London: Printed for J. Roberts, 1733);

The Presbyterians Plea of Merit; In Order to Take off the Test, Impartially Examined (Dublin: Printed & sold by George Faulkner, 1733);

An Epistle to a Lady, Who Desired the Author to Make Verses on Her, in the Heroick Stile. Also a Poem, Occasion'd by Reading Dr. Young's Satires, Called The Universal Passion (London: Reprinted for J. Wilford, 1733);

On Poetry: A Rapsody (London: Reprinted & sold by J. Huggonson, 1733);

A Beautiful Young Nymph Going to Bed. Written for the Honour of the Fair Sex. Pars minima est ipsa Puella sui. Ovid Remed. Amoris. To Which Are Added, Strephon and Chloe. And Cassinus and Peter (London: Reprinted for J. Roberts, 1734);

A Proposal for Giving Badges to the Beggars in All the Parishes of Dublin. By the Dean of St. Patrick's (Dublin: Printed by George Faulkner, 1737);

The Beasts Confession to the Priest, on Observing How Most Men Mistake Their Own Talents. Written in the Year 1732 (Dublin: Printed by George Faulkner, 1738);

A Complete Collection of Genteel and Ingenious Conversation, according to the Most Polite Mode and Method Now Used at Court, and in the Best Companies of England. In Three Dialogues. By Simon Wagstaff, Esq (London: Printed for B. Motte & C. Bathurst, 1738);

Verses on the Death of Dr. Swift. Written by Himself: Nov. 1731 (London: Printed for C. Bathurst, 1739);

Some Free Thoughts upon the Present State of Affairs. Written in the Year 1714 (Dublin: Printed by & for George Faulkner, 1741);

Directions to Servants. By the Revd. Dr. Swift, D.S.P.D. (Dublin: Printed by George Faulkner, 1745);

The Last Will and Testament of Jonathan Swift, D.D. (London: Reprinted & sold by M. Cooper, 1746);

Brotherly Love: A Sermon, Preached in St. Patrick's Church; On December 1st, 1717 (Dublin: Printed by George Faulkner, 1754);

The History of the Four Last Years of the Queen. By the Late Jonathan Swift, D.D.D.S.P.D. (London: Printed for A. Millar, 1758).

Editions and Collections: *The Works of J.S., D.D., D.S.P.D. in Four Volumes* (Dublin: Printed by & for George Faulkner, 1735);

The Works of Dr. Jonathan Swift, 14 volumes (London: Printed for C. Bathurst, 1751);

The Works of D. Jonathan Swift . . . To Which Is Prefixed, the Doctor's Life, with Remarks on His Writings, from the Earl of Orrery and Others, Not to Be Found in Any Former Edition of His Works, 9 volumes (Edinburgh: Reprinted for G. Hamilton & J. Balfour [etc.], 1752);

The Works of Jonathan Swift, Accurately Revised, Adorned with Copper-Plates; with Some Account of the Author's Life and Notes Historical and Explanatory, 16 volumes, edited by John Hawkesworth (London: Printed for C. Bathurst, C. Davis [etc.], 1754-1765);

Works. Arranged, Revised, and Corrected, with Notes, 17 volumes, edited by Thomas Sheridan (London: C. Bathurst, 1784); corrected and revised by John Nichols, 24 volumes (New York: Durell, 1812);

The Works of Jonathan Swift . . . Containing Additional Letters, Tracts, and Poems, Not Hitherto Published; with Notes, and a Life of the Author, 19 volumes, edited by Sir Walter Scott (Edinburgh: Printed for A. Constable, 1814);

The Works of Jonathan Swift . . . Containing Interesting and Valuable Papers, Not Hitherto Published, 2 volumes, edited by Thomas Roscoe (London: Washbourne, 1841);

Gulliver's Travels (1726), edited by Herbert Davis, with an introduction by Harold Williams, revised edition (Oxford: Blackwell, 1959);

Gulliver's Travels and Other Writings, edited, with an introduction and notes, by Louis A. Landa (Boston: Houghton Mifflin, 1960);

Gulliver's Travels, edited by Robert A. Greenberg (New York: Norton, 1970).

On 14 August 1725, Jonathan Swift wrote to his friend Charles Ford: "I have finished my Travells, and I am now transcribing them; they are admirable Things, and will wonderfully mend the World." At the age of fifty-seven, Swift had acquired sufficient experience of human falsehood, cruelty, and pride to harbor few illusions as to the medicinal properties of satire or the perfectibility of the species. "I tell you after all," he wrote to Alexander Pope, "I do not hate Mankind, it is vous autres who hate them because you would have them reasonable Animals, and are Angry for being disappointed." Yet, if *Gulliver's Travels* did not mend mankind, as Swift sardonically suggested it would, it certainly challenged his readers' smug assumptions about the superiority of their political and social institutions, and their assurance that as rational animals they occupied a privileged position in the Chain of Being. Indeed, Swift protested that he would sooner "vex the world . . . than divert it." From the moment of its publication in 1726, *Gulliver's Travels* has done both, charming generations of readers and inspiring more adaptations, answers, and illustrations than any other work of Augustan literature. It has also kindled almost continuous critical debate as to the precise objects of its satire, its moral tendency, and its ultimate significance.

Between 1945 and 1985 nearly five hundred books and articles were devoted to *Gulliver's Travels,* and this critical tide runs on unabated. How to classify a work that has variously been regarded as a children's tale, a fantastic voyage, a moral allegory, and even as a novel is a question that has consistently vexed Swift scholars. For while *Gulliver's Travels* is generally conceded to be the finest prose satire in English, it also stands as one of the most popular works of eighteenth-century fiction, one that has traditionally been linked with *Robinson Crusoe* (1719) for its creation of verisimilitude and its mastery of circumstantial detail. Although written before the full efflorescence of the English novel in the 1740s, *Gulliver's Travels* nonetheless bears a close (albeit idiosyncratic) relationship to that tradition of formal realism exemplified in the works of Samuel Richardson and Daniel Defoe.

At the heart of *Gulliver's Travels* lies Swift's coruscating denunciation of human pride. With relentless irony Swift dramatizes the vanity and moral obliquity of his hero-traveler. At first Gulliver seems merely silly, preening himself upon having been created a *Nardac,* the "highest Title of Honour" among the Lilliputians, and belittling Flimnap the Lord Treasurer, not because of his diminutive size but because he is "only a *Clumglum,* a title inferior by one degree." The reader laughs at Gulliver's martial triumph over a Brobdingnagian rat and his nautical vanity as he grandly sails his little boat around in a Brobdingnagian tub. But one is less amused by Gulliver's purblind condescension to the wise and benevolent king of Brobdingnag, who rightly "observed how contemptible a Thing was human Grandeur, which could be mimicked by such diminutive Insects" as Gulliver. Only after he has acknowledged his kinship with the loathsome Yahoos and has come to admire the virtues of the Houyhnhnms does Gulliver begin "to view the Actions and Passions of Man in a very different Light; and to think the Honour of my own Kind not worth managing." Now Gulliver rejects and vilifies his human form and human nature

Esther Johnson, Swift's "Stella" (portrait by James Latham; National Gallery of Ireland)

with that same single-mindedness that he had previously devoted to their praises: "When I thought of my Family, my Friends, my Countrymen, of human Race in general, I considered them as they really were, *Yahoos* in Shape and Disposition, perhaps a little more civilized, and qualified with the Gift of speech; but making no other Use of Reason, than to improve and multiply those Vices whereof their Brethren in this Country had only the Share that Nature allotted them."

As usual, Gulliver learns the wrong lesson. Instead of seeking to become a better man, he tries to become a horse, going so far as to reject the love of his own family in favor of equine companionship. Of course, Gulliver is not a Houyhnhnm any more than he is a Yahoo; he is a man, and that very pride that had led him to defend the moral enormities of European civilization now convinces Gulliver that, thanks to the tutelage of the Houyhnhnms, he has escaped the human condition. With all the self-righteousness and zeal of a religious convert Gulliver seeks to cast out the mote from his brother's eye while ignoring the beam in his own: "I am not in the least provoked at the Sight of a Lawyer, a Pickpocket, a Colonel, a Fool, a Lord, a Gamester, a Politician, a Whoremunger, a Physician, an Evidence, a Suborner, an Attorney, a Traytor, or the like: This is all according to the due Course of Things: but when I behold a Lump of Deformity, and Diseases both in Body and Mind, smitten with *Pride,* it immediately breaks all the Measures of my patience; neither shall I ever be able to comprehend how such an Animal and such a Vice could tally together." The irony, of course, is that in his dissociation from his fellow mortals, Gulliver reveals how deeply he himself has been "smitten with pride."

The ambiguity of Gulliver's condition has not always been apparent to Swift's critics, however. While Swift's earliest readers greeted *Gulliver's Travels* enthusiastically, critics soon complained that the Voyage to the Houyhnhnms constituted a "real insult upon mankind." Edward Young spoke for many when he accused Swift of having "blasphemed a nature little lower than that of the angels." In large measure, Young's charge that Swift had made a "Monster . . . of the *Human face* divine," arises directly from the benevolent aspirations of the Age of Sensibility. As this faith in the essential goodness and nobility of the human heart ossified into the dogmatic positivism of the Victorians, critics found that they could explain the corrosive satire of the Voyage to the Houyhnhnms only by positing an author who was both misanthropic and mad. Sir Walter Scott, for example, traced Swift's "diatribe against human nature" to that "soured and disgusted state of Swift's mind, which doubtless was even then influenced by the first impressions of that incipient mental disease which in this case, was marked by universal misanthropy."

Although nineteenth-century readers would continue to enjoy Gulliver's adventures in Lilliput and Brobdingnag, they were virtually unanimous in their denunciation of the misanthropy of the Voyage to the Houyhnhnms, lamentations memorably (if melodramatically) offered up by William Makepeace Thackeray. "It is Yahoo language," he fulminated, "a monster gibbering shrieks, and gnashing imprecations against mankind—tearing down all shreds of modesty, past all sense of manliness and shame; filthy in thought, furious, raging, obscene." Since, like his contemporaries, Thackeray assumed that Gulliver and Swift were one and the same, he could only attempt to trace the springs of Gulliver's misanthropy to hypothetical wells of Swiftian depravity. "What had this man done," Thackeray asks, "what secret remorse was rankling at his heart?" In the absence of adequate bi-

ography Thackeray could only guess, and then guess wrong. While Thackeray's treatment of Swift is a triumph of innuendo over evidence, it typifies the desire of nineteenth- and early-twentieth-century biographers to explain Swift's satirical indignation by conjuring up a dark and largely imaginary past.

Now, thanks to the techniques of modern rhetorical criticism, it is possible to separate Swift from Gulliver. Gulliver need no longer be regarded as Swift's alter ego, but can be seen as an ironic persona who fulfills many roles in the course of *Gulliver's Travels*; he is an artfully contrived character who is alternately sage, hero, and buffoon. Perhaps, as well, the atrocities of the twentieth century have made readers less vain about the "human face divine," for *Gulliver's Travels* has gained in popularity as Swift's dark assessment of the human condition has come to be appreciated. Thanks to the efforts of such scholars as Sir Harold Williams, Ricardo Quintana, and Irvin Ehrenpreis, the ghost of the mad dean has finally been laid to rest. In its place they have provided a full portrait of a satirist for whom *Gulliver's Travels* is not merely a symptom of some private pathology but the incarnation of Swift's deepest aspirations and beliefs as patriot, churchman, moralist, and wit.

Swift was born 30 November 1667 in Dublin to Abigail Erick Swift; his father, Jonathan, had died seven months earlier. At the age of six he entered Kilkenny School (the best in Ireland), and in 1682 he was admitted as a pensioner to Trinity College, Dublin, where in 1686 he took the degree bachelor of arts. He spent the years 1689 to 1695 at Moor Park in Surrey, serving as secretary to Sir William Temple, a courtier, statesman, and writer, who was to exert the most powerful influence on Swift's adult life and to serve as the model for the king of Brobdingnag in *Gulliver's Travels.* Swift received his M.A. degree in 1692, and in 1695 he took orders as a priest of the Church of Ireland (Anglican). After spending an unhappy year as prebendary of Kilroot, he returned to Moor Park until 1699. It was there that he met Esther Johnson, or "Stella," who was to become his companion until her death in 1728. These years also witnessed the beginning of Swift's literary career as he first tried his hand at Pindarics and then found his true métier in *A Tale of a Tub* (1704), a satirical tour de force with alternating chapters attacking abuses in learning and religion. Here Swift perfected satirical techniques that he would use again in *Gulliver's Travels*: the adoption of a series of ironic masks; the development of allegory where Martin, his hero (not unlike Gulliver in Houyhnhnmland), stands midway between impossible extremes; and the brilliant exploitation of literary parody.

Upon Temple's death in 1699 Swift was left once more to make his way in the world. In 1700 he was preferred to the prebend of Dunlavin with its livings of three parishes, collectively known as Laracor, in the north of Ireland. He received his D.D. degree the following year. Swift was not cut out for the life of a country parson: he aspired to greater things. For the next ten years he shuttled between Dublin and London on various errands designed to attract the attention of the Whigs in power and to win for Swift the prize he most desired, an English bishopric. Swift wrote numerous pamphlets in defense of the church, yet when *A Tale of a Tub* was published, it was loudly denounced as an impious and scandalous work. Swift's *Account of a Battel between the Antient and Modern Books in St. James's Library* (commonly known as *The Battle of the Books*), a mock-heroic defense of Temple's "Essay of Ancient and Modern Learning" (1690), was published in the same volume and proved to be a major salvo in the war between the Ancients and the Moderns. For years Swift had hoped that the Whigs would find him a suitable place in England, but they disappointed him, as did the Tory government that followed. Even though Swift provided yeoman service as a polemicist, writing the Tory paper *Examiner* from November 1710 until June 1711 and such brilliant pamphlets as *The Conduct of the Allies* (1711) and *The Publick Spirit of the Whigs* (1714), no English bishopric was forthcoming. Instead, in Swift's own words, he was "condemned to live again in Ireland" when the government of Robert Harley and Henry St. John, first Viscount Bolingbroke, finally appointed him dean of St. Patrick's Cathedral, Dublin, in June 1713.

If the years spent in pursuit of preferment brought Swift suspense and disappointment, his efforts as a writer and wit produced greater success. Swift soon joined that Whig literary circle that included Joseph Addison, Richard Steele, and Matthew Prior. He contributed poems and essays to Steele's *Tatler* and gained notoriety as the author of the Bickerstaff Papers (1708-1709), a series of witty burlesques of the person and predictions of John Partridge, an almanac maker. Although Swift would maintain cordial relations with most of these Whig writers after the change

of government in 1710, his loyalties were largely transferred to a new circle of friends, among them those writers—Pope, John Gay, Thomas Parnell, and Dr. John Arbuthnot—who, with Harley, were to form the Scriblerus Club. In the early months of 1714 these wits met weekly (often in Arbuthnot's rooms in St. James's Palace) to write satires on abuses in modern learning. Various scholars have maintained that these early Scriblerian satires formed the nucleus of *Gulliver's Travels*. In *The Memoirs of the Extraordinary Life, Works, and Discoveries of Martinus Scriblerus* (1741) one finds a description of Scriblerus's departure in 1699 (the year Gulliver sets out on his travels) for a land of pygmies, followed by voyages to a land of giants and a land of mathematicians. On his fourth voyage Scriblerus promises to open a "Vein of Melancholy proceeding almost to a Disgust of his Species." It may never be known whether *Gulliver's Travels* is an elaboration of the projected journeys of Scriblerus, or whether, as Ehrenpreis suggests, Pope amended the *Memoirs of Martinus Scriblerus* in order to emphasize its link with *Gulliver's Travels* and to capitalize on the latter's popularity. Certainly *Gulliver's Travels* reveals that same love of jokes and literary hoaxes so characteristic of Scriblerian satire, and Swift's ridicule of modern science in the third voyage closely parallels similar attacks in other Scriblerian works.

On 1 August 1714, Queen Anne died, instantly toppling the Tory government. Swift could only watch from a distance as his old friends Harley and Bolingbroke were impeached by the vengeful Whigs. For the next few years (1714 to 1720) Swift all but vanished from the political stage, concentrating his energies on his duties as dean of St. Patrick's and on the plight of the Irish, who continued to suffer under the mercantilist policies of the English. Swift's anger at English oppression of the Irish found its proper focus in 1724, when he was called upon to rally the Irish people in opposition to a plan to allow William Wood, an English ironmonger, to mint copper coins for Ireland. Writing under the pseudonym of "Mr. B. Drapier," Swift produced a series of pamphlets that galvanized public opposition to Wood's coinage and made a popular hero of the dean when Wood's patent was withdrawn.

In the midst of this controversy Swift wrote *Gulliver's Travels*. The first and second voyages were completed in order in 1721 and 1722; the fourth voyage followed in 1723. The Voyage

Numb. 17.

The EXAMINER.

From Thursday *November* 16, to Thursday *November* 23. 1710.

Qui sunt boni cives? qui belli, qui domi de patria bene merentes,
nisi qui patriae beneficia meminerunt?

I Will employ this present Paper upon a Subject, which of late hath very much affected me, which I have consider'd with a good deal of Application, and made several Enquiries about, among those Persons who I thought were best able to inform me; and if I deliver my Sentiments with some Freedom, I hope it will be forgiven, while I accompany it with that Tenderness which so nice a Point requires.

I said in a former Paper (Numb. 14.) that one specious Objection to the late removals at Court, was the fear of giving Uneasiness to a General, who has been long successful abroad: And accordingly, the common Clamour of Tongues and Pens for some Months past, has run against the Baseness, the Inconstancy and Ingratitude of the whole Kingdom to the Duke of M————, in return of the most eminent Services that ever were perform'd by a Subject to his Country; not to be equal'd in History. And then to be sure some bitter stroak of Detraction against *Alexander* and *Caesar*, who never did us the least Injury. Besides, the People that read *Plutarch* come upon us with Parallels drawn from the *Greeks* and *Romans*, who ungratefully dealt with I know not how many of their most deserving Generals: While the profounder Politicians, have seen Pamphlets, where *Tacitus* and *Machiavel* have been quoted to shew the danger of too resplendent a Merit. Should a Stranger hear these furious Out-cries of Ingratitude against our General, without knowing the particulars, he would be apt to enquire where was his Tomb, or whether he were allow'd Christian Burial? Not doubting but we had put him to some ignominious Death. Or, has he been tried for his Life, and very narrowly escap'd? Has he been accus'd of High Crimes and Misdemeanors? Has the Prince seiz'd on his Estate, and left him to starve? Has he been hooted at as he pass'd the Streets, by an ungrateful Mob? Have neither Honours, Offices nor Grants, been confer'd on Him or his Family? Have not he and they been barbarously stript of them all? Have not he and his Forces been ill pay'd abroad? And does not the Prince by a scanty, limited Commission, hinder him from pursuing his own Methods in the conduct of the War? Has he no Power at all of disposing Commissions as he pleases? Is he not severely us'd by the Ministry or Parliament, who yearly call him to a strict Account? Has the Senate ever thank'd him for good Success, and have they not always publickly censur'd him for the least Miscarriage? Will the Accusers of the Nation join issue upon any of these Particulars, or tell us in what Point, our damnable Sin of Ingratitude lies? Why, 'tis plain and clear; For while he is Commanding abroad, the Queen Dissolves her Parliament, and changes Her Ministry at home: In which *universal Calamity*, no less than *two Persons* allied by Marriage to the General, have lost their Places. Whence came this wonderful Simpathy between the Civil and Military Powers? Will the Troops in *Flanders* refuse to Fight, unless they can have *their own* Lord Keeper, *their own* Lord President of the Council, *their own* chief Governor of *Ireland*, and *their own* Parliament? In a Kingdom where the People are free, how came they to be so fond of having their Councils under the Influence of their Army, or those that lead it? who in all well-instituted States, had no Commerce with the civil Power, further than to receive their Orders, and obey them without Reserve,

When a General is not so Popular, either in his Army or at Home, as one might expect from a long course of Success; it may perhaps be ascribed to his *Wisdom*, or perhaps to his Complexion. The possession of some one *Quality*, or a defect in *some other*, will extremely damp the Peoples Favour, as well as the Love of the Souldiers. Besides, this is not an Age to produce Favourites of the People, while we live under a Queen who engrosses all our Love, and all our Veneration; and where, the only way for a great General or Minister, to acquire any degree of subordinate Affection from the Publick, must be by all Marks of the most *entire Submission and Respect*, to Her Sacred Person and Commands; otherwise, no pretence of great Services, either in the Field or the Cabinet, will be able to skreen them from universal Hatred.

But the late Ministry was closely join'd to the General, by Friendship, Interest, Alliance, Inclination and Opinion, which cannot be affirm'd of the present; and the Ingratitude of the Nation, lies in the People's joining as one Man, to wish, that such a Ministry should be changed. Is it not at the same time notorious to the whole Kingdom, that nothing but a tender regard to the General, was able to preserve that Ministry so long, 'till neither God nor Man could suffer their continuance? Yet in the highest Ferment of Things, we heard few or no Reflections upon this great Commander, but all seem'd unanimous in wishing he might still be at the Head of the Confederate Forces; only at the same time, in case he were resolv'd to resign, they chose rather to turn their Thoughts somewhere else, than throw up all in Despair. And this I cannot but add, in defence of the People, with regard to the Person we are speaking of, that in the high Station he has been for many Years past, his real *Defects* (as nothing Human is without them) have in a detracting Age been very sparingly mention'd, either in Libels or Conversation, and all his *Successes* very freely and universally applauded.

There is an active and a passive Ingratitude; applying both to this Occasion, we may say, the first is, when a Prince or People returns good Services with Cruelty or Ill Usage: The other is, when good Services are not at all, or very meanly rewarded. We have already spoke of the former; let us therefore in the second place, examine how the Services of our General have been rewarded; and whether upon that Article, either Prince or People have been guilty of Ingratitude?

Those are the most valuable Rewards which are given to us from the certain Knowledge of the Doner, that they *fit our Temper best*: I shall therefore say nothing of the Title of *Duke*, or the *Garter*, which the Queen bestow'd the General in the beginning of her Reign; but I shall come to *more Substantial* Instances, and mention nothing which has not been given in the Face of the World. The Lands of *Woodstock*, may, I believe, be reckoned worth 40000 *l*. On the building of *Blenheim* Castle 200000 *l*. have been already expended, tho' it be not yet near finish'd. The Grant of 5000 *l. per Ann.* on the Post-Office, is richly worth 100000 *l*. His Principality in *Germany* may be computed at 30000 *l*. Pictures, Jewels, and other Gifts from Foreign Princes, 60000 *l*. The Grant at the *Pall-mall*, the Rangership, &c. for want of more certain Knowledge, may be call'd 10000 *l*. His own, and his Dutchess's Employments

---

An issue of the Tory paper that Swift produced from November 1710 until June 1711

to Laputa was the last to be completed, and Swift was apparently nearing the end of the third book in April 1724. The controversy over Wood's half-pence intervened, however, so Swift did not complete the work until August 1725, writing to Pope on 29 September 1725 that he was "finishing, correcting, amending, and transcribing my travels, in four parts complete, newly augmented, and intended for the press when the world shall deserve them, or rather when a printer shall be found brave enough to venture his ears."

When Swift left Dublin for London in March 1726 he took the manuscript of *Gulliver's Travels* with him, and, as part of his elaborate ruse to avoid detection as the author, he left England before the work was published. The events leading up to the appearance of *Gulliver's Travels* are worthy of bad detective fiction but perfectly characteristic of Swift's habits of publication. The bookseller Benjamin Motte received a specimen of the manuscript along with a letter from a "Richard Sympson" (who purported to be Lemuel Gulliver's cousin) offering the book for two hundred pounds. Pope reported that "Motte receiv'd the copy (he tells me) he knows not from whence, nor from whom, dropp'd at his house in the dark, from a Hackney-coach." Motte accepted the offer, and *Gulliver's Travels* appeared—under its original title, *Travels into Several Remote Nations of the World. In Four Parts. By Lemuel Gulliver*—to universal applause on 28 October 1726. Gay wrote glowingly: "About ten days ago a Book was publish'd here of the Travels of one Gulliver, which hath been the conversation of the whole town ever since: The whole impression sold in a week." Like Pope, Gay pretended not to know the origins of these wonderful travels, a fiction Swift himself maintained in his letters to England.

To a certain degree Swift's elaborate exercises to assure his own anonymity while guaranteeing that his authorship was known are merely part of that seriocomic mystification that he engaged in whenever a new work of his was published. Certainly Swift wished the book to be successful, and he wished to leave no official clues linking himself with *Gulliver's Travels* until he had full confidence of its success. But beyond mere caution, Swift's Byzantine game of hide-and-seek is but another evidence of his predilection to hide behind masks of various kinds, and is typical of that Swift who remarked in the *Intelligencer*, no. 3 (1728), that he only wished to laugh "with a few friends in a corner." As Ehrenpreis ob-

serves, Swift was simply insuring that the book would be rightly understood when it finally appeared. "He relied on a core of enlightened readers to pick up clues which *hoi polloi* would miss—a chosen few who might join in laughing at the rest." Swift's deadpan denials of his own authorship are of a piece with his tendency to pull his reader's leg, whether it be with the elaborate wordplay on "Master Bates" that opens the first voyage or the seemingly innocent comparison between Gulliver and Sinon (preeminent liar of antiquity) that comes near the end of the fourth. In short, the conditions of the book's publication provide a model for how it must be read. The reader must always remain alert to Swift's shifting ironies and must determine for himself which clues are essential and lead to the heart of the mystery and which are Swiftian red herrings, mere jokes at his expense, like Swift's remark that "a Bishop here said, that Book was full of improbable lies, and for his part, he hardly believed a word of it."

There were also political reasons for Swift's elaborate pretense of anonymity. Given the fate of his friends in government, and the fact that as author of the Drapier letters he had so recently had a price of three hundred pounds on his own head, Swift was understandably nervous about the political satire in *Gulliver's Travels*. As Bertrand A. Goldgar observes, Swift "clearly felt he had angered the Ministry," even though Pope assured him that he found no man of consequence who was "angry at the book" or who accused it of "particular reflections." Readers soon discovered particular political satire nonetheless, and *Gulliver's Travels* came to be seen as part of the growing opposition to Robert Walpole's ministry. Much of the political allegory in the first voyage seems both obvious and harmless. Lilliput is England; Blefuscu is France. Like the English the Lilliputians "labour under two mighty Evils; a violent Faction at home, and the Danger of an Invasion by a most potent Enemy from abroad." The "high-heels" and "low-heels" suggest Tory and Whig, while the king who is determined to use only low-heels in his administrations represents George I. Like the English, the Lilliputians are also divided in matters of religion. One faction argues that the "primitive way of breaking Eggs before we eat them, was upon the larger End," while the king's grandfather commanded thereafter that all eggs should be broken at the little end. "The People so highly resented this Law, that our Histories tell us, there have been six Rebellions raised on that account; wherein one Emperor lost his life, and another his Crown."

There are, however, more specific political reflections in *Gulliver's Travels*. In some measure Gulliver's adventures in Lilliput represent the fortunes of Harley and Bolingbroke at the hands of the Whigs. Interpreted by some as representing the publication of *A Tale of a Tub*, Gulliver's dousing of the flames in the Lilliputian palace with his own urine is more often regarded by modern critics as an allusion to the Tories' negotiation of the Peace of Utrecht. Gulliver's refusal to destroy the fleet of Blefuscu and to stamp out all Bigendians (Catholics) has also been interpreted as referring to the leniency of the peace terms granted the French in 1713. Moreover, the articles of impeachment drawn up against Gulliver clearly echo the formal charges brought against Harley and Bolingbroke by a committee of secrecy headed by Walpole, a figure who is generally seen to be represented by Flimnap, the lord treasurer of Lilliput. The question of "political allegory in *Gulliver's Travels* has occasioned considerable debate. Such scholars as Sir Charles Firth and A. E. Case have outlined an elaborately specific and sustained political allegory throughout the work (the Voyage to Lilliput in particular), while others, such as Phillip Harth and F. P. Lock, have argued that Swift's satire is directed less at English politics and political figures than at the corruptions of European politics in general.

Nevertheless, Swift's satire includes many pointed personal allusions. For example, Gulliver's description of the various methods of discovering plots in "the kingdom of *Tribnia*," where the "Bulk of the People consisted wholly of Discoverers, Witnesses, Informers, Accusers, Prosecutors, Evidences, Swearers," ridicules the uncertain methods used to convict Swift's old friend Bishop Francis Atterbury of treason in 1722. Perhaps most personal of all is the Lindalino episode in the Voyage to Laputa, which seemingly celebrates Swift's victory over Wood's half-pence. Here the tyrannical king of Laputa (George I) attempts to subjugate the rebellious population of Lindalino (Ireland) by stationing the flying island overhead, thus blotting out the sun and rain. In turn, the citizens of Lindalino threaten to wreck the flying island by drawing it down to earth with magnets. Chastened, the king of Laputa withdraws, just as George I had withdrawn Wood's patent. Here indeed was a kind of political satire too dangerous

Portrait of Swift as M. B. Drapier, the pseudonym he used for a 1724 series of pamphlets attacking a plan to allow an English ironmonger to mint coins for Ireland. The plan was defeated, and Swift became a hero to the Irish. The illustration is from the 1735 Faulkner edition of Swift's works.

for publication, and not until the late nineteenth century was this particular episode included in the text of *Gulliver's Travels*. In fact, worried about the political repercussions of publishing the work as it stood, Motte excised or changed several passages. These alterations, in conjunction with a host of other errors introduced into the text, prompted Swift to complain angrily that the style of *Gulliver's Travels* was "debased." There followed a tortuous bibliographical history (outlined by Sir Harold Williams and elaborated by Lock and Clauston Jenkins), the gist of which is that Swift's ultimate intentions for *Gulliver's Travels* were not fully reflected (if then) until the 1735 Dublin edition published by George Faulkner. Although the 1735 version has generally been adopted as a copy text by modern editors, debate continues as to the relative merits of the

Motte and Faulkner editions.

Swift returned to England one last time in 1727, but increasingly his attentions had turned to affairs in Ireland, where the author of the Drapier letters had become a popular hero, and where bonfires were lighted on his birthday. In response to the worsening conditions in Ireland, Swift wrote more pamphlets (several not published until his death), foremost of which was *A Modest Proposal* (1729), in which he suggested using the children of the poor for food. This last great prose satire expressed with grim irony Swift's despair over the plight of the Irish, assailed from without by the cynical exploitation of the English and from within by their own inability or unwillingness to help themselves. Here, as in *Gulliver's Travels*, one encounters that astringent and utterly unsentimental benevolence that marks so many of Swift's satires. Just as Swift had sought to reform that creature man, while holding out scant hope for his reformation, so he struggled to help his fellow Irish who so disgusted him.

Disgust must not be mistaken for misanthropy, however. For while Swift contended that he had "ever hated all Nations professions and Communityes," he also insisted that all his love was "towards individuals." Although troubled throughout his adult life by the periodic deafness and giddiness brought on by Ménière's syndrome, a disorder of the inner ear, Swift reveled in good company, enjoyed the pleasures of cards and conversation, carried on a busy round of visits with his many Irish acquaintances, and maintained a rich correspondence with his old friends in England. Swift was noted for his large charities and left the greater part of his estate for the founding of a lunatic asylum. While he harbored no illusions as to the virtue or comeliness of his beneficiaries, Swift moved with alacrity to relieve the distresses of the needy. Although his health continued to decline, Swift was able to carry out his duties at the cathedral until May 1742, when his physical condition had so deteriorated that he was placed under the protection of a committee of guardians. Unfortunately, rumor mongers soon circulated reports of Swift's lunacy that gradually assumed the status of historical fact. Samuel Johnson was mistaken, however; Swift did not expire "a driveller and a show." Modern biographers (Ehrenpreis preeminently) have shown that if Swift's end on 19 October 1745 was sad, it was not spectacular. At no point was he "mad" as legend would have it, merely old and senile, suffering from aphasia and the effects of Ménière's syndrome that had plagued him for so long.

Swift had worn many masks throughout his life, and played many parts. To paraphrase Pope's tribute to Swift in the *Dunciad* (1728), he had variously been dean, Drapier, Bickerstaff, and Gulliver. To Voltaire, Swift was the "English Rabelais"; to Fielding he was the "English Lucian." Nowhere is Swift's infinite variety made more apparent than in *Gulliver's Travels,* which readers have found as difficult to place as they have found Swift himself. Swift's immediate circle of friends described it as a "wonderful Book," but otherwise regarded it as a travel narrative. For John Boyle, fifth Earl of Cork and Orrery, *Gulliver's Travels* was a "moral political romance"; for Thomas Sheridan, Swift's other contemporary biographer, it was primarily an "apologue." Indeed, discussions of *Gulliver's Travels* have always been plagued by that "bewildering uncertainty of genre" noted by C. J. Rawson. Even though the work includes a yeasty mixture of particular satire, literary parody, moral allegory, and pure fantasy, the temptation to pigeonhole *Gulliver's Travels* has proven irresistible to generations of readers. Indeed, as Robert C. Elliot observes, we "must try to 'place' *Gulliver* as best we can"; we must reach some conclusions about its shaping principle, since generic definitions invariably color our responses to any work of art, particularly one as ambiguous and indeterminate as *Gulliver's Travels.*

Of course *Gulliver's Travels* is satirical, but is it also a novel? "Probably not," Elliot remarks, "although it is not easy to say (except by arbitrary stipulation) why it is not." Part of the problem in classifying *Gulliver's Travels* as a novel arises from Swift's inclusion of large quantities of material that are neither purely narrative nor satirical, but are largely philosophical. Indeed, *Gulliver's Travels* has most often been described as an imaginary or "philosophic" voyage, a subgenre most clearly defined by William A. Eddy as "a didactic treatise in which the author's criticism of society is set forth in a parable form of an *Imaginary Voyage* made by one or more Europeans to a nonexistent or little known country ... together with a description of the imaginary society visited." Among those imaginary voyages whose outlines are visible in *Gulliver's Travels* are Lucian's *True History,* whose mendacious narrator defends his lies as absolute truth and which blends adventure with a "didactic account of some imaginary commonwealth"; Thomas More's *Utopia* (1516),

Frontispiece and title page for Swift's satirical travel narrative

where the narrator's straightforward description of an ideal society serves as a corrective to our own shortcomings; and Cyrano de Bergerac's *Histoire Comique des états et empires de la lune* (1656), where Swift would have found an account of a tiny human traveler captured by lunar giants who first show him for money and then carry him to court, where he debates with the king and queen—clear precedents for the Voyage to Brobdingnag.

Swift may also have had in mind such "rational utopias" as *L'histoire des Sévarambes* (1677-1679) and *La terre australe connue* (1676), contemporary forms of the philosophic voyage that invariably included the discovery of foreign races governed entirely by reason, "natural" men untainted by the corruptions of civilization and actuated by spontaneous virtue. Such works often echoed the new rationalistic and optimistic creed most fully articulated by Baron Gottfried Wilhelm von Leibniz, Francis Hutcheson, and Anthony Ashley Cooper, third Earl of Shaftesbury. As Maynard Mack observes, "Swift, whose aim in

Gulliver is (among other things) to show the fatuity of this creed, deliberately adopts the voyage genre of the enemy and turns it to his own ends. Where Gulliver goes among his fantastic aborigines, he is always encountering, instead of handsome and noble savages, aspects of man as he perennially is, whether in civilized society or in nature."

Imaginary voyages invariably include a wide variety of satirical episodes and philosophical commentary, a formal heterogeneity often explained by invoking the conventions of Menippean satire. According to Northrop Frye, Menippean satire, of which he considers *Gulliver's Travels* to be a primary example, incorporates abstract ideas and theories and "deals less with people as such than with mental attitudes"; its characterization is "stylized rather than naturalistic, and presents people as mouthpieces of the ideas they represent." Frye notes that "at its most concentrated, the Menippean satire presents us with a vision of the world in terms of a single intellectual pattern." While the rich efflorescence of local satirical episodes and shifting points of view makes it difficult to isolate a single pattern in *Gulliver's Travels* as a whole, the Menippean model helps to explain the relationship between the third voyage and the rest of the work, and allows for a kind of unity within the third voyage itself, which has often been discounted. For while the Laputians, the projectors of Lagado, the ghosts of the Ancients, and even the Struldbruggs are certainly personified abstractions, all are related to Swift's satire on intellectual pride and on man's tendency to build airy castles of the mind, whether they be new systems in science and philosophy or fantasies of immortality.

More specifically, the Voyage to Laputa presents an extended satire on modern science, both theoretical and applied. The Laputians, with one eye "turned inward, and the other directly up to the Zenith," personify the abstraction and solipsism of pure mathematics. Their apprehension that the sun will go out satirizes the cosmology of Marin Mersenne and René Descartes (described contemptuously by the ghost of Aristotle as one of the "new Fashions, which would vary in every Age"), while their fear of comets is a satirical jab at William Whiston's *A New Theory of the Earth* (1696). In contrast to those speculative mathematicians of Laputa, the projectors of the Academy of Lagado have rebounded to the inductive extreme, preoccupied with such ludicrous experiments as reducing "human Excrement to its original Food," "plowing the Ground with Hogs," and propagating "the Breed of naked Sheep."

Marjorie Hope Nicholson and Nora M. Mohler have demonstrated that with some satirical license Swift had copied such experiments directly from the *Philosophical Transactions* of the Royal Society. In like manner Gulliver's long and extravagantly detailed explanation of the movement of the flying island of Laputa was based upon William Gilbert's *De Magnete, Magneticisque Corporibus* (1600). Swift's borrowings are seldom straightforward, however, and even his description of the locomotion of the flying island may be part of an elaborate joke. Some critics have suggested that if Gulliver's explanation is examined carefully, it will be found to describe not an island that can hover stationary above the earth, but one that spins perpetually like a top.

On 13 July 1722 (while working on *Gulliver's Travels*), Swift wrote that he had been reading "I know not how many diverting Books of History and Travells," and modern scholars have painstakingly traced those bits and pieces of

Swift's reading that eventually found their way into his own work. Some of the most interesting conjectures concerning Swift's borrowings from actual travel narratives involve the origins of the Yahoos. M. F. Ashley Montagu, for example, suggests that they may derive from the tailless pygmies described in Edward Tyson's *Orang-Outang, sive Homo Sylvestris* (1699). Moreover, both William Dampier's *New Voyage round the World* (1697) and Lionel Wafer's *A New Voyage and Description of the Isthmus of America* (1699) contain accounts of monkeys that resemble the Yahoos. Wafer, for example, describes monkeys skipping "from Bough to Bough . . . chattering, and if they had opportunity, pissing down purposely on our Heads," an account that vividly calls to mind Gulliver's own introduction to the Yahoos.

Of all these travelers, however, it is Dampier with whom Gulliver is most often compared by modern scholars, and with whom Gulliver compares himself. In the prefatory "Letter from Capt. Gulliver to his Cousin Sympson," Gulliver argues that he has been prevailed upon "to publish a very loose and uncorrect Account of my Travels; with Direction to hire some young Gentlemen of either University to put them in Order, and correct their Style, as my Cousin *Dampier* did by my Advice, in his Book called *A Voyage round the World.*" Here, Swift draws attention both to those true accounts of actual voyages such as Dampier's, and to those fictional accounts—such as William Sympson's *A New Voyage to the East Indies* (1715)—that Percy G. Adams has aptly called "travel lies." Throughout *Gulliver's Travels*, Gulliver emphasizes his role as a travel writer and compares himself (quite favorably) with those mountebanks who have corrupted the genre: "I have perused several Books of Travels with great Delight in my younger Days; but, having since gone over most Parts of the Globe, and been able to contradict many fabulous Accounts from my own Observation; it hath given me a great Disgust against this Part of Reading, and some Indignation to see the Credulity of Mankind so impudently abused." Gulliver's remarks clearly reflect that ambiguous attitude toward travel narrative that informs *Gulliver's Travels*, as Swift painstakingly re-creates the very shape and substance of contemporary travel writing while simultaneously parodying its conventions and ridiculing its practitioners and underlying cultural assumptions.

Swift's choice of title, *Travels into Several Remote Nations of the World;* the prefatory letters; the prolix chapter headings; the scientific illustrations; and even the detailed maps are all part of what John J. Richetti has called an "elaborate parody of the documentary apparatus which accompanied the travel book." Scholars have argued over whether the discrepancies between maps and text and the inconsistencies in Gulliver's elaborate chronology are the result of printer's and compositor's errors, or whether such apparent mistakes are really part of Swift's burlesque of the conventions of travel narrative. Swift himself suggests that he may not have been entirely serious when Gulliver protests (too much) that the "Printer hath been so careless as to confound the Times, and mistake the Dates of my several Voyages and Returns." One strongly suspects that Swift's tongue is in his cheek when Gulliver pompously reiterates his "Opinion I have long entertained, that the *Maps* and *Charts* place this Country [New Holland] at least three Degrees more to the *East* than it really is; which Thought I communicated many Years ago to my worthy Friend Mr. *Herman Moll.*" As the original readers of the work would have recognized, Moll was the famous cartographer whose *New Correct Map of the Whole World* (1719) was the model for the maps in *Gulliver's Travels*. One can certainly imagine Swift chuckling at readers perplexed by his cartographical and chronological errors, just as he would have laughed at Arbuthnot's account of that mythical "old Gentleman, who went immediately to his Map to search for Lilly putt."

Swift may have been casting his satirical net wider still: it is possible that in his minute attention to maps and time scheme Swift trains an ironic eye on that new particularity of time and place worked out in such detail by Defoe and noted by Ian Watt as a definitive characteristic of the new "formal realism" of the eighteenth-century novel. Certainly the line between real and fictional travel accounts had become blurred indeed in the early eighteenth century; such works as Defoe's *Robinson Crusoe* (1719) and *Captain Singleton* (1720) made it particularly difficult to determine where travel narrative ended and the novel began. It is often the case, therefore, that even as he defends his own practice as a travel writer, Gulliver also alludes in unmistakable ways to the habits of the modern novelist. "Thus gentle Reader," Gulliver concludes, "I have given thee a faithful History of my Travels for Sixteen Years, and above Seven Months, wherein I have not been so studious of Ornament as of Truth. I could perhaps like others

have astonished thee with strange improbable Tales; but I rather chose to relate plain matter of fact in the simplest Manner and Style, because my principal Design was to inform, and not to amuse thee." Here Swift parodies the most common claims of contemporary travel writers; but in his claims for absolute veracity, his assertion that he seeks more to inform than to amuse, and his having Gulliver take offense that censorious Yahoos have been so "bold as to think my Book of Travels a meer Fiction out of mine own Brain," Swift also echoes the disclaimers of the eighteenth-century fiction writer who was quick to deny that he was a novelist. The joke, of course, is that Gulliver claims to be unlike any other writer living or dead. He *cannot* lie, his residence with the Houyhnhnms having removed that "infernal Habit of Lying, Shuffling, Deceiving, and Equivocating, so deeply rooted in the very Souls of all my Species."

Reflecting on the tendency of his fellow travelers to exaggerate, Gulliver insists that his story contains "little besides common Events, without those ornamental Descriptions of strange Plants, Trees, Birds, and other Animals; or the barbarous Customs and Idolatry of savage People, with which most Writers abound." Here again, Swift toys with his reader. Although he is quick to deny the charge that "the *Houyhnhnms* and *Yahoos* have no more Existence than the Inhabitants of *Utopia*," those "common Events" promised by Gulliver actually comprise the most extraordinary collection of bizarre and impossible adventures in Augustan literature. Throughout *Gulliver's Travels*, Gulliver's authorial persona is characterized by the defense of his own veracity and his earnest efforts to naturalize the preposterous. For example, Gulliver describes how the master Houyhnhnm lifted his hoof so that Gulliver might kiss it. "Detractors are pleased to think it improbable," Gulliver remarks, "that so illustrious a Person should descend to give so great a Mark of Distinction to a Creature so inferior as I. Neither have I forgot how apt some Travellers are to boast of extraordinary Favours they have received." Some critics have argued that Gulliver's actions parody the kissing of the pope's ring and suggest that Gulliver has converted to a false religion. But Gulliver's misplaced emphasis, his naive insistence upon his own veracity, and his earnest description of equine noblesse oblige clearly mark this passage as yet another parodic gibe at the characteristic habits of the travel writer, and as part of an elaborate literary joke.

Page from the manuscript for Gulliver's Travels *(from Edmund Gosse,* English Literature: An Illustrated Record, *1903)*

As Richetti remarks, *"Gulliver's Travels* was inspired in part by Swift's contempt for the vulgar credulity that nourished a popular form like the travel account." Nowhere is Swift's contempt for the credulity of the age more clearly marked than in Gulliver's direct and continuous engagement of the "gentle reader," the "candid reader," and above all the "curious reader," whose avidity for strange adventures is assumed to equal Gulliver's own. Curiosity is what drives Gulliver to travel long after he has achieved relative finan-

cial security, and the reader's curiosity is the standard that guides Gulliver in his choice of narrative details. While he remarks that his descriptions of domestic life in Lilliput are intended to "divert the curious Reader," he also determines not to "trouble the Reader with a particular Account" of his return to England. Like many eighteenth-century narrators, Gulliver seems inordinately self-conscious about the number and kinds of details he includes: "Although I Intend to leave the Description of this Empire [Lilliput] to a particular Treatise," he writes, "in the mean time I am content to gratify the curious Reader with some general Ideas." Here, much in the manner of Defoe, Swift tantalizes the reader with promises of sequels to come. Like a hack novelist, Gulliver whets the reader's appetite for further adventures, even though he has solemnly sworn elsewhere that he never intended for his travels to be published in the first place.

At times Gulliver also invokes the reader's curiosity as the pretext for narrative digression. Of his long description of the Laputians and their flappers Gulliver observes: "It was necessary to give the Reader this Information, without which he would be at the same Loss with me, to understand the Proceedings of these People." Of course, as satire—with its inheritance from Roman *satura lanx* or hodgepodge—*Gulliver's Travels* requires no excuse for its inclusion of diverse materials. That Gulliver apologizes so frequently for his own digressive bent reflects a narrative habit that would become so deeply ingrained in the eighteenth-century novel that by 1760 Laurence Sterne could exploit the narrative digression and its mock defense as a central organizing principle of *Tristram Shandy* (1760-1767). Moreover, those confidential asides later exploited to such advantage by Fielding and his imitators are here burlesqued by Swift, whose implicit attitude toward his readers, according to C. J. Rawson, amounts to a "fundamental unfriendliness." Throughout *Gulliver's Travels,* that "quarrelsome intimacy" that Swift establishes with his readers, and his insistent invocation of their own "curiosity," serve to tweak the noses of his immediate audience while implicating them in Gulliver's folly.

Gulliver's curiosity is special, however. He is not just any wanderer of the world; he is a scientific traveler like Dampier and his fellow explorers sent out by the Royal Society. Gulliver makes close observations and takes precise measurements, going so far as to weigh and measure Brobdingnagian hailstones. Like Sir Hans Sloane and the Fellows of the Royal Society, Gulliver reveals a profound fascination with curious specimens: he attempts to breed his Lilliputian sheep; and he preserves the stings of Brobdingnagian wasps, which he has shown "with some other Curiosities in several Parts of *Europe*"—he has even given "three of them to *Gresham College*." Like other scientific projectors of the age Gulliver consistently poses as a public benefactor. He argues that even the descriptions of his bowel habits "will certainly help a Philosopher to enlarge his Thoughts and Imagination, and apply them to the Benefit of publick as well as private Life; which was my sole Design in presenting this and other Accounts of my Travels to the World; wherein I have been chiefly studious of Truth, without affecting any Ornaments of Learning or of Style." Here, as in his satire on the Academy of Lagado, Swift pokes fun at that craze for "useful knowledge" that marked the activities of the modern scientific virtuoso. But he also burlesques that new style of scientific writing that, according to Thomas Sprat, aspired to describe "so many *things* in an equal number of words." The new science was not alone in its preoccupation with empirical observation and precise denotative description. As Ian Watt argues, the rise of formal realism in the novel was "analogous to the rejection of universals and the emphasis on particulars which characterises philosophic realism." Gulliver's vanity about the clarity and precision of his own style links him both with the new demands of scientific writing (burlesqued in the third voyage) and with those stylistic conventions of formal realism becoming increasingly evident in the eighteenth-century novel.

Watt notes that in the novel, language is more "largely referential" than it is in "other literary forms; that the genre itself works by exhaustive presentation rather than by elegant concentration." Throughout *Gulliver's Travels,* Swift revels in the exhaustive presentation of detail, and in Cousin Sympson's letter to the reader, Swift coyly hints that Gulliver is "a little too circumstantial." In a passage that echoes Dampier, Sympson argues that the volume would have been twice as large if he had not struck out innumerable passages relating to storms, winds, tides, and longitude and latitude. In the light of such claims one is amused to discover at the beginning of Gulliver's second voyage a long and tediously circumstantial description of a storm at sea, copied almost verbatim from *Sturmy's Mariner's Magazine* (1661). Swift's parodies are often marked by an ambiguity of attention, and nowhere is that ambiguity more evident than in his careful elaboration of circumstantial detail. Here, for example, Swift mocks the reader's craving for trifling descriptions even as he panders to that craving. As Ellen Douglass Leyburn observes, "The parody is the more delightful because it is still half actually in the spirit of the original. . . . [Swift's] pleasure in realistic detail is partly what enables him to achieve the circumstantiality that is so often pointed out as giving credibility to his imaginary lands."

Indeed, many have argued that the perennial popularity of *Gulliver's Travels* derives largely from Swift's mastery of circumstantial detail and his maintenance of that "extraordinary illusion of verisimilitude" described by Robert C. Elliot. Certainly Swift renders the fantastic familiar. There is something of the fairy tale about Gulliver's adventures in Lilliput, where the inhabitants are only six inches tall, where the capital city is but five hundred feet square, and where the landscape looks "like the painted Scene of a City in a Theatre"; and yet as Robert Scholes and Robert Kellogg have noted, "the whole tenor of the narrative is set by that delight in verisimilitude for its own sake which unites Swift with his contemporary Defoe."

Readers have always admired the apparent precision with which Swift has calibrated the size differential between the giant Gulliver and the Lilliputians, who can stand on the palm of his hand, lose themselves in his pockets, or fall up to their knees in his snuffbox. In Brobdingnag, Swift looks through the opposite end of the telescope, and now Gulliver is the pygmy among giants, so small that he can be used as an erotic plaything by the maids of honor and so vulnerable that he barks his shin on snail shells, gets pummeled by the wings of a linnet, and is flattened by a falling apple the size of a Bristol barrel. The description of the Yahoos and Houyhnhnms is marked by that same exhaustive presentation of detail that characterizes the earlier voyages. Gulliver painstakingly describes the Houyhnhnms' patterns of speech, their method of building houses, and their "manual" dexterity as they thread needles with pastern and hoof. Quite matter-of-factly Gulliver presents the Houyhnhnms "sitting on their Haunches, upon Mats of Straw, not unartfully made, and perfectly neat and clean." Some critics have argued that such details are introduced to suggest the impossibility and ridiculousness of the Houyhnhnms as a means of undermining their moral authority. If so, Swift provides no certain clues, since the Houyhnhnms are described with the same verisimilitude that prevails throughout the rest of Gulliver's fantastic tale. Other scholars have proved that in the earlier voyages the proportions of the Lilliputians and Brobdingnagians are wrong. But if Swift's mathematics are faulty, the *effect* of his details and their apparent realism remain as convincing as those of a contemporary novel.

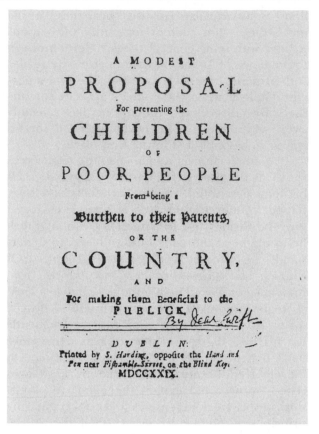

Title page for the notorious pamphlet in which Swift facetiously suggested using the children of the Irish poor for food

Although the realism of *Gulliver's Travels* links it most firmly with the eighteenth-century novel, most readers have not considered its illusion of verisimilitude alone sufficient grounds to classify the work itself as a novel. Part of this difficulty may derive from the absence of a significant plot in *Gulliver's Travels*. Like *Robinson Crusoe*, *Gulliver's Travels* includes episodes of dangerous adventure, shipwreck, abandonment, and solitary survival, and yet as Frederick R. Karl observes, *Robinson Crusoe* is labeled as a novel and *Gulliver's Travels* "rather warily as a kind of mutation, neither novel nor not-novel." *Gulliver's Travels* certainly has a story; the reader is interested in what happens to Gulliver and what he will do next. In this limited sense, as Edward Rosenheim remarks, *Gulliver's Travels* "has a clear plot, however episodic and disjointed it may be." After all, Gulliver "is a *character* whose experiences—rather than postures, beliefs, or literary habits—constitute the major fiction of the work." Yet, if one accepts E. M. Forster's definition of plot as a "narrative of events, the emphasis falling on causality," or R. S. Crane's description of plot as a temporal synthesis of "action, character and thought," whose organizing principle is "completed change," then it becomes more difficult to speak of plot in *Gulliver's Travels*.

Questions of causality never arise in the course of *Gulliver's Travels*: Gulliver's response to the Brobdingnagians is not significantly conditioned by his previous experiences among the Lilliputians, nor does he travel to Laputa *because* he has first been to Lilliput and Brobdingnag. Even in Brobdingnag, Gulliver's reflections on European corruption seem largely unrelated to his particular condition and certainly cannot be said to be the necessary result of his diminutive size. While it is true that Gulliver's adventures are framed by increasingly serious incidents, from shipwreck in the first voyage to mutiny in the last, and as Samuel Holt Monk argues, "so arranged as to attain climactic intensification of tone," intensification is not causation. Nor does framing the narrative constitute a completed change through time.

Instead of a temporal synthesis, "the structural principle of *Gulliver's Travels*," according to Clarence Tracy, "is a series of contrasts, echoes, and anticipations—intersecting links that hold the work together." Perhaps the most obvious of these echoes and anticipations involves the metaphor of perspective. Gulliver's remark that "undoubtedly Philosophers are in the Right when they tell us, that nothing is great or little otherwise than by Comparison," not only articulates the most consistent motif within *Gulliver's Travels* but also links its satire with strategies of comparison so characteristic of eighteenth-century travel literature. Samuel Johnson's famous remark "When once you have thought of big men and little men, it is very easy to do all the rest" oversimplifies Swift's comparative strategy, however. Certainly the reader finds big and little men, but these comparisons are simultaneously physical and moral. Invariably Swift examines analogous phenomena from multiple angles of vision as Gulliver variously observes, attacks, or embodies those vices Swift wishes to anatomize.

Many subjects receive this prismatic treatment in the course of *Gulliver's Travels*. Swift ironically juxtaposes the practical mathematics of the Brobdingnagians with the speculative mathematics of the Laputians, the Struldbruggs' fear of death with the Houyhnhnms' serene acceptance. In all four voyages Gulliver touches on questions of modern degeneracy: in the corrupt constitution of the Lilliputians; in the king of

Brobdingnag's argument that "Nature was degenerated in these latter declining Ages of the World"; in Gulliver's interviews with the ghosts of ancient heroes, who reveal "how much the Race of human Kind was degenerate among us, within these Hundred Years past"; and in the Houyhnhnms' debate as to whether the Yahoos were literally "descended" from an original pair of humans who had been cast ashore on their island. Swift casts this same refracted light on questions of political tyranny: first in Lilliput, where Gulliver is a victim of the petty Machiavellianism of the Lilliputian court; and then in Brobdingnag, where Gulliver himself turns tyrant, offering the king a secret "that would have made him absolute master of the Lives, the Liberties, and the Fortunes of his People." In the third voyage Gulliver celebrates both the heroic Lindalinian resistance to Laputian tyranny and the great leniency of the king of Luggnagg, who indulgently executes a troublesome courtier by having the floor "strowed with a certain brown Powder, of a deadly Composition, which being licked up infallibly kills him in twenty-four hours." These variations find a kind of thematic resolution in the tyranny of the "ruling *Yahoo*," the task of whose first minister is "to *lick his Master's Feet and Posteriors, and drive the Female* Yahoos *to his Kennel.*" That this Yahoo calls to mind both the imaginary Flimnap and the very real Robert Walpole is but an added benefit of Swift's oblique analysis of tyrannical behavior.

Throughout *Gulliver's Travels*, Swift relies upon this prismatic technique to reveal an ever more jaundiced view of European civilization, and an increasingly pessimistic assessment of human nature. In Lilliput the various corruptions of Gulliver's native England are dramatized in miniature. In Brobdingnag the benevolent king listens to Gulliver's passionate defense of those same English institutions only to conclude that the "historical account I gave him of our Affairs during the last Century . . . was only an Heap of Conspiracies, Rebellions, Murders, Massacres, Revolutions, Banishments; the very worst Effects that Avarice, Faction, Hypocrisy, Perfidiousness, Cruelty, Rage, Madness, Hatred, Envy, Lust, Malice, and Ambition could produce." After he has seen the light among the Houyhnhnms and has come to "think the Honour of my own Kind not worth managing," Gulliver repeats this catalogue of intrigue, faction, malfeasance, and luxury for horrified hosts who can only conclude that human "Institutions of *Government* and *Law* were plainly owing to our gross defects in *Reason,* and by consequence, in *Virtue."* The Houyhnhnms are confirmed in their suspicions when they compare Gulliver's own account of human behavior with their observation of the Yahoos, who also suffer from diseases caused by repletion, and who fight among themselves, covetous of "certain *shining Stones* of several Colours." The Yahoos have a primitive legal system whereby if two of them are quarreling over a precious stone, "a third would take the Advantage, and carry it away from them both." They have even found a juicy root that "produced in them the same Effects that Wine hath upon us. It would make them sometimes hug, and sometimes tear one another; they would howl and grin, and chatter, and reel, and tumble, and then fall asleep in the Mud."

This implicit equation of man and Yahoo is but the last in a series of comparisons between man and animal that recur throughout *Gulliver's Travels,* comparisons aimed at locating Gulliver within the chain of being and defining man's place in creation. Like Pope's generic hero in the *Essay on Man* (1733-1734), Gulliver literally finds himself on an "isthmus of a middle state": in size midway between the diminutive Lilliputians and the gigantic Brobdingnagians, in moral faculties somewhere between the bestiality of the Yahoos and the godlike reason of the Houyhnhnms. Gulliver is continually "in doubt to deem himself, a God, or Beast." In Lilliput, Gulliver may be "Great Lord of all things" as tiny armies march between his legs, but in Brobdingnag he is "prey to all," fearing that his captors will "dash me against the ground, as we usually do any little hateful Animal which we have a Mind to destroy." While the queen of Brobdingnag expresses surprise "at so much Wit and good Sense in so diminutive an Animal," the king finds "the Bulk of your Natives, to be the most pernicious Race of little odious Vermin that Nature ever suffered to crawl upon the Surface of the Earth." Throughout *Gulliver's Travels* various observers attempt to determine just what sort of animal Gulliver might be. For the wise men of Brobdingnag he is *lusus naturae,* a freak of nature, while to the Houyhnhnms he is a kind of Yahoo, but "much more cleanly, and not altogether so deformed."

For centuries logic manuals had defined man as *animal rationale,* and at the center of *Gulliver's Travels* lies the question of just what sets man apart from the rest of creation—his appearance, his mental faculties, or his moral essence.

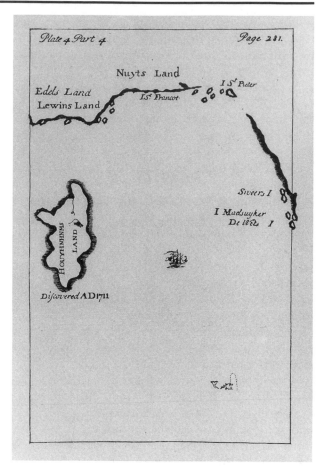

Map of the Houyhnhnms' country from the 1735 Faulkner edition of Gulliver's Travels

As Rosalie L. Colie has pointed out, the eighteenth century saw an active debate over the question of man's essential nature, with John Locke and Bishop Edward Stillingfleet arguing at length over how one might distinguish man as a rational animal from the horse and the ape, which were irrational creatures by definition. Here one finds the three symbolic foci of Swift's trenchant comparison in the fourth voyage. Swift had other sources as well: R. S. Crane argues that Swift was well schooled in such logic manuals as the *Isagoge* of Porphyry, which contrasted man as rational animal with such irrational creatures as the horse. Of course in *Gulliver's Travels* the tables are turned, and as Crane observes, Swift was able to shock "his readers' complacency as human beings by inventing a world in which horses appeared where the logicians had put men and men where they had put horses." While Swift's comparative procedure forces his readers to reexamine their assumptions, his insistence on a satirical method based upon a radical perspectivism has guaranteed that Swift's own final assessment of Gulliver remains ambiguous. Perhaps as near as one can come to Swift's "intentions" is his remark to Pope that he had "got Materials Towards a Treatis proving the falsity of that Definition *animal rationale*; and to show it should be only *rationis capax*" (having the capacity for reason).

Since Gulliver is the only human being that his various hosts have ever seen, however, their judgments of homo sapiens only acquire significance if he is a reasonably representative specimen, an everyman of sorts. This is how Gulliver has often been characterized by scholars and critics, among them John F. Ross, who describes him as a "type of ordinary, normal man," one "capable with his hands, and quick to meet physical emergency . . . essentially a man of good will, friendly, honest, and ethical according to his lights." Such remarks reveal that tendency common among modern readers to search Gulliver's characterization for the outlines of a fully rounded novelistic protagonist. Swift certainly tempts one to treat Gulliver in this fashion; *Gulliver's Travels* overflows with specific details about Gulliver's family, education, places of residence, and occupation. Indeed, the reader knows at least as much about Gulliver's personal background as about that of Richardson's Pamela Andrews. If Gulliver were treated in a novelistic way, one would expect that such information would significantly influence Gulliver's fate, that his middle-class background would color his view of the world in the manner of Crusoe, or that his years at Emmanuel College (that hotbed of Puritanism) might shape his religious beliefs.

Yet, as important as such considerations are in other novels of the period, they hardly seem to matter in *Gulliver's Travels*, functioning rather as part of the superficial apparatus of verisimilitude. For example, Gulliver frequently reminds the reader that he is a surgeon, and yet in the course of his travels he is never seen to treat a wound or prescribe so much as a single pill. His response to the monstrous cancer of the Brobdingnagian peasant seems more that of a horrified tourist than that of a trained surgeon. Even when Gulliver comments on the diseases of the Yahoos and the relative health of the Houyhnhnms, his judgments are moral rather than clinical. Although Gulliver admits to the Houyhnhnms that he has "some Skill in the Faculty" of medicine, this confession only provides Swift the occasion to insert an extended and conventional harangue against modern doctors and the luxury of the

age, a speech that would seem improbable in the mouth of any physician, even one such as Gulliver, who had forgotten how to lie.

Throughout *Gulliver's Travels*, Gulliver's behavior violates the canons of consistent characterization as he blithely contradicts his previous actions or statements of intention. The same Gulliver who humanely refuses to destroy the Blefuscudians provides enthusiastic descriptions of the carnage and mayhem of traditional European warfare. The Gulliver who naively claims that if he had known "the Nature of Princes and Ministers . . . and their Methods of treating Criminals less obnoxious than myself," he would readily have allowed so "*easy* a Punishment" as blinding, seems capable elsewhere of anatomizing European politics with great insight and sophistication. Swift eschews even the simple logic of copy editing. Thus the chastened Gulliver who cannot abide even the sight of his fellow "Yahoos" in England nevertheless sends his manuscript off to the printer complete with the stated wish "for the Tongue of *Demosthenes* or *Cicero*, that might have enabled me to celebrate the Praise of my own dear native Country in a Style equal to its Merits and Felicity." The reader knows that Gulliver is reasonably well read and can converse profitably with the ghosts of Aristotle and Homer; yet at times he seems hardly able to correct his own account of his travels. One might argue, as Clarence Tracy does, that Gulliver "runs through the whole spectrum from dolt to near-genius, from addle-pated projector to man of common sense, from realist to idealist. He is not so much man, as 'all mankind's epitome.'" As long as one regards Gulliver merely as an instrument of Swift's larger satirical purposes in *Gulliver's Travels*, such contradictions and inconsistencies in his characterization pose few problems of interpretation. Once the external object of Swift's satirical attack has been discovered, it becomes possible to determine how Gulliver is being used.

But when *Gulliver's Travels* is treated as a novel, one expects certain narrative conventions to be observed. As Sheldon Sacks argues, one looks for "subtlety and psychological depth of characterization; a discernible connection between the traits revealed about characters and the choices they make," and the "representation of emotional changes in characters as the plausible result of their fictional experiences." Indeed, much of the critical debate over *Gulliver's Travels* centers around just such questions of characterization. While many readers have noted that Gulliver seems emotionally unexpressive and that one gets very little sense of his inner life, others, such as Martin Price, argue that Gulliver's matter-of-factness serves less as a parody of realism than as a critique of character. Gulliver's style of conscious understatement, according to Price, "is calculated (by Swift and not by Gulliver) to reveal sharply just those values it fails to observe or mention; a style that gives itself away." In the same vein other critics have seen Gulliver's inconsistencies as an index to his inner life. If Gulliver says "the thing that is not," they argue, then one is meant to see Gulliver as a liar, or at least as an unreliable narrator whose inconsistencies are traps intentionally laid by Swift to ensnare the uncritical reader. While many have agreed with Robert C. Elliot that "Gulliver's character can hardly be said to develop; it simply changes," many others have concurred with Henry W. Sams that "Gulliver develops in depth and seriousness as his story progresses." Certainly no one has articulated this interpretation of Gulliver's development more memorably than Samuel Holt Monk. "At the outset," he argues, "Gulliver is full of naive goodwill, and though he grows less naive and more critical as a result of his voyaging among remote nations, he retains his benevolence throughout the first three voyages. It is a pity that so fine an example of the bluff, good-natured, honest Englishman should at last grow sick and morbid and should be driven mad."

Of all the problems that have bedeviled readers of *Gulliver's Travels*, none has proven as vexing as the question of how to interpret Gulliver's mad antics upon his return from Houyhnhnmland and his categorical rejection of mankind as noisome and unredeemable Yahoos. Can Gulliver possibly speak for Swift in his "Hatred, Disgust and Contempt" for his own family? Does Swift expect his readers to take seriously a character who talks in a whinny, who trots when he walks, and whose only companions are a pair of garrulous horses? Does Swift intend for his readers to share Gulliver's terrible misanthropy, and to despise themselves as unregenerate Yahoos? Or has Gulliver himself been deceived; has he aspired to an unattainable perfection only to ignore the true humanity he finds in his family and in the ministrations of the kindly Portuguese sea captain who rescues him? Is Gulliver finally only a comic butt at whose foolish misanthropy the reader is meant to laugh? Such questions recur with startling regularity in modern treatments of the fourth voyage, and how they are answered depends in part on how the work is classified—whether it is treated primarily as allegorical satire or as a work of prose fiction.

For one body of critics, dubbed by James L. Clifford as the "soft" school of interpretation, the conclusion of *Gulliver's Travels* is essentially comic. These readers view Gulliver as a madman, a fictional character whose behavior has been conditioned by all that he has seen and known and whose misanthropy is born of that experience. Thus he can hardly be regarded as Swift's satiric alter ego. Gulliver and not Swift is the misanthrope, and therefore the reader is meant to laugh at Gulliver's extreme attitudes. By aspiring to be a Houyhnhnm, such critics might argue, Gulliver has wished for what cannot be, for man is not *animal rationale* after all, but only *rationis capax*. Moreover, the Houyhnhnms represent a false standard, and as Kathleen Williams argues, "the Houyhnhnms are as much subject to ironic treatment" as any other character in *Gulliver's Travels*. Readers generally find the Houyhnhnms "remote, unsympathetic, and in the end profoundly unsatisfying" because Swift deliberately emphasizes their sterile perfection, their stoicism, and their essential coldness; one misses in them that "pity, gratitude, kindness, which makes life bearable in man's fallen world." To find Swift's ideal standard one must look to the benevolent and wise king of Brobdingnag; or to the Portuguese captain Pedro de Mendez, who treats Gulliver with such generosity.

Opposed to this line of interpretation is the "hard" school of critics led by R. S. Crane, who, according to Clifford, emphasize "the shock and difficulty" of *Gulliver's Travels* and insist that "the Houyhnhnms do indeed represent some kind of an ideal" and "are not being satirized or attacked in the same manner as the Yahoos." There is nothing either utopian or hyperrational about the Houyhnhnms' conviction that "*Reason* alone is sufficient to govern a *Rational* creature." Rather, the Houyhnhnms only serve to echo a commonplace of classical and Christian thought familiar to Swift's contemporaries. As Curt A. Zimansky argues, "Swift's readers believed that man is distinguished from the animals by his gift of reason, and is no better than a beast unless he uses that reason." Where the "soft" school cites Pedro de Mendez as Swift's meliorist ideal for human behavior, the "hard" school emphasizes instead the high standard of rational behavior personified by the Houyhnhnms. "There can be no doubt,"

Pages from a letter of 17 July 1735 from Swift to his friend John Boyle, fifth Earl of Orrery (Pierpont Morgan Library) writes George Sherburn, "that for Swift as well as for Gulliver the Houyhnhnms were a *ne plus ultra,*" and there is no evidence to suggest that Swift did not share Gulliver's high opinion of them. Moreover, the apparent comedy of Gulliver's homecoming in no way lessens the severity of Swift's satire or lightens his dark message; fictional events must be separated from moral intentions. As Edward Rosenheim observes, Gulliver's responses are no more than the logical extension of what he has been through and represent only "an artful, final stage in the plot itself."

There may be no way to reconcile such differences of opinion, and perhaps, as Irvin Ehrenpreis suggests, "the more coherence we try to impose on the Houyhnhnms the more awkward we make Swift's procedure." Yet the fact remains that to a far greater degree than the first three voyages, the Voyage to the Houyhnhnms cries out for systematic allegorical interpretation. Allegory by definition requires a doubleness of meaning whereby the moral tenor of the allegory is consistently maintained by its fictional vehicle; it demands at all points that the reader be able to recognize which parts of the fable are purely mimetic, which are representational, and which are both. As Robert Scholes and Robert Kellogg note, however, "the natural tendency is for satire to drift toward mimesis proper, the characters losing their status as generalized types and taking on the problematic qualities we associate with the novel." Certainly this has been the case with *Gulliver's Travels,* where careful readers have often felt uncertainty at various junctures in the tale as to Gulliver's role as satirical spokesman, as abstract representation of ideas, or as fictional protagonist. Indeed, throughout the history of its aesthetic reception, *Gulliver's Travels* has elicited varying responses based in part on how readers have "placed" it, whether they have chosen to emphasize its mimetic texture or its satirical allegory. In this regard as in others, the interpretation of *Gulliver's Travels* has always been profoundly influenced by its ambiguous relationship to the "formal realism" of the eighteenth-century novel.

Scholes and Kellogg argue that the "superiority of Part 4 of *Gulliver's Travels* to the early voyages is partly the result of Swift's growing ability to blend the illustrative, representational, and esthetic elements," but it is also this blending that has led to such confusion among Swift's readers. Of course, one suspects that Swift knew precisely what he was doing. As C. J. Rawson remarks,

Portrait of Swift by Francis Bindon (National Gallery of Ireland)

"the ironic twists and countertwists and the endless flickering uncertainties of local effect suggest that one of Swift's most active weapons is *bewilderment.*" After all, it was Swift's expressed desire to "vex mankind," and he certainly realized that man's moral complacency must first be unsettled before it can be altered. Despite Gulliver's insistence that "seven Months were a sufficient Time" for his travels to "correct every Vice and Folly to which *Yahoos* are subject," Swift understood perfectly how difficult it was to correct a creature as morally complacent as man. As he mordantly observes in the preface to *The Battle of the Books,* "*Satyr is a sort of Glass,* wherein Beholders do generally discover every Body's face but their Own." Therefore, part of Swift's strategy of bewilderment in *Gulliver's Travels* is contrived first of all to make us recognize, however reluctantly, that the face in his satiric glass is none other than our own.

Letters:

The Correspondence of Jonathan Swift, 5 volumes, edited by Harold Williams (Oxford: Clarendon Press, 1963).

Bibliographies:

Louis A. Landa and J. E. Tobin, *Jonathan Swift: A List of Critical Studies Published from 1895-1945* (New York: Cosmopolitan Science & Art Service, 1945);

Herman Teerink, *A Bibliography of the Writings of Jonathan Swift,* second edition, revised and corrected, edited by Arthur H. Scouten (Philadelphia: University of Pennsylvania Press, 1963);

James J. Stathis, *A Bibliography of Swift Studies, 1946-1965* (Nashville, Tenn.: Vanderbilt University Press, 1967);

Richard H. Rodino, *Swift Studies, 1965-1980: An Annotated Bibliography* (New York: Garland, 1984).

Biographies:

John Boyle, fifth Earl of Cork and Orrery, *Remarks on the Life and Writings of Dr. Jonathan Swift, Dean of St. Patrick's, Dublin, in a Series of Letters from John, Earl of Orrery, to His Son, the Honourable Hamilton Boyle* (London: A. Millar, 1752);

Thomas Sheridan, *The Life of the Rev. Dr. Jonathan Swift, Dean of St. Patrick's, Dublin* (London: Printed for C. Bathurst, W. Strahan, B. Collins, J. F. & C. Rivington, L. Davis, W. Owen, J. Dodsley, T. Longman, R. Baldwin, T. Cadell, J. Nichols, T. Egerton & W. Bent, 1784);

Ricardo Quintana, *The Mind and Art of Jonathan Swift* (Oxford: Oxford University Press, 1936);

Irvin Ehrenpreis, *Swift: The Man, His Works, and the Age,* 3 volumes (Cambridge, Mass.: Harvard University Press, 1962-1983);

J. A. Downie, *Jonathan Swift: Political Writer* (London: Routledge & Kegan Paul, 1984);

David Nokes, *Jonathan Swift, A Hypocrite Reversed: A Critical Biography* (London: Oxford University Press, 1985).

References:

Percy G. Adams, *Travellers and Travel Liars 1660-1800* (Berkeley & Los Angeles: University of California Press, 1962);

William Hallam Bonner, *Captain Dampier: Buccaneer-Author* (Stanford, Cal.: Stanford University Press, 1934);

Frederick Bracher, "The Maps in *Gulliver's Travels,*" *Huntington Library Quarterly,* 8 (1944-1945): 59-74;

Frank Brady, "Vexations and Diversions: Three Problems in *Gulliver's Travels,*" *Modern Philology,* 75 (1978): 346-367;

David Bywaters, "*Gulliver's Travels* and the Mode of Political Parallel During Walpole's Administration," *ELH,* 54 (Fall 1987): 717-740;

A. E. Case, *Four Essays on "Gulliver's Travels"* (Princeton: Princeton University Press, 1945);

Larry S. Champion, "Gulliver's Voyages: The Framing Events as a Guide to Interpretation," *Texas Studies in Language and Literature,* 10 (1969): 529-536;

James L. Clifford, "Gulliver's Fourth Voyage: 'Hard' and 'Soft' Schools of Interpretation," in *Quick Springs of Sense,* edited by Champion (Athens: University of Georgia Press, 1974), pp. 33-49;

Merrel D. Clubb, "The Criticism of Gulliver's 'Voyage to the Houyhnhnms,' 1726-1914," *Stanford Studies in Language and Literature* (1941): 203-232;

Rosalie L. Colie, "Gulliver, the Locke-Stillingfleet Controversy, and the Nature of Man," *History of Ideas Newsletter,* 2 (1956): 58-62;

R. S. Crane, "The Houyhnhnms, the Yahoos, and the History of Ideas," in his *The Idea of the Humanities and Other Essays Critical and Historical* (Chicago & London: University of Chicago Press, 1967), II: 261-282;

William A. Eddy, *Gulliver's Travels: A Critical Study* (Princeton: Princeton University Press, 1923);

Irvin Ehrenpreis, "The Meaning of Gulliver's Last Voyage," *Review of English Literature,* 3, no. 3 (1962): 18-38;

Ehrenpreis, "The Origin of *Gulliver's Travels,*" *PMLA,* 72 (1957): 880-899;

Daniel Eilon, "Gulliver's Fellow-Traveller Psalmanazar," *British Journal of Eighteenth-Century Studies,* 8 (Autumn 1985): 173-178;

Robert C. Elliot, *The Power of Satire* (Princeton: Princeton University Press, 1960);

William Ewald, *The Masks of Jonathan Swift* (Cambridge, Mass.: Harvard University Press, 1954);

Sir Charles Firth, "The Political Significance of *Gulliver's Travels,*" *Proceedings of the British Academy,* 9 (1919-1920): 237-259;

R. W. Frantz, *The English Traveller and the Movement of Ideas, 1660-1732* (Lincoln: University of Nebraska, 1934);

Frantz, "Gulliver's 'Cousin Sympson,'" *Huntington Library Quarterly*, 1 (1937-1938): 329-334;

Frantz, "Swift's Yahoos and the Voyager," *Modern Philology*, 29 (1931): 49-57;

Northrop Frye, *Anatomy of Criticism* (Princeton: Princeton University Press, 1957);

Roland M. Frye, "Swift's Yahoos and the Christian Symbols for Sin," *Journal of the History of Ideas*, 15 (1954): 201-217;

Paul Fussell, *The Rhetorical World of Augustan Humanism* (London, Oxford & New York: Oxford University Press, 1965);

Bertrand A. Goldgar, "*Gulliver's Travels*, and the Opposition to Walpole," in *The Augustan Milieu*, edited by Henry Knight Miller and others (Oxford: Clarendon Press, 1970);

Joseph Horrell, "What Gulliver Knew," *Sewanee Review*, 51 (1943): 476-504;

Clauston Jenkins, "The Ford Changes and the Text of *Gulliver's Travels*," *Papers of the Bibliographical Society of America*, 62 (1968): 1-23;

Frederick R. Karl, *A Reader's Guide to the Eighteenth-Century English Novel* (New York: Farrar, Straus & Giroux, 1974);

Charles Kerby-Miller, ed., *Memoirs of the Extraordinary Life, Works, and Discoveries of Martinus Scriblerus* (New Haven: Yale University Press, 1950);

John Lawlor, "The Evolution of Gulliver's Character," *Essays and Studies* (1956): 69-73;

Ellen Douglass Leyburn, *Satiric Allegory: Mirror for Man* (New Haven: Yale University Press, 1956);

F. P. Lock, *The Politics of Gulliver's Travels* (Oxford: Clarendon Press, 1980);

Maynard Mack, "Gulliver's Travels," in *English Masterpieces*, V: *The Augustans*, second edition, edited by Mack (Englewood Cliffs, N.J.: Prentice-Hall, 1961);

George P. Mayhew, *Rage or Raillery: The Swift Manuscripts at the Huntington Library* (San Marino, Cal.: Huntington Library, 1967);

Robert C. Merton, "The 'Motionless' Motion of Swift's Flying Island," *Journal of the History of Ideas*, 27 (1966): 275-277;

Samuel Holt Monk, "The Pride of Lemuel Gulliver," *Sewanee Review*, 63 (1955): 48-71;

M. F. Ashley Montagu, "Tyson's *Orang-Outang, Sive Homo Sylvestris* and Swift's *Gulliver's Travels*," *PMLA*, 59 (1944): 84-89;

J. R. Moore, "The Geography of Gulliver's Travels," *Journal of English and Germanic Philology*, 40 (1941): 214-220;

Marjorie Hope Nicholson and Nora M. Mohler, "The Scientific Background of Swift's *Voyage to Laputa*," *Annals of Science*, 2 (1937): 299-334;

Nicholson and Mohler, "Swift's 'Flying Island' in the *Voyage to Laputa*," *Annals of Science*, 2 (1937): 405-430;

Charles Peake, "Swift and the Passions," *Modern Language Review*, 55 (April 1960): 169-180;

Martin Price, *Swift's Rhetorical Art* (New Haven: Yale University Press, 1953);

Price, *To the Palace of Wisdom* (New York: Doubleday, 1964);

Clive T. Probyn, ed., *The Art of Jonathan Swift* (New York: Barnes & Noble, 1978);

Maurice J. Quinlan, "Treason in Lilliput and in England," *Texas Studies in Language and Literature*, 11 (1970): 1317-1332;

C. J. Rawson, *Gulliver and the Gentle Reader* (London & Boston: Routledge & Kegan Paul, 1973);

Edward J. Reilly, ed., *Approaches to Teaching "Gulliver's Travels"* (New York: Modern Language Association, 1988);

David Renaker, "Swift's Laputians as a Caricature of the Cartesians," *PMLA*, 94 (1979): 936-944;

John J. Richetti, *Popular Fiction Before Richardson: Narrative Patterns 1700-1739* (Oxford: Clarendon Press, 1969);

Edward Rosenheim, *Swift and the Satirist's Art* (Chicago: Univeristy of Chicago Press, 1963);

John F. Ross, "The Final Comedy of Lemuel Gulliver," *Studies in the Comic*, University of California Publications in English, 8, no. 2 (1941): 175-196;

Ross, *Swift and Defoe: A Study in Relationship* (Berkeley & Los Angeles: University of California Press, 1941);

Sheldon Sacks, *Fiction and the Shape of Belief* (Berkeley & Los Angeles: University of California Press, 1967);

Henry W. Sams, "Swift's Satire of the Second Person," *ELH*, 26 (1959): 36-44;

Robert Scholes and Robert Kellogg, *The Nature of Narrative* (London, Oxford & New York: Oxford University Press, 1966);

Arthur Sherbo, "Swift and Travel Literature," *Modern Language Studies*, 9, no. 3 (1979): 114-127;

George Sherburn, "Errors Concerning the Houyhnhnms," *Modern Philology*, 56 (1958): 92-97;

Frederik N. Smith, ed., *The Genres of "Gulliver's Travels"* (Newark: University of Delaware Press, 1990);

John H. Sutherland, "A Reconsideration of Gulliver's Third Voyage," *Studies in Philology*, 54 (1957): 45-52;

Aline M. Taylor, "Cyrano de Bergerac and Gulliver's 'Voyage to Brobdingnag,' " *Tulane Studies in English*, 5 (1955): 83-102;

William Makepeace Thackeray, "Swift," in his *The English Humorists of the Eighteenth Century* (London: Dent, 1912);

Clarence Tracy, "The Unity of *Gulliver's Travels*," *Queen's Quarterly*, 68 (1962): 597-609;

Ernest Tuveson, ed., *Swift: A Collection of Critical Essays* (Englewood Cliffs, N.J.: Prentice-Hall, 1964);

Brian Vickers, ed., *The World of Jonathan Swift: Essays for the Tercentenary* (Cambridge, Mass.: Harvard University Press, 1968);

Milton Voight, *Swift and the Twentieth Century* (Detroit: Wayne State University Press, 1964);

Ian Watt, *The Rise of the Novel* (Berkeley, Los Angeles & London: University of California Press, 1957);

T. O. Wedel, "On the Philosophical Background of *Gulliver's Travels*," *Studies in Philology*, 23 (1926): 434-450;

Sir Harold Williams, *The Text of Gulliver's Travels* (Cambridge: Cambridge University Press, 1952);

Kathleen Williams, *Jonathan Swift and the Age of Compromise* (Lawrence: University of Kansas Press, 1958);

Williams, ed., *Swift: The Critical Heritage* (New York: Barnes & Noble, 1970);

Calhoun Winton, "Conversion on the Road to Houyhnhnmland," *Sewanee Review*, 58 (1960): 20-33;

Curt A. Zimansky, "Gulliver, Yahoos, and Critics," *College English*, 27 (1965): 45-49.

Papers:

Swift manuscripts are widely distributed among English and American repositories. Perhaps the most accessible guides to Swift manuscripts are the secondary bibliographies listed above. One might also consult Herbert Davis, "Remarks on Some Swift Manuscripts in the United States," in Landa and Tobin's *Jonathan Swift: A List of Critical Studies Published from 1895-1945*, pp. 7-16, and Mayhew's *Rage or Raillery: The Swift Manuscripts at the Huntington Library*. The manuscript sources of Swift's letters are listed at the beginning of each volume of *The Correspondence of Jonathan Swift*, edited by Williams, and more specific information regarding Swift's papers may be found in the generous annotations to Ehrenpreis's *Swift: The Man, His Works, and the Age*.

William Wycherley

(March or April 1641 - 31 December 1715)

This entry was written by Rose A. Zimbardo (State University of New York at Stony Brook) for
DLB 80: Restoration and Eighteenth-Century Dramatists: First Series.

BOOKS: *Hero and Leander, in Burlesque* (London, 1669);

Love in a Wood, Or, St. James's Park. A Comedy. As it is Acted at the Theatre Royal, by his Majesties Servants (London: Printed by J. M. for H. Herringman, 1672);

The Gentleman Dancing-Master. A Comedy, Acted at the Duke's Theatre (London: Printed by J. M. for H. Herringman & T. Dring, 1673);

The Country-Wife, A Comedy, Acted at the Theatre Royal (London: Printed for Thomas Dring, 1675);

The Plain-Dealer. A Comedy. As it is Acted at the Theatre Royal (London: Printed by T. N. for James Magnes & Rich. Bentley, 1677);

Epistles to the King and Duke (London: Printed for Thomas Dring, 1683);

Miscellany Poems: as Satyrs, Epistles, Love-Verses, Songs, Sonnets, & c. (London: Printed for C. Brome, J. Taylor, B. Tooke, 1704);

The Folly of Industry; or The Busy Man Expos'd, A Satyr (London: Printed for A. Baldwin, 1704); republished as *The Idleness of Business* (London: Printed for B. Bragg, 1705);

On His Grace the Duke of Marlborough (London: Printed for John Morphew, 1707).

Collections: *The Works of the Ingenious Mr. William Wycherley, Collected into One Volume* (London: Printed for Richard Wellington, 1713);

The Posthumous Works of William Wycherley, esq. in Prose and Verse. Faithfully publish'd from His Original Manuscripts, by Mr. Theobald. In Two Parts. To which are Prefixed. Some Memoirs of Mr. Wycherley's Life. By Major Pack, edited by L. Theobald (London: Printed for A. Bettesworth, 1728);

The Posthumous Works of William Wycherley, Esq; in Prose and Verse. Vol. II. Consisting of Letters and Poems Publish'd from Original Manuscripts, edited by Alexander Pope (London: Printed for J. Roberts, 1729);

The Dramatic Works of Wycherley, Congreve, Vanbrugh, and Farquhar. With Biographical and Critical Notices by Leigh Hunt, edited by Hunt (London: Moxon, 1840);

William Wycherley, edited by W. C. Ward (London: Vizetelly, 1888);

The Complete Works of William Wycherley, 4 volumes, edited by Montague Summers (Soho: Nonesuch Press, 1924);

The Complete Plays of William Wycherley, edited by Gerald Weales (Garden City, N.Y.: Doubleday, 1966);

The Plays of William Wycherley, edited by Arthur Friedman (Oxford: Clarendon Press, 1979).

PLAY PRODUCTIONS: *Love in a Wood*, London, Theatre Royal on Bridges Street, March 1671;

The Gentleman Dancing Master, London, Dorset Garden Theatre, 6 February 1672;

The Country Wife, London, Theatre Royal in Drury Lane, 12 January 1675;

The Plain Dealer, London, Theatre Royal in Drury Lane, 11 December 1676.

OTHER: "The Answer to A Letter from Mr. Shadwell, to Mr. Wicherley," in *Poems on Affairs of State, Part 3* (London, 1689);

"To My Friend Mr. Pope, on his Pastorals," in *Poetical Miscellanies: The Sixth Part* (London: Printed for Jacob Tonson, 1709);

"An Epistle to Mr. Dryden, from Mr. Wycherley. Occasion'd by his Proposal to write a Comedy together," in *Poems on Several Occasions* (London: Printed for Bernard Lintott, 1717).

Satyre lashes Vice into Reformation, and humour represents folly so as to render it ridiculous. Many of our present Writers are eminent in both these kinds; and particularly the Author of the *Plain Dealer*, whom I am proud to call my Friend, has oblig'd all honest and vertuous Men, by one of the most bold, most general, and most useful Satyres which has ever been presented on the English Theatre.

William Wycherley (portrait by Sir Peter Lely; National Portrait Gallery, London)

—so John Dryden wrote in his preface to *The State of Innocence* (1677). Nevertheless, Wycherley's reputation as a playwright and his place in the literary tradition have always been problematic because the history of Wycherley studies hinges upon a bitter paradox. In his own day Wycherley was considered to be a moral satirist of the seriousness and stature of Juvenal; yet from the nineteenth century to the present he has been thought successively to be: a monster of moral depravity; a writer of artificial comedies of manners that are "holidays from the sublime . . . and the real"; a closet Savonarola, who restrained his neurotic rage while he was writing his first three plays only to have it burst forth in his "truly disturbing" last play; and, most recently, a writer of sex farces.

There was no doubt in the minds of his contemporaries that Wycherley was one of the greatest practitioners of moral satire since the ancient Roman masters, Horace and Juvenal. The diarist

John Evelyn, a man of education and taste, expressed the critical consensus of his day when he wrote in his prefatory verse to the 1678 edition of *The Plain Dealer*,

> As long as Men are false and Women vain,
> While Gold continues to be Virtue's bane,
> In pointed Satire Wycherley shall reign.

Dryden, poet laureate during the reigns of Charles II and James II and the greatest literary theorist of his age, used Wycherley's practice to illustrate the delicate balance between satire and humor that must be obtained in moralistic writing. In "The Original and Progress of Satire" (1693), one of the best and most comprehensive examinations of that elusive genre that has ever been written, Dryden argues a similarity between Wycherley and Juvenal, and he uses Wycherley's style to illustrate the "abundance" and *ira* of Juvenal. In 1678, when Charles II offered Wycherley the post of tutor to his son, Charles Lennox, Duke of Richmond, he made the offer in the conviction that Wycherley was the greatest moralist and teacher of the day. The poet, Charles said, had particular "skill in Men and Manners"; he could "pull off the Mask which [men's] several Callings and Pretenses cover them with, and make his Pupil discern what lies at the Bottom of such Appearances." To teach "the Son of a King," Charles believed, he "could make Choice of no Man so proper . . . as Mr. Wycherley." Even Jeremy Collier, in his famous attack upon "the Immorality and Profaneness of the English Stage," exempted Wycherley from his fury and "own[ed] the *Poet* to be an Author of good Sense." Late in his life, when Wycherley was recovering from a near fatal illness, the young Alexander Pope wrote to their friend Henry Cromwell that if Wycherley had died, "our nation would have lost in him as much wit and probity as would have remained . . . in the rest of it." And, in 1709, when "sentiment" was well on the way to replacing satire in English comedy, the father of sentimental comedy himself, Richard Steele, wrote in *The Tatler* no. 3 that the "Moral" of *The Country Wife* was that "there is no Defence against Vice, but Contempt of it," and he called the play a "very pleasant and instructive satire."

It is hard to imagine that Wycherley's widespread and firmly established reputation for morality and skill in teaching moral values could ever be toppled; yet that is precisely what happened. In the two hundred years following his death, gradually but steadily, Wycherley's image changed from that of a stern, fearless moralist to that of a monster of moral depravity whose works were infectious to all who approached them.

In the first half of the eighteenth century Wycherley's two best plays, *The Country Wife* and *The Plain Dealer*, still held the stage steadily—*The Country Wife* hit two high points of popularity: in 1725-1729, when the two theaters staged thirty-three performances of it, and in 1742-1743, when it was shown twelve times. *The Plain Dealer* played perhaps sixty-eight times from the time of its first performance, but printed editions of the play were even more frequent than those of *The Country Wife*. However, in the mid eighteenth century a change began. It occurred first in performance, in bowdlerized versions of the plays, such as David Garrick's *The Country Girl*, which cut Horner and the "ladies of honour" from the script. In order "to clear one of our most cele-

brated Comedies from immorality and obscenity," Garrick said, he was put "to the necessity of lopping off a limb to save the whole from putrefaction." Although the critical reputation of *The Plain Dealer*, always greater than that of *The Country Wife*, remained high in the latter part of the eighteenth century, the play met with much the same fate as *The Country Wife* in performance. Isaac Bickerstaffe staged a much-cut version in 1765, and the famous actor John Philip Kemble put his revised version on for three performances in 1796. In all cases revision pulled the satiric teeth from the plays and reduced them to harmless and, indeed, pointless slapstick farces.

Ironically enough, growing opinion that the plays were "immoral" soon rubbed off on the playwright. In his "Life of Pope" Samuel Johnson, the most highly influential critic of his period, dismissed Wycherley the *man* on moral grounds, saying that he had "had among his contemporaries his full share of reputation, to have been esteemed without virtue, and caressed without good-humour." This strange opinion was taken up and greatly intensified in the nineteenth century. In 1840 Leigh Hunt, in an attempt to reclaim Wycherley and his contemporaries, published *The Dramatic Works of Wycherley, Congreve, Vanbrugh, and Farquhar*. The edition drew the fiery wrath of Thomas Babington Macauley, influential critic for the *Edinburgh Review*. In Macauley's view the works of all four Restoration playwrights were "the most profligate and heartless of human compositions," but among them he singled out Wycherley as the greatest offender, a man depraved in his work, in his life, and in his mind. For Macauley the Restoration period as a whole was "the nadir of national taste and morality," but, in his Bosch-like picture of the age, he conjured no devil more monstrous than Wycherley. Wycherley's plays, Macauley said, were like skunks, safe from critics because they were too filthy to touch. So widely was Macauley's judgment adopted that by the end of the century Wycherley had become a standard against which the relative depravity of other writers of his period was measured. For example, John Doran, writing of Aphra Behn, said, "There is no one that equals this woman in downright nastiness, save Ravenscroft and Wycherley."

From the mid nineteenth to the mid twentieth century, the history of Wycherley criticism was one long contention between critics who dismissed the plays as immoral and those who sought to clear them of that charge. Detractors often damned the plays without granting them the objective consideration that allows a work of art to reveal its moral position in terms of its own aesthetic, while, on the other hand, admirers, in trying to prove the plays harmless, rendered them trivial. Constructing their approaches upon grounds foreign to the plays' aesthetic, they made them either pointless—"holiday[s] from the sublime and the beautiful, from the coarse and the real"—or mindless, photographically realistic reproductions of that carnival of rakes and wenches that "good King Charles's golden days" were supposed to be. Bonamy Dobrée's *Restoration Comedy* (1924) excepted, it was not until the 1950s, in works such as Thomas Fujimura's *The Restoration Comedy of Wit* (1952), Norman Holland's *The First Modern Comedies* (1959), and Dale Underwood's *Etherege and the Seventeenth Century Comedy of Manners* (1957), that objective critical re-evaluation of Wycherley's drama was undertaken in earnest, and it was not until 1965, in Rose A. Zimbardo's *Wycherley's Drama: A Link in the Development of English Satire*, that a serious, book-length study was devoted to placing Wycherley, the satirist, firmly back into English literary history.

How are we to explain so radical a change as that which Wycherley's reputation underwent? Major transformations in epistemology, aesthetics, and social history took place in the centuries following Wycherley's death that caused the changes in critical attitudes toward him. Primary among these was a change in the understanding of how a drama *functions* in relation to its audience. In the Restoration and very early eighteenth century a satiric play was thought to operate by *displaying* vice and folly and *exposing* them to make them ridiculous in the sight of the audience. The play, it was thought, *holds up* images of vice, and the spectator, recognizing them, laughs them to scorn and contempt. The underlying assumption in this kind of moralistic writing was, as Pope put it, that "Vice is a monster of so fearful mien / As, to be hated, needs but to be seen."

However, as the eighteenth century progressed, theories of associationism that had been formulated by John Locke and popularized by Joseph Addison led playwrights and critics to hold an entirely different view of how drama operates upon the minds and sensibility of an audience. From the eighteenth century, we have thought that audiences *imitate* in their own behavior what they see on a stage. Therefore, if we see onstage attractive characters who behave immorally, we are drawn to emulate their behavior with the consequence that we become immoral. We commonly hold this view still, for we think that watching violence in a film makes us violent, or that merry little housewives in television commercials induce passivity and submissiveness in female soap-opera fans.

Concomitant with the notion that audiences identify with dramatic characters was the identification of playwrights with the characters in their plays. As this line of reasoning goes, if Horner is sexually promiscuous and Horner equals Wycherley, or, at the very least, is the spokesman of Wycherley's moral attitudes, then it follows that Wycherley the man was sexually promiscuous—and, indeed, that he wrote his plays in order to seduce *us* into adopting his immoral attitudes.

Wycherley's contemporaries and immediate successors, of course, could never have predicted such a radical transformation in aesthetics, and, most certainly, they could not have imagined that "Manly" Wycherley would one day be accused of encouraging immorality. On the contrary, they saw it as their task to persuade us that a satirist so unflinchingly hard on vice as Wycherley could, in his personal behavior, be an amiable man. In his *Memoirs of the Life of William Wycherley, Esq.; with a Character of his Writings* (1718) one of Wycherley's earliest biographers, George Granville, Baron Lansdowne, felt obliged to reconcile the moral severity of Wycherley the poet with the genial disposition of Wycherley the man:

> As pointed and severe as he is in his writings, in his Temper he has all the softness of the tenderest disposition; gentle and inoffensive to every man in his particular character; he only attacks Vice as a public Enemy, compassionating the wound he is under necessity to probe.

From his earliest appearance on the London scene in 1671 to his last days, when the young poet whose career he helped to launch, Alexander Pope, declared him supreme among his age in "Wit, Probity, and Good Nature," Wycherley was universally valued for his judicious and penetrating wit, for his warm heart, and for his generosity of spirit.

We know very little that is verifiable about Wycherley's life before the success in 1671 of his first play, *Love in a Wood*, rocketed him into the arms of Charles II's then reigning mistress, Barbara Villiers, Duchess of Cleveland, and from

Clive Hall, near Shrewsbury, may have been the birthplace of William Wycherley or his father.

thence into the charmed and enviable circle of the court wits. And, curiously enough, disagreement about Wycherley begins over his very birth. His earliest biographers call him "a Shropshire gentleman" who was born on 28 May 1640; his most recent biographers disagree about whether it was William Wycherley or his father, Daniel, who was born at Clive Hall near Shrewsbury in Shropshire, and they date the son's birth in March of 1641. The firmest evidence indicates that William Wycherley was baptized in Whitchurch, Hampshire, in April 1641, and that the family into which he was born had lived comfortably in Shropshire for more than two centuries. The playwright's father is much easier quarry for a biographer than William because he was a singularly litigious man, and court records make it easier to track him than it is to follow his dazzling son. Daniel Wycherley was high steward in the household of John Paulet, Marquess of Winchester at Basing House in Hampshire. There he met and married Bethnia Shrimpton, lady-in-waiting to the marchioness. William was the eldest of their six children. Less than two years after William Wycherley's birth, civil war broke out, and in 1645 Basing House was invaded by the parliamentary forces under Oliver Cromwell. The marquess was arrested and imprisoned for the duration of the interregnum. During the absence of the marquess Daniel Wycherley remained his stew-

ard and his deputy, and he did very well not only for the marquess but also for himself. He was able to set aside a good deal of money, with which he later bought substantial lands in Shropshire. Daniel Wycherley's two great passions—for land buying and for lawsuits—date from the time of his service to the absent marquess. His passions for litigation, social climbing, and money became prime targets of satire in his son's plays. It is generally accepted that the litigious Widow Blackacre in *The Plain Dealer*, whose passion for the law courts surpasses all other passions and who is ready on the spot to declare her son, Jerry, a bastard to preserve her freedom to sue, is patterned after Daniel Wycherley. More subtle mockery of Daniel's type can be found in Sir Simon Addleplot of *Love in a Wood*, the character who bought his title "of a Court laundress" and who attempts to imitate aristocratic values that he cannot understand, or Sir Jasper Fidget of *The Country Wife*, whose sole "pleasure" is "business." So strong was the playwright's reaction against his father's behavior that, according to B. Eugene McCarthy, his most recent biographer, it formed the mainspring of his characters. In the portrait McCarthy draws, William Wycherley emerges as a decidedly unworldly and certainly unbusinesslike man, a person too easily led by others and too readily duped by them. Wycherley's mocking contempt for "business" and "industry"—the qualities most highly valued by the class that became the ruling class in England in the centuries following his death—is amply demonstrated everywhere in his work, but most pointedly in his poem *The Folly of Industry; or The Busy Man Expos'd* (1704). It is hard to say whether Daniel Wycherley was "the dominating figure in William's life" that McCarthy thinks he was, but certainly self-important, money-hungry social upstarts of the kind that Daniel was are prominent butts in Wycherley's satire.

Predictably, the son of an ardently Royalist family who sent money to the exiled king was sent to France for his education. At the age of fifteen Wycherley was sent to Angoulême in the Charente district, where he became closely associated with Julie d'Angennes, Marquise de Montausier. He had the good fortune—good for any young man, but inestimably valuable for a prospective literary artist—to be "often admitted to the Conversation" of this brilliant intellectual. The Marquise de Montausier, the wife of the provincial governor, was the daughter and the disciple of the celebrated Catherine de Vivonne, Marquise de Rambouillet, in whose salon the cult of exquisitely refined manners, morals, and literary brilliance, *préciosité*, was born and flourished. Kathleen Lynch, in her seminal study *The Social Mode of Restoration Comedy* (1926), has demonstrated the formative influence which *préciosité* exercised upon the philosophical and moral attitudes of the English in the Restoration period. Charles II's mother, Henrietta Maria, herself had had strong connections with the salon de Rambouillet, and it was she who had imported the précieuse cult of "platonic love" into the English Caroline court. The values upheld by this code formed part of the Restoration's inheritance from "before the Flood." Primary among these inherited attitudes was the idea that a generous, passionate love refines the soul and lifts it above the binding coils of commercially contracted marriage and the idea of the ideal of equality and free converse between the sexes. Not only did Mme de Montausier, "the incomparable Julie," introduce the adolescent Wycherley to the brilliant world of French intellectual and social life, but we may also assume that she taught him properly to value women, for "he was equally pleas'd with the Beauty of her Mind, and with the Graces of her Person." Her husband, Charles de Sainte-Maure, Marquis de Montausier, was an equally formative influence upon the young Wycherley. Molière patterned the rigidly honest protagonist

of *Le Misanthrope* (1666), Alceste, upon de Montausier, and the latter was pleased to own his resemblance to the character. A strange anomaly in the court of Louis XIV, de Montausier was a highly successful courtier whose pride it was always to tell the truth despite the social consequences. Gilbert Burnet describes him as "a pattern of virtue and sincerity, if not too cynical in it. He was so far from flattering the King, as all the rest did most abjectly, that he could not hold contradicting him." Whether or not we can say with surety that the young Wycherley patterned his own behavior upon that of this remarkable man, there can be little doubt that aspects of his character went into the making of the protagonist of *The Plain Dealer*.

Between his fifteenth year, when the conversation of Julie d'Angennes polished him into a gentleman, and his thirtieth, when the more raucous voice of the duchess of Cleveland called him "a Son of a Whore" and catapulted him into fame, we lose sight of Wycherley. It is generally believed that during his early twenties he spent some time in Madrid in the household of the poet-ambassador Sir Richard Fanshawe. Wycherley's borrowings from the Spanish drama in his first two plays have been used as evidence for a stay in Spain (J. N. Rundle believes that part of the high plot of *Love in a Wood* is taken from Pedro Calderón de la Barca's *Mañanas de abril y mayo*, and the title of his second play is obviously taken from Calderón's *El Maestro del Danzar*), but Spanish influence upon Wycherley's drama seems negligible. It is well for us to keep in mind that our own provinciality in matters of nationalistic encapsulation and literary borrowing did not obtain in the seventeenth century.

All that is verifiable about Wycherley's life in this vast gap of time is that he returned to England early in 1660 some months before the Restoration of Charles II and began his formal education at Queen's College, Oxford. During his time in France, probably under the influence of the de Montausiers, Wycherley had converted to Roman Catholicism. In his few months at Oxford, he reconverted to Protestantism, probably under the influence of Thomas Barlow, the head of his college, in whose house he lived. Barlow was a distinguished Anglican divine, who had flourished during the Commonwealth period as he did after the return of the king. Wycherley's stay at Oxford was very short. In November of 1660 he enrolled as a student in the Inner Temple. It is doubtful, however, that he ever com-

Joseph Haines, who played Sparkish in the first production of The Country Wife *and Lord Plausible in the premiere of* The Plain Dealer, *was best known for speaking the epilogue in the July 1696 production of Thomas Scott's* The Unhappy Kindness *while seated on a live ass.*

pleted his legal training either, and it is extremely unlikely that he ever practiced the law.

Although we cannot prove it, we may be fairly confident that Wycherley took some part in the naval battle against the Dutch in 1665. Certainly it is true that throughout his writing career he associates aristocratic bravery with heroism at sea. For example, in the epilogue to *The Gentleman Dancing Master* Wycherley mocks the citizens, the "good men o' th'Exchange," who will be the only audience left, for all true "Gentlemen must pack to Sea." More pointedly in *The Plain Dealer* he describes Manly in the list of dramatis personae as being "of an honest, surly, nice humour, suppos'd first, in the time of the *Dutch* War, to

have procur'd the Command of a Ship, out of Honour, not Interest."

We resume sure contact with Wycherley in 1669 when his first work was published anonymously. The poem, *Hero and Leander, in Burlesque*, is a mock-heroic burlesque that is much indebted to the puppet play in Ben Jonson's *Bartholomew Fair*. Although the piece has not much intrinsic value, it does demonstrate that from the beginning of his poetic career Wycherley had a penchant for mock-heroic, that is, for the nice tension between hypsos and bathos that forms the tightrope upon which great satire dances.

Wycherley's first play, *Love in a Wood*, made him famous. It was first performed in 1671 by the King's Company at the Theatre Royal on Bridges Street. A reference to Lent in the dedication (the poet says that his enviers will say the duchess of Cleveland favored the play because it was part of her Lenten self-mortification) leads us to believe that the play premiered in the spring, possibly in March, but it is listed in the *Stationers' Register*, 6 October 1671, and in the *Term Catalogues*, 20 November 1671.

The story of how *Love in a Wood* made Wycherley a star and a member of the charmed company of court wits is so wonderful that, whether or not it is precisely true, it is worth retelling. What is more, the anecdote comes best in the words of the man who first set it down, John Dennis:

The writing of that Play (*Love in a Wood*) was likewise the Occasion of his becoming acquainted with one of King *Charles*'s Mistresses after a very particular manner. As Mr. *Wycherley* was going thro' *Pall-mall* toward *St. James*'s in his Chariot, he met the foresaid Lady in hers, who, thrusting half her Body out of the Chariot, cry'd out aloud to him, *You*, Wycherley, *you are a Son of a Whore*, at the same time laughing aloud and heartily. Perhaps, Sir, if you never heard of this Passage before, you may be surpris'd at so strange a Greeting from one of the most beautiful and best bred Ladies in the World. Mr. *Wycherley* was certainly very much surpris'd at it, yet not so much but he soon apprehended it was spoke with Allusion to the latter End of a Song in the foremention'd Play.

When Parents are Slaves
Their Brats cannot be any other,
Great Wits and great Braves
Have always a Punk to their Mother.

As, during Mr. *Wycherley's* Surprise, the Chariots drove different ways, they were soon at considerable Distance from each other, when Mr. *Wycherley* recovering from his Surprise, ordered his Coachman to drive back, and to overtake the Lady. As soon as he got over-against her, he said to her, *Madam, you have been pleased to bestow a Title on me which generally belongs to the Fortunate. Will your Ladyship be at the Play to Night? Well,* she reply'd, *what if I am there? Why then I will be there to wait on your Ladyship, tho' I disappoint a very fine Woman who has made me an Assignation. So,* said she, *you are sure to disappoint a Woman who has favour'd you for one who has not. Yes,* he reply'd, *if she who has not favour'd me is the finer Woman of the two. But he who will be constant to your Ladyship, till he can find a finer Woman, is sure to die your Captive.* The Lady blush'd, and bade her Coachman drive away. As she was then in all her Bloom, and the most celebrated Beauty that was then in *England,* or perhaps that has been in *England* since, she was touch'd with the Gallantry of that Compliment. In short, she was that Night in the first Row of the King's Box in *Drury Lane,* and Mr. *Wycherley* in the Pit under her, where he entertained her during the whole Play. And this, Sir, was the beginning of a Correspondence between these two Persons, which afterwards made a great Noise in the Town ("To the Honourable Major Pack," 1 September 1720).

Although Dennis's anecdote no doubt embroiders the past, it gives us a window on the world in which Wycherley lived during the whole of his career as a playwright. It was a world that delighted in elegant, playful talk and in sprightly courtship, a world in which men and women alike enjoyed the so-called innocent pleasures of the Town. It was a world in which women were freer in their manners—and only *perhaps* in their morals—than they were to be for the next two hundred years. What is more, it was a world in which women were *valued* for their brains as highly as for their bodies, for their ability to think quickly and to talk wittily as well as for their ability to breed. A great nobleman of the time, the earl of Halifax, advised his daughter that unless wit is *combined* with virtue in a woman's character "the first is so empty and the other so faint, that they scarce have right to be commended." It was a society that held something of the same values as Bernard Shaw's Mrs. Warren, who thinks that it is better to be brave, generous, free, and "immoral," than it is to be respectable and be a slave. Lastly, it was a world in which, literally and figuratively, the playhouse was an important center.

The question has been raised, if Wycherley the man was so swimmingly successful in such a world (as indeed he was until sickness and penury made him too tired to swim), how could he have been a satirist. The very reason that we are led to ask such a question is that we have lost sight of what satire, as the seventeenth century understood it to be, is. For the ancient Romans, as well as for writers, readers, and spectators of the Restoration period, satire "did not . . . denote a specific attitude of mind involving the contemporary scene, but was a term used for an independent literary genre of a particular kind with well-defined limits and a unique profile" (Ulrich Knoche, *Roman Satire* [1975]). In Wycherley's age, satire did not reflect the "real" feelings of an author toward his realistically portrayed society; rather it was a recognized literary genre, just as tragedy, comedy, or epic was. As Maynard Mack showed in his essay "The Muse of Satire," the satiric perspective is a lens which a writer takes up in order to practice his delicate and demanding art. Therefore, it is as irrelevant to ask how a writer who so loved his world and was so well loved by it as Wycherley could write satire as it is to ask how Shakespeare could have written as dark a tragedy as *Hamlet* and as glorious a comedy as *Twelfth Night* in the same year (1600). The inconsistency, if indeed there is one, lies not in the practice of the seventeenth-century writer but in the expectations of a twentieth-century critic, most especially the kind of critic who cannot accept that there has ever been a conception of artistic imitation different from our own.

The conceptual design of satire from Ancient Rome to seventeenth-century England and France consisted in a collision and interplay between contradictory *literary* perspectives upon our timeless human condition. A multivalent mode, satire mocks us for the high-blown heroic, noble, glittering images of ourselves that we spin out of our own feverish imaginations, but, ironically, it also mocks us for not living up to those ideals. It laughs at us for being goats and monkeys, but it also jeers at us for making goats and monkeys of ourselves. It simultaneously elevates what we should be and denigrates what we are. Moreover, satire mocks the satirist himself for the most egregious of follies, that is, thinking that satire can reform anybody. As Wycherley says in *The Plain Dealer* (V.ii), "You [the satirist] rail, and nobody hangs himself: And thou has nothing of the Satyr, but in thy face." Until the eighteenth century, when it came to be thought that the aim

To my LADY B——

Madam,

THO I never had the Honour to receive a Favour from you, nay, or be known to you, I take the confidence of an Author to write to you a Billiet doux Dedicatory; which is no new thing, for by most Dedications it appears, that Authors, though they praise their Patrons from top to toe, and seem to turn 'em inside out, know 'em as little, as sometimes their Patrons their Books, tho they read 'em ont; and if the Poetical Daubers did not write the name of the Man or Woman on top of the Picture, 'twere impossible to guess whose it were. But you, Madam, without the help of a Poet, have made your self known and famous in the World; and, because you do not want it, are therefore most worthy of an Epistle Dedicatory. And this Play claims naturally your Protection, since it has lost its Reputation with the Ladies of stricter lives in the Play-house; and (you know) when mens endeavours are discountenanc'd and refus'd, by the nice coy Women of Honour, they come to you, To you the Great and Noble Patroness of rejected and bashful men, of which number I profess my self to be one, though a Poet, a Dedicating Poet; To you I say, Madam, who have as discerning a judgement, in what's obscene or not, as any quick-sighted civil Person of 'em all, and can make as much of a double meaning saying as the best of 'em; yet wou'd not, as some do, make nonsense of a Poet's jest, rather than not make it baudy: by which they show they as little value Wit in a Play, as in a Lover, provided they can bring t'other thing about. Their sense indeed lies all one way, and therefore are only for that in a Poet which is moving, as they say; but what do they mean by that word moving? Well, I must not put 'em to the blush, since I find I can

†   do't.

The Epistle

do't. In short, Madam, you wou'd not be one of those who ravish a Poet's innocent words, and make 'em guilty of their own naughtiness (as 'tis term'd) in spight of his teeth; nay, nothing is secure from the power of their imaginations; no, not their Husbands, whom they Cuckold with themselves, by thinking of other men, and so make the lawful matrimonial embraces Adultery, wrong Husbands and Poets in thought and word, to keep their own Reputations; but your Ladyship's justice, I know, wou'd think a Woman's Arraigning and Damning a Poet for her own obscenity, like her crying out a Rape, and hanging a man for giving her pleasure, only that she might be thought not to consent to't; and so to vindicate her honour forfeits her modesty. But you, Madam, have too much modesty to pretend to't; tho you have as much to say for your modesty as many a nicer she; for you never were seen at this Play, no, not the first day; and 'tis no matter what Peoples lives have been, they are unquestionably modest who frequent not this Play: For, as Mr. Bays says of his, that it is the only Touchstone of Mens Wit and Understanding; mine is, it seems, the only Touchstone of Womens Vertue and Modesty. But how bold, that Touchstone is equivocal, and, by the strength of a Lady's Imagination, may become something that is not civil; but your Ladyship, I know, scorns to misapply a Touchstone. And, Madam, tho you have not seen this Play, I hope (like other nice Ladies) you will the rather read it; yet, lest the Chambermaid or Page shou'd not be trusted, and their indulgence cou'd gain no further admittance for it, than to their Ladies Lobbies or outward Rooms, take it into your care and protection; for, by your recommendation and procurement, it may have the honour to get into their Closets: For what they renounce in publick often entertains 'em there, with your help especially. In fine, Madam, for these and many other reasons, you are the fittest Patroness or Judge of this Play; for you shew no partiality to this or that Author; for from some many Ladies will take a broad jeast as chearfully as from the watermen, and sit at some downright filthy Play (as they call 'em) as well satisfy'd, and as still, as a Poet cou'd wish 'em elsewhere; therefore it must be the doubtful obscenity of my Plays alone they take exceptions at, because it is too bashful

Dedicatory.

ful for 'em; and indeed most women hate men, for attempting to halves on their Chastity; and Baudy I find, like Satyr, shou'd be home, not to have it taken notice of. But, now I mention Satyr, some there are who say, 'Tis the Plain-dealing of the Play, not the obscenity; 'tis taking off the Ladies Masks, not offering at their Pettycoats, which offends 'em: and generally they are not the handsomest, or most innocent, who are the most angry at being discover'd:

——Nihil est audacius illis
Deprehensis, iram, atq; animos a crimine sumunt.

Pardon, Madam, the Quotation, for a Dedication can no more be without ends of Latine, than Flattery; and 'tis no matter whom it is writ to; for an Author can as easily (I hope) suppose People to have more understanding and Languages than they have, as well as more Vertues: But why, shou'd any of the few modest and handsome be alarm'd? (for some there are who as well as any deserve those Attributes, yet refrain not from seeing this Play, nor think it any addition to their Vertue to set up for it in a Play-house, lest there it shou'd look too much like acting.) But why, I say, shou'd any at all of the truly vertuous be concern'd, if those who are not so are distinguish'd from 'em? For by that Mask of modesty which women wear promiscuously in publick, they are all alike, and you can no more know a kept Wench from a Woman of Honour by her looks than by her Dress; for those who are of Quality without Honour (if any such there are) they have their Quality to set off their false Modesty, as well as their false Jewels, and you must no more suspect their Countenances for counterfeit than their Pendants, tho, as the Plain-dealer Montaigne says, Els envoy leur conscieuce au Bordel, & teinnent leur contenance en regle: But those who act as they look, ought not to be scandaliz'd at the reprehension of others faults, lest they tax themselves with 'em, and by too delicate and quick an apprehension not only make that obscene which I meant innocent, but that Satyr on all, which was intended only on those who deserv'd it. But, Madam, I beg your par-

† 2   don

Dedication to The Plain-Dealer, *from the 1677 edition. Lady B—— was Mother Bennett, a well-known brothel keeper.*

The Epistle

don for this digression, to Civil Women and Ladies of Honour, since you and I shall never be the better for 'em; for a Comic Poet, and a Lady of your Profession, make most of the other sort, and the Stage and your Houses, like our Plantations, are propagated by the least nice Women; and as with the Ministers of Justice, the Vices of the Age are our best business. But, now I mention Publick Persons, I can no longer defer doing you the justice of a Dedication, and telling you your own; who are, of all publick-spirited people, the most necessary, most communicative, most generous and hospitable; your house has been the house of the People, your sleep still disturb'd for the Publick, and when you arose 'twas that others might lye down, and you waked that others might rest; The good you have done is unspeakable; How many young unexperienc'd Heirs have you kept from rash foolish Marriages? and from being jilted for their lives by the worst sort of Jilts, Wives? How many unbewitched Widowers Children have you preserv'd from the Tyranny of Stepmothers? How many old Dotards from Cuckoldage, and keeping other mens Wenches and Children? How many Adulteries and unnatural sins have you prevented? In fine, you have been a constant scourge to the old Lecher, and often a terrour to the young; you have made concupiscence its own punishment, and extinguish'd Lust with Lust, like blowing up of Houses to stop the fire.

Nimirum propter continentiam, incontinentia
Necessaria est, incendium ignibus extinguitur.

There's Latin for you again, Madam; I protest to you, as I am an Author, I cannot help it; nay, I can hardly keep my self from quoting Aristotle and Horace, and talking to you of the Rules of Writing, (like the French Authors,) to shew you and my Readers I understand 'em, in my Epistle, lest neither of you should find it out by the Play; and, according to the Rules of Dedications, 'tis no matter whether you understand or no, what I quote or say to you, of Writing; for an Author can as easily make any one a Judge or Critic, in an Epistle, as an Hero in his Play: But, Madam, that this may prove to the end a true Epistle Dedicatory, I'd have you know 'tis
not

Dedicatory.

not without a design upon you, which is in the behalf of the Fraternity of Parnassus, that Songs and Sonnets may go at your Houses, and in your Liberties, for Guinneys and half Guinneys; and that Wit, at least with you, as of old, may be the price of Beauty, and so you will prove a true encourager of Poetry, for Love is a better help to it than Wine; and Poets, like Painters, draw better after the Life, than by Fancy; Nay, in justice, Madam, I think a Poet ought to be as free of your Houses, as of the Play-houses; since he contributes to the support of both, and is as necessary to such as you, as a Ballad-singer to the Pick-purse, in convening the Cullies at the Theatres, to be pick'd up, and carry'd to Supper and Bed at your houses. And, Madam, the reason of this motion of mine is, because poor Poets can get no favour in the Tiring Rooms, for they are no Keepers, you know; and Folly and Money, the old Enemies of Wit, are even too hard for it on its own Dunghill: And for other Ladies, a Poet can least go to the price of them; besides, his Wit, which ought to recommend him to 'em, is as much an obstruction to his Love, as to his wealth or preferment; for most Women now adays, apprehend Wit in a Lover, as much as in a Husband; they hate a Man that knows 'em, they must have a blind easie Fool, whom they can lead by the Nose, and as the Scythian Women of old, must baffle a Man, and put out his Eyes, ere they will lye with him, and then too, like Thieves, when they have plunder'd and stript a Man, leave him. But if there shou'd be one of an hundred of those Ladies, generous enough to give her self to a Man that has more Wit than Money, (all things consider'd) he wou'd think it cheaper coming to you for a Mistress, though you made him pay his Guinney; as a Man in a Journey, (out of good husbandry) had better pay for what he has in an Inn, than lye on freecost at a Gentlemans House.

In fine, Madam, like a faithful Dedicator, I hope I have done my self right in the first place, then you, and your Profession, which in the wisest and most religious Government of the World, is honour'd with the publick allowance; and in those that are thought the most uncivilized and barbarous, is protected, and supported by the Ministers of Justice; and of you, Madam, I ought to say no more here, for your Vertues deserve a Poem rather than an Epistle,
or

The Epistle

or a Volume intire to give the World your Memoirs, or Life at large, and which (upon the word of an Author that has a mind to make an end of his Dedication) I promise to do, when I write the Annals of our British Love, which shall be Dedicated to the Ladies concern'd, if they will not think them something too obscene too; when your Life, compar'd with many that are thought innocent, I doubt not may vindicate you, and me, to the World, for the confidence I have taken in this Address to you; which then may be thought neither impertinent, nor immodest; and, whatsoever your Amorous misfortunes have been, none can charge you with that heinous, and worst of Womens Crimes, Hypocrisie; nay, in spight of misfortunes or age, you are the same Woman still; though most of your Sex grow Magdalens at fifty, and as a solid French Author has it,

Apres le plaisir, vien't la peine,
Apres la peine la vertu;

But sure an old sinner's continency is much like a Gamester's forswearing Play, when he has lost all his Money; and Modesty is a kind of a youthful dress, which, as it makes a young Woman more amiable, makes an old one more nauseous; a bashful old Woman is like an hopeful old man; and the affected Chastity of antiquated Beauties, is rather a reproach than an honour to 'em, for it shews the mens Vertue only, not theirs. But you, in fine, Madam, are no more an Hypocrite than I am when I praise you; therefore I doubt not will be thought (even by your's and the Play's Enemies, the nicest Ladies) to be the fittest Patroness for,

Madam,

Your Ladyship's most obedient,
faithful, humble Servant, and

The Plain-Dealer.

of literary art was to draw readers or spectators into good moral behavior by making them emulate the good-natured, virtuous characters it portrayed, satire did not portray a standard of good behavior for emulation. It directed its audience to the good only very obliquely and always by indirection. Those of us who have called Wycherley's plays satires have done so in the understanding that Restoration satire does not provide models of good behavior, and that it is, above all, funny. Those who have argued that Wycherley's plays cannot be satires have done so because they think that satirists should be more serious than Wycherley is in "lashing vice" and "ridiculing folly" and in showing us how to behave ourselves.

How can we be sure that Wycherley thought himself to be a satirist? After all, Dryden's essay, which was the first attempt to describe the generic form of satire and trace its development, was written in 1692, almost twenty years after brain fever and consequent loss of memory prevented Wycherley from ever writing another play, and Wycherley, a supreme ironist, would never, of course, condescend to justify his art in literary criticism, except self-mockingly, as when he quotes Tertullian to the famous brothel keeper, Mother Bennett, to whom *The Plain Dealer* is dedicated, and adds:

> *There's* Latin *for you again, Madam; I protest to you, as I am an Author, I cannot help it; nay, I can hardly keep my self from quoting* Aristotle *and* Horace, *and talking to you of the Rules of Writing (like the French Authors,) to show you and my Readers I understand 'em, in my Epistle, lest neither of you should find it out by the Play.*

The message is clear. If we want to understand the satire of this elusive joker, we have to look to his plays, not to critical speculations about them.

In his first play, *Love in a Wood*, Wycherley is light-handed in his satire; he uses it to mock the highly flattering perspective upon our human nature that pastoral romance affords us. The epigraph to the play, "Excludit sanos helicone poetas Democritus" (Democritus excludes those poets who are in their right senses from Helicon), comes from a section of the *Ars Poetica* (296) in which Horace is urging a young poet to try his wings, but also cautioning him to be aware always of the tradition in which he is writing. The epigraph itself is a delicious joke because in this play Wycherley is using for *satiric* purposes one of the most popular plays of the Car-

oline period, one of the first plays to be revived when the theaters were reopened in 1660, and one of the most traditional and rarefied pastoral romances ever written, John Fletcher's *The Faithful Shepherdess* (circa 1608).

Like allegory, satire always "speaks of the *other*"; that is to say, just as it exaggerates *downward* to grotesque effect, a satire must also posit the existence of an equal and opposite *upward* perspective. In a great many satires the indirectly expressed but indispensable upward, *other* perspective is that of pastoral romance. As E. M. Waith, writing about pastoral, puts it in *The Pattern of Tragi-Comedy in Beaumont and Fletcher* (1959), "The satirist . . . portrays with awful vividness the very conditions from which the pastoral poet longs to escape." Looking at the matter from the other side of the coin and writing about satire, Alvin Kernan says in *The Cankered Muse* (1959), "Somehow the satirist seems always to come from a world of pastoral innocence and kindness; he is the prophet come down from the hills to the cities of the plain . . . abroad in the cruel world." Wycherley, the trickster, makes the connection in his work itself and laughs at us while he is making it. There are direct references to Fletcher's play in *Love in a Wood*; for example, the supra-sensuous Cristina, who mourns for her absent Valentine as though he were dead, is twice called "the Faithful Shepherdess." The connection, of course, is to Fletcher's title character, Clorin, who is so elevated of soul and so refined in love that she is married to a dead man, beside whose grave she keeps her bower. There are also direct echoes of Fletcher's play, as when Lady Flippant, a citizen's widow, ranging the park in search of any man who will satisfy her raging sexual appetite, uses words similar to those of Fletcher's Cloe as she ranges the Arcadian wood; Cloe says, "It is impossible to ravish me, / I am so willing." However, the most obvious device Wycherley employs to achieve the necessary satiric-pastoral collision of perspectives is to transfer the pastoral meadows and forests of Arcadia to the middle of Restoration London, to make the pastoral "wood" the most fashionable trysting place in the dear, distracting town, St. James's Park—and then to go a step further and pun on the contradiction in his title. *Love in a Wood* means *both* love in the nowhere-nowhere wood of a wash-tint pastoral landscape *and* love in the mad, muddled whirligig of life in here-and-now fashionable London. The word *wood* is a romantic word for a forest, but it is also a common Restoration word for madness or confusion.

As numerous prefaces and prologues of the 1660s and 1670s testify, the two most powerful influences upon comic and satiric playwrights of the time were "Fletcher" and "Ben" (Jonson). In his first play the fledgling playwright Wycherley follows the Horatian precept that he quotes in his epigraph rather closely. He takes the frame and the high romance plane of his structure from Fletcher, but he takes his downwardly exaggerated humours characters and his low plane of action from Ben. The frame of the play is a pastoral romance ladder of love that stretches from apex in the highly romantic attachment of Cristina and Valentine, where stately postures of the soul and refinements of the debate between love and honor dominate, to nadir in the lecherous Alderman Gripe and the Crossbites, where prurience and greed drive action and hypocritical Puritan cant dominates discourse. One degree less perfect in love and more contemporary in action than the faithful Cristina and her heroic Valentine are Ranger and Lydia. Ranger is a Restoration libertine and Lydia the female wit who cleverly snares him. Their action is typical love chase and their discourse witty banter. The next step down on the Fletcherian scale of love is a step down in social class as well. Dapperwit, a fop and would-be wit, who mistakes backbiting for satire, takes as his partner Martha, the daughter of Alderman Gripe. As is always the case both in pastoral romance and in three-tiered early Restoration comedy, descent into the world is descent into confusion and duplicity—and the further the descent the greater the confusion. Dapperwit is the lover of Martha, but he is also the keeper of Lucy Crossbite, who expects to be elevated by him to success on the stage "where [she] might have had as good luck as others ... good Cloaths, Plate, Jewels." Martha, on the other hand, is pursued by a newly made knight, Sir Simon Addleplot. In the interchanges of Martha and Sir Simon, Wycherley mocks a *real* social phenomenon—the new upstart class that has bought its nobility with money—and a *literary* mode—romance—at the same time:

> SIR SIMON: ... I have freed the Captive Lady, for her long Knight....
> ....
> SIR SIMON: I wou'd have kept the Maiden-head of your lips, for your sweet Knight....
> ....

> MARTHA: My sweet Knight, if he will be Knight of mine, must be contented with what he finds, as well as other Knights.
> ....

> SIR SIMON: ... your Worthy Noble, Brave, Heroick Knight; who loves you only, and only deserves your kindness.

One rung from the bottom of the scale is Wycherley's rendering of Cloe. Lady Flippant, the widow of a Citizen and sister of Alderman Gripe (and consequently among the social climbers and pretenders who are Wycherley's prime targets), nudges her brother's servants into sexual play, relentlessly pursues Dapperwit, who she knows despises her, and hires Mrs. Joyner, the bawd, to get her a husband. When all expedients fail she ranges the park like a predator: "Unfortunate Lady, that I am! I have left the Herd on purpose to be chas'd, and have wandred this hour here; but the Park affords not so much as a Satyr for me, (and that's strange) no Burgundy man, or drunken Scourer will reel my way" (V.i). The discourse of such a passage reveals the subtlety of Wycherley's satire. Language parodies the elevated discourse of pastoral romance; action parodies pastoral action. The Citizen-Lady, a combination oxymoronic in itself, ranges St. James's Park, the favorite site for illicit sexual encounters at that time, in parodic imitation of pastoral's shepherds and shepherdesses who meet at midnight in Arcadian woods to pledge their innocent, platonic loves. The highly literary romantic past collides with the all-too-tarnished present "reality" in the formation of that complex disjunctive unity that is the hallmark of satire.

At the absolute nadir of the scale, exaggerated downwardly to the same degree as Cristina and Valentine are upwardly idealized, are the Jonsonian humours characters, Alderman Gripe, Mrs. Crossbite and her daughter, Lucy, and Mrs. Joyner, the bawd. Their lechery and avarice create the impression of impenetrable materialism to counterbalance the translucent atmosphere of the high plane. However, even their materialism is not simple; it is distorted into grotesque deformity by hypocrisy. "Peace, Plenty, and Pastime be within these Walls!" Alderman Gripe cants upon entering the house of a young wench he means to buy at the lowest possible price. Following Jonson's lead, Wycherley makes his lowest figures—the lecher, the whore, and the pimp—Puritans. It is, in fact, highly probable that his most grossly ridiculous characterizations were created with particular actors in mind, for each of the roles was played by an actor famous for some interpretation of a Jonsonian character. Mrs. Joyner, for instance, was played by Katherine Mitchell Corey, who is referred to by theatrical chroniclers of the time as "Doll Common" because of the excellence of her portrayal of that character in *The Alchemist*. Gripe was played by John Lacey, famous for Sir Politic Would-be, Ananias, and Otter, and Dapperwit was played by Michael Mohun, the Face and Volpone of the Restoration stage.

The geography of *Love in a Wood*, then, is Fletcherian in its heights and Jonsonian in its depths. The new poet has followed the advice of Horace to perfection; he has tried his wings, and yet kept his eye steadily trained upon the traditions in which he was writing.

In composing his second play Wycherley was writing a potboiler, and, what is more, he knew it. Appropriately, the epigraph he chose for this play is "Non satis est risu diducere rictum/ Auditoris; et est quaedam tamen hic quoq; virtus" (It is not enough to make your reader laugh, though there is something even in that). It is taken from Horace's *Satires* (I,x,7-8), and when we go to the Horatian context, we find that in it the Roman theorist-poet is discussing the proper manner of writing moral satire. In choosing the particular passage that he does, Wycherley is apologizing for writing so flimsy a play as *The Gentleman Dancing Master*, acknowledging that it is not worthy work for a satirist, but arguing, almost with a grin, that simply raising a laugh has some merit in it. Nevertheless, even this trifle of a play enjoyed considerable popularity in its time; after its premiere on 6 February 1672, it appeared in three separate editions, in 1673, in 1693, and as late as 1702.

Strictly considered, *The Gentleman Dancing Master* may well be Wycherley's only comedy. Borrowing his central plot device from Calderon's *El Maestro del Danzar*, Wycherley stretches it into a structure, admittedly thin and obvious, that answers the demands of the classic comic formula: the outwitting of a *senex iratus* by a clever innocent, and the triumph of love in an end-scene wedding that unites not just the lovers but all the members of the human community whatever their nature or their initial deviation from the ideal. Perhaps because it so obviously fulfills our expectations of comedy, and Wycherley's drama has so often been labeled "Restoration Comedy," the play has found favor with many critics in this

century and even in the last decades of the last century. A. C. Ward thought the play "less exceptionable and more uniformly pleasing than *The Country Wife*." Montague Summers preferred it to *Love in a Wood*, and in more recent times Virginia Ogden Birdsall and Norman Holland considered the play worthy of close critical attention.

In *The Gentleman Dancing Master* the ideal is the same in *kind* as that in Wycherley's first play (that is, love and virtue), but the ideal does not exist on a high plane of romantic, literary abstraction. The anti-ideal is also the same in kind as that in *Love in a Wood* (hypocrisy and materialism), but whereas in the first play the anti-ideal is exaggerated downward to grotesque satiric effect, in the second it is realized in lightly drawn caricatures of stock comic types—the fop, the prude, the jealous father, the music-hall "foreigner." The play's action is the simplest of one-turn comic plots. Don Diego, an Englishman turned Spaniard, with the caution of his adopted nationality, has locked up his daughter to preserve her virtue, and, by extension, his honor. He intends to marry her to her cousin, Monsieur de Paris, who affects French manners to the same ridiculous degree as his uncle affects Spanish. Hippolita, the bride-elect, is determined not to marry her foolish cousin, but to find means to get herself a husband more to her liking. Playing upon Monsieur's vanity, she tricks him into sending Gerrard, the finest gentleman of the town, to her window. Gerrard and Hippolita fall in love at once, but they are surprised in their first interview by the arrival of Don Diego, who has just returned from Spain, and Mrs. Caution, Hippolita's prudish aunt and duenna. To save Hippolita's honor and her life, Gerrard goes along with her deception that he is a dancing master sent by Monsieur de Paris to instruct his future bride. The rest of the play revolves around the efforts of the lovers to come to an agreement while at the same time maintaining their deception. A subplot concerns the efforts of Don Diego to turn his nephew, the would-be Frenchman, into a would-be Spaniard like himself.

Discourse in this play has none of the double-edged parodic subtlety that we found in *Love in a Wood*. It is the nearest that Wycherley comes in any of his drama to "dialogue," to simulation of contemporary parlance. Similarly, there is very little complexity in character. Characters in satire, of course, are types, but these are not the carefully constructed types of satire. They are simple, stock comic figures. Hippolita is the stock hero-

Agnes Lauchlan as Lady Fidget and Lesley Wareing as Mrs. Margery Pinchwife in a 1934 production of The Country Wife
(photographs by Sasha)

ine of comedy, whose cleverness is sufficiently transparent to reveal the old-fashioned modesty in which it is rooted. For example, she blushes and stutters at her own audacity when she speaks to her lover. Gerrard is a robust, honest Englishman. He cannot dance; he cannot sing any but old English catches; and his speech is plain English, unadorned by foreign locutions. Wycherley is certainly not concerned with lashing vice into reformation in this play, and the folly he ridicules is too preposterous and too simply drawn to have any satiric impact upon an audience. The play may have been intended as a propaganda piece extolling everything that is good, old-fashioned, and English and despising whatever is foreign; and it may have been inspired by the general patriotic enthusiasm that prevailed in preparation for the impending Third Dutch War.

We have some historical evidence that Wycherley fought in that war. George Villiers, Duke of Buckingham, author of *The Rehearsal* (1671), a rollicking parody of the heroic drama of the 1660s, was one of the courtiers in the circle of which Wycherley's success as a playwright and a wit had made him a member. Buckingham

was given a regiment on 20 June 1672, and he commissioned Wycherley as a captain-lieutenant, a position which would have put the playwright into close association with his friend, the colonel. The Third Dutch War was, of course, a naval war, but it is very doubtful that Wycherley saw sea duty in it, because we know that Buckingham spent most of 1673 raising troops in Yorkshire and preparing them for ground combat in the event of invasion on Blackheath Common, just outside of London. Given Wycherley's rank and his friendship with Buckingham, it is likely that he was involved in these activities during the war. When the regiment disbanded at the end of the war, Wycherley was a captain in Buckingham's company. He resigned his commission on 26 February 1674.

Wycherley's two great plays, *The Country Wife* and *The Plain Dealer*, are the works upon which his importance in the history of English drama must be judged. In this writer's opinion, they are among the greatest satires in English, and one of the reasons that we have not generally thought of them in relation to works such as Pope's "To a Lady; On the Character of Women"

(1735) or "Verses on the Death of Dr. Swift" (1731) is that we tend to think of satire as a verse or prose form. As we can see in the quotation from Dryden, which calls *The Plain Dealer* "one of the most bold, most general, and most useful Satyres which has ever been presented on the English Theatre," the seventeenth century made no distinction between verse and drama as suitable media for the expression of the distinct *genre* satire. Both *The Country Wife* and *The Plain Dealer* are satires, but they are quite different from one another in style and in intensity. *The Country Wife* is a comical satire; indeed, most critics would not accept that it is a satire at all, but would rather classify it "Restoration Comedy." *The Plain Dealer* is a darker, more deeply disturbing work, which verges on that end of the satiric spectrum that skirts nihilistic irony. In the former play Wycherley is putting a *particular* Roman model into Restoration dress, Juvenal's *Satire Six*; in the latter he has abstracted the classical structural design of satire, which he fleshes to the contours of his own invention.

Between the beginning and ending of the verse paragraph in Horace from which Wycherley drew epigraphs for his most trivial, second play and his most serious, last play, Horace tells us what style is demanded by moral satire: "You need terseness.... You also need a style now grave, often gay, in keeping with the role, now of orator or poet, at times of the wit who holds his strength in check and husbands it with wisdom" (*Satires* I,x,10-14). Wycherley has been faulted by some twentieth-century critics for not bringing his prose "within the range of realistic conversation." But Wycherley's aim was not to write comic dialogue nor to create naturalistic characters with the interiority and psychology that we novel-conditioned readers expect to find in drama. At his satiric best Wycherley writes almost no dialogue; his discourse is satiric declamation. His style consciously follows the guidance of his theoretical mentor, Horace, for his aim was to write dramatic satire in the classical Roman mode. This he accomplished admirably.

The Country Wife was performed on 12 January 1675, by the King's Company at the Theatre Royal in Drury Lane. It was entered in the *Stationers' Register*, 13 January 1675, and listed in the *Term Catalogues*, 10 May 1675. In the prologue Wycherley calls himself "the late so baffled Scribler," referring to the cold reception which *The Gentleman Dancing Master* had so justly received. *The Country Wife* restored his reputation immediately;

it passed at once into the repertory, where—if we discount the nineteenth-century hiatus as an aberration—it has remained. It is the only one of Wycherley's plays that still enjoys occasional performance.

The epigraph to *The Country Wife*, Wycherley's transcreation of Juvenal's *Sixth Satire* in contemporary dress, is most ingenious, for in it Wycherley makes clear that he is returning to an ancient model and also that he is taking liberties with it, experimenting with its form. The epigraph is taken from the Horatian epistle that concerns itself with the proper approach of a "modern" poet to the ancients: "Indignor quicquam reprehendi, non quia crasse / Compositum illepideve putetur, sed quia nuper: / Nec veniam Antiquis, sed honorem et preamia posci" (I am impatient when any work is censured not because it is coarse or inelegant in style, but because it is modern. What we owe the Ancients is not indulgence but honor and rewards [*Epistles*, II,i,76-78]). Employing a new approach to an ancient model, Wycherley *becomes* Juvenal, and, transversely, Imperial Rome *becomes* Restoration London. Many of Wycherley's characters and scenes—ironically enough, those which have been thought to be particularly "Restoration"—grow from germ ideas and suggestions he found in Juvenal. For example, Pinchwife, the typically Restoration jealous husband, is the shape that Wycherley gives to Juvenal's Ursidius, the old whoremaster, who, despite his knowledge of the world, is driven at last to marry in order to keep a woman to himself (*Satire Six*, 38). Lady Fidget, so adept at acquitting herself when she is surprised by her husband in Horner's arms, finds her origins in Juvenal's women who can employ "the colors of Quintilian" in such a situation. The character of the country wife herself and the pivotal question she presents of whether ignorance and rusticity are any insurance of chastity are Juvenal's (55-59). Margery's goggling over the "player men" comes from Juvenal (63-66), and, in fact, when Dryden translated Juvenal's *Satire Six* in 1693, it is clear that he was remembering Wycherley's Margery:

> The Country Lady in the Box appears,
> Softly she warbles over all she hears;
>   And sucks in Passion, both at Eyes and Ears.

Mrs. Squeamish's keeping a "little tragedian" appears in Juvenal (73-75), as does the drinking party wherein the "virtuous crew" finally drop

Iris Hoey, Edith Evans, and Eileen Peel in a 1936 Old Vic production of The Country Wife *(photograph by Angus McBean)*

their masks and openly acknowledge their sexual voraciousness. However, most striking is the appearance in Juvenal of Horner himself. In Rome, of course, a Horner-figure has a somewhat different way of disguising himself, but he is the same Horner at heart, and he uses his disguise for the same purpose:

> [The cinaedi] do women consult about marriage and divorce, with their society do they relieve boredom, from them do they learn lascivious motions and whatever else the teacher knows. But beware! that teacher is not always what he seems; true he darkens his eyes and dresses like a woman, but adultery is his design. Mistrust him the more for his show of effeminacy; he is a valiant mattress-knight; there Triphallus drops his disguise of Thais.

It would have been impossible to present a sexual stallion disguised as a homosexual transvestite on the Restoration stage, and, therefore, Wycherley re-creates the homosexual disguise of Juvenal's Triphallus as Horner's pretended impo-

tence. Nonetheless, Horner's trick upon husbands is present in the Juvenalian passage, as indeed is the psychology of the Sir Jasper Fidgets of the world, who, too busy to tend to their wives, supply them with sexually disabled male companions as a relief from boredom and a preventive against sexual adventuring.

In *Satire Six*, Juvenal does not follow the usual surface design of Roman verse satire—in which a satiric spokesman and an adversarius survey a "background," the panorama of fools and knaves in satire's fallen city. Rather the satiric spokesman is the narrator's voice and the adversarius is the reader-audience. The design was, therefore, relatively easy to translate into a dramatic medium. The satirist-persona does not appear in the play (as he will in *The Plain Dealer*); the adversarius is the audience; and the scenes presented before us are the satiric background. *The Country Wife* has neither a central character nor a central action. Horner is most often used as a mouthpiece for directly spoken satire, but he is not even present in the majority of scenes. The

A scene from a 1936 production of The Country Wife *starring Ruth Gordon*

play's action itself speaks Wycherley's satire and is only occasionally interspersed with scenes of direct satiric commentary. Horner is not sufficiently detached from the scene to be the satirist's persona. He is distinguished from the other characters by his cleverness, but he is morally of their number. All the characters, including Horner, serve as butts and instruments of satire, examples used by Wycherley, the poet-satirist, to illustrate his vision of the "falling city" of the plain.

The play opens, as a verse satire does, with a declaration of the satiric "thesis" to be argued. The vice in question is lust, which from the Middle Ages to the eighteenth century does not mean sexual activity or even sexual excess, but rather means sexual *exploitation*. However, the vice here is not merely lust; it is lust that disguises itself, assumes one or another mask, not out of deference to morality nor out of shame, but that under the protection of a disguise, it may enjoy greater freedom to operate. The thesis is not directly declared because there is no central satiric persona here; it is presented in the

exchanges of Horner and Quack wherein Horner discloses his plan to pretend that he has been rendered sexually impotent in order to ferret out his prey, women who "love the sport," and to fool their husbands and guardians. Horner is less a character than an emblem, a grotesquely exaggerated "sign" of the moral defect for which we are to watch. In effect, Horner is in himself a graphic declaration of the satiric thesis.

The thesis declared, the argument begins—just as in Roman verse satire. There are three separate actions, of equal importance and maintaining a degree of independence from each other, that attract our attention by turn to the various aspects of the vice under consideration "in something of the way premises are turned about in the octave of a sonnet" (Mary Clare Randolph, "The Structural Design of Formal Verse Satire," *Philological Quarterly*, 21 [October 1942]). This enables the satirist to turn the vice under consideration around on all sides, to attack it from as many angles as possible. Scene after scene is presented in which some new face of the vice is presented, or some aspect already presented is more deeply probed. The movement is circular and continues until what Dryden calls the "members" of the central vice have all been explored to the fullest extent.

The four faces of disguised lust in *The Country Wife* have all made their first appearance by the end of the second act. First Horner is introduced to present lust in the mask of an impotence which secures it freedom. Then Sir Jasper appears with the "ladies of honour," who flaunt their masks of modesty and virtue; Horner sounds their virtue and reveals it to be hollow. The exposure of vice disguised as honor is followed by a brief interlude of satiric commentary. Horner and the company of wits observe and comment upon the lust-hypocrisy that pervades the contemporary social scene. Into this commentary a new aspect of disguised lust is introduced in the person of Pinchwife, who hides and indulges his sexual exploitation under the facade of marriage (I.i):

> HORNER: But prithee, was not the way you were in better, is not keeping better than Marriage?
> PINCH: A Pox on't, The Jades woud jilt me. I coud never keep a Whore to my self.
> HORNER: So then you only marry'd to keep a whore to youself.

Pinchwife's "honor" as a husband is as false as Lady Fidget's virtue or Horner's impotence. In reality Pinchwife is not a husband for he neither trusts, esteems, nor protects his wife; he is the legally sanctioned keeper of a whore, a piece of property that he is anxious to preserve to his exclusive enjoyment. Just like Lady Fidget, he desires to indulge his lust under the cover of a carefully sustained respectability, marriage.

The last face of the vice that is presented to us is lust disguised as innocence. Perhaps *lust* is too strong a word to describe Margery's emotion, as *innocence* is too imprecise to define her ignorance. Her innocence is at first genuine. However, once she has fallen in love with Horner, she develops guile, and she feigns innocence to disguise her passion from Pinchwife in the hope that she will thereby find freedom to satisfy it.

In their first appearance, all four aspects of the vice are purely comic—Horner's knavery, Fidget's affectation, Pinchwife's jealousy, and Margery's rusticity are all at first glance simple follies. However, as the vice is turned around and around, at each successive appearance they assume more serious proportions, and by gradual

steps the comic tone fades to be replaced by the more deeply satiric. For example, consider lust disguised as virtue. Fidget and her company are wholly comic in their first appearance. They are objects of satire only in their exaggeration; theirs is the "humour" of virtue which is exposed by Horner's wit. In act 2 a new dimension of their vice is revealed; their hidden lust, until now only suspected, is uncovered and with it their whole perverted system of morality. Their next appearance in the famous "china scene" is so uproariously funny and so perfectly sustained in its double entendre that we might almost miss its satiric point. The "virtuous gang," who in their first appearance affected exaggerated virtue and in their second appearance could still discuss sexuality only in heroic periphrasis, in their third reverse roles with Horner and become voracious predators upon *him*. (The china scene should remind us that in the seventeenth century the first requirement for satire was to be funny; we must be made to *laugh* our vices to contempt.) In the penultimate appearance of the women (act 4), which Wycherley models closely on Juvenal's description of Roman wives who throw off all restraint in performing the rites of the *Bona Dea*, comic tone vanishes. The women drop their masks and do not bother to pretend virtue. The stylistic tension between heroic/romantic surface of discourse and its underlying satiric intention—which was present in their earlier appearances—is gone. Wine loosens the women's tongues; their tone coarsens and becomes sluttish. They damn their husbands openly, comparing them to "old keeper[s]." They describe themselves as whores, commodities—"women of quality, like the richest Stuffs, lye untumbled and unask'd for." At the climax of the scene, when each of them acknowledges that she has enjoyed Horner, their lust is fully exposed and with it the extent of their hypocrisy. They will form a conspiracy of silence to insure that the "counterfeit" "Jewel," their reputation for virtue, still shines as though it were real.

The same progress from comic to deeply satiric is described in the successive appearances of the other three aspects of the vice. Pinchwife's jealousy is merely ridiculous when he is the butt of the wits' teasing. It becomes a more serious defect when we see him abusing his wife. In his next appearance, when he threatens, "Write as I bid you, or I will write Whore with this Penknife in your Face," it has darkened into cruel sadism. At last it is aggravated into a frenzy that makes him draw his sword on Margery. Her death is averted only when *his reputation* as a husband is rescued by the public assurance that Horner is sexually incapable. Pinchwife's last lines in the play make it clear that *he* knows he has been cuckolded, but, like the "ladies of honor," he is less concerned that his wife has been false than that, false though she is, she has been socially cleared, and, therefore, the false jewel of his "honor" as a husband still shines as though it were real.

Following exactly the same pattern, Margery's disguise, at first so charming, leads to her willingness to sacrifice Alithea's reputation in order that, by saving her own, she may indulge her passion for Horner; and Horner's knavery, at first so devilishly clever and beguiling that it escapes our censure, degenerates into mean duplicity when at last he sacrifices Alithea's true honor to the preservation of his false disguise.

The satiric thesis is complete when we see that in this fallen world of knaves and gulls the gulls are not a jot more sympathetic than the knaves. Sir Jasper as a husband bears resemblance to Pinchwife; it is not his wife he loves but his public image. Sparkish is the male counterpart to Lady Fidget; as she is a would-be lady, he is a would-be man. Her disguise is false modesty; his disguise is false wit and false broadmindedness.

The satiric antithesis of the play (the upward perspective toward the ideal) is presented in Alithea and Harcourt. Antithesis, at first sight, seems stronger here than in most satires, for virtue is presented in the action of the piece, as a human possibility, not, as it would be in *The Plain Dealer*, as a quaint remnant of a mythic literary past. Alithea and Harcourt figure the twin virtues that oppose the double vice of the satiric thesis. Alithea, as her name indicates, is the truth that opposes hypocrisy; Harcourt is the generous, self-sacrificing love that stands against exploitative lust. For every aspect of the vice we are shown, the opposing virtue is held up for comparison in Alithea and Harcourt. For Margery's dishonesty clothed in ignorance is Alithea's sophisticated honesty. For Pinchwife's jealousy is Harcourt's absolute faith that defies social opinion in spite of the most damning evidence. Scenes of vice are underscored by corresponding scenes of virtue. For example, Horner and Fidget's "as perfectly, perfectly?" exchange, in which the two plan an adulterous encounter in the language of heroic romance, is immediately followed by a scene in which Harcourt tries to express his honorable passion for Alithea under the disguise of a double-faced discourse. Even though Harcourt's romantic love is the very opposite of Horner's and Fidget's indiscriminate sexual appetites, Alithea will not allow even honorable love to go masked. Horner, Margery, or Fidget will do harm to others to protect themselves. Alithea sacrifices her own feeling for Harcourt to keep a promise to Sparkish even though she knows he is unworthy of her. Pinchwife will threaten to kill his wife to protect his reputation, and Horner will sacrifice Alithea to preserve his disguise, but Harcourt will stand firm against the "combination against [Alithea's] honour" to prove that his love is stronger and his generosity of spirit greater than his desire for public approval. Alithea and Harcourt end by marrying because it is not marriage that is the object of the satirist's scorn. Quite the contrary, we the audience are made by indirection to *admire* true marriage. What we are made to scorn is marriage as commercial contract (Sparkish's view), marriage as social accoutrement (the view of Sir Jasper and Lady Fidget), and marriage as legalized prostitution (Pinchwife's view).

Nevertheless, great satirists, because their mockery extends even to their own art, would seem to agree with W. H. Auden that "poetry makes nothing happen." In *The Country Wife* the ideal still exists as a possibility in the Restoration present; Harcourt and Alithea survive in the corrupt mob scene of cuckolds, knaves, and fools, but they are hard-pressed. Truth (Alithea) is not only threatened by falsity from without, but it works to its own confounding. (Alithea clings to her contract with Sparkish long after she knows that he is not even aware of the meaning of the contract.) But more important than that, presumably Alithea and Harcourt will live happily ever after in their virtue, but *so will* Horner, Sparkish, the Fidgets, and the Pinchwifes live happily ever after in their vice. Horner has learned nothing more than not to trust his secret with a fool. And to crown this moral ambivalence, the play ends with an ironic twist. Wycherley depends upon our familiarity with the end-scene, stately pairing-dance, and Hymeneal blessing that brings *As You Like It* (circa 1599-1600) to comic closure when he stages his final "Dance of the Cuckolds." He distinctly parodies Shakespeare's *romantic* point-counterpoint choral finale, in which Rosalind sorts out the green world couples ("Good shepherd, tell this youth what 'tis to love . . . "), with his *ironic* choral point counterpoint commentary

Ernest Thesiger as Sparkish in a 1924 production of The Country Wife *(photograph by Bertram Park)*

offered by each of the cuckolds, prospective cuckolds, and cuckold makers in the dance. "There's
doctrine for all Husbands Mr. *Harcourt*," the commentary begins, and in descending order it
moves step by step from Harcourt's idealistic "I
edifie Madam so much, that I am impatient till I
am one," to Pinchwife's final, bitter "But I must
be one—against my will to a Country-Wife, with
a Country-murrain to me." Wycherley pairs ill-
matched city couples to lifelong bondage in satiric parody of the Arcadian harmony to which
he alludes.

Wycherley's last play, *The Plain Dealer*, is his
most classically perfect, as well as his darkest, satire. It was the composition of this "most bold,
most general, and most useful satyre" that
earned him the name "Manly Wycherley" and
the reputation for fearless, incorruptible honesty.
The Plain Dealer was performed on 11 December
1676 by the King's Company at the Theatre

Royal in Drury Lane, in what might have been its
premiere performance. The title page of the first
quarto edition, dated 1677, lists the official licensing of the play as 9 January 1676, and it is listed
in the *Term Catalogues*, 28 May 1677. Even the nim-
blest critics have always been hard put to fit *The
Plain Dealer* into the category "Restoration Comedy," for it is, as James Sutherland calls it in *English Literature of the Late Seventeenth Century*
(1969), "much the grimmest of Wycherley's four
plays." As a satire in the Ancient Roman mold, it
is also much the most perfect, for it not only fulfills in every detail the basic tri-elemental classical verse structure of satirist, adversarius, and background, but it also contains a parody
substructure, so that it is at once a satire and a satiric commentary on satire itself. The epigraph,
drawn from the verse paragraph in *Satires* I. x in
which Horace lays down the rules of composition
for moral satire, forcefully underscores Wych-

erley's intention in this play. The lines he chooses are "Ridiculum acre / Fortus et melius magnas plerumque secat res" (Ridicule often deals more forcefully and more effectively with great matters than severity does). Once again the playwright is pointing to the "rules" that govern the unique genre in which he writes. Once again he is reminding us that it *is* a literary genre, that as a satirist he is not a self-flagellating malcontent with a personality defect that makes him vacillate between love and hatred of his fellow human beings but a quite self-conscious poet who is wrestling with the demands of a difficult and exacting poetic form.

The epistle dedicatory of *The Plain Dealer* is itself a masterly piece of prose satire. In it Wycherley mocks the dedication style of his day, one empty of meaning and crammed with fulsome flattery. He also mocks those playwrights who write critical prefaces by explaining to reader / audiences what they are doing in their works and how closely they are conforming to the trendiest theories of their time. Finally it jeers at those pretenders to virtue who had been shocked by *The Country Wife*. They are Fidget-like hypocrites, scandalized by *words* but not half so put off by the acts they describe—provided they are done in secret.

The play begins with a crashing declaration of thesis. The vice under consideration is hypocrisy. It is ubiquitous, poisoning every sphere of human life, and even a plain dealer, who attacks, or tries to flee from it, is in danger of being overtaken. The thesis is declared both directly, in Manly's spoken rebuke of Lord Plausible, and emblematically: Manly, a personification of the plain dealer, is pursued by Lord Plausible, a personification of the hypocrite. The former figure lashes out at the latter but finds that he is fighting a shadow; the more fierce his attack, the more elaborate the flattery it evokes.

The thesis declared, Wycherley sets the traditional contestants of verse satire, the satirist-persona and the adversarius, to argue it. There has been much critical controversy about these figures. Some critics believe that Manly is a hero and Freeman an opportunist (Dobrée); some believe that Manly is a repressed neurotic and Freeman is a hero (Norman Holland), full of "wild civility" (Birdsall). However, it is well to remember the generic mode in which Wycherley is very consciously and obviously writing. There are no "characters"—in our modern novel-conditioned sense of the term—in satire. Neither Manly nor

Freeman, nor indeed any other character in any of Wycherley's plays, has interiority or "psychology." They are not meant to stimulate "real" people; they are rather meant to designate certain rhetorical positions determined by the poetic form. Manly cannot be a "hero," for his very position as satiric persona requires a certain moral dubiousness (as we have seen, satire mocks satirist-reformers too). As adversarius, Freeman need not have any consistent morality; all that the form requires is that he maintain a rhetorical position opposite to that of the satirist-persona. Freeman's is a type of adversarius common in Roman satire; he is one of the very number that the satirist hates, one who detaches himself from the crowd and draws near to the satirist, where he plays the role of devil's advocate. Freeman does not want to convince Manly that the world is *not* full of hypocrites; rather he argues that hypocrisy is the way of the world and the only course of action available to a man of sense. He is in the play, in effect, to reason the satirist to the side of unreason, to win him to the very vice he stands most firmly against.

In act 1 Wycherley closely adheres to the form of verse satire. Having established the necessary antagonism between satirist and adversarius, he must provide a satiric "background." His first "background" is presented as it is in verse satire, in the conversation of his adversaries. If we examine one of the key act 1 exchanges between Manly and Freeman we discover that it is a classical satire in little. It employs all the rhetorical devices used in verse satire and also figures the pattern of the larger satiric design in miniature. Freeman provokes an attack from Manly with an argument designed to draw the satirist's fire—that is, everybody does it, so it must be right. Then Manly launches his counterargument. To illustrate the rationality of his disgust with the world, he describes a scene that is the usual, moving "background" in verse satire. In it he sketches caricatures of the hypocrites of the world, falling upon every level of society from the bishop to the fishmonger. Finally this minisatire is clinched with a recapitulation of the basic opposing positions of satirist and adversarius (I.i):

> FREEMAN: . . . Observe but any Morning what people do when they get together on the *Exchange*, in *Westminster-hall*, or the Galleries of *Whitehall*.
> MANLY: I must confess, there they seem to rehearse *Bays's* grand *Dance*: here you see a

Bishop bowing to a gaudy *Atheist*; a Judge, to a Door-keeper; a great Lord, to a Fishmonger, or a Scrivener with a Jack-chain about his neck; a Lawyer, to a Serjeant at Arms; a velvet *Physician*, to a thredbare *Chymist*: and a supple Gentleman Usher, to a surly Beef-eater; and so tread round in a preposterous huddle of Ceremony to each other, whil'st they can hardly hold their solemn false countenances.
FREEMAN: Well, they understand the World.
MANLY: Which I do not, I confess.

Manly's attack is upon a simple, harmless kind of flattery, the light oil that keeps the social gears turning. The ferocity of it clearly marks him a humorous character; his attack is overkill, too hot a fire for the harmless folly that provokes it. Wycherley the poet's attack is more complex than his character's. He uses Manly's description of the seats of power—Westminster, Whitehall, and the Exchange—not primarily to ridicule affected manners, but to expose deep-seated social decay. The poet-satirist must not be confused with his character, the satirist-persona. As the play progresses the distance between them widens. Manly, the exposer, will be exposed, first as being a pigheaded fool, mistaken in his judgment, and then as a practitioner of the very vice he most strongly attacks. Wycherley uses Manly as his primary instrument for satiric exposure, but he widens the scope and intensifies the depth of satire in his play beyond his character-persona's limitations.

In act 2 Wycherley proves the spoken satire of act 1 in the scene he sets before us. He broadens our venue to include a new class of society, aristocratic idlers, and he intensifies our focus to reveal the distortions hypocrisy effects in personal life. In act 3 he broadens his scope still further to the widest extent possible, and he intensifies the severity of his attack. The hypocrisy which appeared in act 1 as a simple glossing over of the emptiness of social forms, and deepened in act 2 to become a cover for personal exploitation and spiteful backbiting, is enlarged in act 3 to become the perversion of justice itself. Here hypocrisy is a methodized, culturally determined mechanism for justifying and legitimizing the most brutish self-seeking. When we look back from act 3, we discover that Wycherley has been shaping a perverse platonic progression, tracing hypocrisy from falsity in personal relations, to a poisoning of social and class relations and responsibilities, and finally, to corruption of the principle upon which the government of nations depends, justice. His satire reveals a whole world dancing a Bays's dance to its ruin.

Having widened the scope of satire to the fullest dimension possible in a drama, Wycherley turns our attention in the last two acts to the process by which hypocrisy corrupts the soul of a single man, the plain dealer himself. The deterioration of Manly has been prepared from the beginning of the play. As we have seen, in act 1 his ferocity is such that we rather think him a crank. Act 2 not only reveals how far off Manly's judgment of his beloved mistress, Olivia, and his trusted friend, Vernish, is but it also introduces a parody satiric substructure. Olivia's opening words, "Ah, Cousin, what a World 'tis we live in! I am so weary of it," reveal her to be a tin pot imitation Manly. This mock-satirist-persona engages Eliza, a mock-adversarius, but their moral roles are reversed—that is, Eliza is a plain dealer and Olivia a hypocrite. The parody renders the original suspect. Moreover, Manly's image is further tarnished when we discover that Olivia has tricked him into loving her by playing on his own self-love: "I knew he lov'd his own singular moroseness so well, as to dote upon any Copy of it." We begin to find Manly's, or any satirist's, position questionable. In raging against vice in others, we ask, does not the satirist claim by implication to be above censure? May it not be that his ferocious honesty is founded in pride and self-love?

Wycherley hinges the final deterioration of Manly on these questions. Manly's fall into the vice he detests is pride's fall. When Manly is disenchanted by Olivia, his love turns to ungovernable lust. However, he tries to hide what he feels, especially because he fears Freeman's scorn. At first he finds deception a difficult game—he reflects, "How hard it is to be a Hypocrite!" However, as his lust (hatred combined with sexual desire) is thwarted and becomes increasingly difficult to bear, he falls into greater and greater deceit. He lies to Freeman, pretending to be above a woman's scorn. He lies to Fidelia, pretending that his grotesque efforts to bed Olivia are his way of punishing the wrong she has done him. He lies to Vernish, claiming he has enjoyed Olivia's favors when he has not, in order to enhance his male pride. Finally, Manly reaches the depth of degradation when, since his threat to kill Fidelia if she does not get Olivia for him proves ineffectual, he bribes her with the promise that if she lures Olivia to him, he will allow her to stay with him. Manly has come full circle;

The seventh plate in William Hogarth's The Rake's Progress *(1735), showing Tom Rakewell in Fleet debtors' prison,
where Wycherley was probably confined from 1682 to 1686*

he is what he accused Lord Plausible of being at
the very beginning of the play, "like common
Whores . . . dangerous to those [he] embraces."

Because the satiric thesis of *The Plain Dealer*
is so dark and so pervasive that it even under-
mines itself as an instrument of moral reformation, satiric antithesis is correspondingly more
remote, improbable, and literary-romantic, an
ideal that could exist only in the imagination of
poets. The satiric antithesis exists in a lone emblematic figure, a Morality play "Faithful" tricked
out in Shakespearean garb: a girl named Fidelia,
who dresses up as a boy to follow her beloved
and woos an Olivia for him, even though it
breaks her heart. The ending of the play, which
unites Manly and Fidelia and elicits Freeman's sup-
position that the Plain Dealer has married for
money, is as ironic as the Dance of the Cuckolds
that closes / but does not really close *The Country
Wife*.

The Plain Dealer was Wycherley's last play.
Though he lived on for another forty years, he
never wrote another. His brilliant career as a
dramatist lasted only five short years. Neverthe-

less, his fame, his virtues, and the nickname derived from his most famous character, "Manly,"
lived on with him. John Dennis wrote that the honesty, loyalty, and sincerity of Manly Wycherley
were "long and . . . peculiarly his own." Certainly
the poet demonstrated these qualities against his
own interests in 1677. His friend the duke of Buckingham was sent to the Tower in February of that
year for attempting to force the king to prorogue
Parliament. The poetic epistle which Wycherley
wrote and circulated in Buckingham's defense
began, "Your late Disgrace, is but the Court's
Disgrace"—and this in spite of the fact that
Wycherley's only hope for support depended on
the favor of the king. It is, on the other hand, a
measure of the real goodness of "Good King
Charles" that he not only overlooked the attack
but continued to admire and support the poet
who launched it. When Wycherley fell sick with
the brain fever that was to shatter his memory
and rob him of his creative powers, the king visited him in his lodgings in Bow Street, a demonstration of "Esteem and Affection," as Dennis
tells us, "which never any Sovereign Prince be-

fore had given to an Author who was only a private Gentleman." Moreover, the king gave him five hundred pounds to pay for a rest cure at the famous health resort Montpelier, and proposed that, on his return, Wycherley should become tutor to the duke of Richmond.

Wycherley spent the winter and spring of 1678 in France, but he never fully recovered his health nor his creative ability. In describing his own state of mind in a letter to Etherege, Dryden mentions Wycherley's symptoms and the long trial under which he suffered them: "In short, without apoplexy, Wycherley's long sickness, I forgot everything to enjoy nothing—that is myself." The young Pope later complained that Wycherley "would repeat the same thought sometimes in the compass of ten lines, did not dream of its being inserted but just before. . . . His memory did not carry above a sentence at a time. These single sentences were good, but the whole was without connexion and good for nothing but to be flung into maxims."

The ravages of brain fever were not Wycherley's only problem after 1679. From the time of his first success he had lived the life of a London gentleman, a life which centered around the court, the theaters, the coffeehouses, and all the other places "where youth and wit and bravery keep cost." But, alas, the life of a London wit took money, and Wycherley despised "busy" money brokers and "industrious" country land grabbers with equal asperity. In an age when it was considered ungentlemanly to write for money (only Aphra Behn had the courage to admit that she "wrote for bread"), there were few acceptable ways to get it. One might inherit it, and Wycherley could not do that because Daniel Wycherley was still alive and vigorously spending all his available capital on lawsuits. One could honorably receive a royal appointment or annuity. This Wycherley *almost* did. The king's offer of the position as tutor to his illegitimate seven-year-old son carried a salary of fifteen hundred pounds a year with a liberal annuity after the office terminated. Finally, one could marry it. This Wycherley *thought* he had done, but he proved to be mistaken. On the contrary, it was his marriage that brought on his final financial ruin.

After Wycherley had received the king's offer of a tutorship, he unfortunately took a trip to the fashionable watering place Tunbridge Wells. In a bookstore there he overheard a young widow—noble, beautiful, and reputedly rich—asking for a copy of *The Plain Dealer*. The

friend who accompanied him, Mr. Fairbeard, stepped forward and said, "*Since you are for the* Plain Dealer, *there he is for you,* pushing Mr. *Wycherley* towards her." Wycherley, who seems not to have lost his charm with his memory, complimented the lady in the same sprightly manner he had used on the duchess of Cleveland in his youth. So elegantly witty was the courtship, John Dennis tells us, that Mr. Fairbeard was moved to declare, "*Madam . . . you and the* Plain Dealer *seem design'd by Heaven for each other.*" Mr. Fairbeard was wrong. Whether by the design of a just providence or not, Wycherley's September 1679 marriage to Lady Laetitia-Isabella, Countess of Drogheda, led him to hell. To begin with, it lost him the king's favor as well as the offered post because he rushed into marriage (by his father's command, according to Dennis) without informing the king of his intention. Then, as it turned out, the countess had been living on credit and was deep in debt, even to her maid, when Wycherley met her (a state of affairs that led eventually to the maid's suing the countess and Wycherley). Finally, the estates left to the countess by her late husband were contested by his brother. Henry, the new earl, charged that the late earl had been coerced by his wife into leaving his lands out of his own family. The litigation arising from this suit lasted fifteen years longer than the countess, Mrs. Wycherley, did. At the time of her death the legal dispute, which was to bring Wycherley to final ruin, had only just entered its preliminary stages.

We might chalk off Wycherley's loss of royal patronage and the failure of his expectations in the widow's fortune as among the "little disturbances of man" with which fortune plagues us, but the character of Lady Laetitia-Isabella, Countess of Drogheda, seems to have been designed especially for the torment of William Wycherley, for she was possessed by temperament with the two qualities he most hated. She was fiercely litigious and even more fiercely jealous. Dennis tells us that "she could not endure that [Wycherley] should be one Moment out of her Sight." When he went with his friends from their lodgings in Bow Street to a next door tavern, the *Cock*, "he was oblig'd to leave the Windows open, that the Lady might see there was no Woman in Company, or she would be immediately in a downright raving Condition." Wycherley's willingness to endure her jealousy was part of his code of honor; as Dennis puts it, he "thought that he was oblig'd to humour" his wife because she "had

William Wycherley in the 1690s

bestow'd her Person and her Fortune on him." He believed this even in the teeth of the financial disaster she brought upon him. Wycherley added to his own debts the debts he inherited from her in addition to the staggering costs that accrued constantly from her case in Chancery.

As Wycherley's financial situation grew more desperate, he wrote epistles "To the King" and "To the Duke" in the hope of regaining royal favor. But these were the days of the Popish Plot, the Rye House Plot, and the Exclusion Crisis, and neither of the royal brothers had attention to spare for a destitute playwright, no matter how much they might have liked and admired him. There is no reason to believe that the senti-

ments expressed in Wycherley's *Epistles to the King and Duke*, published in 1683, were mere flattery designed to curry favor. There can be no doubt that Wycherley was a royalist born and bred, and he remained loyal to the Stuart monarchy to his dying day. In fact the poem "To the King My Master; After His Mercy to a Fault, shown to some Conspirators against his Power and Life," which was written on the occasion of Charles's clemency to the perpetrators of the Rye House Plot, was not published until 1704, long after it could have done Wycherley any material good.

Wycherley's creditors had him arrested and committed to Newgate Prison in 1682. He very probably had himself transferred to Fleet Prison, which was a common practice of imprisoned debtors at the time, but we cannot be certain of this, since prison records were not kept before 1685. He remained in debtor's prison for four years, almost the length of time that he was a practicing playwright. None of the friends from his days of glory came to his aid. John Wilmot, Earl of Rochester, was dead, and Charles Sackville, Earl of Dorset, was suffering severe illness. Buckingham and John Sheffield, Earl of Mulgrave, who had given themselves to poetry and criticism in the 1660s and 1670s, were thoroughly involved in the feverish, and sometimes fatal, political machinations of the 1680s. Daniel Wycherley was still alive, but being, as he always was, involved in expensive litigation, he did not feel obliged to come to the rescue of his impecunious son. Wycherley's most recent biographer, McCarthy, has attempted to rescue Daniel from the cliché identity of "stingy and tyrannical senex iratus" imposed on him by earlier biographers, but a man of wealth who allowed two of his sons to languish in debtors' prison at the same time—William and his brother, George, who, it has been said, was committed on his father's complaint and who died in prison—may justly be said to be somewhat wanting in fatherly feeling.

It has been said that the Fleet in the late seventeenth and early eighteenth centuries was no more intolerable than an overcrowded, frowsy inn. Prisoners could bring their furniture, their servants, and their families with them; they could be visited by their tradesmen, their doxies, and their friends. For a price, they could even have their manacles adjusted to a comfortable fit—as in Hogarth's engraving. It was only dreadful, John Strype, the eighteenth-century surveyor of prison conditions, said, "to such poor Men as have parted with their All to their Creditors." We must assume that Wycherley was such a one, for he found life in the Fleet greatly depressing. In a poem he wrote while he was there, "In Praise of a Prison, call'd by its Prisoners their College; and written there," he described himself and his fellow prisoners as "Carcasses of Skin and Bone,/ From which, Life, Soul, Spirit, are dead and gone." He was released from prison in 1686, when the new king, James II, helped to clear his debts and promised him a pension after influential friends had arranged a performance of *The Plain Dealer* at court. Alas, Wycherley was no luckier in his kings than in his wives; when James

fled the country less than three years later Wycherley was once again left penniless.

After this Wycherley lived very modestly, partly in London and partly in Shropshire, with occasional visits to Bath. When he was in London, he was still at the center of the literary world. He was an accepted and admired leader among the poets, critics, and wits who gathered at Will's Coffee House. Dryden remained his constant friend throughout all his misfortune, and he was also much admired by the foremost writers and critics of the younger generation, Congreve, Southerne, Dennis, and Pope.

He had been writing poems off and on throughout his life, and sometime before 1696 he decided to bring out a collection, consisting mainly of new verse. The volume was ready by 1699, but difficulties arose with the publisher. Briscoe advertised it in 1696, but he neither published the book nor gave Wycherley the money he had received in subscriptions. Wycherley had to sue for the return of his manuscript in 1700. The book was finally brought out by Brome, Taylor, and Tooke in 1704 as *Miscellany Poems*. The poet introduced the work in his usual ironic style. The preface was addressed "To my Criticks ... Who were my *Criticks*, before they were my *Readers*," and the book was dedicated "To The Greatest Friend of the Muses, Vanity." The collection was generally condemned. There is no question that for the most part the failure rests with the uneven quality of the poems themselves; Wycherley was no longer capable of the sustained concentration of satiric energy that marked his plays. However, there may be another reason the miscellany had so unfavorable a reception, one which has not been taken sufficiently into account. Wycherley wrote cutting, ironic satire; in style, theme, and tone, he was an artist of the 1670s. The ascension of William and Mary brought a new, decorous, and very bourgeois respectability into fashion. In the miscellany, Wycherley's poems were addressed to an audience thirty years gone.

At about this time Wycherley met the sixteen-year-old Alexander Pope and was much impressed by the elegance of his early pastoral poems. The old "lion of the satire," as Pope called him, took the fledgling poet under his wing and greatly promoted his reputation in literary circles. Pope, who was at first greatly honored to be invited by the famous Mr. Wycherley to help him revise the *Miscellany Poems* that had had such ill success when it appeared in 1704,

was soon driven to distraction by Wycherley's inca-
pacity. He finally told Wycherley to undertake
the revision himself and advised him to cut the
poems into epigrams in the manner of Roche-
foucauld. For a time the friendship cooled, but
Wycherley's great generosity of spirit, which had
never left him, revived it.

Wycherley's end could have been written by
him in a play; it has all the bittersweet satiric ambiguity of one of his end-scenes. His first wife
having died in 1685, he married again at the
age of seventy-four. In 1715 his cousin, Captain
Thomas Shrimpton, advised him to marry a
young woman who could bring with her a cash
dowry sufficient to pay off his debts. The
woman, for her part, would receive the jointure
provided in old Daniel's will should his son re-
marry. The woman, Elizabeth Jackson, was Captain Shrimpton's mistress, and some biographers,
looking at the scene from a romantic perspective, have drawn a dark picture of the wicked
Shrimpton and Jackson getting the poor old
Wycherley drunk and threatening him with debtors' prison if he did not go along with their nefarious scheme. Yet Wycherley "had often told
[Pope], as I doubt not he did all his Acquaintance, that he would Marry as soon as his life was
despair'd of." Wycherley could well have been in
on the scheme from the first, and he may have
found it a wonderful joke—especially on the
ghost of old Daniel. Pope visited him on the day
of his death, twelve days after his wedding day
(19 December 1715), and found him "less peevish in his Sickness than he used to be in his
Health, neither much afraid of dying, nor (which
in him had been more likely) much ashamed of
Marrying." His last request of his young wife
seems to be perfectly in keeping with the sensibility of this great satirist who was withal a most gentle and amiable man. He asked her to make him
a single, simple promise: "My Dear, it is only
this; that you will never marry an old Man
again." The second Mrs. Wycherley, a young
widow with a rich jointure, kept her promise. She
married the young Captain Shrimpton a few
months after the poet's death.

Letters:
*Letters Upon several Occasions: Written by and be-
    tween Mr. Dryden, Mr. Wycherly, Mr. ----, Mr.
    Congreve, and Mr. Dennis,* edited by John
    Dennis (London: Printed for Sam Briscoe,
    1696);

The Correspondence of Alexander Pope, edited by
    George Sherburn, volume 1 (Oxford: Claren-
    don Press, 1956).

Biographies:
Charles Gildon, ed., *Memoirs of the Life of William
    Wycherley, Esq.; with a Character of his Writ-
    ings. By the Right Honourable George, lord
    Lansdowne. To which are added, Some Familiar
    Letters, written by Mr. Wycherley, and a True
    Copy of His Last Will and Testament* (London:
    Printed for E. Curll, 1718);
John Dennis, "Letters on Milton and Wycherley,"
    "Letter 'To the Honourable Major Pack. Con-
    taining some remarkable Passages to Mr.
    Wycherley's Life,'" in *The Critical Works of
    John Dennis,* 2 volumes, edited by E. N.
    Hooker (Baltimore: Johns Hopkins Univer-
    sity Press, 1939, 1943), II: 221-235, 409-
    412;
Gerald Weales, "William Wycherley," *Michigan
    Quarterly Review,* 12 (1973): 45-58;
B. Eugene McCarthy, *William Wycherley: A Biogra-
    phy* (Athens: Ohio University Press, 1979).

References:
Emmett L. Avery, "*The Country Wife* in the Eigh-
    teenth Century," *Research Studies of the State
    College of Washington,* 10 (June 1942): 141-
    172;
Avery, "*The Plain Dealer* in the Eighteenth Cen-
    tury," *Research Studies of the State College of
    Washington,* 11 (September 1943): 234-256;
Avery, "The Reputation of Wycherley's Come-
    dies as Stage Plays in the Eighteenth Cen-
    tury," *Research Studies of the State College of
    Washington,* 12 (September 1944): 131-154;
Virginia Ogden Birdsall, *Wild Civility* (Blooming-
    ton: Indiana University Press, 1970);
Bonamy Dobrée, *Restoration Comedy* (London: Ox-
    ford University Press, 1924);
William Freedman, "Impotence and Self-Destruc-
    tion in *The Country Wife,*" *English Studies,* 53
    (October 1972): 421-431;
A. M. Friedson, "Wycherley and Molière; Satiri-
    cal Point of View in *The Plain Dealer,*" *Mod-
    ern Philology,* 64 (February 1967): 189-197;
Thomas Fujimura, *The Restoration Comedy of
    Wit* (Princeton: Princeton University Press,
    1952);
Charles A. Hallett, "The Hobbesian Substructure
    of *The Country Wife,*" *Papers on Language and
    Literature,* 9 (Fall 1973): 380-395;

Philip A. Highfill, Kalman A. Burnim, and Edward A. Langhans, eds., *A Bibliographical Dictionary of Actors, Actresses, Musicians, Dancers, Managers, and other State Personnel in London, 1660-1800*, 12 volumes to date (Carbondale: Southern Illinois University Press, 1973-   );

Norman Holland, *The First Modern Comedies* (Cambridge, Mass.: Harvard University Press, 1959);

Peter Holland, *The Ornament of Action* (Cambridge: Cambridge University Press, 1979);

Robert D. Hume, *The Development of English Drama in the Late Seventeenth Century* (London: Oxford University Press, 1976);

Anthony Kaufman, "Idealization, Disillusion, and Narcissistic Rage in Wycherley's *The Plain Dealer*," *Criticism*, 21 (Spring 1979): 119-133;

John Loftis, Richard Southern, Marion Jones, and A. H. Scouten, *The Revels History of Drama in English*, volume 5: 1660-1750 (London: Methuen, 1976);

Kathleen Lynch, *The Social Mode of Restoration Comedy* (New York: Macmillan, 1926);

Cynthia Matlack, "Parody and Burlesque of Heroic Ideals in Wycherley's Comedies; A Critical Reinterpretation of Contemporary Evidence," *Papers in Language and Literature*, 8 (Summer 1972): 273-286;

Maximillian E. Novak, "Margery Pinchwife's London Disease; Restoration Comedy and the Libertine Offensive of the 1670's," *Studies in the Literary Imagination*, 10 (Spring 1977): 1-23;

Anne Righter, "William Wycherley," in *Restoration Theater*, edited by J. R. Brown and B. Harris (New York: Capricorn, 1967);

Katharine M. Rogers, *William Wycherley* (New York: Twayne, 1972);

Eric Rump, "Theme and Structure in Wycherley's *Love in a Wood*," *English Studies*, 54 (August 1973): 326-333;

P. F. Vernon, *William Wycherley* (London: Longmans, Green, 1965);

John Harold Wilson, *A Preface to Restoration Drama* (Boston: Houghton Mifflin, 1965);

Rose A. Zimbardo, *Wycherley's Drama: A Link in the Development of English Satire* (New Haven: Yale University Press, 1965).

Index to Volume 2

Index

This index includes proper names: people, places, and works mentioned in the texts of entries for Volume 2. The primary checklists, which appear at the beginning of each entry, are not included in this index. Also omitted are the names London and Dublin, because they appear so frequently. Volume 8 of the *Concise Dictionary of British Literary Biography* includes a cumulative proper-name index to the entire series.

Evelyn, John, 322, 323

Evening's Love, An (Dryden), 69, 126

Every Man In His Humour (Jonson), 74

Every-body's Business, Is No-body's Business (Defoe), 114

Evgeni Onegin (Pushkin), 393

Examen Poeticum: Being the third Part of Miscellany Poems (trans. Dryden), 8, 72

Examiner, The (periodical), 17, 463, 465, 466, 467, 508

"Eyes and Tears" (Marvell), 273

Faber Fortunae (Bacon), 323

Fable of Vertumnus and Pomona (Pope), 338

Fables Ancient and Modern (Dryden), 142, 145

Fables of Aesop, The (L'Estrange, 1692), 379

Faerie Queene, The (Spenser), 292, 310

"Fair Singer, The" (Marvell), 271

Fairfax, Maria, 267, 271

Fairfax, Thomas, third Baron, 264, 266, 267

Fairfax, William, 271

Faithful Shepherd (J. Fletcher), 292

Faithful Shepherdess, The (J. Fletcher), 538

Faithorne, William, 279

False Alarm, The (S. Johnson), 44, 248

False Delicacy (Kelly), 202, 205

Familiar Letters (Richardson), 379, 380, 389

Familiar Letters between the Principal Characters in David Simple (S. Fielding), 169

Family Instructor (Defoe), 183

Fanny Hill (Cleland), 111

Fanshawe, Sir Richard, 533

Fantasia (film), 139

Farquhar, George, 157, 403, 422, 458

"Fatal Sisters, The" (Gray), 220

"Father to a Daughter in Service, on hearing of her Master's attempting her Virtue, A" (Richardson), 379

Fathers, The (Fielding), 415

Faulkner, George, 393, 511, 512

Faust (Goethe), 244

Fawkes, Guy, 130

Female Quixote, The (Lennox), 393, 447

Female Tatler (periodical), 462

Fenton, Elijah, 343

Ferdinand Count Fathom (Smollett), 433, 438, 440, 441, 442, 444, 445, 446, 449, 452

Fermor, Arabella, 337, 339

Ferney, Switzerland, 51

Ficino, Marsilio, 292

Fielding, Anne, 156

Fielding, Beatrice, 156, 157

Fielding, Catharine, 156

Fielding, Charlotte Cradock, 159, 161, 169, 170, 174

Fielding, Edmund (brother), 156, 157

Fielding, Edmund (father), 155, 157, 161, 174

Fielding, Henry, 44, 149-180, 193, 199, 200, 202, 207, 228, 371, 382, 385, 388, 393, 415, 417, 427, 433, 434, 435, 438, 447, 450, 452, 470, 483, 487, 500, 517

Fielding, John, 155, 176

Fielding, Mary Daniel, 169

Fielding, Sarah (sister), 155, 157, 166, 169, 393

Fielding, Sarah Gould, 155, 156

Fielding, Ursula, 156

Fielding and the Woman Question (Smallwood), 154

Financial Times (periodical), 191

Finden, E., 34

Finger, Godfrey, 90

First Anniversary of the Government under O.C., The (Marvell), 275

First Epistle Of The First Book Of Horace Imitated, The (Pope), 360, 364

First Epistle Of The Second Book of Horace, Imitated, The (Pope), 360, 361, 362, 363

First Modern Comedies, The (Holland), 531

First Satire (Juvenal), 458

First Satire Of The Second Book of Horace, Imitated, The (Pope), 360, 361, 364

Firth, Sir Charles, 511

Fisher, John, 302

Fitzgerald, Lord Edward, 420

Flecknoe, Richard, 128, 129, 263

Fletcher, Giles, the Younger, 310

Fletcher, John, 91, 292, 403, 413, 539 538

Florence, Italy, 69, 292, 298

Flying Post (periodical), 107

Foe, Alice, 99

Foe, Henry, 111

Foe, James, 99

Folly of Industry; or The Busy Man Expos'd, The (Wycherley), 533

Fontenelle, Bernard Le Bovier de, 234

Foote, Samuel, 46, 403

Forbes, Sir William, 48

Ford, Charles, 505

Ford, Cornelius, 229

Ford, James, 410

Ford, R., 323

Forster, E. M., 110, 153, 518

Fortunate Mistress, The (Roxana) (Defoe), 112, 113, 116

Fourth Satire of Dr. John Donne, Dean of St. Paul's, Versifyed (Pope), 360

Fox, Charles James, 246, 410, 420

"Fragment in the Manner of Rabelais"(Sterne), 477, 482

Francklin, Thomas 447

Franklin, Benjamin, 395

Frederick the Great (Prussia), 243

Frederick, W., 197

Free Enquiry into the Nature and Origin of Evil, A (Jenyns), 244

Free-holder, The (Addison), 14, 24, 25

Friedman, Arthur, 191

Frye, Northrop, 214, 513

Fujimura, Thomas, 531

Funeral, The (Steele), 458

Funeral of Faction, The, 162

Galileo, 298

"Gallery, The" (Marvell), 271

Garden, The (Marvell), 270, 273

Gargantua (Rabelais), 481

Garrick, David, 31, 34, 39, 46, 202, 205, 206, 229, 230, 239, 241, 254, 255 329, 330, 378, 389, 402, 403, 407, 410, 411, 417, 418, 429, 435, 436, 437, 438, 478, 530

Garth, Samuel, 17

Gascoigne, Henry, 456, 457

Gascoigne, Katherine, 456, 457

Gaubius, 185

Gauden, Dr. John, 283

Gay, John, 16, 17, 157, 166 348, 410, 462, 466, 468, 508, 510

General History of Discoveries and Improvements, in Useful Arts, A (Defoe), 114

General History of the . . . Pyrates, A (Defoe), 108, 113, 116

Geneva, Switzerland, 9, 51

Genoa, Italy, 32

Gentleman Dancing Master, The (Wycherley), 534, 540, 542

Gentleman's Magazine (periodical), 35, 189, 204, 230, 231, 232, 234, 243 376, 377, 343, 450

George I (Great Britain), 24, 106, 108, 123 348, 374, 470, 510, 511

George II (Great Britain), 162, 163, 232, 233, 245 348, 360, 361, 362, 366, 374

George III (Great Britain), 245, 420

George, Prince of Denmark, 458

Georgics (Virgil), 339

"Gerontion" (Eliot), 240

Gibbon, Edward, 228, 420

Gide, André, 371

Giffard, Henry, 382

Gifford, John, 56

Gil Blas (Lesage), 432, 434, 435

Gilbert, William, 514

Gildon, Charles, 108

Gill, Alexander, the Elder, 285

Gill, Alexander, the Younger, 285

Gilray, James, 416

Cumulative Index of Author Entries for
Concise Dictionary of British Literary Biography

Cumulative Index
of Author Entries

ISBN 0-8103-7982-1